THE OXFORD HANDBOOK OF

THE SYNOPTIC GOSPELS

THE OXFORD HANDBOOK OF

THE SYNOPTIC GOSPELS

Edited by
STEPHEN P. AHEARNE-KROLL

OXFORD
UNIVERSITY PRESS

Oxford University Press is a department of the University of Oxford. It furthers
the University's objective of excellence in research, scholarship, and education
by publishing worldwide. Oxford is a registered trade mark of Oxford University
Press in the UK and certain other countries.

Published in the United States of America by Oxford University Press
198 Madison Avenue, New York, NY 10016, United States of America.

© Oxford University Press 2023

All rights reserved. No part of this publication may be reproduced, stored in
a retrieval system, or transmitted, in any form or by any means, without the
prior permission in writing of Oxford University Press, or as expressly permitted
by law, by license, or under terms agreed with the appropriate reproduction
rights organization. Inquiries concerning reproduction outside the scope of the
above should be sent to the Rights Department, Oxford University Press, at the
address above.

You must not circulate this work in any other form
and you must impose this same condition on any acquirer.

Library of Congress Cataloging-in-Publication Data

Names: Ahearne-Kroll, Stephen P., 1967– author.
Title: The Oxford handbook of the synoptic gospels / Stephen P. Ahearne-Kroll.
Description: New York, NY, United States of America : Oxford University Press, [2023] |
Series: Oxford handbooks series | Includes
bibliographical references and index.
Identifiers: LCCN 2022038812 (print) | LCCN 2022038813 (ebook) |
ISBN 9780190887452 (hardback) | ISBN 9780190887476 (epub) |
ISBN 9780190887483
Subjects: LCSH: Bible. Gospels—Criticism, interpretation, etc. |
Synoptic problem.
Classification: LCC BS2555.52 .A37 2022 (print) | LCC BS2555.52 (ebook) |
DDC 226/.06—dc23/eng/20221207
LC record available at https://lccn.loc.gov/2022038812
LC ebook record available at https://lccn.loc.gov/2022038813

DOI: 10.1093/oxfordhb/9780190887452.001.0001

Printed by Integrated Books International, United States of America

Contents

Notes on Contributors   ix
Introduction   xv
    STEPHEN P. AHEARNE-KROLL

PART I THE PROBLEM AND NATURE OF THE SYNOPTIC GOSPELS

1. The History and Prospects of the Synoptic Problem   3
   JOHN S. KLOPPENBORG

2. The Minor Sources and Their Role in the Synoptic Problem   27
   PAUL FOSTER

3. The Use of Sources in Ancient Compositions   44
   JAMES W. BARKER

4. Ancient Rhetoric as an Evaluative Tool for Literary Dependence   63
   ALEXANDER DAMM

5. Paul's Possible Influence on the Synoptics   81
   CAMERON EVAN FERGUSON

6. Oral Tradition, Writing, and the Synoptic Problem: Media Dualism and Gospel Origins   100
   ALAN KIRK

7. Oral Performance of the Synoptics   119
   LEE A. JOHNSON

8. Narrative Design of the Synoptics   136
   MICHAL BETH DINKLER

9. Manuscripts: The Problem with the Synoptic Problem   152
   BRENT NONGBRI

10. The Publication of the Synoptics and the Problem of Dating 175
    MATTHEW LARSEN

11. The Synoptic Gospels and Apocryphal Narratives 204
    JANET E. SPITTLER

12. The Gospel of Thomas and the Synoptics 223
    MELISSA HARL SELLEW

PART II PARTICULAR FEATURES IN COMPARISON

13. Suffering and Sacrifice 245
    CANDIDA R. MOSS

14. Violent Imaginaries 260
    SARAH E. ROLLENS

15. Kingdom, Authority, and Power 278
    MICHAEL PEPPARD

16. Wealth, Poverty, Economy 296
    THOMAS R. BLANTON IV

17. Travel and Itinerancy 320
    TIMOTHY LUCKRITZ MARQUIS

18. Food and Meals 338
    SOHAM AL-SUADI

19. Healing and Exorcism 355
    MEGHAN HENNING

20. Sacred Space 372
    KAREN WENELL

21. History 392
    EVE-MARIE BECKER

22. Apocalyptic Eschatology 412
    ROBYN J. WHITAKER

23. Resurrection and the Afterlife 430
    ALEXEY SOMOV

24. Gospel 451
    JOSHUA D. GARROWAY

25. Jewish Sectarianism 468
    JOHN KAMPEN

26. Gentiles and Their Relations to Jews 486
    MAGNUS ZETTERHOLM

27. Israel's Scriptures 506
    SUSAN E. DOCHERTY

28. Portraits of Women 525
    SUSAN E. MYERS

29. Gender 543
    JOSHUA M. RENO AND STEPHEN P. AHEARNE-KROLL

30. Body 565
    STEPHEN D. MOORE

Index 585

Notes on Contributors

Stephen P. Ahearne-Kroll is the Sundet Family Chair in New Testament and Christian Studies at the University of Minnesota. He is the author of *The Psalms of Lament in Mark's Gospel* (2007); coeditor, with P. A. Holloway and J. A. Kelhoffer, of *Women and Gender in Ancient Religion* (2010); and author of many essays and articles on the Gospel of Mark, including the commentary on Mark in *The Jerome Biblical Commentary for the Twenty-First Century* (2022). He is currently writing *A Chord of Gods: Corinthian Reception of Paul's God and the Origins of the Jesus Movement*.

Soham Al-Suadi is Professor of New Testament Studies at the University of Rostock (Germany). She has published on early Christian rituals with a focus on meals. She is member of the steering committee of the SBL Seminar "Meals in the Greco-Roman World." Her most recent book is *Ritual, Emotion, and Materiality in the Early Christian World* (2021).

James W. Barker is Associate Professor of New Testament at Western Kentucky University. He is a recipient of the Paul J. Achtemeier Award for New Testament Scholarship (2014) and the author of *John's Use of Matthew* (2015) and *Tatian's Diatessaron: Composition, Redaction, Recension, and Reception* (2021). He is currently writing a book on John's use of the Synoptics.

Eve-Marie Becker is Professor of New Testament at the University of Münster and author of numerous books, articles, and essays on a variety of topics in New Testament studies. Most recently, she is author of *Paul on Humility* (2020), *Der Philipperbrief des Paulus: Vorarbeiten zu einem Kommentar* (2020), and *The Birth of Christian History: Memory and Time from Mark to Luke-Acts* (2017).

Thomas R. Blanton IV is Associated Fellow at the Max Weber Centre for Advanced Cultural and Social Studies, University of Erfurt. The author of *A Spiritual Economy: Gift Exchange in the Letters of Paul of Tarsus* (Yale University Press, 2017) and coeditor, with Raymond Pickett, of *Paul and Economics: A Handbook* (Fortress Press, 2017), he is currently writing a monograph on Abraham and circumcision for the Anchor Yale Bible Reference Library.

Alexander Damm is Instructor in the Department of Religion and Culture, Wilfrid Laurier University, Ontario. He is author of *Ancient Rhetoric and the Synoptic Problem* (2013) and editor of *Religions and Education in Antiquity* (2018) and *Gandhi in a Canadian Context* (2016).

Michal Beth Dinkler is Associate Professor of New Testament at Yale Divinity School. Recent publications include *Influence: On Rhetoric and Biblical Interpretation* (Brill) and *Literary Theory and the New Testament* (Yale University Press). She is currently writing *How to Do Things with Stories: Early Christian Narrative as Rhetoric* and *The Gospel of Luke; New International Greek Testament Series*, as well as coediting *The Oxford Handbook of the Gospel of Luke and Acts of the Apostles* with Gregory Sterling.

Susan E. Docherty is Professor of New Testament and Early Judaism at Newman University, Birmingham. She is Chair of the Annual (Hawarden) Seminar on the Use of the OT in the NT and has published widely on the interpretation of scripture in early Jewish and early Christian literature. Her recent publications include *The Jewish Pseudepigrapha* (Fortress, 2015) and, with Beate Kowalski, *Let My People Go: The Reception of Exodus Motifs in Jewish and Christian Literature* (Brill, 2021). Her substantial studies "Israel's Scriptures in the Dead Sea Scrolls" and "Biblical Interpretation in the Apocrypha" are forthcoming.

Cameron Evan Ferguson is Area Coordinator and adjunct faculty at Carroll College. He is the author of *A New Perspective on the Use of Paul in the Gospel of Mark* (Routledge, 2021). He is co-editor with Calvin Roetzel of *Paul: The Man and the Myth, Revised and Expanded Edition* (forthcoming), and a translator for the forthcoming New Tyndale Version (NTV).

Paul Foster is Professor of New Testament and Early Christianity in the School of Divinity at the University of Edinburgh. Recent publications include *Colossians*, BNTC (2016) and *The Gospel of Peter: Introduction, Critical Edition and Commentary*, TENT 4 (2010). He is currently completing a book on the Apostolic Fathers and writing a commentary on the Gospel of Matthew.

Joshua D. Garroway is Sol and Arlene Bronstein Professor of Judaeo-Christian Studies at Hebrew Union College-Jewish Institute of Religion, Los Angeles. He is author of *The Beginning of the Gospel: Paul, Philippi, and the Origins of Christianity* (2018) and *Paul's Gentile-Jews: Neither Jew nor Gentile, but Both* (2012).

Meghan Henning is Associate Professor of Christian Origins at the University of Dayton. She is author of *Educating Early Christians through the Rhetoric of Hell: Weeping and Gnashing of Teeth in Matthew and the Early Church* (2014) and *Hell Hath No Fury: Gender, Disability, and the Invention of Damned Bodies in Early Christian Literature* (2021). Her forthcoming books are *Vivid Rhetoric in the New Testament: Visual Persuasion and Ekphrasis in Early Christian Literature* (coauthor Nils Neumann) and *Apocalypse of Peter: A Commentary* (Hermeneia).

Lee A. Johnson is Associate Professor of Religious Studies at East Carolina University, Greenville, NC. She is the author of numerous articles related to the interface between written texts and oral culture, published in the *Oral History Journal of South Africa, Catholic Biblical Quarterly,* and *Biblical Theology Bulletin* and is completing a monograph on Paul's letters as performed correspondence: *Presenting Paul: Success and Failure of a Letter-Writer in a Non-literate Culture*.

John Kampen is a Distinguished Research Professor at the Methodist Theological School in Ohio, Delaware, OH and professor at Hebrew Union College, Cincinnati and a specialist in the Dead Sea Scrolls, the Gospel of Matthew, and Jewish history of the Greco-Roman period. Most recently, he is author of *Matthew within Sectarian Judaism* (2019) and *Wisdom Literature* (Eerdmans Commentaries on the Dead Sea Scrolls, 2011).

Alan Kirk is Professor of Religion at James Madison University, Harrisonburg, VA. Recent publications include *Memory and the Jesus Tradition* (2019) and *Q in Matthew* (2016). His current work-in-progress is *Gospel Tradition, Gospel Writing, and Jesus Quests: The Synoptic Problem and Scholarship's Long Search for the Authentic Source*.

John S. Kloppenborg is Fellow of the Royal Society of Canada and University Professor at the University of Toronto. His recent publications are *Christ's Associations: Connecting and Belonging in the Ancient City* (2019), *Synoptic Problems* (2014), vols. 1 (with Richard Ascough) and 3 of *Greco-Roman Associations: Texts, Translations, and Commentary* (2011, 2020), and *The Tenants in the Vineyard: Ideology, Economics, and Agrarian Conflict in Jewish Palestine* (2006).

Matthew Larsen is Associate Professor of New Testament at the University of Copenhagen. He is the author of *Gospels before the Book* (2018) and the forthcoming *Ancient Mediterranean Incarceration*, with coauthor Mark Letteney, and *Early Christians and Incarceration: A Cultural History*.

Timothy Luckritz Marquis is Instructional Designer at Virginia Commonwealth University. He is the author of *Transient Apostle: Paul, Travel, and the Rhetoric of Empire* (2013) and other pieces on the intersections of travel, ethnicity, gender, and sexuality in the Roman period. He is currently completing a book on itinerancy and Christian origins.

Stephen D. Moore is Edmund S. Janes Professor of New Testament Studies at the Theological School, Drew University. He is author, editor, coauthor, or coeditor of more than two dozen books, most recently *The Bible after Deleuze: Affects, Assemblages, Bodies without Organs* (2023) and *Decolonial Theory and Biblical Unreading* (forthcoming).

Candida R. Moss is Edward Cadbury Professor of Theology at the University of Birmingham. She is author of *The Other Christs* (2010), *Myth of Persecution* (2013), *Ancient Christian Martyrdom* (2012), *Divine Bodies* (2019), *Reconceiving Infertility* with coauthor Joel S. Baden (2015), *Bible Nation* with coauthor Joel S. Baden (2017). She is currently completing *Mark: A Biography* and a book on enslaved literate workers and the New Testament.

Susan E. Myers is Associate Professor in the Theology Department at the University of St. Thomas, St. Paul, MN. She is author of *Spirit Epicleses in the Acts of Thomas*; editor of *Portraits of Jesus*; and coeditor of *Friars and Jews in the Middle Ages and Renaissance*.

Brent Nongbri is Professor of History of Religions at MF Norwegian School of Theology, Religion and Society, Oslo. He is author of *God's Library: The Archaeology of the Earliest Christian Manuscripts* (2018) and *Before Religion: A History of a Modern Concept* (2013). He is leader of the project The Early History of the Codex: A New Methodology and Ethics for Manuscript Studies (2021–26), sponsored by the Research Council of Norway.

Michael Peppard is Professor of Theology at Fordham University in New York. He is the author of *The Son of God in the Roman World* (Oxford University Press, 2011), *The World's Oldest Church: Bible, Art, and Ritual at Dura-Europos, Syria* (Yale University Press, 2016), and many articles on the Gospels and their reception.

Joshua M. Reno is a Lecturer in the Department of Classics at the University of Illinois Urbana-Champaign. His research covers discourse(s) around sex work in Greek and Roman literature. He is the author of several essays on sex, gender, and the Pauline epistles, most recently "Pornographic Desire in the Pauline Corpus" (*JBL*, 2021). He is currently completing a book on Pauline sexual invective.

Sarah E. Rollens is R. A. Webb Associate Professor of Religious Studies at Rhodes College in Memphis, TN. She is the author of *Framing Social Criticism in the Jesus Movement: The Ideological Project of the Sayings Source Q* (2014). She has written numerous articles and essays on the social worlds and experiences of the earliest Christ followers, as well as on theory and method in the academic study of religion.

Melissa Harl Sellew is Professor Emerita of Classical and Near Eastern Studies at the University of Minnesota and Adjunct Professor of New Testament at United Theological Seminary in St. Paul. Her publications focus largely on the gospels of Mark, Luke, and Thomas, as well as Coptic hagiographical and hymnic texts. She is the editor or coeditor of four collections: *Pauline Conversations in Context* (2002); *The Fabric of Early Christianity* (2006); *Living for Eternity: The White Monastery and Its Neighborhood* (2010); and the forthcoming *Trans Biblical*.

Alexey Somov is Associate Professor of the New Testament at St. Philaret's Orthodox Christian Institute, Moscow, Russia, and Research Fellow at the Department of the Old and New Testament (Faculty of Theology), University of Stellenbosch, South Africa. He is the author of *Representations of the Afterlife in Luke-Acts* (2017). He also works as a translation consultant with the Institute for Bible Translation in Moscow.

Janet E. Spittler is Associate Professor of Religious Studies at the University of Virginia. She is the author of *Animals in the Apocryphal Acts of the Apostles* (2008) and numerous articles on apocryphal Christian narratives.

Karen Wenell is Associate Professor in New Testament and Theology at the University of Birmingham. She is coeditor of *Constructions of Space III: Biblical Spatiality and the Sacred* (2019) and author of *Jesus and Land: Sacred and Social Space in Second Temple Judaism* (2007) and of the forthcoming *Locating the Kingdom of God*. She was Principal

Investigator on the Arts and Humanities Research Council Network Grant "Women, Faith, and Humanitarian Interventions," part of the Global Challenges Research Fund.

Robyn J. Whitaker is Senior Lecturer in New Testament at Pilgrim Theological College, University of Divinity, Parkville, Australia. She is author of *Ekphrasis, Vision and Persuasion in the Book of Revelation* (2015) and has published several articles on the Synoptic Gospels. She is currently coediting a volume of feminist essays on terror and violence in the Bible and writing a book on biblical hermeneutics.

Magnus Zetterholm is Senior Lecturer and Associate Professor of New Testament Studies at Lund University, Sweden. He is coeditor of *Paul within Judaism: Restoring the First-Century Context to the Apostle* (with Mark D. Nanos, 2015) and *The Making of Christianity: Conflicts, Contacts, and Constructions* (with Samuel Byrskog, 2012); author of *Approaches to Paul* (2009); and author of numerous articles and essays on the intersection of early Judaism and the early Jesus movement.

Introduction

Stephen P. Ahearne-Kroll

The field of Synoptic studies traditionally has had two basic foci. The question of how Matthew, Mark, and Luke are related to each other, what their sources are, and how the Gospels use their sources constitutes the first focus. Collectively, scholarship on the Synoptic Problem has tried to address these issues, and recent years have seen renewed interest and rigorous debate about some of the traditional approaches to the Synoptic Problem and how these approaches might inform the understanding of the origins of the early Jesus movement. The second focus involves thematic studies across the three Gospels. These are usually, but not exclusively, performed for theological purposes to tease out the early Jesus movement's thinking about the nature of Jesus, the motivations for his actions, the meaning of his death and resurrection, and his relationship to God. These studies pay less attention to the particular voices of the three individual Synoptic Gospels because they are trying to get to the overall theological character of Jesus.

This book takes a different approach to the study of the Synoptics. Instead of the two traditional foci just described, its two parts are titled "The Problem and Nature of the Synoptics" and "Particular Features in Comparison." A few of the essays in Part I include discussion of the sources for the Synoptics, literary dependence, and the development of the written forms of these Gospels (Kloppenborg, Foster, and Barker [to a certain extent], chapters 1–3 here). At the most basic level, the Synoptic Problem assumes a stable text tradition, usually starting with the Gospel of Mark, although there have been and remain some challenges to Mark's temporal primacy. The work of theorizing dependence happens at the level of individual words, phrases, and pericopae, with the arguments for certain use of one text by another being quite detailed and intricate. Teasing out solutions to the Synoptic problem usually dominates this area of research, and in recent years, there has been an uptick in debate about the Synoptic problem and its solutions. While some form of the two-source hypothesis still holds sway with most scholars, there has been an effort to revisit earlier theories that question the existence of Q and/or the independence of Matthew and Luke.

Other interesting questions have arisen regarding the tools used to evaluate literary dependence beyond that of traditional source criticism and redaction criticism, while maintaining the value of these methods. Creative studies have been performed on the way that sources were used by other ancient authors to contextualize how the Synoptic authors might be using their sources (Barker, chapter 3 here). In addition, ancient rhetoric has been studied as a model for how the gospels present their stories in relation to each other as a way of detecting or confirming dependence (Damm, chapter 4). Therefore, the study of ancient composition practices holds a great deal of potential for providing a deeper understanding of the relationships among Matthew, Mark, and Luke, and so several essays address these issues. The oral nature of the Synoptics also raises questions about the arguments for literary dependence, and the interrelation of orality and writing is precisely the topic of Kirk's essay (chapter 6), while Johnson explores the oral performance of the Synoptics as an integral part of their nature (chapter 7). Two essays take up the analysis of the literary design of the Synoptics and its ramifications for their nature. Ferguson (chapter 5) develops a distinct way of understanding Paul's possible influence on the Gospel of Mark, which in turn affects Matthew's and Luke's appropriation of the Pauline tradition, assuming traditional Synoptic relations along the lines of the two-source hypothesis. And Dinkler (chapter 8) addresses the literary design of the Synoptics through the tools of New Formalism, which focuses its attention on narrative form and structure, while addressing critiques of formalism's earlier iterations.

One also can recognize that the plurality of manuscript traditions has to come into play when thinking about literary dependence and the Synoptic Problem. There has been some creative new work about how to think about the end of the publication process of the Gospels, which Larsen (chapter 10) addresses, and the work of text criticism in this question, which Nongbri (chapter 9) explores. With the plurality of "final" versions a clear phenomenon, what can be said about literary dependence must be raised as a fundamental question regarding Synoptic relationships and the Synoptic Problem. Larsen's and Nongbri's work poses the most fundamental challenges to the Synoptic Problem, along with Kirk's and Johnson's, because all these essays either directly challenge the stability of the early versions of the text or rightly recognize the fluidity of orality as a characteristic of the tradition. Finally, taking the Synoptics a generation or two into the future, Spittler's and Sellew's essays discuss the noncanonical Gospels in relation to the Synoptics to see what light they might shed on the compositional processes (Spittler, chapter 11) and the content of both (in comparison to the Gospel of Thomas; Sellew, chapter 12). While the essays in Part I recognize the importance of the history of scholarship on Synoptic relations, the various ways of understanding the nature of the Synoptics demonstrated in these essays show the complexity of these traditions about Jesus that needs to be grappled with in order to understand more fully the nature of their relationship. This complexity shows that scholars cannot rely on the traditional assumptions that ground the theories of literary dependence in trying to solve the Synoptic Problem.

The studies in Part II fall under the general rubric of thematic studies of the Synoptic Gospels. Traditionally, topics like Jesus, discipleship, justice, love, parables, miracles, and so on are treated thematically across the Synoptics without much attention to the ways that each Synoptic author expresses his own voice through the use of these topics.

In addition, there is usually little attention paid to the greater context of the Synoptics in Judaism and Greek and Roman culture. This gives the impression that the Synoptics were written in a vacuum or that they were major literary works of the ancient world. Neither of these impressions is close to reality, of course, because the Synoptics were minority writings within a minority sect of Judaism, which itself was a diverse minority culture within the dominant Roman culture of the time. Part II takes a different approach to the way topics are handled in Synoptic studies. Most of the essays in Part II are comparative in two ways—among each Gospel and between the Gospels and other expressions of the topic in Jewish, Greek, and Roman contexts. But the essays that keep the discussion mostly on the Synoptics also give voice to each individual Gospel to convey the diversity of expression and preserve the author's perspective as much as possible. Overall, the idea is to capture the similarities *and* differences in the presentation of the topics in each Gospel, and to situate the Gospels in a wider frame of reference.

The topics reflect a combination of some traditional categories and some less traditional categories. Early on a decision was made not to cover many of the traditional categories often found in books on the Synoptics (e.g., parables, discipleship, Christology, etc.). These traditional topics are important to understand, but it was felt that there was already so much written on them that is easily accessible in other books that this book would risk redundancy by including them. Where the essays in Part II do cover more traditional topics (kingdom, suffering, healing, resurrection and afterlife, etc.), the authors have worked to come at the topics in a comparative way that sheds new light on how these features of the Synoptics are not monoliths inserted into the literature but particular expressions of these general topics (e.g., Henning, Whitaker, Somov, chapters 19, 22, 23). And this particularity grounds all of the essays in Part II. Instead of mining the Synoptics for evidence to build abstracted notions of the themes, there is a real and consistent effort in these essays to describe the evidence in the Synoptics in its own context. Each essay topic performs an interesting analysis that brings out the distinct voices of each Gospel, alongside the similarities that exist across the Gospels.

There is a richness to Part II that shows the power of the approach the authors have taken in exploring the Synoptics from a number of different perspectives. They raise important questions of power (Rollens, Peppard, chapters 14 and 15) and the social consequences of it (Moss, Blanton, Luckritz Marquis, and Al-Suadi, chapters 13, 16, 17, and 18). They address the social nature of these traditions (Kampen, Zetterholm, and Reno and Ahearne-Kroll, chapters 25, 26, and 29) and the literary expression of these social realities (Rollens, Myers, Reno and Ahearne-Kroll, and Moore, chapters 14, 28, 29, and 30). And they explore in depth how the traditions of Israel have shaped the concerns of the Synoptic authors (Whitaker, Garroway, Kampen, Zetterholm, and Docherty, chapters 22, 24, 25, 26, and 27). As a whole, the essays in Part II beg the question whether or not "Synoptic" is the best way to describe these three Gospels.

The book as a whole provides thirty studies that substantially contribute to the field of Synoptic studies, moving it forward in interesting ways and providing the groundwork for a new generation of scholars to pursue the directions initiated by the book's contributors.

Many of the essays in this book were written and edited during the deadly global pandemic originating in late 2019 and continuing on up through the final stages of the production of the book. The difficulties the pandemic presented for finishing this book in a timely manner were substantial, and I am deeply thankful to the contributors for their excellent scholarship, prompt responses, and patient endurance as we completed this book. I am also very grateful to Kristofer Coffman and Kristi Lee, who helped a great deal in the formatting and editing of the manuscript. Their futures are bright in Synoptic studies and in the study of religion within the broad landscape of ancient culture.

While Kristofer, Kristi, and all the contributors persevered in their excellent work throughout the pandemic, our efforts do not compare to those of the millions who have suffered and endured real hardship across the globe since late 2019, from the frontline workers of all statuses, who have helped care for, feed, and clothe victims and develop therapies and vaccines, to those who have contracted the virus and struggled for their lives and health. Their work far outshines any scholarship, no matter the level of excellence.

And so this book is dedicated to all those affected by this modern plague, especially the millions who have lost their lives and millions more of their family members who keep their memories alive.

PART I

THE PROBLEM AND NATURE OF THE SYNOPTIC GOSPELS

CHAPTER 1

THE HISTORY AND PROSPECTS OF THE SYNOPTIC PROBLEM

JOHN S. KLOPPENBORG

Early History

DISCREPANCIES among the Synoptic Gospels were noticed almost from the beginning. Origen (c. 184–c. 253 CE) attributed some of the disagreements to the carelessness of copyists but reported that some critics argued that more serious discrepancies were the work of forgers (*radiouroi*; *Comm. Jo.* 32.32, §395). When Origen himself was unable to harmonize the literal sense of one Gospel with another, he resorted to the explanation that such discrepancies pointed to the need for a nonliteral, pneumatic interpretation (*Princ.* 4.3.5).

Origen's apologetic approach did not end the problem. Porphyry (c. 234–c. 305 CE) mounted a concerted attack on Christianity, arguing that Christian teachings were conceptually incoherent, and adduced many seemingly irreconcilable contradictions in parallel Gospel accounts, such as discrepancies in the details of Jesus's death (Porphyry, according to Macarius, *Apocriticus* 2.12). Eusebius, like Origen, responded that when details could not be reconciled at the level of literal meaning, a pneumatic interpretation was intended. But Eusebius's more lasting contribution was his division of the text of the four Gospels into pericopae and his organization of each into one of ten "canons"— lists of pericopae that are attested in all four Gospels, in three Gospels, in two, or singly (Oliver 1959). These canons would come to guide the construction of Gospel harmonies that aimed at a single harmonious narrative which obviated sequential and other discrepancies.

The Eusebian canons informed the construction of Augustine's *De consensu evangelistarum* (c. 400 CE). In Books 2–3 Augustine chose to start with Canons I–VII— the pericopae in which Matthew had a story or saying paralleled in three, two, one or no other gospel., In these pericopae, Augustine argued that disagreements in the sequence of pericopae were only due to the ways in which the evangelists happened to remember those events, since each knew very well the supposedly original sequence. Disagreements in wording were sometimes treated as no more than alternate ways of expressing the same idea. More serious discrepancies might point to the need for spiritual rather than literal interpretation. Book 4 examined the material in Mark and Luke alone (Canon VII), the Luke-John pericopae (Canon IX), and then the *Sondergut* (singly attested material, Canon X), in each case with the intent of showing that there were no real inconsistencies among the Gospels, since disagreements could be relegated to inconsequential variations, different memory choices, or the particular emphases of the evangelists.

Augustine offered several statements that have been taken to imply a primitive solution to the Synoptic Problem. The most widely cited is "Mark followed [Matthew] closely and looks like his attendant and epitomizer [pedissequus et breviator]. For in his narrative he gives nothing in concert with John apart from the others: by himself he has little to record; in conjunction with Luke, as distinguished from the rest, he has still less; but in concord with Matthew he has a very large number of passages. Much, too, he narrates in words almost numerically and identically the same as those used by Matthew, where the agreement is either with that evangelist alone, or with him in connection with the rest" (*Cons.* 1.2.4). The debt to Eusebius is obvious. The supposed lack of Mark's relationship to John or to Luke reflects the facts that Eusebius had omitted assembling canons for Mark-Luke-John or for Mark-John, and that Canon VII (Mark-Luke) had only thirteen items. Augustine seems to have forgotten that Canons I (all four Gospels), II (Matt-Mark-Luke) and IV (Matt-Mark-John), in which Markan material was tabulated, totaled 210 items. This oversight meant that Augustine supposed that Mark's primary relationship was to Matthew, which he assumed without argument was written first.[1]

It is doubtful, however, that Augustine was proposing a solution to the Synoptic Problem comparable to the "utilization hypotheses" of the nineteenth century, although many supposed that Augustine had proposed a literary explanation of the Gospels, with Matthew first, Mark using Matthew, and Luke using both (the so-called Augustinian solution). As a Platonist, he was much less interested in literal disagreements and agreements among the Gospels and literary genealogies than he was in the relationship of all four to the full Gospel of Christ, which each Gospel embodied in a partial and perspectival fashion (de Jonge 1992). For him, Matthew emphasized the royal aspect of Christ, Luke emphasized the priestly aspect, Mark was concerned with neither kingship nor priesthood, and John focused on divinity (*Cons.* 1.6.9).

Augustine's treatise was successful, however, in promoting the idea that a harmony of the Gospels could be constructed. Hundreds of harmonies were produced by the end of

---

[1] In book 4 Augustine (*De consensu* 4.10.11) seems to have recognized the oversight, there opining that while Mark was "preferentially the companion of Matthew" he sometimes "holds a course between the two [Matthew and Luke]."

the eighteenth century (Fabricius 1790–1809: 4:882–89; de Lang 1993). It was, perhaps ironically, the effort to produce a single harmonious narrative of the Gospels that led to the undoing of the effort, and the rebirth of the Synoptic Problem.

The Synoptic Problem, Sixteenth to Nineteenth Century

By the sixteenth century, two basic approaches to Gospel harmonies had been developed. The first adopted one Gospel, typically Matthew or John, as the lead text, and pericopae from the other Gospels were then merged with the lead text. This meant that both sequential and verbal disagreements were obviated. But the other approach, epitomized by the harmony of Alfons Osiander (1537), insisted on respecting the canonical wording and order of each Gospel, and so inevitably repeated stories and sayings. The result was absurd: Jesus was tempted three times; he acted against the temple three times; a centurion's son was healed twice (and a royal official's son once); Jesus was anointed by three different women; and he was betrayed by Judas twice (see de Lang 2019; Dungan 1999, 306).

These harmonizing projects presented easy targets for rationalist criticism. In 1778 Gottfried Lessing published a supposedly anonymous essay in which the author (in fact, Herrmann Samuel Reimarus) attacked the credibility of the Gospel accounts by focusing in detail on their numerous contradictions. These contradictions, he argued, suggested that Jesus's disciples had falsified stories about Jesus, fabricated miracle stories, and invented the entire idea of a resurrection (Reimarus 1778; ET 1970). In their fabrications, they had also produced conflicting and incoherent accounts, which Reimarus took as evidence of fraud. Reimarus's essay sent shock waves through academic circles, since it threatened to undermine the historical and theological value of the Gospels and to render the knowledge of the historical Jesus impossible. The reaction was a series of compositional scenarios that could both account for the differences among the Gospels and yet preserve the possibility of access to the earliest "original" layers of the tradition.

Lessing himself posited the existence of an Aramaic proto-gospel (*Urgospel*) translated into Greek by Matthew in its most complete form, but in different versions by Mark and Luke (Lessing 1784). A more complicated form of the *Urgospel* hypothesis was advanced by J. G. Eichhorn, who hypothesized four intermediate recensions of the *Urgospel* that eventually led to the three Synoptics (Eichhorn 1794). Another approach was to posit an original oral proto-gospel (*Ur-Markus*), which was put into to writing as canonical Mark, expanded and written down as proto-Matthew (later translated into Greek as canonical Matthew), and was in turn revised as Luke (Herder 1796). Neither the *Urgospel* hypotheses nor the oral tradition hypothesis posited a direct relationship between any of the canonical Gospels; the relationship among the three was mediated either by the written *Urgospel*, intermediate recensions, or the oral Gospel. Each of these hypotheses offered ways to account for the differences in sequence and wording of Gospel stories and sayings, tracing the variations to differing translations of the same Aramaic original, to the vagaries of oral transmission, to recensional activities, or a combination of these explanations. Each also made it possible to imagine the recovery of a set of reliable historical traditions about Jesus, even if those traditions were at some remove from the Greek canonical Gospels.

A very different approach was proposed by Johann Jakob Griesbach. Griesbach's signal innovation was the development of a three-gospel synopsis that was intentionally *not* designed to facilitate the creation of a harmonious life of Jesus (1776). Gospels were aligned in three vertical columns, which made it simple to compare the wording of each Gospel with the others. Greisbach's synopsis also allowed each of the Synoptic Gospels to be read continuously in its canonical sequence while at the same time displaying the parallel accounts in the other two Synoptics. Griesbach provided visual indications of sequential agreements and disagreements by means of vertical intercolumn lines alongside any text that was printed out of canonical sequence. This made visible the *internal order* of the Synoptics, that is, where any two of the Synoptics agreed sequentially and where any one Gospel departed from a common sequence. What became clear was that Mark's internal sequence was supported by either Matthew or Luke or both, or, to put it differently, Mark's order of pericopae agreed either with Matthew's or Luke's order but had almost no independent order.

Three developments followed from this. First, J. B. Koppe pointed out that the "Augustinian" sequence of Matthew → Mark → Luke, with Luke using both his predecessors, was unintelligible: for when Mark deviates from Matthew's sequence, he always agrees with Luke (Koppe 1782). This would mean that Luke always preferred Mark's order to Matthew's whenever Mark deviated from Matthew, even though Luke could see Matthew's order of material. But no rationale could be given for such an idiosyncratic procedure. The second development was an alternative, proposed by Gottlob Christian Storr, who contended that Mark was the earliest of the Gospels, used first by Luke, and then by Matthew, who also used Luke (Storr 1786). The phenomenon of order observable in Griesbach's synopsis was explicable on this view, for it meant that sometimes Luke sided with Mark's order, and sometimes altered it, and likewise Matthew usually agreed with Mark but sometimes deviated. Yet Storr's hypothesis that Matthew also used Luke inevitably raised the question, why did Matthew never agree with Luke's sequence against Mark?

The final development was Griesbach's own thesis, which reversed the "Augustinian" relation between Mark and Luke, arguing that Mark had abbreviated and conflated the two other Gospels, but in such a way that whenever he departed from Matthew's sequence, he turned to Luke's (1789–90; ET 1978). Hence, Mark followed one of his sources, then the other, producing a "zigzag" effect.[2]

---

[2] This is visually represented in Meijboom 1991, 152–53.

The important difference between Griesbach and Storr's solutions and those of Lessing and Eichhorn was that the former were "utilization hypotheses" that assumed the direct dependence of one Gospel upon another rather than positing otherwise unknown intermediate texts. This also meant that Griesbach (and Storr) could not rely on such explanations as translation variants to account for the differences among Gospels but had to posit editorial policies on the part of the secondary evangelists. Griesbach, for example, explained Mark's omission of the infancy accounts of Matthew and Luke by asserting that Mark was only interested in Jesus as a teacher. He offered other explanations, mostly deductions from his own hypothesis (hence circular)—that Mark wanted to write a short book and hence omitted the long sermons of Matthew and Luke.

Griesbach's hypothesis (GH) languished for three decades until the thesis of Markan posteriority was revived by De Wette, who rejected Griesbach's view of the relation of Luke to Matthew, proposing instead that both drew on oral tradition and an Aramaic *Urgospel* (de Wette 1826). Until 1860 the GH enjoyed wide acceptance—de Wette counted fifteen major advocates from 1805 to 1853 (1860, 150–52), and the more extensive bibliography of Neirynck and Van Segbroeck (1978) lists almost forty titles before 1880.

For de Wette, the GH exemplified a schema of theological development. Matthew represented Jewish Christianity; Alexandrian or Hellenistic Christianity was epitomized in John and Hebrews; and Pauline Christianity embodied a universalism that had influenced Luke (de Wette 1813, 19–20). A similar scheme had been adopted by the Tübingen school and its doyen, F. C. Baur, who offered a comprehensive theory of the history of dogma based on the fundamental opposition between Jewish Christianity and Paulinism and the eventual resolution of this conflict in catholicism. Matthew's Jewish-Christian Gospel was composed after the Bar Kochba revolt. Luke represented an irenic blend of Pauline and Jewish elements, written in response to Marcion's use of an earlier draft of Luke, but incorporating a decidedly Pauline and universalist outlook. Mark's "indifferent and neutral" character and its harmonistic nature was consistent with a date after the midpoint of the second century (Baur 1847, 567).[3]

By 1860, however, Baur had died, and most of the proponents of the Tübingen school had defected to other synoptic theories and other disciplines.[4] What came to replace the GH owed much to an essay by Friedrich Schleiermacher (1832) and another by the text critic Karl Lachmann (1835; ET 1966–67). Schleiermacher, attracted by the statement of Papias that "Matthew compiled the λόγια [oracles] in the Hebrew language and each interpreted them as they were able" (Eusebius, *Hist. eccl.* 3.39.16), argued that Papias cannot have been speaking about canonical Matthew, which was written in Greek and was hardly a collection of "oracles." Instead, Schleiermacher surmised that Papias knew of a collection of sayings of Jesus that canonical Matthew translated and used in Matthew 5–7; 10; 13:1–52; 18; 23–25. For its narrative materials, canonical Matthew used

---

[3] See also Baur 1851 and Harris 1975, 237, for a convenient summary of Baur's dating of all New Testament books.

[4] The most erudite defense of the GH was by Meijboom 1866, whose Dutch dissertation was never published and was not translated into English until 1991.

another source that Papias had described as Peter's memoirs, collected by Mark and containing the things "said and done by the Lord" (Eusebius, *Hist. eccl.* 3.39.15).

These suggestions proved remarkably durable. In 1835, Lachmann examined the order of the synoptic tradition and concluded that canonical Mark better resembled the order of the primitive narrative gospel than either Matthew or Luke. Lachmann accepted Schleiermacher's conclusions about the λόγια as "obviously true" (Lachmann 1835, 577) as well as his supposition of a narrative source behind Matthew. The content of the synoptic tradition convinced him that Griesbach had underestimated the importance of Mark. When one compared the order of the pericopae, the greatest degree of disagreement was registered between Matthew and Luke; Mark tended to agree with either one or the other. Mark, however, better represented the primitive order than Matthew or Luke. Matthew's divergences from the order of Mark and Luke could be explained by supposing that Matthew, influenced by the sequence of the λόγια, moved some sections from his narrative source so that they might function better in relation to the sayings sources. The converse, that Mark remodeled the narrative source, was unlikely, since his Gospel was uninfluenced by the λόγια source. Thus, there would be no reason for Mark to rearrange narrative materials that he found in Matthew.

In 1838 C. H. Weisse combined the insights of Schleiermacher and Lachmann along with a rejection of the late dating of the Gospels current in the Tübingen school to propose what might be seen as a forerunner to the Two Document hypothesis (2DH): canonical Mark and Papias's Mark were identical, for not only did Mark seem to be the common denominator between Matthew and Luke, but Mark also seemed more primitive. Luke had, like canonical Matthew, used both Mark and the λόγια source (1838, 1:34, 48, 54).

Despite advocating Markan priority, Weisse did not think that Mark always embodied reliable historical memories. On the contrary, it contained stories that had begun as myths that had been historicized as narratives about Jesus. Weisse also expressed some embarrassment over the fact that the two initial pericopae in the λόγια source: Luke 3:7–9, 16–17; 4:1–13 were either not sayings of Jesus or not sayings at all (1838, 2:5). The source also contained a narrative about the centurion's serving boy and the Beelzebul accusation. Weisse had relieved this embarrassment by suggesting that the sayings now attributed to the Baptist were originally Jesus's sayings about John and that the temptation story and the healing of the centurion's serving boy originated as parables of Jesus that had been converted into narratives (1838, 2:8, 17–26, 53–55).

When Weisse revisited the Synoptic Problem in 1856, he felt obliged to modify his hypothesis, reintroducing *Ur-Markus*. Weisse decided, evidently out of loyalty to Schleiermacher's understanding of λόγια as "oracles," that it was better to attribute at least John's sayings (Luke 3:7–9, 16–17), the temptation story, and the story of the centurion to an *Ur-Markus* rather than to the λόγια (1856, 156–57). Hence canonical Mark abbreviated *Ur-Markus*, while Matthew and Luke fused *Ur-Markus* with the λόγια source.

Weisse's 1838 book did not attract followers, and his 1856 work was not much more successful. The turning point in the discussion of the Synoptic Problem came seven years later with the publication of Holtzmann's *Die synoptischen Evangelien* (1863), which is often credited with definitively establishing the 2DH. It is, however, probably more accurate to say that Holtzmann's position triumphed not so much because it had satisfactorily dispatched alternate solutions and had provided compelling arguments for itself as because the thesis of Markan priority was seen to fit with the emerging theological commitments of liberal theology.

Holtzmann was influenced by Weisse's 1856 proposals, in particular the notion of an *Ur-Markus*. Although he supposed that canonical Mark was closer to *Ur-Markus* than the other Synoptics, it differed from *Ur-Markus* (A) in five important respects: (1) at several points Mark contained obscurities that were the result of abbreviation;[5] (2) Mark had legendary—hence secondary—elements not found in the parallel accounts (e.g. Mark 7:24–31); (3) Mark might have shortened the originally longer speeches of John the Baptist and Jesus; (4) the minor agreements of Matthew and Luke against Mark (Holtzmann lists 36) suggested that canonical Mark was secondary to A; (5) at some points Matthaean and Lukan scenes displayed better internal coherence than the Markan parallel (e.g. Mark 10:23; 10:49).

This meant that A contained a longer form of the words of the Baptist (Matt 3:7–12; Luke 3:7–9, 16–17) than was present in Mark, the long form of the temptation story, a version of the inaugural Sermon (Luke 6:20–49), the story of the centurion's serving boy (Matt 8:5–13 // Luke 7:1–10), and an expanded version of the Beelzebul accusation. Holtzmann also assigned the story of the adulterous woman from John (7:53–8:11) and the great commissioning from Matthew (28:9–10, 16–20) to A. Correspondingly, this implied that the other source, the λόγια (Λ), lacked the double tradition material—the material common to Matthew and Luke but absent from Mark—in Luke 3:7–17, 4:1–13, 6:20–49, and 7:1–10.

This conclusion may appear puzzling, since the sermon in Luke 6:20–49 would seem to fit Holtzmann's Λ (sayings source). What had influenced Holtzmann was an alleged "textual gap" detected by Heinrich Ewald at Mark 3:19, 20—the call of the Twelve concluded with "and he went home" (Mark 3:19), but what follows is not an event about Capernaum but the Beelzebul accusation, which has its own introduction, instead. Moreover, neither Matthew nor Luke recorded a parallel to Mark 3:20–21. Ewald surmised that, in the early version of Mark, the Sermon on the Mount and the story of the centurion's serving boy originally filled this gap (1850, 208–9). Holtzmann did not believe that the lengthy Matthaean sermon occurred there but agreed in assigning the substance of the shorter Lukan sermon (6:20–49) and the healing in Luke 7:1–10 to A.

Holtzmann also agreed with Weisse on another crucial point: Λ contained only sayings of Jesus (Holtzmann 1863, 142). To have included in Λ narratives such as the temptation story and the healing in Luke 7 or the sayings of John the Baptist in Luke 3 would have made Λ into an "evangelical narrative" with the very characteristics of the canonical Gospels. Hence, Holtzmann withheld from Λ any narrative elements. He detected,

---

[5] Holtzmann (1863, 60) mentions Mark 1:13, 3:22, and 14:65 ("prophesy"). The last presupposes Luke 22:64, "who struck you?"

nevertheless, a certain appropriateness in having the second source begin with Luke 7:18–35: "just as A began with the appearance of the Baptist, so Λ began appropriately with a statement of Jesus concerning the significance and import of John (Luke 7:18–35 = Matt 11:2–11, 16–19) relating to this ἀρχὴ τοῦ εὐαγγελίου ('beginning of the gospel')" (1863, 143). The lasting influence of Schleiermacher's λόγια can be seen in both Weisse and Holtzmann, dictating a reconstruction of the second synoptic source in accordance with an implicit and wholly undefended notion of generic purity: the λόγια source can only have included sayings. This is ironic in the case of Holtzmann, for notwithstanding his use of the term Λ (which obviously was a gesture toward Papias's λογία), the testimony of Papias played very little role in Holtzmann's argument. Holtzmann's positing of Λ followed from his argument that A was prior to Matthew and Luke, and that Matthew was independent of Luke. This created as its corollary the need to posit a source to account for the material (mostly sayings) that Matthew and Luke had which they did not obtain from Mark. He only considered Papias's testimony, treating it as ancillary confirmation of his proposal, once he had provided the logical grounds for positing a sayings source (1863, 252). Moreover, while previous speculations that the structure of the λόγια source began with Matthew's five well-organized speeches, Holtzmann argued that Matthew appeared to have rearranged the speech material, conflating it with pericopae from A to create those five speeches. Luke better represented the order and character of Λ. Hence, Holtzmann's "second synoptic source" bore little real resemblance to Papias's putative Aramaic "oracles" or to Schleiermacher's collection of Matthaean speeches except insofar as they too were exclusively sayings.

The architecture of Holtzmann's argument for "the Markan hypothesis" left much to be desired. William Farmer complained that Holtzmann's argument and those that followed him were "not based upon a firm grasp of the primary phenomena of the Gospels themselves, but upon an artificial and deceptive consensus among scholars of differing traditions of Gospel criticism" (1964, 38). It is certainly true that Holtzmann did not begin with a detailed analysis of the patterns of agreements and disagreements among the Gospels in sequence and in wording and the logical inferences that these patterns permit. Instead, he proceeded by cataloguing and evaluating the solutions proposed to date: neither Lessing's *Urgospel* hypothesis nor Herder's oral tradition hypothesis was plausible, since the various minute agreements among the Synoptics in the use of rare words (such as ἐπιούσιος in Matt 6:11 // Luke 11:3) or in phrases with complex word-order (e.g., Matt 12:27–28 // Luke 11:19–20) were simply inexplicable on hypotheses that posited independent renditions of oral tradition. Turning to the "utilization hypotheses," he listed all logically possible versions with their adherents but reduced the basic choice to two: either Matthew was primary and Mark secondary, or vice versa, since no one seriously defended Lukan priority.

At this point, Holtzmann invoked what he saw as a consensus of Synoptic scholarship: apart from the GH, which in his view was "without foundation," all agreed that the Synoptics depended upon a common *Grundschrift*. Here the consensus collapsed. Some favored a proto-Matthew, others favored a proto-Mark; some explained Luke with reference to proto-Mark, others with reference to Matthew (1863, 66).

What is problematic about Holtzmann's procedure is that he moved to an exposition of his own solution without resolving the disagreements that he had just enumerated. His procedure was to offer a post hoc rationalization of his own solution without seriously considering the alternatives. Instead, Holtzmann was content to give a plausible accounting of the later evangelists' procedures, given the assumption of their dependence on A and Λ, and only occasionally offered arguments concerning the direction of dependence.

Holtzmann's treatment of citations from the Hebrew Bible was better. He offered more clearly directional arguments, for he observed that whereas all of the citations taken from A were essentially Septuagintal, those added by Matthew showed more affinities with the Masoretic text (MT). For Holtzmann, it was rather unlikely that Mark could have used Matthew but avoided the bulk of Matthew's MT-leaning citations.[6]

Also more persuasive were Holtzmann's remarks on Matthew's and Luke's alterations of A. He noted that Matthew tended to be more concise than Mark but had also made sentences more complete in the interest of clarity. Matthew introduced various improvements, for example, replacing the awkward parenthesis in Mark 11:32 with a participial phrase and replacing Mark's dangling ἀλλ' ἵνα πληρωθῶσιν αἱ γραφαί ("but in order that the scriptures be fulfilled," Mark 14:49) with τοῦτο δὲ ὅλον γέγονεν ἵνα πληρωθῶσιν αἱ γραφαὶ τῶν προφητῶν ("all this happened so that the writings of the prophets would be fulfilled," Matt 26:56). Luke made analogous "improvements," using the optative mood in questions and replacing Mark's direct discourse with the more classical accusative-infinitive construction. Moreover, Holtzmann noted various points where Luke inadvertently betrayed knowledge of what was in Mark, even when he omitted the relevant portions of Mark. For example, Luke omitted Mark's explanation of the reason for Judas's kiss—"whoever I kiss is the one" (Mark 14:44; see Luke 22:47–48). Luke does so because he does not have Judas actually kiss Jesus; he only approaches in order to kiss him. Yet Luke presupposed this explanation by having Jesus say "Judas, do you betray the Son of man with a kiss?" (1863, 331–32).

If one looks to Holtzmann for a systematic proof of the 2DH, one will be disappointed. What he offered was a detailed exposition of Markan priority (or in fact, the priority of A), showing how it might plausibly account for the data. In this it must be said that his solution was coherent, but it must also be made clear that his defense of Markan priority did not logically imply the invalidity of other hypotheses, even if his successors assumed that it did. Eventually, Holtzmann modified the most awkward part of his hypothesis, namely the A (*Ur-Markus*) source. In 1863, he had attempted to explain Mark's omission of the sermon in A (= Luke 6:20–49) because the sermon was "too long for him" (1863, 116). However, Mark's apocalypse (13:5–35) and his parables discourse (4:1–34) are both longer than Luke 6:20–49 (Stoldt 1980, 76). In his 1886 introduction to the New Testament, Holtzmann dropped the idea of an *Ur-Markus* entirely (1886, 363–65;

---

[6] David New's investigation concludes (1) that the evidence of the use of biblical citations is consistent with the 2DH, (2) that none of the evidence clearly favors the GH, and (3) that eleven citations could be argued either way (1993, 121).

1892, 350). Although he did not offer a new catalogue of the contents of Λ, it would presumably now have contained at least some of the double tradition prior to Luke 7:18–35. Abandoning a pre-Markan source, however, also meant that Holtzmann lost a convenient way by which to explain the minor agreements of Matthew and Luke against Mark, and so he speculated on the possibility of sporadic influence of Matthew on Luke.

Holtzmann's case was regarded as so effective that subsequent generations of Synoptic scholars simply took his solution for granted. In the decades between 1863 and William Sanday's *Oxford Studies in the Synoptic Problem* (1911), only Meijboom's dissertation (1866) and Wernle's monograph (1899) qualify as substantial reviews of the problem. Why was the Markan hypothesis embraced as it was? In spite of Holtzmann's positing of a sayings source lying behind Matthew and Luke, there is no evidence that the appeal of Holtzmann's solution lay in a fascination with pre-gospel sources. Indeed it is surprising how little Λ figured in Holtzmann's book. His real interest was A and the way it might serve as the basis for a life of Jesus.

Holtzmann included in his 1863 monograph a sketch titled "The Life of Jesus according to the A Source," in which he used Markan material to circumscribe the development of Jesus's consciousness in seven identifiable stages (1863, 468–96). This he described as the most valuable result of his investigation. Indeed, his portrait of Jesus, as Schweitzer described it, became "the creed and catechism of all who handled the subject during the following decades" (Schweitzer 1906, 203; ET 1910, 204). On Holtzmann's showing, Mark (or A) lacked the "dogmatic" features that were so evident in both Matthew and Luke. The Markan Jesus was the epitome of "the clarity and harmony of what constitutes vigorous persons: the convergence of understanding, emotion, perception, presentiment, genuine simplicity, and innocence in which unrivalled versatility is crystallized with such a wonderful energy as has not been attested empirically elsewhere" (1863, 496; ET 2006, 222). This depiction eminently served the theological goals of liberal theology, with its strong antidogmatic agenda. Indeed, Schweitzer is correct in stating that "the victory . . . belonged, not to the Marcan hypothesis pure and simple, but to the Marcan hypothesis as psychologically interpreted by a liberal theology" (1906, 203; ET 1910, 204).

Between 1863 and 1900 a long string of "lives of Jesus" was published, all capitalizing on Holtzmann's view of Mark: typical of these "lives" was the interpretation of the kingdom of God as a spiritual kingdom of repentance and the conviction, based on Holtzmann's reading of Mark, in which Jesus's messianic consciousness developed, precipitated principally by a "Galilean crisis" in which Jesus faced the failure of his mission. The spell of Mark would not be broken until Wilhelm Wrede demonstrated that the "messianic consciousness" that was so fundamental to the liberal lives was a creation of Mark (Wrede 1901; ET 1971).

As long as the nineteenth-century fascination with the notions of religious genius who embodied ideal humanity held sway, Holtzmann's reconstruction of the historical Jesus appeared self-evidently correct. His Jesus was vigorous, introspective, and nondogmatic and espoused the superior morality of A's Sermon (Luke 6:20–49). It is startling, nevertheless, to note that Holtzmann's treatment passed over Mark 13 in silence—a text that hardly gives the impression of a nondogmatic speaker. It was Johannes Weiss's 1892 "rediscovery" of the apocalyptic strands in the Jesus tradition and its reiteration by Schweitzer (1906)—ironically, Holtzmann's student—that led eventually to the deconstruction of the liberal Jesus. There was, however, no corresponding denouement for Markan priority, as there had been for the Griesbach hypothesis after Baur's death in 1860. The 2DH outlived liberal theology, and insofar as Weiss and Wrede both accepted the 2DH, it played a role in that deconstruction.

The Twentieth Century and Beyond

By the end of the nineteenth century, the two hypotheses of Markan priority and the independence of Matthew and Luke, along with the corollary inference of a sayings document, seemed firmly established. Ever since Weiss, the sayings source, once called τὰ λόγια, now came to be known as Q (for *Quelle* "source") (1890, 557). Three further developments, two in Germany and one in England, finalized a temporary consensus on the Synoptic Problem. First was Paul Wernle's 1899 monograph that argued that it was unnecessary to posit a proto-Mark when Matthew and Luke's direct use of Mark was plausible. This had the corollary that Q was more or less coextensive with the double tradition, along with a few instances of Mark-Q overlaps. The second development was Wrede's 1901 analysis of the messianic secret in Mark, which argued that the Second Gospel, far from being a reliable biography of Jesus, was an apologetically constructed account designed to reconcile the nonmessianic character of the historical Jesus with the messianic beliefs of his followers. Wrede's thesis had the effect of undermining the confidence in Mark that was so fundamental to Holtzmann's use of A to create a psychological portrait of Jesus. Mark's narrative framework was his own editorial invention.

The loss of confidence in Mark as a source for the historical Jesus was followed by a brief period in which attention shifted to Q. Adolf von Harnack opined that Q provided uncontaminated access to the historical Jesus. It was "a compilation of discourses and sayings of our Lord, the arrangement of which has no reference to the Passion, with an horizon which is as good as absolutely bounded by Galilee, without any clearly discernible bias, whether apologetic, didactic, ecclesiastical, national or anti-national" (1907, 121; ET 1908, 171). According to Harnack, Q was qualitatively different from Mark. It was both homogeneous and ancient, unpreoccupied with the miraculous (even in Q 7:1–10!), apologetics, or the "exaggerated" apocalypticism of Mark. Its focus instead was on pure morality (Harnack 1908, 233, 237, 250–51).

The third important development, now in England, was B. H. Streeter's study *The Four Gospels* (1924), the classic British statement of the Two (or Four) Document Hypothesis. Streeter had dispensed with the idea of a proto-Mark, accepting Markan priority and the independence of Matthew and Luke. This meant that Q was represented by the double tradition and some of the Mark-Q overlaps. In addition to Mark and Q, Streeter posited literary sources to account for the special Matthaean (M) and Lukan

(L) materials.[7] Streeter also suggested geographical centers for each of these documents: Mark in Rome, M in Jerusalem; Q in Antioch; L in Caesarea, Matthew in Antioch, and Luke in Corinth (1924, 150). He also proposed that prior to its incorporation into Luke, Q had been joined with L to form "proto-Luke," which was then conflated with Mark to produce the third Gospel.[8]

Questioning Markan Priority

After Streeter there were few challenges to the 2DH. In 1951 B. C. Butler offered a critique of the 2DH, pointing out the illegitimate inference to Markan priority from the observation that Matthew and Luke tended not to agree against Mark in matters of order. He dubbed this the "Lachmann fallacy" even though it is clear that Lachmann did not commit it. But many since Lachmann had, including Streeter: "we note, then, that in regard to (a) items of subject matter, (b) actual words used, (c) relative order of incidents, Mark is in general supported by *both* Matthew and Luke, and in most cases where they do not both support him they do so alternately, and they practically never agree together against Mark. This is only explicable if they followed an authority which is content, in wording, and in arrangement was all but identical with Mark" (Streeter 1924, 162). Butler's counter-argument was that the data Streeter observed permit any inference in which Mark is the connecting link between Matthew and Luke, that is, any arrangement in which Mark is medial.

Butler's entirely correct point was not heeded until much later, probably because the 2DH had proved so useful in underwriting the development of redaction criticism in the wake of World War II. Credible accounts of the editorial profiles of Matthew and Luke had been created assuming the priority of Mark and the independent use of Mark by Matthew and Luke.[9] About the same time as Butler's intervention, Austin Farrer offered an essay advocating Markan priority and the direct dependence of Luke upon Matthew, which eliminated the need to posit Q, since Luke's Q sayings all came directly from Matthew (Farrer 1955). This essay had little immediate effect, perhaps because it was so poorly argued, but it would become a centerpiece of the "Farrer-Goulder hypothesis" or "Farrer hypothesis" (FH), which was revived in the late 1980s.

The most important development since Streeter has been William Farmer's 1964 *The Synoptic Problem*, the first comprehensive survey of the history of the Synoptic Problem since Holtzmann and a devastating critique of previous attempts at a solution. Farmer pointed out the several logical fallacies that had been committed in the construction

---

[7] See Foster, chapter 2 here, for an in-depth discussion of the minor sources in the Synoptic Problem.

[8] Proto-Luke was also espoused by Taylor 1926 but has now largely been abandoned. See Verheyden 2011.

[9] On Matthew: Bornkamm, Held, and Barth 1963; Strecker 1966. On Luke: Conzelmann 1960; Keck and Martyn 1966.

of the 2DH (including the "Lachmann fallacy") and instead revived the Griesbach hypothesis (now called the "Two Gospel Hypothesis" or 2GH). His most important point concerned the phenomenon of order: "Mark's order shows no independence of Matthew and Luke.... This seems explicable only by a conscious effort of Mark to follow the order of Matthew and Luke. Neither Matthew nor Luke could have achieved this alone.... Only someone writing later who was attempting to combine the two narrative documents has the possibility of preserving what order the second preserved from the first and then, wherever the second departed from the first, following the order of either one or the other" (Farmer 1977, 293–94). This statement embodied a fallacy of its own. If it were the case that Mark alternately agreed with Matthew, then Luke, and that when he agrees with one he disagrees with the other, Farmer's inference would be valid. But this is not the case. There are a significant number of instances in which Mark agrees with *both*. These data, as Butler has insisted, permit any arrangement in which Mark is medial, which includes Markan priority, Markan posteriority, and straight line solutions that put Mark between Matthew and Luke, for example Matthew → Mark → Luke or Luke → Mark → Matthew.

The Synoptic Problem in Current Study

Farmer's signal contribution was to reopen the Synoptic Problem as a site for debate. What followed were stout defenses of the 2GH, mounted in a series of conference papers (Corley 1983; Dungan 1990; Farmer 1983; Focant 1993; Strecker 1993; Tuckett 1984) and two important collaborative volumes, one focusing on the relationship of Luke to Matthew (McNicol 1996) and a second on Mark's use of Matthew and Luke (Peabody, Cope, and McNicol 2002).

Only slightly later, the Farrer hypothesis was revived by Michael Goulder (1974; 1989). Since the key problem for this hypothesis was accounting for Luke's direct use of Matthew, Goulder offered a remarkable tour de force, an elaborate commentary on Luke that argued how each Lukan pericope could be understood as either dependent on Mark or on Matthew. The weakest points were his tethering of Luke's editing to a complex lectionary hypothesis—that Luke's editing reflected knowledge of a lectionary cycle—and his theory that Luke worked backward through Matthew. Neither of these two features of the FH has been retained in the several subsequent defenses of the Farrer hypothesis (Goodacre 2002; Goodacre and Perrin 2004; Sanders and Davies 1989). At the end of the century, the 2DH still retained a privileged position, not because it was without difficulties but because the alternate solutions presented serious difficulties of their own. The most problematic datum for the 2DH is the existence of the "minor agreements" (MAs)—points at which Matthew and Luke agree against Mark. On the simplest version of the 2DH, one should not expect such agreements as cannot be explained credibly on the basis of coincidental editing or through the influence of Q. Yet there are some: famously, Matthew 27:68 and Luke 22:64 agree in the words "prophesy, who struck you?" against Mark's "prophesy" (14:65), and both Matthew 9:20 and Luke 8:44 have the woman who was healed of a hemorrhage touching the fringe (κράσπεδον) of Jesus's cloak, whereas Mark's woman only touches the cloak (Mark 5:27). The most comprehensive catalogues of the MAs are Neirynck (1974) and Ennulat (1994). Neirynck offered extensive stylistic analyses designed to show that many of the MAs can be seen as resulting from the editing of Mark by the other evangelists, and that in some cases the editorial decisions coincided, for example, to eliminate Markan parataxis or Markan redundancies. Ennulat did not disagree with this assessment but added that some of the MAs were *post-Markan*, that is, they represented editorial developments or elaborations of Mark. This led Ennulat to suggest that Matthew and Luke used not the version of Mark known as one of the canonical Gospels but rather a *Deutero-Markus*, a slightly expanded version.

The MAs continue to represent a challenge to the 2DH, not because they are technically insolvable but rather because there are too many possible solutions and it is impossible to decide which of these is the better: corruption of Mark's text, textual contamination of Matthew from Luke or vice versa, editing of Mark by Matthew and Luke producing coincidental agreements, post-Markan developments adopted independently by Matthew and Luke, or even the secondary influence of Matthew upon Luke either during Luke's composition or at some stages of its transmission.

The 2GH faces three key challenges: first, why Mark omitted not only minor details from his putative sources, but also the infancy stories, the large Matthaean and Lukan sermons, many parables, and the resurrection appearance stories. Second, Griesbach Mark engaged in conflation, not only at the level of paragraph or section, but at the level of sentence or clause, taking a phrase or a word from Matthew and another from Luke, that is, micro-conflation. But such a procedure is not only very difficult to imagine prior to the development of a writing desk but also unattested in other ancient authors (Derrenbacker 2005; Mattila 1995). And third, the 2GH must also account for Luke's use of Matthew, in particular how Luke worked through Matthew's well-organized speeches in Matthew 5–7; 10:1–42; 13:1–52; 18:1–35; and 24–25 and in many cases disassembled those speeches and shifted sayings into the more heterogeneous section in Luke 9:51–18:13. Moreover, the 2GH also forces one to imagine a Mark who vilified both Jesus's disciples and his family, when both of Mark's sources held them in a more positive light (Kloppenborg 1992).

The challenges for FH have to do not with Matthew or Luke's treatment of Mark but rather with Luke's use of Matthew. First, like the 2GH, the FH posits a direct relationship between Matthew and Luke, and this triggers many of the questions that plague the 2GH. On the FH, Luke has located all of the sayings he shares with Matthew after Matthew 4:16 // Luke 4:16 differently relative to Mark's framework. One expedient is to argue that Luke used Mark's Gospel before he became aware of Matthew, and so worked the Matthaean sayings into his composition differently. This of course does not explain why the Sermon on the Mount was so dramatically shortened by Luke, unless one invokes Goodacre's surmise that Luke did not like long sermons (Goodacre 2002, 81–104). Francis Watson's solution to this conundrum is that Luke saw the Matthaean Sermon on the Mount but copied into a notebook a further thirteen pericopae, which he used later in his composition (Watson 2013). A second challenge to the FH is to explain how Luke could have taken over the Matthaean sayings without Matthew's Markan framing of those sayings. For example, on the FH Luke disengaged the woes against the Pharisees (Luke 11:37–54) from the Markan context that Matthew used in Matthew 23, even though Luke took over that Markan pericope at Luke 20:45–47. Luke also detached the Jerusalem saying (Luke 13:34–35) from its place in Matthew 23, which Matthew locates in Jerusalem, and relocated it to a point in the Lukan story where Jesus is not near Jerusalem at all (MacEwen 2015). Advocates of the FH has only begun to face these difficulties. Third, a more serious challenge is Luke's failure to take over the additions that Matthew effected on Mark (Matthew 3:15; 12:5–7; 13:14–17; 14:28–31; 16:16–19; 19:9, 19b; 27:19, 24). One might argue, as Goodacre does, that Luke knew Mark before he learned of Matthew, and so the basic structure of the Gospel was determined by Mark and additional Matthaean details were only worked into his Gospel later. Still it is odd that none of Matthew's additions found their way into Luke. In fact, Luke shows no awareness of how Matthew joined additional sayings to a Markan anchor (Kloppenborg 2003).

The Ways Forward

At the end of the twentieth century the 2DH, FH, and 2GH remain the best supported hypotheses, along with a handful of more complex hypotheses (Boismard 1990) and such lesser-known options such as "Matthaean posteriority," which reverses the FH's relationship between Matthew and Luke (MacEwen 2015), and the "Jerusalem school," which retains Q but assigns priority to Luke (Lindsey 1963). While the Synoptic Problem should not be treated as a free-for-all of groundless speculation—it requires careful consideration of the relevant data and attention to both logical and technical constraints—there should also be a degree of humility in one's discussions of the Synoptic Problem and avoidance of the hubris that announces that certain hypotheses have been "discredited," when in fact the particular complexion of available data hardly admits the language of deductive testing and disproof.

Significant gaps exist between the putative originals of the Synoptics and their first manuscript attestation. The earliest manuscript of Mark is a century and a half later, in the early third century CE (P^{45}; P.Oxy LXXXIII 5345). The earliest fragment of Matthew (P^{104} = P.Oxy. LXIV 4404) is from the mid-to-late second century, and the earliest manuscript of Luke (P^{75} = P.Bodmer XIV–XV) is dated about 200 CE, that is, more than half a century after its likely date of composition. The fluidity of textual transmission means that it is dangerous to assume that the copies of the Synoptics used for the reconstruction of the Greek texts on which we construct Synoptic Problem hypotheses are identical with the autographs (if indeed there were single autographs). The nature of textual transmission leaves ample room for hypotheses such as Ennulat's *Deutero-Markus* or solutions to the problem of the MAs that appeal to textual contamination. The fact that the wording of any of the Synoptics cannot be known with precision should rule out any dogmatic statements about proofs and disproofs.[10]

Notwithstanding uncertainties about the Synoptic data, it is important to observe at least three critical stages in the construction of arguments on the Synoptic Problem. In the past, the discussion of the Synoptic Problem has often been clouded by confused or skewed descriptions of the Synoptic data and a confusion about what constitutes evidence that counts in favor of any hypothesis.

The architecture of any solution should have three stages: first, a description of the data to be explained, then a discussion of the several arrangements of those data that are logically possible, and, finally, an account of the editorial procedures that must be posited to make sense for any of those arrangements. None of these steps is without complexities. There is no neutral way to align Gospels synoptically. It is not true that the main synopses in use today (Aland 1996; Boismard and Lamouille 1986; Huck and Greeven 1981) are systemically skewed to favor one synoptic theory (Kloppenborg 2011; van Zyl 1997; contrast Dungan 1980). Nevertheless, there are at least three different ways to align the Sermon on the Mount with Mark, at 1:21 (Neirynck 1976), at 1:39 (Griesbach; Huck-Greeven), or at 3:19 (Aland; Boismard-Lamouille; Orchard 1983), and each of these alignments implies something different in respect to Matthew's treatment of Mark (on the FH and 2DH) or vice versa (on the 2GH). There are, moreover, many ways to align words and phrases (and therefore describe those words) within the same pericope. For example in Mark 1:2–6 and parallels, it makes a difference to one's view of the editorial choices of the evangelists whether one chooses the citation of Isaiah 40:3 (Mark 1:2b–3) to anchor the parallel display, or the introduction of John the Baptist (Mark 1:4). On Markan priority, one arrangement implies that both Matthew and Luke moved the introduction of John up relative to Mark's arrangement, while the other suggests that they moved the citation of Isaiah 40:3 to a point after the introduction of John. Aland's arrangement of Matthew 3:7–10 // Luke 3:7–9 implies that both Matthew and Luke supplied an introduction to the oracle of John the Baptist in Q; Boismard's alignment suggests that Luke's introduction comes from Mark 1:5. As was true of Augustine's understanding of the Gospels, the very tools that are used to examine the Synoptic Problem have an effect on the solutions that are proposed.

Second, as Butler made clear, several scenarios are compatible with the basic datum that Matthew and Luke do not agree with each other against Mark in the placing of a particular pericope that is also found in Mark. Any solution in which Mark is medial satisfies this condition. These include several simple solutions and many more complex solutions. One might invoke Ockham's razor—*causae non sunt multiplicandae praeter necessatatem*—to narrow down the options to three or four and to eliminate the complex solutions. But it should also be acknowledged that while simple solutions are heuristically pleasing, history is seldom as simple as one's heuristics suggest. It is extremely

---

[10] See Nongbri, chapter 10 here, for a discussion of the relationship between manuscript traditions and the Synoptic Problem.

doubtful, for example, that on the FH or 2DH Matthew used the autograph of Mark and even unlikely that they used the same copy of Mark. Small (or large) differences among the earliest copies of Mark—differences in vocabulary, scribal corrections and additions, dropped phrases, or minor rearrangements—would inevitably create complexities in the data and make it difficult for a given hypothesis to makes sense of those data. This means that the best that can be hoped for are solutions that address most of the data, most of the time, conceding that all solutions will face data that does not fit. It is true that uncooperative data can always be accommodated by invoking supplementary hypotheses such as textual corruption, or secondary influence of Matthew on Luke, or Watson's notebook of Matthaean sayings. But it must be conceded that any synoptic solution can be made to fit the data provided that sufficient supplementary hypotheses are allowed.

The third stage in the construction of a synoptic hypothesis is to offer an account of what editorial policies each of the evangelists must have adopted in order to produce the Gospels that they did. This stage, in fact, represents the bulk of arguments about the Synoptic Problem, but it is also the most problematic from a logical point of view. These are evidence not of the solution but the editorial procedures that are entailed in the solution. To claim, as Griesbach did, that Mark wanted to write a short Gospel simply converts the datum that Mark's Gospel is shorter than Matthew and Luke into an aesthetic preference and attributes it to Mark. It simply renames the problem. Likewise, when Goulder argues that Luke preferred short sermons as a way to account for the fact that Luke 6:20–49 is shorter than Matthew 5:1–7:27, he simply converts the data about the length of the two sermons into an editorial preference on Luke's part, while also ignoring the fact that Luke tolerates speeches longer than thirty verses. This kind of "explanation" could be invoked to account for anything at all. One could assert that Mark had a preference for avoiding the infancy and resurrection accounts in order to justify the 2GH; or one could posit a Matthaean editorial preference for shorter miracle narratives to support the FH and 2DH, or a Markan preference for longer miracle narratives in order to support the 2GH. These are not explanations; they are the more or less gratuitous positing of aesthetic preferences on one's own part. They prove absolutely nothing because such explanations can be invented to "prove" absolutely anything.

It is doubtful that solutions to the Synoptic Problem can avoid redescriptions of the data masquerading as arguments. Three kinds of considerations might bring one closer to convincing arguments: first, arguments from coherence; second, arguments from physical and technical constraints of composition; and third, arguments based on editorial practices observed in contemporaneous literature.

A plausible argument can be mounted when the datum to be explained (B's transformation of A) can be seen as belonging to a coherent series of analogous transformations in the same document. This still amounts to positing an aesthetic preference of the editor, but at least that aesthetic preference can be related to a network of similar transformations evidenced elsewhere. Unfortunately, coherence arguments can be invoked in support of mutually contradictory theories. The observation that Matthew's wonder accounts are typically much shorter than Mark's and focus on Jesus's speech (Held 1963) might suggest that Matthew has a consistent practice of streamlining Mark's stories. But this argument can be reversed, as it has been by proponents of the 2GH, to the effect that Mark consistently expands Matthaean wonder stories to make the accounts more lively (e.g., Peabody, Cope, and McNicol 2002, 140). In the end, it comes down to which direction of editing one deems to be more plausible, however plausibility is understood.

Second, some Synoptic theories require editorial maneuvers that are unlikely if not impossible. It has already been noted that micro-conflation, which is required by 2GH Mark, is highly unusual since, in the absence of writing surfaces large enough to hold two exemplars as well as the text being composed, it would have been nearly impossible for Mark to maintain constant visual contact with Matthew and Luke in order to effect micro-conflation (Kloppenborg 2019; Mattila 1995). Similarly implausible is Goulder's suggestion that Luke worked backward through Matthew's Gospel and that he had visual access to the whole of the Sermon on the Mount as he moved from Matthew 5:42 (Luke 6:30) to 7:12 (Luke 6:31) and then back to 5:46–48 (Luke 6:32–34, 36) and then on again to 7:2 (Luke 6:37–38), deciding what of the Sermon of the Mount to include and what to delay (1989, 363–66). Downing points out that the physical procedure that Goulder appears to assume—Luke having visual access to the 9,500 characters of Matthew's Sermon—is unlikely, given the fact that the sermon would represent nineteen average-sized columns of text (Downing 1992). No copy stand (even if they existed at the time) would allow visual access to the entire Sermon. Moreover, as Alan Kirk has shown, the construction of scrolls facilitated sequential (forward) movements through a source, not random access or a backward movement (2016, 55–56). Downing's criticism of Goulder does not, of course, affect the versions of the FH that do not rely on Goulder's speculations. The point here is only that attention to the mechanical and physical constraints of composition ought to affect the ways in which we try to solve the Synoptic Problem, at least to rule out procedures that are either otherwise entirely unattested, or that require access to technologies that did not yet exist.

Third, knowledge of the canons of persuasive speech articulated in the *Prosgymnasmata* and other rhetorical manuals can inform one's constructions of synoptic hypotheses (Kennedy 2003). Alexander Damm has shown that the two most commonly recommended rhetorical virtues are clarity (σαφήνεια/*perspecuitas*) and propriety (τὸ πρέπον/*aptum*). Clarity entails both freedom from the risk of obscurity and that the sentence conveys essential information in a way that is not unreasonably delayed. Propriety involves both the skill of inventing and arranging materials to serve the speaker's purpose and matching the "way of speaking" to the content of the argument (Damm 2013, 69–80). If one assumes that editors of the Gospels had these rhetorical virtues in mind, their transformation of source materials should enhance clarity and propriety rather than obscure these virtues. The better direction of dependence is the one that evidences an improvement in rhetorical qualities.

This kind of approach to assessing the competing models of synoptic relationships elevates the argument beyond merely renaming the problem by relating each alteration of the predecessor source to the canons of persuasive speech that is known to have been current in the Hellenistic world. In this way, argument is freed from the subjectivity of what one might think by modern aesthetic standards is a better argument and grounds judgment in what ancient persons thought was a better and more convincing argument (see also Reid 2016).

Expanding the Synoptic Problem

With a few exceptions, the Synoptic Problem has been restricted to the first three canonical Gospels. Yet other Synoptic-like compositions exist—the Gospel of Thomas, the *Didache*, the Gospel citations of Justin Martyr, the Gospel of Peter, and the Longer Gospel of Mark. Some effort has been devoted to ascertaining whether, for example, *Did.* 1:3–2:1 knows and uses both Matthew and Luke or Q or some other collection of sayings of Jesus, and whether and to what extent the Gospel of Thomas is literarily dependent on the Synoptics or whether it embodies earlier forms of synoptic sayings.

These explorations are important not only for establishing a map of the Synoptic tradition, but to the extent that some of these documents embody pre-Synoptic tradition are potentially useful for understanding the history of editorial transformation of the Synoptics. If, for example, it can be shown that *Did.* 16:6–8 is not dependent upon Matthew 24 but rather on the special Matthaean material, which—on the 2DH (and FH)—Matthew fused with Mark 13, then Markan priority would be a more coherent explanation of the origins of Matthew 24 than the contrary, that Mark had extracted Mark 13:24–27 from Matthew but managed to avoided the material in Matthew parallel to *Didache* 16 (Kloppenborg 1979). Likewise, if, as some have argued, some of the sayings in the Gospel of Thomas are independent of, and earlier than, the Synoptics, they may offer some leverage on the Synoptic Problem since they help to show the earliest forms of sayings that now appear also in the Synoptics.

Finally, the recent revival of discussion of Marcion's εὐαγγέλιον, earlier thought to be a revision of Luke, has potential impact on the Synoptic Problem, especially if the theses can be sustained either that Marcion's εὐαγγέλιον was used by Luke or that it was based on an earlier pre-Lukan Gospel that Luke also used (BeDuhn 2013; Klinghardt 1996; 2008; Lieu 2015; Vinzent 2014). For example, Daniel Smith (2018) has recently observed that the reconstructed pre-Marcionite Gospel lacks many of the minor agreements that have plagued the 2DH, including the "fringe" (κράσπεδον) of Jesus's garment in Luke 8:44. If this observation could be sustained, it would suggest that the "fringe" in the canonical version of Luke is due either to the textual corruption of Luke in the course of transmission (Luke being assimilated to Matthew) or perhaps to a secondary influence of Matthew on Luke as Luke edited the pre-Lukan Gospel.

Conclusion

Although the Synoptic Problem has not been solved, nor is it likely to be solved short of other discoveries, it remains a fruitful site for the discussion of the compositional history of the Synoptic Gospels and, more recently, other early Christian writings with contents like the those of the Synoptics. Properly understood, the Synoptic Problem is a laboratory in which scholars engage very complicated sets of literary data and construct hypotheses that aim on making maximal sense of those data, with the help of literary and editorial procedures that take seriously ancient compositional methods and technologies, and that pay attention to other ancient practices in the treatment of sources.

References

Aland, Kurt. 1996. *Synopsis Quattuor Evangeliorum. Griechische Vier-Evangelien-Synopse*. 15th ed., rev. Stuttgart: Deutsche Bibelgesellschaft.

Baur, Ferdinand Christian. 1847. *Kritische Untersuchungen über die kanonischen Evangelien, ihr Verhältnis zueinander, ihren Charakter und Ursprung*. Tübingen: Fues.

Baur, Ferdinand Christian. 1851. *Das Markusevangelium nach seinem Ursprung und Charakter nebst einem Anhang über das Evangelium Marcions*. Tübingen: Fues.

BeDuhn, Jason David. 2013. *The First New Testament: Marcion's Scriptural Canon*. Salem, OR: Polebridge.

Boismard, Marie-Emile, and A. Lamouille. 1986. *Synopsis Graeca Quattuor Evangeliorum*. Louvain: Peeters.

Boismard, Marie-Emile. 1990. "The Multiple Stage Hypothesis." In *The Interrelations of the Gospels: A Symposium Led by M.-E. Boismard— W. R. Farmer—F. Neirynck. Jerusalem 1984*, edited by David L. Dungan, BETL 95, 231–88. Leuven: Peeters.

Bornkamm, Günther, Heinz Joachim Held, and Gerhard Barth. 1963. *Tradition and Interpretation in Matthew*. Translated by P. Scott. Philadelphia: Westminster.

Butler, B. C. 1951. *The Originality of St. Matthew: A Critique of the Two-Document Hypothesis*. Cambridge: Cambridge University Press.

Conzelmann, Hans. 1960. *The Theology of St. Luke*. Translated by Geoffrey Buswell. New York: Harper & Row.

Corley, Bruce, ed. 1983. *Colloquy on New Testament Studies: A Time for Reappraisal and Fresh Approaches*. Macon, GA: Mercer University Press.

Damm, Alex. 2013. *Ancient Rhetoric and the Synoptic Problem: Clarifying Markan Priority*. BETL 252. Leuven: Peeters.

de Jonge, Henk J. 1992. "Augustine on the Interrelations of the Gospels." In *The Four Gospels 1992: Festschrift Frans Neirynck*, edited by F. Van Segbroeck, C.M. Tuckett, G. Van Belle, and J. Verheyden, BETL 100, 2409–17. Leuven: Peeters.

de Lang, Marijke H. 1993. "De opkomst van de historische en literaire kritiek in de synoptische beschouwing van de evangeliën van Calvijn (1555) tot Griesbach (1774)." Dissertation, Rijksuniversiteit te Leiden.

de Lang, Marijke H. 2019. "The Decline of the Gospel Harmony: Loss or Gain?" In *Theological and Theoretical Issues in the Synoptic Problem*, edited by John S. Kloppenborg and Joseph Verheyden, LNTS, 19–35. London: Bloomsbury Academic.

Derrenbacker, Robert A. 2005. *Ancient Compositional Practices and the Synoptic Problem*. BETL 186. Leuven: Peeters.

De Wette, Wilhelm M. L. 1813. *Lehrbuch der christlichen Dogmatik in ihrer historischen Entwicklung dargestellt. Erster Theil: Die biblische Dogmatik Alten und Neuen Testaments*. Berlin: Reimer.

De Wette, Wilhelm M. L. 1826. *Lehrbuch der historisch-kritischen Einleitung in die kanonischen Bücher des Neuen Testaments*. Lehrbuch der Historisch Kritischen Einleitung in die Bibel Alten und Neuen Testaments 2. Berlin: Reimer.

De Wette, Wilhelm M. L. 1860. *Lehrbuch der historisch kritischen Einleitung in die kanonischen Bücher des Neuen Testaments*. 6. Aufl. Edited by Hermann Messner and Gottlieb Lünemann. Lehrbuch der Historisch Kritischen Einleitung in die Bibel Alten und Neuen Testaments 2. Berlin: Reimer.

Downing, F. Gerald. 1992. "A Paradigm Perplex: Luke, Matthew and Mark." *NTS* 38, no. 1: 15–36.

Dungan, David L. 1980. "Theory of Synopsis Construction." *Bib* 61, no. 3: 305–29.

Dungan, David L., ed. 1990. *The Interrelations of the Gospels: A Symposium Led by M.-E. Boismard—W. R. Farmer—F. Neirynck. Jerusalem 1984*. BETL 95. Leuven: Peeters.

Dungan, David L. 1999. *A History of the Synoptic Problem: The Canon, the Text, the Composition, and the Interpretation of the Gospels*. Anchor Bible Reference Library. New York: Doubleday.

Eichhorn, Johann Gottfried. 1794. "Uber die drey ersten Evangelien: Einige Beyträge zu ihrer künftigen kritischen Behandlung." In *Allgemeine Bibliothek der biblischen Literatur* 5, 759–996. Leipzig: Weidmann.

Ennulat, Andreas. 1994. *Die "Minor Agreements": Untersuchung zu einer offenen Frage des synoptischen Problems*. WUNT 2/62. Tübingen: Mohr Siebeck, 1994.

Ewald, Heinrich. 1850. *Die drei ersten Evangelien übersetzt und erklärt*. Göttingen: Vandenhoeck und Ruprecht.

Fabricius, Johannes A. . *Bibliotheca graeca* (1790–1809). 4th ed. Edited by Gottlieb Christophoros Harles. Hamburg: Bohn; reprint Hildesheim: Olms, 1966–1970.

Farmer, William R. 1964. *The Synoptic Problem: A Critical Analysis*. New York: Macmillan.

Farmer, William R. 1977. "Modern Developments of Griesbach's Hypothesis." *NTS* 23, no. 3: 275–95.

Farmer, William R., ed. 1983. *New Synoptic Studies: The Cambridge Gospel Conference and Beyond*. Macon, GA: Mercer University Press.

Farrer, Austin M. 1955. "On Dispensing with Q." In *Studies in the Gospels in Memory of R. H. Lightfoot*, edited by Dennis E. Nineham, 57–88. Oxford: Blackwell.

Focant, Camille, ed. 1993. *The Synoptic Gospels: Source Criticism and New Literary Criticism*. BETL 110. Leuven: Peeters.

Goodacre, Mark S. 2002. *The Case against Q: Studies in Markan Priority and the Synoptic Problem*. Harrisburg, PA: Trinity Press International.

Goodacre, Mark S., and Nicholas Perrin, eds. 2004. *Questioning Q: A Multidimensional Critique*. London: SPCK.

Goulder, Michael D. 1974. *Midrash and Lection in Matthew*. London: SPCK.

Goulder, Michael D. 1989. *Luke: A New Paradigm*. JSNTSup 20. Sheffield: JSOT.

Griesbach, Johann Jakob. 1776. *Synopsis Evangeliorvm Matthaei, Marci et Lucae textum Graecum: ad fidem codicum versionum et patrum emendavit et lectionis varietatem adiecit*. Halle: Curtius.

Griesbach, Johann Jakob. 1789–90. *Commentatio qua Marci Evangelium totum e Matthaei et Lucae commentariis decerptum esse monstratur*. Jena: Goepferdt.

Griesbach, Johann Jakob. 1978. "A Demonstration that Mark was Written after Matthew and Luke." In *J. J. Griesbach, Synoptic and Text Critical Studies, 1776–1976*, edited by Bernard Orchard and Thomas R.W. Longstaff, SNTSMS 34, 103–35. Cambridge: Cambridge University Press.

Harnack, Adolf von. 1907. *Sprüche und Reden Jesu: Die zweite Quelle des Matthäus und Lukas*. Beiträge zur Einleitung in das Neue Testament 2. Leipzig: J. C. Hinrichs.

Harnack, Adolf von. 1908. *The Sayings of Jesus: The Second Source of St. Matthew and St. Luke*. Translated by John Richard Wilkinson. New Testament Studies 2. London: Williams and Norgate.

Harris, Horton. 1975. *The Tübingen School*. Oxford: Clarendon.

Held, Heinz Joachim. 1963. "Matthew as an Interpreter of the Miracle Stories." In *Tradition and Interpretation in Matthew*, by Günther Bornkamm, Heinz Joachim Held, and Gerhard Barth, translated by P. Scott, 165–300. Philadelphia: Westminster.

Herder, Johann Gottfried. 1796. *Vom Erlöser der Menschen: Nach unsern drei ersten Evangelien*. Riga: Hartknoch.

Holtzmann, Heinrich Julius. 1863. *Die synoptischen Evangelien: Ihr Ursprung und geschichtlicher Charakter*. Leipzig: Engelmann.

Holtzmann, Heinrich Julius. 1886. *Lehrbuch der historisch-kritischen Einleitung in das Neue Testament*. 2. Aufl. Freiburg: J. C. B. Mohr [Paul Siebeck].

Holtzmann, Heinrich Julius. 1892. *Lehrbuch der historisch-kritischen Einleitung in das Neue Testament*. 3. verbesserte und vermehrte Aufl. Freiburg: J. C. B. Mohr [Paul Siebeck].

Huck, Albert, and Heinrich Greeven. 1981. *Synopse der drei ersten Evangelien: mit Beigabe der johanneischen Parallelstellen. Synopsis of the First Three Gospels*. 13. Aufl. Tübingen: J. C. B. Mohr [Paul Siebeck].

Keck, Leander E., and J. Louis Martyn, eds. 1966. *Studies in Luke-Acts: Essays Presented in Honor of Paul Schubert*. Nashville: Abingdon.

Kennedy, George A. 2003. *Progymnasmata: Greek Textbooks of Prose Composition and Rhetoric*. Atlanta: Society of Biblical Literature.

Kirk, Alan. 2016. *Q in Matthew: Ancient Media, Memory, and Early Scribal Transmission of the Jesus Tradition*. LNTS 564. London: Bloomsbury T&T Clark.

Klinghardt, Matthias. 1996. *Das älteste Evangelium und die Entstehung der kanonischen Evangelien*. Texte und Arbeiten zum neutestamentlichen Zeitalter 60. Tübingen: Francke.

Klinghardt, Matthias. 2008. "The Marcionite Gospel and the Synoptic Problem: A New Suggestion." *NovT* 50, no. 1: 1–27.

Kloppenborg, John S. 1979. "*Didache* 16,6–8 and Special Matthaean Tradition." *ZNW* 70: 54–67.

Kloppenborg, John S. 1992. "The Theological Stakes in the Synoptic Problem." In *The Four Gospels 1992: Festschrift Frans Neirynck*, edited by Frans Van Segbroeck, C. M. Tuckett, G. Van Belle, and J. Verheyden, BETL 100, 93–120. Leuven: Peeters.

Kloppenborg, John S. 2006. "H. J. Holtzmann's Life of Jesus According to the 'A' Source. Part 2." *JSHJ* 4, no. 2: 203–23.

Kloppenborg, John S. 2003. "On Dispensing with Q? Goodacre on the Relation of Luke to Matthew." *NTS* 49, no. 2: 210–36.

Kloppenborg, John S. 2011. "Synopses and the Synoptic Problem." In *New Studies in the Synoptic Problem*, edited by Paul Foster, Andrew Gregory, John S. Kloppenborg, and Joseph Verheyden, BETL 239, 51–85. Leuven: Peeters.

Kloppenborg, John S. 2019 "Macro-conflation, Micro-conflation, Harmonization and the Compositional Practices of the Synoptic Writers." *ETL* 95, no. 4: 629–43.

Koppe, Johann B. 1782. *Marcus non epitomator Matthaei*. Göttingen: Programm der Universität Göttingen and Fleckeisen.

Lachmann, Karl.1835. "De ordine narrationum in evangeliis synopticis." *TSK* 8: 570–90.

Lessing, Gotthold Ephraim. 1784. "Neue Hypothese über die Evangelisten als bloss menschliche Geschichtsschreiber betrachtet." In *Theologischer Nachlass*, 45–72. Berlin: Voss.

Lieu, Judith M. 2015. *Marcion and the Making of a Heretic: God and Scripture in the Second Century*. New York: Cambridge University Press.

Lindsey, Robert L. 1963. "A Modified Two-Document Theory of the Synoptic Dependence and Interdependence." *NovT* 6: 239–63.

MacEwen, Robert K. 2015. *Matthean Posteriority: An Exploration of Matthew's Use of Mark and Luke as a Solution to the Synoptic Problem*. LNTS 501. London: Bloomsbury T&T Clark.

Mattila, Sharon L. 1995. "A Question Too Often Neglected." *NTS* 41, no. 2: 199–217.

McNicol, Allan J. 1996. *Beyond the Q Impasse—Luke's Use of Matthew: A Demonstration by the Research Team of the International Institute for Gospel Studies*. In collaboration with David L. Dungan and David B. Peabody. Valley Forge, PA: Trinity Press International.

Meijboom, Hajo Uden. 1866. *Geschiedenis en critiek der Marcushypothese*. Proefschrift, Groningen. Amsterdam: Kraay.

Meijboom, Hajo Uden. 1991. *A History and Critique of the Origin of the Marcan Hypothesis, 1835–1866: A Contemporary Report Rediscovered*. Edited and translated by John J. Kiwiet. New Gospel Studies 8. Leuven: Peeters.

Neirynck, Frans. 1974. *The Minor Agreements of Matthew and Luke against Mark: With a Cumulative List*. BETL 37. Leuven: Leuven University Press.

Neirynck, Frans. 1976. "The Sermon on the Mount in the Gospel Synopsis." *ETL* 52: 350–57.

Neirynck, Frans, and Frans Van Segbroeck. 1978. "The Griesbach Hypothesis: A Bibliography." In *J. J. Griesbach, Synoptic and Text Critical Studies, 1776–1976*, edited by Bernard Orchard and Thomas R. W. Longstaff, SNTSMS 34, 176–81, 219. Cambridge: Cambridge University Press.

New, David S. 1993. *Old Testament Quotations in the Synoptic Gospels and the Two-Document Hypothesis*. SCS 37. Atlanta: Scholars Press.

Oliver, Harold H. 1959. "The Epistle of Eusebius to Carpianus: Textual Tradition and Translation." *NovT* 3, no. 1/2: 138–45.

Orchard, Bernard. 1983. *A Synopsis of the Four Gospels in Greek: Arranged According to the Two-Gospel Hypothesis*. Edinburgh: T&T Clark.

Osiander, Andreas. 1537. *Harmoniae evangelicae libri quatuor Graece et Latine*. Geneva: Robert Stephanus.

Palmer, N. Humphrey. 1966–67. "Lachmann's Argument." *NTS* 13, no. 4: 368–78.

Peabody, David L., Lamar Cope, and Allan J. McNicol. 2002. *One Gospel from Two: Mark's Use of Matthew and Luke*. Harrisburg, PA: Trinity Press International.

Reid, Duncan. 2016. *Miracle Tradition, Rhetoric and the Synoptic Problem*. Biblical Texts and Studies 25. Leuven: Peeters.

Reimarus, Hermann Samuel. 1778. "Von dem Zwecke Jesu und seiner Jünger." In *Fragmente des Wolfenbüttelschen Ungenannten*, edited by Gotthold Ephraim Lessing, 3–174. Braunschweig: Schwetschke.

Reimarus, Hermann Samuel. 1970. *Fragments*. Edited by Charles H. Talbert. Translated by Ralph S. Fraser. Lives of Jesus Series. Philadelphia: Fortress.

Sanday, William, ed. 1911. *(Oxford) Studies in the Synoptic Problem*. Oxford: Clarendon.

Sanders, E. P., and Margaret Davies. 1989. *Studying the Synoptic Gospels*. London: SCM Press.

Schleiermacher, Friedrich. 1832. "Über die Zeugnisse des Papias von unsern beiden ersten Evangelien." *TSK* 5: 735–68.

Schweitzer, Albert. 1906. *Von Reimarus zu Wrede: Eine Geschichte der Leben Jesu Forschung*. Tübingen: J. C. B. Mohr [Paul Siebeck].

Schweitzer, Albert. 1910. *The Quest of the Historical Jesus: A Critical Study of Its Progress from Reimarus to Wrede*. Translated by William Montgomery. New York: Macmillan.
Smith, Daniel A. 2018. "The Sayings Gospel Q in Marcion's Edition of Luke." *ETL* 94, no. 3: 481–503.
Stoldt, Hans-Herbert. 1980. *History and Criticism of the Marcan Hypothesis*. Translated by Donald L. Niewyk. Macon, GA: Mercer University Press.
Storr, Gottlob Christian. 1786. *Ueber den Zweck der evangelischen Geschichte und der Briefe Johannis*. Tübingen: Heerbrandt.
Strecker, Georg. 1966. *Der Weg der Gerechtigkeit: Untersuchung zur Theologie des Matthäus*. 2. Aufl. FRLANT 82. Göttingen: Vandenhoeck und Ruprecht.
Strecker, Georg, ed. 1993. *Minor Agreements: Symposium Göttingen 1991*. Göttinger Theologische Arbeiten 50. Göttingen: Vandenhoeck und Ruprecht.
Streeter, B. H. 1924. *The Four Gospels: A Study of Origins, Treating of the Manuscript Tradition, Sources, Authorship, and Dates*. London: Macmillan.
Taylor, Vincent. 1926. *Behind the Third Gospel: A Study of the Proto-Luke Hypothesis*. Oxford: Clarendon.
Tuckett, Christopher M., ed. 1984. *Synoptic Studies: The Ampleforth Conferences of 1982 and 1983*. JSNTSup 7. Sheffield: JSOT.
van Zyl, H. C. 1997. "Objective Display or Textual Engineering? Hermeneutical Aspects in Making and Using a Synopsis of the Synoptic Gospels." *Neot* 31, no. 2: 361–88.
Verheyden, Joseph. 2011. "Proto-Luke, and What Can Possibly Be Made of It." In *New Studies in the Synoptic Problem: Oxford Conference, April 2008, Essays in Honour of Christopher M. Tuckett*, edited by Paul Foster, Andrew Gregory, John S. Kloppenborg, and Joseph Verheyden, BETL 239, 617–54. Leuven: Peeters.
Vinzent, M. 2014. *Marcion and the Dating of the Gospels*. Studia Patristica Supplements 2. Leuven: Peeters.
Watson, Francis. 2013. *Gospel Writing: A Canonical Perspective*. Grand Rapids: Eerdmans.
Weiss, Johannes. 1890. "Die Verteidigung Jesu gegen den Vorwurf des Bündnisses mit Beelzebul." *TSK* 63: 555–69.
Weiss, Johannes. 1892. *Die Predigt Jesu vom Reiche Gottes*. Göttingen: Vandenhoeck und Ruprecht.
Weisse, Christian Hermann. 1838. *Die evangelische Geschichte: Kritisch und philosophisch bearbeitet*. Leipzig: Breitkopf und Härtel.
Weisse, Christian Hermann. 1856. *Die Evangelienfrage in ihrem gegenwärtigen Stadium*. Leipzig: Breitkopf und Härtel.
Wernle, Paul. 1899. *Die synoptische Frage*. Leipzig: J. C. B. Mohr [Paul Siebeck].
Wrede, Wilhelm. 1901. *Das Messiasgeheimnis in den Evangelien*. Göttingen: Vandenhoeck und Ruprecht.
Wrede, Wilhelm. 1971. *The Messianic Secret*. Translated by J. C. G. Greig. Foreword by James M. Robinson. Greenwood, SC: Attic.

CHAPTER 2

THE MINOR SOURCES AND THEIR ROLE IN THE SYNOPTIC PROBLEM

PAUL FOSTER

Introduction

The terminology of "minor source" is in several ways a misnomer. Such language, often used to describe the so-called M and L sources, can give the impression that these proposed sources are less extensive, and consequently less significant, for the reconstruction of the early stages of the Jesus tradition than the better-known hypothetical source Q. However, even a cursory glance at literature shows this not to be the case. Streeter, in his classic work *The Four Gospels* (1924), presented a diagram of his understanding of the Four-Source Hypothesis. Under the diagram Streeter listed the size of each source in terms of verses (see fig. 2.1).

Q is given two estimates—that of Hawkins at 200 verses, and Streeter's own estimate of 270+ verses. Alongside this, Streeter estimates M to have comprised 230+ verses, and L to extend to 400+ verses (Streeter 1924, 150). While size is of significance, it is not the only index of importance. Here again Streeter's perspectives are instructive for revealing what he considered to be at stake in postulating other early sources of Jesus material. For Streeter, the reclamation of more synoptic material as originating with other presynoptic sources was a means potentially of attributing such material drawn from early sources to the historical Jesus. Here it is helpful to cite in full his comment at the end of the two chapters discussing in turn Proto-Luke and M. He states: "thus the final result of the critical analysis which has led to our formulating the Four Document Hypothesis is very materially to broaden the basis of evidence for the authentic teaching of Christ" (Streeter 1924, 270).

It would be wrong to take this statement as the motive for Streeter's formulation of the Four-Document Hypothesis, which consisted of M, L, and the intermediary stage

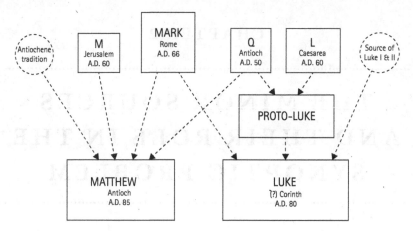

Mark has 661 verses; Matthew 1068; Luke 1149; Proto-Luke c. 700; Q (Hawkins) 200, (B.H.S.) 270+; M 230+; L 400+.

FIGURE 2.1 B. H. Streeter's representation of the Four-Source Hypothesis

designated as Proto-Luke. However, the statement presents an outcome which was, at least to Streeter's mind, highly congenial and theologically reassuring. It was namely that one could have increased confidence that much of the material in the synoptic accounts could be traced back to the historical Jesus with a much stronger level of plausibility.

While the study of pre-Gospel sources has in general seen a waning of interest among scholars, this tendency is nowhere more pronounced than in relation to the two proposed early sources M and L, and the early intermediary stage of Proto-Luke. Given the importance of these three hypothetical sources in theories of the solution to the Synoptic Problem during the late nineteenth century and for most of the twentieth century, it is instructive to trace the emergence of these source-critical hypotheses, to discuss the reasons for the demise of adherence, and to consider whether anything of value endures from these earlier theories.

THE M SOURCE

It had long been recognized that Matthew's Gospel contained material that was unique to it. While suggestions had been made concerning the origins of some of this material, it was not until 1904 that the siglum M was coined as a proposal for a unified source incorporated in Matthew's Gospel. Ernest DeWitt Burton's initial approach was to employ a subtraction method to remove all material from the First Gospel for which parallels exist either in Mark's Gospel or in the shared Lukan material that forms the double tradition (the basis of Q) (Burton 1904, 16, n. 2). The entirety of this material did not constitute Burton's proposed M. This unique material (estimated to be around 381 verses) contains a mixture of narrative and sayings material. Since M was conceived to be primarily a sayings source, like the earliest conception of Q, nonsayings material was largely removed. This resulted in approximately 140–150 verses of largely narrative material (such as the infancy narratives of Matthew 1–2) being removed. The remainder was a source of approximately 230 verses of almost entirely sayings material. While Streeter did not provide a list of the contents of his postulated M, his predecessor Burton had done so, and it appears that it is this list on which Streeter depended for his own views on the extent of M.

Burton chiefly considered material in the five Matthean discourses, that is, material in the following chapters of the Gospel: Matthew 5:1–7:27, 9:36–10:42, 13:1–53, 17:22–18:35, and 23:1–25:46 (using B. W. Bacon's classic division—although the boundaries are defined slightly differently by other scholars; see Bacon 1930, 82, 165–249). A few verses did not belong to these sections of the Gospel, consisting of a few isolated sayings and a couple of extended parables. The material can be presented for convenience as shown in table 2.1.

Counting parts of verses as full verses, this tabulation presents a source comprising material from 235 Matthean verses, of which 171 of the verses are found in the five discourses as classically defined by Bacon, and 64 verses are drawn from material outside those classical discourses. Immediately it is obvious that the extent of much of the

Table 2.1 Ernest Dewitt Burton's list of the contents of M

First Discourse	3:14–15
	5:4, 7–10, 13a, 14, 16, 17, 19–24, 27, 28, 31, 33–39a, 41, 43
	6:1–7, 10b, 13b, 16–18, 34
	7:6, 12b, 15, 22
	9:13a
Second Discourse	10:5, 6, 8a, 16b, 23, 25b, 36, 41
	11:28–30; 12:5–7, 11–12a, 34
Third Discourse	13:14–15, 24–30, 35–53
	15:12–14, 23–24
	16:17–19
Fourth Discourse	17:24–27
	18:4, 10, 14, 16–20, 23–34
	19:10–12, 28
	20:1–15
	21:14–16, 28–32, 43
	22:1–14
Fifth Discourse	23:2, 3, 5, 7b–10, 15–22, 24, 28, 32
	24:10–12, 30a
	25:1–11a, 13, 14–46
	26:52–53

Source: Burton 1904.

material is a single verse or even half-verse intertwined with either double or triple tradition material. In these cases, one now might prefer to consider these verses as editorial or redactional reworking of existing source material by the author of Matthew's Gospel, rather than as preexisting material drawn from a separate unified source. By contrast, some of the larger complexes of material, such as Matthew 18:23–34 and 20:1–15, which are both parables, might be considered to be pre-Matthean material whether or not they were drawn from a single source. By contrast, two further parables Burton attributed to this source, the wedding banquet (Matt 22:1–14) and the talents (Matt 25:14–30), do have parallels in Luke's Gospel (see Luke 14:16–24—the dinner party, and 19:12–27—the 10 minas) albeit with low verbatim agreement. Therefore, it is debatable whether this should be seen as double tradition material and placed within Q, or whether these might be variant Matthean versions with the two parables coming to the first evangelist independently.

Following on from Burton, Streeter was the next to discuss M in a significant manner. Although Streeter did not offer any further comment on the content of M beyond concurring with Burton that its extent was 230+ verses, his contribution was to discuss the character and theological perspective of the source. This was done largely in contrast with Streeter's understanding of the character and locale of Q. In regard to Q, Streeter determined Q to be slightly larger than M, with Q estimated to be approximately 270+ verses. However, the fundamental difference was not size but the related aspects of theological perspective and place of origin. Streeter conceived of Q as having a double origin. Thus, he stated in the *Oxford Studies* volume of 1911 that Q had a Palestinian origin. This view was upheld in his later work *The Four Gospels* (1924): "Q emanated from the (perhaps, freer) atmosphere of Galilee" (Streeter 1924, 233). However, it was precisely that freer spirit that made this material conducive to reception by Gentile believers in Antioch. Describing this second stage of Q's evolution, Streeter stated: "Q may be connected with Antioch. Most probably Q is an Antiochene translation of a document originally composed in Aramaic" (223). While one might legitimately question the degree to which the Greek of Q appears to represent translation rather than composition, Streeter's fundamental observations were clear. Q in its Greek form originated in Antioch, and displayed a somewhat libertine character, especially in regard to Torah matters.

By contrast, Streeter understood the origin of M and its character as significantly different from that of Q. In a series of slightly scattered comments, Streeter's understanding of M becomes apparent. Streeter asserts that "the Judaistic character of much of the material in M suggests a Jerusalem origin" (Streeter 1924, 223). Furthermore, it is argued that this Jerusalem origin accounts both for the anti-Pharisaic attitude coupled with the assertion of the necessity of Torah observance alongside a distinctly anti-Gentile bias. Moreover, it is claimed that M "reflects the spirit and outlook with which in the New Testament the name of James is associated.... The M source will naturally be connected with Jerusalem, the headquarters of the James party" (232). Finally, Streeter saw the separability of what he labeled "Judaistic sayings" from other material in the First Gospel. Such material, he suggested, only occurred in passages unique to Matthew (M) or where such material typically had been conflated with Q material. The conclusions Streeter drew were in some ways harsh and envisaged vastly distinctive outlooks between early centers of the Jesus movement at Jerusalem and Antioch. He stated that "in all these Judaistic passages it is difficult not to suspect the influence of the desire of the followers of James to find a justification for their disapprobation of the attitude of Paul, by inventing sayings of Christ, or misquoting sayings of Christ which, even if authentic, must originally have been spoken in view of entirely different circumstances" (256). Here one detects a tension in Streeter's thinking, for one of the advantages of detecting M was seen to be that of broadening "the basis of evidence for the authentic teaching of Christ" (270). Yet that process of identifying authentic dominical sayings in M is not as unproblematic, even on his own account, as Streeter suggested in this summary statement. Therefore, according to Streeter, M contained sayings of a Jewish character and theological outlook, the material took shape in Jerusalem under the aegis of the group that formed around James prior to the destruction of the Temple, and while the source might contain authentic dominical sayings, those sayings had at times been distorted or even fabricated in order to rebut the form of the message of Jesus being spread by Paul and his followers.

This understanding of the Jewish character of M with its pro-Torah perspective remained influential. A little over a decade later in 1937, T. W. Manson drew upon Streeter's conclusions and expanded the size and significance of the M source. Manson is also to be credited with providing the first commentary treatment of the contents of the M source (Manson 1949, 149–252; for the other commentary-type treatment see S. H. Brooks 1987). Manson initially adopted the same subtraction method as his predecessors. After Markan and Q material had been removed from the contents of Matthew's Gospel, he then grouped the remaining material into four sections: "(i) editorial additions and formulas; (ii) narratives; (iii) testimonia; (iv) teaching" (21). The material that made up the final category, the teaching material, was the basis of Manson's reconstructed M source. However, in his next step he went beyond the work of his predecessors. Manson noted that the arrangement of the teaching material contained in both Q and M corresponded at four points. These four sections were Jesus's preaching, the mission charge, the speech against Pharisaism, and eschatological speech. This led Manson to suggest two possible explanations for this phenomenon. He argued: "either that there is a scheme of the teaching older than M and Q, to which both conform, or that the M material has been incorporated into Q. The latter alternative would involve a kind of Proto-Matthew hypothesis." For Manson, the former option was more plausible. This view concerning the existence of a scheme of teaching material that predated both Q and M allowed Manson to postulate the phenomenon of M/Q overlaps. Consequently, some of the double tradition material was understood to have also been contained independently in the M source, having been drawn from the hypothetical earlier teaching material. Therefore, this led Manson to suggest a larger M source containing the following material: 3:14–15; 5:7–10, (13–16), 17–24, 27–39a, 43, (44a), (44b–48); 6:1–8, (9–15), 16–18, 34; 7:6–13, 15, (16–20), 21–23; 10:5–16, 23–25, 40–42; 11:1, 14, 28–30; 12:5–7, 11, 34a, 36; 13:24–30, 36–53; 15:12, 22–25; 16:2, 17–20; 18:10, 12–35; 19:10–12, 28; 20:1–16; 21:14–16,

28–32, 43, (44); 22:1–14; 23:1–36; 24:10–12, 30a; 25:1–46 (material where there is a level of doubt is included in parentheses). This resulted in an M of approximately 308 verses.

One of the difficulties for the reconstruction of M suggested by Burton and followed by Streeter is its lack of coherence. Reading the 230+ verses in isolation results in a disjointed and broken sequence of material. Manson hinted at this problem in his discussion of the fragments of teaching material that are unique to Matthew's Gospel. Manson presented the issue this way: "in considering these smaller fragments it is necessary to ask the question whether they belong to Mt.'s special source and have been removed by Mt. from their original context to a more suitable place in the chronological scheme of his Gospel, or whether they are editorial additions, or again whether they are fragments of floating tradition not previously incorporated in a collection" (Manson 1949, 149). Manson's solution to his own question is worked out in his extended commentary on the M material. At times, as is the case with the material pertaining to the baptism of Jesus (Matt 3:14–15), Manson was happy to view the saying as a free-floating piece of "early Christian apologetic." He rejected the possibility that this material was editorial composition, and instead saw it as "a fragment of Palestinian Christian oral tradition which Matthew incorporated in his account of the baptism" (149). However, for Manson the appeal to free-floating pieces of tradition was not universally applicable across M. For instance, in regard to mission teaching, Manson noted that the section in Matthew's Gospel consisted of Mark, Q, and M material and that the resultant block of material in the First Gospel was the result of the evangelist's practice of conflating sources. It was the level of "micro-conflation" throughout the Mission Discourse that led Manson to conclude that larger blocks of this material stood in M (Matt 10: 5–16, 23–25, 40–42) even where some of that material is paralleled in other synoptic sources. This also allowed Manson to find coherence in this section of teaching. He observed that "the portions of the Mission Charge which may be assigned to M reflect the aims and aspiration of the Palestinian community" (184).

Manson's overall understanding of M and its theological perspectives was similar to that of Streeter. He saw the source originating with Jewish Christians in Judaea, and again that this group was headquartered in Jerusalem under the leadership of James. In terms of date, on the basis of the saying in Matthew 5:23 and as others had done before him, Manson argued that this was a clear indicator that the Temple was still standing when this antithesis was formulated, and that the Roman destruction was not yet anticipated. Thus, it was suggested, that the date could be located "to a time after A.D. 50 as the time for the compilation of M, and probably nearer 60 than 50" (Manson 1949, 25). Manson added to previous observations by suggesting that M incorporated and was influenced by the teachings of John the Baptist. However, for Manson, like Streeter, M was an "adulterated" source. In fact, Manson saw the source as being doubly polluted both from the anti-Pauline perspectives of Jewish Christian believers in Jerusalem and Judaea and from the teachings of the Baptist (25). Therefore, according to Manson, M did not provide particularly early or reliable access to the pristine teachings of Jesus (26). This was a marked contrast with the ideas of Streeter. In that regard for Manson, Q stood closer to the authentic teachings of Jesus.

For the fifty years following Manson's treatment of M, little attention was focused on the academic study of this putative source. In part, that reflected a swing in interest away from source-critical matters. However, a few scholars made brief references to M. Kilpatrick who stated that there was "no certain means of distinguishing in detail between the remains of M and the handiwork of the editor" (Kilpatrick 1946, 36). Kilpatrick's pared-down M was more limited in size than that of Burton, Streeter, and Manson. Kilpatrick stated that M consisted of at least 170 verses, but that it was smaller than Q, which Kilpatrick estimated as not less than 200 verses. This paucity of material meant it was hard to determine a theological profile for this source. Although the term had not yet been coined, Kilpatrick's shorter M was the result of his application of an embryonic form of redaction criticism. This permitted him to attribute more of the unique Matthean material to the creativity, editorial work, and theological concerns of the evangelist, rather than that material being derived from source material alone. A few years later, Parker found it convenient to retain the siglum M; however, it functioned as no more than a cipher for "those parts of Matt. 3–28 that have no parallel in Mark or Luke" (Parker 1953, 87, n. 1). In place of M and the notion of Markan priority, Parker postulated the existence of a Jewish Christian Gospel written prior to Mark. Parker labeled this document K, and its contents were primarily Mark + M material. According to Parker, Mark removed the so-called M material because of its anti-Gentile perspectives. Parker stated that when Matthew came to compose his Gospel he did not use Mark's Gospel but the K document containing the pro-Jewish M material (4). By contrast, Luke was seen to have used canonical Mark, and therefore does not contain M material (5). This ingenious proposal did not win any widespread support.

Next, in his discussion of Gospel origins, Grant provided a complex diagram of the evolution of the traditions contained in the canonical Gospels. It is interesting to note that M is the only entity that is placed in two possible locations (Grant 1957, 48–49). This attests Grant's uncertainty about the origins of this material. Grant's two possible locations for M in his diagram are represented in one instance with a question mark and in one instance without. It may be presumed that the location without a question mark is seen as the more plausible location, that is, as material arising directly from a Palestinian or Syrian origin. The second, presumably less certain origin stems from a "Palestinian-Syrian Antiochene" origin with M as a medial point on a line connecting earlier Q material with the fully formed Gospel of Matthew. It appears on this model that Q and M are combined before being incorporated into the final form of Matthew's Gospel when Markan material is added to the Q + M complex. Since both Q and M materials arise out of the same environment, it appears that the supposed distinction between pro-Jewish-Christian and pro-Gentile tendencies exemplified by M and Q, respectively, has been abandoned.

Subsequently, interest in M has fallen into virtual abeyance since its zenith during the first half of the twentieth century. Various commentators make reference to M material in their discussions of sources. However, none of the major commentators views the M material as a unified written source in the way proposed by Burton, Streeter, and Manson. Instead such material is understood in a variety of ways. Some have viewed the majority of such material as being due to the redactional work of the evangelist. Others have seen the so-called M material comprising both larger independent blocks of tradition as well as shorter individual traditions. In the first category, some have proposed a pre-Matthean collection of the parables unique to the First Gospel (see Davies and Allison 1988, 125; Luz 2007, 21). This M material has also been seen as circulating in oral rather than written form (Hagner 1993, xlviii).

The one sustained treatment of the M material in the second half of the twentieth century is found in the work of Brooks. For Brooks the use of the symbol M does not require commitment to any source theory. Rather it is simply a means of designating Matthew's unparalleled material (Brooks 1987, 15). As has been noted, after Manson's treatment of the M material, Brooks systematically discusses the same material and comes to fundamentally different conclusions. He states: "the hypothesis of a *single* written source to account for the M sayings traditions is untenable" (112). Brooks sees some of the unique Matthean material as due to the evangelist's redactional creativity. What remains may well be preexisting but disparate traditions. Rejection of a unified source is based on three observations. Such material does not have a coherence that might be expected from a unified source. This problem was already seen, at least in part, by Manson, but his solution was to postulate M/Q overlaps to provide a greater flow to the material. Brooks, however, sees that as a questionable approach and therefore the problem of the lack of unity in the M material remains. The second issue is perhaps the least problematic. Brooks argues that the narrative details appear to be independent of the sayings material. The implication is that the sayings material was free-form, and hence such floating traditions were readily adaptable by the evangelist. The third issue is related to the first. The isolated sayings are seen as lacking a similar style and choice of vocabulary. Hence, according to Brooks, there does not appear to be a single author behind this material. In the end Brooks sees the M material as describing a multiplicity of individual sayings and complexes of sayings that circulated most likely in oral rather than written form (122).

Where does this virtually unanimous rejection of a unified, written M leave scholarship on the unique Matthean material? While the idea of a single M source has been rejected, that does not mean that all the insights concerning that material were without value. While the overarching hypothesis finds few, if any supporters, the theories of Burton, Streeter, and Manson led to a much closer examination of this unique Matthean material. The insights into the ideological character of individual sayings and complexes of material are no longer attributed to a preexisting source but are now to be taken into account as part of the overall message and theology of the first evangelist. A number of the unique sayings, whether redactional creations or transmitted traditions, have a pro-Jewish outlook. The way the evangelist has skillfully woven this material in with the perspectives contained in Mark and Q reveals a creative valuing of various strands of the Jesus tradition, and a more mature outlook that is happy to live with tensions and differences. Closer considerations of the unique Matthean material may also result in a greater degree of humility on the part of scholars. There is a limitation in the methods applied to these traditions, which means that at times it is no longer possible to determine if a saying came to the evangelist as preexisting Jesus material or whether it was part of the Gospel writer's creative work in forming the unified composition of the Gospel of Matthew. Although there has, maybe for this reason, been a tendency to turn away from source-critical questions and to focus on the Gospel as a narrative whole, it may be a mistake to jettison the source-critical enterprise too swiftly. Asking such questions about the origins of material, even if the answer is ambiguous, focuses attention on complexes of tradition in a highly detailed manner. This close examination has served to highlight the skill and genius of the author of the First Gospel, as a figure weaving traditional insights together with new perspectives on the person of Jesus. This is perhaps how the evangelist understood his own task, which he potentially describes as drawing upon treasures old and new from the storehouse of tradition and creative reflection (Matt 13:52).

The L Source and the Proto-Luke Hypothesis

It is more instructive to discuss the role of the L source and the Proto-Luke hypothesis together, since these putative sources are closely related both in scholarly conceptions and in the understanding of the function they play as sources that fed into Luke's Gospel. The traditional understanding of L is that of a unified source comprising the unique (*Sondergut*) material contained in Luke's Gospel, or at least a subset of that material. Proto-Luke is an intermediary source, formed after the composition of L and prior to the Gospel of Luke. It results from the combination of the material in L with the traditions contained in Q. As classically articulated by Streeter, L originated in Caesarea around A.D. 60, and contained material amounting to 400+ verses. When this material was combined with Q traditions, the resultant document was approximately 700 verses in length. This occurred prior to the later combination with Markan material, which then resulted in the formation of the Gospel of Luke around A.D. 80, with the resultant Gospel being 1,149 verses in length. Therefore, in terms of verse count, L represented no less than 34.8 percent of the material in the canonical Gospel, and Proto-Luke contained approximately 60.9 percent of the material in Luke's Gospel. From these figures alone it is possible to see the fallacy of describing either L or the Proto-Luke document as "minor" sources, if the label "minor" is taken as an indication of size. On Streeter's estimate the Markan material contributes around 39.1 percent of the content of Luke's Gospel, which is comparable in size to the 34.8 percent drawn from L, but less extensive than the 60.9 percent of material that reached the redactor of Luke's Gospel in the form of Proto-Luke.

While the existence of material that was unique to the Third Gospel had long been recognized, it appears that the step of labeling such material by employing the siglum L is to be credited to Bernard Weiss (Weiss 1886), with the symbol being used more extensively in his later work on the sources of Luke's Gospel: *Die Quellen des Lukasevangeliums*

(Weiss 1907, 195–276). In this later work, Weiss suggested that the L material formed a continuous and unified document, consisting of the following elements broken down into individual units: Luke 1:5–2:52; 3:10–14, 23–38; 4:16–30; 5:1–11; 6:20–38, 46–49; 7:1–10, 11–17, 18–22a, 36–50; 8:1–3; 9:43–45; 51–56, 61–62; 10:1, 29–37, 38–42; 11.27–28, 37–52, 53–54; 12:1a, 33–34, 35–38, 49–53; 13:1–9, 10–17; 14:1–6, 7–14, 15–24, 25–27, 28–33; 15:1–3, 11–32; 16:14–15, 19–31; 17:3–10, 11–19; 18:9–14, 31–34; 18:43b–19:10; 19:11–28, 37–44, 47–48; 20:20–26, 34–38; 21:12–19, 20–24, 25–28, 34–36, 37–38; 22.1–6, 14–23, 31–34; 22:39–24:49; 24:50b–51 (97–168). As is immediately apparent, Weiss proposed a major source of tradition encapsulating Luke's infancy and Passion narratives. The extent of this proposed source is 646 verses, or 56.2 percent of the contents of the canonical Gospel by verse count.

The major impetus, however, for understanding the unique Lukan material as constituting a separate unified source came in the work of Paul Feine, *Eine vorkanonische Überlieferung des Lukas in Evangelium und Apostelgeschichte* (Feine 1891). In that work Feine proposed that Luke's "peculiar source" (he did not use the siglum L, but described the material as *eigentümlichen Quellenschrift* or *besondere Quellenschrift*) was Jewish Christian in theological character. This proposed source contained infancy and Passion narrative material; it was approximately the same length as the source identified by Weiss, although there was a difference in the material that Weiss and Feine attributed to their respective formulations of L. In fact, it has been calculated that Weiss and Feine agree in 536 of the verses they both attribute to L (for details see Paffenroth 1997, 14, n. 15). Both of the reconstructions of Weiss and Feine are significantly larger than Streeter's later more standard estimate of 400+ verses. In large part, the discrepancy arises because of the inclusion of material drawn from the infancy narratives (Luke 1–2 = 128 verses). If the material contained in the infancy narratives were to be removed from the common material Weiss and Feine attributed to L, the resultant source would then amount to 408 verses. This would consequently be more closely aligned to the classic understanding of L as presented in works written in the early decades of the twentieth century.

Apart from postulating that the unique Lukan material existed as a coherent and unified single source, Feine's major contribution to the study of the Synoptic Problem was his theory that L and Q were combined prior to the formation of Luke's Gospel, which later resulted from the incorporation of material from Mark's Gospel with Proto-Luke. In essence, Feine argued that in Luke's version of the double material, certain traditions revealed a more thoroughgoing Jewish-Christian perspective than the parallels in Matthew's Gospel. From Feine's perspective this would be unexpected if the third evangelist was drawing directly on Q material, since Luke's Gospel was designed for a primarily Gentile audience in comparison with Matthew's Gospel. This Jewish-Christian perspective of the Lukan version of Q material was also characteristic of the unique Lukan (or L) material. Consequently, Feine proposed that it was in the precanonical stage that the increased Jewish Christian orientation was given to the double tradition material when it was combined and aligned with the perspectives of the L material (Feine 1891, 4–12). Hence, the work of Weiss, and to a greater degree that of Feine, gave embryonic articulation to L, and formulated the Proto-Luke hypothesis. These ideas garnered significant attention over the subsequent half century.

The reception of the ideas concerning a special source of Lukan tradition, and the combination of that special source with Q material prior to it being joined with Markan material, was quickly disseminated among British scholars. In an *Expository Times* article of 1900, William Sanday mediated the ideas of Feine to an Anglophone audience (he had in fact mentioned the idea as early as 1893 in his Bampton Lectures). By the time of the publication of the influential 1911 volume *Oxford Studies in the Synoptic Problems*, several of the essays acknowledged an understanding of a special Lukan source and the belief in the Proto-Luke hypothesis. However, in the essay by Vernon Bartlet, "The Sources of St. Luke's Gospel," the most thoroughgoing of the essays in its treatment of the traditions utilized by Luke, there was an important modification to the understanding of L from the way it had been postulated by Feine and Weiss. Bartlet, noting the common point of view he shared with V. H. Stanton, stated: "as to the Nativity in chaps. i–ii (and the connected Genealogy), neither of us sees clear evidence for including it in Luke's 'special source', though it too was composed in Palestine" (Bartlet 1911, 358). This viewpoint became part of mainstream thinking in regard to L. However, another of Bartlet's differing views did not gain widespread acceptance. Bartlet suggested that the Q material had circulated only orally prior to its combination with Luke's special source. Therefore, Bartlet viewed the compositor of Proto-Luke as the figure who first committed Q to a written form. By contrast, according to Bartlet, the manner in which Matthew conflates Q material with Mark's Gospel suggests that Q came to the first evangelist in oral form. This second suggested modification to the Proto-Luke theory failed to convince fellow scholars.

The classic articulation of the L source hypothesis and more particularly the place of Proto-Luke in the formation of Gospel of Luke was to come in the next decade with the works of Streeter (1924) and more fully with Vincent Taylor's monograph *Behind the Third Gospel* (1926). Streeter accepted the fundamentals of the Proto-Luke hypothesis, although following Bartlet he did not attribute the infancy narrative to this document. His own major suggestion concerned the authorship of Proto-Luke. Streeter offered the following proposal: "I suggest that the author of Proto-Luke—the person, I mean, who combined in one document Q and the bulk of the material peculiar to the Third Gospel—was no other than Luke the companion of Paul. And I suggest that this same Luke some years afterwards expanded his own early work by prefixing the stories of the Infancy and by inserting extracts from Mark—no doubt at the same time making certain minor alterations and additions" (Streeter 1924, 218). The value of Proto-Luke, for Streeter, was as an independent and historical third source for the "Life of Christ." Instead of simply two independent sources, it was stated that one "must recognise in Proto-Luke the existence of another authority comparable to Mark" (222). While the historical merit of Proto-Luke was not seen as being unproblematic, it did mean that the unique traditions had to be considered as potentially originating with the historical Jesus.

Without doubt the fullest and most influential work to discuss L and, more particularly, the Proto-Luke hypothesis was Taylor's volume discussing the sources used by the Gospel of Luke. Taylor conceived of the Proto-Luke material being preserved in large blocks in the Gospel of Luke, virtually unmixed with Markan elements. It was for this reason that the Passion narrative proved more difficult to analyze. For while it contained much non-Markan material, it was also mixed at various points with material drawn from Mark. Taylor argued that the earlier blocks of Proto-Luke material required a conclusion and that the Lukan Passion narrative was the sequel or finale to the Proto-Luke document, albeit now surviving in fragmentary form in Luke's Gospel. Using a series of slightly florid mixed metaphors, Taylor stated: "we may justly say that, without the Passion narrative, the non-Markan source would be a torso. We can piece the seven non-Markan sections together, part to part, like the fragments of a broken vase, and if we cannot so easily join the Passion narrative with the rest, it none the less bears clear tokens that it is of the same construction and design" (Taylor 1926, 177). The seven sections, or large blocks of material, preceding the Passion narrative that Taylor saw as making up Proto-Luke were Luke 3:1–4:30; 5:1–11; 6:12–8:3; 9:51–18:14; 19:1–28; 19:37–44; 19:47–48. It appears that the mixing of Markan elements with non-Markan material that was seen to occur in the Passion narrative is also present in Luke 19 to a lesser extent.

Taylor's contribution arose not simply from his reconstruction of the Proto-Luke document based on his own meticulous analysis but also from his consideration of the issues of authorship, date, and place of composition, a reflection on the historical value of Proto-Luke, and a careful examination of the theology of this document. In relation to authorship, Taylor simply stated his opinion that the author of the Third Gospel was Luke the companion of Paul. This led him to address his more substantive question, namely whether the author of the Third Gospel was also the author of Proto-Luke. Consideration of Semitisms led Taylor to see these as characteristic of the Third Gospel as a whole, including the infancy narratives and the Markan sections of the Gospel, as well as being prominent in Proto-Luke material. Therefore, it was argued that this stylistic indicator was impregnated across the whole Gospel. Similarly, the prominent Lukan ideas of concern for the poor and interest in women, outcasts, and sinners are all seen to be present throughout the Gospel. Therefore, on the basis of style, characteristic ideas, connections between sections, and the implications of the preface (Luke 1:1–4), Taylor concluded that in regard to Proto-Luke, "we must think of the evangelist as in the full sense of the term the author of that work" (Taylor 1926, 210). In terms of date, Taylor viewed the composition taking place between the years A.D. 60 and 65. Place of composition was more difficult to fix due to the peripatetic nature of Luke's life, but Taylor opined that one should "look upon Caesarea as the place where the first steps were taken, rather than the actual place of composition" (213). In terms of the historical value of Proto-Luke, Taylor offered no absolute or simplistic answers. He noted places where this third source agrees with other sources (Q and Mark) utilized by Luke and thereby perhaps provides a multiply attested account, as well as other places where it stands in conflict with other sources and thus raises difficult historical questions. On the whole, however, Taylor sees Proto-Luke as one of the earliest sources of generally reliable historical material concerning Jesus. Therefore, he stated: "we have good reason to trust it as an early and reliable historical work" (254).

Taylor treated the theology of Proto-Luke in four parts. The final part is the briefest and considers the theology of Proto-Luke in relation to that of other early Christian authors. The focus of the first three parts is on the presentation of Jesus in Proto-Luke— Jesus's teachings, his portrayal, and the Christology of the work as a whole. Overall the teaching of Jesus in Proto-Luke is seen to reflect the same range of themes and ideas found across the synoptic tradition. It is, however, noted that there is a relative dearth of parables of the Kingdom, and that eschatological teaching is largely segregated in Proto-Luke. Despite these differences, which are viewed as relatively minor by Taylor, it was the range of teaching themes that cover the same gamut as the synoptic material as a whole that confirmed several details of the Proto-Luke hypothesis. According to Taylor, this broad coverage that reflects the "humane character" of Jesus's teachings was viewed as a confirmation that the teaching traditions contained in Proto-Luke depend "on traditions ultimately derived from the women who journeyed with the Apostolic band from Galilee to Jerusalem" (Taylor 1926, 260). In discussing the portrayal of Jesus in Proto-Luke, Taylor saw that characterization as aligning with the unadorned teaching contained in the document and consequently that the alignment between the teaching and the portrayal of the central character attested to the primitiveness of the traits that were attributed to Jesus. Hence, again Taylor found corroboration for the claim that Proto-Luke was an early and reliable source. The Christology of Proto-Luke initially appeared to create difficulties for Taylor's overall argument that the document was an early and reliable source. This was primarily because it uses the term "Lord" (κύριος) with a greater frequency than Mark or Q. Taylor mitigates this apparent difficulty in two ways. First, he seeks to show that such terminology was part of the earliest stages of the Jesus movement, which used the Aramaic title *maran*, which was argued to have quickly been rendered in Greek as κύριος ("Lord"). Second, it is noted that in Proto-Luke the term "Lord" only occurs "in narrative, and does not rise above the level of a term of regard or high respect" (266). Thus, Taylor minimized the impact of any evidence that might suggest the Christology of Proto-Luke indicated a later period, rather than a primitive stage of development.

The importance of Taylor's work in the history of scholarship on the unique Lukan material, and especially on its incorporation in Proto-Luke, is difficult to overstate. Not only was this the classic articulation of the hypothesis but also his ideas represented the full flowering of the study of Proto-Luke during a period when source-criticism was in the ascendancy. Standing at nearly a century's remove, it is possible to detect a clear ideological agenda. There was an obvious desire to unearth sources that predated the Synoptic Gospels themselves. This was undertaken in order to claim that the traditions of which such sources were composed were early and consequently had a greater claim to historical reliability. The supposed outcome was to discover more certain access to the figure of Jesus of Nazareth.

The Proto-Luke theory did not go unchallenged, even during the period when it received classic expression. There was a protracted scholarly debate, with J. M. Creed mounting a sustained rejection of the hypothesis. This resulted in a series of rejoinders between Creed and Taylor (for instance see Creed 1934, 101–7). At a slightly later date, T. W. Manson expressed uncertainty concerning the Proto-Luke hypothesis, although he held that the L source was a body of oral tradition, albeit of unsystematic character, especially in comparison with Q or M. Manson viewed Luke as becoming acquainted with this material during Paul's imprisonment in Caesarea around A.D. 60, and, at some subsequent point, using it in the composition of his Gospel. For Manson the oral character of L and its subtle polemic by means of allusive parables made it harder to determine a unifying theme in this source. He argued that the majority of L material was to be found in the section of Luke's Gospel spanning Luke 9:51–19:44, but that the source did extend in a limited manner into the Passion Narrative (Luke 22:24–33, 35–38; 23:27–31).

Interest in L and Proto-Luke virtually abated during the second half of the twentieth century. This changed in 1997 with the appearance of Paffenroth's monograph, which focused exclusively on L without tying it to the Proto-Luke hypothesis (Paffenroth 1997). After a review of previous scholarship, Paffenroth excluded infancy narrative material from L following the arguments of Streeter and Taylor (27–28). Furthermore, but unlike most of his predecessors, he also excluded the Passion material (29). Paffenroth argued that Luke's Passion narrative was best explained as an editorial adaptation of Mark's Passion narrative (29). This conclusion was easier to defend after the developments in understanding of the evangelists as authors in their own right, which had been discerned through the application of redaction criticism. However, Paffenroth also considered the possibility of Luke having access to a variant Passion narrative. He argued that if this were the case, then the difference from the remainder of the L material made it unlikely that it was part of the same source. Paffenroth commenced his reconstruction of L with an examination of the unique Lukan material in chapters 3–19, and based his reconstruction on the material identified by Feine and Weiss in those chapters. This necessitated consideration of an initial set of 407 verses. Paffenroth analyzed the vocabulary and style, the formal characteristics, and the content of this material to determine material that differed from expected Lukan composition, and simultaneously he considered whether these identified non-Lukan traditions resulted in a set of material with internal similarities. The result was the isolation of twenty-six pericopae making up 164 verses: Luke 3:10–14; 4:25–27; 7:11b–15, 36–47; 10:30–37a, 39–42; 11:5b–8; (12:16b–20); 12:35–38; 13:1b–5, 6b––9, 10–17b, 31b–32; 14:2–5, 8–10, 12–14, 28–32; (15:4–6), 8–9 11–32; 16:1b–8, 9–31; 17:7–10, 12–18; 18:2–8a, 10–14a; 19:2–10 (here 14:8–10, 12–14 are treated as a single pericope; 117–38).

Paffenroth saw this material, without rearrangement or transpositions, as falling into four sections. In turn, these were an introduction presenting preaching to outcasts, a section concerning love and various warnings, a section on honor and the children of Abraham, and a section on the vindication of outcasts. While this arrangement, as Paffenroth presents it, results in the theme of concern for outcasts neatly bookending the document, it may be asked how much coherence is actually contained in the disparate material in each section. Moreover, one may wish to ponder whether the titles attached to each section suggest a greater degree of unity than might be the case (Paffenroth 1997, 144–45).

Based on this reconstruction Paffenroth argued that L was more plausibly understood as a written document than oral tradition. It was argued that this was due to specific details such as names of characters and places being found in this set of L pericopae, which imply written fixity rather than oral fluidity. In terms of origin, it was suggested that "L was composed by Jewish-Christians in Palestine sometime between 40 and 60 CE" (Paffenroth 1997, 156), with Paffenroth seeming to favor an earlier date. The overall message of L is an important indicator that it was indeed a separate source. Paffenroth presented this distinctiveness this way: "this source reveals to us an early community's vision of Jesus that differs markedly from others. L's Jesus is not the suffering Son of Man we have from Mark, nor is he Q's aphoristic teacher of Wisdom, nor is he Luke's universal savior. The L community revered and portrayed Jesus as a powerful ethical teacher who substantiated and revealed the authority of his teaching by acts of healing. They believed that Jesus had come to 'seek' and 'find' the lost, whom he joyously re-established as beloved 'children of Abraham'" (158).

Paffenroth's understanding of L represents a return to understanding the putative source as thematically and theologically distinct from the Gospel of Luke. Such a perspective was characteristic of the original discussions of the L source by Feine and Weiss, who likewise placed it in a Jewish-Christian milieu. The turn taken by Streeter and more fully by Taylor that saw the L material as aligned with Luke's theology and more particularly Proto-Luke as being composed by the third evangelist removed one of the key reasons for isolating L or Proto-Luke material. With the material in the L source or Proto-Luke seen as thematically coherent with the Third Gospel itself, it then became more difficult to explain why Luke could not be understood as the arranger or even composer of L material, and more particularly why the intermediate compositional stage of Proto-Luke was required. If the theological and stylistic indicators were viewed as congruent across the three Lukan sources, then it appeared more plausible to view Luke as compiling Mark, Q, and unique Lukan traditions along with his own redactional perspectives in one compositional stage. This single compositional stage could more simply and straightforwardly explain the creation of the thematic unity found across all strands of material in the Gospel of Luke without recourse to theories of an intermediate stage, which according to Streeter and Taylor displayed few thematic deviations from the Third Gospel as a whole.

Conclusion: The Demise of the Minor Sources

Little significant attention has been devoted to M, L, and the Proto-Luke theory in current studies of the Synoptic Problem. The reasons for this are many. It should be admitted that one of these reasons is fashion. Currently, few people in the guild of New Testament scholarship are interested in the Synoptic Problem, in general, or source criticism, in particular, as areas of research. Fashion alone, however, is perhaps not the key reason for disinterest. Since the heyday of source criticism in the nineteenth and early twentieth centuries, scholars have detected a more active role for the evangelists as active editors and creators of the material contained in the Gospels. Furthermore, there has been a decline in confidence in regard to what can be known in many case about the prehistory of individual synoptic units and sayings. Although there have been significant challenges to the Q hypothesis in recent decades, the fact that such double tradition material is found in both Matthew and Luke requires scholars to provide some explanation for that shared material, be it the dependence of one of those Gospels on the other or the theory of their independent use of a common source. The case is different with singly attested (or *Sondergut*) material. There is little secure basis to differentiate between a unit of material being an editorial creation or a preexistent tradition. Even if the latter is the case, then it is difficult to determine whether it derived from a unified and coherent large source or whether any perceived thematic similarities are due to the later redactional handiwork of an evangelist aligning separate received traditions with the overall theological perspectives of the larger Gospel narrative in which those received traditions are arranged and deployed.

Without doubt, the so-called minor sources have played a significant part in the development of solutions to the Synoptic Problem. In the history of New Testament scholarship significant and substantial works by major figures in former generations are devoted to these sources. Given the fact that scholarship has currently turned away from such theories, this may suggest that such earlier scholarship was a dead end which produced little of lasting value. While on the surface that estimate may appear incontrovertible, it perhaps should not be accepted too quickly. First, those who developed the hypotheses concerning the minor sources also developed methods for the close reading of units of tradition and for the careful consideration of their theological tendencies which are still utilized in New Testament scholarship. Second, while previous scholars may have overdifferentiated the existence of factions or parties in the early Jesus movement and seen them as aligned closely with sources, they have helpfully mapped out the fluidity of understanding in regard to the Jesus traditions that circulated in the early decades of the movement. Third, while there is no widespread sign of it on the horizon, ideas have a strange way of coming back into vogue in New Testament scholarship. At one level, Paffenroth's monograph, published in the late 1990s, is an example of such a tendency. If there is a return to the detailed study of Gospel sources, no doubt the works of previous generations will be scoured, not just for the potentially positive results but also to see if the inherent problems that led to the abandonment of theories of additional synoptic sources can be addressed in the quest to form more robust and better articulated hypotheses of the origins of the traditions contained in the Synoptic Gospels.

References

Bacon, B. W. 1930. *Studies in Matthew*. New York: Holt.
Bartlet, J. V. 1911. "The Sources of St. Luke's Gospel." In *Oxford Studies in the Synoptic Problem*, edited by W. Sanday, 313–63. Oxford: Clarendon.

Brodie, T. L. 2004. *The Birthing of the New Testament: The Intertextual Development of the New Testament Writings.* Sheffield: Sheffield Phoenix.

Brook, S. H. 1987. *Matthew's Community: The Evidence of his Special Sayings Material.* Sheffield: JSOT Press.

Burton, E. de W. 1904. *Some Principles of Literary Criticism and their Application to the Synoptic Problem.* Chicago: University of Chicago Press.

Creed, J. M. 1930. *The Gospel According to Luke.* London: Macmillan.

Creed, J. M. 1934. "Some Outstanding New Testament Problems. II: 'L' and the Structure of the Lucan Gospel. A Study of the Proto-Luke Hypothesis." *ExpTimes* 46: 101–7.

Davies, W. D., and Dale C. Allison. 1988. *A Critical and Exegetical Commentary on the Gospel according to Matthew: Volume I Chapters I-VII.* ICC. Edinburgh: T&T Clark.

Feine, P. 1891. *Eine vorkanonische Überlieferung des Lukas in Evangelium und Apostelgeschichte.* Gotha: Perthes.

Foster, P. 2011. "The M-Source: Its History and Demise in Biblical Scholarship." In *New Studies in the Synoptic Problem: Oxford Conference, April 2008—Essays in Honour of Christopher M. Tuckett,* edited by P. Foster, A. Gregory, J. S. Kloppenborg, and J. Verheyden, 591–616. Leuven: Peeters.

Grant, F. C. 1957. *The Gospels: Their Origin and Their Growth.* London: Faber and Faber.

Hagner, D. A. 1993. *Matthew 1-13.* WBC 33A. Dallas: Word.

Hawkins, J. C. 1911. "Three Limitations to St. Luke's Use of St Mark's Gospel." In *Oxford Studies in the Synoptic Problem,* edited by W. Sanday, 27–94. Oxford: Clarendon.

Kilpatrick, G. D. 1946. *The Origins of the Gospel According to St. Matthew.* Oxford: Oxford University Press.

Luz, U. 2007. *Matthew 1-7.* Translated by James E. Crouch. Hermeneia. Minneapolis: Fortress.

Manson, T. W. 1949. *The Sayings of Jesus.* London: SCM.

Paffenroth, K. 1997. *The Story of Jesus according to L.* JSNTSS 147. Sheffield: Sheffield Academic Press.

Parker, P. 1953. *The Gospel before Matthew.* Chicago: University of Chicago Press.

Sanday, W. 1893. *Eight Lectures on the Early History of the Doctrine of Biblical Inspiration.* Bampton Lectures 1893. London: Longmans and Green.

Sanday, W. 1900. "A Plea for the Logia." *ExpTimes* 11: 471–73.

Streeter, B. H. 1924. *The Four Gospels: A Study in Origins—Treating of the Manuscript Tradition, Sources, Authorship and Dates.* London: Macmillan.

Taylor, V. 1921–22. "Proto-Luke." *ExpTimes* 33: 250–52.

Taylor, V. 1924–25. "The Value of the Proto-Luke Hypothesis." *ExpTimes* 36: 467–68.

Taylor, V. 1926. *Behind the Third Gospel: A Study of the Proto-Luke Hypothesis.* Oxford: Clarendon.

Verheyden, J. 2011. "Proto-Luke, and What Can Possibly Be Made of It." In *New Studies in the Synoptic Problem: Oxford Conference, April 2008— Essays in Honour of Christopher M. Tuckett,* edited by P. Foster, A. Gregory, J. S. Kloppenborg, and J. Verheyden, 617–54. Leuven: Peeters.

Weiss, B. 1886. *Lehrbuch der Einleitung in das Neue Testament.* Berlin: W. Hertz.

Weiss, B. 1907. *Die Quellen des Lukasevangeliums.* Stuttgart: J. G. Cott'schen.

CHAPTER 3

THE USE OF SOURCES IN ANCIENT COMPOSITIONS

JAMES W. BARKER
—*in memory of Larry W. Hurtado*

This essay contextualizes the Synoptic Gospels in terms of ancient writing materials and processes. Greco-Roman writers predominantly used waxed tablets and bookrolls, although codices emerged in the first-century CE. Authors could recall texts from memory, but writers could also maintain visual contact when studying, collating, copying, quoting, or paraphrasing sources. Previous scholarship has highlighted the difficulties of interweaving multiple sources and rearranging their sayings and narratives. However, neither operation was unprecedented or overly complicated, as evinced by Septuagint recensions, Josephus's *Antiquities*, and Tatian's Diatessaron. Some writing processes were more complicated than others, but ancient authors did not always work as simply as possible. Every proposed solution to the Synoptic Problem proves feasible according to ancient compositional practices.

WRITING MATERIALS AND PROCESSES

QUINTILIAN'S (c. 35–c. 96 CE) *Institutio Oratoria* discusses writing materials, processes, and pedagogy. The ability to paraphrase, abridge, and embellish Aesop's fables was prerequisite to rhetorical education (*Inst.* 1.9.1–3), and students were expected to imitate worthy authors when learning composition (*Inst.* 10.2.1). Imitation was associated with memorizing famous sayings and selections by visual copying and repeated reading (*Inst.*

I thank Christopher Begg, Matthew Crawford, Peter Gentry, Mark Goodacre, William Johnson, John Meade, and Elizabeth Meyer for engaging feedback on various sections of this essay. I also thank Marius Gerhardt for providing dimensions of T.Berol. inv. 10508–10512 as well as Kenneth Foushee and Selina Langford for interlibrary loan assistance.

1.1.36; 2.7.2). Students were not typically learning entire literary works by heart (contra Eve 2016, 82–83, and Kirk 2016, 96–97). Quintilian does not recommend dictation, although it was widely practiced (*Inst.* 10.3.18–19). He says to make frequent revisions during writing (*Inst.* 10.3.5–11) and thereafter, specifically to make additions, deletions, and alterations (*Inst.* 10.4.1–2). He recommends that the first draft be written on waxed tablets, which can be erased easily, and some boards should be left empty for corrections and insertions, even material that is out of order [1]

The wooden boards of waxed tablets were 4–6 mm thick, and polyptychs were preferred for literary compositions. The outermost boards served as covers, and the inner boards had 1–2 cm margins surrounding the writing area, which was recessed 1 mm and filled with wax. Diptychs had two covers and two inner pages for writing. Additional inner boards were double-sided, so triptychs had four pages, pentaptychs had eight, and so forth. Polyptychs range in size, but boards from multiple sites measure 14 × 12 cm (see Meyer 2007; Speidel 1996, 24; Tomlin 2003, 41); for comparison, Loeb Classical Library pages measure 16 × 10 cm.

Like codices, tablets were bound inside the long edge. Unlike codices, tablets were typically written horizontally with top and bottom pages rather than *transversa* with left and right pages. A writing area of 12 × 10 cm comfortably fit 300 letters (Tomlin 2003), so the pentaptych in a wall painting at Herculaneum (Turner 1971, 34, pl. 10) could fit 2,000 letters even with one page intentionally left blank; a triptych could easily fit 1,000 letters.[2] Authors also used waxed tablets for excerpting sources at a preliminary writing stage. Pliny the Younger (c. 61–c. 112 CE) tells how his uncle annotated and excerpted while someone was reading (*Ep.* 3.5.10–11), and "a shorthand writer with book and tablets" traveled with him (*Ep.* 3.5.14–15). Tablets could be filled quickly, but they lacked permanence, so contents were transferred to rolls.

The contents of twelve pentaptychs would fill 80 percent of a papyrus roll (340 cm long according to Skeat in Elliott 2004, 65–66), leaving empty columns for further revisions. It would take two days to copy that much text in ink. According to a ninth-century colophon (Munich BSB Clm 14437 f. 109r), two scribes copied for seven days, and another scribe made corrections another day (Gullick 1995, 46–50). Factoring in time for corrections, the scribes averaged 13,000–14,000 letters per day.

The cumbersomeness of reading, writing, or copying bookrolls should not be exaggerated (Hurtado 2014, 327–30). Readers could stand, sit, or lie down, and scrolling with two hands would be automatic (Skeat in Elliott 2004, 82). Bookrolls naturally

---

[1] Waxed tablets were not the only medium for drafts. Quintilian also mentions parchment notebooks (*Inst.* 10.3.31–33), and Catullus (22.5–6) mocks Suffenus for writing everything on new, expensive, papyrus rolls rather than palimpsests. Horace mentions a tablet and stylus (*Sat.* 1.4.15; 1.10.71), but he also began the day with papyrus and pen (*Ep.* 2.1.113), and inked drafts were subject to revision (*Ars* 446–447).

[2] I use the conservative estimate of 2,000 letters per pentaptych throughout this essay, noting here that boards could be smaller or larger and that tablets could contain fewer or additional boards: 250 letters fit an 11.2 × 4.5 cm board (Speidel 1996, 98); 400 letters fit 17 × 14 cm (Kelsey 1923); 500 letters fit 15.5 × 11.9 cm in T.Berol. inv. 10508–10512, which was at least a hexaptych written *transversa* (Calderini 1921, 306–9; Cribiore 1996, 254).

want to roll themselves up (Skeat in Elliott 2004, 71), so they had to be held open. For writing, a roll could be folded under, as depicted in a mosaic of Virgil writing seated in a chair (Martindale 1997, 110–11, pl. 1a). An ancient Egyptian statue depicts a scribe sitting cross-legged on the ground (Metzger 1968, pl. IV), as would be advantageous for copying.[3] A *Vorlage* could be held open with a paperweight if the copyist worked alone, as Hermas describes himself (*Vis.* 2.4), but scribes could have copied via dictation (Parker 2008, 156). There is virtually no artistic representation of Greco-Roman copyists "by *any* method" (Skeat in Elliott 2004, 14; Skeat's emphasis), so "we ... cannot do more than construct theories" (Parker 2008, 156).

Regarding Christian literary activity, Eusebius (c. 260–c. 340 CE) describes Origen's (c. 185–c. 254 CE) early education and later scriptorium. Since childhood Origen learned Christian scriptures by heart through daily recitation (*Hist. eccl.* 6.2.7–8). In adulthood he dictated to more than seven shorthand writers in shifts; at least as many other writers completed drafts and finished works in calligraphy (*Hist. eccl.* 6.23.2). In old age, Origen allowed shorthand transcription of his public discourses (*Hist. eccl.* 6.36.1).

Origen's scripture memorization demands scrutiny. Repeatedly and "almost certainly from memory" (Ehrman et al. 1992, 299), Origen conflates John 12:45 and 14:9c: "He who has seen me has seen the Father who sent me." Yet Origen quotes John 6:51 exactly like Codex Bezae in one place and exactly like Codex Koridethi in another (Ehrman et al. 1992, 173). This is a recurring phenomenon, and Origen expressly identifies textual variants (Metzger 1968, 88–103). Longer quotations agreeing closely with known manuscripts likely entail someone's visual contact with a written source. Origen could read from manuscripts or quote from memory during dictation, and either way someone could revise his quotations later.

The foregoing examples present a range of authorial capabilities and preferences. So when theorizing authors' use of sources, I consider multiple possibilities. Authors could write by themselves or via dictation, and sources could be quoted from memory or through visual contact. Although the scale of authors' enterprises varied, compositions typically developed in stages, beginning with initial drafts on waxed tablets or previously used rolls, and revisions occurred at multiple points. Some processes would have been more efficient than others, but "relatively more difficult" must not be confused with "technically infeasible."

Septuagint Recensions

Septuagint (LXX) recensionists strictly copied and translated, so each Synoptic Gospel evinces more creative rewriting than LXX recensions. Yet the recensionists' use of sources is comparable to the evangelists'. Around the same time as Tatian, Symmachus

---

[3] Regarding the lack of writing desks, see Metzger 1968, 123–37; Derrenbacker 2005, 37–39.

likewise used four *Vorlagen*. *Kaige*, named for its literal translation of וגם ("also") as καίγε ("even"), is the earliest LXX recension, and it consistently interwove two source texts decades before the Gospels emerged.

Along these lines, I elsewhere (Barker 2016, 114–15) adduced the *kaige* Minor Prophets scroll from Naḥal Ḥever (8ḤevXIIgr), which dates to the turn of the era (Tov 1990, 26). Perhaps too briefly, I gave two examples respectively showing *kaige*'s clear dependence on the LXX and proto-Masoretic Hebrew text. Nahum (3:12) compares fortresses to "a fig tree with first fruits," which the LXX oddly translates "fig trees for watchmen" (συκαῖ σκοπούς); since *kaige* reads σκοπ... in column 15, that unusual rendering remained unrevised. Numerous translations were revised, however, and *kaige*'s threefold occurrence of יהוה τῶν δυνάμεων in Zechariah 1:3 matches the Hebrew word count.

Some have objected that *kaige* "hardly requires visual access to a Hebrew text of the 12 Prophets," since the translator habitually replaced the LXX's κύριος παντοκράτωρ ("Lord almighty") with יהוה τῶν δυνάμεων ("YHWH of the troops") for the proto-Masoretic's יהוה צבאות ("YHWH of the armies"; Kloppenborg 2018, 26; see also Kloppenborg 2019, 632, and Kirk 2016, 307). This objection fails to comprehend the particular example of Zechariah 1:3 as well as the general nature of *kaige*. Were the recensionist merely replacing LXX κύριος with the Tetragrammaton and replacing κύριος παντοκράτωρ with יהוה τῶν δυνάμεων, there would be one instance of יהוה τῶν δυνάμεων and one standalone יהוה in *kaige* Zechariah 1:3. On the contrary, 8ḤevXIIgr emphatically uses יהוה τῶν δυνάμεων three times in one verse, just as the proto-Masoretic does.

Similarly, beneath visible blank lines in column 4, an initial lambda is written *ekthesis*, clearly beginning the book of Micah. Whereas the LXX began "And happened a word of the Lord to Micah" (καὶ ἐγένετο λόγος κυρίου πρὸς Μιχαιαν), the Masoretic text commenced "The word of YHWH, which happened to Micah" (דבר יהוה אשר היה אל מיכה). *Kaige* began ΛΟΓΟΣ ה... and Tov's (1990, 33) reconstruction is uncontroversial: "A word of YHWH, which happened to Micah" (λόγος ה[יהוה ὃς ἐγένετο πρὸς Μιχαιαν]). If *kaige*'s Hebrew correspondences were realized from memory, then the recensionist memorized the entirety of the Minor Prophets. Though not impossible, this scenario is implausible in light of Dead Sea Scrolls' scribal tendencies and rabbinic prohibitions of "copying" Scripture from memory (*b. Meg.* 18b; Tov 2004, 11).[4]

The scale of *kaige*'s project required ongoing visual contact with Hebrew and Greek texts, and elsewhere I have elucidated representative examples (Barker 2018, 127–30). *Kaige* Habakkuk 3:14 looks like an independent translation, since the preposition ἐν is the only one of fifteen LXX words left intact. Conversely, in Habakkuk 2:18 *kaige* reproduces twenty of the LXX's twenty-three words; the three alterations align with the Hebrew. In Habakkuk 2:7 *kaige* reproduces ten of the LXX's fifteen words, and again *kaige*'s variations match the Hebrew. In Septuagint studies it is axiomatic that the *kaige* recension of the Minor Prophets resulted from thoroughgoing comparison of written Greek and Hebrew *Vorlagen* (Fernández Marcos 2000, 109; Tov 1990, 102–58).

---

[4] On the similarities between the Dead Sea Scrolls' material production and Maimonides's medieval description, see Poole and Reed 1962, 17–22.

Kaige interwove two source texts by simple collation, and later recensionists maintained and increased the degree of difficulty. Aquila (c. 120 CE) based his recension on *kaige*-Theodotion and made additional revisions toward the Hebrew (Greenspoon 1983, 235–53). Working primarily from Aquila's recension, Symmachus (c. 200 CE) added numerous renderings from the Hebrew while occasionally agreeing verbatim with the LXX and *kaige*-Theodotion (Salvesen 1991, 255–62; van der Meer 2018). In the third century, Origen was producing the Hexapla by collating the Hebrew, LXX, Aquila, Symmachus, and Theodotion, plus three other revisions. A century earlier, Justin Martyr (c. 100–c. 165) conflated the LXX and *kaige* in the Minor Prophets (Barker 2018, 130–39).

Decades before any Gospel, *kaige* unquestionably combined two sources to produce a new text. The question is how the translator(s) worked. One person could read the Hebrew text with another reading Greek and someone writing the revised translation. Alternatively, one person could use two sources simultaneously. The recensionist worked phrase by phrase and only needed one column in view at any time. Even with wide columns like 1QIsaiah and 8HevXIIgr, two juxtaposed *Vorlagen* would measure approximately the same length as an open copy of *Q Parallels* (Kloppenborg 1988).

At a preparatory stage, a recensionist could have collated sources and noted minor alterations on the Greek *Vorlage*. The presence and absence of *kaige*'s definite articles often realign with the proto-Masoretic against the LXX (Tov 1990, 106–8), and other alterations could fit between lines or columns. More complicated revisions could have been drafted on waxed tablets, versos of documentary texts, or ostraca. The sections of *kaige* most closely resembling the LXX could have been drafted onto rolls initially. The entire project also could have been drafted on waxed tablets. Based on Tov's reconstruction (1990, 9), the Minor Prophets would fill three papyrus rolls. The recensionist could draft one book at a time on thirteen pentaptychs; thirteen triptychs would suffice if working through the three longest books one-half at a time. Any of these reverse-engineered materials and processes would have been uncomplicated at the turn of the era.

JOSEPHUS'S *ANTIQUITIES*

Josephus published the *Antiquities* in the last decade of the first century CE, roughly contemporary with the synoptists. Half of the *Antiquities* follows the chronology of the Tanakh, and Josephus condensed, expanded, and reinterpreted while paraphrasing. Although he lacks the synoptists' verbatim agreements, Josephus is comparable because he worked with different books telling the same stories. Gerald Downing and Robert Derrenbacker have examined the *Antiquities*' parallels with Samuel–Kings and Chronicles, but Josephus's redactional work is more complex than has been acknowledged.

Josephus interweaves 2 Samuel and 1 Chronicles throughout *Ant.* 7.46–64 regarding the consolidation of David's reign (Begg 2005, 218–23). Josephus narrates an assassination of Saul's son (*Ant.* 7.46–52 // 2 Sam 4:1–12), which the Chronicler omits.

Samuel–Kings and Chronicles converge for David's anointing at Hebron (2 Sam 5:1–5 // 1 Chr 11:1–3 // *Ant.* 7.53). There Josephus includes the Chronicler's reference to Samuel (1 Chr 11:3), who goes unmentioned in 2 Samuel. Additional *Sondergut* relates the three-day feast (1 Chr 12:23–40), which the Chronicler narrates via flashback. Josephus advances the feast to the proper time and place (*Ant.* 7.54–60), and then David's army captures Jerusalem (2 Sam 5:6–10 // 1 Chr 11:4–9). Only in 2 Samuel (5:6) is David taunted as though hypothetically disabled people could defeat him. Josephus depicts literal, physically disabled people mocking David (*Ant.* 7.61). Only in 1 Chronicles (11:6) does Joab distinguish himself and became a commander; Josephus incorporates Joab's valorous promotion (*Ant.* 7.63–64).

Derrenbacker rightly identifies 2 Samuel as framing Josephus's sequence, but Derrenbacker wrongly denies Josephus's use of the Chronicler's wording (2005, 102–3). Derrenbacker maintains that Josephus does not move "back and forth between sources *within* episodes" (2011, 441, Derrenbacker's emphasis), but that is precisely the case in *Ant.* 7.63–64. Downing more accurately explained the source combinations in this passage (1980, 63), but he characterized Josephus as giving up and writing "a completely fresh account of his own" (1980, 62). Josephus did write a new account, but it straightforwardly combined elements from both sources.

The same is true of Josephus's list of David's descendants (*Ant.* 7.70) via 2 Samuel 5:13–16, 1 Chronicles 3:5–9, and 1 Chronicles 14:3–7. Each biblical list differs from the others, and Josephus diverges yet again (Begg 2005, 223). Josephus's placement corresponds to 2 Samuel's narrative sequence, but two features show dependence on 1 Chronicles 3 (Avioz 2015, 180). Josephus concludes with David's daughter Tamar, who is listed only in 1 Chronicles 3:9. And although Josephus names eleven sons, he says that there were nine. This mistake is explicable, since the Chronicler distinguishes David's four sons by Bathshua (1 Chr 3:5) from his nine other sons (vv. 6–8). Josephus thus found nine sons and one daughter, Tamar, together in 1 Chronicles 3:8–9. Downing granted: "Just occasionally (Josephus) seems to glance across at Chronicles, to check a list of names" (1980, 61). In material terms, Josephus could hardly glance at the Chronicler's first list. Josephus had advanced as far as 1 Chronicles 11:6, if not 14:1–7, so scrolling back to chapter 3 covered a minimum of sixteen wide columns.

Given the scope of Josephus's project, it is highly unlikely that he memorized sources verbatim.[5] Yet I grant that some references could be reminiscences. For example, Josephus notes that Joshua had not expelled the Jebusites from Jerusalem centuries before David (*Ant.* 7.67–68; cf. Josh 15:63). Conversely, the name of Tamar and the solecism of nine sons likely indicate visual contact. Good recollection of texts does not preclude visual contact with manuscripts, for recollection was prerequisite to searching and finding parallels.

Josephus's text reveals unmistakable traces of two sources being combined within one pericope. He could achieve this by writing in a group via dictation. One person

---

[5] The LXX's historical narratives paralleling *Antiquities* 1–10 are longer than the *Iliad* and *Odyssey* combined (> 230,000 words).

could read 2 Samuel, another could read 1 Chronicles, and yet another could write the harmonized version. Regardless, Josephus could have drafted on waxed tablets, the contents of which would be transferred to bookrolls at regular intervals. *Antiquities* 7.1–70 would fill ten pentaptychs or two-thirds of one papyrus roll. Josephus also could have drafted on used bookrolls, three of which would contain book 7.

It is also possible that Josephus worked through sources sequentially by himself. On this model, he could paraphrase what he wanted from 2 Samuel, leave considerable margins in his draft, and later incorporate elements from 1 Chronicles. Or Josephus could have worked economically by himself with both source texts in view. For the conquest of Jerusalem, 2 Samuel 5:6–10 and 1 Chronicles 11:4–9 each comprise less than 600 letters, so a maximum of two columns of each source needed to be unrolled. Assuming wide columns as in 8ḤevXIIgr, each source would stretch 29 cm across, the spatial equivalent of opening two copies of Rahlfs's Septuagint pocket edition side by side.

Downing posited that ancient authors worked "as simply as possible," particularly with "little or no scrolling to and fro" (1991, 111). For Josephus's list of David's descendants, a simpler process would have ignored 1 Chronicles 3 and used the text(s) already in view. Yet Josephus voluntarily traversed one-third the length of a 1 Chronicles scroll to quote the earlier list. Josephus further complicated matters by occasionally conflating Hebrew and Greek versions of the same text.[6] I conclude, then, that Josephus did not work as simply as possible but that he did work simply: collation, conflation, harmonization, moving forward and backward through scrolls, and even working with two scrolls at once would have been relatively simple processes for a first-century author.

Tatian's Diatessaron

In the second half of the second century, Tatian constructed the Diatessaron, one Gospel "out of the four." Since the direction of dependence is certain, Tatian offers valuable insights into the synoptists' compositional practices. Some scholars hesitate to draw this analogy, since none of the Synoptics is a harmony per se (Derrenbacker 2005, 158; Kloppenborg 2019, 639). Thus it is crucial to clarify how Tatian compares to his canonical counterparts. Each synoptist rewrites sources more than Tatian, who quotes the Gospels with barely a trace of paraphrase. Moreover, Tatian includes every episode from each Gospel and adds nothing original.[7] On the whole, none of the canonical Gospels

---

[6] E.g., Josephus combines "ransoming" [= Hebrew] Jonathan with "praying for" [= Greek] him (1 Sam 14:45 // *Ant.* 6.128; Avioz 2015, 199–200; Begg 2009, 25–26), and the ghost of Samuel tells Saul that his children will "fall" [= Greek] in battle and "be with me" [= Hebrew] (1 Sam 28:19 // *Ant.* 6.336; Avioz 2015, 200). Derrenbacker (2005, 115) undervalues Josephus's text-critical conflations.

[7] According to ancient testimonies, the exceptions are omitting Jesus's genealogy, which is present in extant witnesses, and adding light at Jesus's baptism, which is absent from extant witnesses.

is so comprehensive and unoriginal, for each one adds or subtracts something vis-à-vis the others.

The Diatessaron admittedly lacks originality in those regards, yet Tatian hardly lacked innovation. Above all, he fashioned a coherent narrative out of conflicting accounts. And in individual episodes, Tatian generated new meanings by selective omission and creative juxtaposition (Watson 2016, 111). Francis Watson determines: "Tatian's treatment of his sources is on a continuum with Luke's or Matthew's" (2016, 95), and current scholarship considers Tatian an evangelist in his own right. He likely wrote within a century of the Synoptics, and the Diatessaron offers incontrovertible evidence of a subsequent evangelist managing four source texts simultaneously, including the very sources that must be disentangled in the Synoptic Problem.

In the foremost western witness to the Diatessaron, Codex Fuldensis,[8] the feeding of the 5,000 comprises 170 Latin words (f. 73). In fifty lines, the scribe switched sources nine times, excising between three and forty-four words: Matthew 14:15 (3), Luke 9:12 (24), Matthew 14:16 (12), John 6:5–6 (14), Mark 6:38 (6), John 6:8–9 (28), Luke 9:13 (11), Matthew 14:18 (7), Mark 6:39–40 (21), Matthew 14:19–21 (44).[9] The length of this passage is minute within Fuldensis (<0.5 percent), but such intricacy characterizes much of Tatian's work. I approximate the Diatessaron's makeup as follows: harmonization of the Synoptics (55 percent), harmonization of the fourfold gospel (20 percent), long Johannine blocks (19 percent), long Lukan blocks (5 percent), and the Matthean nativity (1 percent).[10] It is thus inaccurate to characterize "the major part of the Diatessaron" as "block-by-block" (contra Mattila 1995, 205), since three-fourths of the time Tatian worked with three or four sources simultaneously.

Before he could harmonize the wording, Tatian had to locate parallels, and he shows remarkable dexterity when traversing sources. Tatian repositions more than twenty medium-sized columns (> 20,000 Greek letters) within each Gospel. He moves from a Matthean Sabbath controversy (Matt 12:2; Arabic 7.38) to the Sermon on the Mount (Matt 5:1; Arabic 8.27) and from the Markan deaf-mute healing (7:31–37; Arabic 21.1–7) to the leprosy healing (1:40–45; Arabic 22.1–8). There Tatian harmonizes with Luke (5:12–16), which was last used for a handwashing controversy (11:37–41; Arabic 20.12–16), and Tatian moves from John's Sukkoth material (ch. 7; Arabic 28) back to the temple disruption (2:14–22; Arabic 32.1–11). Without a standardized numbering system, readers had to scan the text, and these relocations cross between one-fifth and one-third the length of each Gospel.

Adeptly moving forward and backward to and from any point in any Gospel, Tatian even creates narrative sequences disrupting Synoptic unanimity (contra Downing 1992: 36). After the Transfiguration, Jesus exorcises a demon causing epilepsy (Matt 17:1–21 // Mark 9:2–29 // Luke 9:28–43). Rejecting this ready-made sequence, Tatian repositions

---

[8] Fulda MS Bonifatianus 1 (Victor Codex).
[9] Although that may seem complicated, the (western) Fuldensis text represents a simplification of Tatian's original harmonization as represented by the (eastern) Arabic harmony (18.27–43; Hogg 1896).
[10] Estimates come from column counts of Fuldensis.

approximately eighteen columns in a manuscript of Luke (13:31–33) to insert the Pharisees' warning about Herod Antipas (Arabic 24.25–29; Fuldensis ff. 88v–89r).

Tatian relied on his memory, but that does not mean he had the Gospels memorized. Memorization required exponentially more read-throughs than simply composing with source texts in view.[11] Nonetheless, I presuppose that Tatian had read his sources repeatedly and likely made his own copies at some point.[12] Tatian could have composed the Diatessaron using dictation (Mattila 1995, 215). Separate individuals could read each Gospel, and one person could write the harmony after discussing possible combinations. A group of three could have one writer, while two readers managed two Gospels apiece, and numerous other combinations are plausible. Extensive harmonizations would be easier to draft on tablets, although it is conceivable that sections were drafted directly onto rolls.

Tatian also could have composed the Diatessaron by himself. For such passages as the feeding of the 5,000 and the passion narrative, he could indeed manage four sources simultaneously. Four open copies of the pocket edition of NA^{28} occupy approximately the same space as four bookrolls open two columns or four open codices the size of Papyrus 75. Another approach would be first to collate a pericope from any two sources, then to draft a harmony of those two, and finally to revise the draft by incorporating the remaining sources. The trade-off is between juggling and revising: the more sources apprehended at one time, the fewer revisions while drafting, and vice versa. However Tatian worked, the Diatessaron's combination and traversal of sources handily surpasses any synoptist's degree of difficulty as determined by every Synoptic hypothesis.

Writing the Synoptics

Orality and memory are central concerns regarding the synoptists' writing processes. Grounded in Homeric theories, some scholars argue that the Gospels were composed during oral performance (Dewey 2004, 499–500; Wire 2011). Conceivably following centuries of oral transmission, the *Iliad* and *Odyssey* became relatively fixed in writing by 600 BCE (West 2011, 392). By 500 BCE the works of the Epic Cycle might have been composed using "essentially the same poetic language derived from an oral tradition of hexameter verse" (Sammons 2017, 3). According to this model, the Gospels are "written 'transcriptions' of oral narratives that had been composed in performance" (Rhoads 2006, 118), although the performers neither read nor memorized scripts (118, 123). The surviving transcripts came from listeners remembering lengthy performances "with great faithfulness" (124).

---

[11] Though not impossible, such memorization would have been extraordinary, like Augustine's friend Simplicius, who knew Virgil's *Aeneid* forward and backward (*Nat. orig.* 4.7.9; Carruthers 2008, 21–22); the *Aeneid*'s word count (c. 64,000) is comparable to the Greek Gospels (c. 65,000).

[12] For building a library by copying manuscripts yourself, see Houston 2014, 13–14.

I am skeptical that this model applies to the Gospels.[13] Even if the *Iliad, Odyssey,* and Epic Cycle were composed in performance, the Hellenistic period marked a shift. Around 300 BCE the Muses began dictating to solitary poets writing on tablets for eventual readers (Bing 2008, 14–20). Similarly, Apollonius of Rhodes mastered Homeric *imitatio* in the third-century BCE *Argonautica*, but he did not likely compose in oral performance (Hunter 2012, 122). Moreover, the transcript model of Gospel textualization—albeit not impossible—would be highly exceptional, surpassing any memory capability that Quintilian describes. Despite having trained his memory since childhood, Quintilian found it difficult to memorize by listening to someone reading repetitively (*Inst.* 11.2.34), and prose was harder than poetry (*Inst.* 11.2.39).

A more plausible model is that the synoptists, whether by themselves or using dictation, drafted texts on used bookrolls or waxed tablets. It is inaccurate to call tablets unwieldy (contra Eve 2016, 54), and it is misleading to allege their limited capacity (contra Kirk 2016, 49). Works were drafted on waxed tablets from the Hellenistic period through the Middle Ages, and Quintilian's twelve-volume *Institutio Oratoria* is longer than the New Testament; three of Quintilian's books exceed the length of Luke's Gospel. Assuming Quintilian drafted on tablets, his longest book would fill fifty-six pentaptychs spanning approximately 1.7 m spine to spine. It would take eleven days to copy so much content onto bookrolls, so he likely transferred fewer tablets more regularly. We cannot know exactly how many tablets authors typically used, but Anselm of Canterbury had enough to draft the equivalent of nearly half of Luke's Gospel.[14]

Luke would need sixteen pentaptychs to draft the Gospel in one-third increments, as John Poirier (2012, 23) suggests. Or Luke could use twelve pentaptychs and transfer the contents when he could fill most of a bookroll.[15] The more tablets an author filled initially, the more time needed for transferring to rolls eventually, but an author might lose momentum from frequent transference. I infer that ancient authors discovered a range of preferences, and I emphasize that the Gospels are relatively short literary works.[16]

Christians' early adoption of the codex is well attested (Hurtado 2006, 43–93), and the papyri of the Synoptics are from codices. First-century copies could have circulated this way, but that would be remarkably early, since rolls overwhelmingly outnumber codices through the second century (Hurtado 2006, 92). By 85 CE (Citroni 2012, 905) Martial

---

[13] Similar skepticism comes from Hurtado 2014, 335, and Eve 2016, 67–72. Oral composition models may nonetheless illuminate Jesus's original storytelling.

[14] Anselm drafted the *Proslogion* (> 23,000 letters) on tablets, which later disappeared, so he rewrote it on a second set (Rouse and Rouse 1989: 179).

[15] Downing's (2013, 391) estimate of 500 letters per page is plausible, albeit the uppermost limit for a single board (e.g. T.Berol. 14004). However, Downing shows no awareness of polyptychs, thereby vastly overestimating 180–200 tablets for Luke's Gospel or 60–70 for each of Poirier's (2012, 23) divisions; Eve (2016, 144) uncritically accepts these estimates. Similarly Kirk (2016, 49) references Baldric of Bourgueil regarding tablets' limited capacity. In fact, Baldric's poem about his octoptych (Vatican MS Reg. lat. 1351 ff. 24v–25v) reveals that the tablet could fit 3,785 letters (14 pages of 8 lines averaging 33.8 letters).

[16] E.g., Josephus's *Antiquities* is twice as long as the New Testament, and book 7 is longer than Luke's Gospel. In *scriptio continua* this essay is approximately half the length of Luke's Gospel.

(14.184–92) offers the earliest description of parchment codices, although their legal status was debated a few decades earlier (Bülow-Jacobsen 2009, 18), and the earliest material remains are P.Oxy. 1.30, dated c. 100 CE (Mallon 1949, 7). The safest bet is that the synoptists were still using bookrolls.

A key question is how subsequent synoptists accessed sources. Evangelists could work without direct access to texts, particularly when writing *Sondergut*. Luke (7:11–17) casts Jesus in a motif common to Elijah and Elisha, but Luke did not need 1 Kings 17 or 2 Kings 4 in view. Matthew's parable of the dragnet (13:47–50) could be an original composition or reminiscence of oral tradition, neither of which necessitates a written source. Such invention and composition could be "completely mental" (Carruthers 2008, 241), but *Sondergut* contrasts sharply with close verbal agreements elsewhere.

For close verbal agreements, the evangelists could remember content from written sources. Mary Carruthers argues that inexact quotations arise via memory and visual contact alike, so an author might read or recall something precisely while intentionally altering the wording (Carruthers 2008, 111). I do not disagree in general, but in particular cases I consider exactness or inexactness of wording an indication of visual contact or the lack thereof—for example, Origen's long verbatim quotations versus his customary conflation of John 14:9 and 12:45.

I apply this principle to the Gospels as well. Nothing in the Tanakh says that the Messiah "shall be called a Nazorean" (Matt 2:23), so Matthew misremembers something and attributes the phrase to the plural "prophets," like saying "Scripture says somewhere . . ." (e.g. 1 Clem 23.3, 42.5). Conversely, on the supposition of Markan priority, Matthew (13:14–15) adds a verbatim quotation of forty-seven words to Mark's (4:12) allusion to Isaiah 6:9–10. Matthew might have remembered his Old Testament quotations, some of which he reproduced better than others. Or Matthew might have drafted from memory and subsequently checked some quotations against sources while leaving others unrevised. Regardless, I incline further toward visual contact the longer and more precise the verbal correspondence.

To the contrary, Eric Eve suggests, "it is thus possible that the Evangelists had memory command of all their written sources, and so made little or no use of direct eye contact with any of them while composing their own work" (2016, 41). Similarly, Alan Kirk highlights the "memory assimilation of a cultural tradition" via "ruminative reading and recitation" (2016, 94, 96).[17] Yet Kirk does not specify "whatever level of manual and visual engagement Matthew might have with the source" (221). I presuppose that the evangelists relied on memory, in the sense that they knew where to locate parallel pericopes with written texts in view. Given so much verbatim agreement among the Synoptics, I reject memory as the "default working hypothesis" (Eve 2016, 50) and accept instead that the evangelists maintained "regular visual/physical contact with source texts" (Derrenbacker 2017, 221) when composing parallel stories and sayings.

---

[17] Kirk often invokes memory to mitigate the alleged cumbersomeness of bookrolls (e.g. 2016, 165, 218), so it sounds like Matthew memorized sources (Derrenbacker 2017, 218–21; Goodacre 2017, 227–28), yet Kirk stops short of memorization (2017, 235–36, 250).

Synoptists' Visual Contact with Sources

The collection and study of similar works is well attested in the Greco-Roman era (Johnson 2010), and LXX recensions exemplify scholarly projects of collecting and collating earlier editions to produce new ones. Elsewhere I have contextualized the proliferation of Gospels in these terms (Barker 2019).[18] According to this model, subsequent synoptists could write via dictation with multiple readers handling separate sources while someone drafted revised pericopes after study and discussion.[19]

Another model for source combination involves an individual collating two texts and glossing one of them. This process could underlie numerous "minor agreements." For example, when Jesus heals paralysis,[20] Matthew and Luke align against Mark by adding "look!" and specifying that the person was "on a bed"; after the healing they clarify that he "went away into his house." Constituting 1,007 letters in NA[28], Mark 2:1–12 would occupy one full column or two partial ones in a manuscript. At a preparatory stage, Luke could gloss Matthean omissions, additions, and alterations directly on his Markan *Vorlage*.[21] By adding forty-one letters as annotations,[22] the Markan manuscript could be the only one in view, yet Luke's version would combine both sources throughout.

Excerpting is a related process for gathering disparate pieces of one text. Watson (2009, 406) suggests that "in the course of reducing Matthew's Sermon on the Mount to his own Sermon on the Plain, Luke has copied into a notebook those Matthean items he wishes to set aside for subsequent use."[23] Hence Luke's distribution of Sermon on the Mount material does not require "breathtaking" leaps across a manuscript of Matthew (contra Kirk 2016, 150; cf. Goodacre 2017, 229). The reverse process works for Matthean Posteriority: Matthew copies Lukan sayings into tablets and composes his sermon with the tablets of excerpts beside a manuscript open to Luke's Sermon on the Plain. Similarly, for the Two-Source Hypothesis, it is indeed "compositionally feasible" for Matthew to excerpt Q based on multiple readings.[24]

---

[18] E.g., Plutarch's is the lone survivor of nine attested lives of Cato the Younger written within two centuries (Barker 2019, 115–16), and Plutarch used multiple sources. He cites Caesar's accusation of Cato's incest but adds that Cato honorably cared for his widowed sister (*Cat. Min.* 54). Although the exculpating source goes uncited, Plutarch's combination of sources should not be denied (contra Pelling 2002, 21; followed by Derrenbacker 2005, 46; Downing 1988, 72–73; Eve 2016, 57; Kirk 2016, 56–57; Kloppenborg 2019, 638).

[19] Eve (2016, 59–60) mentions dictation as one possibility among others.

[20] Matt 9:1–8 // Mark 2:1–12 // Luke 5:17–26.

[21] I presume that Luke discriminated among Matthean omissions rather than marking them all.

[22] Luke could write ἰδού above and between καὶ and ἔρχονται (Mark 2:3); ἐπὶ κλίνης above παραλυτικόν (v. 3); εἶπεν above λέγει (v. 5); dots under or over τῷ παραλυτικῷ signifying omission (v. 9); ἀπ- above ἐξῆλθεν and εἰς τὸν οἶκον αὐτοῦ interlinear or intercolumnar (v. 12); and φόβος somewhere (v. 12). Such annotations are attested at Qumran (Tov 2004, 178–235) and Oxyrhynchus (Johnson 2010: 179–92).

[23] Eve (2016, 145) also makes this suggestion.

[24] Contra Kirk (2016, 163–64, 168–69); if Kirk means that Matthew recalled Q without visual contact (e.g. 2016, 218), then Matthew must have read Q many more times than are required for scanning and excerpting.

Excerpting is not a necessary postulate, however, for authors could relocate within their source texts in one sitting. Supposing Markan priority, Matthew (10:14, 17–22) moves from Mark 6:11 to 13:9—nearly half the length of the Gospel—to bring apocalyptic sayings into the mission discourse.[25] Luke brings the anointing woman forward from the passion (Mark 14:3–9) and next uses Mark for the parable of the sower (4:1–9; Luke 8:4–8), thereby traversing two-thirds of Mark's Gospel.[26] According to the Two-Source Hypothesis, Mark was the only narrative source for Matthew and Luke, and each literarily dependent synoptist voluntarily rearranged their sources—Matthew more so than Luke.

It takes far more time to write than to read,[27] and the time for repositioning within a manuscript is negligible compared to cogitation and rewriting. Supposing that Matt 8:1–9:26 was initially drafted as is, Matthew transposes two healings (Matt 8:14–17 // Mark 1:29–34; Matt 8:1–4 // Mark 1:40–45), but both Markan stories could be in view with two columns unrolled.[28] Next Matthew scrolls forward eight columns and writes two more miracle stories in 1,053 letters (Matt 8:23–34 // Mark 4:35–5:20). Matthew then scrolls back ten columns to write 1,640 letters for the paralysis healing and subsequent episodes (Matt 9:1–17 // Mark 2:1–22). Finally Matthew scrolls forward eight columns and writes 668 letters for the hemorrhaging woman and Jairus's daughter (Matt 9:18–26 // Mark 5:21–43). Matthew 8:1–9:26 entails three relocations within Mark, each of which could be accomplished in a minute or two. Conversely, the minimum physical writing time of Matthew's shortest rendition was approximately twenty minutes, bracketing altogether the process of cogitation.[29]

Although Matthew's traversals are unproblematic, others worry about the "sheer scale of (Markan) transpositions in Matthew 8 and 9" (Kirk 2016, 248). In this case, one need not presuppose that Matthew's draft proceeded in the same sequence as the published version, for the Gospels were not likely written "in a single pass" (Eve 2016, 143). Matthew could have followed Mark's order initially. Matthew (8:1–9:26) uses less than 3,000 letters from Mark 1–2, which could fill most of two tablets. In a separate pentaptych, Matthew (8:1–9:26) could fit less than 2,000 letters from Mark 4–5. Later, when transferring the tablets to a bookroll, Matthew could easily rearrange the sequence by alternating between tablets. Two juxtaposed 14 × 12 cm polyptychs occupy no more space than an open copy of Kirk's *Q in Matthew* (2016).

Moreover, an individual could feasibly place two manuscripts side by side. It is impossible to hold a bookroll in two hands and copy it at the same, but scribes managed

---

[25] Kirk (2016, 295) deems Matthew's reach from Mark 6:11 to 13:9 "as far as" Matthew ever reaches within Q; Matthew's leap here is actually 50 percent longer than the entirety of Q (Robinson et al. 2000) and more than double Matthew's longest reach within Q (Kirk 2016, 218).

[26] Greg Carey elucidates this as a Lukan redactional *Tendenz*, and he cautions against appeals to memory, since written sources can be in view even for extensive rewriting (2013, 312).

[27] E.g., Matt 1:18–25 NA[28] (775 letters) takes me two minutes to read aloud but fourteen minutes to scribble, reading and writing minuscule with quill and ink on papyrus and with a stylus on wax; reading and writing majuscule in *scriptio continua* takes me twenty-five minutes.

[28] The following calculations approximate 1,000 letters per column, as attested in select prose texts from Oxyrhynchus (Johnson 2004, 217–30); compare c. 1,500 letters per column in 8ḤevXIIgr.

[29] Twenty minutes presumes an exceptionally high rate of c. 13,000 letters per day.

to copy manuscripts by themselves (Hermas *Vis.* 2.4). The simplest solution is that *Vorlagen* were held open by paperweights. It is inconsequential that any such artistic representation (contra Small 1997, 167, and Kirk 2016, 54) is lacking, since there are no ancient depictions of Greco-Roman manuscript copying at all (Skeat in Elliott 2004, 14). Ancient visual art does, however, portray bookrolls open wider than an adult's shoulders (Birt 1907, 155–70). A stretch of 50 cm would expose four or five columns in a single bookroll, but the same span could easily fit two bookrolls open two columns each; for comparison, an open copy of *The Critical Edition of Q* (2000) measures 46 cm across. Objections to simultaneous use of two written sources cannot be sustained.

Conclusion

Authors could remember texts without rereading them, but higher degrees of verbatim agreement increase the likelihood of visual contact. If evangelists are envisioned working predominantly from memory, then no evangelist or hypothesis should be privileged (Barker 2016, 121). Luke can remember Matthew's text (Goodacre 2017, 229) just as Matthew can remember Q (Kirk 2016), and so on. Special pleading should likewise be avoided if the Gospels are imagined circulating in codices in the first century. Matthew could use a codex of Q (Derrenbacker 2005, 25), or Matthew could use a codex of Luke according to Matthean Posteriority, and so forth. Synoptists could draft works on rolls or waxed tablets by themselves or via dictation, and by all means it was feasible to maintain visual contact with multiple manuscripts and to reposition repeatedly within them.

Every solution to the Synoptic Problem requires an evangelist to interweave multiple sources and rearrange their sayings and narratives. The Two-Source Hypothesis is hereby absolved of any charge of impracticality regarding laborious scrolling through source texts.[30] The same absolution for scrolling and, more importantly, for the number of sources regularly combined extends to the Farrer, Griesbach, Augustinian, and Three-Source hypotheses, as well as Matthean Posteriority.

Figure 3.1 diagrams those six theories of Synoptic interrelations, and table 3.1 ranks the modus operandi of real and hypothetical first- and second-century authors from most to least difficult. The primary factor in degree of difficulty is the number of sources regularly used, and a secondary concern is the extents to which sources were reordered; when theories are roughly equal on those grounds, I consider the amount of original composition as a tiebreaker.[31]

---

[30] Exaggerations such as scrolling "furiously" (Kirk 2016, 218) and "absurdly furious" scrolling (Kirk 2017, 250) should thus be avoided.

[31] Elsewhere (Barker 2016, 121) I neglected how much more *kaige* works with two sources simultaneously than does Griesbach Mark. The same applies to Farrer and Augustinian Luke vis-à-vis Two-Source Matthew. I also excluded Matthean Posteriority and Three-Source theories.

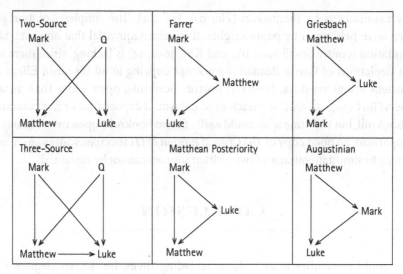

FIGURE 3.1 Six Theories of Synoptic Relations.

Table 3.1 Relative degrees of difficulty for use of sources in first- and second-century texts

1	Tatian	Tatian predominantly works with three or four sources, which are frequently reordered.
2	Symmachus	Symmachus constantly uses Aquila and the proto-Masoretic while occasionally using the LXX and *kaige*-Theodotion.
3	Three-Source Luke	Luke uses Matthew, Mark, and Q in Mark-Q overlap; Matthew and Mark in triple tradition; and Matthew and Q in double tradition.
4	Josephus *Antiquities* 7	Josephus closely coordinates 2 Samuel and 1 Chronicles, even when he alternates between them. Josephus occasionally uses at least one additional source, since he knows Hebrew and Greek versions of 2 Samuel.
5	*Kaige*-Theodotion and Aquila	These recensionists reflect constant, close coordination of the LXX and proto-Masoretic. *Kaige*-Theodotion and Aquila likely reordered the books of the Dodekapropheton, which exceeds the length of each canonical Gospel.
6	Matthean Posteriority Matthew	Matthew uses one fewer source than Three-Source Luke and with more reordering than Farrer or Augustinian Luke.
7	Farrer Luke = Augustinian Luke	Luke uses Matthew and Mark in triple tradition as well as Matthew in double tradition. Both sources are occasionally reordered, and much new material is composed.

Table 3.1 Continued

8	Griesbach Mark	Mark coordinates two sources most of the time, but he sometimes uses them individually and reorders them both. Mark also omits much from each source while adding minimal original material.
9	Two-Source Matthew = Three-Source Matthew	Matthew uses two sources simultaneously for Mark–Q overlap and regularly reorders both sources.
10	Two-Source Luke	Luke uses two sources simultaneously for Mark–Q overlap but otherwise uses one source at a time with occasional reordering of Mark.
11	Griesbach Luke	Luke uses Matthew, and this Matthean material outweighs the Markan material in Farrer Matthew.
12	Farrer Matthew	Matthew uses and reorders Mark more than Matthean Posteriority Luke does.
13	Matthean Posteriority Luke	Luke omits several Markan pericopes and composes more new material than does Augustinian Mark.
14	Augustinian Mark	Mark expands some and omits other Matthean material while adding minimal original material.

Gospel studies have commendably shifted focus to ancient writing practices, but the Synoptic Problem cannot be solved by arguments about compositional conventions. Some operations were demonstrably more complex than others, but none of the synoptists interwove as many Gospel sources, repositioned as many times within them, or rearranged as much material as Tatian did with the very same texts. Josephus and the LXX recensionists also maneuvered more intricately than almost every hypothetical synoptist. And among Synoptic hypotheses, the data evens out. For example, Farrer Luke has it harder than Two-Source Matthew, but Two-Source Luke has it harder than Farrer Matthew. Regarding the use of sources in ancient compositions, every major and minor Synoptic theory entails plausible, attested, and unexceptional means of material production.

References

Avioz, Michael. 2015. *Josephus' Interpretation of the Books of Samuel*. Library of Second Temple Studies 86. London: Bloomsbury T&T Clark.

Barker, James W. 2016. "Ancient Compositional Practices and the Gospels: A Reassessment." *JBL* 135: 109–21.

Barker, James W. 2018. "The Equivalence of *Kaige* and *Quinta* in the Dodekapropheton." In *Found in Translation: Essays on Jewish Biblical Translation in Honor of Leonard J. Greenspoon*, edited by James W. Barker, Anthony Le Donne, and Joel N. Lohr, 127–52. West Lafayette: Purdue University Press.

Barker, James W. 2019. "Tatian's Diatessaron and the Proliferation of Gospels." In *The Gospel of Tatian: Exploring the Nature and Text of the Diatessaron*, edited by Matthew R. Crawford and Nicholas J. Zola, *The Reception of Jesus in the First Three Centuries* 3, 111–41. London: Bloomsbury T&T Clark.

Begg, Christopher. 2005. *Flavius Josephus: Translation and Commentary*. Vol. 4. *Judean Antiquities Books 5–7*. Leiden: Brill.

Begg, Christopher. 2009. "The Adventures of Jonathan According to Josephus." *Sacra Scripta* 7: 7–31.

Bing, Peter. 2008. *The Well-Read Muse: Present and Past in Callimachus and the Hellenistic Poets*. Ann Arbor: Michigan Classical Press.

Birt, Theodor. 1907. *Die Buchrolle in der Kunst: archäologisch-antiquarische Untersuchungen zum antiken Buchwesen*. Leipzig: Teubner.

Bülow-Jacobsen, Adam. 2009. "Writing Materials in the Ancient World." In *The Oxford Handbook of Papyrology*, edited by Roger S. Bagnall, 3–29. Oxford: Oxford University Press.

Calderini, Aristide. 1921. "Commenti 'minori' al testo di Omero in documenti egiziani." *Aegyptus* 2: 303–26.

Carey, Greg. 2013. "Moving Things Ahead: A Lukan Redactional Technique and Its Implications for Gospel Origins." *BibInt* 21: 302–19.

Carruthers, Mary. 2008. *The Book of Memory: A Study of Memory in Medieval Culture*. 2nd ed. Cambridge Studies in Medieval Literature. Cambridge: Cambridge University Press.

Citroni, Mario. 2012. "Martial." In *The Oxford Classical Dictionary*, 4th ed., edited by Simon Hornblower, Antony Spawforth, and Esther Eidinow, 904–6. Oxford: Oxford University Press.

Cribiore, Raffaella. 1996. *Writing, Teachers, and Students in Graeco-Roman Egypt*. ASP 36. Atlanta: Scholars Press.

Derrenbacker, R. A., Jr. 2005. *Ancient Compositional Practices and the Synoptic Problem*. BETL 186. Leuven: Leuven University Press.

Derrenbacker, R. A., Jr. 2011. "The 'External and Psychological Conditions under Which the Synoptic Gospels Were Written': Ancient Compositional Practices and the Synoptic Problem." In *New Studies in the Synoptic Problem: Oxford Conference, April 2008: Essays in Honour of Christopher M. Tuckett*, edited by Paul Foster et al., BETL 239, 435–55. Leuven: Peeters.

Derrenbacker, R. A., Jr. 2017. "Matthew as Scribal Tradent: An Assessment of Alan Kirk's *Q in Matthew*. *JSHJ* 15: 213–23.

Dewey, Joanna. 2004. "The Survival of Mark's Gospel: A Good Story?" *JBL* 123: 495–507.

Downing, F. Gerald. 1980. "Redaction Criticism: Josephus' *Antiquities* and the Synoptic Gospels (I)." *JSNT* 8: 46–65.

Downing, F. Gerald. 1988. "Compositional Conventions and the Synoptic Problem." *JBL* 107: 69–85.

Downing, F. Gerald. 1991. "Actuality versus Abstraction: The Synoptic Gospel Model." *Continuum* 1: 104–20.

Downing, F. Gerald. 1992. "A Paradigm Perplex: Luke, Matthew and Mark." *NTS* 38: 15–36.

Downing, F. Gerald. 2013. "Waxing Careless: Poirier, Derrenbacker and Downing." *JSNT* 35: 388–93.

Ehrman, Bart D., Gordon D. Fee, and Michael W. Holmes. 1992. *The Text of the Fourth Gospel in the Writings of Origen*. Vol. 1. NTGF 3. Atlanta: Scholars Press.

Elliott, J. K., ed. 2004. *The Collected Biblical Writings of T. C. Skeat*. NovTSup 113. Leiden: Brill.

Eve, Eric. 2016. *Writing the Gospels: Composition and Memory*. London: SPCK.

Fernández Marcos, Natalio. 2000. *The Septuagint in Context: Introduction to the Greek Version of the Bible*. Translated by Wilfred G. E. Watson. Leiden: Brill.

Goodacre, Mark. 2017. "Q, Memory, and Matthew: A Response to Alan Kirk." *JSHJ* 15: 224–33.

Greenspoon, Leonard J. 1983. *Textual Studies in the Book of Joshua*. HSM 28. Chico, CA: Scholars Press.

Gullick, Michael. 1995. "How Fast Did Scribes Write? Evidence from Romanesque Manuscripts." In *Making the Medieval Book: Techniques of Production*, edited by Linda L. Brownrigg, 39–58. Los Altos Hills, CA: Anderson-Lovelace.

Hogg, Hope W. 1896. "The Diatessaron of Tatian." In *The Ante-Nicene Fathers*, edited by Alan Menzies, vol. 9, 33–138. New York: Scribner's.

Houston, George W. 2014. *Inside Roman Libraries: Book Collections and Their Management in Antiquity*. Studies in the History of Greece and Rome. Chapel Hill: University of North Carolina Press.

Hunter, Richard L. 2012. "Apollonius Rhodius." In *The Oxford Classical Dictionary*, 4th ed., edited by Simon Hornblower, Antony Spawforth, and Esther Eidinow, 121–22. Oxford: Oxford University Press.

Hurtado, Larry W. 2006. *The Earliest Christian Artifacts: Manuscripts and Christian Origins*. Grand Rapids: Eerdmans.

Hurtado, Larry W. 2014. "Oral Fixation and New Testament Studies? 'Orality,' 'Performance' and Reading Texts in Early Christianity." *NTS* 60: 321–40.

Johnson, William A. 2004. *Bookrolls and Scribes in Oxyrhynchus*. Toronto: University of Toronto Press.

Johnson, William A. 2010. *Readers and Reading Culture in the High Roman Empire: A Study of Elite Communities*. Classical Culture and Study. Oxford: Oxford University Press.

Kelsey, Francis W. 1923. "A Waxed Tablet of the Year 128 A.D." *TAPA* 54: 187–95.

Kirk, Alan. 2016. *Q in Matthew: Ancient Media, Memory, and Early Scribal Transmission of the Jesus Tradition*. LNTS 564. London: Bloomsbury T&T Clark.

Kirk, Alan. 2017. "The Synoptic Problem, Ancient Media, and the Historical Jesus: A Response." *JSHJ* 15: 234–59.

Kloppenborg, John S. 1988. *Q Parallels: Synopsis, Critical Notes and Concordance*. Foundations and Facets. Sonoma, CA: Polebridge.

Kloppenborg, John S. 2018. "Conceptual Stakes in the Synoptic Problem." In *Gospel Interpretation and the Q Hypothesis*, edited by Mogens Müller and Heike Omerzu, LNTS 573, 13–42. London: Bloomsbury T&T Clark.

Kloppenborg, John S. 2019. "Macro-conflation, Micro-conflation, Harmonization and the Compositional Practices of the Synoptic Writers." *ETL* 95: 629–43.

Mallon, Jean. 1949. "Quel est le plus ancien exemple connu d'un manuscrit latin en forme de codex?" *Emerita* 17: 1–8.

Martindale, Charles, ed. 1997. *The Cambridge Companion to Virgil*. Cambridge: Cambridge University Press.

Mattila, Sharon Lea. 1995. "A Question Too Often Neglected." *NTS* 41: 199–217.

Metzger, Bruce M. 1968. *Historical and Literary Studies: Pagan, Jewish, and Christian*. NTTS 8. Grand Rapids: Eerdmans.

Meyer, Elizabeth A. 2007. "Roman Tabulae, Egyptian Christians, and the Adoption of the Codex." *Chiron* 37: 295–347.

Meyer, Elizabeth A. 2009. "Writing Paraphernalia, Tablets, and Muses in Campanian Wall Painting." *American Journal of Archaeology* 113: 569–97.

Novum Testamentum Graece. 2012. Nestle-Aland, 28th ed. Stuttgart: Deutsche Bibelgesellschaft.
Parker, D. C. 2008. *An Introduction to New Testament Manuscripts and Their Texts*. Cambridge: Cambridge University Press.
Pelling, Christopher. 2002. *Plutarch and History: Eighteen Studies*. London: Duckworth.
Poirier, John C. 2012. "The Roll, the Codex, the Wax Tablet and the Synoptic Problem." *JSNT* 35: 3–30.
Poole, J. B., and R. Reid. 1962. "The Preparation of Leather and Parchment by the Dead Sea Scrolls Community." *Technology and Culture* 3: 1–26.
Rahlfs, Alfred. 1979. *Septuaginta*. Stuttgart: Deutsche Bibelgesellschaft.
Rhoads, David. 2006. "Performance Criticism: An Emerging Methodology in Second Testament Studies—Part I." *BTB* 36: 118–33.
Robinson, James M., Paul Hoffmann, and John S. Kloppenborg. 2000. *The Critical Edition of Q*. Hermeneia. Minneapolis: Fortress Press.
Rouse, Richard H., and Mary A. Rouse. 1989. "Wax Tablets." *Language and Communication* 9: 175–91.
Salvesen, Alison. 1991. *Symmachus in the Pentateuch*. Journal of Semitic Studies Monograph 15. Manchester: University of Manchester.
Sammons, Benjamin. 2017. *Device and Composition in the Greek Epic Cycle*. Oxford: Oxford University Press.
Small, Jocelyn Penny. 1997. *Wax Tablets of the Mind: Cognitive Studies of Memory and Literacy in Classical Antiquity*. London: Routledge.
Speidel, Michael Alexander. 1996. *Die römischen Schreibtafeln von Vindonissa: Lateinische Texte des militärischen Alltags und ihre geschichtliche Bedeutung*. Veröffentlichungen der Gesellschaft Pro Vindonissa 12. Brugg: Gesellschaft Pro Vindonissa.
Tomlin, R. S. O. 2003. "'The Girl in Question': A New Text from Roman London." *Brittania* 34: 41–51.
Tov, Emanuel. 1990. *The Greek Minor Prophets Scroll from Naḥal Ḥever (8ḤevXIIgr)*, DJD 8. Oxford: Clarendon.
Tov, Emanuel. 2004. *Scribal Practices and Approaches Reflected in the Texts Found in the Judean Desert, STDJ* 54. Leiden: Brill.
Turner, E. G. 1971. *Greek Manuscripts of the Ancient World*. Princeton: Princeton University Press.
van der Meer, Michaël N. 2018. "Symmachus's Version of Joshua." In *Found in Translation: Essays on Jewish Biblical Translation in Honor of Leonard J. Greenspoon*, edited by James W. Barker, Anthony Le Donne, and Joel N. Lohr. West Lafayette: Purdue University Press, 53–93.
Watson, Francis. 2009. "Q as Hypothesis: A Study in Methodology." *NTS* 55: 397–415.
Watson, Francis. 2016. "Towards a Redaction-Critical Reading of the Diatessaron Gospel." *Early Christianity* 7: 95–112.
West, Martin. 2011. "The Homeric Quest Today." *APSP* 155: 383–93.
Wire, Antoinette Clark. 2011. *The Case for Mark Composed in Performance*. Biblical Performance Criticism Series 3. Eugene, OR: Cascade.

CHAPTER 4

ANCIENT RHETORIC AS AN EVALUATIVE TOOL FOR LITERARY DEPENDENCE

ALEXANDER DAMM

Introduction

THE purpose of this essay is to introduce, evaluate, and illustrate the application of ancient rhetorical insights to investigation of the Synoptic Problem, that is, the problem of the literary sequence among the Synoptic Gospels. The critical study of ancient rhetoric as a tool to evaluate literary dependence has appeared quite recently. I have outlined the story of this developing field elsewhere (Damm 2013, xv–xxxvi). Suffice it to say that roughly the years since 2000 represent a new phase in source-critical applications of rhetoric. This phase began with a call by J. S. Kloppenborg to discover what in ancient literary cultures could explain an evangelist's editorial activity independent of the Gospels themselves. Alleged reasoning for an evangelist's decisions, based simply on tendencies elsewhere in his Gospel, has limited explanatory power: such reasoning denotes only the evangelist's activity (not primarily his reasoning for it) and can be easily influenced by shallow or misinformed literary sensibilities of the investigating scholar (Kloppenborg 2000, 16–17; see Denaux 1995, 117–18).[1] Probing outside the Gospels to facets of ancient thought such as rhetoric reveals conventions—tendencies, rules, and skills—which almost certainly offered the evangelists realistic or plausible explanations and methods for editing their sources. One therefore can judge the relative strength of major source hypotheses that seek to account for the Gospels' sequence, including the

---

[1] In n. 14, Denaux points to earlier research into rhetorically grounded appeals to Gospel sources, including work by Michael Roberts (1985), Robert Morgenthaler (1993), and Vernon K. Robbins (1993). For a summary see Damm 2013, xv–xxxviii.

Two-Document Hypothesis (2DH), the Farrer-Goulder Hypothesis (FH), and the Two-Gospel Hypothesis (2GH).

Ancient Rhetoric and the Synoptic Problem: Three Traditions

There are, in fact, three emerging, related rhetorical traditions which critics have taken up for application to the Synoptic Problem. Each warrants a short introduction and evaluation here. To date, the two more useful traditions (rhetorical activities and forms; *mimesis*) characterize Greek and Roman rhetoric; the latter tradition is biblical or Semitic rhetoric.

Greek and Roman Rhetoric

Many readers will be familiar with studying the New Testament in the light of Greek and Latin rhetoric, the system of communicative conventions which dominated the cultural matrix of the late Roman Empire and early Christian literature. For some decades, New Testament scholars have practiced rhetorical criticism, examining New Testament literature using forms and argumentative patterns typical of Greco-Roman rhetoric. Recognizing that rhetoric was axiomatic to the literary cultures of Greco-Roman antiquity—that it shaped the substance and form alike of both formal speech (or oratory) and of numerous literary genres (like biography and history)—scholars have worked hard to show the indebtedness of the evangelists, the apostle Paul, and other writers to Greek and Roman modes of speech and writing (e.g., Kennedy 1984, 3–38, 144–52; Mack 1990, 19–22, 25–50; Mack and Robbins 1989, 196–97). Their work has provided insight into the arguments these ancient authors sought to highlight, and how they managed to highlight them.

There is good reason to look for signs of Greco-Roman rhetoric in the Gospels. Given that the evangelists wrote in Greek, they invariably had some literate Greek education. Significantly, scholarship recognizes that rhetoric was a key component of ancient education, and even though rhetoric in the sense of judicial speech composition was a summit of education that few students reached, some students achieved a "prerhetorical" level of training, extant in texts called *progymnasmata*. The *progymnasmata* taught fundamental forms of rhetoric, such as the *chreia*, the fable, the narrative, the thesis, and so on, as well as skills in writing and rewriting material, such as paraphrase and elaboration (Cribiore 2001, 220–24; Hock 2001, 58–59; Kennedy 2003, ix–x; Morgan 1999, 70–72). While it is unclear the precise extent to which the evangelists partook of such training, their regular use of rhetorical forms and their thoroughgoing ability to write lengthy Gospels certainly implies some rhetorical influence and skill (see Burridge 1997, 510, 530; Kennedy 2003, ix; see Damm 2013, 16–17).

Rhetorical Activities and Forms

Some studies (Damm 2013, 2016; Gorman 2016; Reid 2016) have sought to establish plausible literary dependence through focusing on the evangelists' appeal to conventions for rhetorical argumentation and rhetorical forms.[2] Rhetorical theory teaches that meaningful writing in its broadest sense entails conventions of argumentation and of precise forms. At their core, these conventions include compelling authors to address three activities: (1) inventing or creating one's material; (2) arranging it according to rules of this or that genre; and (3) expressing it powerfully and appropriately to its content.[3] In addition, an author had to select a form or genre within which to work and then follow more precise conventions for it. In the genre of speeches (oratory), for instance, an author needed to compose each of a speech's five characteristic parts, namely the *exordium*, the *narratio* (or statement of facts), the *propositio* (or statement of case), the *probatio* (or logical proofs for the case), and the *peroratio* (conclusion). In each part of the speech, moreover, there were quite precise conventions for what to argue and how to express oneself. For instance, each part of speech demanded a particular style (plain, or grand, or something in between the two), and there were numerous "figures" of thought and speech on which one could draw (see Kennedy 1984, 12–38; Bonner 1977, 288–308; summarized in Damm 2013, 58–80).

Rhetorical theory is no easy key for inferring literary dependence. For one, different rhetorical conventions are valid in different contexts. For instance, a plain expression might suit one author and his/her narrative and social context, while an ornate style might suit another. For another, the richness and variety of rhetorical conventions makes inferences of literary dependence challenging. If Matthew, for instance, compresses a Markan narrative in a way that is rhetorically appropriate for narratives, that is one thing; but one cannot conclude Matthew has adapted Mark without considering Mark's possibly good rhetorical reasons for adapting Matthew, such as extending and embellishing a particular portrayal of Jesus. Both rhetorical reasons are valid. Thus, to conclude which Gospel has more plausibly adapted the other requires first carefully weighing the number, variety, and quality of alleged rhetorically motivated changes. With these considerations in mind, my own earlier work offered a typology of possible rhetorical reasons for adapting particular rhetorical forms, namely the judicial speech and its elementary form, the elaborated *chreia* (χρεία). These reasons amount to four: (1) to improve a source's argumentation by intensifying or more effectively arranging proofs; (2) to emphasize one's biographical or theological interests; (3) to enhance a source's clarity; and (4) to enhance a source's propriety, namely the "fit" between content and expression in each of the speech's parts; propriety, as I understand it, also implies

---

[2] Gorman has worked on the assumption of Markan priority; Damm and Reid have sought to test Markan priority against the opposing hypothesis of Markan posteriority (the 2GH).

[3] Two further activities, applicable more strictly to speeches, are memory and delivery.

essentially drawing on everything in a source which would contribute to one's cardinal case or thesis (Damm 2013, xxii, 58–60, 68–69, 79–80, 167–70; Damm 2016, 224–26; for detail see Lausberg 1998, §§1060–62).

Rhetorical Imitation or Μίμησισ

In an intelligent new book, Brad McAdon (2018) does not take issue with such rhetorically motivated improvements, such as clarifying and tightening the stylistic propriety of one's source. He shifts focus, though, from specific argumentative, formal, and stylistic conventions for improving sources to a rhetorical practice called μίμησις or *imitatio*: the "practice of engaging, rivalling or transforming an earlier text" (McAdon 2018, 1). According to McAdon, "there are rhetorical relationships between these texts" (i.e., the Synoptic Gospels), "and . . . the Greco-Roman rhetorical . . . practice of *mimesis* seems to be the best explanation for these . . . literary relationships" (3–4). Critical here is that *mimesis* often seeks to improve one's source, usually in the broad sense of "rivaling" it in some way, and indeed scholars indicate that imitation was the context in which ancient students and writers made rhetorical improvements to their sources (Brodie 1984, 19–26, 34–37; Morgan 1999, 251). One of the numerous virtues of McAdon's work is to demonstrate that imitation was thoroughly practiced by Greek authors of the first century CE. Rhetorical assessments of literary dependence must take greater account of it.

I do not wish to critique McAdon for tasks he does not engage: his work does not so much rhetorically evaluate the relative superiority of source hypotheses (e.g., the FH versus the 2DH) as it simply argues that one source hypothesis (the FH) accommodates conventions of *mimesis*. Nonetheless, if employing *mimesis* as an evaluative tool for establishing literary dependence, it's necessary to exercise two cautions. The first, as McAdon and others recognize (McAdon 2018, 39–40), is to be judicious in suggesting *mimesis*. I am not the first to caution that scholarly criteria for detecting *mimesis* do not always seem adequate to describe the evangelists' alleged editorial work (see Downing 2014, 114–15; Verheyden 2014, 154): McAdon's own review of ancient authors leads him to conclude (25) that "acknowledging one's debt (source) . . . constitutes appropriate imitation. . . . Word-for-word borrowing, slavish translation, and claiming another's work as one's own would constitute inappropriate borrowing (imitation) and was thoroughly denounced." These mimetic criteria do not inspire much confidence: the Gospels contain swaths of verbatim and nearly word-for-word parallels that imply slavish translation, and apart from Luke's reference to unnamed predecessors (Luke 1:1–2), the Gospels essentially regard their accounts as their own. These facts do not preclude Gospel *mimesis*, but they should temper one to be cautious in arguing for it. A second caution in use of *mimesis* is reversibility: McAdon states that *mimesis* appears more plausible if "differences are intelligible," that is, if one can detect an imitating author improving—for example, fixing or polishing over potential misunderstandings in—his or her source. To be sure, this criterion allows the scholar to argue that Matthew has imitated Mark (see McAdon 2018, 71–72). But as I indicated earlier, arguments from intelligibility have a reversible quality: alleged changes by Mark to Matthew are arguably as intelligible, in their own way, as changes by Matthew to Mark. This risk of reversibility lurks in appeals to other rhetorical traditions, too.

Biblical Rhetoric

Roland Meynet has been the driving force in studying yet another rhetorical tradition known as biblical rhetoric. According to Meynet, it is not—or at least not principally—Greco-Roman rhetoric that has guided the evangelists. While the evangelists write in Greek, the rhetorical conventions guiding them are biblical, that is to say conventions of Semitic composition—of composition in languages which typify the Old Testament and other ancient Near Eastern literature. Meynet's favored synonym for biblical rhetoric is *composition*, for at its core biblical rhetoric is a compositional art (Meynet 1998, 21–22, 37–38, 172–76, 317–27; Meynet 2002, 200–202, 214; Meynet 2013, 12, 643–45; Meynet 2015, 26–27, 38, 46).

The core conventions of biblical rhetoric are at least three. First, it denotes composition using parallelism on the one hand and concentricity on the other. Operative at the level of sentences, pericopae, sections, and entire texts, biblical rhetoric prioritizes parallel and concentric writing patterns (Meynet 1998, 22–25, 355–56; Meynet 2013, 418–421; Meynet 2015, 38, 46).[4] Second, the cardinal aim of these patterns is to draw readers' attention toward the material which the patterns frame or enclose: parallelism and concentricity always point a reader inward to material at the core of a unit. Third, the material at the center of that unit, while essential, is usually couched in language not entirely explicit. In Semitic languages, ideas often are suggested or indicated without being stated in so many words. Biblical rhetoric favors implication over and above directness (see Meynet 2002, 200–202).[5]

Biblical rhetoric may be illustrated with a text which Meynet has studied and to which I shall return: the story of the healing of blind Bartimaeus in the Gospel of Mark (Mark 10:46–52). Following Meynet, I have shown in distinct fonts (see Table 4.1) some concentric patterns Mark employs to draw attention to the story's central idea of discipleship (in verse 49b). Arranging his pericope into five "parts," Mark concentrically sequences them (A–B–C–B'–A') so that repetitions of synonymous and antonymous words in peripheral parts (examples are in bold, underlined, or italicized text) highlight the message of the center part. Table 4.1 is much simplified but shows some of Mark's concentric patterns.

As the table shows, the story's outer parts (A [10:46] and A' [10:52]) contain sequences of antonyms and synonyms: "blind" (τυφλὸς) opposes "see again" (ἀνέβλεψεν); "sitting" (ἐκάθητο) opposes "followed" (ἠκολούθει); and "on the way" (παρὰ τὴν ὁδόν) in verse

---

[4] Biblical rhetorical critics prefer precise grammatical terms to denote literary units. These include "lexeme," "member," "bi-member," and so forth. For a complete guide see Meynet 2015, 37–39.

[5] On occasion, Meynet has opined that Greco-Roman rhetoric might be relevant for characterizing the evangelists' modus operandi (Meynet 2013, 645). In the main, though, he has thoroughly downplayed the influence of Greco-Roman rhetoric on the New Testament.

> **Table 4.1 The healing of Bartimaeus (Mark 10:46–52)**
>
> A: (46) Καὶ ἔρχονται εἰς Ἰεριχώ. Καὶ ἐκπορευομένου αὐτοῦ ἀπὸ Ἰεριχὼ καὶ τῶν μαθητῶν αὐτοῦ καὶ ὄχλου ἱκανοῦ ὁ υἱὸς Τιμαίου Βαρτιμαῖος,
> **τυφλὸς** προσαίτης, <u>ἐκάθητο</u> *παρὰ τὴν ὁδόν*.
>
> B: (47) καὶ ἀκούσας ὅτι Ἰησοῦς ὁ Ναζαρηνός ἐστιν ἤρξατο κράζειν καὶ λέγειν· υἱὲ Δαυὶδ Ἰησοῦ, ἐλέησόν με. (48) καὶ ἐπετίμων αὐτῷ πολλοὶ ἵνα σιωπήσῃ· ὁ δὲ πολλῷ μᾶλλον ἔκραζεν· υἱὲ Δαυίδ, ἐλέησόν με.
>
> C: (49) καὶ στὰς ὁ Ἰησοῦς εἶπεν· φωνήσατε αὐτόν.
> ***καὶ φωνοῦσιν τὸν τυφλὸν λέγοντες αὐτῷ· θάρσει, ἔγειρε, φωνεῖ σε.***
> (50) ὁ δὲ ἀποβαλὼν τὸ ἱμάτιον αὐτοῦ ἀναπηδήσας ἦλθεν πρὸς τὸν Ἰησοῦν.
>
> B': (51) καὶ ἀποκριθεὶς αὐτῷ ὁ Ἰησοῦς εἶπεν· τί σοι θέλεις ποιήσω; ὁ δὲ τυφλὸς εἶπεν αὐτῷ· ραββουνί, ἵνα ἀναβλέψω. (52) καὶ ὁ Ἰησοῦς εἶπεν αὐτῷ· ὕπαγε, ἡ πίστις σου σέσωκέν σε.
>
> A': καὶ εὐθὺς
> **ἀνέβλεψεν** καὶ <u>ἠκολούθει</u> αὐτῷ *ἐν τῇ ὁδῷ*.

46b is repeated in verse 52c (ἐν τῇ ὁδῷ). Together, these and further parallel and concentric patterns highlight the center part (bold italics), whose focus is discipleship: Mark intends to highlight Jesus's call to people (Meynet 2015, 46–53, 58).

To his credit, Meynet suggests that biblical rhetoric can aid in understanding the Synoptic Problem, helping one determine which evangelist has more plausibly used the others' work and how so. Indeed, Meynet regards it as the proper basis for determining the Gospels' literary relationships. While to date Meynet himself has not engaged in application of biblical rhetoric to the Synoptic Problem, he believes it will be an important source-critical tool (Meynet 2015, 16–17, 23–25, 369). I hope that it will find such application, as his work affords a careful, erudite, and suggestive analysis of Gospel composition. Here I wish to offer two judgments about the potential of biblical rhetoric for studying the Synoptic Problem. First, scholars will need to pair biblical rhetoric with Greco-Roman rhetoric; biblical rhetoric cannot stand on its own as a compositional, let alone source-critical, guide. It has been established beyond a doubt that Greek and Roman rhetorical forms are operative in the Gospels. Vernon Robbins, for instance, has shown conclusively that Mark 3:22–30 is tightly patterned on the *chreia* (a kind of aphorism often buttressed by specific varieties of supporting arguments; Robbins 1989, 171–77). Helpfully, too, it has been shown that Greco-Roman rhetorical forms can play a role alongside Semitic concentric forms: Robbins has articulated the combination of just such forms in the aforementioned work. But there will need to be cooperation; biblical rhetoric alone is inadequate to address literary dependence.

Second, biblical rhetoric has limited relevance for inferring such literary dependence. Unlike Greco-Roman rhetoric, biblical rhetoric lacks ancient theory which commends explicitly how authors should and should not compose texts. Greek and Roman rhetoric affords numerous guidelines for what constitutes "good" or "right" composition—a sort of "how to" guide, located in handbooks by Aristotle, Quintilian, Theon, Hermogenes, and others—and these guidelines are helpful in inferring which of two Gospels draws the other into closer conformity with them. In short, they afford explanatory power for inferring Gospel sequences. In the case of biblical rhetoric, there are no such explicit guidelines; there are only illustrations in biblical texts themselves.[6] While such illustrations can help to infer which of two Gospels has improved the other—for instance, seeing how one evangelist tightens the other's conformity to a concentric pattern—this task is more difficult because of the lack of an explicit "how to" guide. Moreover, Meynet recently has argued for quite precise and elegant, yet highly distinct, concentric patterns in each of the Synoptic Gospels (Matthew, Mark, and Luke). In this context, without an explicit "how to" guide, it would seem hard to infer who is adapting whom. I intend these comments in the spirit of invitations to biblical rhetorical criticism to develop a method for applying itself to the Synoptic Problem.

Whatever the rhetorical tradition with which one engages, one should examine first the relevant primary sources, for instance, *progymnasmata* and rhetorical handbooks by authors including Aristotle, Cicero, Quintilian, and others, as well as modern summaries of them (Lausberg 1998; Martin 1974). Fresh interpretation from primary sources will undoubtedly advance the precision of one's analyses.

Healing of the Blind Men (Mark 10:46–52 // Matthew 20:29–34): Matthew's Adaptation of Mark

It will help to illustrate the fundamental principle with which I began this discussion: grounding inferences about literary dependence in conventions independent of the Gospels themselves. This is the guiding principle behind all appeals to rhetorical traditions. For sake of illustration, I examine Mark and Matthew's pericope of the healing of the blind men (see Table 4.2), suggesting Matthew's adaptation of Mark based on conventions from rhetorical argumentation and forms (discussed earlier). Limitations of space compel consideration of just the editorial scenario of Markan priority (the 2DH and FH). It goes without saying, then, that the following argument is incomplete: it suggests only how Matthew adapts Mark, not how Mark might adapt Matthew. As such, it is hardly determinative for concluding which of the two evangelists more likely adapted the other's work.

Because the illustration concerns the form of *narrative*, I examine conventions of Greco-Roman rhetoric specific to this form. Rhetoric affords two reasons why an author

---

[6] Meynet has shown biblical rhetorical patterns at work in Old Testament texts like the book of Amos (for instance, Meynet 2002, 203–7).

Table 4.2 The Healing of the Blind Men

Matthew 20:29–34	Mark 10:46–52
(29) Καὶ ἐκπορευομένων αὐτῶν ἀπὸ Ἰεριχὼ ἠκολούθησεν αὐτῷ ὄχλος πολύς. (30) καὶ ἰδοὺ δύο τυφλοὶ καθήμενοι παρὰ τὴν ὁδὸν ἀκούσαντες ὅτι Ἰησοῦς παράγει, ἔκραξαν λέγοντες· ἐλέησον ἡμᾶς, [κύριε,] υἱὸς Δαυίδ. (31) ὁ δὲ ὄχλος ἐπετίμησεν αὐτοῖς ἵνα σιωπήσωσιν· οἱ δὲ μεῖζον ἔκραξαν λέγοντες· ἐλέησον ἡμᾶς, κύριε, υἱὸς Δαυίδ. (32) καὶ στὰς ὁ Ἰησοῦς ἐφώνησεν αὐτοὺς καὶ εἶπεν· τί θέλετε ποιήσω ὑμῖν; (33) λέγουσιν αὐτῷ· κύριε, ἵνα ἀνοιγῶσιν οἱ ὀφθαλμοὶ ἡμῶν. (34) σπλαγχνισθεὶς δὲ ὁ Ἰησοῦς ἥψατο τῶν ὀμμάτων αὐτῶν, καὶ εὐθέως ἀνέβλεψαν καὶ ἠκολούθησαν αὐτῷ.	(46) Καὶ ἔρχονται εἰς Ἰεριχώ. Καὶ ἐκπορευομένου αὐτοῦ ἀπὸ Ἰεριχὼ καὶ τῶν μαθητῶν αὐτοῦ καὶ ὄχλου ἱκανοῦ ὁ υἱὸς Τιμαίου Βαρτιμαῖος, τυφλὸς προσαίτης, ἐκάθητο παρὰ τὴν ὁδόν. (47) καὶ ἀκούσας ὅτι Ἰησοῦς ὁ Ναζαρηνός ἐστιν ἤρξατο κράζειν καὶ λέγειν· υἱὲ Δαυὶδ Ἰησοῦ, ἐλέησόν με. (48) καὶ ἐπετίμων αὐτῷ πολλοὶ ἵνα σιωπήσῃ· ὁ δὲ πολλῷ μᾶλλον ἔκραζεν· υἱὲ Δαυίδ, ἐλέησόν με. (49) καὶ στὰς ὁ Ἰησοῦς εἶπεν· φωνήσατε αὐτόν. καὶ φωνοῦσιν τὸν τυφλὸν λέγοντες αὐτῷ· θάρσει, ἔγειρε, φωνεῖ σε. (50) ὁ δὲ ἀποβαλὼν τὸ ἱμάτιον αὐτοῦ ἀναπηδήσας ἦλθεν πρὸς τὸν Ἰησοῦν. (51) καὶ ἀποκριθεὶς αὐτῷ ὁ Ἰησοῦς εἶπεν· τί σοι θέλεις ποιήσω; ὁ δὲ τυφλὸς εἶπεν αὐτῷ· ραββουνί, ἵνα ἀναβλέψω. (52) καὶ ὁ Ἰησοῦς εἶπεν αὐτῷ· ὕπαγε, ἡ πίστις σου σέσωκέν σε. καὶ εὐθὺς ἀνέβλεψεν καὶ ἠκολούθει αὐτῷ ἐν τῇ ὁδῷ.
(29) As they were leaving Jericho, a large crowd followed him. (30) There were two blind men sitting by the roadside. When they heard that Jesus was passing by, they shouted, "Lord have mercy on us, Son of David!" (31) The crowd sternly ordered them to be quiet; but they shouted even more loudly, "Have mercy on us, Lord, Son of David!" (32) Jesus stood still and called them, saying, "What do you want me to do for you?" (33) They said to him, "Lord, let our eyes be opened." (34) Moved with compassion, Jesus touched their eyes. Immediately they regained their sight and followed him.	(46) They came to Jericho. As he and his disciples and a large crowd were leaving Jericho, Bartimaeus son of Timaeus, a blind beggar, was sitting by the roadside. (47) When he heard that it was Jesus of Nazareth, he began to shout out and say, "Jesus, Son of David, have mercy on me!" (48) Many sternly ordered him to be quiet, but he cried out even more loudly, "Son of David, have mercy on me!" (49) Jesus stood still and said, "Call him here." And they called the blind man, saying to him, "Take heart; get up, he is calling you." (50) So throwing off his cloak, he sprang up and came to Jesus. (51) Then Jesus said to him, "What do you want me to do for you?" The blind man said to him, "My teacher, let me see again." (52) Jesus said to him, "Go; your faith has made you well." Immediately he regained his sight and followed him on the way.

might adapt another's narrative: (1) to foster distinctive theological, biographical, or historical interests, and/or (2) to draw the narrative into closer conformity with appropriate conventions of style or expression. And as critics have rightly shown, for narratives an appropriate style entails clarity, conciseness and plausibility (Gorman 2016, 77; Schufer 2003). The more rhetorically motivated changes one can detect in an evangelist's work, the more plausible his adaptation of his source will appear.

In addition to gauging rhetorical motivations, a third rhetorical convention matters: (3) Does an evangelist include everything from his purported source in keeping with his rhetorical motivations, in particular his fundamental interest in the narrative's portrayal? In ancient rhetoric an author of speeches follows a fundamental principle called *utilitas causae*: everything in and about the speech should support its governing case (Lausberg 1998, §1060). When it comes to adapting sources, whether speeches or any other form, this principle still matters; for rhetorically educated authors would almost certainly have asked themselves: "Given my chief rhetorical aims, have I used all material in my source to support them?" That is to say: if an evangelist is seeking to bend a source toward a particular portrayal of Jesus (for instance), then he should not overlook—should not repeatedly and conspicuously miss—source material that would satisfy this very portrayal. To be sure, an evangelist might have good alternative reasons now and again to overlook useful material, rhetorical or otherwise; but repeated and conspicuous neglect of material that would support major aims makes an evangelist's alleged use of a source appear less plausible.

In short, to infer rhetorically how Matthew adapts Mark, three questions should be asked: (1) Does Matthew make changes that appear biographically or theologically motivated? (2) Does Matthew make changes that appear motivated by the intention to enhance the clarity, conciseness, and plausible style of Mark's narrative? (3) Does Matthew include (more or less) everything from Mark that would support these motivations, especially his chief interests in portraying Jesus? Or does his work contain conspicuous oversights? With these questions in mind, I turn to Matthew and Mark's pericope.[7] To anticipate my conclusions, I show that Matthew's adaptations often reflect sound rhetorical reasons for improving narratives.

Outline of the Pericopae

It will help first to know the general and for the most part common contours of the evangelists' versions of this pericope. They are quite similar: the pericope tells of a blind man (in Matthew, a pair of blind men) who not only is given sight by Jesus but also, and it seems consequently, attaches himself to Jesus and becomes, in effect, a disciple.

---

[7] I have tried to arrange the Greek texts approximately following *Synopsis Quattuor Evangeliorum* (1985). I have benefited also from a presentation of texts which highlights specific overlaps and differences between Mark and Matthew's pericopae (Monaghan, 2010, xxviii, 122–23). Unless otherwise noted, all English translations are from the NRSV (2010).

Set outside the city of Jericho, within Jesus's Judean ministry, the narrative opens with a scene of a blind man, a beggar, who learns from passersby that Jesus of Nazareth is approaching along the road beside which he sits (Mark 10:46 // Matt 20:29-30). Aware already of Jesus as at least a healer, the blind man requests Jesus's aid with a sense of desperation, shouting twice at Jesus and his retinue to catch his attention (Mark 10:47-48 // Matt 20:30-31). Aware of the blind man, and despite people around him discouraging the man's request, Jesus asks directly into the blind man's needs and, in apparent response to the man's trust in Jesus's capacity to heal him (Mark) or simply owing to altruism (Matthew), directly follows by healing him. This healing appears to be the motivation in the final verse for the blind man to become a student of Jesus (Mark 10:48-52 // Matt 20:31-34).

Not only are Mark and Matthew's contents similar but also their immediate literary arrangements. Both evangelists situate the story in the later phases of Jesus's Judean ministry, sandwiching it between the disciples' debate on receiving special eschatological favor from Jesus (Mark 10:35-45 // Matt 20:20-28) on the one hand and Jesus's entry into Jerusalem and its public allusions to Jesus as Israel's savior (Mark 11:1-10 // Matt 21:1-9) on the other. Significantly too, the Greco-Roman rhetorical form of Mark's and Matthew's accounts also is similar. According to Klaus Berger, the essential ancient form of these miracle stories is a narrative form called δεήσις or *petitio*: a "petition" or request for aid by one figure to another, found in the works of authors including Philo and Plutarch, and belonging to the rhetorical species called *epideictic*, with its characteristic orientation toward praising or blaming (Berger 2016, 438-39).[8] This point is important for a rhetorical analysis, for like all rhetorical forms the δεήσις/*petitio* requires an appropriate style. In this case it appears that two stylistic considerations especially matter. For one, given that the δεήσις/*petitio* is a narrative, that is, "language descriptive of things that have happened or as though they had happened (Theon *Prog.* 4.78 [trans. Kennedy])," rhetorical theory dictates that it have a *plain* style: a style marked by virtues of "clarity, conciseness, credibility" (Theon *Prog.* 4.79 [trans. Kennedy]). For another, given that the δεήσις/*petitio* typifies the epideictic genus of rhetoric, that is to say the genus which engages in "praise and blame" or amplification of an accepted view (characteristic for example of funeral orations), rhetorical theory dictates that its style have some flourish and ornament, probably fitting for direct discourse that entails praise (see Lausberg 1998, §1079.2 and n. 1). In short, the style of Matthew 10:46-52 // Matthew 20:29-34 should, rhetorically speaking, be sufficiently plain with some flourishes.

Mark 10:46-52

In the view of Joel Marcus, Mark intends his pericope to portray not simply a blind man's petition for healing but more specifically a petition whose success is illustrative of a

---

[8] In addition, Berger locates in Mark 10:46-52 the form of "mandate" in Jesus's closing command (2016, 439, 442) and in Mark 10:47 // Matt 20:30 the form of "acclamation" in the blind man's appeal for mercy (345-46).

learning process among people who follow Jesus—a halting and slow process, to be sure, but nevertheless a process—and which occurs throughout the Gospel. In short, Marcus locates discipleship as a central and key theme of the entire narrative sub-section (Mark 8:27–10:52) to which this pericope belongs. This section significantly opens and closes with stories of successful petitions by blind men for "vision," which is both physical and spiritual, and is centered upon acceptance of Jesus's teachings and Messianic status— in short, centered upon "faith" (Marcus 2009, 589–90, 761, 764–65). Marcus indicates several touches in Mark's narrative which contribute to its emphasis on discipleship: these include the closing phrase "on the way" (ἐν τῇ ὁδῷ; Mark 10:52); and numerous allusions in the story to Christian acceptance of discipleship, i.e., of baptism (for instance, Bartimaeus's "throwing off his garment"; Mark 10:50; Marcus 2009, 760–61, 763, 765). Strikingly, from a quite different rhetorical angle which highlights concentric repetitions of terms, Meynet also locates discipleship as a major theme in Mark 10:46–52 (Meynet 2015, 46–53, 58). It seems fair then to summarize Mark 10:46–52 as arguing for "Bartimaeus . . . as a symbol of the new disciple of Jesus" (Marcus 2009, 765; contrast Gundry 1993, 595–97).[9]

Matthew 20:29–34

While Mark's center of gravity is discipleship, Matthew crafts his narrative with a different emphasis: according to Gundry, Matthew's pericope seeks to portray healing as an illustration of Jesus's *altruism*.[10] Here it is Jesus's "pity" or "compassion" (σπλαγχνισθεὶς) which motivates him to heal the blind men (Gundry 1994, 399, 404, 406). Luz adds that apart from this emphasis on Jesus's altruism, there is a distinct portrayal in Matthew of Jesus's physical modality of healing (he directly touches the blind men; Matt 20:34; see Mark 10:52), and Luz, like Gundry, sees this pericope as an important means to characterize Jesus (Luz 2001, 549–50).

Matthew's Adaptation of Mark (2DH and FH)

In rhetorical terms, why does Matthew change Mark? There appear to be two reasons. The first is to foster a particular biographical portrayal of Jesus. The second is to foster a suitably plainer style. To be sure, in some places Matthew's changes do not appear to have a clear rhetorical reason: sometimes Matthew adds to or replaces words in Mark which commentaries characterize as "Mattheanisms": words Matthew simply "likes."[11]

---

[9] Marcus also indicates that the story portrays Jesus's "Davidic sonship" (2009, 766).
[10] Matthew composed two versions of this pericope; the second appears in Matt 9:27–31. I do not focus in this essay on 9:27–31, though I need to mention it vis-à-vis Matt 20:29–34 from time to time.
[11] According to Gundry (1994, 405–6), these include ἠκολούθησεν (Matt 20:29), καὶ ἰδοὺ (Matt 20:30), λέγοντες (Matt 20:30–31), ὄχλος (Matt 20:31), and the historic present λέγουσιν with asyndeton (Matt 20:33). Other changes for which I cannot at present find a clear rhetorical explanation include Matthew's changing Mark's imperfect tense to the aorist tense in places; and occasional replacement of finite verbs with participles. For these changes see Gundry 1994, 405–6.

I bracket these changes, and on occasion, I find a precise rhetorical reason for them. In any case, strikingly, Matthew often changes Mark's narrative for the two aforementioned rhetorical reasons. His changes to these ends are numerous and varied, a fact which affords hypotheses of Markan priority some plausibility.

Biographical Portrayal

At times Matthew changes Mark in order to foster a different biographical portrayal of Jesus. On the one hand Gundry argues that Matthew seeks to accent Jesus's *altruism*. Matthew's pericope is not—or at least, not so much—an illustration of discipleship, evident for instance in the fact Matthew does not specify that the blind men's faith effects their healing. Rather, Matthew takes pains to specify (Matt 20:34) that the healing comes from Jesus's altruism. To this end, in 20:34 Matthew omits Mark's characterization of the healing as a product of the blind man's faith (ἡ πίστις σου σέσωκέν σε; Mark 10:52) and instead describes it as a product of Jesus's care and love (σπλαγχνισθεὶς δὲ ὁ Ἰησοῦς ἥψατο τῶν ὀμμάτων αὐτῶν; Matt 20:34; Gundry 1994, 399, 404, 406; see Luz 2001, 549–50).[12] According to Gundry, this emphasis makes sense in Matthew's narrative context, for in several pericopae Jesus reaches out to downtrodden figures in gestures of loving inclusion (Gundry 1994, 399, 404, 406; see Luz 2001, 548–49).[13] Similarly to this end, Matthew omits Mark's closing phrase "on the way" (10:52; Matt 20:39), given its emphasis on discipleship and faith.

On the other hand Matthew also changes Mark's portrayal to concentrate more on Jesus *himself*. The critics' emphases differ a little, but they agree that Matthew seeks a more august image of Jesus. According to Gundry, Matthew wants to heighten the portrayal of Jesus as "authoritative"—a shift reflected in such changes as replacing the term "teacher" (ῥαββουνί; Mark 10:51) with "Lord" (κύριε; Matt 20:31) and in substituting the participle καθήμενοι for Mark's ἐκάθητο (Gundry, 1994, 405); as Gundry puts it, "changing Mark's finite verb 'was sitting' to the mere participle 'sitting' makes the stress fall on the blind men's confessional cry," thus augmenting Jesus's authority (405). This motive also appears to explain Matthew's addition of a "large" (πολύς) crowd that "follows" (ἠκολούθησεν) Jesus (Matt 20:29)—after all, a thriving mass of devotees augments Jesus's authoritative image[14]—and to explain Matthew's omission of two whole Markan verses, 10:49–50, where Mark's Jesus dispatches disciples to speak with the blind man: "Matthew's omission concentrates attention on Jesus' call" (406).[15]

---

[12] As Luz (2001, 549), points out, in the earlier version of the same narrative (Matt 9:27–31), Matthew "tells the story as a story of faith," more akin to Mark 10:46–52.

[13] Gundry believes that Matthew (in 20:34) omits Mark's reference to faith as the cause of healing (10:52). In impartial terms, independent of any source hypothesis one can still see Matthew's relative *inattention* to the motif of discipleship or faith.

[14] Gundry's reasoning (2001, 405) differs: Matthew "makes the large crowd 'follow him [Jesus]' . . . to parallel the blind men's following Jesus in 9:27 (see v. 34 here) and portray the large crowd as a vanguard of the many Gentiles who become disciples in the church age."

[15] In a related vein, Luz (2001, 549–50) believes Matthew is most interested in portraying Jesus as forgiving; as the Jewish Messiah; and as having engaged in real and tangible healing miracles.

Clearer, Concise, More Plausible Style

Strikingly, several of Matthew's changes find a common rhetorical explanation in improving Mark's narrative style; in making it more fitting or appropriate for narrative form. Critics already have identified changes that foster clarity. First, Matthew omits Mark's opening clause in service of clarity (καὶ ἔρχονται εἰς Ἰεριχώ; Mark 10:46b), eliminating an awkward juxtaposition of references to Jericho (Luz 2001, 548).[16] A second clarification is omission of Mark's title of Jesus as ὁ Ναζαρηνός, "perhaps ... because the blind men are accepting Jesus, not rejecting him" (this title was earlier cast scornfully at Jesus; Matt 2:23); Luz adds that since Matthew's Jesus was born in Bethlehem, it makes less sense now to call him a Nazarene (Gundry 1994, 405; Luz 2001, 548 n. 3). A third clarification emerges in Matthew's resequencing of Mark's idiosyncratic phrase τί σοι θέλεις ποιήσω (10:51), where the indirect object "you" has an advance position, to the more idiomatic τί θέλετε ποιήσω ὑμῖν (Matt 20:32). Still further linguistic clarifications follow: in Matthew 20:31, "'more greatly' [μεῖζον] replaces 'much rather' [πολλῷ μᾶλλον].... Here [Mark's] 'rather' jars him, for louder yelling does not represent a contrast in kind" (Gundry 1994, 405-6).[17] And at the end of the pericope, Matthew's preference for εὐθέως over εὐθύς is arguably a clarification inasmuch as "εὐθέως is the commoner form in later (i.e., postclassical) Greek" (LSJM, εὐθύς s.v.).[18]

Matthew renders Mark's narrative not only clearer but also more concise. In this regard, Luz's comment that "as often in miracle stories, a number of details are omitted" by Matthew, finds its fuller significance. While omissions do not necessarily imply an effort to economize language, in point of fact Matthew does appear often to economize. First, Matthew makes a major economizing omission in 20:32: while Mark 10:49-50 describes Jesus dispatching his disciples to bring the blind man to him, and only then has Jesus ask the blind man's petition, Matthew omits this dispatch scene entirely; Matthew's Jesus speaks to the blind man directly (Luz 2001, 548). The motivation for this large omission might well be to render Mark's narrative more concise, for Mark's prolonged process of Jesus dispatching intermediaries to consult with the blind man, and of the blind man then approaching Jesus, seems redundant and unnecessary.[19] A second omission, Gundry suggests, also seeks economy: at the narrative's very

---

[16] "In v. 29 Matthew simplifies Mark's confusing geographical statements that speak first of going into, then of leaving Jericho; Jesus has already been in Jericho."

[17] He adds here that "the choice between υἱός [Matt 20:30–31] and υἱέ [Mark 10:47–48] matters little."

[18] An additional clarification, Gundry indicates, comes in Matt 20:32, where trimming Mark's phrase καὶ ἀποκριθεὶς αὐτῷ ὁ Ἰησοῦς εἶπεν (Mark 10:51) down into simply καὶ εἶπεν "stems from ... [Matthew's] observation that the blind men have not yet spoken conversationally to Jesus, but have only yelled" (Gundry 1994, 406). This change also renders Mark's narrative more concise. While in Matt 20:30, ὅτι Ἰησοῦς παράγει ("that Jesus is approaching") is almost indistinguishable from Mark 10:47's ὅτι Ἰησοῦς ... ἐστιν ("that it is Jesus"), Matthew's phrase is a little clearer in the sense it is more descriptive; more precise. According to Gundry, "παράγει replaces ἐστιν in remembrance of [Matt] 9:27" (405).

[19] According to Gundry (1994, 406), Matthew's reasoning is different though related: "Matthew's omission concentrates attention on Jesus' call; i.e., in Mark others issue the call on Jesus' behalf, but

beginning, there is no need to mention Jesus's disciples (Mark 10:46) since Matthew has already set them together with Jesus recently in the larger narrative (Matt 20:17; Gundry 1994, 405).

Numerous further omissions foster conciseness. First, Matthew's omission of Bartimaeus as a "beggar" (προσαίτης; Mark 10:46) fosters conciseness, for first-century readers would have understood the equation of debilitating illness with penury. Second, while Mark 10:47 employs the so-called pleonastic or redundant auxiliary ("began to ... "; Moulton and Turner 1976, 20), Matthew omits it. Third, Matthew economizes by referring to the subject, the blind men, in 20:33 as simply "they" (implied in λέγουσιν); there is no need to repeat, with Mark, the subject τυφλὸς (Mark 10:51). Further still, at the narrative's end Matthew omits Mark's reference to the blind man following Jesus "on the way" (ἐν τῇ ὁδῷ), not only to mute Mark's discipleship motif but also because "on the way" is simply redundant: to "follow" Jesus is to follow him on some way; along some route. The phrase is unnecessary to show that the blind men follow Jesus.[20]

Finally, Matthew renders Mark's narrative rhetorically more plausible—more believable or realistic. The key change in this regard comes in Matthew 20:34 (see Mark 10:51–52), where Matthew adds that ὁ Ἰησοῦς ἥψατο τῶν ὀμμάτων αὐτῶν: "Jesus touched their eyes." While miracle traditions of the first century CE—witness Mark 10:52—do not require physical contact such as touch in order to effect healing, van der Loos reminds us that "touching and laying on of hands play an important part in the New Testament" and indeed in ancient Jewish traditions of healing in the Old Testament (Remus 1992, 860; van der Loos 1965, 313). It is therefore quite attractive to imagine Matthew adding reference to touch in 20:34 precisely to show—in his eyes, at least—the plausibility of Jesus's healing work.

Including Everything Necessary

Matthew's adaptation of Mark on the 2DH/FH is not without problems. In spite of his rhetorically inspired changes, Matthew makes arguable oversights. For one, Matthew doubles Mark's named blind man into two anonymous blind men. The shift seems a little odd, inasmuch as it takes Mark's plausible image of a concrete blind person, Bartimaeus, and converts it into "two blind men," thus anonymizing the reference and paralleling it with quite a similar narrative in 9:27–31, in a way that seems credulous: Is it really plausible, given his Markan source, that Matthew would prefer characterizing Jesus twice encountering and healing two, unnamed pairs of blind men? Is not Matthew

---

in Matthew Jesus himself calls the blind men—directly and authoritatively. Matthew's lordly Jesus dominates the landscape." Gundry immediately adds that this desire to accentuate Jesus's authority explains also the omission of the blind man approaching Jesus in Mark 10:50: "the blind man's throwing aside his garment, jumping up, and coming to Jesus disappear. As a result, the stress falls wholly on Jesus' words."

[20] Gundry comments differently: "the deletion of 'on the road' makes the climactic statement a general description of discipleship rather than a particular reference to the journey toward Jerusalem" (1994, 406).

rejecting Mark's ready-made plausible image? The answer is unclear. Gundry argues that Matthew has a valid biographical-theological motivation: doubling the blind man is part of an effort at "conflating the blind man in Bethsaida (Mark 8:22–26) with the blind man of Jericho, perhaps to get two witnesses . . . [one for] Jesus' lordship and [the other for] Davidic sonship" (1994, 178, 405). But the change still appears suspicious. For another, Matthew misses ready-made word order in Mark which could underwrite his own interest in highlighting Jesus's authority: Mark's blind man calls υἱὲ Δαυίδ, ἐλέησόν με (Mark 10:47), the forward position of "son of David" emphasizing it; Matthew shifts this title back (ἐλέησον ἡμᾶς . . . υἱὸς Δαυίδ; Matt 20:30; see Moulton and Turner 1976, 18; Gundry 1993, 594).[21] An analysis which weighs the number and quality of Matthew's changes on the 2DH against Mark's changes to Matthew on the 2GH must take account of occasions when Matthew seems to miss ready-made material to serve his rhetorical interests. There are other possible oversights, too.[22] The point of this analysis, though, is to argue that there is enough and varied evidence for rhetorically motivated change by Matthew to assign the 2DH and FH some explanatory power.

Summary

In closing, I wish to suggest three cautions or caveats that will help sharpen appeals to rhetoric for inferring plausible literary dependence. First, to infer from a handful of passages that one evangelist adapts another's work rhetorically to improve it does not mean that the reverse scenario is implausible. While Matthew, for instance, has his own range of rhetorical purposes and styles that bear on his changes, Mark too has his own purposes and style. Therefore, often what appears to be a rhetorical improvement of Mark by Matthew could equally be, from the perspective of a different source hypothesis (like the 2GH), a rhetorical improvement of Matthew by Mark. The analyst needs to weigh carefully both the number and quality of changes as a whole before surmising which of two Gospels has more plausibly adapted the other. Second, it should not be assumed that every alleged change to a source is rhetorically motivated. Rhetoric was not the only ancient modality which governed composition (Derrenbacker, 2005), and an author's editorial work might well have further literary and aesthetic motivations. Rhetorical criticism asks which of an evangelist's alleged changes appear grounded in rhetorical conventions for improving sources. Such conventions provide an independent and plausible, that is, historically reasonable or informed, standard against

---

[21] For Matthew's emphasis on Jesus as son of David see Gundry (1994, 176, 405).

[22] Perhaps in Matt 20:32, trimming Mark's phrase καὶ ἀποκριθεὶς αὐτῷ ὁ Ἰησοῦς εἶπεν (Mark 10:51) down into simply καὶ εἶπεν cuts against the image of an authoritative, august Jesus which Matthew otherwise seeks. Perhaps similarly, Matthew's omission of Mark's description of Jesus dispatching people to consult with the blind man, and of the blind man then approaching Jesus, similarly attenuates his effort to portray Jesus in an august, authoritative way.

which one can explain adaptations. Finally, it is important to remember that most Gospel commentaries argue for or assume hypotheses of Markan priority (Peabody, Cope, and McNicol 2002, xiv). These commentaries tend to pay relatively more attention to Matthew and Luke's rhetorical skills vis-à-vis Mark than to skills of Mark vis-à-vis Matthew and Luke, and this bias can predispose an interpreter to favor rhetorical adaptations favoring Markan priority. Again, the interpreter needs take care to imagine and to weigh the number and quality of rhetorically inspired changes and rhetorical oversights on competing hypotheses, before reaching conclusions.

With these cautions in mind, a knowledge of ancient rhetoric(s) can bring much value to answering questions of the Gospels' literary dependence. Using rhetoric as a tool to infer such literary dependence is an exciting and promising application of rhetorical criticism to Gospel studies.

References

Berger, Klaus. 2016. *Forme et Generi nel Nuovo Testamento*, translated by Cristina Esposto. Biblioteca del Commentario Paideia. Brescia: Paideia Editrice.

Bonner, Stanley F. 1977. *Education in Ancient Rome*. Los Angeles: University of California Press.

Brodie, Thomas L. 1984. "Greco-Roman Imitation of Texts as a Partial Guide to Luke's Use of Sources." In *Luke-Acts: New Perspectives from the Society of Biblical Literature Seminar*, edited by Charles H. Talbert, 17–46. New York: Crossroad.

Burridge, Richard A. 1997. "The Gospels and Acts." In *Handbook of Classical Rhetoric in the Hellenistic Period, 330 B.C.–A. D. 400*, edited by Stanley E. Porter, 507–32. Leiden: Brill.

Cribiore, Raffaela. 2001. *Gymnastics of the Mind: Greek Education in Hellenistic and Roman Egypt*. Princeton: Princeton University Press.

Damm, Alex. 2013. *Ancient Rhetoric and the Synoptic Problem: Clarifying Markan Priority*. BETL 252. Leuven: Peeters.

Damm, Alex. 2016. "Ancient Rhetoric as a Guide to Literary Dependence: The Widow's Mite (Mark 12,41–44 par. Luke 21,1–4)." *Biblica* 97, no. 2: 222–43.

Denaux, Adelbert. 1995. "Criteria for Identifying Q Passages. A Critical Review of a Recent Work by T. Bergemann." *Novum Testamentum* 37, no. 2 (April): 105–29.

Derrenbacker, Robert A., Jr. 2005. *Ancient Compositional Conventions and the Synoptic Problem*. BETL 186. Leuven: Peeters.

Downing, F. Gerald. 2014. "Imitation and Emulation, Josephus and Luke: Plot and Psycholinguistics." In *The Elijah-Elisha Narrative in the Composition of Luke*, edited by John S. Kloppenborg and Joseph Verheyden, LNTS 493, 113–29. London: Bloomsbury T&T Clark.

Gorman, Heather M. 2016. *Interweaving Innocence: A Rhetorical Analysis of Luke's Passion Narrative (Luke 22:66–23:49)*. Cambridge: James Clarke.

Gundry, Robert H. 1993. *Mark: A Commentary on His Apology for the Cross*. Grand Rapids: Eerdmans.

Gundry, Robert H. 1994. *Matthew: A Commentary on His Handbook for a Mixed Church under Persecution*. Grand Rapids: Eerdmans.

Hock, Ronald F. 2001. "Homer in Greco-Roman Education." In *Mimesis and Intertextuality in Early Christianity*, edited by D. R. MacDonald, SAC, 56–77. Harrisburg: Trinity Press International.

The Holy Bible. The New Revised Standard Version. 2010. Catholic Edition. Bangalore: Theological Publications in India.

Kennedy, George A. 1984. *New Testament Interpretation through Rhetorical Criticism*. Chapel Hill: University of North Carolina Press.

Kennedy, George A. 2003. Introduction to *Progymnasmata: Greek Textbooks of Prose Composition and Rhetoric*, translated with introductions and notes by George A. Kennedy, SBLWGRW 10, ix–xvi. Leiden: Brill.

Kloppenborg, John S. 2000. *Excavating Q: The History and Setting of the Sayings Gospel*. Minneapolis: Fortress Press.

Lausberg, Heinrich. 1998. *Handbook of Literary Rhetoric: A Foundation for Literary Studies* (1960), edited by David E. Orton and R. Dean Anderson, translated by Matthew T. Bliss et al. Foreword by George A. Kennedy. Leiden: Brill.

Luz, Ulrich. 2001. *Matthew 8–20: A Commentary*, translated by James E. Crouch, Hermeneia. Minneapolis: Fortress Press.

Mack, Burton L. 1990. *Rhetoric and the New Testament*. GBSNTS. Minneapolis: Fortress Press.

Mack, Burton L., and Vernon K. Robbins. 1989. *Patterns of Persuasion in the Gospels*. FFLF. Sonoma, CA: Polebridge Press.

Marcus, Joel. 2009. *Mark 8–16: A New Translation with Introduction and Commentary*. Anchor Yale Bible 27A. New: Yale University Press.

Martin, Josef. 1974. *Antike Rhetorik: Technik und Methode*. HAW 2/3. Munich: Beck.

McAdon, Brad. 2018. *Rhetorical Mimesis and the Migration of Early Christian Conflicts: Examining the Influence That Greco-Roman Mimesis May Have in the Composition of Matthew, Luke and Acts*. Eugene, OR: Pickwick.

Meynet, Roland. 1998. *Rhetorical Analysis: An Introduction to Biblical Rhetoric*. JSOTSS 256. Sheffield: Sheffield Academic Press.

Meynet, Roland. 2002. "The Question at the Center: A Specific Device of Rhetorical Argumentation in Scripture." In *Rhetorical Argumentation in Biblical Texts: Essays from the Lund 2000 Conference*, edited by Anders Eriksson et al., Emory Studies in Early Christianity, 200–214. Harrisburg: Trinity Press International.

Meynet, Roland. 2013. *Traité de rhétorique biblique*. Rhétorique semitique 11. Paris: Gabalda.

Meynet, Roland. 2014. *L'évangile de Marc*. Rhétorique semitique 16. Paris: Gabalda.

Meynet, Roland. 2015. *Le fait synoptique reconsidéré*. Retorica Biblica e Semitica 7. Rome: Gregorian and Biblical Press.

Monaghan, Christopher J. 2010. *A Source Critical Edition of the Gospels of Matthew and Luke in Greek and English*. Vol. 1. *Matthew*. SB 40/1. Rome: Gregorian and Biblical Press.

Morgan, Teresa. 1999. *Literate Education in the Hellenistic and Roman Worlds*. CCS. Cambridge: Cambridge University Press.

Morgenthaler, Robert. 1993. *Lukas Und Quintilian: Rhetorik als Erzählkunst*. Zürich: Gotthelf.

Moulton, James Hope. 1976. *A Grammar of New Testament Greek*. Vol. 4, Style, by Nigel Turner. Edinburgh: T&T Clark.

Peabody, David P., with Lamar Cope and Allan J. McNicol, eds. 2002. *One Gospel from Two: Mark's Use of Matthew and Luke. A Demonstration by the Research Team of the International Institute for Renewal of Gospel Studies*. Harrisburg, PA: Trinity Press International.

Reid, Duncan G. 2016. *Miracle Tradition, Rhetoric and the Synoptic Problem*. BiTS 25. Leuven: Peeters.

Remus, Harold. 1992. "Miracle (NT)." *ABD* 4: 856–69.

Robbins, Vernon K. 1989. "Rhetorical Composition and the Beelzebul Controversy." In Burton L. Mack and Vernon K. Robbins, *Patterns of Persuasion in the Gospels*. FFLF, 161-194. Sonoma, CA: Polebridge Press.

Robbins, Vernon K. 1993. "Progymnastic Rhetorical Composition and Pre- Gospel Traditions: A New Approach." In *The Synoptic Gospels: Source Criticism and the New Literary Criticism*, edited by Camille Focant, BETL 110, 111—147. Leuven: Leuven University Press.

Roberts, Michael. 1985. *Biblical Epic and Rhetorical Paraphrase in Late Antiquity*. Arca Classical and Medieval Texts, Papers and Monographs 16. Liverpool: University of Liverpool Press.

Schufer, Michael. 2003. "Evaluating Luke 22:47–51 as Emulation of Mark 14:53–72." Paper presented at Luke and Mimesis: Imitations of Classical Literature in Luke-Acts, Institute for Antiquity and Christianity, March 15, 2003, Claremont Graduate University, Claremont, CA.

Synopsis Quattuor Evangeliorum: Locis parallelis evangeliorum apocryphorum et partum adhibitis edidit Kurt Aland. 1985. 13th rev. ed. Stuttgart: Deutsche Bibelgesellschaft.

van der Loos, Hendrik. 1965. *The Miracles of Jesus*. NovTSup. 9. Leiden: Brill.

Verheyden, Joseph. 2014. "By Way of Epilogue: Looking Back at the Healing of Naaman and the Healing of the Centurion's Slave—in Response to John Shelton." In *The Elijah-Elisha Narrative in the Composition of Luke*, edited by John S. Kloppenborg and Joseph Verheyden, LNTS 493, 153–67. London: Bloomsbury T&T Clark.

CHAPTER 5

PAUL'S POSSIBLE INFLUENCE ON THE SYNOPTICS

CAMERON EVAN FERGUSON

Introduction

THE question of Paul's influence on the Synoptic Gospels is complicated. In the case of the Gospel of Matthew, for example, some scholars have argued for Matthew's knowledge of and self-conscious attempt to refute Pauline theological ideas within his gospel narrative (e.g., Sim 1998, 188–211; 2002; 2007; 2008; 2009; 2014b), while others maintain either that Matthew stands in relative agreement with Paul (e.g., Luz 2005a, 214–18) or that there is little relationship between the two (e.g., Foster 2011; Stanton 1993, 314; White 2014). In the case of Luke-Acts (presuming single authorship of the two works), the debate revolves around whether or not its author, who clearly shows familiarity with Pauline traditions, makes use of a collection of Paul's letters in the composition of his two-part story (e.g., Goulder 1986; Pervo 2006, 51–147; 2009, 12–14; Walker 1985, 1998). As far as the Gospel of Mark is concerned, arguments for the second evangelist's familiarity with and use of Pauline traditions were in vogue at the turn of the twentieth century, but, after the publication of Martin Werner's seminal monograph (1923), those arguments fell out of fashion. Then, at the dawn of the new millennium, Joel Marcus's "Mark—Interpreter of Paul" ([2000] 2014) made Mark's possible dependence upon Paul a matter of scholarly interest once more (e.g., Adamczewski 2014; Becker et al. 2014; Dykstra 2012; Ferguson 2021; Mader 2020; Nelligan 2015; Wischmeyer et al. 2014). Interestingly (and often overlooked), *if* Mark is influenced by Paul, it would mean that the other Synoptic Gospels, by virtue of their dependence upon Mark, are influenced by Paul, as well. This chapter explores this possibility, and in the pages that follow I present a case for the possible Paulinism of the Gospel of Mark. I then suggest some ways in which Pauline theological ideas, refracted through Mark, are picked up and incorporated into the Gospels of Matthew and Luke. I will conclude with a summary of my argument and select implications for future study.

Mark and Paul: The State of the Question

For the past century, scholars have largely considered Mark's narrative dependent upon traditional materials about Jesus Christ, divorced from Pauline influence. This consensus was established on the basis of Martin Werner's 1923 investigation, *Der Einfluss paulinischer Theologie im Markusevangelium: Eine Studie zur neutestamentlichen Theologie*. In his work, after carefully comparing Mark with Paul on a myriad of important themes in early Christianity (Christology, sacraments, law, etc.), Werner concludes that evidence for dependence of one author upon the other is lacking. According to him, where there are overlaps between Mark and Paul, those overlaps can be attributed to a common Christian tradition shared by the two, and, where Paul presents an innovation, Mark either says nothing or states the exact opposite (Werner 1923, 209).

Though there have been sporadic attempts to bring Mark back into the Pauline sphere of influence since Werner's work (e.g., Bacon 1925; Black 1996; Fenton 1955; Goulder 1991; Marxsen 1969, 117–50; Schenk 1991; Tyson 1961), no one investigation has proved so influential as that of Joel Marcus. Engaging Werner on the level of Christology, Marcus points out that, in order to separate Mark from Paul, Werner "[concentrates] one-sidedly on the picture of Jesus's miracles in the first half of Mark and [ignores] the passion narrative's extraordinary emphasis on Jesus's suffering and weakness [in the second]" ([2000] 2014, 34). For Werner, the defining characteristic of the earthly messiah is the power of the Spirit, as opposed to Paul's emphasis on the weakness of the flesh (34; Werner 1923, 51–60). This does not mean that Jesus's suffering and death plays no role in Mark's narrative, but according to Werner, it does suggest that Jesus's messianism is not contingent upon that death in the way that it is for Paul. Though Christ may ultimately die "for the many" (Mark 10:45), the salvation he has come to offer is already available during his earthly career (e.g., Mark 2:5, 10; Werner 1923, 61–62).

In his response, Marcus argues that one cannot so easily drive a wedge between the first- and second-half characterizations of Jesus in the Gospel nor prioritize one characterization over the other. From the very beginning of Mark's story, and all throughout, the crucifixion is upon the text's horizon (Mark 1:11;[1] 2:18–20; 3:6; 8:31; 9:31; 10:32–33, 45; etc.). Moreover, according to Marcus, Mark's and Paul's understandings of its significance are remarkably similar: the cross is the apocalyptic turning point of the ages wherein God's power and glory is paradoxically made manifest in human suffering, weakness, and death (Marcus [2000] 2014, 36–37). Marcus contends that this position is highly controversial within early Christ-believing communities—Paul's opponents emphasize the glory of the

---

[1] I take Mark's use of the term "beloved" (ἀγαπητός; Mark 1:11) to be a self-conscious invocation of the Aqedah (the binding of Isaac; see esp. Gen 22:2, 12, 16). This invocation, when coupled with the observation that the sequence of events in Mark 1:9–11 mirrors that of Mark 15:38–39, suggests that even Christ's baptism points to his death. For fuller discussion, see Ferguson 2021, 38–44, 105–6.

resurrected Christ, and Matthew, Luke, and John, in different ways, attenuate Jesus's suffering at Gethsemane and Golgotha (38–41)—and, as such, Mark's and Paul's agreement is not so easily resolved on the grounds of a common early Christian tradition. Because Werner's monograph fails to consider fully the scope and nature of Mark's emphasis on the cross (it is a "necessary" [δεῖ] and essential part of salvation history; see Mark 8:31),[2] Marcus is successfully able to call its conclusions into question.

In the wake of Marcus's article, new investigations into the Paulinism of the Gospel of Mark have begun in earnest. So far, however, no one study has proved definitive. Though various thematic overlaps have been recognized (Marcus [2000] 2014, 31–32; Theophilos 2014, 53–61; see also Telford 1999, 169), scholars have failed to offer sufficiently plausible accounts of Mark's hermeneutical approach to Paul. Work thus remains to be done on how Mark thinks about Paul and his mission and the means by which the evangelist connects his narrative to the story of the itinerant apostle.

A Way Forward: Mark's Etiological Hermeneutic

In the first half of the twentieth century, C. H. Dodd argued that the "gospel" (εὐαγγέλιον) is, for Paul, an episodic narrative that tells the story of the life, death, resurrection, and second coming of Jesus Christ "in accordance with the Scriptures" (see 1 Cor 15:3–8).[3]

Through a careful analysis of Paul's letters, Dodd established the following skeletal outline:

1) The prophecies are fulfilled, and the new age is inaugurated by the coming of Christ.
2) He was born of the seed of David.
3) He died according to the Scriptures, to deliver us out of the present evil age.

---

[2] I interpret Mark's δεῖ as a divine mandate, for which I find warrant in Mark 14:21 and 10:45. At Mark 14:21, Jesus says: "the Son of Man goes just as it is written concerning him [καθὼς γέγραπται περὶ αὐτοῦ], but woe to that man through whom [δι' οὗ] the Son of Man is handed over [παραδίδοται]. It would be better for that man if he had not been born." Jesus here relates his death to scriptural fulfillment (καθὼς γέγραπται περὶ αὐτοῦ, a possible allusion to the suffering servant of Isa 53; παραδίδοται; see Isa 53:6, 12), which, taken together with Mark 10:45—"for the Son of Man did not come to be served but to serve and to give his life as a ransom for many [δοῦναι τὴν ψυχὴν αὐτοῦ λύτρον ἀντὶ πολλῶν]"—suggests that Jesus's death is a necessary component in God's salvific plan for the world. For alternative interpretive possibilities, see Ahearne-Kroll 2010, 726–27; Smit 2019. All translations of Greek in this article, unless otherwise noted, are my own.

[3] The first half of this section presents an updated (and more concise) version of the argument I put forth in my monograph (Ferguson 2021, 15–20). The analysis of the foreign exorcist at the end offers a new case study to test my claim.

4) He was buried.
5) He rose on the third day according to the Scriptures.
6) He is exalted at the right hand of God as Son of God and Lord of quick and dead.
7) He will come again as judge and savior of men. (Dodd 1937, 18)

Richard B. Hays has since expanded upon Dodd's work. Agreeing that Paul's letters allude to and reflect a gospel (εὐαγγέλιον) which originates as a "sacred story," Hays contends that "any attempt to account for the nature and method of Paul's theological language must reckon with the centrality of *narrative* elements in his thought" (Hays 2002, 6, emphasis original). It is not just that Paul presumes a sacred story. According to Hays, that story is the "foundational substructure" upon which Paul's occasional arguments (his letters) build (6–7). The episodes of the sacred story are, in other words, the starting point for the theological debates Paul has (see, e.g., 1 Cor 15:3), and, when the apostle adopts a particular position over against that of his interlocutors, he judges his position to be valid on the grounds that he has interpreted the significance of the events of the sacred story properly, whereas his opponents have not.

Margaret M. Mitchell has advanced the theses of Dodd and Hays further. Like these scholars, she maintains that Paul's "gospel" (εὐαγγέλιον) is an episodic narrative to which the apostle alludes but which is only ever partially represented within his letters, and she engages how Paul appeals to and incorporates that narrative into his epistolary arguments. In two interrelated essays (Mitchell [1994] 2017b; [2004] 2017a), Mitchell contends that Paul makes use of what she calls a "synecdochical hermeneutics" in relation to the sacred story. That is, she argues that Paul, employing ancient rhetorical shorthand (βραχυλογία), appeals to the authority of the gospel narrative "through pointed, carefully chosen shorthand references to it" (Mitchell [1994] 2017b, 112, 115). Analyzing 1 Cor 1:17–2:5, where Paul seeks to combat the factionalist boasting of the Corinthians by presenting his own weak persona as mimetic of Christomorphic humility, Mitchell points out that Paul pulls forward a single episode from the gospel narrative, the cross, in order to check the divisive behavior of the community (1 Cor 1:18: "the word of the cross [ὁ λόγος ὁ τοῦ σταυροῦ] is folly to those who are perishing [ἀπολλυμένοις], but to us who are being saved [τοῖς σῳζομένοις ἡμῖν], it is the power of God [δύναμις θεου]"; 117). Though Paul presumes the whole, he has here highlighted one episode—Jesus's humble and obedient death—in order to draw the community into imitation of him as he imitates Christ (see 1 Cor 11:1).

Mitchell then suggests that Paul's gospel is not only contracted through such shorthand references; he is also able to *expand* the story at moments of rhetorical or communal need. That is, though his communities attempt to live their lives in accordance with the sacred story, no narrative is so comprehensive as to cover all eventualities that may occur within the course of a person's daily living. Thus, Paul is able to compose new episodes that speak to the needs of the moment. Mitchell argues, for example, that this is the case with 1 Cor 15:23–28 (and 15:51–55), where the community's doubts around the resurrection have "put the very gospel in question (v.12)" (Mitchell [1994] 2017b, 119). It seems that Paul had provided few concrete details about the nature of the resurrection during his initial preaching activity at Corinth, and this resulted in significant doubt and debate among the faithful. In order to combat their confusion, the apostle takes it upon himself to unpack the future and compose an expanded description of the end-times that counters those who had come to question it (120). Thus, while a certain narrative scaffolding of the gospel subsists (death, resurrection, and resurrection appearances, second coming, etc.), upon that scaffolding new episodes can be and are constructed as a part of Paul's theological and poetic method.

Importantly, it is not the case that Paul's synecdochical hermeneutic is confined to the genre of epistle. Mitchell also contends that Paul takes his very person to be a "rhetorical abbreviation" of the sacred story (Mitchell [1994] 2017b, 123; see also Duff 1991a; 1991b). That is, Paul claims to *embody* the narrative. In his letter to the Galatians, for example, where Paul presents the narrative of his prophetic call to proclaim the good news of Jesus Christ to the Gentiles (Gal 1:13–2:10), the apostle says that God revealed his son ἐν ἐμοί (Gal 1:16). Mitchell points out that this prepositional phrase could be translated one of two ways. Either it could be translated "to me," with Paul being the recipient of an epiphany; or it could be translated "in me," with Paul understanding himself to be "*the epiphanic medium* through whom God's son, Jesus, is revealed to others" (Mitchell [2004] 2017a, 241–42, emphasis original; see also Hooker 1996). For the purposes of her argument, Mitchell defines "epiphany" (ἐπιφάνεια) broadly to mean "a mediated manifestation of the deity," and she suggests that the double entendre in Gal 1:16 is deliberate: Paul both receives an epiphany and presents himself *as* an epiphany (240). Throughout Galatians, as elsewhere, the apostle claims that he is the walking embodiment of the death of Jesus Christ (Gal 2:19–20; 3:1; 4:4; 6:17), and, through the synecdochical manifestation of this one episode in his body, the whole sacred story is evoked for his believing communities (242–43). Indeed, at 2 Cor 4:10, this process is articulated explicitly. Paul carries around the "dying process of Jesus" within his body (τὴν νέκρωσιν τοῦ Ἰησοῦ ἐν τῷ σώματι; 2 Cor 4:10a), in order that the "life of Jesus" might also be made manifest in his body (ἡ ζωὴ τοῦ Ἰησοῦ ἐν τῷ σώματι ἡμῶν φανερωθῇ; 2 Cor 4:10b). In other words, "Paul contends that the necrotic epiphany currently on display in his body actually signals the resurrection epiphany to come" (244). As an icon of Jesus Christ crucified, Paul facilitates an epiphanic encounter between God and believers resulting from their recollection of the whole gospel story through his iconic display of one or more of its parts.

Transitioning to the Gospel of Mark, Mitchell suggests that the Second Gospel also participates in this synecdochical process. Though Mark is a fuller narrative in both form and purpose, it nevertheless presumes more of the sacred story than it narrates. The Gospel of Mark tells the tale of the missionary activity and death of Jesus Christ but does not present to the reader the story of the messiah's birth, his resurrection (there is only the youth at the empty tomb who promises its occurrence; Mark 16:5–7), or his second coming, to name a few examples. Instead, these episodes are either assumed, or they are signaled to the audience through prophetic prediction (Mark 8:31; 9:31; 10:32–3, 45; 13; etc.). According to Mitchell, it is for this reason that Mark concludes at 16:8 and neither Jesus's resurrection nor his resurrection appearances are narrated: it is up to

Mark's audience to recall them as a part of the larger sacred story (Mitchell [2004] 2017a, 246–7).

A similar synecdochical process is at work in miraculous deeds that Jesus accomplishes throughout the narrative. At the level of the story, Mark's characters consistently encounter, but do not comprehend, Jesus's true identity. Mark's audience, however, knows the full gospel plot, and they are able to import that external knowledge into the text (Mitchell [2004] 2017a, 247–48). Thus, based upon Paul's unique religious logic of mediated epiphanies of Jesus Christ crucified, Mark has crafted an extended episodic narrative deliberately designed to be a literary medium for epiphanic display of the crucified Lord: "the oral gospel has become text, a literary icon of the crucified messiah. Mark (the text) is (incorporeal) Paul for all time: Jesus Christ crucified can be seen there" (248).

Taking the foregoing as an interpretive foundation, I suggest that Mark and Paul not only share a synecdochical hermeneutic; *they share the same gospel narrative.* 1 Cor 15:3–8 is the fullest recitation of the gospel that is to be found in any one place in Paul's letters. In its final verse, Paul writes himself into and understands his person and his mission to be constitutive episodes of that narrative: "last of all [ἔσχατον δὲ πάντων], as to an abortion, he appeared also to me."[4] If Mark knows the sacred story, and he knows that Paul is an essential figure within it, the evangelist must compose his narrative such that this figure is a part of what is recalled within the minds of the audience after the conclusion of Mark's sixteen chapters.

Thus, on my reading, the evangelist's goal is not to retroject the figure of Paul into the life of Jesus Christ but, rather, to *anticipate* him. Mark seeks to seed the apostle and his teachings into his text. The evangelist always presumes, though he does not narrate fully, the entirety of the gospel of which Paul and his mission form a part, and his purpose is to tell a story that logically anticipates and concordantly connects with episodes subsequent to his sixteen chapters. In other words, a function of Mark's synecdochical hermeneutic is an etiological hermeneutic vis-à-vis Paul. Knowing that the mission of Paul is a part of the gospel narrative, Mark seeks to create episodic precursors that will bind the missionary activity of the earthly Christ to the eventual teachings of the itinerant apostle, teachings that are themselves affirmed within Mark's community. Depending on the particular Pauline phenomena Mark seeks to seed into his narrative, his literary strategies may be adapted, but his etiological hermeneutic remains the same.

To illustrate, I will compare Paul's self-understanding as one might reconstruct it from his undisputed letters with some of the most important rhetorical emphases of the Markan narrative. I judge Paul's constitutive claims of his person and mission to be as

---

[4] This reading is corroborated by Sim (2014a, 76), who argues that Paul's most complete recitation of the "gospel" (1 Cor 15:3–8) implicitly suggests that the apostle was not originally included in an official list of witnesses to the resurrection of Christ. Instead, the apostle adds himself, and, because he is "last of all" (ἔσχατον δὲ πάντων, 1 Cor 15:8) in the temporal sequence, he effectively becomes the final revelatory word, immune to those who might claim "that they were later visited by Jesus who communicated a message that differed from that of the apostle" (Sim 2014a, 77).

follows: (1) his authority is born of revelation; it is not imparted to him by human beings (Gal 1:1; 15–16; 2 Cor 12:2–4). (2) His mission—to preach the gospel to the Gentiles—is legitimate and divinely necessitated (Gal 1:16; 2:7–8; Rom 11:25–6), and it is a mission over which, if he is not the inaugural leader, his command runs parallel to and is distinct from the mission of the pillar apostles (Gal 2:9). (3) He feels a deep sense of indebtedness to the Jewish roots from which his mission grows (Rom 9:1–5; 11:16–23), manifested both in his insistence on a requited (monetary) gift to the people from whom salvation has come (Gal 2:10; 1 Cor 16:1–4; Rom 15:24–28; etc.), and in the continued expression of Jewish primacy (Rom 1:16; 2:9–10). (4) Because the messiah is crucified, and because Paul understands himself to be an iconic (re)presentation of this episodic "moment," he is called to advance a new ethical pattern in which the weak, despised, and lost become exemplary (1 Cor 1:27–30; 9:19; 2 Cor 11:24–33; 12:10; etc.). (5) Finally, with God's messianic intervention in world history, Paul understands himself to be a herald of the eschaton; not only does he expect an imminent end (1 Thess 4:15–17; 1 Cor 10:11), but he also teaches that the boundary-marking statutes of the Law are effaced (Gal 4:10; 5:2–3; 1 Cor 8:4; 10:25–26; Rom 14:5–6), and distinctions in gender, religious authority, and socioeconomic status are leveled (Gal 3:28; 1 Cor 12:13).

All of these claims are seeded into the Gospel of Mark. In no one place is Paul simply lifted and transposed into Mark's story, but those constitutive claims of his person find literary anticipation in the missionary activity of Jesus Christ. Working backward through the list, Mark also expects the imminent end of the world (Mark 13:30; see also 1:15; 9:1; 14:62; 15:43), and, within the span of its inbreaking, distinctions in gender and status are leveled (Mark 2:15–17; 7:24–30; 14:1–9; 14:41–44), and statutes which separate Jew from Gentile are attenuated (Mark 2:18–22; 23–28; 3:1–6; 7:14–23; 12:28–33).[5] Second, like Paul, the Markan Jesus elevates the lowly, weak, and despised, and he makes them explicit models for behavior (Mark 9:34–7; 10:13–16, 31, 42–4). Third, Mark presumes a deep indebtedness to the Jewish roots of the movement and prioritizes the Jewish mission (Mark 7:27; see also Mark 1:39–45; 6:35–44). Fourth, as in Paul, the mission to the Gentiles is not only legitimized, it is "necessary" (δεῖ; Mark 13:10). While the (pillar) apostles are never overtly represented as hostile to it (but see Mark 8:14–21; Kelber 1979, 30–42), they are famous for their lack of understanding in the Gospel of Mark, particularly when it comes to that which is "necessary" (Mark 8:31–33; 9:30–2). It should come as no surprise, then, that they misunderstand the inclusion of the Gentiles, as well. Finally, the Markan Jesus makes explicit that one does not have to have any contact with him or his disciples to work miracles in his name (Mark 9:38–40). In other words, as with Paul, missionary authority need not be imparted by human beings.

---

[5] As James D. G. Dunn ([1983] 1990a) claims of Paul, I am not here suggesting that Mark categorically rejects the Jewish law. Rather, I suggest that Mark, like Paul, seeks to show that those practices which create identifiable boundaries between Jews and Gentiles (food laws, Sabbath observance, circumcision, etc.) have become matters of indifference.

To show that these overlaps are not simply thematic, but that Mark has self-consciously crafted his story to anticipate the apostle, I will take a closer look at the anonymous exorcist of Mark 9:38–40. His brief appearance in the story runs as follows.

> John said to him, "Teacher, we saw someone [τινα] driving out demons in your name [ἐν τῷ ὀνόματί σου], and we were hindering him [ἐκωλύομεν αὐτόν] because he does not follow us [ὅτι οὐκ ἠκολούθει ἡμῖν]." And Jesus said, "Do not hinder him. For there is no one [οὐδείς] who will perform a powerful deed [δύναμιν] in my name [ἐπὶ τῷ ὀνόματί μου] and [then] swiftly be able to curse me [κακολογῆσαί με]. For he who is not against us is for us [ὃς γὰρ οὐκ ἔστιν καθ' ἡμῶν, ὑπὲρ ἡμῶν ἐστίν]."

The controversy over the exorcist arises soon after the messiah's second passion prediction (Mark 9:30–32). The episode occurs as Jesus journeys to Jerusalem, and it forms a part of a block of sustained teachings on the nature of discipleship (Mark 8:31–10:52; Moloney 2002, 171–72). When John informs Jesus of the disciples' attempt to stop the anonymous miracle worker, he explains that they do so because the man "does not follow *us*" (οὐκ ἠκολούθει ἡμῖν). As R. T. France (2002, 337) notes of John's words, "the expectation that someone should follow *us* (presumably the group associated with Jesus) is new and revealing. . . . What John is looking for is not so much personal allegiance and obedience to Jesus, but membership in the 'authorized' circle of his followers." Jesus responds by asserting that a person need not follow Jesus and the Twelve in order to act in his name. Instead, a true follower of Jesus acts in his name, regardless of his proximity to the disciples, and the confirmation of this is that said person cannot curse the messiah. ("No one . . . will swiftly be able to curse me [κακολογῆσαί με]"; Mark 9:39; compare 1 Cor 12:3.) Mark's Jesus here demonstrates an incredible willingness to accept an outsider as missionary, an acceptance that is elevated to a universal principle with a positive, inclusive articulation of a proverbial statement—"Who is not against us is for us" (ὃς γὰρ οὐκ ἔστιν καθ' ἡμῶν, ὑπὲρ ἡμῶν ἐστίν)—rather than its negative counterpart (e.g., Matthew 12:30: "He who is not with me is against me"; ὁ μὴ ὢν μετ' ἐμοῦ κατ' ἐμοῦ ἐστίν).

I am not suggesting here that the anonymous exorcist functions as some sort of allegorical symbol for Paul (*pace* Volkmar 1870, 464–75, esp. 464–67; see Werner 1923, 17–20). The exorcist does, however, set a precedent. Mark tells the story of an unfamiliar figure casting out demons in Jesus's name in order to introduce and approve within the life of Christ what would subsequently become a contentious aspect of Paul's self-identity: his authority as an outsider, who has never met the earthly messiah, to work effectively in his name. Mark 9:38–40 is thus synecdochical and etiological. It invites the recollection of the full gospel narrative, and, in so doing, it helps to justify Paul's place within it. The episode affirms that, during the time of Christ's mission, a figure like Paul is already operative. Mark has here sought to create literary concordance between the past and his present, a claim that can be made of all the parallels I have listed here. The anonymous exorcist is a figure entirely independent of Paul, but, because the work he executes is approved by Jesus even as he operates independently of the other apostles, Mark implicitly claims that Paul's doing the same is legitimate and already legitimized during Jesus's earthly life.

The Accidental Paulinism of Matthew

If Mark deploys an etiological hermeneutic vis-à-vis Paul, it can now be asked how Mark's anticipation of the evangelist gets picked up in the Gospels of Matthew and Luke. Space is limited, but I hope to provide a couple of illustrative examples that may open avenues of fruitful research. I begin with the Gospel of Matthew.

Though the text of Matthew—conventionally thought to be written around 80 CE in Syria, perhaps in the city of Antioch (Luz 2001–7, 1:56–59)—may bear witness to some theological dispute with Paul, the first evangelist may also affirm Pauline theological ideas unwittingly and as a result of his dependence upon the Gospel of Mark. As is well known, Matthew is a "traditionalist"; he makes use of nearly all of Mark's episodes (Mark 9:38–40 is, tellingly, not an episode he includes), and he follows Mark's emplotted order from chapter 12 onward (Luz 2005b, 5). This implies that Matthew considers the Gospel of Mark to be a largely reliable or authoritative account of the earthly mission of Jesus Christ, regardless of whether or not his own goal in writing a "book" (βίβλος; Matt 1:1) about that mission is to correct or even replace Mark's "gospel" (εὐαγγέλιον; Mark 1:1) that tells the story of the same events (Sim 2014b, 610–12).

As a result of Matthew's cleaving so closely to Mark, I suggest that Paul is able to slip in the back door. Matthew, for example, concludes his narrative with the so-called Great Commission (Matt 28:16–20), wherein the risen Jesus says to the disciples: "Make disciples of all the nations" (μαθητεύσατε πάντα τὰ ἔθνη; Matt 28:19; compare Matt 24:14; Mark 13:10). This injunction is striking given that, earlier in the narrative, Jesus explicitly tells the Twelve *not* to go among the nations. Instead, their mission is to "the lost sheep of the house of Israel" (τὰ πρόβατα τὰ ἀπολωλότα οἴκου Ἰσραήλ; Matt 10:5–6; see also Matt 15:24). To explain the apparent incongruity created by two different commissions with two different targets, Ulrich Luz (2005b, 14–17) has suggested that Matthew is a "two-level story." That is, it is designed to help the Matthean community (1) to process the fact that their mission to Israel has failed, and (2) to understand that, in the wake of their exclusion from the synagogue after the Jewish war of 66–73 CE, their responsibility is now to direct their message of deliverance to the Gentiles. It is for this reason that, though the Gentiles are given access to salvation, no concessions are granted vis-à-vis the law. They, like the Jewish people, are expected to adhere to its statutes (Matt 28:20; see also Matt 5:17–19; White 2014, 355–6; Sim 2008, 386–87). Matthew thus believes that, though the Jewish people may have rejected Jesus (Matt 27:25: "All the people [πᾶς ὁ λαός] said, 'His blood be upon us and upon our children!' "), the commandments of God that they have been given remain eternally valid for all.

Luz's proposal is incisive, but it assumes rather than provides an authoritative warrant for Matthew's abandoning the mission to Israel. Matthew is, after all, the first to narrate Jesus's call to "love your enemies [ἀγαπᾶτε τοὺς ἐχθροὺς ὑμῶν]" and "pray for those who persecute you [προσεύχεσθε ὑπὲρ τῶν διωκόντων ὑμᾶς]" (Matt 5:44; compare Luke 6:27–28; Rom 12:20). It is also Matthew who first tells believers to turn the other cheek (Matt 5:39; compare Luke 6:29) and to forgive the trespasses of others (Matt 6:14; compare Luke 6:37). One might wonder why, then, Matthew does not simply call upon his community to redouble their efforts toward Israel's lost sheep across the Mediterranean rather than direct their attention elsewhere.

The warrant, I suggest, is provided by the Gospel of Mark. The Gentile mission is already embedded in Matthew's source text (Mark 13:10), and it is a mission that Matthew, as a reader of Scripture, can further justify by recourse to biblical prophecy (e.g., Isa 56:1–8; Zech 8:21–3; see White 2014, 368–73). What Matthew does not realize, however, is that Mark's universal mission is deeply indebted to Paul's vision of Gentile inclusion, demonstrated particularly by the fact that the message is distributed to the Jews *first* (πρῶτον: Mark 7:27; see also Rom 1:16; 2:9–10). Far more than a single reference, Mark narratively presents the mission and its Jewish primacy throughout his story via subtle narrative clues (Malbon [1992] 2000, 42–54). The phrase "to the other side" (εἰς τὸ πέραν; Mark 4:35, 5:21; 6:45; 8:13), for example, serves as one of Mark's boundary markers, delineating Jesus's activity in Jewish and then Gentile territory. During his activity on one "side" or the other, contextual elements within the setting signal for the reader the ethnicity of the recipients of the proclamation. Thus, the reader knows that Jesus's confrontation with the Gerasene demoniac takes place in Gentile territory because "there was a great herd of pigs [ἀγέλη χοίρων μεγάλη] feeding next to the mountain" (Mark 5:11) and because the demoniac goes on to proclaim what Jesus has done in the Decapolis (Mark 5:20), a location known for its Hellenistic character (Marcus 2000, 347). Through such careful narrativization, Mark makes it clear that healings and exorcisms always occur among Jewish communities (Mark 1:23–34) before they occur among the Gentiles (Mark 5:1–13; 7:24–37), and proleptic Eucharistic bread is fed to thousands of Jews (Mark 6:35–44) before thousands of Gentiles receive the same (Mark 8:1–9). Jesus's troubling statement to the Syro-Phoenician woman, "let the children be fed first [πρῶτον], for it is not good to take the children's bread and cast it to the dogs" (Mark 7:27), is thus paradigmatic: it is confirmed narratively by Jesus's actions throughout the story.

As a result of his indebtedness to the structure and content of the Gospel of Mark, then, I suggest that Matthew has (re)presented the Pauline mission, even as he significantly modulates its implications. Unlike Mark (and Paul's) attenuation of certain boundary-marking statutes of the law (e.g., food laws: Mark 7:19; Rom 14:20; contrast Matt 15:17), Matthew calls for the adherence to the whole law for all Christ believers, but he does so to the Jew *first*, and then to the Gentile. Matthew has, in other words, unwittingly incorporated the Pauline mission into his narrative even as he updates it according to his own theological agenda.

The Harmonized Paulinism of Luke

Delineating Pauline theological conceptions that come to Luke refracted through Mark is more difficult. First, a couple of historical and literary presuppositions. (1) I take the Gospel of Luke to be an early second-century document (written sometime around 115 CE), composed by an author familiar with a variety of traditions about Paul and with access to a collection of Pauline epistles (Pervo 2006). (2) I presume that Luke is writing in a historiographic mode. That is, in ancient historical composition, evidential priority for the reconstruction of past events is given first to eyewitness testimony (whether of the author himself or of others), followed by various second- and third-order witnesses (see Luc., *Hist. conscr.* 47; see also Thuc. 1.22–23; Josephus, *C. Ap.* 1.1; Irenaeus, *Haer.* 3.3.4; Eusebius, *Hist. eccl.* 3.39.2–7). Though one can debate whether it is more proper to speak of the Gospel of Luke as a biography (Burridge 2004; Robbins 1979), (apologetic) historiography (Callan 1985; Moles 2011; Sterling 1992), or technical composition (*Fachprosa*; Alexander 1986; 1993), it is clear from his prologue that Luke purports to adopt a historical investigative procedure in the composition of his story (see Luke 1:1–4).

Supposing, then, that Luke writes in the early second century and is potentially familiar with a tradition wherein Mark is a follower of Paul (Phlm 1:24; Col 4:10; 2 Tim 4:11) or a tradition wherein he is an interpreter of Peter (Eusebius, *Hist. Eccl.* 3.39.15; 1 Pet 5:13),[6] Mark would not be, for the evangelist, a first-order witness to the earthly life of Christ. If, moreover, Luke had access to a collection of Paul's letters, it follows that, where Luke takes those letters to represent teachings or preserve episodes that derive from the earthly life of Christ, the evangelist would have understood Paul's testimony to rival, in terms of evidentiary authority, the presentation as found in the Gospel of Mark. Indeed, Luke may have taken Paul's testimony to be superior, as the story of Jesus that Paul knows comes both from divine revelation *and* consultation with the apostle Peter (Gal 1:15–18; see Dunn [1982] 1990b). In terms of Pauline influence, then, I suggest that, whereas Matthew unwittingly preserves but attenuates Pauline theological ideas that come to him refracted through the Gospel of Mark, within his two-part story (Luke-Acts), Luke seeks to harmonize Mark's narrative—and, by extension, Mark's Pauline teachings—with the collection of Pauline letters and traditions he knows. To demonstrate this, I will analyze Luke's account of the Last Supper.

Luke's Last Supper (Luke 22:14–20), which contains two cups (Luke 22:17, 20), has a complicated manuscript tradition. Several witnesses excise the second half of Luke 22:19 and all of verse 20, thereby creating a shorter narrative wherein there is only one cup (see Bovon 2002–13, 3:154–56). Scholars generally agree, however, that the longer Lukan formulation (Luke 22:14–20) is the better text based on a preponderance of manuscript

---

[6] Indeed, it may be the case that Luke is familiar with both and implicitly harmonizes the two (see Acts 12:12, 25; 15:37–39).

evidence and the principle of *lectio difficilior* (3:152–56; Fitzmyer 1981–85, 2:1387–89; Johnson 1991, 337; Tannehill 1996, 313–14). To account for the odd repetition of the cup (Luke 22:17, 20), Francois Bovon suggests that Luke is combining two different sources in the narrative of his Last Supper: one biographical and the other liturgical (Bovon 2002–13, 3:156–58). I agree with this assessment, but, whereas Bovon prefers to think of these sources as anonymous, I contend that Luke's "biographical" source is the Gospel of Mark, and his "liturgical" one is 1 Cor 11:23–26.

Leaving aside the first cup for a moment, a strong exegetical case can be made for Luke's harmonization of Mark's Last Supper (Mark 14:22–4) with Paul's (1 Cor 11:23–5) in Luke's description of the breaking of bread and distribution of the *second* cup (Luke 22:19–20). First, in narrating Jesus's words and actions over the bread (Luke 22:19), Luke uses Mark's aorist participle "after taking" (λαβών; Mark 14:22) instead of Paul's aorist indicative "he took" (ἔλαβεν; 1 Cor 11:23), but uses Paul's "after giving thanks" (εὐχαριστήσας; 1 Cor 11:24) instead of Mark's "after blessing" (εὐλογήσας; Mark 14:22; but see Luke 24:30). He then uses "he gave it to them" (ἔδωκεν αὐτοῖς) from Mark 14:23 and the participle "saying" (λέγων) from 1 Cor 11:25, and changes the Greek word order of "this is my body" to follow Mark's formulation rather than Paul's (compare τοῦτό ἐστιν τὸ σῶμά μου; Mark 14:22; Luke 22:19; with τοῦτό μού ἐστιν τὸ σῶμα; 1 Cor 11:24). Luke concludes by using Paul's "on behalf of you" (ὑπὲρ ὑμῶν) and adds his remembrance formula, "do this in remembrance of me" (τοῦτο ποιεῖτε εἰς τὴν ἐμὴν ἀνάμνησιν; 1 Cor 11:24).

Second, in narrating Jesus's words and actions over the cup at Luke 22:20, Luke uses Paul's "in the same way" (ὡσαύτως), "after dinner" (μετὰ τὸ δειπνῆσαι), and "this cup is the new covenant... in my blood" (τοῦτο τὸ ποτήριον ἡ καινὴ διαθήκη... ἐν τῷ αἵματί μου; 1 Cor 11:25), but drops the remembrance formula, and uses Mark's "that which is poured out" (τὸ ἐκχυννόμενον; Mark 14:24). Luke then connects, like Mark, an "on behalf of" (ὑπέρ) statement to the cup, but echoes once again Paul's formula "on behalf of *you*" (τὸ ὑπὲρ ὑμῶν; 1 Cor 11:24). Luke thus continually toggles back and forth between the Markan (Mark 14:22–4) and Pauline (1 Cor 11:23–5) accounts of the Last Supper in his description of Jesus's words and actions over the bread and (second) cup.[7]

Returning to Luke's first cup (Luke 22:17–18), its perplexing introduction is also explained on the basis of Luke's using both Mark and Paul as sources and harmonizing the two. Mark's story of the Last Supper makes it clear that Jesus breaks bread and distributes the cup of the covenant during the Passover meal (Mark 14:22: "while they were eating"; ἐσθιόντων αὐτῶν), but Paul claims that the cup is drunk *after* the meal (μετὰ τὸ δειπνῆσαι; 1 Cor 11:25). To be sure, whether Paul thought the Last Supper was a Passover meal is debated (see Daise 2016, 517–20), but it is in any case clear that Luke

---

[7] For ease of reference, I place the Greek of Luke 22:19–20 here. The words in bold come from Mark, the underlined words come from Paul. Lk 22:19: καὶ **λαβὼν ἄρτον** <u>εὐχαριστήσας</u> **ἔκλασεν καὶ ἔδωκεν αὐτοῖς** <u>λέγων</u>· **τοῦτό ἐστιν τὸ σῶμά μου** <u>τὸ ὑπὲρ ὑμῶν</u> διδόμενον· <u>τοῦτο ποιεῖτε εἰς τὴν ἐμὴν ἀνάμνησιν</u>. Lk 22:20: καὶ τὸ ποτήριον <u>ὡσαύτως μετὰ τὸ δειπνῆσαι, λέγων· τοῦτο τὸ ποτήριον ἡ καινὴ διαθήκη ἐν τῷ αἵματί μου</u> τὸ ὑπὲρ ὑμῶν **ἐκχυννόμενον**.

would be justified in believing that the apostle thought it was (see 1 Cor 5:7). If, for Luke, both Mark and Paul are equally authoritative witnesses to Christ's final meal, the third evangelist finds himself faced with a significant temporal contradiction. His solution is an elegant one: knowing that there are multiple cups during a Passover supper (see, e.g., Thiselton 2000, 756–60), Luke introduces a second cup in order to harmonize Mark's and Paul's statements. On the one hand, Luke agrees with Mark that there is a cup consumed during the meal and at the same time as the bread (Luke 22:17–19), but, according to him, it is *not* the cup over which the words of institution are spoken. Instead, it is a cup to which Jesus attaches an eschatological prophecy. Thus, the Lukan Jesus's words over the first cup—"For I say to you that I shall not drink henceforth from the fruit of the vine [οὐ μὴ πίω ... γενήματος τῆς ἀμπέλου] until [ἕως] [the time] when the Kingdom of God [βασιλεία τοῦ θεοῦ] has come" (Luke 22:18)—are remarkably similar to the Markan Jesus's eschatological formulation over the cup of the covenant: "Truly I say to you that I shall not ever drink from the fruit of the vine [οὐκέτι οὐ μὴ πίω ἐκ τοῦ γενήματος τῆς ἀμπέλου] until [ἕως] that day when I drink it anew in the Kingdom of God [ἐν τῇ βασιλείᾳ τοῦ θεοῦ]" (Mark 14:25). Luke's solution to the temporal contradiction created by Mark's and Paul's accounts is to imagine that Mark has combined two separate Passover cups into one. Luke then separates the two and makes it clear that the cup that is drunk *after* the meal (μετὰ τὸ δειπνῆσαι; 1 Cor 11:25)—Paul's cup—is the true cup of the new covenant. One need look no further than the Last Suppers of Mark and Paul to explain the Last Supper as it is presented in the Gospel of Luke.

Importantly, more than simply creating a story that harmonizes the accounts of Jesus's final meal in Mark and Paul, Luke recognizes that the evangelist and apostle share certain judgments about the significance of that meal, and he incorporates those judgments into his own narratives. For Mark and Paul, celebrating the Eucharist (re)presents for the community the salvific death of Jesus Christ, and the consumption of Christ's broken body serves as the means by which the metaphysical oneness of Christ-believing communities is (re)affirmed. Paul makes this affirmation explicit at 1 Cor 10:17: "Since there is one bread [εἷς ἄρτος], we, the many, are one body [ἓν σῶμα], because we have all partaken of that one bread [ἐκ τοῦ ἑνὸς ἄρτου μετέχομεν]." The one bread (ἄρτος; sc. 1 Cor 11:23) of which believers partake allows Paul to claim that there is one body in which all participate: "For just as the body is one [τὸ σῶμα ἕν ἐστιν] and has many members [μέλη πολλὰ ἔχει], and all the members of the body, though they are many, are one body [ἕν ἐστιν σῶμα], so too is Christ [οὕτως καὶ ὁ Χριστός]" (1 Cor 12:12). According to Paul, after their incorporation into Christ through baptism and the reception of the Spirit (see Gal 3:27–4:6; 1 Cor 12:13; Rom 6:3–8; 8:14–17), Christ believers affirm that incorporation through the act of consuming the Eucharistic bread.

Mark's understanding of the bread, more subtly represented, is similar. The feeding miracles that take place in Jewish (Mark 6:35–44) and then Gentile (Mark 8:1–9) territory proleptically announce the universal unity that will come about through the consumption of Christ's body. It is for this reason that Mark self-consciously crafts these feeding narratives to recall the language of the Last Supper. At both Mark 6:41 and

Mark 14:22, Jesus "takes" bread (λαβὼν τοὺς πέντε ἄρτους/λαβὼν ἄρτον) "blesses" it (εὐλόγησεν/εὐλογήσας), "breaks" it (κατέκλασεν/ἔκλασεν), and gives it to his disciples (ἐδίδου τοῖς μαθηταῖς/ἔδωκεν αὐτοῖς). Similarly, at Mark 8:6 (again compared with Mark 14:22), Jesus "takes" bread (λαβὼν τοὺς ἑπτὰ ἄρτους/λαβὼν ἄρτον), "gives thanks" over it (see Mark 14:23: εὐχαριστήσας), "breaks" it (ἔκλασεν), and gives it to his disciples (ἐδίδου τοῖς μαθηταῖς/ἔδωκεν αὐτοῖς). For Paul, the oneness of believers is affirmed locally through the consumption of the broken body of Jesus Christ, though a universal signification cannot be precluded (see 1 Cor 12:12–13). For Mark, that consumption affirms a universal unity of Christ believers, which, by definition, cannot exclude the local. Mark and Paul thus make the same claim (unity through consuming the [broken] body of Jesus Christ), but they do so at different altitudes (universal/local; for fuller discussion, see Ferguson 2021, 59–80).

Using Mark and Paul as resources, I suggest that Luke also designates the broken bread as the ritualized (re)presentation of the salvific death of Jesus Christ that serves as the means by which believers across the Mediterranean world, baptized and infused with the Holy Spirit (see Acts 2:38–9; compare Gal 3:27–4:6), affirm their bondedness. The importance of the rite is signaled at the end of the Third Gospel. On the road to Emmaus, two disciples encounter the risen Jesus but fail to recognize him (Luke 24:13–16). As they travel together, Jesus discloses to them all that Scripture prophesied concerning his fate (Luke 24:25–7), but they still do not recognize him. Upon reaching Emmaus, the two disciples invite Jesus to stay (Luke 24:28–9), and it is there, as they recline to eat, that "[Jesus], after taking bread [λαβὼν ἄρτον], blessed it [εὐλόγησεν], and, after breaking it [κλάσας], he gave it to them [ἐπεδίδου αὐτοῖς], and their eyes were opened [διηνοίχθησαν οἱ ὀφθαλμοί], and they recognized him [ἐπέγνωσαν αὐτόν]" (Luke 24:30–31; see also Luke 24:35; 22:19). Luke here makes the spectacular claim that Christ is only recognized through the bread rite, implying that "henceforth the risen Christ will be present to his assembled disciples, not visibly (after the ascension), but in the breaking of the bread. So they will know him and recognize him, because *so* he will be truly present among them" (Fitzmyer 1981–85, 2:1559, emphasis original). This significance is also assumed in Acts of the Apostles, where Luke designates the breaking of bread as the essential ritual act in the postbaptismal lives of Christ believers: "They were devoting themselves to the teachings of the apostles and to fellowship [τῇ κοινωνίᾳ]; to the breaking of bread [τῇ κλάσει τοῦ ἄρτου] and to prayer" (Acts 2:41; see also 1 Cor 10:16). Luke even shows the bread ritual occurring among Christ believers across the Mediterranean world (Acts 2:44–47; 20:7, 11; 27:35–36). The result is that, for Luke, the bread not only binds individuals within a given ecclesiological context together through the ritualized (re)presentation of Christ's death (Paul) but also, at the same time, binds communities across the Mediterranean landscape together through participation in a transregional ritual pattern (Mark). Luke may more fully draw out a recognition motif than does Paul or Mark, but the foundation for Luke's thought on the Eucharist is the shared emphasis of the apostle and the second evangelist on the unifying power of the one loaf of which all are invited to partake.

Conclusion

In this paper, I have suggested that Paul's "gospel" is an episodic narrative (the story of the life, death, resurrection, resurrection appearances, and second coming of Jesus Christ "in accordance with the Scriptures"; compare 1 Cor 15:3–8) into which the apostle has inserted himself (1 Cor 15:8). I then argued that Mark shares his gospel with Paul, and, because Paul and his mission occupy a central position within the salvation-historical narrative with which Mark is familiar, that the evangelist seeks to anticipate both within his story of the earthly mission of Jesus Christ. Pauline theological, Christological, and ecclesiological ideas are thus seeded into the Gospel of Mark in order to establish sufficient literary precedent for them such that the larger gospel story that extends from one end of historical time to the other remains fully concordant with itself.

If Mark is influenced by Paul, Mark's Paulinism must then effect those other gospel writers who use the Gospel of Mark as a source. In the case of the Gospel of Matthew, I have suggested that the evangelist inadvertently preserves Pauline theological ideas that he derives from Mark, but, at the same time, he attenuates their more radical implications and conforms them to his own theological agenda. In the case of the Gospel of Luke (and the Acts of the Apostles), I have argued that one sees an active harmonization of Mark and Paul, as Luke considers both the evangelist and apostle to be authoritative witnesses to the teachings and missionary purpose of Jesus Christ. It would be going too far to say that Luke recognizes Mark to be a Pauline text, but he does find Mark and Paul amenable to harmonization, and he uses this to his advantage. Luke's project is, in certain respects, a spiritual successor to Mark's: through the composition of narrative, he seeks to bring his vision of the earthly life of Jesus into harmony with what he takes to be the mission of the apostle Paul.

Should the arguments of this essay prove persuasive, significant new avenues of research are opened. On the one hand, the claim that Mark "seeds" or anticipates Pauline theological, Christological, or ecclesiological ideas into his narrative must be tested fully. Those various thematic overlaps that the apostle and evangelist share (the centrality of Christ's death, the importance of the Gentile mission, an ambivalence toward the [pillar] apostles, etc.) will all need to be read through the lens of a Markan etiological hermeneutic to determine whether they are, in fact, plausibly explained on the grounds of Mark's seeking to establish literary precedent for Paul and his mission within his story of the earthly career of Jesus Christ. On the other hand, if Mark is judged to be Pauline, investigations into how that Paulinism influences the other Synoptic Gospels must be undertaken. I have offered a couple of possibilities, but different ways of reading Matthew and Luke will need to be developed to determine where Pauline ideas, refracted through Mark, are found within these texts and to what ends they have been adapted. The road will no doubt be a long and thorny one, but I hope that I have presented a compelling invitation for its traversal.

References

Adamczewski, Bartosz. 2014. *The Gospel of Mark: A Hypertextual Commentary*. Frankfurt am Main: Peter Lang.

Ahearne-Kroll, Stephen P. 2010. "Audience Inclusion and Exclusion as Rhetorical Technique in the Gospel of Mark." *Journal of Biblical Literature* 129, no. 4 (January): 717–35.

Alexander, Loveday. 1986. "Luke's Preface in the Context of Greek Preface Writing." *Novum Testamentum* 28, no. 1 (January): 48–74.

Alexander, Loveday. 1993. *The Preface to Luke's Gospel: Literary Convention and Social Context in Luke 1:1–4 and Acts 1:1*. Cambridge: Cambridge University Press.

Bacon, Benjamin W. 1925. *The Gospel of Mark: Its Composition and Date*. New Haven: Yale University Press.

Becker, Eve-Marie, Troels Engberg-Pedersen, and Mogens Müller, eds. 2014. *Mark and Paul: Comparative Essays Part II, For and Against Pauline Influence on Mark*. Beihefte zur Zeitschrift für die neutestamentliche Wissenschaft 199. Berlin: De Gruyter.

Black, C. Clifton. 1996. "Christ Crucified in Paul and Mark." In *Theology and Ethics in Paul and His Interpreters: Essays in Honor of Victor Paul Furnish*, edited by Eugene H. Lovering, Jr., and Jerry L. Sumney, 184–206. Nashville: Abingdon.

Bovon, Francois. 2002–13. *Luke*. Translated by Christine M. Thomas, Donald Deer, and James Crouch. 3 vols. Hermeneia. Minneapolis: Fortress.

Burridge, Richard A. 2004. *What are the Gospels: A Comparison with Graeco-Roman Biography*. 2nd ed. Grand Rapids: Eerdmans.

Callan, Terrance. 1985. "The Preface of Luke-Acts and Historiography." *New Testament Studies* 31, no. 4 (October): 576–81.

Daise, Michael A. 2016. "'Christ Our Passover' (1 Corinthians 5:6–8): The Death of Jesus and the Quartodeciman Pascha." *Neotestamentica* 50, no. 2: 507–26.

Dodd, C. H. 1937. *The Apostolic Preaching and Its Developments: Three Lectures*. Chicago: Clark.

Duff, Paul Brooks. 1991a. "Apostolic Suffering and the Language of Processions in 2 Cor 4:7–10." *Biblical Theology Bulletin* 21, no. 4 (November): 158–65.

Duff, Paul Brooks. 1991b. "Metaphor, Motif, and Meaning: The Rhetorical Strategy behind the Image 'Led in Triumph' in 2 Corinthians 2:14." *Catholic Biblical Quarterly* 53, no. 1 (January): 79–92.

Dunn, James D. G. [1983] 1990a. "The New Perspective on Paul." *Bulletin of the John Rylands University Library of Manchester* 65, no. 2 (Spring): 95–122. Reprinted in *Jesus, Paul and the Law: Studies in Mark and Galatians*, edited by James D. G. Dunn, 183–214. Louisville: Westminster John Knox. Citations refer to the John Knox edition.

Dunn, James D. G. [1982] 1990b. "The Relationship between Paul and Jerusalem according to Galatians 1 and 2." *New Testament Studies* 28, no. 4 (October): 461–78. Reprint, *Jesus, Paul and the Law: Studies in Mark and Galatians*, edited by James D. G. Dunn, 108–28. Louisville: Westminster John Knox. Citations refer to the John Knox edition.

Dykstra, Tom E. 2012. *Mark, Canonizer of Paul*. St. Paul, MN: OCABS.

Fenton, J. C. 1955. "Paul and Mark." In *Studies in the Gospels: Essays in Honor of R. H. Lightfoot*, edited by D. E. Nineham, 89–112. Oxford: Blackwell.

Ferguson, Cameron Evan. 2021. *A New Perspective on the Use of Paul in the Gospel of Mark*. Routledge Studies in the Early Christian World. New York: Routledge.

Fitzmyer, Joseph. 1981–85. *The Gospel According to Luke*. 2 vols. Anchor Bible 28. New York: Doubleday.

Foster, Paul. 2011. "Paul and Matthew: Two Strands of the Early Jesus Movement with Little Sign of Connection." In *Paul and the Gospels: Christologies, Conflicts, and Convergences*, edited by Michael F. Bird and Joel Willitts, 86–114. London: T&T Clark.

France, R. T. 2002. *The Gospel of Mark: A Commentary on the Greek Text*. New International Greek Testament Commentary. Grand Rapids: Eerdmans.

Goulder, Michael. 1986. "Did Luke Know Any of the Pauline Letters?" *Perspectives in Religious Studies* 13, no. 2 (Summer): 97–112.

Goulder, Michael. 1991. "Those Outside (Mk 4:10–12)." *Novum Testamentum* 33, no. 4 (October): 289–302.

Hays, Richard B. 2002. *The Faith of Jesus Christ: The Narrative Substructure of Gal 3:1–4:11*. 2nd ed. Grand Rapids: Eerdmans.

Hooker, Morna. 1996. "A Partner in the Gospel: Paul's Understanding of His Ministry." In *Theology and Ethics in Paul and His Interpreters: Essays in Honor of Victor Paul Furnish*, edited by Eugene H. Lovering, Jr., and Jerry L. Sumney, 83–100. Nashville: Abingdon.

Johnson, Luke Timothy. 1991. *The Gospel of Luke*. Collegeville: Liturgical.

Kelber, Werner H. 1979. *Mark's Story of Jesus*. Philadelphia: Fortress.

Luz, Ulrich. 2005a. "The Fulfillment of the Law in Matthew (Matt 5:17–20)." In *Studies in Matthew*, translated by Rosemary Selle, 185–220. Grand Rapids: Eerdmans.

Luz, Ulrich. 2005b. "Matthew the Evangelist: A Jewish Christian at the Crossroads." In *Studies in Matthew*, translated by Rosemary Selle, 3–17. Grand Rapids: Eerdmans.

Mader, Heidrun E. 2020. *Markus und Paulus: Die beiden ältesten erhalten literarischen Werke und theologischen Entwürfe des Urchristentums im Vergleich*. Biblische Zeitschrift—Supplements Band 1. Leiden: Brill.

Malbon, Elizabeth Struthers. [1992] 2000. "Narrative Criticism: How Does the Story Mean?" In *Mark and Method: New Approaches in Biblical Studies*, edited by Janice Cape Anderson and Stephen D. Moore, 23–49. Minneapolis: Fortress. Reprinted in *In the Company of Jesus: Characters in Mark's Gospel*, edited by Elizabeth Struthers Malbon, 1–40. Louisville: Westminster John Knox. Citations refer to the John Knox edition.

Marcus, Joel. 2000. *Mark: 1–8*. Anchor Bible 27. New York: Doubleday.

Marcus, Joel. [2000] 2014. "Mark—Interpreter of Paul." *New Testament Studies* 46, no. 4 (October): 473–87. Reprinted in *Mark and Paul: Comparative Essays Part II, For and Against Pauline Influence on Mark*, edited by Eve-Marie Becker, Troels Engberg-Pedersen, and Mogens Müller, 29–49, Beihefte zur Zeitschrift für die neutestamentliche Wissenschaft 199. Berlin: De Gruyter. Citations refer to the De Gruyter edition.

Marxsen, Willi. 1969. *Mark the Evangelist: Studies on the Redaction History of the Gospel*. Translated by James Boyce, Donald Juel, William Poehlmann, and Roy A. Harrisville. Nashville: Abingdon.

Mitchell, Margaret M. [2004] 2017a. "Epiphanic Evolutions in Earliest Christianity." *Illinois Classical Studies* 29: 183–204. Reprinted in *Paul and the Emergence of Christian Textuality*, edited by Margaret M. Mitchell, 237–55, Wissenschaftliche Untersuchungen zum Neuen Testament 393. Tübingen: Mohr Siebek. Citations refer to the Mohr Siebeck edition.

Mitchell, Margaret M. [1994] 2017b. "Rhetorical Shorthand in Pauline Argumentation: The Functions of 'the Gospel' in the Corinthian Correspondence." In *Gospel in Paul: Studies on Corinthians, Galatians, and Romans for Richard N. Longenecker*, edited by L. Ann Jervis and Peter Richardson, 63–88. Sheffield: Sheffield Academic Press. Reprinted in *Paul and the Emergence of Christian Textuality*, edited by Margaret M. Mitchell, 111–32.Wissenschaftliche

Untersuchungen zum Neuen Testament 393. Tübingen: Mohr Siebek. Citations refer to the Mohr Siebeck edition.

Moles, John. 2011. "Luke's Preface: The Greek Decree, Classical Historiography, and Christian Redefinitions." *New Testament Studies* 57, no. 4 (October): 461–82.

Moloney, Francis J. 2002. *The Gospel of Mark*. Grand Rapids: Baker Academic.

Nelligan. Thomas P. 2015. *The Quest for Mark's Sources: An Exploration of the Case for Mark's Use of First Corinthians*. Eugene, OR: Pickwick.

Pervo, Richard I. 2006. *Dating Acts: Between the Evangelists and the Apologists*. Santa Rosa, CA: Polebridge.

Pervo, Richard I. 2009. *Acts*. Hermeneia. Minneapolis: Fortress.

Robbins, Vernon K. 1979. "Prefaces in Greco-Roman Biography and Luke-Acts." *Perspectives in Religious Studies* 6, no. 2 (Summer): 94–108.

Schenk, Wolfgang. 1991. "Sekundäre Jesuanisierungen von primären Paulus-Aussagen bei Markus." In *The Four Gospels: Festschrift for Frans Neirynck*, edited by F. van Segbroek, C. M. Tucker, G. van Belle, and J. Verheyden, vol. 2, 877–904. Bibliotheca Ephemeridum Theologicarum Lovaniensium 100. Leuven: Leuven University Press.

Sim, David C. 1998. *The Gospel of Matthew and Christian Judaism: The History and Social Setting of Matthew's Community*. Studies of the New Testament and Its World; Edinburgh: T&T Clark.

Sim, David C. 2002. "Matthew's Anti-Paulinism: A Neglected Feature of Matthean Studies." *Hervormde Teologiese Studies* 58, no. 2 (June): 766–83.

Sim, David C. 2007. "Matthew 7.21–3: Further Evidence of Its Anti-Pauline Perspective." *New Testament Studies* 53, no. 3 (July): 325–43.

Sim, David C. 2008. "Matthew, Paul, and the Origin and Nature of the Gentile Mission: The Great Commission in Matthew 28:16–20 as an Anti-Pauline Tradition." *Hervormde Teologiese Studies* 64, no. 1 (March): 377–92.

Sim, David C. 2009. "Matthew and the Pauline Corpus: A Preliminary Intertextual Study." *Journal for the Study of the New Testament* 31, no. 4 (June): 401–22.

Sim, David C. 2014a. "The Family of Jesus and the Disciples of Jesus in Paul and Mark: Taking Sides in the Early Church's Factional Dispute." In *Paul and Mark: Comparative Essays Part I, Two Authors at the Beginnings of Early Christianity*, edited by Oda Wischmeyer, David C. Sim, and Ian J. Elmer, 73–97. Beihefte zur Zeitschrift für die neutestamentliche Wissenschaft 198. Berlin: De Gruyter.

Sim, David C. 2014b. "The Reception of Paul and Mark in the Gospel of Matthew." In *Paul and Mark: Comparative Essays Part I, Two Authors at the Beginnings of Early Christianity*, edited by Oda Wischmeyer, David C. Sim, and Ian J. Elmer, 589–615. Beihefte zur Zeitschrift für die neutestamentliche Wissenschaft 198. Berlin: De Gruyter.

Smit, Peter-Ben. 2019. "Questioning Divine δεῖ: On Allowing Texts *Not* to Say Everything." *Novum Testamentum* 61, no. 1 (December): 40–54.

Stanton, Graham. 1993. *A Gospel for a New People: Studies in Matthew*. Louisville: Westminster John Knox.

Sterling, Gregory E. 1992. *Historiography and Self-Definition: Josephos, Luke-Acts, and Apologetic Historiography*. Novum Testamentum Supplement 64. Leiden: Brill.

Tannehill, Robert C. 1996. *Luke*. Abingdon New Testament Commentaries. Nashville: Abingdon.

Telford, W. R. 1999. *The Theology of the Gospel of Mark*. New Testament Theology. Cambridge: Cambridge University Press.

Theophilos, Michael P. 2014. "The Roman Connection: Paul and Mark." In *Paul and Mark: Comparative Essays Part I, Two Authors at the Beginnings of Early Christianity*, edited by Oda Wischmeyer, David C. Sim, and Ian J. Elmer, 45–71. Beihefte zur Zeitschrift für die neutestamentliche Wissenschaft 198. Berlin: De Gruyter.

Thiselton, Anthony. 2000. *First Corinthians*. New International Greek Testament Commentary. Grand Rapids: Eerdmans.

Tyson, Joseph B. 1961. "The Blindness of the Disciples in Mark." *Journal of Biblical Literature* 80, no. 3 (September): 261–68.

Volkmar, Gustav. 1870. *Die Evangelien, oder Marcus und die Synopsis der kanonischen und ausserkannonischen Evangelien nach dem ältesten Text mit historisch-exegetischem Commentar*. Leipzig: Fues's Verlag (R. Reisland).

Walker, William O., Jr. 1985. "Acts and the Pauline Corpus Reconsidered." *Journal for the Study of the New Testament* 7, no. 24 (May): 3–23.

Walker, William O., Jr. 1998. "Acts and the Pauline Corpus Revisited: Peter's Speech at the Jerusalem Conference." In *Literary Study in Luke-Acts: Essays in Honor of Joseph B. Tyson*, edited by R. P. Thompson and T. E. Philips, 77–86. Macon: Mercer University Press.

Werner, Martin. 1923. *Der Einfluss paulinischer Theologie im Markusevangelium: Eine Studie zur neutestamentlichen Theologie*. Giessen: Verlag von Alfred Töpelmann.

White, Benjamin. 2014. "The Eschatological Conversion of 'All the Nations' in Matthew 28:19–20: (Mis)reading Matthew through Paul." *Journal for the Study of the New Testament* 36, no. 4 (June): 353–82.

Wischmeyer, Oda, David C. Sim, and Ian J. Elmer, eds. 2014. *Paul and Mark: Comparative Essays Part I, Two Authors at the Beginnings of Early Christianity*. Beihefte zur Zeitschrift für die neutestamentliche Wissenschaft 198. Berlin: De Gruyter.

CHAPTER 6

ORAL TRADITION, WRITING, AND THE SYNOPTIC PROBLEM
Media Dualism and Gospel Origins

ALAN KIRK

Introduction

THE question of gospel origins is bound up with the Synoptic Problem, which arises out of the peculiar patterns of variation and agreement displayed by Synoptic parallels. Assumptions about orality and writing that critics bring to their analyses profoundly affect their proposed solutions. From the outset the default premise has been a media dualism: conceiving orality and writing as mutually exclusive modes of transmission, with variation the index property of the oral medium and close agreement the index property of the written medium. The effect has been to place one-sided documentary and oral solutions in opposition to each other or, alternatively, to distribute Synoptic parallels out among various written and oral sources.

This media dualism appeared right at the commencement of critical Synoptic Problem research, in Gotthold Ephraim Lessing's proposal for a written *Urgospel* (1784) and Johann Gottfried Herder's counter-proposal for an oral *Urgospel* (1796–97). In permutations of greater or less complexity it has persisted since then. Critics advance primarily oral or literary utilization hypotheses, or shaded combinations of these, depending upon whether they view Synoptic variability or Synoptic agreement as the more determinative. Strictly documentary hypotheses face the difficulty of accounting for Synoptic variability, oral hypotheses the difficulty of accounting for the patterns of Synoptic agreements.

Lessing's and Herder's essays simply reconnoitered the media terrain. Lessing's theory was taken up and given full exposition by Johann Gottfried Eichhorn (1796; 1820) and

Herder's by Johann Carl Ludwig Gieseler (1818). With Christian Gottlob Wilke (1838), *redaction* emerged as the primary factor adduced to account for Synoptic variation in strictly documentary solutions. To summarize, the first fifty years of Synoptic source criticism saw the emergence of the main approaches taken to the problem down to the present. I will give particular attention to these five scholars, using their analyses to get a grasp on the media problematic in Synoptic Problem criticism. I will then show how their respective media-driven solutions, in various guises, simply recur in more recent source criticism. The essay concludes by outlining an emerging media model that places orality and writing in a closely interfacing relationship, thereby overcoming the media binary and—potentially—the current impasses. No particular utilization hypothesis will be privileged; the point will be to show the determinative effects of a particular set of media assumptions on solutions to the Synoptic Problem and the corollary accounts of Synoptic Gospel origins.

Early Synoptic Scholarship

Lessing versus Herder

Lessing posited the early appearance of a written Aramaic *Urgospel*. Anonymous "Nazarenes" spontaneously collected and wrote down orally transmitted stories and sayings that they had heard directly from living apostles and other eyewitnesses. This *Urgospel* came to circulate in Palestine, alongside oral tradition, in expanded, abbreviated, textually variant, and differently ordered forms. The breakout of the movement into the Greek-speaking world precipitated the Synoptic Gospels. Each evangelist (the apostle Matthew being the first) extracted directly from the Aramaic *Urgospel* in whatever form it happened to be available to him (Mark's version of the *Urgospel*, for example, being less complete). Each made his own selections and each translated in his own style (Lessing [1784] 1957, 66–79). Hence the patterns of agreement and variation: they arise in the written medium out of the contingencies of collection, copying, extraction, translation, and stylistic shaping. Oral tradition for Lessing equates to the immediate oral instruction by living apostles, grounded in their eyewitness testimony, to the "Nazarenes" of Palestine; the role of this body of oral instruction is limited to providing these anonymous collectors, via their recollections of this testimony, the raw material for their written *Urgospel*. It is the *Urgospel*, in its written tangibility, that bridges the gap between Christ's death and the Synoptic Gospels (66–70).

Herder in his reaction expressed skepticism that utilization of a written *Urgospel* source—and a single one at that—could have generated the observable range of Synoptic variation. He posits a cohesive *oral Urgospel*, whose genesis lies in the oral preaching of Christ himself, but more immediately in the apostles' preaching of the gospel in its kerygmatic outline (Herder, [1796–97] 1994, 670–79). With its origins in a unitary preaching and instructional enterprise, the oral *Urgospel* took on a cohesive Gestalt, comprising a common fund of episodes, healing stories, parables, and sayings that like the *Urgospel* itself had assumed stable traditional forms. This "apostolic Saga" was narrated by the apostles and evangelists in quite uniform ways, at times extending so far as verbatim agreement. On the other hand these "gospel rhapsodes" exercised freedom in their oral enactments of the *Urgospel*. Given this powerful factor producing variation, the difficulty, Herder admits, is the patterns of agreement. Parables and sayings are inherently stable. The sufficient factor maintaining the oral *Urgospel* as a whole in durable cohesion, he argues, was its kerygmatic schema (686–97; [1797] 1829, 7–14, 31, 57–58).

The likely setting for the appearance of the written Synoptics would have been baptismal preparation. There was nothing to prevent a catechumen from writing down some version of the oral *Urgospel* conveyed in this setting, and the Prologue to Luke's Gospel explicitly locates its origins in convert instruction. Mark and Luke belonged among the "apostolic helpers," evangelists, by definition competent in the oral *Urgospel*. The Gospel of Mark is the earliest and the most primitive. It is very close to the form of the primitive Palestinian *Urgospel*, as it existed prior to its modifications and secondary expansions in the course of its oral transmission and dissemination. This means that a not inconsiderable quantity of the supplementary materials found in Matthew and Luke is not original to the oral *Urgospel*. The primitive oral *Urgospel* (best conserved in Mark), therefore, is the basis, the "center column," for agreements in order and wording in the common tradition of the three Synoptics ([1796–97] 1994, 679–85; [1797] 1829, 7–24, 61–66).

The distinction of being the first written Gospel, however, goes to the Aramaic Gospel of the Nazarenes (or Hebrews), fragmentarily attested in patristic citations but more fully, albeit only approximately, represented in Greek translation by the Gospel of Matthew. Like the Gospel of Mark, this Gospel, perhaps composed by the apostle Matthew himself (thus Herder interprets Papias's reference to Matthew's λόγια), took the primitive *Urgospel* as its basis (hence the agreements between Matthew and Mark). The medial term between Mark's and Luke's Gospels was likewise the oral *Urgospel*. But Herder thinks it probable that Luke also used the Gospel of the Nazarenes. This accounts for the double tradition that Luke shares with the Gospel of Matthew. Alternatively, if Luke did not know the Gospel of the Nazarenes—as is suggested by his quite different arrangements of this material—he had direct access to the individual narratives and sayings that it comprised ([1796–97] 1994: 26–29, 63–66; [1797] 1829, 678–84). With what amounts to a mixed oral gospel/written gospel utilization account, Herder, more so than Lessing, brings to light the tangled media problematic that besets all scholarship on the Synoptic Problem.

Eichhorn's *Urschrift*

Eichhorn followed Lessing's lead. Appeal to common oral tradition, he argued, cannot account for Synoptic agreements; these indicate written, documentary mediation.

Owing to their wide divergences in wording and order, however, the evangelists could not have directly utilized each other. Therefore they must have been drawing from a common written *Urgospel*, an Aramaic *Urschrift* (Eichhorn, 1794, 766–75, 841–42). Where the order of all three Synoptics agrees in their common episodes, and where two out of three agree against the other (and a reason can be given for latter's divergence), one is in touch with this *Urschrift*. It was a primitive first draft of the gospel message, with bare-essentials content and clumsy episodic arrangements. Because the Synoptics alternate in the primitivity of their common tradition, none preserves the *Urschrift* in its original purity. Doubly attested (Mark // Matt and Mark // Luke) pericopes found in the common triple sequence (without a reason for the odd Gospel out omitting these materials) are subsequent additions to the *Urschrift* in the course of its written transmission. The *Urschrift* therefore has descended to the evangelists in branching stemmata of three different exemplars: an exemplar used by Matthew with additions (A), an exemplar used by Luke with different additions (B), and an exemplar used by Mark (C) that had combined the additions found in the A and B exemplars, respectively (797–826, 961–62).

In effect Eichhorn parses out Synoptic variation among proliferating exemplars plotted on complex stemmata connecting the Synoptics back to the *Urschrift*. The *Urschrift*'s primitive, truncated pericopes invited expansion in its variegated course of transmission; exemplar A used by Matthew best preserves the *Urschrift*'s short-pericope character. Token instructional elements in the *Urschrift* triggered supplementations with analogous materials. Copyist-tradents frequently supplemented their exemplars with materials from their own memories, direct or mediated, of the life of Jesus, or sometimes exchanged an element in the text with a variant current in the tradent's immediate context. At times they substituted a favorite expression for the one in their exemplar, and on occasion they let their historical contexts affect their copying (1794, 790–96, 823–37, 877–90). The apostle Matthew, though not the author of the *Urschrift*, redacted an early exemplar in the stemma descending to the Gospel of Matthew, occasionally correcting its order and wording on the basis of his eyewitness knowledge of events. Inserting additions into an exemplar required that a tradent edit adjacent materials, which created further variants. The principal factor that produced variation in wording, however, was translation variants—again a strictly editorial operation performed upon written texts. Each evangelist independently translated his *Urschrift* exemplar into Greek. Matthew's tauter, more concise Greek comes from his more literal translation of the Aramaic text; Mark's verbose periphrastic style from his freer approach to translation (780–84, 930–49; 1820, 437–38). The translation-variant expedient, in concert with the variations that developed among the A, B, and C exemplars through a multibranched stemmatic transmission, allows Eichhorn to reconcile the Synoptics' widely variant wording with their broad agreement in order, one of the most puzzling enigmas in Synoptic criticism.

The translation-variant theory showed serious strains already when Eichhorn first advanced it in 1794. It had difficulty coping with contradictory variants, but more seriously it could not explain the extensive close or verbatim agreements in wording, and especially in Greek citations of the Old Testament that diverged from the LXX text and in rare Greek words. In subsequent explications of his hypothesis Eichhorn introduced an amendment. Shortly after the appearance of the Aramaic *Urschrift*, a bilingual Christian teacher and companion of the apostles carried out a Greek translation. Just like the Aramaic *Urschrift*, this Greek translation was copied and disseminated along various stemmata and came down to the evangelists who used it as an aid as they translated their respective Aramaic exemplars. They followed their Greek version of the *Urschrift* where its text still matched closely the text of their respective Aramaic exemplars, but they translated directly from their Aramaic exemplars where these diverged from the Greek text. This produced the Synoptic patterns of alternating agreement and variation (1820, 196–200).

This proposed remedy actually further exacerbated the principal difficulty of Eichhorn's writing-only utilization hypothesis: the uncontrolled proliferation of intermediating written sources that are needed to cope with the range of Synoptic variation. In addition to their Aramaic exemplars—A (used by Matthew), B (used by Luke), and C (used by Mark)—each evangelist had a Greek translation of the *Urschrift* which similarly had come down though them along diverse stemmatic routes. Eichhorn now also posits a D source—a version of the *Urschrift* used by Matthew and Luke that contained their double tradition expansions. He tries to simplify this by proposing an Aramaic Matthew E, a combination of A and D, subsequently translated into Greek (1820, 366–70). In short, his account collapses under the load of sources he must postulate to prop it up. It cannot cope with the range of Synoptic variation, for each variant requires some documentary action. The problem is that Eichhorn has difficulty conceiving written source utilization other than in the mode of manuscript transmission: close copying with only the narrowest range for editorial modifications, and variants accumulating down long stemmata of transmission.

What role does oral tradition play in this account? Oral tradition for Eichhorn is simply a subsidiary term for direct apostolic eyewitness testimony, thus a phenomenon pertaining uniquely to the individual apostles. He attributes no cohering artifactual form to it other than "oral instruction." The radius of its effective range is those within earshot of the apostles or other eyewitnesses. Accordingly, the primitive *Urschrift* appears immediately upon the carrying of the movement beyond the borders of Palestine by apostolic helpers and teachers. The *Urschrift* is subliterary and artless in its form, the artifact of uneducated individuals unpracticed in composition, a minimalist sketch of the life of Jesus, but on the other hand the virtually unfiltered expression of unmediated apostolic memory (1794, 177–78; 1820, 548–49, 778).

Notwithstanding the cul-de-sacs Eichhorn's theory leads him into, his singular focus on a documentary solution paved the way for important source-critical developments. He recognizes that the common narrative order of the triple tradition is the narrative order of the *Urschrift*. By comparing Mark // Matthew parallels with Mark // Luke parallels, he recognizes that the version of the *Urschrift* used by Mark is medial and the most primitive (1794, 828). Against Eichhorn's media horizon, however, the evangelists do not exercise the level of redactional autonomy that would make Matthew's and Luke's direct utilization of Mark even a theoretical possibility. The double tradition materials also catch Eichhorn's attention. These are only explicable if Luke and Matthew are drawing these materials from a common written source, whose primitive order is better represented in Luke (992–93; 1820, 365, 544–45, 647–50, 965–67). It is Eichhorn's recognition of the properties of the written medium, in particular its ability to stabilize wording and order, that allows him to make these observations.

Gieseler's Oral *Urgospel*

Given the problems with Eichhorn's hypothesis, the sharp swing to the oral medium in Gieseler's analysis was inevitable. Gieseler argued that the Synoptic Gospels were independent realizations of a wholly oral *Urgospel*. Orality, he points out, pervaded the ancient world. The rabbis of Jewish Palestine, who transmitted their traditions orally, are a case in point. If orality dominated the practices of the elite literate rabbis, how much more the primitive Palestinian community, composed of simple people? The free charismatic vitality of the primitive community's orality, moreover, was the antithesis of the lifeless artificiality of writing. Their "living memory" of Jesus, uttered in enthusiastic fervor, would hardly have been "chained" to "dead letters." The oral tradition itself emerged direct from the eyewitness testimony of the apostles. In their inspired teaching their memories of the details of Jesus's life and his sayings converged with messianic interpretation of the Old Testament to form the primitive tradition. To counter the powerful centrifugal forces of orality, these oral traditions were given tight, cohesive narrative forms (Gieseler 1818, 60–80, 102). A comprehensive oral *Urgospel* nucleated in their apostolic preaching. More to the point, this oral Gospel emerged in quasi-fixed (*feste*) form such that it could account for Synoptic agreements in order and wording. How did this happen, given orality's innate tendency to variation? It was of "highest importance" to the apostles that the oral Gospel follow historically correct order (88). Through repeated rehearsal this order became fixed. The tight oral forms assumed by the constituent traditions put limits on the range of variation in wording. The apostles, moreover, "always repeated things in the same words" (95). Aramaic's poverty in synonymous expression also conduced to lexical uniformity, as did the "oriental simplicity" of the apostles and the primitive community. The "high importance" of the matters to which the episodes bore witness was likewise a formidable factor strengthening lexical cohesion (94, 97).

Given these factors generating *feste Form* uniformity, how does Gieseler explain the differential levels of Synoptic agreement? The high-agreement narrative pericopes were regarded as more important than the low-agreement pericopes, hence were more frequently rehearsed and thereby more exactly imprinted in memory. The contents more than the forms of the less important narratives was preserved. Similarly, owing to their particular importance, sayings elements consistently display high agreement, an additional factor being their tight, memorable forms. Like the disciples of the rabbis, moreover, those sitting under the apostles would have repeated their teachings with exactitude (Gieseler 1818, 90–99). In addition (and on the face of it in tension with the latter scenario), the oral *Urgospel* was uttered in the midst of the primitive community by eyewitnesses in a state of charismatic exultation. The traditions resounded in the deepest being of the earliest Christians, aroused their affects to a high pitch, and—the effects magnified by the intensity of their community life—deeply imprinted their memories (92–99). The oral *Urgospel*, thus immunized against orality's innate tendency to variation, shaped in forms sanctioned by usage, and cultivated in cultural contexts accustomed to passing down cultural tradition by memory, was rendered capable of durable, long-term transmission. Its *feste Form* was apt for quick memory assimilation by nonapostolic evangelists whose travels disseminated it beyond Palestine (68–69, 88–97, 105–7). Its tight coherence in order and wording surfaces in the striking patterns of the agreements of the Synoptic Gospels.

Given his insistence on the oral Gospel's baked-in resistance to variation, how does Gieseler explain the extensive Synoptic variation? His claim that the *Urgospel*'s constituent episodes fell on a scale of greater or less "importance," the latter being rehearsed less often and thus more variable except in essential elements, was his preemptive response to this difficulty. In its individual pericopes the oral Gospel disseminated from Jerusalem was therefore just "more or less" fixed in its profile. Another factor was the rise of the Gentile mission, which generated diverging vectors of the *Urgospel*'s development. For example, in the Gentile mission *Urgospel*, passages that seemed to teach Jewish exclusivity fell away (Gieseler 1818, 103–10). To further explain variant wording Gieseler falls back on Eichhorn's expedient: translation variants. Owing to the presence of Hellenists in the Jerusalem community the apostles themselves decided on an oral Greek version of the *Urgospel*, though initially this was fully realized in Antioch under the auspices of Hellenistic believers such as Barnabas who were involved in the Gentile mission. This Antioch version omitted Jewish-exclusive passages of the *Urgospel* and rendered its Aramaic *Vorlage* into a more fluent idiomatic Greek. It was the oral Gospel that passed into the Pauline mission, and thus to Luke. Later, the Jerusalem apostles, Matthew and Peter in particular, also moved by the impetus to ministry beyond Palestine, worked up an oral Greek version of the oral *Urgospel* that, because of their lack of facility in Greek, bore a more pronounced Semitic linguistic complexion. This explains why Matthew and Mark (i.e. Peter) agree more closely with each other in wording than with Luke (113–16, 123–27).

Given this versatile, easily assimilated, and transmissible oral *Urgospel*, the relatively quick appearance of the written Synoptics seems anomalous. Gieseler gives the only account he can of this phenomenon: their appearance was completely adventitious. With the *Urgospel*'s wide dissemination in the more literate Greek world there would inevitably be some to whom it occurred to write it down, among whom were the writers of the Synoptics. There was no higher purpose in these writing projects; they were merely for private use (*Privatschriften*), handy aids for assimilation of the *Urgospel* to memory or for use as performance prompts (Gieseler 1818, 116–17). The oral Gospel copiously contained all Synoptic content; the evangelists drew upon it independently and selectively, guided by the needs of their respective audiences. Their divergences in order were due to the natural freedom of variation that "an oral narrative schema" permits (87–89).

Gieseler seems very contemporary in his grasp not just of the pervasiveness of orality in the ancient world but also of the cultural reliance upon the oral medium. But if Eichhorn had difficulty accounting for Synoptic variation, Gieseler's oral hypothesis has difficulty with the patterns of agreement. *Prima facie* dubious is his main explanation: the more "important" a tradition, the more it is rehearsed, the higher the level of agreement. Moreover, once its units are differentiated on the basis of importance and frequency of rehearsal, the oral Gospel's *feste Form*, so essential to the success of Gieseler's hypothesis, is compromised. The oral tradition effectively breaks back up into distinct units. In addition, if the evangelists were at liberty to be selective in appropriating the *Urgospel* and in some cases altered its order, why not tradents of the oral *Urgospel*? If an "oral narrative schema" allows the evangelists freedom to vary order in their writing projects, how did the oral Gospel maintain the same order down through decades of solely oral transmission? The oral hypothesis leads to the odd consequence that less variation occurs in the oral medium than in the written medium.

As it was for Eichhorn, the root of Gieseler's difficulties is a set of media premises that construe orality and writing as mutually exclusive modes of transmission. In Gieseler's case the media dualism is intensified by his romanticization of orality and the primitive Palestinian community, setting these in structural antithesis to the lifeless artificiality of writing and elite literacy. Brute Synoptic realities, however, force him in effect to impute the text-stabilizing properties of the written medium to the oral *Urgospel* and the variation tendencies of the oral medium to the evangelists. Ironically, his oral *Urgospel* is better at accounting for agreements than for variation. It fails at explaining the phenomenon that should give an oral hypothesis the least difficulty.

Wilke: Evangelists as Redactors

Christian Gottlob Wilke represents the unequivocal turn back to documentary solutions (though of course he had predecessors). By imputing significant redactional freedom to the evangelists Wilke is able to avoid getting bogged down in the morass of intermediating sources that doomed Eichhorn's documentary hypothesis and, at the same time, to argue that the Synoptics stand in direct source relations with each other. Close agreements in narrative elements of Synoptic parallels, he points out, indicate the effects of the written medium. So does the striking agreement in order of episodes, an order that forms, moreover, a coherent narrative arc (Wilke 1838, 28–30, 110–24). These phenomena depend upon the properties of writing—its capacity to hold heterogeneous materials together in spatial extension in the materiality of the medium—and, by the same token, detached authorial reflection for their realization. Oral traditions on the other hand are unformed, the immediate afflatus of recollection and feeling (*Gefühl*). The division between oral tradition and writing is as sharp as between *Natur* and *Kunst* (artifice). Oral traditions were the immediate recollections of the first Christian preachers; they had no stable, marked forms that would persist in transmission and into the written medium. The exception is the sayings, which would stick immediately in the memories of those who heard Jesus utter them. Accordingly they are the secure memory elements of the tradition. The narrative episodes of the Synoptics on the other hand, do not reflect the naïve immediacy, the realism, the idiosyncratic detail of individual recollection. Therefore they are products of the reflective authorial artifice requisite to give inchoate recollections of the events their narrative form and style. Not just their coherent overall ordering but their very form originates in authorial activity. The sayings of Jesus usually appear as the dominant element of these short narratives, which frequently serve to give sayings their narrative occasions (28–41, 122–33).

In short, Synoptic patterns of agreement and variation come into existence because the evangelists are exercising reflective authorial freedom in their operations upon a common source or sources. Wilke makes calculated authorial redaction virtually the exclusive factor in the rise of Synoptic variation, breaking with the earlier assumption that close copying is the normative mode of written source utilization (1838, 305–17, 472–75, 520–21). He grounds this claim in close study of the parallels, arguing that redactional intent can be seen in "the effort to give the material a more precise expression, or to strengthen or improve the connections, or in the case of additional material being inserted, to further elaborate upon an element in the common text, or to substitute an alternative" (299). All these operations are accompanied by editorial modifications to connect inserted materials coherently into the context, as well as stylistic modifications attributable to the preferences of the evangelists. A set of coherent redactional principles is readily imputable to an evangelist from observation of his modifications. Nevertheless, Wilke admits, in passing, that a portion of the Synoptic variants appears unmotivated: no redactional rationale can be given for them (292, 658–59).

How does Wilke's recourse to redaction affect his source criticism? Matthew and Luke, he observes, generally agree in the order and disposition of their triple tradition materials. But they frequently diverge in the way these individual materials are redactionally connected to one another. Similarly, in individual pericopes Matthew's and Luke's observable redactional traits only show up in the respective variations. The inference: a common *Vorlage*, an *Urtext*, "a coherent whole constituted of intelligibly ordered materials" (Wilke 1838, 560). The *Urtext* emerges in the patterns of three-way agreements and two-way agreements in wording and order. Mark, Wilke observes, is the middle term in these patterns of agreement (293–97). Matthew and Luke display alternating primitivity in their triple tradition (ruling out either being dependent on the other in these materials), with Mark consistently coattesting the primitive reading. When both Matthew and Luke simultaneously offer clarifying variants in these materials, neither shows awareness of the redaction of the other. Once one recognizes that the evangelists are bold redactors, Wilke says, a different profile of the *Urtext* emerges, one very close to the text of Mark (384–93). In fact, no meaningful distinction exists between the *Urtext* and the Gospel of Mark. Though final certainty is not possible (because of solely Markan elements), Mark is probably the *Urevangelist* (417–29, 551, 655).

Wilke recognizes that the postulate of Markan priority must reckon with the extensive Matthew // Luke agreements against Mark. He observes that the double tradition bears a pronounced instructional profile. It constitutes a "distinctive sphere" vis-à-vis the mostly narrative materials of the Markan tradition (Wilke 1838, 11, 19–20). In Matthew these materials are "braided around" and "attached" to the narrative stem of the triple-agreement materials; in Luke they appear mostly as block insertions interrupting the narrative sequence, and the units fall into a very different order from the order in Matthew (12, 170–71). The constituent sayings of the double tradition are closely woven into didactic sequences. These sequences therefore are products of authorial reflection and require the fixing properties of the written medium. They must come from some written source. Wilke thinks, however, that when abstracted out from their Matthean and Lukan contexts, these sayings materials cannot be seen to fall together into any cohering, connected source (128–29, 685). It follows that either Luke or Matthew is taking these materials from the other—Wilke decides that Matthew takes them from Luke.

Wilke recognizes the distinctive media properties of writing: that it has the capacity to consolidate and dramatically stabilize in its material substratum an extended, complex text, and that such a work, requiring meditated reflection detached from the immediacy of oral enactment, can only be realized in the written medium (1838, 121–23). This insight powers his critique of the oral hypothesis and leads him to his important documentary inferences. Over against this, however, stands a defective understanding of oral tradition. In his view early Christian oral traditions, sayings excepted, possessed no stable transmissible forms; Synoptic episodic pericopes are not residues of oral traditions. So sharp is his media antithesis that Wilke is not able to bridge the gap between the tradition and Synoptic writing; he cannot work out a theory of the relationship between the tradition and the reflective writing activities of the evangelists. Only the sayings cross the span from one to the other; other information comes more indeterminately via "rumors" and "reports" (160, 304).

Wilke's defective model for oral tradition forces him to reduce all Synoptic variation to redaction, to meditated editorial operations, though he must concede that a quantity of variants resist redactional explanation. His own acute observations, however, manage at times to escape these mono-media constraints. Certain incongruities in the texts of Matthew and Luke—for example πρὸς πάντας in Luke 9:23—come from their having the Markan text in memory even while they redacted it (Wilke 1838, 380). On a few occasions Wilke comes close to dismantling the media binary and recognizing oral forces at work in the utilization of written tradition. Reflecting on the "Metamorphosen" of Mark in Matthew and Luke he writes: "the way in which the base text has been rendered in other forms is not unlike the way someone re-narrates by ear and memory: in the mouth of the narrator the words undergo all sorts of re-combinations and coalesce into a unique form" (1838, 406). Wilke also recognizes that Matthew and Luke act more like tradents in their treatment of Mark than like independent and autonomous authors. They treat their written materials as a tradition, something that they have received and are constrained by, something that even in the transformations they visit on it they strive to mediate faithfully and comprehensively (18–29, 299, 468–71). These inferences arise out of his close observation of the redactional factor in producing Synoptic patterns of variation and agreement. The weakness of his account lies in its lack of a robust model for oral tradition and orality in Synoptic source utilization.

Summing Up

One can see that from its inception Synoptic source criticism revolved around the media problematic and was driven by a categorical media dualism. The inherent problems of the oral hypothesis along with recognition of the redactional factor opened the way for subsequent nineteenth-century scholarship (with a few exceptions) to pursue simple documentary solutions: in this respect Wilke's analysis can serve to represent an inflection point. The media dualism itself persisted, however, and now with the marginalization of the oral factor. Like Wilke, subsequent nineteenth-century source criticism lacked a robust model for oral tradition and for orality. It was not inclined to reflect on or theorize the phenomenological distinction between apostolic recollection and oral tradition. Though frequently just ignored, both the range and the patterns of Synoptic variation therefore continued to be nagging anomalies.

Heinrich Julius Holtzmann, for example, assigned a kind of primordial, urprimitivity to the oral tradition, which circulated as a disconnected aggregate of individual episodes and sayings. Like Wilke, he construed it as the immanent expression of apostolic memory (Holtzmann 1863, 52–53). The oral tradition embodied the naïve directness of eyewitness recollection; it was a "conglomeration" of individual recollections (Holtzmann 1901, 20–25). Very early, pre-Synoptic written collections of these materials appeared that were not ontologically distinct from the oral tradition (1863, 25, 244). These pre-Synoptic written collections, among which are Holtzmann's Logia source and his Source A (*Urmarcus*), were the principal means through which the primordial tradition was mediated to the evangelists (104, 160–63). For Holtzmann, in other words, oral tradition was significant insofar as it served as a temporary placeholder for primordial apostolic memory, and insofar as it found its way very early into written collections.

In contrast to Holtzmann, in Paul Wernle one finds little reflection at all on oral tradition and its connections to memory. Indeed, Wernle claims that Synoptic Problem analysis "should be completely separated from the question of the origin and history of the gospel tradition" (Wernle 1899, vi). Source criticism is a matter of written Greek sources and their literary relationships. The forerunner to these sources, Wernle notes, was "the Aramaic oral tradition," but he regards this is terra incognita (233). His utilization account therefore is dominated by written sources and writing. Oral tradition serves as a placeholder for the obscure early phase of the tradition, and as a parallel source for *Sondergut* materials.

In Synoptic scholarship also around the turn of the twentieth century, however, one observes a heightened awareness of oral tradition as an autonomous phenomenon—this comes to full, even exaggerated display in form criticism. There is no scope here to survey these developments; instead I will use source-critical reflections of Oxford source critics John Hawkins and B. H. Streeter as a springboard to the more recent scene, which has seen a resurgence in Synoptic source-critical analysis. Through a selective survey of scholars (representing the Two Document Hypothesis, the Oral Hypothesis, the Multiple-Source Hypothesis, the Griesbach Hypothesis, and the Farrer Hypothesis), I will show that a categorical media dualism, and with it the media problematic, simply reappear in contemporary source criticism.

Persistence of Media Dualism in Synoptic Scholarship

The Two Document Hypothesis

John Hawkins associated high-agreement Synoptic parallels with documentary transmission and low-agreement parallels with oral transmission. Identities of wording, he observed, "are so many and so close . . . that the use of written Greek documents is *prima facie* suggested by them" (1909: 54). On the other hand the large number of high-variation parallels remains "inexplicable on any exclusively documentary theory" (67). These indicate the influence of oral transmission. The double tradition and the triple tradition therefore reflect the combined effects of oral and written transmission (216–17). The problems, however, that will plague binary solutions like Hawkins's—distributing the synoptic materials out among written and oral sources—is first the range of variation (falling on a continuum from 100 percent to about 8 percent), and second that agreements and variations rarely occur unmingled. Hawkins seems to sense these difficulties when he admits that "we may be unable . . . to explain how [oral and written transmission] accompanied or succeeded one another" (217).

In *The Four Gospels* B. H. Streeter similarly argued that low-agreement parallels were oral traditions that had come separately to the evangelists (Streeter 1936, xiv–xv). For the double tradition this induced him to adopt the theory of a minimalist written Q that was limited to close-agreement double tradition parallels, with higher variation passages assigned their more proximate origins in a separate sphere of oral tradition. So text-oriented was Streeter, however, that it was difficult for him to imagine a utilization scenario that featured anything other than copying from written sources. Though on occasion he seems to countenance the possibility of the evangelists accessing "different cycles of oral tradition" directly, he usually conceives oral tradition being mediated to the evangelists via written sources, notably M and L (185, 237–39, 281–88). In short, orality and oral tradition serve Streeter as an ad hoc expedient to explain the origin of variants, after which he shifts back to a closed documentary world.

With the post–World War II flourishing of redaction criticism (largely predicated on the Two Document Hypothesis) came a temporary eclipse of source criticism and, along with it, marginalization of the oral factor. Subsequently—and more recently—scholarship has increasingly lost confidence that redaction criticism alone can account for the range and patterns of Synoptic variation, a reality already quietly conceded by Wilke. Thomas Bergemann's 1993 analysis of the Q tradition represents this loss of confidence. He assumes, however, that textual fixation, with a narrow margin accorded to redaction, is the marker of written transmission and that variation is the marker of oral tradition. On this media-binary basis he infers that the majority of the parallel passages of the Sermon on the Mount and the Sermon on the Plain could not have come from a common written Q (1993, 10–11, 171–202). As it was for Streeter, for Bergemann Q is a document limited to the higher-agreement Matthew/Luke parallels.

The more widespread expedient among Two Document Hypothesis scholars (one that goes back at least to Paul Wernle) for dealing with the anomaly of high variation double tradition parallels running in a common order is to propose two recensions of Q: Q^{Lk}/Q^{Mt}. Ulrich Luz adopts this strategy, while admitting that it is a contrivance born of necessity, the alternative being the "dissolution of the hypothesis of a documentary Q" (1998, 205–6). This is effectively Eichhorn's strategy of positing ad hoc another written source when redaction cannot plausibly account for the profile of variation. It breaks variation down into editorial stages, keeping Synoptic written tradition effectively insulated from oral-traditional forces. Franz Neirynck is uncomfortable with this strategy of proposing "intermediate stages" and, as Wilke did 150 years earlier, argues for attributing double tradition variation to Matthew's creative redaction (Neirynck 1990, 591).

Media dualism appears in James D. G. Dunn's treatments of the Synoptic Problem, though with the important difference that he pays much greater attention to the effects of the oral medium. Dunn has a heightened awareness of the pervasively oral environment in which Gospel formation took place and, correspondingly, of the limitations of narrow written-medium approaches to source-critical problems. Nevertheless he continues to separate oral from written modes of transmission. He argues that in high-agreement passages Matthew and Luke are copying from a document, Q, whereas in low-agreement passages they are drawing from cycles of oral tradition that occasionally overlap with the written pericopes; these he designates "q" (Dunn 2003a, 164; 2003b, 233–37). On Dunn's accounting, for example, three quarters of the Sermon on the Mount is q. This is full circle back to Hawkins's oral and written Synoptic sources and Streeter's Q/not Q. Nor is Dunn any more able than Hawkins to offer an account of how the coordination of oral and written sources might have produced the observable patterns of Synoptic variation and agreement. The challenge facing the "oral source or written source" solution is to identify the threshold at which variation is such that a given passage is to be categorized as oral tradition instead of redacted written tradition. Since agreement rates in the double tradition move incrementally from very high to very low agreement, it is difficult to draw a defensible line between Q and q material. At one point, however, Dunn suggests—not unlike the way Wilke did—that Matthew and Luke on occasion might "retell" a written pericope "in an oral mode" (2003a, 163–16; 2003b, 214–22, 231–33; 2005, 59). This is an intimation of a different media model, one that breaks down the oral/written binary; one that might overcome the difficulties that the Two Document Hypothesis runs up against explaining Matthew's and Luke's utilization of Q and Markan material.

In this connection John Kloppenborg, Alex Damm, and Duncan Reid argue that the evangelists apply established Greco-Roman rhetorical techniques in their source utilization (Damm 2013; Kloppenborg 2007; Reid 2016). Rhetoric by definition is an oral practice; accordingly, this is a promising model for conceiving how the Synoptic written tradition might have interacted with oral practices to produce patterns of variation. It is not clear, however, that this model is capable of providing a comprehensive explanation of Synoptic variation, or for that matter can account satisfactorily for the patterns of agreements.

The Griesbach Hypothesis

After a period of revival the Griesbach Hypothesis has again a much diminished presence in source-critical debates. For my purposes it is nevertheless instructive to take a brief look at its media scenario. Since the major postulate of the hypothesis is that Mark is a textual excerption and combination of Matthew and Luke, the advocates for this hypothesis's revival paid little attention to questions of pre-Synoptic oral tradition. One finds at most perfunctory reflection on media factors. As noted, the Griesbach Mark is an epitomator and conflater; both of these are by definition visually enabled editorial operations, rather wooden ones at that, on written source texts. In William Farmer's words, Mark has "both the texts of Matthew and Luke before him," comparing and conflating the wording of the parallel passages (1964, 264). Peabody, Cope, and McNicol sharply distinguish oral from literary factors in Synoptic source relations, making a token gesture to the former before adverting exclusively to the latter (Peabody, Cope, and McNichol 2002, 12; McNichol 1996, 26).

The Oral Hypothesis

This hypothesis has found a contemporary advocate in Armin Baum, whose starting point is again the failure of closed documentary utilization hypotheses to account comprehensively for the remarkable range and inhomogeneity of patterns of agreement (Baum 2008, 54). Baum argues that this variation profile corresponds not only to indexical features of oral tradition but also to characteristic features of materials reproduced out of memory as identified in experimental studies in cognitive science (187–95). In short, the oral Gospel hypothesis, now grounded in contemporary research in orality and experimental research on memory, accounts for Synoptic relationships: Mark, Matthew, and Luke draw their double and triple tradition materials independently from a common body of oral tradition.

Baum's analysis remains obligated to a pronounced media dualism. He assumes that close, visually executed copying, with some margin for editing and redaction, is in fact the mode of documentary source relationships. This is why he finds the unpredictably varying levels of Synoptic agreement inexplicable on a documentary theory, for why would an evangelist copy at randomly different rates of agreement (2008, 241-42)? His operative media binary leaves him no way to conceive how variation might enter into the transmission of written tradition beyond the narrow margin for editorial modification. Conversely, he puts oral tradition's property of multiformity down to the imprecisions of memory functionality. Baum is then confronted, just as his predecessor Gieseler was, by the problem of explaining how independent utilization of a common body of oral tradition can account for Synoptic agreements. In what amounts to an update of Gieseler's response, Baum follows Birger Gerhardsson and takes rabbinic practices of memorization and recitation as the template for the existence and transmission of oral tradition in memory. Like Gieseler, Baum in effect must impute documentary properties to the oral Gospel, assimilating it to the norms of the written medium. Correspondingly he brings much of the variation under the *Gedächtnisfehler* (memory errors) rubric. In accordance with this media model the first written Gospel, Mark, is more or less the mirror of its oral exemplar. Subsequently the oral Gospel underwent additional condensation, dropping of details, and word changes, phenomena attested for memory reproductions of written texts in experiments. Thus when Matthew and Luke come to write down the oral Gospel, their versions differ from Mark's Gospel in these respects (252, 304, 395–411). It is because the oral Gospel behaves like a written text that Baum can thus accommodate Markan priority within the oral Gospel hypothesis.

The Multiple-Source Hypothesis

As was the case with Eichhorn's analysis, contemporary multiple-source hypotheses deal with Synoptic variation by distributing it out among proliferating intermediating documents. M.-E. Boismard argues that multiple written sources, existing at various intermediate and primitive "redactional levels," and interconnected in complex stemmata by crisscross copying, issue in "a final redaction, a definitive edition" of Matthew, Mark, and Luke, respectively (Boismard 1972, 15–17; 1990, 235). Sources such as "intermediate" Matthew, Mark, and Luke, and yet more primitive documents A, B, C, and Q still do not encompass the full number of pre-Gospel documents. Q itself is likely just a convenient rubric for a number of distinct sources (55). Boismard has no working conception of a preliterary tradition; prior to the redactional levels the tradition existed in written collections organized on the principle of genre (55). Repeated copying and redaction therefore is the principal agent in the rise of Synoptic variation.

The model comes from text-criticism: incremental accumulation of variants down extended stemmata of copying, editing, and conflation of documents. Delbert Burkett similarly resolves patterns of variation and agreement in the Synoptics back into multiple written sources that over an extended history of scribal copying and compilation accrued into the Gospels. In his account oral tradition is hardly to be found even as preliterary placeholder or adduced ad hoc to fill explanatory gaps. Patterns of variation for Burkett are the cumulative effect of this history of compilations and conflations of written sources. As already with Eichhorn, to fully parse the strands of variation and agreement back into parallel and overlapping documents requires a proliferation of sources. When finished, Burkett has rectified the history of the triple tradition into Matthew, Mark, Luke, Proto-Mark, Proto-Mark A, Proto-Mark B, sources B, C, K, L, M, Parable Discourse, Lord's Supper Sayings, Trial Source, Elements of a Passion Narrative, and Mission-Miracle source, in total seventeen sources plotted on intersecting stemmata (Burkett 2004).

The Farrer Hypothesis

This hypothesis owes its present visibility to Michael Goulder's and Mark Goodacre's effective advocacy. What media premises inform their theorizing? In a manner reminiscent of Wilke, Goulder conceives Matthew and Luke as full-fledged authors. They rewrite old materials and create new ones ingeniously and often spontaneously, cued by motifs in the text of the source before them. In other words, for Goulder the principal factor in generating much of the tradition itself, as well as its patterns of variation and agreement, is individual authorial creativity (Goulder 1974, 4–5, 64; 1989, 87–88, 543–44; see Goodacre 1996, 25, 237–38, 363). Goulder therefore hardly needs oral tradition even as an ad hoc expedient (1996, 673). He has no working conception of oral processes and the properties of oral tradition. The pre-Markan oral tradition is more or less inert, a static consolidation (with some "erosions" and "additions") of apostolic memories (Goulder 1974, 138–52, 297; 1989, 22–23). This conception of oral tradition accounts for Goulder's default to individual authorial inspiration as the force driving change and development in the tradition. It also accounts for his confidence that the double tradition can be explained as Matthew's free rewriting of Mark. The text of Mark is the originating matrix for all developments in the tradition, supplying the cues for the flashes of inspiration of the subsequent authors. Non-Markan material comes to the evangelists from written sources, such as the Jewish scriptures or the epistles of Paul (1974, 4).

Goodacre for his part follows Goulder in identifying creative authorial agency as the principal factor in source relations, particularly when it comes to accounting for Luke's utilization of Matthew (Goodacre 2002, 122–23). To explicate Luke's literary conception and design is per se to answer the source utilization question. In a departure from Goulder, however, Goodacre invokes the oral tradition factor, not just in view of the incredibility of some of Goulder's accounts of Matthew's and Luke's generation of new tradition from motifs in their written sources but also to explain the anomaly that Luke sometimes has the more primitive version of a double tradition passage (1996, 259–60, 284–91; 2001, 138; 2002, 64–66).

OVERCOMING THE MEDIA BINARY

The foregoing analysis does not set out to privilege any particular utilization hypothesis. Rather, it shows how media assumptions continue to be a determinative factor in source-critical theorizing and in the stubborn persistence of impasses in Synoptic Problem scholarship. A sharp dualism between oral and written transmission has been the unvarying premise from the earliest phase of critical scholarship to the contemporary period. It is hardly unexpected, therefore, that the hypotheses produced in the early period simply reappear in various mutations in contemporary analyses and along with them the old impasses and anomalies.

In consequence of cross-disciplinary research on orality, writing, and ancient media practices, however, the contemporary period has also seen advances in media understanding and ancient media practices that are auspicious for Synoptic source criticism and the corollary question of Gospel origins. The long-entrenched media binary is in the process of being displaced by approaches that position ancient orality and writing in close interface with each other, while taking full account of their distinctive media properties. These approaches conceive orality and writing as distinct communication "channels," or "registers," that cannot be insulated from each other (Foley 1999, 3–5; also Finnegan 1988, 141; Thomas 1992, 5). In societies where a predominant orality coexists with long-standing but limited literacy, as in the ancient Mediterranean world, a constant interaction between oral and written registers comes into play. Written artifacts, such as the Synoptic Gospels, produced in cultural contexts with high ambient orality will participate in this complex media reality. The particular profile of the Synoptic Gospels displays characteristics of works that John Miles Foley classifies as "oral-derived" texts: written works that emerge in close connection with a foundational oral tradition, and whose use is characterized by heightened and complex interactions of orality and writing (1991, 15). The "oral-derived" rubric conceives of a spectrum of ways and proportions in which writing and orality, authorial initiative and practices of tradition transmission, might interact with each other in the origins of a work—and in source utilization operations. On a spectrum running from "author" at one end to "tradent" at the other (a relative not categorical distinction), the evangelists would be positioned more toward the "tradent" end: exercising authorial and rhetorical initiative, but bound to the tradition, committed to its consolidation, cultivation, enactment, and transmission (Kirk 2016, 40–42). In low-literacy cultures, written artifacts are aligned to the dominant modalities of orality and aurality. In the ancient world, the spoken word infused not only the creation but also the utilization of written artifacts. The indistinctness of the boundary between the written medium and the oral medium was emblematic of manuscript culture. Oral practices affected the cultivation of written tradition, and utilization of a written tradition amounted to an actualization of that tradition within a particular set of exigent social and historical realities. Accordingly, in its utilization and transmission a written, manuscript-based tradition, particularly one still in the process of consolidation like the Synoptic Gospel tradition, would come to display some of the qualities of an oral tradition. In other words variation, the index feature of oral tradition, can persist into manuscript tradition, though modified and controlled by the properties of the written medium (Kirk 2016, 93–150).

The pertinence of this media model for analysis of Synoptic source criticism is evident. Though no one should think that with its application all source-critical difficulties will suddenly evaporate, it has the potential to account for the most controverted feature of the Synoptics—their wide range and uneven levels of variation and agreement. Nor does the approach *prima facie* privilege one of the currently contending hypotheses over the other. What it does is provide a sound media basis for hammering out details of proposed hypotheses, for putting them to the proof, and for the critical debate among them. Nor does it displace redaction-critical analysis of Synoptic parallels; rather, it locates it within a broader media and cultural framework in which redaction is an essential mode for cultivation and transmission of a normative written tradition. These new media conceptions are currently making their presence felt in Synoptic scholarship, though it is still too early to foresee the full consequences of their application.

References

Baum, Armin D. 2008. *Der mündliche Faktor und seine Bedeutung für die synoptische Frage.* Tübingen: Francke.
Bergemann, Thomas. 1993. *Q auf dem Prüfstand: Die Zuordnung des Mt/Lk-Stoffes zu Q am Beispiel der Bergpredigt.* Göttingen: Vandenhoeck und Ruprecht.
Boismard, M.-E. 1972. *Synopse des quatre évangiles in francais.* Vol 2. Paris: Cerf.
Boismard, M.-E. 1990. "Théorie des niveaux multiples." In *The Interrelations of the Gospels*, edited by David L. Dungan, BETL 95, 231–43. Leuven: Leuven University Press.
Burkett, Delbert. 2004. *Rethinking Gospel Sources: From Proto-Mark to Mark.* New York: T&T Clark.
Damm, Alex. 2013. *Ancient Rhetoric and the Synoptic Problem: Clarifying Markan Priority.* BETL 252. Leuven: Peeters.
Dunn, James D. G. 2003a. "Altering the Default Settings: Re-envisaging the Early Transmission of the Jesus Tradition." *New Testament Studies* 49 (2003): 139–75.
Dunn, James D. G. 2003b. *Jesus Remembered.* Grand Rapids: Eerdmans.
Dunn, James D. G. 2005. "Q^1 as Oral Tradition." In *The Written Gospel*, edited by Markus Bockmuehl and Donald A Hagner, 45–69. Cambridge: Cambridge University Press.
Eichhorn, Johann Gottfried. 1794. "Ueber die drey ersten Evangelien: Einige Beyträge zu ihrer künftigen kritischen Behandlung." In *Allgemeine Bibliothek der biblischen Literature*, vol. 5, 760–996. Leipzig: Weidmann.
Eichhorn, Johann Gottfried. 1820. *Einleitung in das Neue Testament.* Vol 1. 2nd ed. Leipzig: Weidmann.
Farmer, William R. 1964. *The Synoptic Problem: A Critical Analysis.* New York: Macmillan.
Finnegan, Ruth. 1988. *Literacy and Orality: Studies in the Technology of Communication.* Oxford: Blackwell.
Foley, John Miles. 1991. *Immanent Art: From Structure to Meaning in Traditional Oral Epic.* Bloomington: Indiana University Press.
Foley, John Miles. 1999. *Homer's Traditional Art.* University Park, PA: Pennsylvania State University Press.
Goodacre, Mark S. 1996. *Goulder and the Gospels: An Examination of a New Paradigm.* JSNT Suppl. 133. Sheffield: Sheffield Academic Press.
Goodacre, Mark. 2001. *The Synoptic Problem: A Way through the Maze.* London: T&T Clark.
Goodacre, Mark. 2002. *The Case against Q: Studies in Markan Priority and the Synoptic Problem.* Harrisburg, PA: Trinity Press International.

Goulder, Michael. D. 1974. *Midrash and Lection in Matthew*. London: SPCK.
Goulder, Michael D. 1978. "On Putting Q to the Test." *New Testament Studies* 24: 218–34.
Goulder, Michael D. 1989. *Luke: A New Paradigm*. JSNT Supp. 20. Sheffield: JSOT Press.
Goulder, Michael D. 1996. "Is Q a Juggernaut?" *Journal of Biblical Literature* 115: 667–81.
Gieseler, Johann Carl Ludwig. 1818. *Historisch-kritischer Versuch über die Entstehung und die frühesten Schicksale der schriftlichen Evangelien*. Leipzig: Engelmann.
Hawkins, John C. 1909. *Horae Synopticae. Contributions to the Study of the Synoptic Problem*. 2nd ed. Oxford: Clarendon.
Herder, Johann Gottfried. [1797] 1829. "Regel der Zusammenstimmung unsrer Evangelien, aus ihrer Entstehung und Ordnung. JSNT Suppl. *Sämmtliche Werke: Religion und Theologie, erster Theil*, edited by Johann Georg Müller, 1–68. Carlsruhe: Büreau der deutschen Classiker.
Herder, Johann Gottfried. [1796–97] 1994. "Vom Erlöser der Menschen: nach unsern drei ersten Evangelien." In *Johann Gottfried Herder Theologische Schriften; Johann Gottfried Werke 9/1*, edited by Christoph Bultmann and Thomas Zippert, 609–724. Frankfurt am Main: Deutsche Klassiker Verlag.
Holtzmann, Heinrich Julius. 1863. *Die synoptischen Evangelien: Ihr Ursprung und geschichtlicher Charakter*. Leipzig: Engelmann.
Holtzmann, Heinrich Julius. 1901. *Hand-Commentar zum Neuen Testament*. Vol. 1. *Die Synoptiker*. 3rd ed. Tübingen: Mohr.
Kirk, Alan. 2016. *Q in Matthew: Ancient Media, Memory, and Early Scribal Transmission of the Jesus Tradition*. LNTS 564. London: Bloomsbury T&T Clark.
Kloppenborg, John S. 2007. "Variation and Reproduction of the Double Tradition and an Oral Q?" *Ephemerides Theologicae Louvanienses* 83: 53–80.
Lessing, Gotthold Ephraim. [1784] 1957. "New Hypothesis concerning the Evangelists Regarded as Merely Human Historians." In *Lessing's Theological Writings*, translated by Henry Chadwick, 65–81. Stanford: Stanford University Press.
Luz, Ulrich. 1998. "Matthäus und Q." In *Von Jesus zum Christus: christologische Studien; Festgabe für Paul Hoffmann zum 65. Geburtstag*, edited by Rudolf Hoppe and Ulrich Busse, 201–15. Berlin: De Gruyter.
McNicol, Allan J., with David L. Dungan and David P. Peabody. 1996. *Beyond the Q Impasse: Luke's Use of Matthew*. Valley Forge, PA: Trinity Press International.
Neirynck, Frans. 1990. "Synoptic Problem." In *The New Jerome Bible Commentary*, edited by Raymond E. Brown, Joseph A. Fitzmyer, and Robert E. Murphy, 587–95. Englewood Cliffs, NJ: Prentice Hall.
Peabody, David B., with Lamar Cope and Allan J. McNicol. 2002. *One Gospel from Two: Mark's Use of Matthew and Luke*. Harrisburg, PA: Trinity Press International.
Reid, Duncan. 2016. *Miracle Tradition, Rhetoric, and the Synoptic Problem*. Biblical Tools and Studies 25. Leuven: Peeters.
Streeter, Burnett Hillman. 1936. *The Four Gospels: A Study of Origins*. London: MacMillan.
Thomas, Rosalind. 1992. *Literacy and Orality in Ancient Greece*. Cambridge: Cambridge University Press.
Wernle, Paul. 1899. *Die synoptische Frage*. Tübingen: Mohr.
Wilke, Christian Gottlob. 1838. *Der Urevangelist, oder exegetisch kritisch Untersuchung über das Verwandtschaftsverhältniß der drei ersten Evangelien*. Dresden: Gerhard Fleischer.

CHAPTER 7

ORAL PERFORMANCE OF THE SYNOPTICS

LEE A. JOHNSON

The Problem

UNTIL the latter decades of the twentieth century, the search for origins of the New Testament gospel writings was intertwined with the "quest for the historical Jesus"; to understand the Gospels was to understand Jesus himself. The basic framework for the study of the New Testament was form criticism-source criticism-redaction criticism (Bultmann 1963; Dibelius 1971 Gerhardsson 1961; Wellhausen 1885), which led biblical studies down an ever-reductive path toward the "original text," thus the original words and deeds of Jesus. Even though form- and source-critical pioneers recognized that they were working in the murky world of what was described as the "oral period," they invariably relied upon the literary forms to define the oral tradition. Walter Ong defined this tendency in biblical studies as a "chirographic bias" of the West (1982, 140). The simplified progression from Jesus to sacred Gospel was: Jesus spoke—people remembered and repeated—gospels were composed in writing—texts were codified and officially viewed as inspired by God.

The Response

The hegemony of textually focused gospel hermeneutical approaches faced opposition from various corners of biblical criticism in the 1980s. Most notable was Werner Kelber's challenge (in *The Oral and Written Gospel* [1983]) to the stranglehold that previous critical methodologies held on biblical interpretation. Influenced by narrative and literary criticisms, he viewed Mark as a crafted narrative rather than a "string of beads," an influential designation of the Gospel coined by Schmidt (1919), who used form criticism to argue that there was no narrative structure in Mark's Gospel. Kelber's groundbreaking work brought to the fore the notion of the orally dominated world of the New Testament and challenged the ingrained assumptions of form, source, and redaction criticisms.

Concurrent with Kelber's influence arose the impact of innovative methodologies in the arena of biblical studies. The Context Group, founded in 1986, was initially involved in the Jesus Seminar, under the leadership of Robert Funk, in their work on the "historical Jesus." The Context Group resigned (or was ejected) from the Jesus Seminar in large part because of their insistence that the search for Jesus must have a broader investigative field than the texts themselves (Elliott 1986; Malina 1981; Rohrbaugh 1996; Stegemann and Stegemann 1999). Thinking about the Gospels "in context," these scholars challenged the notion that the primary way to understand Jesus or his words was through the printed text; rather, their focus was upon social science models that helped explain the dynamics behind the context of Jesus's life and teachings and those of the communities of the gospel writers.

In addition to the Context Group, the 1980s and 1990s saw an ever-widening field of critical methodologies brought to bear upon biblical interpretation. The Bible in Ancient and Modern Media Group formed within the Society of Biblical Literature, consisting of scholars with an interest in the oral presentation and aural reception of the biblical message, spearheaded by noted storyteller and scholar Thomas Boomershine (1988). In opposition to the deconstruction of the gospels that was encouraged by the application of form and source criticisms, scholars began to look at the gospels as constructed narratives in their entireties (Rhoads and Michie 1982).

Outside the arena of biblical studies, historian William Harris's influential work *Ancient Literacy* (1989) inspired questions about the composition, reception, and dissemination of written texts in the oral-dominated world of the New Testament. Although challenges have arisen against Harris's estimates (1989, 175–284) that no more than 10 percent of the urban population and less than 5 percent of the rural population of the ancient Mediterranean world was literate (Johnson and Parker 2009), Harris' findings brought the issue of literacy to the forefront of biblical interpretation (Herzer 2001); long-held assumptions about biblical texts were questioned. Scholars soon recognized that current definitions of literacy would not correlate to the ancient world. Even within the most affluent strata of society, there would not have been standard levels of literacy education. Capability in reading and writing did not necessarily imply utility in the work of handwriting or document production (Dewey 2013, 5–14; Herzer 2001; Woolf 2009). In addition to the educational differences, it is clear that the Greco-Roman world perceived the printed word as secondary to the oral message. Discussions from ancient rhetorical handbooks reveal a cultural bias against orators who relied upon written notes or lawyers who delivered speeches in court by reading passages (Jaffee 2001, 16–17; Johnson 2017, 65; Rhoads 2006b, 122). Composition in the ancient world was by and large an oral process; if writing was employed at all, it only occurred in the last stage of a work (Botha 2005, 632). The decades-long work of cultural historian and anthropologist Jack Goody on texts, authority, and oral cultures became a significant conversation partner with the renegades in biblical studies (1968; 1987; 2000). As biblical scholars were forced to address the conundrum of the orality of the ancient world and the myopic textual methods that were applied to biblical interpretation, the startling differences between modern textually based Western society and the world of the New Testament were brought into sharp focus.

Finally, another significant impact upon traditional biblical interpretation came from the theatrical arena. In the 1980s, several biblical scholars experimented with performances of the Gospel of Mark. David Rhoads, Tom Boomershine, and Whitney Shiner found that many of their long-held assumptions about the Gospel pericopes were dismantled when exposed to oral presentation. Their multiple public presentations of Mark's Gospel in its entirety spawned scholarly publications on the value of oral performance of the biblical text (Boomershine 1988; Rhoads 2004; Shiner 2003). Although in its infancy, a hermeneutic of performance was forming within the world of biblical scholarship.

Defining Performance Criticism

As attention to the oral context of the ancient Mediterranean world emerged in biblical studies, so did the proliferation of organized scholarly study groups with such foci as orality and textuality, memory, and performance within the Society of Biblical Literature. Scholars sought to define literacy in the Greco-Roman world (Botha 2012; Carr 2005; Loubser 2013), the relationship between oral culture and written word (Goody 1987; Niditch 1996; Rodríguez 2014; Thomas 1992), and the impact of written text in a nonliterate culture (Furniss 2004; Kelber and Byrskog 2009; Horsley 2013; Person 2016). Biblical scholars reached out to include methodologies from other disciplines to expand the discussion around oral traditions and the dissemination of information, communal stories, and lore. It was the research of classicist Milman Parry, founder of the discipline of oral tradition, that had the most dramatic impact upon the emerging work in biblical studies. Parry argued that Homer was an oral poet, finding parallels with the epic poets in the Slavic regions in the 1930s. Linguist Alfred Lord collaborated with and expanded upon Parry's work on epic poetry. Lord's doctoral work produced the highly influential work *The Singer of Tales* (1960), which expanded the application of Parry's theory to other literary works, such as *Beowulf*. The Parry-Lord approach to oral traditions inspired John Miles Foley to clarify and expand their insights into numerous current oral cultures with ancient roots, for example Native American and African cultures. Foley was also a pioneer in applying his findings to the Hebrew Bible and New Testament (1991; 1995). These scholars' insights have provided conversational entrées into the problematic questions of the interplay between the oral tradition and written texts that does not originate within the biblical texts themselves, thus moving away from the quagmire of the form-source-redaction methodological box.

The greatest impact upon the formulation of a hermeneutic of performance arose from a discipline that prior to the twenty-first century had little interaction with biblical studies. Performance studies as a discrete discipline and methodology had its origins in two different geographical regions and from two different backgrounds. New York University's performance studies department formed in 1980 out of the intersection of theater, dance, performance art, and the social sciences, later widening its scope to include the disciplines of gender and queer studies, poststructuralism, postcolonial studies, and critical race theory. In 1984, Northwestern University in Evanston, Illinois, formulated its performance studies department out of the disciplines of oral interpretation, communication, speech-act theory, and ethnography, later broadening its reach into personal narrative, literature, culture, technology, and performance theory. Although New York University has roots related more to fine arts and Northwestern University more to communication and rhetoric, both strains of performance studies share the ethos of widening circles of discussion as they seek to understand the meaning and impact of performance on society.

Richard Schechner, considered a pioneer of the field, published in 2002 what is still considered the defining work on performance studies, currently in its third edition. Although notoriously difficult to define, "performance" is generally thought of in terms of what it includes rather than what it excludes. Schechner provides the following list life events in which performances occur: (1) everyday life, (2) the arts, (3) sports and other popular entertainments, (4) business, (5) technology, (6) sex, (7) ritual—sacred and secular, and (8) play (2013, 31). What may be called a performance does not depend upon the act itself but upon how that action is received and the location where it occurs. Schechner delineates the functions of performance as: (1) to entertain, (2) to create beauty, (3) to mark or change identity, (4) to make or foster community, (5) to heal, (6) to teach or persuade, and (7) to deal with the sacred and the demonic (46).

The expansive reach of performance studies as a discipline provides a welcome correlative to the widening vision of biblical studies. Dwight Conquergood, the initial force behind the performance studies department at Northwestern University, speaks of the radical posture that performance critics take against the tendency of the academy to segregate disciplines. He describes this phenomenon as an "apartheid of knowledge that plays out inside the academy as the difference between thinking and doing, interpreting and making, conceptualizing and creating. . . . The division of labor between theory and practice, abstraction and embodiment, is an arbitrary and rigged choice" (2002, 153). Peter Perry's *Insights from Performance Criticism* (2016) avoids a narrow definition of "performance," embracing the contested nature of performance as a benefit to the study of the Bible (2016, 29).

Biblical scholars began to employ the insights from performance critical methodology to the biblical texts with a paradigm of thinking about the circumstance, setting, intent, impact, and audience of the texts of the Bible. Recognizing that meaning is derived from so much more than written words in today's world, they explored how those dynamics shed light on the transmission of sacred texts in antiquity.

Biblical Performance Criticism

The roots of performance are most evident in the Hebrew Bible. Long before the advent of performance criticism, biblical interpreters were considering the composition and presentation of the prophetic texts, approaching both these writings and the psalms as collective expressions between God and God's people. It is Only in recent years, however, has performance criticism been applied as a systematic methodology for interpretation of these writings (Doan and Giles 2005; Mathews 2012; Person 2010).

The prophetic writings do not have a strong narrative plot structure; rather the focus is upon the medium (Levy 2000, 2–5). The setting, audience, and situation are more self-evident in prophetic composition. Note that in most of the prophetic texts in the Hebrew Bible the particular details are provided: the individual call of the prophet, the prophet's reaction to the call, the circumstance behind the call, and the community to whom the message is directed. With these obvious cues provided within the text, future audiences readily envision a messenger called by God, his or her reaction to that vision, his or her presentation of God's words to a select audience, and their compliance with or rejection of that presentation. The prophetic books of the Hebrew Bible invite future audiences to engage in new presentations of these prior performances, drawing parallels with their own circumstances (Mathews 2012, 7–9; Sweeney 2000, 488).

The specific discipline of biblical performance criticism was the result of conversations in the Bible and Ancient and Modern Media section of the Society of Biblical Literature. David Rhoads defined this study in his two-part article "Performance Criticism: An Emerging Methodology in Second Testament Studies" (2006a, 2006b). Performance critics focus upon the embodiment of culture, recognizing that speech is more than vocalization, and realizing the range of questions that need to be asked of the ancient texts prior to presenting their content. The performer must be concerned with the setting, the audience, the power dynamics of the situation, the identity of performer, the composition of the audience, and the characters, symbols, and so on in the texts themselves. In preparation for performance, the presenter becomes a self-conscious analyst of the text, realizing that embodiment of the story involves innumerable interpretive choices.

Perry describes the process of performance of biblical texts as a three-step process: (1) preparation, (2) internalization, and (3) performance (2016, 41–72). The preparation process is where the depth of intersectionality that performance criticism demands of its adherents quickly becomes apparent. The "world behind the text" is explored. For a pericope such as Mark 5:25–34, where a woman encounters Jesus in a crowd and touches him, the world behind the text requires a performer to have predetermined the answers to such questions as: (1) What size would be considered a "large crowd" in the first century in the area by the lake described in this scene? (2) What would be the expectations for an unaccompanied woman in public? (3) What would the stipulations be on "touching," particularly instigated by a woman upon a man with whom she is unfamiliar? (4) What is the expected religious, ethnic, class background of the woman? (5) What is known about the affliction of the woman? (6) What is known about the medical practices of the day? (6) What would the crowd around have expected from the woman and from Jesus during this encounter? (7) Does Jesus's response break any social customs? (8) Similarly, what does the woman's physical reaction convey to Jesus and the onlookers? These questions require investigation into various disciplines such as archaeology, the social sciences, and anthropology.

The next step in performance preparation is the "world of the text." Much of this segment of preparation is derived from narrative criticism. The passage in Mark 5 has two main actors: Jesus and the woman; two groups: the large crowd and Jesus's disciples; and one implied but unmentioned character: Jairus, a leader from the synagogue from the story that sandwiches this one. The setting is by the lake and in the midst of a crowd. The action is told through the woman's thoughts, then through Jesus's response, and finally through his disciples' reaction. The performer must consider whether each of these actors is reliable, honorable, or untrustworthy. In addition to narrative critical questions, the world of the text includes a linguistic analysis of the passage, more in the familiar arena of traditional biblical interpretation. If the performer is not familiar with the Greek text, various translations can be consulted to determine if there are phrases in dispute. For instance, the translations of the woman's condition in 5:25 vary from "flow of blood" to "severe bleeding" to "hemorrhages" across English versions; and in 5:29 it is said she was "healed of her affliction," "freed from her suffering," or "cured from her scourge"; or "she was well." The presenter will also need to consider the context of the pericope in Mark. This particular passage is one of several of such constructions in Mark wherein two stories are intertwined in order for the hearer to imagine these events as connected. The woman in Mark 5 interrupts the interchange with Jairus, who is leading Jesus to tend to his ailing daughter. Knowing that there is another daughter in this story impacts the portrayal of the woman who touches Jesus herself.

Performance preparation also requires an examination of the "world in front of the text." The performer also must analyze the setting for the performance. That analysis would include a search for cues as to: Which venues in the ancient world would invite a performance of this passage? What kind of audience would appreciate this story or perhaps find it objectionable? In this exploration, the performer imagines the current audience and their expectations. The setting and audience dictate such choices as apparel, gestures, level of emotional expression, and desired impact upon the listeners. Should the performer dress in normal street clothes or try to replicate a wardrobe from the ancient world? How emphatic should the gestures and emotional expression be? Depending upon the setting, the appropriate level of theatrics increases or diminishes. What is the point of the performance? If audiences are made up only of women, how would the presentation change? As the performer considers these aspects of audience and purpose in his or her own setting, it compels contemplation of the myriad of prior settings and audiences before which this same passage has been performed and the innumerable performative choices that have been made by each of the people who have presented this same Markan passage.

After the exhaustive preparation of step 1, step 2 is "internalization" of the passage (Perry 2016, 70–71). Rather than rote memorization, the practitioners of biblical storytelling offer various (often communal) ways of increasing familiarity with the passage, moving toward a natural embodiment of the events of the narrative that allow for natural gestures, intonation, and emotional responses (Swanson 2004; Ward and Trobisch 2013). The final step is the performance itself. Although the language of "performance" sounds formal, Schechner and other performance critics make it clear that something as mundane as a telephone conversation should be defined as a performance. The caller needs to determine a mood to portray, how familiar the address will be, the length of conversation, the topic(s) covered, and the expected response. If the one who is called is familiar to the caller, she can determine the mood with a single "hello." So the performance of a biblical passage can range from a dramatic performance with costumes, formal actors, and a paying audience in a theater to a single lector reading the passage during the church worship service. As Perry aptly notes, the more preparation the performer has put in, the less effort is required from the listener (72). If the performer has spent time in the world behind the text, in the text itself, and the world in front of the text, the listener can engage with what might be a familiar biblical story in fresh, new ways.

Performance and the Synoptic Gospels

The rise of performance criticism and the New Testament had its roots in storytelling traditions. The Network of Biblical Storytellers, in existence since the 1970s, was made up of biblical scholars, pastors, and laypeople who committed to learning and telling the stories of the Bible. The network's founder, Tom Boomershine, sought to link biblical scholarship with the performance of biblical texts. His work began to attract attention from various corners of the academic world, leading to the formulation of the Bible in Ancient and Modern Media group within the Society of Biblical Literature. One of the earliest fruits of those academic conversations was a series of *Semeia* studies on orality (Dewey 1995; Silberman 1987). Other biblical scholars began to explore evidence of the oral culture and communication world of the ancient texts (Botha 2012; A. Dewey 2009; Dunn 2013; Hearon 2006; Rodríguez 2014).

It was David Rhoads, New Testament scholar and ordained Lutheran (Evangelical Lutheran Church in America) pastor, who began to bring structure to the discipline of performance criticism. His two-part article in *Biblical Theology Bulletin* proposed the establishment of performance criticism as a "discrete discipline in New Testament studies" to address the blind spot in biblical criticism such that people analyze writings composed "in and for oral performance" without ever experiencing these texts in a performance (2006a; 2006b). Prior to these publications, Rhoads had a reputation for his inspiring performances of the complete Gospel of Mark. Another noted biblical scholar who performed Mark's gospel, Whitney Shiner (2003), claims his inspiration from seeing Rhoads's performance, as has Phil Ruge-Jones (2009).

Mark

Mark's Gospel was a predictable choice as an entrée into the performance-critical discussion. Scholars had long noted the "oral nature" of Mark's Gospel through such features as the frequent use of paratactic καί, the common adverb εὐθύς, and the use of the verbal present tense. Kelber and Botha find oral cues in the use of "folkloric triads" in Peter's denial (Mark 14:66–72), the disciples' failure in the Garden of Gethsemane (Mark 14:32–42), and the three passion predictions (Mark 8:31, 9:31, 10:33–34; Botha 2012, 170–81; Kelber 1983, 66). Prior to their specific application of performance criticism to Mark's Gospel, David Rhoads, Joanna Dewey, and Donald Michie embraced the coherent narrative structure of Mark, interpreting the gospel with social science insights regarding honor-shame peasant societies, kinship, and purity in their influential work *Mark as Story* (1999). Their commentary examined the characters, setting, plot, and points of view of both the players in the story and the hearers of the stories within the story. Vernon Robbins responded with his exploration "Interfaces of Orality and Literature in the Gospel of Mark" (2006), part of a larger volume on Mark, orality, and memory. He situates the Gospel in a rhetorical framework. The work of Antoinette Clark Wire pushed the discussion further, arguing that the Gospel of Mark was not only an oral composition but also the "story of a community told by several favored oral performers" (2011, 5). Wire's theory of Mark as a multiple-authored work allows for composition over a lengthy period of time rather than at a single point in history. This view eases the pressure to impose a consistent vision across the work, linked to one social setting. Although Wire's argument envisions a much more malleable development of the Gospel, whose parameters change with every performance, she claims that the strong oral tradition that precedes a work as well-known and beloved as Mark's Gospel enforces accountability upon the various performers to adhere to the established oral tradition (5–6).

Scholars-cum-performers attest to the insights that this medium brings to the biblical texts; as they seek to embody the narrative, they recognize that performance is interpretation. Performers of the Gospels relate common insights from their experiences. First, the medium brings meaning. Face-to-face communication involves gestures, facial expressions, sounds, pace, posture, pauses, and emotions. One can imagine the possibilities that a performer has before her when she returns to the sleeping disciples a third time in Gethsemane (Mark 14:41–42). Is the response sarcastic, disappointed, or grief-stricken? Perhaps there is an element of humor in the epic failure of Jesus's closest friends. Facial expressions and body language can convey the difference even though the dialogue remains the same. Second, performance not only is interpretive but also exposes the level of implicit interpretation that underlies any reading of the text. For example, the story of John the Baptist's beheading by a reluctant Herod describes the pleasure that Herodias brought to Herod and his guests by dancing for them (Mark

6:14–29). Classical paintings represent this "pleasure" as erotic in nature from a voluptuous daughter, but as viewers of Rhoads's performance of Mark will observe, his interpretation is a father's proud reaction to his young child's darling dance. The text offers no clues as to the source of their pleasure; a performer is compelled to interpret the scene. A third shared insight from performing Mark is the impact that the audience has on the meaning of the story. Depending upon the makeup of the audience, the size of the group, and the proximity of the performer to the listeners, the presentation varies. To a women-only group, the performer relates the story of the anointing woman (Mark 14:3–9)—her shame and Jesus's defense of her—with a level of empathy that would not be as easily related to a mixed audience. These insights reveal that these same dynamics are at play for each performance across place and time (Perry 2016, 143–53; Rhoads 2006a).

Performances fill in the narrative gaps with "sounds, gestures, facial expressions, glances, pace, pauses, pitch, volume, movement, posture, body language, and proximity to audience" (Rhoads 2006b, 174). There is no better passage than Mark 15:39 to demonstrate the impact of performance criticism upon interpretation. The centurion's immediate reaction to Jesus's death is to utter, "truly, this man was God's son." In stage 1 preparation, the performer would determine the intent of this comment—is the centurion radically changed because he has witnessed Jesus's last breath "in this way," or because he is impressed by Jesus's strength, or dignity, or endurance, or all of the above? If so, the performer will present the statement in awe, perhaps with sympathy, or pensively, with profound respect. But it is entirely possible that the performer could interpret the centurion's statement as a sarcastic remark, noting how "ungodly" this scene of Jesus's crucifixion was. The soldier might have been watching to see if anything unusual would happen at the crucifixion of Jesus, having heard some comments about Jesus's innocence, or noting the inscription "King of the Jews" over Jesus's head. His sarcastic remark, then, would be the exclamation point in a long line of taunts from the soldiers (v. 18–20), the passers-by (v. 29–30), the chief priests and scribes (v. 31–32a), and those crucified with Jesus (v. 32b). Either performance option can be readily conveyed through tone of voice, volume of pronouncement, and accompanying gestures. A posture of "awe" will be visibly different from a posture of derision. The impact of this performance choice at the climax of the narrative is profound. Jesus's death has either inspired a "conversion" of a hardened military leader who oversaw his torture and death or has provoked in Jesus yet one more moment of pain at the hands of his unfeeling captors (Iverson 2011).

Whitney Shiner's work on Mark and performance explores first-century audience reactions to scenes in the story. Evidence from ancient rhetorical discussions such as Cicero's *De oratorio* and Quintilian's *Institutes* reveals a much more emotional and vocally reactive audience in the Greco-Roman world as opposed to current-day audiences (Johnson 2017, 68–72; Shiner 2003, 153–56) who would not have to be goaded into participating in a performance. Shiner identifies "applause markers" in Mark's Gospel that indicate where listeners would openly express their feelings either by shouting or with applause. Some markers include places where Jesus gets the better of his opponents, accompanied by clever, pithy sayings, such as: "Give to the emperor the things that are the emperor's, and to God the things that are God's" (Mark 11:17). Similarly, within the conflict stories in Mark 2, Jesus defeats his opposition with an applause-worthy line: "The sabbath was made for humankind, and not humankind for the sabbath; so the Son of Man is lord even of the sabbath" (2:27–28).

One might imagine that applause would ensue at Peter's response to the question Jesus poses: "who do you say that I am?" (Mark 8:29); but Shiner notes the terseness of Peter's response—"You are the Messiah"—and the lack of a natural pause in narrative following the statement. Both of these characteristics are indications of audience cues against a show of approval (2003, 166–68). In contrast, the parallel scene in Matthew 16 does provoke audience vocal approval. Not only is Peter's reply to the question embellished ("You are the Messiah, the Son of the living God" [16:16]) but also Jesus's affirmative reply is extensive—both clear applause markers.

Performance criticism also offers insights into the abrupt ending of Mark at 16:8— "and they said nothing to anyone, for they were afraid." This "unsatisfying" conclusion has proved a compositional conundrum for centuries of biblical scholars. Of those who do not accept that verse 8 is the intended ending of the Gospel, some propose that the work was not completed, and others imagine that the final ending was lost (Bultmann 1968, 285, n. 2, 441–42; Elliott 2000, 586–87; Metzger 1971, 126 n. 7; Wire 2011, 164–65). Antoinette Wire interprets the abrupt ending as evidence of Mark's composition out of performance and consistent with the themes of fear, misunderstanding, and secrecy throughout the Gospel. Ending in fear and silence tends to provoke the audience to respond, perhaps even question the women's disobedience. Yet the ending prompts the question "Why didn't they respond?" Their fear of association with a resurrected enemy of the Roman Empire, their fear of not being believed, would surely resonate with early followers of Jesus who struggled with the same threats from authorities. According to Wire, the power of Mark's Gospel ending without action inspired communities of faith under pressure with its provocative performance for centuries (2011, 171–74). That pressure is best revealed when the ending is performed rather than read.

Matthew, Luke, and Q

As stated previously, performances and performance-critical scholarship are dominated by application to Mark's Gospel. Mark is an obvious choice because its composition carries markers of orality, because Mark is the shortest, and therefore more readily memorized and performed in one sitting, and finally because Mark is considered the earliest of the canonical gospels and thus enjoys a reputation as having less adulterated theological agendas than later compositions. In addition, any foray into the remaining Synoptic traditions requires wading into the congested waters of the Synoptic Problem and the various hypotheses for its solution.

It is precisely in this arena of biblical scholarship that performance criticism has received its most staunch opposition, and not surprisingly, for performance theory sets forth another solution to the Synoptic Problem that does not rely upon redaction of printed texts. Many scholars have contributed to this conversation, but three notable examples will be summarized here.

First, James Dunn's work—*Jesus Remembered* (2003)—examines the oral tradition of the Gospels along with the Pauline evidence to reconstruct the transmission and preservation of the Jesus stories. Relying upon Kenneth Bailey's theory of informal controlled oral tradition derived from his observation of Middle Eastern oral culture, Dunn concludes that oral presentations of the same story differ not because the performers are "editing" a previous performance. Rather, "each telling is a performance of the tradition itself" (Bailey 1991; Dunn 2003, 209). Dunn does not reject the influence of a textual tradition entirely but elevates the role of oral performance in the composition of the Gospels. Claiming both stability and variability as dynamics within the performance arena, Dunn imagines that elements of subject and theme and key details would remain constant, but he allows for variations in minor details and elaborations in performances. Dunn is confident that the Synoptics reflect "surprising immediacy to the heart of the first memories of Jesus" (2003, 254).

Dunn's book invited significant responses to the lacuna in his investigation, well summarized by Eric Eve (2014, 108–15). Richard Horsley attempts to address Dunn's lack of treatment of the workings of memory in the transmission of the tradition, noting that Dunn seems to move from Jesus's speech to his followers' performance of those words without comment on the process in between those two stages. Horsley incorporates the work of John Miles Foley in social memory theory to construct a model of oral tradition that explains the process in which Jesus's words were received, interpreted, and transmitted in an oral culture (Foley 1988; Horsley 2008). Furthermore, Horsley, along with Jonathan Draper, brings insights from cultural anthropological, socioeconomic, and political studies to help reconstruct the first-century context of the Gospels (Horsley and Draper 1999). In his wide-ranging work, Horsley develops a theory of Q as a collection of speeches delivered in the rural Galilean region that were faithfully transposed—described by Foley as an "oral-derived text" (Foley 1995, 60–98; Horsley and Draper 1999, 46–60). Situating the speeches of Jesus in the Israelite tradition, Horsley describes the Markan Jesus as a prophetic leader of a covenant renewal movement. The Q speeches confirm that vision—they confront social and economic injustices and employ "kingdom of God" language to provoke challenges against the imperial rule.

Horsley began to explore how the arenas of social memory and oral transmission inform the study of the Gospels but left a number of unanswered questions, which the work of Rafael Rodríguez, *Structuring Early Christian Memory*, sought to answer (2010). Relying more upon social memory theory than his predecessors, Rodriquez wants to change the focus and nomenclature of the historical Jesus scholarship of "authenticity" when it comes to Jesus's teachings and deeds to a broader consideration of the Gospel material in context (2010, 213–25). He brings the notion of the audience's role in the performance of the Gospel; listeners need to have a grounding in the "metonymic reference," or sociocultural context of the speech, so that the implied meaning is conveyed. In this manner, the boundaries of the tradition limit interpretations and applications in performance. Alongside the audiences' context, experience, and expectation come guidelines for oral performances. Rodríguez requires that a study of Gospel composition include a study of Gospel reception (88–102; see Eve 2014, 123–31).

Impact and Influence of Performance Criticism

Performance critics have been instrumental in the elevation of the problem of interpreting written texts that arise from largely nonliterate cultures. The most recent "quest for the historical Jesus" that attempted to clarify the disputed criteria for determining the authenticity of sayings and deeds recorded in the four canonical gospels and the Sayings Gospel of Thomas has lost momentum over the past twenty years. Critics of the quest point out that despite clarified criteria, the same model of inquiry, developed from form criticism, is mired in the text and ignores the emerging evidence from literacy studies and sociolinguistic models of nonliterate cultures. Chris Keith summarizes the problem as competing models of interpretation (2016, 426–55). The older model, arising out of textually focused methodologies from the 1950s, examines texts for authenticity; it cuts away the layers of theology and bias that the followers of Jesus have imposed upon the original message. Keith and others advocate for a new model that begins the search for Jesus outside the texts. Insights from historiography, memory theory, and social science models define the context within which speech from Jesus, interpretation of his speeches, and transmission of those speeches occurs. Proponents of a new model have shifted the goal from "finding the historical Jesus" to constructing models of the early followers, interpreters, and transmitters of messages about Jesus. The portrait of the "real Jesus" is unattainable, but hypotheses about Jesus can be structured "as part of a larger process of accounting for how and why early Christians came to view Jesus in the ways that they did" (430–31).

Of course, the cracks in the textually based methodologies of form-source-redaction criticism have been brought about by the larger surge of discussion arising from disciplines such as ancient media studies, social memory theory, rhetorical studies, and oral tradition studies. Enough doubt has been cast upon the traditional methods of biblical criticism that future studies of the Gospels will be hard-pressed to limit their discussion to the translation and interpretation of the extant Greek manuscripts. The messy problem of the oral message can no longer be ignored.

Performance criticism stands in the midst of this problem. Although it is but one method in the burgeoning arena of biblical criticism, it does make some unique contributions to the discussion. First, performance criticism opens a new avenue of intersection and engagement for biblical studies. Schechner's development of performance criticism out of the convergence of theater, performance art, and social sciences provides a framework upon which inquiries about the transmission of ancient biblical stories may be constructed. With the expanded view of the function of performance—to entertain, create beauty, mark or change identity, make or foster community, heal, teach or persuade, and deal with the sacred and demonic—interpreters of the Gospels have a new paradigm for exploring the oral culture of the Gospel writings. If people find Jesus through his early followers, as Keith claims, then defining a Gospel scene as an identity-changing performance sheds light on the community who interpreted it as such in their transmission of the scene. For example, the parallel scene in Mark 8 and Matthew 16, where Jesus asks his disciples what others are saying about him, Peter's answer and Jesus's reaction fall under different performative functions in the two Gospel accounts. Mark's terse answer and harsh reaction can best be viewed as a performance to persuade the audience to a certain response. Since Peter is not affirmed for his reply, Jesus's harsh order must be viewed as a rebuke of sorts that would stand as a cautionary moment for the listeners in the Markan community. Conversely, Matthew's scene displays an event of changing identity. Peter's proclamation reveals his understanding of Jesus's true identity, and Jesus's lengthy and positive response culminates with Jesus bestowing a new identity upon Peter. He moves from "Simon" to "Rock," from unsteady follower to the foundation of the church in this scene. Reading the two texts with this performance paradigm is enlightening; observing the performance of these two scenes as a member of a larger audience produces even more profound insights. These two communities interpreted and conveyed this scene in markedly different ways. Performance criticism provides a new platform upon which a sketch of these followers of Jesus may be drawn. By definition, performance is not the act itself but how that action is received and the location in which it occurs.

A second profound insight that performance criticism brings is an exegetical ethos for biblical interpretation. The development of performance as a discipline is an apt demonstration of this issue. Northwestern University was a second birthplace of performance criticism that developed concurrently, but separately, from the movement at New York University under Schechner. Rather than a confluence of theater and social science, the Northwestern University performance studies' roots were in communication and literature. Both institutions were grappling with the interconnectivity of the areas of human interaction, communication, and understanding and ended up expanding the field of discussion around "performance" well beyond a single discipline of study. Critics cite the amorphous and undefined nature of performance studies, which is an issue not lost on these departments (Hurtado 2014). However, they resist the pressure to be defined and constrained by a singular discipline. Schechner provides a defining range for performance, leaving it open for future adaptation; Conquergood demands that the arbitrary boundaries set by the academy be challenged.

Out of this radical vision of ever-expanding fields of possible intersection, this malleable model of performance criticism speaks to the same objections that have arisen in the field of biblical interpretation over the past two decades. The arbitrary boundaries of "authentic" and "inauthentic" and the tunnel vision of text-oriented discussions appear hollow and ineffective to those oriented to current scholarship trends. Performance criticism does not endorse existing methodologies that then will serve as the new hermeneutical standard for the Bible. Rather, it embraces ever-widening circles of discussion in order to find points of connection between different cultures, settings, performers, and audiences as a circle of interpretation of the Bible.

Predictably, diverse avenues of scholarship under the auspices of biblical performance criticism have emerged. Sound mapping uses discourse analysis and study of pronunciation of ancient biblical languages to explore how sound manifested in pitch, intensity, intonation, and so on impacts audiences (Lee and Scott 2009; Nasselqvist 2015, 2018). Person (2010, 2011), Rodriguez (2014), and Keith (2014) study ancient media cultures to shed light upon the interaction of performer, text, and audience in the biblical world. The study of social memory attends to the reception, shaping, and dissemination of oral traditions (DeConick 2008; Rodriguez 2014; Thatcher 2006). Perry has recently applied relevance theory, from the arena of cognitive linguistics, to the New Testament as a means to explore modes of communication across cultures (Perry 2019).

Performance criticism is demanding of its adherents. It is difficult to imagine a mastery of the field in an arena that is ever-expanding and intentionally defies definition. However, stepping within this methodology prepares the biblical scholar for the unknowable aspects of the first-century oral culture within which Jesus performed, audiences reacted, communities remembered, and stories were performed anew. Biblical scholars must face the difficult truth that the gospels do not have Jesus's unadulterated teachings. The comfort of certainty is not to be found in the Gospels. However, a world of possibilities for connection between the voices of the first-century followers of Jesus awaits through the magic of performance. The embodiment of the message is truth as surely as are the familiar texts themselves.

References

Bailey, Kenneth. 1991. "Informal Controlled Oral Tradition and the Synoptic Gospels." *Asia Journal of Theology* 3: 34–54.

Boomershine, Thomas. 1988. *Story Journey: An Invitation to the Gospel as Storytelling.* Nashville: Abingdon.

Botha, Pieter. 2005. "New Testament Texts in the Context of Reading Practices of the Roman Period: The Role of Memory and Performance." *Scriptura* 90: 621–40.

Botha, Pieter. 2012. *Orality and Literacy in Early Christianity.* Eugene, OR: Cascade.

Bultmann, Rudolf. 1921. *Die Geschichte der synoptischen Tradition.* Göttingen: Vandenhoeck und Ruprecht.

Bultmann, Rudolf. 1968. *The History of the Synoptic Tradition.* Translated by John Marsh. New York: Harper & Row.

Carr, David. 2005. *Writing on the Tablet of the Heart: Origins of Scripture and Literature.* Oxford: Oxford University Press.

Cicero, Marcus Tullius. 2001. *Cicero on the Ideal Orator (De Oratore).* Translated by James May and Jakob Wisse. New York: Oxford University Press.

Conquergood, Dwight. 2002. "Performance Studies: Interventions and Radical Research." *Drama Review* 46, no. 2 (Summer): 145–56.

DeConick, April. 2008. "Human Memory and the Sayings of Jesus: Contemporary Experimental Exercises in the Transmission of Jesus Traditions." In *Jesus, The Voice, and the Text: Beyond the Oral and the Written Gospel*, edited by Tom Thatcher, 135–79. Waco: Baylor University Press.

Dewey, Arthur. 2009. "Competing Gospels: Imperial Echoes, A Dissident Voice." In *The Bible in Ancient and Modern Media: Story and Performance*, edited by Holly E. Hearon and Philip Ruge Jones, 64–79. Eugene, OR: Cascade.

Dewey, Joanna, ed. 1995. *Orality and Textuality in Early Christian Literature*. Semeia 65. Atlanta, GA: SBL Press.

Dewey, Joanna. 2013. *The Oral Ethos of the Early Church: Speaking, Writing, and the Gospel of Mark*. Eugene, OR: Cascade.

Dibelius, Martin and Bertram Lee Woolf. 1971. *From Tradition to Gospel:* Die Formgeschichte des Evangeliums. Cambridge: Lutterworth Press.

Doan, William, and Terry Giles. 2005. *Prophets, Performance, and Power*. London: Continuum.

Dunn, James. 2003. *Jesus Remembered*. Grand Rapids: Eerdmans.

Dunn, James. 2013. *The Oral Gospel Tradition*. Grand Rapids: Eerdmans.

Elliott, John, ed. 1986. *Social-Scientific Criticism of the New Testament and Its Social World*. Semeia 35. Atlanta, GA: SBL Press.

Elliott, John. 2000. "Mark 1.1–3—A Later Addition to the Gospel?" *New Testament Studies* 46: 584–88. Cambridge: Cambridge University Press.

Eve, Eric. 2014. *Behind the Gospels: Understanding the Oral Tradition*. Minneapolis: Fortress.

Foley, John Miles. 1988. *The Theory of Oral Composition: History and Methodology*. Bloomington: Indiana University Press.

Foley, John Miles. 1991. *Immanent Art: From Structure to Meaning in Traditional Oral Epic*. Bloomington: Indiana University Press.

Foley, John Miles. 1995. *The Singer of Tales in Performance*. Bloomington: Indiana University Press.

Furniss, Graham. 2004. *Orality: The Power of the Spoken Word*. New York: Palgrave.

Gerdhardsson, Birger. 1961. *Memory and Manuscript: Oral Tradition and Written Transmission in Rabbinic Judaism and Early Christianity*. Translated by Eric J. Sharpe. Grand Rapids: Eerdmans.

Goody, Jack, ed. 1968. *Literacy in Traditional Societies*. Cambridge: Cambridge University Press.

Goody, Jack. 1987. *The Interface between the Written and the Oral*. Cambridge: Cambridge University Press.

Goody, Jack. 2000. *The Power of the Written Tradition*. Washington, DC: Smithsonian Institution Press.

Harris, William. 1989. *Ancient Literacy*. Cambridge, MA: Harvard University Press.

Hearon, Holly. 2006. "Implications of Orality for the Studies of the Biblical Text." In *Performing the Gospel: Orality, Memory, and Mark*, edited by Richard Horsley, Jonathan Draper, and John Miles Foley, 3–20. Minneapolis: Fortress.

Herzer, Catherine. 2001. *Jewish Literacy in Roman Palestine*. Tübingen: Mohr Siebeck.

Horsley, Richard. 2008. *Jesus in Context: Power, People, and Performance*. Minneapolis: Fortress.

Horsley, Richard. 2013. *Text and Tradition in Performance and Writing*. Eugene, OR: Cascade.

Horsley, Richard, and Jonathan Draper. 1999. *Whoever Hears You Hears Me: Prophets, Performance and Tradition in Q*. Harrisburg: Trinity Press International.

Hurtado, Larry. 2014. "Oral Fixation and New Testament Studies? 'Orality,' 'Performance' and Reading Texts in Early Christianity." *New Testament Studies* 60, no. 3: 321–40.

Iverson, Kelly. 2011. "A Centurion's 'Confession': A Performance-Critical Analysis of Mark 15:39." *Journal of Biblical Literature* 130, no. 2: 329–50.

Jaffee, Martin S. 2001. *Torah in the Mouth: Writing and Oral Tradition in Palestinian Judaism 200 BCE–400 CE*. Oxford: Oxford University Press.

Johnson, Lee. 2016. "Paul's Letters as Artifacts: The Value of the Written Text among Non-literate People." *Biblical Theology Bulletin* 46, no. 2: 25–34.

Johnson, Lee. 2017. "Paul's Letters Reheard: A Performance-Critical Examination of the Preparation, Transportation, and Delivery of Paul's Correspondence." *Catholic Biblical Quarterly* 79: 60–76.

Johnson, William A., and Holt N. Parker. 2009. *Ancient Literacies: The Culture of Reading in Greece and Rome*. Oxford: Oxford University Press.

Keith, Chris. 2014. *Jesus against the Scribal Elite: The Origins of the Conflict*. Grand Rapids: Eerdmans.

Keith, Chris. 2016. "The Narrative of the Gospels and the Historical Jesus: Current Debates, Prior Debates and the Goal of Historical Jesus Research." *Journal for the Study of the New Testament* 38, no. 4: 426–55.

Kelber, Werner. 1983. *The Oral and Written Gospel: The Hermeneutics of Speaking and Writing in the Synoptic Tradition, Mark, Paul, and Q*. Philadelphia: Fortress.

Kelber, Werner, and Samuel Byrskog, eds. 2009. *Jesus in Memory: Traditions in Oral and Scribal Perspectives*. Waco: Baylor University Press.

Lee, Margaret, and Brandon Scott. 2009. *Sound Mapping the New Testament*. Santa Rosa, CA: Polebridge.

Levy, Shimon. 2000. *The Bible as Theater*. Brighton, UK: Sussex Academic Press.

Lord, Alfred. 1960. *The Singer of Tales*. Cambridge, MA: Harvard University Press.

Loubser, J. A. 2013. *Oral and Manuscript Culture in the Bible*. Eugene, OR: Cascade.

Malina, Bruce. 1981. *The New Testament World: Insights from Cultural Anthropology*. Atlanta: John Knox.

Mathews, Jeanette. 2012. *Performing Habakkuk: Faithful Re-enactment in the Midst of Crisis*. Eugene, OR: Pickwick.

Metzger, Bruce. 1971. *Textual Commentary on the Greek New Testament*. London: United Bible Societies.

Nässelqvitch, Dan. 2015. *Public Reading in Early Christianity: Lectors, Manuscripts, and Sound in the Oral Delivery of John 1–4*. Leiden: Brill.

Nässelqvitch, Dan. 2018. "Unexplored Benefits of Sound Mapping in New Testament Exegesis." In *Sound Matters: New Testament Studies in Sound Mapping*, edited by Margaret Lee, 120–32. Eugene, OR: Cascade.

Niditch, Susan. 1996. *Oral World and Written Word*. Louisville: Westminster John Knox.

Ong, Walter. 1982. *Orality and Literacy: The Technologizing of the Word*. London: Methuen.

Perry, Peter. 2016. *Insights from Performance Criticism*. Minneapolis: Fortress.

Perry, Peter. 2019. "Biblical Performance Criticism: Survey and Prospects." *Religions* 10, 117. doi:10.3390/rel10020117.

Person, Raymond. 2010. *The Deuteronomistic History and the Book of Chronicles: Scribal Works in an Oral World*. Atlanta: SBL Press.

Person, Raymond. 2011. "The Role of Memory in the Tradition Represented by the Deuteronomic History and the Book of Chronicles." *Oral Tradition* 26, no. 2: 537–50.

Person, Raymond. 2016. *From Conversation to Oral Tradition: A Simplest Systematics for Oral Traditions.* New York: Routledge.

Quintilian. 2015. *Quintilian on the Teaching of Speaking and Writing: Translations from Books One, Two & Ten of the Institutio Oratoria.* Edited by James Murphy and Cleve Wiese. Carbondale: Southern Illinois University Press.

Rhoads, David. 2004. *Reading Mark: Engaging the Gospel.* Minneapolis: Fortress.

Rhoads, David. 2006a. "Performance Criticism: An Emerging Methodology in Second Testament Studies—Part I." *Biblical Theology Bulletin* 36, no. 3: 118–33.

Rhoads, David. 2006b. "Performance Criticism: An Emerging Methodology in Second Testament Studies—Part II." *Biblical Theology Bulletin* 36, no. 4: 164–84.

Rhoads, David, Joanna Dewey, and Donald Michie. 1999. *Mark as Story: An Introduction to the Narrative of a Gospel.* 2nd ed. Minneapolis: Fortress.

Rhoads, David, and Donald Michie. 1982. *Mark as Story: An Introduction to the Narrative of a Gospel.* Minneapolis: Fortress.

Robbins, Vernon. 2006. "Interfaces of Orality and Literature in the Gospel of Mark." In *Performing the Gospel, Orality, Memory and Mark,* edited by Richard Horsley, Jonathan Draper, and John Miles Foley, 125–46. Minneapolis: Fortress.

Rodríguez, Rafael. 2010. *Structuring Early Christian Memory: Jesus in Tradition, Performance and Text.* London: T&T Clark.

Rodríguez, Rafael. 2014. *Oral Tradition and the New Testament.* London: Bloomsbury.

Rohrbaugh, Richard L., ed. 1996. *The Social Sciences and New Testament Interpretation.* Peabody, MA: Hendrickson.

Ruge-Jones, Philip. 2009. "The Word Heard: How Hearing a Text Differs from Reading One." In *The Bible in Ancient and Modern Media: Story and Performance,* edited by Holly E. Hearon and Philip Ruge Jones, 101–13. Eugene, OR: Cascade.

Schechner, Richard. 2013. *Performance Studies: An Introduction.* 3rd ed. New York: Routledge.

Schmidt, Karl. 1919. *Der Rahmen der Geschichte Jesu: Literarkritische Untersuchungen zur ältesten Jesusberlieferung..* Berlin: Trowitzsch & Sohn.

Shiner, Whitney. 2003. *Proclaiming the Gospel: First-Century Performance of Mark.* Harrisburg: Trinity Press International.

Silberman, Louis, ed. 1987. *Orality, Aurality, and Biblical Narrative.* Semeia 39. Atlanta, GA: SBL Press.

Stegemann, Ekkehard S., and Wolfgang Stegemann. 1999. *The Jesus Movement: A Social History of Its First Century.* Translated by O. C. Dean, Jr. Minneapolis: Fortress.

Swanson, Richard. 2004. *Provoking the Gospel: Methods to Embody Biblical Storytelling through Drama.* Cleveland: Pilgrim.

Sweeney, Marvin. 2000. *The Twelve Prophets.* Vol. 2. Collegeville: Liturgical.

Thatcher, Tom. 2006. *Why John Wrote a Gospel: Jesus—Memory—History.* Louisville: Westminster John Knox.

Thomas, Rosalind. 1992. *Literacy and Orality in Ancient Greece.* Cambridge: University Press.

Ward, Richard, and David Trobisch. 2013. *Bringing the Word to Life: Engaging the New Testament through Performing It.* Grand Rapids: Eerdmans.

Wellhausen, Julius. 1885. *Prolegomena to the History of Israel.* With preface by W. Robertson Smith. Edinburgh: Adam and Charles Black.

Wire, Antoinette Clark. 2011. *The Case for Mark Composed in Performance.* Eugene, OR: Cascade.

Woolf, Greg. 2009. "Literacy or Literacies in Rome?" In *Ancient Literacies: The Culture of Reading in Greece and Rome,* edited by William A. Johnson and Holt N. Parker, 46–68. Oxford: Oxford University Press.

CHAPTER 8

NARRATIVE DESIGN OF THE SYNOPTICS

MICHAL BETH DINKLER

INTRODUCTION

STUDENTS of the New Testament (NT) have long been accustomed to thinking of the Synoptic Gospels as the products of ancient theologians, historians, and/or redactors and collectors. The so-called literary turn in late twentieth-century Gospel scholarship brought special attention to the writers of the Gospels—hereafter Matthew, Mark, and Luke—as thoughtful, intentional storytellers, as well. In 2010, Kelli O'Brien reflected on the shift: "in the last 30 years or so, literary critics have sought and found connections between pericopes with literary devices such as setting, characterization, and use of symbols" (2010, 2).[1] The Gospel of Mark, O'Brien concludes, "is now considered a work of considerable story-telling skill and theological insight" (2). The same can be said, of course, about Matthew and Luke.

When proponents of NT "narrative criticism" began interpreting in a self-consciously synchronic way, they drew heavily from the subfields of literary formalism and structuralism, both of which (though in different ways) focused on constitutive components of story like plot, character, setting, and time. Indeed, the "close reading" advocated by the literary formalist approach known as New Criticism entails slow, scrupulous, discerning reading that attends to the text's rhyme and rhythm, meter and metrics, tropes and techniques, ideally in isolation from the circumstances in which the text originated.[2] The New Critics, that is, refused to define meaning solely in terms of a text's

---

[1] O'Brien also suggests that this trend began with Wrede.
[2] The phrase "New Criticism" was first used by Joel E. Spingarn in a lecture at Columbia University in 1910 (see Spingarn 1917). T. S. Eliot, William Empson, and I. A. Richards were influential in the development of New Criticism in England in the 1920s, though its popularity really rose following Ransom (1941).

sociohistorical context or authorial intent, instead analyzing each literary work as "a new and independent expression" (Spingarn 1917, 29).

The biblical scholars who first adopted this formalist approach argued that the Synoptic Gospels ought to be read not (to use an oft-repeated description) simply as "pearls on a string," nor as compilations of pre-existing fragments, but as carefully crafted unified narratives, valuable as literary creations in their own right. As such, Matthew, Mark, and Luke have now been profitably foraged for literary techniques like irony, first person versus third person narration, direct versus indirect speech, peripeteia, and denouement. This chapter will not rehearse this work in detail, since it is readily available elsewhere. Instead, I presuppose and build on the insights of previous narrative critics.

Specifically, I advocate renewed engagement with the field of literary studies, wherein so-called New Formalists have moved beyond the formalist perspectives of earlier generations.[3] The first section of the chapter introduces New Formalism in more detail. The key New Formalist question is "how to hone form (back) into a viable theoretical shape and to (re)assign it a critically interventive power," to which New Formalists offer not one, but a "myriad of answers and kaleidoscopically fragmented visions" (Thiele 2013, 16). I, too, wish to entertain a "myriad of answers" regarding how readers might "hone form (back) into a viable theoretical shape" in Synoptic studies. Toward that end, the second section of the chapter brings New Formalist approaches to bear on the narrative design of the Synoptic Gospels.

New Formalism

By the end of the twentieth century, in theory, if not always in practice, formalist approaches like New Criticism had fallen into disrepute. In 2002, Richard Strier went so far as to say that formalism had become a "dirty word" in literary studies; yet, Strier also insisted, "we can't do without it." Form is inescapable, ubiquitous. Formalism, wrote Paul de Man, "is an all-absorbing and tyrannical muse" (de Man 1979, 4). Thus it is that, while some were busy rebranding the study of literature as "literary *and cultural* studies" and rightly challenging the possibility and desirability of the New Critics' demand for ahistorical "objectivity," the New Formalists were rethinking purported formalist/ historicist dichotomies altogether.

In 2007, Marjorie Levinson wrote an essay titled, "What Is New Formalism?" in which she identifies two distinct types of New Formalism. On the one hand, an activist strain of New Formalism works to wed literary formalism more closely to historical inquiry

---

[3] According to Bruster (2002), Heather Dubrow first used the phrase "New Formalism" in a 1989 MLA session titled, "Toward the New Formalism: Formalist Approaches to Renaissance New Historicism and Feminism." Dubrow and others kept developing the idea of New Formalism after her 1989 address, but the movement truly gained traction in the first decade of the twenty-first century.

(e.g., Hunter 2000; Rooney 2000). On the other hand, a normative strain distinguishes clearly between history and literary art, insisting that aesthetic form is and ought to remain separate from historical context (e.g., Bérubé 2000; Harpham 2006). Levinson summarizes: "in short, we have a new formalism that makes a continuum with new historicism and a backlash new formalism" (2007, 559). Annette Federico typifies activist New Formalists as "seek[ing] a compromise between the New Critical bent toward non-historical and aesthetic reading and the important work of historicists, Marxists, and feminists from the 1980s and after" (Federico 2016, 19). The "important work" to which Federico refers is marked by the view that form and content are shaped by particular social and historical contexts; thus, unlike an "old" formalist approach, activist New Formalists ask if there is "a way to combine a wish to delve into the aesthetic complexity of a literary work with a concern for its life in politics and history" (19). Despite normative and activist New Formalists' divergent perspectives vis-à-vis history, both strands of New Formalism aim to revive the formalist attention to textual form and structure while addressing critiques of formalism's earlier iterations. Two such critiques are particularly relevant for scholarship on the Synoptic Gospels.

The first challenge to "old" formalism comes from New Formalists themselves and concerns the task of critical inquiry. New Formalists explicitly reject two axiomatic New Critical tenets: the "intentional fallacy," which appeals to authorial intention as determinative of meaning, and the "affective fallacy," which appeals to readerly response as an interpretive key (Wimsatt and Beardsley 1946; 1949).[4] According to literary critic William Wimsatt and philosopher Monroe Beardsley, the intentional fallacy confuses "the poem and its origins," while the affective fallacy confuses "the poem and its *results*"; consequently, "the poem itself, as an object of specifically critical judgment, tends to disappear" (Wimsatt and Beardsley 1949, 21; my emphasis). New Formalists argue, on the contrary, that "a text's formal features, its aesthetics, in close conjunction with cultural context, convey a politically and historically significant literary experience that is *both intentional and affective*" (Thiele 2013, 16; my emphasis).

Importantly, New Formalists do not advocate a return to authorial intent as it was conceived prior to the twentieth-century linguistic turn. Against those who would psychologize authors and define meaning in terms of a writer's original intent, New Formalists maintain that it is impossible to recover the original intent of any author, especially those who died long ago; even if we could speak with ancient authors, they themselves might not know their own motivations and intentions fully. Furthermore, New Formalists recognize that, as deconstructionists emphasized, the selectivity, ambiguity, and iterability of all language means that texts have the potential to exceed or fall short of authorial intentions. Intentionality in a New Formalist sense refers, rather, to the purposiveness of a text—that is, it is a recognition that a narrative has been designed by some individual or group (usually called the implied author) for someone

---

[4] See the staunch defense of authorial intention in Hirsch 1967, and the discussion of Hirsch in Lentricchia 1980.

(usually called the implied audience) and did not fall randomly into coherent sentences all on its own.

Most Gospel critics today will concede that, as Mark Allen Powell puts it, "the meaning of literature transcends the historical intentions of the author" (Powell 1990, 12). Even so, many continue to proceed as though the linguistic turn never occurred, focusing primarily on authorial intent as constitutive of meaning. Bock and Fanning, for example, first declare that "one does not try to reproduce what the author must have been thinking at a given point or why he wrote," but the very next sentence bespeaks their true aim: "rather the interpreter's goal is to ascertain *what the writer wanted to communicate* through the terms he chose for his message" (Bock and Fanning 2006, 137; my emphasis). Later, they assert, "the concern of the exegete is the meaning of the author's mind" (2006, 137). This conception of textual meaning is shaped by a "celebrated analogy" to which Russian Formalist Yury Tynjanov had already objected – namely, that "form-content = glass-wine" (1981, 32).

New Formalists would describe this analogy as dependent on "restrictive ideas of form's *givenness* (whether as container, or adornment, or genre, or verse-form, or speech act)" (Bogel 2013, 85; my emphasis). In NT studies, historical-critical, sociocultural, and anthropological approaches typically pay little attention to the Synoptic stories' literary form, but even approaches that do attend to form (like form criticism and narrative criticism) tend to ascribe to "restrictive ideas of form's *givenness.*" New Formalists, in contrast, see form as dynamic and constructed; as such, narrative design performs certain kinds of work, shaping the potentialities of a text.[5] Assuming that a narrative text functions merely as a container (a wine glass) for an author's extractable message (the wine) renders its design inconsequential or incidental.

This is why New Formalist Fredric Bogel calls critics to "pay closer attention to the cultural significance or valence of literary forms and conventions. Onto the preformalist and formalist interest in genres and conventions has been grafted an attention to their cultural, social, and political weight" (2013, 76). New Formalism, that is, sees narrative as participating in the social and cultural discourses of its day as a literary form. New Formalists insist that form is not static or given. The form itself has a "critically interventive power" (Thiele 2013, 16). Not only that, but New Formalists recognize that multiple kinds of form are always operating simultaneously, intersecting and overlapping in any given text.

The second New Formalist critique of "old" formalism is especially relevant for scholars of the Synoptic Gospels. Unlike prior formalist approaches, New Formalism is fundamentally a "pluralistic approach, which allows for multiple perspectives" (Schwarz 2008, xiii). As such, New Formalists consciously embrace multiple—sometimes contradictory—possible readings. This is a crucial point for NT scholars, whose overwhelming tendency has been to entertain multiple possible factors in the reading

---

[5] In this, the New Formalists harken back to work by Russian Formalists like Yury Tynjanov (2014, 33), who argued in the early twentieth century that "all fixed, static definitions of [literature] are swept away by the fact of evolution."

process and then to choose between them in order to argue for the "best" single, integrated interpretation. New Formalism suggests that the step of isolating a single reading loses something essential to the textual exchange. Portraying the possible as inevitable reduces the power of narrative.

In line with the above New Formalist views, I will not argue for one or another interpretive possibility as the definitive "right" reading. This should not be misconstrued as an endorsement of interpretive relativism or anarchy. One of the most significant contributions of New Formalism is its recognition that narrative form circumscribes our interpretive options even as it gives rise to multiple potential meanings. Working out the precise ways in which texts employ various kinds of form (social, cultural, and, indeed, literary) is no small task. Forms are complex. But the answer is neither to isolate nor to ignore them. As Caroline Levine avers, "literary formalists have precisely the tools to grasp this formal complexity and, with them, to begin to imagine workable, progressive, thoughtful relations among forms" (2015, xiii).

Toward that end, I adopt two conceptual resources from Levine's 2015 volume *Forms*. First, Levine argues convincingly for a capacious definition of form: "'form' always indicates *an arrangement of elements—an ordering, patterning, or shaping*. . . . Form, for our purposes, will mean all shapes and configurations, all ordering principles, all patterns of repetition and difference" (2015, 3; my emphasis). Levine recognizes that some will object to her expansive conceptualization of form. "Why," she asks, "adopt such a broad definition? The stakes," she explains, "are high. It is the work of form to make order. And this means that forms are the stuff of politics" (3). Second, Levine borrows the concept of *affordances* from design theory (referring specifically to Norman 1990). Designers discuss materials and forms in terms of the potentialities they afford. A doorknob, for example, creates the possibilities of turning, pushing, or pulling a door. It cannot, however, offer fluidity or the cleaning capabilities of a running faucet. "Affordance," Levine explains, "allows us to think about both constraint and capability—that is, what actions or thoughts are made possible or impossible by the fact of a form" (152 n. 15). With these tools in hand, I turn to the narrative form of the Synoptic Gospels.

Narrative Design and the Synoptic Gospels

Were this a traditional formalist essay about the Synoptic Gospels' narrative design, I would at this point introduce the Aristotelian principle that "a narrative without a plot is a logical impossibility" (Chatman 1978, 47). I might cite Jack Dean Kingsbury, who explicitly connects plot with order and arrangement—that is, with narrative form: "the plot of a story has to do with the way in which the author arranges the events" (1991, 34). Certain (sometimes substantial) divergences notwithstanding, Matthew, Mark, and Luke arrange events in a similar general order; events in the story unfold according to the same basic shape, a macro-structure known in narrative theory as "Freytag's pyramid" (Freytag 1984). All three Synoptics set the stage (exposition) by recounting Jesus's preparation for ministry (with Matthew and Luke adding unique birth narratives), including the introduction of John the Baptist, Jesus's baptism, and his subsequent temptation by the devil in the desert (Mark 1:2–13//Matt. 3:1–4:11//Lk. 3:1–4:13). All three devote the bulk of the story to Jesus's ministry—his call for others to follow him as disciples, and then his teachings and miracles performed in response to those in need; this public work begins in Galilee (Mark 1:14–8:26//Matt. 4:12–16:12//Lk. 4:14–9:50), and eventually moves out and on toward the seat of Jewish religious and political power, Jerusalem (Mark 9:9–10:52//Matt. 17:9–20:34//Lk. 9:50–19:27).

Tracing this pyramidal progression, an "old" formalist treatment would mention that narrative plots require some kind of disequilibrium, a conflict or change of the status quo, and that in the Synoptics, this rising action is accomplished through Jesus's repeated conflicts with and hostility from the Jewish people. Ultimately, these antagonistic interactions culminate in Jesus provocatively "cleansing" the Jerusalem Temple, which precipitates unbridled opposition from the Jewish leaders and directly sets in motion the events of his passion (Mark 11:1–14:11//Matt. 21:1–26:16//Lk. 19:28–22:6). Here, too, the Synoptics depict the climactic events in the same basic order: Jesus's last Passover supper with his disciples, his betrayal, arrest, and trial, and finally, the crucifixion (Mark 14:12–15:47//Matt. 26:17–27:66//Lk. 22:7–23:56). The falling action, or concluding denouement, of all three Gospels is Jesus's resurrection from the dead, including the women's discovery of the empty tomb (Mark 16:1–8//Matt. 28:1–20//Lk. 24:1–53, with Matthew and Luke adding post-resurrection appearances to his disciples).

Were this a standard account of Synoptic narrative design, I would discuss, along with plot, the importance of temporal succession and the related narratological distinction between *story*, or *fabula* ("the *content* of the narrative expression"), and *discourse*, or *sjuzet* ("the *form* of that expression"; Chatman 1978, 23).[6] Specifically, the Synoptic Gospels use the ratios and distribution of direct discourse (quoted speech) versus third-person narration to regulate the rhythm of their stories. Here is a clear example: compare Luke 4:33–37, which recounts a dialogical exchange between Jesus and a demon in ninety-two Greek words, with Luke 4:40–41, which speedily summarizes multiple exorcisms in only fifty-two Greek words (with just one directly quoted outburst in 4:41). Because quoted speech between characters slows the narrative and simple narration speeds it up, these otherwise similar Lukan accounts differ with respect to the length of time it takes to tell them (*Erzählzeit*).

---

[6] The Russian Formalist terms *fabula* and *sjuzet* were popularized by Jurij Lotman (1977, 231–39). One also finds the French structuralist terms *histoire* (the content or chain of events) and *discours* (the expression of the contents; see Todorov 1980, 3–36). Many scholars use Genette's three-tiered model: "histoire/diégèse" (translated in English as "story," i.e. the chronological order of events that must be inferred by the reader); "récit" (translated as "narrative," i.e. the story in the order that it is presented to the reader); and "narration" (translated as "narrating," i.e. how the story is told).

The Synoptics all make liberal use of direct discourse; Matthew and Luke actually contain more cited dialogue than they do narration (by some estimates, 58–66 percent). However, Mark's storyline moves at the fastest clip, in part because it includes the least direct discourse. (This is also in part the consequence of Mark's paratactic style; commentators frequently point to Mark's repetition of the words καί and εὐθύς.) The Gospel of Matthew creates more of a balanced rhythm by alternating narration and direct speech. Mirroring the five books of the Pentateuch, Matthew is structured around five dominant discourses (the Sermon on the Mount Discourse, 5–7; Instructions on Mission, 9:36–10:42; Parable collection, 13:1–53; Instructions on Community, 17:22–18:35; Eschatology Discourse, 23–25),[7] each of which ends with a variation of the formula καὶ ἐγένετο ὅτε ἐτέλεσεν ὁ Ἰησοῦς τοὺς λόγους τούτους (7:28, 11:1, 13:53, 19:1; 26:1). And Luke, for its part, distributes discourse and narration fairly evenly, although roughly twenty of the Gospel's twenty-four parables, many of which are uniquely Lukan, occur during the so-called Travel Narrative, Jesus's journey to Jerusalem between 9:50 and 19:27.[8]

Systematic discussion of identifiable formal conventions like plot, narration, and rhythm is hardly new in NT scholarship. What New Formalism contributes is a commitment to attending to the ways that literary or aesthetic forms interact with—Levine would say "encounter"—other kinds of forms, such as social, temporal, or political organizing principles. Some of these forms affirm, reflect, and reinforce one another, while others collide and conflict. By way of illustration, I offer the following case study.

The Sense of (Suspended) Endings: Mark 16:1–8 in New Formalist Perspective

Above, I outlined the broad similarities in the Synoptics' plots, including the fact that the plots of all three end with an empty tomb, signifying Jesus's resurrection. Here, I wish to explore one way that the formal designs of these endings noticeably diverge: whereas Matthew and Luke include scenes of the risen Jesus appearing to and communing with his disciples, Mark's Gospel closes with a famously puzzling scene, in which the women who visit Jesus's empty tomb flee, saying "nothing to anyone, for they were afraid" (Mark 16:8). While there is some truth to Daniel Marguerat's claim that "the ending of Mark is judged incomplete only by dint of a comparison with Matthew 28 and Luke 24" (1993, 75), Mark 16:8 remains enigmatic even without the comparison. Why, for instance, do the women remain afraid and silent at the end of a narrative labeled "good news" (Mark

---

[7] Based on Bacon 1930, especially 264–335.
[8] The exact definition of a parable differs depending on the scholar, and thus, so does the number of pericopes identified as parables in the Gospel of Luke. See the discussion of the difficulties of categorizing parables in Bultmann 1963, 174.

1:1)? Why do Jesus and the other disciples never reappear? Why does the sentence end unusually, with a conjunction (γάρ)?

Widely believed to be the earliest ending of Mark's Gospel, the evocative closing scene of Mark 16:1–8 has provoked a steady stream of scholarly suggestions, ranging from historical, materialist, textual, and/or manuscript-based proposals to linguistic, literary, and/or rhetorical interpretations. (For helpful overviews, see Lincoln 1989; Williams 1999, 26–35; Collins 2007, 796–818.) What is fascinating is the extent to which, despite the differences between them, these suggestions are predicated upon a common ("old") formalist premise: namely, the view that totality is commensurate with narrative form.[9] Even historically-minded scholars, so often cast as enemies of (formalist) literary criticism, assume the "givenness" of narrative closure when they explain (away) the Markan ending as evidence of lost or damaged scrolls (e.g., Kenyon 1939; Klein 1926; Wright 2003) or compare it with other ancient narratives ending in γάρ (e.g., van der Horst 1972). New Formalism's distinctive characteristics will be clearer by contrast if I briefly mention several prominent prior proposals.

One common strategy for explaining the Markan open ending is to resituate narrative closure, relocating it from the purview of the text or author to that of readers. J. Lee Magness, for instance, argues that Mark's open ending provokes an "existential crisis of following" for readers, explaining: "the suspension creates the necessity of choosing among these various options, of providing a resolution to the story in the experience of the reader rather than in the text" (2002, 125). Similarly, the classic formalist-inspired work of NT narrative criticism, *Mark as Story*, declares that Mark 16:8 provides "no satisfying ending, no resolution, no closure," especially "for those of us so used to stories with a resolution" (Rhoads et al. 1999, 143), but nevertheless concludes: "the ideal readers are called to finish the story, to proclaim what happened. The readers alone will have remained faithful to the last and are now left with the choice to flee with the women or to proclaim boldly in spite of fear and death. And the ideal reader will choose to proclaim!" (143). This interpretive move makes sense. After all, Frank Kermode famously argued in his landmark twentieth-century work, *The Sense of an Ending*, that a story's end unifies and organizes the entire narrative, thereby giving rise to the story's sense, or meaning; from this perspective, it is human nature to use narrative as a way of imposing form upon the chaos of time (Kermode 1966, 45). The point here is to notice the resilience of the assumption that narrative form intrinsically creates (or should create) wholeness and closure; even when the text itself does not clearly do so, critics presume that readers must.

More recently, Elizabeth Shively has argued from a cognitive-linguistic perspective that a first-century audience "would have recognized the Gospel [of Mark] as a *gestalt* schema"—that is, an organized whole—and that they would have seen it as an example

---

[9] Of course, this valuing of closure did not originate in the modern era. Ancient writers also extolled the virtues of finishing one's account with a sense of completion. The historian Dionysius of Halicarnassus, for example, laments the fact that Thucydides "left off his history unfinished" (*On Thucydides* 16.847). See the discussion in Troftgruben 2010, esp. 61–113.

of Greco-Roman biography "even when it violates default values [such as] providing suitable closure" (Shively 2018, 283, 278). In contrast, Matthew Larsen (2018), writing from the markedly different perspective of a cultural historian, argues that the earliest readers would not have considered Mark to be a narrative (διήγησις) at all, but rather an example of ὑπομνήματα (ancient unfinished collections of notes). Yet, both Shively and Larsen discuss the oddness of Mark's ending, over and against the "givenness" of narrative closure. Larsen puts it baldly: Mark 16:1–8 "is a bad conclusion to a narrative" (2018, 133). The foregoing interpretations, regardless of theoretical starting point, share the "old" formalist premise that narrative form requires at least some degree of boundedness, resolution, or closure.

One finds here an example of what Bogel terms "the Fallacy of Formal Generalization": "the mistaken assumption that the meanings, or associations, or symbolic valences of a given formal feature are intrinsic to it and thus inseparable from it in any given appearance" (2013, 117). Resolution and finality are hardly intrinsic to or inseparable from narrative form. In my view, privileging totality may be intuitive given the way we are taught to interpret stories, but doing so effaces the particularized *affordances* of the Markan narrative form. The latter claim, of course, coheres well with poststructuralist approaches like those of Jacques Derrida and Roland Barthes, who held the philosophical view that language itself is inherently indeterminate. Some NT scholars have advanced poststructuralist interpretations of the Gospels; George Aichele, for instance, reads Mark's Gospel as a Barthesian "writerly" text, one that "resists decidable coherence" (Aichele 1996, 127; see Barthes 1990, 4).

Still, as amenable as New Formalism is to poststructuralist leanings regarding language, it generally resists the urge toward the "asymptotic unreachability" of the poststructuralist interpretive posture (Bogel 2013, 113). Instead, the New Formalist asks "what actions or thoughts are made possible or impossible by the fact of" a particular narrative configuration (Levine 2015, 152 n. 15). Standard treatments present Mark's readers with an apparently inescapable choice: either Mark's ending is prematurely aborted (as familiar historical-critical and literary approaches typically suggest), or its meaning is indeterminate and self-contradictory (as poststructuralists would aver). New Formalism pushes beyond the putative choice by rendering the Markan ending its own kind of critical tool—that is, its own means of communicating, its own politics of representation.

Structurally speaking, the Gospel of Mark does not end. It suspends. Its design creates, in one sense, a permanent narrative pause—more like a moth stuck in amber than a caterpillar thwarted while exiting its cocoon. This sustained liminality begins with Jesus's climactic crucifixion, which is widely seen as creating theological or socio-communal conundrums, but also poses a narratological problem. Jesus's death fractures the formal architecture of the narrative by depriving the plot of its main contiguous figure. While the Markan messenger in the tomb declares that Jesus has returned (and prophecies throughout the prior narrative have implied that this is true), the figure of Jesus himself remains "offstage," out of sight of the women and of their readers. What does a perpetually suspended plot like this *afford* that another (more "closed") ending might not?

To proffer an answer, it will help to take a wider view and situate this story in its historical Sitz im Leben. Because New Formalists see form and content as embedded in particular social and historical contexts, they appreciate references to external background information where their New Critical predecessors would not. Typically, the Gospel of Mark is dated to the period during, or immediately following, the Roman-Jewish War of 66–70 CE.[10] Many historians have claimed that the narrative's intended first-century audience was experiencing persecution and suffering for their beliefs. Certainly, suffering is central to the Markan narrative as a literary theme (see Dinkler 2016). It is no accident that Martin Kähler's famous comment that the Gospels are "passion narratives with extended introductions" is most commonly invoked to describe Mark specifically.[11]

Still, historians such as G. E. M. de Ste. Croix have demonstrated that in the first century CE, "official publication of imperial constitutions [was] an extremely inefficient and haphazard process," and individual governors held a considerable degree of localized freedom (Ste. Croix 1963, 14; see also Selinger 2004). Evidence of systematized and widespread persecution of Christians does not appear until later. Further, since Mark is the earliest formal written narrative about Jesus's life and death, the institution of the church had not yet developed and could hardly have stood as an organized threat to the totalizing conceits of Rome. In short, the certainty of earlier historians' claims about Mark's audience has been tempered, while assertions about suffering in and "behind" the Markan text tend now to be both more nuanced and more expansive.

Postcolonial and trauma theorists have helpfully illuminated the complex social and political landscapes of marginalization and mourning in which the earliest Christians were located. Maia Kotrosits and Hal Taussig (2013), for example, advocate "re-reading" Mark's Gospel as a dramatic depiction of a people still in the throes of a different kind of suffering –namely, the catastrophic but nebulous pain, trauma, and loss experienced by a community post-war. In the first century CE, moreover, structures of empire generally, and the criminalizing implications of execution by crucifixion specifically, worked together to impose certain kinds of political order and colonializing kyriarchies. The earliest followers of Jesus faced multiple competing allegiances, intersecting hierarchies of privilege, and varying truth claims (e.g., divine, emotional, sensory, political, criminal). It is in that world, subjected to forms and forces largely outside their control, that Mark's characters and audience suffer. This kind of suffering is far less specific than literal physical torture or martyrdom, but still remains grounded in the historical realities of a particular people and context. How, then, recalling Federico's question from above, might one "delve into the aesthetic complexity of" Mark's Gospel in light of (this version of) "its life in politics and history"?

---

[10] For more on the implications of dating vis-à-vis Mark's intended audience, see Marcus 1992.

[11] Kähler 1964, 80 n.11. It is true that Mark packs an extraordinary amount of Jesus's life and teaching into thirteen quick chapters and then decelerates to spend the last three chapters on just a few days. Still, as Richard Burridge insists, "to see over 80% of a work as mere introduction [gives] insufficient importance to these earlier sections" (1992, 195).

I begin by noting that the unpredictability that inheres in the final Markan scene fits well the precarity of its characters. Many NT scholars have recognized that the women at the tomb are marginal figures, both within the story and in its broader ancient setting. New Testament scholars also regularly discuss how, on the level of the story, Jesus is characterized through conflict (ἀγών) with his adversaries (see, e.g., Malina and Neyrey 1991). Fewer, however, have explored how these points come together in and through narrative form, as characters compete not just within the story, but also on the level of its discourse (a point suggested by the etymology of the word *protagonist* itself, proto-agonist; see Dinkler 2017). The formalist work of literary critic Alex Woloch is illuminating here.

Woloch (2003) argues that every narrative gives rise to a "distributional matrix," by which "the discrete representation of any specific individual is intertwined with the narrative's continual apportioning of attention to different characters who jostle for limited space within the same fictive universe" (2003, 13). In other words, the space allocated to any one character only arises relative to, and in asymmetric relationship with, the attention afforded to other characters. The crucifixion and subsequent emptiness of Jesus's tomb thus give rise to a formal emptiness: Jesus's empty character-space creates a void in the character system. Other figures must then fill that void.

In Luke and Matthew, the void created by Jesus's bodily absence is only temporary. In both accounts, Jesus transitions first "from a somatic to a linguistic presence" as the women tell the tale to other disciples, and then Jesus returns as a bodily presence and formal focus (Tilborg and Counet 2000, 117). With the reentry of the protagonist, formal continuity is restored. In Matthew and Luke, the ordering impulse toward narrative closure is on full display. In Mark's closing scene, however, the disruption of this ordering impulse through Jesus's continued absence facilitates—indeed, it is precisely what enables—the final focus on the frightened female disciples. By making this claim, I echo what Eugenie Brinkema articulates in a different context; Brinkema, drawing together form and affect, calls critics "to think the absent center as something other than a loss, think loss as something other than absence, and take seriously the creativity generated by affirming the undoing of presence" (Brinkema 2014, 45).

Previous speculation regarding the women's frightened silence at the end of Mark has analyzed its significance within the story itself. To some NT scholars, like Joel Williams, the women's silence indicates their redeemable but condemnable "disobedience" (1999, 22). For many, the absence of the women's voices represents failed discipleship, in much the same way that the absence of Jesus's return in Mark represents a failed ending. Others explain the women's silence as a lack of power—a sign, Gayatri Spivak (1988) would say, of their subaltern status. As Liew summarizes, the assumption underlying this view is that "not speaking is to be mute, without a voice, without agency, and without fight" (Liew 2016, 101). Certainly, patterns of speech and silence can betoken power dynamics in which dominant groups render minority groups ideologically voiceless through censoring or oppression. But disobedience and powerlessness on the part of the women are not the only interpretive options.

Attending to the form of the Markan discourse opens up new possibilities. Think again of Mark's unusual final γάρ. Scott Elliott describes this as Mark "signing off with an abrupt interruption of silence in the narrative's final sentence (16:8)" (2015, 2), in other words, a silence interrupted—a silence in the story, silenced by the story. In this narrative moment, form and content encounter—that is, they organize, refract, and creatively construct—one another. The open space, or void, of an empty tomb with its stone unexpectedly rolled away from the entrance (Mark 16:3–4) generates a similarly surprising emptiness of form: as a narrative, Mark's Gospel disrupts codified desires for closure or meaning by resisting the sense imposed by the final(ized) formal endings of Matthew and Luke. The disruption of narrative progress thereby mimics on the level of form the ways that the women's raw phobia (φοβέω) disrupts their forward movement on the level of the story.

In Mark, the absence of the first-agonist affords space for a different agony: the existential agony of a multiply-marginalized group, terrorized by their circumstances. The closing words "they said nothing to anyone" can plausibly be read as a formal instantiation of the affectual response the text ascribes to the women: they flee and remain silent, the text says, because they are seized by τρόμος and ἔκστασις—terror and ecstasy. Liew is right: "since *ekstasis* in Greek literally means 'out of one's place, one's stance, or one's standing' ... one may say that the women's ecstatic experience at the empty tomb disturbs, disorients, or even displaces them" (2016, 103). They are, put differently, beside themselves (ἐκ + στασις) with fear, arrested by trauma.

To push the matter yet further, New Formalism points up intricate and contradictory connections between the body *of* the text (i.e., its form) and the bodies *in* the text. The body of the Markan text freezes the women's bodies mid-flight. Without stipulating any final destination, the narrator simply says that "they fled" (ἔφυγον) from the tomb (Mark 16:8). This is, in fact, the third instance of such destinationless flight (φεύγω) in the Markan passion narrative. The first two occur in the Garden of Gethsemane, just after Judas betrays Jesus. Jesus makes it clear that he will not resist arrest, and then, the text says, "they all abandoned him and fled (ἔφυγον)" (Mark 14:50). The exception appears to be one young man, wrapped in a linen cloth, who begins to follow Jesus, but then, after being seized, the text simply says: "he fled naked [γυμνὸς ἔφυγεν]" (Mark 14:51). In Matthew, an angel appears to Joseph and instructs him to take Mary and Jesus and "flee to Egypt (φεῦγε εἰς Αἴγυπτον)" (Matt 2:13). In Mark, in contrast, the narrator does not stipulate where these fleeing characters go. They simply disappear.

As the third of three such flight scenes, Mark 16:1–8 shows the women embodying an *ek-stasis* of another kind. Consider the fact that the messenger in the tomb instructs the women to go back to Galilee, where they will find Jesus (Mark 16:6–7). Of course, unlike the Gospels of Matthew and Luke, Mark's story of "good news" begins with an adult Jesus, "who came from Nazareth in Galilee" (Mark 1:9). In other words, the young man charges the women to return to the beginning of the story, to retrace Jesus's steps and their own, to *re*-member (in the sense of recreating the whole). Their refusal or inability to do so disrupts not only the cyclical nature of the messenger's instructions, but also the forward flow of narrative time.[12]

The disruption is apropos; the women have just been given the shocking message that their leader, recently executed as a criminal by the Roman imperial machine, has disrupted the quotidian carceral laws of the Roman Empire. Not only that, but the undead absent Jesus has also disrupted the more fundamental, elemental laws of the natural human life cycle. But perhaps this is constitutive of the "good news" for Mark. Drawing on the Lacanian notion of *jouissance*, Liew suggests that trauma is never unidimensional; there can be joy or satisfaction in the suffering, and vice versa: "what the women experience at the end of Mark's Gospel, let me suggest, is the *jouissance*, or the unspeakable traumatic enjoyment in the recognition that a tomb, with or without a corpse, cannot prevent Jesus and Jesus's story from being kept alive in this world, and that story's effectual bursting of the pax Romana bubble" (Liew 2016, 114).

The women's silence, and their flight to nowhere, together create and reflect a disruption of multiple ordering forms and forces. I contend that the overall result of this narrative design is that Mark's particular ending affords ways of contemplating the disruptive, disorderly nature of this "good news" that the endings of Matthew and Luke do not.

Conclusion

After introducing New Formalism, this essay briefly outlined traditional discussions of Synoptic narrative design. The final section explored how New Formalism's openness of interpretation might illuminate the formal openness of Mark's suspended ending. I suggested that, just as Mark's ending defies resolution, it also defies reduction of meaning. In sum, the essay has argued, based on New Formalist principles, that allowing for capacious considerations of the Gospels' narrative design—and the polyvalent affordances of narrative form—can expand and deepen our conceptions of how the Synoptic Gospels work literarily as narrative structures.

References

Aichele, George. 1996. *Jesus Framed*. Biblical Limits. London: Routledge.
Barthes, Roland. 1990. *S/Z*. Translated by R. Miller. Oxford: Blackwell.
Bérubé, Michael. 2000. "Aesthetics and the Literal Imagination." In *Falling into Theory: Conflicting Views on Reading Literature*, edited by David Richter, 391–98. Boston: Bedford.
Bock, Darrell L., and Buist M. Fanning, eds. 2006. *Interpreting the New Testament Text: Introduction to the Art and Science of Exegesis*. Wheaton, IL: Crossway.

---

[12] On the appropriateness of Mark's suspended ending for an apocalyptic text, see King 2015.

Bogel, Fredric V. 2013. *New Formalist Criticism: Theory and Practice*. New York: Palgrave Macmillan.

Brinkema, Eugenie. 2014. *The Forms of the Affects*. Durham, NC: Duke University Press.

Brooks, Peter. 1992. *Reading for the Plot: Design and Intention in Narrative*. Cambridge, MA: Harvard University Press.

Bruster, Douglas. 2002. "Shakespeare and the Composite Text." In *Renaissance Literature and Its Formal Engagements*, edited by Mark David Rasmussen, 43–66. Basingstoke: Palgrave.

Bultmann, Rudolf. 1963. *The History of the Synoptic Tradition*. Rev. ed. Translated by John Marsh. New York: Harper & Row.

Burridge, Richard. 1992. *What Are the Gospels?: A Comparison with Graeco-Roman Biography*. Cambridge: Cambridge University Press.

Chatman, Seymour. 1978. *Story and Discourse: Narrative Structure in Discourse and Film*. Ithaca: Cornell University Press.

Collins, Adela. 2007. *Mark: A Commentary*. Hermeneia. Minneapolis: Fortress Press.

de Man, Paul. 1979. *Allegories of Reading: Figural Language in Rousseau, Nietzsche, Rilke, and Proust*. New Haven: Yale University Press.

de Ste. Croix, G. E. M. 1963. "Why Were the Christians Persecuted?" *Past and Present* 26: 6–38.

Dinkler, Michal Beth. 2016. "Suffering, Misunderstanding, and Suffering Misunderstanding: The Markan Misunderstanding Motif as a Form of Jesus' Suffering." *JSNT* 38: 316–338.

Dinkler, Michal Beth. 2017. "Building Character on the Road to Emmaus: Lukan Characterization in Contemporary Literary Perspective." *JBL* 136: 687–706.

Dubrow, Heather. 2013. Foreword to *New Formalisms and Literary Theory*, edited by Verena Theile and Linda Tredennick, vii–xviii. New York: Palgrave Macmillan.

Elliott, Scott S. 2015. "Time and Focalization in the Gospel According to Mark." In *The Oxford Handbook of Biblical Narrative*, edited by Danna Nolan Fewell, 296–306. Oxford: Oxford University Press.

Federico, Annette. 2016. *Engagements with Close Reading*. London: Routledge.

Freytag, Gustav. 1894. *Freytag's Technique of the Drama: An Exposition of Dramatic Composition and Art*. Translated by Elias J. MacEwan. Chicago: Griggs.

Harpham, Geoffrey. 2006. *The Character of Criticism*. London: Routledge.

Hirsch, E. D. 1967. *Validity in Interpretation*. New Haven: Yale University Press.

Hunter, J. Paul. 2000. "Formalism and History: Binarism and the Anglophone Couplet." *MLQ* 61: 109–29.

Kähler, Martin. 1964. *The So-Called Historical Jesus and the Historic, Biblical Christ*. Translated and edited by Carl E. Braaten. Philadelphia: Fortress Press.

Kenyon, Frederic G. 1939. "Papyrus Rolls and the Ending of St. Mark." *JTS* 60: 56–57.

Kermode, Frank. 1966. *The Sense of an Ending: Studies in the Theory of Fiction*. New York: Oxford University Press.

King, Karen. 2015. "Endings: *The Gospel of Mark* and *The Gospel of Judas*." In *Early Christian and Jewish Narrative: The Role of Religion in Shaping Narrative Forms*, edited by Ilaria Ramelli and Judith Perkins, 55–72. Tübingen: Mohr Siebeck.

Kingsbury, Jack Dean. 1991. *Conflict in Luke*. Minneapolis: Augsburg Fortress.

Klein, R. O. 1926. "The Lost Ending of the Gospel According to Mark." *JBL* 45: 81–103.

Kotrosits, Maia and Hal Taussig. 2011. *Re-reading the Gospel of Mark amidst Pain and Loss*. New York: Palgrave.

Larsen, Matthew. 2018. *Gospels before the Book*. Oxford: Oxford University Press.

Lentricchia, Frank. 1980. *After the New Criticism*. Chicago: University of Chicago.

Levine, Caroline. 2015. *Forms: Whole, Rhythm, Hierarchy, Network*. Princeton: Princeton University Press.

Levinson, Marjorie. 2007. "What Is New Formalism?" *PMLA* 122, no. 2: 558–69.

Liew, Tat-siong Benny. 2016. "Haunting Silence: Trauma, Failed Orality, and Mark's Messianic Secret." In *Psychoanalytic Mediations between Marxist and Postcolonial Readings of the Bible*, edited by Tat-siong Benny Liew and Erin Runions, 99–128. Atlanta: SBL Press.

Lincoln, Andrew. 1989. "The Promise and the Failure: Mark 16.7, 8." *JBL* 108, no. 2: 283–300.

Lotman, Jurij. 1977. *The Structure of the Artistic Text*. Ann Arbor: University of Michigan Press.

Magness, J. Lee. 2002. *Marking the End: Sense and Absence in the Gospel of Mark*. Eugene, OR: Wipf and Stock.

Malina, Bruce, and Jerome Neyrey. 1991. "Honor and Shame in Luke-Acts: Pivotal Values of the Mediterranean World." In *The Social World of Luke-Acts: Models of Interpretation*, edited by Jerome H. Neyrey, 25–65. Peabody, MA: Hendrickson.

Marcus, Joel. 1992. "The Jewish War and the *Sitz im Leben* of Mark." *JBL* 111: 441–62.

Marguerat, Daniel. 1993. "The End of Acts (28, 16–31) and the Rhetoric of Silence." In *Rhetoric and the New Testament: Essays from the 1992 Heidelberg Conference*, edited by Stanley E. Porter and Thomas H. Olbricht, JSNTSup 90, 74–89. Sheffield: Sheffield Academic Press.

Miller, J. Hillis. 1978. "The Problematic of Ending in Narrative." *Nineteenth-Century Fiction* 33: 3–7.

Norman, Donald. 1990. *The Psychology of Everyday Things*. New York: Basic Books.

O'Brien, Kelli S. 2010. *The Use of Scripture in the Markan Passion Narrative*. London: T&T Clark.

Powell, Mark Allan. 1990. *What Is Narrative Criticism?* Minneapolis: Fortress.

Ransom, John Crowe. 1941. *The New Criticism*. Norfolk, CT: New Directions.

Rhoads, David, Joanna Dewey, and Donald Michie. 1999. *Mark as Story: An Introduction to the Narrative of a Gospel*. 2nd ed. Philadelphia: Fortress Press.

Rooney, Ellen. 2000. "Form and Contentment." *MLQ* 61: 17–40.

Schwarz, Daniel. 2008. *In Defense of Reading*. Malden, MA: Blackwell.

Selinger, Reinhard. 2004. *The Mid-Third Century Persecutions of Decius and Valerian*. 2nd ed. Frankfurt: Peter Lang.

Shively, Elizabeth. 2018. "Recognizing Penguins: Audience Expectation, Cognitive Genre Theory, and the Ending of Mark's Gospel." *CBQ* 80: 273–92.

Spingarn, Joel E. 1917. "The New Criticism." In *Creative Criticism: Essays on the Unity of Genius and Taste*, 3–46. New York: Holt.

Spivak, Gayatri Chakravorty. 1988. "Can the Subaltern Speak?" In *Marxism and the Interpretation of Culture*, edited by Cary Nelson and Lawrence, 271–313. Chicago: University of Illinois Press.

Strier, Richard. 2002. "How Formalism Became a Dirty Word, and Why We Can't Do without It." In *Renaissance Literature and Its Formal Engagements*, edited by Mark David Rasmussen, 207–16. New York: Palgrave.

Thiele, Verena. 2013. "New Formalism(s): A Prologue." In *New Formalisms and Literary Theory*, edited by Verena Thiele and Linda Tredennick, 3–26. Basingstoke: Palgrave.

Tilborg, Sjef Van and Patrick Chatelion Counet. 2000. *Jesus' Appearances and Disappearances in Luke 24*. Leiden: Brill.

Todorov, Tzvetan. 1980. "The Categories of Literary Narrative." Translated by Joseph Kestner. *Papers on Language and Literature* 16: 3–36.

Troftgruben, Troy M. 2010. *A Conclusion Unhindered: A Study of the Ending of Acts within Its Literary Environment.* Tübingen: Mohr Siebeck.

Tynjanov, Yury. 1981. *The Problem of Verse Language.* Trans. Michael Sosa and Brent Harvey. Ann Arbor: Ardis.

van der Horst, P. W. 1972. "Can a Book End with Gar? A Note on Mark XVI.8." *JTS* 23: 121–24.

van Tilborg, Sjef, and Patrick Chatelion Counet. 2000. *Jesus' Appearances and Disappearances in Luke 24.* Leiden: Brill.

Wimsatt, W. K., and M. C. Beardsley. 1949. "The Affective Fallacy." Repr. In *The Verbal Icon: Studies in the Meaning of Poetry,* 21–39. Lexington: University of Kentucky Press, 1954.

Wimsatt, W. K., and M. C. Beardsley. 1946. "The Intentional Fallacy." Repr. In *The Verbal Icon: Studies in the Meaning of Poetry,* 3–18. Lexington: University of Kentucky Press, 1954.

Williams, Joel. 1999. "Literary Approaches to the End of Mark's Gospel." *JETS* 42: 21–35.

Woloch, Alex. 2003. *The One vs. the Many: Minor Characters and the Space of the Protagonist in the Novel.* Princeton: Princeton University Press.

Wright, N.T. 2003. *The Resurrection of the Son of God.* Minneapolis: Fortress Press.

CHAPTER 9

MANUSCRIPTS

The Problem with the Synoptic Problem

BRENT NONGBRI

Introduction

THE texts traditionally known as the Gospels According to Matthew, Mark, and Luke are so similar that, if they lacked these traditional names, they would probably simply be classified as different versions of the same text—a shorter recension of the *Life of Jesus* and two longer recensions of the *Life of Jesus*. But the fact is that these texts do bear these traditional names and came to be thought of as three distinct works by at least as early as the late second century. Both ancient and modern readers have thus understandably treated them as discrete compositions that can be compared and contrasted with each other.[1] One of the typical goals of such comparison is resolving the issue of dependence. That is to say, because these texts are so very similar, often displaying near exact verbal agreement, modern scholars regularly speak of the composers of two of these three texts "being dependent upon" or "using" one or more of the others.

The very detailed comparisons of the similarities and differences among these texts undertaken in order to determine these relationships constitute the so-called Synoptic Problem, one of the central building blocks of the study of the Gospels and the historical Jesus over the last century. Yet the kinds of comparisons that New Testament scholars carry out under the heading of the Synoptic Problem often presume that these texts (the Gospel According to Matthew, the Gospel According to Mark, and the Gospel According

---

Thanks to Hugo Lundhaug and the Faculty of Theology at the University of Oslo for the invitation to present an earlier version of this material at the Oslo Lectures in New Testament and Early Christian Studies in April 2019. I am also grateful to AnneMarie Luijendijk and Mark Goodacre for providing very useful feedback to an earlier version of this essay and to Mary Jane Cuyler for insightful discussion of several points.

[1] Awareness of literary relationships among the gospels goes back at least to Augustine of Hippo, who described Mark as something like an epitomizer (*breviator*) of Matthew (*Cons.* I.2.4 and I.3.6).

to Luke) each existed in a stable, finalized form, akin to what we find in modern printed editions. But, like all ancient literature, the Gospels were preserved in manuscripts, individual copies made by hand, each with unique characteristics. In the case of the Gospels, thousands of manuscripts have survived with many thousands of variations.[2] For the last few centuries, textual critics of the New Testament have attempted to sort through these variations and determine the earliest recoverable text of each of the Gospels, and in doing so, they often adopt particular approaches to the Synoptic Problem. At the same time, one's approach to the Synoptic Problem is determined by the analysis of the editions established by textual critics. While most New Testament scholars would agree that we can be reasonably confident about the results of the text-critical enterprise, it is simply a fact that the ancient manuscripts of the Gospels show myriad variations. That is to say, these are *not* the kinds of stable texts necessary for detailed synoptic comparison.[3] The difficulties of dealing with any single ancient text preserved in multiple different manuscripts with textual variation are increased threefold when attempting to compare and contrast these three Gospels. This is not a reason for despair so much as a call for vigilance and an invitation to view the Synoptic Problem as an opportunity for exploring the complex transmission and transformation of Gospel texts.

My task in this essay is to provide a series of observations from a material perspective that may be of interest to those engaged in research related to the issue of "dependence" among the Synoptic Gospels. I attempt to demonstrate the ways in which textual fluidity and the practicalities of manuscript culture complicate both the search for solutions to the Synoptic Problem and the very idea of "dependence." To more fully appreciate the ways that manuscripts affect these discussions, however, we need to begin by having a very clear sense of what the Synoptic Problem is and how scholars have tried to "solve" the problem.[4] The first portion of the chapter is thus a general overview of the Synoptic Problem, and the second portion is a more technical look at Greek manuscripts of the Synoptic Gospels and the ways editors have worked with them.

What Is the Synoptic Problem?

It has long been recognized that the Gospels According to Matthew, Mark, and Luke agree closely not only in general contents but also in the exact wording of their Greek texts. This agreement occurs both in direct quotations of characters in the Gospels and in narrative exposition, which suggests that these three Gospels have some kind

---

[2] For an assessment of the levels and types of variation in New Testament manuscripts, see Holmes 2013.

[3] The challenge that the multiplicity of Gospel manuscripts presents to students of the Synoptic Problem has long been known. For an excellent overview of scholarship at the turn of the twentieth century and reflections on the symbiotic relationship between textual criticism of the Gospels and the Synoptic Problem, see Head 2011. For further incisive commentary, see Parker 1997, 103–23.

[4] For more detailed and nuanced treatments of the Synoptic Problem, see Sanders and Davies 1989 and Goodacre 2001. For a history of the Problem, see Kloppenborg, chapter 1 here.

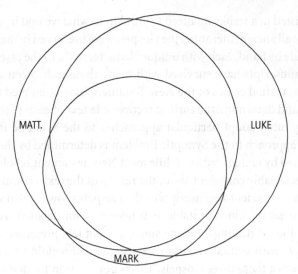

FIGURE 9.1 Venn diagram showing shared material in Matthew, Mark, and Luke (design by Joe Weaks)

of literary relationship. We can get some sense of this overlap with a basic Venn diagram (see fig. 9.1). There are a variety of different ways one might choose to "count" agreement and overlap among the Synoptic Gospels that will differ in some degree, but this diagram, based on a rough count of the shared stories in Matthew, Mark, and Luke, provides a good general idea of overall relations.[5]

The overlaps show the material common to the Gospels. Matthew contains a little over 90 percent of Mark. Luke contains just under 90 percent of Mark. Matthew and Luke share very roughly about 75 percent of their material.[6]

How did the Gospels come to share these commonalities? The opening sentence of Luke in fact suggests a likely reason: "Since many have undertaken to set down an orderly account [διήγησις] of the events that have been fulfilled among us . . ." That is to say, the composer of Luke knew of and very likely made use of other written accounts or narrations of the life of Jesus. The same is presumably true of the composers of Matthew and Mark. That is to say, there is a literary relationship among these Gospels. There is really no other convincing way to explain the similarities among these three texts. They are so alike, in fact, that they are often called the "Synoptic Gospels," for they can

---

[5] Thanks to Joe Weaks for the design of the graphic, which is based on a survey of the *Conspectus locorum parallelorum* index in Aland 1997, 567–91. Thanks also to Mark Goodacre for pointing out that this way of representing synoptic data takes no account of the order of stories in the Gospels and therefore can misrepresent the actual degree of similarity among the three.

[6] Different methods of comparison (for instance, comparing words or verses rather than stories) will yield different percentages but do not radically alter the overall picture. See, for instance, Honoré 1968. B. H. Streeter's estimate that "Luke omits more than 45%" of the subject matter of Mark results from his presumption that Luke used "a non-Markan source" for some of his "Markan" material (Streeter 1930, 159–60).

Table 9.1 The calling of Matthew/Levi (NSRV)

Matthew 9:9	Mark 2:14	Luke 5:27-28
As Jesus <u>was walking along</u>, he saw a man called Matthew sitting at the tax booth; and he said to him, "Follow me." And he got up and followed him.	<u>As</u> he *was walking along*, <u>he</u> **saw** *Levi* son of Alphaeus **sitting at the tax booth,** **and he said to him,** **"Follow me."** And he got up **and followed him.**	After this he went out and **saw** a tax collector named *Levi* **sitting at the tax booth;** **and he said to him,** **"Follow me."** And he got up, left everything, **and followed him.**

be productively viewed syn-optically, that is, side by side. Thus one of the ideal tools for studying these Gospels is a synopsis, a text that prints the Gospels side by side in columns in order to highlight where they align and where they are different.[7]

In fact, using a synopsis is the best way to get a sense of the degree of similarity among these Gospels. I will begin by looking at a single verse (table 9.1). The English translation used here is the New Revised Standard Version.

The material in bold is the same, word for word, in all three Gospels. The underlined words are common to Matthew and Mark, and the italicized words are common to Mark and Luke. It is clear that the central elements of the story and the quotation of Jesus are exactly the same, but the framing differs slightly among the three. Matthew and Mark agree in saying that Jesus was walking along, while Mark and Luke agree that the name of the man at the tax booth was Levi, while in Matthew, the man at the tax booth is called Matthew. In Luke, there is the detail that this man from the tax booth "left everything" to follow Jesus. But, overall we can see that this kind of close verbal similarity can really only be explained by a literary relationship among these three Gospels.

So when scholars talk about the Synoptic Problem, what they mean is *"the study of the similarities and differences of the Synoptic Gospels in an attempt to explain their literary relationship"* (Goodacre 2001, 16). How we resolve this literary relationship has ramifications both for the study of the historical Jesus and for the study of the early Christians who produced and used the Gospels. So there is actually quite a lot at stake with how we think about the Synoptic Problem. When it comes to explaining this literary relationship among the Synoptic Gospels, there are some clues that help us determine at least some of the lines of influence. I noted earlier that roughly 90 percent of the material in Mark is contained in Matthew. That means about 10 percent of the material in Mark is not present in Matthew. Most of this material is also absent from Luke. Examining some of these passages provides insight into why they might be in Mark but not in Matthew or Luke. Consider a healing story unique to Mark (Mark 8:22–36; table 9.2).

---

[7] Gospel synopses are plentiful. A good English edition is Throckmorton 1992. The standard Greek texts are Aland 1997 and Huck and Greeven 1981.

Table 9.2 Mark 8:22–36 (NSRV)

Matthew	Mark 8:22–26	Luke
	They came to Bethsaida. Some people brought a blind man to him and begged him to touch him. He took the blind man by the hand and led him out of the village; and when he had put saliva on his eyes and laid his hands on him, he asked him, "Can you see anything?" And the man looked up and said, "I can see people, but they look like trees, walking." Then Jesus laid his hands on his eyes again; and he looked intently and his sight was restored, and he saw everything clearly. Then he sent him away to his home, saying, "Do not even go into the village."	

There are no parallels in Matthew and Luke for this story in Mark. One can imagine why. We have an account of Jesus using his own spit to perform a healing, at first unsuccessfully. Jesus gets it right on the second try but then tells the healed man not to say anything about it. It is a somewhat uncomfortable story. And it turns out that much of the material that is unique to Mark seems a bit strange. To take just one other example, consider Mark 14:48–52 (table 9.3).

For much of the account there is significant verbal overlap among the three, especially between Matthew and Mark, but Mark closes with the words in bold italics, a bizarre little story of a naked man fleeing the scene. These odd features unique to Mark raise the question: Are these stories the kind of thing one imagines Mark adding to Matthew or Luke? Or are they the kind of thing one imagines Matthew and Luke deleting from Mark? Most scholars think the latter. That is to say, most scholars agree that the best way to account for these similarities and differences is to suppose that Mark seems to have served as a source for the composers of Matthew and Luke.[8] While the majority of students of the Synoptic Problem basically agree on this point, there is significantly more disagreement when it comes to determining other synoptic relationships, specifically the material that is not present in Mark.

Once one has accounted for the "triple tradition," that is, the overlapping material present in Matthew, Mark, and Luke, one is left with a substantial amount of parallel material that is common only to Matthew and Luke. And we often find a high level of verbal agreement in these passages. Consider the preaching of John the Baptist (table 9.4).

---

[8] There are of course others reasons in addition to the unique contents of Mark that have led a majority of scholars to agree on Markan priority. For a clear summary of the relevant evidence, see Goodacre 2002, 19–45. A minority of scholars argue that Matthew was the oldest composition and was used by the composers of Mark and Luke. For a discussion of the strengths and weaknesses of this position, see Sanders and Davies 1989, 84–92.

Table 9.3 The young man in the garden (NSRV)

Matthew 26:55-56	Mark 14:48-52	Luke 22:52-53
At that hour **Jesus said to** the crowds,	Then **Jesus said to** them,	Then **Jesus said to** the chief priests, the officers of the temple police, and the elders who had come for him,
"Have you come out with swords and clubs to arrest me as though I were a bandit? Day after day I sat in the temple teaching, and you did not arrest me. But all this has taken place, so that the scriptures of the prophets may be fulfilled." Then all the disciples deserted him and fled.	"Have you come out with swords and clubs to arrest me as though I were a bandit? Day after day I *was with you* in the temple teaching, and you did not arrest me. But let the scriptures be fulfilled." All of them deserted him and fled. *A certain young man was following him, wearing nothing but a linen cloth. They caught hold of him, but he left the linen cloth and ran off naked.*	"Have you come out with swords and clubs as if I were a bandit? When I *was with you* day after day in the temple, you did not lay hands on me. But this is your hour, and the power of darkness!"

Table 9.4 The preaching of John the Baptist (NSRV)

Matthew 3:7-10	Mark	Luke 3:7-9
But when he saw many Pharisees and Sadducees coming for baptism, he said to them,		John said to the crowds that came out to be baptized by him,
"You brood of vipers! Who warned you to flee from the wrath to come? Bear **fruit** worthy of repentance. Do not **presume** to say to yourselves, 'We have Abraham as our ancestor'; for I tell you, God is able from these stones to raise up children to Abraham. Even now the ax is lying at the root of the trees; every tree therefore that does not bear good fruit is cut down and thrown into the fire."		"You brood of vipers! Who warned you to flee from the wrath to come? Bear **fruits** worthy of repentance. Do not **begin** to say to yourselves, 'We have Abraham as our ancestor'; for I tell you, God is able from these stones to raise up children to Abraham. Even now the ax is lying at the root of the trees; every tree therefore that does not bear good fruit is cut down and thrown into the fire."

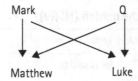

FIGURE 9.2 The Two-Source Hypothesis

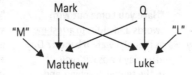

FIGURE 9.3 The Four-Source Hypothesis

The narrative framing is slightly different, but the words of John the Baptist are almost identical, showing nearly perfect verbal agreement (only the words printed in bold are different). So we seem to be dealing with a literary relationship beyond just Mark as a common source. The evidence has led many scholars to adopt what is called the Two-Source Hypothesis or Two Document Hypothesis, which states that Matthew and Luke independently used Mark and also a second source, usually called Q (from the German word for "source," *Quelle*), a hypothetical document that has not survived but is thought to have contained the material that is common to Matthew and Luke but absent from Mark.[9] This proposed set of relationships is generally set out in a diagrammed fashion as shown in figure 9.2.

Sometimes the material that is unique to Matthew and that which is unique to Luke is also represented, designated by "M" and "L," as shown in figure 9.3.

Thus Matthew and Luke are supposed to have composed their Gospels by independently using Mark and Q along with additional material available to each of them.[10] This is the most widely accepted solution to the Synoptic Problem today.

But matters are not quite so neat as such graphics imply, because there are several instances when Matthew and Luke actually agree with each other against Mark.[11] Table 9.5 gives an example of this phenomenon in the Parable of the Mustard Seed.

---

[9] John Kloppenborg defines the hypothesis as follows: "stated succinctly, the Two Document hypothesis proposes that the Gospels of Matthew and Luke independently used Mark as a source. Since Matthew and Luke share about 235 verses that they did not get from Mark, the 2DH requires that they had independent access to a second source consisting mainly of sayings of Jesus. This, for want of a better term, is the 'Sayings Gospel,' or, 'Q' " (Kloppenborg Verbin 2000, 12–13).

[10] In more advanced studies of the Synoptic Problem, the relationships are acknowledged to be more complex. See, for example, Kloppenborg Verbin 2000, 37, and Sanders and Davies 1989, 100–109.

[11] In what follows, I speak of "agreements between Matthew and Luke against Mark" because I regard this description as both accurate and neutral. Advocates of the Two-Source Hypothesis tend to describe this material under separate headings that derive from the Two-Source Hypothesis itself. Some of these agreements are said to be "Mark-Q overlaps" while others are "minor" agreements. The result of this way of classifying is an obfuscation of the full measure of agreements between Matthew and Luke against Mark. See further Goodacre 2002, 163–65, and Goodacre 2018.

Table 9.5 The Parable of the Mustard Seed (NRSV)

Matthew 13:31–32	Mark 4:30–32	Luke 13:18–19
He put before them another parable:	He also said,	He said therefore,
"The kingdom of heaven is like a mustard seed *that someone took and sowed in his* field;	"With what can we compare *the kingdom of God*, or what parable will we use for it? *It* is like a mustard seed, which, when sown upon the ground,	"What is *the kingdom of God* like? And to what should I compare it? *It* is like a mustard seed *that someone took and sowed in his* garden;
it <u>is the smallest of all the seeds</u>, but when it has grown it is	<u>is the smallest of all the seeds</u> on earth; yet when it is sown it grows up and becomes	it grew
<u>the greatest of shrubs</u> and becomes *a tree*, *so that* the birds of the air come and <u>make</u> nests in its *branches*."	<u>the greatest of</u> all <u>shrubs</u>, and puts forth large branches, <u>so that</u> the birds of the air can <u>make</u> nests in its shade."	and became *a tree*, and the birds of the air made nests in its *branches*."

Notice the word-for-word agreements (in bold italics) between Matthew and Luke against Mark. These kinds of agreements pose a problem for scholars who hold to the Two-Source Hypothesis.[12] If Matthew and Luke both adapted this passage from copies of Mark, then it is incredible that they both changed it in such similar fashions. Scholars holding to the Two-Source Hypothesis have tried to explain this phenomenon in different ways. Some propose that Matthew and Luke preserve an earlier and more primitive version of Mark's Gospel that differs in some substantial ways from the versions of Mark that have survived in the manuscript tradition.[13] This solution is possible, but it forces advocates of the Two-Source Hypothesis to depend upon a second hypothetical document in addition to Q. Many more scholars have suggested that passages like this one must have been preserved both in Mark and in Q, and that Matthew and Luke have both followed the Q version rather than the version in Mark. This notion of Mark-Q overlaps is of course possible. Since Q is a hypothetical document, its contents cannot be known with certainty. But allowing for the existence of Mark-Q overlaps also creates problems for the Two-Source Hypothesis. One of the arguments that necessitates hypothesizing Q in the first place is the claim that neither Luke nor Matthew reproduces

---

[12] I choose this example for its brevity. For a list of other examples, see Sanders, 1973.

[13] In one sense, this observation is self-evident: it is unlikely, bordering on impossible, that the composers of Matthew and Luke "used" copies of Mark that were identical to each other, or to any surviving manuscript of Mark. That said, it is not possible to know the precise wording of any manuscripts of Mark that predate the earliest surviving extensive copies, which date to the fourth century.

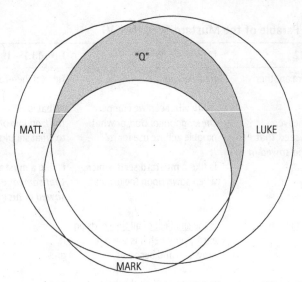

FIGURE 9.4 Venn diagram showing shared material in Matthew, Mark, and Luke, with Q material shaded (design by Joe Weaks)

the other's changes to Mark (which one would expect, if either Luke used Matthew or Matthew used Luke).[14] The very existence of Mark-Q overlaps refutes that claim. We can visualize this difficulty by adjusting the Venn diagram of Synoptic relations. First, figure 9.4 adapts it to the Two-Source Hypothesis by identifying the material common to Matthew and Luke but absent from Mark as Q.

Then, notice what happens if we allow for overlaps between Mark and Q, as shown in figure 9.5.

Q begins to look more and more like the Gospel According to Matthew (and, to a slightly lesser degree, Luke). Indeed, we could shade in even more of the "triple tradition" space in deference to the observation of E. P. Sanders that "those who wish to explain all or most of the agreements between Matthew and Luke against Mark by attributing them to the influence of Q are simply arguing for an Ur-Gospel which very closely resembles Matthew. *Virtually every single pericope in the triple tradition has some such agreements*" (Sanders 1973, 454, my emphasis). Problems like this have led some scholars to dispense with the hypothetical Q-source and argue instead that Luke made use of Mark and Matthew. This approach to the Synoptic Problem is most commonly known as the Farrer Hypothesis.[15] It is usually diagrammed in a manner similar to figure 9.6.

The Farrer Hypothesis remains a minority opinion in current scholarship, but my sense is that an increasing number of scholars are open to entertaining it as a viable solution to the Synoptic Problem.[16]

---

[14] See further Goodacre 2018.
[15] The clearest articulation of this viewpoint can be found in Goodacre 2002.
[16] See, for instance, Watson 2013.

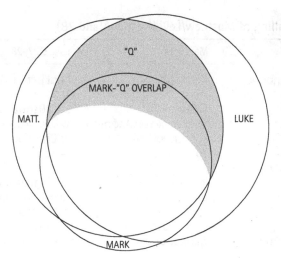

FIGURE 9.5 Venn diagram showing shared material in Matthew, Mark, and Luke, with Q and a sample of Mark-Q overlap material shaded (design by Joe Weaks)

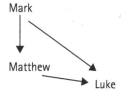

FIGURE 9.6 The Farrer Hypothesis

It is important to emphasize that in several of the examples provided here, small differences of just one or two words here and there really do matter. Although they may seem insignificant when examined individually, cumulatively they are important factors for scholars seeking to resolve the Synoptic Problem.

The Problem: Manuscripts

As I noted at the outset, advocates of these traditional approaches to the Synoptic Problem often proceed as if there were singular, stable texts of Matthew, Mark, and Luke.[17] Recall Goodacre's definition of the Synoptic Problem: "the Synoptic Problem might be defined

[17] I am not the first to make this point. D. C. Parker characterizes the situation as follows: "the study of the Synoptic Problem as normally conducted includes the agreement between practitioners that the text of Nestle-Aland is, to all intents and purposes, what Matthew, Mark and Luke originally wrote" (Parker 1997, 115). Parker also helpfully observes that "solutions" to the Synoptic Problem are actually models, which by definition simplify the phenomena they describe.

Table 9.6 The calling of Matthew/Levi (Nestle-Aland 28)

Matthew 9:9	Mark 2:14	Luke 5:27-28
Καὶ παράγων ⌜ὁ Ἰησοῦς ἐκεῖθεν⌝ **εἶδεν** ἄνθρωπον καθήμενον ἐπὶ τὸ τελώνιον, Μαθθαῖον λεγόμενον, καὶ **λέγει** αὐτῷ· ἀκολούθει μοι. καὶ ἀναστὰς ⌜**ἠκολούθησεν** αὐτῷ.	Καὶ παράγων **εἶδεν** ⌜Λευὶν τὸν τοῦ Ἁλφαίου καθήμενον ἐπὶ τὸ τελώνιον, καὶ **λέγει** αὐτῷ· ἀκολούθει μοι. καὶ ἀναστὰς **ἠκολούθησεν** αὐτῷ.	⌜Καὶ μετὰ ταῦτα ἐξῆλθεν καὶ **ἐθεάσατο** τελώνην ὀνόματι Λευὶν⌝ καθήμενον ἐπὶ τὸ τελώνιον, καὶ ⌜**εἶπεν** αὐτῷ· ἀκολούθει μοι. καὶ καταλιπὼν πάντα ἀναστὰς ⌜**ἠκολούθει** αὐτῷ.
⌜ εκειθεν ο Ιησους D N Θ f¹³ 565; Eus ¦ ο Ιησους ℵ* L bo^ms ¦ ο κυριος ημων Ιησους ο Χριστος /844. /2211 ¦ ⌜ ηκολουθει ℵ C^vid D f¹ 892	⌜ (3,18) Ιακωβον D Θ f¹³| 565 it ¦ Λευι ℵ* A K Γ Δ 28. 33. 2542 pm aur q vg^cl co? ¦ txt 𝔓⁸⁸ ℵ² B C L W 1. 579. 700. 892. 1241. 1424. /2211 pm f 1 vg^st	⌜ p) και ελθων παλιν παρα την θαλασσαν τον επακολουθουντα αυτω οχλον εδιδασκεν· και παραγων ειδεν Λευι τον του Αλφαιου D | ⌜ p) λεγει ℵ D f¹³ | ⌜ p) ηκολουθησεν ℵ A C K N Γ Δ Θ Ψ f¹·¹³ 33. 565. 579. 1241. 1424. 2542. /844. /2211 m ¦ txt B D L W Ξ 700. 892 a

as *the study of the similarities and differences of the Synoptic Gospels in an attempt to explain their literary relationship*" (Goodacre 2001, 16). In this formulation, the phrase "Synoptic Gospels" is really a shorthand. What are actually being compared are reconstructed Greek texts of each of the Synoptic Gospels. Table 9.6 shows the call of the tax collector in Matthew 9:9 (the simple example given in table 9.1) in an eclectic Greek text.

The first obvious difference is the presence of a critical apparatus showing a number of textual variants in this verse in all three Gospels. I will return to some of the details of the apparatus later. For now, notice the first line of the Greek text. Looking back at the English translation of this passage, we find agreement across all three Gospels with the word "saw," but notice that this covers up a difference in the Greek of Luke. There is εἶδεν in Matthew and εἶδεν in Mark, but ἐθεάσατο in Luke. The same thing happens with the verb "saying" further down. There is the historical present λέγει in Matthew and Mark and the aorist εἶπεν in Luke. The same thing happens yet again with the final verb in the passage. In the English translation, there is triple agreement with the word "followed," but the Greek text has an instance of Matthew and Mark agreeing on the aorist form ἠκολούθησεν against Luke's imperfect ἠκολούθει. It is clear that in order to notice the small differences present in the manuscripts, it is necessary to work with a Greek text.

This observation in turn raises the question: *Which* Greek text should be used? The foregoing parallels are drawn from the twenty-eighth edition of Nestle-Aland's *Novum Testamentum Graece*, the standard eclectic Greek text in use today among scholars.[18] But it is certainly not the only Greek text of the Gospels. Earlier generations of scholars also regularly consulted the *Synopsis* of Albert Huck (now the Huck-Greeven *Synopsis*).[19] Table 9.7 shows the same passage in the Huck-Greeven *Synopsis*.

The two printed Greek texts are very close, but notice what happens with the last verb. In the Huck-Greeven *Synopsis*, we find triple agreement with the imperfect form ἠκολούθει. The editors have chosen to print the imperfect form in Matthew and Mark rather than the aorist ἠκολούθησεν that the editors of Nestle-Aland preferred. This particular choice for the text of Mark 2:14 is striking, because the Nestle-Aland text and apparatus give no indication of variation for this word in Mark 2:14. But as the apparatus for the Huck-Greeven *Synopsis* indicates, the imperfect form does occur in manuscripts of Mark, including one of earliest surviving Greek manuscripts of Mark, Codex Ephraemi Syri Rescriptus. Readers using only Nestle-Aland would never know that in one of the most ancient surviving manuscripts of Mark, this verse reads ἠκολούθει. Nor would they know that in the judgment of at least some scholars, that reading represents the earliest recoverable text, resulting in an instance of triple agreement here.

Of course, this is a very small difference, but it is just one of many that can be found by comparing different synopses.[20] Consulting different synopses provides a salutary reminder that even the Greek text itself is unstable. Over the last couple of decades, scholars have come to realize that the idea of a single, stable, original text is a highly problematic notion.[21] Ancient production and transmission of literature was a far cry from the publication of modern works mass-produced by printing presses. What modern readers might call "rough drafts" of pieces of literature sometimes circulated outside authors' control in antiquity. Works were revised and circulated multiple times in different forms. Using the surviving manuscripts to try to triangulate an earlier version of any single text is thus a hazardous undertaking. The difficulty is only compounded when we seek to compare *three* such reconstructed texts. The idea can be expressed in mathematical terms. If there is, say, 80 percent certainty that the eclectic

---

[18] I have elected to generate my own synopsis from the twenty-eighth edition of Nestle-Aland in order to make use of its revised critical apparatus. The most recent printing of Aland's *Synopsis Quattuor Evangeliorum* was made in 2001 and employs an older form of the apparatus that cites fewer witnesses.

[19] Huck and Greeven 1981. Since the newest edition of this synopsis appeared in 1981, it does not reflect the most recent papyrological discoveries, but in fact these discoveries have had very little impact on the printed Greek text in modern editions. See Petersen 1994, 138: "it is simply a fact that *nowhere* in the *entire* apparatus for the Gospels in Nestle-Aland^{27}/UBS^{4} is there a single instance where a reading supported *just* by the papyri, or by *just* the papyri and Patristic evidence has been adopted as the text."

[20] To judge from most studies of the Synoptic Problem, the comparison of multiple different Greek synopses does not seem to be a frequent practice. J. K. Elliott has, however, repeatedly stressed the importance of such work in a series of articles: Elliott 1980; 1986; 1992; and 1993. These essays have been reprinted in Elliott 2010, 385–467.

[21] On these points, see the seminal works of D. C. Parker (Parker 1997), Eldon J. Epp (Epp 1999), and Matthew D. C. Larsen (Larsen 2017, 2018).

Table 9.7 The calling of Matthew/Levi (Huck–Greeven *Synopsis*)

Matthew 9:9	Mark 2:14	Luke 5:27–28
Καὶ παράγων ὁ Ἰησοῦς ἐκεῖθεν εἶδεν ἄνθρωπον καθήμενον ἐπὶ τὸ τελώνιον, Μαθθαῖον λεγόμενον, καὶ λέγει αὐτῷ· ἀκολούθει μοι. καὶ ἀναστὰς **ἠκολούθει** αὐτῷ.	Καὶ παράγων εἶδεν Λευὶν τὸν τοῦ Ἀλφαίου καθήμενον ἐπὶ τὸ τελώνιον, καὶ λέγει αὐτῷ· ἀκολούθει μοι. καὶ ἀναστὰς **ἠκολούθει** αὐτῷ.	Καὶ μετὰ ταῦτα ἐξῆλθεν, καὶ ἐθεάσατο τελώνην ὀνόματι Λευὶν καθήμενον ἐπὶ τὸ τελώνιον, καὶ εἶπεν αὐτῷ· ἀκολούθει μοι. καὶ καταλιπὼν πάντα ἀναστὰς **ἠκολούθει** αὐτῷ.
omit εκειθεν ||p: ℵ* L φ ƒ547 σ71–692 *Lvg*¹ *Cb*¹ | λεγομ.] ονοματι ||Lk: S Eu *L*<k[e]> *Ss*[c]p Eu *C* ηκολουθησεν || 420p.22Lk511Jo137 *Rpl* Eu Or *LS*, j Eu *C*	παρ. + ο Ιησους ||Mt: 1604 φ230–346 σ27–179–267–945–1194–1223–1391–1402 F G H Γ Ω *al* + εκειθεν ||Mt: φ 174 1093 *Geo* | Λ.] Ιακωβον ||3₁₈: Θ–565 Φ<346–983> D Pho *Le*[k] abcff²r¹ vg¹ Δa Eᵃ | ηκολουθησεν || 1₁₈ Mt4₂₀.₂₂pJo1₃₇: 𝔓⁸⁸ *Rpl* L *S*[sc],j *C*	και² + παραγων ||p: φ/547 D | εθ.] ειδεν ||p: 544 σ945–990–1223 A D Πᶜ *pc* | τελ. ον. Λ.] Λευι τον του Αλφαιου ||Mk: D | ειπ.] λεγει ||Mt Mk: ℵ φ<124> D *pc* /50 /184 /1627 *Arm* | αναστ.] και αν.||p: 2145 | ηκολουθησεν || 5₁₁pJo1₃₇: *Rpl L*¹ *Ss*ᵛ[c]phj *C*

text of each of the three Synoptic Gospels represents the earliest recoverable text in a basically accurate fashion, then we would be only about 50 percent certain that any given set of parallels in the triple tradition all represent the earliest recoverable text (0.8 × 0.8 × 0.8 = 0.512).

How might we then proceed with comparison of the Synoptic Gospels? One way is to look at the parallels one manuscript at a time. Let us turn to the parallel texts for our simple example of the call of the tax collector in Codex Sinaiticus, a manuscript generally agreed to have been produced in the fourth century.[22] It is perhaps the earliest surviving version of a number of the synoptic parallels (table 9.8). Agreements across all three Gospels are in bold, agreements between Matthew and Mark against Luke are underlined, and agreements between Matthew and Luke against Mark are in italics.

To begin, I want to draw attention to the correction in the first line of Matthew 9:9. Notice that in the apparatus of the Nestle-Aland text, the reading attributed to the copyist of Sinaiticus (ℵ*) is simply ὁ Ἰησοῦς εἶδεν. The same is true of the Huck-Greeven

---

[22] The text is drawn from the transcription at codexsinaiticus.org. For a recent overview of the manuscript, see Parker 2010.

Table 9.8 The calling of Matthew/Levi (Codex Sinaiticus)

Matthew 9:9	Mark 2:14	Luke 5:27–28
και παραγων ο ις εκιθε(ν) ειδεν ανον	και παραγων ειδε(ν) λευει τον του αλφαιου	και μετα ταυτα εξηλθεν και εθεασα το τελωνην ονοματι λευειν
καθημενον	καθημενο(ν)	καθημενον
επι το τελωνιον	επι το τελωνιον	επι το τελωνιον
μαθθαιον λεγομενον κ(αι)	και	και
λεγι αυτω	λεγει αυτω	λεγει αυτω
ακολουθι μοι	ακολουθι μοι	ακολουθι μοι
και	και	και καταλιπων απαντας
αναστας ηκολουθει αυτω	αναστας ηκολουθησεν αυτω	αναστας ηκολουθησεν αυτω

FIGURE 9.7 Codex Sinaiticus, Matthew 9:9 (image: codexsinaiticus.org)

Synopsis. In both synopses, then, the "original" reading of Sinaiticus is said to lack the word ἐκεῖθεν. Indeed, if we look closely at the line in question, we can see that the word does appear to be a secondary addition, as it was inserted in a smaller script above the end of a line. (See the top line in fig. 9.7.)

But the question is: *When* was this addition inserted? In this instance, the correction is actually attributed to one of the same copyists who copied the text.[23] That is to say, the correction happened at or near the time of copying and may in fact be a *better* representation of the exemplar, the manuscript that was being copied, than the so-called original reading of the manuscript marked with the asterisk in the Nestle-Aland apparatus. Thus, even when one consults multiple different Greek synopses, the manuscripts themselves continue to present a more nuanced picture. One can begin to see some of the problems with the notion of what constitutes the "best" text of a passage.

---

[23] According to the website of the Codex Sinaiticus Project, a correction like this one (identified as "S1") is "a correction made in the production process, as part of the revision of the text after it had been copied, or a correction by the scribe in the copying process. These cannot always be distinguished" (http://www.codexsinaiticus.org/en/project/transcription_detailed.aspx).

Table 9.9 The calling of Matthew/Levi (Codex Bezae)

Matthew 9:9	Mark 2:14	Luke 5:27–28
και παραγων εκειθεν ο ιης ειδεν ανθρωπον καθημενον επι το τελωνιον Μαθθαιον λεγομενον και λεγει αυτω ακολουθει μοι και αναστας *ηκολουθει* αυτω	και παραγων ειδεν ϊακωβον *τον του αλφαιου* καθημενον επι το τελωνιον και λεγει αυτω ακολουθει μοι και αναστας ηκολουθησεν αυτω	και παραγων ειδεν λευει *τον του αλφαιου* καθημενον επι το τελωνιον και λεγει αυτω ακολουθει μοι και καταλιπων παντα αναστας *ηκολουθει* αυτω

To get a better sense of the levels of possible variation in the manuscripts, it is useful to examine the same passage in another manuscript, Codex Bezae, a diglot likely produced in the fifth century.[24] The Greek and Latin texts of the Gospels and Acts are presented on facing pages. If we look at the text of our passage in this manuscript, we find a number of differences (table 9.9). Agreements are formatted as in table 9.8, with the addition of bold-italics for agreements of Matthew and Luke against Mark.

Perhaps the most striking characteristic is that the name of the tax collector differs across the three Gospels—Matthaios, Iakobos, and Levi. On the other hand, notice how the framing material in the Gospel of Luke more nearly matches the framing of Matthew and Mark. The synoptic relations here differ in fairly substantive ways from the relations in Codex Sinaiticus.

Examining two actual manuscripts side by side demonstrates that it is not the case that the variant readings in the apparatus just intrinsically belong down at the bottom of the page below the main body of our critical editions. Any one of these readings may be the earliest recoverable text. Every variant represents an editor's decision, a choice made between multiple possible readings. And that leads to a central question: how exactly do editors choose between variants? They look at many factors. Editors have traditionally referred to the differing quality of the manuscripts in which readings appear. They consider the age of the manuscripts. They determine the degree to which a given variant matches an author's style. But in the Synoptic Gospels, there is an added issue that is crucial for our topic, a phenomenon called synoptic harmonization. In the opinion of most textual critics of the New Testament, the copyists who produced the surviving manuscripts often eliminated small differences among the Synoptic Gospels, usually assimilating Mark to Matthew or Luke. Kurt and Barbara Aland have phrased it this way:

> Particularly frequent are harmonizations between parallel texts with slight differences. In the Synoptic Gospels this could be quite unintentional. The scribe

[24] For details on the manuscript, see Parker 1992.

knew the text of the Gospels by heart, and when copying a pericope the details from a parallel passage would be suggested automatically. But again it could also be intentional, because it was impossible that sacred texts should not be in agreement. The text of the Gospel of Mark (which was the 'weakest,' i.e., used least extensively among the churches) was particularly susceptible to influence from parallel texts in the course of manuscript transmission" (Aland and Aland 1995, 290).

Textual critics are in general agreement on this point, and they stress its importance as a factor in establishing the earliest recoverable Greek text. Thus, Bruce Metzger and Bart Ehrman have argued that "since scribes would frequently bring divergent passages into harmony with one another, in parallel passages (whether involving quotations from the Old Testament or different accounts of the same event or narrative) *that reading is to be preferred which stands in verbal dissidence with the other*" (Metzger and Ehrman 2005, 303, emphasis mine).[25]

These claims are not without problems. The biggest is the assumption that one can know with certainty when any given reading actually is an instance of harmonization (rather than, say, simple coincidence). But I want to set aside such problems and examine the implications of these claims. If, as a general rule, editors of the Synoptic Gospels have opted to favor unparalleled readings as more original, then the eclectic text produced by such a process will provide a version of the Gospels with *the least possible* verbal agreement among the three Synoptic Gospels. What this means is that, even if editors do an excellent job, at least some instances of agreements among the Synoptic Gospels will probably be lost in the production of an eclectic Greek text.

It will be helpful to illustrate some of the complexity of the editorial decisions that translate manuscripts with variants into a readable critical synopsis. Take, for example, a saying of Jesus in the triple tradition, the Son of Man is the Lord of the Sabbath. Table 9.10 presents the saying as printed in the Huck-Greeven *Synopsis*.

Table 9.10 The son of man is Lord of the Sabbath (Huck–Greeven *Synopsis*)

Matthew 12:8	Mark 2:28	Luke 6:5
κύριος γάρ ἐστιν τοῦ σαββάτου ὁ υἱὸς τοῦ ἀνθρώπου.	ὥστε **κύριός ἐστιν** ὁ υἱὸς τοῦ ἀνθρώπου καὶ τοῦ σαββάτου.	ὅτι **κύριός ἐστιν** ὁ υἱὸς τοῦ ἀνθρώπου καὶ τοῦ σαββάτου.
του–αν.] ο–αν. και του σαβ. || p: 33–892 Φ-1604 λ1–1582 φ788 σ7–349–517–945–1424 **047** 157 *al* /48 /49 *Llz* vg¹–*txt* (*prm* και): *Rpl* (*pm*) Or *Lvl*¹[e](f vg¹) *S*¹(h) *C,f*		~ 6–10.5 *cf. ad* 4: D Mcn | *omit* οτι || Mk: 𝔓⁴ᵛ א* BW–579 700 λ<118>–1582–2193 σ954 157 872/32 *S*[sc]j *Arm Aeth* | ο–σαβ.] • του σαβ. ο υι. τ. αν. || Mt 𝔓⁴ א BW *S*[sc]pj *C*(*prm* και: sb¹)

[25] So also Elliott 1980, 231: "It is a useful and valuable rule of thumb in textual criticism to accept as the original text the variant which makes parallel passages more dissimilar, and to explain the secondary text as scribal harmonization."

Table 9.11 The son of man is Lord of the Sabbath (Nestle-Aland)

Matthew 12:8	Mark 2:28	Luke 6:5
κύριος γάρ **ἐστιν τοῦ σαββάτου ὁ υἱὸς τοῦ ἀνθρώπου.**	ὥστε⌐ κύριός ἐστιν ὁ υἱὸς τοῦ ἀνθρώπου καὶ τοῦ σαββάτου.	⸓καὶ ἔλεγεν αὐτοῖς· ⌜κύριός **ἐστιν ⸀τοῦ σαββάτου ὁ υἱὸς τοῦ ἀνθρώπου⸁.**
	27/28 ⌐ λεγω δε υμιν οτι το σαββατον δια τον ανθρωπον εκτισθη ωστε W (sy⁵) ¦ λεγω δε υμιν D (it)	⸓ vs 5 p. 10 D ¦ ⌜οτι ℵ² A D K L Γ Δ Θ Ψ f¹³ 33. 565. 892. 1241. 1424. 2542 𝔪 latt ¦ txt 𝔓⁴ᵛⁱᵈ ℵ* B W f¹ 579. 700 ¦ ⸀(p)ουιος του ανθρωπου και του σαββατου A D K L Γ Δ Θ Ψ f¹·¹³ 33. 579. 700. 892. 1424. 2542 𝔪 lat syʰ sa boᵖᵗ; Mcionᴱ ¦ txt ℵ B W 1241 syᵖ boᵖᵗ

In Huck-Greeven we find agreement between Mark and Luke against Matthew in terms of the order of words (marked in bold in table 9.10), although substantive variants are listed for both Matthew and Luke. When we turn to the Nestle-Aland parallels, however, we encounter a different situation (table 9.11).

The editors of Nestle-Aland have produced exact verbal agreement between Matthew and Luke against Mark (highlighted in bold in table 9.11) by choosing to print a different text of Luke 6:5. The reasoning for choosing to print this Lukan text is provided by Bruce Metzger: "It is rather more probable that copyists inserted καί before τοῦ σαββάτου, thus giving more point to the saying (and assimilating it to the parallel in Mk 2:28), than that καί should have been deleted from early representatives of several text-types. The non-Markan word order is likewise to be preferred" (Metzger 1994, 117). In this instance, the Nestle-Aland text has the virtue of lining up precisely with some of the earliest surviving manuscripts across all three Gospels. Codex Vaticanus, for instance, a codex of the full Bible likely produced in the fourth century, supports the Nestle-Aland reading for each of the Gospels in this passage, as does Codex Sinaiticus. It is, however, surprising that the Nestle-Aland apparatus for these verses lacks any indication of variation in the manuscripts of Matthew. As noted above, the Huck-Greeven *Synopsis* apparatus for this passage reports that some later manuscripts preserve an alternative reading in Matthew that matches the text of Mark. This is in addition to the fairly strong support for the Markan reading among manuscripts of Luke.[26] Thus, if the editors of the Nestle-Aland edition have in fact correctly identified the earliest recoverable reading for all three Gospels, then it is interesting that so many manuscripts of both Matthew and Luke have been *independently*

---

[26] The apparent stability of the saying in Greek manuscripts of Mark is impressive, although it is interesting to note that in the Old Latin Codex Vercellensis the saying in Mark 2:28 is followed directly by a version of Mark 3:21 ("et cum audissent qui ab eo exierunt detinere eum dicebant enim quia extitit mente").

harmonized *to the text of Mark* in this passage, especially given the Alands' characterization of Mark as the "weakest" of the three Gospels when it comes to harmonization.

For an even more striking example of the problem of assimilation and the creation of a critical text, we can look at the end of Matthew 21. Table 9.12 presents the

Table 9.12 The stone that the builders rejected (Nestle–Aland)

Matthew 21:42–46	Mark 12:10–12	Luke 20:17–19
42 οὐδέποτε ἀνέγνωτε ἐν ταῖς γραφαῖς· **λίθον ὃν ἀπεδοκίμασαν οἱ οἰκοδομοῦντες, οὗτος ἐγενήθη εἰς κεφαλὴν γωνίας**· παρὰ κυρίου ἐγένετο αὕτη καὶ ἔστιν θαυμαστὴ ἐν ὀφθαλμοῖς ⌜ἡμῶν⌝; 43 διὰ τοῦτο λέγω ὑμῖν °ὅτι ἀρθήσεται ἀφ' ὑμῶν ἡ βασιλεία τοῦ θεοῦ καὶ δοθήσεται ἔθνει ποιοῦντι τοὺς καρποὺς αὐτῆς. 44 ⌐[καὶ *ὁ πεσὼν ἐπὶ τὸν λίθον τοῦτον συνθλασθήσεται· ἐφ' ὃν δ' ἂν πέσῃ λικμήσει αὐτόν.*]⌐ 45 ⌜Καὶ ἀκούσαντες⌝ οἱ ἀρχιερεῖς καὶ οἱ Φαρισαῖοι τὰς παραβολὰς αὐτοῦ ἔγνωσαν ὅτι περὶ αὐτῶν λέγει· 46 **καὶ** ζητοῦντες αὐτὸν κρατῆσαι **ἐφοβήθησαν** τοὺς ὄχλους, ⌜ἐπεὶ ⌜εἰς προφήτην αὐτὸν εἶχον.	10 Οὐδὲ τὴν γραφὴν ταύτην ἀνέγνωτε· **λίθον ὃν ἀπεδοκίμασαν οἱ οἰκοδομοῦντες, οὗτος ἐγενήθη εἰς κεφαλὴν γωνίας**· 11 παρὰ κυρίου ἐγένετο αὕτη καὶ ἔστιν θαυμαστὴ ἐν ὀφθαλμοῖς ἡμῶν; 12 **Καὶ** ἐζήτουν αὐτὸν κρατῆσαι, καὶ **ἐφοβήθησαν** τὸν ὄχλον, ἔγνωσαν γὰρ ὅτι πρὸς αὐτοὺς τὴν παραβολὴν εἶπεν. ⌐καὶ ἀφέντες αὐτὸν ἀπῆλθον.⌐	17 τί οὖν ἐστιν τὸ γεγραμμένον τοῦτο· **λίθον ὃν ἀπεδοκίμασαν οἱ οἰκοδομοῦντες, οὗτος ἐγενήθη εἰς κεφαλὴν γωνίας**; 18 πᾶς *ὁ πεσὼν ἐπ' ἐκεῖνον τὸν λίθον συνθλασθήσεται· ἐφ' ὃν δ' ἂν πέσῃ, λικμήσει αὐτόν.* 19 **Καὶ** ἐζήτησαν ⌜οἱ γραμματεῖς καὶ οἱ ἀρχιερεῖς⌝ ἐπιβαλεῖν ἐπ' αὐτὸν τὰς χεῖρας ἐν αὐτῇ τῇ ὥρᾳ καὶ **ἐφοβήθησαν** τὸν λαόν, ἔγνωσαν γὰρ ὅτι πρὸς αὐτοὺς ⌜εἶπεν τὴν παραβολὴν ταύτην⌝.

(continued)

Table 9.12 Continued		
Matthew 21:42-46	Mark 12:10-12	Luke 20:17-19
42 ⌐ υμων D* f¹·¹³ 1424 sa mae 43 ° ℵ B* Θ 565. 700. 892 ¦ txt B² C D K L W Z Δ 0102 f¹·¹³ 33. 579. 1241. 1424. /844 m; Ir^lat 44 □ D 33 it sy^s; Or Eus^syr ¦ txt ℵ B C K L W Z Δ (– και Θ) 0102 f¹·¹³ 565. 579. 700. 892. 1241. 1424. /844 m lat sy^c.p.h co 45 ⌐ ακουσαντες δε ℵ L Z 33. 892 aur sa bo ¦ txt B C D K W Δ Θ 0102 f¹·¹³ 565. 579. 700. 1241. 1424. /844 m lat sy^p.h mae 46 ⌐ επειδη C K W Δ 0102 f¹³ 565. 579. 700. 1241. 1424. /844 m ¦ txt ℵ B D L Θ f¹ 33. 892 ⌐ ως C D K W Δ 0102 f¹³ 33. 565. 579. 700. 892. 1241. 1424. /844 m sy co ¦ txt ℵ B L Θ f¹	12 □ W	19 ⌐ 4 5 3 1 2 ℵ D N Γ Δ Ψ 565. 579. 700. 892. 1241. 1424 m lat sy^s.c.p sa ¦ οι γραμματεις και οι Φαρισαιοι C ¦ txt A B K L W Θ f¹·¹³ 33. 2542 e sy^h bo	⌐ 2-4 1 A C K N W Γ Δ Θ Ψ f¹ 33. 565. 700. 1241. 1424 m sy^h ¦ 2 3 1 579 ¦ ειρηκεν την παραβολην αυτην D ¦ txt ℵ B L f¹³ 892. 2542 latt

Nestle-Aland text for that portion of Matthew along with the parallel passages in Mark and Luke.

In all three versions, a citation of Psalm 118 is followed by a saying of Jesus with nearly a full sentence of material common to Matthew and Luke but absent in Mark. But note verse 44 in Matthew. It is annotated with a small square, the Nestle-Aland symbol indicating omitted text. If we look down in the apparatus for verse 44, we can see that this verse is indeed lacking in a very small group of witnesses. But the editors have decided to place verse 44 in brackets, indicating that "the authenticity of the text enclosed in brackets is dubious." In fact, the editors regarded this passage not just as dubious but as definitely a later addition to the text of Matthew, as Metzger explained in his commentary:

> Many modern scholars regard the verse as an early interpolation (from Lk 20:18) into most manuscripts of Matthew. On the other hand, however, the words are not the same, and a more appropriate place for its insertion would have been after ver. 42. Its omission can perhaps be accounted for when the eye of the copyist passed from αὐτῆς (ver. 43) to αὐτόν. *While considering the verse to be an accretion to the text, yet because of the antiquity of the reading and its importance in the textual tradition, the Committee decided to retain it in the text, enclosed within square brackets.* (Metzger 1994, 47, my emphasis)

The editors acknowledged that the text was "an accretion," they nevertheless opted to print it (in brackets) because of its "importance in the textual tradition." If we turn to the Huck-Greeven *Synopsis*, we find that the verse is simply missing entirely from their text.

These are interesting decisions. If we look at the evidence in the Nestle-Aland apparatus, we find that the manuscripts generally regarded as the earliest and most reliable contain the verse. It is present in Codex Vaticanus, Codex Sinaiticus, and Codex Ephraemi Syri Rescriptus, not to mention the Coptic versions and what are usually considered as the most important minuscules. On the other hand the small group of witnesses lacking the verse includes Codex Bezae and the Old Latin.[27] This passage thus provides a vivid example of how editorial decisions can lead to, depending on one's perspective, the disappearance of a fairly major agreement of Matthew and Luke against Mark that is present in many of the earliest surviving manuscripts, or the creation of such an agreement that is absent in some important witnesses.

The significance of such textual decisions divides scholars of the Synoptic Problem, and they generally treat such matters, if at all, as an afterthought.[28] Yet these kinds of editorial decisions are foundational to the whole enterprise of the Synoptic Problem. Very small differences of word choice or word order in the critical text that are sometimes ignored by exegetes take on special significance with reference to the Synoptic Problem because it is exactly questions of precise diction and word order that allow scholars to argue for or against, say, the Two-Source Hypothesis or the Farrer Hypothesis. That the creators of Matthew and Luke each relied on a manuscript (or manuscripts?) of Mark still seems like a safe conclusion. But in light of the realities of manuscript variation and transmission, deciding firmly between the Two-Source Hypothesis and the Farrer Hypothesis becomes more challenging.[29]

Conclusions

Where, then, do these observations leave us? It is sobering to acknowledge the sheer complexity of trying to balance the textual criticism of the individual Synoptic Gospels with the determination of synoptic relationships. Without a set of stable texts to compare, how can this kind of work take place responsibly?[30] One thing that seems

---

[27] It has been suggested that a more recently published papyrus from Oxyrhynchus, P.Oxy. 64.4404 (P104), supports the omission of verse 44. For the fullest discussion of the matter, see Lanier 2016 and the literature cited there. This papyrus is sometimes assigned to a date as early as the second century, so it is regarded by some as an especially important witness. The text of the papyrus, however, is highly uncertain and thus of limited usefulness in this discussion. And in any event, the date of this papyrus relies solely on paleographic evidence and is therefore subject to doubt. On the scant evidence used to establish the second-century date for P.Oxy. 64.4404, see Nongbri 2018, 245.

[28] For contrasting views, see Kloppenborg Verbin 2000, 36, and Goodacre 2002, 162.

[29] It does appear that the more widely held Two-Source Hypothesis, which requires nonagreement of Matthew and Luke against Mark, may be especially liable to scrutiny in light of editors' preferences for favoring dissimilar readings in parallel passages.

[30] A good example of a piece of scholarship that really wrestles with the problem productively is Holmes 1990.

clear is that traditional printed Greek synopses, while necessary for doing work on the Synoptic Problem, are not adequate for carrying out such work seriously. New tools are needed. At minimum, a critical parallel Gospel text with fuller citation of witnesses is required. Fortunately, the producers of the *editio critica maior* have produced a prototype of this kind of complex synopsis that is highly promising.[31] But more innovative tools will be helpful as well: the recently published synopsis of Matthew, Mark, and Luke with the texts of Codex Vaticanus and Codex Bezae on facing pages offers one example of a useful set of parallels that recenters our focus on the manuscripts.[32]

Finally, a work like the Vaticanus-Bezae parallels also helpfully reminds us that the earliest surviving manuscripts of the Synoptic Gospels that preserve extensive parallel passages date to *the fourth and fifth centuries*, meaning that the critical synopses are based on manuscripts that are the result of at least *two centuries* of textual transmission and intermingling.[33] What we can know with confidence about the text(s) of the Gospels in the period before the fourth century is, I think, more limited than we have sometimes imagined. Conflicting trends in composition and transmission in those prior centuries pull in different directions. The creative rewriting of Mark by Matthew and Luke in the first or second century suggests a willingness to freely change, cut, and expand "Gospel" material.[34] But developments in the second and third centuries, such as the emerging argument for a four-Gospel canon and the production of harmonies of the Gospels, suggest an impulse toward harmonization in the period before the earliest surviving manuscripts.[35] This should probably make us humble about any and all conclusions we make about issues of "dependence" among the Synoptic Gospels.

References

Aland, Kurt. 1997. *Synopsis quattuor evangeliorum*. 15th ed. Stuttgart: Deutsche Bibelgesellschaft.

Aland, Kurt, and Barbara Aland. 1995. *The Text of the New Testament: An Introduction to the Critical Editions and to the Theory and Practice of Modern Textual Criticism*. 2nd ed. Translated by Erroll F. Rhodes. Grand Rapids: Eerdmans.

Elliott, J. K. 1980. "Textual Criticism, Assimilation, and the Synoptic Gospels." *New Testament Studies* 26: 231–42.

Elliott, J. K. 1986. "An Examination of the Text and Apparatus of Three Recent Greek Synopses." *New Testament Studies* 32: 557–82.

---

[31] Strutwolf and Wachtel 2011.

[32] Read-Heimerdinger and Rius-Camps 2014. One could also imagine a parallel text in the form of Reuben Swanson's New Testament Greek Manuscripts series.

[33] While one fairly extensive manuscript of the Synoptic Gospels is sometimes assigned to the third century (the Chester Beatty codex of the Gospels and Acts, P45), the number of parallel passages preserved is limited, and the dating of the codex to the third rather than the fourth century may be overly optimistic; see Nongbri 2018, 134–38.

[34] On this point, see the fascinating work of Larsen (2018).

[35] See further Parker 1997, 120–21.

Elliott, J. K. 1992. "Printed Editions of Greek Synopses and Their Influence on the Synoptic Problem." In *The Four Gospels 1992: Festschrift for Frans Neirynck*, edited by F. van Segbroeck et al., 337–357. Leuven: Leuven University Press.

Elliott, J. K. 1993. "Resolving the Synoptic Problem Using the Text of Printed Greek Synopses." *Filología Neotestamentaria* 11: 51–58.

Elliott, J. K. 2010. *New Testament Textual Criticism: The Application of Thoroughgoing Principles: Essays on Manuscripts and Textual Variation*. Leiden: Brill.

Epp, Eldon J. 1999. "The Multivalence of the Term 'Original Text' in New Testament Textual Criticism." *Harvard Theological Review* 92: 245–81.

Goodacre, Mark S. 2001. *The Synoptic Problem: A Way through the Maze*. London: Continuum.

Goodacre, Mark S. 2002. *The Case against Q: Studies in Markan Priority and the Synoptic Problem*. Harrisburg: Trinity Press International.

Goodacre, Mark S. 2018. "Taking Our Leave of Mark-Q Overlaps: Major Agreements and the Farrer Theory." In *Gospel Interpretation and the Q Hypothesis*, edited by Mogens Müller and Heike Omerzu, 201–22. Library of New Testament Studies. London: Bloomsbury.

Head, Peter M. 2011. "Textual Criticism and the Synoptic Problem." In *New Studies in the Synoptic Problem, Oxford Conference, April 2008: Essays in Honour of Christopher M. Tuckett*, edited by Paul Foster et al., 115–56. Leuven: Peeters.

Holmes, Michael W. 1990. "The Text of the Matthean Divorce Passages: A Comment on the Appeal to Harmonization in Textual Decisions." *Journal of Biblical Literature* 109: 651–64.

Holmes, Michael W. 2013. "From 'Original Text' to 'Initial Text': The Traditional Goal of New Testament Textual Criticism in Contemporary Discussion." In *The Text of the New Testament in Contemporary Research: Essays on the Status Quaestionis*, 2nd ed., edited by Bart D. Ehrman and Michael W. Holmes, 637–88. Leiden: Brill.

Honoré, A. M. 1968. "A Statistical Study of the Synoptic Problem." *Novum Testamentum* 10: 95–140.

Huck, Albert, and Heinrich Greeven. 1981. *Synopsis of the First Three Gospels with the Addition of the Johannine Parallels*. 13th ed. Tübingen: Mohr Siebeck.

Kloppenborg Verbin, John S. 2000. *Excavating Q: The History and Setting of the Sayings Gospel*. Minneapolis: Fortress Press.

Lanier, Gregory R. 2016. "A Case for the Assimilation of Matthew 21:44 to the Lukan 'Crushing Stone' (20:18), with Special Reference to P104." *TC: A Journal of Biblical Textual Criticism* 21. http://jbtc.org/v21/TC-2016-Lanier.pdf.

Larsen, Matthew D. C. 2017. "Accidental Publication, Unfinished Texts and the Traditional Goals of New Testament Textual Criticism." *Journal for the Study of the New Testament* 39: 362–87.

Larsen, Matthew D. C. 2018. *Gospels before the Book*. New York: Oxford University Press.

Metzger, Bruce M. 1994. *A Textual Commentary on the Greek New Testament*. 2nd ed. London: United Bible Societies.

Metzger, Bruce M., and Bart D. Ehrman. 2005. *The Text of the New Testament: Its Transmission, Corruption, and Restoration*. 4th ed. New York: Oxford University Press.

Nongbri, Brent. 2018. *God's Library: The Archaeology of the Earliest Christian Manuscripts*. New Haven: Yale University Press.

Pardee, Cambry G. 2019. *Scribal Harmonization in the Synoptic Gospels*. Leiden: Brill.

Parker, D. C. 1992. *Codex Bezae: An Early Christian Manuscript and Its Text*. Cambridge: Cambridge University Press.

Parker, D. C. 1997. *The Living Text of the Gospels*. Cambridge: Cambridge University Press.

Parker, D. C. 2010. *Codex Sinaiticus: The Story of the World's Oldest Bible.* Peabody, MA: Hendrickson.

Petersen, William L. 1994. "What Text Can New Testament Textual Criticism Ultimately Reach?" In *New Testament Textual Criticism, Exegesis, and Early Church History: A Discussion of Methods*, edited by Barbara Aland and Joël Delobel, 136–52. Kampen: Kok Pharos.

Read-Heimerdinger, Jenny, and Josep Rius-Camps. 2014. *A Gospel Synopsis of the Greek Text of Matthew, Mark, and Luke: A Comparison of Codex Bezae and Codex Vaticanus.* Leiden: Brill.

Sanders, E. P. 1973. "The Overlaps of Mark and Q and the Synoptic Problem." *New Testament Studies* 19: 453–65.

Sanders, E. P., and Margaret Davies. 1989. *Studying the Synoptic Gospels.* London: SCM.

Streeter, Burnett Hillman. 1930. *The Four Gospels: A Study of Origins.* Rev. ed. London: MacMillan.

Strutwolf, Holger, and Klaus Wachtel. 2011. *Novum Testamentum Graecum Editio Critica Maior: Parallel Pericopes.* Stuttgart: Deutsche Bibelgesellschaft.

Throckmorton, Burton H., Jr. 1992. *Gospel Parallels: A Comparison of the Synoptic Gospels.* 5th ed. Nashville: Thomas Nelson.

Watson, Francis. 2013. *Gospel Writing: A Canonical Perspective.* Grand Rapids: Eerdmans.

CHAPTER 10

THE PUBLICATION OF THE SYNOPTICS AND THE PROBLEM OF DATING

MATTHEW LARSEN

BUILDING BLOCKS OF SYNOPTIC GOSPEL STUDIES

CRITICAL scholarship on the Synoptic Gospels, from its beginnings in the eighteenth century up through the present, operates with a few fundamental assumptions that serve as building blocks for constructing knowledge about textualized gospel tradition, its publication, and dependence.[1] These building blocks are the ideas of author, book, and publication. These ideas hang together to form a cohesive framework: that of an author publishing a finished book. In the scenarios of the Synoptic Gospels, the author is an evangelist. The book is called a Gospel. Consequently, a Gospel is a book that an author writes, finishes, and "publishes" at a concrete point that—anachronistically speaking—could be geo-tagged and time-stamped. These building blocks constitute the primary material from which the architecture of the field of Synoptic Gospels has been built. In this chapter, I consider each of these assumptive building blocks individually.

Gospels as Authored Texts

The assumption of a historical personage as an author-figure is so fundamental to the field of Synoptic studies, so deeply entrenched within centuries of scholarship, and so ubiquitously and subconsciously deployed that it is unclear what it would look like to

---

[1] On the eighteenth century and the beginnings of the New Testament, see Baird 1992, xix–30.

marshal evidence demonstrating its history and influence. Nevertheless, I can point to a couple of key frames. With the dawn of the Enlightenment, critical scholars began to study "the Bible" just like any other piece of literature. Enlightenment thinkers were reacting historically to the religious idea that the Christian scriptures were a single book authored by the Christian God. In reaction to the claim of the divine authorship, a binary alternative was taken for granted: the Gospels were not written by a deity but by human authors. Thus, the idea still ever-present within biblical studies was born; namely, that the Gospels had real, historical human authors, even if the names of such authors now attached to the traditions were not taken to be correct.

To cite a scholar deploying the idea of Gospels as produced by authors is unproductive. In fact, the current "best practices" of the field even restrict scholars from thinking outside of the framework of the author-figure. For instance, the *SBL Handbook of Style* is the authoritative guide to citation in the field of biblical studies. It dictates that when someone cites from one of the textualized traditions that is now called the Gospel according to [Name], one simply cites "Name," even though the titles were added later and usually follow the format of "According to [Name]" (Collines, Buller, and Kutsko 2014). According to the *SBL Handbook of Style*, not evoking the idea of the author is forbidden when discussing the Gospels.

The subtle work done by this elision—[Gospel] according to [Name] > Gospel of [Name] > Name—conflates the textual tradition, with its pluriform complexities and authorial subtleties, with the figure of an author, thereby reifying the idea of an author and foreclosing other possibilities of textual production. Similar to the effect of drawing the gas giants of Jupiter or Uranus, which have no terra firma surface on which one could walk, on a two-dimensional children's map of the solar system, the textualized gospel traditions—with all their multiform, fluid constellations—are flattened and bounded into books that human authors wrote.

Gospels as Books

The current scholarly apparatus inherits and reproduces the assumption of Gospels as books. At the beginnings of the critical study of the Gospels was the need to establish "the original text" of each Gospel. The production of critical editions began with the assumption of the Gospels according to Matthew, Mark, Luke, and John as separate books, and with each new printing extended the idea further. When a critical edition ends the Gospel according to Matthew on one page and begins the Gospel according to Mark on the next, it intimates concrete physical and visual "evidence" that corroborates the idea that gospels are discrete books. It imports assumptions about boundedness, discreteness, and wholeness that may prove unsupported or inappropriate, especially given the fragmentary nature of the earliest gospel manuscripts.

For instance, lost in the scandal around the papyrus formerly known as "First Century Mark" (now 𝔓137 or *P.Oxy.* LXXXIII.5345) was the fact that the papyrus contains only a handful of fragmentary lines from a few verses (Mark 1:7–9, 16–18) in a textual tradition that is now called the Gospel according to Mark. It is misleading to assert that the 4.4 x 4 cm fragment is in fact a "copy of Mark's Gospel" (Obbink and Colomo 2018, 5); to make this assertion is a subtle sleight of hand that demonstrates the deeply ingrained assumptions about the gospel traditions within the field. The seemingly obvious move of calling it a "copy of Mark's Gospel" smuggles in the assumption that it is a copy of a book, that book is a Gospel, and that Gospel was produced by an author eponymously called Mark, when in reality the artifact is a tiny fragment of only a handful of words.

Gospels as Published

While scholars do not always use the language of "publication" or refer to Gospels as "published," the logic is ubiquitous in modern scholarship on the Gospels. It is taken as perfunctory that, before commentators can comment historically on a passage, they must first locate when, where, and to whom a Gospel was written. In so doing, the commentator treats the Gospel as a literary product (rather than a complex process). The point of locating when the literary product came to an end is to allow the scholar to situate the text historically between author and audience.

To see how the idea of publication or finishing a book works in the scholarship, it is instructive to consider a famous debate about whether the Gospels were written "for all Christians" or for particular communities. Richard Bauckham put forth the idea that, contra the practices of certain redaction critics who want to see each Gospel as a window into a particular early Jesus-believing community, the canonical Gospels were written with the goal of circulating widely among different Christian communities, not for a single, specific audience (1998, 9–48). Margaret M. Mitchell published a response to Bauckham's theory, showing how early Christian writers imagined Gospels as published for specific audiences, thus challenging the view that Gospels were "for all Christians" (2005, 36–79). Assumed in either position, however, is a moment of publication in which a Gospel-book was presented as a finished product to a public, even if the public was a local and specific one. Implied is that author's intention and the finished product are linked, which allows the commentator to triangulate historically and thus "discover" the meaning of the book.

For the past few decades, Harry Y. Gamble's *Books and Readers in the Early Church* has remained the most lengthy and authoritative discussion of publication and early Christian scriptures. He devotes an entire chapter to the publication and circulation of early Christian writings (1995, 82–143). He claims that the Gospels circulated widely at an early stage and speculates that "broader dissemination in Christian circles, if not beyond, must have been intended from the outset" (1995, 102). Here Gamble seems to use the term "dissemination" to refer to the ancient publication practice of distributing a text among a nonspecific, anonymous public readership.[2]

---

[2] See also Alexander 1998.

Reference to multiple editions of the Gospels have been common among scholars, yet even in the midst of such discussion, a particular moment of publication when the product was finished has usually been given priority. The more complex processual aspects of the textual growth are quickly whisked away in favor of a singular and self-contained moment of "actual publication" (e.g. Gamble 1995, 286). At issue here is the definitive version of the book and the intention of the author. One wonders, however: what happens when an ancient authors' works are made public without their consent or when they purposely issue multiple different versions at different times for authorized circulation, as is known frequently to have happened?

The Architecture of Synoptic Studies

The architecture of the field of Synoptic Gospel studies has a framework built from the assumptive building blocks of author, book, and publication. While many different and important methods have emerged in the last few decades, the approaches of source, redaction, and text criticism remain foundational. Each is constituted from ideas of author, book, and publication as weight-bearing components of its approach. While each approach of source, redaction, and text criticism has recent proponents pushing in new and productive directions, the history of each is difficult to imagine without the presumption of authors publishing books.[3]

Source Criticism of the Synoptic Gospels

Source criticism of the Synoptic Gospels is a centuries-old endeavor, heavily burdened with scholarly publications. Arguably, the question of how the canonical Gospels relate literarily to each other is as old as Augustine of Hippo in the fifth century (see Watson 2013, 13–61). The so-called Synoptic Problem asked which Gospel "used" which as a source. While efforts have been made recently move away from anachronistic concepts like books made by authors, it would be difficult to account for the history of the "Synoptic Problem" apart from first assuming that each Gospel as a discrete literary

---

[3] For source criticism, see, for example, Kirk 2016. For redaction criticism, see Doole 2013. For text criticism, see Knust 2008; Knust and Wasserman 2019; Luijendijk 2008; Lin 2016; Epp 1999; 2007; Ehrman 1996.

unit produced by different author-figures. (See also the issues raised by Nongbri, chapter 9 here.)

Redaction Criticism of the Synoptic Gospels

The realm of investigation where the ascendancy of the author is perhaps clearest is redaction criticism. As the Gospels came to be regarded as pieces of literature, those who produced the Gospels came to be literary producers—which is to say, authors. While the form critics interrogated the way the collectors of gospel tradition gather together prior oral proclamations, the redaction critics delineated how the author—not a collector or editor—produced a piece of literature (Dibelius 1935, 59). Norman Perrin in his 1969 book *What Is Redaction Criticism?* defined redaction criticism as "studying the theological motivation of an author as this is revealed in the collection, arrangement, editing, and modification of tradition material, and in the composition of new material or the creation of new forms within the traditions of early Christianity" (1969, 1–2). The "prime requisite" is the existence of an author and the ability to discern the discrete textual sources used by the author, who in turn is producing his own separate piece of literature (see Perrin 1969, 1–20).

Text Criticism of the Synoptic Gospels

As traditionally practiced over the last few centuries, text criticism of the Synoptic Gospels has set its goal as recovering the "original" text of the individual Synoptic Gospels. The famous example of this goal is the title of Westcott and Hort's 1881 book *The New Testament in the Original Greek*. The notion that scholars can recover the original Greek, however, has been abandoned by many, who now prefer to use the term "initial text," which David Parker defines as "the text from which the readings in the extant manuscripts are genealogically descended" (2011, 15).[4] Nonetheless, the idea of books (Gospels) produced by authors (evangelists) remains a fundamental assumption of text criticism of the Synoptic Gospels. Another way to get at this idea is to ask: what makes text criticism not redaction criticism? Both are fundamentally about tracking textual change. Bluntly summarized, redaction criticism tracks changes made by authors leading up to the finished book; text criticism tracks changes made by scribes to the text in the subsequent transmission of the finished literary product (see Larsen 2017, 362–87). If the difference between a scribe and an author is removed, the traditional goal of textual criticism becomes a chimera, and other approaches to textual scholarship of the Gospels must be used.

---

[4] See also Mink, 2004, 25.

Problems with the Current Architecture of the Field of Synoptic Studies

The discreteness of these Gospels, their finished literary qualities, and their connections with authors are weight-bearing presuppositions in the architecture of Synoptic studies. Yet there are problems with applying all three of these ideas to gospel tradition prior to the end of the second century. Removing such assumptions has implications concerning—among other things—the publication and dependence of the Synoptic Gospels.

Textual Unfinishedness in Ancient Writing Practices

Occasionally the idea of publication is described explicitly in Synoptic studies. Harry Gamble offers this view of publication in antiquity in *Books and Readers in the Early Church*:

> authors who wished to make their work public had several ways to do so. They might make or have made at their own expense, several copies of a draft, which they would distribute to friends. This alone did not amount to publication but constituted what we might think of as a referee procedure: the author expected a private reading and response from the recipients, with a view to revising and improving the work. Alternatively, they might invite a small group of friends to a reading (*recitatio*), at which the work, or parts of it, would be read by the author and discussed by the gathered company. In these ways an author made his work known, but only to a small and sympathetic circle of acquaintances. The work remained essentially private, under the author's direct control, and was still subject to revision.
>
> Only after the author had tentatively proffered a composition and then revised it would he or she make it available to a larger audience. Literature (as distinct from technical, scholarly work), and above all poetry, was traditionally made public not by multiplying and distributing copies of the text, but in oral performance, a practice that continued into the first century. (1995, 83–84)

I identify a few integral assumptions in Gamble's framework: (1) the documents in question are "literature"; (2) the author's control and intention both predicate and authorize the publication moment; (3) the publication moment is a singular and contained event in time; (4) the official version of the text is the one that the author decides to "proffer" to public readership; and (5) the published and authorized piece of literature, consequently, only exists in one version. Each of these assumptions is uncertain when it comes to the Synoptic Gospels.

Unfinished or less authored para- (or pre-) literary texts (ὑπομνήματα in Greek; *commentarii* in Latin) were common in ancient Greek, Roman, Jewish, and Christian contexts—probably even more common than "literature" (Larsen 2018b, 11–36). While written documents were everywhere, not nearly all of them were finished pieces of literature. Moreover, the phenomena of accidental publication, postpublication revision, and multiple authorized versions of the same work trouble the connection between the author's intention, a singular and contained text, and the public life of a textual tradition. There was a good deal of potential for slippage between the authorial intent and a singular publication moment. In addition, it was not uncommon for someone (whether the same writer or someone else) to create and release (intentionally or unintentionally) multiple versions of the same work. The Greek and Hebrew editions of Jeremiah or Esther, Ovid's *Amores*, Apollonius of Perge's *Conics*, Tertullian's *Against Marcion*, and Augustine's *On the Trinity* come immediately to mind. It is hardly clear that the Gospels were produced or read from the beginning as formal pieces of literature, and it is clear that they were not initially treated as books published by authors (see Larsen 2018b, 37–78; 79–120).

Earliest Evidence of Gospels as Books Published by Authors

While scholars working on the Synoptic Gospels routinely operate with the textual metaphor of books published by authors to describe textualized gospel tradition, the earliest evidence of someone using such ideas in relation to the Gospels come from Irenaeus of Lyons, writing around 190 CE.[5] In *Against Heresies* 3.1.1, Irenaeus details when, where, by whom, and for whom his four canonical Gospels were written.[6] Thus, the earliest evidence for the Gospels as discrete, published books produced by different authors does not come until the end of the second century CE—roughly a century after their supposed "publication." Throughout the first several centuries of the Common Era, there were other ways of thinking about gospel textuality, ways of thinking which continued to persist well into the fourth and fifth centuries (see

---

[5] I distinguish "books published by authors" from "books," and from the identification of gospel tradition as recorded in βιβλία, as opposed to a family of terms like ὑπομνήματα, ἀπομνημονεύματα, etc. Gospel tradition is marked as βιβλία/βίβλοι. Matt 1:1 refers to the textual tradition we have now come to call the Gospel according to Matthew as a βίβλος, which indicates how the producer(s) of the Gospel according to Matthew understood the gospel tradition they were producing. The words βίβλος/βιβλίον must not immediately be taken to mean "book" in a modern sense. The words can also refer to a piece of papyrus, a scroll, a tablet, a paper, or such documents. For example, the only other use of a βιβλ* word in the Gospel according to Matthew comes in Matt 19:7, where the text refers to a "certificate of divorce" (βιβλίον ἀποστασίου): a legal document and not a "book." If Matt 19:7 is any indication of the meaning of βίβλος in Matt 1:1, it is wrong to read the sense of "book" into the term.

[6] For a fuller discussion of Irenaeus, see Larsen 2018b, 93–96.

Larsen and Letteney 2019; Larsen 2018b, 96–98; 150–51). In this sense, it is—strictly speaking—anachronistic to speak of Gospels as books published by authors prior to the end of the second century.

Without the ideas of author, book, and publication, the questions about source, redaction, and text criticism of the Synoptic Gospels change significantly from the way they have historically been pursued. The historically prevailing architecture of the field of Synoptic studies is ill-equipped to describe the fluid, mushrooming constellations of textualized gospel traditions prior to the end of the second century. Approaching textualized gospel tradition as open, unfinished, multiform, and processual textual tradition raises problems for thinking about the Gospels' publication and dependence, as such topics have been traditionally conceived.

Variance, (In)stability, and the Problem of Synoptic Dependence

The state of the text in the second century of what became the New Testament has long been a matter of debate, in which the text of the Synoptic Gospels has played a central role. Scholars like Helmet Koester and William L. Petersen have made the case that the text of the Gospels in the second century was in flux (Koester 1989, 19–37; Petersen 2002, 33–65). They take as evidence the quotations of gospel tradition from second-century writers. On a more theoretical level, Eldon Epp argues that the Gospels would not have been issued in a definitive form and David Parker has written that Gospels were not the kinds of texts that would have had "originals" (Epp 1999, 245–81; Parker 1997, 7). On the other hand scholars like Charles Hill and Larry Hurtado have argued that the fluidity seen in the citation of gospel tradition from second-century writers is commensurate with or even more conservative than the citation practices of other second-century contemporaries (Hill 2012, 261–81; Hurtado 2018, 14–18). Michael W. Holmes considered the manuscript data of the Gospels and concluded that they exhibit micro-level variance and macro-level stability (Holmes 2013, 637–88). That is, Holmes contends—contra Petersen, Koester, and (in particular) Parker—that there is variance on the level of words, phrases, and sentence structure, but the overall structure of each individual book demonstrates textual stability.

Holmes's intervention in the field, while judicious and carefully argued, nonetheless illustrates the depth of the problems created by the faulty assumptive building blocks of the field—and in particular how rethinking these problematic ideas relates to the questions of publication and dependence of the Gospels. First, there is precious little evidence about textualized gospel tradition from manuscripts in the second and third centuries, and none from the first century. The more one takes the current trend of redating many important manuscripts into account, the more difficult it is to speak with conviction about the text of the New Testament before the third or fourth centuries CE (see Nongbri 2011; 2014; 2016; 2018; 2019; Kruger 2012; Orsini 2015). With only a handful of fragmentary glimpses of gospel tradition from the second and third centuries, and these not securely dated, the extant manuscripts of the Gospels essentially provide data about the micro-level variance and the macro-level stability of their textual transmission in the post-Constantinian era, not the first centuries CE. Speaking about the manuscript evidence of the Gospels in the first three centuries, apart from piecemeal evidence from a handful of fragmentary papyri and perhaps citations, may in large part ending up being a guessing game.

There is, however, a second and more fundamental problem with Holmes's claim about micro-level variance and macro-level stability. Namely, it is possible to argue for macro-level stability, only if one has already presupposed that the textual traditions now called the Gospel according to Matthew, Mark, and Luke are in fact discrete books existing in the first century in a definitive form produced by distinct authors. After all, these textual traditions are remarkably similar by ancient standards, and it seems likely that the Gospels originally circulated anonymously and without titles (see Reed 2002, 11–46; Ehrman 2013, 51; Gamble 1995, 153–54). Moreover, many early Christian writers referred to textualized gospel tradition not as books but as unfinished notes, that is, ὑπομνήματα or *commentarii* (Larsen 2018b, 79–120). Thus, it seems more historically appropriate, from the perspective of the earliest readers, to view the Gospel according to Matthew not as a separate book from the Gospel according to Mark nor as created by a separate author but as itself a clear piece of evidence of the macro-level fluidity of the same textualized gospel tradition. If one does not presuppose that the Gospels according to Mark and Matthew are separate books, the very existence of the textual tradition that is now called The Gospel According to Matthew is itself concrete evidence of macro-level fluidity of gospel tradition. The same argument would hold for the Gospels according to Luke, John, Thomas, and Peter, according to the Hebrews, according to the Egyptians, the Egerton Gospel, Tatian's Gospel, Marcion's Gospel, the Dura gospel fragment—just to name a few examples. From such a "before the book" point of view, there is widespread and undisputable evidence of macro-level fluidity and textual openness in early gospel traditions within the first few centuries.

Advances in Gospel Studies and Adjacent Fields

Before offering a view of the publication and dependence of the textualized gospel traditions that takes ancient writing and reading practices into account, it is necessary to gesture to a few important advances in the field of gospel studies as well as adjacent fields. These advances offer trajectories for thinking beyond the search for origins of singular texts, and consequently beyond the metaphor of the author, the book, and publication.

From "New Testament and Christian Origins" to "New Testament and Early Christianity"

Over the past few decades, there has been a shift to viewing the documents that came to be included in late antiquity in the canon of the New Testament within the context of the development of what became Christianity in the first few centuries of the Common Era. The textual tradition now called the Gospels according to Matthew, Mark, Luke, and John has traditionally been dated to between 70 and 100 CE. The chronological direction in which one looks from that 70–100 CE time frame sets one's scholarly agenda, and within the trends of the field of Synoptic studies this direction of focus has begun to change. The focus for much of the nineteenth and twentieth centuries was how one could come to understand what happened prior to the writing of the Gospels: tracing historical traditions about Jesus, his birth, his life as an apocalyptic prophet, and his execution (around 30 CE) and how these traditions changed up to 70 CE, when the Gospels began to be written. In the past few decades, however, scholars have begun to chart more and more the forward-moving historical trajectories from the era associated with the New Testament documents (70–100 CE) into the first several centuries of Christian history, rather than pursuing backward-facing searches for origins.

Signs of this shift are now clear. Even as recently as 2010, however, it was still necessary for the founding editors of the journal *Early Christianity* to write the following in their editorial manifesto:

> in this journal, then, "early Christianity" is taken to cover not only the first Christian century but also the second. Until recently, it has been widely assumed that the early second century marks the dividing-line between two academic fields (New Testament studies and patristics), rather than an area of overlap. . . . Only recently has the crucial concept of reception begun to attract serious attention from New Testament scholars, as the necessary counterpart to the conventional emphasis on production. By viewing the New Testament as the creation of the second century as well as the first, we intend this journal to contribute to a long overdue reorientation. (Frey, Rothschild, Schröter, and Watson 2010, 1–2)

One of the founding editors of *Early Christianity* was Francis Watson, and his *Gospel Writing* exemplifies this shift of direction mentioned by these editors (2013). Watson charts how Gospels were written not only in the first century but up through the fifth. Similar trajectories can be seen in the adjacent fields of Hebrew Bible and ancient Judaism (see Najman 2009, Breed 2014, Mroczek 2016).

From Tradition Philology of Variants to New Philology of Variance

Establishing the original text of the Gospels is an unproblematic goal for only a few critical scholars today. It is still customary, however, to try to establish as old a version of the text as possible. In such a frame, ancient manuscripts containing gospel traditions are viewed as a means to an end of constructing a critical edition. Manuscripts are not treated as late antique objects in their own right. Thus, what Codex Washingtonianus allows scholars to surmise about the state of the text of the Gospels in the first century has traditionally been regarded as more important than what it indicates about the social and cultural histories of fourth- to fifth-century Christians and their reading practices.

New Philology, however, focuses on manuscripts as objects, not as a means to an end. Bernard Cerquiglini's famous remarks about medieval manuscripts have proved a productive axiom for many other fields as well: "medieval writing does not produce variants; it is variance" (1999, 111). Liv Ingeborg Lied and Hugo Lunghaug's essay "Studying Snapshots: On Manuscript Culture, Textual Fluidity, and New Philology," outlines an approach to ancient Jewish and Christian manuscript research that treats manuscripts as primary objects of study rather than mere containers of text and flawed witnesses to now-gone texts (2017). Their introductory essay and their book as a whole draw together scholars from across various subfields engaged in material (rather than traditional) philology.

This effort is not new. Eldon Jay Epp's *Theological Tendency of Codex Bezae Cantabrigiensis in Acts* (1966) remains exemplary both for its findings and for its methodological approach to studying Codex Bezae as a material object (see also Epp 2007). More recently, Jennifer Knust's and Tommy Wasserman's book *To Cast the First Stone: The Transmission of a Gospel Story* (2019) shows the breadth of possibilities of shifting philological focus. They trace the transmission of a single story from gospel tradition (the so-called *Pericope Adulterae*), telling a story that is at least as much about the developing manuscript culture and changing writing and reading practices of ancient Christianity well into late antiquity as it is about the first-century textual tradition now identified as the Gospel according to John.

An adjacent development is telling the cultural "biography" of gospel texts—a shift that moves the field from conjecture about lost (disembodied) texts to papyrological analysis of the lives of artifacts. AnneMarie Luijendijk's *From Gospels to Garbage: Christian Reading Practices in Late Antique Egypt* (forthcoming) charts a new path that fundamentally reframes what it means to do textual studies of the Gospels by looking at the life cycle of Gospels, from creation to destruction. Roberta Mazza's "Papyri, Ethics, and Economics: A Biography of *P.Oxy.* 15.1780 (P 39)," exemplifies the benefits of treating manuscript objects in their own right, as well as the adjacent ethical issues (2015; see also Nongbri 2018).

From Writing as Contained Literary Product to Open-Ended Textual Process

In line with treating writing as variance, rather than variants, as well as tracing forward moving trajectories from the first-century gospel traditions in later centuries, is the work done by scholars considering ancient texts not as singular and contained product but as part of an ongoing process of growth and change. Whereas textual scholars of the Gospels have treated variants as textual "problems" to be solved, others consider vitality a positive sign (see Najman 2012).

The language about shifting from product to process comes out clearly in the work of Eva Mroczek. Surveying a variety of texts, she argues that ancient Jewish writers used metaphors other than contained books and finished literary products. They often thought of their own writing practices as running rivers and other images of movement and change. About Ben Sira's textual metaphors specifically, she concludes: "the imagery of movement and progression—channels and rivers, growing trees, and gleaners after grape harvesters—places Ben Sira's textual activity in a longer history that is both ancient and ongoing. It is as if the text itself was highlighting, or even enabling, its own openness, as a moment in a long process of writing, reading, and collection" (Mroczek 2016, 113). Ben Sira does not produce a unified literary product. He participates in a textual process that has neither origin nor telos (113). Mroczek argues that ancient Jewish readers thought similarly about the Psalms. There were thousands of Psalms of David, but no Book of the Psalms (19–50). The idea of constellations of textual traditions rather than books as circumscribed containers is more in line with the metaphors used by ancient Jewish writers to describe their own textual activities.

Similar work has been introduced to gospel tradition by David Parker. As noted, he argues that Gospels were not the kinds of texts that had originals (Parker 1997, 7). The effort to establish a single, original, authorial, or finished version of a Gospel is wrongheaded. He furthermore concludes that the early period of gospel tradition was characterized by great diversity and fluidity, and that "the further back we go, the greater seems to be the degree of variation" (188). The Gospels are not initially self-contained and finished books. Rather "what we have is a collection of interpretive rewritings of a tradition" (93). He views the textual tradition of the Gospel(s) as dynamically alive.

Synthesizing Remarks

Taken together, these developments move scholarly attention (1) from a backward-orienting search for origins to a forward-oriented tracing of trajectories, (2) from viewing manuscripts as a means to an end (of establishing "original" texts) to manuscripts as material objects of value in their own right, and (3) from viewing ancient textual culture as producing contained and finished literary products to ancient textual producers as participating in an ongoing textual process. I draw these three developments together to gesture toward a new way of discussing the publication and dependence of the Synoptic Gospels. These advances offer trajectories for thinking beyond the search for origins of singular texts, and consequently beyond the metaphor of the author, the book, and publication. They have the advantage (1) of mapping on a wider variety of ancient writing and reading practices, (2) of attending more closely to the extant material data, and (3) of being more historiographically honest and humble about what can (and cannot) be determined from the data.

Given the diverse iterations of textualized gospel tradition and the generic expectations of the earliest readers of gospel tradition, the new framework I suggest forgoes the search for the single, original, authorial, or finished version of a particular Gospel book. It views the earliest gospel tradition as a mushrooming constellation with different instantiations written and used by local producers. It considers publication not as a particular, isolated moment in time but as a complicated and often lengthy process. It gives priority not to a speculated moment of publication but to the material, paratextual, and reader-oriented expectations of a published work. It then redescribes what it might mean to talk about dependence of the Synoptic tradition, which ends up looking more like a rhizomatic process, simultaneously passing on while also reworking previous textualized gospel tradition.

Publication as Complex Social Process

When scholars have approached the question of publication in antiquity, they have tended to give priority to the one facet that looks most like modern publication. The broader picture of publication in antiquity was far messier. It was social and notional yet also material and paratextual. It involved the process of bringing a text to a public and anonymous readership. As is clear from the few examples mentioned, this involves the perceptions of readers just as much as or, perhaps, more than the intentions of authors. It could happen at a singular moment but often was a series of moments. There was a cultural habitus associated with recognizing a published text. It had a series of markers. The presence or absence of such markers contributed to how someone read a document as well as what someone felt authorized to do to it.

Internal Markings of a Published Text

Perhaps the most salient markers that distinguished a published text from an unpublished one were the presence of titles and the ascription of authorship. Such would usually be written directly on the manuscript itself. The two often went hand-in-hand, with a common aspect of the title being the ascription of authorship. Galen in his little treatise *On My Own Books* lays out a framework (*taxis*) of his writings. Some documents were designed for Galen's private use or as notes given personally to a particular individual.

Such writings were not intended for publication (οὐ πρὸς ἔκδοσιν)—whether they arrived in the hands of a public readership is a separate question. Other documents were intended for "common publication" (πρὸς κοινὴν ἔκδοσιν; Galen, *Libr. Propr.* 6). Such a distinction frames Galen's opening story of *On My Own Books*, set in the Sandalarium area of Rome, where many booksellers were concentrated, about Galen witnessing people arguing about the authenticity of a document, rather ambiguously titled *Galen the Doctor*. An unnamed learned man reads the first two pages, determines the work does not reflect Galen's style, and concludes that the title and ascribed authorship are wrong. Galen moves on from the opening story to claim that many of his unpublished, unfinished writings circulated in many different countries, and that they have been altered and reworked significantly, with parts changed, sections added, others removed, and so forth. He then writes:

> well, as for the fact of my books being published by many people under their own names, my dearest Bassus, you know the reason yourself: it is that they were given without *title* (χωρὶς ἐπιγραφῆς) to friends or pupils, having been written with no thought for publication, but simply at the request of those individuals, who had desired a written record of lectures they had attended. When in the course of time some of these individuals died, their successors came into possession of the writings, liked them, and began to pass them off as their own [. . .] Taking them from their owners, they returned to their own countries, and after a short space of time began to perform demonstrations in them, each in some different way. (Galen, *Libr. Propr.* preface)[7]

In addition to an imagined sketch of how textual pluriformity happens, as well as the ongoing and complex social process of publication, the anecdote shows the work performed by the title and the ascribed authorship in antiquity. It is a key differentiating mark between a published and unpublished text. The title expresses the identity of the author, identifies the author's intention for the work, and seeks to guide the reader's approach to the text (Mansfeld 1994, 119).

Another key internal feature to a published text was the presence of a preface detailing how the work was composed, why it was written, who wrote it, for whom it was written, and what sources it used. Arrian, the late first/early second-century CE disciple of Epictetus, wrote down *hypomnēmata* of his teacher's discourses. He created them not as literature but as unpublished notes for his own personal use. His notes, however, were published without his knowledge or consent. In response to their accidental publication, Arrian wrote a preface (in the form of a letter) to his now published work; it states who he is and in what context his notes were produced, describes their purpose, and defends their style to an anonymous public readership (Epictetus, *Diatr. praef.* 1–8). Galen similarly claims that his *hypomnēmata* on Hippocrates's *Epidemics* were initially created for individuals, but he changed course and felt the need to append "these

---

[7] Translated from Singer 1997, 3–4, with modification.

particular preliminary remarks [about the style of writing and its textual origins] because it [his *hypomnēmata*] had percolated to the general public" (Galen, *In librum vi Epidemiarum*, 5.2–3; see Mansfeld 1994, 140). The prospect of a public anonymous readership demanded a prefatory account that situated what the text was and what it was created to do. The preface could involve appending a biography of the person in question (Mansfeld 1994, 108–16).

Publishing a previously unpublished text could also involve adding chapter divisions or other paratextual aids to help readers navigate the work. This is another way for someone publishing a text to attempt to control the reading of an anonymous public. Porphyry was the one responsible for publishing the teachings of his teacher, Plotinus's *Enneads*. Plotinus did not write down his teachings for the first ten or so years of his career as a philosopher. Rather, his disciple Amelius wrote down Plotinus's teachings in notebooks (Porphyry, *Vita Plot.* 3–4). Porphyry encouraged Plotinus to write, and so Plotinus did, but he never cared to revise his writings or even bothered to read them over even once to correct them. The task of correcting and publishing his rough, unedited writings fell to Plotinus (Porphyry, *Vita Plot.* 7–8). In the process of revising them, Porphyry had to address several paratextual issues. He had to select an appropriate arrangement or framework (*taxis*) of the books that would be legible and useful to an anonymous readership. He had to attach a preface, which contained a story of Plotinus's life and mapping his writings onto the various moments of his life. Porphyry also added numbered κεφάλαια (chapters or chapter summaries) to each book of Plotinus's (except one that he didn't have access to), and he mentions his intention to add punctuation (τάς . . . στιγμὰς) and correct any mistakes with respect to diction or style (κατὰ λέξιν). Such chapter divisions, summaries, and punctuation were readers' aids that often accompanied the process of publication.

External Markings of a Published Text

An important external marking of a public text was the establishment of an authoritative edition. Unpublished, unfinished sorts of works could exist in many versions or multiple forms. The more these traditions were used, the more they changed, as fluidity is an essential part of the energy of vibrant traditions (see Bryant 2002, 59–63, 94). Part of the process of establishing a published version of a previously unfinished, unpublished, and, especially, oral tradition involved dealing with textual pluriformity. Readers took the pluriform textual traditions, removed excessive or problematic lines, and published corrected editions. A good example of publishing corrected editions of a previously oral and pluriform textual tradition is the Homeric epics. Margalit Finkelberg writes: "as the evidence provided by the papyri demonstrates, after ca. 150 B.C.E. variants and especially additions, found in abundance in the earlier papyri (the so-called 'wild' or 'eccentric' papyri), suddenly disappear. This coincides with the activity of Aristarchus of Samothrace, who undertook to purge the text of Homer of extra lines, in particular repetitions, which had accumulated in the course of centuries" (2006, 234). Scholars debate the exact causes behind this transition from wild to more stable textual traditions, but it is clear that it roughly coincides with Aristarchus of Samothrace, the rise of his scholarly activity in Alexandria, and the appearance of published corrected editions of the Homeric texts (see West 2001). Connected with the publication of corrected editions of a text is the rise of commentarial tradition on a text.

How readers describe a textual tradition offers important information about its perception as a published text. When readers describe a text as πρὸς ἔκδοσις rather than οὐ πρὸς ἔκδοσις, it is being marked as a published text. Similarly, when ancient readers compared texts marked as συγγράμματα with those marked as ὑπομνήματα, they often did so in order to distinguish between finished and unfinished texts. When readers ascribe the text to an identifiable human author-figure (as opposed a deity or mythical person from the past), it is being marked as a published text. When readers refer to a text being published in a specific time and place, it is being marked as a published text. When readers refer to a text as being a discrete part of a recognizable literary canon, it is being marked as published literature.

These internal and external signs of a published text are not a rigid set of criteria that any text must fully meet in order to be regarded as published. They are a Wittgensteinian constellation of family resemblances about how published texts look. Not all texts regarded as published necessarily meet all the signs, and vice versa. Moreover, publication as a process can occur at various moments over a text's life. Authors might publish a text multiple times, in multiple ways throughout their lifetimes, and even after their lifetimes, meeting various markers of publication at different moments. In short, publication was a complex, social process, involving both writers and readers, who looked for expected material and paratextual features.

The Publication Process of the Gospel(s)

The traditional way of describing publication in antiquity has relied heavily on comparanda from elite Greek and Roman authors. The models of Pliny the Younger hosting events of reading or of Cicero sending his manuscripts to Atticus for formal distribution are clearly not useful models for thinking about how the Gospels were published, with the possible exception of the Gospel according to Luke. Rather it is more useful to think of a composite process, analogous to the emergence of the Homeric tradition, Hippocratic medical writings, or the Hebrew Bible, that occurred over a long period of time involving a web of textual producers, writing communities, public readers, liturgical performances, textual correctors, paratextual development, commentarial tradition, and so forth.

All of the textual traditions that are now called the Synoptic Gospels were anonymous. As a point of comparison, take the openings of Herodotus's *Histories*, Plutarch's *On Tranquility of the Soul*, Seneca the Elder's *Controversies*, Josephus's *Jewish War*, or the conclusion of Ben Sira. The authors of all these works signed their names in their works, a common practice among Greek, Roman, and Hellenistic Jewish writers. None of the

Gospels, however, are signed in this way. Even the Gospel according to Luke (the only Synoptic Gospel with a preface) noticeably is not signed with an author's name.

The earliest evidence of the titles "according to [name]" comes from Irenaeus of Lyons, near the end of the second century. Prior to Irenaeus there were a wide variety of ways and metaphors for making sense of textualized gospel tradition. For instance, when Theophilus of Antioch (c. 170–80 CE) used gospel tradition in his argument in *To Autolycus* 3.13–14, he did not use the "book published by author" metaphor. Instead, he imagined gospel tradition as coming directly from "the gospel voice" (ἡ ... εὐαγγέλιος φωνὴ ... λέγουσα). In that particular context, the gospel voice functions like the voices of other author-figures such as Isaiah, Jeremiah, Hosea, Joel, and Zechariah (3.12). The gospel tradition Theophilus cites in *Autol.* 3.13–14 looks similar to elements of the textual traditions that are now called the Gospels according to Matthew and Luke (Matt 5:28, 32, 44, 46; Luke 6:28; 32–33; 16:18), yet it does not appear that Theophilus used either one as a "source." In *Autol.* 3.13–14, the gospel itself is personified, functioning with its own agency, and somehow self-authorizing. This is quite different from a "book published by (human) author" metaphor.[8] Similarly, Celsus and Justin Martyr both use metaphors of the gospel tradition not as discrete books but as a fluid, in-flux constellation of textual traditions.[9] The *Didache* and 2 Clement simply refer to the Lord (= Jesus) speaking in his gospel as a metaphor for textualized gospel, seeming to view it as still primarily a speech genre that also happens to have been textualized. The *Martyrdom of Polycarp* discusses dying a death "in accordance with the gospel" (*Mart. Pol.* 1), which, based on its clear allusions to gospel tradition, includes dying in a way that parallels Jesus's death. Thus, it seems to refer to the gospel not as a singular book but as a narrative pattern of Jesus's life and death exhibited in a constellation of textual traditions. The title formula "according to [Name]" itself also indicates another textual metaphor. "According to [Name]" was not a way of denoting authorship in antiquity. Rather it was used to indicate the corrector, editor, or translator of a pluriform textual tradition, for example the editors of Homer or Hippocrates. In this light, the formula attached to early Christian Gospels is further evidence that these titles were not created by their "authors" but by later revisers of the tradition (see Larsen 2018a, 78–104).

According to Simon Gathercole, the earliest manuscript evidence of the titles of the Synoptic Gospels comes from a flyleaf with the title of the Gospel according to Matthew found among the fragments known as 𝔓4, which he dates to the late second or early

---

[8] Elsewhere in his treatise *To Autolycus*, Theophilus does refer to the author-figure "John" speaking in reference to gospel tradition (Ἰωάννης λέγει· "Ἐν ἀρχῇ ἦν ὁ λόγος ... κτλ.), although he does not use the term *gospel* there, when he cites the opening of the prologue of the Gospel according to John (*Autol.* 2.22.5–6). This is different from both the metaphor of "book published by author" and the metaphor of personified, self-authorizing gospel deployed in 3.13. Thus, Theophilus does not operate with a single metaphor of gospel textuality in his *To Autolycus* but uses multiple metaphors to configure gospel tradition.

[9] On Celsus's account of gospel textuality and pluriformity, see Origen, *Contra Celsum* 2.27. Justin customarily refers to ἀπομνημονεύματα τῶν ἀποστόλων many times. See *1 Apol.* 66.3 where the term is connected with the gospels. See also treatment of these passages in Larsen and Letteney 2019.

third century CE, and 𝔓75, a manuscript he dates to the third century containing the titles "the Gospel according to Luke" followed immediately on the same page by "the Gospel according to John" (Gathercole 2013, 33–76). Brent Nongbri has recently demonstrated, however, that 𝔓75 fits more comfortably in the fourth century, which would make it roughly contemporaneous with the great codices Vaticanus and Sinaiaticus, both of which date to the fourth century CE and also provide titles of the Gospels. When one takes Nongbri's argument about the limits of paleography, the secure manuscript evidence for the titles of the Gospels before the fourth century becomes rather thin (Nongbri 2016, 405–37.[10]

There are no other manuscripts with alternative titles to the Synoptic Gospels apart from "according to [Name]." Given their uniform appearance in such an unusual form, David Trobisch rightly concludes that the "possibility that the titles were independently formulated this way by the authors of the Gospels may be safely ruled out" (2000, 38). Rather, the literary and manuscript evidence suggests a publication process of giving titles to the pluriform gospel and attaching different iterations of the gospel to different named figures beginning in the later part of the second century, with Irenaeus being the first evidence.[11]

Describing Gospels as Books Published by Authors

Prior to Irenaeus, people used metaphors other than book-author-publication to figure out how to make sense of textualized gospel. While Irenaeus also uses different metaphors throughout the rest of his *Adversus Haereses* (written near the end of the second century, c. 190 CE), in the beginning of book 3 he deploys the book-author-publication metaphor in a way quite distinct from prior readers of textualized gospel tradition. He speaks of the publication, in specific contexts, of three of his four canonical Gospels and connects each of them with apostolic heritage. It is important to bear in mind that the appearance of Irenaeus's new way of thinking about textualized gospel did not mean that everyone else in the Mediterranean reading the Gospels post-190 CE regarded them as published books. Other nonbook metaphors continued to be deployed for centuries.

The Preface(s) of the Gospel(s)

Apart from the opening verses of the textual tradition now called the Gospel according to Luke (Luke 1:1–4), the Synoptic Gospels do not have prefaces, and even the

---

[10] The earliest material evidence for the titles of the Gospel according to John comes from 𝔓66, which dates to sometime between the late second and fourth centuries CE. See Nongbri 2014. Nongbri suggests that a date in the fourth century is more plausible.

[11] On the claim that the uniformity of the titles must indicate their circulation of titles from an early stage, see the historical counter-evidence in Porphyry, *Vita Plot.* 4, in which certain titles prevailed after a period of titular pluriformity.

opening to the Gospel according to Luke does not perform the role an ancient reader would expect from a preface. It is more truncated and ambiguous concerning important details that ancient readers would expect from a preface. For instance, in addition to failing to name an author, it does not name or describe the sources the work uses, apart from labeling them as "narrations" (διηγήσεις) that are flawed in specific ways: not well-ordered or lacking a proper framework, not addressing the topic "from the top" (ἄνωθεν), nor "following closely" (παρηκολουθηκώς) the subject matter, nor sufficiently careful (ἀκριβῆς). By comparison, the prefaces to Philostratus's *Life of Apollonius* and Papias's *Exegeses of the Dominical Logia* discuss in greater detail the origins of their preliterary sources for their literary creation.[12] Moreover, the creation of this preface fits comfortably in the back-and-forth alteration of the Gospel according to Luke vis-à-vis Marcion's *Gospel*, and thus itself likely reflects a second-century growth and alteration of the Gospel.

So, when do the sort of prefaces that ancient readers might expect to accompany a published text (e.g. the *Life of Plotinus and Arrangement of His Books*) begin to appear in relation to the Gospel(s)? The earliest evidence comes from the so-called *Muratorian canon* (the *quibus tamen interfuit* fragment) found in the seventh- or eighth-century Codex Muratorianus. Scholars debate whether the fragment represents a tradition from the fourth century or from the second half of the second century CE (Ferguson 1982, 677–83; Hahneman 1992; Sundberg 1973, 1–41). Clare K. Rothschild, however, has recently put forth a persuasive solution, arguing the Muratorian fragment is a fourth-century Roman fake of a second-century text (Rothschild 2018).[13] The fragment contains biographical information about the authors and situation of writings of much of the New Testament in a way reminiscent of the preface-*cum*-biography traditions seen elsewhere in antiquity (as discussed earlier). Similar prefaces exist in the so-called Anti-Marcionite and Monarchian prologues, which scholars tend to date to the fourth or fifth centuries. These prefaces offered an anonymous public readership the kind of data they would have expected from published texts about important persons. Thus, it is possible to point to a series of moments in the publication process of the Gospels in the fourth century that correspond to the received prefaces that readers would have expected in published works.

Furthermore, the Muratorian fragment as well as the Anti-Marcionite and Monarchian prologues gesture to another element of the publication of the Gospel. As has been pointed out by David Trobisch and David Parker, the Gospel as a published book is not four Gospels but one fourfold Gospel. By the late second century and into the third, the Gospels are most often published not as individual books. It is a singular Gospel with four constituent parts: *The Gospel*, according to Matthew, according to Mark, according to Luke, and according to John.

---

[12] Papias's comments in his preface (Eusebius, *Hist. eccl.* 3.39) or the preface of Philostratus's *Life of Apollonius* (*Vita Apoll.* 1.1–3), both of whom name the source used and explain how they use them.

[13] Rothschild draws on Irene Peirano Garrison's work on the Roman fake; Peirano 2012, 3–4.

Adding Taxis to the Gospel(s), Incorporation into a Literary Canon, and Commentary

Part of producing a published work was placing the various components of the work in order (*taxis*). If a work is, for example, a history, such arrangement is straightforward. But when it involves bringing together a series of lectures, treatises, letters, or other similar compositions, the issue of *taxis* is a critical part of making the published work legible to an anonymous readership. Papias, bishop of Hieropolis in the first part of the second century, mentions that someone named Mark textualized the *logia* (which in the context means not "oracles" in an oracular sense but broadly stories about Jesus and the early apostolic leaders) that lacked *taxis*, but that Matthew added *taxis* to the *logia*. The *logia* exist in a variety of forms, ranging from unarranged to arranged. This sense of order or arrangement refers to an internal component of polishing the stories into a more literary order.

More evidence comes, however, about how the fourfold Gospel should be arranged. The traditional *taxis* of the fourfold Gospel is *According to Matthew*, *According to Mark*, *According to Luke*, and *According to John*. This seems to rely in part on Irenaeus's discussion of the Gospels in *Against Heresies* 3.1.1. This is, however, not the only way of arranging the Gospel. The oldest manuscript bearing witness to a fourfold Gospel arrangement is 𝔓45, which has traditionally been dated to 200–250 CE, though Nongbri has (again) called such a date into question, with a fourth-century date also being possible and even more likely (2018, 135–38). The manuscript is badly damaged, but it likely contained the "Western" order of Matthew-John-Luke-Mark, followed by the Acts of the Apostles (Hurtado 2004, 132–48). The "Western" arrangement of the Gospels moves from the corrected editions of the Gospel associated with apostles, John-Matthew, to those associated with followers of the apostles, Luke-Mark (see Crawford, 2018). Codex Bobiensis, which originally had more gospel material, now contains the second half of the Gospel according to Mark followed immediately by the Gospel according to Matthew, which represents a break from the traditional as well as the "Western" arrangements (Larsen 2021). The manuscript evidence of the Old Syriac Curatorian Gospels, which has been dated on the basis of paleography to the fifth century CE, offers the arrangement Matthew-Mark-John-Luke (Metzger 1977, 36–37). This would seemingly be the case so as to allow the Gospel according to Luke to come immediately before its sequel, the Acts of the Apostles. All of these arrangements are a part of the publication history of the gospels. It is clear that there was not one "right" way to arrange the gospel as a published work in late antiquity. In each case, the Gospels according to Matthew, Mark, Luke, and John are treated as a published unit, with each offering a different approach to the *taxis* of the Gospels. Each effort represents another link in the complex process of publication.

Part of the process of publishing a work in the ancient world involved situating it within a larger literary canon. It needed a place to belong within a library—both figuratively and often literally. The larger literary canon to which the Gospels belonged was the New Testament. While many of the writings that came to make up what are now called the New Testament took their nascent forms in the first and early second centuries, the idea of a literary corpus called the New Testament came later. The collocation of καινὴ διαθήκη to refer to a corpus of books is clearly established by the time of Eusebius of Caesarea in the early fourth century. The first unambiguous evidence of the use of the collocation καινὴ διαθήκη as a corpus of books comes from Clement of Alexandria, in his *Stromateis*, written at the very beginning of the third century (*Strom.* 3.11, 18; 5.13). When Origen picks up the collocation, however, in the middle of the third century CE, he often does so with some reservation. In his *De principiis* and his *Commentary on John* he uses the phrase "so-called New Testament,"[14] with his language showing some hesitation with the titling of the corpus as the "New Testament."[15] Part of the problem with calling the literary collection of books the "New Testament" was that it implied the outdatedness of the "Old Testament," as Origen makes explicit in *hom. Num.* 9.4 and *frag. Ioh.* 49 (see Kinzig 1994, 541–42). The explanation for the anxiety of the literary title "New Testament" proposed by Wolfram Kinzig is that Marcion was the first to designate an Old Testament vis-à-vis a New Testament.

Other important elements in the history of the publication of the Gospel are chapter divisions (κεφαλαία), the Eusebian (and Ammonian) canons, and other paratextual interpretative signs (σημεια) all of which seek to create a "map" for an anonymous reading public through the text of the Gospel(s) (see Coogan 2017). Porphyry indicated that part of his process of preparing Plotinus's lectures for publication was adding chapter headings (κεφαλαία). The key actors in the publication process of adding such paratextual features with respect to the Gospels were Origen, Ammonius, Eusebius, and Euthalius. The nature of the manuscript evidence is incomplete, yet it seems clear that the third and fourth centuries were pivotal moments in this aspect of the publication history (Fewster 2019, 178).

One of the final elements of the process of publication is the rise of commentarial tradition. For example, shortly after the time when the pluriform, oral-yet-textualized traditions of Homer began to appear in published corrected editions, commentarial tradition also began to appear. Commentary can signal that a text has become public, less changeable, and more fixed, and thus one would be inclined, in order to offer solutions (λύσεις) to textual problems (προβλήματα), to offer commentary rather than textual revision.

When does the commentarial tradition appear in relation to the Gospel(s)? Irenaeus has a reference to the "commentaries" (*commentarios*) of the disciples of Valentinus, and he mentions a certain Ptolemy. The reference is complicated, however, by the facts that

---

[14] *De princ.* 4.1.1: διαθήκης καὶ τῆς καλουμένης καινῆς: *Comm. John*: τὴν ὀνομαζομένην καινήν. For a gathering of the evidence, see Kinzig 1994. The term διαθήκη does perhaps refer to a collection of books in Clement of Alexandria, writing earlier than Origen in the third century, but the usages are ambiguous and not connected with the term καινή.

[15] See Kinzig 1994, 532–33. He notes that the same hesitation still exists in Augustine in the fifth century. Origen does use the phrase "Books of the New Testament" with the "so-called" qualifier in *Comm. John* 1.32: Καὶ ταῦτα μὲν ἀπὸ τῶν τῆς καινῆς διαθήκης βιβλίων ἐλέγετο ὑπ' αὐτοῦ περὶ ἑαυτοῦ.

(1) the writings of Ptolemy are not extant, and (2) the term *commentarii* (ὑπομνήματα) can refer to commentaries in a strict sense but also notes and a wide variety of other things. From Irenaeus's comments elsewhere (e.g. *Adv. haer.* 1.8.5), it would appear that Plotemy did not write commentary in a strict sense (lemma and explanation) so much as a blend of exposition and rewriting. Elsewhere, Jerome records that Theophilus of Antioch (c. 170–80 CE) wrote "commentaries [called] *On the Gospel* and *On the Proverbs of Solomon*" (*in Evangelium et in Proverbia Salomonis Commentarios*), but Jerome thinks the style of such works does not correspond to the other known works of Theophilus. Moreover, as with its Greek counterpart ὑπομνήματα, the term *commentarii* can refer to commentary as well as notes, rough drafts, memoranda, legal records, and so forth. Even still, it is important that the commentary ascribed to Theophilus is on the gospel, not the Gospels, and that the gospel is not ascribed to an author, as the proverbs are ascribed to Solomon. This fits with concepts of the gospel as an authorless constellation of textual tradition. The earliest evidence of a commentary (in a narrow sense of the term) on the text of the Gospel(s) comes from Origen. He wrote commentaries on the Gospels according to Matthew and John, and there are extant fragments of Origen's *Homilies on Luke*.

The commentarial situation related to the Gospel according to Mark, however, is different. The text *In Catena in Marcum* is frequently attributed to Victor of Antioch (c. 400; contemporary of John Chrysostom), but William R. S. Lamb has recently shown that it is an "open book" that "emerged at the beginning of the sixth century" (2012, 27, 51, 60). Furthermore, it is not a commentary per se but catenae excerpted from commentaries on other gospels and various other writings. The first proper commentary on the Gospel according to Mark comes from either an anonymous Latin commentary (*Expositio Evangelii secundum Marcum*), which may date to the seventh century, or, more securely, from Bede in the early eighth century. (On the Latin commentary, see Cahill 1998; on Bede, see Hurst 1960.)

Concluding Remarks on the Publication of the Gospel(s)

The Synoptic Gospels have traditionally been treated as books that were published sometime between the years 70 and 90 CE. Such a claim relies on a heavily abstracted, ahistorical, and ambiguous use of the term "publication." A more accurate restatement of the claim would be as follows: the Synoptic Gospels, if an author-book-publication framework is presupposed, may productively be read against the historical backdrop of the trauma of the destruction of the Second Temple in Jerusalem by the future emperor Titus in 70 CE. Then, source criticism is used to determine their respective chronology. In reality, however, none of the foregoing has to do with ancient publication practices in a strict sense.

There are a couple problems to explicate here. First, as I have shown, the very existence of the Synoptic and other early gospel tradition is evidence of macro-fluidity in the first and second centuries, and consequently this tradition's existence serves as concrete evidence that the text of the earliest gospel tradition was in flux and thus something of a moving target. Furthermore, within each of the overlapping constellations of textualized gospel tradition that is now called the Synoptic Gospels, there is further evidence of ongoing textual revision.[16] The moment one chooses to prioritize within a fluid and changing tradition is subjective. Second, such a view of publication is undertheorized and fails to take account of ancient readers' expectations of published works and the material and paratextual features associated with published works in antiquity. It conflates the "initial text" or earliest version of a work with the finished or complete one, which is not how ancient writing practices necessarily worked. It imagines an evangelist curating a publication moment when he brought forth his polished literary product to some form of a public (whether "for all Christians" or more local), which is a scenario more suited for elite Roman authors than those who produced the Gospels. A material, social, paratextual, and reader-oriented account of the publication process of the Gospels does not validate viewing them as published within a specific and contained moment in time.

Based on the criteria listed here of expected material and paratextual elements of a published work, I propose an alternative model for discussing the publication history of the Gospels. The publication process of the Gospels did not begin until toward the end of the second century CE. The Gospels took a more published shape throughout the third and fourth centuries. The process of establishing the Gospel according to Mark, in particular, as a public text continued into the seventh or eighth centuries CE.

From yet another point of view, the publication history of the Gospels extends well beyond the eighth century and into the present moment. From a book-historical perspective, each new publication of the Gospels, whether designed for historical research, liturgy, or devotional use, is a part of their publication history. In addition, the future of the publication history of the Gospels is unfinalizable. For instance, it is not hard to imagine someone producing a version of the Synoptic Gospels for readers interested in the historical study of early Christianity that placed the Gospel according Mark before the Gospel according to Matthew and had a way of presenting textual pluriformity that doesn't literally minimize textual "variants."

The appearance of the "gospel as book published by author" discourse does not immediately result in the disappearance of prior discourses (Larsen 2018b, 79–98). Gospel tradition was called ὑπομνήματα well into the fourth century (Larsen and Letteney 2019). The *Acts of Timothy* 8–10, for instance, in the fifth century shares a story about texts that are now called the Synoptic Gospels as a loose disorganized assemblage of sheets of papyrus. Thus, the complex history of the publication of the Gospels is neither geographically nor chronologically clean-cut.

---

[16] On the Gospel according to Mark, see Larsen 2018a; on the Gospel according to Matthew, see Broadhead 2017; on the Gospel according to Luke, see Tyson 2006.

At this point, it will be clear that a more historically nuanced and materially grounded approach to publication of the Gospel(s) will have important ramifications for the question of dependence of the Synoptic Gospels. Thus, the traditional framework for thinking about the dependence of the Gospels (source criticism) must be retooled for new questions and perspectives. It is not so much that the solutions are wrong; it is that the question itself is flawed.

Paths for Future Research on the Textuality of the Gospel(s)

In lieu of a conclusion, I offer five suggestions for future work on gospel textualization and publication. First, scholars need to develop new language and analytical tools for describing textualized gospel tradition in the earliest centuries without anachronistically making recourse to metaphors of books, authors, and published/finished texts. The names one uses ("Mark," "Matthew," and so forth) have a predetermining effect on the questions one can ask and the conclusion we can draw. Each time one writes or says "Luke says . . . " in regard to a first-century historical textualized gospel tradition, one further entrenches oneself in an anachronism. In order to work on gospel tradition in the earliest centuries, one must at this point resist use of the book-author-publication metaphor to refer to first- or early second-century texts. Gospel writing is not a case of authors publishing books called Gospel but of the proliferation of textualized constellations of gospel tradition producing the need for author-figures.

Second, educators must reimagine how to teach the "Synoptic Problem." No longer can one draw boxes, write names inside the boxes, and draw arrows connecting them as a way of visualizing how gospel traditions relate to each other. In so doing, one imports book-author-publication metaphors of textuality that are not native to the first century. Rather, as I have suggested elsewhere, what is needed is a 3D time-lapse video of proportional Venn diagrams of the overlapping constellations of the Gospels according to Mark, Matthew, Luke, Thomas, John, Peter, and Mary, and Tatian's *Gospel*—just to name a few—from the year 70 CE up through the end of the second century, growing like a bulbous rhizome (Larsen 2018, 149–54).

Third, scholars need to be more upfront in their scholarship and teaching about the fact that the Greek critical editions they work with (e.g. NA28, USB) are scholarly constructions of a text that never existed prior to its creation and furthermore that it is based more on the third/fourth century (and later) evidence than on evidence from the first or second centuries.

Fourth, as has already begun, scholars must pay attention to the materiality and social history implied by particular textual artifacts (manuscripts). In so doing, however, scholars are often hamstrung by an author-scribe dichotomy that sees authors as creative, active, and brilliant and scribes as passive and almost mindless tradents of tradition.

While some manuscripts of the Gospels in late antiquity do seem to be produced by automaton-like scribes, I want to suggest micro-authors as useful term for describing the person or people who produced and used and reused manuscripts such as the so-called Egerton Gospel, the Dura Gospel fragment, or Codex Bobiensis. They are not authors in a formal, literary sense of the term. They are, however, presumably the ones who produced the Gospel in textual form for their local communities. To the degree that they felt liberty to remake the textual tradition, "micro-author" seems fruitful language to describe their actions.

Fifth, the observations of scholars working on social and cultural memory (e.g. Hübenthal 2014) need to be heeded, but it must be understood that the relevance of their observations and conclusions does not stop in 70 CE but continues for several centuries. In order to study the documents now identified as early Christian Gospels, scholars must not focus exclusively on the first century but must become historians of late antiquity.

References

Alexander, Loveday. 1998. "Ancient Book Production and the Circulation of the Gospels." In *The Gospels for All Christians*, edited by Richard Bauckham, 71–105. Grand Rapids: Eerdmans.

Baird, William. 1992. *The History of New Testament Research. Vol. 1. From Deism to Tübingen*. Minneapolis: Augsburg Fortress.

Bauckham, Richard. 1998. "For Whom Were Gospels Written?" In *The Gospels for All Christians: Rethinking the Gospel Audiences*, edited by Richard Bauckham, 9–48. Grand Rapids: Eerdmans.

Bovon, François. 1988. "The Synoptic Gospels and the Noncanonical Acts of the Apostles." *Harvard Theological Review* 81, no. 1: 19–36.

Breed, Brennen W. 2014. *The Nomadic Text: A Theory of Biblical Reception*. Indiana Studies in Biblical Literature. Bloomington: Indiana University Press.

Broadhead, Edwin K. 2017. *The Gospel of Matthew on the Landscape of Antiquity*. WUNT 378. Tübingen: Mohr Siebeck.

Bryant, John. 2002. *The Fluid Text: A Theory of Revision and Editing for Book and Screen*. Ann Arbor: University of Michigan Press.

Cahill, Michael. 1998. *The First Commentary on Mark: An Annotated Translation*. New York: Oxford University Press.

Cerquiglini, Bernard. 1999. *In Praise of the Variant: A Critical History of Philology*. Translated by Betsy Wing. Baltimore: Johns Hopkins University Press.

Collins, Adela Yarbro. 2009. *Mark: A Commentary*. Hermeneia. Minneapolis: Fortress.

Collines, Billie Jean, Bob Buller, and John F. Kutsko, eds. 2014. *SBL Handbook of Style: For Biblical Studies and Related Disciplines*. 2nd ed. Atlanta: SBL Press.

Coogan, Jeremiah. 2017. "Mapping the Fourfold Gospel: Textual Geography in the Eusebian Apparatus." *Journal of Early Christian Studies* 25, no. 3: 337–57.

Crawford, Matthew. 2018. "A New Witness to the 'Western' Ordering of the Gospels: GA 073 + 084." *Journal of Theological Studies* 69, no. 2: 477–83.

Dibelius, Martin. 1935. *From Tradition to Gospel*. Translated by Bertram Lee Wolf. New York: Scribner.

Doole, J. Andrew. 2013. *What Was Mark for Matthew? An Examination of Matthew's Relationship and Attitude to His Primary Source*. WUNT II 344; Tübingen: Mohr Siebeck.

Ehrman, Bart D. 1996. *The Orthodox Corruption of Scripture: The Effect of Early Christological Controversies on the Text of the New Testament*. Oxford: Oxford University Press.

Ehrman, Bart D. 2013. *Forgery and Counterforgery: The Use of Literary Deceit in Early Christian Polemics*. New York: Oxford University Press.

Epp, Eldon Jay. 1966. *The Theological Tendency of Codex Bezae Cantabrigiensis in Acts*. Cambridge: Cambridge University Press.

Epp, Eldon Jay. 1999. "The Multivalence of the Term 'Original Text' in New Testament Textual Criticism." *Harvard Theological Review* 92: 245–81.

Epp, Eldon Jay. 2007. "It's All about Variants: A Variant-Conscious Approach to New Testament Textual Criticism." *Harvard Theological Review* 100: 275–308.

Ferguson, Everett. 1982. "Canon Muratori: Date and Provenance." *Studia Patristica* 17, no. 2: 677–83.

Fewster, Gregory Peter. 2019. "Finding Your Place: Developing Cross-reference Systems in Late Antique Biblical Codices." In *The Future of New Testament Textual Scholarship: From H. C. Hoskier to the Editio Critica Maior and Beyond*, edited by Garrick E. Allen, WUNT 417, 153–77. Tübingen: Mohr Siebeck.

Finkelberg, Margalit. 2006. "Regional Texts and the Circulation of Books: the Case of Homer." *Greek, Roman, and Byzantine Studies* 46: 231–48.

Frey, Jörg, Clare K. Rothschild, Jens Schröter, and Francis Watson. 2010. "An Editorial Manifesto." *Early Christianity* 1, no. 1: 1–4.

Gamble, Harry Y. 1995. *Books and Readers in the Early Church: A History of Early Christian Texts*. New Haven: Yale University Press.

Gathercole, Simon. 2012. "The Earliest Manuscript Title of Matthew's Gospel (BnF Suppl. gr. 1120 ii 3 / P4)." *Novum Testamentum* 54: 209–35.

Gathercole, Simon. 2013. "The Titles of the Gospels in the Earliest New Testament Manuscripts." *Zeitschrift für die neutestamentliche Wissenschaft* 104, no. 1: 33–76.

Hahneman, Geoffrey Mark. 1992. *The Muratorian Fragment and the Development of the Canon*. Oxford: Oxford University Press.

Hill, Charles E. 2012. "'In These Very Words': Methods and Standards of Literary Borrowing in the Second Century." In *The Early Text of the New Testament*, edited by Charles E. Hill and Michael J. Kruger, 261–81. Oxford: Oxford University Press.

Holmes, Michael W. 2013. "From 'Original Text' to 'Initial Text': The Traditional Goal of New Testament Textual Criticism in Contemporary Discussion." In *The Text of the New Testament in Contemporary Research: Essays on the Status Quaestionis*, 2nd ed., edited by Bart D. Ehrman and Michael W. Holmes, 637–88, NTTSD 46. Leiden: Brill.

Hübenthal, Sandra. 2014. *Das Markusevangelium als kollektives Gedächtnis*. Göttingen: Vandenhoeck & Ruprecht.

Hurst, David, ed. 1960. *Bedae Venerabilis Opera. Pars 2.3. Opera Exegetica: In Lucae Evangelium Expositio; In Marci Evangelium Expositio*. CChrSL 120: Turnhout: Brepols.

Hurtado, Larry. 2004. "P45 and the Textual History of the Gospel of Mark." In *The Earliest Gospels: The Origins and Transmission of the Earliest Christian Gospels—The Contribution of the Chester Beatty Gospel Codex P45*, edited by Charles Horton, 132–48. London: T&T Clark International

Hurtado, Larry. 2018. "The New Testament in the Second Century: Text, Collections and Canon." In *Texts and Artifacts: Selected Essays on Textual Criticism and Early Christian Manuscripts*, 14–18. New York: Bloomsbury T&T Clark.

Kinzig, Wolfram. 1994. "Καινὴ διαθήκη: The Title of the New Testament in the Second and Third Centuries." *Journal of Theological Studies* 45, no. 2: 519–44.

Kirk, Alan. 2016. *Q in Matthew: Ancient Media, Memory, and Early Scribal Transmission of the Jesus Tradition*. LNTS 564. London: T&T Clark.

Knust, Jennifer. 2008. "In Pursuit of a Singular Text: New Testament Textual Criticism and the Desire for the True Original." *RC* 2: 1–15.

Knust, Jennifer, and Tommy Wasserman. 2019. *To Cast the First Stone: The Transmission of a Gospel Story*. Princeton: Princeton University Press.

Koester, Helmut. 1989. "The Text of the Synoptic Gospels in the Second Century." In *Gospel Traditions in the Second Century*, edited by William L. Petersen, 19–37. Notre Dame, IL: University of Notre Dame Press.

Kopytoff, Igor. 1986. "The Cultural Biography of Things: Commoditization as Process." In *The Social Life of Things: Commodities in Cultural Perspective*, edited by Arjun Appadurai, 64–91. Cambridge: Cambridge University Press.

Kruger, Michael J. 2012. "The Date and Content of P. Antinoopolis 12 (0232)." *New Testament Studies* 58: 254–71.

Lamb, William R. S. 2012. *The Catena in Marcum: A Byzantine Anthology of Early Commentary on Mark*. Leiden: Brill.

Larsen, Matthew D. C. 2017. "Accidental Publication, Unfinished Texts and the Traditional Goals of New Testament Textual Criticism." *Journal for the Study of the New Testament* 39, no. 4: 362–87.

Larsen, Matthew D. C. 2018a. "Correcting the Gospel: Putting the Titles of the Gospels in Historical Context." In *Beyond Authority: Authorship, Law, and Transmission in Jewish and Christian Tradition*, edited by A. J. Berkovitz and Mark Letteney, 78–104. New York: Routledge.

Larsen, Matthew D. C. 2018b. *Gospels before the Book*. New York: Oxford University Press.

Larsen, Matthew D. C. 2021. "The Real-and-Imagined Biography of a Gospel Manuscript." *Early Christianity*, no. 12.1: 103–131.

Larsen, Matthew D. C., and Mark Letteney. 2019. "Christians and the Codex: Generic Materiality and Gospel Tradition." *Journal of Early Christian Studies* 27, no. 3: 383–415.

Lied, Liv Ingeborg, and Hugo Lundhaug, eds. 2017. *Snapshots of Evolving Traditions: Jewish and Christian Manuscript Culture, Textual Fluidity, and New Philology*. Texte und Untersuchungen zur Geschichte der altchristlichen Literatur 175. Berlin: De Gruyter.

Lin, Yii-Jan. 2016. *The Erotic Life of Manuscripts: New Testament Textual Criticism and the Biological Sciences*. New York: Oxford University Press.

Luijendijk, AnneMarie. 2008. *Greetings in the Lord: Early Christians and the Oxyrhynchus Papyri*. Harvard Theological Studies 60. Cambridge, MA: Harvard University Press.

Luijendijk, AnneMarie. Forthcoming. *From Gospels to Garbage: Christian Reading Practices in Late Antique Egypt*.

Mansfeld, Jaap. 1994. *Prolegomena: Questions to be Settled before the Study of an Author, or a Text*. Leiden: Brill.

Mazza, Roberta. 2015. "Papyri, Ethics, and Economics: A Biography of P.Oxy. 15.1780 (P 39)." *Bulletin of the American Society of Papyrologists* 52: 113–42.

Metzger, Bruce. 1977. *The Early Versions of the New Testament*. Oxford: Oxford University Press.

Mink, Gerd. 2004. "Problems of a Highly Contaminated Tradition, the New Testament: Stemmata of Variants as a Source of a Genealogy of Witnesses." In *Studies in Stemmatology*, vol. 2, edited by Pieter van Reenen et al., 13–86. Amsterdam: John Benjamins.

Mitchell, Margaret M. 2005. "Patristic Counter-evidence to the Claim That 'The Gospels Were Written for All Christians.'" *New Testament Studies* 51, no. 1: 36–79.

Mroczek, Eva. 2016. *The Literary Imagination in Jewish Antiquity*. New York: Oxford University Press.

Nagy, Gregory. 1996. *Poetry as Performance: Homer and Beyond*. Cambridge: Cambridge University Press.

Najman, Hindy. 2009. *Seconding Sinai: The Development of Mosaic Discourse in Second Temple Judaism*. Leiden: Brill.

Najman, Hindy. 2012. "The Vitality of Scripture within and beyond the 'Canon.'" *Journal for the Study of Judaism* 43: 497–518.

Najman, Hindy. 2013. "Traditionary Processes and Textual Unity in 4 Ezra." In *Fourth Ezra and Second Baruch: Reconstruction after the Fall*, edited by Matthias Henze and Gabriele Boccaccini, 99–118. Leiden: Brill.

Nongbri, Brent. 2005. "The Use and Abuse of P52: Papyrological Pitfalls in the Dating of the Fourth Gospel." *Harvard Theological Review* 98: 23–48.

Nongbri, Brent. 2011. "Grenfell and Hunt on the Dates of Early Christian Codices: Setting the Record Straight." *Bulletin of the American Society of Papyrologists* 48: 149–62.

Nongbri, Brent. 2014. "The Limits of Palaeographic Dating of Literary Papyri: Some Observations on the Date and Provenance of P.Bodmer II (P66)." *Museum Helveticum* 71: 1–35.

Nongbri, Brent. 2016. "Reconsidering the Place of Papyrus Bodmer XIV–XV ($\mathfrak{P}$75) in the Textual Criticism of the New Testament." *Journal of Biblical Literature* 135, no. 2: 405–37.

Nongbri, Brent. 2018. *God's Library: The Archeology of the Earliest Christian Manuscripts*. New Haven: Yale University.

Nongbri, Brent. 2019. "Palaeographic Analysis of Codices from the Early Christian Period: A Point of Method." *Journal for the Study of the New Testament* 42: 84–97.

Obbink, D., and D. Colomo. 2018. "5345. Mark i 7–9, 16–18." In *The Oxyrhynchus Papyri Vol. LXXXIII*, edited by P. J. Parsons and N. Gonis, Graeco-Roman Memoir 4–7, 104. London: Egypt Exploration Society.

Orsini, Pasquale. 2015. "I papiri Bodmer: Scritture e libri." *Adamantius* 21: 60–78.

Parker, David C. 1997. *The Living Text of the Gospels*. New York: Cambridge University Press.

Parker, David C. 2011. "Is 'Living Text' Compatible with 'Initial Text'? Editing the Gospel of John." In *The Textual History of the Greek New Testament: Changing Views in Contemporary Research*, edited by Klaus Wachtel and Michael W. Holmes, 13–22. Atlanta: Society of Biblical Literature.

Parker, David C. 2012. *Textual Scholarship and the Making of the New Testament*. Oxford: Oxford University Press.

Peirano, Irene. 2012. *The Rhetoric of the Roman Fake: Latin Pseudepigrapha in Context*. Cambridge: Cambridge University Press.

Perrin, Norman. 1969. *What Is Redaction Criticism?* Philadelphia: Augsburg Fortress.

Petersen, William L. 2002. "The Genesis of the Gospels." In *New Testament Textual Criticism and Exegesis: Festschrift J. Delobel*, edited by A. Denaux, BETL 161, 33–65. Leuven: Peeters.

Reed, Annette Yoshiko. 2002. "ΕΥΑΓΓΕΛΙΟΝ: Orality, Textuality, and the Christian Truth in Irenaeus' *Adversus haereses*." *VC* 56: 11–46.

Rothschild, Clare K. 2018. "The Muratorian Fragment as Roman Fake." *Novum Testamentum* 60: 55–82.
Schironi, Francesca. 2012. "The Ambiguity of Signs: Critical Σημεια from Zenodotus to Origen." In *Homer and the Bible in the Eyes of Ancient Interpreters*, edited by M. R. Niehoff, 88–100. Leiden: Brill.
Singer, P. N. 1997. *Galen: Selected Works*. Oxford: Oxford University Press.
Sundberg, Albert C. 1973. "Canon Muratori: A Fourth-Century List." *Harvard Theological Review* 66, no. 1: 1–41.
Trobisch, David. 2000. *The First Edition of the New Testament*. Oxford: Oxford University Press.
Tyson, Joseph B. 2006. *Marcion and Luke-Acts: A Defining Struggle*. Columbia: University of South Caroline Press.
Watson, Francis. 2013. *Gospel Writing: A Canonical Perspective*. Grand Rapids: Eerdmans.
West, Martin L. 2001. *Studies in the Text and Transmission of the Iliad*. Munich: K. G. Saur.
Westcott, Brooke Foss and Fenton John Anthony Hort. 1881. *The New Testament in the Original Greek*. Cambridge and London: MacMillan and Co.

CHAPTER 11

THE SYNOPTIC GOSPELS AND APOCRYPHAL NARRATIVES

JANET E. SPITTLER

INTRODUCTION

It is necessary, at the outset of this essay on the Synoptic Gospels and apocryphal Christian narratives, to acknowledge my debt to François Bovon, one of very few scholars of early Christianity who has made substantial and equal contributions to our understanding of both canonical and noncanonical texts and—what's more—has brought scholarship on the noncanonical texts to bear upon our understanding of the canonical. In two essays that have perhaps not received the scholarly engagement they deserve, Bovon suggests three distinct ways in which attention to apocryphal texts might contribute specifically to our understanding of the Synoptic Gospels and their early interpretation.

First, in "The Apocryphal Reception of Luke's Gospel and the Orthodox Reading of the Apocryphal Acts of the Apostles," Bovon points to apocryphal texts as providing key evidence of the reception of canonical texts (2003a, 293–301). Apocryphal texts occasionally provide some of our earliest evidence that a canonical text is in circulation and is being read. Beyond just evidence of their circulation, however, apocryphal texts provide fascinating examples of what second-century authors are doing with the canonical texts, above all the Synoptic Gospels. Apocryphal narratives, particularly infancy gospels and apocryphal acts, frequently take up scenes and sayings from the Synoptics, adapting them to new contexts and retelling them from different perspectives. Second, in "The Synoptic Gospels and the Noncanonical Acts of the Apostles," Bovon points to a second point of comparison: apocryphal acts in particular provide an analogy for the compositional process of the Synoptic Gospels, particularly for the ways in which the authors of Matthew and Luke worked with the Gospel of Mark (2003b, 209–25). Apocryphal narratives in general (and apocryphal acts in particular) are "fluid" texts: these narratives were continually reworked by successive redactors who improved, reshaped, pruned, and added to them. While the canonical Gospels would soon be assigned authors and invested with authority, in the early period (certainly to the end of the first century and first half of the second), they were treated by redactors in much the same way that apocryphal acts always would be. As Bovon puts it: "at this earlier time the gospels were what the apocrypha never ceased to be" (210). Third, Bovon notes that apocryphal texts provide evidence not just of the reception of the content of the Synoptic Gospels but also of traditions concerning the composition of the Synoptic Gospels by Matthew, Mark, and Luke (2003a, 299–300).

In this essay, I take up each of these points, to which Bovon first drew attention. I will offer one sample case for each, taking up (1) the "transfiguration" scene in the *Acts of John* as an example of a reception of the Synoptic transfiguration account, (2) two recensions of a passage from the *Acts of John in Rome* as an analogy for the compositional process of the Synoptics, and (3) a passage from the *Acts of Timothy* as an example of apocryphal traditions reflecting on the compositional process of the Synoptics. These are offered not as exhaustive accounts of the contributions the study of apocryphal narratives might make to the study of the Synoptic Gospels but as an effort to illustrate the potential and to amplify Bovon's initial call for more research in these areas.

The Reception of the Synoptic Gospels in Apocryphal Narratives

Scholars of the Synoptic Gospels have most frequently engaged with apocryphal texts to the extent that they represent potentially early witnesses to the status and circulation of the canonical works. Leaving aside the well-known example of the Gospel of Thomas (which is treated elsewhere in this book), we might point to the engagement of Lukan scholars with the apocryphal *Protevangelium of James*, composed in the second century CE, which Bovon himself has argued may indeed provide some of the earliest evidence of use of the Gospel of Luke (2003a; see also Gregory 2003, 103–12, 153–72). J. Keith Elliott, like Bovon a scholar whose work bridges the canonical and apocryphal (also bringing the latter to bear on the former), has rigorously evaluated the extent to which apocryphal texts can contribute to text-critical studies of the canonical New Testament, likewise calling for more attention to the ways in which later authors used and adapted canonical sources (e.g. 1997, 265–71; 2010, 33–34).[1] This work has not,

---

[1] See, for example, Elliott 1997; see also Elliott 2010, particularly 33–34, where Elliott writes: "obviously, as these apocryphal texts are not copies of the canonical books, text-critics cannot use this evidence as if they were manuscript witnesses, but what they can and should do is to see how a particular saying of Jesus (for example) was adjusted in different retellings. The synoptic parallels reveal their own differences and similarities especially if we are alert to the *apparatus criticus*; similarly, the same parallels found in non-canonical sources, apocryphal and in some cases patristic, usually exhibit still further variations. What all this tells the textual critic of the Greek New Testament is that we are dealing with

however, been carried out as fully as it might be. In this section, I will take as an exemplary case the transfiguration narrative (Mark 9:2–8, Matt 17:1–8, and Luke 9:28–36), in part because apocryphal versions of the transfiguration have received substantial treatment in contemporary canonical scholarship. I hope to illustrate, on the one hand, some of the pitfalls that have hindered a full consideration of apocryphal sources in the past and, on the other hand, the potential for apocryphal texts to enrich our understanding of the Synoptic episode.

Modern scholarship on the Synoptic transfiguration episode has been dominated by two main theories, recently and neatly summarized by Delbert Burkett as follows: "either Jesus' transformation was an epiphany, that is, an unveiling of the divine nature that he already possessed, or it was a preview, that is, a revelation of the divine glory that he would possess in the future" (2019, 414).[2] Much, if not all, of this scholarship responds to the suggestion (made early on by both J. Wellhausen and G. Volkmar) that the transfiguration narrative was originally a resurrection narrative (see Blinzler 1937; Baltensweiler 1959; Stein 1976). It is in connection with this idea that significant attention has been paid to apocryphal texts: in particular, the apocryphal *Apocalypse of Peter* was introduced as comparandum, either as an early transfiguration account that is clearly a resurrection-ascension narrative (see Goetz 1927) or as a (not necessarily early) transfiguration account that places Jesus's transfiguration in a parousia-context (e.g. Boobyer 1942).

This emphasis on identifying pre-Synoptic versions of the episode that might shed light on its "original" form and meaning is carried over into the evaluation of the transfiguration as it appears elsewhere, that is, in the apocryphal *Acts of Thomas*, *Acts of John*, and *Acts of Peter*—all of which have received some attention in monographs and articles on the canonical transfiguration accounts. Consider, for example, Joseph Blinzler's comparison of the transfiguration in the *Acts of John* 90–91 with the Synoptic accounts. After offering a fairly detailed analysis of the similarities and differences, Blinzler emphasizes moments where the *Acts of John* is not just different but is in fact contrary to the canonical accounts. He writes: "während bei den Synoptikern, bei Mk ausdrücklich in erster Linier, die Kleider umgestaltet werden, erscheint in den Akten—wohl dem antiken Geschmack des Verfassers zuliebe—Jesus als unverhüllt. Statt des Antlitzes, wie Mt und Lk, hebt der Autor der Akten die Beleuchtung der Füße hervor. Unser modernes Empfinden ist in Anbetracht derartig trivialisierender Züge (vgl. dazu auch das burleske Wort von den Stockschlägen) fast geneigt, die Erzählung als Parodie zur evangelischen aufzufassen. Aber eine polemische Absicht wird den Akten hier fernliegen: Unbedenklich reihen sie zum Erhabenen das Lächerliche (vgl. K. 60f)" (1937,

---

traditions which were transmitted with a relative degree of freedom in the first one hundred years of their existence. Here again that word 'freedom' is used of the 2nd century. All the important variants that we can identify in our manuscripts were in existence in the 2nd century.... Perhaps originally there were more in existence. We cannot know. All that one can say is that there was a flexibility, a diversity in that 2nd century text."

[2] For an alternative summary, see Rothschild 2005, 133–34.

64). To my mind, Blinzler here makes some very good observations: the shift of focus from the character of Jesus's clothing to his total nakedness and from his shining face to his shining feet does suggest a trivialization, which, combined with Jesus's transformation into a grumpy, beard-pulling old man, does indeed approach a parody of the canonical accounts. Blinzler sees this in the text but cannot really entertain the possibility because he cannot bring himself to attribute any serious intentionality to the author's use of humor. For Blinzler, this author simply piles up "ridiculous" stories "uncritically" (196–10).[3] Blinzler concludes that the transfiguration as recorded in the *Acts of John* has nothing to offer for our understanding of the Synoptic versions: "daher können auch sie die kanonischen Berichte nicht erhellen oder bereichern, selbst wenn man die frühest mögliche Datierung (etwa Mitte des 2. Jh.) annehmen wollte" (64; see also Baltensweiler 1959, 21).

But what if we were to both set aside the hunt for an early, independent version of the transfiguration and, contrary to Blinzler, entertain the possibility that the author of the *Acts of John* was in fact thinking, was in fact doing critical work?[4] What could we do with Blinzler's own observations? Is it possible that the *Acts of John* presents a parody of the Synoptic transfiguration accounts and, if so, what would the significance of that be? A handbook essay is not quite the place to pursue these questions at length, but we might briefly look at the transfiguration account in the *Acts of John* with an eye toward this underlying question: can a later version of a narrated episode shed light on and enrich our understanding of earlier versions?

The transfiguration in the *Acts of John* is somewhat longer than the Synoptic accounts, but because its details are likely not familiar to all readers of this handbook I present it here in full:

90. ἄλλοτε δέ ποτε παραλαμβάνει με <καὶ> Ἰάκωβον καὶ Πέτρον εἰς τὸ ὄρος ὅπου ἦν αὐτῷ ἔθος εὔχεσθαι, καὶ εἴδομεν <ἐν> αὐτῷ φῶς τοιοῦτον ὁποῖον οὐκ ἔστιν δυνατὸν ἀνθρώπῳ χρωμένῳ λόγῳ φθαρτῷ ἐκφέρειν οἷον ἦν. πάλιν ὁμοίως ἀνάγει ἡμᾶς τοὺς τρεῖς εἰς τὸ ὄρος λέγων· Ἔλθατε σὺν ἐμοί. Ἡμεῖς δὲ πάλιν ἐπορεύθημεν, καὶ ὁρῶμεν αὐτὸν ἀπὸ διαστήματος εὐχόμενον· ἐγὼ δὲ οὖν, ἐπειδὴ ἐφίλει με, ἠρέμα ὡς μὴ ὁρῶντος [αὐτὸς] αὐτοῦ ἐγγίζω αὐτῷ καὶ ἵσταμαι ἀφορῶν [αὐτὸν] εἰς τὰ ὀπίσθια αὐτοῦ· καὶ ὁρῶ αὐτὸν ἱμάτια μὲν μηδὲ ὅλως ἠμφιεσμένον, γυμνὸν δὲ τούτων <τῶν> ὁρωμένων ὑφ' ἡμῶν, ἄνθρωπον δὲ οὐδὲ ὅλως· καὶ τοὺς μὲν πόδας [ποίας] χιόνος λε υκοτέρους, ὡς καὶ τὴν γῆν ἐκείνην καταλάμπεσθαι ὑπὸ τῶν ποδῶν· τὴν δὲ κεφαλὴν εἰς τὸν οὐρανὸν ἐρειδομένην, ὡς φοβηθέντα με κραυγάσαι, αὐτὸν δὲ ἐπιστραφέντα μικρὸν ἄνθρωπον ὀφθῆναι καὶ κρατήσαντά μου τὸ γένειον ἀνασπάσαι καὶ εἰπεῖν μοι· Ἰωάννη, μὴ γίνου ἄπιστος ἀλλὰ πιστὸς καὶ μὴ περίεργος. Καὶ εἶπον αὐτῷ· Τί

---

[3] Here, Blinzler cites *Acts of John* 60, the story of the obedient bedbugs. This is no doubt an amusing episode, but it is not without serious content. See Spittler 2008, 96–110.

[4] I wish I could write here that Blinzler's view on the "uncritical" nature of the *Acts of John* is no longer commonly held. It is certainly the case that scholars of apocryphal Christian literature no longer view texts like the *Acts of John* in this way; see, for example, Nicklas 2019; 2007. It is, however, not entirely clear to me that a majority of nonspecialists have adopted this perspective.

γὰρ ἐποίησα, κύριε; Λέγω δὲ ὑμῖν, ἀδελφοί, οὕτως πεπόνηκα τὸν τόπον ἐκεῖνον ὅθεν μου τοῦ γενείου ἐλάβετο ἡμέρας τριάκοντα, ὥστε με εἰπεῖν αὐτῷ· Κύριε, εἰ τὸ τίλμα σου παίζοντος τοιαύτην ἀλγηδόνα πεποίηκεν, τί εἰ ῥαπίσμασίν με ἔλαβες; Καὶ αὐτός μοι εἶπεν· Σὸν λοιπὸν ἤτω μὴ πειράζειν τὸν ἀπείραστον. 91. Ὁ δὲ Πέτρος καὶ Ἰάκωβος ἐμοῦ ὁμιλοῦντος τῷ κυρίῳ ἠγανάκτουν διανευόμενοί με ὅπως παραγένωμαι πρὸς αὐτοὺς ἀπολιπὼν μόνον τὸν κύριον. καὶ ἐπορεύθην καὶ εἶπον μοι ἀμφότεροι· Ὁ τῷ κυρίῳ προσομιλῶν γέρων ἐπὶ ὕψους τίς ἦν; καὶ γὰρ ἠκροώμεθα ἀμφοτέρων λαλούντων. Καὶ συννοήσας τὴν πολλὴν χάριν αὐτοῦ καὶ πολυπρόσωπον ἑνότητα καὶ σοφίαν ἄληκτον εἰς ἡμᾶς ἀποβλέπουσαν εἶπον· Μαθήσεσθε αὐτοῦ τοῦτο αὐτὸν ἐξετάσαντες. (Junod and Kaestli 1983, 193, 195, 197)

90. 'Another time, he had James, Peter, and me accompany him to the mountain on which he used to pray. There we saw upon him a kind of light that a mortal using perishable speech could not possibly describe. Similarly, at another time, he led the three of us up the mountain saying, "Come with me." Again we went, and stood at some distance watching him pray. And then, because he loved me, I quietly approached him, supposing that I was not detected, and stood gazing at him from behind. He was quite without clothing, devoid of the garments we usually saw him wearing; in fact, he wasn't like a regular person in any way. His feet were whiter than snow—so bright that they illumined the ground beneath him. His head extended up to the sky. I cried out in terror. He turned around, like a small person in appearance, seized my beard, and gave it a tug. "John," he said, "don't be skeptical but be a believer; and don't be such a busy-body!" And I said to him, "Well, what did I do, Lord?" And I'm telling you, brothers, I suffered so much at the place where he took hold of my beard for thirty days that I said to him, "Lord, if your joking tug has caused such pain, what [would it be like] if you took hold of me with slaps?" He answered, "From now on do not test the untestable!" 91. But, while I was conversing with the Lord, Peter and James got irritated, beckoning to me that I come to them and leave the Lord alone. And I went, and they both said to me: "Who was the old man conversing with the Lord on the mountain? For indeed we heard them both speaking." And after reflecting on his great grace and many-faced oneness and wisdom unceasingly gazing at us, I said: "You will learn this from him if you ask him."' (*Acts of John* 90–91)[5]

Multiple elements shared with the Synoptic accounts are immediately evident: The incident involves Peter, James, and John, whom Jesus specifically takes aside (παραλαμβάνει) onto a mountain (ὄρος); as in Luke's account, the *Acts of John* notes that Jesus is there to pray (εὔχεσθαι).[6] The passage describes a great light (φῶς), which is perhaps closest to Matthew's notice that Jesus's face "shone like the sun" and that his garments became "white as light" (λευκὰ ὡς τὸ φῶς). As in the Synoptic accounts, fear is narrated (though

---

[5] Unless otherwise noted, all translations from Greek are my own, though, for the *Acts of John*, with reference to those of Pervo with Hills 2016, Elliott 1993, and James 1924. Here I largely follow Pervo's.

[6] These elements alone are more than enough to indicate that the author of this passage is familiar with one or more versions of the Synoptic transfiguration. As discussed below, this section of the *Acts of John* (chapters 87–93, all contained in a single manuscript) also renarrates Jesus's initial calling of the disciples, again with clear knowledge of one or more versions of the Synoptic accounts.

notably differently in each of the four accounts). As in the Synoptics, particularly Mark's version, Jesus's gloriously bright manifestation comes to an abrupt end. And also as in the Synoptics, the narrative proceeds with bickering among the disciples.

There are also some notable differences, places where (as Blinzler suggests), specific elements of the Synoptic accounts seem to be played with. Each of the Synoptic accounts specifically refers to the transformation of Jesus's garments (ἱμάτια): in Mark, the transformation of his garments to a dazzling white is, in fact, the only element of Jesus's transfiguration that is explicitly described; in Matthew and Luke, this element remains but is preceded by a description of some change to his face. The author of the account in the *Acts of John* also specifically refers to Jesus's garments (ἱμάτια) but only to make it explicitly clear that it is not Jesus's garments that are changed; to the contrary, the narrative emphasizes that Jesus is not wearing any garments at all! In a similar vein, it is not Jesus's face that becomes radiant white but rather his feet; his face—perhaps not visible, as his head reaches into the heavens—is not described. Further, while each of the Synoptic accounts narrates the transfiguration as a single occurrence taking place at a particular time, in the author of the *Acts of John* emphasizes the iterative nature of Jesus's transformations: the experience of Peter, James, and John is broken up into two distinct occurrences that took place "another time" (ἄλλοτε) and then "again" (πάλιν). Moreover, these are just two of some twelve instances within chapters 87–93 in which Jesus gives the impression of taking multiple forms, beginning with the initial call of James and John, in which the two brothers see Jesus as a child and man, respectively, and including John's experience reclining at dinner against Jesus's chest, which feels alternately hard as stone and squishy (see Junod and Kaestli 1983, 474–90; Lalleman 1995, 97–118).

These observations on specific points of both contact and disconnect lead to broader observations of the particular interests of this new account. Above all, we note that the "transfiguration" as narrated in the *Acts of John* is, in fact, devoid of any vocabulary of transformation. The verb μεταμορφόω, used in Mark and maintained in Matthew, is absent, but so is any vocabulary of change or difference (cf. Luke's turn of phrase in 9:29). Taking one further step back, we observe that the same holds true for all of the descriptions of Jesus's taking of multiple forms in chapters 87–93: here we have a polymorphic deity who continually "appears"[7] or whom the disciples "saw" in multiple forms but is never explicitly described as changing or transforming. Moreover, there is little sense that any of the individual forms is his real form, nor indeed is there much sense that any other forms are a disguise. In depicting Jesus as appearing polymorphically from beginning to end, the text instructs the reader to reject any single form as either more or less true. To be sure, John is depicted as continually trying to discover information about Jesus: does he ever close his eyes? does he leave footprints? John's view of Jesus on the mountain is itself a result of this curiosity: he has approached Jesus from behind, without him seeing. The reader might understand the form Jesus appears in

---

[7] Note that the usage of ὤφθη in this episode is further evidence that the word is not in fact a *terminus technicus* for resurrection appearances, as claimed by Weeden 1971, 119; see discussion by Stein 1976, 80–83.

here as closest to a "true" form (a giant with radiant feet and a head stretching into the heavens, stripped of the normal clothes Jesus usually wears), but the narrative does not say so. To the contrary, that notion is immediately undercut, as Jesus appears in the form of a short old man, who tugs John's beard and commands him (with a line from the Thomas episode in John 20:27) to be faithful rather than unbelieving, and—what's more—not so inquisitive (περίεργος)!

This brings us to a consideration of the characterization of John throughout the passage. At this point, it is helpful to broaden our scope and consider the longer episode, which begins in medias res in 87 with a crowd of questioning Christians, at a loss for how to understand a report from one of their contemporaries of Jesus's polymorphy. John reassures them, saying:

Ἄνδρες ἀδελφοί, οὐδὲν ξένον πεπόνθατε οὐδὲ παράδοξον περὶ τῆς εἰς τὸν <κύριον> ἐκδοχῆς, ὅπου γε καὶ ἡμεῖς, οὓς ἐξελέξατο ἑαυτῷ ἀποστόλους, πολλὰ ἐπειράσθημεν· ἐγὼ μὲν ὑμῖν <οὔτε> προσομιλεῖν[8] οὔτε γράψαι χωρῶ ἅ τε εἶδον ἅ τε ἤκουσα· καὶ νῦν μὴν δεῖ με πρὸς τὰς ἀκοὰς ὑμῶν ἁρμόσασθαι, καὶ καθ' ἃ χωρεῖ ἕκαστος ἐκείνων ὑμῖν κοινωνήσω ὧν ἀκροαταὶ δύνασθε γενέσθαι, ὅπως ἴδητε τὴν περὶ αὐτὸν δόξαν ἥτις ἦν καὶ ἔστιν καὶ νῦν καὶ εἰς ἀεί.

Men, brothers: you have experienced nothing strange or miraculous in this perception of the Lord, inasmuch as even we, whom he selected for himself as apostles, were tested in many ways. I, for my part, although conversing with you, am neither able to write what I saw nor what I heard. Well, even now it is necessary for me to adapt to your hearing; indeed, I will communicate with you according to the capacities of each of you who are able to be hearers, so that you might know the glory about him— which was and is, both now and forever. (*Acts of John* 88:1-8)

John then recounts his multiple experiences with a polymorphic Jesus, beginning with an account from the apostle's own perspective of the calling of the first disciples (Mark 1:16-20 and parallels). The overarching story John tells of his experiences of Jesus is one of increasing confusion, not recognition, as he makes quite plain in 89: "Then, having followed him, we were both more and more confused as we contemplated the matter" (εἶτα ἑπόμενοι αὐτῷ ἀμφότεροι κατ' ὀλίγον ἠπορούμεν ἐννοούμενοι τὸ πρᾶγμα). This

---

[8] This is Junod and Kaestli's emendation of text; the manuscript lacks the initial οὔτε and does not have the infinitive προσομιλεῖν but rather πρὸσόμιλὸν, which (correcting the orthography) I take to be the nominative masculine singular present active participle. I do not think the emendation is required. While one might want a coordinated οὔτε . . . οὔτε construction, this is not strictly necessary (see Denniston 1950, 508-11). Without it, there is no need to emend προσομιλῶν to προσομιλεῖν to make the two οὔτε clauses correspond; instead, I take προσομιλῶν as a concessive—but not negated— circumstantial participle (and translate as such). This construal has the added benefit of corresponding to the actual situation narrated: John *is in fact conversing* with his audience. There is an interesting meta-analysis to be made here as well: John expresses an inability to write down what he saw and heard, but can adapt his speech to the capacities of his audience; the author of the text must, of course, write these things down, but he compromises by presenting the material in direct discourse.

confusion continues as John, who reclines against Jesus, notices that his chest is sometimes hard, sometimes soft (89.11–15). There follows the transfiguration account (divided, as noted, into two separate occasions), John's largely unsuccessful attempt to observe Jesus during the night while the other disciples were sleeping (92), another report on the shifting quality of Jesus's body, and, finally, John's observation that Jesus never left footprints in the earth. The larger episode spanning 87–93 closes with this summative statement: καὶ ταῦτα ὑμῖν ἔτι ὥσπερ προτροπῆς ἕνεκεν, ἀδελφοί, τῆς ἐπ᾽ αὐτὸν πίστεως ὁμιλῶ· τὰ γὰρ μεγαλεῖα αὐτοῦ καὶ τὰ θαυμάσια τὸ νῦν σεσιγήσθω, ἄρρητα ὄντα καὶ τάχα οὐ δυνάμενα οὔτε λέγεσθαι οὔτε ἀκούεσθαι. "Indeed I am saying these things to you as I do, brothers and sisters, for the purpose of incitement of faith in him; for as to his great deeds and miracles, one must now be silent, since they are unspeakable and, perhaps, not at all able to be spoken or heard" (*Acts of John* 93:14–17). Keeping in mind that this story is narrated in John's own voice, it is important to note that, while he does indeed present himself as having special access to Jesus, John does not present himself as having special knowledge of Jesus's true identity. To the contrary, John presents himself as knowing—better than anyone else—that he does not know Jesus's true form.

This central paradox is narrated in what I take to be a light, even humorous tone. It is notoriously difficult to prove that an ancient text—particularly one for which we have little evidence of reception—was intended to be funny; that said, many modern readers of the *Acts of John* have found evidence of humor in multiple episodes (see Spittler 2017, 209–25). I would not go so far as to confirm Blinzler's suggestion that the episode is a literary parody of the Synoptic account; I do not find enough direct points of connection to make that argument. I would say, however, that the characterization of John stands in stark ironic contrast to the characterization of Peter in both the Synoptic and apocryphal accounts. The Synoptic Peter displays his lack of understanding through a series of mistakes that are rebuked by Jesus; later Petrine accounts (in 2 Peter, the *Apocalypse of Peter*, and the *Acts of Peter* 20–21) have notable apologetic tendencies, generally omitting any reference to Peter's mistakes (see Lee 2009, 183; Neyrey 1980, 504–19). The *Acts of John* presents John as describing his own mistakes in literally painful detail, including a comedic punishment by Jesus (see Spittler 2017, 222).[9] His lack of understanding is depicted less as a problem to be overcome than as a state to be accepted.

And so what, if anything, does reflection on the transfiguration in the *Acts of John* add to our thinking about the Synoptic transfiguration accounts? In the first place, it should underscore both the flexibility of the basic story and the rigidity of modern categories of interpretation. In this section of the *Acts of John* we have an early reception and renarration of the scene that is neither an epiphany nor a preview of the Parousia—and certainly not a misplaced resurrection account. Here, the "transfiguration" is not really a transformation at all; or, rather, "transfiguring" is Jesus's constant state, evident to his disciples (particularly, but not exclusively, John) within his lifetime on earth, and

---

[9] See discussion in Spittler 2017, 222. For examples of comic beard-pulling, see Lucian, *Symposium (or The Lapiths)*, 33 and 43, *The Dead Come to Life*, 12, *Zeus Rants*, 16; Persius, *Satire 1*, lines 132–34, *Satire 2*, lines 26–29; Horace, *Satire 1*, lines 133–34; Martial, *Epigram 10*, lines 9–10.

continually evident to Christians of the next generation (like Drusiana, whose vision of a polymorphic Jesus launched the entire episode and frames John's recounting of his own experiences). Moreover, John's attempts to gather information about Jesus's form (secretly observing him, checking for footprints, watching to see if he closes his eyes) are presented as comically ineffectual: at the moment when the reader might think they are hearing a description of Jesus as he really is (brighter than light, larger than life), Jesus appears as a short old man, giving John's beard a playful yet painful tug and telling him not to be so curious. The effect, particularly with John narrating these stories about himself, is on the one hand to depict curiosity and speculation about Jesus's true form as understandable yet on the other hand to underscore the fact that any single notion of Jesus's true form is at best inadequate. That a Christian, perhaps as early as the mid-second century CE, could think of the transfiguration in this way should give us some pause before too quickly narrowing the list of possible "original" meanings and contexts of the Synoptic accounts. That a Christian, perhaps actually writing centuries later, could think of the transfiguration in this way should also give us pause before judging "earlier" or more "original" accounts to be more theologically interesting or sophisticated.

Apocryphal Acts as an Analogy for the Compositional Process of the Synoptic Gospels

As noted above, concerning the state of the Synoptic Gospels before the second half of the second century Bovon writes: "at this earlier time the gospels were what the apocrypha never ceased to be" (2003b, 20). Apocryphal narratives were continually—right up to the modern period—reworked, reshaped, added to, subtracted from, and recombined.[10] These are the same redactional activities that resulted in the three distinct Synoptic Gospels: reworking, reshaping, adding to, subtracting from, and recombining are precisely what the redactors who produced Matthew and Luke did with Mark, and the Gospel of Mark may itself be the result of such activities. These activities ground to a halt once these three Gospels were invested with authors and canonical authority; without the stabilizing effect of authorship and, above all, canonicity, these activities simply continued in the case of apocryphal narratives.[11] Thinking in the opposite

---

[10] Bovon notes that at the same time Tischendorf, Lipsius, and Bonnet were preparing the critical editions of apocryphal apostle narratives, the Greek monk Joasaph of the S. Sabba monastery was retelling the same stories in his own style as he produced a new manuscript. See Bovon 2003b, 19–20.

[11] That is, the large-scale editing that the Gospel of Mark was submitted to by the author/editors of Luke and Matthew seems to have come to an end; smaller scale changes (as evident in, for example, the various endings of Mark) continued. The attribution of authorship alone, however, does not seem to have been enough to put a halt to textual fluidity; several apocryphal texts (e.g. the *Acts of John by Prochorus*) are attributed to authors but continue to be reshaped and recombined with other material.

direction, we could also, perhaps more provocatively, say that if the Synoptic Gospels had not been invested with authors and canonical authority, modern scholarship would not regard them as three distinct texts; instead, we would deal with them as three recensions of a single gospel.[12] Many, if not most, apocryphal narratives, particularly apocryphal acts, exist in multiple recensions, and these individual recensions often differ more significantly than the individual Synoptic Gospels differ from each other. This insight should give scholars of apocryphal narratives pause, and indeed it has: a significant body of recent scholarship, particularly that influenced by New Philology, emphasizes attention to individual recensions "as they have been preserved in actual manuscripts, in all their idiosyncratic glory," noting that what we take to be copies of the same text may in fact have "never been associated with the earlier writings by anyone other than their modern editors" (Lundhaug and Lied 2017, 16, 10). The upshot for scholars of the Synoptic Gospels is this: the multiple recensions of "single" apocryphal texts provide us with useful comparanda when thinking about how early Christian editors were working with preexisting source material. Questions of how "Matthew" and "Luke" dealt with "Mark" or "Q" can be raised in the context of how early Christian editors of narrative in general dealt with sources.[13]

The usefulness of this almost too-broad context can be increased if the points to be compared are framed narrowly. Consider, for example, the following passage from the *Acts of John in Rome* (table 11.1), a text that exists in two recensions (presented here synoptically), both narrating the arrest of John in Ephesus, his transport to Rome, his trial before the emperor, and his exile to the island Patmos.[14] We pick up here in chapter 7, when John arrives at Rome and first meets with the emperor; this episode culminates in a quotation from the Old Testament/LXX, and it is in this respect—in the quotation of scripture across multiple versions of the same episode—that I would like to compare the episode with the Synoptic Gospels.

We can describe these two passages as two versions of the same episode, inasmuch as they share a basic emplotment in a larger narrative (in both cases this is John's initial meeting with the Roman emperor), a key piece of action (John kisses the emperor), and a quotation of the LXX (Prov 20:2). Yet in every other detail, they are substantially different. The identity of the emperor is different: in the γ recension, the emperor is Domitian; in the β recension, the emperor is Hadrian. While the action (the kiss) is nearly the same in the two recensions, its immediate context—the situation that prompted it—is rather different: in the γ recension, Domitian is told a miraculous report about John, and therefore attempts to kiss the apostle; John dodges this attempt, instead kissing the emperor's chest, prompting Domitian's questioning of his action. In the

---

[12] I have profited from great conversations with my doctoral student Jonathan D. Holste on this topic.
[13] The same applies, of course, regardless of which solution to the Synoptic Problem one finds most convincing. I suspect, in fact, that a broader sense of how *most* early Christian narratives were continually redacted might lead most scholars to either a more relaxed attitude toward the so-called Problem or much less confidence in individual "solutions" based on the limited source material.
[14] The two Greek recensions along with commentary can be found in Junod and Kaestli 1983, 835–86.

Table 11.1 Two recensions of the *Acts of John in Rome*

γ	β
Now, when much time had elapsed, they finished the journey, with John still fasting in this way. So, bringing him to the king, they said, "Augustus Domitian, we bring before you John, a god not a human being—for from the hour that we arrested him up until now, he has not tasted bread." Domitian, astounded by these things, stretched his face forward, wishing to greet him with a kiss on account of this miracle. But John, dropping his head, kissed his chest. And Domitian said, "Why did you do that? Do you not think me worthy to kiss you?" And John said to him, "It is right first to kiss the mouth of the king. For it is written in the holy books: 'A king's heart is in God's hand'" (Prov 20:2 LXX).	As soon as they arrived in Rome, they brought the apostle to the king. And the apostle, having come face-to-face with the king and drawing near, kissed him on the chest and on the head. The king said to him, "How is it that you have kissed me? For I am a human being, but you—as I hear—teach all human beings to kiss and worship a heavenly god." But the theologian said to the king, "Since it is written: 'A king's heart is in God's hand' (Prov 20:2 LXX), and again 'The Lord's hand is upon the king's head,' on account of this I have kissed your chest and head."

β reception, the emperor is not told of John's miraculous diet (although the apostle has similarly fasted throughout the journey from Ephesus); instead, John simply initiates the kiss, this time on both chest and head, though this action still prompts questioning by the emperor. While the prompts and rationales are somewhat different, in both instances the emperor's question amounts to "why did you do that?" John's answer, in both instances, is a quotation of Proverbs 21:1 LXX.

Scholarship on the *Acts of John in Rome* (what little is available) has focused on the relationship between the two recensions. Early scholarship by R. A. Lipsius regarded the two recensions as independent redactions of the same source, which he supposed to be lost episodes from the *Periodoi of Leucius* (i.e., the text scholars now refer to as the early *Acts of John*). Junod and Kaestli, however, have argued convincingly that the β recension is dependent upon the γ recension, inasmuch as the characteristic elements of the β recension can be explained largely as the effort of a redactor to harmonize the γ recension with the *Acts of John by Prochorus*, yet another Johannine apocryphon into which this redactor recombined the *Acts of John in Rome* (Junod and Kaestli 1983, 837–40). A key element of this redactional effort is the downplaying of the emphasis on Christ's power over the emperor in favor of an emphasis on the divine investiture of imperial power. We can clearly see this difference at play in our episode: whereas in the γ recension John rejects an initial attempt at a kiss from Domitian, instead offering his own biblically sanctioned version (reasoning via Proverbs that a kiss on the king's chest is tantamount to kissing God's hands), in the β recension it is the emperor who questions the kiss initiated by God, suggesting his own unworthiness of a kiss from the apostle. As is no doubt clear, then, scholarship on the *Acts of John in Rome* has proceeded very much like (and certainly under the influence of) scholarship on the Synoptic Gospels. We have raised and answered questions of literary dependence, ultimately using the perceived redactional efforts of one author/editor to underscore both his own theological interests and the elements he found unacceptable in his *Vorlage*, just as we have done with Mark and Matthew, Mark and Luke, and/or Matthew, Luke, and their hypothetical common source.

But could texts like the *Acts of John in Rome* be brought back to bear on our understanding of the editorial work we find in the Synoptics? I think the potential is there. The exchange between the apostle and the emperor calls to mind, for example, the episode concerning the "Greatest Commandment" at Mark 12:28-37, Matthew 22:34-40, and Luke 10:25-28—an episode that similarly hinges on the quotation of the Old Testament/LXX. There we find precisely the same kinds of differences we noted above: the identity of the hero's interlocutor shifts between versions; the situation that prompts the quotation of scripture modulates; the relationship between the hero and the interlocutor is variably adversarial (with the relationship between Jesus and his Jewish interlocutor growing more adversarial from Mark to Luke and Matthew, and the relationship between John and his imperial interlocutor growing less so from the γ to the β recension). While there is variation as to the precise formulation of the quotations of scripture, the central element is stable in both sets of recensions and serves as the culminating moment of the exchange.[15] Much ink has been spilled on the use of the Old Testament/LXX in the New Testament, including numerous books and essays specifically dedicated to the Synoptic Gospels, even one monograph and one major essay dedicated explicitly to the question of Old Testament/LXX quotations and the Synoptic Problem (see New 1993; Goodacre 2011). To my knowledge, however, no attention has been paid to the comparable use of the Old Testament/LXX across multiple recensions of apocryphal texts. What would such comparanda add to our understanding of the Synoptics? We won't know until we actually make the comparisons. The particular value of the apocryphal texts as comparanda will likely be their sheer bulk: I do not expect that the analysis of a single apocryphal episode will dramatically change our understanding of any Synoptic text; I do expect, however, that a comprehensive study of apocryphal episodes quoting the Old Testament/LXX that exist in multiple recensions—that is, a study of how editors treat scriptural quotations when producing new versions of texts—would shed significant light on the activities of the author-editors who produced the Gospels of Matthew and Luke.

---

[15] The two accounts of the apostle's kiss also, perhaps, call to mind the Synoptic episode of the anointing woman in Mark 14:3-9, Matt 26:6-13, and Luke 7:36-50: both sets of episodes include descriptions of a significant action, whose significance is variable. Just as the γ and β recensions differ as to the significance of John's kissing the emperor's chest (has he potentially insulted the emperor by rejecting his own kiss, or has he honored the emperor by spontaneously offering the kiss?), the three versions of the anointing woman episode differ on the reason for performing the action (is she preparing Jesus's body for burial, or is she demonstrating her great love for Jesus?) as well as the problematic aspect of the action (is she wasting money, or is she a polluted woman whose touch he should reject?). I thank David Moessner for noting this comparandum (in conversation at the University of Regensburg's Beyond Canon Center (directed by Tobias Nicklas), October 7, 2019).

An Apocryphal Account of the Redaction of the Synoptic Gospels

The thread that connects the material presented in the two preceding sections is the recognition of the fluidity, flexibility, and perhaps general messiness of early Christian narratives, including the Synoptic Gospels. Early Christian author-editors clearly felt free to borrow, to excise, to adapt, to rearrange, and to rewrite existing narratives; moreover, the extant texts indicate that virtually all Christian narratives, whether canonical or apocryphal, received this treatment. Particularly interesting in this context is an apocryphal account of this very process, that is, of the redacting of the Synoptic Gospels. Eusebius's account of the composition of the canonical Gospels is well known: he writes that John, noting that the Gospels of Matthew, Mark, and Luke all lacked material describing the beginning of Jesus's ministry (before John the Baptist's arrest), wrote his own Gospel as a supplement.[16] A similar but rather more developed account is found in the *Acts of Timothy*, likely composed in Ephesus in or around the fifth century CE.[17] This short text in fact relates only one "act" of Timothy: his protest at a "pagan" religious festival in Ephesus (the Katagogia) and his resultant martyrdom. This report, moreover, is told quite briefly and represents less than half of the total text. The remainder of the text has to do with the apostle John, narrating his arrival at Ephesus, the composition of the Fourth Gospel, and his exile to and return from Patmos—all the while underscoring the fact that Timothy was also *his* disciple (i.e., not just a disciple of Paul). As in Eusebius, here John writes his Gospel last and as a supplement to the other three, which he has read. Notably, however, in the *Acts of Timothy*, John is not just the author of the Fourth Gospel but is in fact the editor of the Synoptics! The relevant passage is both brief and extremely interesting, and so I quote it in full:

8. ὅτε καὶ οἱ ἐπακολουθήσαντες τοῖς μαθηταῖς τοῦ κυρίου ἡμῶν ἰησοῦ χριστοῦ τοὺς παρ' αὐτῶν σποράδην συνταγέντας χάρτας διαφόροις γλώσσαις συντεταγμένους τῶν γενομένων ἐπ' αὐτῶν θαυματουργημάτων ὑπὸ κυρίου ἡμῶν ἰησοῦ χριστοῦ οὐκ ἐγνωκότες συνθεῖναι, παραγενόμενοι ἐπὶ τῆς ἐφεσίων κατὰ κοινὴν γνώμην ἰωάννῃ τῷ πανευφήμῳ θεολόγῳ αὐτοὺς προσήγαγον· 9. ὅστις πάντα κατανοήσας καὶ ἐξ αὐτῶν ὁρμηθεὶς τὰ μὲν παρ' αὐτῶν εἰρημένα ἐν τοῖς τρισὶν εὐαγγελίοις ἐνθεὶς κατὰ τάξιν ματθαίου καὶ μάρκου καὶ λουκᾶ ἀπεγράψατο, τὰς τούτων ὀνομασίας ἐνθεὶς τοῖς εὐαγγελίοις· 10. εὑρὼν δὲ αὐτοὺς τὰ τῆς οἰκονομίας τῆς ἐνανθρωπήσεως

---

[16] See Eusebius, *Historia Ecclesiae* 3.24; cf. 6.14.7.

[17] This previously neglected apocryphon has received a small flurry of attention in the last decade or so, no doubt spurred by the new edition of Claudio Zamagni (2007). Cavan Concannon has produced an English translation and introduction (2016a, 395–405) as well as a substantial article on the context and purpose of the text (2016b). See also Kensky 2019 and Nicklas 2018, and most recently Jan Bremmer (2021).

γενεαλογήσαντας,[18] ὅτε τὰ ἐκ τοῦ θείου στήθους ἀναμαξάμενος τὰ ἐκείνοις οὐκ εἰρημένα αὐτὸς θεολογεῖ, ἀναπληρώσας καὶ τὰ ἐλλιπῶς αὐτοῖς εἰρημένα ἐν τοῖς κεφαλαίοις θεῖα θαυματουργήματα· ὅθεν τὸ τοιοῦτον σύνταγμα εἴτουν εὐαγγέλιον τῷ ἑαυτοῦ ἐπετέθεικεν ὀνόματι. (Zamagni 2007)

8. At that time, those who had followed the disciples of our Lord Jesus Christ, because they did not know how to piece together sheets of paper (composed scatteredly by them in different languages and comprising the miracles accomplished in their time by our Lord Jesus Christ) and because they also were present at the city of the Ephesians, by communal decision brought [the sheets of paper] to the entirely-praiseworthy theologian, John— 9. who indeed, after observing everything well and beginning from them, on the one hand, after putting the things said by them into three gospels, designated them in order as Matthew's, Mark's, and Luke's, putting their names onto the Gospels. 10. On the other hand, having found that they described the process of his becoming human in terms of human generations, whereas he had received from the divine breast things not told by them, he himself gave an account in divine terms, also supplementing the divine miracles inadequately told by them in their chapters.[19] In the end, the resulting composition—that is, the Gospel—he attributed to his own name.[20]

There is much to take note of in this short passage. First is perhaps the impact of the imagined physical form of the writings of the early compositions: these are loose sheets of paper, whose sequencing must be determined.[21] The work of arranging the Synoptic Gospels—both internally and externally as a corpus—is John's; prior to his efforts, the material that would make up the Synoptics is imagined as completely amorphous. That

---

[18] Zamagni's text reads γενεαλογήσαντες here, while Usener has γενεαλογήσαντας. Neither editor notes any variants. Given the syntactical call for an accusative here, I suspect Zamagni's text is a typo.

[19] There are multiple ways to take this sentence, particularly the phrase ἐν τοῖς κεφαλαίοις. In translating it as "in their chapters," I am drawing a connection with the practice in fifth-century (and beyond) manuscripts of dividing the Gospels into chapters (κεφάλαια) and prefixing tables of κεφάλαια to the Gospels. In the first half of the sentence (εὑρὼν δὲ αὐτοὺς τὰ τῆς οἰκονομίας τῆς ἐνανθρωπήσεως γενεαλογήσαντας, ὅτε τὰ ἐκ τοῦ θείου στήθους ἀναμαξάμενος τὰ ἐκείνοις οὐκ εἰρημένα αὐτὸς θεολογεῖ) the author is describing differences between the genealogies found in Matthew and Luke and John 1, where the incarnation of Jesus is indeed described in terms of human generations and in more divine terms, respectively. While contemporary synopses of the four Gospels do not generally place John 1 in a parallel column alongside the genealogies of Matthew and Luke, it is important to remember that Eusebius's Canon Tables do just that. In fact, I would argue that the *Acts of Timothy* is, at this point, influenced by the Canon Tables. In the second half of the sentence (ἀναπληρώσας καὶ τὰ ἐλλιπῶς αὐτοῖς εἰρημένα ἐν τοῖς κεφαλαίοις θεῖα θαυματουργήματα), where the emphasis is on the broader supplementation of information, the emphasis is on "the chapters," that is, the remainder of the narratives.

[20] The final translation choices here are my own, but I benefited immensely from the input of Jan Bremmer, Janet Downie, Jörg Frey, David Moessner, Tobias Nicklas, Anna Oracz, Mara Rescio, Julia Snyder, and Luigi Walt at a translation seminar organized through the University of Regensburg's Beyond Canon Center on October 9, 2019.

[21] I thank Jan Bremmer for this observation, made in conversation at the University of Regensburg's Beyond Canon Center (directed by Tobias Nicklas) on September 17, 2019.

situation, moreover, is imagined as untenable: second- and third-generation Christians are depicted as recognizing the need for order, for arrangement; John's suitability to do this work is attributed to his repute as a theologian. The fact that he was the Beloved Disciple, and thus had special access to certain information (particularly regarding the incarnation), is offered as a rationale for the composition of his own Gospel. The verb used to describe this special access is particularly evocative: ἀναμαξάμενος (ἀναμάσσω) refers quite clearly to physical contact, meaning "wipe off" (as one might smear a liquid or other substance on someone's skin) or "receive an impression of" (as clay receives a stamp). Miracle reports are already present in the sheets of paper brought to John, but he finds them insufficient, and thus includes miracles in his own Gospel that are not present in the Synoptics. In this passage, then, we have a really interesting representation of how Christians in subsequent centuries imagined the compositional process of canonical texts. For the author of the *Acts of Timothy*, at least, the Synoptic Gospels did not emerge fully formed from the minds of Matthew, Mark, and Luke; to the contrary, they emerged over decades, and their final forms were the result of an editor. In other words, the *Acts of Timothy* imagines a compositional process that is, in very broad strokes, accurate.

Reflection on the composition of early Christian narrative is not, however, limited to this section of the *Acts of Timothy*. Elsewhere, the text refers explicitly to Luke-Acts, noting that Timothy's parentage (a Greek father and Jewish mother) is known "from the treatise concerning the catholic Acts compiled by the most holy evangelist Luke" ἐκ τῆς συνταγείσης παρὰ λουκᾶ τοῦ ἁγιοτάτου εὐαγγελιστοῦ πραγματείας τῶν καθολικῶν (*Acts of Timothy* 3; cf. Acts 16:1). In addition to this direct reference, the prologue of the *Acts of Timothy* is laced with ideas and vocabulary drawn from Luke's prologue:

> ἴσμεν πολλοὺς ἱστορίας τε καὶ βίους ἤθη τε καὶ πολιτείας καὶ τελευτὰς θεοφιλῶν καὶ ὁσίων ἀνδρῶν συγγραψαμένους, ἀφ᾽ ὧν αὐτοὺς τοῖς μετὰ ταῦτα γνωρίμους κατεστήσαντο· τοιγαροῦν οὐκ ἔξω τοῦ δικαίου καὶ ἡμεῖς τὸ τοιοῦτον νομίσαντες μνήμῃ παραδοῦναι τόν τε βίον καὶ τὴν πολιτείαν καὶ τελευτὴν τοῦ ἁγίου ἀποστόλου τοῦ πρώτου πατριαρχήσαντος τῆς ἐφεσίων μεγαλοπόλεως τιμοθέου ἐσπουδάσαμεν.

> We know that many have composed both histories and biographies concerning the character, conduct, and death of men who were holy and friends of God, through which they made these men known to those [who lived] afterward. For that very reason also we, regarding such a thing to be not unjust, were eager to hand down to memory [i.e. to record] the life, conduct, and death of the holy apostle and first patriarch of the great city of Ephesus, Timothy. (*Acts of Timothy* 2)

Here we see that the text begins, like Luke's prologue, with a reference to the "many" who composed earlier, similar texts (cf. Luke 1:1); it continues, also like Luke's prologue, with a justification of this effort as an attempt to make information available to successive generations of Christians (cf. Luke 1:2–3). Whereas Luke positions his account against other, presumably less reliable, versions, the *Acts of Timothy* positions itself (in a μὲν clause) as a supplement to the information contained in the canonical Acts, even pointing the reader to that text as source:

> ὅσα μὲν οὖν αὐτῷ ἔν τε διδασκαλίαις καὶ θαυματουργίαις καὶ ἰάσεσιν καὶ πολιτείαις ὑπερβαινούσαις ἀνθρωπίνους λογισμοὺς πέπρακται, ἐξὸν ἑκάστῳ ἐκ τῶν διαφόρως εἰς αὐτὸν εἰρημένων ἐν ταῖς τῶν ἁγίων ἀποστόλων πράξεσιν καταμαθεῖν.

> And so, on the one hand, as much as was accomplished by him in teachings, wonders, healings, and conduct that exceeded human understanding, it is possible for anyone to learn from the things excellently told concerning him in the Acts of the holy apostles. (*Acts of Timothy* 5; translation adapted from Concannon 2016a, 402–403)

The new information to be revealed, however, is immediately underscored (in the δὲ clause that completes the thought):

> ἡμᾶς δὲ δίκαιον παραστῆσαι, ὅτι γε δὴ ὁ αὐτὸς ἁγιώτατος ἀπόστολος καὶ πατριάρκης τιμόθεος οὐ νόνον τοῦ ἀοιδίμου παύλου τοῦ ἀποστόλου, ἀλλὰ καὶ τοῦ ἐνδόξου θεολόγου ἰωάννου τοῦ ἐπὶ τὸ στῆθος ἀναπαυσαμένου τοῦ μεγάλου θεοῦ καὶ σωτῆρος ἡμῶν ἰησοῦ χριστοῦ αὐτόπτης τε καὶ αὐτήκοος γεγένηται.

> On the other hand, it is right for us to show that—indeed—the same most holy apostle and patriarch Timothy was not only an eyewitness and ear-witness of the famous apostle Paul but also of the illustrious theologian John, the one who rested upon the breast of our great God and savior Jesus Christ. (*Acts of Timothy* 6; translation adapted from Concannon 2016a, 403)

If one were to read only Acts, one would have the mistaken impression that Timothy was only the disciple of Paul. According to the author of this text, he also had a close connection with John.

In the immediate context of the *Acts of Timothy*, the importance of connecting Timothy with John no doubt relates to the text's primary goal of promoting the importance of the city of Ephesus, particularly at a time (likely the fifth century CE) when Constantinople had dramatically overshadowed it (see Kensky 2019, 103–19). As Meira Kensky puts it, the *Acts of Timothy* should be understood as "an attempt to revitalize the city and invest it with meaning during the waning ecclesiastical and economic fortunes of Ephesus in the fifth century CE in the shadow of *Nova Roma* right down the road." Further, "rather than understanding the *Acts of Timothy* as an attempt to claim Ephesus for Timothy, we should understand this text as an attempt to claim not only Timothy but also John *and the creation of the tetraevangelium* itself for Ephesus, part of a strategy to assert Ephesus's continuing relevance, sacrality, and vibrancy in order to lure pilgrims and other religious travelers and tourists to the city" (94).

Particularly interesting for the present purposes, however, is the cohesion of the passages in which the author describes his own rationale in composing the *Acts of Timothy* and the passages in which s/he describes John's rationale in composing the

Fourth Gospel. The rationales presented are essentially the same: to supplement and, to some extent, correct the record. This is, to be sure, more or less what authors like Eusebius write with regard to the canonical Gospels. What is notable, however, is that the author of the *Acts of Timothy* clearly regards this process of composition as ongoing: this author-narrator self-consciously presents her/himself as doing precisely what the author-editors of the first and second centuries did.

CONCLUSIONS

I hope the reader will already have concluded that apocryphal literature is surely of interest to those working primarily with the Synoptic Gospels: apocryphal narratives continue to retell Synoptic episodes, providing evidence not just of how later Christians were reading these episodes but also of what they were doing with them, that is, what potential they saw for new directions of theological thinking. Apocryphal narratives that exist in multiple recensions (as so many do) also supply comparanda for thinking about the relationship between the Synoptics; as Bovon puts it: "one and the same literary practice is shared by the Evangelists and by their successors. It is by observing the successors at work—and the workshop is still open—that we will be able to reconstruct the practice of the Evangelists whose workshop is now closed" (Bovon 2003b, 211). Finally, apocryphal narratives occasionally reflect directly on the production of the Synoptic Gospels, as the *Acts of Timothy* does. This is perhaps the most eye-opening aspect of the material I've presented here. In this text we find a fifth-century author who seems to recognize the difficult nature of the Synoptic Gospels, in terms of their relationships to each other and to the Fourth Gospel, and offers an explanation that—again, in broad strokes—approximates contemporary conclusions: for this author, the Synoptic Gospels emerged over at least two generations, and their final forms were the result of careful editorial work, rather than the whole-cloth compositions of Matthew, Mark, and Luke.

REFERENCES

Baltensweiler, Heinrich. 1959. *Die Verklärung Jesu: Historisches Ereignis und synoptische Berichte*. Zürich: Zwingli Verlag.

Blinzler, Joseph. 1937. *Die neutestamentlichen Berichte über die Verklärung Jesus*. Münster: Verlag der Aschendorffschen Verlagsbuchhandlung.

Boobyer, G. H. 1942. *St. Mark and the Transfiguration Story*. Edinburgh: T&T Clark.

Bovon, François. 2003a. "The Apocryphal Reception of Luke's Gospel and the Orthodox Reading of the Apocryphal Acts of the Apostles." In *Studies in Early Christianity*, edited by François Bovon, translated by Laura Beth Bugg, 293–301. Tübingen: Mohr Siebeck.

Bovon, François. [1988] 2003b. "The Synoptic Gospels and the Noncanonical Acts of the Apostles." *Harvard Theological Review* 81: 19–36. Reprinted in *Studies in Early Christianity*, edited by François Bovon, 209–25. Tübingen: Mohr Siebeck, 2003.

Bremmer, Jan. 2021. "Timothy, John and Ephesus in the *Acts of Timothy*." In *The Apostles Peter, Paul, John, Thomas and Philip with their Companions in Late Antiquity*, edited by Jan Bremmer, Tobias Nicklas, and Janet E. Spittler, 215–39. Leuven: Peeters.

Burkett, Delbert. 2019. "The Transfiguration of Jesus (Mark 9:2–8): Epiphany or Apotheosis?" *JBL* 138, no. 2: 413–32.

Concannon, Cavan. 2016a. "The Acts of Timothy." In *New Testament Apocrypha: More Noncanonical Scriptures*, edited by Tony Burke and Brent Landau, 395–405. Grand Rapids: Eerdmans.

Concannon, Cavan. 2016b. "In the Great City of the Ephesians: Contestations over Apostolic Memory and Ecclesial Power in the *Acts of Timothy*." *JECS* 24: 419–46.

Denniston, J. D. 1950. *The Greek Particles*. 2nd edition, revised by K. J. Dover. Oxford: Oxford University Press.

Elliott, J. Keith. 1993. "Acts of John." In *The Apocryphal New Testament*, edited by J. Keith Elliott, 303–46. Oxford: Clarendon.

Elliott, J. Keith. 1997. "The Influence of the Apocrypha on Manuscripts of the New Testament." *Apocrypha* 8: 265–71.

Elliot, J. Keith. 2010. *New Testament Textual Criticism: The Application of Thoroughgoing Principles: Essays on Manuscripts and Textual Variation*. Leiden: Brill.

Goetz, K. G. 1927. *Petrus als Gründer und Oberhaupt der Kirche und Schauer von Gesichten nach der altchristlichen Berichten und Legenden*. Leipzig: J. C. Hinrichs.

Goodacre, Mark. 2011. "The Evangelists' Use of the Old Testament and the Synoptic Problem." In *New Studies in the Synoptic Problem. Oxford Conference, April 2008. Essays in Honour of Christopher M. Tuckett*, edited by Paul Foster et al., 281–98. Leuven: Peeters.

Gregory, Andrew. 2003. *The Reception of Luke and Acts in the Period before Irenaeus*. Tübingen: Mohr Siebeck.

James, M. R. 1924. "Acts of John." In *The Apocryphal New Testament*, edited by M. R. James, 228–70. Oxford: Clarendon.

Junod, Eric and Jean-Daniel Kaestli. 1983. *Acta Iohannis*, CCSA 1–2. Turnhout: Brepols.

Kensky, Meira. 2019. "Ephesus, *Loca Sancta*." In *The Narrative Self in Ealry Christianity: Essays in Honor of Judith Perkins*, edited by Janet E. Spittler, 103–19. Atlanta: SBL Press.

Lalleman, Pieter J. 1995. "Polymorphy of Christ." In *The Apocryphal Acts of John*, Studies on the Apocryphal Acts of the Apostles 1, 97–118. Kampen, Netherlands: Kok Pharos.

Lee, Simon S. 2009. *Jesus' Transfiguration and the Believers' Transformation*. Tübingen: Mohr Siebeck.

Lundhaug, Hugo, and Liv Ingeborg Lied. 2017. "Studying Snapshots: On Manuscript Culture, Textual Fluidity, and New Philology." In *Snapshots of Evolving Traditions. Jewish and Christian Manuscript Culture, Textual Fluidity, and New Philology*, edited by Hugo Lundhaug and Liv Ingeborg Lied. 1–19. Berlin: De Gruyter.

New, David S. 1993. *Old Testament Quotations in the Synoptic Gospels, and the Two-Document Hypothesis*. SBL Septuagint and Cognate Studies 97. Atlanta: Scholars Press.

Neyrey, Jerome H. 1980. "The Apologetic Use of the Transfiguration in 2 Peter 1:16–21." *CBQ* 42, no. 4: 504–19.

Nicklas, Tobias. 2007. "'Écrits apocryphes chrétiens.' Ein Sammelband als Spiegel eines weitreichenden Paradigmenwechsel in der Apokryphenforschung." *Vigiliae Christianae* 61: 70–95.

Nicklas, Tobias. 2018. "Christian Apocrypha as Heterotopias in Ancient Christian Discourse: The *Acts of Timothy*." *Proceedings of the Irish Biblical Association (PIBA)* 41: 60–74.

Nicklas, Tobias. 2019. "Absonderlich und geschmacklos? Antike christliche Wundererzählungen zwischen 'kanonisch' und 'apokryph.'" In *Between Canonical and Apocryphal Texts*, edited by Jörg Frey et al., 415–40. Tübingen: Mohr Siebeck.

Pervo, Richard I., with Julian V. Hills. 2016. *The Acts of John*. Early Christian Apocrypha 6. Salem, OR: Polebridge Press.

Rothschild, Clare. 2005. *Baptist Traditions and Q*. Tübingen: Mohr Siebeck.

Spittler, Janet E. 2008. *Animals in the Apocryphal Acts of the Apostles*. Tübingen: Mohr Siebeck.

Spittler, Janet E. 2017. "Joking and Play in the Acts of John." In *Delightful Acts*, edited by Harold W. Attridge, Dennis R. MacDonald, and Clare K. Rothschild, 209–25. Tübingen: Mohr Siebeck.

Stein, R. H. 1976. "Is the Transfiguration (Mark 9:2–8) a Misplaced Resurrection Account?" *JBL* 95/1: 79–96.

Usener, Hermann. 1877. *Acta S. Timothei*. Bonn: Georgi.

Weeden, Theodore J. 1971. *Mark—Traditions in Conflict*. Philadelphia: Fortress Press.

Zamagni, Claudio. 2007. "Passion (ou Actes) de Timothée. Étude des traditions anciennes et edition de la forme BHG 1487." In *Poussières de christianisme et de judaïsme antiques. Études réunies en l'honneur de Jean Daniel Kaestli et Éric Junod*, edited by Albert Frey and Rémi Gounelle, Publications de l'Institut Romand des Sciences Bibliques 5, 341–75. Lausanne: Éditions du Zèbre.

CHAPTER 12

THE GOSPEL OF THOMAS AND THE SYNOPTICS

MELISSA HARL SELLEW

A Different Sort of Gospel

SINCE the discovery and first publication of elements of the Gospel of Thomas, there has been a rich and vibrant discussion among scholars as to how it might relate to the Synoptic Gospels of the New Testament. The conversation began well over a century ago. English classicists digging in the trash heaps of Oxyrhynchus, a city of Greco-Roman Egypt (Parsons 2007), discovered three small fragments of Greek papyri with brief sayings ascribed to Jesus, which they termed *logia* (Grenfell and Hunt 1897). These statements showed an intriguing pattern of similarity and contrast with verses well known from the New Testament. A few examples will make the point.

The opening lines of the first fragment (labeled Papyrus Oxyrhynchus 1 = P. Oxy. 1) contain the conclusion of a pithy moral exhortation well known from the programmatic speech Jesus makes in Matthew 5–7 and Luke 6: "and then you will see clearly to cast out the speck in your brother's eye" (P. Oxy. 1.1–4, now known as Gos. Thom. 26b; Greek text in Attridge 1989, 96–128; Coptic in Layton 1989, 52–93). The wording of this partial sentence is precisely the same in Greek as in Matthew 7:5b (with a small variation in word order in Luke 6:42b). But when one reads the very next lines on the fragment, Jesus's statements are unfamiliar from the canonical Gospels, though the vocabulary is found in and outside the Bible. Jesus says, "If you do not fast with regard to the world, you will surely not find the Kingdom of God; and if you do not keep the sabbath [as] the sabbath, you will not see the Father" (P. Oxy. 1.4–11 = Gos. Thom. 27). Jesus says, "I stood in the midst of the world, and was seen by them in the flesh, and found all of them drunk and no one thirsty among them, and my soul was pained for the children of humanity, because they are blind in their heart and [do not] see" (P. Oxy. 1.11–21 = Gos. Thom. 28). Soon, however, on the other side of the fragment, we find the familiar aphorism "A prophet is not acceptable in his town" (P. Oxy. 1.30–35 = Gos. Thom. 31, see Mark 6:4a; Matt 13:57; Luke 4:24; John 4:44).

This unexpected appearance of a "lost gospel" aroused public excitement as well as scholarly scrutiny. Two more papyri fragments from separate manuscripts were soon published as well, but still without indication of their literary context. Half a century later a complete copy of this text was found elsewhere in Egypt, in 1945—not in Greek, but instead in Coptic translation, entitled the "Gospel of Thomas," and inscribed in a late fourth-century manuscript buried across the Nile from the modern town of Nag Hammadi (Nag Hammadi Codex II; Layton 1989). When read in its full version, the newly discovered Gospel now appeared to resemble the Synoptic Gospels quite closely in some respects, in that more than half of Jesus's statements in Thomas have counterparts there (Koester 1989, 46–48); yet the new Gospel differs dramatically from the New Testament writings in some significant ways, including its structure, view of the world, connections to Scripture, soteriology, and theology. How are we to explain this combination of close equivalence and considerable distance?

Scholars have struggled to answer the questions that consumed them at first with anything like consensus (recent treatments of the history of research in Patterson 2013, 93–118; Gathercole 2014, 91–184; Miroshnikov 2018, 25–37). In what ways does Thomas relate to the canonical Gospels? Does it represent an early and possibly autonomous witness to "authentic" Jesus traditions, or is it better understood as a late patchwork of secondary citations lifted from the (ultimately) canonical texts mixed with unbiblical notions? How do we best understand its unusual structure, consisting of a series of statements ascribed to Jesus (114 *logia* in the conventional numeration), with little or no apparent narrative design? What are its views of the person and role of Jesus, its anthropology and theory of salvation, or its connection with Judaism? What was its original language and place of composition?

Patterns of Familiarity and Independence

Debates over the relative antiquity of Thomas, or its secondary dependence on the Synoptic Gospels, have been intimately connected to contrasting views over the nature of Christian origins, including one's preferred construal of the "historical Jesus" (Cameron 2004; Patterson 2013, 119–39; Gathercole 2014, 176–84). It is not difficult to sense that many who propose either a first-century or a later origin of Thomas, or at least for much of its content, have done so because this Gospel could then support their preferred views of the formative Jesus movement. Since Thomas lacks the apocalyptic imagery of the Synoptic Jesus, for example, this fact might be explained as attesting to its very early composition, before a putative redirecting by Paul of the Jesus traditions toward a more eschatological direction (Crossan 1985; Koester 1971). Thomas has been claimed by others to rely on early Jewish–Christian traditions (DeConick 1996; Lelyveld 1987; Quispel 1974/75) or to fit within Near Eastern wisdom traditions, based on its format and tone (Davies 1983; Patterson 1993; 2013, 141–74), in either case in contrast to the strains of proto-orthodox Christianity that show a more urgent eschatological outlook, such as is found in Paul, the Synoptic Gospels, or the Apocalypse of John.

From another point of view, scholars have argued that Thomas is a second-century and secondary text that derives its seemingly earlier content from the protocanonical Gospels, with sayings of Jesus that were extracted from them either directly, or possibly indirectly, or both, as for example via oral traditions (Gathercole 2012; Goodacre 2012; see Uro 1998a). These more "authentic" sayings were then combined with newly created material, apparently in service of some ultimately less orthodox portrayal of Jesus, whether that be termed Gnostic or mystical or Encratite. Scholars who pressed the "dependence" model usually found their interpretive context for Thomas not in first-century Palestinian Judaism, or Hellenistic Wisdom, or in comparisons with the Sayings Source Q, but rather mostly among so-called Gnostic writings bound and buried with the Coptic translation of Thomas in the late antique Nag Hammadi codices (Grant et al. 1960; Haenchen 1961; see Popkes 2007). Scholars taking this position argue that far from reflecting some preapocalyptic moment in the earliest Jesus tradition, the lack of apocalyptic symbolism results from Thomas's deliberate rejection and excision of the sort of first-century Jewish and Christian eschatology seen in Paul or Mark.

The question of the dependence or autonomy of Thomas with regard to the Synoptic tradition is difficult to solve using the methods of classical source criticism (Gathercole 2012, 1–16). There is no clearly visible connection of content and sequence between Thomas and the New Testament Gospels that is at all comparable to the relationships of the three Synoptic Gospels with each other, however those are explained, or even to their somewhat less obvious connection with the Gospel of John. In addition to the close verbal connections and sequencing of events seen in many parallel passages and individual verses among the Synoptics, all four canonical Gospels adopt a semibiographical narrative format. Their stories feature the same general plotline and many specific themes, running from Jesus's encounter with the prophet John the Baptist, calling of twelve disciples, engagement in public teaching and works of wonder, adversarial encounters with Jewish opponents, and eventual arrest, trial, crucifixion, burial, and reported resurrection. None of these key elements of the canonical story of Jesus is developed in Thomas, apart from bare snippets (e.g., a reference to John the Baptist as a marker of the age in Gos. Thom. 46). Despite similarities in the wording of individual sayings, there are only a relatively few, and comparatively minor, cases of agreement in their sequence in Thomas as compared with the Synoptics.

Thus, a reader of Thomas who did not know the New Testament texts would have little ability to reconstruct or perhaps even imagine the story of Jesus presented there. Consideration of early gospels beyond the Synoptic three helps make this point. Readers who knew only John's Gospel or the Gospel of Peter (Crossan 1985; Hill 2004; Koester 1980; Sellew 1992b; Wiles 1961) would nonetheless find the same narrative thrust presented in the Synoptic texts, though of course presented with a different tone and theological emphasis, and somewhat variant content. The surviving portion of the Gospel of Peter, for all its distinct character, is visibly telling more or less the same story of Jesus's passion and resurrection as do the New Testament four.

The Jesus of Thomas, in great contrast, though he speaks proverbs, macarisms, and parables alike to those of his Synoptic counterpart, nonetheless performs no deeds of power, encounters no opposition from either Jewish or Roman leaders, makes no threats or warnings of imminent divine judgment or eschatological crisis. Only by foreknowledge of the New Testament Gospels (or for argument's sake, the Gospel of Peter) would a reader of Thomas realize that Jesus was to meet a gruesome death at the hands of the Romans, framed as a divinely required sacrifice to redeem the world of sin, and yet was somehow able to transcend death through resurrection. In other words, the "Jesus Christ crucified, and him alone" preached by Paul (1 Cor 2:2) is not the subject of the Gospel of Thomas.

Arguments about Thomas's relative autonomy from, familiarity with, or dependence on other gospels thus necessarily adopt a more granular compositional approach (Gathercole 2012; Goodacre 2012; Kloppenborg 2006; Patterson 1993). It is noteworthy, for example, that parables spoken by Jesus in Thomas are presented without the interpretive introductions or summary moralizing found in the Synoptics, beginning with Jesus's decoding of the *Fate of the Seeds* in Mark 4:14–20 and parallels (contrast Gos. Thom. 9). This absence of explanations by Jesus or the author can be construed as evidence that the parables were taken up by Thomas without knowledge of those Synoptic interpretive interventions (Jeremias 1972; Scott 1989); just as well, however, one could imagine Thomas or its traditions omitting any such explanations known to them in service of the text's opening challenge: to avoid "tasting death" by finding the meaning of Jesus's mysterious words for oneself (Gos. Thom. 1). Some illustrative cases are treated in more detail in the section "Parables" here.

A more productive path through this perennial controversy is emerging from several quarters, an approach that avoids limiting our thinking to the methods of classical source criticism and canonical criticism. Instead of framing the issue starkly as reliance of a later writing on one or more authoritative predecessors, one can instead apply the lens of intertextuality, along with other possible models of familiarity with shared traditions. Such an approach sets aside any privileging of works found within the biblical canon on seemingly unexamined assumptions that they have a priori claims to antiquity or "authenticity" compared with other early texts, including Q or Thomas. Stating that Thomas is somehow less relevant to one's construal of Jesus or of Christian origins because it relies on other gospels for some of its content, or because it may be from the second century, appears to be rather an odd perspective, given what we know about the connections among the New Testament Gospels themselves. Few disregard the Gospel of Luke simply because it openly reveals its knowledge of (and implies its partial dependence on) earlier writings (Luke 1:1–4) or because it (along with its companion text, Acts) may well also be an early second-century composition (Matthews 2017, 103-4; Reasoner 2017, 174–75; Reid and Matthews, 2021).

Perhaps one could look to discussions of the Gospel of John's relation to the Synoptic tradition as something of a model for how we might imagine Thomas's connections with Luke, among other possibilities. Over the decades, scholarly views on John's relationship with the Synoptics have swung back and forth (Smith 2001). A theory of Johannine independence dominated scholarship through most of the twentieth century, based largely on the canons of form criticism; this allowed (or required) that some prominent aspects of Mark, Matthew, and Luke that are shared by John, such as a cycle of miracle stories or the Passion Narrative, "must" have had pre-Markan origins, potentially in a putative oral tradition. But the hypothesis of John's independent access to such material via oral traditions has come to seem less and less likely in recent work, as scholars have adopted a more expansive approach to questions of sources and influence (MacKay 2004; Viviano 2004). When one drops the presumption that John wrote without knowledge of other gospels, in some sense at least, the simpler and more elegant explanation for John's incorporation of the Synoptic plotline and major characters is some sort of intertextual connection. At places it seems as though John has read or heard another gospel; mostly, it is a matter of shared themes and topics that could have been drawn one way or another from shared traditions. So too with Thomas.

The Genre of Thomas

One fundamental difference with the Synoptics is Thomas's adoption of a wisdom-book style of presentation, along with a radical disinterest in employing the biographical mode that was apparently pioneered by Mark. Thomas consists of a brief opening remark from its author (incipit + Gos. Thom. 1), followed by a series of statements ascribed to Jesus, punctuated here and there by questions or observations by others. These statements employ a range of formats, including conventional proverbs, ethical demands, beatitudes, parables, and puzzling allusions and metaphors. In strong contrast to the New Testament Gospels, in Thomas virtually all the statements of Jesus lack placement in a chronological or travel narrative. The occasional introductory notes to a statement in Thomas, reflecting the style of apophthegmatic *chreiai* or pronouncement stories, such as at Gos. Thom. 22 ("Jesus saw infants being suckled") or Gos. Thom. 60 ("[He saw] a Samaritan carrying a lamb on the way to Judea") offer only a scattered and unhelpful set of data from which one might imagine an "original setting" for any particular pronouncement, even less usefully than do such comments in the New Testament Gospels.

Thomas's format as a wisdom-book or sayings gospel can be helpfully compared and contrasted with the Sayings Source Q in several ways. An early point stressed by supporters of the two-source solution to the Synoptic Problem was that the discovery of Thomas challenged the assertion by Q skeptics that a "gospel" must have certain narrative and Christological features; Thomas has even less of a visible narrative structure than does the Q material, though its manuscript calls it a gospel, and it is labeled as such even by its ancient critics (Sellew 1992a; see testimonia in Gathercole 2014, 34–61). The similarities extend to some aspects of their theologies as well: neither has a Passion Narrative, indeed neither displays any interest in the Pauline/Markan emphasis on the redemptive power of Jesus's suffering and death. On the other hand there are stark differences between Thomas and Q that make any claims of close correspondence between the two seem strained. A fundamental contrast is that the Q material sets Jesus firmly and decisively into the context of Jewish prophetic and apocalyptic teaching, and includes frequent and significant appeals to the Jewish Scriptures to explain Jesus's person and role, while Thomas eschews any direct appeal to biblical traditions and seems rather removed from any actual connection with contemporary practice of Judaism (e.g., Gos. Thom. 52–53).

Thomas's manner of presentation lends itself well to the inquiring minds of readers who seek inspiration of a more probing sort in Jesus's words and may have less need (for whatever reason) for narration of events in his life. Thomas has been well compared to gnomological texts, which could suggest its use in a school setting (Arnal 2021; Kloppenborg 1987, 289–306; 2014, 228–31). In terms of its reception, as distinct from its original composition, whose circumstances remain opaque, a text like Thomas would have had much appeal to solitary ascetics who sought to make progress on a spiritual path of self-scrutiny and improvement (Sellew 2018). In this sense, in terms of its usage, the Gospel of Thomas could be characterized as a spiritual guide (Sellew 1997a; see Valantasis 1997) that activates a "hermeneutical soteriology" (Sellew 1997b).

The frequent use of paradox and of contrasting symbols and images, leading at times to outright contradiction, a feature found throughout Thomas, coupled with the lack of interpretive narrative context or framings, forces its readership to think for themselves. Many of the instances of this paradoxical tone are familiar from the Synoptics, such as Gos. Thom. 4b: "Many who are first will become last" (see Mark 10:31 // Matt 19:30; 20:16 // Luke 13:30); Gos. Thom. 5b: "There is nothing hidden that will not be made manifest" (Mark 4:22 // Matt 10:26 // Luke 8:17; 12:2); Gos. Thom. 20: "The smallest of all seeds... produces a great plant" (Mark 4:32 // Matt 13:32 // Luke 13:19); or such beatitudes as Gos. Thom. 54: "Blessed are the poor, for yours is the Kingdom of Heaven" (Luke 6:20 // Matt 5:3), or Gos. Thom. 68a: "Blessed are you when you are hated and persecuted" (Luke 6:22 // Matt 5:11). But Thomas takes this tendency of spinning out oppositions further, as in the conclusion to Gos. Thom. 3: "The Kingdom is inside of you *and it is outside of you*" (see Luke 17:20–21), or Gos. Thom. 18: "Have you discovered *the beginning* that you look for the end?" Contrasting pairs of darkness and light, body and soul, flesh and spirit, above and below are woven throughout the text (esp. Gos. Thom. 22) as it calls its readers to look away from their material existence to find their authentic spiritual character.

"Whoever finds the meaning of these words will not taste death. Let the person who is seeking keep on seeking until they find" (Gos. Thom. 1–2a). The process of searching for meaning leads to difficulty, wonder, and ultimately to self-mastery and rest (Gos. Thom. 3). The text's lack of concern for presenting Jesus's sayings in even the modified sort of biographical story seen in the New Testament Gospels could be explained in various ways. Perhaps, as some argue, Thomas stems from a Syrian context, where the suffering messiah and eschatological message of Paul (and Jesus?) carried little currency (e.g. Patterson 2013, 9–32; but see Given 2017), or from a more exegetically engaged Alexandrian environment (Brown 2019). Or, more plausibly, Thomas shares with John's Gospel an interest in a more transcendent theology and soteriology, unconnected to physical location, and influenced in part by popularized Platonism (Asgeirsson 2006; Miroshnikov 2018; Patterson 2013, 32–91; Sellew 2020); Thomas achieves this move more thoroughly than does John by abrogating the Markan plotline entirely.

The Character of Jesus: Speaker of Divine Mysteries

At a very basic level, one could say that both Thomas and the New Testament Gospels feature Jesus as their protagonist. As such, his personality shares some features across all five texts: he can speak with misdirection and opacity; he can show impatience with his listeners' difficulty in understanding his comments, instructions, or symbolic speech. But the differences in characterizing their main figure far outweigh these basic similarities. Jesus's role in Thomas is fundamentally as a speaker of mysterious sentences (Gos. Thom. incipit; 38; 62), whose authority arises from his status as the "Living One" (Gos. Thom. incipit; 52; 59) who is the "son of the Living One" (Gos. Thom. 37) and "exists from the Undivided" (Gos. Thom. 61). There are indications, such as Gos. Thom. 28 ("I took my place in the midst of the world, and I appeared to them in flesh"), of Jesus having come from a nonmaterial plane. The place that Jesus has arrived from is not Galilee or Nazareth, nor is his destination Jerusalem, but his home is where the divine Light exists. Gos. Thom. 77a: "Jesus said, 'It is I who am the light which is above them all; it is I who am the all.'" This portrait offers interesting analogies with John's view of Jesus as God's enfleshed Word and Light that shone in the darkness (John 1:1–18), having arrived from and soon returning to the divine realm; similarly, in Thomas, Jesus "is seen both as a preexistent and as a divine human being" (Marjanen 2006, 212).

Thomas has no interest in showing Jesus moving about in the world in ordinary ways (walking or boating from place to place, as so often in the Synoptics) or in display of unusual powers of sudden appearance and disappearance, as seen in both biblical and noncanonical postresurrection scenes (Matthew 28; Luke 24; John 20 and 21; Gospel of Judas). The contrast with the New Testament Gospels is quite strong in this regard. Jesus performs no healings, whether miraculous or not, and, like John, no exorcisms. The grave attention paid to Satan and the demonic in the Synoptics (and later monastic texts) is conspicuously absent from Thomas.

The Jesus of Thomas has occasional things to say about ritual behaviors, but seemingly only in response to questions from the disciples, and not clearly with any intention to establish community rules (but see Moreland 2006). Indeed, in stark contrast to the

Synoptics, this Jesus seems mostly uninterested in pious practices like prayer, fasting, almsgiving, or dietary rules (Gos. Thom. 14; 89), including even circumcision (Gos. Thom 53), apart from warnings that these can encourage the sin of hypocrisy (Gos. Thom. 6; 104; Marjanen 1998b; Sellew 1994). Lively conversation and debate with other forms of Jewish life and practice are staged throughout the canonical Gospels and Paul, but in Thomas disagreements over pious practice lack a sense of tension or immediacy, suggesting little connection to a putative community struggling with issues of its identity within Judaism, despite a few disparaging remarks thrown that way (Gos. Thom. 39; 43; 102; Sellew 2000).

A fundamental contrast with the Synoptics is Thomas's lack of messianic titles or expectations for Jesus's return. The term *Christ* as either a name or a title with the meaning "messiah" never appears (an interesting absence shared with the Q material), nor does Thomas place Jesus in the context of a specifically Israelite prophetic tradition; indeed the "prophets" of the Jewish Scriptures are dismissed as "dead" (Gos. Thom. 52). The Jesus of Thomas is less a character in his own story than a spiritual guide tied to no specific historical, biographical, or geographical locale; he speaks directly to his audience in the form of challenges and riddles that can be pondered in many situations. The confusion and incomprehension of his "student" audience in the text stands in for the reader or audience even more clearly than does the cadre of disciples and other followers in the canonical Gospels.

PARABLES

Jesus speaks more than a dozen parables in Thomas, eleven of which are closely paralleled in the Synoptics, along with three that are not: the *Children in the Field* (Gos. Thom. 21); the *Woman with a Jar of Meal;* and the *Assassin* (Gos. Thom. 97–98; Cameron 1986; Crossan 1973; Dodd 1961; Jeremias 1972; Scott 1989). The text does not say why he adopts this discursive mode, though it fits both with his persona of a speaker of mysteries and the rich use of metaphor and simile throughout the text. Mark's Gospel, of course, explains Jesus's parabolic speech with its theory of the messianic secret: Jesus deploys symbolic stories as a tool to separate out faithful from more wobbly believers: "With many such parables he spoke the word to them, as they were able to hear it; he did not speak to them except in parables, but he explained everything in private to his disciples" (Mark 4:33–34; Sellew 1990).

Matthew and Luke, in their own ways, represent the parables as tools of a master teacher. As was suggested earlier, all three Synoptics reinforce this approach by having either Jesus or the narrator, or both, offer interpretations of the parables to other characters within the narrative, or else directly to their readers and listeners through the introductory or summarizing attachment of moral or ethical meaning. In Luke, for example, one sees such framing comments surrounding the *Good Samaritan*, 10:29, 36–37; the *Rich Fool*, 12:13–15, 21; the *Banquet*, 14:15, 24; the *Lost and Found* sheep and coin,

15:1–2, 7, 10; the *Shrewd Manager*, 16:8b–13; and the *Unjust Judge*, 18:1, 6–8; as well as the deployment of interior monologue (Dinkler 2015; Sellew 1992b). The readers of Thomas are given no such interpretive guidance but instead are challenged to unlock the significance of these symbolic vignettes for themselves, as seen in the repeated call for the audience to play close attention at the close of parables: "The one with ears to hear had better listen!" (Gos. Thom. 8; 21; 63; 65; 96; see 24). Closer examination of a few examples will illustrate Thomas's tendency toward sparseness of narration and explanation.

First, a story of *A Catch of Fish*, known from two early sources, Gos. Thom. 8 and Matthew 13:47–50. These are clearly performance variations of the same basic story of an experienced fisherman's discernment in separating out the better from the inferior fish, an ordinary task of the trade. Both Gospels show that Jesus intends to have his listeners draw a lesson, but that lesson diverges dramatically. In Thomas, a wise individual will know how to discard the unimportant and less useful aspects of life, symbolized as "small," in favor of concentration on one "large" and desirable prize (similarly in the parable of the *Lost Sheep*, Gos. Thom. 107). Rather than spelling out the lesson, Thomas has Jesus add its favorite tagline about having ears to hear, to draw attention to the necessity of scrutiny and thought. In Matthew on the other hand the two types of fish are characterized in moral terms, as either "good" or else "bad" and "evil." Some are chosen and others are discarded, leading to one of Matthew's signature applications of Jesus's words: they are to be heard as warnings or threats of fiery divine punishment of wicked people. Thomas seemingly speaks of a timeless occurrence, where for Matthew the story is a vehicle for pressing its vision of apocalyptic, eschatological, and violent judgment.

Another parable known only from Matthew and Thomas is the *Weeds among the Wheat* (Gos. Thom. 57 and Matt 13:24–30). Thomas includes a less elaborate telling of the tale, or perhaps an abbreviated version. Matthew has Jesus offer his disciples an explanation a bit later "in the house" (Matt 13:36–43), where he decodes the details of the parable as pointing to "the end of the age" (13:40–43). Thomas of course lacks this interpretive material; but in other ways its rendering of the parable reads to some as truncated. There is seemingly no preparation in Gos. Thom. 57 for the farmer's address to an unnamed audience, which Goodacre sees as fitting a pattern of abbreviated parables in Thomas (with omitted details) that he interprets as revealing familiarity with Matthew's or Luke's longer versions, as well as revealing a narrative deficiency that exposes the author as a lesser literary talent (Goodacre 2012, 73–80).

A third such example is the *Rich Fool*, found only in Gos. Thom. 63 and Luke 12:15–21. Luke's telling is more detailed and is introduced and concluded with moralizing commentary. Here Goodacre makes a stronger case for Thomas presenting an abbreviated version of the story that shows familiarity with its parallel in Luke, as opposed to the notion that it offers a more archaic, simpler telling that Luke has elaborated. In this case, the brevity of the narration in Thomas creates no inconcinnity, at least to my ear, though Goodacre numbers this parable among those that he argues have "a missing middle" of the story (2012, 109–12).

What may be more telling is Thomas's mention of the foolish person's inner thoughts, though they are not directly quoted. This feature, even if quite attenuated, nonetheless appears to be inspired by Luke's signature device of using interior monologue to lay bare the intentions and private thoughts of characters in parables—particularly those of rather dubious moral standing, such as the *Prodigal Son*, the *Shrewd Manager*, the *Unjust Judge*, or this parable's self-satisfied and clueless landowner (Goodacre 2012, 89–90, drawing on Sellew 1992b; but see the critique in Kloppenborg 2014, 216). As Dinkler puts it, "The narrative rhetoric suggests that he has read his situation too myopically; the interior monologue demonstrates his foolish thinking" (2015, 386). Interesting from a more directly theological perspective is the absence of God as an active character in Gos. Thom. 63, or indeed in any part of this Gospel. The foolish landowner's death has come unexpectedly to him in both versions, revealing his misplaced confidence about his fate; Luke takes the opportunity to provide an ethical lesson, about how followers of Jesus must order their priorities: "So it is with those who store up treasures for themselves but are not rich toward God" (Luke 12: 21). Throughout their Gospels, Thomas and Luke share a strong critique of misbegotten or misdirected wealth and a consistent concern for the poor, so their inclusion of this parable fits the tendencies of both.

A fourth and final comparison of parables presented in Thomas and in the Synoptics is the *Tenants of the Vineyard*. Here the differences, some obvious and others subtle, reveal much about Thomas's perspective. In all three Synoptic versions, Jesus is speaking in a fraught environment of challenge and dangerous opposition in the Jerusalem temple precinct, as seen immediately beforehand in Mark 11:27–33, where the "chief priests, the scribes, and the elders" question his authority. We have just been told that these leaders "kept looking for a way to kill him, for they were afraid of him" (Mark 11:18 // Luke 19:47). After Jesus speaks the parable, appending an interpretive citation of Scripture (Psalm 118 [117 LXX]; Mark 12:10–11), the narrator tells us: "When they realized that he had told this parable against them, they wanted to arrest him, but they feared the crowd" (Mark 12:12). In Thomas we get no hint of such a frightening confrontation, in accordance with its lack of interest in Jesus's violent death.

Even more interesting is what the sequence of parable and biblical citation shows about Thomas's attitude to Scripture in contrast to that of the Synoptics. Mark 12:1 and Matthew 21:23 make specific allusions to the symbolic vineyard planted by the Lord in Isaiah 5, with their reference to the surrounding fence, the wine press, and the watchtower (Isa 5:2 LXX); Luke 20:9 and Thomas 65 do not include these details. In Isaiah, God decides to destroy the vineyard after it fails to produce the proper grapes, that is, in place of the expected justice and righteousness God saw bloodshed and lamentation (Isa 5:7). In the four witnesses known today to Jesus's version of the story, it is the workers in the vineyard who are to blame for the owner not receiving his due, and who are destroyed. Still, there is an interesting intertext in Gos. Thom. 40: "A grapevine has been planted outside of the Father, but being unsound, it will be pulled up by its roots and destroyed," but without any direct mention of the biblical metaphor.

In the Synoptics it is clear to the reader, and even to the characters in the story, that Jesus "told this parable against" the leaders of Jerusalem. This makes his remark "Have you not read this Scripture, 'The stone that the builders rejected has become the cornerstone'?" (Ps 118:22–23) that much more piquant. Thomas also has Jesus refer to the rejected stone becoming the cornerstone in a separate statement placed immediately after the parable of the *Tenants* (Gos. Thom. 66), a juxtaposition whose similarity is too prominent to likely be explained by coincidence. Some proponents of Thomas's autonomy from the Synoptics ascribe the placement of the cornerstone remark here to a secondary stage in the Gospel's transmission history, perhaps on the occasion of its translation from Greek into Coptic (e.g., Patterson 1993, 51). But a different approach may be more satisfying. The lack of allusion to Isaiah 5 in Thomas's telling of the parable, combined with no indication in Gos. Thom. 66 that Jesus is quoting from the Psalms, suggest a deliberate distancing of the Gospel from reliance on the Bible as a support or source of information about Jesus and the meaning of his words and deeds. This disconnect between Scripture and Jesus is one of the greatest contrasts between Thomas and virtually the entire New Testament collection (Baarda 2003; Goodacre 2012, 187–91).

When Luke presents the parable, he adds a telling and rather shocking adverb to the owner's speech when he sends out his "beloved son" after his previous messengers to the wicked tenants have been met with violence. The owner says: "*Perhaps* they will respect him" (Luke 20:13). This statement strikes one as chilling for a loving parent to make in these dangerous circumstances: does the owner care more about his profits than his cherished son's life? (Sellew 1992b, 248; see also Dinkler, 392). But the remark's retrospective symbolism is clear. Luke means that the priests and elders of Jerusalem should have respected Jesus and given him his due as God's son, and Luke's readers know that they did not. The owner in Mark and Matthew does not express this attitude of apparent uncertainty or unconcern; he simply asserts "they will respect my son" (Mark 12:6 // Matt 21:37). The addition of the single word in Luke makes a powerful impression. Quite interestingly, Thomas 65 has the owner show this same attitude twice: "*Perhaps* he did not know them" (said of the first messenger who was nearly killed). And then: "*Perhaps* they will show respect to my son." This agreement with Luke in expressing this rather surprising landowner's perspective is best explained by supposing a literary connection. Since Luke has presumably modified the story from Mark, the stunning addition of the word "perhaps" is Luke's contribution, and thus its double appearance in Gos. Thom. 65 indicates familiarity with the Lukan version (Gathercole 2012, 188–94).

Disciples in Thomas

Occasionally Thomas has Jesus speak with interlocutors, mostly said to be "his disciples." Often it is they who open a brief exchange with a question or challenging remark, starting with Gos. Thom. 6; frequently their comments and Jesus's dismissals or ripostes reveal their lack of understanding (e.g., Gos. Thom. 12, on leadership; Gos. Thom. 18 and 51, on eschatology; Gos. Thom. 52, on the pertinence of Jewish Scripture). All the individuals explicitly named in Thomas, including James (Gos. Thom. 12), Judas Thomas (Gos. Thom. incipit; 13), Simon Peter (13; 114), Matthew (13), Mary (21; 114), and Salome (61), appear in one or more of the Synoptics. Precisely why these individuals are interacting with Jesus as their teacher, however, is never explained. For all one can tell, until the disciples' first, unprepared appearance in Gos. Thom. 6, Jesus is speaking into the void, or, more likely, directing his words mostly to an implied audience outside the text.

In Gos. Thom. 19, Jesus clarifies that "listening to his words" is necessary to become his disciple and to avoid death. Yet there are no scenes of initial encounters or "calls" of people like Peter, James, or Levi to follow him as one sees them in the Synoptics (Mark 1:16–20 // Matt 4:18–22, cf. Luke 5:1–11 and John 1:35–51; 21:1–11; Mark 2:14 // Luke 5: 27–28, cf. Matt 9:9; Mark 3:13–19 // Luke 6:12–16, cf. Matt 10:1–4). Jesus explicitly refuses the role of his followers' teacher or master within a scene of apostolic competition in Gos. Thom. 13, where Thomas succeeds by silence over Matthew's and Peter's attempts to characterize Jesus properly. "Leaders" who claim to explain the Kingdom had already been dismissed as misguided as early as Gos. Thom. 3. These and similar factors contribute to a strong sense of "masterless discipleship" in Thomas (Marjanen 1998a; 2006; Uro 2003, 80–105; Zöckler 1999, 245–47). The disciples' interest in seeking an apostolic authority (Gos. Thom. 12), renewed even in the face of Jesus's refusal of the title of teacher and praise of Thomas's silence in Gos. Thom. 13, is striking (Sellew 2017). In combination with the naming of Judas Didymus Thomas as scribe in the incipit, this scene may suggest a literary development from (earlier) anonymous gospels to those depending on "eyewitness" authority, moving in the direction of "authorial fiction" such as one sees in Luke 1:1–4; John 21:24–25, and here in Thomas (Dunderberg 1998a, 80–88; 2006). It may be that the implied rejection of Matthew's and Peter's construals of Jesus and his role in Gos. Thom. 13 reflects knowledge of other gospels' claims to authority (Goodacre 2012, 174–79).

Two women appear on the margins of those called disciples, and their names are also familiar from the canon: a person named Mary, who asks Jesus to characterize his disciples (Gos. Thom. 21), suggesting that she is not among them, and Salome. Both women's status appears contingent, despite Salome's self-assertion "I am your disciple" (Gos. Thom. 61; Marjanen 1998c). An unnamed woman shouts out a blessing on the womb and breasts of the unnamed mother of Jesus, a blessing that he immediately rejects, adding a denigration of reproduction and child rearing (Gos. Thom. 79; see other rejections of parents and family in Gos. Thom. 99; 101; 105). The demand by Simon Peter at the conclusion of the Gospel (Gos. Thom. 114) that Mary be excluded from the group on the grounds of her female gender seems mostly to reflect concerns over preconditions of salvation (see section "Salvation in Thomas" here) rather than controversies over reproduction or women's place as leaders in a particular community (Cwikla 2019; Sellew 2020), though such disputes are of course well attested from the letters of Paul and his followers, as well as texts like the second-century *Acts of Paul and Thekla* and the Gospel of Mary (King 2003; Tuckett 2017).

Though some of the specifics differ, Thomas shares the theme of incomprehension on the part of the disciples as to Jesus's intentions and teaching with Mark and, notably, with John. The bewilderment and repeated misunderstandings of the male disciples of course make up a major theme of the Synoptics, tied closely to Mark's theme of the hidden destiny of Jesus as messiah and son of God. Thomas's deployment of this feature more closely resembles that of John's Gospel, where irony and misdirection serve to fuel the literary effects of Jesus as a "man of mystery" and the incarnate Son of God (Dunderberg 1998b; 2006). In Thomas, the function of the theme of incomprehension serves to underline one of the Gospel's central topics and purposes: to encourage the reader or listener to scrutinize the meaning of Jesus's words as a means of enlightenment, self-discovery, and salvation from our world of death.

Salvation in Thomas: The World, the Body, and Authentic Human Existence

Thomas's approach to the means and meaning of salvation differs markedly from that of the Synoptics and entails understanding of authentic human existence. For Thomas, faith or belief in Jesus is not a precondition or a means to salvation, as it is for the New Testament Gospels and for Paul. When asked to provide information so that people "may believe in you," Jesus says, "you have not recognized the one who is before you, and you do not know how to read this moment" (Gos. Thom. 91). Instead of Mark's sharp focus on the salvific suffering of Jesus and his death on the cross, followed by his resurrection, Thomas (and Q) make only a single oblique reference to (hypothetical) crucifixion: followers or disciples are told to "pick up their cross"—not as a means of salvation but as a metaphor for radical commitment (Gos. Thom. 55b; see Mark 8:34 and Q = Luke 14:27 // Matt 10:38). Though Thomas was likely aware of the manner of Jesus's death, salvation for this gospel does not require the self-sacrificial martyrdom of Jesus, or its ritual reenactment; instead, each individual must achieve return to the divine realm through self-knowledge, so as to overcome their material existence in favor of a unified essence called variously being a "solitary," a "Living Spirit," and a "person of Light" (Gos. Thom 24; 49; 114; Marjanen 2006; Sellew 1997b; 2020; Valantasis 1997; cf. Litwa 2015). This path is what Thomas would understand "following Jesus" could mean.

The Gospel of Thomas has a view of human origins and destiny that is shared by at least some of its contemporaries, with several of its statements finding particular resonance with the Prologue to John, as well as with Platonizing biblical exegesis of the Genesis creation myths as known from Philo of Alexandria (Brown 2019; Davies 1992; Miroshnikov 2018; Pagels 1999; Patterson 2013, 33–92). For Thomas, authentic human being descends from a place of eternal divine Light; Jesus calls on his audience to live as persons of the Light, as does he, and reveals that their destiny is to return to the place of Light where he and they first originated as Living Spirits. "When you have found the beginning, then you will know the end" (Gos. Thom. 18; 24; 49–50). The soul or the spirit is the locus of one's divine identity, whereas the physical body, as part of the material world, shares in its corruption, division, and mortal condition. So in Gos. Thom. 29: "If the flesh came into being because of spirit, it is a wonder. But if spirit came into being because of the body, it is a wonder of wonders. Indeed, I am amazed at how this great wealth has made its home in this poverty." Thomas never expresses the biblical view of a good, divinely created order brought into being by a benevolent deity; instead, the world is a dead thing, a corpse (Gos. Thom. 56, 80; Miroshnikov 2018; Sellew 1997a; 2006) that those who follow the example of Jesus should prepare to escape (Gos. Thom. 49–50).

Quite interesting in Thomas is its view of authentic human existence as somehow transcending the limitations of embodiment, including especially the divisions marked by sex or gender (Sellew 2020). Salvation entails transformation that parallels the "rebirth" of John 3. So Gos. Thom. 22b: "When you make the two one, and when you make the inside like the outside, and the outside like the inside, and the above like the below, and when you make the male and female one and the same, so that the male not be male nor the female be female; and you fashion eyes in place of an eye, and a hand in place of a hand, and a foot in place of a foot, and a likeness in place of a likeness, then you will enter [the Kingdom]." When the human soul returns to the place of its origin, the divine realm of Light, it will not be conveyed in a material form exhibiting sexual difference but instead be transformed (back) into the incorporeal, undivided, nonsexual, spiritual character that represents divine humanity. Thomas here shares in broader interpretive traditions of the biblical creation narratives that are still visible in Philo, and others: original and authentic human existence, after the image and likeness of God, had no gender, until the first human, Adam, was divided into male and female, a fatal event (Miroshnikov 2018; Sellew 2020; Valantasis 1997). And so Gos. Thom. 85: "Adam came into being from a great power and a great wealth, but he did not become worthy of you. For had he been worthy, [he would] not [have tasted] death."

The contrast with the Synoptic view of human existence and its destiny is quite strong: Mark, Matthew, and Luke portray people riven by conflict between the divine and the demonic, and a Jesus who fights to expel evil forces from within humans and grants power to others to do likewise. This struggle rises above the mundane to involve cosmic combat between Satan, God's opponent, and Jesus, as God's representative, champion, and son. Much of this picture emerges more or less directly from Jewish apocalyptic prophecy. For Thomas, which depends only indirectly if at all on the Hebrew Scriptures, the struggle is individual and internal: the need to scrutinize the self, to come to recognize one's identity as a person of Light, just like Jesus, undivided by gender, and ultimately to find oneself as part of God—this is what salvation involves.

Thomas and Eschatology

Developed apocalyptic imagery is lacking in this Gospel, though there are a few remarks that evoke or echo apocalyptic eschatological discourse, such as in Gos. Thom. 11: "this world will pass away." The similar statement in Gos. Thom. 111 ("the heavens and the earth will be rolled up in your presence") is immediately qualified by the remark that "the one who lives from the Living One will not taste death" (see Gathercole 2011). The reference to the "son of human being" in Gos. Thom. 86 signifies, as its Synoptic parallels suggest (Luke 9:58 // Matt 8:20), the dilemma of people caught between heaven and earth, rather than invoking the angelic heavenly being of Mark 13 and other apocalyptic texts. In determining the interpretive context of these phrases, Patterson points usefully to the polyvalent character of prophetic pronouncements, whether those be of a "wisdom" or an "eschatological" type (Patterson 2013, 211–36). Reference to the rolling up of the heavens or passing away of the earth, then, can function in an apocalyptic drama but can also at times function as hyperbolic metaphorical gestures toward an indefinite future, as it appears in Matthew 5:18—not one iota of the Law of Moses will fall off the page before heaven and earth disappear.

Most likely this muted use of apocalyptic vocabulary or themes represents a disavowal and partial redirection of the usage seen in the Synoptics. Here the Gospels of John and Thomas seemingly agree in moving away from a historical or social-group approach to eschatology in the direction of a more individualized path to salvation: "belief in Jesus" and "birth from above" for John, return to divine "unity" or "singleness" in Thomas.

Conclusion

What Thomas Tells Us about the Synoptic Gospels

Moving away from fraught questions of dependence or autonomy, we have seen that comparison of the texts' style and content is quite fruitful for understanding both Thomas and the Synoptics. When one reads the Synoptics against Thomas, some of the central characteristics of Mark, Matthew, and Luke stand out in higher relief. Differences in theology, narrative structures, genre, and approaches to community formation, among other features, combine to reveal that early gospel writers had a variety of choices about their modes of representation of the meaning(s) of Jesus. One sees that there was nothing inevitable about the narrative pattern originating in the Gospel of Mark and taken over by Matthew, Luke, and John in distinct ways. Mark's story of Jesus on the way to the cross in order to save the world from sin through his sacrificial death, punctuated by encounters with the diseased and demonic, was remarkably influential. But neither of the two rituals central to Pauline communities that are narrativized in the Synoptics, baptism and the Lord's Supper, features in Thomas, a lack that is seemingly paralleled by the Q material. As part of its pattern of distance from Judaism, Thomas shows that it was possible to present Jesus as somehow removed or distant from the thought world of Scripture, even as a source of revelatory or prophetic information. Nor is Jesus set into the context of Israelite or Judean history and strife, be that with internal or external opponents. Concern over the fall of Jerusalem and its temple, an event that looms large over the Synoptic story line, is remarkably absent. This is a stunning departure from the other portrayals we have. It is thanks to Thomas than one can see that the

Synoptic presentation of Jesus and his meaning was not inevitable but was fundamentally a matter of choice and circumstance.

Future Directions

Future work on Thomas can build on recent advances in reading its distinctive portrait of Jesus in conversation with its canonical and extracanonical partners with less concern for the "authenticity" or "dependence" or "autonomy" of its material. What are the social implications of a gospel that found early Christian readers drawn to its style of paradox and challenge? What does Thomas's disinterest in the martyrdom of Jesus (and his followers) suggest about the circumstances of this gospel's composition or reception? What does its rejection of the relevance of Jewish ritual, prophecy, and apocalyptic for understanding Jesus, or the means of salvation, tell us about the varieties of Christian communities, and their preoccupations? Furthermore, what aspects of the Synoptic style of portraying Jesus can emerge more distinctly, once we see more clearly that their presentations must also have been in deliberate service of specific goals, be those theological, ecclesiological, or ethical? What was gained by adopting a biographical format to explain Jesus and his importance? These and assuredly many other questions remain open to continued collective work on this fascinating and most enigmatic Gospel.

References

Arnal, William E. 2021. "Minding the Margins: 'Scholia' in the Text of the Gospel of Thomas." *JECS* 29:1–30.
Asgeirsson, Jon Ma. 2006. "Conflicting Epic Worlds." In *Thomasine Traditions in Antiquity: The Social and Cultural World of the Gospel of Thomas*, edited by Jon Ma Asgeirsson, April D. DeConick, and Risto Uro, NHMS 59, 155–74. Leiden: Brill.
Asgeirsson, Jon Ma, April D. DeConick, and Risto Uro, eds. 2006. *Thomasine Traditions in Antiquity: The Social and Cultural World of the Gospel of Thomas*. NHMS 59. Leiden: Brill.
Attridge, Harold W. 1989. "The Greek Fragments [of the Gospel of Thomas]." In *Nag Hammadi Codex II, 2–7*, vol. 1, edited by Bentley Layton, 96–128. Leiden: Brill.
Baarda, Tjitze. 2003. "The Gospel of Thomas and the Old Testament." *PIBA* 26:46–65.
Brown, Ian Phillip. 2019. "Where Indeed Was the Gospel of Thomas Written? Thomas in Alexandria." *JBL* 138: 451–72.
Cameron, Ron. 1986. "Parable and Interpretation in the Gospel of Thomas." *Forum* 2.2: 3–39.
Cameron, Ron. 2004. "Ancient Myths and Modern Theories of the Gospel of Thomas and Christian Origins." In *Redescribing Christian Origins*, edited by Ron Cameron and Merrill P. Miller, 89–108. Atlanta: SBL.
Crossan, John Dominic. 1973. *In Parables: The Challenge of the Historical Jesus*. New York: Harper.
Crossan, John Dominic. 1985. *Four Other Gospels: Shadows on the Contours of Canon*. Minneapolis: Seabury.

Cwikla, Anna. 2019. "There's Nothing about Mary: The Insignificance of Mary in the Gospel of Thomas 114." *Journal of Interdisciplinary Biblical Studies* 1, no. 1: 95–112.

Davies, Stevan L. 1983. *The Gospel of Thomas and Christian Wisdom*. New York: Seabury.

Davies, Stevan L. 1992. "The Christology and Protology of the *Gospel of Thomas*." *JBL* 111: 663–82.

DeConick, April D. 1996. *Seek to See Him: Ascent and Vision Mysticism in the Gospel of Thomas*. VCSup 33. Leiden: Brill.

Dinkler, Michal Beth. 2015. "'The Thoughts of Many Hearts Shall Be Revealed': Listening in on Lukan Interior Monologues." *JBL* 134:373–99.

Dodd, C. H. 1961. *Parables of the Kingdom*. Rev. ed. New York: Scribner.

Dunderberg, Ismo. 1998a. "*Thomas* and the Beloved Disciple." In *Thomas at the Crossroads: Essays on the Gospel of Thomas*, edited by Risto Uro, 65–88. Edinburgh: T&T Clark.

Dunderberg, Ismo. 1998b. "*Thomas*' I-Sayings and the Gospel of John." In *Thomas at the Crossroads: Essays on the Gospel of Thomas*, edited by Risto Uro, 33–64. Edinburgh: T&T Clark.

Dunderberg, Ismo. 2006. *The Beloved Disciple in Conflict? Revisiting the Gospels of John and Thomas*. Oxford: Oxford University Press.

Gathercole, Simon. 2011. "'The Heavens and the Earth Will Be Rolled Up': The Eschatology of the *Gospel of Thomas*." In *Eschatologie—Eschatology*, edited by H.-J. Eckstein, C. Landmesser, and H. Lichtenberger, WUNT 272, 280–302. Tübingen: Mohr Siebeck.

Gathercole, Simon. 2012. *The Composition of the Gospel of Thomas: Original Language and Influences*. SNTSMS 151. Cambridge: Cambridge University Press.

Gathercole, Simon. 2014. *The Gospel of Thomas: Introduction and Commentary*. TENT 11. Leiden: Brill.

Given, J. Gregory. 2017. "'Finding the Gospel of Thomas in Edessa." *JECS* 25: 501–25.

Goodacre, Mark. 2012. *Thomas and the Gospels: The Case for Thomas's Familiarity with the Synoptics*. Grand Rapids: Eerdmans.

Grant, Robert M., David Noel Freedman, and William R. Schoedel. 1960. *The Secret Sayings of Jesus*. Garden City: Doubleday.

Grenfell, B. P., and A. S. Hunt. 1897. *ΛΟΓΙΑ ΙΗΣΟΥ: Sayings of Our Lord from an Early Greek Papyrus*. London: Egypt Exploration Fund.

Haenchen, Ernst. 1961. *Die Botschaft des Thomas-Evangeliums*. Berlin: Töpelmann.

Hill, Charles E. 2004. *The Johannine Corpus in the Early Church*. Oxford: Oxford University Press.

Jeremias, Joachim. 1972. *The Parables of Jesus*. 2nd edition. New York: Scribners.

King, Karen L. 2003. *The Gospel of Mary Magdalene: Jesus and the First Woman Apostle*. Santa Rosa, CA: Polebridge Press.

Kloppenborg, John S. 1987. *The Formation of Q: Trajectories in Ancient Wisdom Collections*. Philadelphia: Fortress Press.

Kloppenborg, John S. 2006. *The Tenants in the Vineyard: Ideology, Economics, and Agrarian Conflict in Jewish Palestine*. WUNT 295. Tübingen: Mohr Siebeck.

Kloppenborg, John S. 2014. "A New Synoptic Problem: Mark Goodacre and Simon Gathercole on Thomas." *JSNT* 36: 199–239.

Koester, Helmut. 1971. "One Jesus and Four Primitive Gospels." In *Trajectories through Early Christianity*, by James M. Robinson and Helmut Koester, 158–204. Philadelphia: Fortress Press.

Koester, Helmut. 1980. "Apocryphal and Canonical Gospels." *HTR* 73: 105–30.

Koester, Helmut. 1989. "Introduction [to the Gospel of Thomas]." In *Nag Hammadi Codex II, 2–7*, vol. 1, edited by Bentley Layton, 38–51. Leiden: Brill.

Koester, Helmut. 1990. *Ancient Christian Gospels: Their History and Development*. Philadelphia: Trinity Press International.

Layton, Bentley. 1989. *Nag Hammadi Codex II, 2–7: Together with XIII,2*, Brit. Lib. Or. 4926(1), and P. Oxy. 1, 654, 655*. Vol. 1. NHS 20. Leiden: Brill.

Lelyveld, Margaretha. 1987. *Les Logia de la vie dans l'Évangile selon Thomas: À la recherche d'une tradition et d'une rédaction*. NHS 34. Leiden: Brill.

Litwa, M. David. 2015. "'I Will Become Him': Homology and Deification in the *Gospel of Thomas*." *JBL* 133:427–47.

MacKay, Ian D. 2004. *John's Relationship with Mark: An Analysis of John 6 in the Light of Mark 6–8*. WUNT 2/182. Tübingen: Mohr Siebeck.

Marjanen, Antti. 1998a. "Is *Thomas* a Gnostic Gospel?" In *Thomas at the Crossroads: Essays on the Gospel of Thomas*, edited by Risto Uro, 107–39. Edinburgh: T&T Clark.

Marjanen, Antti. 1998b. "Thomas and Jewish Religious Practices." In *Thomas at the Crossroads: Essays on the Gospel of Thomas*, edited by Risto Uro, 163–82. Edinburgh: T&T Clark.

Marjanen, Antti. 1998c. "Women Disciples in the Gospel of Thomas." In *Thomas at the Crossroads: Essays on the Gospel of Thomas*, edited by Risto Uro, 89–106. Edinburgh: T&T Clark.

Marjanen, Antti. 2006. "The Portrait of Jesus in the *Gospel of Thomas*." *Thomasine Traditions in Antiquity: The Social and Cultural World of the Gospel of Thomas*, edited by Jon Ma Asgeirsson, April D. DeConick, and Risto Uro, NHMS 59, 209–19. Leiden: Brill.

Matthews, Shelly. 2017. "Fleshly Resurrection, Wifely Submission, and the Myth of the Primal Androgyne." In *Delightful Acts: New Essays on Canonical and Non-canonical Acts*, edited by Harold W. Attridge, Dennis R. MacDonald, and Claire K. Rothschild, 101–17. WUNT 391. Tübingen: Mohr Siebeck.

Miroshnikov, Ivan. 2018. *The Gospel of Thomas and Plato: A Study of the Impact of Platonism on the "Fifth Gospel."* NHMS 93. Leiden: Brill.

Moreland, Milton. 2006. "The Twenty-Four Prophets of Israel Are Dead: *Gospel of Thomas* 52 as a Critique of Early Christian Hermeneutics." In *Thomasine Traditions in Antiquity: The Social and Cultural World of the Gospel of Thomas*, edited by Jon Ma Asgeirsson, April D. DeConick, and Risto Uro, NHMS 59, 75–91. Leiden: Brill.

Pagels, Elaine H. 1999. "Exegesis of Genesis 1 in the Gospels of Thomas and John." *JBL* 118: 477–96.

Parsons, Peter. 2007. *City of the Sharp-Nosed Fish: Greek Lives in Roman Egypt*. London: Weidenfeld & Nicolson.

Patterson, Stephen J. 1993. *The Gospel of Thomas and Jesus*. Sonoma, CA: Polebridge Press.

Patterson, Stephen J. 2013. *The Gospel of Thomas and Christian Origins: Essays on the Fifth Gospel*. NHMS 84. Leiden: Brill.

Popkes, Enno Edzard. 2007. *Das Menschenbild des Thomasevangelium*. WUNT 206. Tübingen: Mohr Siebeck.

Quispel, Gilles. 1974–75. *Gnostic Studies I–II*. Istanbul: Nederlands Instituut.

Reasoner, Mark. 2017. "The Open Stage of Luke and Acts." In *Delightful Acts: New Essays on Canonical and Non-canonical Acts*, edited by Harold W. Attridge, Dennis R. MacDonald, and Claire K. Rothschild, 159–76. WUNT 391. Tübingen: Mohr Siebeck.

Reid, Barbara E., O.P., and Shelly Matthews. 2021. *Luke 1–9*. Wisdom Commentary 34A. Collegeville: Liturgical Press.

Scott, Bernard Brandon. 1989. *Hear Then the Parable: A Commentary on the Parables of Jesus*. Minneapolis: Fortress Press.

Sellew, Melissa [née Philip] Harl. 1990. "Oral and Written Sources in Mark 4. 1–34." *NTS* 36: 234–67.

Sellew, Melissa Harl. 1992a. "Eusebius on the Gospels." In *Eusebius, Christianity, and Judaism*, edited by Harold W. Attridge and Gohei Hata, 110–38. Leiden: Brill

Sellew, Melissa Harl. 1992b. "Interior Monologue as a Narrative Device in the Gospel of Luke." *JBL* 111: 239–53.

Sellew, Melissa Harl. 1994. "Pious Practice and Social Formation in the Gospel of Thomas." *Forum* 10: 47–56.

Sellew, Melissa Harl. 1997a. "Death, the Body, and the World in the Coptic Gospel of Thomas." *StPat* 33: 530–35.

Sellew, Melissa Harl. 1997b. "The *Gospel of Thomas*: Prospects for Future Research." In *The Nag Hammadi Library after Fifty Years*, edited by John D. Turner and Anne McGuire. NHMS 44. Leiden: Brill.

Sellew, Melissa Harl. 2000. "Thomas Christianity: Scholars in Search of a Community." In *The Apocryphal Acts of Thomas*, edited by Jan M. Bremmer, 11–35. Leuven: Peeters.

Sellew, Melissa Harl. 2006. "Jesus and the Voice from beyond the Grave: *Gospel of Thomas* 42 in the Context of Funerary Epigraphy." In *Thomasine Traditions in Antiquity: The Social and Cultural World of the Gospel of Thomas*, edited by Jon Ma Asgeirsson, April D. DeConick, and Risto Uro, NHMS 59, 39–73. Leiden: Brill.

Sellew, Melissa Harl. 2017. "James and the Rejection of Apostolic Authority in the Gospel of Thomas." In *Delightful Acts: New Essays on Canonical and Non-canonical Acts*, edited by Harold W. Attridge, Dennis R. MacDonald, and Claire K. Rothschild, 193–207. WUNT 391. Tübingen: Mohr Siebeck.

Sellew, Melissa Harl. 2018. "Reading Jesus in the Desert: The *Gospel of Thomas* Meets the *Apophthegma Patrum*." In *The Nag Hammadi Codices in Late Antique Egypt*, edited by Hugo Lundhaug and Lance Jannot. STAC 110. Tübingen: Mohr Siebeck.

Sellew, Melissa Harl. 2020. "Reading the Gospel of Thomas from Here: A Trans-centered Hermeneutic." *Journal of Interdisciplinary Biblical Studies* 1, no. 2: 61–96.

Smith, Dwight Moody. 2001. *John among the Gospels*. 2nd ed. Columbia: University of South Carolina Press.

Tuckett, Christopher M. 2017. "Women in the *Gospels of Mark* and *Mary*." In *Connecting Gospels: Beyond the Canonical/Non-canonical Divide*, edited by Francis Watson and Sarah Parkhouse, 142–62. Oxford: Oxford University Press.

Uro, Risto. 1998a. "*Thomas* and Oral Gospel Tradition." In *Thomas at the Crossroads: Essays on the Gospel of Thomas*, 8–32. Edinburgh: T&T Clark.

Uro, Risto. 1998b. *Thomas at the Crossroads: Essays on the Gospel of Thomas*, edited by Risto Uro. Edinburgh: T&T Clark.

Uro, Risto. 2003. *Thomas: Seeking the Historical Context of the Gospel of Thomas*. London: T&T Clark.

Valantasis, Richard. 1997. *The Gospel of Thomas*. London: Routledge.

Viviano, Benedict T. 2004. "John's Use of Matthew: Beyond Tweaking." *RB* 90: 209–37.

Wiles, Maurice F. 1961. *The Spiritual Gospel: The Interpretation of the Fourth Gospel in the Early Church*. Cambridge: Cambridge University Press.

Zöckler, Thomas. 1999. *Jesu Lehren im Thomasevangelium*. NHMS 47. Leiden: Brill.

Further Reading

DeConick, April D. 2005. *Recovering the Original Gospel of Thomas: A History of the Gospel and Its Growth*. LNTS 286. London: T&T Clark.

DeConick, April D. 2006. *The Original Gospel of Thomas in Translation with a Commentary*. LNTS 287. London: T&T Clark.

Frey, Jörg, Enno Edzard Popkes, and Jens Schröter, eds. 2008. *Das Thomasevangelium: Entstehung—Rezeption—Theologie*. Berlin: De Gruyter.

Pagels, Elaine. 2003. *Beyond Belief: The Secret Gospel of Thomas*. New York: Random House.

Plisch, Uwe-Karsten. 2008. *The Gospel of Thomas: Original Text with Commentary*. Translated by Gesine Robinson. Stuttgart: Deutsche Bibelgesellschaft.

Pokorny, Peter. 2009. *A Commentary on the Gospel of Thomas: From Interpretations to the Interpreted*. London: T&T Clark.

Schröter, Jens. 1997. *Erinnerung an Jesu Worte: Studien zur Rezeption der Logienüberlieferung in Markus, Q, and Thomas*. WMANT 76. Neukiurchen-Vluyn: Neukirchener Verlag.

Snodgrass, Klyne. 1989–90. "The Gospel of Thomas: A Secondary Gospel." *Second Century* 7: 19–38.

Tuckett, Christopher M. 1988. "Thomas and the Synoptics." *NovT* 30: 132–57.

Turner, H. E. W., and Hugh Montefiore. 1962. *Thomas and the Evangelists*. London: SCM.

Uro, Risto. 2006. "The Social World of the Gospel of Thomas." In *Thomasine Traditions in Antiquity: The Social and Cultural World of the Gospel of Thomas*, edited by Jon Ma Asgeirsson, April D. DeConick, and Risto Uro, NHMS 59, 19–38. Leiden: Brill.

Valantasis, Richard. 1999. "Is the *Gospel of Thomas* Ascetical? Revisiting an Old Problem with a New Theory." *JECS* 7: 55–81.

PART II

PARTICULAR FEATURES IN COMPARISON

CHAPTER 13

SUFFERING AND SACRIFICE

CANDIDA R. MOSS

INTRODUCTION

IN the history of the study of religion it is customary to attempt to trace the origins of religious traditions back to their earliest and simplest iteration, as if locating a kernel of an idea in the foggy dawn of recorded history would yield some special insight about the nature of religion itself. Surely every theological interest is vulnerable to this kind of reduction, because very few concepts are intrinsically novel. Suffering, and speculation about the necessity, value, and cause of suffering in the world, is no different. Before Jesus trod the dusty roads of Galilee, Jews already cherished the memories of the Maccabean martyrs and hypothesized about the identity of the "suffering servant" described by Isaiah. And yet, with the crucifixion, suffering took on a new, almost architectural role in the worldview of the first followers of Jesus. The cross was the scaffolding upon which a host of interrelated concepts—theodicy, martyrdom, discipleship, and eschatology—would hang.

Prior to the crucifixion, the execution of the leader of a religious movement would almost certainly have entailed the end of that movement and the dispersal of its members. Broadly speaking, suffering was conceived as the result of a deity that was either angered by the disobedience and sinfulness of human beings or incapable of assisting them. In 2 Maccabees 7, for example, one of the seven brothers who goes to his death insists to Antiochus Epiphanes IV that their experience of torture and martyrdom is the consequence of their own sinfulness. The final brother states that he and his brothers suffer because of their own sins and that their executions function to "punish and discipline" them (2 Macc 7:33) (van Henten 1997, 116–24, 144–51).

For those who lived in the ancient world, the terms "sacrifice" and "suffering" could mean a whole range of things. "Sacrifice" was most frequently used as a technical term to invoke an array of specific rituals and thought-systems connected to placating and pleasing the regents of the material world.[1] The language of sacrifice also had a broader application for those who died noble deaths and gave up their lives for city, family, or deity. As the title of this essay places sacrifice in concert with suffering, I will focus on sacrifice in its broader, less technical meaning: as a means of describing hardships and physical violence for the sake of a perceived greater good (Breytenbach 1989).

The writers of the Synoptic Gospels lived in a world of sufferers: illness, war, taxation, famine, and violence were just some of the ways that people might expect to suffer. It is noteworthy that while English translations tend to interpolate the language of "suffering" into descriptions of physical ailments (e.g., NRSV Mark 5:34 and Luke 8:43), in the Greek text the evangelists themselves tend to reserve it for the experience of political and social violence (e.g., Luke 9:22; Matt 27:19). Nevertheless, each of the Synoptic writers wrestled in his own particular ways with the question of how to reconfigure the suffering of Jesus, the expectation of the suffering of others, and the existence of suffering in the world.

This essay considers in turn the related themes of (1) suffering in the world due to illness and other causes; (2) predictions of the suffering and sacrifice of Jesus; (3) the presentation of Jesus's suffering; (4) predictions about the suffering of Jesus's followers; and (5) predictions about end-time suffering within each of the Synoptic Gospels.

Illness as Suffering

The three Synoptic evangelists agree on the basic point that the experience of illness or disability is a form of suffering that necessitates endurance. This analysis is only rarely made explicit. In Mark 5:25–34, Jesus encounters a woman with a flow of blood. The woman had suffered from this ailment for ten years. The text says that "she had endured (παθοῦσα) much under many physicians, and had spent all that she had; and she was no better, but rather grew worse" (NRSV Mark 5:26). Matthew and Luke, while repeating the story, simply note that the woman had a flow of blood (Matt 9:23; Luke 8:43). But on a different occasion it is Matthew who explicitly uses the language of pathos to describe ordinary human ailments. In Matthew 17:15, when a man with a son who experiences seizures implores Jesus for help, he says, "Lord, have mercy on my son, for he is an epileptic and he suffers terribly (καὶ κακῶς πάσχει, πολλάκις); he often falls into the fire and often into the water" (NRSV Matt 17:15). Mark and Luke do not explicitly describe this as suffering. Matthew, however, is the only evangelist to mention falling in the fire, and it is

---

[1] See Young 1979; Daly 1978. Most twentieth-century scholars would agree that the killing of an animal or human being is the foundation of sacrificial ritual, e.g., Girard 1972; see the anthropological theory of Walter Burkert, which states that sacrificial killing in the classical world is the precondition for the preservation of society (1972). The same basic principle was applied to biblical texts in Gese (1983, 85–106).

likely that it is this additional experience of being burned that is identified as the source of suffering.

Luke does not use the language of pathos for physical ailments but instead tends to reserve it for instances of political and social oppression and mistreatment. Luke does this most notably with respect to the suffering of Jesus (discussed later) but also in Luke 13:2, in a description of the mistreatment of the Galileans at the hands of Pilate: "He asked them, 'Do you think that because these Galileans suffered in this way they were worse sinners than all other Galileans?'"

It is, however, implicit in Luke, as it is in the other Gospels, that physical ailments cause suffering and pain that Jesus can and does alleviate. Throughout the Synoptic Gospels, one might say, Jesus acts as a kind of "cathartic scourge and as the Kingdom of God breaks into the world of Mark's Gospel, disability is systematically removed from it" (Moss 2010, 519). Everyone who faithfully encounters Jesus in the Synoptic Gospels is healed; thus salvation and healing essentially coalesce.

Predictions of the Suffering and Sacrifice of Jesus

More usually, the language of suffering is reserved for predictions and descriptions of political brutalization. On three occasions in Mark, Jesus predicts his future suffering and death (Mark 8:31; 9:31; 10:33–34). Matthew and Luke rehearse these predictions with some emendations (Matt 16:21; 17:22–23; 20:18–19; Luke 9:22; 18:31–33). On a further occasion, Jesus's suffering is specifically referred to as a "ransom" (λύτρον) for the people (Mark 10:45 // Matt 20:28).

In each of the passion predictions in Mark, Jesus takes the disciples aside for special and secret instruction about the culmination of his ministry. In 1901, William Wrede argued that these sayings form part of a "Messianic Secret" in Mark in which the identity of Jesus is concealed in order to explain how Jesus came to be crucified (Wrede 1971).[2] The content of the first prediction is that "the Son of Man must undergo great suffering, and be rejected by the elders, the chief priests, and the scribes, and be killed, and after three days rise again" (Mark 8:31). The use of the passive voice in the first passion prediction may well be suggestive of the "divine passive," which is similarly used of the Servant of the Lord in Isaiah 53. In Isaiah, the Servant is handed over to death, accounted among the lawless, "bore the sins of many," and was "handed over on account of their sins" (LXX Isaiah 53:12, 6).

---

[2] There are different interpretations of the function of the Messianic Secret. Martin Dibelius, for example, focused on the way that the secret would explain Jesus's rejection by the Jews (Dibelius 1935, 223).

The same language of handing over is similarly used of the Son of Man in Mark 9:31 (Collins 1994, 492–93). By the third passion prediction, the scope of the handing over of Jesus has expanded and the description of that suffering has grown more detailed: "the Son of Man will be handed over to the chief priests and the scribes, and they will condemn him to death; then they will hand him over to the Gentiles; they will mock him, and spit upon him, and flog him, and kill him; and after three days he will rise again" (10:33–34). The reference to "the Gentiles" for the first time alludes to the eventual handing over of Jesus to Pilate, and the passage explicitly gestures to the humiliation and torture he will receive at the hands of Roman soldiers in 15:16–20.

In a sequence that layers content gradually, the first passion prediction begins by connecting the mysterious nature of the kingdom of God (4:11) to suffering and briefly situates that mystery in the narrative of Mark by referring to the "elders . . . chief priests . . . and scribes" (8:31). The second passion prediction focuses on death and resurrection as well as gesturing to the concept of being handed over. The final prediction serves to build suspense: it foreshadows the passion narrative and prepares the audience for the events that will unfold (Collins 2007, 486).

As one would expect, Matthew and Luke make some changes to Mark's predictions. They agree against Mark in changing "after three days rise" to "on the third day be raised."[3] Matthew makes the same change in the second and third passion predictions (Matt 17:23 // Mark 9:31; Matt 20:19 // Mark 10:34) but Luke does not. In the final passion prediction, Luke 18:33 agrees with Matthew in reading "on the third day" but follows Mark in including the verb "he will rise" (ἀναστήσεται). Mark's original formula appears to be a paraphrase of LXX Hosea 6:2, but Matthew and Luke prefer to include the Pauline formulation of 1 Cor 15:4: "was raised on the third day in accordance with the scriptures" (Collins 2007, 405).

As is typical of the First Evangelist, Matthew also subtly shifts the context in which the passion predictions appear. In contrast to Mark's statement that Jesus taught "them" (Mark 8:31), Matthew focuses emphatically on him showing "his disciples" (Matt 16:21). As with so many of Matthew's changes to Mark, his focus here is on the instruction imparted to the disciples.[4]

Luke's interpretation of the predictions of the suffering of Jesus expands beyond the basic passion predictions. He interjects an explanatory note into the so-called "Little Apocalypse" of Mark 13: before the Son of Man appears almost like lightning, "first he must endure much suffering and be rejected by this generation" (Luke 17:25). The amplification of the theme of suffering, and its introduction into passages predicting the judgment of others explicitly ties expected future judgment to the suffering of Jesus.

The clearest explanation and theological account of the death of Jesus and its function is found in both Mark and Matthew in a reprimand to the sons of Zebedee. Having cryptically crushed their expectations of power, Jesus states, "the Son of Man came not to be

---

[3] For a summary of views about this redactional relationship see Perry 1986, 637–54.
[4] For a classic exposition of Matthew's redactional interest in the disciples see Bornkamm 1963, 52–57.

served but to serve, and to give his life a ransom (λύτρον) for many" (Mark 10:45 // Matt 20:28). The striking use of the term λύτρον clarifies some of the more opaque imagery of suffering that proceeded this statement (Mark 10:38–39). It also has some similarities to Isaiah 53:10b–12 and the notion that the Servant of the Lord will "bear the sins" of the many.[5]

As a term, *ransom* (λύτρον) appears in references to compensation (Prov 6:35) and the manumission of slaves (Lev 19:20). In Exod 21:29 the term is used to refer to money paid as a substitution for the execution of a criminally liable person (in Exod 21:29, the owner of a murderous ox). The language also appears in connection with the Levites in Num 3:11–13, which suggests that the Levites must dedicate their firstborns to God in exchange for their delivery from the land of Egypt. Read through this lens, "the implication would be that the death of Jesus is a substitute for the deaths of many others" (Collins 2007, 502; see 501–3).

In non-Jewish sources, ransom language appears in inscriptions in which slaves are dedicated to the gods as ransoms for unspecified sins. In such examples the meaning appears to be propitiatory: the ransom makes the deity more favorably inclined toward the one paying it.[6] A similar notion about the death of Jesus appears outside of Mark and Matthew in Rom 3:24–25, in which Jesus's death serves a ransoming and expiatory purpose. Romans does not appear to have been the source for this tradition but rather serves as evidence of a broadly held idea that Jesus's death could be understood in terms of cultic rituals of expiation (Collins 1997).

Whereas Mark and Matthew are content to place Jesus's death within the context of ritual exchange, Luke sees the death of Jesus in light of ancient Greco-Roman concepts about noble death. Thus, it is interesting, although largely unsurprising, that Luke omits this statement altogether. With these distinctions in mind, I turn now to the passion narratives.

The Suffering of Jesus

In 1 Corinthians Paul states: "We preach Christ crucified, to the Jews a cause of offense and to the Gentiles foolishness" (1 Cor 1:23), and Paul's summary appears correct. By the second century, Romans like Celsus were able to openly ridicule the idea of a religious movement headed by a leader who suffered and died (Origen, *Contra Celsus* 6.10).[7] The crucifixion of Jesus was, quite clearly, an embarrassment that even rhetorically slick

---

[5] For the argument that Mark 10:45 relies on Isaiah 53 see Watts 1998, 125–51.

[6] For the notion that "ransom" rituals are always being constructed and a sophisticated analysis of the ways in which narrative descriptions of rituals serve to construct those rituals rather than simply describe them see Feldman 2017, 1–35.

[7] For Christian awareness of the problem of the cross see Justin Martyr, *1 Apol* 13.4; Lactantius, *Inst.* 4.26 and *Epit.* 50–51.

preachers like Paul had difficulties smoothing over. It was not simply the fact of the crucifixion, however, but Jesus's comportment during his crucifixion that was the cause of the problem.

Mark

Mark's account of the suffering of Jesus spares no details of his mental anguish. While the bloodiness of the physical torture and pain is rarely noted, Mark lingers over the descriptions of Jesus's inner turmoil, relaying words of despair that no eyewitness was present to hear. The mental suffering of Jesus is portrayed chiefly in two scenes: the Gethsemane "agony" and the crucifixion itself. In the former, Jesus asks his disciples to stay awake with him, only to realize, repeatedly, that they have fallen asleep (Mark 14:37, 40, 41). At first he is described as "distressed and agitated" (14:33) and tells Peter, James, and John that he is "deeply grieved, even to death" (14:34). It is precisely his grief that leads him to ask them to stay awake. He moves on "a little farther, and throwing himself on the ground" he prays that "the hour might pass from him" (14:35). The content of the prayer, too, is shaded with despair: "Abba, Father, for you all things are possible; remove this cup from me; yet, not what I want, but what you want" (14:36). While Patristic authors would later emphasize Jesus's submission to the will of God in this moment, early modern readers would embrace the conflict Jesus experienced in the garden (Origen, *Contra Celsus* 2.24; More 1993, 15–16).

Lingering beneath the surface of the Gethsemane agony, and throughout Mark's passion narrative as a whole, is a biblical script furnished primarily from the Old Testament psalms of lament.[8] The repeated allusion to this cluster of texts aligns Jesus with King David, the traditional "author" and voice of the Psalmist. Jesus's association with David was clearly established at the Triumphal Entry into Jerusalem (11–12), and now his kingship is redefined. Jesus is the Davidic King, but one whose monarchic aspirations are "realized through suffering and death rather than through violent, military triumph" (Ahearne-Kroll 2007, 193). In his detailed study of this motif, Stephen Ahearne-Kroll argues that the allusion to the psalms of lament and, in particular, Psalms 41–42, which position King David as a sufferer crying out to God, explain a great deal about the Gethsemane agony: "Jesus' distress is at least in part colored by the sense of abandonment and the inaction on God's part in the face of suffering that is communicated in Psalm 41–42" (180).

Ahearne-Kroll goes on to argue that Jesus's prayer in Mark 14:36 invokes David's own cry to God to alleviate his suffering. The prayer, so despised by Celsus, is not one of desperation but, rather, "a search for understanding with respect to God's will for Jesus to suffer and die" (Ahearne-Kroll 2007, 180). The resulting intertextual reading "results in

---

[8] On the use of passages and motifs from the Hebrew Bible in Mark see, in particular, Marcus 1992. For a summary of the history of this kind of work with respect to Mark and the passion narrative in particular see Ahearne-Kroll 2007, 3–23.

a complex understanding of the scriptural basis for Jesus' suffering and death . . . one that upholds both an expression of God's will for Jesus to suffer and a challenge to the need for suffering to occur" (2007, 180). The prayer evokes not only the Davidic themes in Psalms 41–42 but also Psalm 6, Sirach 37:2, and Jonah 4:9. In addition, Eileen Schuller has noted the similarity between Jesus's prayer and that of Joseph in 4Q Apocryphon of Joseph (Schuller 1990, 349–76). In this text about the patriarch Joseph, the hero asks, "My father and my God, do not abandon me in the hands of gentiles" (4Q372 frg 1, lines 15–16).

In addition to highlighting the association with David, several scholars have noticed Mark's distinctive language of the "cup" as a means of describing the suffering that Jesus is about to experience. This is not the first invocation of this image: it recalls Mark 10:38, when the sons of Zebedee request that they be allowed to sit at the left hand and right hand of Jesus in glory. The image of the cup is reminiscent of the Old Testament prophetic language of the "cup of wrath." Isaiah 51:17, for example, rouses sleepy Jerusalem, identifying the people as those "who have drunk the cup of wrath from the hand of the Lord," and in Jeremiah 25:15–29 the prophet is told to give the cup of wrath first to Jerusalem and then to the nations.[9] In this reading, Jesus, an innocent sufferer, would take upon himself the suffering justly deserved by others, an idea found also in Mark 14:24 and the ransom saying of 10:45.

As one would expect, the suffering of Jesus only intensifies in the hours preceding his death. Mark describes the humiliation Jesus received at the hands of the soldiers (15:16–20), only briefly mentions the flogging (15:15), and notes Jesus's physical frailty when Simon of Cyrene is pressed into service to carry the wooden beam of the cross (15:21).

At Golgotha, immediately before he is crucified, the soldiers offer Jesus wine mixed with myrrh, which Jesus refuses (15:23). A number of scholars have hypothesized that myrrh is an analgesic designed to dull the physical effects of death. Certainly, ancient medics were willing to prescribe narcotics at the end of life in order to produce a painless death, and it is possible that ancient readers would have read this scene in the same way.[10] That Jesus rejected the drink would, in this reading, highlight in a somewhat indirect way the physical pain experienced by Jesus during the crucifixion (Dormeyer 1974, 193). As Collins has put it, "for those in the audiences familiar with the noble death tradition, the gesture would still carry the connotation of disdaining pain and any effort to minimize it" (Collins 2007, 743).

Jesus is crucified and, despite the taunts of those who are there, remains silent. His only and final words are repeated in Aramaic and Greek: "'Eloi, Eloi, lema

---

[9] For a discussion of the origins and use of this image in Mark see Collins 2007, 496–98, 680.

[10] On the analgesic properties of wine see Prov 31:6–7; *m. Sanh* 6.1, and Dioscorides, *De materia medica* 1.64.3, and discussion in Collins 2007, 743. Imbibing drugs seems to have been a practice among imprisoned North African Christians. Tertullian writes disapprovingly of one man who was drugged up with doctored wine during his torture and death (*De ieiunio* 12.3). The Christian martyr-bishop named Fructuosus was offered "spiced" wine by his friends before his execution (*Martyrdom of Fructuosus* 3.1–3).

sabachthani?' which means, 'My God, my God, why have you forsaken me?'" (Mark 15:34). He utters a final "loud cry" and dies (15:37). This final scene emphasizes, more than any other moment in Mark, the frailty and humanity of Jesus in Mark. It is likely that the final words of Jesus were added by Mark himself, who once again presses the scripture into the mouth of Jesus, citing directly from LXX Psalm 21:2a, an individual psalm of lament: "O God, my God, give heed to me; why have you forsaken me?" Matthew, here, follows Mark in allowing Jesus to express a wrenching sense of abandonment in his final moments (Matt 27:46).

The expression of despair and abandonment so palpable in this scene starkly contrasts with the standards for noble death held by both ancient Jews, Greeks, and Romans. That those who are "standing nearby" (Mark 15:35) misunderstand his words and think he is calling for Elijah is a final reference to both the mockery experienced by Jesus and the misunderstandings about his messiahship held by so many actors in the narrative. The final cry of dereliction frustrates the efforts of others to force him to drink and marks the fulfillment of the pain predictions of his death (8:31; 9:31; 10:45). The statement of the nearby centurion, rather than being mocking, is an ironic commentary on the scene: "The real Son of God, the real ruler of the world, has died a shameful and horrifying death on a cross" (Collins 2007, 769).

Luke

Luke's version of the passion narrative diverges wildly from the example offered in Mark. The framing of the suffering of Jesus, in particular, is so different that François Bovon questioned whether or not Luke used a different source for the Gethsemane agony and the cross (Bovon 1993, 413–15).[11] Regardless of whether or not Luke possessed another literary source, it is clear that Luke has radically altered the presentation of Jesus's suffering.

The first major difference is the calm approach to death that Jesus takes, an approach that some scholars label stoic.[12] Gone is the "howling" in Gethsemane and on the cross that so irked Celsus, and in its place one finds a different character entirely. Whereas Mark's Jesus requests that the disciples "stay here while I pray," Luke's Jesus instead instructs the disciples to "pray that you are not put to the test" (Mark 14:32 // Luke 22:40). Instead of Mark's Jesus being "deeply distressed unto death" (Mark 14:34), Luke explains that it was the disciples who were "sleeping out of distress" (Luke 22:45). In this way the Gethsemane agony appears completely reoriented, such that rather than focusing on the testing of Jesus it instead focuses on the disciples: the problematic mental anguish of Jesus is here displaced onto the disciples.

---

[11] For the view that Luke redacted Mark more strongly here see Matera 1985, 469–85. For the view that Luke rewrote Mark with his own concerns in mind see Soards 1987 and Brown 1994, 1:64–67, 75.

[12] My argument here closely follows that of Neyrey 1980, 153–71, Neyrey 1985, 49–68, and Sterling 2001, 395.

In the same way, Luke eliminates three Markan statements that gesture to the emotional turmoil experienced by Jesus in the garden: "and he began to be disturbed and agitated" (Mark 14:33); "My soul is distressed, even to the point of death" (14:34); and the opening of the prayer: "If it is possible, let this hour pass from me" (14:35). And Luke reorients Jesus's body language so that instead of "falling" onto the ground and praying as he does in Mark, Jesus now gets down on his knees (Mark 14:35 // Luke 22:41). Luke does not want readers to think that Jesus collapsed.[13]

The same pattern emerges in Luke's redaction of the crucifixion. Not only the cry but also the entire episode that prompts the agonizing cry of derelict, "My God, my God, why have you forsaken me" (Mark 15:34), is omitted in Luke. Interestingly, Luke chooses to conclude, as Mark does, with a citation from the Psalms. Instead of Psalm 22:2, however, he employs Psalm 31:6: "Father, into your hands I entrust my spirit" (Luke 23:46). It has been argued that the alteration is motivated by a desire to avoid both the use of Aramaic and predictions about the return of Elijah; Luke regularly omits Aramaicisms from Mark.[14] At the same time, the omission of the psalm of lament and its replacement with a psalm of fidelity and dedication reverses the tone of Jesus's final statement and removes any hint of suffering from the scene.

In the history of scholarship, Luke's elimination of the suffering of Jesus from his final hours has not gone unnoted. In the first decades of the twentieth century, Schmidt and Dibelius suggested that these differences were the result of Luke modeling the death of Jesus on (Jewish) martyrological narratives.[15] The manner in which one should conduct oneself at the moment of one's death was the subject of great conversation and speculation in the ancient world.

In his work on this subject, Sterling has suggested that Luke's elimination of the suffering of Jesus in the passion narrative is intended to present Jesus as a Socratic figure who approaches his death with all of the calm self-assurance of the famous Greek philosopher (Sterling 2001). As he notes, in the *Phaedo*, Socrates states that "the true practitioners of philosophy practice dying and death as less fearful to them than for any others" (Plato, *Phaedo* 67E). In particular Sterling points to the similarity between Jesus's and Socrates's acknowledgment of the importance of the will of God/the gods (Luke 22:42 // Plato, *Crito* 43D).

---

[13] As Sterling has noted, the potential exception to this rule is the strengthening angel that appears in Western manuscripts of Luke 22:43–44. It is highly unlikely that these verses are original to the text and run counter to Luke's interpretative program here. For discussion see Ehrman and Plunkett 1983, 401–16, and Sterling 2001, 396.

[14] See also Mark 3:17 // Luke 6:14; Mark 5:41 // Luke 8:54; Mark 11:9–10 // Luke 19:38; Mark 14:36 // Luke 22:42; Mark 15:22 // Luke 23:33. See Acts 1:19, which adds an Aramaic term.

[15] On the similarities between the Lukan passion narratives and later Christian martyrologies see Schmidt 1918, 114–16, and Schmidt 1919. The first to advance the hypothesis that Luke's passion narrative was based on Jewish martyrological models was Dibelius 1935, 178–217. The theory was more fully developed by his student Surkau 1938, 98–100.

A wealth of scholarship has followed Dibelius and Surkau, including Ernst 1977, 643; Grundmann 1961; Lagrange 1927, 593; and Stöger 1969, 4–8. For the view that Luke was not the first to introduce the martyrological motifs see Surkau 1938, 90. For a more recent summary see Beck 1981, 28–47.

Even before the composition of Luke, generations of Greeks and Romans had adapted and reinterpreted the death of Socrates, thereby creating a composite portrait of Socrates focused on the good death (Moss 2012, 25). Beyond Socrates, many ancient philosophers and heroes were commended for their dispassionate and accepting attitude to death. The insensibility to or disregard of pain, which becomes a feature in later Christian interpretations of the death of Jesus in Luke, is an important element of the portrayals of the deaths of philosophers like Anaxarchus and Zeno (both of whom bite off their own tongues) in defiance of tyranny (Diogenes Laertius, *Lives* 9.26–28, 9.59).[16] These traditions had a profound impact: the story is twice referred to by Cicero, is discussed by Plutarch, and is cited by the Roman historian Valerius Maximus (Cicero, *Tusculan Disputations* 2.52 and *On the Nature of the Gods* 3.23; Plutarch, *On Talkativeness* 505D; Valerius Maximus, 3.3). In the same vein, Philo commends those who bite off their own tongues rather than divulge their secrets (Philo, *The Worse Attacks the Better* 176). Even in a case in Seneca involving a would-be assassin who failed to execute his mission, the fact that a young man placed his own arm into the flames and "extracted his own penalty" made him worthy of honor (Davis 1990, 109). The ability to withstand or embrace pain in obedience to the gods of Greco-Roman philosophical principles made one worthy of respect. Luke's redaction of the passion narrative brings the death of Jesus into line with narratives like these and strips from his source any hint of physical or psychic distress. The elimination of the experience of suffering during the crucifixion brings the death of Jesus into line with generally agreed-upon conventions about how heroes die.

PREDICTIONS OF THE SUFFERINGS OF JESUS FOLLOWERS

In both Matthew and Mark, Jesus is explicitly identified as an example for his followers: he was the model for calling disciples (Mark 3:13–19; Matt 28:18–20), prayer (Mark 1:35–39; Matt 6:9–13), performing healings (Matt 8:1–17), answering the charges of opponents (Mark 2:1–3:27), and relating to one's family (Mark 3:31–35). As Philip Davis noted, for Mark, the teachings of Jesus take a backseat to the exhortations to follow the example of Jesus. He begins his Gospel by appealing to the "way of the Lord" (1:1–3) and repeatedly describes the journey from Caesarea Philippi to Jerusalem in the same terms (8:27; 9:33–34; 10:32). Mark's Gospel "can be read as a blueprint for the Christian life: it begins with baptism, proceeds with the vigorous pursuit of ministry in the face of temptation and opposition, and culminates in suffering and death orientated toward an as-yet unseen vindication" (Davis 1990, 109).

---

[16] See also Pliny, *NH* 7.23: "in viris Anaxarchi, qui simili de causa cum torqueretur pracrosam dentibus linguam unamque spem indici in tyranny os expuit."

The theme of imitating Jesus by suffering is made explicit in Mark 8:22–10:52, where the role of the disciple and the true nature of discipleship become preoccupying themes for the evangelist. Toward the beginning of this section, Jesus instructs the disciples in what it means to follow him:

> And he called to him the multitude with his disciples, and said to them. . . . If any man would come after me, let him deny himself and take up his cross and follow me. For whoever would save his life will lose it; and whoever loses his life for my sake and the gospel's will save it. For what does it profit a man, to gain the whole world and forfeit his life? For what can a man give in return for his life? For whoever is ashamed of me and of my words in this adulterous and sinful generation, of him will the Son of Man also be ashamed, when he comes in the glory of his Father with the holy angels. (Mark 8:34–38)

There has been considerable debate about Mark's specific meaning here.[17] Some have argued that the instruction be read literally as an exhortation to martyrdom, while others have advocated for a figurative interpretation about the hardships of discipleship in general (Gundry 1993, 433–40; Moss 2010, 31).

Early readers of Mark were aware of and in some cases supported literal interpretations of the call to take up the cross. Luke's redaction of this pericope quite explicitly rejects such an interpretation: "Then he said to them all, 'If any want to become my followers, let them deny themselves and take up their cross daily and follow me'" (Luke 9:23) The addition of the phrase "daily" (καθ' ἡμέραν) here transforms the saying, such that it cannot be read as a prescription for martyrdom or as a call to suffering (Moss 2010, 31). The redaction betrays a Lukan anxiety about the demands of discipleship.

The same redactional tendency is at work in Luke's redaction of Jesus's rebuke of the sons of Zebedee in Mark 10. In response to the somewhat brazen request to sit at his right hand and left hand, Mark's Jesus asks, "Are you able to drink the cup that I drink, or to be baptized with the baptism with which I am baptized?" (Mark 10:38). The ambiguous reference to the cup will, as already discussed, only be clarified in the Garden of Gethsemane. The sons of Zebedee are not entirely certain what they are agreeing to. While a minority has read this passage eucharistically, it is more probable that Jesus is inviting the men to a form of discipleship that, practically speaking, involves the acceptance of suffering (Theissen 1991, 197–98). It is precisely this passage that leads Jesus to refer to his own death as a ransom (Mark 10:45).

Luke, by briefly summarizing the passage, once again, tempers the expectation that followers of Jesus must suffer and die. Instead of a passage about the unexpected nature of discipleship, Luke reconfigures it into a narrative about leadership and service (Luke

---

[17] Since the early twentieth century a majority of scholars have attributed the passage to Jesus himself. I follow Menzies and Branscomb in seeing the reference to the cross as the product of the evangelist. See Menzies 1901; Branscomb 1937.

22:24–27). Matthew, for his part, softens the story so that it is the mother of the sons of Zebedee who makes the embarrassing request (Matt 20:20–21).

In the case of both Mark and Matthew, there is an expectation that the suffering experienced by Jesus's followers would confer rewards. Mark's Jesus promises a whole host of eschatological rewards for those who leave behind families and belongings (Mark 10:29–30). The statement is picked up by Matthew and Luke, but Matthew's version of the Beatitudes expands the promise of future rewards to include those who are persecuted (Matt 5:10–11). Suffering, while difficult, comes with the expectation of rewards.

Predictions of Eschatological Suffering

Even if only Matthew and Mark agree that the cost of discipleship involves suffering for and like Jesus, all three Synoptic authors agree that in the eschaton and at Jesus's return, the world will experience a period of great suffering. Apocalyptic anguish is, of course, something of a feature of the genre of "apocalypse" of which Mark 13, the basis for these predictions, is often considered a part. "In those days," Mark relates, "there will be suffering, such as has not been from the beginning of the creation that God created until now, no, and never will be" (13:19).

Mark's own description of this era of suffering is elaborate and detailed. He instructs his audience that when they see the desolating sacrilege they should flee to the hills (13:14), to pray that they will not be pregnant (13:17), to expect false messiahs (13:21), and to anticipate arrests and persecution (13:11). The majority of this concert of destruction and suffering is adapted by Matthew and Luke (Matt 24:15–22 // Luke 21:20–24). For Luke the reference to the "desolating sacrilege" is shifted to specifically identify the warning as the Roman attacks on the city of Jerusalem and the impending destruction of Jerusalem (Luke 21:20). Luke also, as already noted, elsewhere explicitly links the destruction of Jerusalem to the suffering of Jesus. The apocalyptic destruction of the city is, in this way, understood in terms of divine punishment for the mistreatment of Jesus (Luke 17:24).[18]

Conclusion

In general, each of the Synoptic writers envisions the world as a place in which suffering is powerful, predictable, and meaningful. Each expects that, in the future, followers of

---

[18] See Whitaker, chapter 22 here, for an extended discussion of apocalyptic eschatology in the Synoptics.

Jesus will experience hardships and that people in general will experience suffering in the apocalypse. To paint in broad nuance-obscuring stripes, each author reveals his own thematic interests. While Luke sets his gaze on the Jews who rejected Jesus as responsible for their own downfall, Mark and Matthew take a less deterministic approach to the death of Jesus. The suffering of Jesus is not only necessary; it serves as a redemptive suffering in expiating the sins of "the many." For Luke, the death of Jesus adheres to the model of the self-controlled and respectable death of a philosopher. For Mark, Jesus's suffering is uncomfortably close and present; the reader cannot look away from the Gethsemane agony or cry of despair from the cross. For Matthew, such moments serve pedagogical roles; they offer moments of instruction for the disciples and, by extension, for the audience itself.

References

Ahearne-Kroll, Stephen P. 2007. *The Psalms of Lament in Mark's Passion: Jesus' Davidic Suffering*. SNTS Monograph Series 142. Cambridge: Cambridge University Press.

Beck, Brian E. 1981. "'Imitatio Christi' and the Lukan Passion Narrative." In *Suffering and Martyrdom in the New Testament: Studies Presented to G. M. Styler by the Cambridge New Testament Seminar*, edited by William Horbury and Brian McNeil, 28–47. Cambridge: Cambridge University Press.

Bornkamm, Günther. 1963. "The Stilling of the Storm in Matthew." In *Tradition and Interpretation in Matthew*, edited by Günther Bornkamm, Gerhard Barth, and Heinz Joachi Held, 52–57. London: SCM Press.

Bovon, François. 1993. "Le récit lucanien de la passion de Jésus (Lc 22–23)." In *The Synoptic Gospels: Source Criticism and the New Literary Criticism*, Bibliotheca ephemeridum theologicarum Lovaniensium, edited by E. Focant, 393–423. Louvain: Peeters.

Branscomb, Bennett Harvie. 1937. *The Gospel of Mark*. Moffatt New Testament Commentary Series 2. New York: Harper.

Breytenbach, Cilliers. 1989. *Versöhnung: Eine Studie zur Paulinischen Soteriologie*. Wissenschaftliche Monographien zum Alten und Neuen Testament 60. Neukirchen-Vluyn: Neukirchener.

Brown, Raymond E. 1994. *The Death of the Messiah: From Gethsemane to the Grave, A Commentary on the Passion Narratives in the Four Gospels*. 2 vols. Anchor Bible Reference Library. New York: Doubleday.

Burkert, Walter. 1972. *Homo Necans: Interpretationen Altgriechischer Opferriten und Mythen*. Religionsgeschichtliche Versuche und Vorarbeiten, bd. 32. Berlin: De Gruyter.

Collins, Adela Yarbro. 1994. "From Noble Death to Crucified Messiah." *NTS* 40: 481–503.

Collins, Adela Yarbro. 1997. "The Signification of Mark 10:45 among Gentile Christians." *HTR* 90: 371–82.

Collins, Adela Yarbro. 2007. *Mark: A Commentary*. Edited by Harold W. Attridge. Hermeneia. Minneapolis: Fortress Press.

Daly, Robert J. 1978. *Christian Sacrifice: The Judaeo-Christian Background before Origen*. Washington, DC: Catholic University of America Press.

Davis, Philip. 1990. "Christology, Discipleship and Self-Understanding in the Gospel of Mark." In *Self-Definition in Early Christianity: A Case of Shifting Horizons. Essays in Appreciation of*

Ben F. Meyer from His Former Students, edited by David Hawkin and Tom Robinson, 101–19. Lewiston, ME: Mellen.

Dibelius, Martin. 1935. *From Tradition to Gospel*. 2nd ed. New York: Scribner's.

Dormeyer, Detlev. 1974. *Die Passion Jesu als Verhaltensmodell: Literarische und theologische Analyse der Traditions-und Redaktionsgeschichte der Markuspassion*. Neutestamentliche Abhandlungen 11. Münster: Aschendorff.

Ehrman, Bart D., and Mark A. Plunkett. 1983. "The Angel and the Agony: The Textual Problem of Luke 22:43–44." *CBQ* 45: 401–16.

Ernst, Josef. 1977. *Das Evangelium nach Lukas*. RNT 3. Regensburg: Pstet.

Feldman, Lianne Marquis. 2017. "Ritual Sequence and Narrative Constraints in Leviticus 9:1–10:3." *JHS* 17: 1–35.

Gese, Hartmut. 1983. "Die Sühne." In *Zur Biblischen Theologie: Altestamentliche Vorträge*, edited by Hartmut Gese, 85–106. Tübingen: Mohr Siebeck.

Girard, René. 1972. *La violence et le sacré*. Paris: B. Grasset.

Grundmann, Walter. 1961. *Das Evangelium nach Lukas*. Berlin: Evangelische Verlagsanstalt.

Gundry, Robert Horton. 1993. *Mark: A Commentary on His Apology for the Cross*. Grand Rapids: Eerdmans.

Käsemann, Ernst. 1980. *Commentary on Romans*. Grand Rapids: Eerdmans.

Lagrange, Marie-Joseph. 1927. *Évangile selon Saint Luc*. Paris: Gabalda.

Marcus, Joel. 1992. *The Way of the Lord: Christological Exegesis of the Old Testament in the Gospel of Mark*. Louisville, KY: Westminster/John Knox.

Matera, Frank J. 1982. *The Kingship of Jesus: Composition and Theology in Mark 15*. SBL Dissertation Series. Atlanta: SBL Press.

Matera, Frank J. 1985. "The Death of Jesus According to Luke: A Question of Sources." *CBQ* 47: 469–85.

Menzies, Allan. 1901. *The Earliest Gospel: A Historical Study of the Gospel According to Mark*. London: Macmillan.

More Thomas. 1993. *De Tristitia Christi*, volume 14 of the *Complete Works of St. Thomas More*. New Haven: Yale University Press. Reprinted as *The Sadness of Christ*. New York: Scepter.

Moss, Candida R. 2010. *The Other Christs: Imitating Jesus in Ancient Christian Ideologies of Martyrdom*. New York: Oxford University Press.

Moss, Candida R. 2012. *Ancient Christian Martyrdom*. New Haven: Yale University Press.

Neyrey, Jerome H. 1980. "The Absence of Jesus' Emotions: The Lucan Redaction of Lk. 22, 39–46." *Bib* 61: 153–71.

Neyrey, Jerome H. 1985. *The Passion According to Luke: A Redaction Study of Luke's Soteriology*. New York: Paulist.

Perry, John H. 1986. "The Three Days in the Synoptic Passion Predictions." *CBQ* 48: 637–54.

Schmidt, Karl L. 1918. "Die literarische Eigenart der Leidensgeschichte Jesu." *Die christliche Welt* 32: 114–16.

Schmidt, Karl L. 1919. *Der Rahmen der Geschichte Jesu: Literarkritische Untersuchungen zur ältesten Jesusüberlieferung*. Berlin: Trowtsche und Sohn.

Schuller, Eileen. 1990. "4Q372 1: A Text about Joseph." *RevQ* 14: 349–76.

Soards, Marion L. 1987. *The Passion According to Luke: The Special Material of Luke 22*. JSNTSup 14. Sheffield: Sheffield Academic Press.

Sterling, Gregory E. 2001. "*Mors Philosophi*: The Death of Jesus in Luke." *HTR* 94: 383–402.

Stöger, Alois. 1969. "Eigenart und Botschaft der lukanischen Passionsgeschichte." *Bibel und Kirche* 24, no. 1: 4–8.

Surkau, Hans-Werner. 1938. *Martyrien in jüdischer und frühchristlicher Zeit.* FRLANT 36. Göttingen: Vanderhoeck und Ruprecht.

Theissen, Gerd. 1991. *The Gospels in Context: Social and Political History in the Synoptic Tradition.* Minneapolis: Fortress Press.

Van Henten, Jan Willem. 1997. *The Maccabean Martyrs as Saviours of the Jewish People: A Study of 2 and 4 Maccabees.* Supplements to the Journal for the Study of Judaism 57. Leiden: Brill.

Watts, Rikki E. 1998. "Jesus' Death, Isaiah 53, and Mark 10:45: A Crux Revisited." In *Jesus and the Suffering Servant: Isaiah 53 and Christian Origins*, edited by William H. Bellinger, Jr., and William R. Farmer, 125–51. Harrisburg, PA: Trinity Press international.

Wrede, William. 1971. *The Messianic Secret.* Translated by James C. G. Grieg. Cambridge: James Clark.

Young, Frances M. 1979. *The Use of Sacrificial Ideas in Greek Christian Writers from the New Testament to John Chrysostom.* Patristic Monograph Series 5. Cambridge, MA: Philadelphia Patristic Foundation.

CHAPTER 14

VIOLENT IMAGINARIES

SARAH E. ROLLENS

Introduction

THE Synoptic Gospels feature some of the most well-known episodes from the life of Jesus. Many of the stories have served as proof-texts for centuries of Christian charity or formed the basis of ideologies of peace and nonviolence, arguably found in such places as the Sermon on the Mount. The focus on nonviolence in the Synoptic Gospels, however, must be reconciled with the explicit language of violence that often occurs alongside such irenic imagery. This chapter thus explores language of violence in the Synoptic Gospels and treats it as an important intellectual resource that the authors intentionally deployed for rhetorical purposes.

Violence is a complicated topic to analyze within texts. For one, all scholars have access to are textual representations of violence. The representations of violence that authors create within texts can have manifold relationships to the reality of such violence. Through the textual medium, authors can reflect on real violent circumstances that they or others experience, but conversely, they can also use the space of the text to exaggerate or downplay those phenomena. And, of course, authors can fabricate experiences of violence altogether (e.g. Duff 2001, 14–15). Complicating matters even more is the fact that ancient peoples' attitudes toward violence could, in some cases, be fundamentally different from those of today; that is, they may have considered some forms of violence socially appropriate in ways that no one would today (see Fagan 2011).[1] This means that when readers try to expose the logic behind some representations of violence, they will admittedly do so without agreeing with the ancient author's assumption

---

[1] Much of this is what may be deemed "sanctioned violence." Following Randall Caroline Forsberg (2001), Warren Carter explains that sanctioned violence is "often legal, socially accepted, and widely practiced. Such violence is facilitated by obedience to authority, the seeking of social approval, a reduced sense of agency or responsibility, dehumanization of the victims, and, especially, internalized learned justifications" (Carter 2017, 284).

that it is a just or unjust deed. Moreover, since it is challenging to connect language of violence to its social reality, this chapter focuses instead on how the imagery contributes to and functions within texts. It considers violence as a literary device that an author chooses to deploy for particular reasons.

Though violence is an enormous category that can encompass all sorts of individual, communal, and structural phenomena, for the purposes of this analysis, I aim for a relatively simplistic way of thinking about violence. I define it as: acts of force or compulsion against others, meant to either positively enact physical damage to the person or their property, or to preclude them, by means of force, from attaining resources and opportunities that they need or want. To supplement this, I incorporate Warren Carter's insightful remarks: "violence is the sanctioned or unsanctioned destructive assertion of power against the will and interests of others. It violates the personhood of individuals and/or groups to their physical and/or psychological/emotional detriment and harm. Violence can be expressed in interpersonal as well as structural/systemic and societal realms. It can take multiple forms—physical-rhetorical, psychological, emotional, legal, military, institutional, administrative, symbolic, ideological, religious, etc." (Carter 2017, 285). Again, it must be emphasized that the violence I discuss here is encountered in the textual realm. As such, violent language must also be considered a productive, creative intellectual resource. It has, in addition, the ability to generate certain affective dispositions in audiences, which contribute to the project of persuasion.

As other contributors to this book have discussed at length (e.g., Kloppenborg, Foster, and Kirk, chapters 1, 2, and 6 here, respectively), both here and in numerous other publications, there are various ways of thinking about the compositional relationships of the Synoptic Gospels to one another. This chapter takes for granted the cogency of the Two-Document/Source Hypothesis (2DH or 2SH), which I have argued for in several other publications (Rollens 2010; 2014).

Violence against the Envoys of God

The most explicit scene of violence in the canonical Gospels is the death of Jesus, stylized in the so-called passion narratives. There have been countless academic studies on the passion narratives, exploring such aspects as how Matthew and Luke have developed Mark's relatively brief account or how Jesus's suffering is variously represented by the different authors. So as to not reinvent the wheel, here I would instead like to focus on contextualizing Jesus's death within a wider ideological frame, one in which the envoys of God suffer violence by those to whom they have been sent. This theme is present in all three Synoptic Gospels to different degrees, as well as in Matthew and Luke's source Q. Q, in turn, depends on an ideology that was widespread in earlier Jewish texts, a point to which I return later.

Though Q does not contain a passion narrative, it knows of Jesus's death and situates it within a broader scheme of the people of Israel rejecting God's prophets. For instance,

Q 11:49–51 includes a judgment spoken by the Wisdom of God, which was regularly personified as a feminine entity in late antique Jewish texts (Johnson-DeBaufre 2005). "I will send them prophets and sages," Wisdom bemoans, "and some of them they will kill and persecute, so that a settling of accounts for the blood of all the prophets poured out from the founding of the world may be required of this generation, from the blood of Abel to the blood of Zechariah, murdered between the sacrificial altar and the House.... An accounting will be required of this generation!"[2] This reflection refers to a series of sages and prophets whom God sent to reform the people of Israel and who were consistently and violently rejected. It is crucial to realize that this violence does not reflect any specific events in the Jewish Scriptures (Kloppenborg 2000, 121). Rather, it is Q's hyperbolic judgment on the disobedience of the people of Israel, which helps the followers of Jesus who engaged with Q make sense of Jesus's death. The logic is thus: not only have the people of Israel murdered innocent and divinely endorsed great men but also they did so in an explicitly sacrilegious way (literally within the sanctity of the temple space in Jerusalem). Again in Q 13:34–35, the speaker (presumably Jesus this time) voices a similar anxiety to Q 11:49–51: "O Jerusalem, Jerusalem, who kills the prophets and stones those sent to her! How often I wanted to gather your children together, as a hen gathers her nestlings under her wings, and you were not willing! Look, your house is forsaken!" In this case, Jerusalem (whether it stands for the elite rulers or the Jewish people more generally) is lamented for its violent rejection of those sent to her with good intentions. In the earliest text about Jesus, then, his death is but one instantiation of a range of experiences of violence suffered by those commissioned by God.

Given the legacy of rejection that Q already presupposes, the gruesome death of John the Baptist becomes more explicable. The author of Mark provides an extensive narrative that explores the specific details and injustice of John the Baptist's death. According to Mark, John's fate is sealed when he criticizes Herod Antipas's marriage. (Antipas's wife, Herodias, was previously married to his brother Philip; Mark 6:17–18.) To put an end to this unwelcome critique, Antipas has John captured and locked in prison (Mark 6:17). Yet Mark specifies that it is really Herodias who is plotting against John; it is she who "had a grudge against him and wanted to kill him" (Mark 6:19).[3] Her opportunity comes when her daughter (Mark calls both mother and daughter by the name Herodias, but the daughter is traditionally deemed Salome to distinguish the two) dances for Antipas and his guests at a banquet, for which Antipas, in gratitude, offers to fulfill one of her wishes. Under the direction of her mother, the daughter approaches the king and requests, "I want you to give me at once the head of John the Baptist on a platter" (Mark 6:25). The drama is intense: Antipas cannot damage his honor in front of his guests by refusing to honor her request (Mark 6:26). He immediately disposes a soldier to do the deed; the daughter receives his head and turns it over to her mother. John's disciples then

---

[2] All passages from Q are drawn from the International Q Project's reconstruction and translation (Robinson et al. 2000) and are, as is custom, cited accordingly to Lukan versification.

[3] All biblical texts are from the NRSV translation unless otherwise noted.

come and collect his decapitated body, though Mark is unclear about the fate of his head (Mark 6:29).

While the complicity for John's death is focused on Herod Antipas (Herodias and Salome, of course, share the blame), the notion of a wider coterie of prophetic envoys is clear in these texts. Indeed, just prior to relating the scene of John's death, Mark brings up the ambiguity of Jesus's, John's, and Elijah's identities and their relationship to one another—regardless of these ambiguities, they are all emissaries of God. Indeed, both Mark and Q underscore the similarities among Elijah's, John's, and Jesus's activities (Q 7:18–23; Mark 8:27–28). Despite acknowledging that there are strong similarities between the figures of Elijah, John, and Jesus, Q specifies that the "age of Jesus" experiences a distinct kind of violence. In an enigmatic formulation, Q states that "the law and the prophets were until John. From then on the kingdom of God is violated and the violent plunder it" (Q 16:16). The import of such a saying is not automatically clear, but for my purposes, one can observe its basic conclusion: after the time of John the Baptist (i.e., during the time of Jesus), the kingdom of God experiences violence at the hands of the "violent" (βιασταί; Aichele 1998, 74).

In general, Mark tends to contain rougher and more vivid imagery of violence than Matthew and Luke. The latter authors typically replace Mark's violent or harsh imagery with softer vocabulary items or remove it altogether (see Rollens 2018). One can observe these tendencies in how Luke and Matthew treat the tradition of John's death. Luke does not retain Mark's graphic account of John's fate in his Gospel; only Matthew decides to work with these violent resources. Matthew, as is characteristic of his redactional policy regarding Mark, generally prunes some details in this story so that his version is much more brief. Even so, he still retains the details that Antipas seized and bound John before imprisoning him, and the request for John's head on a platter still comes from Herodias through her daughter. The primary difference in Matthew's account is that Matthew has removed all the excess dialogue between Antipas and the daughter and then between the daughter and Herodias. In some ways then, Matthew has muffled the drama of this scene by curtailing it. That Matthew places this story directly after the scene of Jesus being rejected by his fellow villagers in Nazareth (Matt 13:53–58) underscores that Matthew, like Mark and Q, situated the rejection of Jesus and John in a wider framework of violence enacted against all the prophets of God. And this legacy of violence extends forward in time as well as backward; the fate of John the Baptist, Brown observes, "is a warning of what the fate of Jesus is likely to be—and the fate of those sent to carry on his work" (Brown 1997, 136).

The assumption that those whom God sends to reform his people will suffer rejection and violence is famously encapsulated in the Parable of the Tenants in the Vineyard found in Mark 12:1–12 (Kloppenborg 2006, 57–60). The parable tells of a vineyard owner who furnishes his estate with a well, a wine press, and a water tower before leasing it to tenants while he is away in another country. When the harvest comes, the owner sends a slave to extract a portion of the produce, which is a typical strategy in an agricultural tenancy arrangement. The vineyard workers attack the first slave, leading the owner to send a second slave to accomplish what the first had not been able to. The second slave is treated similarly, as is the third. The vineyard owner nevertheless continues to send an unspecified number of slaves to demand the portion of the harvest. After achieving no success with his subordinates, he eventually opts to send his beloved son, whom the workers—unsurprisingly at this point in the story—murder. In response, the owner returns in person to "destroy" the tenants and transfer the lease of the vineyard to others. Despite some important differences, most commentators argue that in its Markan instantiation, the parable works allegorically to show the sequence of rejection that the prophets and Jesus experienced (Kloppenborg 2006, 50–70).[4]

The extremely violent imagery in this narrative episode is immediately evident, especially when commentators rely on a pre-Markan version of the parable, stripped of all its allegorizing details adapted from Isaiah and elsewhere (as in Herzog 1994 98–101). Under careful examination, one sees that the physical violence becomes increasingly cruel at each stage of the story. According to Mark, when the first servant arrived, the tenants "took him and beat him" (Mark 12:3) but nevertheless allowed him to leave. The second servant was "wounded in the head" (Mark 12:4) and treated with contempt; Mark's narrative does not state whether he escaped as the first did. The third servant, however, was outright murdered, as were numerous ones after him. The use of violent imagery ramps up the stakes at each stage of the tale. Rejection of the teachings/warnings of Jesus and the other prophets is thus recast as physical violence and eventual murder of emissaries who are supposed to be welcomed and respected.

Imagery of force and coercion works in a different way in this parable, as well: it exposes the violence and injustice involved in ancient socioeconomic power dynamics. In general, the world presupposed in the Gospels "was dominated by Roman power exerted through structural violence" (Carter 2017, 285), for example, the kind that forced peasants to sell off their land and enter into precarious tenancy arrangements. And here, it is important to realize that depending on one's social location in the ancient world, the appropriateness of the characters' actions would be understood rather differently. From the elite vantage point, the servants and the son are legally owed the produce, and the laborers are thus acting both illegally and illogically according to normal economic exchange practices. From the subelite vantage point, however, this scene reflects the oppressive demands of sharecropping practices, which required tenants to surrender part of their harvest, sometimes on top of other rent payments, taxes, and other financial obligations. The envoys thus represent unwelcome surveillance and a constant threat to the laborers' livelihoods; attacking the messengers may have sounded to nonelite ears like a reasonable reaction in order to protect one's labor and surplus produce. Herzog, for instance, sees in this parable a codification of a spiral of agrarian violence that often ended up in outright revolt; peasants, pushed to the edge of subsistence, rebelled against the consistent exploitation of their labor and extraction of their produce by elite landowners (Herzog 1989, 98–113).

---

[4] The earliest version of the parable, however, may not have functioned allegorically (Kloppenborg 2006, 70).

On the other hand in the Synoptics' version of the story, which adapts details from Isaiah and leaves no ambiguity that the vineyard owner is meant to represent God, readers are meant to sympathize with the unjust rejection of the envoys of God and to agree that the owner's eventual actions (destroying the tenants and leasing it to others) are acceptable. This contributes to the Christian myth of supersessionism that has unfortunately vilified Jews for centuries. Violence here thus acts to demonstrate the irrational, inexplicable rejection of Jesus, who is an honorable representative of God. The next section explores other examples of violence in the Synoptic parables, but for now I focus on how the violence in this particular parable is part of a wider ideology of violence in ancient Judaism.

The framework of rejection this section has been exploring thus far is part of a wider theological schema that scholars call Deuteronomistic theology (Kloppenborg 2000, 121; 2006, 58–59; Steck 1967; see Jacobson 1982). According to this theology, "the history of Israel is depicted as a repetitive cycle of sinfulness, prophetic calls to repentance (which are ignored), punishment by God, and renewed calls to repentance with threats of judgment" (Kloppenborg 2000, 121). The Parable of the Tenants is a clear exposition on this schema. The Deuteronomistic theological framework interprets the landowner as God, the servants as prophets, the vineyard workers as the people of Israel (or their leaders), and the son as, of course, Jesus. Crucially, this theological framework accounts for the predictable rejection of those who envision themselves as prophets sent by God: it gives a ready-made, mythic-explanatory reason for why early followers of Jesus were rejected. That is, if an early follower of Jesus experienced some sort of negative reaction from an outsider (rejection, hostility, mocking), they already had a template by which to make sense of it: since the Israelite prophets, John the Baptist, and Jesus were not welcomed by those to whom they were sent, it is "natural" for people sanctioned by God to experience rejection. Perhaps this is why Paul, or someone emending his letter (Rollens 2016), could easily insert 1 Thessalonians 2:14–16 into the First Letter to the Thessalonians; it is a myth that helps make sense of social experience (i.e., perceived rejection) that many early Christians no doubt experienced.

Of course, the most obvious example of violence against an envoy of God concerns the fate of Jesus. The violence of the crucifixion is obvious and has been explored by numerous scholars (Aitken 2004; Carrol and Green 1989; Carter 2017, 292–94; Crossan 1988; Green 1988), but it is nevertheless worth investigating for further insights about this influential scene of violence. Religious systems based on sacrifice and atonement are inherently violent (Girard 1977; Burkert et al. 1988; Yoder Neufeld 2011, 73–98), and indeed, they require such violence for their religion to be properly performed. Curiously, Christianity manages to hold two forms of violence in tension in its myth about Jesus: that God intentionally sent his son to die a violent death and that Jesus unjustly suffered violence at the hands of his enemies, who failed to properly comprehend his teachings. As noted, the violent experience of Jesus also becomes an important myth for later social formation, helping followers of Jesus understand their own rejection, lack of success, or dishonor (Dube 2013; Kelhoffer 2010; Mack 1988; Middleton 2014). The suggestion that this cosmic drama had been intended by God alleviated the anxieties of the first

Christians, who were still holding out hope that their ideas would be preached to the "ends of the earth" and that outsiders would come to see how they had been right all along in their devotion to Jesus.

Since its early literary expressions in the first century, the crucifixion has informed nearly two millennia of imaginative theology about the violence Jesus suffered during his last hours, even though the Gospels are rather sparse about the details. What I want to underscore is that in the Synoptic Gospels, this episode of violence culminates a series of other encounters in which Jesus and others are objectified, victimized, and treated as passive objects. It is within this context of violent consequences for God's envoys that one should view the death of Jesus, instead of fixating on it as a unique occurrence. What is different, of course, about Jesus is that he is understood to be the son of God, and therefore a very special envoy of God. His rejection then becomes all the more grave for those familiar with this story. However, it is important to ground this scene of violence within the wider ideological framework present in the Synoptics in order to fully appreciate the drama unfolding within the accounts.

VIGNETTES OF VIOLENCE: SYNOPTIC PARABLES

The Parable of the Tenants in the Vineyard (Mark 12:1–12) is but one of many parables that Jesus is purported to have told in his life. Indeed, many scholars believe that a good portion of the parables stem from Jesus himself (e.g. Crossan 1991). I am less convinced of that (Berg and Rollens 2008), but I do agree that a number of the parables reflect the relatively coherent worldview of subelites in a rural environment, though they may have ultimately been embedded in more elite literary products.[5] Here I examine three parables drawn from the Synoptic Gospels in order to show that they often reflect a world both structured and stoked by visible violence and injustice. In this sense, they draw upon violent language as a literary resource in order to achieve persuasion. This persuasion banks on the audience recognizing the features of the world under discussion in the parables and affirming its danger. Put differently: violence is often integral to the parables of Jesus because the argumentative thrust, indeed, the point of many of the parables, would be lost without the inclusion of the violent language.

The parable in Matthew 18:23–35, for instance, is a chilling account in which a slave is indebted to a king for the outlandish sum of 10,000 talents (Snodgrass 2008, 66). When the king demands the debt be settled and discovers that the slave is unable to pay, the king orders that the slave, his family, and his possessions be sold. The slave begs for time to repay the debt, and remarkably, the king not only acquiesces, but then also cancels the debt altogether. The slave, in turn, goes out to find a fellow servant indebted to him

---

[5] On nonelite literary traditions embedded in elite literature, see Rollens 2014.

(for a mere 100 denarii) and demands settlement by seemingly inappropriate force (i.e., he starts choking him [ἔπνιγεν]). It is worth noting that this is exclusively Matthean vocabulary. The New Testament only contains three instances of this term and its variations; all are in Matthew. The indebted servant makes the same request of him that he had made of the king, but the original servant refuses his request. When the king finds out, he angrily sends the original servant to the torturers "until he should pay back all he owed" (Matt 18:34), which implies that the king reinstated the initial debt. Matthew's Jesus sums up this parable with the abrupt conclusion: "This is how my heavenly Father will treat each of you unless you forgive your brother or sister from your heart" (Matt 18:35).

The structural violence of this parable is striking: the rigid hierarchy of ancient society renders various people under the control of their superiors; elite rulers literally held the power of life and death over their human property; and casual, physical violence appears to be routine in both the economic and legal spheres, at many different levels of social interaction. The violence that was inherently built into the master-slave relationship especially seems to determine the subordinate's vicious treatment of his fellow servant. Curiously, note that the king's mercy seems to have no effect on the servant's actions, perhaps because such forgiveness was so out of the ordinary in a world so plagued with inequality. And this entire scenario, as Matthew explains in the preface of the parable, is meant to illuminate something about how forgiveness works in the kingdom of heaven (Matt 18:21–23).

In William Herzog's interpretation of this parable, the point of this story banks on the inherent violence involved in ancient politics (Herzog 1994, 131–49). The story also relies on a portrait of God/Jesus that, Hector Avalos has observed, blatantly draws upon imagery of imperial, and sometimes cruel, power (Avalos 2015). It underscores the vast inequality of the Roman Empire and the violence that characterized it and sustained it (see also Carter 2017, 294–95). The unrealistic nature of the scenario, including the exorbitant amount of wealth involved in the first debt, is likely "meant to evoke the virtually unlimited power and incalculable wealth of the ruler" (139). Warren Carter makes similar observations: the story is "a parable about forgiveness (or more accurately, unforgiveness), the kingdom/empire of the heavens is compared to imperial structures of tax or tribute collection presided over by a kingly tyrant and peopled by subservient slaves or officials" (2016, 84). The eventual reaction of the king (to submit the slave to torture until his debt is paid) can be understood as function of shame, in this case, the king's need to reassert his power and honor in the face of the servant's shaming actions (Herzog 1994, 140–46). Torture, moreover, while violent to the modern reader, is precisely the legal action thought to yield the best results when slaves were involved (Gale and Scourfield 2018, 7–8). In this politically inclined interpretation, the theological thrust is rather troubling to the modern reader; if God is likened to a slave-owning king or master here, the implication is that he can enact or initiate great violence against his subjects, seemingly capriciously. Though the parable might ultimately champion the "unlimited range of God's forgiveness," it does so, ironically, by "invoke[ing] divine judgment on those who refuse to repent" (Brown 1997, 193). If God is not meant to be likened to the king, Snodgrass has noted, the interpretations fail. "If the king is a ruthless oppressor not representing God, from where does any expectation of messianic forgiveness come, and what would motivate such a costly act?" (2008, 70). These commentators illustrate how the violence among the parable's key characters has provided a significant stumbling block for interpreters. Perhaps it was for this reason that C. H. Dodd wrote: "I have failed to find any specific link between this parable (Mt. xviii. 23–35) and the idea of the Kingdom of God, apart from the general notion of judgment" (1961, 19, n. 2), and Joachim Jeremias referred to its ethic as "a forgiveness which passes all understanding" (1954, 145).

Some have tried to argue that the parable instead promotes nonviolence. In seeking to rehabilitate the parable, Thomas Yoder Neufeld extracts some wider theological ideas from the story: "that forgiveness is an act of power.... The one whom much was forgiven was expected to emulate his master's treatment of him.... The slave who owed much did not emulate his master's breathtaking generosity" (2011, 50). Eventually, he falls back on suggesting that the parable has "limited function" (54). Michel Desjardins also maintains that the parable overall emphasizes pacifism, though it does so with a violent imagery. Matthew, he argues, used the parable to highlight "forgiveness, humility and the willingness to accept suffering even unto death" (Desjardins 1997, 49). While forgiveness is clearly the ideal of the parable, the way it goes about promoting the importance of it, I would argue, nevertheless relies on threats of violence at the hands of an all-powerful deity, an arguably "unflattering" depiction (Snodgrass 2008, 61, 71). Thus, one can see that the violent contours of this story have been apparent to most, even those who ultimately want to salvage a nonviolent theological core for modern Christians.

The Parable of the Entrusted Money, also known as the Parable of the Pounds, in Q 19 (Matt 25:14–30 // Luke 19:11–27)[6] also illustrates how the parables of Jesus deployed in imagery of violence and force for their persuasive effects. The parable in Q tells of a wealthy master who wants to take a trip, and before going, he entrusts his slaves with a certain amount of money while he is away. When the master returns, he begins to settle his accounts with the slaves. Two slaves have apparently done something productive with the money, earning ten times the money's full value and five times its full value in profit or interest, respectively. The third (arguably bold) slave returns the original amount to the master, saying, "I knew that you are a hard person, reaping where you did not sow and gathering from where you did not winnow; and scared, I went and hid your mina in the ground. Here, you have what belongs to you" (Q 19:21). The enraged master chastises him for not producing any interest on the money and wrests the original money away from him to give to the others. The Q version of the parable concludes with this unsatisfactory platitude: "For to everyone who has, will be given; but from the one who does not have, even what he has will be taken from him" (Q 19:26).

At first glance, this is not an overwhelmingly violent scenario. There is no explicit physical violence; rather, the violence exists at the level of social structure, particularly

---

[6] See also Mark 13:33–37 for a brief version of this parable.

in how it sustains the inequality between the master and his slaves and imprints a deadly fear of the master onto the slave. Brown gives the parable a metaphorical interpretation: "the thrust of the parable is to challenge the disciples to make profitable use of all that Jesus has revealed to them about the kingdom" (1997, 252–53). Rather differently, Herzog once again gives a darker interpretation that focuses on the sociopolitical dynamics in the world of Jesus. Instead of being a parable that encourages proper use of "wealth" (even if wealth is interpreted metaphorically, à la Brown), Herzog argues that the takeaway of the parable has to do with the vulnerability of subelite figures within an elite household. The key to the proper interpretation involves understanding the contours of an aristocratic household. The household was "organized hierarchically, the most competent and trusted retainers rising to the highest level" (Herzog 1994, 157). Household retainers navigated a precarious space within these power dynamics: "the trick was not to become too visible but to remain discreet while accumulating whatever wealth one could muster" (157). When the third slave buries his lot instead of investing it, he takes what economically vulnerable subelites would have considered "the best available precaution against theft and liability" (164). His response when questioned is not meek; it is a form of shaming, and thus resistance, which exposes the mechanics of exploitation that propped up elites in the ancient world (164–65). Therefore, the master, embarrassed by being called out so unexpectedly (in addition to the slave not having increased his wealth), explodes in an angry outburst.

Importantly, aristocratic household management was a conscious imitation of "imperial bureaucracy" (Herzog 1994, 164). Since the power and presence of Rome was also sustained with various forms of physical and institutional violence, one can analogously conclude that a similar kind of invisible violence sustained elite households. The characters of the parable do not neatly correspond to anything, for Herzog, but rather, the entire story is about the violence and the "merciless oppression" that elites used to sustain their social and political positions in the ancient world (165).

Crossan suggests reading this parable somewhat differently, attuned to the negative connotations of economic interest in Jewish traditions (Crossan 2012, 98–106). Having done so, he interprets the parable as a commentary on the kind of world that the hearer wants to imagine: "what about interest and gain? Whose law do you follow? ... Do you accept God's laws or Rome's customs?" (Crossan 2012, 106). He discourages a simplistic mapping of God onto the slave-owning master. "It would make God admit to being 'harsh,'" he points out, "would have God say, 'I reap where I did not sow, and gather where I did not scatter'" (106). Jeremias also finds it difficult to imagine that Jesus would have compared himself (or God) with "a rapacious man, heedlessly intent on his own profit" (Jeremias 1954, 49), concluding that it is only the surrounding frame of the parable that forces the interpretation of Jesus/God as the harsh master (Luke 19:26).[7]

---

[7] Luke, more than Q, explicitly links the master to Jesus. Luke connects this parable with another story about a ruler who was hated and rejected by his constituents. As Brown points out, this second story is obviously a commentary on Jesus's rejection in Jerusalem (Brown 1997, 253), but in such close

For other commentators, though, "Jesus does not need to be protected from harshness" (Snodgrass 2008, 540).

I would argue that taken as a whole, biblical texts have absolutely no qualms about presenting the divine with violent metaphors (such as a parent or spouse), nor do they shy away from depicting the divine along the lines of other ancient figures of power, often claiming other people as property and punishing them at a whim. As Herzog notes, "postexilic Judaism's understanding of God" is quite often "stern and harsh" (1994, 153). It is only theological anxieties, in my opinion, that have caused so many people to be uncomfortable with these depictions of God. Realizing how prevalent imagery of violence is in the Synoptics, there seems to be no compelling reason to pretend that the authors did not know full well the implications of their chosen imagery.

To underscore this point of the implicit violence of God in the Synoptics even more, I examine one final example in Q's Parable of the Faithful or Unfaithful Slave (Matt 24:45–51 // Luke 12:42–46). This parable also imagines that a slave owner is absent from his household for a period of time. Instead of tasking his slave with doing business in his absence, this time he simply entrusts the slave with maintaining the household in good working order (i.e., those in the household are fed and cared for, and the household is maintained). The parable then envisions a situation where the master is delayed and the slave in charge of the household descends into depravity: he begins to beat the other slaves and banquet with "the drunkards" (Q 12:45). If the master returns unexpectedly, he will "cut him into pieces and give him an inheritance with the faithless" (Q 12:46).

The scenario is similar to the Parable of the Entrusted Money: there is an aristocratic estate with various slaves involved in the running of the household economy, sometimes in the absence of the owner. What is striking about this parable is the vividly precise imagery of violence that is used to describe the slave's punishment. The Greek term in Q is διχοτομήσει, which literally means to cut something apart or bisect it. Both Matthew and Luke retain this vocabulary in their Gospels. The parable is obviously about Jesus's Parousia, which is confirmed both by the preceding unit on the Son of Man's coming (Q 12:39–40), as well as by how Matthew and Luke understood and deployed the story. Luke places it in a wider series of units on how to properly understand and prepare for what will happen during the end-times (Luke 12:1–51), while Matthew locates it even more explicitly in a discussion about watching for Jesus's return (Matt 24:26–51). This means that the reader must surmise that Jesus is the master who can potentially bisect the disobedient slave; this is perhaps some of the most explicit (potential) violence associated with Jesus in New Testament.[8] Yoder Neufeld sums up the import of such language aptly: "the evangelists do not depict Jesus as shy about using the language of violence to describe his mission and its effect. Conflict, division and terrifying judgment are not anomalies in the parables of Jesus or in his teaching as a whole. In a real sense, parables are by their very nature a way of bringing 'division'" (Yoder Neufeld 2011, 40). Desjardins likewise

proximity to the Parable of the Entrusted Money, it suggests that Jesus is reflected, in some way or another, as the harsh master.

[8] Other good candidates are Mt 10:34–36 and Rev 14:14–20.

aligns this parable with others that "allude to the coming horrors" (Desjardins 1997, 71) involved in God's future judgment.[9]

Other commentators have made even more of the violence and conflict embedded in this story. John S. Kloppenborg observes that this parable is both "gruesome" and unfortunately "realistic" (2014a, 615) in terms of feasible options available to elite slave owners. Given that, as noted earlier, the parable is closely tied to the preceding unit about the coming of the Son of Man, the only reasonable conclusion is that the threat of lethal violence from Jesus himself should keep his constituents constantly vigilant for his return: "the Son of Man becomes a man of violence not only against demons but against his own disobedient partisans" (620). Such a frightening threat was likely an answer to the increasing skepticism about Jesus's delayed return: "that there may well be no delay at all" (620).

These parables all seem to stem from a rather coherent social setting: one in which agricultural activities and related labor were the norm for most people; one in which a laborer's activities were often regulated by a more powerful figure; one in which, accordingly, the world was sorted into elites and subelites; and one in which the power differential between these groups was conspicuous, with the potential to erupt into violent confrontations. Many of the most powerful figures in the parables are symbols for God and/or Jesus, which raises the uncomfortable specter that early followers of Jesus assumed that both Jesus and God (whether or not they merged them into a single actor, as many contemporary Christians do) were capable of extreme violence. Though the parables do not always entail physical violence, they are rife with situations of inequality and injustice, especially if read from a subelite perspective. In other words, they reflect the institutional violence that lower classes experienced on a routine basis in the ancient world. Especially if some of these parables can be traced to the historical Jesus, the implication is that some of the earliest teachings of Jesus reflected a dangerous, cutthroat world, where one's safety and livelihood were never secure. In many ways, some other key teachings of the Jesus movement, especially those that speak of the providential care and debt relief available in the kingdom of God (e.g. Q 11:2–4 and 12:22–31), offer relief from the routine struggles embodied in the parables. In this way, one sees how important imagery of violence is to some of the central teaching of the Synoptic Gospels.

THE ESCHATOLOGICAL VIOLENCE IN THE SYNOPTIC "APOCALYPSE(S)"

Eschatology (i.e., contemplating "the end," no matter how it is imagined) pervades the Synoptic Gospels. Though none of the Gospels is an apocalypse in terms of genre, they

---

[9] Desjardins, following Jeremias among others, notes that this parable seems to be aimed at those who hold positions of leadership among Christ groups (Desjardins 1997, 71; Jeremias 1954, 124).

nevertheless embody many characteristics of an apocalyptic worldview. They envision the current world order gone terribly awry; they sort the populace of the cosmos into binary and opposing camps; they look forward to future divine intervention, presuming that the righteous are unable to right their own circumstances; and they imagine that those righteous followers of Jesus are guaranteed a reward, while their opponents are destined for punishment. As Kloppenborg rightly observes, usually insiders are spared from this violence: "apocalyptic literature is rife with imagined scenes of torture and brutal punishment—persons being cast into flaming pits, or being devoured by animals and vomited up only to be devoured again. The typical victims of such tortures are fallen stars, kings and landlords, sinners, and the wicked" (Kloppenborg 2014a, 618). In other words, apocalyptic violence serves an important function of justifying the plight of the in-group while vilifying the out-group. Yet the Synoptics, as I have shown in the examination of the parables, differ from the usual pattern in assuming that divine, apocalyptic violence can affect insiders as well. Many of the parables discussed here function as illustrations for apocalyptic scenarios of judgment (e.g., the return of the absent master is an apocalyptic trope often evoking the second coming of Jesus), and while I will not revisit them here, I can note that unlike apocalyptic scenarios in such texts as the Apocalypse of John or Daniel 7–12, the apocalyptic violence of the parables has potentially violent consequences for followers of Jesus. By not questioning the appropriateness of this violence, moreover, the Synoptics implicitly sanction this "misery-inducing violence" (Carter 2017, 295).

Apocalyptic violence in the Synoptic Gospels extends well beyond the parables, however. Mark 13, for instance, has sometimes been called a "Little Apocalypse" and contains some of the most classic apocalyptic imagery in the New Testament, outside of the Apocalypse of John. In this chapter, Jesus lectures his disciples in the shadow of the Second Jewish Temple. His first apocalyptic prediction is that the end-times will involve the destruction of the Temple (Mark 13:2), depicting the end as part of a violent collapse. The disciples inquire about signs that will foretell when this destruction will happen. Unlike other passages in the Synoptics in which Jesus says that no signs will accompany the end (e.g., Matt 12:39–41, 16:1–4; Luke 17:20–21), in Mark 13 Jesus offers a virtual checklist of things that will take place during the end-times. Many of these involve violence and suffering endured by the followers of Jesus, perpetrated both by opponents and also by God (Aichele 1998, 78–79). Jesus warns first that there will be deceivers who try to lead the disciples astray (Mark 13:6). In addition, there will then be natural disasters that will cause suffering: earthquakes and famines (Mark 13:8). Hector Avalos has deemed the depiction of Jesus here as "eco-hostile" (an interesting form of violence aimed at nonhumans) as he meticulously outlines his "eco-destruction" (Avalos 2015, 346). Even so, much of the violence and suffering in Mark 13 (e.g., wars and persecution) is initiated by humans, and the general sense is that humans have brought much of this eschatological suffering upon themselves.

There will also be various forms of human conflict involving violence. Jesus tells his followers to be on the lookout for war and political conflicts: "For nation will rise against nation, and kingdom against kingdom" (Mark 13:8). More troubling are the localized conflicts: the followers of Jesus will experience resistance and challenges from outsiders (likely understood as "persecution"; Rollens 2015), some in formal legal settings (Mark 13:9, 11) while others play out in the context of the household (Mark 13:12). Jesus emphasizes the acute violence of this eschatological drama by claiming that this tribulation will be like nothing that has existed since Creation (Mark 13:19). In order to illustrate this moment even more clearly, Mark's Jesus employs the most cosmically "apocalyptic" language in the Synoptics (Mark 13:24–27), picking up on language originally in the book of Daniel (Daniel 7:9–14).

Matthew and Luke have both eagerly taken over Mark's Little Apocalypse, retaining much of it verbatim, but they have made a few curious redactions that show that they were interested in its violent imaginaries in different ways. For instance, Matthew, who relocates part of Mark 13 in chapter 24 and part in chapter 10, takes over Jesus's statement that the followers of Jesus will be beaten in synagogues and will "stand" before government and kings. However, he changes Mark's "you will be beaten" to "they will flog you" (Matt 10:17), and instead of merely "standing" before rulers, Matthew emphasizes that the followers of Jesus will be "dragged" (Matt 10:18). In addition, he prefaces his comments on persecution in Matthew 24 with the warning: "Then they will deliver you up to tribulation and put you to death" (Matt 24:9). This seems to be a Matthean invention, since the statement is nowhere in his source, Mark. Perhaps these additions imply that Matthew was keener to illustrate the vivid force that followers would experience (flogging and forcible dragging, instead of being beaten and standing). Luke on the other hand shows signs of a desire to ameliorate this violent imagery. Instead of warning of beating or flogging, Luke merely warns his disciples that his opponents will "lay their hands on you" (Luke 21:12). And whereas both Mark and Matthew commend endurance through all of these trials (Mark 13:13; Matt 24:13), Luke's Jesus assures them that "not a hair of your head will perish" (Luke 21:18), thus downplaying the threat of potential violence.

Matthew and Luke both reflect apocalyptic violence outside of their use of Mark 13. In fact, some of the apocalyptic violence that they incorporate can be traced back to their other source, Q. Even in Q, which contains very little narrative material, a violent apocalyptic timetable is in view, demonstrating that even the earliest written form of the Jesus tradition imagined an impending, violent intervention by God. Violence is in view in the opening verses of Q, which features John the Baptist as the speaker. John's heated remarks mobilize language of an agricultural harvest to pronounce eschatological judgment on those who do not repent. He announces that no one can run from the "impending rage" (i.e., the wrath of God) and that judgment is now so near that "every tree not bearing healthy fruit is to be chopped down and thrown into the fire" (Q 3:7–9). He then compares this reckoning process to separating the valuable wheat from the useless chaff during a harvest (Q 3:17). While these are all routine agricultural activities involved in separating the valuable part of crops from the useless or unproductive parts, they take on a much more sinister tone when applied to the bodies of believers: those who do not demonstrate proper value to God will receive a fiery punishment. Harvest imagery, moreover, implies "a necessary violence" (Aichele 1998, 76).

Complete apocalyptic annihilation is also in view in Q 10:10–15, a unit which chastises the Galilean towns that have rejected the envoys of Jesus. For those who do not receive them positively, "it shall be more bearable on that day for Sodom than for that town" (Q 10:11). In other words, the burning sulfur that the Lord sent upon Sodom is somehow better than what he has in store for the Galilean towns. Furthermore, for Capernaum in particular, its inhabitants are relegated to the depths of Hades (Q 10:15). Indeed, God is a source of great destruction in Q. Q 12:4–5 counsels that one should not fear those who can damage the body (i.e., opponent, persecutors, etc.) but rather that one should fear "the one who is able to destroy both the soul and the body in Gehenna" (i.e., God [or Jesus]). It was, in fact, Jesus, after all, who implicitly threatened in some of the aforementioned parables to cut his slaves to pieces (Matt 24:45–51 // Luke 12:42–46).

Thus, while the Synoptics as a whole feature apocalyptic violence, and indeed depend on it to underscore the urgency of Jesus's teaching, one can see that the seeds of such violence existed as early as Q. And since, for many scholars, Q might be a potential link to the original teachings of Jesus (Robinson 2005), it becomes all the more critical to examine how violent imagery functions in this source.

Conclusion

The violent imagery in the Synoptic Gospels thus goes well beyond the cruelty involved in the crucifixion. It targets other envoys of God; it is embedded in the stories Jesus tells; and it imbues the apocalyptic teachings within the Gospels. Its functions are multifold. Yet few scholars have opted to dwell on this language of violence. In part, this is because the study of the New Testament has often been closely connected to theological concerns, for which it is not fruitful to emphasize the explicit violence and force in the texts. To do so means confronting the notion that some early followers of Jesus imagined their god as a violent patriarchal figure who could extinguish his subordinates' lives on a whim if he was displeased.

In the last several decades, scholars of early Christianity have managed to distinguish themselves from theologians proper, so that they can ask different sorts of questions, those unconcerned with confessional interests or the need the present a flattering portrait of Christian origins. Within this context, these scholars have been able to focus on difficult topics, such as the presence of slavery in Christian origins, the gender inequality, and as I have here, the deployment of violent language in the texts for persuasive ends, which demonstrates unquestionably violent theological imaginaries. In this way, this chapter has explored numerous expressions of violent language in the Synoptic Gospels, focusing particularly on violence aimed at envoys of God in the narratives, violence presupposed in the world of the parables, and violence entailed in apocalyptic expectations. It is crucial to point out that these forms of violence are explicit. There are numerous other forms of interpersonal violence—discrimination, emotional abuse, denial of personhood—that I have not been able to cover here. My intention is rather to initiate a conversation about violent language as an intellectual resource for ancient authors.

REFERENCES

Aichele, George. 1998. "Jesus's Violence." In *Violence, Utopia, and the Kingdom of God: Fantasy and Ideology in the Bible*, edited by George Aichele and Tiny Pippin, 72–91. London: Routledge.

Aitken, Ellen Bradshaw. 2004. *Jesus's Death in Early Christian Memory*. Göttingen: Vandenhoeck & Ruprecht.

Avalos, Hector. 2015. *The Bad Jesus: The Ethics of New Testament Ethics*. Bible in the Modern World 68. Sheffield: Sheffield Phoenix Press.

Berg, Herbert, and Sarah E. Rollens. 2008. "The Historical Muhammad and the Historical Jesus: A Comparison of Scholarly Reinventions and Reinterpretations." *Studies in Religion/Sciences Religieuses* 32, no. 2: 271–92.

Brown, Raymond E. 1997. *An Introduction to the New Testament*. Anchor Bible Reference Library. New York: Yale University Press.

Burkert, Walter, René Girard, and Jonathan Z. Smith. 1988. *Violent Origins: Walter Burkert, René Girard, and Jonathan Z. Smith on Ritual Killing and Cultural Formation*. Edited by Robert G. Hamerton-Kelly. Stanford: Stanford University Press.

Carrol, John, and Joel Green. 1989. *The Death of Jesus in Early Christianity*. Peabody, MA: Hendrickson.

Carter, Warren. 2016. "An Imperial-Critical Reading of Matthew." In *An Introduction to Empire in the New Testament*, edited by Adam Winn, Resources for Biblical Studies 64, 71–90. Atlanta: SBL Press.

Carter, Warren. 2017. "Sanctioned Violence in the New Testament." *Interpretation* 71, no. 3: 284–97.

Crossan, John Dominic. 1988. *The Cross That Spoke: The Origin of the Passion Narrative*. San Francisco: Harper & Row.

Crossan, John Dominic. 1991. *The Historical Jesus: The Life of a Mediterranean Jewish Peasant*. San Francisco: HarperCollins.

Crossan, John Dominic. 2012. *The Power of Parable: How Fiction by Jesus Became Fiction about Jesus*. New York: HarperCollins.

Desjardins, Michel. 1997. *Peace, Violence and the New Testament*. Biblical Seminar 46. Sheffield: Sheffield Academic Press.

Dodd, C. H. 1961. *The Parables of the Kingdom*. New York: Scribner.

Dube, Zorodzai. 2013. "Jesus's Death and Resurrection as Cultural Trauma." *Neotestamenica* 47, no. 1: 107–22.

Duff, Paul B. 2001. *Who Rides the Beast? Prophetic Rivalry and the Rhetoric of Crisis in the Churches of the Apocalypse*. Oxford: Oxford University Press.

Fagan, Garret G. 2011. "Violence in Roman Social Relations." In *The Oxford Handbook of Social Relations in the Roman World*, edited by Michael Peachin, 467–95. Oxford: Oxford University Press.

Farmer, William. 1976. *The Synoptic Problem: A Critical Analysis*. Dillsboro: Western North Carolina Press.

Forsberg, Randall C. 2001. "Socially-Sanctioned and Non-sanctioned Violence: On the Role of Moral Beliefs in Causing and Preventing War and Other Forms of Large-Group Violence." In *Konflikt Und Gewalt in Der Globalisierten Welt*, edited by Ruth Stanley, 201–30. Opladen: Westdeutscher Verlag.

Gale, Monica R., and J. H. D. Scourfield. 2018. "Introduction: Reading Roman Violence." In *Texts and Violence in the Roman World*, edited by Monica R. Gale and J. H. D. Scourfield, 1–43. Cambridge: Cambridge University Press.

Girard, René. 1977. *Violence and the Sacred*. Translated by Patrick Gregory. Baltimore: Johns Hopkins University Press.

Goodacre, Mark. 2002. *The Case against Q: Studies in Markan Priority and the Synoptic Problem*. Harrisburg: Trinity Press International.

Green, Joel. 1988. *The Death of Jesus*. Tübingen: Mohr Siebeck.

Herzog, William R., II. 1994. *Parables as Subversive Speech: Jesus as Pedagogue of the Oppressed*. Lousiville: Westminster/John Knox.

Jacobson, Arland. 1982. "The Literary Unity of Q." *Journal of Biblical Literature* 101, no. 3: 365–89.

Jeremias, Joachim. 1954. *The Parables of Jesus*. Translated by S. H. Hooke. London: SCM Press.

Johnson-DeBaufre, Melanie. 2006. *Jesus among Her Children: Q, Eschatology, and the Construction of Christian Origins*. Cambridge, MA: Harvard University Press.

Juergensmeyer, Mark, Margo Kitts, and Michael Jerryson, eds. 2013. *The Oxford Handbook of Religion and Violence*. Oxford: Oxford University Press.

Kelhoffer, James A. 2010. *Persecution, Persuasion and Power*. 1st ed. Vol. 270. Wissenschaftliche Untersuchungen Zum Neuen Testament. Tübingen: Mohr Siebeck.

Kloppenborg, John S. 2000. *Excavating Q: The History and Setting of the Sayings Gospel*. Minneapolis: Fortress Press.

Kloppenborg, John S. 2005. "Evocatio Deorum and the Date of Mark." *Journal of Biblical Literature* 124, no. 3: 419–50.

Kloppenborg, John S. 2006. *The Tenants in the Vineyard: Ideology, Economics, and Agrarian Conflict in Jewish Palestine*. WUNT 195. Tübingen: Mohr Siebeck.

Kloppenborg, John S. 2014a. "The Representation of Violence in the Synoptic Parables." In *Synoptic Problems: Collected Essays*, edited by John S. Kloppenborg, WUNT 329, 600–29. Tübingen: Mohr Siebeck.

Kloppenborg, John S. 2014b. *Synoptic Problems: Collected Essays*. Mohr Siebeck.

Mack, Burton L. 1988. *A Myth of Innocence: Mark and Christian Origins*. Philadelphia: Fortress Press.

Middleton, Paul. 2014. "Suffering and the Creation of Christian Identity in the Gospel of Mark." In *The T&T Clark Handbook to Social Identity in the New Testament*, edited by Coleman Baker and Brian Tucker, 173–89. London: T&T Clark.

Robinson, James M. 2005. *The Gospel of Jesus: In Search of the Original Good News*. San Francisco: HarperOne.

Robinson, James M., Paul Hoffmann, and John S. Kloppenborg, eds. 2000. *The Critical Edition of Q: A Synopsis Including the Gospels of Matthew and Luke, Mark and Thomas with English with German and French Translations of Q and Thomas*. Hermeneia Supplement Series. Minneapolis: Fortress Press.

Rollens, Sarah E. 2010. "'Why Do You Not Judge for Yourselves What Is Right?': A Consideration of the Synoptic Relationship between Mt 5,25–26 and Lk 12,57–59." *Ephemerides Theologicae Lovanienses* 86, no. 4: 449–69.

Rollens, Sarah E. 2014. *Framing Social Criticism in the Jesus Movement: The Ideological Project in the Sayings Gospel Q*. WUNT II 374. Tübingen: Mohr Siebeck.

Rollens, Sarah E. 2015. "Persecution in the Social Setting of Q." In *Q in Context II: Social Setting and Archaeological Background of the Sayings Source*, edited by Markus Tiwald, BBB, 149–64. Bonn: Bonn University Press.

Rollens, Sarah E. 2016. "Inventing Tradition in Thessalonica: The Appropriation of the Past in 1 Thessalonians 2:14–16." *Biblical Theology Bulletin* 46, no. 3: 123–32.

Rollens, Sarah E. 2018. "From Birth Pangs to Dismembered Limbs: The Anthropology of Bodily Violence in the Gospel of Mark." In *The Gospels and Their Stories in Anthropological Perspective*, edited by John S. Kloppenborg and Joseph Verheyden, WUNT 409, 53–68. Tübingen: Mohr Siebeck.

Snodgrass, Klyne R. 2008. *Stories with Intent: A Comprehensive Guide to the Parables of Jesus*. Grand RapidsI: Eerdmans.

Steck, Odil H. 1991. *Der Abschluss der Prophetie im Alten Testament: ein Versuch zur Frage der Vorgeschichte des Kanons*. Vol. 17. Biblisch-theologische Studien. Neukirchen-Vluyn: Neukirchener Verlag.

Steck, Odil Hannes. 1967. *Israel und das gewaltsame Geschick der Propheten. Untersuchungen zur Überlieferungen des deuteronomistischen Geschichtsbildes im Alten Testament, Spätjudentum und Urchristentum*. Wissenschaftliche Monographien zum Alten und Neuen Testament 23. Neukirchener-Vluyn: Neukirchener Verlag.

Yoder Neufeld, Thomas. 2011. *Killing Enmity: Violence and the New Testament*. Grand Rapids: Baker Academic.

CHAPTER 15

KINGDOM, AUTHORITY, AND POWER

MICHAEL PEPPARD

INTRODUCTION

THE themes of power and authority, whether on earth or in heaven, permeate the Synoptic Gospels, being expressed from Jesus's inaugural proclamation about the "Kingdom of God" to his ultimate destiny as a parodic "king" and royal "son of God." In between, the narratives of and about Jesus explore: the power to control land, human bodies, and material goods through persuasion and threat; the authority to regulate the appropriate use of bodies and religious rituals; the power and authority to punish those who resist regulation and control; alternatively, the power and authority to liberate someone from another's control; and the clash of different forms of authority—when institutional authorities, such as kings and priests and governing councils, struggle for power against charismatic authorities, such as prophets and healers and wonder-workers.

Contemporary scholars have approached these narratives with diverse methodologies—especially political theology, feminist criticism, liberation theology, Marxist analysis, and postcolonial criticism—to interrogate how earthly and heavenly power shaped: the interaction between Jesus and the political powers of his day, the historical subjugation of marginalized groups by Romans, the economic conditions of first-century Palestine, the spread of Christianity through modern colonialism, and subaltern interpretations generated through such patterns of colonization. These approaches enable readers to: understand the historical context of the emergence of Christianity; clarify theological imagery and doctrine; reveal Christianity's inextricable relationship to struggles over earthly power; unveil collusion between religious and political power in empires; liberate present-day marginalized groups; and generally challenge the social locations via which contemporary readers "read themselves into" the narratives of the Gospels.

Some of the "empire-critical" interpretations of the Gospels rely on well-known methods of biblical criticism, especially historical, narrative, redaction, and social-scientific criticism. Many of these scholars also employ poststructuralist approaches that do not presume stable, self-conscious authorial intentions behind the texts or stable, coherent structures within the texts. Rather, these scholars point out that the Gospels, born from sites of colonial encounter, "are enmeshed in elaborate ideological formulations, and hence intricate networks of contradiction, that exceed and elude the consciousness of their authors" (Moore 2006, 6). Matthew, Mark, and Luke each have particular stances toward the interaction of earthly and heavenly power—and each is uniquely receptive to some modes of scholarly criticism more than others—but all three Synoptics are engaged with the topic from beginning to end.

Power on Earth, Power from Heaven

Each of the Synoptic Gospels situates the opening of its narrative at the nexus of earthly and heavenly rule. Luke does so most explicitly and systematically, in the model of ancient historiography. He precisely dates his story according to various ruling powers, listed in descending order of rank, from the Romans (the emperor Tiberius and Pontius Pilate as governor of Judea) to the Romans' appointed rulers over the regions (the Herodian tetrarchs) to the local high priests of the Jerusalem Temple (Luke 3:1–2). Amid these earthly powers, ruling from their various cities, a heavenly power came to John—not a king on a throne or a priest in a temple but a prophet in the wilderness (Luke 3:2). Luke labels him the "son of Zechariah," his father who had power at the nexus of heaven and earth as "a priest" in Jerusalem "in the days of King Herod of Judea" (Luke 1:5). In contrast to his father, John's charismatic power, the prophetic "word of God," came from outside these institutional authorities and was thus inherently challenging to them.

Matthew's opening characterization of earthly rule during the Greco-Roman era is less neutral. Immediately after Jesus is born in Judea, "in the days of King Herod" (Matt 2:1), the king dispatches the magi as informants to find the special boy whom an omen and prophecy predicted would threaten his earthly rule (Matt 2:6–7). But when heavenly power intervenes through dreams to warn both the magi and the boy's parents about Herod's deviousness, the boy is saved by flight from the land ruled by Herod—ironically to Egypt, a land associated with the prior oppression of their people (Matt 2:12–15). The earthly ruler becomes enraged and uses the ultimate political power: the power to destroy the body. He orders the massacre of infant boys in Bethlehem (Matt 2:16), an irrational self-genocide that recalls the slaughter in Egypt and also foreshadows what will become the Roman client-king's main response to prophetic power: spasmodic, extravagant, public violence. Even after King Herod's death, the fear of Roman-allied governance remained: the family avoids Judea also under his successor, Archelaus (Matt 2:22). Indeed, the only positive image of earthly rule mentioned in this opening sequence is the lineage of distant Israelite kings in the genealogy of Jesus, who came from "David the king" (Matt 1:6). In the Roman-era present, however, Jesus would fulfill the different prophetic call of John the Baptist, whose first announcement proclaims the imminent "kingdom of heaven" (Matt 3:2).

Mark's opening scenes invoke the nexus of heavenly power and earthly power the most subtly, sotto voce, but an attuned listener hears the points of connection. The inbreaking of the heavenly power is not the subtle part: God announces the "sending of a messenger" to "prepare the way of the Lord" (Mark 1:2), the way for "one who is more powerful" (Mark 1:7); then when that anointed one arrives, he saw "the heavens torn apart" with a descending dove and a voice from heaven (Mark 1:10–11). Heavenly power in the form of God's Spirit has ripped apart the firmament, and the beloved Son then declares a new kind of "kingdom" (Mark 1:15). All this occurs so quickly in the narrative that one might miss the language that resonates with the ideology of earthly rule. The baptismal voice's allusion to Psalm 2:7 carries with it the whole context of that psalm for a royal Israelite coronation, as does the opening declaration of Jesus as the "Christ" (anointed one, Mark 1:1 and Ps 2:2). Divine sonship was a central marker of authorized rule in terms of both Jewish and Roman royal ideology. For Roman political theology, claims to earthly rule were secured through divine ancestry, recent genealogy (natural or adoptive), and divine election, with Augustus and emperors after him propagating the specific title "son of god." In addition to this rare and resonant title of divinely authorized earthly power, Mark narrates the bird omen as a kind of augury, a form of divination widely acknowledged by Roman culture with respect to eagles and the rightful accession of earthly rulers. The dove and the eagle make up a contrasting pair of birds, a recognizable juxtaposition of natural enemies (like the wolf and the lamb) in which one is a mighty predator and the other a sacrificial victim (Peppard 2011, 118). All of these signifiers are enveloped between proclamations of the "beginning" of the "good news" (εὐαγγέλιον, Mark 1:1, 14–15) that arrives with Jesus, a term which was known to herald also the arrival of a new emperor, as with both Augustus and Vespasian. In the important Priene Inscription, for example, "the Greeks of Asia" made a formal decree to praise Augustus as, among other things, the "savior" and to describe "the birthday of the god" Augustus as that which "began for the world the good news that happened because of him" (Evans 2000).

Mark's opening narrative seems prima facie to be less interested in precise dating of events on a political calendar (see Luke) or direct contrast with tyrannical rulers (see Matthew), despite its resonances with the language of earthly power. Yet, hiding in plain sight, Mark discreetly pinpoints the nexus of the two kingdoms; it is less overt than in Matthew or Luke but no less significant. At what point, in earthly time, does Mark say Jesus arrives to announce the "kingdom of God?" He does so "after John had been arrested" (1:14)—when John had been seized and subsequently executed by Herod Antipas, the earthly ruler whom Mark calls "king" Herod in the later narration of John's execution (6:14–29). Thus Mark's opening scenes characterize Jesus in terms of both Israelite royal ideology and Roman imperial ideology, while juxtaposing his incipient kingdom of nonviolent power with the violent king who decapitated his forerunner.

Imperial Power and Resistance

The broad setting of the Synoptic Gospels is often called the Greco-Roman world, a modern designation for an era in the Mediterranean region during which various forms of Greek urban culture flourished within geopolitical demarcations governed and administered by Roman imperial rule. The regions of Judea and Galilee, where most of the Gospel narratives occur, were distant from the center of empire, to be sure. But for over two hundred years, Greek language and culture had been established in their urban areas, while the impact of Roman rule—in the forms of military presence, extractive taxation, and client-kingship of the Herods—had been felt already for a few generations. Residents of Judea and Galilee, especially in and around the cities, were to some degree dominated by Greek power in their culture and Roman military power over their land.

More specifically, social-scientific historical analysis describes Roman rule over Palestine during the time of Jesus as an aristocratic, extractive empire. Aristocrats—a "nonlaboring, privileged, ruling class" drawn from both Roman provincial officials and local elites—worked together to "rule agrarian peasants and live from the peasants' labor" (Hanson and Oakman 2008, 63). Through an exploitative economic system, peasant families were kept to subsistence wages and frequently trapped in spirals of debt (Horsley 2009, 89–91). Locally sourced tax collectors made sure that resources were extracted from peripheral provinces and directed toward the center of empire or used to bolster regional infrastructure that benefited local elites (Hanson and Oakman 2008, 64). The overextensions of King Herod's building programs exacerbated the primary economic problem in Roman-era Palestine, which was "acute lack of land, that is, a shortage of agriculturally usable land *per capita* of population. . . . At the same time, confiscations and the oppressive tax burden narrowed the possibility for self-sufficiency, and thus more and more small farmers lost their land. . . . The indebtedness of small farmers and expropriation of their land are the hallmarks of this Roman epoch" (Stegemann and Stegemann 1995, 112). The power of local aristocrats was propagated not only through ownership of land and laborers but also through social networks of honor and shame.

The Gospels refract this socioeconomic world through the stories of and about Jesus. He tells parables of absentee landlords (Mark 12:1), debt spirals (Matt 18:23–25), day laborers (Matt 20:1), and stark contrasts of wealth and poverty (Luke 16:19–31). One imagined character goes to a far-off land to acquire "a kingdom for himself" and returns to punish violently any who deny his royal claims (Luke 19:12–27). Jesus meets corrupt tax collectors who surprise with their contrition (Luke 19:1–8) but also wealthy owners of estates who regret nothing (Mark 10:22). Considering the economic systems of first-century Galilee, the family of that particular "rich young man" (Mark 10:17–22) had almost certainly gained their many estates through expropriation of peasant land, followed by defrauding workers of rightful wages. Jesus's invocation of God's commandment "do not defraud" (Mark 10:19) was thus a prophetic word of resistance against the aristocratic empire (Peppard 2015).

Ancient economic conditions within a zero-sum economy went out of focus for much of the modern period in the West, as economies focused on growth through colonization, industrialization, and, most recently, the dramatic expansion of finance capital. Contemporary biblical scholars, however, have demonstrated how the Gospel narratives about economic and political power are interpreted differently by readers, especially those from the Global South, whose current conditions resemble the ancient Mediterranean world more than that of the West. Side-by-side exegetical comparisons of interpreting Jesus's parables, for example, show that the meaning of a moral tale depends on how one's social location of empowerment enables a person to read him- or herself into that story (Herzog 1994; Ukpong 1996). Landlords of large estates do not come off very well—and they are certainly not always understood to be allegories for God (West and Zwane, 2013). In contemporary South Africa, reading the story of the rich young man with different status groups demonstrated that peasant laborers of agrarian society viewed him as implicated in systemic, sinful exploitation. These readers clearly identify "social structures which produced wealth for the man and poverty for the people, in the same way that the social system of apartheid empowered white South Africans to become wealthy and pushed black South Africans into poverty. So even if the man had worked for his property or had inherited his wealth, he was still part of a sinful social structure" (West 1993, 177).

Shifting back to Roman-era Palestine: with such social conditions and limited opportunities for living with a moderate surplus, not even to mention upward mobility, it was inevitable that a revolutionary spirit animated the countryside outside the cities. Full-blown revolutionaries like Judas the Galilean were rare (Acts 5:37; Josephus, *Ant.* 18.1–10), but smaller groups of organized resistance were more common. The memory of the Maccabean era of Judean self-governance lived on strongly, as witnessed by popular names of men at the time. Many of Jesus's closest disciples—Simon, Judas, John, Matthew—were named after the Maccabees themselves.

With no ability to overcome the dominant cultural and economic forces backed by Roman military might, some Judeans and Galileans turned to social banditry. Social bandits emerge in many times and places as a rural phenomenon, when peasants are ruled corruptly by a foreign power and thus band together in nimble groups around charismatic leaders in order to "provide tangible goods, protection, or redress of injustices for their villages" (Hanson and Oakman 2008, 83). Within such a context, it is less difficult to understand why a Judean crowd might call for the release of Barabbas, a bandit and murderer, instead of the rabbi from Nazareth (Luke 23:19). Bandits were regarded positively by some because "they rob the monopoly of violence from the rich and distribute it to the poor, and, more significantly, they rob aristocratic and structural violence of the veneer of morality under which it operates" (Crossan 1991, 304).

While Jesus himself was not a social bandit, some features of his origin and behavior would have associated him with banditry: he was from peasant village roots; he was a known associate of John the Baptist, who had been executed as a potential threat

(Mark 6:14–29; Josephus, *Ant.* 18.118–19); as an adult he was a charismatic itinerant with followers but no home or land; he "associated with a variety of people who were disreputable by urban elite standards"; and he publicly pronounced about Roman taxation and the financial transactions at the Temple (Hanson and Oakman 2008, 83). It is no wonder that the Roman authorities considered him a bandit or a threat to their political stability; even his disciples seem to have been confused up to the end. When Jesus commanded them about the coming crisis that "one who does not have a sword should sell his cloak and buy one," the disciples responded immediately: "Lord, look, there are two swords here" (Luke 22:36, 38). Then at the moment of his arrest, some thought the attack should commence: "Lord, shall we strike with a sword?" (Luke 22:49). The events of Jesus's final days, combined with the repeated contrast of his coming "kingdom" with the ruling elites of this world, led ultimately to the parodic kingship of the passion narrative and the crucifixion. He hung as a "king" like Herod and "son of god" like the emperor—hung between two bandits.

Empire-Critical Approaches

The foundational teaching of Jesus in the Synoptic Gospels is the "kingdom of God": its prediction in prophecy, depiction in parable, and enactment in deeds of power. From the opening lines of Mark to the last lines of Acts, the kingdom of God is the message of Jesus and his followers. But has "kingdom" lost its rhetorical force for contemporary listeners? And if salt loses its saltiness, how shall it be restored? Relatively few contemporary readers and listeners have a real-life point of contact for the ancient concepts of "king" or "kingdom." For inhabitants of most modern democracies, the referents of these signifiers exist only in an imagined past or the realm of fantasy fiction. Therefore, some have begun translating βασιλεία as "reign" of God, which emphasizes the temporal activity of sovereignty more than a static, bordered region ruled by a sovereign. Those using "reign" of God have been usually identified with social liberationist and antipatriarchal modes of translation (Ruether 1983). Some feminist critics prefer instead not to translate βασιλεία at all but to redefine its content in the quest for a Christian discipleship of equals that subverts all forms of oppression (Schüssler Fiorenza 1984). Another option, preferred by biblical scholars attuned to the dominance of Roman imperial ideology in the time of Jesus, is to render βασιλεία as "empire" of God. While this translation also risks facile associations with either modern empires (Japanese, British, etc.) or fantasy fiction of galaxies far, far away, it nonetheless expresses a crucial historical fact: the vast population of Greek-speaking subjects of the eastern Roman empire did use the word βασιλεία to refer to Rome's sovereignty and βασιλεύς for its sovereign. The translation "empire of God" has begun to appear more frequently due to such historical arguments, along with the astute observation that "kingdom" has become "innocuous" for most modern readers of the Bible, as a word whose "political edge has been all but rubbed smooth by centuries of theological usage" (Moore 2006, 37).

Scholarly approaches that inhabit and critique the ancient imperial contexts of power—resharpening the "political edge" of the early Christian message—now cover the entire New Testament (Winn 2016). Regarding the Synoptic Gospels, most scholars view Luke-Acts as a text generally accommodating toward earthly political power, even while its plot is governed from above by the heavenly power of the Holy Spirit and it subtly critiques the kingdom of this world. Mark and Matthew, on the other hand, have received sustained attention from empire-critical scholars, especially at the most evident episodes of political interface: the infancy narratives, the casting out of "Legion," the beheading of John the Baptist, the activities of tax collectors and Roman centurions, the encounter with Pilate, the title "son of God." Beyond these pericopes, empire-critical scholars have listened anew to entire Gospel narratives with Roman imperial ideology as the dominant setting, the foreground not the background of the plot, like a cantus firmus establishing the tonal system for a performance.

Mark

One of the first such "political readings" to break through and affect both the scholar's classroom and the church's pulpit was the thoroughgoing narrative interpretation *Binding the Strong Man* (Myers 1988). Inspired by liberation theology and his social activism alongside the firebrand Berrigan brothers—Daniel Berrigan wrote the foreword for his book—Myers presents Mark's Jesus as a subversive, constructive, prophetic pedagogue of the oppressed peasants of occupied Galilee. Writing from the *"locus imperium"* of "white North American Christianity," Myers finds in Mark a full-throated expression of the goals and idioms of a "Christian Left" that seeks liberative praxis, "to take the side of the Hebrews even though citizens of Egypt" (Myers 1988, 7). This Jesus was a prophet who "disdained the collaborationist aristocracy *and* Romans equally, and who repudiated Qumranite withdrawal *and* Pharisaic activism on the grounds that neither addressed the roots of oppression in the dominant symbolic order" (Myers 1988, 86). Bringing a "logic of solidarity among the poor" to the peasant villages of Galilee through "civil disobedience," Mark was "sympathetic to the socio-economic and political grievances of the rebels," who wanted to overthrow Rome by force. But in the end, Mark understood Jesus's struggle of liberation to be "restorationist" and "counterrevolutionary" (Myers 1988, 87). The pivotal political episodes of the Parable of the Tenants and the controversy about Roman taxation show, for Myers, that Mark "strongly asserts the ideology of nonalignment, a rejection of both the Roman colonial presence and the revolt" (Myers 1988, 314). This nonalignment with the earthly powers of either colonizer or revolutionary constitutes the "radical discipleship" of Mark, which leads inevitably to "failure and disillusionment," to losing one's life in order to save it (Mark 8:36; Myers 1988, 456). Though Myers intends to be hopeful, his study is—as a faithful reading of Mark's narrative—nonetheless infused with its apocalyptic darkness about delayed eschatology. This Jesus is not far from that of Albert Schweitzer's famous parable of Synoptic eschatology, of the Son of Man who "lays hold of the wheel of the world to set it moving on that last revolution which is to bring all ordinary history to a close. It refuses to turn, and He throws Himself upon it. Then it does turn; and crushes Him.... The wheel rolls onward, and the mangled body of the one immeasurably great Man, who was strong enough to think of Himself as the spiritual ruler of mankind and to bend history to His purpose, is hanging upon it still. That is His victory and His reign" (Schweitzer 1968, 370–71). Myers keeps that wheel of Jesus's reign rolling—not with Jesus as a revolutionary, but a revolution nonetheless.

Richard Horsley continues the tradition of interpreting Mark as an antiimperial narrative, likewise blending social-scientific and Marxist analysis with an eye toward contemporary American empire and the mystification of its oppressive systems. Beyond Jesus's many sayings about the kingdom of God, which challenged "the new world disorder," he was also "practicing or implementing the kingdom of God in healings, exorcisms, feedings, and covenantal teachings" (Horsley 2003, 14). This kingdom "had two broad aspects: the kingdom of God as judgment of rulers and the kingdom of God as the renewal of Israel" (14). Horsley argues, based primarily on Mark, that Jesus was radically concerned with this-worldly judgment and justice, leading a movement rooted in the peasant villages of the Galilean countryside and the covenantal principles of Torah. "In the crisis of social disintegration under Roman imperial rule and drawing on the Israelite tradition of prophetic renewal of the people, particularly renewal of covenantal cooperation and justice, Jesus assumed the role of a prophet like Moses and/or Elijah, founder and renewer of the people, in healing the debilitating effects of Roman imperialism and renewing the covenantal community life of the people" (125). Horsley calls upon modern Americans, "the society now at the apex of the new imperial disorder," to acknowledge the urgent political message of Jesus against empire (149).

Others are not so sure the Jesus of Mark's Gospel is as antiimperial as Myers and Horsley think he is. Postcolonial criticism has made a substantial impact on the study of the Synoptic Gospels and the Bible overall (Sugirtharajah 1998). Scholarship enlivened by postcolonial sensibilities draws from the voices and stories of colonized people throughout history, illuminating how sustained relationships of power are never simply imposed from one culture onto another. Power relations that last never come unilaterally from the top, and there are many points on a spectrum between utter domination and armed resistance. Power relations are more often characterized by collusion, incoherence, codependence, mimicry, and innovation into a "third space" that emerges from the nexus of colonial encounter (Bhabha 1994; Moore 2006). The colonized always retain some power, some agency, though it is often an agency enacted, in part, through the particular modes of expression by which they have been oppressed.

Tat-siong Benny Liew approaches Mark's Gospel with a "diasporic consciousness," a "sensitivity to colonization and refusal of idealization" based on his own experiences of imperial power relations on two continents (Liew 1999b, 12). He argues that "despite all of Mark's anti-authority and barrier-breaking rhetoric," the author has "indeed internalized the imperialist ideology of his colonizers" by attributing absolute authority to Jesus, preserving an insider-outsider binary, and presenting Jesus's authority as an overwhelming show of force—a "might-is-right ideology" that glories in the imagined, ultimate annihilation of wicked enemies (Liew 1999a, 93, 107). Liew's arguments are a salutary challenge to the antiimperial reading of Mark. They would apply indubitably to the book of Revelation, but the Gospel of Mark seems to be neither plainly antiimperial nor a reinscription of colonial, imperial ideology. Perhaps Mark's narrative is counter-imperial similarly to how musical counterpoint relates to a dominant melody: a contrapuntal musical line is independent from but not directly or always opposed to the melodic line. It is sometimes consonant, sometimes dissonant, but always interacting with and drawing energy from the motifs of the main melody. For the listeners, the dominant and contrapuntal lines resonate together in the theater—in this case, the theater of discourse about ancient power, authority, and rule.

Stephen Moore interprets Mark's rhetoric of the "kingdom" (βασιλεία), which he prefers to translate as "empire," as a counterpoint to Roman *imperium* that is neither antiauthoritarian nor a mirroring of it. He asks whether Mark's βασιλεία "may be deemed a stunning example of what the postcolonial theorist Gayatri Spivak has dubbed *catachresis*, originally a Greek rhetorical figure denoting 'misuse' or 'misapplication' ... a practice of resistance through an act of usurpation" (Moore 2006, 37). The answer is yes and no, depending on how apocalypticism is construed in Mark. The apocalyptic discourse of Mark 13 does gesture toward a fearsome Revelation-style destruction and tribulation, a colonial mimicry of Roman imperial power, with promised "power and glory" from above (Mark 13:26). Instead, Moore cleverly shifts focus to the two women who envelop the apocalyptic discourse: the widow of the "widow's mite" (Mark 12:41–44) and the anointing woman who "wastes" the costly ointment (Mark 14:3–9). These are "the real site of apocalypse in Mark" because the "voluntary self-divestment" of these women exceeds "Jesus' own self-emptying"; each "may be read as an act of epiphanic extravagance whose immeasurable immoderation thrusts it outside every conventional circle of economic exchange," that is, Derrida's "gift beyond reciprocity," which is the real kingdom breaking through (42–43). Nevertheless, Mark fails to learn from these women, leaving the listener with cacophonous messages about power. These women prepared the way, they planted the seed, but the Gospel could not fully "relinquish its dreams of empire" (44).

Matthew

The Gospel of Matthew has not been a site of empire-critical readings as often as Mark has, but Warren Carter has deftly explained its imperial context and counternarratives of power. For late-twentieth-century scholarship, the traditional fault lines for exploring Matthew's context had been Jewish-Gentile relations (incipient Jewish-Christian relations) in first-century Antioch. Carter's research, however, establishes the robust Roman imperial presence in Antioch, exemplified by administrative officials, buildings, visits of emperors, and heavy taxation to support the enormous military presence in and around the city (2001, 35–53). In this context, the characterization of soteriology through Jesus means a rejection of Roman imperial theology and choosing membership instead in "God's Empire," which entails the destruction of Rome. Salvation includes deliverance "from the sinful sociopolitical and economic structures of Roman imperialism that manifest Satan's rule" (Carter 2001, 76). Carter analyzes through re-presentation a series of Matthean "counternarratives" about empire. First, the Isaiah citations in the Gospel's opening chapters, which in their original context "address a situation of imperial threat," establish "an analogy with the situation of the Gospel's authorial audience" and "give content to God's salvific promise" against the current empire (97). Later in the Gospel, the invitation to take on Jesus's yoke (Matt 11:29–39) evokes for the implied audience "political control, particularly the imposition of harsh imperial power" (122). Third, Carter argues that the query about paying the Roman tax (Matt 22:15–22) would have called to mind the post-70 *fiscus Judaicus* and thereby "remind[ed] the Gospel's audience in Antioch that Roman power, which must be taken seriously as a daily reality, is not, though, the final or determinative reality" (143). Finally, the interactions between Pilate, Jesus, and the people of Judea (Matt 27:11–26) show the Roman "elite's control masked under claims of benefit for and responsiveness to the ruled. . . . The hand washing and pronouncement of his own innocence are part of the same deception" (167).

Carter admits that Matthew is not straightforwardly an antiimperial narrative. He draws from the insights of postcolonial theory at several crucial moments of exegesis, but what others call "postcolonial" or "colonial mimicry" he often calls "irony" or "imperial imitation," perhaps having in mind some of his intended readership who act allergic to terminology drawn from social theory. Nonetheless, Moore and others would concur with Carter's final evaluation of Matthew's empire of heaven. The Gospel "cannot find an alternative" to the imperial "sovereignty model of power," and the Matthean imaginary "testifies to just how pervasive and deep-seated is the imperial paradigm" (Carter 2001, 90, 129). Even as much as Matthew's Jesus resembles the Jesus of Horsley's covenantal resistance movement—Matthew "glimpses something of the merciful inclusion of the non-elite in God's love and life-giving reign for all"—even so, this Gospel "cannot, finally, escape the imperial mindset" (171). Like Horsley's, Carter's analysis has an eye to the world in front of the text too, especially an implied American Christian reader. Using the Gospel of Matthew, Carter wants to "train contemporary readers to be suspicious of the structures and actions of all ruling powers," to encourage implicated modern imperialists to renounce the benefits of being agents of domination (like the tax collector, Matt 9:9) and to find transformation at the crux of Jesus and empire (like the centurion, Matt 27:54).

Not all empire-critical readings offer their critique from within the dominant contemporary cultural paradigm. The most powerful ones emerge from scholars inhabiting multiple worlds, enunciating new paradigms from hybridized sites of encounter. Probably the most significant postcolonial intervention into biblical scholarship on Matthew has come from Musa Dube, as part of her programmatic work, *Postcolonial Feminist Interpretation of the Bible* (Dube 2000). Her book was methodologically pioneering—if such a colonizing compliment can be excused—by bringing together Western European scholastic knowledge with indigenous and hybridized forms of biblical reflection from the women of African Independent Churches (AICs). Primarily the book depicts and justifies a fierce decolonial method, spending well over half its pages pulling the weeds and tilling the soil of an overgrown field of Euro-American biblical scholarship; following that, she cultivates exegetical seeds about the conquest narrative in Joshua and a pericope in Matthew. She chooses Jesus's encounter with the Canaanite woman (Matt 15:21–28) as her model of how to decolonize "white Western male and feminist interpretations" of the Bible (Dube 2000).

Readers of "sub-Saharan African origin" attest powerfully to the inextricable connection between "biblical mission passages and imperialism" (Dube 2000, 128). She regards Jesus's encounter with the Canaanite woman as "a type-scene of land possession," and her "decolonizing feminist reading therefore seeks to illumine and problematize the power relations entailed in the construction of mission, empire, gender, and race ... that have become so normalized and are hardly questioned even by the most critical and liberation-oriented readers" (144). While many interpreters of this passage have focused on the gender and ethnic dynamics, Dube rightly notes Matthew's geographical designations that label the beginning and end of the story—and, of course, label the woman too. The Canaanite and her daughter "represent foreigners who appear in stories they did not write," and she is marked to be "invaded, conquered, annihilated" or to "survive only as a colonized mind, a subjugated and domestic subject" (147). Whereas Mark foreshadowed the mission to the Gentiles by calling her "a Greek" (Mark 7:26), a woman living among those "who were never mythologized as conquest targets of Israel," Matthew's "Canaanite" evokes those "who must be conquered and dispossessed" (148). Moreover, the Matthean narrative mystifies its intentions and forms of oppression. Even though Matthew's Gospel "has shown interest in the nations from the start," the outsiders "must not only be characterized as evil and dangerous, womenlike and worthless dogs but also be seen as those who beg for salvation from a very reluctant and nationalistic Jesus" (153). The story is ripe for Dube's deft decolonizing because "an unsuspecting reader" could easily "blame the victims" and "miss the tactics of the narrative" (153).

This pericope "has enjoyed popularity among white Western feminist readers," yet Dube's readings with women of AICs have shown her that white feminist readers have not often allowed the Canaanite woman to "speak with her own voice"; rather, they "imprison her to a story that is written about her but nevertheless against her" (Dube 2000, 170). For her fieldwork in 1994, Dube recorded sermons and administered questionnaires with specific exegetical queries about the meanings of each part of the story. One poignant response captures the "liberating interdependence" that Dube identified, when a reader described the Canaanites and Israelites: "'Israelites were taken from Egypt, where they were enslaved,' said the respondent, 'and sent to Canaan, a land that flowed with milk and honey. This Canaanite woman with great faith illustrates for us what it means that their land flowed with milk and honey'" (193). Dube relishes this "subversive postcolonial interpretation," which professes that "the land of the Canaanites, or the colonized, was rich both materially and spiritually" (193). Drawing from indigenous biblical knowledge and experience, this reader offered an inductive, decolonial interpretation.

While Dube has mediated the interpretive contributions of nonacademic women in African churches, other scholars have begun to decolonize their scholarship by laying bare the colonial mindset of nineteenth-century European scholarship and missionary literature. Writing from Sweden and engaged with his own tradition's history of missionary activity, Hans Leander aims to re-present "a colonial heritage of biblical scholarship that, unless monitored, risks becoming reproduced in contemporary scholarship" and to show that "what is seen as ordinary biblical exegesis is in fact an expression of a particular culture with its dominating regimes of knowledge" (Leander 2013b, 289). Specifically, Leander examines both nineteenth-century European biblical scholarship, which essentialized a "Greek/Semitic" philological binary into a main categorization of interpreting "son of God" in Matthew and Mark, and nineteenth-century European missionary tracts, which emphasized the Matthean "Great Commission" (Matt 28:19–20) in the propagation of the binary "Christian/Heathen" (Leander 2013b). His provocative analyses begin to fill a large gap in the production of knowledge about how Gospel narratives shaped the colonizing efforts over minds and lands—and vice versa (Leander 2013a; see Prior 1997).

Dube and Leander confront readers with the presentness of the imperial past, collapsing the faux-objectivity of European biblical scholarship—the false binary in twentieth-century exegetical handbooks of observer and observed, of "what it meant" and "what it means." Readers of the ancient Bible and a contemporary interpretation are thus forced to see both texts always already as "what it means." American Christian readers who feel unfamiliar with, and unimplicated in, what the Bible means for colonial exploits around the world might turn instead to their own recent past. A fitting confrontation comes in the form of an inaugural exhibit at the National Museum of the American Indian, the most recent museum (2004) on the National Mall in Washington, DC. One poignant section of the "Our Peoples: Giving Voice to Our Histories" exhibit juxtaposes historical artifacts of three types: guns, Bibles, and treaties, three contact zones of colonial encounter. Guns and Bibles fill two sides of a central, room-dividing wall, displayed as fraught and hybridized tools. One apparently designed for domination and the other for salvation, in fact both artifacts enacted both modes of power (see Cobb 2005, 486). Among the nearly two hundred versions and excerpts of the Bible displayed in about 175 Native American languages, the Gospels of Matthew and Mark feature prominently. In many instances, Matthew (for its influence) and Mark (for its brevity) were the only texts ever written down in the language of a particular tribe. Especially well executed is a Cherokee Gospel of Matthew, written just a few years after the development of a Cherokee syllabary and possibly written during the forced relocation of the Cherokee people on the Trail of Tears (1836–39). Was someone even reading the apocalypse of Matthew or Mark while on this death march, hearing wars and rumors of wars, with famines and familial ruptures, not having been able to get their belongings, pregnant or nursing, and praying that it not happen in winter?

In 2017 a different, triumphalist Museum of the Bible opened a few blocks away, but empire-critical scholars would argue that it is superfluous. A Bible exhibit had already been there in the nation's capital, hand in hand with an exhibit of guns, as an apocalypse past and present. Guns and Bibles make up the "museum of the Bible" that the United States always already needed. "Whether you read Third World scholars or not," says Musa Dube to her fellow biblical scholars, "you are already stuck in the framework of modern colonial history" (Offenberger 2011).

Spiritual Power, Healing, and Exorcism

Besides the power expressed by the domination of rulers over subjects—and the diverse responses of the dominated—several other forms of power pulse throughout the Synoptic Gospels. All three consistently describe the empowerment of individuals by the Holy Spirit, a superhuman being who seems to function as God's immanent expressed power through human beings on earth and also as a unitive power that binds together the followers of Jesus, who each possess it. Its appearance on earth comes both through Jesus's birth (Matthew and Luke) and his unique baptism (Matthew, Mark, and Luke), and later in the book of Acts it becomes the primary protagonist of the early Christian movement, guiding the plot forward through history. Luke's Gospel emphasizes Jesus's empowerment by the Spirit most readily. Jesus's life begins with a distinctive annunciation narrative to Mary about the conception by the Holy Spirit (Luke 1:35) and, in turn, her rejoicing in spirit (Luke 1:47). Later Jesus receives again the Holy Spirit at his baptism (Luke 3:22), he is "filled with the Holy Spirit" and "led by the Holy Spirit" (Luke 4:1) from the Jordan, and his first public declaration after his baptism and reclusive time in the desert is "The Spirit of the Lord is upon me" (Luke 4:18).

His Spirit-empowerment from heaven relates to earthly powers too. By calling to mind certain prophecies of Isaiah 58 and 61, "Luke's Jesus declares himself as the Messiah who by the power of the Spirit will create a restored Israel in which justice and compassion for the poor will prevail.... The announcement in the synagogue at Nazareth is a declaration that Jesus has been empowered by the Spirit to inaugurate the liberation of God's people" (Hays 1996, 116). The Spirit that empowered healings and the breaking of chains around Galilee will continue to do the same for the disciples beyond, after they receive the power of the Holy Spirit (Acts 1:8; 2:17) and threaten "to turn the world upside down" (Acts 17:6–7; Rowe 2009). While these expressions of Spirit-empowerment in Luke are not as overtly opposed to earthly powers, especially the Roman Empire, as those in Mark, scholars have argued that the liberative actions of Jesus and his disciples as depicted by Luke would still have constituted a danger to the empire, somewhat akin to Gandhi's nonviolent resistance in imperial-era India (Cassidy 1978). The challenging of social stratifications and structures of earthly authority implied new and better patterns of human interaction that would necessitate the dismantling of the older ones. Recalling Horsley's interpretation of Mark, such a reading of Luke shows how "the purpose of God's outpouring of the Spirit is to establish a covenant community in which justice is both proclaimed and practiced" (Hays 1996, 135). This mustard seed of liberation will grow beyond all expectation, even reaching the "end of the earth" (Acts 1:8), the heart of empire where "the kingdom of God" will be proclaimed (Acts 28:31).

Animated by the Holy Spirit, Jesus reveals heavenly power through miraculous dominance over nature—walking on water, stilling the storm—and epiphanic transfigurations of superhuman glory. Most significant for the people of Galilee, though, was Jesus's power of healing, perhaps his most illustrious attribute in his own day. He twice calls himself a "doctor" (Luke 4:23; Mark 2:17 and parallels), and more than twenty healing stories are proclaimed in the Gospels—not counting exorcisms. People seem to have sought Jesus primarily as a healer, secondarily as a teacher. And even his opponents did not question his healing powers, though some found them "strange" (Luke 5:26). Others were threatened by this power and sought to destroy him (Mark 3:6), but they did not deny the powers themselves. This legacy continued in early Christianity, especially in Syria, where "healer" and "physician" remained central aspects of Christology (as in Ignatius of Antioch, the *Acts of Thomas*, and Ephrem). The first few centuries of Christian art memorialized and propagated many healing stories from the Synoptic Gospels too, including the healings of the paralytic, the blind men, and the woman with the flow of blood (Jefferson 2014).

The power relations between Jesus and those healed by him have begun to be reinterpreted with insights drawn from disability studies. While there is textual evidence to support the traditional interpretations—that "disability is a problem that is fixed by Jesus, provided that the disabled person has the requisite amount of faith"— attention and imagination show how often "it is people with disabilities who possess the ability to recognize who Jesus is" (Moss 2017, 299). These include the blind, those possessed by unclean spirits, amputees, and the disfigured. For example, the woman with the flow of blood has been considered multiply oppressed, weakened by her porous physical condition and her loss of financial resources (Mark 5:25–34). But this woman "initiates her own healing by pulling power from an unsuspecting Jesus," and "like the flow of blood, the flow of power is something embodied and physical; just as the woman feels the flow of blood dry up, so Jesus feels—physically—the flow of power leave his body" (290). Whereas contemporaneous medical perspectives on the body regarded porousness as weakness, Mark's narrative presents the porous body as "leaky and vulnerable" but "nonetheless powerful" (291).

Jesus's exorcisms of demons and unclean spirits constitute an overlapping but distinct set of stories from the healings. Undoubtedly these exorcisms signify Jesus's "authority and power" to manipulate bodies and spirits (Luke 4:36) and manifest his "kingdom of God." One of them even presents an explicit interface between the realms of spiritual and political struggle, when a man possessed by "unclean spirits" declares their name to be "Legion" (Mark 5:9). To listeners attuned to the political context of the Gospels, the Latin military loan-word λεγιών pierces the air, an undeniable evocation of Roman colonial occupation in the guise of demonic possession. The natural follow-up question, then, is whether the clarity and length of this extended narrative (Mark 5:1–20) signify for the implied reader that the demons were "to be identified analogically with the Roman 'army of occupation'" and whether "the demoniac may be identified in turn as the land and people under occupation—which, it may be argued, is why the demons earnestly entreat the exorcist 'not to send them out of the land'" (Moore 2006, 26). And if so, does this make λεγιών a "hermeneutical key" for the whole Gospel of Mark? (27).

Virtually every Markan interpreter and every empire-critical scholar has weighed in on these questions, which cannot be resolved here. Suffice it to say that a scholarly consensus has emerged on at least this point: the Latin military loan-word λεγιών alludes in some way to Roman occupation of the region. It would be as if a tale circulated in Iraq during the US occupation in which a possessed man said in Arabic: "*ismi* Marines *li'annana kathirun*," meaning "my name is Marines, for we are many" (Garroway 2009, 61). Some scholars thus take "Legion" as the clue to the allegory that reveals the overall antiimperial message of Mark (Horsley 2003, 99–103; Myers 1988, 190–94). Others go further to read Mark as a political allegory or invective commentary (Incigneri 2003; Winn 2008). Compelling interpretations of the episode have come from a combination of historical criticism (regarding Vespasian's activities in the region), narrative criticism (connecting this episode especially to the preceding seed parables), and postcolonial criticism (regarding the mimicry and subversion in the plot), thus demonstrating how the study of the Synoptic Gospels continues to blend diverse methods (Garroway 2009, Leander 2013a; Moore 2006). The expulsion of the "Legion" is, however, not the end of the story. Following the satirical drowning of the army, "the invaded becomes the invader as the cured demoniac, like a solitary mustard seed, reenters the community from which he has been expelled and preaches a message that rapidly proliferates. The colonial ideology of invasion is thus mimicked and invoked, but also subversively altered. The might of an occupying kingdom is conquered, as expected, with even greater might, yet against expectations the ensuing kingdom invades in a most *unmighty* manner—through the planting of a single, meager seed" (Garroway 2009, 60; see Leander 2013a, 201–19).

Conclusion and Future Directions

Each in its own way, the Synoptic Gospels situate Jesus's coming kingdom of God in the context of earthly authorities and diverse modes of power. Recent scholarship has attended especially to the Roman imperial presence in first-century Galilee and Judea: the ways in which its colonial dominance affected peasant villagers, manipulated aristocratic collaborators, and catalyzed conscientious resistance. While Luke has usually been interpreted as a text accommodating to Roman imperial power, both Matthew and Mark have been read in part as subversive narratives of resistance. Empire-critical scholars, informed especially by postcolonial theory, bring nuance to these views, showing how texts produced at sites of colonial encounter struggle to cleanly disavow the modes of power experienced by their authorial communities. Their leader wore a thorny crown, but it was a crown nonetheless.

As empire criticism develops further, it will continue to move beyond historical interpretations of past empires and toward self-critical redescriptions of present-day empires. Following the path charted by scholars like Dube and West, more mediation of the interpretive juxtapositions possible in contemporary colonial encounter will be undertaken. In addition to the exegesis of the Gospels from culturally hybridized regions of sub-Saharan Africa, opportunities for similar research abound in South and Central America, the "base communities" from which liberation theology—at root, a biblical theology—was born. Scholars will likely continue to pursue decolonial interpretations of the biblical understanding of land and dispossession as well. For already scholars know that the Legion-possessed man has not been interpreted only as a Roman occupation from the distant past. In nineteenth-century European interpretation, there was "a strong tendency among orthodox, pietist, and critical commentaries alike to take the demon-possessed man as an image of the wretched heathen who needs to be rescued by Christian mission" and who becomes, in turn, the first missionary to the heathen (Leander 2013b, 306). This character in the Synoptic Gospels thus lives on as a cipher, a signifying site for multiple encounters of authority and power: spiritual and physical, prophetic and militaristic, Jewish and gentile, Christian and heathen, colonizer and colonized, antiimperial and postcolonial. Here is the mustard seed of Jesus's growing kingdom—and of the continual interpretation of that kingdom.

References

Bhabha, Homi. 1994. *The Location of Culture*. London: Routledge.
Carter, Warren. 2001. *Matthew and Empire: Initial Explorations*. Harrisburg: Trinity Press International.
Cassidy, Richard J. 1978. *Jesus, Politics, and Society: A Study of Luke's Gospel*. Maryknoll, NY: Orbis Books.
Cobb, Amanda J. 2005. "The National Museum of the American Indian as Cultural Sovereignty." *American Quarterly* 57: 485–506.
Crossan, John Dominic. 1991. *The Historical Jesus: The Life of a Mediterranean Jewish Peasant*. San Francisco: HarperCollins.
Dube, Musa W. 2000. *Postcolonial Feminist Interpretation of the Bible*. St. Louis, MO: Chalice Books.
Evans, Craig A. 2000. "Mark's Incipit and the Priene Calendar Inscription: From Jewish Gospel to Greco-Roman Gospel." *Journal for the Study of Greco-Roman Christianity and Judaism* 1: 67–81.
Garroway, Joshua. 2009. "The Invasion of a Mustard Seed: A Reading of Mark 5.1–20." *Journal for the Study of the New Testament* 32: 57–75.
Hanson, K. C., and Douglas E. Oakman. 2008. *Palestine in the Time of Jesus: Social Structures and Social Conflicts*. 2nd ed. Minneapolis: Fortress Press.

Hays, Richard B. 1996. *The Moral Vision of the New Testament: Community, Cross, New Creation; A Contemporary Introduction to New Testament Ethics*. San Francisco: HarperSanFrancisco.

Herzog, William R. 1994. *Parables as Subversive Speech: Jesus as Pedagogue of the Oppressed*. Louisville: Westminster John Knox Press.

Horsley, Richard A. 2003. *Jesus and Empire: The Kingdom of God and the New World Disorder*. Minneapolis: Fortress Press.

Horsley, Richard A. 2009. *Covenant Economics: A Biblical Vision of Justice for All*. Louisville: Westminster John Knox Press.

Incigneri, Brian J. 2003. *The Gospel to the Romans: The Setting and Rhetoric of Mark's Gospel*. Leiden: Brill.

Jefferson, Lee M. 2014. *Christ the Miracle Worker in Early Christian Art*. Minneapolis: Fortress Press.

Leander, Hans. 2013a. *Discourses of Empire: The Gospel of Mark from a Postcolonial Perspective*. Atlanta: Society of Biblical Literature Press.

Leander, Hans. 2013b. "Mark and Matthew after Edward Said." In *Mark and Matthew II, Comparative Readings: Reception History, Cultural Hermeneutics, and Theology*, edited by Eve-Marie Becker and Anders Runesson, 289–309. Tübingen: Mohr Siebeck.

Liew, Tat-siong Benny. 1999a. *Politics of Parousia: Reading Mark Inter(con)textually*. Leiden: Brill.

Liew, Tat-siong Benny. 1999b. "Tyranny, Boundary, and Might: Colonial Mimicry in Mark's Gospel." *Journal for the Study of the New Testament* 73: 7–31.

Moore, Stephen D. 2006. *Empire and Apocalypse: Postcolonialism and the New Testament*. Sheffield: Sheffield Phoenix Press.

Moss, Candida R. 2017. "Mark and Matthew." In *The Bible and Disability: A Commentary*, edited by Sarah J. Melcher, Mikeal C. Parsons, and Amos Young, 275–301. Waco: Baylor University Press.

Myers, Ched. 1988. *Binding the Strong Man: A Political Reading of Mark's Story of Jesus*. Maryknoll, NY: Orbis Books.

Offenberger, Bernhard. 2011. "Interview mit Musa Dube." http://www.befreiungstheologisches-netzwerk.de/?page_id=2143.

Peppard, Michael. 2011. *The Son of God in the Roman World: Divine Sonship in Its Social and Political Context*. New York: Oxford University Press.

Peppard, Michael. 2015. "Torah for the Man Who Has Everything: 'Do Not Defraud' in Mark 10:19." *Journal of Biblical Literature* 134: 595–604.

Prior, Michael. 1997. *The Bible and Colonialism: A Moral Critique*. Sheffield: Sheffield Academic Press.

Rowe, C. Kavin. 2009. *World Upside Down: Reading Acts in the Graeco-Roman Age*. New York: Oxford University Press.

Ruether, Rosemary Radford. 1983. *Sexism and God-Talk: Toward a Feminist Theology*. London: SCM Press.

Schüssler Fiorenza, Elizabeth. 1983. *In Memory of Her: A Feminist Theological Reconstruction of Christian Origins*. New York: Crossroad.

Schweitzer, Albert. 1968. *The Quest of the Historical Jesus: A Critical Study of Its Progress from Reimarus to Wrede*. Translated by W. Montgomery. New York: Collier Books.

Stegemann, Ekkehard W., and Wolfgang Stegemann. 1995. *The Jesus Movement: A Social History of Its First Century*. Translated by O. C. Dean, Jr. Minneapolis: Fortress Press.

Sugirtharajah, R. S., ed. 1998. *The Postcolonial Bible*. Sheffield: Sheffield Academic Press.

Ukpong, Justin. 1996. "The Parable of the Shrewd Manager (Luke 16:1–13): An Essay in Inculturation Biblical Hermeneutic." *Semeia* 76: 189–208.

West, Gerald O. 1993. "The Interface between Trained Readers and Ordinary Readers in Liberation Hermeneutics. A Case Study: Mark 10:17–22." *Neotestamentica* 27: 165–80.

West, Gerald O., and Sithembiso Zwane. 2013. "Why Are You Sitting There? Reading Matthew 20:1–16 in the Context of Casual Workers in Pietermaritzburg, South Africa." In *Matthew*, edited by Nicole Wilkinson Duran and James P. Grimshaw, 175–88. Minneapolis: Fortress Press.

Winn, Adam. 2008. *The Purpose of Mark's Gospel: An Early Christian Response to Imperial Propaganda*. Tübingen: Mohr Siebeck.

Winn, Adam, ed. 2016. *An Introduction to Empire in the New Testament*. Atlanta: Society of Biblical Literature Press.

CHAPTER 16

WEALTH, POVERTY, ECONOMY

THOMAS R. BLANTON IV

DEFINING MULTIVALENT TERMS: WEALTH, POVERTY, ECONOMY

Wealth and Poverty

The English terms "wealth" and "poverty," the related adjectives "rich" and "poor," and, for different reasons, the term "economy" are multivalent signifiers whose connotations vary widely depending on the author and context in which they are used. Moreover, the connotations of the English terms do not correspond exactly to those of the vocabulary of wealth and poverty in ancient Hebrew, Greek, and Latin. This is in part due to expected differences in the semantics of the various languages, but also because the "economy" is conceptualized very differently in the twenty-first century from the way it was in antiquity.

Wealth is generally assessed positively in the Hebrew Bible. The great wealth attributed to Solomon, for example, was described in positive terms and paired with wisdom among his noteworthy traits (1 Kgs 4:22–34; see Matt 6:29 // Luke 12:27; Matt 12:42). Deuteronomisic texts associate wealth, in the form of productive fields and livestock, with observing the precepts of the law, while poverty is associated with failure to adhere to the law (Deut 7:12–16; 8:11–13; 28:11–12, 38–44). Second and Third Isaiah imagine a future in which Israel would accrue wealth from other nations in the form of tribute (Isa 45:14; 60:5, 11; 61:6; 66:12).

In some apocalyptically oriented texts, for example the Epistle of Enoch (1 En 92–105), the rich are characterized as those who trust in wealth rather than Israel's God to provide security and who have amassed their fortunes through oppressing others (1 En 94:6–9;

I thank John Kloppenborg, David Fiensy, Tony Keddie, David Hollander, and Giovanni Bazzana, whose incisive comments have materially improved this chapter. I am entirely responsible for any remaining faults or omissions.

95:6–7; 96:6–7; 102:9; 103:11–15).[1] The older Deuteronomistic association of wealth with following the law is reversed: the wealthy are characterized as sinners who do not follow the law and oppress the righteous poor (1 En 94:11; 95:7; 96:1, 4; 97:7).

In Greek literature, Aristotle paints a picture of the landed aristocrat who, living from the surplus produced by a landed estate (*oikos*), was able to devote time to philosophy and politics within the confines of the polis (*Pol.* 1.2–3; Leshem 2014). The person who did not control an estate could by way of contrast be described as a *penēs*, "one who is obliged to work for a living: poor."[2] Distinct from the *penēs* was the *ptōchos*, the "destitute" person who depended on others for support. This distinction is generally observed in the Greek translation of the Pentateuch, where the typical day laborer could be described as "poor and in need" (*penēs kai endeēs*; Deut 24:14 LXX) but still expected to repay a loan (assumed in Deut 24:12) or to offer Yahweh a lamb and some flour mixed with oil (Lev 14:21).[3] In contrast, the *ptōchos* is the beneficiary of laws prohibiting harvest at the margins of fields, permitting those without resources to glean what little remained (Lev 19:10; 23:22). The distinction is not uniformly maintained, however, and the significance of the terms is reversed in other texts.[4]

Jinyu Liu (2017, 32–33) points to the range of Latin terms used to refer to poverty and poor persons, including *paupertas* ("poverty"), *pauper* ("poor"), *inops* ("destitute"), *indigens* ("needy"), and *mendicans* ("begging"), which, like their Greek counterparts *penia*, *penēs*, *ptōchos*, *endeēs*, and *prosaitōn*, are "indicative of wanting, lacking, and absence." Liu points to a small number of epitaphs inscribed on commemorative monuments identifying the deceased as a *pauper* or experiencing *paupertas*. The tombstones on which epitaphs were inscribed ranged in price; the lowest-priced tombstone recorded in Italy was valued at 120 sesterces (Duncan-Jones 1982, 128; see, however, Graham 2006, 66). The families and friends who commemorated the "poor" with epitaphs thus controlled some surplus, albeit modest.

Latin writers use terms such as *egens* ("needy") and *pauper* to indicate relative differences in wealth; from the perspective of the hyperwealthy Seneca the Younger (ES 1 on the economic scale; see table 16.1), less wealthy beneficiaries of his largesse, although themselves situated among the Roman elite (e.g., equestrians at ES 2), could be described as "poor" in comparison (e.g., *Ben.* 4.10.4–5; see Parkin 2006, 62). Greg Woolf (2006, 97) notes the loose way in which the poet Martial uses the term "poor": "Gaurus in [*Epig.*] 4.67 is described as poor, possessing only HS 300,000 and denied the balance needed to acquire equestrian status by his praetorian friend who preferred to patronize charioteers." Martial (ES 2) likewise described himself as poor, especially in epigrams asking for donations from his literary patron (98–99). Notions of wealth and poverty can thus be deployed to register relative differences between elite members of Roman society. The corresponding terms are therefore highly imprecise and offer little

---

[1] On economic issues in the Epistle of Enoch, see Nickelsburg 2001, 426–27. See Keddie (2018) for similar examples.
[2] LSJ, s.v. πένης.
[3] Translations are my own unless noted otherwise.
[4] Keddie 2018, 107 n. 63.

Table 16.1 Friesen-Longenecker Economic Scale

Scale	Description	Includes
ES 1	Imperial elites	Imperial dynasty, Roman senatorial families, a few retainers, local royalty, a few freed persons
ES 2	Regional or provincial elites	Equestrian families, provincial officials, some retainers, some decurial families, some freed persons, some retired military officers
ES 3	Municipal elites	Most decurial families, wealthy men and women who do not hold office, some freed persons, some retainers, some veterans, some merchants
ES 4	Moderate surplus	Some merchants, some traders, some freed persons, some artisans (especially those who employ others), military veterans
ES 5	Stable near subsistence level (with reasonable hope of remaining above the minimum level to sustain life)	Many merchants and traders, regular wage earners, artisans, large shop owners, freed persons, some farm families
ES 6	At subsistence level (and often below minimum level to sustain life)	Small farm families, laborers (skilled and unskilled), artisans (especially those employed by others), wage earners, most merchants and traders, small shop/tavern owners
ES 7	Below subsistence level	Some farm families, unattached widows, orphans, beggars, disabled, unskilled day laborers, prisoners

The table is a modified version based on Pickett (2017, xv), which in turn reproduces Longenecker (2010, 45), itself based on Friesen (2004, 341) with slight modification.

information about the actual economic conditions experienced by those to whom they were applied; the Greek terms are similarly imprecise.

The Friesen-Longenecker Economic Scale

In order to overcome the simplifying dichotomy between "rich" and "poor," Steven Friesen (2004) proposed a system of classification involving seven distinct "levels" on an economic scale. Friesen's scheme has been subjected to criticism (Oakes 2004; Welborn 2012), but it has also been elaborated and refined (Brookins 2017; Longenecker 2010, 36–59; Scheidel and Friesen 2009). I reproduce here a modified version of Friesen's "poverty scale," which Bruce Longenecker later renamed an "economic scale"; the latter is indicated by the acronym ES in table 16.1.

This "economic scale" does not take into account a number of issues relevant to the assessment of resources available to an individual or household, most notably the size, location, arrangement, and decoration of household space (Oakes 2009), nor does it purport to describe the sociopolitical relations that largely generate one's "position" on the economic scale (i.e., class relations between exploiter and exploited; see Boer and Petterson 2017, 25–40, 68–73; Welborn 2017); nevertheless, it serves the important heuristic function of disaggregating people and groups who enjoyed differential access to resources in antiquity but who might otherwise be classed together as either "rich" or "poor."[5] Timothy Brookins (2017, 72) notes that "scalar models ... have begun to offer sufficient nuancing to account for diversity in ancient experiences."

A few caveats ought to be registered, however, along with an explanation of the way in which the scale will be employed in this investigation. The Friesen-Longenecker scale apparently combines three different types of organizational principles. First: the designations ES 1–3 are based on the Roman status system in which senators occupy the highest rung, followed by equestrians and decurions. This sociopolitical ranking system is (however imperfectly) correlated with gradations in wealth, which at least partly justifies its inclusion in an economic scale.[6] Second: the designations ES 4–7 employ a different logic based on resource availability measured in relation to subsistence, as the notations in the middle column of the table make explicit. Third: the designation ES 7 employs an additional criterion. Except for farm families and day laborers, all of the groups listed in ES 7 presumably are understood to depend on the generosity of others for their survival (e.g., prisoners must be fed by captors, family, or friends; beggars depend on donations, etc.), implying that they do not themselves control resources sufficient to attain subsistence-level maintenance. Following C. R. Whitaker, Friesen (2004, 344) describes this group as "incapable of earning a living" and "permanently in crisis."

The placement of widows and orphans in the single category of ES 7, however, is misleading, as widows likely existed across the economic spectrum, from the extremely wealthy Cornelia Africana, mother of Tiberius and Gaius Gracchus, to Babatha of Maoza in Nabatea, who more modestly controlled four date orchards (P.Yadin 16; on Babatha, see Lewis 1989; Czajkowski 2017; Hanson 2005). One must not be misled by the story of the poor widow in Mark 12:41–44 to assume that all widows fell into the same category. The same holds true for orphans. Persons with disabilities could in many cases hold jobs, while beggars could develop successful (if sometimes coercive or deceptive) strategies to elicit donations (Parkin 2006), indicating that not all members of those groups necessarily fell below subsistence level at all times. Finally, no prior assumptions can be made about where a given craftsperson or merchant is to be placed on the scale since a great deal of variation existed within those groups. The scale as presented in table 16.1 is thus constructed as a hodgepodge of different considerations, not all of them equally cogent.

The more elaborate scale of Scheidel and Friesen (2009), which relies on measures of income translated into equivalent values in wheat, facilitates useful observations about the distribution of resources and consumption across different segments of the population. The lack of detailed income data, however, renders very difficult the placement of

---

[5] For additional critiques of binary economic models, see Scheidel 2006.
[6] See further Scheidel and Friesen 2009, 79.

the various characters as depicted in the Synoptic Gospels on that scale of measurement. For that reason and despite its flaws, the seven-tiered scale is more useful in categorizing the characters and implied audiences of the Gospels. The Friesen-Longenecker economic scale is employed in this essay as a heuristic tool to register differences in the relative amounts of resources attributed both to characters in the narratives and to the implied audiences of the Synoptic Gospels and Q, and to register discrepancies between the economic portrayals sketched by the various sources.

Defining Ancient "Economy"

A number of studies of ancient Greece, Rome, and Palestine have followed the modern discipline of economics in assuming that the market and its activity constitute the primary area of concern (e.g., Safrai 1994; Temin 2001). The more recent integration of insights from the field of New Institutional Economics has helped to broaden this narrow focus based on the recognition that institutional and ideological factors play significant roles in shaping economies (e.g., North 1981, 1990; Scheidel, Morris, and Saller 2008; see, however, the critiques by Blanton and Hollander 2019).

Peter Bang (2007, 2012) has argued that the economic predation entailed in Roman imperialism needs to be given a prominent place in the study of the ancient Roman economy: "redistribution of wealth and economic resources [through plunder, confiscation of agricultural lands, and taxation] was staggering and must easily have been the single most significant and dynamic factor shaping economic developments" (2012, 201). Philip Kay (2014) convincingly argues that economic predation and mercantile activity are closely related, as Roman predation provided wealth that subsequently stimulated markets. The influx of money and resources from conquered states provided Rome with a steady income in the form of war indemnities (*phoros* or *stipendium*), *manubiae* ("plunder" or "booty"), and natural resources claimed by Rome. Rome also benefited from the imposition of taxes in the form of fixed sums (*vectigalia*), agricultural tithes (*decumae*), and *portoria*, or "customs dues," paid as a percentage of the value of items transported for sale on the market. In addition, persons taken captive in pacified regions could be transported to Rome and sold as slaves; Walter Scheidel (2005) estimates that by the end of the first century BCE, there were around 1.2 million slaves in Italy.

The influx of such immense wealth, combined with the productive capacity inherent in slave labor, stimulated massive building projects in Rome beginning in the second century BCE, which in turn provided employment for architects, laborers, craftsmen of various sorts, and those involved in water transport (Kay 2014, 216–26). Moreover, with the influx of wealth in Rome came an increased demand for luxury items and foodstuffs imported from abroad, including fish processed near the sea of Galilee.

In this essay, "economy" will be understood broadly to concern (1) the provisioning of human need and/or desire, (2) the sociopolitical systems by which resources are produced, allocated, and extracted, and (3) the ideological factors associated with those sociopolitical systems, whether legitimizing, decrying, or attempting to modify them.

(See also Boer 2015; Boer and Petterson 2017; Dalton 1971, xlii; Fitzgerald 2019; Leshem 2014; Blanton 2017a, 280–86.)

The Economic Concerns of the Gospels

The imperial economy of Rome marked the Synoptic Gospels and Q, documents reflecting the periods that preceded and followed the First Jewish Revolt against Rome in 66–73 CE. The Gospel of Mark is examined first here, as it indicates many of the structures of the "ancient economy" that are relevant to the investigation of the Synoptics; Q, with its more limited palette of economic concerns, is treated second; Matthew and Luke follow in that order.

The Gospel of Mark

Water and food rank among the most basic of human needs, and their provisioning constitutes the basis of all economies (see Earle 2008, 6). Although in Aristotle's view the landed estate provided the resources to sustain households, homo sapiens foraged and hunted long before they cultivated crops. The notice in Mark 1:6 that John the Baptizer survived in the desert by foraging honey and locusts thus indicates the most primitive form of economic provisioning encountered in this Gospel.[7]

More advanced, agrarian forms of provisioning are presupposed in Mark 2:23–28, where Jesus and his disciples are portrayed as harvesting small amounts of grain on the Sabbath. In Mark 4:1–9, the practice of sowing seed and harvesting the produce for a yield thirty to one hundred times greater than the amount planted is taken as a metaphor indicating a positive response to Jesus's preaching (Mark 4:10–20). These numbers, however, are fantastic; "apart from areas under irrigation (such as Egypt or lower Mesopotamia) or well-watered by other means," yields averaged between 4:1 and 5:1, although "regional variations were significant," and yields up to 8:1 were possible (Boer and Petterson 2017, 59 and n. 46).

Larger-scale agricultural operations are presupposed in Mark 12:1–12, where an absentee landlord has tenant farmers plant a vineyard with its own wine press (see Fiensy 2014, 98–117). The vineyard is overlooked by a tower, which, in addition to providing a vantage point for guards monitoring the field's perimeter, also provided shelter for laborers. The reference to a millstone in Mark 9:42 points to the grinding of wheat into meal on a scale beyond that of a single household, for whose needs a simple handheld grindstone would be sufficient.

---

[7] See Kelhoffer (2005) on the consumption of locusts and honey in antiquity.

The resources of the sea were exploited as well as those of the earth. The musht (or "St. Peter's fish," a type of tilapia), barbels (or "Biny fish"), and sardines that could be harvested from the Sea of Galilee were economically important in antiquity (Firmage 1992, 1146–47; Troche 2015, 33–37). Situated midway between Capernaum and Tiberias on the western shore of the Sea of Galilee was Magdala, whose Greek name, Taricheae, was derived from the verb ταριχεύειν, referring to the salting or smoking of fish. Fish preserved in Taricheae were known as far away as Rome, as Strabo indicates (*Geogr.* 16.2.45; see further Zapata Meza 2013).

Mark 1:16–18 depicts the brothers Simon and Andrew as fishermen (ἁλιεῖς) "throwing nets" (ἀμφιβάλλοντας) in the Sea of Galilee near Capernaum (Mark 1:21). The two were probably understood to be casting smaller, circular nets (the ἀμφίβληστρον; see Oppian, *Halieutica* 3.78–84; Matt 4:18) that could be launched from shore, while standing in shallow water, or from a boat. Unlike James and John, however, Simon and Andrew are not said to possess a boat. The small casting nets involved "a minimal economic investment" (Troche 2015, 52). In Mark 1:29–31, the brothers are described as possessing a house and hosting Jesus, James, and John for a meal, all suggesting a placement on Friesen's economic scale at ES 6 or ES 5.

James and John, the sons of Zebedee, are likewise portrayed as fishermen, although with a boat and a larger gill net that could be let down into the water. John Kloppenborg (2018, 577–78) notes that the ancient boat found near Kibbutz Ginnosar on the Sea of Galilee was made largely of imported cedar and was probably constructed by professional shipbuilders. Moreover, when Jesus calls them, the brothers leave their father "in the boat with the hired men" (ἐν τῷ πλοίῳ μετὰ τῶν μισθωτῶν; Mark 1:18–20). The control of a boat, a gill net, and the means to hire workers suggests a placement for Zebedee's family at ES 4.

Instead of working to derive resources directly from earth or sea, others sold products or services. Jesus is described as a τέκτων in Mark 6:3, indicating a profession as a builder who worked with wood or perhaps stone (MM, s.v. τέκτων). The *tektōn* was typically "skilled in fashioning wood projects, such as furniture, tools, agricultural implements, water wheels for irrigation, scaffolding for houses, and perhaps even ships"; the trade necessitated an investment in tools, including "axes, chisels, drills, [and] saws" (Fiensy 2014, 25). Limited opportunities may have forced craftsmen from small villages like Nazareth to seek employment on the larger building projects characteristic of cities such as Sepphoris, Tiberias, and even Jerusalem (26–29). As a laborer sometimes employed by others who could nevertheless afford his own tools, the Markan Jesus falls under category ES 5 or ES 6.

Jesus's instructions to his disciples to take no bread, purse, or money during stints of itinerant preaching in Mark 6:10 points to an important aspect of ancient economies: hospitality. Jesus says: "Whenever you enter a house, remain there until you depart from that place" (Mark 6:10), implying that the disciples accept both food and lodging when on tour. Jesus instructs them to take "neither bread, nor pouch, nor small change in [their] belts" (Mark 6:8). Networks of paths and roads crisscrossed the Galilee, and it was possible to walk from one village to the next in a few hours' time, so it was not unreasonable to travel with no provisions (see Strange 2014). Simon and Andrew host Jesus, James, and John in their home in Capernaum (Mark 1:29–31); from Mark 1:32 and 1:35 it can be inferred that the group lodged there for the night (Guelich 1989, 63). Closely related to hospitality is the invitation to dine; Jesus is portrayed as dining in the homes of Levi the toll collector (Mark 2:15) and Simon "the leper" (Mark 14:3–10).

Herod the Great (37 BCE–4 CE) and his successors could host dinner guests on a more lavish scale. Herod imposed land and property taxes (*tributum soli*) in his realms in Judea, Samaria, Galilee, and Perea and collected vast revenue from tolls and duties on transported goods. Moreover, he benefited from multiple sources of "personal wealth," including his own landed estates; treasures, land, and palaces confiscated from the Hasmoneans; and interest on large loans (Udoh 2005, 159–206). Those sources of revenue enabled him and his successors to act as patrons to a retinue of supporters, designated as clients or euphemized as "friends" (i.e., the "Herodians" mentioned in Mark 3:6; 12:13). (On patronage, see Osiek 2009; on the Herodians, see Yarbro Collins 2007, 210 and n. 175.) Patrons typically invited their "friends" to dinner, as in Mark 6:21–29, where Herod Antipas invites "his high-ranking officials, military tribunes, and the leading men of Galilee" to a birthday banquet.

The Gospel of Mark brings taxation by the Jerusalem Temple into close association with Roman imperial taxation.[8] In Mark 12:13–17, Pharisees and Herodians ask Jesus: "Is it lawful to pay the tax to Caesar or not?" to which Jesus famously responds: "Repay to Caesar what belongs to Caesar, and to God what belongs to God." Udoh (2005, 224) argues that, contrary to what has become "an orthodoxy among ancient historians and New Testament scholars," Jews did not pay the *tributum capitis*—a poll tax on each qualifying individual—to Rome under Herod and his successors. Nor is there evidence that Roman denarii were in common circulation in Judea prior to 69 CE; before that time, Tyrian coinage was the predominant type (Udoh 2005, 223–38). Udoh concludes that the only per capita tax on Jews in the early Roman period was paid to the Jerusalem Temple. After the capture of Jerusalem in 70 CE, Vespasian redirected the temple tax to Rome as the *fiscus Iudaicus* (Josephus, *J.W.* 7.218). Some sixty-nine tax receipts from the Egyptian city of Apollinopolis Magna (modern Edfu) written on ostraca from 72 to 116 CE record payments of this "two-denarius tax on Jews" (τιμῆς δηναρίων δύο Ἰουδ[αίων]; *CPJ*, nos. 169–229; see also Incigneri 2003, 200–201, n. 164).

Brian Incigneri (2003, 194–202) plausibly argues that Mark 12:13–17 reflects the period after the temple tax had been redirected to Rome. Adela Yarbro Collins's (2007, 553) suggestion, based on a pre-70 CE dating of the Gospel of Mark, that "Jesus' request for a denarius does not signify a literal payment of a tax in coin," is unlikely since the denarius is specified and the temple tax is brought into direct relation to a Roman *tributum capitis* (see κῆνσος; Mark 12:14), a conjunction that occurred only when Vespasian converted the temple tax into the *fiscus Iudaicus*.

---

[8] On priestly and royal extraction, see Boer 2015, 146–56.

At the low end of the economic spectrum is Mark's "poor widow" (χήρα πτωχή), who "contributed everything that she had, her whole means of subsistence" (πάντα ὅσα εἶχεν ἔβαλεν ὅλον τὸν βίον αὐτῆς) to the temple treasury (Mark 12:41–44). The widow is portrayed as situated at ES 6 or ES 7, since the donated sum amounted only to "two *lepta*; that is, a [Roman] *quadrans*" (Mark 12:42). A *leptos* was a copper coin worth 1/128 of a denarius; two were thus worth 1/64 to 1/32 of a day's wage for a laborer.[9] The contrast drawn in the narrative is economic, not moral: the poor widow gives "everything that she had" "out of her lack" (ἐκ τῆς ὑστερήσεως αὐτῆς), whereas the rich donors at the temple, although they "gave a lot" (ἔβαλλον πολλά), are presumed to have donated a smaller proportion of their resources: they gave "out of their abundance" (ἐκ τοῦ περισσεύοντος αὐτοῖς). The Markan Jesus thus does not assess donations to the temple in terms of absolute value but as a proportion of total wealth (see Seneca, *Ben.* 1.6.3).

The Q Material[10]

John Kloppenborg's (2000, 200–201) suggestion that Q was produced by village scribes in Galilee has been elaborated in studies by William Arnal (2001, 168–72) and Giovanni Bazzana (2015), among others. Scribes served important functions in royal and imperial bureaucratic administrations, often by keeping records on produce extracted in the form of in-kind taxation, although they also directly served the populace by drafting loan agreements, marriage contracts, and other documents (Czajkowski 2017).

The Beatitudes occur in different forms in Matthew and Luke (Matt 5:3–12 // Luke 6:20–26). Harry Fleddermann (2005, 281) reconstructs the Q version as follows: "Blessed are the poor [οἱ πτωχοί], because God's royal administration [ἡ βασιλεία τοῦ θεοῦ] belongs to them. Blessed are those who hunger, for they will be fed."[11] Reconstructing the Q text is difficult, however, since Matthew uses third person forms ("the poor"/ "theirs"/"they"), while Luke uses the second person ("you poor"/"yours"/"you"); it is unclear whether the poor are addressed or merely referred to. The reference to "those who hunger" may indicate a state of chronic poverty (i.e., ES 7) but more likely reflects the insecurity of agrarian production; bad harvests are expected occasionally, resulting in periodic but not chronic food shortages (see Scott 1976). Thus "hunger" may indicate

---

[9] Kloppenborg (2018, 597, n. 94) notes that wages varied from 1/2 denarius to 1 denarius per day. There was of course wide variation over time and in different geographic regions; unskilled workers are paid 25 denarii per day in Diocletian's Edict on Maximum Prices, issued in 301 CE.

[10] In light of the current ferment in Synoptic Gospel studies, I note that the discussion of Q material is included here not because I think that the Q hypothesis necessarily provides the best solution to the Synoptic Problem, but because the excellent work that has been done on economic issues in Q is highly germane to the present topic.

[11] My trans. of Fledderman's reconstructed Greek text, which provides the basis of all citations of Q herein.

a periodic rather than a chronic condition, and the beatitude therefore may be directed to persons at ES 5–6.

The probability that periodic rather than chronic hunger is in view is raised by the fact that "hunger" is closely linked to "royal administration" (βασιλεία) in Q, which suggests the opening of royal granaries to feed the populace during times of famine; the administration was expected to ensure that the populace did not starve. As an example of ancient famine relief, Bazzana points to the Canopus decree, issued in Egypt in 238 BCE, which indicates that in response to a drought that adversely affected grain production, Egypt's sovereigns, "putting themselves providentially in defense ... [of the] inhabitants of the country ... brought grain, which they had bought at higher prices, to the country (of Egypt) from Syria and Phoenicia and Cyprus and many other places; they saved the inhabitants of Egypt, leaving an immortal benefaction ... to those who are now living and to posterity."[12] With its assurance that the hungry will be fed, God's royal administration in Q is portrayed as functioning in a manner analogous to that of royal administrations from Egypt to Rome. The future tense of the verb χορτασθήσονται, "they will be fed," however, looks forward to an apocalyptic banquet hosted by Israel's God (see Bergmann 2016).

Anthony Keddie (2018, 238) notes that the addressees of Q are invited to forgive loans (Q 11:2–4), implying the control of resources adequate to extend loans, while Q 6:30 assumes the control of surplus that could be donated to others. Kloppenborg (2000, 198) reasons that "the addressees include smallholders and handworkers." The "poor" audience of Q is thus characterized as living in the range of ES 4–6, indicating the flexibility with which that term could be used.

The Lord's Prayer (Matt 6:9–13 // Luke 11:2–4) reads in part: "Give us today our bread [sufficient] for the day, and cancel our debts for us [καὶ ἄφες ἡμῖν τὰ ὀφειλήματα ἡμῶν], as we, too, have forgiven those who owe us." Heinz Heinen (1990; see, however, Bazzana 2015, 191–93) has plausibly argued that this saying refers to the practice of apportioning the *sitometria* ("measured allowance of grain") by which slaves, hirelings, or members of the household were given a daily food ration (see Luke 12:42). God serves as the distributive agent in the Q logion.

The statement on forgiving "those who owe us" indicates that some of Q's addressees could conceivably remit debts; the debts owed may be associated with unpaid loans, rent by tenants, or bills for goods sold (see Luke 16:1–9; Goodrich 2012b). When bad harvests interfered with his tenants' ability to pay rents, Pliny the Younger (ES 1) lowered their rent (*Ep.* 9.37.2–4; 10.8.5); after the death of a certain Calvina's father, Pliny paid all the outstanding loans of the deceased and forgave what he had owed Pliny (*Ep.* 2.4).[13] Similarly, Ben Sira advocated extending loans even when the prospect of repayment was highly uncertain (Sir 29:1–7; Goff 2013, 77). The Lord's Prayer assumes an audience some of whom are to be placed at least at ES 4–5.

---

[12] Bazzana 2015, 187–202; citation 189; Bazzana's trans. of *OGIS* 156, 13–20.
[13] On Pliny's finances, see Duncan-Jones 1982, 17–59.

Jesus's injunction not to be anxious about the provisioning of food and clothing (Matt 6:25–33 // Luke 12:22–31) is based on an argument from the lesser to the greater (*a minore ad maius*): just as God feeds the ravens and splendidly "clothes" the lilies, how much more will God feed and clothe the hearer. Therefore, Jesus reasons: "Don't be anxious, saying, 'What will we eat?' and 'What will we drink?' and 'What will we wear?'" The theme that God provides for human need is found also in Ps 104:27–28 and 4Q416 2 I–II, 1.22–2.3; Q thus draws on traditional motifs. As Roland Deines (2014, 348–49) notes, this advice can only be directed to those who may reasonably expect to remain at or above subsistence level; if addressed to those at ES 7, who really lack any assurance that they will have access to food, drink, and clothing on a daily basis, this could be taken as insensitive at best and as a form of mockery at worst (see James 2:15–16).

The directive not to be anxious (μὴ μεριμνᾶτε) about one's material circumstances (Matt 6:25–33 // Luke 12:22–31) echoes themes found in Greek and Latin authors. Seneca writes: "It is a bad sort of existence that is spent in apprehension. Whoever has largely surrendered himself to the power of Fortune has made for himself a huge web of disquietude, from which he cannot get free" (*Ep.* 74.5–6; trans. Grummere, LCL). Moreover, Horace writes that "as money grows, it is attended by worry [*cura*] and a craving for more" (*Odes* 3.16; trans. Rudd, LCL). Seneca advocates avoiding anxiety about one's wealth by cultivating a disposition of philosophical detachment, and Horace by constraining desire so that one is content with "just enough" (see Prov 30:8), while Q's Jesus advocates *pistis* ("trust") in God's providence (see ὀλιγόπιστοι; Matt 6:30 // Luke 12:28). Whereas in Q anxiety is associated with securing basic necessities whose procurement was periodically threatened, in Horace it is associated with the pursuit of riches, gold, and luxury items. A wide gulf separates Horace's addressees, the Roman beneficiaries of vast systems of imperial exploitation situated at ES 1 and ES 2, and the addressees of Q, situated at ES 4–6.

The desire to protect and/or augment one's wealth is also described as a form of enslavement in Greco-Roman literature: "he who craves riches feels fear on their account.... In short, he ceases to be master [*dominus*] and becomes a manager [*procurator*]" (Seneca, *Ep.* 14.18; trans. Grummere, LCL, slightly modified). The person who desires to increase his wealth is not served by his business interests but rather serves them as a slave or estate manager. A Q saying expresses a similar sentiment: "No one [i.e., no slave] is able to serve two masters; ... you are not able to serve [δουλεύειν] God and mammon" (Matt 6:24 // Luke 16:13). Seneca understood business interests to imply goals antithetical to those involved in the study of philosophy; in parallel fashion, Q posits that the desire for mammon, a transliteration of the Hebrew (מָמוֹן) or Aramaic (מָמוֹנָא) word for "wealth," is antithetical to the service of Israel's God. The danger attributed to serving as a slave to the interest of wealth accumulation is faced not by the destitute, who are concerned with acquiring daily necessities, but by persons who have both resources and time to direct toward accumulative pursuits, for example, by lending at interest, buying properties, or investing in markets, thus presupposing a situation at least at ES 5 or ES 4.

The Gospel of Matthew

Whereas the economic advice that Jesus offers his addressees in Q could conceivably be followed by persons situated at ES 4 or ES 5, in the Gospel of Matthew, counterfactual economic scenarios advance theological narratives. In what follows, I examine a selection of material appearing only in Matthew (i.e., M material) under the headings of labor, amassing treasure in heaven, hoarding and hiding, and the temple economy.

Labor: Slaves, Tenants, Daily Wage Earners

The parable of the weeds sown in the field in Matthew 13:24–30 deploys economic motifs, albeit in a highly unusual configuration, to develop a theological point. The parable portrays "a man" who sows wheat in a field that he controls: the field is "his" (ἐν τῷ ἀγρῷ αὐτοῦ), and he is referred to as "master of the estate" (οἰκοδεσπότης). While the man sleeps, "enemies" sow darnel (ζιζάνιον; prob. *Lolium temulentum*) in the field; the presence of the weed is later detected and reported to the estate owner by his slaves.[14] The term *zizanion* may be a Semitic loanword; it is identified with the more commonly used Greek term *aira* ("darnel") by both the *Suda* and the *Geoponica* (BDAG, s.v. ζιζάνιον). It is highly unusual that the "master of the estate" himself is portrayed as performing the manual labor of sowing seed, while his agricultural slaves, who would normally be expected to perform such work, are reduced to the role of field inspectors and informants. The unusual allocation of labor is explained in the parable's interpretation: the "master of the estate" serves as a thinly veiled reference to Jesus (Matt 13:37; similarly in Matt 10:25), while the "enemy" refers to Satan (Matt 13:39). As in Matthew 13:1–9, 18–23, Jesus plays the role of the sower; thus the "master of the estate" himself does the planting. The parable's counterfactual allocation of agricultural labor serves as a vehicle for Matthew's theology. The narrative conveys the idea that good and evil, indicated by the wheat and darnel, are mixed until the time of the apocalyptic judgment, another one of Matthew's favored themes (e.g., Matt 13:47–50; 22:10; 25:31–33; see Meier 2016, 195–96).

Two additional parables in which theological motifs similarly color economic descriptions may briefly be summarized. In Matthew 18:23–35, a king wishes to settle accounts with his *oikonomoi*; that is, slaves, freedmen, or free persons entrusted with the operational and fiscal management of an estate (e.g., Xenophon, *Oec.* 1.4; Goodrich 2012a, 71–102). Counterfactual economic aspects of the parable are the products of Matthean theologizing: the "loan" and its unusually high amount—10,000 talents, a sum equivalent to 60 million denarii (Davies and Allison 1988–97, 2:798; by way of comparison, see *Ant.* 17.318–20)—likely derive from the notion that "sin" is analogous to a debt owed to God (Matt 6:12). Moreover, instead of a king, one might have expected to encounter an *oikodespotēs* ("estate owner") or *kyrios* ("master") interacting with his

---

[14] Darnel grows in the same climatic zones as wheat and closely resembles it; it is easily distinguishable from wheat only after the grain ripens. Theophrastus believed that wheat could spontaneously transform into darnel since the weed often appeared in fields in which it was not planted (*Hist. plant.* 8.7.1).

managerial slaves; the "king" of Matthew 18:23 is in fact later replaced by a "master" (Matt 18:32, 34). The out-of-place reference to the king is probably redactional (Davies and Allison 1988–97, 2:796–97) and may be influenced by Matthew 22:1–10 (from Q) and Matthew 22:11–13 (M), where a kingly figure serves as a metaphor for God. Finally, the statement in Matthew 18:34 that the master "handed [the slave] over to the torturers" is a "transparent symbol of eschatological judgment" (Davies and Allison 1988–97, 2:803).

Similarly unexpected economic behavior is seen in the parable of the day laborers in the vineyard in Matthew 20:1–16. All the wage-earning day laborers (ἐργάται) are paid 1 denarius (understood as a typical daily wage for a laborer),[15] regardless of the actual time they spent working. The reference to the "estate owner" and his characterization as "good" offer clues that God is the referent. (God is also the estate owner in Matt 21:33–41 [Luz 1989, 3:39], and Matt 19:17 [see Mark 10:18] implies that God is good.) The concluding statement that the payment (μισθός) should be made "beginning from the last and proceeding to the first" points toward the last judgment (see Matt 19:30; 21:16; on μισθός: Matt 5:12; 6:16; 10:41–42).

Amassing Treasure in Heaven

Nathan Eubank (2013) has shown that Matthew understands sin as a form of debt owed to Israel's God. Performing good deeds such as giving alms resulted in the accrual of "wages" to be "paid" by God in the form of "heavenly treasure," which could be utilized to "pay off" the debt incurred as the result of sin; thus often-repeated claims that "the Matthean Jesus wanted the disciples to forsake any thought of recompense are entirely untenable" (Eubank 2013, 105).

Enduring persecution and slander due to one's association with Jesus results in a "great reward [μισθός] in the heavens" (Matt 5:11–12; derived from Q). Matthew 5:46 implies that love displayed toward one's enemies, instantiated in prayer on behalf of persecutors, results in a heavenly reward. Conversely, engaging in an action to receive honor from humans does not accrue rewards in heaven (Matt 6:1, 2, 5, 16). Matthew 19:21, albeit derived from Mark, indicates that those who give alms accrue treasure in heaven. The notion that one may be rewarded with "treasure in heaven" sometimes assumes a more concrete form, as Jesus's disciples are said to "sit on twelve thrones judging the twelve tribes of Israel" at the time of the apocalyptic "restoration" (ἐν τῇ παλιγγενεσίᾳ); that is, when Jesus as the Danielic Son of Man takes the throne in a newly established theocratic kingdom (Matt 19:28; see Dan 7:13–14; Matt 20:21).

Hoarding and Hiding: Treasure and the Precious Pearl

In light of the interdiction against hoarding in Matthew 6:19–21 (// Luke 12:33–34), it is surprising that hoards of wealth in the form of coinage, precious metals, and luxury items would play a positive role in Matthew. A positive evaluation of wealth in the form of precious metals or coinage stored in a treasure box or chest (θησαυρός) occurs, however, in

---

[15] See n. 9 here.

Matthew 13:44, where the "kingdom of the heavens" is likened to a box of treasure found hidden in a field; to acquire it, the finder joyfully "sells all that he possesses and purchases that field." In Matthew 13:45–46, the kingdom of the heavens is likened to a merchant who, after locating a "very precious" pearl, "sold everything that he had and purchased it." The economic metaphors involving the hiding and finding of treasure and a luxury item (i.e., the pearl) suggest an evaluative system that privileges the pursuit of the "kingdom of the heavens" above all other endeavors (see "God and mammon" earlier here).

Another Matthean logion follows: "Every scribe [γραμματεύς] instructed concerning the kingdom of the heavens [τῇ βασιλείᾳ τῶν οὐρανῶν] is like a man who owns an estate [ἀνθρώπῳ οἰκοδεσπότῃ], who withdraws from his treasure chest[16] things new and old" (Matt 13:51–52). This saying implies that special "instruction" "concerning the kingdom of the heavens" was available to some scribes. Matthew 13:51-52 indicates the manner in which "heavenly" scribal administration was understood: scribes "withdraw" from the "treasure chest" of tradition both older material (παλαιά), including scriptural texts (see, e.g., Matt 1:23; 2:6, 18), and newer material (καινά) recently developed within associations of Jesus-followers (see Matt 9:14–17). The inclusion of this logion suggests that the author of the Gospel of Matthew had knowledge of such scribal groups (or himself belonged to one), which may have been similar to those that produced Q.[17]

The Temple Economy

Matthew expresses considerable interest in the temple economy, including taxation, votive offerings, and the temple as a site of wealth accumulation. In Matthew 17:24–27, Jesus indicates that taxes and tolls are collected not from the families of kings (i.e., "sons") but from subject peoples (i.e., "others"), implying that as "sons" of the God of Israel (see Matt 5:9, 45), he and his disciples are not obliged to pay the annual didrachma to the Jerusalem Temple. In order to appease collection agents, however, he orchestrates a miracle by which Peter is able to extract a stater (equal in value to 2 didrachmas) from the mouth of a fish, enough to pay the temple tax for them both.

The 10 percent tithe on agricultural produce is referred to in Matthew 23:23 (albeit derived from Q [Luke 11:42]; see Deut 14:22; Mal 3:8; Tob 1:7), where Pharisees are said to subsume even spices such as mint, dill, and cumin, which are harvested in small quantities, under the law of tithing. The standard for weighing spices in the Palestinian Talmud is the *kelah* (כְּלָה), a shortened form derived from *'uklah* (עוּכְלָה), "a small measure of capacity" or weight (Jastrow 1992, s.v. כְלָה and עוּכְלָה). Ze'ev Safrai (1994, 146) estimates that the *kelah* equaled between 50 and 100 grams. While paying scrupulous attention to tithing quantities of spices measurable in grams, Matthew's Jesus charges that Pharisees neglect the "weightier matters of the law," justice, mercy, and loyalty.

In the context of a discussion about valid and invalid oaths, Matthew 23:18–19 refers to freewill or thank offerings (see also Matt 5:23–24; 8:4; 15:5), while Matthew 23:16–17

---

[16] Or: "storage room," "magazine," "treasury" (θησαυρός); see Duling 2016.
[17] On the scribes of Q, see Kloppenborg 2000, 200–201; Bazzana 2015. On scribes in Matthew, see Foster 2016.

points to the wealth accumulated at the sanctuary in the form of precious metals. As an indication of the wealth amassed in the temple, Josephus (*Ant.* 14.4.4, 7.1) writes that in 54 BCE, Crassus despoiled the temple of 2,000 talents in coinage, 8,000 talents in gold, and a gold beam weighing 300 minas (1 mina = 1/60 talent). Josephus (*J. W.* 7.148–52, 161–62) describes the spoils taken from the Jerusalem Temple and displayed during Vespasian's triumphal procession in Rome, and depicted on the Arch of Titus (see Fine, Schertz, and Sanders 2017). In sum, economic themes in the Gospel of Matthew tend to be used to illustrate Matthean theological and halakic motifs.

The Gospel of Luke

The speech of Mary, mother of Jesus, introduces a theme that will persist throughout the Gospel of Luke: in an apocalyptic reversal of fortunes, the "hungry will be filled, and the rich [πλουτοῦντας] sent away empty" (Luke 1:46–55). Moreover, the Lukan Jesus understands his own work as a fulfillment of Isaiah 58:6 and 61:1–2: "The Spirit of the Lord is upon me; for this reason, he has anointed me to proclaim glad tidings to the poor [εὐαγγελίσασθαι πτωχοῖς]" (Luke 4:16). Luke 7:22 draws on a congenial saying from Q [see Matt 11:5] to express a similar sentiment: as the result of Jesus's miraculous healings and proclamation, "The poor receive good tidings" (πτωχοὶ εὐαγγελίζονται).

The poor appear again in a parable found only in Luke (16:19–31) in which a certain "rich man" (ἄνθρωπος ... πλούσιος) is described as wearing purple and fine linen, signs of affluence and conspicuous consumption, and "daily celebrating [εὐφραινόμενος] in splendid fashion," implying sumptuous banqueting (see Luke 12:19; Eccl 8:15). Meanwhile a poor man (πτωχός), Lazarus, lay outside the front gate of the rich man's compound hoping to receive some scraps of food. Instead, he himself is fed upon: dogs licked the exudates that emanated from his leprous sores (Luke 16:21). Both men subsequently die, whereupon Lazarus is conducted by angels "to the bosom of Abraham" (εἰς τὸν κόλπον Ἀβραάμ; a banquet scene may be presupposed; see John 13:23),[18] while the unnamed rich man suffers torment in Hades, with no means to quench his severe thirst. Abraham explains the logic of the situation to the rich man: "You received your good things during your life, and Lazarus likewise received bad things, but now he is comforted here, and you are suffering." By this logic, one's reward or punishment in the afterlife is meted out in inverse proportion to the material wealth at one's disposal during life. Consequently, the one who enjoyed an abundant surplus of "good things" during life suffers want (expressed as unquenched thirst) in the afterlife, whereas he who experienced "bad things" during life (i.e., by suffering want) is "comforted" (i.e., by gaining access to surplus) in the hereafter.

Luke's theology of inverse proportionality in the afterlife is in keeping with the Lukan form of the beatitude "Blessed are the poor. ... Blessed are those who hunger

---

[18] See BDAG, s.v. κόλπος.

now, for you will be fed" (Luke 6:20b–21a). The poor are pronounced "blessed" not because of their present circumstances but because their present lack will be recompensed with future abundance. Moreover, Luke's version of the beatitudes adds a woe oracle that finds no parallel in Matthew: "But woe to you who are wealthy [τοῖς πλουσίοις], for you have received your comfort; woe to you who are full now, for you will be hungry" (Luke 6:24–25a). Like the Lazarus narrative, the logion indicates that the present surplus of the wealthy (i.e., "comfort") will be recompensed by future lack (i.e., "hunger").

Given its strong emphasis on the poor, it is notable that the addressees presupposed by the Gospel of Luke seem to range from ES 3 to ES 6; the indigent of ES 7 are talked *about* in the Gospel, but they are rarely talked *to*. At the high end of the economic scale, the elite and very wealthy figures associated with ES 1–2, that is, kings (βασιλεῖς), rulers (ἀρχαί), authorities (ἐξουσίαι), provincial governors (ἡγεμόνες), and civic benefactors (εὐεργέται), are generally viewed as distant figures before whom members of early Christian assemblies could conceivably be brought for examination (Luke 7:25; 10:24; 12:11; 21:12; 22:25; see Pliny the Younger, *Ep.* 10.96). Conversely, the poor of ES 7 appear alongside captives, the blind, the deaf, and the lame (Luke 4:18; 7:22) as persons who could, at least in theory, be invited to dinner parties (Luke 14:13, 21) and who depended on the donations of others for their sustenance (Luke 16:19–31; 18:22; 19:8; but see 21:2). The bulk of the L (i.e., found only in Luke) material in the Gospel, however, concerns persons and groups who have a modest surplus, as the following indicates.

Survey of Direct Addressees in L Narratives

In this section, I examine L material containing second person verb forms—Jesus's direct addresses to individuals or groups in the Gospel—and make inferences about the economic situations of the various (fictive or actual) addressees. In the context of the "Sermon on the Plain," Jesus states: "And if you lend to those from whom you hope to receive, what kind of favor [χάρις] are you doing? Even sinners lend to sinners to receive back the same amount" (Luke 6:34). The saying suggests that loan forgiveness ought to be extended to borrowers; the repayment of the loan is not foregone, however, but relocated and deferred: "Your repayment will be great [ὁ μισθὸς ὑμῶν πολύς], and you will be children of the Most High" (Luke 6:35b). It is not the borrower but God who is imagined as "repaying" the loan by offering a μισθός ("reward") in the apocalyptic future. The ability to extend loans assumes a surplus of resources at ES 5 or higher. If the ability to sustain losses resulting from unrepaid loans without thereby experiencing economic ruin is presupposed, a situation at ES 4 or perhaps even ES 3 is envisioned.

In Luke 6:38, Jesus states: "Give, and it will be given to you; they will place a good measure, pressed down and shaken, spilling over, into the fold of your garment." The logion presupposes a system of reciprocity between friends or neighbors in which grain is the medium of exchange, in amounts small enough to fit into the fold of an outer garment, used as a pocket; this requires only a minimum of ES 5–6.[19] Similarly in Luke 11:5–8, a man who has received a visitor late in the evening asks a neighbor for three loaves of bread to serve his guest; both hospitality and reciprocity are evident. Friends are united by a socioeconomic bond of give and take that Seneca the Younger likened to the "dance of the Graces."[20] Only a minimal surplus is involved in the donation of a few loaves, suggesting ES 5 or 6.

In Luke 10:30–37, a traveler from Samaria cares for an injured person by tending his wounds and paying 2 denarii plus expenses to house and feed the man at an inn. Although Jesus's exhortation to "go and do likewise" is directed specifically toward the legal adviser (νομικός) introduced in Luke 10:25, the parable is almost certainly meant to provide an example to be followed by Luke's addressees. A minimal surplus of a few denarii would be required to "do likewise"; a situation at ES 5 or better is therefore envisioned.

Luke 12:13–15 relates to issues of inheritance, presupposing a situation in which a father owned a house and/or lands to bequeath to his children. The petitioner asks Jesus to "tell" his brother to divide the inheritance with him, apparently wishing to settle his claim out of court. Jesus responds that he has no legal authority in such matters and counsels the man to "be on guard against every form of greed," suggesting that "a person's life does not consist of the abundance of his possessions." The reference to the "abundance of possessions" implies either that the petitioner enjoys a moderate surplus and greedily seeks more (assuming ES 4–5) or that he exists near subsistence and wishes to acquire a surplus by claiming part of the inheritance that had devolved to his elder brother (assuming ES 5–6).

In the context of a banquet scene, Luke's Jesus advises the guests not to sit in the "position of honor" directly to the right of the host at a wedding banquet, since the guest then runs the risk that a more honored invitee may arrive later and he would be forced to move "down" a position to make way for the new arrival, thus suffering humiliation (Luke 14:7–10). Similarly, Luke 14:12, although directed in the narrative to the banquet's Pharisaic host, likely applied also to Luke's own audience: "When you host a morning meal or dinner [ὅταν ποιῇς ἄριστον ἢ δεῖπνον]. . . . When you host a banquet [ὅταν δοχὴν ποιῇς] . . ." (Luke 14:12–14). Hosts are enjoined to invite the poor, the lame, and the blind to dine: "Because they do not have the means to repay you, you will be repaid at the resurrection of the righteous" (Luke 14:14). The saying indicates that debts incurred on earth as the result of unrequited giving will be "repaid" in the apocalyptic future (i.e., "at the resurrection").

In Luke 14:14, those who "do not have the means to repay" are to be invited to banquets in preference to one's "friends, siblings, relatives, and rich neighbors [γείτονας πλουσίους]." The mention of "friends" may imply close neighborly relations (see on Luke 6:38; 11:5–8 earlier), or it may be taken in its more technical sense to indicate a

---

[19] On the "pocket" mentioned, see BDAG, s.v. κόλπος 2.
[20] On the "dance of the Graces" as a metaphor for gifting, see Blanton 2017b, 16–18.

patron-client relationship, as clients (*clientes*) could be euphemistically referred to as friends (*amici*/φίλοι; Saller 1989). Those who would attend and host banquets to which they could conceivably invite "rich neighbors" would fit comfortably within the range of ES 3-4.

Luke 17:7-8 assumes that addressees own slaves who would serve them at table: "Who among you, if you have a slave . . ." (Τίς δὲ ἐξ ὑμῶν δοῦλον ἔχων). Moreover, Jesus's injunctions to "make friends for yourselves using unjust mammon so that when it runs out, you may be welcomed into eternal tents" (Luke 16:9) and to "sell your goods and give alms" (Lk 12:33) both presuppose that addressees control a surplus of resources. Similarly, the advice to "be on guard against dissipation, drunkenness, and the worries of life" (Luke 21:34) in what is likely a Lukan insertion into Q material (Lk 21:34-36 // Matt 24:43-51) applies to those whose business interests threaten to eclipse other aspects of their lives (see on Matt 6:25-33 // Luke 12:22-31 earlier; also Luke 14:15-20). The reference to "dissipation and drunkenness" implies both surplus resources and the leisure to enjoy them. (See Luke 15:11-31; also Rom 13:13; Gal 5:21, where μέθη, "drunkenness," is paired with κώμη, "carousing," recalling *kōmos* scenes described in Greek literature and depicted on vases.)[21] These sayings pertain to persons situated at ES 4 or better, at least some of whom probably owned slaves. Surplus resources are also assumed in Jesus's exhortation to give alms in Luke 12:33 (similarly Luke 11:41, unless it is metaphorical).

The L material briefly surveyed here suggests that the disposition of surplus resources among those at ES 3-6 on the Friesen-Longenecker economy scale is of special interest to the author/editor of this material. Aside from Luke 6:20, which many scholars attribute to Q, the poor are not directly addressed in the Gospel. The poor are typically referred to in the third person ("they") and do not appear as direct addressees (e.g., Luke 14:21; 16:20); they are instead the recipients of the addressees' largesse (Luke 14:13; 18:22; 19:8).

If one plausibly supposes that hortatory material addressed to characters in the narrative is meant to apply to the immediate audience of the Gospel of Luke, then it follows that most or all members of the audience fall within the categories of ES 3-6. This is supported by the fact that the only specifically named addressee, Theophilus (whether an actual or fictive person), is addressed like a literary patron ("most excellent"; κράτιστε Θεόφιλε) who had previously received some "instruction" (κατηχήθης; the term may carry overtones of catechesis) in early Christian traditions (Luke 1:1-4).[22] The indication in Luke 1:4 that the Gospel itself is intended to further Theophilus's instruction suggests that its hortatory material is capable of application by the Lukan audience. The "economic profile" of the Lukan assembly would then be similar to but slightly

---

[21] For example: Komos scene, black-figure amphora, Vulci, c. 560 BCE, Staatliche Antikensammlungen (Inv. 1432), Wikimedia Commons: https://en.wikipedia.org/wiki/Komos#/media/File:Komos_Staatliche_Antikensammlungen_1432.jpg.

[22] On Theophilus: Bovon 2002-13, 1:9, 22-23; Fitzmyer 1981, 1:288-89, 299-300; Bock 1994, 1:63-64. On "instruction": BDAG, s.v. κατηχέω (see Rom 2:18; Acts 18:25); Bock 1994, 1:65-66.

higher than those posited for Pauline assemblies in the 50s and 60s CE (i.e., ES 4–6; see Friesen 2004; Longenecker 2010; Brookins 2017, 83).

The Lukan Jesus teaches that surplus ought not be retained solely for oneself or one's immediate household (see Luke 12:13–21, where a "rich man" is censured for "storing up for himself" [θησαυρίζων ἑαυτῷ]) but rather should be passed along to the poor through benefaction, most notably through almsgiving and invitations to dine. The picture is complicated, however, by the fact that, except for the counterfactual image presented in the parable in Luke 14:16–24, the poor are never said to be present at any dinner attended by Jesus and his disciples. Moreover, all mention of the poor is absent in the book of Acts, where donations are directed either internally to members of early Christian assemblies, which did not typically include persons at ES 7 (Acts 4:32–5:11; 11:29–30), or to the Jewish people in the form of alms (Acts 10:2, 4, 31; 24:7), although in one case the recipients are unclear (Acts 10:36). This suggests that the function of Lukan narratives about giving to the poor were not designed primarily to encourage addressees to give to persons at ES 7 but instead to give to assemblies of Jesus-devotees, with Acts 4:32–5:11 providing the paradigmatic examples. (Ananias and Sapphira are struck dead for withholding funds from the community.)

In light of this, the Lukan narratives about the poor, the theology of inverse proportionality, and the repeated exhortations to give without return all appear to serve a single purpose: to spur addressees at ES 3–6 to reflect on what surplus they controlled and to channel that surplus toward assemblies of Jesus-devotees. These assemblies contained members who could themselves be labeled "poor," either because they were relatively worse off than well-placed donors (e.g., at ES 5–6 rather than ES 3–4) or because they worked for a living at ES 4–6. One may recall that working persons at ES 4–6, who would make up the majority of most early Christian assemblies, were typically described as "poor" in the sources. Greg Woolf (2006, 99) notes that "eloquent poets [like Martial], whose education and manners proclaim their status, play at paupers to amuse and tease their hosts and to extract from them a little of the wealth about which they have been made to feel uneasy." Judging from the narratives in Luke-Acts, it appears that evangelists could deploy similar tactics to elicit donations among givers and recipients placed far lower on the economic scale.

Concluding Remarks

This brief survey indicates that economic issues play important roles in Mark, Q, Matthew, and Luke. Because the binary classification system involving "rich" and "poor" occludes more than it reveals, this essay has employed the Friesen-Longenecker economic scale in the hope that its use might introduce greater precision into discussions about economic issues in the Synoptic Gospels. The use of this scale helps to expose subtler economic differences between, for example, the Markan Jesus, situated at ES 5–6, and James and John, the sons of Zebedee, situated at ES 4. By another measure, all three could be classified as "poor," but this would obscure the slight difference in the control of resources as Mark portrays it. The use of the economic scale likewise reveals that Luke includes material relevant to persons situated at ES 3–6, whereas Q, for example, includes material relevant to those situated at ES 4–6. Luke seems to envision an audience whose economic concerns reflect a slightly greater degree of affluence. This difference may be attributed in part to Q's rural setting versus Luke's urban milieu, although more work needs to be done to address this issue.[23] Additional work also needs to be done to assess the economic situation presupposed for Matthew's addressees. Despite its penchant for counterfactual economic scenarios, it is likely that an investigation of the exhortations in Matthew's Gospel would, as with the Gospel of Luke and Q, yield useful information.

Moreover, economic concerns animate Q's exhortations, which could feasibly be followed by villagers living at ES 4–6, Matthew's counterfactual economic scenarios that contribute to the elaboration of theological narratives, Luke's emphasis on the poor and theology of inverse proportionality, and Mark's concession that the *fiscus Iudaicus* should be paid to Rome. Just as each Gospel writer developed a particular theological agenda—a fact that has long been recognized—each also promoted a distinctive economic agenda, and the two are in fact inseparable aspects of "the social order in which all human practice is immersed."[24]

References

Arnal, William E. 2001. *Jesus and the Village Scribes: Galilean Conflicts and the Setting of Q*. Minneapolis: Fortress.

Bang, Peter Fibiger. 2007. "Trade and Empire: In Search of Organizing Concepts for the Roman Economy." *Past and Present* 195: 3–54.

Bang, Peter Fibiger. 2012. "Predation." In *The Cambridge Companion to the Roman Economy*, edited by Walter Scheidel, 197–217. Cambridge: Cambridge University Press.

Bazzana, Giovanni B. 2015. *Kingdom of Bureaucracy: The Political Theology of Village Scribes in the Sayings Gospel Q*. BETL 274. Leuven: Peeters.

Bazzana, Giovanni B. 2017. "From *Thesauroi* to Purses: Wealth and Poverty between Q and Luke." In *Luke on Jesus, Paul and Christianity: What Did He Really Know?*, edited by Joseph Verheyden and John S. Kloppenborg, BTS 29, 193–217. Leuven: Peeters.

Bergmann, Claudia D. 2016. "Identity on the Menu: Imaginary Meals and Ideas of the World-to-Come in Jewish Apocalyptic Writings." In *Burial Rituals, Ideas of Afterlife, and the Individual in the Hellenistic World and the Roman Empire*, edited by Katharina Waldner, Wolfgang Spickermann, and Richard Gordon, 167–88. Stuttgart: Steiner.

Blanton, Thomas R., IV. 2017a. "The Economic Functions of Gift Exchange in Pauline Assemblies." In *Paul and Economics: A Handbook*, edited by Thomas R. Blanton IV and Raymond Pickett, 279–306. Minneapolis: Fortress.

---

[23] The detailed treatment of Bazzana (2017) provides a foundation for further study.
[24] Citation from Bourdieu 2005, 1, discussing the category "economy."

Blanton, Thomas R., IV. 2017b. *A Spiritual Economy: Gift Exchange in the Letters of Paul of Tarsus*. Synkrisis: Comparative Approaches to Early Christianity in Greco-Roman Context. New Haven: Yale University Press.

Blanton, Thomas R., IV, and David B. Hollander. 2019. "The Extramercantile Economy: An Assessment of the New Institutional Economics Paradigm in Relation to Recent Studies of Ancient Greece and Rome." In *The Extramercantile Economies of Greek and Roman Cities: New Perspectives on the Economic History of Classical Antiquity*, edited by David B. Hollander, Thomas R. Blanton IV, and John T. Fitzgerald, 8–28. London: Routledge.

Bock, Darrell L. 1994. *Luke*. 2 vols. BECNT 3A–B. Grand Rapids: Baker Books.

Boer, Roland. 2015. *The Sacred Economy of Ancient Israel*. LAI. Louisville: Westminster John Knox.

Boer, Roland, and Christina Petterson. 2017. *Time of Troubles: A New Economic Framework for Early Christianity*. Minneapolis: Fortress.

Bourdieu, Pierre. 2005. *The Social Structures of the Economy*. Translated by Chris Turner. Malden, MA: Polity.

Bovon, François. 2002–13. *Luke: A Commentary on the Gospel of Luke*. 3 vols. Hermeneia. Translated by Christine M. Thomas. Minneapolis: Fortress.

Brookins, Timothy A. 2017. "Economic Profiling of Early Christian Assemblies." In *Paul and Economics: A Handbook*, edited by Thomas R. Blanton IV and Raymond Pickett, 57–88. Minneapolis: Fortress.

Czajkowski, Kimberly. 2017. *Localized Law: The Babatha and Salome Komaise Archives*. Oxford Studies in Roman Society and Law. Oxford: Oxford University Press.

Dalton, George. 1971. Introduction to *Primitive, Archaic, and Modern Economies: Essays of Karl Polanyi*. Edited by George Dalton. Boston: Beacon.

Davies, W. D., and Dale C. Allison, Jr. 1988–97. *The Gospel According to Saint Matthew*. 3 vols. ICC. Edinburgh: T&T Clark.

Deines, Roland. 2014. "God or Mammon: The Danger of Wealth in the Jesus Tradition and in the Epistle of James." In *Anthropologie und Ethik im Frühjudentum und im Neuen Testament: Wechselseitige Wahrnehmungen*, edited by Matthias Konradt und Esther Schläpfer, 327–85. Tübingen: Mohr Siebeck.

Duling, Dennis C. 2016. "The Scribe 'Disciplined' for the Kingdom of the Heavens and the ΘΗΣΑΥΡΟΣ of the Head of the Household (Matthew 13,52)." In *Scribal Practices and Social Structures among Jesus Adherents: Essays in Honor of John S. Kloppenborg*, edited by William E. Arnal, Richard S. Ascough, Robert A. Derenbacker, Jr., and Philip A. Harland, BETL 285, 351–76. Leuven: Peeters.

Duncan-Jones, Richard. 1982. *The Economy of the Roman Empire: Quantitative Studies*. 2nd ed. Cambridge: Cambridge University Press.

Earle, Timothy. 2008. "Economic Anthropology." In *The New Palgrave Dictionary of Economics*, 2nd ed., vol. 2, edited by Steven N. Durlauf and Lawrence E. Blume, 1538–43. London: Palgrave Macmillan.

Eubank, Nathan. 2013. *Wages of Cross-Bearing and Debt of Sin: The Economy of Heaven in Matthew's Gospel*. BZNW 196. Berlin: De Gruyter.

Fiensy, David A. 2014. *Christian Origins and the Ancient Economy*. Eugene, OR: Cascade.

Fine, Steven, Peter J. Schertz, and Donald H. Sanders. 2017. "True Colors: Digital Reconstruction Restores Original Brilliance to the Arch of Titus." *BAR* 40, no. 3: 28–35, 60–61.

Firmage, Edwin. 1992. "Zoology (Fauna)." *ABD* 6: 1109–67.

Fitzgerald, John T. 2019. "Early Greek Economic Thought." In *The Extramercantile Economies of Greek and Roman Cities: New Perspectives on the Economic History of Classical Antiquity*, edited by David B. Hollander, Thomas R. Blanton IV, and John T. Fitzgerald, 29–50. London: Routledge.

Fitzmyer, Joseph A. 1981. *The Gospel according to Luke: Introduction, Translation, and Notes*. 2 vols. AB. Garden City, NY: Doubleday.

Fleddermann, Harry T. 2005. *Q: A Reconstruction and Commentary*. BTS. Leuven: Peeters.

Foster, Paul. 2016. "Scribes and Scribalism in Matthew's Gospel." In *Scribal Practices and Social Structures among Jesus Adherents: Essays in Honor of John S. Kloppenborg*, edited by William E. Arnal, Richard S. Ascough, Robert A. Derenbacker, Jr., and Philip A. Harland, BETL 285, 157–82. Leuven: Peeters.

Friesen, Steven J. 2004. "Poverty in Pauline Studies: Beyond the So-Called New Consensus." *JSNT* 26, no. 3: 323–61.

Goff, Matthew J. 2013. *4QInstruction*. Atlanta: Society of Biblical Literature.

Goodrich, John K. 2012a. *Paul as an Administrator of God in 1 Corinthians*. SNTSMS 152. Cambridge: Cambridge University Press.

Goodrich, John K. 2012b. "Voluntary Debt Remission and the Parable of the Unjust Steward (Luke 16:1–13)." *JBL* 131, no. 3: 547–66.

Graham, E.-J. 2006. "Discarding the Destitute: Ancient and Modern Attitudes towards Burial Practices and Memory Preservation amongst the Lower Classes of Rome." In *TRAC 2005: Proceedings of the Fifteenth Annual Theoretical Roman Archaeology Conference, Birmingham 2005*, edited by Ben Croxford, Helen Goodchild, Jason Lucas, and Nick Ray, 57–72. Oxford: Oxbow Books.

Guelich, Robert A. 1989. *Mark 1:1–8:26*. WBC 34A. Dallas: Word Books.

Hann, Chris, and Keith Hart. 2011. *Economic Anthropology: History, Ethnography, Critique*. Cambridge: Polity.

Hanson, Ann Ellis. 2005. "The Widow Babatha and the Poor Orphan Boy." In *Law in the Documents of the Judean Desert*, edited by Ranon Katzoff and David Schaps, JSJSup 96, 85–103. Leiden: Brill.

Heinen, Heinz. 1990. "Göttliche Sitometrie: Beobachtungen zur Brotbitte des Vaterunsers." *TTZ* 99: 72–79.

Horace. *Odes and Epodes*. 2015. Translated by Niall Rudd. LCL. Cambridge, MA: Harvard University Press.

Incignieri, Brian J. 2003. *The Gospel to the Romans: The Setting and Rhetoric of Mark's Gospel*. BibInt 65. Leiden: Brill.

Jastrow, Marcus. 1992. *A Dictionary of the Targumim, the Talmud Babli and Yerushalmi, and the Midrashic Literature: With an Index of Scriptural Quotations*. New York: Judaica Press.

Kay, Philip. 2014. *Rome's Economic Revolution*. Oxford: Oxford University Press.

Keddie, G. Anthony. 2018. *Revelations of Ideology: Apocalyptic Class Politics in Early Roman Palestine*. JSJSup 189. Leiden: Brill.

Kelhoffer, James A. 2005. *The Diet of John the Baptist*. WUNT 176. Tübingen: Mohr Siebeck.

Kloppenborg, John S. 2000. *Excavating Q: The History and Setting of the Sayings Gospel*. Minneapolis: Fortress.

Kloppenborg, John S. 2018. "Jesus, Fishermen and Tax Collectors: Papyrology and the Construction of the Ancient Economy of Roman Palestine." *ETL* 94, no. 4: 571–99.

Leshem, Dotan. 2014. "The Ancient Art of Economics." *European Journal of the History of Economic Thought* 21, no. 2: 1–29.

Lewis, Naphtali. 1989. *The Documents from the Bar Kokhba Period in the Cave of Letters*. JDS. Edited by Naphtali Lewis, Yigael Yadin, and Jonas C. Greenfield. Jerusalem: Jerusalem Exploration Society.

Liu, Jinyu. 2017. "Urban Poverty in the Roman Empire: Material Conditions." In *Paul and Economics: A Handbook*, edited by Thomas R. Blanton IV and Raymond Pickett, 23–56. Minneapolis: Fortress.

Longenecker, Bruce W. 2010. *Remember the Poor: Paul, Poverty, and the Greco-Roman World*. Grand Rapids: Eerdmans.

Luz, Ulrich. 1989. *Matthew: A Commentary*. Translated by James E. Crouch. Hermeneia. 3 vols. Minneapolis: Fortress.

Meier, John P. 2016. *Probing the Authenticity of the Parables*. Vol. 5 of *A Marginal Jew: Rethinking the Historical Jesus*. New Haven: Yale University Press.

Nickelsburg, George W. E. 2001. *1 Enoch 1: A Commentary on the Book of 1 Enoch Chapters 1–36; 81–108*. Hermeneia. Minneapolis: Fortress.

North, Douglass C. 1990. *Institutions, Institutional Change and Economic Performance*. Cambridge: Cambridge University Press.

North, Douglass C. 1981. *Structure and Change in Economic History*. New York: Norton.

Oakes, Peter. 2004. "Constructing Poverty Scales for Graeco-Roman Society: A Response to Steven Friesen's 'Poverty in Pauline Studies.'" *JSNT* 26: 367–71.

Oakes, Peter. 2009. *Reading Romans in Pompeii: Paul's Letter at Ground Level*. Minneapolis: Fortress.

Osiek, Caroyln. 2009. "The Politics of Patronage and the Politics of Kinship: The Meeting of the Ways." *BTB* 39, no. 3: 143–52.

Parkin, Anneliese. 2006. "'You Do Him No Service': An Exploration of Pagan Almsgiving." In *Poverty in the Roman World*, edited by Margaret Atkins and Robin Osborne, 60–82. Cambridge: Cambridge University Press.

Pickett, Raymond. 2017. Introduction to *Paul and Economics: A Handbook*, edited by Thomas R. Blanton IV and Raymond Pickett, xiii–xxxvi. Minneapolis: Fortress.

Safrai, Ze'ev. 1994. *The Economy of Roman Palestine*. London: Routledge.

Saller, Richard. 1989. "Patronage and Friendship in Early Imperial Rome: Drawing the Distinction." In *Patronage in Ancient Society*, edited by Andrew Wallace-Hadrill, 49–62. London: Routledge.

Scheidel, Walter. 2005. "Human Mobility in Roman Italy, II: The Slave Population." *JRS* 95: 64–79.

Scheidel, Walter. 2006. "Stratification, Deprivation, and Quality of Life." In *Poverty in the Roman World*, edited by Margaret Atkins and Robin Osborne, 40–59. Cambridge: Cambridge University Press.

Scheidel, Walter, and Steven J. Friesen. 2009. "The Size of the Economy and the Distribution of Income in the Roman Empire." *JRS* 99: 61–91.

Scheidel, Walter, Ian Morris, and Richard P. Saller, eds. 2008. *The Cambridge Economic History of the Greco-Roman World*. Cambridge: Cambridge University Press.

Scott, James C. 1976. *The Moral Economy of the Peasant: Rebellion and Subsistence in Southeast Asia*. New Haven: Yale University Press.

Seneca the Younger. 1920. *Epistles*. Translated by Richard M. Grummere. 3 vols. LCL. Cambridge, MA: Harvard University Press.

Strange, James F. 2014. "The Galilean Road System." In *Life, Culture, and Society*, vol. 1 of *Galilee in the Late Second Temple and Mishnaic Periods*, edited by David A. Fiensy and James Riley Strange, 263–71. Minneapolis: Fortress.

Temin, Peter. 2001. "A Market Economy in the Early Roman Empire." *JRS* 91: 169–81.

Troche, Facundo Daniel. 2015. "Il sistema della pesca nel lago di Galilea al tempo di Gesù: Indagine sulla base dei papiri documentari e dei dati archeologici e letterari." PhD diss., Università di Bologna.

Udoh, Fabian E. 2005. *To Caesar What Is Caesar's: Tribute, Taxes, and Imperial Administration in Early Roman Palestine (63 B.C.E.–70 C.E.)*. BJS 343. Providence, RI: Brown Judaic Studies.

Welborn, L. L. 2012. Review of *Remember the Poor: Paul, Poverty, and the Greco-Roman World*, by Bruce W. Longenecker. *RBL* 07/2012. http://www.bookreviews.org/pdf/7899_9350.pdf.

Welborn, L. L. 2017. "Marxism and Capitalism in Pauline Studies." In *Paul and Economics: A Handbook*, edited by Thomas R. Blanton IV and Raymond Pickett, 361–96. Minneapolis: Fortress.

Woolf, Greg. 2006. "Writing Poverty in Rome." In *Poverty in the Roman World*, edited by Margaret Atkins and Robin Osborne, 83–99. Cambridge: Cambridge University Press.

Yarbro Collins, Adela. 2007. *Mark: A Commentary*. Hermeneia. Minneapolis: Fortress.

Zapata Meza, Marcela, ed. 2013. "El Proyecto arqueológico Magdala: Interpretaciones preliminaires bajo una perspectiva interdisciplinar." Special issue, *El Pensador monográficos* 5, no. 1. https://issuu.com/revistaelpensador/docs/el_pensador_n___5.

CHAPTER 17

TRAVEL AND ITINERANCY

TIMOTHY LUCKRITZ MARQUIS

INTRODUCTION

THE travels of Jesus and his followers drive the narratives of the Synoptic Gospels perhaps more than any other plot point. In addition, the sayings of Jesus that make up much of the Synoptic tradition frequently speak of travel, homelessness, departure from households, and hospitality toward strangers. Moreover, travel conditioned both the origin and spread of the Synoptic traditions and the way in which those traditions constructed the social imaginary of the people who first produced and used them. Yet while travel has played a central role in some renowned scholarly reconstructions of the early history and ideologies of the first Christ-believers, it is often taken for granted as a major factor in the origins and goals of earliest Christian traditions. Travel as a theme both pervades and eludes interpretation of the Gospels for the same reasons it complicates study in other contexts.

Focusing simply on travel in the first century CE, ancient historian Laurens Tacoma notes that travel and migration under the Roman Empire was "an unruly phenomenon indeed" (2016, 48), blurring boundaries between voluntary and forced mobility, permanent and temporary migration, and journeys between relatively local and distant settlements. Similarly, in reading the Synoptic tradition, scholars debate whether passages depicting travel refer to actual practices or to idealized situations, to planned itineraries or to homeless wandering, to material realities or to figurative, narrative constructs. In examining Synoptic travel, this essay in part argues that this elusiveness of narrative and material travel (as in any context, but perhaps especially in gospel traditions) stems from the way in which human mobility bridges on the one hand perceived spheres of social, material, and geographic context and on the other hand social imagination. For this reason, theorizing travel in the Synoptics can be understood as a subset of a more widespread effort in the humanities and social sciences to schematize more precisely the ways in which material realities, social formations, and ideologies organize social life and meaning. Moreover, the social and ideological assemblages generated at Christian origins, in part produced through their complex engagements with Roman material and ideological domination, can be seen as continuing to travel through history, in turn guiding and generating new social imaginaries, such as the Western concept of universality and its offshoots.

After putting forth some main observations about early Christian travel within its ancient contexts, I synthesize and contribute to the expansive debate about the role of itinerancy within the Synoptic sayings source ("Q"), treating the question as a microcosm of the larger issue of travel at the roots of the Jesus tradition. I move on to interpret how travel as a literary trope allows Mark, Matthew, and Luke to trace their own, new epistemological and social paths, paths that influence later Christian traditions and later Western ideological constructs.

Travel: Roman Empire and Galilee

Assessment of how travel affected the production, dissemination, and reception of the Synoptic traditions must take into account local and international socioeconomic contexts—that is, both the Galilean and Judean roots of Jesus traditions and their more far-flung dispersion as reflected in the production of the Synoptic Gospels themselves. The relative ease, speed, and safety of travel that occasioned the expansion of Roman rule across the Mediterranean did not immediately impact the rural environment of first-century Galilee. International flows of trade did not require construction of major Roman roads through the region (Chancey 2002, 160). Many reconstructions of Galilean village social life depict small groups of houses cooperatively working agricultural fields within a five-to-ten-mile radius around the residential grouping (the radius kept close to maximize crop yields in relation to feed amounts consumed by beasts of burden walking out to the fields they worked; see Arnal 2001, 115–19). In such a compact environment, the journeys from village to village reflected in numerous passages of the Synoptic tradition would, in reality, be so short as to have the character of "morning walks" (to cite the famous characterization in Kloppenborg 1993, 22). At the same time, the close-knit nature of village work and culture may well have meant that visitors would have been received, even if with hospitality, as strangers and outsiders, regardless of distance traveled (Destro and Pesce 2012, 102–3).

Scholarship on the historical Jesus and the earliest spread of his traditions has focused on understanding the impact of Galilean urbanization projects during the period—specifically, the renovation of Sepphoris (around 3 BCE) and construction of Tiberias (around 18 CE). Jonathan Reed has argued (2010) that normal demographic instability experienced in premodern societies would have been exacerbated by the introduction and expansion of urban centers, as the increased urban mortality rate caused by pathogen vectors in areas with higher population density would have drained population from the surrounding villages. The migration of rural labor forces to fill opportunities in Sepphoris or Tiberias may well have disrupted village networks, both in terms of local cultures as well as in terms of Roman local administration. In the absence of textual and epigraphic evidence for rural mobility in most places in the Roman world (Tacoma 2016; Zerbini 2016), such demographic modeling becomes vital for reconstructing travel and migration patterns outside urban centers.

On a more international level, the increased ease of travel under Rome, which could similarly be framed as a type of instability, is usually described as economic and social "opportunity" in the historical record and more modern historiography. As in analysis of intraregional mobility, international migration is often seen as conditioned by various "push-pull factors" that encourage uprooting and resettling. The aforementioned notion that cities would pull migration to themselves due to higher mortality rates (referred to as "urban graveyard theory") takes on different significance when discussing migration across further distances. Specifically, a modification of the theory holds that the gender and marital status of travelers impacted mobility far more than pathogen vectors; migrants tended to be male, single, and without families, and were so transient (or sufficiently remained at the outskirts of city society) that they did not marry local inhabitants and procreate. They thus died at a rate that outstripped the birth rates of local families. (See the discussion in Tacoma 2016, 144–52.) While historians and demographers debate the global validity of "urban graveyard theory" in its various forms, the ways in which it attempts to coordinate mortality, procreation, sexuality, economics, and mobility should prompt historiographers of earliest Christianity to confront the number of social factors implicated in travel and mobility. Specifically, researchers must confront how Jesus-sayings on itinerancy, marriage, economics, and life and death must be considered as a complex nexus heavily impacted by travel and migration.

Across the Mediterranean, politicians, merchants, preachers, and pilgrims found increased opportunity to travel on safer seas and more reliable roads. And while the arrival and departure of travelers was common in a city, strangers and ethnic minorities would have been a noticeable presence. Monumental inscriptions from wealthy travelers bear witness to outsiders trying to gain a foothold in local society (Bitner 2015; Nasrallah 2017). Voluntary societies dedicated to foreign communities in diaspora provided support for newcomers but also allowed individuals and groups to maintain foreign ethnic identities after many generations in a city (Harland 2013, 26–28; Tacoma 2016, 232–37). Indeed, it was in urban environments that traveling outsiders made the biggest mark on the historical record (whether in documents or inscriptions), not simply due to the amount of evidence they left to extol their impacts on their new homes but also because urbanites were more likely to name prominently in documents and inscriptions their cities of origin and foreign inhabitation (Zerbini 2016). Even on a material level, ideological presentations conditioned how travelers impacted the social landscape.

Regardless of schemata for mobility, there are always, as Tacoma (2016) has noted, overlapping spectrums of travel activity: journeys that are more or less distant, more or less circular, more or less motivated by economic necessity, more or less voluntary. It was up to actual travelers, managing their social contexts, to present both their travels and themselves as travelers as a way of reacting to and manipulating their surroundings. The many facets of mobility force upon scholars of early Christianity new methodologies for imagining travel and its ideological presentation in the earliest literary sources, however reconstructed. Tracing travel in the Synoptic tradition offers an opportunity for such theorization.

Q, THE SYNOPTICS, AND ITINERANCY

Itinerancy has, at times, lain at the heart of major reconstructions of the Synoptic sources, and particularly so in the last 150 years of discussion of the hypothetical Synoptic sayings source.[1] Adolf von Harnack's strong reading—heavily influenced by the recent discovery of a complete copy of the Didache and Max Weber's theories of "charismatic" leadership—depicted wandering "prophets, teachers, and apostles" (the Didache's language) who must have produced and used the sayings source (Harnack 1908). Harnack's theory took new form in the 1970s in Gerd Theissen's introduction of social-historical approaches to Christian origins. For Theissen, the social emergence of the Jesus movement and its literature is best explained by the emergence of "wandering radicals" who rejected housing and property in service of Christ's message. This rejection of material support and sustenance is crucial for his depiction, in that it reads quite literally Synoptic injunctions to leave behind home and possessions as reflecting a deliberate, voluntary poverty and wandering among the first Jesus preachers. Like Cynic philosophers of the day (a comparison later developed by many others; see Downing 1992), Q preachers intentionally abandoned possessions, wandered homeless, and challenged convention with their teachings and behavior.

Critiques of Theissen's thesis took at least a couple of forms. Richard Horsley saw in the reconstruction, in part, a continuation of liberal, academic, and late-capitalist ideals of social change through radical individualism (Horsley 1991, 1999) that, like Harnack, circularly relied on a Weberian reading of the Didache when Weber's reading had itself been inspired by the Didache's discovery (Draper 1991). Like most other ancient individuals, the Q preachers must have been necessarily poor by virtue of the wider socioeconomic environment and Roman patterns of oppression (Horsley 1999; Schottroff and Stegemann 1986). Less like Cynic philosophers and more akin to the prophets of Jewish scriptural tradition, the Q people sought the restoration of Israel rather than radical, individualistic moral conversion. Rather than abandon their homes, they strove to rehabilitate their communities. In such a context, the oral transmission of gnomic

---

[1] I assume the Four Source Hypothesis as a working solution to the Synoptic Problem, including the positing of Q as lying behind "double-tradition" material. At times, however, I will note how the Farrer Hypothesis (which has increased in scholarly support over the past couple of decades) might affect my readings. Since much of the discussion of early Jesus-movement itinerancy centers around reconstructions and contextualizations of Q, discussion of the Q scholarship is, at the very least, unavoidable for the purposes of this essay.

wisdom circulated among Galilean villages as an attempt to construct a social alternative to the elite, scribal, Judean-Roman coalition of oppression.

Similar critiques were leveled by scholars variously associated with the International Q Project who questioned the material, contextual likelihood of a group of wandering disciples spreading and expounding upon inspired, orally disseminated sayings (Arnal 2001, 2013; Kloppenborg 1993;). Since reconstructions of Q and its use by Matthew and Luke necessitate a text (and, indeed, something with some literary structure as opposed to a random set of notes), Kloppenborg and followers posit that the Q people must have had access to some resources to support the materials and education needed for writing and, moreover, were unlikely to be "radically" itinerant (a modifier they read as incoherent in their reconstruction), as such a lifestyle would seem to impede literary aspirations (Arnal 2013, 44). Any possible references to travel (e.g., in Q 9:57–10:24) refer to planned journeys and not radical homelessness, or else use the figure of homelessness to drive home hyperbolically the singular focus required by the gospel and its dissemination. Thus, references to destitution and transience in Q are "metaphors" (Arnal 2013, 42–43) meant to be understood as "ideological," (37), and should be regarded as "superficial" (Arnal 2001, 61), "hyperbole" (92), and "ethereal" (101). Such figures were instead used rhetorically by settled, scribal administrators who were firmly ensconced in the village settings their writings largely address.

Work on Q over the past few decades has rightly attempted to read its rhetorical program in light of material realities. Yet too often such studies proceed as if rhetoric or ideology can be extracted from social context. The notion that metaphor or ideology can be an ethereal fog blown away by the scholar to reveal a stable, material truth misconstrues the social makeup of reality. A project of persuasion cannot be divorced from social context any more than future is disconnected from present. While the language of equality surely must be understood as aspirational rhetoric, critiques of Theissen's "radical itinerancy" oddly conflate Q's program with descriptions of the material realia of the time. As such, Theissen's instinct that earliest preachers used their lifestyle to reach for a future incommensurate with their present circumstances while working in and through those same circumstances, and that this reaching forward through action was a central aspect both of their program of persuasion and of their lives lived on the ground, deserves revisiting. Such a question demands theorization of materialism and imagination, of context and (re)presentation, of life and lifestyle. Since Theissen, scholars have theorized this tension with recourse to queer theory and subversive performativity (see Moxnes 2003), to the role of political theology in constructing social cohesion (see Bazzana 2015), to Lacanian sublimation (see Myles 2014 on homelessness in Matthew), to more general attempts to read how Q scribes might have attempted to represent a marginalized community through productively ambiguous rhetorical programs (Rollens 2014).

One example of this work can be found in the scholarly tracing of one possible subject position behind the production of this literature (again, with specific focus on Q).[2] Kloppenborg (1993) once briefly suggested that the social role of κωμογραμματεύς or

---

[2] I think it is clear, however, that the production of the Synoptic literary tradition, and, indeed, the production of the earliest, non-Pauline textual traditions, demands the sort of social type outlined here,

"village scribe," best known from Ptolemaic Egyptian documentary papyri, would encapsulate the sorts of material requirements of a producer of such literature. This suggestion was later developed by William Arnal (2001; 2013) and Willi Braun (1999) but recently found extensive exploration in a book by Giovanni Bazzana (2015). The village scribe thesis provides a literate functionary who is nevertheless fully ensconced in village life. Such a scribe was often simply a villager who participated in agricultural work yet monitored and reported on a circuit of villages for the provincial administration as the first line of an empire's or kingdom's bureaucracy. Inspection tours of a scribe's village circuit were a planned, official aspect of the scribe's job, as he recorded accounts of agricultural yields, fielded complaints from locals about abuses suffered from fellow villagers and other administrators, and promised the protection (even σωτηρία) of the βασιλεία, a promise in which local inhabitants could place their trust or πίστις.

In terms of status (if not class, per se), such officials can be termed "middling" in a way that resonates with Theissen's proclivity toward writers somewhere in between poverty and power. If village scribes are behind the production of Q, their situation cannot be explained in terms of voluntary impoverishment but rather displacement caused by the shifting Herodian administration of the region (largely through the urbanization of Sepphoris and Tiberias), which may have deprived the scribes of their positions. Such displacement could have been the first wave of Roman readministration of the region that accompanied increased urbanization (Arnal 2013, 67–68; Bazzana 2015, 53).

Positing κωμογραμματεῖς as the producers and disseminators of the Synoptic sayings material makes sense of a number of the material problems the sayings present. In addition to the Q mission speech (at its greatest extent, partitioned off as Q 9:57–10:24), many of the sayings Q scholars have read as reflecting a sedentary village lifestyle actually work better as appeals from outsiders for hospitality. After this mission discourse, Jesus teaches the disciples how to pray (complete with a plea for "daily bread"), while the subsequent instructions about asking and trusting God depict villagers receiving people knocking on doors and expecting welcome (Q 11:5–10). Finally, Q compares following Jesus not simply to the rejection of household: "Whoever does not hate father and mother cannot be my disciple. And whoever does not hate son and daughter cannot be my disciple. Whoever does not take up his cross and follow after me cannot be my disciple" (Q 14:26–27). In multiple sections of Q, discipleship occurs not just on the road but also apart from homes, sustenance, and lodging. As in the readings of Moxnes (2003), the abandonment of the household and reliance on hospitality during a divinely sanctioned, "bureaucratic" tour of homes expected to receive evangelical scribes and their message would be a way in which such scribes might touch micro-locations of power with the alternative vision of God's βασιλεία (as in Bazzana's political-theological reading).

Such observations present a way to bridge the gap, noted earlier, between context and presentation. While the normal practice of (perhaps displaced) village scribes

regardless of preferred theory of Synoptic literary dependence.

would be a prescribed and defined circuit of inspection, they could have portrayed their displacement as social and material deprivation and, thus, some sort of poverty and homelessness on behalf of a new kingdom. This (re)presentation, this reframing, of their administrative practice shifting allegiances toward a new βασιλεία perhaps constituted a way of reflecting the impoverished situation around them, albeit reflected through their own loss of status. Even the observation by Kloppenborg and Arnal that Christ-believing village scribes played with imperial administrative ideology to create meaning makes fuller sense in Bazzana's overall reading (2015) within a political-theological frame that acknowledges the pervasive nature of sovereign power, as administrative journeys for God's kingdom play essentially on the necessity and freedom of movement characterizing imperialism. As Musa Dube (2000) has persuasively argued, travel and its imagination are an essential aspect of imperial conquest in its material and narrative aspects.

In contextualizing travel within the political aspects of the earliest Jesus movement, focusing on how the central, brutal, and political event of the earliest Jesus story—the crucifixion—fits within the social context of early Christian ideologies helps make better sense of how Jesus's travel spoke both to material contexts as well as to imagined social programs. Scholars frequently observe that Q has no narrative of Jesus's death and, thus, surmise that the cross plays no role in the hypothetical text's "theology." (See Kloppenborg Verbin 2000, 369–74, for a more nuanced appraisal.) The cross does appear in Q, however, wandering into its series of sayings in connection with itinerancy: "Whoever does not take up his cross and come after me will not be my disciple" (Q 14:27). This well-attested Jesus saying both participates in broader ancient associations of travel with death and generates in Q (as in other texts) a link between apostolic travel and participation in Jesus's passion. (For a similar point about Paul's letters, see Luckritz Marquis 2013; for the role of travel in the publicization of the gospel of the crucifixion, see Luckritz Marquis 2012, 23–25.) Far from the sublimation of impoverished wandering (Myles 2014), itinerancy in light of the cross engages the economic and social abjection of life under Rome by framing travel as death. This nexus between the crucifixion and itinerancy functions as an epistemological center not just in the Synoptic tradition but also in multiple strands of the earliest Jesus traditions.

Mark and Mobility

The Gospel of Mark provides the basic itinerary for the Synoptic Jesus, a schema by which Jesus's early ministry wanders in and out of Galilee, shifting to a pivotal set of events near Caesarea Philippi, and culminating in a straight trip, structured around three predictions of Jesus's death, through Galilee to Judea and Jerusalem for the passion narrative. This final trip to the crucifixion serves Mark's focus on the cross so well that it has no easy claim to historicity. (The Fourth Gospel's more frequent trips to Jerusalem could as easily reflect Jesus's actual life and movements; his connections to Bethany needed to be formed somehow [Stewart 2009, 2–5]). A quick impression from the way Mark follows Jesus is that the reader is supposed to follow him, too. As modern readers, this implicit invitation to follow would imply the ability to plot his path on a map. Such mapping is impossible, however, as some of Mark's itineraries seem wildly implausible and his named locations either imprecise or nonexistent. Mark's mention in 5:1 of a "region of the Gerasenes" near the coast of the Sea of Galilee confused scribal copyists and the author of Matthew, as the city of Gerasa is rather far from the Sea. At 8:1, Mark names an otherwise unknown "Dalmanutha," which Matthew corrects to "Magdala." And Jesus's purported path (in Mark 7:31) of going from Tyre to the Decapolis via Sidon and the Sea of Galilee is somewhat akin to traveling from St. Louis to Miami via Chicago (without the "logic" of modern airline layovers; for an explanation of this path, see Yarbro Collins 2007, 369).

While attention to the accuracy of Mark's geography has been used to support reconstructions of the location of the text's writing (whether inside or outside Palestine), it is also instructive to note how Mark's Gospel asks its readers to trace Jesus's strange pathways among various, putatively specific locations. One theory devises a scheme whereby Jesus's constant crossing of the boundaries of his native Galilee (understood as a majority Jewish region) represents Jesus's transition and transgression from Jewish roots to Gentile audiences, with his journey to Jerusalem marking, in part, the decisive point at which the Gospel comments on its Jewish qua Jerusalemite nature. (See the discussion of past scholarship in Stewart 2009, 2–15.) Simultaneously, his frequent departures from Galilee (understood as part of scriptural Israel) resonates with the travels of Elijah in 1 and 2 Kings, so much so that the author's attempt to replicate the historical portions of Jewish scripture offers the key to understanding the generic aspects of this "first Gospel" (following the argument of Yarbro Collins 2007, 42–43). Finally, Jesus's frequent departures from cities and households implicate his message and lifestyle in the construction of alternate visions of family, gender, and power, as Jesus can alternately be understood as dissolving existing households, creating new fictive households, taking on active, masculine roles in public, or adopting less masculine positions akin to the poor, homeless people, and bandits (Lieu 2003; Moxnes 2003; Ruiz 2018; Thurman 2003). Indeed, the contrast between named cities or villages and unspecified wilderness produces a malleable Jesus—a shepherd among sheep engaged in a process of anthropogenesis, the creation of a new (type of) people.

This creation of newness must also be an aspect of mobility in Mark, though exactly what new thing Mark is driving at is up for debate. As with most aspects of modern Markan scholarship, readers explore the eschatological implications of Mark's itineraries. Again, the relationship between Galilee and Judea/Jerusalem comes to the fore, with earlier debate wondering which region represented Mark's implicit, expected location of the parousia (Stewart 2009, 5). The argument may be misguided, as the most explicit account of the parousia in Mark (in many ways similar to 1 Thess 4:16–17) never clearly has him touch the ground, as the angels with him gather the scattered elect from his station in the clouds (Mark 13:26–27). The impersonal "they" who witness his arrival could conceivably be anywhere, looking up at the sky—though those in the vicinity of the tribulation around Jerusalem circa 70 CE are in view for most of Mark 13.

At the same time, Jesus seems to be a location of holiness and power unto himself, apart from Temple, city, or household (Moxnes 2003; Stewart 2009.) The Temple itself, once destroyed, is replaced by a Temple "not made by human hands," seemingly indicating the community of Christ-followers as a human sanctuary (in the mode of the Qumranic eschatology and that of other apocalyptic texts; Marcus 2009, 814–15, 1014–15) or else the true, heavenly Temple (Yarbro Collins 2007, 703), insofar as the action of the final eschatological battle is, in the cosmological indications of Mark 13:24–25 and 15:33, a heavenly affair (Marcus 2000, 72–73). This dialectic between Jesus as the presence of God and the Temple as the former location of God's presence, then, presents the problematic situation of the Gospel's first readership, stretched between the post-70 movement and the expected return of Christ and reestablishment of a Temple. This dialectic, whereby Christ and the Temple feed meaning to each other, is spatially represented by the sort of "proximate marginality" of Jesus's kingship (Luckritz Marquis 2012), most starkly portrayed in the basic passion narrative, climaxing when Jesus's death just outside the city limits coincides with the rending of the Temple veil, portending the sanctuary's demise and the departure of God's presence and protection. Such proximate marginality is more than just the spatial cognate to the temporal "already–not yet" of modern Christian attempts to theologize earliest eschatology. The tension between the past and future of Jerusalem and the narrative present of the Christian movement becomes figured in atopic locations, particularly the wilderness, the sea, the mountain (of Transfiguration and of Olives), where, at times, the reader is alone with Jesus (or with a small group of disciples) to see and hear mysteries only known to a few. This wilderness becomes the space of the movement community, a post-resurrection Exodus, Elijanic exile, or Way of the Lord, once and for all to culminate in the final restoration of a heavenly Temple, composed of the followers who, in the meantime, are scattered in diaspora yet simultaneously structured in Jesus's proleptic presence. Jesus's journeys in and around Galilee and finally to the heart of Jerusalem mirror the readership's sense of nearness to a promised, imminent end and, thus, also evoke a sense of community despite physical diaspora and temporal distance from past and future.

Matthew and Mission

Two main issues condition discussions of travel (usually framed as "mission" or "commission") in Matthew. First, through appropriations of Q material, Matthew insists not only on Jesus's wandering, even "homeless" ministry (see, e.g., Luz 2001, 71–72) but also on his prescription of travel for his followers, particularly in Matthew 8:18–22 (near the beginning of the plot of his ministry, close after the first sermon of Matt 5–7) and the commission of the Twelve in Matthew 9:35–11:1. Second, and following upon the topic of commission passages, Matthew's two instances of sending followers seem programmatically distinct, with the aforementioned Matthew 10 ordering (quite symbolically of the Tribes of Israel) twelve disciples: "Do not travel on roads leading to Gentile cities,[3] and do not enter a Samaritan city. Instead, travel to the lost sheep of the house of Israel" (Matt 10:5–7). This sending thus exclusively targets Jewish people living in Galilee, avoiding Gentile cites, and moreover recommends an impoverished wandering from village to village, with apostles packing neither money, traveling bag, second cloak, sandals, nor staff (Matt 10:9–10). The second commission, at the Gospel's conclusion, instead sends the disciples to "make disciples of all nations" (Matt 28:19). It is likely the two commissions reflect two stages in the Jesus movement, with the author of Matthew set firmly in the second, reflecting on the postresurrection effort to convert Gentiles to Jesus's brand of Pharisaic Judaism. (Centuries of controversy underlie this point; see the discussion in White 2014.) At the same time, the plot of Matthew before the commission in Matthew 28 does, at times, look forward to the postresurrection international mission. At one point in Matthew 23:15, the narrative of Jesus's ministry acts as a counterpart to (post-70?) non-Christ-believing Pharisaic missionary activity, likely geared toward converting Jewish people to the Pharisaic mode of Torah observance (Goodman 2007, 69–74).

To a large extent, the foregoing observations about wandering radicalism in Q pertain similarly to depictions of impoverished mission in Matthew. Matthew 19 contains a series of stories encapsulating the various facets of this wandering apostleship. Itinerant disciples are likely celibate (Matt 19:10–12) and have left behind family and all possessions (Matt 19:27–30) as a prerequisite for perfection and rulership in the age to come (Matt 19:12, 21, and 28; see 5:48). Robert Myles, in his important study on homelessness in Matthew (2014), argues that the material constraints of poverty and homelessness experienced by Jesus become ideologically sublimated in Matthew's depiction. As I have noted, it's entirely possible that such sublimation of economic and political realia were sublimated much earlier, either by Jesus's first followers or even by Jesus himself. At the same time, it is clear that Matthew's viewpoint on this wandering, rural mission is largely retrospective and memorializing. Matthew's commissions seem to require the explicit and extensive blessing of Jesus, making the two, distinct programs seem more functional than lifestyle-oriented, much more like the commission of the rabbinic *shaliach* that would coincide with a specific task and itinerary (Draper 1998, 558–60).

Indeed, Matthew's contestation with scribes and Pharisees constitutes an attempt more explicitly to assume for its textual producers the role of traveling scribes and, thus, much more like the κωμογραμματεύς or scribe as literate, scriptural expert that may well lay behind the Synoptic tradition and Mathew more specifically. Similarly, it is possible that scribal travel characterized activity among Pharisaic sages and students. While

---

[3] On this interpretation, see Davies and Allison 1991, 165, and Luz 2001, 72 n. 18.

caution must be taken in retrojecting mishnaic discussions into the first century CE, there is plenty of evidence for rabbinic travel, both for economic and scholarly reasons, as well as discussions and debates about the nature of such travel and its impact on rabbinic authority and domestic ethics (Boyarin 1995, 134–67; Heszer 2011). Moreover, traveling practitioners of cultic wisdom considered by Romans to be "Eastern" (e.g., Chaldean astrologers or interpreters of Orphic oracles) often used scribal expertise in their own ethnic texts to prove their authority (Wendt 2016). Thus, the sorts of traveling Jewish scribes Matthew seems to reflect would fit well within Judaism of the time and its larger Roman context.

Also tangible in Matthew, but often overlooked, is the connection between Jesus's homeless travel and his death. As Sarit Kattan Gribetz (2017) has noted, rabbinic halakhic discussions of special prayer routines and formulae during travel acknowledge the dangers of the journey; rabbinic prayer not only protected against threats to life on the road but also warded off the ideological threat represented by Roman built and protected roads and the pervasive domination they represented. Similarly, Matthew's narrative presents the way the suspicions against a traveler such as Jesus could result in his execution (Myles 2014, 163–91). Itinerancy is precarious because it entails not just poverty but also abject status and social death.

Thus, while Matthew vividly deploys its sense of the significance of homeless wandering in its depiction of Jesus, it is far from clear that the lifestyle it traces in any way reflects the practices of the people who produced and first used this Gospel. The final commission scene, proposing journeys and preaching to new territories and peoples (in distinction to the mission to only Jewish people in Matthew 10), might also imply a mission with a new notion of travel and its provisions. At the same time, suspicion directed toward wandering preachers could be indicated by Matthew 7:15–20, which encourages the testing of false prophets based on the "fruit" they bear, a sentiment more explicitly applied to wandering apostles in the Didache, an early milestone both for Matthean reception and growing wariness among Christ-believing communities toward itinerancy. The deployment of parables of the kingdom also points to the foreclosing of an apostolic era, though this closing occurs not so much with the resurrection appearance at the Gospel's close but rather with the destruction of the Temple. Both the parable of the tenants and the parable of the wedding feast (Matt 20:33–46 and 22:1–14) depict the sending of servants (and a son, in the tenants parable) who are killed, resulting in the destruction of the residents and the inclusion of new people. Similarly, the sayings about the "blood of the prophets" (Matt 23:27–39) indicate that God will send prophets (Matt 23:34 and 37) who will be persecuted and killed by the scribes and Pharisees of Jerusalem, even chasing them from city to city (Matt 23:34, resonating with the original commission in chapter 10; see Matt 10:23). This city-to-city, village-to-village mission has likely, in Matthew's view, ended with the Temple's destruction, and the Gospel now views the movement from Antioch as a more international, cosmopolitan operation. Matthew memorializes an image of the homelessness of Jesus and his disciples as a thing of the past.

Luke-Acts and Universality

At least in terms of Jesus's own mobility, Luke focuses more on his radical poverty and the nature and meaning of his mobility rather than his actual itinerary (Stegemann 1984). Specific locales, villages, and interstices of time between events are unspecified, effectively idealizing Jesus's village activity in Galilee. This vagueness is deceptively and notoriously true for Luke's most distinctive narrative structure, his expansion of the Markan journey to Jerusalem in Luke 9:51–19:27 (or 19:44, or perhaps later), which is less an itinerary than a framing for instruction loosely strung across a handful of themes. (For discussion of the abundant scholarship on Luke's travel narrative, see Noël 2004.) While Lukan journeys are not quite as detached from context as they might initially appear, they work in complex ways to outbid material and ideological modes of domination in ways that created new ideological formations that, in later hands, would come to characterize Christianity and its impact on the West.

Luke's central travel narrative, like the Markan construct it accentuates, places focus on the cross. Jesus prepares for the journey by discussing it with Moses and Elijah as his "exodus" or "departure" (9:31), which refers both to the journey to Jerusalem and the death to which it leads. Jesus's discourses during the journey focus on this mortal departure (see the predictions taken from Mark, as well as Luke 13:32–25 and 14:27). For Luke, this focus plays into its larger geographic outline, centering the significance of Jesus around Jerusalem at the beginning and ending of the Gospel, a structure partially mirrored in Acts (taking into account Paul's disastrous return to the Temple, Jerusalem, and Palestine in Acts 21–26 before his final journey to Rome). In both books, the Temple is a place of promising origins that is returned to as a site of rejection and transformation. The Lukan journey narrative similarly establishes a pattern whereby later preachers will take momentous journeys leading to physical danger, often because of mistaken identity (especially Paul, with his Roman citizenship playing a notable role in the accounts; see his first trip to Europe and his beating in Philippi in Acts 16, his return to Jerusalem and long imprisonment in Acts 21–26, and his final trip to Rome and shipwreck in Acts 27–28).

As elsewhere in Luke, the travel narrative is multivocal and pulls on a variety of traditions. Jesus's march toward the holy city seems to fulfill multiple scriptural prophecies about the climactic "Way of the Lord" in places such as Isaiah 40:3 and especially Malachi 3:1, while the narrative is also strung among a number of "Deuteronomic" posts—the appearance of Moses and Elijah at its outset, discussion of the Torah and its fulfillment in Luke 10:25–37, laments of Jerusalem mirroring the curse sections of Deuteronomy (Luke 13:33–34 and 19:41–44), and the journey's culmination in the Temple in Luke 19. (See the discussion of scholarship in Denaux 2010.) Again, this journey as "exodus" recalls Mosaic redemption—in this case, from the apocalyptic situation of bondage to evil. (See Garrett 1990; in the debate regarding the eschatological or apocalyptic nature of Luke's ideology, I read Luke-Acts as basically reflecting an imminent apocalyptic eschatology.) This redemption takes place through the death of Jesus initiated by the journey he is about to take (much like the Exodus) but also through his ascension to heaven. The transfiguration is also an ἀνάληψις (9:51) foretelling the time when he will be "taken up" to heaven (ἀναλαμάνω in Acts 1:11 and 22; Carroll 2012, 228–29; Feldmeier 2017). That the journey predicts Jesus's "departure" foreshadows the time when the followers of Jesus will be on their own, both in Acts and in the generation of the Gospel's readership. It is telling that the final parable before Jesus's arrival in Jerusalem pertains to how followers will invest their spiritual "wealth" when "a certain nobleman traveled to a distant country to receive kingship and then returned" (Luke 19:12). Luke makes evident that Jesus's teachings on the road to Jerusalem relate both to the apostolic era narrated in Acts and to the post-70 situation of the Gospel's audience through its emphatic focus on the demise of Jerusalem (Luke 13:34–35, 19:41–46). As the other Synoptics do in their own ways, Luke's travel narrative collapses the crisis of the movement's loss of its messianic leader with the crisis of the loss of the center of Judaism four decades later.

Thus, Jesus's march to Jerusalem enacts the prophetic "way of the Lord" resulting in the judgment and destruction of the city, in turn predicting later, eschatological judgment (Luke 21:25–28). The string of sayings and parables that make up the travel narrative, however, do not simply point toward a future transformation but also attempt to parse out the logics by which such transformations will occur. Scholars have long noted the prominence of economic imagery in the travel narrative, particularly imagery dealing with money and its exchange (Metzger 2007; Moxnes 1988). Such imagery is often deployed as a metaphor for the type of consideration one needs to take with regard to discipleship and how it rearranges social relationships, especially family. The ethical import of many of these stories emphatically teaches against the utility or worth of wealth or property. For example, borrowing from Q, Luke has the commissioned disciples carry neither bag nor purse (10:4). Luke does not categorically dispense with the evangelical value of money, however, signaling at the close of the Last Supper discourse (Luke 22:35–36) that money will be crucial to the postresurrection phase of the movement (and, truly, after the initial, Jerusalem phase of Christian communism; Acts 2:42–47, 4:32–37).

More important, Luke in his travel narrative retains the logic of economic exchange in its discussion of the cost of following Jesus. In the banquet parable, invited guests turn down the feast in favor of existing social relationships framed as economic and familial ties (Luke 14:18–20). Later in the journey, Jesus asserts that to build restorative relationships with people, one must act like a sinful, dishonest estate manager who cancels the debts of his master's clients—that is, forgive their sins (to provide a quick interpretation of the notoriously troublesome parable of the dishonest manager; Luke 16:1–13). Immediately following the banquet parable, the rejection of family in favor of following Jesus to Jerusalem (which grounds the initial journey in Luke 9:57–62; see also 18:28–30) also receives an economic interpretation. As Jesus progresses southward, he turns to his followers to impart two well-known sayings from the tradition: the directive to leave family (which Luke frames as "hating" them) and the injunction to "take up their cross and follow me" (Luke 14:26–27). Two brief parables explain what is at stake in the decision to follow Jesus: a person should not build a tower without sufficient funds, and a king should not start a war without enough troops. "So then," Jesus concludes, "any of you who does not renounce all their possessions cannot be my disciple" (Luke 14:33). Following Jesus is a reckoning akin to a large, risky, but beneficial financial enterprise, an exchange of family and possessions for life.

Part of the reason this figurative economic logic works is due to the fact that money travels. In both the dishonest manager story and the tale of the nobleman departing to become king, the abandonment of money or financial responsibility figures a commission stretched across space and time, and one that is expected to be transformative and itself transformed. The commission of discipleship should not only result in growth (in some stories, the money is invested and increases) but also create new social bonds and communities. Money, which governs social relationships in these sayings and parables, is exchanged for new social relationships. Family is rejected for a new sort of kinship. New bonds transgressing normal boundaries of status (see, e.g., the critiques of the Pharisees and their economic and social relationships in Luke 11:37–54, 14:7–14, and 16:14–18) are in fact signs of the incursion of the kingdom. Traveling with Jesus involves the dissolution and exchange of the old in favor of the transformed new.

As Luke liquidates familial bonds, so, too, does it simultaneously dissolve ethnic bonds. A look at the flow of sayings in Luke 11 helps highlight how Luke targets family within the broader context of ethnicity. At the outset of the chapter, Luke deploys Q sayings about prayer that figure it through travel and household images as begging from door to door or as constituting communication to a superior "Father" (Luke 11:5–13). Next, a dispute over the origin of Jesus's exorcism power leads Jesus to defend himself using the imagery of broken households (Satan's house attacked by Jesus in Luke 11:21–22 and the cryptic tale of the demon reinvading a house in 11:24–26; see Moxnes 2003, 125–41). This is followed by a uniquely Lukan tale rejecting traditional family bonds: in response to a woman blessing his mother, Jesus instead blesses "those who hear the word of God and keep it" (Luke 11:27–28). Here, the breaking of traditional household bonds through travel results in a new family and kingdom.

Luke 11 also sees polemic with Pharisees increase, so that the dissolution of family pairs with a condemnation of Jewish leaders that, in its imagery, parallels the journey undertaken in the larger travel narrative. For Luke's Jesus, the failure of the Pharisees and scribes to accept his message will result in a final judgment on Jerusalem, framed as a punishment for spilling "the blood of the prophets" (Luke 11:50). This passage in its Q context, without the escalating animosity between Jesus and the other Jewish teachers or the journey to the crucifixion (not to mention its context in a pre-70 situation), expresses the urgency of Wisdom's call to accept its new message, open to all (Johnson-DeBaufre 2005, 78–80).[4] In Luke, by contrast, the creation of new families

---

[4] Within the context of the Farrer Hypothesis, one might read Luke then altering Matthew's intra-Jewish polemic to condition a more radical split between the Jewish people and a new movement.

narratively performed by the journey of Jesus and all who would follow him away from their households extends to the macro-context of ethnic groups. Such a reading enters another contested location in Lukan studies (again, to show how central travel is to the way the work makes meaning): the projected soteriological fate in Luke-Acts of the Jewish leaders or people as a whole. I read Luke's travel narratives as establishing a set of overlapping crises—Jesus's crucifixion, Stephen's execution (Acts 7), Paul's rejection at the Temple (Acts 21–22), and the destruction of the Temple itself—that in turn present the matrix of prophecies behind the journey as foretelling the transfer of God's promise from the Jewish people to the "nations," including only the remnant of Jewish people who follow Jesus on the Way (Luke 11:29–54, Luke 19:41–44, Acts 7:48–53, Acts 13:46–47, Acts 28:25–28). More important for this essay's purposes, the narratological fact that Luke-Acts portrays this transfer through a logic of *mobility* and *exchange* differs from other ideologies of the expansion of an ethnic people by which the group assimilates or accommodates other peoples (as in the other Synoptics, or Paul's letters, or in Roman ideologies of the expansion of *romanitas* and citizenship; Dench 2005) to something more abstracted from social contexts. In an effort to outflank Roman ideologies of peoplehood, the path cut by Jesus and his first followers becomes in Luke-Acts the way by which Western notions of universality began to flow, with its attendant creations and destructions. Just as Jesus's crucifixion occasions a departure from the center of Judaism, the successive journeys of Luke-Acts trace an itinerary without a center, leaving an open expanse to be explored, one only fully mapped as "the Way" progressed ever closer toward Constantine. As such, Lukan travel sketches the first marks on the Western map of universality, paths worn, paved, and still present today.

References

Arnal, William. 2001. *Jesus and the Village Scribes: Galilean Conflict and the Setting of Q.* Minneapolis: Augsburg Fortress Press.

Arnal, William. 2013. "The Trouble with Q." *Foundations and Facets Forum*, 3rd series, 2, no. 1: 7–78.

Bazzana, Giovanni Battista. 2015. *Kingdom of Bureaucracy: The Political Theology of the Village Scribes in the Sayings Gospel Q.* Leuven: Peeters.

Bitner, Bradley. 2015. *Paul's Political Strategy in 1 Corinthians 1:1–4:6: Constitution and Covenant.* Cambridge: Cambridge University Press.

Boyarin, Daniel. 1995. *Carnal Israel: Reading Sex in Talmudic Culture.* Berkeley: University of California Press.

Braun, Willi. 1999. "Socio-mythic Invention, Graeco-Roman Schools, and the Sayings Gospel Q." *Method and Theory in the Study of Religion* 11: 210–35.

Carroll, John T. 2012. *Luke: A Commentary.* New Testament Library. Louisville: Westminster John Knox Press.

Chancey, Mark A. 2002. *The Myth of a Gentile Galilee: The Population of Galilee and New Testament Studies.* Cambridge: Cambridge University Press.

Davies, W. D., and Dale C. Allison. 1991. *Matthew 8–18.* ICC. Edinburgh: T&T Clark.

Denaux, Adelbert, 2010. *Studies in the Gospel of Luke: Structure, Language and Theology*. Münster: Lit Verlag.

Dench, Emma. 2005. *Romulus' Asylum: Roman Identities from the Age of Alexander to the Age of Hadrian*. Oxford: Oxford University Press.

Destro, Adriano, and Mauro Pesce. 2011. *Encounters with Jesus: The Man in His Time and Place*. Minneapolis: Fortress Press.

Downing, Francis Gerald. 1992. *Cynics and Christian Origins*. Edinburgh: T&T Clark.

Draper, Jonathan A. 1991. "Wandering Charismatics and Scholarly Circularities." In Horsley, Richard A., with Johanthan A. Draper. *Whoever Hears You Hears Me: Prophets, Performance, and Tradition in Q*, 29–45. Harrisburg: Fortress Press

Draper, Jonathan A. 1998. "Weber, Theissen, and 'Wandering Charismatics' in the *Didache*." *JECS* 6, no. 4: 541–76.

Dube, Musa W. 2000. *Postcolonial Feminist Interpretation of the Bible*. St. Louis, MO: Chalice Press.

Feldmeier, Reinhard. 2017. "The Wandering Jesus: Luke's Travel Narrative as Part of His Hermeneutical Strategy of 'Double Codification.'" In *Journeys in the Roman East: Imagined and Real*, edited by Maren R. Niehoff, 343–53. Tübingen: Mohr Siebeck.

Garrett, Susan, R. 1990. "Exodus from Bondage: Luke 9:31 and Acts 12:1–24." *CBQ* 52, no. 4: 656–80.

Goodman, Martin. 2007. *Rome and Jerusalem: The Clash of Ancient Civilizations*. New York: Vintage Books.

Harland, Phillip A. 2013. *Associations, Synagogues, and Congregations: Claiming a Place in Ancient Mediterranean Society*. 2nd rev. ed. Ontario: Phillip Harland. http://philipharland.com/publications/Harland%202013%20Associations-Synagogues-Congregations.pdf

Harnack, Adolf von. 1908. *The Sayings of Jesus*. Translated by J. R. Wilkinson. London: Williams and Norgate.

Heszer, Catherine. 2011. *Jewish Travel in Antiquity*. TSAJ 144. Tübingen: Mohr Siebeck.

Horsley, Richard A. 1991. "The Q People: Renovation, Not Radicalism." *Continuum* 1: 40–63.

Horsley, Richard A., with Jonathan Draper. 1999. *Whoever Hears You Hears Me: Prophets, Performance, and Tradition in Q*. Harrisburg: Fortress Press.

Johnson-DeBaufre, Melanie. 2005. *Jesus among Her Children: Q, Eschatology, and the Construction of Christian Origins*. Cambridge, MA: Harvard University Press.

Kattan Gribetz, Sarit. 2017. "'Lead Me Forth in Peace': The Origins of the Wayfarer's Prayer and Rabbinic Rituals of Travel in the Roman World." In *Journeys in the Roman East: Imagined and Real*, edited by Maren R. Niehoff, 297–328. Tübingen: Mohr Siebeck.

Kloppenborg, John S. 1993. "The Sayings Gospel Q: Recent Opinion on the People behind the Document." *Currents in Research: Biblical Studies* 1: 9–34.

Kloppenborg Verbin, John S. 2000. *Excavating Q: The History and Setting of the Sayings Gospel*. Edinburg: T&T Clark.

Lieu, Tat-siong Benny. 2003. "Re-Mark-able Masculinities: Jesus, the Son of Man, and the (Sad) Sum of Manhood?" In *New Testament Masculinities*, edited by Stephen D. Moore and Janice Capel Anderson, 93–136. Leiden: Brill.

Luckritz Marquis, Timothy. 2012. "Crucifixion, State of Emergency, and the Proximate Marginality of Christ's Kingship." In *Portraits of Jesus: Studies in Christology*, edited by Susan E. Myers, 99–123. Tübingen: Mohr Siebeck.

Luckritz Marquis, Timothy. 2013. *Transient Apostle: Paul, Travel, and the Rhetoric of Empire*. Synkrisis. New Haven: Yale University Press.

Luckritz Marquis, Timothy. 2018. "Movement, Performance, and Choice in Earliest Christianity." *Interpretation* 72, no. 2: 163–74.

Luz, Ullrich. 2001. *Matthew: 8–20*. Hermeneia. Minneapolis: Fortress Press.

Marcus, Joel. 2000. *Mark 1–8: A New Translation with Introduction and Commentary*. AB 27A. New York: Doubleday.

Marcus, Joel. 2009. *Mark 9–16: A New Translation with Introduction and Commentary*. AB 27A. New Haven: Yale University Press.

Metzger, James A. 2007. *Consumption and Wealth in Luke's Travel Narrative*. Leiden: Brill.

Moxnes, Halvor. 1988. *The Economy of the Kingdom: Social Conflict and Economic Relations in Luke's Gospel*. Eugene, OR: Wipf & Stock.

Moxnes, Halvor. 2003. *Putting Jesus in His Place: A Radical Vision of Household and Kingdom*. Louisville: Westminster John Knox Press.

Myles, Robert J. 2014. *The Homeless Jesus in the Gospel of Matthew*. Sheffield: Sheffield Phoenix Press.

Nasrallah, Laura. 2017. "Imposing Travelers: An Inscription from Galatia and the Journeys of the Earliest Christians. In *Journeys in the Roman East: Imagined and Real*, edited by Maren R. Niehoff, 273–98. Tübingen: Mohr Siebeck.

Noël, Filip. 2004. *The Travel Narrative in the Gospel of Luke: Interpretation of Lk 9,51–19,28*. Brussels: Voor Wentenschappen en Kunsten.

Reed, Jonathan L. 2010. "Instability in Jesus' Galilee: A Demographic Perspective." *JBL* 129, no. 2: 343–65.

Rollens, Sarah E. 2014. *Framing Social Criticism in the Jesus Movement: The Ideological Project in the Sayings Gospel Q*. WUNT 2.374; Tübingen: Mohr Siebeck.

Ruiz, Gilberto A. 2018. "'Out of Egypt I Have Called My Son': Migration as a Male Activity in the New Testament Gospels." In *Latinxs, the Bible, and Migration*, edited by Efrain Agosto and Jacqueline M. Hidalgo, 89–107. Cham: Palgrave Macmillan.

Schotroff, Louise, and Wolfgang Stegemann. 1986. *Jesus and the Hope of the Poor*. Translated by Matthew J. O'Connell. New York: Orbis.

Stegemann, Wolfgang. 1984. "Vagabond Radicalism in Early Christianity? A Historical and Theological Discussion of a Thesis Proposed by Gerd Theissen." In *God of the Lowly: Sociohistorical Interpretations of the Bible*, edited by Willy Schotroff and Wolfgang Stegemann, translated by Matthew J. O'Connell, 148–68. Maryknoll, NY: Orbis Books.

Stewart, Eric C. 2009. *Gathered around Jesus: An Alternative Spatial Practice in the Gospel of Mark*. Cambridge: James Clarke.

Tacoma, Laurens E. 2016. *Moving Romans: Migration to Rome in the Principiate*. Oxford: Oxford University Press.

Tacoma, Laurens E., and Rolf A. Tybout. 2016. "Moving Epigrams: Migration and Mobility in the Greek East." In *Migration and Mobility in the Early Roman Empire*, edited by Luuk de Ligt and Laurens E. Tacoma, 345–89. Leiden: Brill.

Theissen, Gerd. 1978. *Sociology of Early Palestinian Christianity*. Translated by John Bowden. Philadelphia: Fortress Press.

Theissen, Gerd. 1992. *Social Reality and the Early Christians: Theology, Ethics, and the World of the New Testament*. Translated by Margaret Kohl. Minneapolis: Fortress Press.

Thurman, Eric. 2003. "Looking for a Few Good Men: Mark and Masculinity." In *New Testament Masculinities*, edited by Stephen D. Moore and Janice Capel Anderson, 138–62. Leiden: Brill.

Wendt, Heidi. 2016. *At the Temple Gates: The Religion of Freelance Experts in the Roman Empire*. Oxford: Oxford University Press.

White, Benjamin L. 2014. "The Eschatological Conversion of 'All the Nations' in Matthew 28.19–20: (Mis)reading Matthew through Paul." *JSNT* 36, no. 4: 353–82.

Yarbro Collins, Adela. 2007. *Mark: A Commentary*. Hermeneia. Minneapolis: Fortress Press.

Zerbini, Andrea. 2016. "Human Mobility in the Roman Near East: Patterns and Motives." In *Migration and Mobility in the Early Roman Empire*, edited by Luuk de Ligt and Laurens E. Tacoma, 305–44. Leiden: Brill.

CHAPTER 18

FOOD AND MEALS

SOHAM AL-SUADI

Introduction

Food and meal communities belong directly together when one looks at the Synoptic Gospels and the sociohistorical context behind them. These meals communities are two sides of the same coin that should not be underestimated either from a literary or a sociohistorical perspective. In portrayals of food and meal communities, the boundaries between the social-historical content and the theologically unique selling point of the literary meaning are often fluid. This is mainly due to the matter itself, because both food and communities are suitable for idealization, differentiation, and exceptional descriptions. This essay presents the sociohistorical background against which the reports on food and meal communities in the Synoptic Gospels can be understood. In the first part, the basics are described, drawing attention to the fact that the literary use of this topic must be viewed in a differentiated way. In the second part, the meaning of food and meal communities in the Synoptic Gospels is pointed out. Here, I seek an internal comparison as well as a comparison between the Synoptic Gospels. Finally, some Synoptic features are examined in the light of ritual-scientific categories.

Meals in the Greco-Roman World

At the time of the New Testament, the communal meal was held in small groups of eight to twelve people, where the participants lay down at dinner as a sign of a high social status. Besides the festive meals in communities, eating and drinking also took place in taverns, food stalls, and food booths on the streets (Al-Suadi and Altman 2019). The texts of the New Testament illustrate these very different ways of eating and drinking. Some stories explicitly refer to festive food, while others are implicitly dedicated to the values and practices of communal eating. Communal eating and drinking was a cultural practice influenced by social, political, and religious aspects of the so-called Hellenization of the Mediterranean. "Hellenization" refers to the adaptation of non-Greek people and cultures to Greek cultural practice. The process of Hellenization began with Alexander the Great, who ruled from 334 to 324 BCE. Beginning with the influence of Greek culture under the political rule of Alexander and his successors, and continuing under Roman rule, "Hellenistic" came to designate a cultural framework that was independent from other socioreligious formations. As the Hellenistic influences in the ancient Mediterranean influenced the life of everyday people, one can speak of a "globalization" of everyday life, including the organization of the community. As a result, the practices of communal meals were identical in regard to the overall cultural frame, which allows the locating of Roman and Jewish writings about food and meals of the second/third centuries CE within Hellenized cultures. (See the writings at Qumran, e.g., 1QS, and Justin's Apology, 1Apol 67; Al-Suadi and Altman 2019.) One of the culturally established activities of ancient societies was to organize themselves into associations. Associations made it possible for people to meet with like-minded people who did not necessarily correspond only to their social classes. Matthias Klinghardt (1996) and Dennis Smith (2003) elaborate in detail on the establishment of associations that led to the holding of community meals that included very different social classes (Al-Suadi 2011, 36).

Klinghardt highlights the distinction between private and association meals. In this context, the term "private meal" does not imply that the meal was eaten alone with family or friends but that it was financed privately. The "association meal" refers to the communal meal of an association which was able to meet in public (Klinghardt 1996, 29). Although the distinction between "private" and "public" seems clear-cut, it must be stressed that the boundaries between a private and a non–privately financed meal were fluid. In Taussig's studies, therefore, the distinction between private and public meetings is no longer made, since this differentiation cannot do justice to sociohistorical circumstances. For him, these are semiprivate assemblies. The term "semiprivate" is more appropriate, since it describes the simultaneity of individual and socially relevant characteristics and highlights that the location of the meal is not dependent on the structures of the association system (Taussig 2009, 68). "The semiprivate nature of the meals suggests that they were in some ways social laboratories. They were protected enough to allow for real experiments, yet open enough for the larger society to notice what occurred within them. Hellenistic society straddled an historical gap in which neither the artificially and forcefully imposed social institutions of Rome nor the decimated social remains of national or tribal associations held sway. In this gap, the meal developed a strong loyalty and an extended field of influence" (35). The reading of letters, writings, or the teaching of common topics was an important focus of semiprivate associations. Thus, the first writings to the early Christian communities were also written, read, performed, or sung in this semiprivate space.

Food in the Greco-Roman World

At first glance information about food and meals seems to be easily accessible in New Testament texts. However, lists of foods and drinks may provide information about agricultural products, but reading these text parts requires interpretation and analysis in order to draw valuable conclusions about the sociohistorical setting. It is therefore vital not only to take food descriptions at face value but to remember that most texts associate idealized social values with the description of food.

At the ideal banquet male (and female) diners would be propped on downy couches, would be adorned with floral wreaths, and would relax while before them slaves scurried to bring in elegant, leonine-legged tables covered with delectable foods: figs and nuts, later fish and pork glistening in garum sauce. Beautiful, youthful male slaves circulated wine in handsome cups, while sweet-tempered child slaves sat at their mistresses' feet. Flute-players, harpists, and slaves, male and female, likewise danced and sang at the guests' pleasure (Daniel-Hughes 2012, 216).

Matthias Klinghardt describes how much the author's intention plays a role in describing the food: "it is safe to assume that several courses typically were served in such a dinner. Naturally, the table included a wide variety of foodstuffs, whose range depended on the host's or the respective meal group's financial means and cultural backgrounds. One must realize, however, that unlike today in the same part of the world, meat (and fish where available) was regularly consumed by the wealthy only. Most of the population during the Greco-Roman era primarily had diets of grains and vegetables" (Klinghardt 2012, 10).

In the elite Greek tradition, two courses were distinguished from each other. The first course was a conventional dinner with meat, fish, and vegetables. The second course was the symposion, which was mainly drunk (Smith 2003, 52). During the symposion, desserts (nuts, fruits, cakes, and sometimes eggs) were served in addition to wine. It can be assumed that bread, fish, vegetables, and wine were among the simplest dishes served at a meal. Bread was mainly used as cutlery. Among the vegetables, onion and cabbage were particularly popular because they could be served either raw or cooked. They were eaten as salads with vinegar and oil or with honey (Klinghardt 1996, 52–57). Small fish and other seafood, such as mussels, were also popular as a side dish because they were inexpensive and widespread. Meat did not belong to the basic meal, because it was very expensive and could be eaten by poorer households only at sacrificial celebrations. In Roman times, the two-course menu was extended by an appetizer before the meal. It is evident from the sources that the spectrum was also relatively large for poor semiprivate banquets and that one can disregard the idea of meal that consisted only of bread and wine.

Food and Meals in the Synoptic Gospels

Even if eating and drinking was possible outside a meal community and determined the everyday life of people in antiquity, it can be assumed that the texts on food and meals refer to (festive) meal communities. This is likely because the scenes in the Gospels describe eating and drinking as ritual acts set in complex social settings. The term ἐσθίω, therefore, normally refers to a ritualized eating practice that always has the same characteristics, regardless of social embedding (but see Matt 12:1 and Mark 7:28). Hence, ἀναπίπτω, ἀνακλίνω, ἀνάκειμαι, κατακεῖμαι, συνανακεῖμαι, and συνεσθίω describe the common meal or practice of sitting down to dinner. (See Matt 9:10; 14:19; 22:10; 26:7, 20; Mark 6:26; 14:18; 16:14; Luke 7:37; 9:15; 22:27; John 6:11; 12:2; 13:23, 28.) Guests of a meal are also referred to as ἀνακειμένους.

The Hellenistic meal practice is characterized by Hal Taussig (2009, 26) with a clear typology of five points. I will discuss each in turn.

1. The reclining of (more or less) all participants
2. The order of a supper (*deipnon*) of eating, followed by an extended time (*symposion*); of drinking, conversation, and/or performance
3. Marking the transition from *deipnon* to *symposion* with a ceremonial libation
4. Leadership by a "president" (*symposiarch*) of the meal
5. A variety of marginal personages

(1) The importance of the seating arrangement should not be underestimated, because it depicts essential characteristics of the meal and society. The act of reclining in itself was a mark of one's rank in society: only free citizens were allowed to recline. Women could occasionally lie down to eat, but children and slaves were not allowed to do so. If they were allowed to participate, they could only do so sitting. Those who reclined were further ranked by the places assigned to them at the table. Though the positions might vary based upon local custom or table arrangement, there was almost always an honored place at any table. Others were ranked according to their position relative to the honored place (Smith 2003, 11).

In the New Testament, the participants in the communal meal are described in various places. Luke 14:7–11, in which the order of rank at the meal and the right guests are mentioned, is one of the most detailed stories, along with Mark 2:13–17 (parr. Matt 9:9–13; Luke 5:27–32), the so-called public dinner (Al-Suadi and Altman 2019).

(2) The order of *deipnon* and *symposion*, with eating during *deipnon* and *symposion* reserved for drinking, conversations, and/or performances, was an integral part of the Hellenistic dining culture. It is to be assumed that the mass of the population usually ate poorly and did not benefit from the luxury of the Greco-Roman food culture. For these poor communities, it meant that the *deipnon* consisted mainly

of bread and/or side dishes. Vegetables and fish or seafood, such as mussels, were part of the diet of many meal communities. Meat was eaten when it was available for sacrifice. On the other hand wealthy hosts not only dined more delicately but also had the opportunity to engage chefs for an evening. Delicacies could also be served in addition to the basic food, depending on financial leeway. As a rule, the meal consisted of three parts: starter, main course, and dessert. The main course could consist of several dishes. It can also be assumed that the meal communities, which met in associations, offered staple foods such as fish and, rarely, meat. References to bread and wine (Irenaeus, *Haer.* 5.33.3; 5.1.3; 1.13.2), which have often led to the conclusion that some meal communities were particularly poor or lived ascetically, are less often related to social situations. Rather, they refer to the fact that bread and wine were everyday foods, and bread and wine is to be understood as typical, since the limitation to "Eucharistic" elements can only be observed from the third century onward (McGowan 1999).

The meal was followed by the *symposion*, which was distinguished from the *deipnon* by a solemn libation. It is striking that pure drinking is not documented and that the *symposion* was always preceded by a satiation meal. Musical performances, but also poetry and the reading of writings, were among the activities held during the *symposion*. In addition, the dessert (nuts, cakes, cheese, or salads) was served at the *symposion* (Klinghardt 1996).

In the New Testament δεῖπνον refers to a festive meal that was usually held in the evening (see Luke 14:12, 16, 17, 24; John 13:2, 4; 21:20; 1 Cor 11:20; plural: Matt 23:6; Mark 12:39; Luke 20:46); δειπνέω is the associated verb). The alternation between *deipnon* and *symposion* is primarily associated with the so-called words of institution. In the preliminary remarks to the "words of institution" (Mark 14:18–21; Luke 22:21–23; Matt 26:21–25) the Synoptic Gospels say very clearly that bread was eaten at the *deipnon*.

(3) Typically, the *symposion* began with a libation, which was understood as the honoring of one or more gods and was often performed by the *symposion* leader (Taussig 2009, 74). Songs and hymns were associated with the libation but also with the *symposion*. During the libation the hymns were sung together, while during the *symposion* the hymns and songs were mostly performed by professional musicians (Stein 2008, 44).

> Looking at the multiplicity of gods receiving libations as reproductive of the larger quest for identity can help one understand the conation of libations to gods and libations to guests of honor at the meal. Associating oneself libationally with an important personage at the meal itself communicated important aspects of identity—that is, if one sees the pivotal libations as subliminal explorations of identity (to whom do you belong?), raising a cup to a person of honor at the meal one was attending encouraged a sense that you and the honored person belong together, that the respective identities reinforced each other. (Taussig 2009, 78)

In Mark 14:22–25; Luke 22:15–20 and Matthew 26:26–29, the "words of institution" illustrate the social and religious aspects of the libation(s), which are also reproduced in Paul's account of the Lord's Supper (1 Cor 11:23–25).

(4) Both the host and the *symposiarch* played special roles in the meal. While the host provided the space and infrastructure, the *symposiarch* was responsible for the smooth running and coordination of the guests and, if necessary, the artist. The host could also be the *symposiarch*, but not infrequently the two tasks were assigned to different people. In other words, the person who invited the guests to the meal gladly left the tasks of the *symposion* to another person. Why? Isn't it a matter of course that the person who invited the guests would also be the man/woman to determine the courses, the atmosphere, and the topics of conversation? This was not the case, however: at the time of the New Testament, the office of the *symposiarch* resembled that of a supervisor who was repeatedly criticized during the course of the meal. The hierarchy increased from left to right, so that the one who was at the far right was the host, the *symposiarch*, or the guest with the highest status (within the meal community). The head seat of the *symposion* was a privileged place, which did not have to correspond with one's social status outside the meal community and was not fixed to one person (Al-Suadi 2011, 184).

(5) Marginal personages were slaves, performers, children, and uninvited guests. Smith elaborates the different roles of the marginal people at the meal. It is said that the food was brought in by the slaves, if the tables were the normal portable kind, or on trays if the tables were permanent (Smith 2003, 28). Performers played instruments. Carly Daniel-Hughes demonstrates how satires envision ribald meals that highlight the presence of marginalized subjects, freedmen, slaves, and courtesans. She argues that their presence critiques Roman constructions of elite subjects as self-controlled and virtuous (Daniel-Hughes 2012, 219).

Similarities and Differences between the Gospels

The Beginnings in Mark, Matthew, and Luke and in John the Baptist

Although the birth of a child, service in the temple, and the homage of a god are directly related to food and meal fellowship in the Hellenistic world, the first chapters of Matthew and Luke do not connect the subjects. It is striking that in the reports before the beginning of Jesus's ministry the subject is not present. However, it is present in the negative: fasting is emphasized in the cases of the prophet Anna and John the Baptist. The renunciation of food and thus of fellowship seems to make them especially God-fearing. Luke relates that Anna never left the temple but worshiped there with fasting and prayer night and day (Luke 2:36). Anna reflects what the angel tells Elizabeth about her son: John must never drink wine or strong drink and will be filled with the Holy Spirit (Luke 1:15). The prophecies about John are fulfilled, at least if one takes the evidence from Matthew and Mark into consideration. Mark 1:6 and Matthew 3:4 say that John baptized and that he ate locusts and wild honey. Luke refers to John proclaiming a baptism of repentance for the forgiveness of sins (Luke 3:3) but, despite his detailed reports about Anna and the prophecy, omits any mention of the Baptist's diet. It seems that Luke wants to keep fasting as an expression of closeness to God.

The Beginnings of Jesus's Ministry

Luke remains faithful to the motif of fasting. When describing the temptation, he says that Jesus eats nothing (Luke 4:2). Matthew tells it slightly differently, stating that afterward Jesus was famished. Any modern reader will not be surprised to read that Jesus was famished after his fasting. Isn't hunger expected after forty days of fasting in the desert? In the Gospels, however, the reference does not serve only for the identification of the reader with the physical needs of Jesus. In addition, the reference leads to texts (Luke 9 and Luke 24) in which food and meal communities play an important role. With the background that so far in the Synoptic Gospels neither food nor a meal community have played a role, Luke 4:2 is a central verse. Mark remains silent about the conditions of temptation, which makes the extension of the content by fasting and the subsequent hunger even more essential for Matthew and Luke.

The Galilean Ministry

Only beginning with the work of Jesus in Galilee are the social-historical context and the theological relevance of food and meal communities thematized. In Mark 2:13–17, Jesus is the one who invites publicans and sinners to a meal, although the meal does not take place in the house of Jesus but in the house of Levi the publican. In response to the protest of the scribes and Pharisees, Jesus says that he has not come to call the righteous but rather the socially stigmatized: to call sinners to repentance and those who are socially weak to community. In the spirit of Luke's theology, Luke adds to Jesus's answer that he came to call sinners to repentance (Luke 5:32). Matthew adds that Jesus's behavior is a sign of mercy (Matt 9:13) (Al-Suadi and Altman 2019). In Luke 5:29 κατακεῖμαι is used to refer to the taking of the seating order. This verb occurs a total of twelve times in the New Testament and refers to the lying down of several sick people (Mark 1:30; 2:4; Luke 5:25; John 5:3.6; Acts 9:33; 28:8) as well as to participation in a meal (Mark 2:15; 14:3; Luke 5:29; 7:37; 1 Cor 8:10). The anointing by a woman, the awakening of the daughter of Jairus, and the feeding of the 5,000 can be understood to describe the role of women in detail. In Mark 14:3–9, Matthew 26:5–13, and Luke 7:36–50 the woman's anointing is described in detail, suggesting that it is a washing of the feet during a meal. Luke does not mention women at the feeding of the 5,000, but Matthew 14:21 and 15:38 mention women explicitly. Contrary to the expectation that in the Gospel of Luke the rights of the weak are strengthened in social contexts, the evangelist expresses himself critically on the role of women. In Luke 4:39; 7:36–50; 10:40, the author relegates the participation of women to that of servants at the meal. Susan Marks, Dennis Smith, Kathleen Corley, and Matthew Roller challenged the view that women participated as slaves, or only at the side of their husbands (Corley 2002; Roller 2006; Smith 2003; Taussig and Marks 2014). Women could be invited and would sit before their own tables. Were the tables for women in the same space as those for men? Dennis Smith and Kathleen Corley both cite Lucian (second century CE) as an example of women (including the bride) sharing a couch (and thus a table?) with each other while apparently occupying the same room as the men (Marks 2012, 129).

In Mark's case, at Herod's feast (Mark 6:14–29), it becomes clear that women who are given power at the feast are viewed critically, based on the fact that the equal participation of women was probably not a matter of course but nevertheless a familiar picture. While women usually took part in the meal with their husbands and also benefited from their social status, they also had an emancipated participation in the meal—even if this behavior was viewed critically. Typical actions such as serving, washing feet, or anointing, which belonged to the meal, are of course associated with the participating women.

The awakening of the daughter of Jairus reveals interesting differences among the Synoptic Gospels. While in Luke and Mark it is explicitly reported that the child eats after the awakening, this detail is missing in Matthew. In 9:25, Matthew writes: "But when the crowd had been put outside, he went in and took her by the hand, and the girl got up."

The reference to flute-players (Matt 9:23) and the crowd that was worried might indicate in Matthew that Jesus wanted to prevent a funerary meal. Matthew is the only evangelist who mentions the flute-players next to the weeping and worried group. This simplifying tendency to avoid narrating social interaction is also reflected in the description of the interaction between Jesus and the girl. While Mark and Luke talk about Jesus talking to the girl and asking her to stand up, Matthew reflects about Jesus taking the girl by the hand and healing her. Apart from the community aspect, Mark and Luke also differ from Matthew in that they do not "prove" that the girl is alive. Food stands for life and community. Jan Bremmer makes it clear that in this context it is also about the demarcation between people and spirits. "We may even wonder if the eating refers back to the resurrection of Jairus's daughter (Luke 8), who also receives food after her resurrection, presumably as definitive proof that she is really alive and not a kind of ghost" (Bremmer 2019, 203).

The story of the Baptist's death is about a feast (Mark 6:14–29; Matt 14:1–11; Luke 3:19–20). Here also a difference between the Synoptic Gospels becomes clear. I agree with Markus Ebner that in Mark the difference between the meal of Jesus and the meal of a worldly ruler should be especially noted:

> Herod eats with his "great ones" only. Jesus, however, whose meal has started out in the same way (vv. 30–32), opens it up for nameless "little ones": for the "many" who

are "like sheep without a shepherd" (vv. 33–34). At Jesus's meal, the fare is simple: bread and fish, poor people's food. At Herod's meal, in the end the head of John the Baptist is passed around on a meat dish (πίναξ, v. 28)—against Herod's wishes, to be sure (v. 26). Herod is, however, forced to follow through on the wish of his daughter, given that he has made a promise to her under oath, made in front of his table fellowship of courtiers and followers. He has to give the order to produce the head of the Baptist. By contrast, Jesus remains in charge vis-à-vis of his "great ones." (Ebner 2019, 96)

But eating with the "little ones" also involves the same difficulty, as it is signposted at Herod's meal: different interests and demands. Matthew shows that the meal can still be understood as a link between social classes and cultural contexts (in the diaspora). This can be seen very impressively in the story of the feast for Herod's daughter. "Similarly, the story of Herodias's daughter entertaining at a meal hauntingly holds the execution of John the Baptist, the festivity of Jesus's own meals and the ethnic tension around Herod's recent marriage together" (Taussig 2019, 131).

Luke omits mentioning the feast of Herod. This is understandable if one strives for a Synoptic comparison with regard to thematic completeness. The social difference within meal communities is described by Luke in various other places in relation to Jesus's meal communities. The description of meal communities from different religious or cultural contexts is discussed in Luke especially with regard to Jewish and non-Jewish meal participants. In other words, Luke does not need Herod's meal to develop his theological profile.

Ministry to the Gentile Regions

When Jesus acts outside Galilee and returns to Galilee, Matthew and Mark share the narratives of Jesus's criticism of the Pharisees and the feeding of the 4,000. Luke does not mention the feeding of the 4,000 and incorporates the criticism of the Pharisees at a different place.

In Jesus's criticism of the Pharisees (Mark 7:1–13; Matt 15:1–9) and Luke's woes against the Pharisees (Luke 11:37–54), the fundamental problem is that the Pharisees criticize people's failure to wash before a meal. In Matthew and Mark, it is the disciples who do not wash. In Luke 11:37–54, it is Jesus himself. Since the meal communities met in the evening or late afternoon, washings were an important part of the ancient culture. Public bathhouses and thermal baths were available for these purposes. Anointing with precious oils was also part of the rite. While cleansing at the beginning had a ritual character, washing one's hands after a meal also involved cleansing food leftovers. In Matthew and Mark reference is made to the tradition of the elders, which the disciples were expected to follow. Although the Jewish cleansing actions regarding washing hands before eating and after visiting the market, as well as cleaning drinking vessels, jugs, kettles, and benches, are named as the basis for criticizing Jesus's disciples (Mark

7:3–4), there is no doubt from a sociohistorical perspective that these were actions that preceded every meal. In other words, washing hands and other utensils to eat food is not a decidedly religious but a ritual and pragmatic act (Al-Suadi and Altman 2019).

The feedings of 5,000 (Matt 14:13–21; Mark 6:31–44; Luke 9:12–17; John 6:1–14) or 4,000 (Matt 15:32–39; Mark 8:1–9) are traditionally regarded as literary motifs, freeing them from the need for historical reconstruction. "The miraculous feeding stories, like other miracles in the Jesus tradition, are problematic if assumed to be historical events. Their function is to idealize Jesus, much as the meal texts in general do. Consequently, they will be analyzed as components of the literary motifs of the Gospel narratives" (Smith 2003, 223). The historical reconstruction is hindered by simple choices. First, "both Mark and Matthew have parallel stories of five thousand and four thousand, while Luke and John both only have one story each. The food in these stories is bread and fish. These texts seem to place little emphasis on the significance of the food itself" (Taussig 2009, 43). Second, "the various uses of reclining verbs ... indicate that the gospels mean these outdoor meals of fish and bread to be understood as commentaries on actual Hellenistic meals indoors" (43, referring to Smith 2003). Third, "the breadth of mention of food and drink that references the meal gatherings of the early Christians testifies to the intense interest in these meals as a central social institution for early Christianity" (43).

Turning away from questions about the historical content and, by extension, about the historical Jesus, the theological dynamic between Jesus and his disciples becomes clear. In the Synoptic Gospels, the food becomes a sign of recognition at this moment, because the disciples could not yet believe what they saw.

The Journey to Jerusalem

The story of Jesus on the way to Jerusalem is especially marked by many meal scenes in the Gospel of Luke: Luke 12:35–39 (watchful slaves), Luke 12:40–48 (the faithful or unfaithful slave), Luke 14:7–14 (humility and hospitality), Luke 14:15–24 (the parable of the great dinner), and Luke 15:11–32 (the parable of the prodigal and his brother). On the basis of Hellenistic meal practice, it becomes clear at this point how meal practice coincides above all with an ethical discussion. In Luke 14 a double frame is described in the context of a meal community. The Lukan Jesus tells a parable of a wedding feast to those present at a meal. He feels challenged to do so because places of honor were chosen for the meal in the customary way. In the parable Jesus puts his listeners in the situation of a person who was invited to a wedding feast and chooses a place for this occasion. Jesus advises against choosing the place of honor, since someone who is more respected might be invited. Eric Ottenheijm relates Luke 14 and rabbinical texts to each other: "the crucial connection is how spatial imagery is pervasive both for the etiquette and the ethical message: ending up 'higher' happens when someone is humble enough to start at a 'low' level. These teachings inculcate a sense of modesty in the pupil or believer, paradoxically by awarding them with greater visible honour in the dining hall or academy" (2019, 79). It is revealing at this point to include space as a category, because the socioethical focus describes a society that changes spaces in terms of their use. Ottenheijm observes that the transition from an amorphous society to a well-established meal community takes place in the reception room (2019, 84). This means that the spatial descriptions in the Synoptic Gospels represent not just sociohistorical but, above all, theological explications. Especially with regard to the narratives in Jerusalem and the Passion, these adaptations and receptions of early Christianity become clear.

This clear focus in Luke is only reflected in the approach of Matthew and Mark to the narrative of the demands of John and James, a scene without parallel in Luke. In Mark 10:35–45 and Matthew 20:20–28, the discussion centers on the seats of the disciples at the eschatological meal with Jesus. When asked what the two disciples expect from Jesus, they answer: "Grant us to sit, one at your right hand and one at your left, in your glory" (Mark 10:37). Jesus does not believe that they have understood the extent of their question and so asks them whether they are able to drink the cup he drinks or to be baptized with the baptism with which he was baptized, to which they answer yes. Their willingness to do according to him is related to the meal. Jesus concludes by stating that "to sit at my right hand or at my left is not mine to grant, but it is for those for whom it has been prepared (Mark 10:40). Matthew 20:23 adds the gloss "by my Father." Mark and Matthew make it clear that Jesus describes a theology in which drinking from a common cup, having experienced a common baptism, can be negotiated among the Christ believers in the community. Ebner connects this theology with the question of "the first": "from the point of view of the rule of God, this is the way for all who would like to be 'first.' The two Zebedaides, who proudly answer 'yes, we can!' to Jesus's question, are told by him, in a yet mysterious manner, 'The cup that I drink you will drink; and with the baptism with which I am baptized, you will be baptized.' (Mark 10.39) In other words 'go ahead with your wishes!'" (Ebner 2019, 98). Looking forward to the last supper of Jesus with his disciples, the seating order is destined by God. It will have to be clarified in the Passion reports why this detail is not taken up again.

The Passion and Death of Jesus

The entry into Jerusalem is the last Synoptic narrative to be found in all three Gospels without reference to food or meal fellowship. References to food and meal fellowship resume with the activity of Jesus in Jerusalem. While Luke already mentions the parable of the great feast in Luke 14:15–24, Matthew only takes it up in 22:1–14. Matthew's location of the meal within the Passion narrative distinguishes it from comparable Lukan stories which are located early in the work of Jesus (beside Luke 14:7–14 also 7:36–50; Heilmann 2019, 265 no. 5.) The main difference between Luke 14 and Matthew 22 is that it is not the excuses of the guests that are described but their behavior toward the slaves of the Lord and his reaction to their excuses (Ottenheijm 2019, 83). As was already apparent in Matthew 20, another crisis of a festive meal community goes hand in hand with lying at the table. In Matthew 22, it is added that access to the banquet without appropriate clothing is questioned by the king. The first crisis, namely that the invited guests did not appear, seemed to be resolved by the fact that the king's slaves invited everyone who met them (Matt 22:9–10). But the certainty that no unworthy guests would attend the meal did not ease the situation. Beginning in Matthew 22:11 it is described how the king looks at the guests and finds that someone is not wearing the right clothes and is already lying down for the meal (Matt 22:12). With regard to the importance of the seating arrangement for the community, it is relevant that the king does not ask the slaves but the servants of the meal (διακόνοις) to tie up this guest's hands and feet and throw him into the darkness. Thus, the guest is neither taken outside by those who invited him (that would be the slaves) nor released to where he came from (that would be the main streets of the city). Instead, he is taken by those responsible for the meal and thus also for the cohesion of the community to a place from which he will not return to such a community. It can therefore be assumed that the placement of this narrative is particularly relevant. While Luke clearly focuses on the aspect of discipleship and avoids the second crisis, Matthew makes it clear that there is now no turning back to escape the wrath of God and that even those who made it to the meal cannot be sure of their position.

Matthew takes the meal as a motif in Jesus's eschatological discourse. In contrast to Luke and Mark, who give no indication of food or mealtimes in this section, Matthew plays on the theme in three passages: Matthew 23:1–37 (Jesus denounces scribes and Pharisees), Matthew 24:36–44 (the necessity for watchfulness), and Matthew 24:45–51 (the faithful or the unfaithful slave). In the speech against the Pharisees and scribes, the relevance of the places of honor at the meal and in the synagogue is discussed. Jesus warns his disciples and the people not to conform to the example of the scribes and Pharisees, who did not act according to what they said. Yet Jesus instructs people to listen to them and, above all, to keep their word (Matt 23:1). The places of honor are only problematic if they are combined with arrogance. Matthew 23:12 clearly shows that in the worldview of Jesus, the one who exalts himself will be humbled and the one who humbles himself will be exalted. The goal, however, for both groups is exaltation but not with the same means. Matthew 24:37–44 deals only indirectly with the topic of food and meal sharing. In the retelling of the Flood (Gen 6:11–13), eating and drinking serve as a symbol for everyday life and are based on the naivete of the people, which is dramatically changed by the flood. The parable of the good servant and the evil servant (Matt 24:45–51) is another story Luke places much earlier in the narrative of Jesus (Luke 12:42–46). In Matthew, the parable and the question of who is the faithful and wise servant, whom the Lord sets over his servants to give them food at the right time, is a question of the Lord. For the servant who gives food and drink to the other servants represents the Lord. The choice of the servant is therefore a representation of the Lord. Here, too, eating and drinking is a matter of everyday life.

The Last Supper Tradition

From the previous evidence on food and meal fellowship, differences between the Synoptic Gospels was particularly clear in the placement of the narratives in the Gospels and the additions. However, from various perspectives, a description of a last meal between Jesus and his disciples is obvious in every Gospel. In Mark, because the disciples already drank from the cup (Mark 14:23—καὶ ἔπιον ἐξ αὐτοῦ πάντες; Ebner 2019, 98), in Matthew, because the meal participants have a social obligation to each other (Taussig 2019, 123), and in Luke, because a cup is given to God so that the community can experience the New Covenant, "the cup that is 'poured out for you' is an offering addressed to God. Although not mentioned at all, God is implied as the logical subject and is expected to bestow his gift (the New Covenant) on the beneficiaries (i.e. the apostles, mentioned in the ὑπέρ-phrase)" (Klinghardt 2019, 115).

The similarities and differences in the Synoptic findings can be summarized briefly: "while the interpretation of the meal proper in the 'word over the bread' seems to be identical or at least very similar in all four accounts (Matt. 26.26; Mark 14.22; Luke 22.19; 1 Cor. 11.24), the word over the cup in Mark and Matthew does clearly not relate to the libation (as in Luke and in Paul): Here, the cup is not poured out. Instead, Jesus asks the disciples to conjointly drink from one single cup (Mark 14.24; Matt. 26.27–28)" (Klinghardt 2019, 116). The difference is due to the following ritual difference: "this [cup] refers to the proposis, a less common, yet well-attested ritual gesture. . . . The proposis functions like a toast and expresses the esteem one symposiast holds for another one ('Here's to you!'). If all participants drink from one and the same cup, they express their mutual esteem, each one for the others, thus evening out any possible differences of social status within the group" (117).

At the beginning of this essay I briefly mentioned that the Synoptic Gospels contextualize the meal scene of the "Last Supper" very differently, which describes a meal of Jesus with his closest circle of disciples. It should not go unmentioned that in every instance a Christology is expressed. Smith makes it clear that these are Christological speculations.

When Mark takes up the Last Supper text in his narrative of the life of Jesus, it becomes embedded in his larger theme in which Jesus has foreknowledge of his death and provides a soteriological interpretation of it. This literary and theological formula that originates in Mark is then taken up by all of the Gospels until it reaches its culmination in John. Since the Last Supper story has no existence in the existing data apart from Christological speculation, it quite likely originated as a form of such speculation. Such a process of speculation, even in its earliest, originating form, is best understood as an attempt by the followers of Jesus to give him enduring significance after his death. To say that Jesus was the one who started such speculation about himself is to ignore the nature of the data, in which Christological speculation is always a process under development. The process does not begin with certain knowledge or fact; rather, in its very beginning it is speculation, and as speculation it is subject to continuing reinterpretation (Smith 2003, 226).

To describe this process as "Christological speculation" does not necessarily put the subject of the events in the right light. Taussig responds to this phenomenon by describing the efforts of the first Christian faith communities as an "experiment." Both terms perceive that there is no uniform or normative interpretation but that the texts in their plurality must be taken seriously. This plurality is encountered not only in the comparison of the reconstructed versions of the Synoptic Gospels, which are regarded as original, but above all in the richly varied tradition of the texts. The text-critical analysis of the so-called Last Supper Paradadosis also connects the Synoptic Gospels with the Pauline tradition. Of particular importance are the words spoken over the bread. In 1 Corinthians 11:24 the following text is documented: "καὶ εὐχαριστήσας ἔκλασεν καὶ εἶπεν· ᵀ τοῦτό ⸂μού ἐστιν⸃ τὸ σῶμα °τὸ ὑπὲρ ὑμῶν ᵀ· τοῦτο ποιεῖτε εἰς τὴν ἐμὴν ἀνάμνησιν" ("and when he had given thanks, he broke it and said, 'This is my body that is for you. Do this in remembrance of me'"). Four text-critical variants are listed for this verse: (1) the insertion of λαβετε φαγετε before the first τοῦτό in C3 Ψ 𝔐 t vgcl sy; (2) the testimony of μού ἐστιν in 𝔓46 and Latin manuscripts; (3) the omission of τὸ in 𝔓46; and (4) the insertion of (a) κλωμενον in ℵ2 C3 D2 F G Ψ 1739mg. 1881 𝔐 sy, (b) θρυπτο μενον in D*, and (c) διδομενον in co. Of these variants, mainly 1 and 4c are interesting with respect to the Synoptic Gospels.

The insertion of λαβετε φαγετε is an important variant, because it refers to Matthew 26:26, which reads: "⸂Ἐσθιόντων δὲ αὐτῶν⸃ λαβὼν ὁ Ἰησοῦς ᵀ ἄρτον ⸀καὶ εὐλογήσας⸃ ἔκλασεν καὶ ⸀δοὺς τοῖς μαθηταῖς⸃ εἶπεν· λάβετε φάγετε, τοῦτό ἐστιν τὸ σῶμά μου" ("While they were eating, Jesus took a loaf of bread, and after blessing it he broke it, gave it to the disciples, and said, 'Take, eat; this is my body'"). Although the text exhibits many variant readings, all sources state λάβετε φάγετε. One must therefore ask how the similarity between 1 Corinthians 11:24 in C3 Ψ 𝔐 t vgcl sy and Matthew 26:26 can be explained, since for both texts "Take, eat; this is my body" has been preserved. Since the two imperatives can be understood as an invitation to ritual action, the scientific network "Mahl und Text" has argued that this connection between 1 Corinthians and Matthew is due to liturgical developments. This would mean that from a ritual scientific perspective the variants of 1 Corinthians and Matthew refer to the same liturgical form or tradition. The second variant, which points to the interdependence between the Synoptic Gospels and the Pauline letters, is similar. If one places the word διδόμενον before the second τοῦτο, then the proximity to Luke 22:19 becomes clear: "Καὶ λαβὼν ἄρτον εὐχαριστήσας ἔκλασεν καὶ ἔδωκεν αὐτοῖς λέγων· τοῦτό ἐστιν τὸ σῶμά μου ⸆τὸ ὑπὲρ ὑμῶν διδόμενον· τοῦτο ποιεῖτε εἰς τὴν ἐμὴν ἀνάμνησιν" ("Then he took a loaf of bread, and when he had given thanks, he broke it and gave it to them, saying, 'This is my body, which is given for you. Do this in remembrance of me'"). Now here there might be a ritual correspondence between the two cup words in 1 Cor 11:24 and Luke 22:19, for the addition διδόμενον clearly indicates the given character of the bread. It is not unlikely that in the Coptic tradition this aspect would be particularly emphasized, but the network has, on the basis of little testimony, argued that this is more of a literary than a ritual approximation.

The Resurrection and Ascension of Jesus

In the resurrection reports, Mark 16:14–18 (with the eleven at the table), Luke 24:30–32 (Jesus breaks bread with the two on the road to Emmaus), and Luke 24:33–43 (Jesus appears to the eleven plus the two from Emmaus) will be addressed. In Mark 16:14–18 Jesus reveals himself to the eleven disciples, while in Luke 24:30–35 two disciples first meet Jesus on the way to Emmaus. In Luke 24:30–35 a Luke speciality is expressed, which Taussig thematizes: "Luke-Acts refers to what it calls the 'breaking of bread' three explicit times, once at the end of the story when the disciples encounter the risen Jesus at a meal (Luke 24:30–35), again in a picture of the early postresurrection believers in Jerusalem gathering for meals (Acts 2:46), and in a story about Paul at a meal on the first day of the week in Troas. In Acts 27:35, Paul is portrayed as convening a meal on a threatened ship, wherein only the breaking of bread is portrayed as social act" (2009, 42). These reports make it clear that the description of the ritual act or the description of the table community in the Hellenistic sense expresses an interest in the social, ethical, and ritual significance of the meal community (e.g., 2009, 43). In Luke 24:42 the community is constituted in a different way. Here the eating of the grilled fish is a sign that the risen Christ is not a spirit. With such a spirit, as the story suggests, a (meal) fellowship would be excluded.

Conclusion

This essay has looked at the theme of eating and meal fellowship from a literary and ritual-scientific perspective and has understood communal eating as an everyday, cultural practice, influenced by social, political, and religious aspects of the so-called Hellenization of the Mediterranean. The dependence of ritual-scientific aspects of the stories on their literary character is due to the fact that the communities are semiprivate where the writings have been read, edited, and distributed. Hence, texts on food and meals refer to (festive) meal communities. In order to compare the Synoptic Gospels, the meal scenes from different points in the Gospel narratives have been compared with each other.

The beginnings of Mark, Matthew, and Luke, as well as the narrative of John the Baptist reveal that Luke wants to keep fasting as an expression of closeness to God. As Mark narrates the beginnings of Jesus's ministry, fasting does not take place as a condition of the temptation, but fasting and the following hunger are essential for Matthew and Luke. Luke's special consideration of the socially vulnerable is highlighted in the Galilean Ministry. Here he points out that Jesus came to save the socially weak (Luke 5:32); Matthew adds that Jesus's behavior is a sign of mercy (Matt 9:13). The Synoptics also show that the equal participation of women, though not a matter of course, was a familiar picture. Some stories show a simplifying tendency to avoid narrating social interaction, such as the interaction between Jesus and Jarius's daughter. While Mark and Luke narrate Jesus talking to the girl and asking her to stand up, Matthew shifts the narrative to Jesus taking the girl by the hand and healing her. Concerning the ministry to the Gentile regions, I have argued that it is more revealing to question the theological context between Jesus and his disciples, than to debate the historical content. The journey to Jerusalem highlights that Mark and Matthew make it clear that Jesus describes a theology in which drinking from a common cup, having experienced a common baptism, can be experienced among the Christ believers in the community. Further on, the Passion and death of Jesus include a description of a meal between Jesus and his disciples in every Gospel: in Mark, the disciples already drank from the cup (Mark 14:23; Ebner 2019, 98); in Matthew, the meal participants have a social obligation to each other (Taussig 2019, 123); and in Luke, a cup is given to God so that the community can experience the New Covenant (Klinghardt 2019, 115). Although the connotations of the meal differ from one Gospel to the other, it is justifiable to claim that descriptions of common meals and Jesus's Passion are inseparable.

This ritual-scientific exegesis allows a look at the texts beyond text reconstruction. I have focused not on the traditionally Synoptic comparisons but on the ritual comparison of the texts, which show their characteristic literary and ritual imprint on the subject of food and meal. The resurrection and ascension of Jesus revealed the ritual significance of the meal community. The Synoptic findings have shown that "Synoptic" cannot only be a literary category, but also a ritual one: The texts were compared on the basis of the ritual contextualization, and no limitation was made by limiting source theories, which emphasizes a simultaneity of the sources.

References

Al-Suadi, Soham. 2011. *Essen als Christusgläubige—Ritualtheoretische Exegese paulinischer Texte*. Vol. 55, TANZ. Tübingen: Francke.
Al-Suadi, Soham, and Peter Altmann. 2019. *Essen und Trinken*. Edited by Markus Öhler and Alexandra Grund. Lebenswelten der Bibel. Gütersloh: Gütersloher Verlagshaus.
Bremmer, Jan N. 2019. "Eucharists and other Meals in the Apocryphal Acts of John and Acts of Andrew." In *T&T Clark Handbook to Early Christian Meals in the Greco-Roman World*, edited by Soham Al-Suadi and Peter-Ben Smit, 197–210. London: T&T Clark.
Corley, Kathleen E. 2002. "Women and Greco-Roman Meals." Paper presented at the annual meeting of the Society of Biblical Literature, Toronto.
Daniel-Hughes, Carly. 2012. "Bodies in Motion, Bodies at Rest: Corporeality, Status, and the Negotiation of Power at the Meal." In *Meals in the Early Christian World: Social Formation, Experimentation, and Conflict at the Table*, edited by Hal Taussig and Dennis Smith, 215–27. New York: Palgrave Macmillan.
Ebner, Martin. 2019. "The Gospel of Mark—The Commitment of the 'Unleavened' to the Kingdom of God Agenda of Jesus." In *T&T Clark Handbook to Early Christian Meals in*

the Greco-Roman World, edited by Soham Al-Suadi and Peter-Ben Smit, 93–107. London: T&T Clark.

Heilmann, Jan. 2019. "Meals in the Johannine Letters." In *T&T Clark Handbook to Early Christian Meals in the Greco-Roman World*, edited by Soham Al-Suadi and Peter-Ben Smit, 258–68. London: T&T Clark.

Klinghardt, Matthias. 1996. *Gemeinschaftsmahl und Mahlgemeinschaft: Soziologie und Liturgie frühchristlicher Mahlfeiern*. Vol. 13, *TANZ*. Tübingen: Francke Verlag.

Klinghardt, Matthias. 2012. "A Typology of the Communal Meal." In *Meals in the Early Christian World: Social Formation, Experimentation, and Conflict at the Table*, edited by Hal Taussig and Dennis Smith, 9–22. New York: Palgrave Macmillan.

Klinghardt, Matthias. 2019. "Meals in the Gospel of Luke." In *T&T Clark Handbook to Early Christian Meals in the Greco-Roman World*, edited by Soham Al-Suadi and Peter-Ben Smit, 108–20. London: T&T Clark.

Marks, Susan. 2012. "Present and Absent: Women at Greco-Roman Wedding Meals." In *Meals in the Early Christian World: Social Formation, Experimentation, and Conflict at the Table*, edited by Hal Taussig and Dennis Smith, 123–48. New York: Palgrave Macmillan.

McGowan, Andrew Brian. 1999. *Ascetic Eucharists: Food and drink in early Christian Ritual Meals*. Oxford Early Christian Studies. Oxford: Oxford University Press.

Ottenheijm, Eric. 2019. "'Prepare Yourself.' Spatial Rhetoric in Rabbinic and Synoptic Meal Parables." In *T&T Clark Handbook to Early Christian Meals in the Greco-Roman World*, edited by Soham Al-Suadi and Peter-Ben Smit, 75–92. London: T&T Clark.

Roller, Matthew B. 2006. *Dining Posture in Ancient Rome: Bodies, Values, and Status*. Princeton: Princeton University Press.

Smith, Dennis E. 2003. *From Symposium to Eucharist: The Banquet in the Early Christian World*. Minneapolis: Fortress Press.

Stein, Hans Joachim. 2008. *Frühchristliche Mahlfeiern. Ihre Gestalt und Bedeutung nach der neutestamentlichen Briefliteratur und der Johannesoffenbarung*. WUNT II. Tübingen.

Taussig, Hal. 2009. *In the Beginning Was the Meal: Social Experimentation and Early Christian Identity*. Minneapolis: Fortress Press.

Taussig, Hal. 2019. "The Primary Role of Meals in Matthew's Construction of Diasporic Identity." In *T&T Clark Handbook to Early Christian Meals in the Greco-Roman World*, edited by Soham Al-Suadi and Peter-Ben Smit, 121–35. London: T&T Clark.

Taussig, Hal, and Susan Marks, eds. 2014. *Meals in Early Judaism: Social Formation at the Table*. New York: Palgrave Macmillan.

CHAPTER 19

HEALING AND EXORCISM

MEGHAN HENNING

INTRODUCTION[*]

ADOLF von Harnack, in his 1906 commentary, argued that Luke was distinctive among the Synoptic authors because he "mentions only the healings [in the summaries] and makes a sharp distinction between natural and demonic diseases" (1906, 136). He adds that Luke makes this distinction between natural and demonic disease because "the latter required a quite different medical treatment."[1] Harnack's attempt to distinguish between types of diseases is emblematic of scholarship of this era, allowing scholars to differentiate between healing and exorcism or, as in the case of Harnack, to see Luke himself making that "sharp distinction" on the basis of medical knowledge. Harnack is so eager to apply the scientific methods of higher criticism to the New Testament that he can't help but imagine that Luke is also employing differential diagnosis in telling the stories themselves. This application of contemporary scientific precision to the New Testament miracle stories would enliven much of twentieth-century scholarship. But that same emphasis on modern scientific epistemology would also continue to elide both the bodily world of the modern New Testament critic and that of the ancient authors and texts themselves.

Some of the earliest critical scholarship on the healing and exorcism stories in the Synoptic Gospels was focused on form- and source-critical questions (Bultmann 1968 [1921]; Dibelius 1982 [1933]). Within this line of inquiry, the "form" of the story is tightly connected to its verisimilitude, distinguishing between the historically implausible

---

[*] I would like to thank Stephen Ahearne-Kroll, Dustin Atlas, John David Penniman, and the editorial team at Oxford University press for their careful reading and editorial attention to this essay. I would especially like to thank Candida R. Moss, who offered ongoing conversation, critical feedback and intellectual companionship at key moments of the writing process.

[1] As Theissen, 1983, 92, argues, the overall thesis regarding the uniqueness of Luke's distinction between healing and exorcism is "certainly wrong as regards Mark."

"wonders" and the miracles which scholars deem more likely to have originated from factual accounts (Bultmann 1968 [1921], 209–20; Dibelius 1982 [1933], 99–103; Theissen 1983, 34). The method of form criticism allowed scholars to compare healing stories across the Synoptics, and classify them using literary diagnostic criteria to distinguish between different literary genres (exorcisms, healings, rule miracles, etc.) and the social setting (Sitz im Leben) that made the transmission of each literary form possible. Paradoxically, this application of modernist scientific approaches to miracle stories in order to categorize them has typically precluded any concerted attention to ancient medicine or disease theory (Hengel and Hengel 1959, 348; Theissen 1983, 90, 93). Even in recent form-critical work, medical insights are still seen as ancillary, a phenomenon that Annette Weissenrieder calls "unsettling" (2017, 266).

Current scholarship on healing and exorcism has shifted from focusing exclusively on questions about the texts and their visions of reality to questions about the bodies which are described in those texts, and the ancient culture of the body that produced these textual artifacts. This shift has expanded the scope of inquiry to question some of the starting assumptions of the healing and exorcism stories themselves (Avalos 1995; Avalos 1999; Kee 1986; Moss and Schipper 2011; Melcher, Parsons, and Yong 2017; Wainright 2006; Weissenrieder and Etzelmüller 2016). This line of inquiry is led by scholars who are informed by disability studies, ancient medicine, classics, and material and epigraphic evidence from the Asclepieia, as well as critical theoretical work on space, the body, and gender. These scholars are simultaneously interrogating the assumptions of the texts around bodies, while also historicizing those claims using philology, material culture, and ancient medicine (Alkier and Weissenrieder 2013; Kelley 2011; Moss 2010; Moss and Schipper 2011; Weissenrieder 2017).

Healings and exorcisms in the Synoptic Gospels are best understood as part of early Christian engagement with broader cultural ideas about the body. These vignettes reveal not only the theological aims of the Gospel authors but also the ways in which those authors were reproducing, resisting, or providing nuance to ancient understandings of bodies and bodily transformation in service of their overall theological agendas. In particular these stories replicate ancient tropes of healing as a demonstration of power and faith and replicate, resist, and give nuance to ideas about the sick or demon-possessed body.

Exorcisms

Exorcisms have been distinguished from healings on the basis of the presence of a demon, the battle or conversation between the demon and the exorcist, and the destructive activity of the demon (Bultmann 1968 [1921], 223, 231–32; Theissen 1983, 85–90). As Walter Wilson has noted, the social assumptions about the demonic are never "an isolated phenomena but contribute to an array of complex processes according to which cultural norms, boundaries, and limits are negotiated and enforced" (Wilson

2014, 119). In particular, many scholars have pointed to the diverse ways in which the demonic is frequently associated with whatever is identified as marginal in a given context (Dochorn, Rudnig-Zelt, and Wold 2016; Keith and Stuckenbruck 2016; Ronis 2017; Witmer 2012, 27). Nevertheless, as disability studies scholarship has demonstrated, in the first century CE the demonic is not the only way that authors use bodies to talk about boundaries. Sickness and bodily difference are used by ancient authors to demarcate boundaries, enforce cultural norms, and emphasize that which is marginal. What is more, daimons, divine agents, and gods are active agents in other ancient contexts of sickness and healing, as evidenced in medical authors like Galen or at the shrines devoted to Asclepius (Avalos, Melcher 2007, and Schipper; Carter 2011; Henning 2011; Kelley 2011; Moss and Schipper 2011, 2–4). There is also a strong tradition by the first century CE that links illness and the demonic (Kee 1986, 22–23; Kelley 2011). When the demonic is understood in this broader context of ancient assumptions about the body and healing activities, exorcism hardly stands out as its own form, but rather as another ancient healing story. Here I identify the places where each of the Gospel authors refers to demon possession and exorcism, acknowledging that in their ancient context these references to the demonic occupy much of the same space as the healing narratives.

Exorcism is right at home in the apocalyptic schema of the Gospel of Mark (Collins 2007, 156; Marcus 2000, 71–75; Skinner 2016, 102–4, 107–19; Twelftree 2007, 101–28). Immediately after the calling of the first disciples, Jesus casts out an unclean spirit from a man in a synagogue, demonstrating from the outset of his ministry that even the demons recognize him, and that he and his disciples will be victorious in the cosmic battle between God and the forces of evil (Mark 1:21–28). Mark also contains two passing references to Jesus or the disciples casting out many demons in the first chapter, giving the reader the impression that this was a frequent occurrence and a central component of Jesus's earthly ministry (Mark 1:34, 39). At the call of the twelve disciples, Jesus appoints them to have the authority to cast out demons, among other things (Mark 3:15; Matt 10:2). The authority with which Jesus himself casts out demons becomes an issue in the Beelzebul controversy of Mark 3:22–27 (Matt 12:22–24; Luke 11:14–23). Mark contains the most expansive telling of the stories of the Gerasene demoniac (Mark 5:1–20; Matt 8:28–34; Luke 8:26–39), the story of the Syrophoenician women's daughter (Mark 7:24–30; Matt 15:21–38), the healing of the boy with the unclean spirit (Mark 9:14–29; Matt 17:14–21; Luke 9:37–43), and the exorcist who casts out demons in Jesus's name but is not a disciple of Jesus (Mark 9:38–41; Luke 9:49–50). Within Mark's cosmology, Jesus's exorcisms not only demonstrate his superior power over the forces of evil but also announce the inbreaking of the kingdom of God. Nevertheless, many of Mark's stories are retold in Matthew and Luke (if abbreviated), and Matthew and Luke both contain additional exorcism material that is not in Mark. Thus all three of the Synoptic authors appear to have an interest in retelling exorcism stories.

Matthew contains all of the Markan exorcism stories except for the story of the man with the unclean spirit in the synagogue and the passage about the anonymous exorcist (Mark 1:21–28; Mark 9:38–41). Matthew includes the story of the exorcism of the Syrophoenician woman's daughter and abbreviates the story of the Gerasene demoniac and the healing of the boy with the unclean spirit. In addition to the Markan exorcism material, Matthew also contains the Q source stories about the return of the unclean spirit (Matt 12:43–45; Luke 11:24–26) and the doublet of the demoniac who was a non-speaking person (Matt 9:32–34; Matt 12:22–24). Some have hypothesized that Matthew's redaction reflects ambivalence or animosity toward exorcism stories (Koskenniemi 2013, 93–97; Twelftree 2011, 62–63) or an interest in drawing a distinction between exorcism and healing stories (Theissen 1983, 90–91).

Yet Matthew includes as many distinct exorcism stories as he excises, and in the exorcism stories that are included Matthew blurs the lines between healing and exorcism. For example, in Matthew's telling of the story of the exorcism of the Syrophoenician woman's daughter (Canaanite woman for Matthew), the author of Matthew shifts the focus of the ending to the faith of the woman (πίστις Matt 15:28) and the daughter's healing (ἰάθη, Matt 15:28) rather than the expulsion of the demon (τὸ δαιμόνιον ἐξεληλυθός, Mark 7:30). Whereas Mark refers to the demon or unclean spirit three times in the telling of the story, Matthew mentions the word *demon* once to set the scene as an exorcism but then concludes with an emphasis on the daughter's healing. Matthew stops short of removing all traces of exorcism but instead retells the story so that it is a healing story in which the impairment is identified as demon possession. Matthew (and Luke) take a similar approach in their redaction of Mark 9:14–29 (Matt 17:14–20; Luke 9:37–43a), the healing of the boy with the unclean spirit, telling the exorcism story with an emphasis on healing (Sterling 1993, 476). Similarly, Matthew treats exorcism as a type of healing in the special section of the Gospel that is devoted to healing stories (Matt 8–9). Here the author of Matthew groups the story of the non-speaking person possessed by a demon (9:32–34) along with other healing stories, even though this story is a doublet that is repeated later in Matthew 12:22–24. Matthew depicts exorcism as a kind of healing, and making a distinction between healing and exorcism does not appear to be a priority.

In Luke, exorcisms are presented alongside healings as "signs and wonders" that qualify Jesus as a prophet or a Son of God, and the disciples as prophets. The earliest mention of exorcism, Luke 4:31–37, is grouped with other healing stories and is arranged by Luke so that it precedes the call of the disciples in Luke 5, establishing exorcism and healing as emblematic of the power and justice that characterized Jesus's prophetic activity and authority (Bovon 2002, 161–62; Johnson 1991, 85–86). Like the elevation of the poor, women, sinners, tax-collectors, and the sick, the demon-possessed are elevated as a part of the prophetic hospitality of Luke's Jesus (Jipp 2013, 49–53, 266–68). Of the Markan material, Luke omits the story of the Syrophoenician women's daughter and the commission to cast out demons in the calling of the twelve. Luke does include the stories of the man with the unclean spirit in the synagogue (Mark 1:21–28; Luke 4:31–37), the Gerasene demoniac (Luke 8:26–39), and the Beelzebul controversy (Luke 11:14–23). Luke abridges the stories of the boy with the unclean spirit (Luke 9:37–43) and of the exorcist who casts out demons in the name of Jesus but is not a disciple (Luke 9:49–50). In addition to these Markan stories, Luke contains the Q story about the return of the unclean spirit (Luke 11:24–26) and the two exorcism stories that are unique to Luke: the submission of the demons when the seventy return (Luke 10:17) and the pericope in which Jesus tells the disciples to go tell Herod that he will be busy casting out demons and performing cures today and tomorrow (Luke 13:31–33).

Whereas Harnack made a sharp distinction between Luke's depictions of exorcism and healing, reasoning that Luke distinguished between the two because they required different treatments, the author of Luke does not appear to share this concern. For example, in Luke 4:31–37, the author of Luke redacts Mark so that the exorcism "does him no harm" (μηδὲν βλάψαν αὐτόν 4:35), changing the wording of Mark 1:26, which has the unclean spirit convulsing and screaming on its way out. The language Luke uses is not only less dramatic than Mark's classically violent exorcism scene but also a possible allusion to the broadly held cultural idea that medical treatments should "do no harm," depicting the exorcism in Luke as a medical treatment and Jesus as physician (Hippocrates, *Epidemics* 1.11; Hippocrates, *The Oath*, lines 18–19, 28).[2] In the story which immediately follows, the healing of Peter's mother-in law, Luke edits the moment of healing so that the healing shares the same mechanics as the preceding exorcism. In both stories Jesus "rebukes" the demon/fever (ἐπετίμησεν; Luke 4:35, 39, 41), the demon/fever leaves, and the person being healed is good as new (Bovon 2002, 163–64; Johnson 1991, 85).

Luke also reshapes the summary material that follows the healing of Peter's mother-in-law, so that sickness and demon possession are not just described alongside one another (as they are in Mark and Matthew) but demon possession is mentioned as a type of sickness. Luke edits Mark's mention of "all who were sick or possessed with demons" to simply say that people brought "any who were sick with various kinds of diseases" to Jesus (Luke 4:40a; Mark 1:32). Whereas Mark describes curing the sick and casting out demons as two separate but related activities (Mark 1:34), Luke describes exorcism (4:41) as the continuation of the treatment of "various kinds of diseases" via the laying on of hands which brought about a cure (Luke 4:40b). After this statement of cure, Luke adds: "Demons also came out of many, shouting 'You are the Son of God!'" and Jesus again "rebukes" the demons (ἐπιτιμῶν; Luke 4:41). Here Luke omits Mark's statement that Jesus "cast out many demons" in favor of a description of demons simply coming out of the "many," as if the expulsion of demons is simply the logical continuation of Jesus healing people of a variety of ailments in the previous verse. In Luke 4, casting out demons is itself a healing activity, and one that helps to identify Jesus as "Son of

---

[2] Luke and the oldest recoverable Greek version of the Hippocratic Oath use different Greek verbs to talk about harm avoidance. Whereas Luke uses βλάπτω, the Hippocratic Oath has ἀδικία and φθορία (Hippocrates, *The Oath*, lines 18–19, 28). Although the exact phrase "do no harm" does not occur in the Hippocratic Oath, a closer formulation does appear in Hippocrates, *Epidemics* 1.11, which, like Luke, uses μὴ βλάπτω ("the physician ... must have two special objects in mind with regard to disease, namely to do good or to do no harm"). The idea that physicians should endeavor not to harm the patient was not only mentioned multiple times in the Hippocratic Oath; it appears elsewhere in the medical literature, suggesting that this was a broadly held component of ancient medical thinking which might have been known by Luke and his audience. Authorship of texts attributed to Hippocrates is a difficult question, and so references to "Hippocrates" simply refer to the group of texts that are attributed to Hippocrates in antiquity, the Hippocratic corpus.

God." The Lukan redaction of the exorcism and healing stories in chapter 4 appears to intentionally read exorcism and healing as the same kind of activity, activity which establishes Jesus as a prophetic Son of God who uses his power to reverse the social status of the sick.

Healings

Healings can be identified as a literary form in the Synoptic Gospels, one that is characterized by a description of the illness and the healing, and sometimes mentioning a healing touch, the healer's power, the use of healing agents, and the reactions of onlookers (Bultmann 1968 [1921], 218–31; Dibelius 1982 [1933], 70; Theissen 1983, 90–94; Wilson 2014, 5–8). The healing stories not only represent a prominent literary form within the Synoptic tradition, they also represent a prominent feature of early Christianity: its engagement with ancient ideas about the body. In addition to forty-one healing stories, the Synoptic Gospels also contain summary statements like the one found in Mark 1:34 stating that "he cured many who were sick with various diseases, and cast out many demons." These summary statements help to give the reader of the Gospels the impression that healing was a major activity in the life of Jesus.

Why was healing so central to the retelling of the story of Jesus's earthly ministry? Some scholars have hypothesized that the primary concern in telling healing stories was to demonstrate the power of Jesus and announce the kingdom of God, viewing them largely as literary devices (Bultmann 1968 [1921], 209–44). Others have argued that this reading strategy obscures the bodily realities of first-century life, like those of increasing urbanization (and subsequent rise in sickness), economic barriers to health care, and other available understandings of healing (Avalos 1999, 4–7, 117–19; Cotter 1999; Kee 1986; Pilch 2000; Wainright 2006). Reading the healing stories in conjunction with the lived reality of their ancient context means that they must be appreciated as stories that describe a healthcare encounter, one that was sometimes in concert with other ancient healthcare practices and at other times offered an alternative approach to healing.

Mark concentrates the bulk of his healing material in the first ten chapters of the Gospel, so that at least one healing or exorcism occurs in each of the first ten chapters. In chapter 1, Peter's mother-in-law is healed first (Mark 1:29–31; Matt 8:14–15; Luke 4:38–39), followed immediately by the unnamed group of the sick who were healed in the evening (Mark 1:32–34; Matt 8:16–17; Luke 4:40–41) and the healing of the leper (Mark 1:40–45; Matt 8:1–4; Luke 5:12–16). After the healing of the sick in the evening and the healing of the leper, Jesus commands the demons not to speak and the leper not to say anything. These peculiar commands are characteristic Markan injunctions to silence that are meant to highlight the special knowledge that Mark's audience has about Jesus's identity. (This Markan emphasis on the "Messianic Secret" is left out in Matt 8:16–17; Matt 8:1–4; Luke 5:12–16; Wrede 1901.) Since these injunctions to silence occur in the first chapter of Mark, after some of the first healing activities of Jesus they not only establish his identity as one with the power to heal but also invite the audience to identify with the sick. In Mark, the sick, and the audience with them, are able to recognize Jesus's power because of their vulnerability, not in spite of it, reversing existing cultural narratives about power and knowledge.

Once these initial scenes of healing have helped to characterize the Markan Jesus as an extremely popular and sought-out healer, "who could no longer go out into a town openly" (Mark 1:45), Jesus continues this activity in subsequent chapters, healing a leper (Mark 2:1–12; see healing of paralytic Matt 9:1–8; Luke 5:17–26), a man with a withered hand (Mark 3:1–6; Matt 12:9–14; Luke 6:6–11), and the multitudes (Mark 3:7–12; Matt 12:15–21; Luke 6:17–19). By interspersing the healing stories amid the narrative, the Gospel of Mark invites the reader to draw connections between the wounded bodies of the sick and the wounded body of Jesus that is depicted in the three passion predictions and the final passion narrative (Mark 8:31–33; 9:30–32; 10:32–34; Moss 2017, 283–99; Remus 1997, 27–29). But even as the passion predictions invite the audience to reflect upon the soon to be wounded body of Jesus and his powerlessness, the emphasis on Jesus's power to heal increases as the narrative moves toward the crucifixion. For the readers of Mark, Jesus is depicted as a wounded healer, exhibiting a great power to heal that is in tension with his full acknowledgment of his powerlessness in the face of his impending crucifixion.

In Mark 5–10 the power to heal is articulated through a series of intercalated stories that emphasize the role of touch in the healing encounter and progress toward increasingly more intimate bodily contact. In Mark 5, Jesus heals Jairus's daughter and the hemorrhaging woman, who is healed by simply touching the garment of Jesus, draining him of his power (Mark 5:21–43; Matt 9:18–26; Luke 8:40–56; Moss 2010). Similarly, the healings at Gennesaret in chapter 6 occur through people touching the hem of Jesus's cloak (Mark 6:53–56; Matt 14:34–36). In chapter 7, the healing touch becomes more intimate, with Jesus inserting his fingers in the ears of the deaf person who speaks differently (Mark 7:31–37). And in chapters 8–10, two stories of Jesus healing blindness in chapters 8 (Mark 8:22–26) and 10 (Mark 10:46–52; Matt 20:29–34; Luke 18:35–43) and the story of the healing of the boy possessed by a spirit in chapter 9 (Mark 9) demonstrate Jesus's power over unseen ailments that were internal and associated with the soul. Blindness, which was thought to reside in the soul, is healed in Mark 8 through a touch and application of saliva to the eyes, but by Mark 10 Jesus is able to heal Bartimaeus's blindness with words (see Matt 6:22–23; Luke 11:33–36; Henning 2017; Moss 2011). In Mark 8–10 Jesus's impending suffering and death is juxtaposed with his ability to access the wounded bodies of others in increasingly more intimate ways.

Whereas Mark has interspersed healing narratives throughout his Gospel in service of a broader narrative about wounded bodies, the author of Matthew arranges many of the healing and exorcism stories together, in a special narrative section (Matt 8–9) between the Sermon on the Mount (Matt 5–7) and the Missionary Discourse (Matt 10).[3] Matthew

---

[3] There are a few healing stories that occur in Matthew outside of this special section as well, including the healing of the man with the withered hand (Matt 12:9–14) and the healing of many sick people (Matt 15:29–31).

begins this special section with the healing of the leper (Matt 8:1–4; Mark 1:40–45; Luke 5:12–16), the healing of the centurion's servant (Matt 8:5–13; Luke 7:1–10), the healing of Peter's mother-in-law (Matt 8:14–15; Mark 1:29–31; Luke 4:38–39), a summary statement, and a fulfillment quotation from Isaiah (Matt 8:16–17; see Isa 53:4; Mark 1:32–34; Luke 4:40–41). The remainder of chapter 8 is devoted to pronouncement stories, a sea rescue, and an exorcism (Matt 8:19–34). Chapter 9 returns to the topic of healing, beginning with the healing of the paralytic (Matt 9:1–8; Mark 2:1–12; Luke 5:17–26), the revival of the official's daughter (Matt 9:18–19, 23–26; Mark 5:21–43; Luke 8:40–56), the healing of the hemorrhaging woman (Matt 9:20–22; Mark 5:24–34; Luke 8:42b–48), the healing of two blind men (Matt 9:27–31; doublet Matt 20:29–34; Mark 10:46–52; Luke 18:35–43) and a non-speaking person possessed by a demon (9:32–34; doublet Matt 12:22–24), and a final summary statement and instructions for the disciples (Matt 9:35–38). Matthew also includes the call of Levi and a question about fasting in the midst of the healing stories of chapter 9 (9:9–17; Mark 2:13–22; Luke 5:27–39).

The Gospel of Matthew presents healing activity as central to the ministry of Jesus and the disciples. Matthew's unique arrangement depicts healing activity as an outgrowth of the ethical instruction of the Sermon on the Mount and a routine activity of the disciples, who receive their instruction immediately after the rapid succession of different types of healing encounters. The elements that are uniquely Matthean offer key insights into the way that healing functions in the first Gospel. The fulfillment quotation of Isaiah 53:4 depicts healing activity as vicarious suffering: "He took our infirmities and bore our diseases." The summary statement of Matthew 9:35 juxtaposes teaching at the synagogues in every city with "healing every disease and sickness." Likewise a few verses later, as the disciples are being commissioned, they are not only given authority over the unclean spirits (as in Mark 6:7) but also in Matthew and Luke receive the authority to "heal every disease and every sickness" (Matt 10:1). In both of these passages the NRSV translation renders the verb θεραπεύω as "cure," a translation that renders the iterative healing encounters to be primarily about total transformation of bodies rather than treatment or care. While the immediate context of Matthew 8–9 might suggest a translation of θεραπεύω that refers to total transformation, the word itself can mean to serve, to take care of, or to heal, and I would submit that those definitions help one to exhibit more care in distinguishing between what is going on in the ancient context and today's hypermedicalized world that is preoccupied with the "cure." (For distinction between healing and cure see Moss 2017.)

Like Mark, Luke intersperses healing stories throughout his Gospel rather than grouping them together. Luke contains all of the Markan healing stories except the healings at Gennesaret (Mark 6:53–56) and the deaf person who spoke differently (Mark 7:31–37). Luke 4–8 contains the healing of Peter's mother-in-law, the leper, the paralytic, the man with the withered hand, the multitudes, and Jairus's daughter and the hemorrhaging woman (Luke 4:38–39; 5:12–16; 5:17–26; 6:6–11; 6:17–19; 8:40–56). The special Lukan section contains several healing stories that are unique to Luke, spread throughout Luke 7–13 (Luke 7:11–19; 8:40–56; 13:10–17; 14:1–6). The final healing story in Luke is the healing of Bartimaeus (Luke 18:35–43).

Luke also uses the bodily realities of sickness and healing to depict Jesus as a prophet or physician with a particular political orientation. A number of the healing encounters in Luke frame Jesus as the active agent of healing. In the healing of Peter's mother-in-law, Jesus does not take her by the hand (as in Mark and Matthew); he stands over her and rebukes the fever, a depiction of Jesus as a powerful agent of healing who is able to heal with only his words (Luke 4:38–39; Cotter 1999, 179–83). In both of the healing stories that are unique to Luke, the healing of the woman with a mobility impairment (Luke 8:40–56) and the healing of the man with dropsy (Luke 14:1–6), the pattern of people bringing sick persons to Jesus is interrupted (as in other Synoptic healing stories, like the healing of the paralytic in Matt 9:1–8, Mark 2:1–12; Luke 5:17–26). Instead, Jesus goes to the person in need of healing. Both of these healing stories in Luke 8 and 14 occur on the Sabbath, situating Jesus as a healer who is willing to transgress the boundaries of his social world in order to heal. Similarly, the healing of the ten lepers, which is also unique to Luke, emphasizes the faith of the Samaritan who returns to praise Jesus (Luke 7:11–19). Again, Luke seems to use Jesus's bodily engagement with the lepers to transgress not only purity boundaries but also social and political boundaries that would have marked the Samaritan as an outsider.

Even as Luke's depiction of Jesus overlaps with ancient ideals of the physician, this portrait is far from the neutral practitioner of medicine who was idealized in the post-Enlightenment world. Jesus's engagement with the body in Luke, like the other Synoptic Gospels, is characterized by Luke's own emphasis on Jesus's theopolitically charged engagement with the material world. In the healing of the woman with a mobility impairment Jesus describes the woman as "a daughter of Abraham whom Satan bound for eighteen years" and proclaims that she has been "set free from this bondage on the sabbath day" (Luke 13:10–17). This conflation of disease and apocalyptic imagery recurs in the Synoptic apocalypse, in Luke 21:11, in which Luke adds "plagues" to the list of signs of the end of the age (contrast Mark 13:8; Matt 24:7). Ostensibly, Luke may have done this to make the allusion to the prophetic rereading of Exodus from the previous verse stronger (see Isa 19:2; Luke 21:10), yet the end result is that Luke aligns disease with temporal and other-worldly disruption and with the forces of evil. For Luke, disease is a sign of the ending of the old age, and Jesus is the powerful prophet-physician who is able to bind it, simultaneously constraining the power of Satan and challenging the power structures of his own world that would restrict this activity.

Demonstrations of Power and Allegiance

Modern studies of the healing accounts have emphasized both the power (*dunamis*) of Jesus and the faith or trust (*pistis*) in Jesus as healer (Bultmann 1968 [1921], 219–21; Theissen 1983, 91–92). Within the context of the Synoptic Gospels one can certainly find evidence of these themes, and their repetition within healing stories. But these themes were not unique to Synoptic healing stories.

Outside the Synoptic Gospels, the emphasis on the power of the healer and the trust of the sick person were common elements in many different kinds of ancient healing encounters. At the Asclepieia, ancient healing shrines devoted to the god Asclepius, there is a tight connection between the allegiance and trust of the suppliant, the power of the god to heal, and the suppliant achieving his or her desired outcome, usually an outcome related to bodily wholeness (Avalos 1999; Henning 2011; Wickkiser 2008). The Asclepius cult thrived from the fourth century BCE to the fifth century CE, with more than one hundred shrines in the ancient Mediterranean, each with distinctive features based upon its geographic and historical context (Cilliers and Retief 2013, 70–75; Rüttimann 1986, 11–21; Wells 1998, 19–83). Despite the differences among the shrines, the written evidence reveals a general pattern (Cilliers and Retief 2013, 70–75; LiDonnici 1995, 20–39).[4]

The inscriptions, which were recorded on stone by priests at the shrine, offer a lasting witness in the space, testifying to the idea that allegiance and trust in the god led to encountering his power in a way that transformed one's body from sick to well.[5] For example, one inscription records the story of a man who entered the shrine with nine paralyzed fingers and scoffed at the inscriptions and "expressed his incredulity regarding the cures." While he slept at the shrine that evening, Asclepius appeared to the man and stretched out the man's fingers, telling him that from now on his name would be "Incredulous"; the man wakes up and leaves the temple "sound" (*IG* IV 1.121–22 Stele 1.3). That Incredulous is healed interrupts the link between the man's belief and the power of Asclepius to heal. Several other inscriptions at the Asclepieia tell of suppliants who, like Incredulous, were described as bad patients by ancient standards—they did not trust in the god-healer, they did not do as they were told, or they did not ask for a specific outcome (see, e.g., *IG* IV 1.121–22 Stele 2.36; *IG* IV 1.121 Stele A2). These patients, however, do not receive bodily transformation until they mend their ways, exhibiting trust in the divine physician. A number of inscriptions, like that of Diophantus of Sphettus at the Athenian shrine, describe the suppliant's trust in the god through "earnest prayer," expound upon Asclepius's power, and report a healing encounter that results from their faith in the god (IG II² 4514). In another inscription the god offers direct instruction that the patient exhibit endurance or trust in the divine physician. At the shrine in Lebena, Asclepius orders Poplius Granius Rufus to "be a steadfast patient" (καρτερεῖν) while he awaits healing of his shoulder pains (IC I 17.18). Similarly, in the ancient medical authors

---

[4] The shrines at Epidaurus, Athens, Kos, and Pergamon yield the most written evidence. Wells 1998, 17. For an overview of this evidence see Edelstein and Edelstein 1945.

[5] Because the inscriptions follow a predictable pattern, scholars have classified them as folk-material (LiDonnici 1995, 70–73) or propaganda that was designed to support the temple infrastructure (Wells 1998, 21). In either case it is important to think about them as mediated accounts that reveal more about ancient attitudes toward sickness, health, and the body than they do about individual experiences (Henning 2011, 192; Schäffer 2000, 260; Cilliers and Retief 2013).

there is a link being made between the behavior of the patient and the efficacy of the treatment (Nutton 2013, 88,102–3; see for instance Hippocrates, *The Art of Medicine* 11.1–41; *Regimen* 3.71.19–23). Even for the earthly physician, healing power could not be unlocked unless the patient exhibited trust in the physician.

Embodiment and the Tyranny of Transformation

The ancient emphasis on the power of the healer and the faith or trust of the suppliant has far-reaching effects, not only on the Synoptic healing stories but also on their readers today. In this narrative frame of the healing story, Bultmann argues, it is logical that the emphasis is on Jesus as healer: "since *pistis* involves the acknowledgement of Jesus, all the light falls on him who deserves such acknowledgement, instead of on the sick person" (Bultmann 1968 [1921], 219). Bultmann's statement here takes for granted the ancient logic around sickness and health, assuming that it is logical to place emphasis on the well, powerful body of the healer and to focus on the body of the sick person only when describing the seriousness of the person's illness, "so as to bring the act of the healer into its proper light" (221). In the texts themselves the result of this ancient emphasis on the power of the healer is the objectification and individualization of the sick body.

Throughout antiquity, healing encounters are narrated in ways that fix the reader's gaze upon the sick person's body, offering high levels of detail about the sick body relative to other bodies. At the Epidauran Asclepeion, in the *Sacred Tales* of Aelius Aristides, in the ancient medical literature, and in the Synoptic Gospels there are depictions of sick bodies that reveal them as fundamentally weak, less desirable, and in need of transformation (Avalos 1999; Avalos, Melcher, and Schipper 2007; Henning 2011; Moss 2017; Moss and Schipper 2011; Watson 2017). For example, two inscriptions placed next to each other on the same stele at Epidaurus tell the story of a blind man who was completely missing an eyeball who came to have his sight restored alongside another story of a baggage carrier who broke a cup and took it to the sanctuary, where Asclepius "made the cup whole" (*IG* IV 1.121 Stelae A9 and A10). In both stories, the blind man and the boy are initially mocked by others but are evaluated as "wise" because of their trust in the ability of Asclepius to heal. Here, the body of the blind man is intentionally juxtaposed with the broken cup, objectifying the disabled body and equating a lack of faith with the large percentage of ancient persons who would have found themselves in possession of "broken bodies." In the light of this tendency in the broader culture, it is not surprising that many of the Synoptic healing stories begin with a highly individualized description of the sick person. Read in their ancient historical context, these descriptions of the sick are not just a generic feature of Synoptic healing stories, they are part of a dichotomous cultural discourse about the body that juxtaposed abnormal/normal, sick/well, broken/

whole, unwise/wise, weak/strong, unnatural/natural, nonfunctioning/functioning, and was intimately related to other discursive frames of the body, like female/male and slave/free. The bodies in these pairs with relatively less power were frequently acted upon and objectified by those with more power, and healing encounters were emblematic of this normative discourse of the body, not exceptional.

For the interpreters of the Synoptic Gospels, these ancient hermeneutics of the body raise important questions about the sick body and its relationship to δύναμις and πίστις, then and now. As recent scholarship has observed, modern readers of the Synoptic healing stories frequently collapse ancient and today's hermeneutics of the body, misreading the healing stories in a variety of ways. Demon possession offers a great example of the way in which ancient and contemporary discourses around the body differ. As I have argued here, demon possession was treated much like a disease in the Synoptic Gospels, albeit a condition that was difficult to identify as a disability, an impairment, or an entirely separate phenomenon (Cotter 1999, 75–127; Kelley 2011, 2017; Ronis 2017; Witmer 2012). In the face of this ambiguity, contemporary readers of exorcism texts have mapped onto the demonic a contemporary category of the body that is characterized in the contemporary world as ambiguous and difficult to pin down: cognitive difference. To be sure, the demonic and the cognitively different are bodily categories that are theorized in similar ways in the ancient and contemporary world. Both are able to function negatively and positively, either to externalize evil and marginalize the body in question (as in Mark 5) or to fetishize it as extraordinarily adept at creative pursuits (as with Aelius Aristides, *Sacred Tales* 2.259; see Moss 2017, 287). But there are major differences between a demon-possessed body in the ancient world and a cognitively different body in the contemporary world. Inattentiveness to these differences further reinforces the idea that standards of neuronormativity are universal and compounds the social stigma applied to those with emotional and neurological disabilities.

Where ancient standards of bodily normativity overlap with our own, there is the risk of using ancient standards of bodily normativity to reinforce contemporary ones, and the healing stories become "texts of terror" for persons with a disability in the contemporary world (Betcher 2013, 165; see Koosed and Schumm 2011; Trible 1984). In the contemporary world the disabled or sick body is often valued negatively or objectified, leading to difficulty noticing when the healing stories of the Synoptic Gospels present the sick or disabled body as an object and the disabled person as marginal. For instance, in the story of the deaf man who speaks differently in Mark 7:31–37, the man never speaks or seeks healing himself. He is brought to Jesus, the crowd begs Jesus to lay his hand on him, and Jesus puts his fingers in the man's ears, spits on his tongue, and utters a magic word. Once the man "speaks plainly" Jesus turns and addresses the crowd, and the crowd exclaims "he even makes the deaf to hear and the non-speakers to speak." The reader never learns whether the man himself was seeking healing or how he responded to the encounter, but the response of the crowd interprets his speech impediment (μογιλάλον) as lack of speech (ἀλάλους). Here, the deaf man is not a character in the story, he is a vessel for his impairment, an impairment that allows the crowds and the audience of Mark to experiment with Jesus's power to transform. Attending to the historically and culturally bound nature of the deaf man's healing enables readers to see that a transformed body is not always a better body, and that they have the choice to resist the tyranny of transformation.

The objectification of the sick body is so widely accepted as normative by both ancient and modern readers that interpreters have also frequently overlooked the distinctive ways in which some of the healing stories transgress the ancient hierarchical dualisms of the body. Interpreters who have begun to attend to the discourses around the body that are operative in these healing stories are able to notice the way in which some them flip the ancient discourses of the body, depicting sick, disabled, and female bodies as active agents in the healing encounter (Moss 2010, 514–19; Wainright 2006, 186–89; Wilson 2014, 316–19).

Conclusion

In his influential work on miracle stories, Gerd Theissen distinguished between exorcism and healing by appealing to the closeness between healing stories and the "dawn of medicine": "the mere absence of demonological motifs is not a distinctive feature of healings as opposed to exorcisms; what is distinctive is that the motifs of conflict are replaced by images of the transmission of healing power, images which doubtless bring us closer to the dawn of medicine than do the powerful words of exorcism" (Theissen 1983, 90). As I have argued, both the exorcism stories and the healing stories do have some real resonances with ancient medical thinking and practices, and these resonances would have framed the activity of Jesus as consonant with other ancient understandings of the body. Yet Theissen's statement that these images "bring us closer to the dawn of medicine" also gives pause, revealing a teleological hermeneutic that privileges modern medical ways of knowing and reading as the "goal."

A teleological hermeneutic of the body when applied to the Synoptic healing stories obscures the way that ancient audiences, who did not have modern medicine in mind as their telos, would have encountered these stories. One example of this that I have explored in this essay is the way scholarship from the enlightenment to today has resisted seeing a real overlap between exorcism and healing in the Synoptic Gospels. I have argued instead that exorcisms are healing stories that use ancient language and categories of embodiment and sickness to frame the healing encounter. Perhaps most disastrously, this teleological hermeneutic of the body also prevents interpreters from seeing the places where there are real continuities between the ancient and modern understandings of the body, leading moderns to assume that culturally constructed ideas about the body are universal simply because they are shared. This appears in the way that healing stories have typically been read merely as literary devices to demonstrate transformation and healing power. When reading all of the healing stories through this lens, it becomes easy to ignore the power dynamics between the sick and the well that buttress this narrative frame, and the often unseen tension between this understanding of the body and the other themes of the Synoptic Gospels. In part, this tension is easy to overlook, not only because the "healing power of Jesus" narrative is so totalizing but also because it fits very well with present day cultural fantasies of medical practitioners as powerful agents who enact total bodily transformation, even in the face of an awareness of medicine's limitations. By paying attention to questions of ancient body hermeneutics the interpreter is able to ask a new set of questions: How does the narrative frame of "bodily transformation" fit with the themes of power amid powerlessness, solidarity with the marginalized, and political resistance that are also present in the Synoptic Gospels, even sometimes within the healing stories themselves?

With these questions in mind, it becomes apparent that sometimes the Synoptic healing stories tell the story of a healing encounter using the narrative frame of bodily transformation and offer today's readers a glimpse of the way in which early Christians recapitulated familiar stories with Jesus at the center. While some of the flat readings of post-enlightenment scholarship have actually amplified the tyranny of transformation, historicizing the narrative frame of bodily transformation allows for an opportunity to perform counter-readings that name and resist the various impulses to read sick bodies through a wide range of hierarchical dualisms. At other points in the Synoptic tradition, healing stories that (at least in part) model such a reading strategy occur, telling stories of bodily transformation while also resisting the body hermeneutics of their own day. Sick persons who exhibit agency, a healer who is weak, or a narrative frame that disrupts other existing power structures appear in these stories. With an awareness of these tensions that exist within the Synoptic healing stories themselves, interpretation becomes a much richer exercise. The complexity of the Synoptic healing tradition itself challenges the contemporary exegete to identify and analyze the hermeneutics of the body within the text, and to retell those stories in ways that do not simply prop up current understandings of the body.

REFERENCES

Alkier, Stefan, and Annette Weissenrieder. 2013. *Miracles Revisited: New Testament Miracle Stories and Their Concepts of Reality*. Berlin: De Gruyter.

Avalos, Hector. 1995. *Illness and Health Care in the Ancient Near East: The Role of the Temple in Greece, Mesopotamia, and Israel*. Atlanta: Scholars.

Avalos, Hector. 1999. *Healthcare and the Rise of Christianity*. Peabody, MA: Hendrickson.

Avalos, Hector, Sarah Melcher, and Jeremy Schipper. 2007. *This Abled Body: Rethinking Disability and Biblical Studies*. Atlanta: Society of Biblical Literature.

Betcher, Sharon. 2013. "Disability and the Terror of the Miracle Tradition." In *Miracles Revisited: New Testament Miracle Stories and Their Concepts of Reality*, edited by Stefan Alkier and Annette Weissenrieder, 161–81. Berlin: De Gruyter.

Bovon, François. 2002. *Luke 1: A Commentary on the Gospel of Luke 1:1–9:50*. Edited by Helmut Koester. Translated by Christine M. Thomas. Hermeneia. Minneapolis: Fortress.

Bultmann, Rudolf. 1968 [1921]. *The History of the Synoptic Tradition*. 2nd rev. ed. Oxford: Oxford University Press.

Carter, Warren. 2011. "The blind, lame and paralyzed" (John 5:3): John's Gospel, Disability Studies, and Postcolonial Perspectives." In In *Disability Studies and Biblical Literature*, edited by Candida R. Moss and Jeremy Schipper, 205–22. New York: Palgrave Macmillan.
Cilliers, Louise, and François Retief. 2013. "Dream Healing in Asclepieia in the Mediterranean." In *Dreams, Healing, and Medicine in Greece: From Antiquity to the Present*, edited by Steven M. Oberhelman, 69–92. Farnham: Ashgate.
Collins, Adela Yarbro. 2007. *Mark: A Commentary*. Edited by Harold W. Attridge. Heremeneia. Minneapolis: Fortress.
Cotter, Wendy. 1999. *Miracles in Greco-Roman Antiquity: A Sourcebook for the Study of New Testament Miracle Stories*. New York: Routledge.
Dibelius, Martin. 1982 [1933]. *From Tradition to Gospel*. 2nd rev. ed. Cambridge: James Clark.
Dochorn, Jan, Susanne Rudnig-Zelt, and Benjamin Wold. 2016. *Das Böse, der Teufel und Dämonen—Evil, the Devil, and Demons*. WUNT 2, 412. Tübingen: Mohr Siebeck.
Edelstein, Emma J., and Ludwig Edelstein. 1945. *Asclepius: A Collection and Interpretation of the Testimonies*. 2 vols. Baltimore: Johns Hopkins Press.
Harnack, Adolf von. 1906. *Lukas der Arzt: der Verfasser des dritten Evangeliums und der Apostelgeschichte*. Leipzig: J. C. Hinrichs.
Hengel, Martin and Rudolf Hengel 1959. "Die Heilungen Jesu und medizinisches Denken." In *Medicus Viator*, edited by Paul Christian and Dietrich Rössler, 331–61. Tübingen: Mohr Siebeck.
Henning, Meghan R. 2011. "In Sickness and in Health: Ancient 'Rituals of Truth' in the Greco-Roman World and 1 Peter." In *Disability Studies and Biblical Literature*, edited by Candida R. Moss and Jeremy Schipper, 205–22. New York: Palgrave Macmillan.
Henning, Meghan R. 2017. "Metaphorical, Punitive, and Pedagogical Blindness in Hell." *Health, Medicine, and Christianity in Late Antiquity*. Jared Secord, Heidi Marx-Wolf, Christoph Markschies, eds. *Studia Patristica* 81, no. 7 (Fall): 139–52.
Jipp, Joshua. 2013. *Divine Visitations and Hospitality to Strangers in Luke-Acts: An Interpretation of the Malta Episode in Acts 28:1–10*. Leiden: Brill.
Johnson, Luke Timothy. 1991. *The Gospel of Luke*. Sacra Pagina. Collegeville, MN: Liturgical Press.
Kee, Howard Clark. 1986. *Medicine, Miracle, and Magic in New Testament Times*. Cambridge: Cambridge University Press.
Keith, Chris, and Lorent T. Stuckenbruck. 2016. *Evil in Second Temple Judaism and Early Christianity*. Tübingen: Mohr Siebeck.
Kelley, Nicole. 2007. "Deformity and Disability in Greece and Rome." In *This Abled Body: Rethinking Disability and Biblical Studies*, edited by Hector Avalos, Sarah Melcher, and Jeremy Schipper, 31–45. Atlanta: Society of Biblical Literature.
Kelley, Nicole. 2011. "'The Punishment of the Devil Was Apparent in the Torment of the Human Body': Epilepsy in Ancient Christianity." In *Disability Studies and Biblical Literature*, edited by Candida R. Moss and Jeremy Schipper, 205–22. New York: Palgrave Macmillan.
Koosed, Jennifer L., and Darla Schumm. 2011. "Out of the Darkness: Examining the Rhetoric of Blindness in the Gospel of John." *Disability in Judaism, Christianity, and Islam: Sacred Texts, Historical Traditions, and Social Analysis*, edited by Darla Schumm and Michael Stoltzfus, 77–92. New York: Palgrave Macmillan.
Koskenniemi, Erkki. 2013. "Miracles of the Devil and His Assistants in Early Judaism and Their Influence on the Gospel of Matthew." In *Evil and the Devil*, edited by Ida Fröhlich and Erkki Koskenniemi, 84–97. London: Bloomsbury.

LiDonnici, Lynn R. 1995. *The Epidaurian Miracle Inscriptions: Text, Translation and Commentary*. Texts and Translations: Graeco-Roman Religion Series. Atlanta: Scholars.

Marcus, Joel. 2000. *Mark 1–8: A New Translation with Introduction and Commentary*. AB 27. New York: Doubleday.

Melcher, Sarah J., Mikeal C. Parsons, and Amos Yong. 2017. *The Bible and Disability: A Commentary*. Waco: Baylor University Press.

Moss, Candida R. 2010. "The Man with the Flow of Power: Porous Bodies in Mark 5:25–34." *Journal of Biblical Literature* 129: 507–19.

Moss, Candida R. 2011. "Blurred Vision and Ethical Confusion: The Rhetorical Function of Matthew 6:22–23." *CBQ* 73: 757–76.

Moss, Candida R. 2017. "Mark and Matthew." In *The Bible and Disability: A Commentary*, edited by Sarah J. Melcher, Mikeal C. Parsons, and Amos Yong, 275–302. Waco: Baylor University Press.

Moss, Candida R., and Jeremy Schipper. 2011. *Disability Studies and Biblical Literature*. New York: Palgrave Macmillan.

Nutton, Vivian. 2013. *Ancient Medicine*. 2nd ed. New York: Routledge.

Pilch, John. 2000. *Healing in the New Testament: Insights from Medical and Mediterranean Anthropology*. Minneapolis: Augsburg Fortress.

Remus, Harold. 1997. *Jesus as Healer*. Cambridge: Cambridge University Press.

Ronis, Sara. 2017. "Space, Place, and the Race for Power: Rabbis, Demons, and the Construction of Babylonia." *Harvard Theological Review* 110, no. 4: 588–603.

Rüttimann, René Josef. 1986. *Asklepios and Jesus: The Form, Character and Status of the Asklepios Cult in the Second Century CE and Its Influence on Early Christianity*. Cambridge, MA: Harvard University Press.

Schäffer, Daniel. 2000. "Traum und Wunderheilung im Asklepios-Kult in der griechisch-römische Medizin." In *Heilkunde und Hochkultur, I: Geburt, Seuche, und Traumdeutung in den antiken Zivilisation des Mittelmeerraumes*, edited by Axel Karenberg and Christian Leitz, 259–74. Münster: Lit Verlag.

Skinner, Christopher W. 2016. "Overcoming Satan, Overcoming the World: Exploring the Cosmologies of Mark and John." In *Evil in Second Temple Judaism and Early Christianity*, edited by Chris Keith and Loren T. Stuckenbruck. Tübingen: Mohr Siebeck: 101–120.

Sterling, Gregory E. 1993. "Jesus as Exorcist: An Analysis of Matthew 17:14–20; Mark 9:14–29; Luke 9:37–43a." *Catholic Biblical Quarterly* 55, no. 3 (July): 467–93.

Theissen, Gerd. 1983. *Miracle Stories of the Early Christian Tradition*. Edinburgh: T&T Clark.

Trible, Phyllis. 1984. *Texts of Terror: Literary-Feminist Readings of Biblical Narratives*. Minneapolis: Fortress.

Twelftree, Graham H. 2007. *In the Name of Jesus: Exorcism among Early Christians*. Grand Rapids: Baker.

Twelftree, Graham H. 2011. "Deliverance and Exorcism in the New Testament." In *Exorcism and Deliverance*, edited by William K. Kay and Robin Parry, 45–68. Milton Keynes: Paternoster.

Wainright, Elaine M. 2006. *Women Healing/Healing Women: The Genderization of Healing in Early Christianity*. Translated by Francis McDonagh. London: Equinox.

Watson, David F. 2017. "Luke-Acts." In *The Bible and Disability: A Commentary*, edited by Sarah J. Melcher, Mikeal C. Parsons, and Amos Yong, 303–32. Waco: Baylor University Press.

Watson, Duane F. 2012. *Miracle Discourse in the New Testament*. Atlanta: Society of Biblical Literature.

Weissenrieder, Annette. 2017. "Disease and Healing in a Changing World: 'Medical' Vocabulary and the Woman with the 'Issue of Blood' in the *Vetus Latina* Mark 5:25–34 and Luke 8:40–48." *Religion in the Roman Empire* 3, no. 2 (June): 265–85.

Weissenrieder, Annette, and Gregor Etzelmüller. 2016. *Religion and Illness*. Eugene, OR: Cascade.

Wells, Louise. 1998. *The Greek Language of Healing from Homer to the New Testament Times*. Berlin: De Gruyter.

Wickkiser, Laura Bronwen. 2008. *Asklepios, Medicine, and the Politics of Healing in Fifth Century Greece: Between Craft and Cult*. Baltimore: Johns Hopkins University Press.

Wilson, Walter T. 2014. *Healing in the Gospel of Matthew: Reflections on Method and Ministry*. Minneapolis: Fortress.

Witmer, Amanda. 2012. *Jesus, the Galilean Exorcist: His Exorcisms in Social and Political Context*. London: T&T Clark.

Wrede, William. 1901. *Das Messiasgeheimnis in den Evangelien: Zugleich ein Beitrag zum Verständnis des Markusevangeliumsn*. Göttingen: Vandenhoeck & Ruprecht.

CHAPTER 20

SACRED SPACE

KAREN WENELL

SYNOPTIC ENCOUNTERS WITH SACRED SPACE

ONLY once in the Synoptic Gospels is the physical creation, or making (*poieō*; Mark 9:5 and parallels) of sacred space explicitly considered. This occurs in the so-called transfiguration narrative, present in all three Synoptics, where Peter, James, and John suggest the construction of three tabernacles to mark their mountain experience of seeing Moses and Elijah appear alongside Jesus, who was transformed in his clothing and appearance (Matt 17:1–13; Mark 9:2–13; Luke 9:28–36). Jesus does not affirm the disciples' tabernacle-building suggestion in the story, and their request is interrupted by a divine parental voice coming from a cloud in heaven. (Jesus is called "my beloved son" in Matthew 17:5 and Mark 9:7 and "my son, my chosen" in Luke 9:35.) In each account the disciples are said to tell no one of what they have seen. None of the texts offers any suggestion that the disciples should return to the idea of building tabernacles at a later time when they do not need to keep silent (after the Son of Man is raised from the dead in Mark 9:9 and Matthew 17:9/after "those days" in Luke 9:36). The interruption of the divine voice seems to put a stop to the idea of marking physical space as a potential response to the experience of hierophany.

This is a fascinating account, and one that provides interesting information about sacred space from the perspective of the Synoptic Gospels. It shows a lack of focus on building specific, physical structures to mark the presence of the sacred, which is fitting with the historical setting of the Synoptic Gospels in a time when there were no "purpose-built" Christian structures, and groups likely made use of different types of existing domestic and public spaces for communal gathering (Adams 2013; Billings 2011; Horrell 2004). Only later, into the third and fourth centuries CE, did purpose-built structures appear, as well as developing interest in pilgrimage to sites associated with Jesus, which, once it "emerged as a form of devotion among Christians . . . became an enduring feature of Christian piety" (Wilken 1992, 101–25). These activities are some distance in time from the appearance of the Synoptic Gospels.

Despite a lack of evidence for the construction of specific sacred spaces in the period in which the Gospels were written, there is no shortage of evidence pertaining to attention to the location of God and to divine interaction with the physical world. Some of the most interesting evidence in this regard is found in the Synoptic Gospels. The transfiguration account in particular gives God a heavenly locus, as affirmed by the hierophany of the voice in the cloud, also recalling the synoptic accounts of the baptism of Jesus by John. The notion of the heavenly realm as God's domain was common for this period of Jewish thought, and part of an accepted spatial division between the earth and the heavens (Gooder 2011, 2–11). Furthermore, the mountain location of the transfiguration has a pedigree as the type of physical space that could be conducive to experience of the presence of God, as indeed both Moses and Elijah were "known to have benefited from a vision of God after having climbed a mountain" (1 Kgs 19; Exod 2; Guijarro 2017, 97). In addition, each account is prefaced by a statement about some not tasting death before seeing the Kingdom of God (Matt 16:28; Mark 9:1; Luke 9:27). One possible interpretation would be to view the transfiguration, where representative disciples both see and hear a manifestation of the sacred, as agreement among the synoptic authors that the transfiguration was a sensory experience of the (normally not physically visible) Kingdom via sight and sound (e.g., Davies and Allison 1988–97, 2:677; Green 1997, 376).

Clearly there are a range of interactions between the sacred and space that are prominent in the transfiguration narrative, making it a key text for thinking about this topic in the Synoptic Gospels. Several points are brought into focus. One is that scholars should not limit this investigation to physical, visible spaces but should also consider questions of where the sacred is being located in and through the texts, which may include particular attention to invisible (or at times invisible) or otherworldly realms. As Thomas Tweed argues, nonmaterial spaces like heaven or the Kingdom can be as significant as material spaces like a mountain or temple (Tweed 2011, 119). Though Christianity may be somewhat unusual in the ancient world for not initially establishing its own sacred sites, the transfiguration cautions one that avoidance of marking physical space does not indicate a lack of concern with the location of God and the divine realm in the physical world. Like other ancient groups, early Christians appear to have had quite a developed orientation to an invisible sacred realm where humans connect with God and where everyday activities and group belonging have their sacred orientation. The Synoptic Gospels attest to this.

The transfiguration is an important beginning point for a discussion of sacred space as a theme in the Synoptic Gospels precisely because of the various ways it allows one to engage with the nonmaterial quality of the sacred and its manifestation in the material world. One is reminded that the terminology of sacred space can be elusive and abstract. One helpful way to think about sacredness in relation to space is to theorize the sacred precisely as a quality (Anttonen 2007), and one that is not so much applied but discovered and lived in relation to place (Ingold 2001, 138; though Ingold is not here concerned with the sacred as such). The ability to perceive the sacred can be viewed as a skill that may or may not be developed in humans in different times and places, depending on the shaping of their environments (142; again, Ingold is not focused on the sacred in particular). In the transfiguration narrative, one sees evidence of the sacred having been distinguished in the different interactions between God, people, and place that unfold in the texts. An approach that can accommodate investigation of the nonmaterial quality of the sacred is needed.

Synoptic Architecture

Neither traditional approaches to the Synoptic Problem nor purely literary approaches to the texts are easily suited to an investigation of sacred space. Approaches to synoptic relationships are in any case necessarily uncertain when it comes to questions of the order and priority between the accounts. So, for instance, a recent survey of the Synoptic Problem by Christopher Tuckett concludes about the various theories of synoptic relationships: "we are (hopefully) all now much more aware of the provisional nature of any alleged 'solutions' to the Synoptic Problem, and are aware too that between our (sometimes neat and simple) solutions and historical reality may lie an unbridgeable chasm. We are aware too of the strengths—and weaknesses—of all our hypotheses" (2011, 49–50). This suggests that uncertainty itself as a significant feature of any investigation. Although one way forward is to take Tuckett's point as a necessary caveat and proceed with one's preferred theory, another approach can be envisioned which values the very fact of uncertainty, and works with it to investigate the texts. Being less concerned with dating and order can work very well with a spatial approach, where the presence of particular features of space and attention to the location of the sacred are not necessarily precise or dependent on a chronological sequence of writing. The benefit of loosening the connection to traditional questions of order and dating mirrors the benefit of taking a "spatial turn" in many disciplines, in that it allows for the prioritization of matters of space over those of time and (sequential) history (Massey 2005). A spatial approach to the Gospels that allows for uncertainty may be compared to aspects of uncertainty in archaeology, where an "original" building may be difficult to distinguish with any precision from other layers of its own existence in the ground, and one building of a certain age and type may not be identifiable on a timeline in relation to a similar example in its vicinity. Open questions about a structure do not prevent an investigation which tries to understand its features. With the Synoptics, their preservation "above ground" has its own history of additions and modifications, constituting the data that text critics concern themselves with tracing, in a parallel move to the archaeologist. The "original" text is a disappearing entity when one tries to excavate it (Parker 1997, 4), yet the texts still provide valuable information and insight into the material and nonmaterial spaces of the past and the perception of the sacred where it has left no physical mark in the environment for the archaeologist to discover. Being less concerned with traditional questions of synoptic relationships and generally less precise about dating and order does not preclude the possibility of gaining significant insight into the spaces of the past.

Another possible approach to the study of sacred space in the Synoptic Gospels would be to analyze all the references to spaces in the texts in a literary study. Something like Elizabeth Struthers Malbon's significant work *Narrative Space and Mythic Meaning in Mark* (1991) could be expanded to an investigation of Matthew and Luke from a structuralist perspective, setting out oppositions within, and development of, spaces present in the narratives. This would undoubtedly reveal insights into the texts. However, although m many meaningful spaces may be referenced in the texts—from Galilee to a city/country distinction to mountains and seas—not all of these necessarily constitute a locus for the sacred in the text, even where they are part of a wider mythic narrative. A sociological approach is also valid, and fits with wider emphases in spatial theoretical work on human interactions with space (Økland, de Vos, and Wenell 2016, xv). A sociological study allows for a focus on the spaces in the texts that are the most meaningful in terms of group formation and identity, and the setting out of relationships between the divine and human realms. There is great potential for the study of the location of the sacred in the Synoptics, drawing on Kim Knott's spatial approach to the study of religion, where she proposes a very open approach to the question of the location of the sacred, rather than focusing on traditional "religious" spaces in society (2005). A careful investigation of where the sacred is being located also avoids the potential pitfall of sacralizing every socially meaningful space encountered in the texts.

Historical, literary, and social insights need not be exclusive, and may all contribute to an approach to the Synoptic Gospels that is well suited to an investigation into sacred space. Potentially relevant is social anthropologist Tim Ingold's notion of an "education of attention" in different environments, where skilled practitioners enskill others in matters of importance, orienting them to their surroundings, wherein they make their own discoveries (2001). Thinking about the Synoptic Gospels, the texts themselves are a certain type of evidence of an "education of attention", orienting hearers to the location of the sacred, and at the same time, opening up the possibility for extending the story to successive generations through representation. There may, after all, be numerous ways to answer the significant question "what are the Gospels?" (Burridge 2004) which are not necessarily primarily literary or historical. From a spatial perspective, the Gospels can be seen as part of an "education of attention" to the sacred in the environment, and clues to where the sacred was located and perceived or discovered by ancient people. This perspective is still respectful of historical and literary insights, yet it is less concerned with the emphasis on origins and sequence that can dominate studies of the gospels.

The Synoptic Gospels are a fascinating resource, precisely because of the amount of shared material they contain, and this can open up one's awareness of matters that were seen as core to the spatial perception of the sacred, and those matters that were more variously understood, or even controversial, as where divergences are noted in the synoptic view of the texts. Nowhere else in the New Testament corpus is such comparative evidence available. What emerges from the Synoptic Gospels is not shared concepts of the sacred as such but a shared environment where different traditions were available and incorporated into distinctive and purposeful narratives where one can detect clues to the location of the sacred.

Returning to a comparison between texts and physical spaces in the environment, if one were to study examples of the "four-room house" within a roughly similar geographic area and time period, the likely focus of the analysis would be on the common features (not necessarily consistently present), as well as any distinctive features of the particular examples (Faust and Bunimovitz 2003). An analyst would be unlikely to try to establish any particular individuals as "architects" or a precise order of appearance or directionality in terms of "copying" of features. A similar approach could be taken to the Synoptic Gospels, considering the common features of sacred space they evidence (in triple tradition), as well as distinctive features (in double tradition and special material). Smaller differences and minor agreements in the common features would not seem unusual in an examination of physical buildings of a common era; indeed, they would be expected. I take this approach to key synoptic spaces in the sections to follow, focusing on common and distinctive features where relevant. I begin with the Kingdom of God as a potentially important response to the question of where the sacred is located. I go on to consider the "negative sacred space" of the Kingdom of Satan, as well as potential connections to the spaces of land and temple.

The Kingdom of God as Sacred Realm

The very terminology of the Kingdom of God/*basileia tou theou* indicates its relevance to the question of the location of the sacred. Though Gustaf Dalman's insistence (1902) on the "rule not realm" definition of the Kingdom has held enormous influence (Aalen 1962; Brown 2001), the time has come to appreciate the spatial importance of the Kingdom (Moxnes 2003) and to value its role in setting out relationships between God, people, and place. As in the transfiguration narrative, spatial relationships to the divine sphere may not be focused on physical marking of the environment and may not have a material manifestation but may nonetheless evidence a high concern with orienting to the sacred in the world. Certainly, "rule" or "dominion" are among the possible translations of *basileia*, but the exclusivity of Dalman's interpretation goes too far, insisting that the meaning is "always the 'kingly rule' never the 'kingdom'" (Dalman 1902, 94; based on the meaning of *malkut*). Consideration of a more spatial aspect to the Kingdom opens up possibilities for engagement with the (potentially nonphysical) realm to which such a rule belongs. The Kingdom is arguably the central concern of the Synoptic Gospels in terms of a sacred locus for divine engagement. With this in mind, I consider some of the common and distinctive features of the Kingdom in the synoptic accounts.

Common Features of the Kingdom: Inside/Outside and Point of Entry

Although sacred space need not necessarily have a clear boundary, in the sense that it could be universal, incorporating all known space, the Kingdom is clearly spoken of in boundary terms across all three synoptic accounts. In the parable of the Sower, there is the statement about the mystery of the Kingdom, which is given to the disciples but not to "those outside/them/others" (Mark 4:11; Matthew 13:11; Luke 8:10), suggesting the presence of a boundary between groups in relation to the Kingdom. Also significant are the references to entering the Kingdom "as a little child" (Mark 10:15; Luke 18:17) or becoming "like children" (Matthew 18:3) and concerning the difficulty for the rich to enter the Kingdom (Mark 10:23–25; Matt 19:23–24; Luke 22:24–25). In these texts, occurring in core material across all three Synoptics, there is a sense of an inside/outside division and also a point of entry, though with difficulties in gaining entry.

Parables, as a form, are themselves a common feature of the proclamation of the Kingdom across the Synoptic Gospels. The Sower, as the "parable of parables," is accompanied by a metalevel reflection on what the parables achieve in terms of the identity of the hearers. The saying about those inside and outside is key, and France emphasizes the "general tone of these verses" which "does not encourage us to attempt specific designation" (2002, 198). That is, in specific terms, identifications of insiders and outsiders are not made, but in general terms there is a setting out of "two classes of people" (France 2007, 511). By framing the boundary language between people using the Kingdom of God terminology, a group aspect emerges which is defined in relation to proximity to God, either inside God's realm, or outside. Joel Marcus points out that entering is not physical: "almost all ["entering" statements] speak not of physical movement into a real realm but of participation in the already-inaugurated explosion of God's power into the world" (1988, 674). The lack of physicality need not be a matter of concern in relation to the locus of the sacred, and connection with God's power at work in the world is sufficient to mark the necessity of the movement "into" the Kingdom and among the correct "class" of people. The realm is spoken of as "real" even if not "physical." Entering carries with it the idea of distinct groups, and the described entry is not universal entry of all people (though Luke's statement that "everyone tries to enter by force" in 16:16 may indicate that "all are being urged to enter"; Johnson 1992, 251) but instead relates to receiving the Kingdom as a child (Mark 10:15 // Luke 18:17); becoming like children (Matt 18:3). It is also possible, but difficult, for those who have wealth (Mark 10:23–25 // Luke 22.24–5 // Matt 19.23–4) to enter. The Kingdom "belongs" to children, but is difficult (though not impossible) to gain entry to for rich adults. Children appear as a (seemingly passive) model for adults who wish to gain entry. The children do not do anything in particular in order to belong (though in Matthew, the child is humble—Matthew 18:4). With regard to wealth, it is attached to the person: they "have wealth" or "are rich." Their possession of wealth/riches inhibits their entry into the realm of God. The idea that "with God all things are possible" gives the sense that God is not barring the rich from entry but they themselves have a challenge to overcome if they desire to enter. Not all sacred places restrict access to the divine, but it does seem that the language used to describe the Kingdom includes this feature of restricted access of space "set apart." Children may freely enter, but the rich only with difficulty.

Common Features of the Kingdom: Organic Growth and Experience through the Senses

Another feature of the Kingdom that the synoptic accounts agree on is that the Kingdom is like a small mustard seed that grows into a large tree/shrub (Mark 4:30–32; Matt 13:31–32; Luke 13:18–19; also Gospel of Thomas 20). The organic imagery fits with that of the parable of the Sower, where seeds grow and produce depending on their reception in a range of soils. The "strange co-existence" (Marcus 2000, 297) of good and bad soils and the presence of a productive crop is revealing of the mystery of the Kingdom. Spatially in terms of size, it would seem that the synoptic accounts agree that the realm of the Kingdom is able to produce what would be "considered quite remarkable" growth (296). In relation to Matthew and Luke's "Q" version of the mustard seed parable, Halvor Moxnes points out that the size aspect is not emphasized, though "the strange transformation from a vegetable seed into a tree" suggests a strange juxtaposition of two different places—the garden where a vegetable seed is thrown, and the ground that would be suitable for a substantial tree (Moxnes 2003, 112–13).

Organic growth is seen, or observed, in the growth of crops to maturity in harvest, and in the transformed mustard seed, having become a tree. Sight is also significant to the transfiguration narrative, where the statement about some not tasting death before seeing the Kingdom of God is followed by the "sight" of the transfiguration event. The idea of anticipating sight in this way constitutes an interesting perspective on how the sacred realm is perceived in terms of its visibility and invisibility in the created world. In relation to "taste," Lawrence notes that the links between taste and death, and particularly Jesus's death (in Mark, but this can be extended to parallel synoptic sayings) indicate a sense-based response where "the link between taste and memory is a dynamic aspect of Mark's sensorium" (2011, 389). The senses connect to the physical, material world of experience and memory. The Kingdom is also connected to the sense of taste and consumption in the reference to drinking "the fruit of the vine" in the Kingdom (Mark 14:25; Matt 26:29; Luke 22:15). Jesus identifies his final activity of drinking prior to drinking in the Kingdom. As drinking and eating are regular, physical activities, there is a sense of imminence in this statement that parallels the statement about some not tasting death. Drinking "new" connects to the memory of Jesus's earlier drinking with Eucharistic overtones. Rather than focusing on eschatology and the timing of the "new" Kingdom, as did scholars of a previous generation (Willis 1987), it is possible to emphasize the transformational nature of this sacred realm, where the texts indicate the hope of immanent future visibility and experience of taste.

Distinctive Features: Doors and Cities

Going beyond the common features of the Kingdom, Matthew seems to extend a bit further in relation to the development of the inside/outside and point of entry, in describing a kind of door (France 2007, 869). The scribes and Pharisees are said to "not enter," to "try and stop others from entering," and to be "locking others out" (Matthew 23:13). Righteousness exceeding that of the scribes and Pharisees is required for entry in Matthew (5:19–20). Matthew also mentions that Peter has been given the keys to the Kingdom (16:19). Margaret Davies views this as a "role of opening" for Peter, alongside the idea of his binding and loosing on earth/heaven in 16:20 and 18:18 (1993, 159). In these different ways, the Kingdom is described in spatial terms, a realm in which dwelling with God can be attained, though regulated by others (i.e. Peter, or scribes and Pharisees).

Another interesting feature of the Kingdom that would seem to be distinctive rather than agreed is that of the reception or rejection of the Kingdom by entire cities. Matthew and Luke both address this question, though in different ways. There is a concern with correct positioning in relation to the Kingdom, as highlighted by material Luke includes as part of the sending-out of the seventy (Luke 10:8–12). (The question of whether seventy or the variant reading of seventy-two should be preferred has a complex history; see Metzger 1958–59.) For those who welcome those bearing the message of the Kingdom, its nearness is convivial and restorative; for those who do not welcome the seventy, the message of the nearness of the Kingdom stands as a threat: "Whenever you enter a town and its people welcome you, eat what is set before you; cure the sick who are there, and say to them, 'The Kingdom of God has come near to you.' But whenever you enter a town and they do not welcome you, go out into its streets and say, 'Even the dust of your town that clings to our feet, we wipe off in protest against you. Yet know this: the Kingdom of God has come near'" (Luke 10:8–11).

Here, the message of the Kingdom is moving to entire towns, and this continues with specific examples in Luke 10:13–15; if those who already "belong" to the Kingdom (the seventy/seventy-two) are welcomed, the "town and its people" can share in the reassurance of the nearness of the Kingdom. If they are not welcomed, the proximity of the Kingdom stands as a warning that the town will be like Sodom (Luke 10:12) and so presumably face destruction or even a "worse fate" (Knight 1998, 105), though how or when is not clear. The aspect of correctly positioning oneself in relationship to God and the Kingdom is elevated to the level of entire towns, which seem to have the possibility of being "exalted to heaven" or "brought down to Hades" (Luke 10:15). More than some sort of divine zip code lottery, this emphasizes the need for even geographic areas to be on the correct side of the boundary in relation to the Kingdom. There is no universal sense of all people and places belonging to God but a clear need to accept those who bear the message in relation to the Kingdom. The insistence that things could be more tolerable for Tyre and Sidon than for Galilean towns (Luke 10:13–15) indicates that the traditional associations of sacred space—that is, Galilee as part of the wider traditional notion of "the land"—are not a guarantor of safety from judgment.

Matthew's comparable text is the sending-out of the twelve (Matthew 10:5–16). The address to the twelve in particular is seen as significant in terms of confining the mission to Israel, with the twelve here connecting to the idea of Israel in twelve tribes, according to Davies and Allison (1988–97, 2:167). Specification is provided as to the locale where they are instructed by Jesus to preach the good news that the Kingdom has come near: "Go nowhere among the Gentiles, and enter no town of the Samaritans, but go rather to the lost sheep of the house of Israel" (Matt 10:5–6; see Matt 28:18–20). There is a timing issue that emerges here, but it is not the timing issue of present/future manifestation of the Kingdom. Rather, the controversy over timing seems to center on whether, in the context of Jesus's ministry prior to his death and resurrection, there had been any hope expressed for Gentile (or Samaritan) towns, or conversely judgment on Jewish towns. Matthew has Jesus avoiding Gentile and Samaritan locations, but Luke does not absolutely exclude Tyre and Sidon from Jesus's concern.

This point leads to larger questions about spokespersons, controversies, and the expectation of transformed space in the new world coming. Marcus identifies a group of sayings that indicate the motion of the Kingdom: the Kingdom moves, rather than people moving in relation to it (1988, 663; see references in n. 2). This is not an insignificant point, and one can push it even further to say that the Kingdom as a sacred space is something that is continually in motion (Wenell 2012). This is not to say that the Kingdom is not capable of relating to "real" life "on the ground" and more concrete boundaries, for even a physical building made of bricks and mortar can be thought of as a building-in-motion when controversies surround it and individuals (sometimes representing groups) speak out in relation to it (Yaneva 2010).[1] The controversies of the Kingdom in the ancient world attracted spokespersons, including the authors of the Synoptic Gospels, who undertook the task to define the contours and boundaries of the Kingdom. The relationships that are established between God, people and space are performed, setting out boundaries of definition in relation to the sacred. The group—and the Kingdom—rely on the activity of spokespersons to set out the God-people-space relationship, and this is why the Synoptic Gospels work so well to illuminate where and how this work is being done.

Distinctive Features: The Kingdom of Heaven

In many of the examples already discussed here which occur across the Synoptic Gospels, the terminology used by Matthew is the "Kingdom of Heaven" (*basileia tōn ouranōn*) rather than the "Kingdom of God" (*basileia tou theou*). In relation to the

---

[1] Yaneva speaks of the Whitney Museum in New York as a "building-in-motion" that actively gathers controversies and reactions to various proposed extension plans.

location of the sacred, it is important to consider why Matthew has used this terminology where otherwise the text is in agreement with Mark and Luke. Once again, the point is not about the order of writing and sources but the distinctiveness of features which occur. Each accepts certain features as central to the Kingdom, but Matthew most commonly throughout his narrative names the sacred realm the Kingdom of Heaven.

Though Gustaf Dalman's views on the "rule not realm" meaning of the Kingdom have persisted, his view on the reasons for Matthew's Kingdom of Heaven terminology have not held the same levels of acceptance. Dalman's view was that Matthew was using a term which was more original to the teachings of Jesus, suggesting that it was more common to avoid the divine name and use Kingdom of Heaven as a circumlocution (Dalman 1902). Casey rejects the circumlocution argument and argues instead that the phrase Kingdom of God is original, going so far as to actually change references in Matthew to the Kingdom of Heaven and reconstruct them with Kingdom of God inserted in its place. So, from Casey: "to see what Jesus said, we must turn Matthew's editorial 'kingdom of heaven' back into 'kingdom of God'" (2010, 203). This is quite a shocking and destructive attitude toward distinctive ancient texts. Yet, one is still left with the question of why Matthew uses this term. Casey's, and earlier Chilton's (1984, 3:513) view that there is no difference between Kingdom of God and Kingdom of Heaven needs revisiting. If Kingdom of Heaven is not a circumlocution, or merely a stylistic preference, then what significance does it have? Pamment (1981) argued that the Kingdom of Heaven indicated where the future aspect of the Kingdom was emphasized, with the Kingdom of God indicative of the present reality, but Robert Foster is correct to note where this does not bear out in the references within the Gospel (2002). One can agree with Foster even further that Matthew's narrative on the whole utilizes Kingdom of Heaven language as intentional, and "part of a larger 'heavenly' discourse in the Gospel" (2002, 489). Matthew emphasizes the idea of the Father in Heaven, thereby specifically locating both God and the Kingdom in relation to Heaven. Mark's Gospel on one occasion refers to the "Father in Heaven" (Mark 11:25), but the emphasis is not as strong throughout Mark's Gospel as it is in Matthew. As already noted in relation to the transfiguration narrative where God spoke from the heavens in the cloud, the divine realm and natural dwelling place was precisely in the heavenly realm, which was more physical and spatial than spiritual in biblical terms (Gooder 2011).

For Matthew to emphasize this realm may, as Yarbrough suggests, indicate a tension between heaven and earth and God and humanity which looks toward eventual eschatological resolution (2012, 109). Foster picks up on aspects of identity orientation to heaven, noting that Matthew's language serves to "reaffirm to Jesus' disciples that their identity, affirmation, and goal were in heaven and not on earth." (2002, 490). With twenty unique Kingdom of Heaven sayings in Matthew, this theme is clearly important (see references in Duling 1992, 57–58), and in terms of the location of the divine, it is doubly spatial in that it uses a spatial term ("kingdom") and combines it with an emphasis on location ("heaven"). If Casey and others are correct that Matthew's use of this particular terminology is not circumlocution, then other possibilities for meaning must be explored, including that this particular language constitutes a strong identification with sacred space, and the orientation of the sacred on earth in parity with heaven, where identity is to be focused (Schreiner 2018, 36–37).

The association of God's name with place indicates God's presence in that place (Black 2014, 7), in this case heaven. Ulrich Simon indicates that "the Bible views Heaven and Earth as one world. If the earth is spatial, so is Heaven" (1958, 126; see also Gooder 2011, 9–11). Heaven is directional, and "above" in relation to earth. It is the realm of God, but it is at least partially hidden from the view of humans, and requiring imaginative language for comprehension (Gooder 2011, 9). Importantly, it is also created space, intended to enable proximity between God and humans but also capable of being renewed, just as the earth is capable of being renewed. Though "Kingdom of God" can also indicate God's location in heaven, "Kingdom of Heaven" places a particular emphasis on this directionality and spatial reality above. This spatial emphasis is distinctive to Matthew, and gives one a sense of an author who is concerned to connect Jesus very closely to the sacred realm beyond human sight and material experience. In analytical terms, one can say that Matthew orients Jesus's life and mission especially to the sacred dimension of life and created order that is connected to, but at the same time above, human life on earth. Matthew, in effect, makes the Kingdom more clearly spatial and oriented to the realm of the sacred.

Negative Sacred Space: The Kingdom of Satan

The so-called Beelzebul controversy is a key text found in each of the Synoptic Gospels which gives a clear view of opposing space to the Kingdom of God. Satan's Kingdom is in view and is discussed at some length. Eliade's classic phenomenological treatment of sacred space in *The Sacred and the Profane* treats the two categories as requiring each other for definition. The profane is the other side of the coin, the designation for what is sacred "in the wrong way" (Eliade 1959; Smith 1987). Though this may be critiqued for proposing a dualistic view of the world which is not always in operation, there are nonetheless times and places where this sort of dualism is discernible, and one such example could be where one finds this in the Synoptic Gospels. The Beelzebul controversy illustrates this most strongly, and has a solid basis in each of the Synoptic Gospels, with some variations and additions. Although not explicitly commented on as such in scholarship, the Beelzebul controversy begins with a spatial "rule" or principle: one that I would propose to call the "spatial collapse principle." That is, Jesus in the texts sets out the clear idea that divided spaces cannot stand (Mark 3:24–25, Matt 12:25), are laid waste (Matt 12:25), or become a desert, with "house falling on house" (Luke 11:17). Luke's interesting image of a transformation to an uninhabited, or uninhabitable, space of the desert is intriguing, as is the idea of "a house falls on a house," which Marshall's commentary deems "unclear" but potentially indicative of a kind of continual, domino-like destructive movement in falling, as "house after house collapses" (1978, 474). All three accounts work with some form of the "spatial collapse principle": divided spaces move toward destruction and collapse or desertion. This spatial principle is applied to Satan, and his real, though seemingly not physically visible, Kingdom. If Satan's Kingdom is divided, it will not be able to stand. However, rather than showing the weakness and collapse of Satan, the reductio ad absurdum is that Satan's Kingdom/house is not divided and his end has not come (Marcus 1999, 2000, 273–74; 280–82). This rather discouraging implied application of the spatial rule nonetheless proves the point that Jesus could not possibly be exorcising demons on account of his possession by an "unclean spirit" (Mark 3:30), namely Beelzebul (Mark 3:22). The strength of Satan's unified Kingdom proves Jesus's lack of connection to it.

Davies and Allison point out that Jesus's reductio ad absurdum "affirms Satan's rational behaviour" (1988–97, 2:337) or, as Barrett puts it, "Satan is not such a fool" (1947, 61). But Marcus is also correct to critique this, and to point out that the text does not seem to focus on the perspective of Satan as seen in the *ei* + aorist grammatical construction (Marcus 1999, 256–60). Although Marcus goes on to dismiss this interpretation, he does so too quickly. There *is* a question of rational behavior here, but this is firmly directed against *the critics* in the passage. Jesus presents such critics with a logical argument to refute their *own reasoning*, not Satan's. The critics are the ones who have been so "foolish" as to not recognize the rational argument of the "spatial collapse principle," and therefore they have made an irrational accusation to begin with. The reality and power of the two realms remains untouched—the Kingdom of God and the Kingdom of Satan are clear and accepted by all involved, as is the possibility of exorcism and the ability of the exorcist, with power derived from a source. Jesus's accusers have applied faulty logic in making their accusation. The weakening of Satan through exorcism must, of course, come from outside Satan's Kingdom.

As Moxnes points out in *Putting Jesus in His Place*, the language here is very much of two kingdoms fighting over a territory (2003, 125–41). Jesus's activity in casting out demons constitutes hope in response to the implied discouraging application of the spatial rule; that is, although Satan's Kingdom remains strong, there is hope in the idea that a "strong man" can be tied through the activity of exorcism with power authority deriving from the "spirit" (Matt 12:28) or "finger" (Luke 11:20) of God, and indicative of the coming of the Kingdom of God. There is no question that Satan is being attacked in the activity of exorcism (demons are part of Satan's group/house/Kingdom), but the attack is not an uprising from within; rather, it indicates presence of another Kingdom and another power. The controversy is over the power and realm to which that activity can be attributed. What cannot physically be seen is the location of that activity, as the realms themselves are invisible to the eye. They must be discerned by their results or manifestations in the physical world. The Synoptic authors are doing significant work here to clarify these realities. Satan's Kingdom/house/castle is sacred "in the wrong way" and associated with the language of impurity, suggesting a struggle "between demonic impurity and divine holiness" (Kazen 2002, 333). Conversely in the Gospels,

Jesus's activity is sacred "in the right way" and associated with the power of God and his Kingdom.

While Horsley may be correct to point out that all these terms are for spaces that are political in some regard, it may be questioned whether this is "the point of the discussion" (2003, 101). Though there may be political implications and even connections, what is most prominent is a sense of the articulation of two distinct nonphysical realms, powerful in their own right, and in conflict and competition with each other. This is core to the construction in each synoptic account of the Beelzebul controversy. There is an extended interest in the practice of casting out demons in Matthew and Luke that makes a specific association with the Spirit of God and the presence of the Kingdom (Matt 12:28; Luke 11:20). Demons, as seen in a comparative text such as Jubilees 10:2, are not spatially contained entities and are capable of violating earthly boundaries. The continuation of the Beelzebul controversy in Matthew and Luke indicates that the exorcism of demons is only a temporary solution. An unclean spirit may return to a house swept in order and, bringing friends, make things worse for that person than when that person was first possessed by the spirit (Luke 11:24–26; Matt 12:43–45). Within the physical space of the earth and Jesus's ministry in the Gospels, dualistic nonphysical entities are in competition, yet there is also the hope that the Kingdom of God will prevail. The Kingdom of Satan is not just "sacred in the wrong way," or opposite in terms, but actively evil and opposing. This reinforces the realities of the nonphysical realms active in the created world of heaven and earth. The synoptic authors agree that these realities are present, real, and active. While there may be political connections to make, the primary focus is on the felt power of these unseen entities, and not their political connection(s).

Land as Common Feature?

A focus on the theme of land, or the Abrahamic land promise, has a strong textual history in the Hebrew Bible traditions and within texts of the Second Temple Period. Yet scholars have noted, since W. D. Davies's significant study *The Gospel and the Land* (1994), this theme's overall absence from the Synoptic Gospels. The reason for its lack of prominence cannot be determined with certainty. The relative silence on the theme could be attributed just as plausibly to the potential political danger of emphasizing a theme that could be perceived as an attempt to claim rights (Halpern-Amaru 1994, 1986) as to a general acceptance of the theme's importance without the need for special comment or clarification with new insight. Unfortunately, interpreters from a distance lack the ability to give a definitive reason for the lack of attention to the land as sacred space.

There is, however, one common feature of the three Synoptic Gospels which is intriguing for its relevance to the theme of land, and this is the presence of the group of the twelve. Twelve is a highly symbolic number in terms of a tribal configuration—denoting all the people in all the land. The number twelve could be evoked to recall such a configuration, and in the broader context of Josephus's so-called sign prophets (i.e. Theudas, *Ant.* 20:97–99; the Egyptian, *Ant.* 20:169–72; *War* 2:261; Acts 21:38) it would seem reasonable to assume that the inclusion of the twelve is not accidental but symbolic of the whole group in the whole (sacred) land—broadly, if not specifically, recalling foundational sacred narratives of exodus and entry (Wenell 2007b, 116–17). While each Synoptic Gospel includes the fact of the twelve as a group, none gives a full explanation of the significance of the twelve in spatial terms. Eric Stewart makes the point that the twelve are called to be "with him," that is, with Jesus, in the narrative (2009, 210–14) and so locates sacred presence around the figure of Jesus himself.

Looking beyond this common feature of the basic presence of the twelve, Matthew and Luke give the added feature of a ruling scenario, where the twelve have twelve thrones and a role in judgment. These thrones have no physical substance in the present world but are part of an envisioned future space. Matthew uses the significant, but rare in the New Testament, term παλινγενεσία (Matt 19:28), pointing to a renewal of the created order, which can include both heaven and earth and can have material or immaterial referents, as in Philo's use of the term to refer to the soul's journey to immortality (Burnett 1983). Matthew has articulated a sacred reality that is yet to materialize, providing an extension of the space of the present and strengthening the relationship between the group of the twelve and the presence of God in the anticipated space of the future. If the land itself is a promise and a covenant between God and the descendants of Abraham, the divine throne room can be viewed as a promised space for the group of the twelve in a reading of Matthew and Luke. Mark does not have the specific scenario of the twelve thrones but does speak of James and John and the "other ten," so there is a hint of this feature in Mark, but Matthew and Luke have developed the vision of this ruling space with greater detail in relation to the twelve. The idea of twelve tribal rulers looks to renewed space in the future, with suggestive reference to tribal land as the location of the sacred.

One final point is worth noting in relation to the land, and that is the quotation from Psalm 37 in Matthew's Sermon on the Mount, appealing to the promise of inheritance of the land: "Blessed are the meek, for they shall inherit the land" (Psalm 37:11; Matt 5:5). This more accurate translation "inherit the land" utilizes a phrase that occurs in the LXX and was at this time "the standard formula to express the promise of the land to Abraham and his descendants" (Wilken 1992, 7). English translations like "inherit the earth" hide this connection to the land from view. Of the three synoptic authors, Matthew would appear to have the most interest (in a slim field) in the land as a feature of the sacred landscape. Though references are not abundant and Beavis is correct to caution against the idea that the twelve indicate a literal restoration of the tribes (2006, 98), there is at least some evidence of reflection on the promise of inheritance of the land, and on the twelve as a symbolic group with possible significance in terms of future spatial arrangements and a land-modeled vision of ideal sacred space.

The Temple and the Location of the Sacred

In a way, land and kingdom have a considerable degree of similarity as sacred spaces. Both are concerned with the identity of the whole group in relation to God and a sacred realm. They are not in themselves concerned with the concentration of sacredness in particular built structures. They are more relevant to outer boundaries and the inside of the group as distinguished from the outside; those who belong and those who do not. In spatial terms, the Kingdom sometimes points to distinctions between heaven and earth. For the land, the twelve provide a symbolic association with a territorial arrangement of space. With the temple, the sacred is identified with a specific built structure. References to the temple occur in core synoptic material, where they do not seem to be focused on boundary work of defining insiders and outsiders in relation to that structure. In comparison, Jonathan Z. Smith's analysis of the hierarchy of the temple as described in Ezekiel (1987, 47–73) shows very distinct hierarchical and group associations with different parts of temple space which are distinguished. In the Synoptics, the temple is identified as a location for teaching by Jesus (Mark 11:17, 12:35; Matt 21:23; Luke 19:47, 20:1, 21.37), a question about Jesus's authority (Mark 11:27–33; Matt 21:23–27; Luke 20:1–8), protest (Mark 11:15–18; Matt 21:12–13; Luke 19:45–46), and one of the events accompanying the death of Jesus, where the temple curtain is torn in two (Mark 15:38; Matt 27:51, Luke 23:45). In Mark and Matthew, this action originates from above/the heavens, as the temple curtain is torn "from top to bottom" (Mark 15:8; Matt 27:51). Mark and Matthew include derision of Jesus prior to his execution with the charge "you who would destroy the temple and build it in three days, save yourself!" (Mark 15:29; Matt 27:40).

Studies of the temple in other contemporary texts, in architecture, and in broader social-historical enquiry reveal a considerable amount about the structure of the temple, and its significance in ancient thought and practice (e.g. Day 2007). Its prominence is formidable, and the temple was clearly a focus of an "education of attention" to sacredness in this era. Some of this attention is seen in the Gospels. All three Synoptic Gospels include Jesus and his disciples eating a Passover meal together in Jerusalem. Nowhere in the Synoptic Gospels is the specific celebration of Passover in Jerusalem in connection to the temple criticized in any way. Luke extends this feature of accepted and uncritical performance of ritual connected to the temple when sacrifices are presented at the birth of Jesus. Simeon comes to the temple where Jesus's parents are presenting him, and Luke 2:40–42 indicates a family practice of attendance in Jerusalem for the Passover, noted as a "usual" practice (Luke 2:42: "according to custom"; see Green 1997, 154). The inclusion of the sacrifices at the birth of Jesus in Luke's Gospel gives this sense of normal, expected practices carried out in the temple.

However, one common feature across the three synoptic accounts is more critical, namely, the incident in the temple whereby Jesus overturns the tables of the money changers and those buying and selling (Mark 11:15–19; Luke 19:45–48; Matt 21:12–14).

Here, the angry performance of Jesus sets out a divine purpose for the temple which is contrasted with current practice, through the quotation of Isaiah 56:7 and Isaiah 7:11, pitting one name for the temple "house of prayer" against another "den of thieves" (Wenell 2007a). Mark and Matthew include a predictive (even if after the fact) statement by Jesus to indicate that "not one stone will be left here upon another" (Mark 13:2 // Matthew 24:2). These constitute attention to the temple and its role in society, but in a way that is critical of at least some aspects of current practice.

The tearing of the temple curtain does nothing to affirm the continuing location of the sacred in the temple after the death of Jesus from the perspective of the Synoptic Gospels. Although there is no voice from heaven as in the transfiguration narrative, this action, seemingly originating with God (due to the tearing starting from the "top" as Mark and Matthew indicate), responds to Jesus's death with an action that renders ineffective an object (the curtain) intended to mark out the divine presence in the temple. Overall, the temple is connected to positive activities of a sacred economy in the Synoptics (sacrifice, Passover, teaching), yet more critical aspects connected to its sacred purpose are also given attention in the texts.

Synoptic (or Seen Together) Views of Sacred Space

In the experience of many in the (Western/westernized) world today, the skill of distinguishing the sacred and discovering its place in relation to material and immaterial worlds is diminished or missing. The more awareness there is of the significance of human emplacement in the world, the more humans are able to connect to, and consider themselves part of, a shared environment. In the ancient environment in which the Synoptic Gospels were produced, what in today's terms are understood as environmental issues were not live in the same way they are today as humans face the need to address the effects of damage to their world. What was more prominent in that ancient setting was the relationship between the nonmaterial sacred world and the physical world of day-to-day life. Emplacement meant more than physical orientation, and the issues and struggles of daily life were interconnected with other, nonvisible realities. The realm of the gods was present and active in day-to-day life and day-to-day dwelling in the physical world. There were points of connection between the sacred world of the gods and the world of humans, as in the performance of sacred groves (Barnett 2007) or attention to Mount Olympus, and in the Synoptic Gospels through events like hierophany.

There were ways to consider and care for the environment in the ancient world, just as there are ways to consider the immaterial sacrality of space in the contemporary world. These matters of concern are not constrained to one time period or another. In the Synoptic Gospels, there is evidence of concern for the sacred in relation to place. Some of this relates to the meaning of physical structures like the temple in Jerusalem—the most significant Jewish central sacred space of its time—or of land as physical space signifying the whole group in relationship to God. Other matters relate to unseen realms, and to consideration of the meaning of the Kingdom of God, or the significance of heaven as God's domain. All these various interactions between the sacred and space are important to consider in relation to the Synoptic Gospels.

Focusing on material that is core, or common to all three synoptic accounts, has the advantage of showing specific instances where a level of ancient agreement on matters of space occurred, as well as showing extensions and modifications of ideas. Mark Goodacre encouraged scholars to envision a "world without Q" where it was possible to value the "literary artistry of the evangelists," "tempered by the encouragement to take oral tradition even more seriously" so that it was possible to think more creatively about "the way that people lived, engaging with texts and listening to the living voice" (2004, 179). With matters of space, it is possible to think more creatively and openly about lived experience and interactions with the sacred, whether through physical or nonmaterial manifestations in the environment. These are social as much as historical or literary questions, and moving away from an emphasis on order and sources has the potential to open up new ways of working with the texts and thinking about ancient interactions between God, people, and place.

REFERENCES

Aalen, Sverre. 1962. "'Reign' and 'House' in the Kingdom of God in the Gospels." *New Testament Studies* 8, no. 3: 215–40.

Adams, Edward. 2013. *The Earliest Christian Meeting Places: Almost Exclusively Houses?* Library of New Testament Studies. London: T&T Clark.

Anttonen, Veikko. 2007. "Rethinking 'Religious' Cognition: The Eliadean Notion of the Sacred in the Light of the Legacy of Uno Harva." *Temenos* 43, no. 1: 53–72.

Barnett, Rod. 2007. "Sacred Groves: Sacrifice and the Order of Nature in Ancient Greek Landscapes." *Landscape Journal* 26, no. 2: 252–70.

Barrett, C. K. 1947. *The Holy Spirit and the Gospel Tradition*. London: SCM Press.

Beavis, Mary Ann. 2006. *Jesus and Utopia: Looking for the Kingdom of God in the Roman World*. Minneapolis: Fortress Press.

Billings, Bradly S. 2011. "From House Church to Tenement Church: Domestic Space and the Development of Early Urban Christianity — The Example of Ephesus." *Journal of Theological Studies* 62, no. 2: 541–69.

Black, CC. 2014. "Whose Kingdom? Whose Power? Whose Glory?" *Horizons in Biblical Theology* 36, no. 1: 1–20.

Brown, Rick. 2001. "A Brief History of Interpretations of 'the Kingdom of God' and Some Consequences for Translation." *Notes on Translation* 51, no. 1: 3–23.

Burnett, Fred W. 1983. "Palingenesia in Matt 19:28: A Window on the Matthean Community?" *Journal for the Study of the New Testament* 17: 60–72.

Burridge, Richard. 2004. *What Are the Gospels? A Comparison with Graeco-Roman Biography*. 2nd ed. Grand Rapids: Eerdmans.

Chilton, B. 2006–2009. "Kingdom of God/Kingdom of Heaven." In New Interpreter's Dictionary of the Bible, edited by KD Sakenfeld. Nashville: Abingdon.

Chilton, Bruce, ed. 1984. "The Kingdom of God in the Teaching of Jesus." In *Issues in Religion and Theology*, edited by Douglas Knight and Robert Morgan. Philadelphia: Fortress Press and SPCK.

Dalman, Gustaf. 1902. *The Words of Jesus, Considered in the Light of Post-biblical Writings and the Aramaic Language*. Translated by David Miller Kay. Edinburgh: T&T Clark.

Davies, Margaret. 1993. *Matthew*. Sheffield: Sheffield: JSOT.

Davies, W. D. 1994. *The Gospel and the Land: Early Christianity and Jewish Territorial Doctrine*. Biblical Seminar 25. Sheffield: JSOT Press.

Davies, W. D., and Dale C. Allison. 1988–97. *A Critical and Exegetical Commentary on the Gospel According to Saint Matthew*. 3 vols. Edinburgh: T&T Clark.

Day, John, ed. 2007. *Temple and Worship in Biblical Israel*. London: Continuum.

Duling, Dennis C. 1992. "Kingdom of God, Kingdom of Heaven." In *The Anchor Bible Dictionary*, edited by David Noel Freedman, 49–69. New York: Doubleday.

Eliade, Mircea. 1959. *The Sacred and the Profane: The Nature of Religion*. Translated by Willard R. Trask. San Diego: Harcourt.

Faust, A., and S. Bunimovitz. 2003. "The Four Room House." *Near Eastern Archaeology* 66, nos. 1–2: 22–31.

Foster, Robert. 2002. "Why on Earth Use "Kingdom of Heaven"?: Matthew's Terminology Revisited." *New Testament Studies* 48, no. 4: 487–99.

France, R. T. 2007. *The Gospel of Matthew*. NICNT. Grand Rapids: Eerdmans.

Goodacre, Mark. 2004. "A World without Q." In *Questioning Q*, edited by Mark Goodacre and Nicholas Perrin, 174–79. London: SPCK.

Gooder, Paula. 2011. *Heaven*. London: SPCK.

Green, Joel B. 1997. *The Gospel of Luke*. NICNT. Grand Rapids: Eerdmans.

Guijarro, Santiago. 2017. "The Transfiguration of Jesus and the Easter Visions." *Biblical Theology Bulletin* 47, no. 2: 95–99.

Halpern-Amaru, Betsy. 1986. "Land Theology in Philo and Josephus." In *The Land of Israel: Jewish Perspectives*, edited by Lawrence A. Hoffman, 63–93. Notre Dame: University of Notre Dame Press.

Halpern-Amaru, Betsy. 1994. *Rewriting the Bible: Land and Covenant in Post-biblical Jewish Literature*. Valley Forge, PA: Trinity Press International.

Horrell, David G. 2004. "Domestic Space and Christian Meetings at Corinth: Imagining New Contexts and the Buildings East of the Theatre." *New Testament Studies* 50, no. 3: 349–69.

Horsley, Richard A. 2003. *Jesus and Empire: The Kingdom of God and the New World Disorder*. Minneapolis: Fortress Press.

Ingold, Tim. 2001. "From the Transmission of Representations to the Education of Attention." In *The Debated Mind: Evolutionary Psychology Versus Ethnography*, edited by Harvey Whitehouse, 113–53. Oxford: Berg.

Johnson, Luke Timothy. 1992. *The Gospel of Luke*. Sacra Pagina. Collegeville: Liturgical Press.

Kazen, Thomas. 2002. *Jesus and Purity Halakhah: Was Jesus Indifferent to Impurity?* Coniectanea Biblica New Testament Series 38. Stockholm: Almqvist & Wiksell International.

Knight, Jonathan. 1998. *Luke's Gospel*. London: Routledge.

Knott, Kim. 2005. *The Location of Religion: A Spatial Analysis*. Durham, UK: Acumen.

Lawrence, Louise. 2011. "Exploring the Sense-scape of the Gospel of Mark." *Journal for the Study of the New Testament* 33, no. 4: 387–97.

Malbon, Elizabeth Struthers. 1991. *Narrative Space and Mythic Meaning in Mark.* Sheffield: JSOT Press.

Marcus, Joel. 1988. "Entering into the Kingly Power of God." *Journal of Biblical Literature* 107, no. 4: 663–75.

Marcus, Joel. 1999. "The Beelzebul Controversy and the Eschatologies of Jesus." In *Authenticating the Activities of Jesus*, edited by Bruce Chilton and Craig A. Evans, 247–77. Leiden: Brill.

Marcus, Joel. 2000. *Mark 1–8: A New Translation with Introduction and Commentary.* Anchor Bible 27. New York: Doubleday.

Marshall, I. Howard. 1978. *The Gospel of Luke: A Commentary on the Greek Text.* Exeter, UK: Paternoster Press.

Massey, Doreen. 2005. *For Space.* Los Angeles: SAGE.

Metzger, Bruce M. 1958–59. "Seventy or Seventy-Two Disciples?" *New Testament Studies* 5: 299–306.

Moxnes, Halvor. 2003. *Putting Jesus in His Place: A Radical Vision of Household and Kingdom.* Louisville: Westminster John Knox Press.

Økland, Jorunn, Cornelis de Vos, and Karen Wenell. 2016. Introduction to n *Constructions of Space III: Biblical Spatiality and the Sacred*, edited by Karen Wenell, Jorunn Økland, and Cornelis de Vos, xii–xvi. London: Bloomsbury.

Pamment, Margaret. 1981. "The Kingdom of Heaven According to the First Gospel." *New Testament Studies* 27, no. 2: 211–32.

Parker, David C. 1997. *The Living Text of the Gospels.* Cambridge: Cambridge University Press.

Schreiner, Patrick. 2018. *The Body of Jesus: A Spatial Analysis of the Kingdom in Matthew.* Paperback ed. London: T&T Clark.

Simon, Ulrich E. 1958. *Heaven in the Christian Tradition.* London: Rockliff.

Smith, Jonathan Z. 1987. *To Take Place: Toward Theory in Ritual.* Edited by Jacob Neusner, William Scott Green, and Calvin Goldscheider. Chicago Studies in the History of Judaism. Chicago: University of Chicago Press.

Stewart, Eric C. 2009. *Gathered around Jesus: An Alternative Spatial Practice in the Gospel of Mark.* Cambridge: James Clarke.

Tuckett, Christopher. 2011. "The Current State of the Synoptic Problem." In *New Studies in the Synoptic Problem: Oxford Conference, April 2008: Essays in Honour of Christopher M. Tuckett*, edited by Paul Foster, Andrew Gregory, J. S. Kloppenborg, and J. Verheyden, 9–50. Leuven: Peeters.

Tweed, Thomas A. 2011. "Space." *Material Religion* 7, no. 1: 116–23.

Wenell, Karen. 2007a. "Contested Temple Space and Visionary Kingdom Space in Mark 11–12." *Biblical Interpretation* 15, no. 3: 323–37.

Wenell, Karen J. 2007b. *Jesus and Land: Sacred and Social Space in Second Temple Judaism.* Edited by Robert L. Webb. Library of Historical Jesus Studies/Library of New Testament Studies 334. London: T&T Clark.

Wenell, Karen. 2012. "'Ears to Hear': The Bible, the Sower and Performative Christianity." In *New Perspectives on Religious and Spiritual Education*, edited by Theo van der Zee and Terence J. Lovat, 117–32. Münster: Waxmann.

Wilken, Robert L. 1992. *The Land Called Holy: Palestine in Christian History and Thought.* New Haven: Yale University Press.

Willis, Wendell. 1987. "The Discovery of the Eschatological Kingdom: Johannes Weiss and Albert Schweitzer." In *The Kingdom of God in 20th-Century Interpretation*, edited by Wendell Willis, 1–14. Peabody, MA: Hendrickson.

Yaneva, Albena. 2010. "A Building's Trajectory." In *Coping with the Past: Creative Perspectives on Conservation and Restoration*, edited by Pasquale Gagliardi, Bruno Latour, and Pedro Memelsdorff, 17–45. Firenze: Olschki.

Yarbrough, Robert W. 2012. "The Kingdom of God in the New Testament: Matthew and Revelation." In *The Kingdom of God*, edited by C. W. Morgan and R. A. Peterson, 95–123. Wheaton: Crossway.

CHAPTER 21

HISTORY

EVE-MARIE BECKER

"History" has been a subject of multiple studies and research quests regarding the Synoptic Gospels. For example: (1) Mark, Matthew, and Luke(-Acts) act as historical sources to the history of Palestine in the first century CE (Roman Near East studies). (2) The Synoptic Gospels act as biographical sources to the historical Jesus figure (Jesus research). (3) The Synoptic Gospels act as literary witnesses to the beginnings of the Jesus-movement and the emergence of Christ-believing communities (history of early Christianity studies). (4) The Synoptic Gospels act as historiographical narratives in which historical data and events around Jesus's ministry in Palestine in the first century CE are presented in a narrative form: by means of literary memory, the Synoptic Gospels construe "history." Initiated by Mark, the Synoptic Gospel writers present the mission and fortune of Jesus of Nazareth as an *arche*-narrative of global historiographical meaning (historiography approach).

This article addresses this last research quest in "history" and the Synoptic Gospels.

Writing "History" in Hellenistic-Roman Times

The writing of *historiography* and the construction of *history* go hand in hand. What proves to be true in general, for nearly three millennia of human history, especially applies to Hellenistic-Roman times. Even if monuments, sculptures, Greco-Roman architecture, and all kinds of art can produce and reproduce various forms of historical memory, the medium of history writing has a specific conceptual value for saving memories about the past and construing "history" out of it. In particular, historiographical accounts about past events allow for a comprehensive interpretation of *time* (see Becker 2017a; and see hereafter).

The Synoptic Gospel writers participate in the Hellenistic culture of history writing—they construe history by historiographical means. Mark initiates the gospel genre as historiographical literature by creating a narrative about how the history of the gospel proclamation started during Jesus's ministry and brutal death in Jerusalem around 30 CE. Mark reports a sequence of events in Galilee and Jerusalem, which is, at first, of marginal importance for global history or even the history of the Roman Near East in the first century CE—the gospels are rather seen as testimonies of "popular religious consciousness" (Millar 2001, 342). According to Mark's depiction (see hereafter), which was composed shortly after 70 CE—probably in the aftermath of the First Jewish-Roman War—that history about the "beginnings of the gospel proclamation" (Mark 1:1), however, is of universal significance (Mark 13:10; 14:9) since it has a cosmic significance (Mark 13:24–27; 15:33). Without being a contemporary historian, as for example Flavius Josephus, Mark connects his history programmatically to political history of the surrounding world (Mark 15:1; see also 6:14)—even though sparely.

Mark's narrative concept of an *arche*-history, which is of historiographical nature and significance, was further developed by Luke. Within two books, Luke carves out and underscores the historiographical dimensions of the gospel-narrative he found in Mark (see hereafter). When placing the Synoptic Gospels in the broader frame of Greco-Roman and Hellenistic-Jewish historiography, no supposition is made that ancient historiography would solely consist of *bruta facta* accounts. Fact and fiction, myth and history constantly interact in the narrative world(s) of ancient history writing. According to Quintilian, history writing comes close to poetry. As a poem without verses, history writing aims at narrating, not at proving ("ad narrandum, non ad probandum"; *Inst.* 10.1.31).

In addition, the gospel writings—even though they do contain valuable historical data and information (see, e.g., *titulus crucis*: Mark 15:26 parr.)—tell their stories in light of fictitious amplification (see, e.g., the prodigy: Mark 15:38) and theological interpretation (see, e.g., Mk 8:31 etc.). Accordingly, the *arche tou euanggeliou* in Mark 1:1 defines the literary and historical beginnings of the gospel story. At the same time, the opening phrase shapes an imagination of the mythical origin of the gospel story in the desert region (Mark 1:4). As Greco-Roman historians do (Bowersock, 1994), Mark and his successors Luke and Matthew mix fact and fiction when providing their historiographical accounts.

General Remarks on the Synoptic Gospels and Ancient Histor(iograph)y

Historiography of various generic forms typically functions in several ways. (1) It shapes *chronological* conjunctions of individual historical data and events, somehow dated and linked to world history. (2) History writing offers *causal* explanation for the story told. (3) In historiography, the chronology-based narrative appears in *prose* form. (4) Historiography *evaluates* past events in their historiographical significance, and (5) builds narrative storylines through which *chronotopes* are (re)produced as hermeneutical keys to the temporal and spatial character of historical events. (6) In doing so, history writing is the most ambitious cultural concept of storing and reproducing historical memory as *literary memory*.

Among the Synoptic Gospels, the Markan and the Lukan gospel narratives share these features of history writing: Mark and Luke offer a storyline about the beginnings of the gospel proclamation which is chronologically structured, is intentionally dated, and serves the narrative evaluation of the past events for present purposes. Herein lies an etiological dimension of (pre)historiographical texts as *arche*-narratives (Walter 2020).

Periodization: Gospel Writings *as* Hellenistic Literature

The literature of Hellenistic-Roman times is the richest of all kinds of historiographical writings—this applies to the Greco-Roman as well as to the Jewish world(s); see overview in Becker 2011; 2015). Recently, the historian and classical scholar Angelos Chaniotis has emphasized that herein lies a characteristic feature of Hellenistic-Roman times: "the 'long Hellenistic Age' is the golden age of historiography, at least as far as quantity goes; it is also the golden age of commemorative anniversaries, historical monuments and mythography" (Chaniotis 2019, 399–400). It is not accidental then that Josephus also—like many of his Greco-Roman contemporaries—chooses the genre of history writing as a central mode of literary self-expression.

How does one define the "Hellenistic Age"? There are good reasons for following Chaniotis in revising Johann G. Droysen's (1808–84) prominent concept of "Hellenism" (Droysen 2008; see also Gehrke 2008), both in terms of its heuristics and its periodization. Droysen's concept of Hellenism, even though well-received for a long time, is periodically and heuristically limited—it concentrates on political history and reaches up to the year 219 BCE (Gehrke 2008, XII). Chaniotis, instead, suggests taking the even longer time span which stretches from 336 BCE—that is, from Alexander the Great's government takeover—up to Hadrian's death in 138 CE as a coherent period of political, military, and cultural history of the Mediterranean world (Chaniotis 2019, 3). When this is done, the rise of New Testament literature during the first and second centuries CE falls into Hellenistic times. Consequently, New Testament literature, including the Synoptic Gospels, appears to be a phenomenon of Hellenistic culture.

In and beyond its affiliation to the Hebrew and Jewish tradition of constructing history as God's history with his people, gospel literature has to be circumscribed within the broad field of Hellenistic literature. (On Jewish literary culture and Hellenism see Hengel 1988, esp. 152; Becker 2011, 1798.) Even though gospel literature was composed in a period of time that might best be classified as "Early Roman Imperial" time in geopolitical terms and as Flavian in terms of time period (see hereafter), this literature contributes to the rich market of Hellenistic history writing in its broader sense.

The Synoptic Gospels as Prehistoriographical Accounts

Gospel Writings *as* Historiography

Genre criticism is an inevitable tool whenever discussing the generic place of gospel writings within their ancient literary settings (Becker 2017b, 17; see also various contributions in Calhoun, Moessner, and Nicklas 2020). Many scholars tend to classify the gospel literature *as* biography—in analogy either to Hellenistic-Jewish (as, e.g., Helmut Koester), or Greco-Roman (e.g., Charles H. Talbert; Richard A. Burridge; M. R. Licona 2017) biographical forms (see Licona 2017, 3). The more the analogy to Greco-Roman literature is pointed out, the more emphasis is put on the level of the rhetorical education the gospel writers might have gained through, for instance, *progymnasmata* teaching (see Licona 2017, 197).

In light of genre classifications made in the field of classics, especially those classifications proposed by the classical scholar Hubert Cancik (1991), I have suggested that the gospel writings not be read *as* biographies but be related to the *macro*-type of ancient historiography. Put in the macro-setting of historiography, the gospel writings appear—in terms of their micro-type—to be a genre sui generis. The gospel writings present a new type of a narrative, a person-centered history about a sequence of events, which finally reaches back to the beginnings (*arche*) of the gospel proclamation (see Mark 1:1; Luke 1:1–4; Becker 2017a: 69).

The classification of the Synoptic Gospel genre as a distinct micro-type within the expansive macro-type of Hellenistic historiography explains why the gospel writings were successful early on. On the one hand the gospels found their particular place in a booming Hellenistic-Roman book market. From the period of Alexander the Great onward and up to Early Roman Imperial literature, the highly diversified writing and reading culture of Hellenistic-Roman times is progressively interested in the lives of emperors and Caesars, such as Augustus and his successors (see, e.g., Nicolaus of Damascus, Suetonius, Plutarch), or military leaders, such as Philopoemen (see, e.g., Polybius, Plutarch). The pluriform Hellenistic-Roman tradition of person-centered accounts like "de viris illustribus" (see, e.g., Nepos) is later programmatically continued by ancient Christian authors (see, e.g., Jerome). On the other hand the gospel writings carry on the rich and manifold (early) Jewish traditions of person-centered historiography, where protagonists from the past—like Moses—are subjects of narrative accounts. Those narratives constantly circulate between history writing and legendary stories or novellas as they are found among the writings of Deuterocanonical and cognate literature (see, e.g., Artapanus).

In his collection of memorable doings and sayings (*Facta et Dicta Memorabilia*), written in Tiberian times (*Praef.*), the Roman rhetorician Valerius Maximus reflects the value of literary memory: he considers deeds and sayings to be "worthy of memorial of the Roman city and external nations" (translation: LCL 492: 13). In his literary work, Valerius not only provides important insight into history-oriented literary activity in the first century CE but also signifies basic parameters of how cultural memory is established and stored. The memorial interest in collecting and presenting sayings (*logia/dicta*) and deeds (*erga/facta*) once more points to why historiographical memory in Hellenistic-Roman times is preferably about people—powerful men, political leaders, or prominent philosophers. In Hellenistic times, history writing approaches history as narratives about events caused by human action.

Rather than being composed as biographies, the Synoptic Gospel writings are a genre sui generis in the broader frame of Hellenistic-Roman history writing. As such, the gospel writings do contribute to the increasing value of person-centered historiographical memory.

The Gospel Writings as Part of Hellenistic Culture and Literary Products of Early Roman Imperial Times

Gospel literature originates from Hellenistic times and appears as a natural part of Hellenistic culture with its strong emphasis on historiographical literature. What is attested by the variety of person-centered historiographical forms and literary microtypes, also applies in linguistic terms. As all New Testament writers and cognate authors (e.g., Philo; Josephus) do, the synoptic gospel writers choose Koine Greek as their first literary language. More precisely, the gospel writings were composed in the Early Roman Imperial time, or the "Principate," more particularly, in the last third of the first century CE. This time span might best be called the "Flavian period"—a time span of first-century CE (literary) history that is currently gaining increasing attention in antiquity studies (see, e.g., Bessone/Fucecchi 2019). What does this context mean for the composition of the Synoptic Gospels?

(1) Flavian ideology is specifically embodied by Vespasian and Titus's suppression of the Jewish revolt in 66–70/73 CE. If ever the history of Palestine mattered in global terms, it was during the reign of the Flavian Emperors (69–96 CE)—exactly that period of time where the Synoptic Gospels emerged. In this very time period, Flavius Josephus most impressively showed how to make the project of writing history about the war and the Jewish people "profitable." The gospel writers, instead, do not explicitly take up contemporary history but look back into Tiberian (Luke 3:1) or even Augustan (Luke 2:1) times.

(2) The Flavian period has generated its specific topics and types of literature, which can be analyzed in historical and ideological dimensions (see, e.g., Pfeiffer 2009; Augoustakis et al. 2019). Part of the *Zeitgefühl* (sense of time) is dominated by a *metus temporum* (angst of the times; see Tacitus, *Hist.* 1.49.3; 2.72.1; Pliny, *Ep.* 5.1.7; 7.19.6; 9.13.3; Kneppe 1994, 49).

Besides the factor of contemporary political history and its ideological implications and impacts on *Zeitgefühl*, the Early Roman Imperial setting has at least five more effects on the rise of the gospel writings as historiographical literature, as follows.

(3) Roman historiographical culture is closely connected to the concept of *memoria*. To the Romans, history and historiography have memorial value and function (Quintilian, *Inst.* 10.1.31: "ad memoriam posteritatis"). They even emanate from memory in the form of lists: Roman *fasti* are forerunners of historiographical accounts (see Rüpke 2012). While the Greeks "tend to link the present to the past through practices of representation," the Romans "memorialize people, duties, and deeds for posterity" (Becker 2017a, 2—with reference to Price 2012, 15). Gospel writers share the Roman interest in shaping a memorial culture by creating historiographical thinking.

(4) Since the Augustan period at least, historiography had gained specific attraction in Roman society. History writing is sometimes called a crucial "occupation of a cultural Roman" (Price 2005, 103; see Pliny, *Ep.* 5.8; Juvenal, *Sat.* 7.98–104; Quintilian, *Inst.* 10.1). By providing a historiographical narrative about the origins of the gospel proclamation, the synoptic authors thus contribute to the Roman curiosity regarding *memoria* and history writing.

(5) As, for instance, Quintilian shows in his *Institutio Oratoria*, Romans consider themselves in continuity with and in competition with their Greek forerunners (see, e.g., Baier 2019). According to the expectations of their literary audience, Roman authors shall match, or better supersede, the literary concepts and stylistic features of the Greek-Hellenistic preceding literary culture (*Inst.* 10.1.101). As the Romans do, Christ-believing authors in the early Roman Empire, like the evangelists, place their historiographical narratives in continuity with and in some competition with the precedent early Jewish prose tradition: "all ancient poets were bound by the principle of *imitatio*" (Vessey 1982, 65). The idea of literary competition exists not only in a transcultural dimension but also in an intracultural sense: literary authors who belong to the same "cultural cluster" see themselves in constant competition with each other (see, e.g., Josephus and Justus of Tiberias; Luke 1:1–4). As a memorial practice, historiographical accounts even produce "counter memory" enduringly (Becker 2017a: 19—with reference to Foucault 1977).

(6) Roman literary culture allows—much more than was the case in Greek-Hellenistic literary culture—for a promotion of nonprofessional literary authors. This again, also applies to the wide-range field of historiography: Valerius Maximus (see earlier), who initially came from lower social status, is a good example of successful advancement as a literary author in Tiberian times. Two further examples are even more illustrative: Suetonius mentions a man named Cornelius Epicadus, a former slave, as the person who finally completed Sulla's memoirs (*Gramm.* 12.1). Velleius Paterculus remembers a certain Pomponius as an inventor of new kind of a literary genre (2.9). Social promotion and literary innovation go hand in hand. In Roman times, especially among the movement of the so-called Neoterics, literary innovation was highly appreciated, if not defined as a literary objective.

Here, again, lies a possible "structural analogy" to how literary activity began in early Christian times, and to how early Christian writers like the synoptic authors defined their self-understanding. According to the *Zeitgeist* of late Republican and Principate literary culture, the gospel writers do not necessarily have to come from an upper-class background and/or a well-established literary tradition. The gospel writers, nevertheless, might not come from a low social status group either: the Synoptic Gospels rather show certain compositional and rhetorical elements that seemingly point to a *progymnasmata*-education of their authors (see Martin and Parsons 2018). Luke's usage of *diegesis* (Luke 1:1), for instance, clearly points to a concept of history writing that follows the literary theory as defined in the *progymnasmata* handbooks (see Aelius Theon; Hermogenes in Kennedy 2003).

(7) The idea of the Imperium Romanum as a concept of global governance likewise inspires global or "ecumenical" thinking. As Paul intends to reach Spain (Rom 15:24, 28) and thereby wishes to bring the gospel proclamation up to the borders of the known world of his time, the synoptic authors develop programmatic ideas of the global spreading of the *euaggelion*. According to the synoptic gospel writers, it was not only the group of Jesus-followers, disciples, or apostles who would have finally decided upon a global missionary strategy. Mark, Luke, and Matthew rather emphasize that already Jesus himself—either during his earthly ministry (Mark 13:11; 14:11) or as the risen one (Matt 28:19; Acts 1:8)—has given such instruction for a universal mission that exceeds the boundaries between the Jewish and the Gentile world (e.g., Acts 18:6).

To sum up: the gospel writings originate from Hellenistic times, and they are part of Hellenistic culture. In many ways, they reflect some of the *Zeitgefühl* (*metus temporum*) and *Zeitgeist* of Early Roman Imperial culture according to which global thinking, literary continuity and competition, and social promotion and literary innovation have become legitimate patterns in the field of literary activity, in which history writing, in turn, has developed as a dominant area of literary self-expression.

In contrast to how the Synoptic Gospels reflect Hellenistic-Roman *Zeitgeist* in various ways, they show less concrete interest in contemporary history (Becker 2022), as Josephus does (see *Bellum Judaicum*). Neither do the Synoptic Gospels reflect clear tendencies of antiimperialist thinking. Such an antiimperialist thinking, however, has been assigned to texts like, for instance, Mark 13, by more recent scholarship (e.g., Gelardini 2016; Blatz 2016). According to an "empire-critical reading," Mark appears as "reactionary literature towards a disastrous war" (G. Gelardini 2016, 1). One might assume that the events of the Flavian period were decisive for the composition of the gospel writings as histories about sequences of events in Palestine. However, there is less evidence for antiimperialism encapsulated in the gospels than there are hints at how the gospel writers understood their task in structural analogy to Hellenistic-Roman historiographers: the period of the Principate as such offers a range of conceptual opportunities even for "outsider historians" such as Mark and Luke.

The Synoptic Gospels, Time Mastery, and the Birth of Christian History

As I have extensively pointed out elsewhere (Becker 2017a), historical memory evokes historiography and finally the narrative shape of history. Especially in Mark and Luke's concept of a gospel narrative, the dimensions of memory, time, and history cooperate closely. In other words, historiography and history specifically serve the purpose of time mastery. The hermeneutical key to Mark and Luke's gospel concepts lies in their interest in presenting the history about the *past* as a constitutive mode of coping with *present* and *future* needs. How do people in Hellenistic-Roman times in general approach past time and the role that history writing plays herein? How do they manage time? What kind of time mastery strategy do the synoptic gospel writers offer?

Disclosing the Past: The Historian's Task Then and Now

Seneca, the Stoic philosopher and contemporary of Paul who lived in Neronian time, denies the possibility of accessing either past or future time ("Et quae praeterierunt et quae futura sunt, absunt; neutra sentimus"; *Ep.* 74.34). Elsewhere he points out how future plans nevertheless depend on the past ("Hoc nos pessimos facit, quod nemo vitam suam respicit. Quid facturi simus cogitamus. Atqui consilium future ex praeteritio venit"; *Ep.* 83.2). Historians, in some contrast to moral philosophers like Seneca, want to make the past accessible for the present audience and its current needs. In particular the prologues in ancient history writing frequently express the idea of how the historian—by depicting a story about the past—primarily wants to address *contemporary* readers, for the purpose of providing historical information and/or moral teaching.

The Lukan prologues (Luke 1:1–4; Acts 1:1 see Wolter 2009) are especially evident examples of how the historian spans past and present. The prologues, in other words, are historiographical metatexts or, better yet, "paratexts" (Becker 2017a, 102) which reflect the temporality of "then" and "now." Following his first prologue, Luke ties the "history" of Jesus to the history of Judaea (Luke 1), to the Roman imperial history and its rule in Palestine (Luke 2), and to the history of God with his people (Simeon and Hanna). In the genealogy (Luke 3:23–38), Jesus is presented as a descendant of David and Abraham.

Modern historians claim that the depiction of the past helps to anticipate the future. According to the great historian Eric Hobsbawm, the crucial function of history writing is foreseeing: historians "are constantly foreseeing, if only retrospectively. Their future happens to be the present or a more recent past compared to a more remote past" (1997, 57). Hobsbawm's definition entails two crucial insights into the phenomenon of history writing—both ancient and (post)modern. First, Hobsbawm's concept of history allows for uncovering intentionality and ideology behind history writing. The historian wants to disclose the past in order to "manage" time. Second, since history writing is much more than a source for the past, it always transcends the time that lies behind. It continuously aims at reaching present time by making sense of the past. In this "motion sequence," historians de facto tend to look ahead, and to prepare for times to come, which is their own and their audience's time, reaching out for the pending future.

Some of those foreseeing elements appear in the Markan Gospel. Mark is obviously very interested in "time mastery." In Mark 9:1; 10:38-40 and Matthew 29:22, Jesus makes predictions about the future that de facto refer to the readers' present time or recent past. In these passages Mark intends to bridge the gap between the past = level of the story = narrated time and the present time of (himself and) his readers = time of the narrative. By looking at a complex text like Jesus's eschatological speech in Mark 13, one learns more about Mark's historiographical technique of "foreseeing." Partly, the historian's foreseeing is simply a literary device. Depending on how to classify the literary form of Jesus's speech (e.g., teaching sequence; eschatological speech; prophecy; *vaticinia ex eventu*) the temporal scope varies as to how far the historian still "foresees" the future retrospectively or looks ahead prospectively. In the case of Mark 13, it is highly debated where exactly (v. 14?) Mark's account of past and present events changes over to the evangelist's pure speculation about future time (e.g., v. 24). Partly, the historiographical technique of "foreseeing" the future retrospectively is the historian's heuristic mode of disclosing the past for a future audience, which consists of his present audience and probable posterior readers. Another example is Mark 14:9. In this passage, Mark explicitly foresees the future value of the memory from the past which is encapsulated in and preserved behind the tradition in its literary form (Mark 14:3-9 // Matthew 26:6-13 // Luke 7:36-50; John 12:1-8).

As far as it is possible to see, Mark is the first Christian author who is interested in such a literary strategy of foreseeing the future by retrospective means. In the beginnings of early Christian literary activity, the technique of a historiographical foreseeing does not yet exist. In his letter writing, Paul does not shape a comprehensive account about past events as such. Neither does the apostle intend to foresee the future retrospectively. Rather, wherever Paul makes diverse recourses to the past in terms of autobiography (e.g., Gal 1-2), salvation history (e.g., 1 Cor 10; Gal 4), or missionary history (e.g., 1 Thess 2; Becker 2014), he primarily works on the legitimization of his present apostolic ministry. Paul starts with present community life, while Mark, comparable to a historian, backtracks his story into the past.

Shaping and Transforming Literary Memory: From Paul to Mark

In material terms, Mark's historiographical practice of foreseeing builds on two types of early Christian memorial groundwork. First, at the time when the Markan Gospel emerged, there was already a nearly four-decade running tradition of preserving oral memories about Jesus. The oral memorial material must have been extensive and highly diverse (e.g., passion; miracles; sayings). Second, at the same time, an early Christian literary culture existed—as documented by Pauline epistolography. In his letter writing, Paul defined a standard of how to memorize the past by literary means for present purposes (e.g., 1 Cor 15:1–5; 11:23). Even during Paul's lifetime there was a growing concern among Christ-believers that the content of the gospel message was no longer a sufficient object of oral memory or kerygmatic proclamation (e.g., 1 Thess 2:13; Rom 10:17; Gal 3:2). Rather, oral memories about Jesus and the beginnings of faith in Christ gradually became an object of written communication and literary interpretation. By his letter writing, Paul established literary memory as a mode of a highly intellectual interaction among Christ-believing communities.

For various needs, Paul transformed the mechanisms of oral memory into literary memory around 50 CE (see 1 Thess). By using literary texts he had to interpret and to frame the essence of the gospel proclamation (e.g., 1 Cor 15:3b–5; Rom 10:9; Phil 2:11b). By doing so, Paul had to conflate traditions about Jesus of Nazareth (e.g., 1 Cor 11:23–25) and the Jesus-Christ-message as the essence of the gospel kerygma. In order to conflate various types of (oral) memories adequately, Paul chooses a prehistoriographical concept, as is shown in the case of Phil 2:6–11, which is an exemplum-like story about the humiliation and exaltation of Christ as a "myth-historical" memory of Christ's fortune—interpreted by Paul as the constitutive, eventful foundation of ecclesial identity. By pointing to the exemplary, partly eventful character of Jesus's fortune, the passage shows an awareness of a historical incidence. Since the passage, however, lacks any more detailed information about Jesus's biographical origins and the concrete time, place, or circumstances of his crucifixion, it remains a mythical memory embedded in a paraenetic frame (Phil 1:27; see Becker 2020).

Less than two decades later (c. 70 CE), in postapostolic times, the purpose of retelling the past changes dramatically. When the generation of those who were eyewitnesses of Jesus's mission (e.g., Peter) and/or the Easter events (e.g., Paul; James) had ultimately passed away, the earliest Christian *memoria* culture adjusted. The selective approach to traditions from the past for present ecclesial and ethical purposes, which was typical of Paul's shaping of literary memory, became insufficient. At a time when the "guarantors" of the proper preservation of (oral) memories (see also: John 21:24; 1 John 1:1) were no longer alive, the need to reshape the memorial culture by literary means became an increasing demand.

In postapostolic times, then, attempts were made to (1) collect and fix all extant memories about Jesus. At the same time, the gospel writers developed (2) literary concepts for construing these memories in such a way that they were potentially accessible for a wider audience, possibly for all readers at any time. In other words, the gospel genre emerged as a response to a crucial narrative desideratum. Christ-believing readers of later generations demanded a story about the actual origins or the genesis of the gospel-proclamation. By shaping a comprehensive story about the *arche tou euaggeliou* the gospel writer Mark fills out this lack. While the basic need of reaching back to the actual "beginnings," again, is a motif/motive of authoritative writing already expressed in Paul's letter writing (Phil 4:15), the narrative concept of defining the beginnings of the gospel proclamation particularly in Jesus's (or even John the Baptist's) earthly ministry (Mark 1:4) itself has to be seen as a (literary) invention of Mark. In shaping his outline of a gospel narrative, Mark might have been stimulated or provoked by the literary collection of Jesus-sayings as provided at the time by the Q-document (see Becker 2018). In a sense, the Markan Gospel appears to be a "counter concept" or a counter memory (see earlier) to the Q-collection.

In a generic sense, the comprehensive story about the *arche tou euaggeliou* as "invented" by Mark has formed a stable "prototype" of a history-oriented narrative (see Matthew, Luke, and John). In a conceptual sense, Mark's narrative interpretation of the past had defined a persistent demand: in its written form, the story about the *arche tou euaggeliou* was in an even stronger need of being continuously retold and reinterpreted—not least because the conditions of time mastery changed over time. The *parousia* and the cosmic end of time were more and more delayed (e.g., Mark 13:24). The delay of the end of time, indeed, forced Christ-believers early on to reconsider their perception of time. From Mark to Luke-Acts different historiographical modes of foreseeing the future retrospectively were developed.

The guiding principle of the gospel concept as invented by Mark consists of a stable spatially structured narrative frame (Jesus in Galilee, Jesus in Jerusalem, crucifixion, post-Easter events), which—at the same time—allows for significant reinterpretation. Both mechanisms—generic stability and hermeneutical reinterpretation—are two sides of the same coin.

Creating History: Mark's Literary Invention

In the earliest Christian times, historiographical thinking could emerge when literary memory arose. The rise of Christian historical thinking fits well into the vividness of Roman *memoria* culture. How does Mark mold early Christian literary memory? Mark composes his gospel narrative partly on the basis of oral memory and partly by means of semiwritten tradition, such as the passion narrative (Mark 14), which was an *exitus*-report prior to Mark. Mark (1) combines the complexes of oral and written Galilean (e.g., Mark 2–3) and Jerusalem (e.g., Mark 11) traditions, and (2) makes a coherent and logical narrative out of it. (3) In Mark's gospel narrative, the seams between oral and written material, between material coming from Galilean and from Jerusalem origins, and between tradition and Markan redaction are only visible occasionally (e.g., Mark 3:6). (4) By incorporating and conflating various traditions, Mark has refined their generic outline. As an *exitus*-report close to biographical forms, the passion story became part of a historiographical narrative once included in the gospel narrative. The final product of Mark's Gospel has moved beyond the oral-written divide, and it has generated a new micro-type of history writing. The Markan Gospel appears as a cohesive concept of literary memory (e.g., reading instruction in Mark 13:14).

New Testament scholarship has tended to assume that orality transmits the past more reliably than literacy. The latter opens up for possibility of literary creativity, including history writing (see various contributions in Kirk and Thatcher 2005). Sociology demonstrates how oral memory differs from literary modes of memorization especially regarding the concepts of time mastery. The "oral transmission of the past means that the past is bound to the present for its survival. The past exists only in so far as it continues to be held in living memory, and it is so remembered only as long as it serves present needs" (Misztal 2003, 28). In oral culture, the perception of time and concepts of time management thus are rather limited: "due to the limitations of memory ... such societies' response to time is limited to an annual cycle and therefore cannot be used to differentiate longer periods than seasons" (28).

In other words, while "oral memory constantly makes the past present, literary memory is not limited by temporality" (Becker 2017a, 13). Oral "memory implies a rather cyclic or static—that is, immobile—perception of time, whereas literary memory can provide a much more detailed (narrative) approach to diverse temporal settings and progressions" (13). Literary memory, in contrast, "prepares for a distinctive perception of time in its temporal progress" (13). The literary memory about Jesus's ministry and the beginnings of the gospel proclamation as found in the Markan Gospel provide a complex narrative concept of time and temporality—the reader is prepared "for a distinctive perception of time in its temporal progress" (13).

Mark is the first Christian author who prepares for such a complex concept of time mastery and hereby exceeds how Jesus-traditions were memorized around 30–70 CE. The oral memorization of Jesus-traditions repeated and represented the past in the present. During these processes, there was no sufficient distinction between past and present times. In oral memorization processes, a rather cyclic or static understanding of temporality was proposed. Such a concept of memory must have also been behind a document like Q, and probably also behind the Gospel of Thomas. Literary memory provided by a narrative, by contrast, prepared for a comprehensive perception and depiction of time. In literary memory, the distinction between various periods of the past and the present was enforced. The construct of literary memory, put into a narrative frame of prose literature, thus creates and provides complex concepts of temporality and time mastery.

How does Mark create literary memory? What concept of time mastery does he offer? Mark gives a concise structure to the temporal progress behind the narrative outline—it reaches from John the Baptist to Jesus's ministry in Galilee (1:14) and in Jerusalem (Mark 11–15). In his compositional outline, Mark shapes, right from the beginning (1:1–3), an oscillation between a narrative depiction about the origins of the gospel proclamation and the display of that proclamation itself (Mark 1:1–15). Consequently, on the one hand Jesus appears as a historical agent, operating in a particular historical setting (Palestine in the first century CE). On the other hand Jesus is presented as the one who himself announces and accelerates—as a prophet-like eschatological or messianic figure—the closeness of God's *basileia*, which exceeds any limits of past time and historical space. Not accidentally, then, as the gospel message does in prophetic times and throughout John the Baptist's ministry (Mark 1:3 [see Isa 40:3 LXX]), Jesus's mission also (Mark 1:9 and 1:12) starts from the desert area—an uninhabited space that resists proper historical dating and placing.

In Mark's case, the memory of and about Jesus and the story about the beginnings of the gospel proclamation—put into the narrative frame of the gospel story—are evidently of past and present value. Mark's story line consists of a conflation of memories about Jesus and of kerygmatic traditions—the latter probably influenced by Pauline theology (on Paul and Mark, see Wischmeyer, Sim, and Elmer 2014/2017; Becker, Engberg-Pedersen, and Müller 2014/2017). The story which results from this conflation, about the origin and the initial history of the gospel proclamation, is essentially of historiographical nature. At the same time, the story is itself reshaped as a kerygmatic message. Especially in Mark 1, the Jesus-figure of the gospel narrative is a historical agent or a protagonist of a historiographical account and is a *hic et nunc* messenger of the kingdom of God.

As a "historian," Mark does not refrain from approaching the past by transmitting and storing Jesus-traditions as a collective memory. As an early Christian author who stands in line with Paul's concept of literary memory, Mark reshapes the kerygmatic claim of the gospel message. Jesus and the memory about him are, in Mark's case, both of past and present value. One could speak of "bitemporality" here: on the compositional level, Mark's historiographical concept of foreseeing by retrospectively approaching the past aims at revealing the present meaning of Jesus's gospel proclamation from the past.

The early reception history of the Markan Gospel shows how Mark's concept of bitemporality had opened up two major paths of gospel writing. These two paths lead in very different directions: the author of Luke-Acts follows up the history-oriented account. The author of the Fourth Gospel chooses another avenue—John provides a narrative display of Jesus as God's *hic et nunc* messenger. John pursues the literary strategy of a revelatory narrative (on Mark and John, see Becker, Bond, and Williams 2021). By contrast, the author of the Matthean Gospel neither develops the historiographical path nor chooses the revelatory concept. Matthew refrains from refining the gospel concept as such. Rather, Matthew restricts himself to enlarging the Markan *Vorlage* in order to "suppress" it (discussed later).

Developing the Historiographical Concept: Luke's Transformation of Mark

In contrast to certain other scholars, who see Luke as the first Christian historian (see, e.g., Marguerat 2004), I have worked out how Mark in his gospel writing has prepared the conceptual floor for a history-oriented approach to the past. Already Mark paves the way for the beginnings of "Christian history" (Becker 2017a).

In this article, I want to show in more detail how time mastery works and how Mark practices the historian's mode of foreseeing the future when approaching the past.

Mark still envisions a future that is identical with his audience's present. The Markan Gospel remains an "eschatological monograph" (Yarbro Collins 2007). In consequence, Mark's Jesus has what one could call a "bitemporal face": Mark constantly—and up to the ending of his story (Mark 16:7)—oscillates between presenting a narrative account about the past and proclaiming a kerygmatic message in the present. Herein lies Mark's literary proposal of bridging past and present times.

In his gospel account, Luke made use of the Markan *Vorlage*: Mark is a basic literary source for Luke. By using Mark, Luke follows Mark's basic narrative concept. At the same time, Luke makes some substantial literary amendments and narrative alterations (see, e.g., Luke 1–2). In contrast to Mark, Luke's historiographical concept limits itself to a narrative about the past. Luke makes Jesus a historical protagonist of the past only. In contrast to Mark, Luke focuses more systematically on the depiction of past events, since he presupposes for his reading audience(s) a time to come, in which the story about the past is a constant and sufficient source of learning for the present time (Luke 1:1–4).

To Luke, past and present are distinct periods. Here lies the actual premise for Luke when assuming that time continues and "history" develops. Luke rejects the eschatological approach to time he found in Mark. To Luke, time and temporality evolve in longer periods—Luke appears as a congenial author of Hellenistic times (see earlier). Luke perceives history as a *historia continua*. According to Luke, the continuity in history rests upon God's enduring promise of salvation and mercy (e.g., Luke 1:50). In Jesus's ministry, however, a temporal caesura is reached: from now on, the gospel message on God's *basileia* is preached (Lk 16:16). In Luke 16:16, Luke apparently takes a Jesus-logion from Q (see Matt 11:12; Q 16:16), which he redacts according to his own historiographical intentions. Luke understands history as God's salvific history with his people—in short: as salvation history (see J. Schröter 2005).

In compositional terms, Luke transforms the Markan *Vorlage* toward his concept of historiography in multiple dimensions. (1) By inserting prologues (Luke 1:1–4; Acts 1:1), Luke creates paratexts with which he reflects his role as a historian (Luke 1:1) and with which he summarizes the historiographical account of the first volume (Acts 1:1–3). (2) By inserting synchronisms (Luke 1:5; 2:1; 3:1), Luke relates to world history—even more programmatically than was the case in Mark—the history of events around John the Baptist, Jesus, and his disciples in Judea, Galilee, and Jerusalem. (3) By structuring his gospel narrative around an itinerary in which he presents Jesus programmatically on his way to Jerusalem (Luke 9:51–19:27), Luke adapts a literary element of ancient historiography (*itinerarium*) that Mark only hints at by means of his Galilee-Jerusalem divide (Mark 1–10; 11–16). In Acts, Luke will intensely utilize that literary pattern (Acts 13) in order to show how Paul fulfills the instruction which was given to the disciples by the risen Christ (Acts 1:8). Luke in fact works out a "spatial concept" of historiography.

(4) Luke intentionally adds a second volume to the gospel story in order to continue his narrative up to Paul's arrival in Rome (Acts 28). In his second volume, Luke reaches out much closer to the contemporary time of his reading audience. (5) In and

throughout both volumes, Luke extends the time frame of his narrative significantly. He begins his narrative in the time of Herod the Great in Jerusalem (Luke 1:5) and closes his narrative in the time of Festus (Acts 24:27; 25:1) and with Paul's arrival as a prisoner in Rome (Acts 28:16–31). Luke stretches that time frame even more by inserting three hymnic, psalm-like texts in Luke 1–2 in which God's long history with his people is remembered (Luke 1:46; 1:67; 2:28), in line with Septuagint language.

(6) In his gospel narrative Luke restricts himself to presenting Jesus as an orator using only the speeches he already found in the Markan *Vorlage* (Luke 8:4 par. Mark 4; Luke 21:5 par. Mark 13)—Luke does not further develop the image of Jesus as an extensive speaker. Nor does Luke transform Q-material as consistently into a comprehensive teaching unit as Matthew does (see Matt 5–7 par. Luke 6:20). During the travel account Jesus appears as a *kyrios* (e.g., Luke 10:1) who, being on his way to Jerusalem, invites followers for discipleship (e.g., Luke 10:1; 10:38) and talks steadily in allegories or parables to his followers and opponents (e.g., Luke 10:25; 11:5; 12:16).

In the book of Acts, in contrast, parables are absent. Instead, speeches gain a specific value for Luke's interpretation of history. In Acts, Luke continuously provides speeches held by the apostolic protagonists. With these speeches, Luke either connects together programmatically the time of the current missionary history with the history of God's promises or the narrative about Israel's past (e.g., Acts 2:14; 7:1; 13:16). Alternatively, Luke makes his protagonists interpret themselves in relation to current and future times (Acts 20:17)—even beyond the temporal scope that Luke himself offers. In his farewell speech to the Elders from Ephesus, Paul foresees the future oppressions and brutal actions against him (Acts 20:22), whereas Luke himself as narrator refrains from telling Paul's martyrdom in Rome to his readers.

In Luke, historiographical foreseeing comes up through a *historia continua*: during the course of history, God's promises are kept and verified. The historian does not need to hide behind a messenger who would—by looking back into the past—foresee the future as his and his readers' contemporary time. In contrast to Mark, Luke himself acts as a learned interpreter of past events and literary sources (especially the Septuagint) which he considers to be sources of knowledge about God's steadiness during history. By studying history and God's salvific plan with his people, the protagonists of Luke's story and his readers will finally foresee their salvific future and thereby accomplish time mastery.

Suppressing the *Vorlage*: Matthew's Transformation of Mark

In Luke-Acts, Mark's draft of a "bitemporal narrative," in which the depiction of past events and the proclamation of the gospel message constantly oscillate, is transformed into a historiographical account, in which the historian carefully gives structure to past, present, and future times. Luke's *historia continua* account is linear and progressive. It is supposed to encourage the readers' learning about God's unfailing salvific plan with his people, which ultimately comes true in and throughout history.

Matthew, in contrast to Luke, sticks to Mark's "bitemporal" outline. Matthew provides a narrative account about past events—an account which is enlarged significantly in material terms, compared to what is found in the Markan *Vorlage* (see especially Matt 1–2; 28:8–20). At the same time, Matthew lays high emphasis on presenting Jesus as a powerful teacher, a talented speaker, and a sapient interpreter of the Torah (see especially Matt 5–7). By composing Jesus's speeches (Matt 5–7; 10; 13; 18; 23–25), Matthew wants to show the enduring meaning and value of Jesus's teaching as presented in the story. Herein lies the crucial difference between Matthew's Gospel and the literary character and outline of the Didache as a nonnarrative writing, both works having probably derived from the same community milieu (Draper 2009, 20).

Matthew does not redefine the Markan concept of history writing as such—although he surpasses Mark in quantitative terms (Doole 2013). Matthew obviously intends to suppress the Markan *Vorlage* (Sim 2011). Does Matthew refine the Markan understanding of history? Matthew does adhere to the Markan idea of bitemporality—like Mark, Matthew has Jesus speaking in and through the gospel narrative. However, while Jesus, according to Mark, acts as an eschatological messenger (Mark 1:14), who announces time and ensures the acceleration of time, Jesus according to Matthew appears as a teacher who is remarkably "timeless."

In his gospel account, Mark wants to tell a history which gives causal explanation for how Jesus in his teaching, deeds, and passion announces and accelerates time (Mark 8:31) and thereby finally appears as God's truthful son (Mark 15:39). Luke, in continuation of Mark, wants to depict a history about Jesus's ministry as a central period of God's salvific history with his people. Matthew, in contrast to Luke, has no further historiographical ambition that would exceed Mark, nor does he reject a history-oriented approach to the gospel story as the Gospel of John does. To Matthew, Jesus's ministry is situated in the past and can be approached throughout a narrative from and about the past. Throughout that very narrative, Jesus appears as a valuable teacher whose instruction still awaits fulfillment and verification among present readers (Matt 28:16–20).

The story about Jesus's birth (Matt 1–2) might well be an example of how Matthew wants to address his readers: as the birth story fulfills long-lasting prophetic predictions (see, e.g., Matt 1:22; 2:5), Matthew's *biblos geneseos* (Matt 1:1) still awaits verification among present Jesus-followers. In and beyond his speeches, Jesus—according to Matthew—teaches his audience(s), then and now, how such verification will be reached. While Mark aims at giving historiographical explanation for Jesus's brutal death on the cross (see Mark 3:6; 8:31; 15:26), Matthew—even though not dismissing or remolding the Markan *explananda,* as Luke tends to do—focuses on showing Jesus as the enduring teacher: the teaching of Jesus, empowered as the risen one (Matt 28:16–20), throughout the gospel narrative is of timeless meaning.

Conclusion

How does early Christian history writing emerge from Mark to Luke-Acts? What is "history" according to the synoptic authors?

Mark, Luke, and Matthew present a narrative about past events. The gospel narratives (especially Mark and Matthew) present the life and death of Jesus as God's ultimate history with his people and put that history more (Luke) or less (Mark) evidently in the frame of world history. The gospel stories arrange historical events in a chronological and causal order. All three synoptic writers evaluate the past for present needs. Mark, followed by Matthew, provides a bitemporal approach to the gospel concept, where narration and proclamation oscillate. In Matthew, the eschatological vanishing point of Markan bitemporality is transformed into the image of Jesus as a timeless teacher. Luke, in both of his books, shapes a periodization of time – from Israel's past to the contemporary time of mission and witnessing. Seen as *historia continua*, history is a source of constant learning to Luke and his readers. Beginning with Mark, the Synoptic Gospels shape certain chronotopes (e.g., Galilee and Jerusalem) through which time and space merge. Luke further develops the concept of spatiality (see itineraries in Luke-Acts and especially Acts 1:8). By presenting a narrative about the beginnings of the gospel story, all three synoptic writers aim at identity formation among Christ-believing readers and communities (see Becker 2016). The Synoptic Gospels present historiography-like narratives, which generate a new literary genre in the broader frame of Hellenistic historiography. The history-oriented approach to the past, as chosen initially by Mark and climaxing in Luke-Acts, is composed *ad narrandum* and *ad memoriam posteritatis* (Quintilian, *Inst.* 10.1.31). In short, these texts are composed as literary memory, not as *bruta facta* report. Even though Christians might have failed to adapt to historiography in its narrower sense as defined by Greco-Roman historians (Cameron 1991), from Mark to Luke-Acts one encounters an increasing historical awareness. More particularly, one encounters an awareness of the urgent need to give narrative shape to the memory of the common past. By pushing subaltern events in Palestine around 30 CE into the front lines of their distinct historiographical accounts, the Synoptic Gospels make a significant contribution to Hellenistic history writing. Henceforth, their "history" becomes a crucial part of the world history of the first century CE.

References

Augoustakis, Antony, et al., eds. 2019. *Fides in Flavian Literature*. Toronto: University of Toronto Press.

Baier, Thomas. 2019. "Quintilian's Approach to Literary History via *Imitatio* and *Utilitas*." In *The Literary Genres in the Flavian Age. Canons, Transformations, Reception*, edited by F. Bessone and M. Fucecchi, 47–61. Berlin: De Gruyter.

Becker, Eve-Marie. 2011. "Historiographical Literature in the New Testament Period (1st and 2nd Centuries CE)." In *Handbook for the Study of the Historical Jesus*, vol. 2, *The Study of Jesus*, edited by T. Holmén and S. E. Porter, 1787–1817. Leiden: Brill.

Becker, Eve- Marie. 2014. "Die Konstruktion von 'Geschichte': Paulus und Markus im Vergleich." In *Paul and Mark: Comparative Essays Part I. Two Authors at the Beginnings of Christianity*, edited by O. Wischmeyer, D. C. Sim, and I. J. Elmer, BZNW 198, 393–422. Berlin: De Gruyter.

Becker, Eve-Marie. 2015. "Historiography: II. Greco-Roman Antiquity." *EBR* 11: 1129–35.

Becker, Eve-Marie. 2016. "Shaping Identity by Writing History: Earliest Christianity in its Making." *Religion in the Roman Empire* 2: 152–69.

Becker, Eve-Marie. 2017a. *The Birth of Christian History. Memory and Time from Mark to Luke-Acts*. AYBRL. New Haven: Yale University Press.

Becker, Eve-Marie. 2017b. *Der früheste Evangelist. Studien zum Markusevangelium*. WUNT 380. Tübingen: Mohr Siebeck.

Becker, Eve-Marie 2018. "Mark with and against Q: The Earliest Gospel Narrative as a Countermodel." In *Gospel Interpretation and the Q-Hypothesis*, edited by M. Müller and H. Omerzu, LNTS 573, 151–63. London: Bloomsbury T&T Clark.

Becker, Eve-Marie 2020. *Paul on Humility*. Translated by Wayne Coppins. BMSEC. Waco: Baylor University Press.

Becker, Eve-Marie 2022. "Zeitgeschichtsschreibung im entstehenden Christentum (ca. 30-100 n.Chr.)." In *Écrire l'historire de son temps, de Thucydide à Ammien Marcellin. Neuf exposés suivis de discussion*, edited by V. Fromentin in collaboration with P. Derron, Entretiens sur l'Antiquité Classique LXVII, 241–82. Genève: Fondation Hardt.

Becker, Eve-Marie, T. Engberg-Pedersen, and M. Müller, eds. 2014/2017. *Mark and Paul: Comparative Essays Part II: For and against Pauline Influence on Mark*. BZNW 199. Berlin: de Gruyter.

Becker, Eve-Marie, H. Bond, and C. Williams, eds. 2021. *John's Transformation of Mark*. London: Bloomsbury.

Bessone, Federica and Marco Fucecchi, eds. 2019. *The Literary Genres in the Flavian Age. Canons, Transformations, Reception*. Berlin: De Gruyter.

Blatz, H. 2016. *Die Semantik der Macht. Eine zeit- und religionsgeschichtliche Studie zu den markinischen Wundererzählungen*. NTA 59. Münster: Aschendorff.

Bowersock, G. W. 1994. *Fiction as History. Nero to Julian*. Berkeley: University of California Press.

Calhoun, Robert M., David P. Moessner, and Tobias Nicklas, eds. 2020. *Modern and Ancient Literary Criticism of the Gospels*. WUNT 451. Tübingen: Mohr Siebeck.

Cameron, A. 1991. *Christianity and the Rhetoric of Empire: The Development of Christian Discourse*. Berkeley: University of California Press.

Cancik, H. 1991. "Geschichtsschreibung." *NBL* 1: 813–22.

Chaniotis, A. 2019. *Age of Conquests. The Greek World from Alexander to Hadrian 336 BC–AD 138*. London: Profile Books.

Doole, J. A. 2013. *What Was Mark for Matthew? An Examination of Matthew's Relationship and Attitude to His Primary Source*. WUNT 2.344. Tübingen: Mohr Siebeck.

Draper, Jonathan A. 2009. "Die Didache." In *Die Apostolischen Väter. Eine Einleitung*, edited by W. Pratscher, 17–38. Göttingen: Vandenhoeck & Ruprecht.

Droysen, J. G. 2008. *Geschichte des Hellenismus. Geschichte Alexanders des Grossen*. Vol. 1, edited by E. Bayer. Introduction by H.-J. Gehrke. Darmstadt: Wissenschaftliche Buchgesellschaft.

Foucault, Michel. 1977. *Language, Counter-memory, Practice: Selected Essays and Interviews*, edited by D. F. Bouchard and S. Simon. Ithaca: Cornell University Press.

Gehrke, H.-J. 2008. "Einleitung." In *Geschichte des Hellenismus. Geschichte Alexanders des Grossen*. Vol. 1, edited by E. Bayer, introduced by H.-J. Gehrke, v–xv. Darmstadt: Wissenschaftliche Buchgesellschaft.

Gelardini, G. 2016. *Christus Militans: Studien zur politisch-militärischen Semantik im Markusevangelium vor dem Hintergrund des ersten jüdisch-römischen Krieges*. NTSupp 165. Leiden: Brill.

Hengel, M. 1988. *Judentum und Hellenismus. Studien zu ihrer Begegnung unter besonderer Berücksichtigung Palästinas bis zur Mitte des 2. Jh.s v.Chr.* Tübingen: Mohr Siebeck.

Hobsbawm, E. 1997. *On History*. London: Abacus.

Kennedy, G. A. 2003. *Greek Textbooks of Prose Composition and Rhetoric*. Writings from the Greco-Roman World 10. Atlanta: Society of Biblical Literature.

Kirk, A. and T. Thatcher, eds. 2005. *Memory, Tradition, and Text: Uses of the Past in Early Christianity*. Semeia Studies 52. Atlanta: Society of Biblical Literature.

Kneppe, A. 1994. *Metus temporum: Zur Bedeutung von Angst in Politik und Gesellschaft der römischen Kaiserzeit des 1. und 2. Jhdts. n. Chr.* Stuttgart: Franz Steiner Verlag.

Licona, M. R. 2017. *Why Are There Differences in the Gospels? What We Can Learn from Ancient Biography*. Oxford: Oxford University Press.

Marguerat, D. 2004. *The First Christian Historian: Writing the "Acts of the Apostles."* SNTS.MS 121. Cambridge: Cambridge University Press.

Martin, M. W., and M. C. Parsons. 2018. *Ancient Rhetoric and the New Testament. The Influence of Elementary Greek Composition*. Waco: Baylor University Press.

Millar, Fergus. 2001. *The Roman Near East 31 BC–AD 337*. Cambridge, MA: Harvard University Press. (4th printing)

Misztal, B. A. 2003. *Theories of Social Remembering*. Maidenhead: Open University Press.

Pfeiffer, S. 2009. *Die Zeit der Flavier. Vespasian—Titus—Domitian*. Darmstadt: Wissenschaftliche Buchgesellschaft.

Price, J. J. 2005. "The Provincial Historian in Rome." In *Josephus and Jewish History in Flavian Rome and Beyond*, edited by J. Sievers and G. Lembi, JSJS 104, 101–18. Leiden: Brill.

Price, S. 2012. "Memory and Ancient Greece." In *Historical and Religious Memory in the Ancient World*, edited by B. Dignas and R. R. R. Smith, 15–36. Oxford: Oxford University Press.

Rüpke, J. 2012. *Religiöse Erinnerungskulturen. Formen der Geschichtsschreibung in der römischen Antike*. Darmstadt: Wissenschaftliche Buchgesellschaft.

Schröter, J. 2005. "Lukas als Historiograph. Das lukanische Doppelwerk und die Entdeckung der christlichen Heilsgeschichte." In *Die antike Historiographie und die Anfänge der christlichen Geschichtsschreibung*, edited by E.-M. Becker, BZNW 129, 237–62. Berlin/New York: de Gruyter.

Sim, D. C. 2011. "Matthew: The Current State of Research." In *Mark and Matthew I: Comparative Readings: Understanding the Earliest Gospels in Their First-Century Setting*, edited by Eve-Marie Becker and A. Runesson, WUNT 271, 33–51. Tübingen: Mohr Siebeck.

Valerius Maximus. 2000. *Memorable Doings and Sayings. Books 1–5*, edited and translated by D. R. Shackleton Bailey. LCL 492. Cambridge, MA: Harvard University Press.

Vessey, D. W. T. C. 1982. "Flavian Epic." In *The Cambridge History of Classical Literature*, vol. 2, pt. 4, *The Early Principate*, edited by E. J. Kenney, 62–100. Cambridge: Cambridge University Press.

Walter, A. 2020. *Time in Ancient Stories of Origin*. Oxford: Oxford University Press.

Wischmeyer, O., D. C. Sim, and I. J. Elmer, eds. 2014. *Paul and Mark: Comparative Essays Part I. Two Authors at the Beginnings of Christianity*. BZNW 198. Berlin: De Gruyter.

Wolter, M. 2009. "Die Proömien des lukanischen Doppelwerks (Lk 1,1-4 und Apg 1,1-2)." In *Die Apostelgeschichte im Kontext antiker und frühchristlicher Historiographie*, edited by J. Frey, C. K. Rothschild, and J. Schröter, BZNW 162, 476–94. Berlin/New York: de Gruyter.

Yarbro Collins, A. 2007. *Mark. A Commentary*. Hermeneia. Minneapolis: Fortress Press.

CHAPTER 22

APOCALYPTIC ESCHATOLOGY

ROBYN J. WHITAKER

INTRODUCTION

THE terms *apocalyptic* and *eschatology* are both contested, notoriously difficult to define, and used by scholars in a variety of ways. Apocalyptic is sometimes narrowly associated with a particular genre (apocalypse) or used more broadly to denote a worldview, which is the approach taken here. Most apocalyptic literature is eschatological, whereas not all eschatology is apocalyptic. *Eschatology*, a term coined in the seventh century, refers to ideas about the "end-times" or "last things," that is, what happens at the end of human history (Frey 2011, 6–7). Biblical ideas and theology associated with end-times can vary greatly, ranging from the redemption of Israel within human history to abrupt, cataclysmic, and cosmic disaster that inaugurates a new era. Eschatology, therefore, is a way of referring to a variety of future hopes about the coming of God's kingdom.

This essay places the Synoptics in conversation with one another regarding their apocalyptic eschatologies as well as with a wider range of early Christian literature from the first and second centuries CE. I briefly outline how the ideas associated with apocalyptic eschatology emerged in Second Temple Judaism, prior to the writing of the Synoptics. I then look at how such ideas were reshaped in light of the Christ event by the authors of the Synoptics. Recent scholarly developments, particularly in relation to Luke's Gospel and eschatology, are examined as well as timeless themes that have informed Christian thought. I begin by defining the terms.

DEFINING *APOCALYPSE*, *APOCALYPTIC*, AND *APOCALYPTIC ESCHATOLOGY*

Apocalyptic and *eschatology* were once understood to mean quite different things but now are treated as virtually synonymous by many. Therefore, *apocalyptic eschatology* requires some definitional work, as neither of these views is adequate. Apocalyptic (*apokalypsis*) is a descriptor that points to something hidden being revealed or disclosed to a human recipient. In apocalyptic texts, what is revealed usually relates to the mysteries of the heavenly realm or the future of human history; thus revelation has both a spatial and temporal element. The former aspect includes tours of heaven and hell, or mystical journeys. It is the latter, temporal aspect that is my focus here. This temporal aspect of apocalyptic texts unveils what will happen in the future or at the end of time. Typically, these eschatological ideas in apocalyptic texts are communicated through images of a final battle, judgment scenes, rewards and punishment, and/or visions of an afterlife.

There is ongoing scholarly debate about how best to define the genre "apocalypse," a genre traditionally associated with the canonical books of Daniel and Revelation as well as numerous noncanonical works. For my purposes here, it is important to note that apocalyptic eschatology is not limited to the genre "apocalypse" (Collins 2014, 5).[1] The Synoptic Gospels, for example, are not apocalypses, yet they contain considerable apocalyptic theology; in addition, they include smaller sections of text often dubbed "mini apocalypses" due to the density of apocalyptic language and ideas therein (see Mark 13). Hence, one might describe the Synoptic Gospels as "apocalyptic" in their worldview while not being apocalypses in genre. Similarly, apocalyptic eschatology is found throughout Paul's letters and other New Testament writings, something scholars are increasingly recognizing as important (Frey 2011, 20–22).[2]

"Apocalyptic eschatology" refers to a collection of eschatological ideas typically found in apocalypses. It might best be described as the revelation of God's plan and promises about the end. Loren Stuckenbruck defines it as "a speculative hope that the God of Israel will deliver God's people and the world at large from manifestations of evil at the end of history, whether that end is imminent or remote in time from the present" (2016, 144). In this sense it differs from other kinds of eschatology, including prophetic eschatology, that envisage God's reign and restoration occurring within human history. Apocalyptic ideas are often dualistic and deterministic, reflecting an intense interest in angelic and demonic activity and in the division of humanity into the righteous and the wicked. Apocalyptic eschatology can be highly symbolic. It imagines history as divided into periods, envisages a post-mortem judgment for humanity, a final battle between good and evil, and rewards or punishments for individual humans.

"Apocalyptic eschatology" will be used here as a shorthand way of referring to a range of ideas and imagery related to eschatological anticipation, drawn from the observance of common traits in apocalyptic literature. While the focus is on the eschaton, it is a perspective that is not exclusively concerned with the future but makes sense of current events through particular interpretations of the past, insights about the present, and

---

[1] Collins notes that there is some debate about the modern definition of the genre "apocalypse," but the current widely agreed-on definition that emerged from SBL sessions on the matter in the 1980s assumes eschatology as a core feature of the genre.

[2] There was a shift toward recognizing apocalypticism in the twentieth century, after a period of downplaying apocalyptic in the New Testament.

hopes about the future. That is, the future is imagined on the basis of God's past faithfulness and the fulfillment of past promises. In many cases the envisaged future reign of God is imagined as a return to a primordial world or Edenic life where humans and God lived together in harmony, free from evil and sinfulness.

When it comes to the Synoptic Gospels, apocalyptic eschatology is expressed through key themes, each of which I discuss here: the kingdom of God (kingdom of heaven); dualism; judgment, including rewards and punishments in the afterlife; messianic expectation and the Son of Man; and the second coming. For each of these traits I compare the particular features of apocalyptic eschatology as found in the Synoptic Gospels, noting similarities and differences. I then situate these features of the Synoptics in their wider context to see how the Synoptics reflect, adapt, or differ from other ancient texts in their conception of apocalyptic eschatology.

Precursors to the Apocalyptic Eschatology of the Synoptics

The apocalyptic eschatology of the New Testament cannot be understood apart from the Jewish context in which these texts emerged. One must be cautious in discussing Jewish apocalyptic eschatology as if it were a consistent or monolithic worldview. John Collins warns against oversimplifying the different types of apocalypses and the different types of eschatology therein (Collins 1998, 11). Recognizing that diversity, one can, however, identify certain themes that emerge in these Second Temple texts.

Apocalyptic eschatology emerged in conjunction with a shifting social setting, religious oppression, and emerging ideas of the righteous sufferer exemplified by biblical characters like Daniel or martyrs like Eleazar (2 Macc 6). The theological logic is that hope in future vindication and reward sustains a life of righteousness in the present, even in the face of inevitable suffering or death. As such, apocalyptic eschatology is predominantly about transcendence over death, be it through resurrection or transformed status (such as becoming an angel). It is clearly future focused, but in a way that informs and transforms the present. God's impending judgment offers vindication for the righteous and punishment or defeat of evil and oppressive powers.

One of the major innovations during this period is the idea of individual resurrection and individual judgment. Daniel 12:2 is arguably the earliest extant Jewish reference to the future resurrection of dead individuals and their judgment to either eternal life or eternal shame (see also Isa 24–27). This contrasts with earlier images of resurrection, such as the famous vision of the bones in Ezekiel 37, that imagine a nation revived and restored. The difference lies not only in the communal versus individual nature of resurrection but also in the time in which it is imagined. Prophetic eschatology generally depicts restoration as something that occurs within human history in the earthly realm, whereas Daniel, 1 Enoch (104:2–6), and other apocalypses associate judgment and renewal with a future time outside history or in the heavenly sphere.

Another dominant apocalyptic theme found in several Jewish apocalyptic texts is the concept of two ages. The first age, or present age, is characterized by the presence of evil, often portrayed as primeval evil (Noah and the flood, Adam and Eve) or the fall of angelic beings who continue to roam on earth (1 En 6–19; Jub 4:15–22; 2 Bar 56). The account of the "sons of God" descending to pursue earthly women in Genesis 6:1–6 lies behind the latter tradition. According to the *Book of Watchers* (1 En 1–36), fallen angels are to blame for all of the earth's present wickedness. Other texts refer to the Adam and Eve story to locate the source of the human rebellion and wickedness of the present age (Jub 3, 2 Bar 54).

The transition from the present evil age to a future good age is typically mediated through some kind of cosmic, apocalyptic event. This period can be marked by tribulation or increased conflict between good and evil (sometimes featuring angels and demons), prior to God's intervention to judge and issue rewards or punishments. This event inaugurates a second or new age, marked by theocratic rule, justice, and an eternal or permanent nature.

The dualism of two ages is only one part of a larger dualistic worldview in apocalyptic eschatology. As a postexilic phenomenon, possibly influenced by Persian religion (Zoroastrianism), apocalyptic eschatology contains abundant dualisms that may be cosmic, spiritual, anthropological, ethical, or eschatological, such as, the idea of two ages. For example, the *Book of Watchers* (1 En 10–36) displays a cosmic dualism in dividing the world into two spheres of heaven and earth, each separate and with distinct characteristics. Many of the Dead Sea Scrolls from the Qumran community likewise reveal a dualistic worldview now acknowledged to have influenced New Testament texts (e.g. *War Scroll* 1QM). In a monotheistic religion like Judaism, divine dualism is always tempered. Hence, while the figure of Satan and the activity of evil is portrayed as battling with God, Satan or evil is never God's equal in these texts.

Finally, one cannot discuss apocalyptic eschatology without mentioning determinism. This is the idea that history unfolds toward a designated end point. One way of denoting this is the periodization of history. The idea of two ages is closely associated here, but several apocalypses have multiple and complex periodization of history and time (e.g. *Apocalypse of Weeks*).

The *Two Spirits Treatise* (1QS 3:13–4:26) offers an excellent example of the deterministic worldview so common to apocalyptic theology: "Before things come to be, he [God] has established all their plans and when things come to be at their ordained time they will fulfil all their work in accordance with his glorious plan" (1QS 3:14–15). Jubilees phrases it differently, but equally strongly, portraying the periods of time as written on heavenly tablets (6:35). Such texts point to a divinely ordained, predetermined sequence of events that will lead up to and inaugurate the end of history.

Apocalyptic Eschatology in the Synoptic Gospels

The apocalyptic eschatology of the Gospels would not exist nor make sense without the aforementioned emergence of Jewish apocalypticism and the shift in eschatological ideas that occurred in the few centuries prior to Jesus. Jesus's preaching and John the Baptist's message are unimaginable without the apocalyptic ideas that preceded them. While there is much continuity between Jewish apocalyptic texts and the New Testament when it comes to apocalyptic eschatology, one of the fundamental differences is that Jewish hopes tend to be wholly future oriented,[3] whereas Christians interpreted the Christ event as the beginning of the kingdom, or the beginning of the end, even if not yet fulfilled or complete. For early Christian writers, the eschaton had begun, at least in some sense, because of Jesus and their belief that Jesus was the promised Messiah.

Here I explore several key themes or images associated with apocalyptic eschatology in the Synoptics, comparing each Gospel's use of that particular idea. I begin each time with Mark's Gospel on the assumption that it is the earliest of the Synoptics and was a source for both Matthew and Luke. Matthew and Luke both modify their source, but in different directions. I argue against the common view that Luke is less eschatological, and I show that while his framing of apocalyptic themes may differ from that of Mark and Matthew, it is no less eschatological.

The Kingdom of God

In all three Synoptic Gospels, Jesus proclaims the nearness of the kingdom of God (or kingdom of Heaven). How each of the Gospel writers presents the kingdom and what each means by it is not only central to Jesus's message but also essential for understanding Synoptic eschatology. A large part of the discussion of this concept among scholars centers on the meaning of the nearness of the kingdom. Is the kingdom something already present in the ministry and life of Jesus, or is it something Jesus proclaimed as still in the future even if now closer in time somehow? Scholarly opinions are divided, partly because the texts themselves are not always clear.

In Mark, the nearness of the kingdom is the very first thing Jesus proclaims (1:14). The kingdom is associated with "good news" and a certain understanding of time "fulfilled" or "completed." Mark's Gospel is strongly apocalyptic in its entirety, and the connection

---

[3] Exceptions include the Thanksgiving Hymns from Qumran, which express a sense of present reality as marked by end-time righteousness (1QH), and Jubilees 5:12. Future expectation may include the immediate future.

between kingdom and fulfillment is in keeping with Jewish apocalypses that emphasize fulfillment of prophecies as a sign of God's ongoing faithfulness. Elsewhere in the Gospel, the kingdom is made present through Jesus's deeds of power, table fellowship, and his teaching through the use of parables (e.g. Mark 4:30–32). Mark describes the kingdom as "near" yet not fully present. Salvation is implied in the ministry of Jesus (Mark 4:35–41; 5:25–42; 9:20–24; 10:13–15) but will manifest fully in the future when the Son of Man comes in glory (Mark 9:1; 11:10; 13:26–27; 14:25).

Matthew and Luke similarly portray Jesus beginning his ministry with a proclamation that the kingdom has come near (Matt 4:17 // Luke 4:43). Matthew generally prefers the phrase "kingdom of heaven" to "kingdom of God," but the concept is the same. Matthew, however, uses kingdom language approximately twice as many times as Mark. This is particularly evident in the parables about the kingdom, which increase dramatically in Matthew. In the parables, the kingdom is like yeast (Matt 13:33), hidden treasure (Matt 13:44), a fishing net (Matt 13:47), an overly generous landowner (Matt 20:1), and a wedding banquet (Matt 22:2), to name a few examples. Several of these images suggest that the kingdom is something that needs to be sought after; it is not easy to find or easy to enter. Through the use of parables, Matthew depicts the kingdom as associated with the rampant, unexpected generosity of God and with judgment for the unworthy. In a similar manner, Luke too uses parables to describe the kingdom, and all three Synoptics are explicit that the kingdom is a "secret" not all will understand (Mark 4:11 // Matt 13:11 // Luke 8:10).

The prayer commonly known as the Lord's Prayer appears only in Matthew and Luke. The phrase "let your kingdom come . . . on earth as it is in heaven" (Matt 6:10 // Luke 11:2) reflects a typical Jewish eschatological understanding of the kingdom as something that will come and ultimately transform the earthly sphere. The kingdom then is not escape to another realm nor synonymous with heaven but is about God's rule on earth. This view is consistent throughout Matthew, who depicts the kingdom as something that will transform the earthly sphere.

Luke depicts the kingdom as something that has already begun in the ministry of Jesus, signified in Jesus's power over the demonic and his proclamation on the cross that "today you will be with me in paradise" (Luke 11:20; 17:20; 23:42–43). Luke adapts the speculation about the Messiah appearing in Mark 13:2 (Matt 24:23), adding the phrase "the kingdom of God is among you" (Luke 17:21). Luke's infancy narrative likewise proclaims that the liberation associated with the reign of God and the nearness of the kingdom has already begun. Perhaps the most startling aspect of Luke's apocalyptic eschatology is his emphasis on the ascension. Luke uniquely narrates, twice, the ascension of Jesus (Luke 24:50–53; Acts 1:9–11). It is only after the ascension that Jesus is worshiped as God (Luke 24:52) and that the Spirit is given to his followers to equip them for ministry (Acts 1:5; 2:1–4). Hence, the ascension of Jesus ushers in the new era marked by the activity of the Spirit. In the logic of Luke, this can only occur because Jesus now sits "with power" at the right hand of God, a position from which he can share the power of the Spirit and hence begin his reign (Luke 22:69; 24:49).

Dualism

A dominant trait of apocalyptic eschatology is its dualistic outlook. This manifests in several ways, for example the contrasts between death and resurrection, good and evil, and reward and punishment. A dualistic worldview not only divides history, space, and time itself into two ages (the current age and the age to come) but also tends to divide people, powers, and states into neat categories of good and evil, righteous and wicked.

The classic doctrine of "two ages" is one of the principal ideas associated with apocalyptic eschatology. This view imagines time as divided into two periods: a present age in which evil is active and thus tribulation experienced, and an age where peace and justice are evident because evil has been destroyed and God's rule has begun. All three Synoptic Gospels refer to this concept of two ages.

In Mark 10:30 Jesus promises his followers that those who have made sacrifices for the Gospel in this life will be rewarded "in the age to come" (see Luke 18:29–30). Matthew repeats this dichotomy in 12:32 when discussing forgiveness. The age to come is associated with eternal life and thus has a markedly different character from present life or "this age." Awareness of two ages is also at the heart of speculation about the timing of the end. Matthew makes this clearest in his phrasing of the question from the disciples "What will be the sign of your coming and of the end of the age?" (Matt 24:3 // Mk 13:4 // Luke 21:7).

Apocalyptic eschatology, however, does not always assume a linear progression of two ages or such a neat binary. Many eschatological visions imagine a return to an idealized primordial age rather than something entirely new (see Rev 21–22; Jub 5). This division of time into two eras therefore is not exclusively about temporality—present versus future, or, impermanent versus eternal—but also juxtaposes the current, natural world with a future redeemed or recreated world. It is a way of assuring readers that the present reality is not the ultimate reality and that God will deal with evil. It is closely related with determinism, the idea that there is a fixed end point or a divine plan unfolding.

Other dualisms envisage humanity or spiritual beings divided into two categories. Such dualistic spiritual conflict can be seen most distinctly in Mark, although all three Gospels describe angelic and demonic activity. The setting and stage for Jesus's ministry in Mark's Gospel is conflict between good and evil, between Jesus and the demonic. This observation has led scholars like Joel Marcus and Adela Yabro Collins to call Mark's Gospel thoroughly "apocalyptic" in its outlook and theology (Marcus 2000, 71; Yabro Collins 1992, 27–28). Immediately after defeating Satan in the wilderness by resisting temptation (Mark 1:12–13), Jesus continues his battle with evil in his first miraculous deed. The first miracle in Mark is an exorcism: an act which reveals his power and identity through the silencing of an unclean spirit that has taken possession of a man (Mark 1:21–27). Salvation is framed as liberation from the forces of evil and sin, something only God can do (Mark 10:26–27). In contrast, Matthew describes Jesus as teaching and healing sickness when he begins his ministry, omitting explicit reference to exorcism and shifting the focus to general healing (Matt 4:23–25). Whereas Jesus's authority in Mark is a direct result of his power over unclean spirits (Mark 1:27), in Matthew authority is tied to his teaching (Matt 7:28–29). Luke is more in keeping with Matthew, emphasizing Jesus both as teacher and as prophet (Luke 4:14–21).

As part of his construction of the conflict between Jesus and the demonic, Mark places the Beelzebub story early in his Gospel (Mark 3:22–30), whereas both Matthew and Luke locate it later. In doing so, Mark reinforces the idea of Jesus in conflict with Satan as key to Jesus's early ministry in Galilee. The metaphor of a divided house is striking in a setting wherein Jesus's own family is at odds with him and he effectively reconstitutes a new family of the basis of belief (Mark 3:21, 31–35). The kingdom of God is depicted as a new household, a familial structure based on belief and allegiance rather than biology.

Angels play a pivotal role in the dualism of apocalyptic eschatology, where they can be both good and wicked. For the most part, the Gospel writers portray angels as good or on the side of Jesus, preferring terms like "unclean spirit," "demon," or "the Devil" for the powers that oppose Jesus, although Matthew acknowledges that the Devil has angels too (Matt 25:41).

Mark's Gospel places the emphasis on demonic activity, with the angels playing a minor role in serving Jesus after his temptation (Mark 1:13) or accompanying the Son of Man at the eschaton (Mark 8:38; 13:27). Matthew and Luke, however, both contain a more developed conception of angelic activity. The obvious example is that both include angelic messengers in their respective infancy narratives as well as resurrection scenes. These angels reveal God's plans and interpret events in a manner consistent with other apocalyptic texts.

In Matthew, angels play a significant role in accompanying the Son of Man at the end or assisting in judgment, a role in keeping with the Gospel's amplification of final judgment. Matthew uniquely describes the angels belonging to the Son of Man (Matt 13:41; 16:27; 24:31). Twice in parables about the kingdom, angels are credited with separating the evil from the righteous and meting out eternal punishment for the wicked (Matt 13:41, 49). On the positive side, they play a role in gathering the elect (Matt 24:31) and accompanying the Son of Man as he takes up his reign in glory (Matt 25:41). Angels are Jesus's personal military in Matthew's Gospel, a heavenly host prepared to wage war in the anticipated battle and judgment of evil (Matt 26:53).

Angels in Luke play a kind of cheerleader role, praising God and rejoicing at repentant sinners (2:13; 15:10). Luke shifts Matthew's emphasis from angelic agents of judgment and condemnation to beings that protect and strengthen the faithful (4:10; 16:22; 22:43). Luke uniquely refers to the tradition that Satan was a fallen angel when he quotes Jesus as saying "I saw Satan fall from heaven like a flash of lightning" (Luke 10:18). This biblical tradition has its roots in Genesis 6 and is a way of explaining the presence of evil on earth that simultaneously affirms God's ultimate power over Satan and functions as a sign that the eschaton is near (see Isa 14:12; 1 En 6–7; Rev 12).

Matthew is perhaps the most dualistic of the Gospels, particularly when it comes to humanity (Sim 1996, 79–85). Humans fall into one of two categories: children of the kingdom or children of the evil one (13:38), the righteous or the wicked (13:41–42; 24:45–51), sheep or goats (25:32–33). Only the righteous inherit the kingdom of heaven, and harsh judgment awaits the rest.

While Matthew and Luke place their emphasis in different places, the basic dualisms that are part of the worldview of apocalyptic eschatology are present in all three Synoptic Gospels. A belief in two ages, conflict between good and evil spirits, and, in Matthew's case, the division of humanity into two categories indicate how steeped these authors were in the apocalyptic milieu of Second Temple Judaism.

Judgment, Reward, and Punishment

A final judgment, followed by rewards for the faithful and accompanying punishments for the wicked, is one of the ways apocalyptic eschatology addresses concerns about justice and theodicy. One of the significant differences between the apocalyptic eschatology of the Gospels and that of earlier Jewish texts is a focus on salvation as something that has begun in Christ, rather than as a distant end (Sim 1996, 79–85). Matthew, in particular, highlights the role of Christ as eschatological judge, and both Matthew and Luke explicate the rewards and punishments that await humans, showing some development of this tradition in the three Synoptic Gospels.

Mark does not use the terms for judgment (*krisis, krino*) at all in his Gospel. Similarly, there is only a minor emphasis on repentance when compared to the rest of the New Testament. Mark's Jesus does call "sinners" to repentance, and the baptism of John is a baptism of repentance for the forgiveness of sins (Mark 1:4, 15; 6:12), but judging humanity is not Mark's major concern. Mark's Jesus is engaged in a battle with evil rather than a judge concerned to confront humanity. (See earlier discussion on dualism.) Matthew, however, could not be more different on this issue, as he amplifies the element of judgment at the eschaton (Matt 25:31–46). The judgment scene described in Matthew 25 reflects the aforementioned theological dualism but also indicates the depth of Matthew's ethical concern (Henning 2014). Judgment is inextricably tied to one's ethical action in relation to care for the sick, the hungry, the imprisoned, and the stranger.

Matthew contrasts a person's two prospective fates as either eternal life or eternal punishment, in keeping with his strongly dualistic perspective (Matt 25:46). The explicit reference to eternal punishment (*kolasis*) is rare in the New Testament. More common for Matthew is the threat of fire as the fate of the wicked or unfruitful (3:12; 5:22; 7:19; 13:40; 18:8). Matthew replaces Mark's "Gehenna" (9:45) with "eternal fire" in his discourse on dealing with the causes of sin (18:8). Another image almost exclusive to Matthew is "weeping and gnashing of teeth" to describe the fate of the wicked. Matthew uses this phrase six times (8:12; 13:42, 50; 22:13; 24:51; 25:30). Elsewhere it only appears once in Luke (13:28) and is not in Mark. Only Matthew highlights the role of the Son of Man as presider over the final judgment (Matt 7:21–23; 19:28; 25:31; Sim 1996, 116). Taken as a whole, Matthew's emphasis on Christ as judge and his vivid depictions of the fates that await evildoers—fire, weeping, gnashing of teeth, eternal punishment—demonstrates how dualistic and dominant these ideas of eschatological judgment and reward/punishment were for this author.

Heavenly or eternal rewards lie in the future (Matt 5:12; 6:5), and, while assured, they can be also be lost (9:41; 10:44). These rewards are granted by a God who sees what happens "in secret" (6:6, 18). Luke follows Matthew in mentioning future rewards but does so only twice in the narrative that follows the beatitudes and woes (Luke 6:23, 25), indicating that reward, like punishment, is a less important concern for Luke. Luke's Gospel, however, includes one of the most explicit scenes of reward and punishment in the whole New Testament. The story of the rich man and Lazarus graphically depicts the reversal of fortunes in the afterlife for those who are not living righteously (Luke 16:19–31). Much like the judgment scene in Matthew 25, which gives prominence to the ethical behaviour of those being judged, Luke highlights the wealth disparity between Lazarus and the rich man on earth along with the rich man's lack of compassion. The vivid description of their prospective afterlives acts as a moral exhortation in the manner of other apocalyptic tours of heaven and hell (1En. 5–7; *Apoc. Peter* 7–12). Luke unusually includes fire in his description of Hades (Luke 16:24) as well as explicit, immediate rewards and punishments, showing the influence of Hellenistic depictions of the afterlife (Lehtipuu 2007, 41). Like Jesus's statement on the cross—"today you will be with me in paradise"—Luke envisages immediate retribution or reward after death. Such Lukan eschatology leaves readers with an unresolved tension between the immediacy of individual destiny and the communal judgment and final eschaton that lies in the future.

When it comes to judgment, reward, and punishment, one can see a development in the Synoptic Gospels. Mark shows little interest in these themes or the eternal fate of humanity generally. Matthew on the other hand appears to have an intense interest in judgment as well as the various rewards and punishments that will be metered out at the eschaton. Luke lies somewhere in between the two, downplaying Matthew's emphasis on reward and punishment yet able to use the idea of fate after death to press for ethical behavior and concern for the poor.

The Son of Man and Messianic Expectation

Closely related to expectations regarding the kingdom are messianic expectations associated with the Son of Man. "Son of Man" is arguably the most eschatological of the christological titles used for Jesus in the Gospels, adopting imagery from Daniel 7:13–14 and the prophecy therein about the Son of Man coming with the clouds.

In Mark's Gospel, messianic expectation is amplified through the depiction of John the Baptist as an Elijah figure (see 2 Kgs 1:8). Elijah, in Jewish tradition, was expected to precede the "great and dreadful day of the Lord" (Malachi 4:5–6; see Mark 9:12). Mark's preferred title for Jesus, Son of Man, is therefore closely related to messianic expectation and is used throughout Mark's Gospel in three different ways: by Jesus in reference to himself as Son of Man in his earthly ministry (Mark 2:10, 28; 8:31; 10:45); by Jesus in reference to his impending death and resurrection (Mark 8:31; 9:9, 31;10:33); and by Jesus in relation to his second coming or the parousia (Mark 8:38; 13:26; 14:62). The vision in Daniel 7:9-14 is, of course, the antecedent for this parousia imagery of the Son of Man coming with the clouds in glory.

Matthew follows Mark in using Son of Man as Jesus's public title. He uses a greater diversity of christological titles, including Messiah/Christ and son of David, which underscore his emphasis on fulfillment of prophecy. Matthew, however, is distinct in linking Son of Man with the role of judge (see earlier). Luke follows Matthew and Mark fairly closely in his use of Son of Man. Appearing first in Luke 5:24, Son of Man is absent from Luke's infancy narratives and other special Lukan material.

The Synoptic Gospels show remarkable consistency in their use of Son of Man as a title for Jesus. The fact that they do so points to a shared apocalyptic worldview that associated Jesus of Nazareth with the anticipated Messiah of the Jewish tradition and, moreover, the apocalyptic eschatology of Daniel 7. Theologically, this undergirds their view that the kingdom has come near in Jesus and that the end has somehow begun.

Parousia

Closely related to Son of Man Christology is the idea of Jesus's second coming or parousia. The parousia (the coming or presence) is only used as a technical Greek term in Matthew's Gospel, where it is part of the apocalyptic discourse about the end (Matt 24:3, 27, 37, 39). Mark and Luke do not use the term at all, although they do, like Matthew, anticipate a future return of the Son of Man (Mark 8:28; 13:26; 14:62; Luke 9:26; 12:40).

As noted, Mark's conception of the future coming of the Son of Man is heavily indebted to Daniel 7:13-14. The Son will come with heavenly accoutrements (clouds or angels) as well as with power and glory. This distinguishes his future coming from other references to the Son of Man in the text that are self-references by Jesus to his earthly deeds or actions. Matthew adds detail to the Markan account, expanding expectations about the future coming of the Son of Man to emphasize his role as judge (Matt 13:41; 16:27; 19:28). As a result, in Matthew, Christ's future coming is associated with mourning and woes for many on earth as they face judgment (Matt 24:30).

Delayed parousia (or return of Christ) was one of the significant theological shifts that occurred within earliest Christianity. As communities grappled with the fact that Jesus had not returned as soon as expected, ideas about Christ's return became situated more vaguely in the future, even if that future was still very close. Of the three Synoptics, Luke's Gospel has garnered the most attention when it comes to his treatment of the delayed parousia. Thanks to the influence of Hans Conzelmann, the dominant scholarly view for much of the twentieth century, and until very recently, was that delayed parousia is a significant concern for Luke.[4] Conzelmann argued that Luke is concerned with salvation history (*Heilsgeschichte*) and that his division of history into three periods of salvation—the period of Israel, the period of Christ, and the period of the church—is his solution to the delay of parousia and an accompanying lack of eschatological expectation. Conzelmann's influence, and this basic paradigm for Luke, has meant that scholars have tended to describe Luke as less eschatological and more interested in history than Matthew and Mark.

There have been various critics of Conzelmann over the years; the most recent charge has been led by Kylie Crabbe, who argues that Luke's concern with the periodization of history is deeply eschatological when read in its ancient context but has been "obscured by assumptions about the incompatibility of history and eschatology" (Crabbe 2019, 336).[5] The juxtaposition of history and eschatology creates a false dichotomy and a misunderstanding of the nature of apocalyptic eschatology. Many Jewish apocalyptic texts show an intense interest in history or describe history as divided into periods of time. One well-known example is the *Apocalypse of Weeks* (1 Enoch 93:1–10; 91:11–17), which divides history into ten "weeks" that map onto key periods in Israel's history, for example the Abrahamic covenant or exile. (See also Dan 9:20–27, 12:7; Jer 25:12; 4 Ezra 11–12.) This division of time is a way of making sense of the past in order to anticipate God's action and the fulfillment of God's promises in the future. It reflects the determinism so common in apocalyptic literature, as well as hope in God's judgment and recreation, or reordering, of the world to address evil and injustice. In the *Apocalypse of Weeks*, for example, the last three "weeks" describe future judgment and a new heaven or cosmos.

When read in the context of other Second Temple literature, Luke's periodization of history only reinforces his theological view that God has acted and will act. His eschatological determinism is guided by his sense of history and prophecy fulfilled. Luke points to both imminent and delayed parousia being held in balance (Luke 12:35–40; 13:6–9; 18:1–8; 24:48–49). The heightened role of the Holy Spirit in Luke-Acts has also traditionally been offered as a solution to the delayed parousia, although it is not quite that simple. The fulfillment of prophecy and promises along with the giving of the Spirit serve to reassure readers that the plan of God and promise of Christ's return is in motion. Indeed, the presence of the Spirit and the ongoing miraculous activity associated with it are signs that the final period of history has begun. Hence the Spirit itself, along with the resurrection and ascension of Jesus, is an eschatological sign in Luke, an assurance that the final period has begun. Luke maintains a certain urgency in his narrative through his idea that the end-time is under way and the parousia is near.

All three Synoptic authors, then, balance an awareness that Christ has not yet returned at the time they are writing with an assurance that because other promises of God have

---

[4] For a fuller history of this scholarship see Gaventa 1982, 27–28, or Crabbe 2019.

[5] Conzelmann interpreted Luke's interest in history as evidence for a lack of eschatological speculation, setting history against eschatology. Crabbe demonstrates, through appeal to other contemporary literature, how interest in the periodization of history is a particular feature of apocalyptic eschatology.

been fulfilled, Christians can be assured that Christ will return in glory as promised. Luke emphasizes the role of the Spirit as both fulfiller of promises and place-holder for Christ while the community waits, but Luke is equally eschatological in his outlook and expectation.

The Apocalyptic Eschatology of the Synoptics in Wider Context

In the second part of this essay I briefly reflect on how the apocalyptic eschatology of the Synoptic Gospels, as outlined here, relates to other early Christian literature. The question is, are the Synoptics reflecting the general apocalyptic eschatology of the first-century early Jesus movement, or do they differ in some way from other early Christian voices or their Jewish predecessors? The answer is both yes and no.

Kingdom

Paul writes earlier than the Synoptic Gospels and his letters show markedly less use of the concept of the kingdom of God. In Romans, Paul briefly describes the kingdom as a spiritual place, experienced in the present through the spirit and spiritual gifts (Rom 14:17). In contrast, in 1 Corinthians the kingdom is something believers will inherit once they enter an imperishable, resurrected state at the eschaton (1 Cor 6:9; 15:24–50). This is contingent on Christ "handing over" the kingdom to God in the final defeat of all evil and even death (1 Cor 15:24).

John has very little mention of kingdom, and his eschatology differs from the other Gospels and Paul in his emphasis on glory and the repeated assertion that "the hour is coming" (John 5:25–28; 16:25) or "had come" (John 12:23; 13:1). John uses language of "eternal life" rather than kingdom to describe a future potential status (John 3:15; 5:24; 6:27, 40). Eternal life in John is juxtaposed with either death (to perish) or eternal wrath (John 3:36; 5:24). Such life comes from the Son of Man and is based on belief in him (John 6:27, 40). When it comes to this idea, John exhibits the same tension between future and realized eschatology that the Synoptics do. On the one hand eternal life is already experienced in the present through belief in Jesus (John 17:3), but on the other it is promised as a future gift "on the last day" (John 6:54). The death and resurrection of Jesus are, of course, key to this promised access to eternal life in John (11:25–26).

Kingdom language is also prevalent in Revelation, the only New Testament text considered to fit the genre "apocalypse." There the kingdom of God is juxtaposed and compared with the kingdom of the beast, a symbol for Rome (Rev 16:10; 17:17). As such, the author is comparing an earthly kingdom to a heavenly kingdom, or a present kingdom to a future one. The future kingdom is imagined as shared rule with the resurrected Christ (Rev 5:10) and is ultimately located on earth as a replacement for the present earthly kingdom (Rev 11:15).

None of the Apocryphal Gospels nor Apocryphal Acts use kingdom language as frequently as the Synoptic Gospels do, although the idea persists in a less dominant way. Even if one credits Mark, as the earliest Gospel, with establishing the term, it does not explain why both Matthew and Luke use it even more avidly. Kingdom of God (or heaven) remains an eschatological concept to describe Christ's future reign that is most strongly associated with the Synoptic Gospels.

Dualism

Dualisms are found throughout the New Testament pointing to the general apocalyptic nature of much of the canonical text. John's Gospel is known for its juxtaposition of light and dark (John 3:19), a pairing found also in Matthew and Luke (Matt 4:6; 10:27; Luke 1:79; 12:3) as well as several Pauline epistles. The concept of two ages is strong in Pauline literature (1 Cor 2:6; Gal 1:4; Eph 1:21; 2:7) but lacking in Johannine texts, where it is replaced by the concept of "eternal life."

The most dualistic text in the New Testament is, perhaps unsurprisingly, the book of Revelation. Here some of the dualistic ideas introduced in the Synoptics are developed more fully: God versus Satan; angels versus beasts; earthly versus heavenly kingdoms; true witnesses and false prophets; evildoers versus the righteous, the Whore of Babylon and the Bride of Christ (New Jerusalem); earth versus heaven; and resurrection versus eternal death. The difference between this text and the Synoptic Gospels is largely one of genre.

Judgment, Reward, and Punishment

The Synoptic Gospels acknowledge but downplay expectations about a cosmic battle that precedes final judgment. This stands in contrast with earlier texts, for example Qumran's *War Scroll* (1QM) and the contemporaneous Book of Revelation, which both envisage a final battle of cosmic proportions taking place prior to divine judgment. The Synoptics do, however, continue the tradition of rewards and punishments also found in these other texts.

The judgment motif that is so strong in Matthew is similarly evident in other New Testament texts. Paul's letter to the Romans addresses judgment more explicitly than his other epistles do. Paul describes judgment as God's (Rom 2:1–3), in part to reject humans' judgment of one another (Rom 14:3–13) and in part because God's judgment is related to God's righteousness for Paul. John's Gospel is more similar to that of Matthew in describing judgment as one of the roles of the Son of Man, although one shared with God (John 5:22, 27; 8:16). Even when not amplified as in Matthew, New Testament texts generally assume divine judgment as inevitable at some point.

The paraenetic function of future reward and punishment, made explicit in Matthew and Luke, continued in later Christian texts such as 1 Clement (28-29). Sometimes this paraenetic function is served by even more vivid depictions of the rewards and punishments that await humanity after death. James 5:3, Hebrews 10:27, and Revelation 14:10; 19:20; 20:9-15 all use the image of fire as eschatological punishment or fate for evildoers. Revelation balances graphic depictions of judgment and destruction with an equally powerful positive image of the heavenly banquet in New Jerusalem that awaits those who persevere and remain faithful to God (Rev 19-22). *The Apocalypse of Peter*, a second-century CE Christian text, likewise vividly describes the fates of the dead, indicating the popularity and development of this tradition in early Christianity. These texts, however, primarily serve a moral exhortatory function. The point is not to give an accurate depiction of the afterlife, even if the author could know such a thing, but to persuade readers to act faithfully and morally in the present.

Messianic Expectation and the Son of Man

"Son of Man" as a title for Jesus is not attested in Christian literature prior to the Gospels: Paul does not use it in his epistles, nor does it appear in any later epistolary canonical literature. Paul prefers the title "Christ" for Jesus, and although this should not be interpreted as any less apocalyptic, it possibly has less of an eschatological focus. In the Book of Revelation, "Son of Man" appears twice as a descriptor for the resurrected Jesus in imagery that closely echoes the apocalyptic Son of Man in Daniel 7 (Rev 1:13; 4:14). John's Gospel narrative, much like the Synoptics, exhibits messianic expectation in the questions about whether Jesus is Elijah or the Messiah (John 1:21-27). The disciples are more aware of Jesus's status throughout (see John 1:45), and while John's Gospel uses the title Son of Man, his Christology is expressed differently through the use of "I am" statements by Jesus, as well as images of Lamb, light, bread, and so on.

That narratives that discuss Messianic expectation, and the accompanying "Son of Man" title, are more prevalent in all four Gospels can be explained by genre. The nature of Revelation and the New Testament epistles means that they are primarily concerned not with describing Jesus's earthly life but with presenting what the Christ event means. They write from a perspective that assumes Christ's messianic status and resurrection rather than narrating it, unlike the Gospels.

Parousia

The tension between imminent expectation and awareness of the delay of Christ's second coming is found throughout the New Testament. *Parousia*, as a term, is present in several Pauline epistles prior to Matthew (1 Thess 2:19, 3:13; 1 Cor 15:23). While 1 Thessalonians 4:17 points to imminent expectation about the end, 2 Thessalonians shows awareness of the delay of the parousia, something the author addresses directly in 2:1–12, asking the community not to panic and telling them explicitly that "the day" has not yet come. Likewise, 2 Peter addresses the delay directly, quoting opponents who scoff and ask "where is the promise of his coming?" (2 Pet 3:4). The author's theological answer is that the delay is in order that more may repent and therefore not perish on the day of judgment (2 Pet 3:9).

This theological solution to the gap between Jesus's ascension and his anticipated return is also a concern in the second-century *Shepherd of Hermas*. A combination of visions, paraenetic sections, and parables, *Shepherd* is a deeply eschatological text. Like 2 Peter, the author posits that the delay is to give people time to repent so that they are not "cast out" (Par. 9.26.6–8). At the other end of the spectrum is a strand of Christian eschatology preserved in the critique of Hymenaeus and Philetus in 2 Timothy 2:17–18, which claims that the resurrection (of people) has already taken place. While a minority report, this idea persists in a few so-called gnostic texts that speak of a predeath resurrection and claim that the fullness of God's reign has already occurred.[6]

Overall, however, eschatology in the second century CE became increasingly future focused as communities accepted the reality of a potentially longer period of waiting before the return of Christ. The prime example of this shift is 2 Clement, exhibiting an almost entirely future-focused apocalyptic eschatology. Classic markers of apocalyptic eschatology remain in this text—a day of judgment (16:3; 17:6), a kingdom associated with eternal life (5:5; 17:5), an increase of evil before the end (16:2; 18:2), and an imminent contest (7:1–3)—but the author has placed an emphasis on future realization. Current life is marked by a perishable and temporary nature, as opposed to future "good" and "imperishable" things (6:6). While waiting for the future kingdom, Christians are exhorted to "endure patiently," living with love and righteousness (11:5; 12:1–2).

Conclusion

This essay has sought to demonstrate that the Synoptic Gospels are thoroughly steeped in apocalyptic eschatology. There is much they share with the Jewish apocalyptic texts that preceded them: hope in a future kingdom of God's reign, expectation of tribulation or increased conflict before the end, and rewards and punishments following God's judgment. However, adaptations of these traditions are also evident. Messianic expectation has been adapted, in light of Jesus's death and resurrection, as something now fulfilled and is offered as evidence of God's faithfulness in fulfilling divine promises.

Each of the Synoptic Gospels, however, has its own emphasis. Mark portrays an apocalyptic Jesus as the binder of the strong man whose primary battle is with the forces of evil. Matthew offers the most dualistic worldview, categorizing humans into sheep

---

[6] Irenaeus to Menander (*Haer.* 1,23.5–24.5) and the second-century *Epistle to Rheginus* (NHC I, 4). See Niklas 2011, 604–5.

and goats, the righteous or the wicked, and emphasizing the impending judgment all will face. Luke divides history into periods, not to diminish apocalyptic expectation but rather to show how prophecy is being fulfilled and the eschaton is near. It is not that one has more apocalyptic eschatology than another but that they reflect some of the diversity of the tradition, as well as great continuity.

Further questions and possibilities for scholarly work remain. Why do the Synoptics use kingdom language so strongly and why does it disappear from later texts? How does the eschatology of the Synoptics compare with later apocryphal Gospels? And, if Luke knows Matthew, in what way is he reshaping the judgment emphasis there and imagining salvation differently?

References

Aarde, Andries van. 2011. "'On Earth as It Is in Heaven': Matthew's Eschatology as the Kingdom of the Heavens That Has Come." In Jan G. van der Watt, ed., *Eschatology of the New Testament and Some Related Documents*, WUNT 2, 315. Tübingen: Mohr Siebeck, pp. 35–63.

Carey, Greg. 2005. *Ultimate Things:* An Introduction to Jewish and Christian Apocalyptic Literature. St Louis: Chalice Press.

Collins, Adela Yarbro. 1992. *The Beginning of the Gospel: Probing Mark in Context*. Minneapolis: Fortress.

Collins, John J. 1974. "Apocalyptic Eschatology as the Transcendence of Death." *Catholic Biblical Quarterly* 36: 21–43.

Collins, John J. 1998. *The Apocalyptic Imagination: An Introduction to Jewish Apocalyptic Literature*. 2nd ed. Grand Rapids: Eerdmans.

Collins, John J., ed. 2014. The Oxford Handbook of Apocalyptic Literature. Oxford Handbooks. New York: Oxford University Press.

Crabbe, Kylie. 2019. *Luke/Acts and the End of History*. BZNW 238. Berlin: De Gruyter.

de Boer, Martinus C. 1988. *The Defeat of Death: Apocalyptic Eschatology in 1 Corinthians 15 and Romans 5*. Sheffield: Sheffield Academic Press.

Gaventa, Beverly Roberts. 1982. "The Eschatology of Luke-Acts Revisited." *Encounter* 43: 27–42.

Henning, Meghan. 2014. *Educating Early Christians through the Rhetoric of Hell*. WUNT 2, 382. Tübingen: Mohr Siebeck.

Keith, Chris, and Loren T. Stuckenbruck, eds. 2016. *Evil in Second Temple Judaism and Early Christianity*. WUNT 2, 417. Tübingen: Mohr Siebeck.

Lehtipuu, Outi. 2007. *The Afterlife Imagery in Luke's Story of the Rich Man and Lazarus*. NovTSup 123. Leiden: Brill.

Marcus, Joel. 2000. *Mark 1–8*. The Anchor Yale Bible. New York: Doubleday.

Niklas, Tobias. 2011. "Gnostic 'Eschatologies.'" In Jan G. van der Watt, ed., *Eschatology of the New Testament and Some Related Documents*, WUNT 2, 315. Tübingen: Mohr Siebeck, pp. 601–628.

Perrin, Norman. 1963. *The Kingdom of God in the Teaching of Jesus*. London: SCM Press.

Rowland, Christopher. 2002. *The Open Heaven: A Study of Apocalyptic in Judaism and Early Christianity*. Eugene, OR: Wipf and Stock.

Shively, Elizabeth E. 2012. *Apocalyptic Imagination in the Gospel of Mark: The Literary and Theological Role of Mark 3:22–30*. Berlin: De Gruyter.

Sim, David. 1996. *Apocalyptic Eschatology in the Gospel of Matthew*. SMTSMS 88. Cambridge: Cambridge University Press.

Stone, Michael E. 2011. *Ancient Judaism: New Visions and Views*. Grand Rapids: Eerdmans.

Stuckenbruck, Loren T. 2016. "How Much Evil Does the Christ Event Solve? Jesus and Paul in Relation to Jewish 'Apocalyptic' Thought." In Chris Keith and Loren T. Stuckenbruck, ed., *Evil in Second Temple Judaism and Early Christianity*, WUNT 2, 417. Tübingen: Mohr Siebeck, pp. 142–68

Van der Watt, Jan G., ed. 2011. *Eschatology of the New Testament and Some Related Documents*. WUNT 2, 315. Tübingen: Mohr Siebeck.

CHAPTER 23

RESURRECTION AND THE AFTERLIFE

ALEXEY SOMOV

DIFFICULTIES IN DEFINING RESURRECTION IN THE SYNOPTICS

VIEWS on resurrection, as they are reflected in the Synoptic Gospels, are linked to the evangelists' understanding of the afterlife, which can be generally defined as a belief in continued existence after physical death. However, it is not an easy task to give a more precise definition of what resurrection means in the Synoptics. Of course, in a very general sense it can be seen as the return of the departed from the realm of death back to life. However, a certain afterlife existence can be achieved via (1) receiving eternal life (Jesus's resurrection in Mark 16:1–8; Matt 28:1–10; Luke 24:1–10); (2) eschatological resurrection (Mark 12:18–27; Matt 22:23–33; Luke 20:27–40); or (3) a temporary return to physical life (e.g., the resurrection of Jairus's daughter in Mark 5:38–43; Matt 9:23–25: Luke 8:51–55; see John 11:1–45). All of the Synoptics speak about resurrection and share the ambiguities mentioned earlier, but it seems that for Luke issues of the afterlife and the destiny of the individual are of much more importance than for Mark or Matthew (Somov 2017). Luke not only retains the accounts from Mark and traditions which he shares with Matthew but also adds his own material (e.g., Luke 16:19–31; 23:39–43). For this reason, this article sometimes focuses on Luke's views on the afterlife more than on those of Mark and Matthew. In addition, in order that one might hear the individual voice of each of the Synoptics, this article does not discuss in detail the issue of the evangelists' sources, leaving aside such questions as the Two Source Hypothesis or the interdependency of Matthew and Luke.

Further, the term "resurrection" itself does not automatically indicate what form of afterlife existence (a bodily existence, the resurrected soul, or the spirit) is meant. Such an ambiguity surrounding resurrection was inherited by the Synoptics from common beliefs and traditions in their cultural-religious milieu, with all their diversity and complexity. This article describes these diversities and complexities in each Synoptic Gospel and then offers some new approaches that could bring today's readers to a new level of understanding of these issues. The main question addressed here is whether there is univocacy or polysemy in the Synoptics' views on resurrection as a bodily afterlife existence. While some apparent discrepancies in the views on resurrection (such as the bodily resurrection of Jesus in Luke 27:39 and the angel-like resurrection of the righteous in 20:36) may puzzle a modern reader of the Gospels, did this create any tension for the authors of these texts?

Until at least the middle of the twentieth century it was a commonplace in theological and biblical scholarly works to speak about a more or less homogeneous understanding of the corporeality of resurrection in early Jewish and New Testament views on the afterlife, regarding these views as opposed to Greco-Roman ones. Oscar Cullmann, who represents this typical position (Cullmann 1958), stated that while for Greeks death was a gateway to eternity and liberation of the soul from the burdens of the physical life, and, therefore, a way to blessed immortality, for Jews and early Christians death was a terrible enemy, in which one died and could not be a full personality anymore. In this framework, one had to distinguish between a supposedly single New Testament view on resurrection and the pagan idea of immortality (Mattill 1979). This approach, however, was criticized as too simplistic (e.g., Collins 1960, 410–16; Nickelsburg [1972] 2006, 219–23), because the authors of the Synoptic Gospels as well as other New Testament writers had much more diverse views on the afterlife, in general, and on resurrection, in particular, than was earlier presupposed.

Is there really a need to strictly contrast Greek immortality and Jewish resurrection, as if these ideas were polar opposites? Although this traditional contrast between Greek and Jewish views can sometimes still be found among researchers (e.g., Perkins 1984, 56–63; Segal 2004, 534; Wright 2003, 82–83), most modern scholarship, which tends to emphasize the diversity of views on the afterlife in Greco-Roman, Jewish, and early Christian literature, regards these ideas as less doctrinal and much more multifaceted. First, the Judaism of the first century CE, especially in the Greco-Roman diaspora, was affected on all sides by Hellenistic and Roman culture. Judaism of this period was "an ethnic subculture within the hegemonic culture of the Hellenistic Mediterranean" (Martin 1995, xiv). This idea goes back to Martin Hengel, who pointed out that Judaism was affected by Hellenistic culture already in the Hellenistic period (starting from c. 334 BCE; Hengel 1974). This means that in the first century CE Hellenism was the most important and influential cultural, religious, and ideological system for the whole area of the eastern Mediterranean world (Endsjø 2009, 16). This culture, religion, and ideology had been successfully introduced to the non-Greek populations of this area, including Jews. Second, the previous scholarly consensus on the homogeneity of Greek views on immortality has to be reconsidered. On the one hand in the most ancient and traditional Greek views on the afterlife, resurrection to eternal life was impossible (e.g., Homer, *Il.* 24.550; Aeschylus, *Eum.* 648), and, according to Plato, only the immortality of the soul was a desirable form of afterlife. On the other hand many Greeks considered the existence of the soul without a body to be insufficient. As Dag Øistein Endsjø, whose approach is opposite that of Cullmann, shows that for many Greeks immortality did not mean being a disembodied immortal soul (the view that was virtually a commonplace in previous scholarship) but having an eternal union of body and soul (Endsjø 2009, 24, 39, 57). This idea, as well as traditional Greek religion with its comprehensive worldview, continued to exist as part of Hellenistic views on the matter. Moreover, as Erwin Rohde demonstrated, the influence of Plato's views on the immortality of the soul were popular only in some isolated sects and philosophical schools (Rohde 1925, 254, 538; see Segal 2004, 204). Nevertheless, as Outi Lehtipuu rightly notes, resurrection terminology, which in contrast to early Jewish texts was used virtually only for temporary resuscitation but not for the resurrection to eternal life, was something new for Greco-Roman audiences. After all, the Greco-Roman world had many attitudes toward the afterlife and the possibility/impossibility of resurrection (Lehtipuu 2015, 63–64).

Further, as most modern scholarship agrees, the Jewish concept of resurrection itself appeared, probably, not earlier than during the Hellenistic period. It was shaped both by the theological ideas of the Hebrew Bible (e.g., that God was the Lord over death and life [Deut 32:39] or collective retribution [Deut 28; Lev 26] and individual retribution [Jer 21:28–30; Ezek 18:38]) and by Hellenistic and even Zoroastrian ideas, which were characterized by a dualistic view of the world, the idea of a beatific afterlife, and resurrection (a belief attested as early as the fourth century BCE; Segal 2004, 173). The basic points of this Persian influence on the Jewish concept of resurrection have been discussed in a number of scholarly works (see, e.g., Martin-Achard 1956, 148–55).

In addition, there was no single Jewish view on the form of afterlife existence or on what happened after death. Jews may have believed in resurrection not only in a corporeal form but also in a certain angelomorphic existence, or even in an incorporeal form as the immortality of the soul. The latter belief was characteristic of those Jewish Hellenistic writers who were heavily influenced by Plato's views on the immortality of the soul (Segal 2004, 204), such as Philo of Alexandria, Josephus, and the author of the Wisdom of Solomon. A few Jewish groups, who were influenced by popular Epicurean philosophy (like the Sadducees), did not believe in any postmortem existence at all (see Josephus, *Ant.* 18.16; *J.W.* 2.165). These religious ideas were often mixed and molded into more complex views. All this demonstrates a much more diverse picture of what Greeks and Jews could believe about the afterlife than was presupposed by the traditional scholarly opposition between immortality and resurrection. The New Testament authors inherited this diversity of beliefs about the afterlife. This means that although the Synoptics most often deal with resurrection, traces of other concepts are also sometimes evident in their writings. Therefore, the statement that Jesus's resurrection was unambiguously bodily because that was the only kind of resurrection understood at the time (e.g., Brown 1973, 70, n. 121; Wright 2003, 314) needs at least further clarification, if not outright refutation.

Different Types of Resurrection

When speaking about resurrection as the dominant form of the afterlife in the Synoptics, one should have in mind at least three types of resurrection in early Jewish literature. The first and the second types are, respectively, associated with Isaiah 26:19 and Daniel 12:2–3. These passages are, among others, usually regarded as the most significant representations of Jewish views on resurrection (e.g., Cavallin 1974, 26–27, 106–7; Lehtipuu 2015, 33–34; Martin-Achard 1956, 106–18; Nickelsburg 2006, 23–42; Segal 2004, 259–65; Somov 2017, 108–9, 112–13). In Isaiah 26:19, which in its original context may have indicated national revival and restoration rather than resurrection (Nickelsburg 2006, 31) but later was reinterpreted as related to resurrection, it appears as a reward for the righteous. Following this idea, many later Jewish texts depict resurrection as an eschatological event that takes place after the last judgment and rewards of the righteous with eternal life (*1 En.* 22:13; 102:4–8; 103:4; 104:2–6; 108:9–12; *Pss. Sol.* 3:10–12; *Jub.* 23:30–31; 4Q521 fr.7, 6). In Daniel 12:2–3, which is usually accepted as an indubitable account of the eschatological resurrection, a collective resurrection intended for both the righteous and the wicked is followed by the final judgment. After the judgment, the resurrected righteous will be granted eternal life, while the wicked will be punished. Many Jewish texts present this type of resurrection (e.g., *1 En.* 51:1–2; *4 Ezra* 7:31–38; *2 Bar.* 30:1–5; 42:8; *Sib. Or.* 4:181–82; *L.A.B.* 3:10; *T. Ben.* 10:6–10; *T. Jud.* 25:1–2; *L.A.E.* 13:3b–6). In addition to these two types of resurrection, in some other Jewish documents the issue of the last judgment is not so important or is simply not mentioned. Such an understanding of resurrection, which can be defined as the third type of resurrection, deals with the resurrection of an individual righteous person who has suffered from the wicked oppressors. It can directly relate to the most ancient understanding of Jesus's resurrection, because the ancient church seems to have adopted the Jewish idea of martyrdom (although it was never literally called martyrdom in the early Jewish texts) in relation to Jesus (Downing 1963, 279–93).

The proponents of this idea often call this type of resurrection "martyrological resurrection" and "a resurrection to heaven," which is linked to "the heavenly vindication of the martyr," that is, his/her immediate elevation to heaven after death (de Jonge 1991; Holleman 1996; Kellermann 1979; Pollard 1972). Several Jewish texts are taken as proving this idea (e.g., 2 Macc 7; *4 Macc.*; Wis 1–6; *Pseudo-Philo, T. Job*). The problem with this list, however, is that not all of these documents actually mention resurrection. For instance, *4 Maccabees* 9:22; 14:5; 16:13 and Wisdom 3:2–7; 4:7; 5:5, 15–16 narrate a more general view of immortality. Nevertheless, the advocates of the idea of the martyrological resurrection correctly indicate that these texts do speak about the persecution and the subsequent vindication of the martyr. George W. E. Nickelsburg demonstrates that the literary motif of the persecution and vindication of the righteous who suffered from the wicked is present in many biblical and cognate texts (Nickelsburg 2006, 119–40). Certain features of this motif are found in the story about Joseph and his brothers (Genesis

37–45), Isaiah 52–53, the book of Esther, Daniel 3 and 6, the story of Susanna, Wisdom 1–6, 2 Maccabees 7, 1 Enoch 62–63, 4 *Maccabees*, and in some other texts. But again, most of them do not actually mention resurrection. Among those that do, 2 Maccabees 7 and Daniel 12:2–3 are the most prominent. While the former directly proclaims the future bodily resurrection for Jewish righteous sufferers with no direct reference to the end of time, the latter believes that resurrection, which will be granted to both the righteous and the wicked, is appointed in the eschatological future. For the righteous it will be a gift of blessed eternal life, but for the wicked it will be to their shame and everlasting contempt. In contrast to bodily resurrection for the Maccabean martyrs, in Daniel the righteous ones are like the brightness of the firmament and the stars. Several attempts have been made, however, to associate the resurrection in 2 Maccabees 7 with that of Daniel 12:2–3 (Goldstein 1983, 306; Kellermann 1989, 51–70; Wright 2003, 150–53). Kellermann even argued that the "martyrological resurrection" in 2 Maccabees 7 is really a further development of Daniel 12:2–3 (Kellermann 1989, 52). However, as Holleman states, there is not enough evidence for such connections between these texts (Holleman 1996, 155). Further, Ezekiel 37:1–14 is also sometimes regarded as related to the bodily resurrection. However, in its immediate context, it prophesies about a restoration of Israel (Johnston 2002, 223). Moreover, its imagery of the revived bodies is too natural and earthly and was not widely used as evidence of the resurrection until the second century CE (see Justin, *1 Apol.* 52.3–5; Tromp 2007 contra Allison 2011, 155–61).

The issue of the resurrection of the innocent righteous sufferer, which does not directly relate to the final future consummation at the end of times, can be seen broader than is considered by proponents of the idea of the martyrological resurrection. It is still opposed to the collective resurrection at the end of time, but it may be seen not only as the resurrection of a single righteous individual (e.g., 2 Macc 14:46) but also as a small group of the righteous (e.g., 2 Macc 7). It is not necessary to place it only immediately after death, as this would take place in a certain period of time, though not at the end of time.

Further, while the resurrection of the righteous sufferer was most likely regarded as a bodily one as in 2 Maccabees 7, the nature of the eschatological resurrection remains more complicated. It seems that *1 Enoch* 22:13 speaks about the resurrection of the spirits of the righteous. In Daniel 12:3 the resurrected and glorified righteous are associated with the stars: "Those who are wise shall shine like the brightness of the sky, and those who lead many to righteousness, like the stars forever and ever" (NRSV). However, due to the very general description of this resurrection, it is uncertain whether they were originally regarded as being literally exalted to the heavens to become stars or as being transformed into a celestial form like angels. These ambiguities triggered many Jewish interpretations of the nature of resurrection in Daniel 12:2–3. For instance, in the Additions to the Book of Enoch the resurrected righteous are called "the lights of heaven" (*1 En.* 104:2), "the generation of light" (108:11). They will have joy as great as that of the angels, and they will be their companions (104:4). Moreover, in the Book of Parables, Enoch himself is taken to the highest part of the heavens to the heavenly house of fire (71:5–6) and his flesh is dissolved, while his spirit is transformed before the Head of Days (71:11). The other righteous will be also transformed, vindicated, and glorified (50:1; 71:16) and will be given garments of glory (*1 En.* 62:13–16). In *2 Baruch* the resurrection of the body of both the righteous and the wicked (probably, the physical body; 30:1–5; 42:8), which Cavallin calls "the most explicit expression concerning a spiritually resurrected body which can be found in the Jewish literature" (1974, 88), is a transitional step to the final transformation (Lehtipuu 2015, 37–38; Seim 2009, 28–29). After this resurrection everybody will be judged according to their deeds (50:2–3), and the forms of those who will be found guilty will be changed to become more evil than they were during their earthly life (51:1–2, 5), while the forms of those who are justified will be glorified and transformed to the light and the splendor of angels (51:3,5), with their bodies becoming the radiance of glory so that they can resemble the celestial beings (51:10; see *4 Ezra* 7:36–38; *T. Benj.* 10:6–10).

Further, the idea of the angelomorphic transformation, though without explicit mention of the resurrection, is found in some Qumran writings. John J. Collins indicates that, according to 4Q417 2 I.15–18, the righteous were created in the likeness of the angels (Collins 1999, 609–18). The Qumranites may have assumed that the angels were present in their community during the liturgical worship (Frennesson 1999). Moreover, as Fletcher-Louis states, the Qumranites believed that some members of the community (namely priests) may have been actually transformed into angels (Fletcher-Louis 1996). These views appear to conform to the idea found in *1 Enoch* 69:11 that humanity was originally created to be like angels.

Beliefs in a celestial afterlife were widespread not only in Jewish writings but also in Greco-Roman literature. Allan Scott's extensive study of the astral and celestial afterlife in Hellenistic culture demonstrates that the idea that after death the soul goes back to the stars had been known since the fifth century BCE (Scott 1991, 4). The view that the soul was a celestial substance became a part of Hellenistic popular beliefs as well as the teachings of several philosophical schools (24–38).

All these diverse ideas and views were a part of the cultural-religious milieu that formed the worldview of the eastern Mediterranean world at the time when the Synoptic Gospels were written. The evangelists inherited these views with all their diversity and complexity.

Jesus's Resurrection in the Synoptics

Marinus de Jonge states that Jesus's death was "that of an envoy of God rejected by Israel" (see Luke 11:49–51; Matt 23:34–36; Luke 13:34–35; Matt 23:37–39; Mark 12:1–9; 1 Thess 2:14–16; de Jonge 1988, 143). In addition, as many studies show, Jesus was understood as God's suffering righteous one (Mark 8:31; 9:31; 10:32–34; e.g., Ruppert 1972; Kleinknecht 1984; de Jonge 1988). Then, the early followers of Jesus may have seen him as the Son of God who was delivered to suffering and death and then was resurrected and vindicated (de Jonge, 1988, 143–45). The literary motif of the persecution and vindication of the righteous, which Nickelsburg discusses in Jewish literature, has been also successfully applied to the Synoptic Passion narrative (Nickelsburg 2006, 236–42, 245–46, 259–63). According to this approach, Jesus receives his body back, because it was unjustly taken away from him, as it has been promised to those Jewish righteous sufferers (e.g., the Maccabean martyrs) who have innocently died for their faithfulness to the Lord. This idea is especially prominent in Luke (Ehrman [1997] 2000, 117, 133), where Jesus's innocent death is a result of a miscarriage of justice and is similar to the destinies of the prophets before him (Luke 11:47–51; 13:33–34; see Acts 7:51–52; Lehtipuu 2010, 161). Matthew could also support this idea, as his allusion to Wisdom 2:18 (which Nickelsburg regards as relating to the motif of the persecution and vindication) about the deliverance of the righteous one from his adversaries in Matthew 27:43 demonstrates. For this evangelist, Jesus is vindicated in his claim to be the Son of God through his obedient death.

In contrast to such understanding of Jesus's resurrection as related to the individual resurrection of the righteous sufferer, it is often argued that already in the earliest period his resurrection was perceived as being linked to the eschatological general resurrection (e.g., Davies and Allison 1997, 629; Waters 2003, 492–94). Indeed, one can find such a link in 1 Corinthians 15:12–19 (see John 11:25), where Paul calls Jesus "the first fruit" of those who will be raised at the end of time (15:20). Joost Holleman argues that it was Paul who developed this idea (1998, 137). This would mean that the eschatological understanding of Jesus's resurrection was known long before the Synoptics. However, even if it were so, how can one prove that although Paul is the earliest known witness of the belief in Jesus's resurrection and the eschatological resurrection and although he claims that his understanding of Jesus's resurrection is based on the apostolic authority (1 Cor 15:3–8), everyone in the ancient church was unconditionally preoccupied with Paul's idea? Another option which cannot be discarded: while for the contemporaries of Paul it would have been evident that Jesus's resurrection had initiated the eschatological resurrection, which was expected soon, for the generations of Matthew and Luke it would have been already less evident (Lehtipuu 2010, 161), though the period of this delay would be debatable (Maddox 1982, 105–23). Indeed, although it is important for Matthew to emphasize that both Jesus's death and resurrection were accompanied by certain eschatological signs, such as the earthquake and the splitting of the rocks, and even the resurrection of certain saints (see 27:51–53), would this mean that one should regard Jesus's resurrection not as a preeschatological but as a present-oriented eschatological event? Some have attempted to state the same about the resurrection in Matthew 27:52–53, the story which is unique for the Synoptics. Kenneth L. Waters argues that this passage is a pre-Matthean early Christian apocalyptic insertion, which deals with the eschatological resurrection at the end of time. In his opinion, these saints are Christian martyrs from the book of Revelation (Rev 20:4, 6) who will appear in the new Jerusalem (Rev 21:2; Waters 2003, 489–515). However, it could be difficult to prove the dependence of Matthew on the book of Revelation or vice versa. Dale C. Allison declares that this resurrection refers to Christ's descent to hell and releasing the righteous dead from the captivity of death, the popular idea in early Christianity (see Irenaeus, *Haer.* 4.7.2;

Allison 2008, 353). However, it looks that in early Christian writings, this passage was never used as a proof of this idea (Luz 2005, 564). Nolland calls these raised saints "a 'supporting cast' to Jesus as his own resurrection and appearances are enacted: their resurrections and appearances are miniatures of his own" (Nolland 2005, 1216). Even if the resurrection of the saints in Matthew 27:52–53 was accompanied by certain eschatological signs, its nature is emphasized as corporeal. Such a feature links it to Jesus's resurrection as a preeschatological resurrection of the righteous sufferer. Matthew could have understood Jesus's resurrection as a trigger of the resurrection of those pious Jews who unjustly died before him (Borg and Crossan 2006, 174). This evangelist, who is always very conscious of the fulfillment of prophecies, could have taken very seriously the promise of bodily resurrection for the righteous sufferers (first of all that in 2 Macc 7; Somov 2021 379-380).

As for Luke, he may be (if, as most scholars believe, Luke and Acts were written by the same author) aware of Paul's view on Jesus's resurrection as the first step of the general resurrection in Acts 26:23, but he acknowledges a tension between these two types of resurrection (Lehtipuu 2010, 162).

In addition, Joost Holleman states that the earliest Christian concept of Jesus's resurrection is expressed by the formula ἀνίστημι/ἐγείρω ἐκ (τῶν) νεκρῶν (raise up/wake up from [the] dead), meaning that he has been taken from the realm of the dead (Holleman 1996, 142). Indeed, Mark uses ἐκ νεκρῶν for both Jesus's resurrection and eschatological resurrection (Mark 6:14; 9:9, 10; 12:25). Does this mean that the righteous are thought to share in Jesus's resurrection?

However, the use of the expression νεκρῶν/ἐκ (τῶν) νεκρῶν (of the dead/from [the] dead) in the context of resurrection is not consistent in the New Testament in general or in the Synoptics in particular. Matthew prefers to use ἐγείρω ἐκ/ἀπό (τῶν) νεκρῶν for Jesus's resurrection (14:2; 17:9; 27:64; 28:7) and reserves ἡ ἀνάστασις τῶν νεκρῶν (22:31) for the eschatological resurrection. Luke modifies the Marcan phrase ἐκ νεκρῶν ἀναστῶσιν ("they rise from the dead"; Mark 12:25) to τῆς ἀναστάσεως τῆς ἐκ νεκρῶν ("the resurrection from the dead") in Luke 20:35 for referring to the eschatological resurrection of the righteous. This ἡ ἀνάστασις ἡ ἐκ νεκρῶν (20:35) with ἐκ can be distinguished from ἀνάστασις νεκρῶν ("the resurrection of the dead") in Acts 17:32; 23:6; 24:21; 26:23. The latter usually refers to the general eschatological resurrection. François Bovon compares the use of ἀνάστασις νεκρῶν in Luke-Acts with the book of Revelation (Rev 2:11; 20:5–6; see 20:12–13) and argues that in the Lucan context it may refer to the general eschatological resurrection, in which the destiny of the righteous differs from that of the wicked, while the form with ἐκ is reserved for the resurrection of the righteous only (Bovon 1996, 495). This argument would be plausible but for the fact that Luke uses the expression with ἐκ νεκρῶν in the context of the preeschatological resurrection as well (Luke 9:7; 16:31; 24:46; Acts 3:15; 4:2, 10; 10:41; 13:30, 34; 17:3, 31). It is safe to state that the expressions with νεκρῶν/ἐκ (τῶν) νεκρῶν are basically interchangeable in the Synoptics.

Further, there is a general scholarly consensus that Jesus's resurrection, which happens on the third day after his death on the cross and burial, is clearly a bodily one.

Moreover, this resurrection is "a unique incidence of a full bodily resurrection" and continuation of Jesus's earthly life and ministry (Fletcher-Louis 1997, 70). The Synoptics speak about its features and its corporeality in several ways.

First, the presence of the story of the empty tomb in all the Synoptics (it first appears in Mark 16:1–8, whether received from the earlier tradition [e.g., Bultmann 1931, 308; Dibelius 1971, 104, 190] or was created by the evangelist himself [Hamilton 1965]), indicates that they agree that Jesus's body disappeared from the tomb on the third day after his death (Matt 28:6; Mark 16:6; Luke 24:3). In Mark (in which 16:9–20, as most scholars believe, is a late addition), the empty tomb is a sort of promise of the appearance of Jesus in bodily resurrected form. In Matthew and Luke, this story serves as a preparation scene for an appearance of the resurrected Jesus in a corporeal form (Hamilton 1965, 416). Matthew goes further and in 28:2 supplies this passage with an epiphany sign of the great earthquake, which accompanies the descent of the angel from heaven to roll away the stone from Jesus's tomb. This earthquake is sometimes associated with the earthquake in Matthew 27:51 (McNeile 1915, 424), but it is more reasonable to regard them as two separate events (Hagner 1998, 850). Moreover, Matthew probably adds the story told by Jesus's opponents about his body being stolen (28:11–15) specifically in order to give more credibility to his resurrection (Weren 2011, 194).

Moreover, Matthew narrates actual appearances of the risen Jesus, first to the women (28:9–10) and then to the disciples (28:16–20). Describing Jesus's appearance to the women, Matthew clearly reports that they could touch his resurrected body (28:9). This may indicate the evangelist's intention to articulate that the risen Jesus does have a body (Lehtipuu 2015, 43).

Luke emphasizes the bodily nature of this resurrection perhaps more than Matthew and Mark, especially in Luke 24:36–43. Several traditions may lie behind this episode. It has some connections with Mark 16:14–15 and Matthew 28:16–20 and also relates to John 20:19–23 and 1 Corinthians 15:5. However, it is doubtful that the person who composed the so-called long ending of Mark was familiar with the Lucan account (Bovon 2008, 580). The language and style of the Lucan episode and Mark 16:14–15 are too different to be dependent on each other.

Whatever it was, in Luke 24:36–43 the risen Jesus appears in the midst of his disciples to demonstrate that he is alive and is a real human being, though with a resurrected body. While his disciples are in a panic (24:37; see 21:9; 24:5), thinking that they are seeing a ghost (πνεῦμα), he declares that in contrast to a ghost, he has "flesh and bones" (σάρκα καὶ ὀστέα; 24:39). Indeed, "flesh and bones" is a biblical synecdoche for the whole body (e.g., Gen 2:23; 29:14; Judg 9:2; 2 Sam 5:1; 19:13; 1 Chron 11:1; Ps 37:4; 101:6; Prov 3:22; Job 2:5; 19:20; 33:21; Mic 3:2; Lam 3:4). Nolland states that in such a way Luke emphasizes the solidity and rigidity of the human body (1993b, 1213).

Moreover, in demonstrating that Jesus is not simply a ghost but a human, Luke may be referring to Greco-Roman views of ghosts, as he applies the same vocabulary that Homer used for the souls of the dead, whose nature was regarded as similar to that of a ghost (*Od.* 11.207; 11.219). In the Greco-Roman world the appearance of ghosts was explained as a consequence of improper burial or no burial. (Jesus's disciples may not have known if he had a proper burial, as they did not participate in it; see Luke 23:53–55.) It was believed that the souls of innocent victims appeared in order to punish offenders (see Suetonius, *Otho* 7) and to seek vengeance for their murders (Plutarch, *Sera* 555c; Cicero, *Div.* 1.27.57; Somov 2017, 138). In addition, similarly to the Matthean account, the Lucan Jesus invites his disciples to touch his body to identify him and to prove that he is a real human. In doing so, he lets them examine his hands and feet (Luke 24:39). Moreover, Jesus demonstrates his ability to eat (24:41–43), which could be regarded as a sign of his corporeality (Ellis 1974, 279; Lehtipuu 2015, 44–45). Therefore, all of the Synoptics deliberately emphasize the corporeal character of the resurrection of Jesus, which was a feature of the individual resurrection of the righteous sufferer in Jewish traditions.

In addition to telling their readers about the corporeal character of Jesus's resurrection, the Synoptics also note his supernatural abilities after resurrection. In Matthew, Jesus can appear suddenly (28:9). The Lucan Jesus appears and disappears, may be at times unrecognizable, or even invisible, and finally ascends to heaven (Luke 24:13–51; see Acts 1:9). Here Luke may be combining Jewish ideas about individual and eschatological types of resurrection. As shown earlier, in some Jewish texts the final state of the resurrected righteous at the end of time presupposes their glorification and transformation. This makes it possible to perform miracles, healings, and have other supernatural abilities. This feature of resurrection is known to Mark, who refers to popular Jewish beliefs ascribing these abilities to the resurrected: if John the Baptist were raised from the dead, miraculous powers would be at work in him (6:16). Matthew retains the rumor about the resurrected John the Baptist (Matt 14:2), while Luke also indicates this to his readers in Luke 9:7–9 and then in 9:19.

Moreover, in contrast to Mark and Matthew, in Luke, Jesus's resurrection seems to be an intermediate step in Jesus's vindication and exaltation in heaven (Lehtipuu 2010, 162; 2015, 46) and has to be considered in connection with his ascension. Although there are some parallels between Jesus's ascension and the stories about ascensions of Roman emperors and other noble persons (e.g., Plutarch, *Rom.* 27.5–28.2), latter ones do not include their bodies (McDonald 2013, 310–11). Was this event perceived as similar to the ascension of Elijah (Davies 1958; Pesch 1986, 72–77) or as a rapture-type ascension (Lohfink 1971)? Should it be seen as Jesus's final departure after the series of post-Easter appearances (Conzelmann 1954, 177) or Luke's editorial attempt to fight with docetic tendencies in the early church (Talbert 1974, 58–65, 112–16)? Arie Zwiep shows that Jesus's ascension does not separate his exaltation and resurrection and may be seen simply as "a description of the last post-resurrection appearance of Jesus" (Zwiep 2010, 63; see Zwiep 1997, 164–65).

Thus, while there are some variations in how the Synoptics speak about Jesus's resurrection and the features of his resurrected body, they basically agree that it is a case of corporeal afterlife existence, although not identical to the life in the physical body. However, the discussion of resurrection in the Synoptics includes not only Jesus's resurrection but also the eschatological resurrection; as I will show, the Synoptics are less clear about the form in which this will happen.

The Corporeality and Incorporeality of Eschatological Resurrection in the Synoptics

Mark mentions the resurrection at the end of time but with no reference to the final judgment, which may indicate that he is speaking about the resurrection of the righteous only (Mark 12:25; see 13:27): "For when they rise from the dead, they neither marry nor are given in marriage, but are like angels in heaven" (NRSV). Mathew retains Mark's material about the resurrection of the righteous (Matt 22:30), but also admits the general resurrection of both the righteous and the wicked in 12:41–42, which reports about the people of Nineveh and the queen of the South who will rise up together with those who did not believe in Jesus. For Matthew, the resurrection of the wicked opens the way to their further destruction (Matt 7:13–14; Lehtipuu 2015, 50). Luke speaks about "the resurrection of the righteous" (ἡ ἀνάστασις τῶν δικαίων) in Luke 14:14 and develops Mark 12:25 in Luke 20:35–36 but on the other hand refers to the general resurrection of both the righteous and the wicked in Acts 24:10–21. This can be explained by the fact that the resurrection of the righteous was seen simply as the positive half of the general resurrection, as it comes, for instance, in Acts 24:15 (Evans 2008, 572; Nolland 1993a, 751).

All in all, the central piece of evidence of the eschatological resurrection in the Synoptics is the aforementioned Marcan story about Jesus's controversy with the Sadducees (Mark 12:18–27). Here, the resurrected righteous are like the angels in the heavens (ὡς ἄγγελοι ἐν τοῖς οὐρανοῖς; 12:25). Many commentators believe that in its original context, this meant that the life of the resurrected ones would be like that of the angels in the sense that they would not need marriage in its present meaning (Cranfield 1959, 375; Gould 1912, 229; Wessel 1984, 736). Matthew retains ὡς ἄγγελοι (Matt 22:30) and basically follows Mark in his version of this story. Luke, however, deliberately changes this expression to ἰσάγγελοι ("like angels," "equal to angels"; Luke 20:36), a word unique in the New Testament. It is interesting that the replacement of ὡς ("like," "as") with ἰσ- seems to be due to the resemblance of ἰσάγγελοι to ἴσος ἀγγέλοις ("equal to angels") in Philo, *De Sacrificiis Abellis et Caini* 1.5, or ἰσαστέροι ("star-like") in *4 Maccabees* 17:5. Philo equates the "incorporeal and happy souls" of Abel, Abraham, Isaac, and Jacob with the angels ("having become equal to the angels") because they have passed over to "the immortal and perfect genus" (*Sacr.* 1.5–7). In *4 Maccabees* 17:5 the afterlife of the Maccabean martyrs is likened to the lives of the stars, regarding this as a celestial postmortem existence. In addition, in Luke 20:36b the author considers the resurrected to be υἱοί θεοῦ (literally, "sons of God"), a term often associated with angels or celestial beings in Jewish sources (Gen 6:2, 4; Deut 32:8; Job 1:6; 2:1; 38:7; Pss 29:1; 82:6; 89:6; Wis 5:5).

Further, the Lucan πάντες γὰρ αὐτῷ ζῶσιν ("for everybody is alive to him") in Luke 20:38 is an expression that is more appropriate to the language of immortality and is similar to *4 Maccabees* 7:19 and 16:25, which directly connects the destiny of the righteous with a celestial postmortem existence: ζῶσιν τῷ θεῷ ("they are alive to God"). It therefore seems that for Luke, the patriarchs Abraham, Isaac, and Jacob have ascended to heaven (Lehtipuu 2015, 52).

Crispin H. T. Fletcher-Louis (1997, 78–86) develops the point that Luke understands the eschatological resurrection in terms of a certain angelomorphic state of the resurrected ones. Fletcher-Louis finds potential angelomorphic traditions not only in Luke 20:27–38 but also in several other Lucan passages, for example, Luke 5:1–11; 9:28–36; 15:7, 10; 15:11–32; 24:13–43; Acts 6:15; 7:53; 23:8–9 (33–107). Indeed, as shown earlier, in this period the idea of the eschatological resurrection was often expressed in terms of celestial and angelomorphic imagery. Nevertheless, as Lehtipuu states, to be like the stars does not necessarily just indicate an actual turning into the stars but may also mean taking a leading position among the other resurrected ones (Lehtipuu 2015, 34). On the other hand one has to consider the idea of *1 Enoch* 69:11, which states that humanity was originally created to be like angels, which in this context means to be immortal. This idea may a key for understanding the reference to angels in Jesus's controversy with the Sadducees. It is found in all of the Synoptics, but it is especially emphasized by Luke: a transformed existence of the resurrected corresponds to humanity's immortal state at creation. In other words, Luke 20:27–38 aims to demonstrate that, first of all, the righteous and the patriarchs are equated with the angels in their immortality. That is what the Lucan remark "they cannot die anymore" in 20:36 would mean (Somov 2017, 173–74).

Further, while Matthew, who basically follows Mark in representing Jesus's controversy with the Sadducees (Matt 22:23–33), speaks about the future resurrection of the righteous, Luke goes further and converts the whole discourse to the present tense, as if the eschatological resurrection were already accomplished and those who are worthy of being resurrected have already been raised up (Luke 20:35). Lucan addition to Mark 12:25 in Luke 20:38b puts ζάω ("live") in the present tense, which also may indicate the present, not the future, state of the patriarchs. This emphasis on the importance of the present state of believers has been further analyzed in several ways. First, it initiates certain ascetical interpretations of the present state of the resurrected ones in Luke 20:34–38. Turid Karlsen Seim suggests that Luke's alteration of Mark's story initiates an essential shift in meaning and makes the opposition between "children of this age" and "children of the resurrection" as not temporal but moral. "Children of the resurrection" may refer to those believers who do not marry and therefore are equal to the angels. In this case, resurrection, as Seim argues, could be a present state which is attained by practicing the ascetical discipline in the early Christian groups (Seim 1994, 216–22; 1999, 119–20).

However, such a shift in the traditional understanding of temporal aspects of eschatology is probably connected with Luke's view of the Kingdom of God as already a present reality and with his understanding of salvation as already experienced in this world (Maddox 1982, 132–45; see Bultmann 1951, 4–11; Ladd 1974, 195–217). These issues, in turn, relate to Luke's understanding of repentance. This is visible, for instance, in Luke 9:60 (see Matt 8:22): those who have repented and are following Jesus are, in some sense, already resurrected or live as if they were resurrected. They already participate in the Kingdom of God as the blessed reality of the righteous being ruled by God and relating to salvation (Luke 13:23–30; 18:18–27). Thus, in Luke, repentance brings salvation, which is already in action and will continue in the age to come. Some expectations about the end have been partly fulfilled, and Jesus's disciples already participate in the new life (Lehtipuu 2007, 256–62). In contrast, those who do not repent and do not receive salvation will be punished in Hades (Luke 10:9–15; 16:22–23; see 13:1–5) or Gehenna (12:5), which probably has a similar meaning for Luke (Lehtipuu 2007, 272–74 contra Milikowski 1988). Nonetheless, Lucan Jesus does not give a clear answer about whether this punishment is eternal or not (see Mark 9:43–48; Matt 10:28; Rev 21:8).

The significance of the present state of the believers also signifies how the destiny of the individual directly after death is important for Luke. In the Parable of Lazarus and the Rich Man (16:19–31), which has been the subject of extensive interpretation and research since Hippolytus of Rome (*Univ.* 33) and Tertullian (*An.* 7.3; *Marc.* 4.34.11–14; e.g., Jülicher 1899, 617–41; Gressmann 1918; Plummer 1896, 393; Bultmann 1931, 212–13, 220–22; Jeremias [1954] 1972, 182–87; Schweizer 1982, 173; Ellis 1974, 201–2; Mattill 1979, 26–40; Fitzmyer 1985, 1124–36; Hock 1987; Bauckham 1991; Somov 2014, 59–62; 85–86; 98–100; 181; 215–16; 2017; Somov and Voinov 2017). The destiny of the righteous and the wicked is defined immediately after death without any possibility of subsequent change. Outi Lehtipuu (2007) in her extensive research on this parable demonstrates that although Luke supports basic points of traditional Jewish collective eschatology, he also applies elements of individual eschatology that deal with an immediate entry into the otherworld. Some details of this parable seem to refer to the corporeality of the postmortem states of the rich man and Lazarus. Indeed, the former is in torments and flame in Hades, which designates the place of the final punishment in Luke 16:23–24, rather than a temporal abode of the dead (Mattill 1979, 29–31; Somov 2017, 85–86; contra Jeremias [1954] 1972, 185), and wants Lazarus to cool his tongue with water on the tip of his finger (16:24). The imagery of Abraham's bosom, which only Luke uses, may imply sleeping with one's ancestors (Lehtipuu 2007, 207–8) or Abraham's active afterlife state receiving the souls of the righteous (Fitzmyer 1985, 1132) but also may indicate that Lazarus is feasting at a heavenly banquet along with Abraham (Esler 1987, 193; Lehtipuu 2007, 215; Marshall 1978, 636; Meyer 1966, 825; Smith 2003, 260; Somov and Voinov 2017). If the latter suggestion is correct it does not mean that both Lazarus and Abraham are in a corporeal state in the afterlife in this parable. As Lehtipuu demonstrates, the mention of parts of the physical body (Lazarus's finger and the rich man's tongue) does not necessarily refer to real corporeality but "makes the story alive and more immediate" (2007, 228). Moreover, in pagan and Jewish sources the souls of the deceased did have some corporeal and physical characteristics (223–28). Indeed, many Greek philosophers considered the soul in some way material (e.g., Euripides, *Suppl.* 531–36, 1140; *Hel.* 1014–16). This feature of the soul may have affected the descriptions of postmortem existence in a corporeal manner. Thus, in Luke 16:22–23 Abraham and Lazarus's postmortem existence is not explicitly associated with resurrection. Moreover, in contrast to the rich man, who seems to be fully conscious in Hades, Lazarus is passive in his afterlife.

Thus, critical approaches to resurrection demonstrate that in the Synoptics the corporeality of the eschatological resurrection is less evident and consistent than in the case of Jesus's resurrection. Nevertheless, all of the Synoptics use more or less the same terminology regarding the afterlife and resurrection, which is most frequently represented by forms of the Greek verbs ἀνίστημι and ἐγείρω. The extensive use of the forms of these verbs (81 percent) predominates over other more general terms (19 percent; Somov 2017, 196). However, ἀνίστημι and ἐγείρω, which usually relate to the idea of rising, standing up, waking, or getting up from sleep, do not automatically refer to the resurrection to eternal life or the corporeal character of such a resurrection. Indeed, the Synoptics apply the same terminology not only to the resurrection to eternal life but also to the restoration of physical life, merely a temporal return to the earthly body, which has to die again (e.g., Matt 19:25; Mark 5:41; Luke 8:54). Lehtipuu is fully justified in asking: "if the key terminology is partly the same, how would people have understood a difference between the 'resurrection' of Jesus and, say, the 'reviving' of Lazarus?" (2010, 157). Therefore, the next question that needs to be examined is what kind of afterlife reality and existence is described by resurrection terminology.

A Cognitive Approach to the Ambiguity of Resurrection in the Synoptics

An important step forward can be taken in the discussion of the ambiguity of the representation of the afterlife existence by examining resurrection vocabulary in the Synoptics in the context of its metaphorical features. Indeed, in the ancient Mediterranean worldview resurrection is not exactly the same thing as getting up from bed (Pokorný und Heckel 2007, 17). Nevertheless, linguistically, these concepts share the same terminology in Jewish and early Christian texts. This leads to the necessity of positioning resurrection in the framework of the Jewish and early Christian religious system, which is predominantly metaphorical (like any other ancient religious system) since it allows the articulation of abstract, divine, and supernatural concepts "by using finite expressions derived from the experiences of human existence" (Perdue 1991, 22). In other words, "if a person wants to speak about the D/divine it should be done by means of metaphors. Although human concepts are used, reference is made to a divine reality (which differs from the ordinary referents of the concepts)" (van der Watt 2000, 22).

Further, classical theories of language see metaphor only as a matter of language (Lakoff 2007, 267). Therefore, at the linguistic level metaphor can be defined as "that figure of speech whereby we speak about one thing in terms which are seen to be suggestive of another" (Soskice 1985, 15). However, such a view of metaphor was criticized already by I. A. Richards (1936) and Max Black (1962) and further by E. R. MacCormack, who regarded metaphor as a feature of cognition (1985). In 1980 American cognitive linguists George Lakoff and Mark Johnson developed a theory called *cognitive metaphor theory* or *conceptual metaphor theory* (CMT). In this theory, metaphor is not simply a verbal device that works only on the linguistic level but is a broader phenomenon in which one conceptual domain is systematically structured in terms of another. In cognitive linguistics, a concept is a fundamental unit of knowledge necessary for the perception and categorization of the world. Each concept is a part of a conceptual system, which is the repository of concepts available to human beings (Evans 2007, 38) and can be encoded and externalized via a language system (Pereira 2007, 47–83). Lakoff and Johnson regard metaphor as an integral part of the process of human thinking and acting. This feature of metaphor allows people to comprehend some aspects of a more abstract concept in terms of another, "lower level" concept from everyday human experience. In such a context, "metaphor means metaphorical concept" (Lakoff and Johnson 1980, 6) and is called cognitive/conceptual metaphor. Cognitive metaphors, which are often universal for many cultures, can be further represented on the linguistic level by several verbal metaphors, which are more culturally motivated. One of the further developments of CMT is *conceptual blending theory* (CBT), developed by Gilles Fauconnier and Mark Turner (2002).

While CMT regards metaphors as stable and systematic relationships between two concepts or conceptual domains, CBT deals with mental spaces—partial and temporary representational structures during thinking or communicating. Conceptual integration or blending is a basic human cognitive operation that constructs partial matches between two or more mental spaces (inputs). It projects these matches into a new "blended" mental space. The combination of CMT and CBT helps to explain how the concept of resurrection is represented in the Synoptic Gospels. Both theories demonstrate the importance of humans' embodied experience in cognitive structuring of meaning. This is expressed by *image-schemas*, a term used in cognitive lingusitcs, which denotes *preconceptual primitives* or basic structural elements that establish the process of thinking and understanding and that are associated with particular types of human embodied experience (Johnson 1987, 44–79). The representation of resurrection through the metaphors of waking up and rising up relates to the ancient Mediterranean view that "death could be spoken of in terms of sleep, a sleep from which one did not awake" (McAlpine 1987, 149). Indeed, in the Hebrew Bible death is called "eternal sleep" (Jer 51:39, 57) from which there is no way to awake (Job 14:12). After death everybody goes to the underworld (Sheol) to exist there as if asleep. In addition to this, as is seen in Xenophon, *Memorabilia* 1.4.11.4; Plato, *Phaedrus* 247b–c; Aristotle, *De partibus animalium*. 686a; Cicero, *De natura deorum* 2.140.4–11; Philo, *De posteritate Caini*. C. 27.2–6, *De gigantibus* 49; and Plutarch, *Apophthegmata laconica* 234, in ancient anthropological views, the ability to stand upright, which relates to the concept of standing up and is sometimes represented by similar terms, is a distinctively human capacity given by the gods marking humanity's special relations with divinity and the celestial world as well as a participation in immortality. In the Greco-Roman world, the human standing posture also relates to the restoration of physical life in terms of a process of waking up from the sleep of death (Claudius Aelianus, *De Natura Animalium* 9.33; Pausanias,

Descr. 2.26.6.1). Therefore, in order to be alive, the individual has to be awakened and raised from this sleep of death. This process is represented by the cognitive metaphors DEATH IS DOWN, DEATH IS SLEEP, LIFE IS UP, and RESURRECTION IS RISING, because in many cultures the physical basis for personal happiness, health, and life, is often expressed as MOVING/BEING UP, and misery, disease, and death as MOVING/BEING DOWN (Somov 2017, 201–2; Tappenden 2016, 46–54). These metaphors are structured by the image-schema UP-DOWN. Further, resurrection itself can be metaphorically described as RESURRECTION IS CONSCIOUSNESS, in which resurrection is structured "in relation to the basic human experience of waking to consciousness" (Tappenden 2012, 206–9), or RESURRECTION IS WAKEFULNESS (Somov 2017, 201, n. 41). All these metaphors are at work in the New Testament conceptual system and are most often represented by forms of ἀνίστημι and ἐγείρω on the linguistic level, thereby shaping the basis of its resurrection vocabulary. These metaphors represent the process and result of revivification either to earthly life or to eternal life in general, which is opposite to the process and result of dying and going to the underworld. Therefore, they cannot emphasize the corporeal character of resurrection automatically. This is why the Synoptics use similar terminology for Jesus's resurrection, eschatological resurrection, and the restoration of physical life.

The metaphor RESURRECTION IS CONSCIOUSNESS/WAKEFULNESS, as opposed to DEATH IS UNCONSCIONESS/SLEEP, is sometimes structured by the framework of PERSECUTION, as in 2 Maccabees 7 or the Synoptics' accounts about Jesus's death and resurrection. This allows the metaphor to include the embodied state of the resurrected ones as it projects some components of the domain NATURAL LIFE, which includes such element as an earthly body, onto the domain RISEN LIFE, in which a risen body is understood as a transformed earthly one (Tappenden 2016, 51–52, 69). In other words, the corporeality of resurrection has to be additionally marked, as in the case of Jesus's resurrection in Luke 24:36–43 or the resurrection of the saints in Matt 27:52–53. Frederick Tappenden also introduces the metaphor RESURRECTION IS CELESTIAL LUMINOSITY (52), in which UP/DOWN-structured concepts include the opposition between light and darkness, which are, in turn, associated with the states of being awake and being asleep. This metaphor is at work in texts like Daniel 12:2–3 or *1 Enoch* 58:2–6, where the resurrected ones are represented as elevated and shining like celestial beings, and is also applicable to those accounts from the Synoptics that deal with eschatological resurrection. In this case, the state of the raised righteous in the eschatological resurrection is likened to the angelic/celestial state in order to demonstrate their immortality and eternal life. Since they were not martyred like Jesus or the Maccabean martyrs, there is no need for additional emphasis on the corporeality of this resurrection (Somov 2017, 214).

Finally, the metaphors LIFE IS UP and DEATH IS DOWN explain a quasi-spatial difference between the postmortem dwellings of the righteous and the wicked. As a rule, the abode of the righteous is represented in the Synoptics as a certain exalted position—as either in heaven (e.g., Luke 6:23; 10:20; 12:33; 16:9; 18:22) or just in a higher position than others (16:23). In Luke 16:23 the wicked and the righteous are separated in the otherworld not only by altitude but also by distance: the rich man looks up to see Abraham, who is far away, together with Lazarus in his bosom. The spatial difference metaphorically represents the difference in the afterlife status: the lower is worse. Moreover, this metaphorical differentiation correlates with the view of a "three-story universe" that was common in ancient cosmology: the dead (especially the wicked) are in the underworld (DOWN), the living are on the earth (MIDDLE), while God, the celestial world, and the blessed righteous are in the heavens (UP; Somov 2017, 218). Taking this view metaphorically, it is worth stating that "being in heaven" is rather a marker of belonging to the divine, celestial, or blessed realm than a geographical location.

REFERENCES

Allison, Dale C. 2008. "'After His Resurrection' (Matt 27,53) and the Descens ad inferos." In *Neutestamentliche Exegese im Dialog. Festschrift für Ulrich Luz zum 70. Geburtstag*, edited by Peter Lampe, Moisés Mayordomo, and Migaku Sato, 335–54. Neukirchen-Vluyn: Neukirchener.

Allison, Dale C. 2011. "The Scriptural Background of the Matthean Legend: Ezekiel 37, Zechariah 14, and Matthew 27." In *Life Beyond Death in Matthew's Gospel: Religious Metaphor or Bodily Reality?*, edited by Wim Weren, Huub van de Sandt, and Joseph Verheyden, Biblical Tools and Studies 13, 153–88. Leuven: Peeters.

Bauckham, Richard. 1991. "The Rich Man and Lazarus: The Parable and the Parallel." *New Testament Studies* 37: 225–46.

Black, Max. 1962. *Models and Metaphors*. Ithaca: Cornell University Press.

Borg, Marcus J., and John Dominic Crossan. 2006. *The Last Week: What the Gospels Really Teach about Jesus's Final Days in Jerusalem*. New York: HarperCollins.

Bovon, François. 1996. *Das Evangelium nach Lukas: 2. Teilband Lk 9,51–14,35*. Zürich: Benziger Verlag.

Bovon, François. 2008. *Das Evangelium nach Lukas: 4. Teilband Lk 19,28–24,53*. Neukirchen-Vluyn: Neukirchener Patmos.

Brown, Raymond E. 1973. *The Virginal Conception and Bodily Resurrection of Jesus*. London: Geoffrey Chapman.

Bultmann, Rudolf. 1931. *Die Geschichte der synoptischen Tradition* (1921). Göttingen: Vandenhoeck & Ruprecht.

Bultmann, Rudolf. 1951. *Theology of the New Testament*. Translated by K. Grobel. New York: Scribner's.

Cavallin, H. C. C. 1974. *Life after Death: Paul's Argument for the Resurrection of the Dead in 1 Cor 15. Pt. 1. An Enquiry into the Jewish Background*. Lund, Sweden: CWK Gleerup.

Collins, John J. 1960. "Reflections on Cullmann's Immortality of the Soul." *Catholic Biblical Quarterly* 22, no. 40: 410–16.

Collins, John J. 1999. "In the Likeness of the Holy Ones: the Creation of Humankind in a Wisdom Text from Qumran." In *The Provo International Conference on the Dead Sea Scrolls*, edited by Donald W. Parry and Eugene Ulrich, 609–18. Boston: Brill.

Conzelmann, Hans. 1954. *Die Mitte der Zeit. Studien zur Theologie des Lukas*. Tübingen: Mohr Siebeck.

Cranfield, C. E. B. 1959. *The Gospel According to St. Mark*. Cambridge Greek Testament Commentary. Cambridge: Cambridge University Press.

Cullmann, Oscar. 1958. *Immortality of the Soul or Resurrection of the Dead? The Witness of the New Testament*. London: Epworth.

Davies, J. G. 1958. *He Ascended into Heaven: A Study in the History of Doctrine*. London: Lutterworth.

Davies, W. D., and Dale C. Allison, J. 1997. *A Critical and Exegetical Commentary on the Gospel According to Saint Matthew*. Vol. 3. *Commentary on Matthew XIX–XXVIII*. International Critical Commentary. Edinburgh: T&T Clark.

Dibelius, Martin. 1971. *From Tradition to Gospel*. Translated by B. L. Woolf. Library of Theological Translations. Cambridge: James Clarke.

Downing, John. 1963. "Jesus and Martyrdom." *Journal of Theological Studies* 14, no. 2: 279–93.

Ehrman, Bart D. [1997] 2000. *The New Testament: A Historical Introduction to the Early Christian Writings*. Oxford: Oxford University Press.

Ellis, Earl E. 1974. *The Gospel of Luke*. Greenwood, SC: the Attic Press.

Endsjø, Dag Øistein. 2009. *Greek Resurrection Beliefs and the Success of Christianity*. New York: Palgrave Macmillan.

Esler, Philip Francis. 1987. *Community and Gospel in Luke-Acts: The Social and Political Motivations of Lucan Theology*. Society for New Testament Studies. Cambridge: Cambridge University Press.

Evans, C. F. 2008. *Saint Luke*. London: SCM Press.

Evans, Vyvyan. 2007. *A Glossary of Cognitive Linguistics*. Edinburgh: Edinburgh University Press.

Fauconnier, Gilles, and Mark Turner. 2002. *The Way We Think: Conceptual Blending and the Mind's Hidden Complexities*. New York: Basic Books.

Fitzmyer, Joseph A. 1985. *The Gospel According to Luke X–XXIV: Introduction, Translation and Notes*. Anchor Bible 28a. New York: Doubleday.

Fletcher-Louis, Crispin H. T. 1996. "4Q374: A Discourse on the Sinai Tradition: The Deification of Moses and Early Christology." *Dead Sea Discoveries* 3: 236–52.

Fletcher-Louis, Crispin H. T. 1997. *Luke-Acts: Angels, Christology and Soteriology*. Tübingen: Mohr Siebeck.

Frennesson, Björn. 1999. *In a Common Rejoicing: Liturgical Communion with Angels in Qumran*. Studia Semitica Upsaliensia. Uppsala: Uppsala University.

Goldstein, Jonathan A. 1983. *II Maccabees: A New Translation with Introduction and Commentary*. Anchor Bible 41A. New York: Doubleday.

Gould, Ezra P. 1912. *The Gospel According to St. Mark*. International and Exegetical Commentary. Edinburgh: T&T Clark.

Gressmann, Hugo. 1918. *Vom reichen Mann und armen Lazarus: Eine literargeschichtliche Studie*. Abhandlungen der Königlich preussischen Akademie der Wissenschaften: Philosophisch-historische Klasse 1918, no. 7. Berlin: Verlag der königlich Akademie der Wissenschaften.

Hagner, Donald A. 1998. *Matthew 14–28*. Word Biblical Commentary 33B. Dallas: Word.

Hamilton, N. Q. 1965. "Resurrection Tradition and the Composition of Mark." *Journal of Biblical Literature* 84, no. 4: 415–21.

Hengel, Martin. 1974. *Judaism and Hellenism: Studies in Their Encounter in Palestine during the Early Hellenistic Period*. Translated by J. Bowden. Philadelphia: Fortress.

Hock, R. F. 1987. "Lazarus and Mycyllus: Greco-Roman Backgrounds to Luke 16:19–31." *Journal of Biblical Literature* 106, no. 3: 447–63.

Holleman, Joost. 1998. *Resurrection and Parousia: A Traditio-historical Study of Paul's Eschatology in 1 Cor. 15:20–23*. Leiden: Brill.

Jeremias, Joachim. [1954] 1972. *The Parables of Jesus*. New York: Scribner's.

Johnson, Mark. 1987. *The Body in the Mind: The Bodily Basis of Meaning, Imagination, and Reason*. Chicago: University of Chicago Press.

Johnston, Philip S. 2002. *Shades of Sheol: Death and Afterlife in the Old Testament*. Downers Grove, IL: InterVarsity Press.

Jonge H.J. de. 1991. "De opstanding van Jezus. De joodse traditie achter een christelijke belijdenis." In *Jodendom en vroeg Christendom: Continuïteit en discontinuïtet*, edited by T. Baarda, H. J. de Jonge & M. J. J. Menken, 47–61. Kampen: Kok.

Jonge, Marinus de. 1988. "Jesus' Death for Others and the Death of the Maccabean Martyrs." In *Text and Testimony: Essays on New Testament and Apocryphal Literature in Honour of A. F. J. Klijn*, edited by T. Baarda, A. Hilhorst, G. P. Luttikhuizen, and A. S. van der Woude, 142–151. Kampen: Uitgeversmaatschappij J. H. Kok.

Jülicher, Adolf. 1899. *Die Gleichnisreden Jesu. Zweiter Teil: Auslegung der Gleichnisreden der drei ersten Evangelien*. Freiburg: Mohr Siebeck.

Kellermann, Ulrich. 1979. *Auferstanden in den Himmel. 1 Makkabäer 7 und die Auferstehung der Märtyrer*. Stuttgarter Bibel-Studien 95. Stuttgart: Katholisches Bibelwerk.

Kellermann, Ulrich. 1989. "Das Danielbuch und die Märtyrertheologie der Auferstehung." In *Die Entstehung der Jüdischen Martyrologie*, edited by J. W. van Henten, 51–75. Studia Post-Biblica. Leiden: Brill.

Kleinknecht, Karl Theodor. 1984. *Der leidende Gerechtfertigte: die alttestamentlich-jüdische Tradition vom 'leidenden Gerechten' und ihre Rezeption bei Paulus*. Tübingen: Mohr Siebeck.

Ladd, George Eldon. 1974. *The Presence of the Future: The Eschatology of Biblical Realism*. Grand Rapids: Eerdmans.

Lakoff, George. 2007. "The Contemporary Theory of Metaphor." In *The Cognitive Linguistics Reader*, edited by Vyvyan Evans, Benjamin K. Bergen, and Jörg Zinken, 264–315. London: Equinox.

Lakoff, George, and Mark Johnson. 1980. *Metaphors We Live By*. Chicago: University of Chicago Press.

Lehtipuu, Outi. 2007. *The Afterlife Imagery in Luke's Story of the Rich Man and Lazarus*. NovTSup 123. Leiden: Brill.

Lehtipuu, Outi. 2010. "Biblical Body Language: The Spiritual and Bodily Resurrection." In *Anthropology in the New Testament and Its Ancient Context*, edited by Michael Labahn and Outi Lehtipuu, 151–68. Leuven: Peeters.

Lehtipuu, Outi. 2015. *Debates over the Resurrection of the Dead: Constructing Early Christian Identity*. Oxford Early Christian Studies. Oxford: Oxford University Press.

Lohfink, Gerhard. 1971. *Die Himmelfahrt Jesu. Untersuchungen zu den Himmelfahrts- und Erhöhungstexten bei Lukas*. Studien zum Alten und Neuen Testament. Munich: Kösel.

Luz, Ulrich. 2005. *Matthew 21–28*. Translated by J. Crouch. Hermeneia. Minneapolis: Fortress.

MacCormack, E. R. 1985. *A Cognitive Theory of Metaphor*. Cambridge, MA: MIT Press.

Maddox, Robert. 1982. *The Purpose of Luke-Acts*. Göttingen: Vandenhoeck & Ruprecht.

Marshall, I. Howard. 1978. *The Gospel of Luke: A Commentary on the Greek Text*. New International Greek Testament Commentary. Grand Rapids: Eerdmans.

Martin, Dale B. 1995. *The Corinthian Body*. New Haven: Yale University.

Martin-Achard, Robert. 1956. *De la mort a la Résurrection d'après l'Ancien Testament*. Neuchatel: Delachaux & Niestlé.

Mattill, A. J., Jr. 1979. *Luke and the Last Things: A Perspective for the Understanding of Lukan Thought*. Dillsboro: Western North Carolina Press.

McAlpine, Thomas H. 1987. *Sleep, Divine and Human, in the Old Testament*. JSOTSup. Sheffield: JSOT Press.

McDonald, L. M. 2013. *The Story of Jesus in History and Faith: An Introduction*. Grand Rapids, MI: Baker Academic.

McNeile, Alan Hugh. 1915. *The Gospel according to St. Matthew*. London: Macmillan.

Meyer, R. 1966. "Κόλπος." In *Theological Dictionary of the New Testament*, edited by Gerhard Kittel and Gerhard Friedrich, translated by Geoffrey W. Bromiley, vol. 3, 824–26. Grand Rapids: Eerdmans.

Milikowski, C. 1988. 'Which Gehenna? Retribution and Eschatology in the Synoptic Gospels and in Early Jewish Texts', *NTS* 34: 238–49.

Nickelsburg, George W. E. [1972] 2006. *Resurrection, Immortality, and Eternal Life in Intertestamental Judaism and Early Christianity*. Expanded ed. Cambridge, MA: Harvard University Press.

Nolland, John. 1993a. *Luke 9:21–18:34*. Word Biblical Commentary 35B. Dallas: Word Books.

Nolland, John. 1993b. *Luke 18:35–24:53*. Word Biblical Commentary 35C. Dallas: Word Books.

Nolland, John. 2005. *The Gospel of Matthew: A Commentary on the Greek Text*. New International Greek Testament Commentary. Grand Rapids: Eerdmans.

Perdue, Leo G. 1991. *Wisdom in Revolt: Metaphorical Theology in the Book of Job*. JSOTSup. Sheffield: JSOT Press.

Pereira, Francisco Câmara. 2007. *Creativity and Artificial Intelligence: A Conceptual Blending Approach*. Berlin: De Gruyter.

Perkins, Pheme. 1984. *Resurrection: New Testament Witness and Contemporary Reflection*. Garden City, NY: Doubleday.

Pesch, Rudolf. 1986. *Die Apostelgeschichte (Apg 1–12)*. Evangelisch-katholischer Kommentar zum Neuen Testament 5.1. Neukirchen: Neukirchener.

Pokorný, Petr, and U. Heckel. 2007. *Einleitung in das Neue Testament: Seine Literatur und Theologie im Überblick*. Tübingen: Mohr Siebeck.

Plummer, Alfred. 1896. *Gospel According to S. Luke*. International Critical Commentary. Edinburgh: T&T Clark.

Pollard, T. E. 1972. "Martyrdom and Resurrection in the New Testament." *Bulletin of the John Rylands Library* 55, no.1: 240–51.

Richards, I. A. 1936. *The Philosophy of Rhetoric*. New York: Oxford University Press.

Rohde, Erwin. 1925. *Psyche: The Cult of Souls and Belief in Immortality among the Greeks*. Translated by W. B. Hillis. London: Kegan Paul, Trench, Trubner.

Ruppert, Lothar. 1972. *Jesus als der leidende Gerechte? Der Weg Jesu im Lichte eines alt- und zwischentestamentlichen Motivs*. Stuttgart: Katholisches Bibelwerk.

Schweizer, Eduard. 1982. *Das Evangelium nach Lukas*. Göttingen: Vandenhoeck & Ruprecht.

Scott, Alan. 1991. *Origen and the Life of the Stars: A History of an Idea*. Oxford: Clarendon.

Segal, Alan F. 2004. *Life after Death: A History of the Afterlife in the Religions of the West*. New York: Doubleday.

Seim, Turid Karlsen. 1994. *The Double Message: Patterns of Gender in Luke-Acts*. Edinburgh: T&T Clark.

Seim, Turid Karlsen. 1999. "Children of the Resurrection: Perspectives on Angelic Asceticism in Luke-Acts." In *Asceticism and the New Testament*, edited by Leif E. Vaage and Vincent L. Wimbush, 115–25. New York: Routledge.

Seim, Turid Karlsen. 2009. "The Resurrected Body in Luke-Acts: The Significance of Space." In *Metamorphoses: Resurrection, Body and Transformative Practices in Early Christianity*, edited by Turid Karlsen Seim and Jorunn Økland, 19–39. Berlin: De Gruyter.

Smith, Dennis Edwin. 2003. *From Symposium to Eucharist: The Banquet in the Early Christian World*. Minneapolis: Fortress.

Somov, Alexey. 2014. "'He Lifted Up His Eyes': Translating Luke 16:23 in the Context of Cognitive Interpretation." *Journal of Biblical Text Research* 35: 291–309.

Somov, Alexey. 2017. *Representations of the Afterlife in Luke-Acts*. International Studies on Christian Origins. London: Bloomsbury T&T Clark.

Somov, Alexey. 2021. "Resurrection of the Righteous Sufferers in the New Testament: The Case of Matt 27:52–53." In *The Gospel of Matthew in Its Historical and Theological Context. Papers from the International Conference in Moscow, September 24 to 28, 2018*, edited by Mikhail Seleznev, William R. G. Loader, and Karl-Wilhelm Niebuhr, 365–80. Wissenschaftliche Untersuchungen zum Neuen Testament. Tübingen: Mohr Siebeck.

Somov, Alexey, and Vitaly Voinov. 2017. "Translating 'Abraham's Bosom' (Luke 16:22–23) as a Key Metaphor in the Overall Composition of the Parable of the Rich Man and Lazarus." *Catholic Biblical Quarterly* 79, no. 4: 615–33.

Soskice, Janet Martin. 1985. *Metaphor and Religious Language*. Oxford: Clarendon Press.

Talbert, Charles H. 1974. *Literary Patterns, Theological Themes, and the Genre of Luke-Acts*. SBL Monograph Series 20. Missoula: Scholars Press.

Tappenden, Frederick S. 2012. "Luke and Paul in Dialogue: Ritual Meals and Risen Bodies as Instances of Embodied Cognition." In *Resurrection of the Dead: Biblical Traditions in Dialogue*, edited by Geert van Oyen, Tom Shepherd, Bibliotheca Ephemeridum Theologicarum Lovaniensium 249, 201–28. Leuven: Peeters.

Tappenden, Frederick S. 2016. *Resurrection in Paul: Cognition, Metaphor, and Transformation*. Early Christianity and Its Literature 19. Atlanta: SBL.

Tromp, Johannes. 2007. "'Can These Bones Live?' Ezekiel 37:1-14 and Eschatological Resurrection." In *The Book of Ezekiel and Its Influence*, edited by Henk Jan de Jonge and Johannes Tromp, 61–78. Burlington, VT: Ashgate.

Van der Watt, Jan G. 2000. *Family of the King: Dynamics of Metaphor in the Gospel According to John*. Biblical Interpretation Series. Leiden: Brill.

Waters, Kenneth L. S. 2003. "Matthew 27:52-53 as Apocalyptic Apostrophe: Temporal-Spatial Collapse in the Gospel of Matthew." *Journal of Biblical Literature* 122, no. 3: 489–515.

Weren, Wim. 2011. "Matthew's Stories about Jesus' Bural and Resurrection (27:55-28:20) as the Climax of His Gospel." In *Life Beyond Death in Matthew's Gospel: Religious Metaphor or Bodily Reality?*, edited by Wim Weren, Huub van de Sandt, and Joseph Verheyden, Biblical Tools and Studies 13, 189–200. Leuven: Peeters.

Wessel, Walter W. 1984. "Mark." In *The Expositor's Bible Commentary*, vol. 8, *Matthew, Mark, Luke*, edited by Frank E. Gaebelein, 603–793. Grand Rapids: Zondervan.

Wright, N. T. 2003. *The Resurrection of the Son of God*. Minneapolis: Fortress.

Zwiep, A. W. 1997. *The Ascension of the Messiah in Luke Christology*. NovTSup. New York: Brill.

Zwiep, A. W. 2010. *Christ, the Spirit, and the Community of God*. WUNT 2. Tübingen: Mohr Siebeck.

CHAPTER 24

GOSPEL

JOSHUA D. GARROWAY

INTRODUCTION

In Christian circles today, few words rival "gospel" in their ubiquity. There are gospel choirs, gospel churches, gospel meetings, and gospel ministries. There is gospel music and gospel art. Pastors and missionaries preach the gospel; churchgoers hear the gospel; and, of course, there are the Gospels themselves: Matthew, Mark, Luke, and John. The term has even acquired currency in non-Christian contexts. Information from a trusted source is often said to be taken "as gospel," while any constellation of beliefs and commitments zealously adhered to might be deemed a gospel. Samuel Hays's *Conservation and the Gospel of Efficiency* (1999), for example, has nothing to do with Christianity.

The pervasiveness of "gospel" in contemporary English stands in stark contrast with the relative rarity of the word in the Greek-speaking world in which Christianity emerged. "Gospel" comes from the Old English *godspel*, a medieval rendering (by way of Latin) of the Greek εὐαγγέλιον. Though not unheard-of in classical Greek, the εὐαγγελ- root was hardly common parlance. Of the approximately 20,000 occurrences of such words known from ancient Greek texts, nearly all of them are found in Christian sources after the first century (Mason 2008). Only a smattering come from the likes of Homer, Demosthenes, the Septuagint, Josephus, Philo, or Plutarch. Christianity, in other words, turned a somewhat obscure Greek term into the foundation of its faith and, over time, into a household word.

When, where, how, and why this linguistic phenomenon occurred have drawn the attention of biblical scholars for more than a century. The answer, though complicated, can ultimately be summed up in two names: Paul and Mark.

Gospel BCE

In Greek sources prior to the rise of Christianity, the rare occurrences of εὐαγγελ- terminology describe activity related to a εὐάγγελος, a messenger bearing news—sometimes "good" (εὐ-) news, but not necessarily (Bultmann 2007; Dickson 2005; Friedrich 1964; Koester 1990). The verb εὐαγγελίζομαι describes the act of proclaiming the messenger's tidings; the noun εὐαγγέλιον refers either to the news itself or to the reward the messenger receives. The message often has to do with military success. Plutarch (*Sert*.11.4), for example, speaks of Quintus Sertorius's peculiar habit of parading a garlanded doe before his troops upon hearing the good news of a triumph, while elsewhere (*Glor. Ath.* 3 [347D]) he remarks on the Spartan custom of providing meat to the man who brings news of victory from the battlefield. The translators of the Septuagint deploy the term similarly when rendering the Hebrew root בשר in the Former Prophets. The Amalekite hopes for a reward (בשרה/εὐαγγελία) when reporting the good news (מבשר/εὐαγγελιζόμενης) of Saul's death to David (2 Sam 4:10; 18:22), while Jonathan, son of Abiathar, ironically brings the good news (מבשר/εὐαγγέλισαι) of Solomon's anointing to Adonijah's feast (1 Kgs 1:42).

The distribution of the εὐαγγελ- root in non-Christian Greek is noteworthy. Among the nouns, the plural εὐαγγέλια outnumbers the singular. The singular, neuter noun occurs but seven times in non-Christian Greek. Even more remarkably, all but one of those occurrences lack the definite article; the lone example of the singular, articular noun comes in Plutarch's account of a messenger sent by Demetrius bearing news of a victory at Cyprus (*Demetr.* 17.5). Plutarch composed *Parallel Lives* in the first two decades of the second century, which means that the singular, articular, neuter noun may not even have existed when the earliest Christian author whose work survives today, Paul, used it a whopping forty-three times in his uncontested epistles. Where, then, did Paul acquire this neologism, and why did it emerge within the Christian community?

The Gospel CE

Scholars have spent more than a century debating the merits of the two most likely derivations of εὐαγγέλιον. (1) One group contends that the earliest followers of Jesus, and perhaps even Jesus himself, used the Hebrew term בשורה, or the Aramaic בשורתא, to denote the coming kingdom about which they preached, and their Hellenistic associates subsequently rendered the word in Greek with εὐαγγέλιον. (2) Another group points to the εὐαγγελ- terminology in the propaganda that sustained the Roman imperial cult.

The first view is often associated with Adolf von Harnack, who defended it in an influential essay at the close of *The Constitution and Law of the Church in the First Two*

Centuries (1910).¹ Since then, many others have refined the arguments (Bird 2014; Burrows 1925; Horbury 2005; Stuhlmacher 1968). They note, for example, that the earliest account of the ministry of Jesus—namely, Mark—portrays Jesus proclaiming the "gospel of God" and instructing his listeners to believe in it (Mark 1:14–15). Moreover, several of the prophecies in Second Isaiah that appear to have shaped first-century Jewish eschatology describe the reign of God and the salvation of Israel with verbal forms of בשר (Bird 2014; Dunn 1998). If the earliest followers of Jesus drew upon these prophecies to account for their experience of Jesus, they might well have characterized their message as בשורה/בשורתא.

Reservations are in order, however. In the first place, redactional analysis of Mark indicates that the appearance of the word εὐαγγέλιον on the lips of Jesus more likely stems from an editorial hand than from sayings originating with Jesus (Marxsen 1969). Considering also that the term is absent in Q, one finds no convincing evidence of a tradition in which Jesus uses the word. A further problem is the terminology in Isaiah itself. Whereas verbal forms of בשר abound, the noun never appears. Even if the first followers of Jesus described their activity using the verbal forms of בשר—and I will suggest that they probably did—there would be no prophetic precedent for labeling their proclamation using the noun בשורה and no biblical precedent whatsoever for the articular noun הבשורה. Still further, in the unlikely event that they did call their proclamation (ה)בשורה or בשורתא, their Greek-speaking associates would scarcely have rendered this expression with τὸ εὐαγγέλιον. Had they drawn on the Septuagint, these Hellenistic Jews would have chosen the peculiar feminine singular εὐαγγελία; had they drawn on the wider Greek milieu, they would have chosen the far more popular neuter plural, εὐαγγέλια. Tracing Christian usage of εὐαγγέλιον back to a Semitic antecedent and/or to the Septuagint thus hypothesizes a sequence of possible, but unlikely, linguistic developments (Koester 1990).

Situating the origin of εὐαγγέλιον in Christian appropriation of language from the Roman imperial cult has also been both promising and problematic. Frequently cited to corroborate this approach is the so-called Priene inscription, one of many proclamations posted throughout Asia in the first century BCE instituting the new Julian calendar.² In it, the birthday of Augustus is celebrated as "'good news' for the world." Gospel appears here in the neuter plural (εὐαγγέλια), as it does in several other inscriptions and literary sources related to the imperial cult (Horsley 1983; Stanton 2004). At first glance, these uniformly plural forms might appear to undermine the likelihood that Greek-speaking followers of Jesus, who used the singular form exclusively, took their gospel terminology from the cult; yet the discrepancy might rather reflect a polemical appropriation. Whereas imperial propaganda would speak of multiple glad tidings in the life of a Caesar—birth, accession, military triumph, and so on—followers of Christ made but one bold proclamation about their redeemer, and they highlighted this distinction

---

[1] The scholarly pedigree for this view stretches back at least as far as Hugo Grotius (Horbury 2005).
[2] Stanton (2004, 325–33) offers a brief, helpful overview of the Priene inscription as well as other literary and epigraphic evidence related to the use of the εὐαγγελ- root in the imperial cult.

by shifting to the singular form. As Graham N. Stanton puts it, "the life, salvation, and resurrection of Jesus was God's 'once for all' disclosure of 'the one glad tiding'" (2004, 34). Amid the numerous imperial gospels (τὰ εὐαγγέλια), followers of Jesus laid claim to the one, true gospel (τὸ εὐαγγέλιον).

The shortcoming of this approach is obvious: neither Paul, nor Mark, nor Matthew, nor any other early Christian author mentions the imperial gospels or defines his own understanding of εὐαγγέλιον against them. Is it possible that imperial propaganda stands in the background? Of course. But absent any explicit connection in Christian sources, and in light of the shift from the (almost) exclusively plural usage in the cult to the exclusively singular usage among Christians, a measure of suspicion is inescapable. Even Stanton (2004, 35), a staunch proponent of this view, concedes that the evidence allows one to say only that the gospel terminology of early Christianity would have been "heard against the backdrop of the imperial cult." As for the origin of Christian usage, he goes on to say: "I do not think that we can be certain."

The same is true of the first approach. Once Christians began to use gospel terminology, surely some of them would have heard that proclamation against the backdrop of Isaiah's prophecies; however, the evidence does not warrant a confident claim about the Hebrew בשורה as the origin of εὐαγγέλιον. For good reason, it seems, Ernst Käsemann (1980, 6–7) wrote in his commentary on Romans: "in spite of much solid research in the last generation, the derivation and concrete meaning of the singular τὸ εὐαγγέλιον used absolutely have still not been satisfactorily explained" (see also Bultmann 2007 and Frankemölle 1988).

A New Way Forward: Paul as Founder and Proprietor of the Gospel

A third alternative has emerged recently that focuses squarely on the earliest witness to the word εὐαγγέλιον in a Christian context, namely Paul. What if Paul himself coined the neologism? Moreover, what if he deployed the word not as a descriptor of the general message about Christ that he shared with other apostles but rather to distinguish his own preaching from that of his peers?

Steve Mason championed both of these propositions in a provocative 2008 essay.[3] He paid particular attention to the peculiarly proprietary language Paul employs when speaking about the gospel. In letter after letter, Paul mentions "my gospel" (Rom 2:16; 16:25), "our gospel" (1 Thess 1:5), "the gospel that I preached" (1 Cor 15:1), and the gospel

---

[3] Mason was not the first to suggest that Paul introduced the term εὐαγγέλιον to believers in Christ. Dunn (1998, 168) suggested as much a decade earlier, and reiterated that view subsequently (Dunn 2013, 291–93). Bultmann (2007, 1:87–88) hints at it: "whether the absolute use is earlier than Paul cannot be said with certainty."

with which he and his colleagues were "entrusted" (1 Thess 2:4; Gal 2:7). He sees it as his personal mission to preach the gospel (Gal 2:2) and to defend it (Gal 2:5; Rom 1:16; Phil 1:7) against those who would oppose it (Gal 1:6–7; 2:14). In his letter to the Romans, Paul complements this proprietary language with an insistence that the teaching of rival preachers in Christ's name does not constitute the gospel. They offer rather "some sort of teaching" (Rom 6:1), which is why the Gentiles in Rome remain to be "reaped" (Rom 1:13) by the gospel.

Mason recognized that two passages from Paul's pen, 1 Corinthians 15:1–3 and Galatians 2:7–9, require attention before concluding that Paul's proprietary language about the gospel means that he saw the gospel as exclusively his own (2008, 289–91). In the first, Paul tells the Corinthians that "the gospel I preached to you" was "that which I also received." Paul's language of "receiving and delivering" the gospel corresponds to Greek and rabbinic texts describing chains of tradition, leading most commentators to assume that Paul here acknowledges that he received the gospel from the apostles who preceded him (Conzelmann 1975; Fee 1987; Hays 1997). On the contrary, Mason shows, Paul elsewhere proclaims with unmistakable emphasis that he received the gospel directly from Christ: "I want you to know," he tells the Galatians, "that the gospel preached by me is not from a human being. I did not receive it from a human being; nor was I taught it, but it came to me through a revelation from Jesus Christ" (Gal 1:11–12). Against the objection that Paul could not have believed that he received from Christ so detailed a kerygma as the one put forth in 1 Corinthians 15:3–7, Mason observes that Paul claims to have experienced several revelations over the course of his career, some of which revealed detailed knowledge (1 Thess 4:13–18; 1 Cor 11:23–26; 1 Cor 15:51–58; 2 Cor 12:2–9). Accordingly, 1 Corinthians 15:1–3 need not imply that Paul received the gospel from a human source.

Likewise, Galatians 2:7–9 does not require that Paul acknowledged the right of apostles outside his orbit to preach the gospel. Although translators often make these verses say something like "I had been entrusted with the gospel for the uncircumcised, just as Peter had been entrusted with the gospel for the circumcised" (NRSV), Paul never explicitly associates Peter with gospel. He says, rather, "I had been entrusted with the gospel for the uncircumcised, just as Peter . . . for the circumcised." Paul might have elided the second "gospel" for the sake of brevity, as many commentators suppose (e.g., Betz 1979; Martyn 1997), but he also might have done so intentionally to avoid conceding that Peter's message is, in fact, the gospel. Indeed, Paul includes a parallel ellipsis in the following verse, faltering before identifying himself as an apostle: "He who worked through Peter for the apostleship to the circumcision also worked through me . . . for the Gentiles." Interpreters sometimes assume that Paul hesitates here intentionally, a tacit admission that the pillars had not recognized him as a legitimate apostle at the Jerusalem Conference (e.g., Betz 1979; Martyn 1997). If so, then perhaps the ellipsis in the preceding verse reflects Paul's reciprocal unwillingness to recognize Peter's preaching among Jews as a legitimate manifestation of the gospel. Paul uses the elisions to suggest that his gospel corresponds to Peter's apostleship. Peter no more preaches the gospel than Paul preaches as a deputized apostle. On this reading, Galatians 2:7–9 becomes evidence favoring, not opposing, the view that Paul considered the gospel to be uniquely his.

If it is true that Paul conceived and named the gospel sometime during his career as a preacher in Christ, when and where would this momentous development have taken place? Paul may provide precise answers to these questions in his epistle to the Philippians. He closes that letter by recalling the support the Philippians provided him during and after his initial visit to their city, a time he labels "the beginning of the gospel" (ἐν ἀρχῇ τοῦ εὐαγγελίου). The statement forms an *inclusio*, or rhetorical framing, with Philippians 1:5, in which Paul opens the letter by praising the Philippians for their "fellowship in the gospel from the first day until now" (ἐπὶ τῇ κοινωνίᾳ ὑμῶν εἰς τὸ εὐαγγέλιον ἀπὸ τῆς πρώτης ἡμέρας ἄχρι τοῦ νῦν). Although translators and commentators typically render the phrase in Philippians 4:15 as "the early days of the gospel" (NRSV), "the early days of your acquaintance with the gospel" (NIV), or some other expression intimating that Paul's visit to Philippi did not mark the initial launch of the gospel itself, Paul appears to say straightforwardly that his ministry in Macedonia was the "beginning," or the "first day," of the gospel.[4] In other words, the gospel came into existence around the time Paul first trekked westward through Macedonia. This is probably why Paul (or pseudo-Paul) refers to the believers in Thessaloniki, the Macedonian city just to the west of Philippi, as the "first-fruits of salvation" (2 Thess 2:13)—that is, the first-fruits of the gospel.

Presuming the sort of Pauline chronology put forth in recent years by Robert Jewett (1979), Gerd Luedemann (1984), Jerome Murphy-O'Connor (1996), and Douglas Campbell (2014), in which Paul's initial sojourn in Macedonia occurred after his departure for Syria and Cilicia (Gal 1:21) but before his return to Jerusalem fourteen years later (Gal 2:1), Paul will have arrived in Philippi with the gospel following several years of preaching in Arabia, Damascus, Syria, Cilicia, and possibly southern Galatia. What, then, was Paul preaching about in those early years, if not the gospel? How did the gospel differ from his original message? Paul again appears to provide specific answers, this time in his letter to the Galatians. Responding to the curious accusation that he encourages circumcision (despite his vociferous objection to it in the letter), Paul says: "if, brethren, I still preach circumcision, why am I still being persecuted?" (Gal 5:11). The adverb ἔτι ("still") packs a punch, for it implies that Paul had, in fact, promoted circumcision at an earlier point in his career (Campbell 2009). Is it possible that Paul, following the revelation in which he turned from persecutor of Christ to follower, initially instructed his Gentile charges to enter the covenant of Israel by submitting to the yoke

---

[4] According to Delling (1964, 1:481–82), "in the NT ἀρχή is most frequently used for 'beginning' ... so that it simply denotes the first point of time according to the context." Commentators often suppose that Paul means "the beginning of the gospel" for the Philippians (Bruce 1983; Fee 1995; Michaelis 1935). Others say Paul meant the beginning of his ministry in Europe (Lohmeyer 1953) or without Barnabas (Gnilka 1976). Capper (1993) argues that Paul saw his departure from Philippi as the beginning of the gospel because in that city he had forged an agreement ensuring the financial support needed to press westward. Suggs (1960) suggests that Paul's ministry actually began in Philippi, an intriguing proposal that nonetheless fails to account for Gal 1:21–23.

of Torah? Is it possible that the upshot of the gospel Paul eventually conceived was to announce, by contrast, that Gentiles baptized into Christ enjoy freedom from the Law and circumcision?

Paul's epistles indicate as much. First and foremost is the letter to the Galatians, a diatribe against circumcision couched as a defense of the gospel. There are no other gospels, Paul insists, and to circumcise a baptized Gentile, as his adversaries in Galatia would do, represents a fundamental breach of the gospel's proclamation. Paul highlights this point by acclaiming his refusal to circumcise Titus as a valiant act of defiance that exemplified "the freedom we have in Jesus Christ" and preserved "the truth of the gospel" (Gal 2:4-5). Similarly, when Peter withdrew from the communal table in Antioch, thereby indicating that Gentiles would have to become circumcised should they wish to enjoy table fellowship with him and his Jewish colleagues, Paul claims to have reprimanded Peter for controverting "the truth of the gospel" (Gal 2:14). Romans also presents itself as a vigorous defense of the gospel, and it, too, constructs an elaborate argument to demonstrate the foolishness of Gentile submission to the Torah. Paul's other letters, though less polemical in the main, likewise feature segments in which Paul addresses the obsolescence of the Law (2 Cor 3), the folly of Gentile circumcision (Phil 3:2), and the shortcomings of rivals who preach phony, Law-oriented alternatives to the gospel (2 Cor 11).

All in all, then, a welter of evidence supports the hypothesis that Paul, midway through his career, coined the term "gospel" to designate his novel insight regarding the availability of salvation through Christ outside the Law. Drawing upon Paul's autobiographical remarks in Galatians 1:11-2:14, the following sequence of events suggests itself. (1) Following the crucifixion, the original disciples of Jesus began to publicize their belief in the resurrection amongst Jews in Judea and Galilee, drawing upon the biblical verb בשר to describe their eschatological activity. (2) Soon thereafter, believers in Greek-speaking venues used the verb εὐαγγελίζομαι to describe the same activity. (3) Within a few years, and probably in Damascus or Antioch, believers began to approach Gentiles with the report of Christ's imminent return, encouraging these Gentiles, many of whom were affiliated with synagogues already, to join Israel in the final hour by submitting to the yoke of the Torah. (4) Paul joined the ranks of this Gentile mission following a purported revelation (Gal 1:15-16) and pressed its cause in Syria, Cilicia, and possibly southern Galatia—the enterprise he would later call "preaching circumcision" (Gal 5:11), "preaching Christ" (Gal 1:16), and "preaching the faith" (Gal 1:23). (5) While engaged in this mission, Paul experienced another revelation (Gal 1:11-12), in which Christ told him that Gentiles need not submit to the Law or be circumcised to be saved. (6) Drawing on the verb εὐαγγελίζομαι, Paul labeled this momentous innovation τὸ εὐαγγέλιον, "*the* gospel," and sought out a virgin mission field in which to proclaim it. (7) Paul introduced the gospel in Philippi, Thessaloniki, Athens, Corinth, and possibly elsewhere (Phil 4:15) before returning to Jerusalem to defend the gospel against its detractors in the East (Gal 2:1). (8) the recognition of the gospel Paul secured in Jerusalem (Gal 2:7-10) was undermined shortly thereafter when Peter withdrew from the table in Antioch, thereby suggesting that uncircumcised Gentile men could not participate fully in believing communities (Gal 2:11–14). (9) Paul and his adversaries traded barbs as they competed for the allegiance of Gentile believers in Asia, Macedonia, and Achaea, the period during which all seven uncontested epistles originated. (10) Paul arranged a visit to Rome and dispatched a thoroughgoing defense of the gospel in advance.

What happened to Paul thereafter is anyone's guess, except to say that he died within a few years of composing Romans. When he did, the gospel was still closely identified with him. Already by the early to mid-50s CE, Paul's rivals were capitalizing on his success and on the currency of the new term by calling their competing messages gospels, as Galatians 1:6–9 and 2 Corinthians 11:4 suggest; yet anyone familiar with the events of the preceding decade would have known that *the* gospel was Paul's gospel, the liberating message of salvation through Christ outside the Law.

Gospel in the Gospels

In time, of course, the term *gospel* would lose its association with Paul. By the middle of the second century, εὐαγγέλιον would refer alternatively to the general message of Christianity, to the preachment of Jesus himself, and to the several books in which the teachings and deeds of Jesus were recorded. Much as the first stage in the development of "gospel" in Christianity traces back to a single figure, Paul, so, too, the next stage owes its development to one person, namely Mark.

Mark

Writing a decade or so after the death of Paul, Mark opens his account of the ministry, death, and resurrection of Jesus with the statement "the beginning of the gospel of Jesus Christ" (Mark 1:1). He goes on to use the term six more times, in each case as a part of the teaching of Jesus himself. Jesus arrives in Galilee preaching the gospel and urging listeners to believe in it (Mark 1:14–15); he praises those who would lose their lives or abandon their families for the sake of the gospel (Mark 8:35; 10:29); he speaks of the gospel being "preached to all nations" when the disciples face persecution (Mark 13:10); and he says that the deed of the woman who anoints him will be told in remembrance of her "wherever the gospel is preached in the whole world" (Mark 14:9).

By most accounts, Mark's incorporation of "gospel" into his arrangement of Jesus traditions signals a transformation in the semantic range of the word. Whereas εὐαγγέλιον had referred, as Adela Yarbro Collins puts it, to "the oral announcement and explanation of the salvific significance of the life and work of Jesus, especially his death and resurrection" (2007, 130), Mark uses the word to refer also to the deeds and teachings of Jesus. Mark by no means obviates the original meaning, as indicated in his account by the prominence of the passion narrative, the threefold prediction of Christ's suffering and death, and the several other adumbrations of the passion interspersed throughout (Dunn 2013). In other words, Mark styles his account "the gospel of Jesus Christ" in part because it gives written expression to the oral proclamation about the death and resurrection of Jesus already in circulation. At the same time, Mark suggests, it is also "the gospel of Jesus Christ" because it includes the message imparted by the recorded deeds and sayings of Jesus. Still further, it is "the gospel of Jesus Christ" because it constitutes the very message of Jesus himself (Dunn 2013; Pekorný 2013).

Why Mark undertook so radical a recasting of the gospel is not clear. Some interpreters resolve this conundrum by proposing that Mark's treatment of the term was not as groundbreaking as it seems. Already before Mark, it is argued, perhaps even as early as Jesus himself, followers of Jesus understood the sayings and deeds of Jesus as components of the gospel (Bird 2014; Dunn 2013; Stanton 2004). Mark merely represents developments that had taken shape before him. Underplaying Mark's apparent creativity fails to account for two crucial pieces of evidence, however. First, as noted earlier, neither Q nor the Jesus traditions inherited by Mark featured the word εὐαγγέλιον, an unlikely prospect if the sayings and deeds of Jesus had been connected to the gospel before Mark picked up his pen. Second, the figure so closely associated with the gospel in extant writings, Paul, appears famously unconcerned with stories about Jesus or sayings attributed to him.

Once it is recognized that the gospel was not the general proclamation about Jesus preached by early believers but was Paul's specific announcement about salvation through Christ outside the Law, then Mark's novel deployment of εὐαγγέλιον makes sense. Mark, it turns out, may well have been an admirer of Paul.[5] If so, his integration of the gospel into the Jesus tradition reflects his effort to defend Paul's legacy, to reinforce the validity of the gospel by attributing it to Jesus himself rather than to a one-time persecutor whose apostolic credentials were never fully acknowledged. It was not Paul who first conceived the gospel, Mark tells his readers; it was Jesus. Jesus knew the gospel, taught the gospel, and tried to impart the gospel to his disciples.

Unfortunately, as Mark demonstrates ad nauseam, the disciples proved too dimwitted to understand the gospel when it was first revealed. Mark's unflattering representation of the disciples remains one of the most curious aspects of his account.[6] Beginning with their failure to understand the parables (Mark 4:13), the disciples appear unceasingly obtuse: in Mark 4:40, they fail to recognize that Jesus can still the storm; in Mark 6:37, they do not understand that Jesus can multiply food; in Mark 6:52, they do not understand the loaves; in Mark 8:4, they fail—again—to recognize that Jesus can multiply food. Then, on three separate occasions—Mark 8:27-33, 9:30-32, 10:33-45—they misunderstand a

---

[5] The influence of Paul on Mark has resurfaced as a contentious issue. Twentieth-century scholarship was largely guided by Martin Werner's claim that "not in the least can there be the influence of Pauline theology in the Gospel of Mark" (1923, 209). Since then, a measure of Pauline influence has been proposed by Bacon (1925), Fenton (1957), Goulder (1991), Telford (1999), and most notably Marcus (2000). Recent consideration of the issue appears in Wischmeyer et al. (2014) and Becker et al. (2014). See Ferguson chapter 5 here.

[6] Similarly noteworthy is the unflattering treatment Mark affords the family of Jesus. Recently, see Sim 2014.

prediction of the passion. Following the transfiguration, they fail to grasp the meaning of resurrection from the dead. They are routinely branded as faithless and hard-hearted (Mark 4:40, 6:52, 8:17–18; 9:19–20). By the book's end their leader, Peter, has been called Satan by his master (Mark 8:33), has denied his master three times (Mark 14:72), and has joined the other disciples in deserting their master in the final hour (Mark 14:50). It is a devastating defamation from start to finish, which Mark brings into even bolder relief by peppering his account with minor characters—the centurion, for example—who readily demonstrate faith and discernment.[7]

Interpreters disinclined to see Mark's vilification of the disciples as an end in itself often suggest that the unflattering portrayal serves a more noble purpose. The obtuseness of the disciples provides Jesus with opportunities to repeat and elaborate on his teachings, it is said, while their cowardice and faithlessness give strength to believers in Mark's community who struggle similarly in their new faith.[8] Such explanations fail to convince, however, given the unrelenting nature of Mark's disparagement and the simple fact that the disciples are not rehabilitated in the end. In Mark, recall, the disciples do not return in the final chapter to witness the resurrected Jesus, a reconciliation that might encourage readers to think that all has been forgiven. Instead, Mark's witless disciples abandon Jesus, never to be heard from again.

Mark's treatment of the disciples makes more sense if he was bent on making the disciples look bad, pure, and simple. What sort of author would entertain such a hope? Certainly not someone well-disposed toward the leadership of the Jerusalem community. A devotee of Paul on the other hand might be inclined to criticize the likes of Peter and John, the Jerusalem pillars who failed to understand the gospel when Jesus taught it to them, and failed just the same when Paul shared it with them years later.

Were this the case, one would expect Mark to include in his account, in addition to the suffering, death, and resurrection of Jesus, the two uniquely Pauline tenets of the gospel—to wit, the annulment of the ceremonial requirements of the Law and a mission to Gentiles. Sure enough, both materialize in the middle of the narrative, the one leading to the other. In Mark 7:1–23, he construes Jesus's enigmatic maxim about purity as a declaration that all foods are clean. Mark's interpretation is probably inaccurate, but whatever this saying originally meant, and whether Jesus ever said it, Mark needed to find something in the Jesus tradition that he could spin into a rejection of the dietary restrictions in the Law. Having declared all foods clean, Jesus departs for Tyre to initiate a mission in Gentile territory (Mark 7:24–30), an enterprise for which Mark previously had paved the way with the exorcism of the Gerasene demoniac (Mark 5:1–20).

---

[7] See Cook 2018. A full list of such minor characters might include: the centurion (Mark 15:39); Simon of Cyrene (Mark 15:21); Joseph of Arimathea (Mark 15:43–46); the eager crowds (Mark 5:25; 6:34; 11:18; 12:37); the father of the demoniac (Mark 9:23–24); the anointing woman (Mark 14:3–9); the young man at Gethsemane (Mark 14:51–52); and the women at the tomb (Mark 16:1–8).

[8] As an example of the former, "pedagogical" approach, see Best 1977; of the latter, "pastoral" approach, see Tannehill 1977.

The abrogation of the Law, the Gentile mission, the disparagement of the undiscerning Jerusalem pillars, the gospel preached "in the whole world" (Mark 14:9) and "to all nations" (Mark 13:10)—the shadow of Paul hangs over Mark because the account is not a mere arrangement of Jesus traditions as Mark found them; it is a carefully crafted defense of Paul and the gospel. A younger Mark no doubt knew of the treatment Paul endured in the late 40s and early 50s, when the gospel was dismissed by Paul's opponents as the unsanctioned creation of a belated and uncredentialed apostle. Au contraire, Mark insists, the gospel had been proclaimed and acted out by Jesus himself, and Christ's eventual recruitment of Paul would have been unnecessary if only the so-called pillars had proved capable of understanding it. As such, the "beginning of the gospel" (Phil 4:15) did not occur when Paul first entered Philippi preaching it; rather, "the beginning of the gospel" (Mark 1:1) occurred when Jesus first entered Galilee preaching it.

Not everyone was convinced by Mark, however. When they recast Mark's narrative toward the end of the second century, both recognized what Mark had done. Luke, the historian, took issue with the historical inaccuracy of attributing the gospel to Jesus; Matthew, representing a community with Jewish origins, took issue with the notion that Jesus would have promoted the annulment of the Law. Both authors adjusted Mark's account accordingly.

Luke

Luke's deployment of the εὐαγγελ- root has confounded interpreters for years (Fitzmyer 1981; Harnack 1910). In his first volume, Luke carefully expunges all seven instances of the noun he found in Mark, at the same time peppering his narrative with the verb. He continues using the verb in the second volume but adds the noun twice, at Acts 15:7 and 20:24.[9] Why would Luke have steered clear of the noun so conscientiously in his descriptions of Jesus and of the postcrucifixion missions of Peter, John, Barnabas, and Paul, only to introduce it at the momentous Jerusalem Conference?

The answer is simpler than commentators have imagined: Luke knew the historical course of events. He gets the origin of the gospel exactly right. In the process of investigating the events that preceded him (Luke 1:3), he discovered—if he did not know it already—that Paul had coined the term "gospel" midway through his career to describe his Law-free mission among the Gentiles. Accordingly, Luke utilizes the verb liberally to describe the preaching of his protagonists until the time when the noun entered history; he introduces it at that point.

---

[9] The relationship between Luke and Acts is a matter of contention. The long-standing consensus that Luke-Acts constitutes a unified, two-part work (Cadbury 1927; Tannehill 1986–90) has been challenged by Mikeal Parsons and Richard I. Pervo (1993), who see Acts as a sequel to Luke that differs in its characters, themes, and theological emphases. This essay assumes that Acts is a sequel to Luke, but one whose general content was envisioned even as Luke was being written.

Luke's concern for historical accuracy does not mean that he is above tinkering with the truth, however. To represent history accurately would have required Luke to portray the heated controversies so transparent in Paul's epistles, while Luke prefers to depict the early church as irenic. To represent the origin of the gospel accurately would also have required Luke to credit Paul, a latecomer to the scene, with that important development, while Luke prefers to centralize authority in the original twelve apostles in Jerusalem. Luke therefore tweaks the story.

In the first place he acclaims Peter, not Paul, as the originator of the gospel. The timing of the gospel's origin, if not the personality, is spot on. Luke introduces the gospel following Paul's initial ministry in southern Galatia (Acts 13:13–14:20) but before his arrival in Macedonia (Acts 16:11). Rather than having Christ reveal the gospel to Paul out in the mission field, however, Luke has Paul race back to Jerusalem for a conference at which Peter defends the notion of Gentile inclusion without circumcision and designates it "the gospel." To give the gospel such apostolic sanction, Luke must also advance the Jerusalem Conference to an earlier juncture in Paul's ministry, thereby producing the extra trip to Jerusalem that does not fit into a chronology based on Paul's epistles. Were one to cordon off Acts 14:26–16:10 as the Lukan artifice required to get Paul back to Jerusalem, provide the gospel apostolic imprimatur, and return Paul to the mission field, then Luke's chronology corresponds to an epistolary chronology almost exactly. Missing, obviously, is the falling out in Antioch reported by Paul in Gal 2:11–14, but this omission reflects Luke's reluctance to depict hostility in the earliest church.

In sum, then, Luke's delay in deploying the word "gospel" until midway through his second volume reflects his knowledge about the history of the word. The way in which he manipulates the story to suit his interests would have a lasting impact, however. Future readers of Luke and Acts, unfamiliar with the uniquely Pauline origin of the term, would associate the gospel with Peter and the church in Jerusalem as much as with Paul. Were they to read Mark along with Luke, as Christians eventually would do, it would be difficult to escape the conclusion that the gospel was the message not only of Paul, Peter, and the other apostles but of Jesus as well. Luke, however, was not the only reviser of Mark. Matthew, too, understood what Mark had done with the gospel, and he strove to undo it.

Matthew

Despite his affiliation with a community of believers that subscribed to Torah observance, Matthew did not object to the gospel per se.[10] Writing at the end of the first

---

[10] Scholars have long debated what sort of believer Matthew was and for what sort of community he wrote. Solutions to those questions must account for Matthew's paradoxical treatment of Mark. Matthew esteems Mark enough to reproduce approximately 90 percent of his content, while at the same time undermining many of his key themes—e.g., Jesus's abrogation of the Law (Matt 5:18; 23:23; 24:20), Jesus's Gentile mission (Matt 10:6), the disparagement of the disciples (Matt 13:16–17; Matt 16:17–19). This essay presumes a situation similar to the ones proposed by Odil Hennes Steck (1967) and Ulrich Luz (2005): Matthew represents a community of Jewish followers of Jesus who, following the sack of Jerusalem and

century, he recognized that the incorporation of Gentiles who did not adhere to the Law represented the unavoidable destiny of the new faith. The great commission of Matthew 28:19–20 thus endorses the Gentile mission full bore.

Matthew's frustration results rather from Mark's portrayal of Jesus as the originator of the gospel. Matthew's Jesus never abrogates the Law, nor does he endorse a Gentile mission until after the crucifixion; yet, instead of scrapping εὐαγγέλιον from his revision of Mark, as Luke does, Matthew appropriates the Pauline term but changes its content. Matthew preserves four of Mark's seven instances of εὐαγγέλιον, but he expands three of them to say "the gospel of the kingdom" (4:23; 9:35; 24:14). On the lips of Matthew's Jesus, the gospel is detached from its association with Paul's circumcision-free Gentile mission and connected to a topic Jesus probably discussed frequently in his ministry, namely the kingdom of God (or Heaven). Matthew thus capitalized on the currency the word εὐαγγέλιον had achieved by the end of the first century, especially in the wake of Mark, but recast it in a way that undid the linkage of Jesus to Paul that Mark had sought to create.

Adding "kingdom" to the gospel was only one of the ways Matthew disentangled Jesus from Paul. The other innovation transformed the word εὐαγγέλιον more dramatically. The one place Matthew does not expand Mark's "gospel" into "the gospel of the kingdom" comes in his account of the anointing woman. Matthew nonetheless modifies "the gospel" in Mark 14:9 in another important respect: Jesus says "this gospel" (τὸ εὐαγγέλιον τοῦτο), not "the gospel" (τὸ εὐαγγέλιον). "Wherever this gospel is preached in the whole world" (Matt 26:13), the deed of the anointing woman will be remembered. He also adds the near demonstrative pronoun to "this gospel of the kingdom" (τοῦτο τὸ εὐαγγέλιον τῆς βασιλείας) in Matthew 24:14.

So, what is this gospel, as opposed to the gospel? Matthew is probably referring to the account he is writing. In other words, he means to say that the very pages he is composing will be "preached to the whole world as a testimony to all the nations" amid the disciples' persecution (Matt 24:14); and when it is, the deed of the anointing woman "will be told in remembrance of her" (Matt 26:13). Why might Matthew have figured that an account of the ministry of Jesus should be called a Gospel?[11] The most likely answer is that Matthew thought Mark was titled "The Gospel," either because it circulated originally under that title or because it was accorded that title, on account of its opening line, when it was acquired, copied, and/or recirculated.[12] In composing his new and improved version of "the Gospel," Matthew hoped to supplant

---

the demise of the Jewish mission, had assimilated into a predominantly Gentile community of believers. See Kampen's (2019) recent estimation of Matthew in the light of the Dead Sea Scrolls, where Kampen views Matthew as "the work of a writer who is advocating a distinctive Jewish sectarianism, rooted in the Jesus movement, probably in Galilee toward the end of the first century" (2019, 6).

[11] In this essay, the capitalized "Gospel" refers to a written work about Jesus.

[12] Martin Hengel (1985, 72–81) explains why one should assume that Mark had acquired a title. Titles were both a practical necessity and a cultural expectation. Even if Mark did not circulate with a title originally, it would have been given one in short order.

his predecessor and presumed that his Gospel, *this* Gospel, would be the one to sweep over the world.

How long it took for Matthew's innovative use of εὐαγγέλιον with reference to a written work about Jesus to catch on in Christian circles is difficult to determine. The earliest unambiguous and undisputed reference to such writings as Gospels comes from the middle of the second century, when Justin Martyr refers to the "memoirs of the apostles" as "Gospels" (pl. εὐαγγέλια). Most historians agree, however, that Marcion had called his edited version of Luke a Gospel a decade or so before (c. 140), thereby establishing a terminus ante quem. Accordingly, scholars have debated extensively whether εὐαγγέλιον was first used to describe a written work about Jesus as early as Matthew's "this Gospel," the position taken here, or whether this usage did not emerge until Marcion a half century later—or, whether, of course, it happened sometime in between.[13] Complicating the matter is dispute not only over the meaning of "this Gospel" in Matthew but also over the meaning of εὐαγγέλιον in sources composed between 90 and 140 CE, especially the letters of Ignatius and the Didache.[14]

Conclusion

Whether it was Matthew or Marcion who did it first, by the close of the second century εὐαγγέλιον was widely recognized as the name for a written record about Jesus—in particular, one of the four Gospels that would eventually constitute the first part of the New Testament. This was hardly the only meaning, of course. According to Harnack, the church fathers use εὐαγγέλιον in four discrete ways:

> (i) It remains a general expression for the Christian preaching; (ii) it receives the meaning "tidings of the Crucified and Risen Christ," because this preaching of Christ crucified is its heart and core ... (iii) it receives the meaning "gospel history" (deeds and sayings of Jesus), or it denotes the history of Jesus recorded in a fourfold written work (εὐαγγέλιον κατὰ Ματθαῖου, κ.τ.λ.), or each individual part of this written work (*evangelii libri*, "Gospel of Matthew, etc."; "gospels"); (iv) finally, "gospel" denotes the nature and influence of the new religion as the religion of grace and freedom in distinction from the Old Testament stage of law and bondage. (1910, 327–28)

As such, the original association of the gospel with Paul was lost. Ironically, it was the handiwork of an ardent defender of Paul and the gospel who led the charge. By calling

---

[13] The earliest end of the spectrum is staked about by Collins (2007) and Dunn (2011), who suggest that Mark refers to his own work as a Gospel in Mark 14:9. The latest end is usually associated with Koester (1990).

[14] On the question of whether Ignatius and/or the Didache used εὐαγγέλιον to refer to a Gospel, specifically to Matthew, see now Garroway 2018.

his account "the beginning of the gospel" and by placing Paul's signature term on the lips of Jesus, Mark obscured the true origin of the term. Luke and Matthew followed suit, the one by attributing the gospel to, of all people, Paul's rival Peter, the other by altering the content of the gospel and by assigning to gospel the altogether new meaning of a written work about Jesus. In light of this welter of development, no wonder εὐαγγέλιον came to acquire so broad an array of meanings in medieval Christianity, a legacy that continues today.

References

Bacon, Benjamin W. 1925. *The Gospel of Mark: Its Composition and Date.* New Haven: Yale University Press.
Becker, Eve-Marie, Troels Engberg-Pedersen, and Mogens Müller, eds. 2014. *Mark and Paul: Comparative Essays Part II: For and against Pauline Influence on Mark.* BZNW 199. Berlin: De Gruyter.
Best, Ernest. 1977. "The Role of the Disciples in Mark." *NTS* 23, no. 4: 377–401.
Betz, Hans Dieter. 1979. *Galatians: A Commentary.* Hermeneia. Minneapolis: Fortress.
Bird, Michael F. 2014. *The Gospel of the Lord: How the Early Church Wrote the Story of Jesus.* Grand Rapids: Eerdmans.
Bruce, F. F. 1983. *Philippians.* Good News Commentary. San Francisco: Harper & Row.
Bultmann, Rudolf. [1951] 2007. *Theology of the New Testament.* Translated by Kendrick Grobel. Reprint, Waco: Baylor University Press.
Burrows, Millar. 1925. "The Origin of the Term 'Gospel.'" *JBL* 44, no. 1/2: 21–33.
Cadbury, Henry. 1927. *The Formation of Luke-Acts.* London: Macmillan.
Campbell, Douglas A. 2009. *The Deliverance of God: An Apocalyptic Rereading of Justification in Paul.* Grand Rapids: Eerdmans.
Campbell, Douglas A. 2014. *Framing Paul: An Epistolary Biography.* Grand Rapids: Eerdmans.
Capper, Brian J. 1993. "Paul's Dispute with Philippi: Understanding Paul's Argument in Phil 1–2 from His Thanks in 4.10–20." *Theologische Zeitschrift* 49, no. 3: 193–214.
Collins, Adela Yarbro. 2007. *Mark: A Commentary.* Hermeneia. Minneapolis: Fortress.
Conzelmann, Hans. 1975. *1 Corinthians: A Commentary.* Translated by James W. Leitch. Hermeneia. Philadelphia: Fortress.
Cook, Michael J. 2008. *Modern Jews Engage the New Testament: Enhancing Jewish Well-Being in a Christian Environment.* Woodstock, VT: Jewish Lights.
Delling, Gerhard. 1964. "ἀρχή." *TDNT* 1: 479–84.
Dickson, John P. 2005. "Gospel as News: Εὐαγγελ- from Aristophanes to the Apostle Paul." *NTS* 51, no. 2: 212–30.
Dunn, James D. G. 1998. *The Theology of Paul the Apostle.* Grand Rapids: Eerdmans.
Dunn, James D. G. 2011. "How Did Matthew Go About Composing His Gospel?" In *Jesus, Matthew's Gospel and Early Christianity: Studies in Memory of Graham N. Stanton*, edited by Daniel M. Gurtner, Joel Willits, and Richard A. Burridge, 39–58. LNTS 435. London: T&T Clark.
Dunn, James D. G. 2013. "The Gospel and the Gospels." *Evangelical Quarterly* 85, no. 4: 291–308.
Fee, Gordon D. 1987. *The First Epistle to the Corinthians.* NICNT. Grand Rapids: Eerdmans.
Fee, Gordon D. 1995. *Paul's Letter to the Philippians.* NICNT. Grand Rapids: Eerdmans.

Fenton, John C. 1957. "Paul and Mark." In *Studies in the Gospels: Essays in Memory of R. H. Lightfoot*, edited by Dennis E. Nineham, 89–112. Oxford: Blackwell.

Fitzmyer, Joseph A. 1981. *The Gospel According to Luke: Introduction, Translation, and Notes*. AB 28. Garden City, NY: Doubleday.

Frankemölle, Hubert. 1988. *Evangelium. Begriff und Gattung: Ein Forschungsbericht*. Stuttgarter biblische Beiträge 15. Stuttgart: Katholisches Bibelwerk.

Friedrich, Gerhard. 1964. "Εὐαγγέλιον." *TDNT* 2: 721–36.

Garroway, Joshua D. 2018. *The Beginning of the Gospel: Paul, Philippi, and the Origins of Christianity*. Cham, Switzerland: Palgrave Macmillan.

Gnilka, Joachim. 1976. *Der Philipperbrief*. Herders theologischer Kommentar zum Neuen Testament. Freiburg: Herder.

Goulder, Michael D. 1991. "Those Outside (Mk 4.10–12)." *NovT* 33, no. 4: 289–302.

Harnack, Adolf von. 1910. *The Constitution and Law of the Church in the First Two Centuries*. Translated by F. L. Pogson. New York: Putnam.

Hays, Richard B. 1997. *First Corinthians*. Interpretation. Louisville: John Knox.

Hays, Samuel P. 1999. *Conservation and the Gospel of Efficiency: The Progressive Conservation Movement, 1890–1920*. Pittsburgh: University of Pittsburgh Press.

Hengel, Martin. 1985. *Studies in the Gospel of Mark*. Philadelphia: Fortress.

Horbury, William. 2005. "'Gospel' in Herodian Judea." In *The Written Gospel*, edited by Marcus Bockmuehl and Donald A. Hagner, 7–30. Cambridge: Cambridge University Press.

Horsley, G. H. R. 1983. *New Documents Illustrating Early Christianity*. Vol. 3. Sydney: Ancient History Research Centre, Macquarie University.

Jewett, Robert. 1979. *A Chronology of Paul's Life*. Philadelphia: Fortress.

Kampen, John. 2019. *Matthew within Sectarian Judaism*. New Haven, CT, and London: Yale University Press.

Käsemann, Ernst. 1980. *Commentary on Romans*. Translated by Geoffrey W. Bromiley. Grand Rapids: Eerdmans.

Koester, Helmut. 1990. *Ancient Christian Gospels: Their History and Development*. Philadelphia: Trinity International.

Lohmeyer, Ernst. 1953. *Die Briefe an die Philipper, an die Kolosser und an Philemon*. KEK 9. Göttingen: Vandenhoeck & Ruprecht.

Luedemann, Gerd. 1984. *Paul: Apostle to the Gentiles: Studies in Chronology*. Translated by F. Stanley Jones. Philadelphia: Fortress.

Luz, Ulrich. 2005. *Studies in Matthew*. Translated by Rosemary Selle. Grand Rapids: Eerdmans.

Marcus, Joel. 2000. "Mark—Interpreter of Paul." *NTS* 46, no. 4: 473–87.

Martyn, J. Louis. 1997. *Galatians: A New Translation with Introduction and Commentary*. AB 33A. New York: Doubleday.

Marxsen, Willi. 1969. *Mark the Evangelist: Studies on the Redaction History of the Gospel*. Translated by Roy A. Harrisville. Nashville: Abingdon.

Mason, Steve. 2009. *Josephus, Judea, and Christian Origins: Methods and Categories*. Peabody, MA: Hendrickson.

Michaelis, Wilhelm. 1935. *Der Brief des Paulus an die Philipper*. THNT 11. Leipzig: Deichert.

Murphy-O'Connor, Jerome. 1996. *Paul: A Critical Life*. Oxford: Oxford University Press.

Parsons, Mikeal C., and Richard I. Pervo. 1993. *Rethinking the Unity of Luke and Acts*. Minneapolis: Fortress.

Pekorný, Petr. 2013. *From the Gospel to the Gospels: History, Theology and Impact of the Biblical Term "Euangelion."* BZNW 195. Berlin: De Gruyter.

Plutarch. 1919. *Lives: Sertorius and Eumenes. Phocion and Cato the Younger*. Translated by Bernadotte Perrin. LCL. Cambridge, MA: Harvard University Press.

Plutarch. 1920. *Lives: Demetrius and Antony. Pyrrhus and Caius Marius*. Translated by Bernadotte Perrin. LCL. Cambridge, MA: Harvard University Press.

Plutarch. 1936. *Moralia*. Vol. 4. Translated by Frank Colel Babbitt. LCL. Cambridge, MA: Harvard University Press.

Sim, David C. 2014. "The Family of Jesus and the Disciples of Jesus in Paul and Mark: Taking Sides in the Early Church's Factional Dispute." In *Paul and Mark: Comparative Essays Part I: Two Authors at the Beginnings of Christianity*, edited by Oda Wischmeyer, David C. Sim, and Ian J. Elmer, Beihefte zur Zeitschrift für die neutestamentliche Wissenschaft 198, 73–97. Berlin: De Gruyter.

Stanton, Graham N. 2004. *Jesus and Gospel*. Cambridge: Cambridge University Press.

Steck, Odil Hannes. 1967. *Israel und das gewaltsame Geschick der Propheten. Untersuchungen zur Überlieferung des deuteronomistischen Geschichtsbildes im Alten Testament, Spätjudentum und Urchristentum*. Wissenschaftliche Monographien zum Alten und Neuen Testament 23. Neukirchen-Vluyn: Neukirchener Verlag.

Stuhlmacher, Peter. 1968. *Das paulinische Evangelium: I. Vorgeschichte*. FRLANT 95. Göttingen: Vandenhoeck & Ruprecht.

Suggs, M. Jack. 1960. "Concerning the Date of Paul's Macedonian Ministry." *NovT* 4, no. 1: 60–68.

Tannehill, Robert C. 1977. "The Disciples in Mark: The Function of a Narrative Role." *JR* 57, no. 4: 386–405.

Tannehill, Robert C. 1986–90. *The Narrative Unity of Luke-Acts: A Literary Interpretation*. 2 vols. Minneapolis: Fortress.

Telford, W. R. 1999. *The Theology of the Gospel of Mark*. New Testament Theology. Cambridge: Cambridge University Press.

Werner, Martin. 1923. *Der Einfluss paulinischer Theologie im Markusevangelium: eine Studie zur neutestamentlichen Theologie*. BZNW 1. Giessen: A. Töpelmann.

Wischmeyer, Oda, David C. Sim, and Ian J. Elmer, eds. 2014. *Paul and Mark: Comparative Essays Part I: Two Authors at the Beginnings of Christianity*. BZNW 198. Berlin: De Gruyter.

CHAPTER 25

JEWISH SECTARIANISM

JOHN KAMPEN

INTRODUCTION

THE utilization of a sectarian analysis in the study of ancient texts is rooted in the discipline of sociology. A sustained attempt to employ sociology in the analysis of NT texts is evident in the work of Rudolf Bultmann: "the *Sitz-im-Leben* is . . . a typical situation or occupation in the life of a community. In the same way, the literary 'category', or 'form' through which a particular item is classified is a sociological concept and not an aesthetic one" (Bultmann 1972, 4). The tendency to identify these forms as discrete types within the emerging Christian movement rather than placing the NT texts within the broader Hellenistic world of its time and particularly within its Jewish literature resulted in limitations in the ability of the sociological methods to yield significant results (Holmberg 1990, 1). These developments were also the result of the limited and uninformed use of Jewish literature of the era and the negative perceptions of it held by many of the NT interpreters. It was the NT texts themselves that were used in the identification of the various forms and their contexts in this endeavor (Theissen 1992, 9). The broader social movements of which these texts were a part were outside the parameters of these sociological endeavors. This turn inward toward the Christian materials as the sole context for their own interpretation was entrenched in the discipline with the shift toward redaction criticism: "interest was turned toward the individual evangelist and his specific theology, and the social life of the receiving communities was left far aside. . . . This meant that New Testament studies around 1970 suffered from a fifty-year deficit on social history and sociological perspectives" (Holmberg 1990, 2). Composition criticism and then narrative criticism built and expanded upon these same impulses.

Influential in the reorientation to the questions of sociology was the work of Theissen with his article on itinerant radicalism (Theissen 1975). Differences in methodological issues were highlighted a decade later in Horsley's extensive critique of Theissen's employment of structural functionalism in support of his thesis of itinerant radicalism (Horsley 1989, 9–64). The assumption in both sociological studies was that it is possible to say something meaningful about the nature of the Jesus movement prior to its descriptions in the gospel accounts. In both cases an analysis of the NT materials proceeded without sustained engagement with the literary and archaeological evidence from the Jewish world of the first century.

In the meantime, advances in Jewish studies were to have an impact on the utilization of sociological methods in gospel studies, including a new level of attention to sectarianism. On the one hand archaeological work in the Galilee that began in the late 1960s had an impact on the traditional views of Jewish history of the Galilee and Judea. At the same time, the critical methodology employed by Jacob Neusner in the study of rabbinic materials was beginning to have a significant impact on Jewish studies. Both Morton Smith and Jacob Neusner used the word "sect" to describe their portrayal of the Pharisees, as well as other groups from the late Second Temple period: "the rabbinical traditions of the Pharisees may be characterized as self-centered. They are the internal records of a sect concerning its own life, sectarian laws, and partisan conflicts" (Neusner 1973, 90; Smith 1961). Without substantive definition, the employment of the term "sect" as a meaningful analytical category rather than merely the most convenient translation of the term αἵρεσις in Josephus had been established.

These two new perspectives had a substantive influence on the emerging directions to be taken in the study of Matthew, the "most Jewish" Gospel. This new approach to the study of Matthew was most evident in a conference held at Southern Methodist University in 1989 and in a study published one year later by Overman (Balch 1991; Overman 1990). In a summary of the major points of a resulting portrait of the Matthean community drawn from the presentations at the conference, a few are significant for the purposes of this essay: (1) the Matthean community is best thought of as a sect within Judaism; (2) at the center of the quarrel with Pharisaic Judaism was the interpretation and practice of the Jewish law; and (3) while encompassing Gentile converts, the ethnic makeup of the Matthean community was predominantly Jewish Christian (Kingsbury 1991, 264–65).

Defining *Sect*

The social-scientific approach advanced in the aforementioned study as the basis of a sectarian reading of antique texts proceeds on the basis of the presupposition that a Gospel text can be identified with a community: "that the gospel traditions and texts were transmitted and written down within—and served the needs of—specific communities as these groups interpreted their beliefs in specific cultural contexts and addressed specific problems" (Runesson 2008, 95, n. 1).

In the first pages of his book, Overman advanced his understanding of a sect: "while avoiding a comprehensive definition of the term *sect*, we follow J. Blenkinsopp in taking the term *sectarian* to mean a group which is, or perceives itself to be, a minority in relation to the group it understands to be the 'parent body.' The sect is a minority in that it is subject to, and usually persecuted by, the group in power. The dissenting group is in opposition to the parent body and tends to claim more or less to be what the dominant body claims to be" (Overman 1990, 8–9; referencing Blenkinsopp 1981, 1–2). While reflecting the state of the discipline at the time of its publication, this description is limiting in its potential for developing a convincing sociological portrait of social relations in first-century Judaism. As noted already by Esler, it is not clear that the Pharisees can easily fit the same sociological category as the Matthean community or most of the other groups in first-century Judaism that are currently known (Esler 1993). In his work, Overman adopted the term "formative Judaism," used by Neusner to describe the link between the developments attributed in part to the Pharisees and later rabbinic Judaism (Overman 1990, 2–3). Overman suggested that "formative Judaism and the Matthean community may have been roughly equal in size and shape" (155). Such a proposal does not seem viable based upon the apparently complex nature of the makeup and functioning of Jewish communities in southern Syria and the Galilee at the conclusion of the first century CE.

The extensive history of the development and critique of this concept in sociology and religious studies from Max Weber to the present day is beyond the scope of this essay (Chalcraft 2007). For its modern usage in American sociology, Johnson moved the discussion from a historical and theological analysis rooted in the Reformation and developed by Ernst Troeltsch to a theoretical foundation for the analysis of the religious movements of the twentieth century (Johnson 1963, 1971). It was in his work that Stark and Bainbridge found the category "tension" and applied it to their sociological analysis of new religious movements. Wilson also attempted to come to terms with the limitations of the category *sect* derived from the term's Protestant European origins (Wilson 1973, 1990). He wanted to free the study of sect within the sociology of religion from that inherited ideological bias (1973, 18–28). However, his categories are of greater value for purposes of explanation than for description or definition (Luomanen 2002, 120; Wassen and Jokiranta 2007, 208; but see Jokiranta 2009). His categories do not provide a substantive basis for the identification of sectarian Jewish groups within the texts of the NT or of their role in Jewish society.

The category of tension with the surrounding environment adopted by Stark and Bainbridge informs the definition developed by Baumgarten in his seminal study: "a voluntary association of protest, which utilizes boundary marking mechanisms—the social means of differentiating between insiders and outsiders—to distinguish between its own members and those otherwise normally regarded as belonging to the same national or religious entity" (Baumgarten 1997, 7). Noting that the conflict has its basis in the claims of the deviant group to represent the ideals or beliefs of the dominant body is a helpful clarification in the attempt to comprehend this social phenomenon. Baumgarten's definition highlights the "boundary marking mechanisms" of the group itself, thereby permitting the analyst to find the distinction between the group and its opposition within the sectarian literature itself. The focus is not on a minority group separating from a majority group but on a group who set some kind of boundary or barriers between themselves and others with the same national or religious identity.

In her study of the materials from Qumran, Jokiranta concluded that the best candidates for use as criteria for sectarianism are the tension with the sociocultural environment and the tendency for a group to view themselves as uniquely legitimate, or the tendency to establish boundaries against another group (Jokiranta 2001, 228–30, 236–39; Nickelsburg 2003, 181–82). She turned to the categories developed by Stark and Bainbridge, who sought to provide further specificity for the criterion of tension with the sociocultural environment (Baumgarten 1997, 6, n. 17; Kampen 2019, 47–50). Their understanding of sect formation as a type of subcultural deviance consists of three elements: difference, antagonism, and separation (Stark and Bainbridge 1985, 49–67). These are to be understood not as independent axes or dimensions each capable of separate evaluation but as the interdependent categories by which tension is created and sustained (66). The level of tension with the sociocultural environment is to be understood as a continuum rather than in binary categories. Difference indicates the extent to which sectarians advocate or practice deviant norms of behavior. These norms vary from those followed by the average members of the society or from the standards advocated or practiced by the powerful members of the society. Antagonism is expressed in the attitudes toward other religious groups or society, usually evident in particularistic beliefs denying the legitimacy of other competing groups. These other groups may be representative of the majority or a leadership group, but this need not necessarily be the case. The antagonism may also find expression in attitudes toward other marginal groups who do not share in the particularistic viewpoints that characterize the life of the sect under study. This normally results in the sect's rejection by these other groups. Separation concerns the extent to which there are restrictions on social relations to mainly in-group members. Group norms, behavioral expectations, and demands for communal engagement may limit contacts and relationships with members outside the group, whether a majority body or some competing marginal entity. The examination of these three elements provides the best basis presently available for the study of sectarianism in Second Temple literature.

In his 1991 essay, Saldarini employed the sociology of deviance in his analysis of the Matthean community. He noted: "the Gospel of Matthew and the community behind it are Jewish in that they accept all the fundamental commitments of first-century Judaism, but argue about their interpretation, actualization, and relative importance" (1991, 48). He then classified the innovations attributed to Jesus in the Matthean account under five headings: core symbols, cosmology, boundaries, laws, and social structure. In his subsequent book, his appropriation of the sociology of deviance is informed by the assertion that it is a broader theoretical concept of which sect is a subordinate category, thereby providing a firmer foundation upon which to base an understanding of this group in antiquity (Saldarini 1994, 108).

Accepting the premises of Overman and Saldarini, Sim argued that this sectarian composition was speaking into the tensions that were arising from disagreement about the place of Judaism within the early Christian movement (Sim 1998; 2011). Sim accepted the sectarian identity of Matthew vis-à-vis Judaism and built upon the three central indicators identified by Overman: sectarian language, hostility toward the Jewish leadership, and the centrality of the law. Sim also added a list of items indicating sectarian tendencies: egalitarian inclination, the structure of the scribal leadership and organization, the nature of the expectations of the future, and their religious practices (1998, 110–50). Then Sim sought to establish that the variety of Christian Judaism reflected in Matthew was the result of James's victory over Paul in Antioch. In Sim's view the Christian Judaism portrayed in Matthew fades from history and is absorbed later by the Gentile church, while evidence of some of its anti-Pauline tendencies can be found in the later law-observant Christian heresies.

Two studies by Matthean scholars accept the sectarian identity already discussed but then give it a surprising turn. Stanton asserts that the sectarian analysis provides evidence for an independent identity: "both the Damascus Document and Matthew's gospel explain and sustain the separate identity of communities which have parted company painfully with parent bodies" (Stanton 1992, 106). Matthew appears after a parting of the ways (113–281). In his more recent work Foster also holds that the Matthean community recently had made a decisive break with the synagogue (Foster 2004, 253). Matthew 5:17–20 establishes Jesus as the authoritative interpreter of the law, who is not destroying it as his opponents charge (80–217). Both Stanton and Foster understand the Gentile mission to be a challenge to Jewish law as it was understood in the first century (218–52). The posited break with Judaism undercuts the tension of the sectarian argumentation that this essay proposes was characteristic of the Matthean community. The points of tension in this argumentation rather suggest a sectarian body *within* Judaism. If that body is separated from Judaism, the argument over the manner in which Jews should live in consort with the will of God is no longer as necessary, or at least the justification of the existence of the separated group proceeds in a different manner.

That this Matthean community emerged out of a split from a Pharisaic "association" has been more recently proposed by Runesson. Using the classification of "denomination," from the sociology of religion, he suggests that there is limited evidence for the Pharisees of tension with their surrounding environment. He then defines the Matthean group as a sect in relationship to the Pharisees (Runesson 2008). Language of "association" emerges from his analysis, in which he differentiates between "public" and "association" synagogues, evidence for which can be found in Matthew with references to Pharisaic synagogues (Matt 10:17; 12:9; 23:34). Runesson's evidence concerning the Pharisees is too dependent upon the Gospel of Matthew itself, a composition that wants to place blame for the problems of the Jewish community upon the Pharisees but does not constitute evidence of the community's actual situation independent of that argument.

An examination of Greek and Roman materials permits Jewish sectarian organizations to be placed within the broader context of the voluntary associations of the Greco-Roman world. Gillihan observes that voluntary associations throughout the Roman Empire tended to replicate the organizational patterns, laws, and self-descriptive language of the state. The civic ideologies of these associations resulted in the production of counter-ideologies in sectarian groups that contested the claims of the state. In so doing, they critiqued the state or society as a whole for failing to live up to their stated ideals and offered an alternative to it (Gillihan 2012).

The Gospel of Matthew

Upon the basis of the predominant Two-Source Hypothesis to explain the compositional history of the Synoptic Gospels, it is possible to identify distinctive portions and features of the text of Matthew.[1] The significance of these sections stands out in light of the observation that the plot of the narrative of Matthew is heavily dependent upon Mark. The former includes about 90 percent of the latter's content, with additional material used in the more lengthy composition, including the genealogy as well as the birth and resurrection narratives. A few of these distinctive sections include the Sermon on the Mount (Matt 5–7), Jesus as wisdom (Matt 11), and the paragraph on community discipline (Matt 18:15–20).

While the Sermon on the Mount is by no means composed only of material unique to Matthew among the Synoptics, its distinctive literary structure and some elements of its rhetoric distinguish it from Q and the related portion in Luke 6:17–49. Scattered elements from a Q source present in the Matthean sermon also appear elsewhere in Luke. The Sermon on the Mount is the first of the five distinctive didactic portions of the composition and the most substantive, in both length and content, addressed to the adherents of this Matthean community. As such, the Sermon on the Mount constitutes a major statement on the identity and lifestyle expectations of the followers of Jesus addressed therein: the contribution of a Matthean Jew to the legal (or halakhic) debates within Judaism of the late Second Temple era and its immediate aftermath.

The Sermon on the Mount begins with a section of eleven macarisms (or beatitudes) (Matt 5:3–12; Kampen 2019, 77–84). Significant connections in content can be identified with the sectarian compositions from Qumran (Brooke 2005, 224–33). References to the poor in spirit, the meek, and those who mourn from Matthew 5:3–5 are apparent in 1QH^a (Thanksgiving Hymns; Evans 2012, 103–6; Flusser 1988, 102–25). In Pesher Ps 37, wherein "the meek shall inherit the earth," the meek are identified as the "assembly of the poor" (4Q171 1–10 II, 10). This body is also called "the assembly of his elect," thereby making the explicit connection with sectarian membership. These sectarian authors identify themselves as the "poor," "meek," and "humble." The "poor" in particular are attested throughout the sectarian texts, for example in Pesher Habakkuk, the War Scroll, and the Thanksgiving Hymns. Within these macarisms, Matthew employs designators utilized by other sectarian groups in the late Second Temple period to directly address the members of the Matthean community. It is apparent that these designators are

---

[1] Substantial portions of the following discussion of Matthew are based upon Kampen 2019.

being employed in the service of the formation and support of the social identity of the members of that group (Esler 2014).

The next macarism designates "those who hunger and thirst for righteousness" (5:6). It can be demonstrated that the term "righteousness" is used to describe the expectations of a Jewish way of life in Matthew and some other sectarian texts of Second Temple Judaism (Evans 2011; Kampen 1997). "Righteousness" is relatively rare in the other Gospels, found only in Luke 1:75 and John 16:8, 10. Of some significance here is the reference in Matthew 5:10 to the anticipation of persecution and in 5:20, "unless your righteousness exceeds that of the scribes and Pharisees," one of the most important verses in the composition. As in the Damascus Document, the term is used here to designate the sectarian way of life in contrast to the practices advocated by other leaders and influential groups in the Jewish community (Stanton 1992, 85–107). It was this sectarian way of life that Matthew wanted the members of the sect (and therefore all Jews) to aspire to, but which also was the basis for persecution. In crafting an argument for a higher standard, the author actually was arguing for a distinctive identity within the Jewish world at that time.

Purity is a central concern of the explicitly sectarian Dead Sea Scrolls, as well as other compositions of that corpus. The "pure in heart" of the next verse (Matt 5:8) is a descriptor equally at home in the sectarian scrolls as in the first Gospel. In the scrolls it represents a central aspiration of the sectarian lifestyle. In CD 6:17–18 the initiate brought into the new covenant is "to distinguish between the pure and the impure, and to make known the distinction between the holy and profane" (my translation). Of some significance is the observation that the approach to impurity represented in the Qumran texts is distinctive in Second Temple Judaism in that "ritual and moral impurity were melded into a single concept of defilement, which had both ritual and moral implications" (Klawans 2000, 90). This means that the terms טמא ("impure," "defiled") and טהור ("clean," "pure") are relatively absent from the Tannaitic literature, the writings of the earlier rabbinic traditions (117). Matthew has here adopted a term to designate the Matthean community that is characteristic of a sectarian viewpoint.

The tension between peace and violence is a common feature of apocalyptic literature, for example the manner in which violence and bloodshed is decried in 1 Enoch 6–11, presumably during the early period of the Hellenistic empire (Kampen 2016, 225; Nickelsburg 2001, 169–71; Wyse-Rhodes 2014). Bloodshed is linked with injustice in Jubilees 7:23–25, 11:2–6. The explicitly sectarian context for this macarism may be evident later in Matthew 5 in one of the antitheses: "You have heard that it was said, 'You shall love your neighbor and hate your enemy'" (Matt 5:43). Elsewhere I have suggested that this is an explicit response to other Jewish sectarian viewpoints such as those reflected in 1QS I, 9–11: "those admitted to the covenant shall walk perfectly and love all the Children of Light—each commensurate with his rightful place in the council of God—and to hate all the Children of Darkness, each commensurate with his guilt and the vengeance due him from God" (Kampen 2019, 109). The simultaneous desire for relief from conflict and for harmonious relationships coupled with the expectation that there will be conflict getting to such a place is not unusual in apocalyptic literature

(Davies and Allison 1988–97, 457–58; Evans 2012, 133–34). This feature of the Matthean composition can be identified as representative of a sectarian viewpoint. That a utopian desire for peace and an accompanying mandate for its membership to be peacemakers can readily be attributed to a sectarian group displaying a high level of tension with its surrounding environment is not exceptional. From a sectarian perspective, the features of separation and difference identified here as features of this tension are necessary for a sectarian self-understanding as peacemakers. That in this process of differentiation the sect exhibits antagonism toward those coreligionists who do not have such an understanding of peace should not be a surprise. The identity of the group as peacemaker is solidified as all other Jewish groups outside the sect are deemed deficient with regard to this aspect of Jewish life, regardless of their actual practice and teaching.

The eighth macarism introduces the topic that continues into the concluding section: "those who are persecuted for righteousness's sake" (Matt 5:10). That persecution is assumed to be part of the experience of Jews as it is expressed in sectarian literature and in the broader swath of apocalyptic literature is well attested: "In the days of our tribulation, we toiled laboriously, and every tribulation we saw, and many evils we found. We were consumed and became few, and our spirits small, and we were destroyed and there was no one to help us with word and deed; we were powerless and found nothing" (1 En 103:9–10). The portrayal of the situation of the righteous in 1 Enoch and Daniel is evidence of the manner in which these authors understood the persecution and oppressive nature of Hellenistic rule and the associated Judean aristocracy (Nickelsburg 2001, 41, 62–64, 426–28; Portier-Young 2011, 140–216; Smith-Christopher 1996, 23–33). These apocalyptic themes continue in Jewish literature well into the Roman era and after the destruction of the temple. It has been demonstrated that the evidence for the persecution of "Christians" in the first century has been considerably overestimated (Moss 2012; 2013, 123–87). It is necessary to evaluate this as a topos particularly prominent in the apocalyptic and sectarian literature of Second Temple Judaism rather than evidence of historical experience (Boyarin 1999). This does not negate the possibility that the topos found continuing resonance due to Jewish experience in the Hellenistic and Roman empires. This is another theme employed in Matthew as a significant indicator of identity that is not present in the other Synoptic Gospels.

A different dimension of the sectarian aspect of Matthew 5:3–12 becomes apparent when it is compared with the set of macarisms found in 4Q525 (Beatitudes) 2 II + 3, 1–10 (Brooke 2005, 217–34; Kampen 2011, 307–49). The extant text includes four macarisms plus one extended macarism as a conclusion, similar to the eight of Matthew with the conclusion in 5:11–12. This text from the Qumran corpus does not contain any obvious sectarian indicators and so does not provide immediate evidence of sectarian identity associated with those compositions. What the text does contain in the extended concluding macarism is a statement on the centrality of the law: "Blessed is the man who has obtained wisdom. He walks in the law of the Most High and prepares his heart for her ways" (2 II + 3, 3–4). This is followed by an indication of the adherent's loyalty during affliction, distress, and hardship, resulting in a crown of pure gold upon his head and a place seated among the kings. The structure of the argument is similar to

Matthew 5:11–12, with the exception that in the latter the persecution is rather ἕνεκεν ἐμοῦ ("for my sake"), that is, for Jesus's sake (also Matt 10:18, 39; 16:25; 19:29). Here they are persecuted because of their adherence to Jesus rather than to the law. A similar case is apparent in the commissioning of the disciples when Jesus warns them that "they will be hated by all for my name's sake" (Matt 10:22). Their persecution is anticipated in the next verse (Matt 10:23). This comparative example highlights the manner in which the sectarian way of life and Jesus as its central authority define the Jewish sect addressed in the first Gospel.

The sectarian self-definition also is central to the antitheses that follow in the latter portion of Matthew 5. It has been demonstrated that "You have heard that it was said, . . . But I say to you . . ." constitutes a style of argumentation not characteristic of later rabbinic exegesis but is based in a claim for exclusive authority characteristic of sectarian biblical interpretation (Kampen 2019, 92–111). Jesus is the central authority for the interpretation of the law. It is other sectarian groups' misunderstandings of biblical texts that are addressed in this section.

The chapter concludes with the verse on perfection: "Be perfect, therefore, as your heavenly Father is perfect" (Matt 5:48). The appeal to the criterion of perfection suggests that this is not the conclusion of the sixth antithesis but rather the summation and conclusion of all six. The connection with the Father points back to earlier references in the macarisms (Matt 5:9) and the antitheses (Matt 5:45), along with significant allusions elsewhere, for example the wisdom references of Matthew 11:25–27. Being perfect is a very important consideration in the legal and communal discipline texts from Qumran (Davies and Allison 1988–97, 1:561–63; Strawn and Rietz 2007). This sectarian injunction concludes a section whose heading was an injunction for righteousness, an equally sectarian directive (Matt 5:20).

Matthew's introduction to the treatment of the law precedes the six antitheses (Matt 5:17–20). Those six proclamations about issues in the practice of Judaism in the Second Temple period are within the scope of materials considered to be "Torah." These proclamations are authoritative interpretations of biblical law and narrative that may include but are certainly broader than the material included in the Pentateuch. It is known today that within Judaism of the Second Temple era, "Torah" was important when talking about communal structure, identity, and ethics (Najman 2010; Tso 2010, 76–87). This trajectory through Second Temple literature is evident in the Qumran literature as well as most other exemplars (Kampen 2012). The purpose of these four verses in Matthew is to place these sectarian provisions into the ongoing Mosaic discourse of Second Temple Judaism. While references to Torah and the revelation to Moses appear throughout that literature, beginning with Nehemiah 8–10 with Ezra as an expert in Mosaic law and continuing into the sectarian legislation of the manuscripts of the Community Rule and the Damascus Document, ample evidence that these authoritative appeals include legislation not found in any Hebrew texts of the Pentateuch demonstrate the importance of the authoritative appeal over any specific content. The Temple Scroll and Jubilees are premier exemplars of compositions of Mosaic law not limited to the content of the Pentateuch. Of particular relevance for a sectarian reading is the use of the phrase תורת מושה (law of Moses) in the oaths of those joining the sect in both the Community Rule and the Damascus Document. In both instances the law of Moses includes the stated requirements of sectarian membership. It is the recognition of the continuation of the Mosaic discourse into sectarian Jewish life that permits a sectarian reading of these introductory verses in Matthew.

In these four verses Matthew asserts the sectarian continuity with the Mosaic discourse by placing the argument for continuity in the mouth of Jesus: "I have not come to abolish the law ... but to fulfill." The term "fulfill" here does not have the sense of completion, a meaning the verse acquires in later Christian history, but the recognition that Jesus teaches the only way in which the law can be fully observed. The exclusive sectarian hold on the correct interpretation of the law is the point of the injunction in Matthew 5:19: "whoever breaks one of the least of these commandments, and teaches others to do the same, will be called least in the kingdom of heaven; but whoever does them and teaches them will be called great in the kingdom of heaven." This sectarian reading of the Torah causes its adherents to stand out from competing Jewish groups in the first century and to advance claims for their understanding of the Jewish future.

The sectarian nature of the appeal to wisdom in Matthew is also apparent. Jesus as the exclusive source of wisdom is evident in 11:25–30 (Kampen 2019, 113–30). This entire chapter provides the basis for the claim to exclusive wisdom on the part of the Matthean sect, analogous to the sectarian texts from Qumran. The opening lines of the Community Rule follow the same extended infinitive structure as the introduction in Proverbs 1:1–6, thereby establishing the wisdom context for communal life and expectations (Newsom 2004, 109). The same feature is evident in the Damascus Document, where the Cairo A version begins with the line "Now listen all who know righteousness and understand the works of God" (CD 1:1). This same literary structure introduces the next sections of the composition at CD 2:2 and 2:14, always incorporating the offer of revealed knowledge. In both instances the introduction indicates the wisdom orientation of its exclusive sectarian aspirations. Sectarian claims to exclusive wisdom are not novel in Jewish life by the time of the composition of the gospel literature.

Matthean indebtedness to Jewish sectarianism attested in the Qumran literature can be demonstrated in the procedures for communal discipline (Kampen 2019, 131–55). One of the distinctive features of Qumran legislation is an extended penal code in multiple documents (Hempel 1997; 2013, 141–44; Schiffman 1986; 2010, 180). This detailed attention to communal order and punishment suggests that the disciplinary procedures of Matthew 18:15–20 have a specific context within the history of the interpretation of Lev 19:15–18. The authoritative nature of the judgments of this community is established already in the commissioning of Simon Peter (Matt 16:16–19). The point of connection between this attribution and the discipline procedures is evident in the parallel structure of Matt 16:19 and 18:18.

The evidence for sectarian Judaism within early literature of the movement attributed to Jesus is most apparent in Matthew. The justification for a sectarian reading of this material is most dependent upon the paraenetic portions that can be defined as representative of the author's distinctive voice. From that evidence a sectarian reading of the first Gospel as a whole can then be advanced. The level of tension with the surrounding sociocultural environment expressed within Matthew is considerable, making claims to the same national or religious identity. Of the three features of sectarianism that have been identified here, some of the characteristics of the sect which separate it from its Jewish competitors are developed in the Sermon on the Mount, with some claims for this separation identified in the Sermon's conclusion (Matt 7:13-29). The sect's separation is apparent in its claims for exclusive wisdom and for Jesus as the authoritative interpreter of the law. The sect's distinctive procedures for community discipline and the justification for those practices also points to the difference of the sect as well as its separation from the larger sociocultural context. Since Matthew is a narrative betraying elements of the construction of a story, it should not come as a surprise that the antagonism is most vigorous as the reader approaches the climax of the story. The level of violence in the encounters and parables (see earlier) of Matthew 21-25 indicate a high level of antagonism between the Matthean community and its surrounding environment, a tension that continues into the trial and execution. Matthew's sectarian nature is evident in the trial when responsibility for the verdict of death is shifted more intensely onto the shoulders of the Jewish leadership than is evident in either Mark or Luke. This is most apparent in some notable additions to the Markan narrative (Matt 27:19, 24-26). The so-called blood curse verses, which provide the basis for the repeated Christian assertion that the Jewish people are responsible for the death of Jesus, with tragic consequences, is one of the high points of tension in the narrative, a sectarian statement of hostility directed toward a sect's coreligionists. Sectarian antagonism is on full display in the Matthean shaping of the execution narrative. How does this reading impact one's understanding of the other Synoptic Gospels?

The Remainder of the Synoptic Evidence

The justification for reading Mark or Luke as sectarian Jewish compositions in the same manner as Matthew is not apparent. Whether a movement or a group of followers gathered around a figure called Jesus should be regarded as sectarian also is not self-evident, particularly since the determination of which literature to include in the evaluation would be somewhat arbitrary. One point does merit attention. Mark's portrait of Jesus points to a relationship between that portrayal and the life of John the Baptist. While the hypothesis that he was an Essene continues to resurface, the limited evidence about his life is certainly insufficient to make the case. Mark points to John's placement within the context of the prophetic tradition rooted in the imagery of Elijah. His central message is a call for repentance based upon Isaiah 40:3 and the role of Elijah and the "messenger" of Mal 3:1 and 4:5-6. This alignment with the prophetic tradition is linked to an apocalyptic theme via the emphasis on John as the forerunner to Jesus and his proclamation of the kingdom of God (Mark 1:14–15). That this was the proclamation of the fulfillment of the hope for God's eschatological rule and realm, when the divine will would be done on earth, is evident from the apocalyptic development of this theme already present in Daniel (2:44; 7:14, 18, 27) and some compositions from Qumran (4Q246 [apocDan ar] 2, 2–7; 4Q521 [Messianic Apocalypse] 2 II + 4, 7–9; 1QSb [Messianic Blessings] 4, 25–26) as well as in other apocalyptic texts of this period (Sib. Or. 3.46–47, 767–71; 3 Bar. 11:2; Pss. Sol. 17:3; 2 Esd. 12:13). There is no indication that these apocalyptic allusions approach the level of tension characteristic of sectarian materials.

The same can be said for the manner in which the kingdom of God functions as the center of the sayings of Jesus as portrayed in Q. That Q was a "sayings gospel" was advanced by Helmut Koester, who compared its wisdom orientation to the Wisdom of Solomon and proposed its similarity to the Gospel of Thomas (Koester 1980, 112–14). Both Q and the Gospel of Thomas attest to an earlier wisdom source that is supplemented with apocalyptic Son of Man imagery in Q and with further development of a Gnostic theology in the Gospel of Thomas (Koester 1982, 2:47, 147–49). Further study of wisdom material in Second Temple Judaism has demonstrated the intimate relationship between wisdom and apocalyptic literature, including its eschatological perspectives (Wright and Wills 2005). These perspectives provide the basis for Kloppenborg's reading of Q, in which he demonstrates that its theological center is the reign of God, even when it does include Son of Man imagery. Apocalyptic tendencies are in evidence, particularly in its second phase, according to Kloppenborg (2000, 379–95), but this also does not betray the heightened level of tension with the sociocultural environment that would permit Q's consideration as sectarian literature.

The same can be said for a group or movement associated with the historical Jesus. Whether this is the Jesus who proclaimed the kingdom of God as a prophet in an eschatological context (Allison 2008, 272–74; Dunn 2003, 383–761; Sanders 1985) or acting as a Galilean peasant (Crossan 1991), the evidence for an explicitly sectarian movement is lacking. The possibility that this was initially a sectarian movement is a reasonable hypothesis and is widely assumed; however, it is impossible to delineate the evidence for its specific shape and character during the lifetime of Jesus. The problem can be illustrated in the massive study of Dunn. Having reviewed how the kingdom of God would have been viewed in the Judaism of Jews living in the first century CE, Dunn comments: "we need to recall that many of the texts covered in the above review are sectarian in character." Other Jews, "other Jewish sects, often fell under the condemnations or were excluded from the hopes expressed in these documents" (2003, 397). It is evident that Dunn labels the literature of "Jewish factionalism" as sectarian (281–86). When this literature should be classified as sectarian demands more nuance than Dunn's characterization permits. There is insufficient evidence to evaluate whether a group associated with the historical Jesus was sectarian or whether he was making sectarian claims.

The historical context of the Gospel of Mark has been a contested subject for the last decades, particularly since the resurgence of interest in the history of the Galilee driven by the archaeological work of the last five decades. The attraction of the "simpler" of the Gospels, informed by perceptions influenced by more than a century of the dominance of the Two (or four) Source Hypothesis for the formation of the Synoptic Gospels, has led to the proposition of Galilee as a less complicated, more rural environment for Mark's composition (Freyne 2011; 2014, 280–95). It is not clear that such a portrait for the composition of Mark is adequate. As demonstrated by Collins, this "new" composition (or genre) fits within the literary tradition of Hellenistic biography. She classifies it as being of a didactic nature, like Philo's *Life of Moses* and *On the Pythagorean Way of Life* by Iamblichus. The purpose of these compositions is to instruct readers about the way of life of the group's founder. This compostion also resembles historical biographies that demonstrate the implicit manner in which divine agency is at work in the world and indirectly controls events (Collins 2007, 15–43). The environment for the production of such works would more likely be a cosmopolitan context, such as Alexandria in the case of Philo or Rome with regard to Josephus. The eastern Mediterranean context finds support in the cultural nuances of the composition that lead some to suggest a Galilean provenance. This recognition suggests the cosmopolitan context of Antioch as the more likely venue for its composition than Rome, the site traditionally and most commonly proposed (Collins 2007, 7–10, 96–102).

The didactic and historical nature of this composition does not betray elements of sectarian competition. While the common interpretation of the parenthetical remark in Mark 7:19, "for he declared all foods clean," as indicating that the followers of Jesus did not need to observe the kosher food laws could be seen as controversial, this remark's Markan context does not indicate that it is part of a sectarian argument. This argument was much more likely to have been about the postbiblical Jewish requirement for the washing of hands than about kosher foods (Boyarin 2012, 106–27). Mark does portray it in the context of an argument of Jesus with the Pharisees. These episodic encounters in Mark are one portion of the developing conflict that results in the death of Jesus and has implications for the way of life anticipated for his followers. Addressed to Jewish and Gentile followers, the appeal of this story is to the followers of Jesus, not to the adherents of a new Jewish sect.

For the purposes of this examination, the case of Luke/Acts is rather clear. Whether intended for a Gentile audience or a Hellenized Jewish audience, the latter more likely, a less argumentative tone than that of either Matthew or Mark is evident throughout the two volumes of this composition. I assume the same authorship for both Luke and Acts. The less argumentative tone is a necessary part of an argument which advances the case that the movement founded in the name of Jesus, dubbed "the way" in Acts (9:2; 18:25–26; 19:9, 23, etc.), is the direct continuation of the history of Israel and the natural successor to that legacy. Whether the author was a Greek by birth who turned to Judaism early in life and then encountered the followers of Jesus (Bovon 2002, 8–9) or whether he was even born a Jew (Oliver 2013, 448), the argument is one for continuity with the tradition. The sense of continuity frequently attributed to this composition originates in that argument (Culpepper 1995, 21–31). Of significance here is the reminder that Judaism of the Hellenistic era contains diverse literatures written in multiple languages and participating in a variety of literary traditions. Suggestions that the primary audience might have been Hellenized Jews makes it no less Jewish. Philo and Josephus were no less Jewish than the largely hypothetical Hillel. What is at stake in the identification of sectarianism within the Jewish materials is the question of what type of Jews was this literature written for and by, and what was the nature of the specific argument made by the composition within the Jewish world. The Gospel of Luke does not inject a sectarian argument into the debates of the Jewish community (or communities) of the first century CE.

Conclusion

The application of sociological methodologies to the study of NT texts resulted in more attention to the sectarian dimensions of that study as they became more prominent in the study of the literature of Second Temple Judaism. This aspect of study received more attention after the larger corpus of texts from Qumran became available in 1991, demonstrating a greater diversity than had previously been understood to characterize that collection. This attention to sectarianism as an integral part of the study of Second Temple Jewish religious life found expression in the examination of Matthew among the Synoptic Gospels. The sociological method utilized here adopts categories employed in the study of new religious movements. It evaluates the level of tension with the sociocultural environment evident within the specific phenomenon under investigation. In the case of antiquity, this entails the examination of a person's or group's literary production. With regard to Matthew it can be demonstrated that the level of tension evaluated through the categories of difference, separation, and antagonism, is evidence of a sectarian orientation not apparent in Q, Mark, or Luke or in the material attributed to the historical Jesus in various academic studies. These features are most apparent in those sections of Matthew—such as the Sermon on the Mount, the treatment of wisdom, the discussion of communal discipline, and portions of the trial narrative—that appear to be additional to the vast portion of the composition that follows the text of the biographical narrative of Mark. This evidence suggests that Matthew displays a different relationship to the Jewish community(ies) in which it originated or that it was produced in Jewish communities considerably different from those of the other Synoptic Gospels.

References

Allison, Dale C., Jr. 1993. *The New Moses: A Matthean Typology*. Minneapolis: Fortress.
Allison, Dale C., Jr. 2008. "Jesus Christ." In *New Interpreters Dictionary of the Bible*, 5 vols., edited by Katherine Doob Sakenfeld, 3:261–93. Nashville: Abingdon.
Balch, David L., ed. 1991. *Social History of the Matthean Community: Cross-disciplinary Approaches*. Minneapolis: Fortress.

Baumgarten, Albert I. 1997. *The Flourishing of Jewish Sects in the Maccabean Era: An Interpretation*. JSJSup 55. Leiden: Brill.

Becker, Eve-Marie, and Anders Runesson, eds. 2011. *Mark and Matthew. Comparative Readings I: Understanding the Earliest Gospels in Their First-Century Settings*. WUNT 271. Tübingen: Mohr Siebeck.

Blenkinsopp, Joseph. 1981. "Interpretation and the Tendency to Sectarianism: An Aspect of Second Temple History." In *Jewish and Christian Self-Definition*, 3 vols., edited by E. P. Sanders, 2:1–16. Philadelphia: Fortress.

Bovon, François. 2002. *Luke 1: A Commentary on Luke 1:1–9:50*. Translated by Christine M. Thomas. Hermeneia. Philadelphia: Augsburg Fortress.

Boyarin, Daniel. 1999. *Dying for God: Martyrdom and the Making of Christianity and Judaism*. Stanford: Stanford University Press.

Boyarin, Daniel. 2012. *The Jewish Gospels: The Story of the Jewish Christ*. New York: The New Press.

Brooke, George J. 2005. *The Dead Sea Scrolls and the New Testament*. Minneapolis: Fortress.

Bultmann, Rudolph. 1972. History of the Synoptic Tradition, translated by J. Marsh. Oxford: Blackwell.

Chalcraft, David J., ed. 2007. *Sectarianism in Early Judaism: Sociological Advances*. London: Equinox.

Collins, Adela Yarbro. 2007. *Mark*. Hermeneia. Minneapolis: Fortress.

Crossan, John Dominic. 1991. *The Historical Jesus: The Life of a Mediterranean Jewish Peasant*. San Francisco: Harper Collins.

Culpepper, R. Alan. 1995. "Luke." In *The New Interpreters Bible*, 12 vols., edited by Leander E. Keck et al., 9:3–490. Nashville: Abingdon.

Davies, W. D., and Dale C. Allison, Jr. 1988–97. *A Critical and Exegetical Commentary on the Gospel According to Saint Matthew*. 3 vols. Edinburgh: T&T Clark.

Dunn, James D. G. 2003. *Jesus Remembered*. Christianity in the Making 1. Grand Rapids: Eerdmans.

Esler, Philip Francis. 1993. Review of *Matthew's Gospel and Formative Judaism* by J. Andrew Overman, *BibInt* 1: 255–58.

Esler, Philip Francis. 2014. "Group Norms and Prototypes in Matthew 5.3–12: A Social Identity Interpretation of the Matthaean Beatitudes." In *T&T Clark Handbook to Social Identity in the New Testament*, edited by Brian J. Tucker and Coleman A. Baker, 147–71. London: Bloomsbury.

Evans, Craig A. 2011. "Fulfilling the Law and Seeking Righteousness in Matthew and the Dead Sea Scrolls." In *Jesus, Matthew's Gospel and Early Christianity: Studies in Memory of Graham N. Stanton*, edited by Daniel M. Gurtner, Joel Willitts, and Richard A. Burridge, 102–14. LNTS 435. London: T & T Clark.

Evans, Craig A. 2012. *Matthew*. New Cambridge Bible Commentary. New York: Cambridge University Press.

Flusser, David. 1988. *Judaism and the Origins of Christianity*. Jerusalem: Magnes Press, Hebrew University.

Foster, Paul. 2004. *Community, Law and Mission in Matthew's Gospel*. WUNT 177. Tübingen: Mohr Siebeck.

Freyne, Sean. 2011. "Matthew and Mark: The Jewish Contexts." In *Mark and Matthew. Comparative Readings I: Understanding the Earliest Gospels in their First-Century Settings*, edited by Eve-Marie Becker and Anders Runesson, 179–203. WUNT 271. Tübingen: Mohr Siebeck.

Freyne, Sean. 2014. *The Jesus Movement: Meaning and Mission*. Grand Rapids: Eerdmans.

Gillihan, Yonder Moynihan. 2012. *Civic Ideology, Organization, and Law in the Rule Scrolls: A Comparative Study of the Covenanters' Sect and Contemporary Voluntary Associations in Political Context*. Leiden: Brill.

Hempel, Charlotte. 1997. "The Penal Code Reconsidered." In *Legal Texts and Legal Issues. Proceedings of the Second Meeting of the IOQS Cambridge 1995. Studies Presented in Honour of J. Baumgarten*, edited by Moshe Bernstein, Florentino García Martínez, and John Kampen, 337–48. STDJ 23. Leiden: Brill.

Hempel, Charlotte. 2013. *The Qumran Rule Texts in Context: Collected Studies*. TSAJ 154. Tübingen: Mohr Siebeck.

Holmberg, Bengt. 1990. *Sociology and the New Testament: An Appraisal*. Minneapolis: Fortress.

Horsley, Richard A. 1989. *Sociology and the Jesus Movement*. New York: Crossroad.

Johnson, Benton. 1963. "On Church and Sect." *ASR* 28: 539–49.

Johnson, Benton. 1971. "Church and Sect Revisited." *JSSR* 10: 124–37.

Jokiranta, Jutta M. 2001. "'Sectarianism' of the Qumran 'Sect': Sociological Notes." *RevQ* 20: 223–39.

Jokiranta, Jutta M. 2009. "Learning from Sectarian Responses: Windows on Qumran Sects and Emerging Christian Sects." In *Echoes from the Caves: Qumran and the New Testament*, edited by Florentino García Martínez, 177–209. STDJ 85. Leiden: Brill.

Kampen, John. 1994. "The Sectarian Form of the Antitheses within the Social World of the Matthean Community." *DSD* 1: 338–63.

Kampen, John. 1997. "'Righteousness' in Matthew and the Legal Texts from Qumran." In *Legal Texts and Legal Issues. Proceedings of the Second Meeting of the IOQS Cambridge 1995. Studies Presented in Honour of J. Baumgarten*, edited by Moshe Bernstein, Florentino García Martínez, and John Kampen, 461–88. STDJ 23. Leiden: Brill.

Kampen, John. 2011. *Wisdom Literature*. ECDSS. Grand Rapids: Eerdmans.

Kampen, John. 2012. "'Torah' and Authority in the Major Sectarian Rules Texts from Qumran." In *The Scrolls and Biblical Traditions: Proceedings of the Seventh Meeting of the IOQS in Helsinki*, edited by George J. Brooke, Daniel K. Falk, Eibert J. C. Tigchelaar, and Molly M. Zahn, 231–54. STDJ 103. Leiden: Brill.

Kampen, John. 2016. "Wisdom, Poverty, and Non-violence in Instruction." In *The War Scroll, Violence, War and Peace in the Dead Sea Scrolls and Related Literature: Essays in Honour of Martin G. Abegg on the Occasion of His 65th Birthday*, edited by Kipp Davis, Dorothy M. Peters, Kyung S. Baek, and Peter W. Flint, 215–36. STDJ 115. Leiden: Brill.

Kampen, John. 2019. *Matthew within Sectarian Judaism*. New Haven: Yale University Press.

Kingsbury, Jack Dean. 1991. "Conclusion: Analysis of a Conversation." In *Social History of the Matthean Community: Cross-disciplinary Approaches*, edited by David L. Balch, 259–69. Minneapolis: Fortress.

Klawans, Jonathan. 2000. *Impurity and Sin in Ancient Judaism*. New York: Oxford University Press.

Kloppenborg Verbin, John S. 2000. *Excavating Q: The History and Setting of the Sayings Source*. Minneapolis: Fortress.

Koester, Helmut. 1980. "Apocryphal and Canonical Gospels." *HTR* 73: 105–30.

Koester, Helmut. 1982. *Introduction to the New Testament*. 2 vols. Berlin: De Gruyter.

Luomanen, Petri. 2002. "The 'Sociology of Sectarianism' in Matthew: Modeling the Genesis of Early Jewish and Christian Communities." In *Fair Play: Diversity and Conflicts in Early Christianity: Essays in Honor of Heikke Räisänen*, edited by Ismo Dundenberg, Christopher Tuckett, and Kari Syreeni, 109–30. NovTSup 103. Leiden: Brill.

Moss, Candida. 2012. *Ancient Christian Martyrdom: Diverse Practices, Theologies, and Traditions*. AYBRL. New Haven: Yale University Press.

Moss, Candida. 2013. *The Myth of Persecution: How Early Christians Invented a Story of Martyrdom*. New York: Harper One.

Najman, Hindy J. 2010. "Torah and Tradition." In *Eerdmans Dictionary of Early Judaism*, edited by John J. Collins and Daniel C. Harlow, 1316–17. Grand Rapids: Eerdmans.

Neusner, Jacob. 1973. *From Politics to Piety: The Emergence of Pharisaic Judaism*. Englewood Cliffs: Prentice-Hall.

Newsom, Carol A. 2004. *The Self as Symbolic Space: Constructing Identity and Community at Qumran*. STDJ 52. Atlanta: SBL.

Nickelsburg, George W. E. 2001. *1 Enoch 1: A Commentary on the Book of 1 Enoch*. Hermeneia. Minneapolis: Fortress.

Nickelsburg, George W. E. 2003. *Ancient Judaism and Christian Origins: Diversity, Continuity, and Transformation*. Minneapolis: Fortress.

Oliver, Isaac W. 2013. *Torah Praxis after 70 CE: Reading Matthew and Luke-Acts as Jewish Text*. 2nd ser. WUNT 355. Tübingen: Mohr Siebeck.

Overman, J. Andrew. 1990. *Matthew's Gospel and Formative Judaism: The Social World of the Matthean Community*. Philadelphia: Fortress.

Portier-Young, Anathea. 2011. *Apocalypse against Empire: Theologies of Resistance in Early Judaism*. Grand Rapids: Eerdmans.

Runesson, Anders. 2008. "Rethinking Early Jewish-Christian Relations: Matthean Community History as Pharisaic Intragroup Conflict." *JBL* 127: 95–132.

Saldarini, Anthony J. 1991. "The Gospel of Matthew and Jewish-Christian Conflict." In *Social History of the Matthean Community: Cross-disciplinary Approaches*, edited by David L. Balch, 38–61. Minneapolis: Fortress.

Saldarini, Anthony J. 1994. *Matthew's Christian-Jewish Community*. Chicago: University of Chicago Press.

Sanders, E. P. 1985. *Jesus and Judaism*. Philadelphia: Fortress.

Schiffman, Lawrence H. 1986. "Reproof as a Requisite for Punishment in the Law of the Dead Sea Scrolls." In *Jewish Law Association Studies II: The Jerusalem Conference Volume*, edited by Bernard S. Jackson, 59–74. Atlanta: Scholars Press.

Schiffman, Lawrence H. 2010. *Qumran and Jerusalem: Studies in the Dead Sea Scrolls and the History of Judaism*. Grand Rapids: Eerdmans.

Schwartz, Seth. 2006. "*Political, Social, and Economic Life in the Land of Israel, 66–c. 235.*" In *The Late Roman-Rabbinic Period*, edited by Steven T. Katz, CHJ, 4:23–52. Cambridge: Cambridge University Press.

Schwartz, Seth. 2014. *The Ancient Jews from Alexander to Muhammad*. KTAH. Cambridge: Cambridge University Press.

Sim, David C. 1998. *The Gospel of Matthew and Christian Judaism: The History and Social Setting of the Matthean Community*. Edinburgh: T&T Clark.

Sim, David C. 2011. "Matthew: The Current State of Research." In *Mark and Matthew. Comparative Readings I: Understanding the Earliest Gospels in Their First-Century Settings*, edited by Eve-Marie Becker and Anders Runesson, WUNT 271, 33–51. Tübingen: Mohr Siebeck.

Smith, Morton. 1961. "The Dead Sea Sect in Relation to Ancient Judaism." *NTS* 7: 347–60.

Smith-Christopher, Daniel L. 1996. "The Book of Daniel." In *The New Interpreters Bible*, 12 vols., edited by Leander E. Keck et al., 7:17–152. Nashville: Abingdon.

Stanton, Graham N. 1992. *A Gospel for a New People: Studies in Matthew*. Edinburgh: T&T Clark.

Stark, Rodney, and William Sims Bainbridge. 1985. *The Future of Religion: Secularization, Revival and Cult Formation*. Berkeley: University of California Press.

Strawn, Brent A., and Henry W. Morisada Rietz. 2007. "(More) Sectarian Terminology in the Songs of the Sabbath Sacrifice: The Case of *Temime Derekh*." In *Qumran Studies: New Approaches, New Questions*, edited by Michael Thomas Davis and Brent A. Strawn, 53–64. Grand Rapids: Eerdmans.

Theissen, Gerd. 1975. "Itinerant Radicalism: The Tradition of Jesus Sayings from the Perspective of the Sociology of Literature." *Radical Religion* 2, nos. 2–3: 84–93. Translation of "Wanderradikalismus: Literatursoziologische Aspekte der Überlieferung von Worten Jesu im Urchristentum," *ZTK* 70 (1973): 245–71.

Theissen, Gerd. 1992. *Social Reality and the Early Christians. Theology, Ethics, and the World of the New Testament*. Translated by Margaret Kohl. Minneapolis: Fortress.

Tso, Marcus K. M. 2010. *Ethics in the Qumran Community: An Interdisciplinary Investigation*. WUNT, 2nd ser., 292. Tübingen: Mohr Siebeck.

Wassen, Cecilia, and Jutta Jokiranta. 2007. "Groups in Tension: Sectarianism in the *Damascus Document* and the *Community Rule*." In *Sectarianism in Early Judaism: Sociological Advances*, edited by David J. Chalcraft, 205–45. London: Equinox.

Werrett, Ian C. 2007. *Ritual Purity and the Dead Sea Scrolls*. STDJ 72. Leiden: Brill.

Wilson, Bryan. 1973. *Magic and the Millennium: A Sociological Study of Religious Movements of Protest among Tribal and Third-World Peoples*. New York: Harper & Row.

Wilson, Bryan. 1990. *The Social Dimensions of Sectarianism: Sects and New Religious Movements in Contemporary Society*. Oxford: Clarendon.

Wright, Benjamin G., III, and Lawrence M. Wills, eds. 2005. *Conflicted Boundaries in Wisdom and Apocalypticism*. SymS 35. Atlanta: SBL.

Wyse-Rhodes, Jackie. 2014 "Sex, Knowledge, and Evil: Violence and Peace in the *Book of the Watchers*." In *Struggles for Shalom: Peace and Violence Across the Testaments*, edited by Laura L. Brenneman and Brian D. Schantz, 114–24. Studies in Peace and Scriptures 12. Eugene: Pickwick, 2014.

CHAPTER 26

GENTILES AND THEIR RELATIONS TO JEWS

MAGNUS ZETTERHOLM

The General Situation during the First Century CE

The Jewish population in the Roman Empire constituted a considerable minority, although the exact number is unclear (McGing 2002). Most Jews distinguished themselves from other ethnic groups, since Jews commonly insisted on continuing to observe their ancestral customs, which were not always compatible with the Greco-Roman religio-political system. The main obstacle, which occasionally led to political complications, was the Jewish reluctance to get involved in what from a Jewish perspective was defined as "idolatry." Apart from participation in cultic activities in pagan temples or during pagan festivals, this could involve anything connected to Greco-Roman culture or religion, such as consuming food that had been used in sacrificial rites or even prepared by Gentiles, or handling objects, for instance in business transactions, intended for sacrificial purposes (Tomson 1990, 151–76).

Jewish texts from the Second Temple period and onward often designate Gentiles with the stereotyping label "sinners," implying that all Gentiles share a common nature leading to the worship of "idols" and in turn to immorality (Novenson 2022). Because of their involvement in "idolatry," Gentiles were thus typically considered "morally impure" during the Second Temple period (Hayes 2002, 54–58), and as a result, Jews were expected to avoid close contacts with Gentiles. The source of this negative view of Gentiles is found in the Hebrew Bible, in texts that envisage the eschatological destruction of the Gentile nations or their subordination to Israel (see, e.g., Amos 1:3–2:3; Isa 13:1–19:15; Jer 46:1–50; Ezek 25:1–30:26). The same theme is prevalent also in texts from the Second Temple period (see, e.g., Jub. 23:30; 1 En. 91:9, Bar. 4:25, 31–35; Sib. Or. 3:669–701, T. Mos. 10:7; 1QM 1:6, 11:11–17, 12:10–12, 14:5–7).

Paradoxically, however, the opposite idea is also found both in the Hebrew Bible and in later Jewish literature in texts which foresee a time when the Gentile nations will turn to God (see, e.g., Isa 2:2–3; Jub. 4:26; Pss. Sol. 17:34; Sir 36; T. Levi 14:4; Tob 13:11). Thus, the morally impure status of Gentiles was generally not considered intrinsic, as it was primarily connected to abominable actions connected to "idolatry." If a Gentile ceased worshiping "idols" and turned to the god of Israel, he or she could, accordingly, be considered morally pure (Hayes 2002, 56–57).

Indeed, Greeks and Romans held corresponding views of Jews (and other ethnic groups, such as Egyptians, Phoenicians, Carthaginians, and Syrians, among others). Both Greeks and Romans regarded themselves as superior to any people they had defeated, and stereotypes sometimes ran both ways—Romans, for instance, perceived Greeks as barbarous and considered contemporary Greeks decadent, while at the same time admiring classical Greek culture (Barchiesi 2009; Phang 2016).

It could, however, be argued that Gentiles' relations to Jews and Judaism was of a different kind. Peter Schäfer has suggested that the label "anti-Semitism" is applicable to Greek and Roman attitudes toward the Jews, which he describes as "the amalgamation of Egyptian and Greek prejudices" (Schäfer 1997, 206). What distinguishes "anti-Judaism" from "anti-Semitism," Schäfer claims, is the presentation of Jews as a constant threat to the civilized world, allegations which are directed toward all Jews, not some Jews, irrespective of what Jews actually do or do not do, thus crossing the line from the "justifiable" to the "unjustifiable" (206). For Rome, Schäfer argues for a more complex situation. Whereas Greek attitudes toward Jews are straightforwardly negative, Roman attitudes display an "ambivalence between dislike and fear, criticism and respect, attraction and repulsion, which responds to the peculiar combination of exclusiveness and yet success that characterizes Judaism in the eyes of the Roman authors." This Schäfer labels "Judeophobia" (210).

The root of these negative views of Jews is predominantly found in their alterity. A quotation from Tacitus (*Hist*. 5.4.1; Moore, LCL) is illustrative: "to establish his influence over this people for all time, Moses introduced new religious practices, quite opposed to those of all other religions. The Jews regard as profane all that we hold sacred; on the other hand, they permit all that we abhor." Because of their strange, from a Roman perspective, customs and religious views, Jews were profoundly criticized and ridiculed. Jewish exclusive monotheism, however, appears not to have incurred much criticism, but to have been seen as something positive (Gruen 2002, 42–43; see, e.g., Tacitus, *Hist*. 5.5.4; Plutarch, *Quaest. conv*. 4.6; Cassius Dio, 37.17.2), while Jewish dietary regulations, especially the prohibition against eating pork, were seen as proof of Jewish unsociability. Roman authors typically regarded the Sabbath as idleness, and male circumcision was perceived as an abnormal mutilation, often with sexual overtones (see, e.g., Tacitus, *Hist*. 5.5.2; on various accusations against the Jews see Isaac 2004; Schäfer 1997). Note, however, that such negative views, even though they probably were shared by many ordinary people, were primarily the opinions of the elite.

Even though it is true that a certain Jewish reluctance to socialize with Gentiles existed, social relations between Jews and Gentiles must nevertheless have been common, especially in the Diaspora. In some places, like Rome and Alexandria, Jews were admittedly confined to live in certain designated areas (Barclay 1996, 29, 290), but in other places, for example Antioch-on-the-Orontes, the sources seem not to indicate the existence of similar areas. Given the size of the Jewish population in the Diaspora, especially in the large cities, it is quite natural to imagine that considerable social interactions took place.

There is also ample evidence that Judaism attracted great interest from Gentiles, especially from the upper ranks of society (Murray 2004, 15–21), and that at least some Jews approved of that. In a slightly hyperbolic statement, Josephus even claims that "there is not one city of the Greeks, nor a single barbarian nation, where the custom of the seventh day, on which we rest, has not permeated, and where our fasts and lighting of lamps and many of our prohibitions with regard to food have not been observed" (*C. Ap.* 2.282, Barclay).

In his extensive study, Terence Donaldson has identified a number of Jewish attitudes to Gentiles, indicating the existence of a kind of Jewish universalism (Donaldson 2007). First, Donaldson mentions Gentiles who in various forms expressed sympathy with Judaism. This can range from very generalized positive statements to more specific activities, such as honoring the temple in Jerusalem, attending synagogue services, adopting certain Jewish customs and observances, honoring the god of Israel, or even recognizing the Jewish God as the supreme deity. Second, sympathy, taken to its extreme, could occasionally result in someone's conversion to Judaism. Such a person was expected to observe the Torah and to exclusively worship the god of Israel. According to Donaldson, "Jews in both Judea and the Diaspora believed that it was possible for Gentiles to join the Jewish community as converts, that conversion was a positive thing and converts were to be welcomed" (2007, 491). The third pattern of Jewish universalism Donaldson labels "ethical monotheism": the idea that the Torah represents an articulation of a monotheistic ethic that is accessible by all humans. With some Jewish authors this can mean presenting the Jewish law as a general monotheistic ethical principle, or equating the Torah with Greek philosophy, which sometimes means downplaying the specific Jewish identity markers.

From a Roman elite perspective, Gentiles' involvement in Jewish affairs was not looked upon favorably. Gentile sympathizers and above all proselytes were typically seen as traitors, a dangerous phenomenon, threatening the Roman spirit, especially since converts abandoned the religion of their ancestors and could no longer participate in the religious ceremonies of the *polis*, thereby risking the peace of the gods, *pax deorum* (Champion 2017). Seneca's famous statement, preserved by Augustine, is telling: "the customs of this accursed race have gained such influence that they are now received throughout the world. The vanquished have given laws to their victors" (*Civ.* 6.11; Green, LCL). Occasionally, Rome took action against Gentile "Judaizers." Tacitus (*Ann.* 13.32; Jackson, LCL) reports that under Nero, a woman of high standing, Pomponia Graecina, was accused of "alien superstition" and "was left to the jurisdiction of her husband," who, after due investigation, declared her innocent. According to Dio Cassius (67.14; Cary, LCL), Domitian, in the aftermath of the Jewish War, carried out purges in the imperial family: some were executed, others were deprived of their property and banished. The charges were "atheism" and having "drifted into Jewish ways."

Jewish Privileges

In general, however, Roman authorities appear to have been rather indifferent to Jewish affairs. Erich Gruen has drawn attention to the fact that the expulsion of Jews from Rome in 19, under Tiberius, and around 49, under Claudius, were not aimed at Jews only—several other groups were also targeted—and that actions taken against the Jews (and other groups) "came only when it might benefit the government's image—and even then it was largely performance and ceremony" (Gruen 2002, 29–41).

Jews were commonly permitted to practice their religion as a result of the Roman ideology of allowing conquered people to follow their own laws and practice their ancestral religion. According to Cicero (*Leg.* 2.8.19; Keyes LCL) Romans should worship "those gods whose worship they have duly received from their ancestors." This was true, of course, as long as foreign cults were not perceived as a threat to Roman values or believed to be the source of public disorder. In such cases, the imperial government did not hesitate to take action, as in the case with the Isis cult, which was expelled from Rome in 19 CE (Rüpke 2014, 474).

There was, however, one impediment with regard to the Jews. As mentioned earlier, the *pax deorum* was an important consideration for Roman authorities: beginning with Augustus, all inhabitants in the Roman Empire were expected to participate in the official cult, for instance by honoring the official gods of the empire, including deified emperors, and by participating in religious festivals and rituals (Beard, North, and Price 1998, 214–36). In the imperial Greek *poleis*, the situation involved an additional aspect: inhabitants were expected to participate also in the cult of the city. For Jews who wanted to be true to their ancestral traditions, this caused considerable complications. The problem was, however, recognized by Rome, as it had been previously in the Greek East during the Seleucid period, and resulted in a series of concessions that were not granted to any other ethnic group, concessions that sometimes led to tensions with the Gentile population.

The Romans thus inherited a system where Jews had negotiated certain privileges in relation to the authorities of the Greek city-states and were aiming at maintaining a status quo regarding Jewish rights to live in accordance with their customs. A collection of decrees preserved by Josephus (*A.J.* 14.185–267; 301–23; 16.31–64; 16:160–78;19.280–91; 19:303–11) indicates that a Roman charter where the Jewish privileges were laid down probably did not exist. Instead, the decrees form a series of ad hoc actions taken to guarantee Jewish privileges in various locations whenever they were under attack (Rajak 1984).

According to the documents collected in Josephus's *Antiquitates*, the privileges granted to the Jews included the right to assemble weekly for Sabbath services and a limited autonomous administrative organization. A few decrees mention permission to build places to assemble. Connected to this was the right to observe the Sabbath and other religious festivals, which, for instance, meant that Jews did not have to appear in court on the Sabbath. Also permitted was the collection of the temple tax, which on several occasions had been seized by the Greeks. The permission to observe dietary laws is rarely mentioned, but Greek cities could occasionally be forced by Roman authorities to guarantee that food suitable for Jews was available. Although Jews could be compelled to enlist in the army on certain occasions, they were normally exempted from military service, which was based on voluntariness. Two main reasons are given: that Jews were prevented from carrying weapons or to march on the Sabbath and the difficulties of obtaining food suitable for Jews. Finally, Jews were exempted from participation in the imperial cult, which followed from their right to live in accordance with their customs. Instead, Jews found other acceptable ways to express their loyalty to the empire and to the emperor—prayers and sacrifices for the welfare of the emperor were offered, and dedicatory inscriptions in honor of the emperor were set up in the synagogues (Tellbe 2001, 37–51). One such example is the Mindius Faustus inscription (second century) from the synagogue in Ostia, which reads: "For the safety of the Emperor. Mindius Faustus with his family built and made (it) from his own gifts, and set up the ark for the holy law" (*JIWE* 1.13).

Thus, despite the existence of reciprocal stereotyping, hostility, and prejudice among Jews and Gentiles, it must be concluded that positive relations also existed within some strata of the population. Some Gentiles expressed sympathy for Judaism to various degrees, and some even adopted a Jewish lifestyle of sorts. In some other cases, this Judaizing process culminated in a full conversion to Judaism. From a Jewish perspective, interest in Judaism was seen as a positive thing, and converts were welcomed, although not everyone would have shared this attitude. Furthermore, there is little evidence of systematic repression of Jews by either Romans or Greeks, although local skirmishes occasionally occurred, for example the events in Alexandria in 38–41 CE, which developed into a hideous riot with devastating consequences for the Jewish population (Barclay 1996, 48–60; Gambetti 2009).

When the imperial government took action against Jews, it rarely concerned only Jews but also involved Chaldeans, Egyptians, or magicians and should rather be seen in the context of matters of the state (Gruen 2002, 15–104). It was not in the interest of Rome to have a bad relationship with the Jewish community, and even in the aftermath of the Jewish War, Rome was eager to normalize relations. Josephus (*B.J.* 7.100–110; Thackeray LCL) writes about events that took place in Antioch in connection with the end of this war. Titus was evidently passing through Syria, and when the people of Antioch heard that he was approaching they welcomed him warmly, but they also made the request that Titus expel the Jews from the city. Titus refused and left the city and, on his return shortly after, they repeated their request, which was once more denied. According to Josephus, the people of Antioch then made a second request—that the brass tablets on which the privileges of the Jews were inscribed should be removed. Titus also refused to grant this petition, Josephus states, "and leaving the status of the Jews of Antioch exactly as it was before, he set out for Egypt."

Notwithstanding Josephus's tendency to present Titus in a favorable light, the essence of the story appears to be historically accurate and demonstrates the official Roman attitude to the Jews of the empire quite well. When needed, Rome protected the rights of the Jewish people, which very well could lead to strained relations on the local level. In general, however, the system seems to have worked quite well.

Spaces of Interaction

The fact that Gentiles and Jews interacted raises questions of where such interactions took place. One obvious answer is business transactions, and it is worth mentioning that the Mishnah devotes a good part of the tractate Avodah Zarah to this topic. Then, of course, there were synagogues. The term "synagogue" is not as unambiguous as it may seem. One complication was that the designation was not only used for Jewish groups but was a common term used by many other associations. The same is true regarding the title "leader of the synagogue" (ἀρχισυνάγωγος), which was a very common designation for the president of an association (Kloppenborg 2019, 28). Recent research has also challenged the traditional view of "the synagogue" as ethnic-based groups where Jews practiced Judaism and that such groups functioned to preserve Jewish traditions. Such "synagogues" did indeed exist, but other forms of Jewish institutions, for instance craft guilds, did as well, but they are usually distinguished from "synagogues" in most scholarship. As a consequence, synagogue scholarship is today considering new ways of referring to such institutions. Richard Last, for instance, has suggested "Judean-deity groups/associations" instead of "synagogues," which foregrounds the identity of the patron deity of a group rather than the precise nature of that group (Last 2016a, 344).

In order to understand Jewish-Gentile interaction, various forms of Jewish associations are of enormous importance. They were modeled upon similar kinds of networks, like Greco-Roman associations and could be typologized on the basis of five sources of membership: (1) household networks; (2) ethnic connections; (3) inhabitants of a common neighborhood; (4) occupational networks; and (5) cult affiliations (Harland 2003, 28–29). According to Richard Last, "most associations recruited individuals from neighborhood or street based network" (2016a, 344). These categories should be used loosely: an occupational association could very well also be a neighborhood association and include members who happened to live on the same street where the occupational association had its workshops, and many household, ethnic, and neighborhood associations also had cultic functions (Kloppenborg 2019, 25).

The important thing here, however, is that even though some "synagogues," where membership was primarily based on devotion to the god of Israel, may have been ethnically homogenous, other forms of Jewish associations were not. Thus, such groups, for instance neighborhood or occupational associations, provided a space where Jews and Gentiles socially interacted and where the god of Israel was the patron deity or simply one among others (Last 2016b, 34–37). There is plenty of evidence of Gentiles worshiping the god of Israel together with Jews. Josephus, for instance, writes that the Jews of Antioch "were constantly attracting to their religious ceremonies multitudes of Greeks, and these they had in some measure incorporated with themselves" (*B.J.* 7.45; Thackery LCL). In addition, Luke mentions the presence of Greeks in "synagogues" (see, e.g., Acts 14:1, 17:1–4, 18:4). In Acts 11:19–20, Luke describes how some of those who had been forced to flee Jerusalem as a result of the stoning of Stephen (Acts 7:54–60) came to Antioch and "spoke to the Hellenists also, proclaiming the Lord Jesus." (All English translations of the Bible here, unless otherwise noted, are from the NRSV.) Even though Luke does not mention in what setting this took place, some form of association, perhaps a neighborhood or occupational association, is the most likely location.

To conclude, various forms of associations provided a shared space where Gentiles and Jews could socially interact. As John Kloppenborg has pointed out, the designation "voluntary" association is somewhat misleading, since "membership in occupational guilds was likely a pragmatic necessity ... membership was practically obligatory" (Kloppenborg 2019, 23; see also Last and Harland 2020, 9–13). Thus, despite negative mutual stereotyping, the Jewish tendency to keep separate, and the critique from the Roman elite, Jews and Gentiles did in fact socialize, and cultural exchange most likely went in both directions.

THE EARLY JESUS MOVEMENT— PAUL AND HIS OPPONENTS

The earliest sources of the Jesus movement are the undisputed letters of Paul, written during the 50s. Whereas the historical Jesus seems to have had a limited interest in the salvation of the nations (Sanders 1985, 218–21), the situation is quite different some twenty years later. Evidently, as Sanders has pointed out, "Jesus started a movement which came to see the Gentile mission as a logical extension of itself" (220). During the period when Paul was active, various representatives, often involved in serious disputes, were engaged in an extensive mission to the Gentiles. It appears as if Jews within the Jesus movement agreed that Gentiles were also affected by the Jesus-event and thus were subject to some form of inclusion in the final salvation, but they disagreed on what terms. On a general level, the interest in the Gentile world on the part of the Jewish Jesus movement should be seen against the background of the universalistic trend present within first-century Judaism, as presented here.

What distinguished the Jesus movement from other universalistic expressions was the eschatological urgency. Jews who had a positive attitude to Gentiles interested in Judaism presumably had some notion that the god of Israel, in a distant future, would also have mercy on the Gentile nations. But the early Jesus movement firmly believed that this time had come. Through the death and resurrection of Jesus, the messianic age had already begun—the Kingdom of God was at hand. This, I believe, is what triggered the use of certain texts from the Hebrew Bible and other Jewish works mentioned above, texts like Isaiah 2:2–4, which deals with the eschatological pilgrimage (Wagner 2003). In this way, the mission to the Gentiles could be seen as a form of legitimization process; when Gentiles turned to the god of Israel, this functioned as a confirmation of the idea that the end-time had come.

How one understands Paul's view of Gentiles and the relation between Jews and Gentiles is profoundly dependent on how Paul's relation to Judaism is understood. Up until the 1980s, the dominant hermeneutical key for interpreting Paul was that of conflict. After his so-called conversion on the road to Damascus, Paul was understood as standing outside Judaism, resulting in his repudiation of traditional Jewish identity markers and—above all—the Torah. According to many traditional mainstream interpretations, Paul ceased being a Jew when he became a "Christian." One peculiar effect of this paradigm was the idea that Paul in reality created a religious group beyond ethnic categories, "the Christians," separate from Jews and Gentiles (e.g., Sanders 1983, 171–79; see also Zetterholm 2009), meaning that the question of ethnicity played a subordinate role, if any, in most Pauline scholarship at the time. "The Christians" were believed to consist of former Jews and Gentiles now joined together by their "Christian" faith and characterized by a common, non-Jewish religious behavior.

Beginning with E. P. Sanders's now classic reconstruction of ancient Judaism (Sanders 1977), Pauline scholarship has undergone a dramatic development and has resulted in a gradual "re-Judaization" of the apostle, culminating in scholarly trends that locate Paul fully within Judaism. In sharp contrast to the view of ancient Judaism then prevalent, Sanders reached the conclusion that Judaism was not a legalistic religion but a religion of grace, a religious system where Torah observance functioned in a covenantal context, that is, what Sanders labeled "covenantal nomism" (422). The process of bringing Paul closer to Judaism has also affected how scholars imagine the relation between Jews and Gentiles within the early Jesus movement. In the decades that followed the publication of Sanders's magnum opus, Paul's Jewish identity was increasingly acknowledged, which naturally led to a problematization of the ethnic categories of the Jesus movement. Just to mention two examples: according to Philip F. Esler, Paul aimed at creating a common Christian identity while at the same time striving at maintaining the original identities of the two subgroups, Jews and Gentiles (Esler 2003). According to James D. G. Dunn, Paul overcame the merging of Jewish and Gentile identities by redefining "Israel" to mean "the called of God," thus creating a new common identity built solely on the relation to God, while still claiming that ethnic Israel had not lost its relation to the eschatological Israel (Dunn 1998). This clearly shows that scholars began to take ethnic categories seriously.

However, the process of reevaluating Paul's relation to Judaism that started with Sanders and was further developed by scholars mainly belonging to the scholarly tradition known as "the New Perspective on Paul" was hard to stop. Some scholars began to explore the possibility that Paul not only was Jewish in an ethnic sense, or had a Jewish background, but was as Jewish as any other Diaspora Jew. Pamela Eisenbaum has pertinently described this shift as the difference between considering Paul Jewish *kata sarka* or Jewish also *kata pneuma* (Eisenbaum 2005).

This scholarly tradition, known as the Paul-within-Judaism perspective (Nanos and Zetterholm 2015), rests upon two fundamental assumptions (Zetterholm 2020), which quite dramatically change how the relations between Jews and Gentiles within the Jesus movement are understood. First, if Paul is considered Jewish that means that he most likely also practiced Judaism. Admittedly, there are examples of Jews who seem to have abandoned Judaism (Josephus, *B.J.* 7.50; 1 Macc. 1:11–15), but this seems not to be the case with Paul, who repeatedly emphasizes his Jewishness and his loyalty with the people of Israel (Gal 1:12, 2:15; Rom 9:3, 11:1). There is, of course, no way of determining exactly how or to what degree Paul should be considered Torah observant, but that is true for virtually every other first-century Jewish person (Hedner Zetterholm 2015). However, it seems more likely that someone who claims to be "circumcised on the eighth day, a member of the people of Israel, of the tribe of Benjamin, a Hebrew born of Hebrews; as to the law, a Pharisee" (Phil 3:5) practices Judaism than not.

So why does Paul write all those negative things about the Torah (see, e.g., Gal 3:13, 3:23–24, Rom 7:5–6)? The answer from Paul-within-Judaism scholars is connected to the second major assumption: Paul, the apostle to the Gentiles, writes precisely to Gentiles—not Jews. It is undisputed that Paul presents himself as the apostle to the nations (Rom 1:5, 11:13; Gal 2:8). This means that he predominantly deals with questions that concern the salvation of the nations and that his letters are mainly directed to Gentiles, even though he occasionally also touches upon aspects relevant for Jews and deals with the relation between Israel and the Gentiles in the new economy of salvation. In short: Paul's main problem is not the Jews but the Gentile nations.

The main issue, and the major source of conflicts between different factions of the Jesus movement, concerned on what terms Gentiles should be connected to the Jesus movement. There seem to have been at least two major options. In Paul's letter to the Galatians, the focal problem seems to be that Gentiles are under pressure to become Jews. Paul apparently has a different opinion as he labels his opponent "false brothers" (Gal 2:4; my translation), and the Galatians bewitched fools (Gal 3:1). Acts, although significantly later, may give an idea of what was going on. Luke writes that people had come down from Judea to Antioch, claiming that the Gentiles had to be circumcised in order to be saved. This led to intense discussions, and it was decided that the issue should be discussed with the apostles in Jerusalem.

This meeting, later known as the Apostolic Council, took place around 49 and concerned precisely on what terms Gentiles should be allowed into the Jesus movement. According to Luke, "some believers who belonged to the sect of the Pharisees stood up and said, 'It is necessary for them to be circumcised and ordered to keep the law of Moses'" (Acts 15:5). Apparently, this was one serious option the early Jesus movement had to consider. Luke reports that the council reached the decision, the so-called Apostolic Decree, that Gentiles should not convert to Judaism but should "abstain only from things polluted by idols and from fornication and from whatever has been strangled and from blood" (Acts 15:20). In Galatians 2:1–10, Paul seems to refer to the same event, confirming that his faction won the day, while those arguing for conversion to Judaism lost.

Now, the Apostolic Decree has often been taken as an example of how the early Jesus movement exempted Gentiles from observing the Torah, especially the food regulations (Dunn 2020; Haenchen 1971, 449) or has been taken as meant to facilitate table-fellowship between Jews and Gentiles (Conzelmann 1987, 118). However, as noted by many scholars (see, e.g., 118–19; Haenchen 1971, 469), the Apostolic Decree is built on the Holiness Code in Leviticus 17–18 and includes precisely those laws that are applicable not only to Israel but also to the *gerim*, the resident stranger in the Land of Israel. Thus, the Apostolic Decree explicitly declared for all Gentile followers of Jesus the regulations that the Hebrew Bible had already imposed on Gentiles residing in the Land of Israel (Oliver 2013, 370–98; Zellentin 2018, 131). It is true that the Decree presumes that Gentile followers of Jesus should remain Gentiles and thus not be obliged to observe the Torah in its entirety. However, according to the Decree, they were expected to eat food acceptable to Jews and observe certain purity regulations, that is, to some extent behaving "Jewishly" (Nanos 2014). Jewish food laws and purity regulations seem to have played a vital part in the early Jesus movement. As Paula Fredriksen has pointed out, this seems to be "a much more radical form of Judaizing than diaspora synagogues ever requested, much less required" (Fredriksen 2017, 111).

The reason for this stricter attitude to Gentiles within the Jesus movement is probably found in problems caused by the assumed moral impurity of Gentiles. Even though Jews accepted that Gentiles were involved in Greco-Roman religion (Goodman 1995, 39–59), and, as I have shown, could also participate in associations where pagan deities were present, within the Jesus movement social interaction between Jews and Gentiles was taken to a whole new level. Gentiles were no longer seen as predominantly "idol worshipers" but as part of the people of God, aimed for salvation through the work of Jesus. Thus, completely new demands were placed on social interaction, and questions of to what extent Gentiles could be trusted naturally came up. One must keep in mind that it was not entirely possible for a Gentile to avoid involvement in "idolatry," unless he or she completely withdrew from society. The whole Greco-Roman society was permeated with religion, participation in the official religion was expected, certain rituals had to be performed in connection with births and deaths, and both business transactions and normal social relations involved cultic aspects (Price 1999; Turcan 2000). Thus, far from representing a liberation from the law, the Apostolic Decree placed an enormous burden on Gentile adherents to the movement, which for the majority was not completely possible to live up to. Thus, more intimate social relations in connection with suspicions that Gentile followers of Jesus were still involved in some Greco-Roman cultic activities may very well have affected some Jewish sensibilities.

From these points of departure, the demand from some within the Jesus movement to turn Gentiles into Jews seems logical, as that would take care of the whole problem with the assumed moral impurity of Gentile adherents to the movement. As Jews, former Gentiles would be obliged to observe the Torah in the way Jews within the movement did, and they would also enjoy legal protection for doing so. Recall that Jews were normally permitted to practice their religion.

Paul, however, insisted, in accordance with the apostles in Jerusalem, that Gentiles should remain Gentiles and that they should not observe the Torah. This last aspect is somewhat confusing; as I have noted, the Apostolic Decree is built on the Torah. Even if it is highly probable that Paul knew and endorsed the Decree (Sandt and Flusser 2002, 245), it cannot be certain that he knew it exactly in the form it appears in Acts. It is, however, undisputable that his instructions to Gentiles are based on Torah ethics, which also appears in the Decree, especially the prohibitions of "idolatry" (e.g., 1 Cor 5:11, 10:14) and "sexual immorality" (πορνεία; e.g., 1 Cor 5:11, 6:13, 6:18). So while Paul's instruction to Gentiles could be defined as "Torah teaching," at the same time he emphatically encourages them not to put their trust in the Torah. How is this contradiction to be resolved? The key, I believe, is to take Paul's audience into consideration.

It is almost completely certain that those Gentiles who were attracted to the Jesus movement had previously been in contact with Jews and Judaism, either in ethnic-based "synagogues" or in ethnic heterogenous associations. It is also highly probable that they had learnt that the Torah provided wisdom, even a way to achieve self-mastery (ἐγκράτεια), one of the most valued virtues in Greco-Roman culture (Stowers 1994, 58–65). It is thus likely that Paul encountered Gentiles who, to varying degrees, could be described as Torah observant. Paul's attitude to Gentile Torah observance makes most sense if one assumes that he, unlike many other Jews, believed the Torah was the most precious gift to the Jewish people, not intended for Gentiles, an idea one finds later in early rabbinic literature (Hirshman 2000). If Gentiles thus imitated a Jewish lifestyle, claiming a special relationship to God by observing the Torah, they would enter a path to salvation not intended for them, which in effect would prevent them from being saved: "You who want to be justified by the law have cut yourselves off from Christ; you have fallen away from grace" (Gal 5:4). For Paul it seems to have been imperative to preserve the ethnic distinction between Jews and the Gentile nations. According to the divine plan, humanity is to be saved as Jews and Gentiles, which may have been a result of the notion that God is the God of the whole world: if Gentiles were to become Jews, God would no longer be the God of Jews only, and his oneness would thus be compromised (Rom 3:29–30; Nanos 1996, 9–10). As argued by Matthew Thiessen (2011), it is possible that Paul even believed that conversion to Judaism was impossible for genealogical reasons—only those circumcised on the eighth day belong to the covenant, an idea also found in Jubilees 15:26, and which effectively prevents conversion to Judaism (Livesey 2010). In addition, Christine Hayes has recently suggested that Paul's negative statement on Torah observance is a rhetorical strategy using the ancient Greco-Roman dichotomy between divine law and human law in order to dissuade Gentiles from observing the Torah in a Jewish way (Hayes 2017).

Although Paul probably shared a negative view of Gentiles in general (Rom 1:18–32; Gal 2:15), he firmly believed that through Christ, the God of Israel had provided a way for Gentiles also to be accepted by God. Once, even Paul's Gentiles had been lost because of their evil deeds, fornication, idolatry, adultery, and so on, but now they had been "washed" (ἀπελούσασθε), "sanctified" (ἡγιάσθητε), and "justified" (ἐδικαιώθητε) in the name of the Lord Jesus Christ and in the Spirit of our God" (1 Cor 5:11), clearly a reference to baptism. According to Paul, Gentiles in Christ were now as holy and pure as Israel, since ethnicity, social status, or gender no longer mattered for a relationship with God (Gal 3:28). If such Gentiles behaved, that is, observed the Apostolic Decree, they could be saved. For Paul, the social implication is that such Gentiles could be trusted. This could, for instance, manifest itself at common meals, where Gentiles perhaps were allowed to bring food and seating was arranged in order to minimize social and ethnic status (Nanos 2002). Thus, Paul's theological conviction was transformed into a social reality that challenged normal Jewish social conventions on how to socially interact with Gentiles.

The main cause of the harsh conflicts within the movement was, accordingly, the question of how to relate to Gentiles in Christ. Should they remain Gentiles and observe the Apostolic Decree, as Paul and the apostles in Jerusalem had agreed on, or should they simply become Torah observant Jews, as "some believers who belonged to the sect of the Pharisees" argued (Acts 15:5)? Or should they remain Gentiles but observe as much of the Torah as possible (especially "food offered to idols"), which seems to be the suggestion of Didache 6:2–3? Furthermore, even when there was agreement that Gentiles should not become Jews, the question of how Jews and Gentiles should relate to each other was not settled, which is evident from the so-called Antioch incident (Gal 2:1–11), where Paul rebukes Peter for having withdrawn from table-fellowship with Gentiles because Peter was under pressure from people from Jerusalem (Zetterholm 2016).

To sum up, the sources reveal an ongoing negotiation regarding the status of the Gentiles within the early Jesus movement, and various positions can be identified. The common denominator is probably the assumed moral impurity of the Gentiles because of the possibility that they were still engaged in some form of "idolatry." The various positions one finds in the sources can be said to constitute strategies to handle the problem of Gentile impurity.

The Gentiles in the Synoptic Gospels

The recent trend of placing the early Jesus movement in a Jewish setting has also affected the study of the canonical gospels—hitherto with the exception of the Gospel of Mark. Traditionally, Mark's Gospel is believed to have been written in Rome, for a Roman Gentile audience (see, e.g., Taylor 1966). In addition, more recent studies favor a Roman origin (see, e.g., Incigneri 2003), while some scholars suggest an Eastern location, in Syria (Antioch) or in the Land of Israel (see discussion in Yarbro Collins 2007, 7–10, 96–102). Most scholars, however, conclude that Mark addressed a Gentile audience mainly because he wrote in Greek and because of his explanations of Jewish customs and translations of Aramaic terms and phrases (e.g., Cranfield 1959, 8).

In 1995, Eric K. Wefald suggested that Mark's Jesus in fact conducts a separate mission to the Gentiles in parallel to the mission to the Jews (1995). More recently, this idea was further developed in a monograph by Kelly R. Iverson (2007). Iverson notices that little interest has been devoted to the Gentiles in Mark and identifies eleven Gentile characters in Mark: the crowd by the sea (Mark 3:7–12), the Gerasene demoniac (5:1–20), the Syrophoenician woman (7:24–30), a deaf man (7:21–37), the 4,000 people (8:1–9), a blind man (8:22–26), the father with a demon-possessed son (9:14–29), Pilate (15:1–15, 42–47), soldiers (15:16–41), Simon of Cyrene (15:21), and the centurion (15:39, 44–45).

Iverson connects these Gentile characters to Jesus's four journeys into Gentile territory, during which he encounters some of the aforementioned characters, and to the events during the trial and execution of Jesus. Gentiles are typically presented positively and as recipients of Jesus's compassion, Iverson claims, and are characterized by desperation, faith, and understanding, even though there are exceptions, especially in the Passion narrative, where some Gentiles act as opponents of Jesus. Taken together, however, the four journeys form a sequence of events that reveals a theological progression, Iverson states, which culminates in the gospel being handed over to the Gentiles: "the Gospel has been passed from the Jews to the Gentiles in accordance with the divine plan" (Iverson 2007, 186).

In stark contrast to Iverson's traditional, even supersessionist perspective, John Van Maaren (2019; see also Van Maaren 2022) has offered a new interpretation that clearly also places the Gospel of Mark in a Jewish setting and significantly affects Gentile-Jew relations. Using social-scientific theories of ethnicity, Van Maaren argues that Mark's narrative assumes a basic binary between Israel and Gentile nations and an Israel-centric vision of the future kingdom of God. Van Maaren also questions the idea of clear-cut Gentile territories: in all the places Jesus visits there is a substantial Jewish population, and it may very well be the case that Jesus is targeting the Jewish residents in, for instance, Tyre, Sidon, Caesarea Philippi, and the cities of the Decapolis area.

As for the story of the Syrophoenician woman (Mark 7:24–30), Van Maaren claims that the narrative *reinforces* the Jew/Gentile boundary. He notices that since the daughter's healing is dependent on the woman's acceptance of the hierarchical difference between Israel and the nations, the power inequality depicted as the privilege of children over dogs is not overturned in the narrative. Furthermore, according to Van Maaren, Mark includes no indication of a future mission to the Gentiles. The proof text for the existence of such a mission is Mark 13:9–10, usually translated "and you will stand before governors and kings because of me, as a testimony to them. And the good news must first be proclaimed to all nations." This translation assumes that the phrase "to all nations" (εἰς πάντα τὰ ἔθνη) modifies the following sentence. Van Maaren, however, argues that for grammatical reasons εἰς πάντα τὰ ἔθνη should instead be linked to the preceding phrase: "you will stand for my sake for witnesses to them and to all the nations." If this is correct, there are no signs of a future mission to the Gentiles in Mark.

Mark is certainly not unaware of a mission to the Gentiles, or antagonistic to such a project, Van Maaren concludes, but the peripheral role Gentiles play in the future kingdom could indicate that Mark assumes that Jesus's mission was directed to Jews.

And since obedience to God is directly connected with Torah observance in Mark's Gospel, as Van Maaren claims, it is possible that Torah observance would be required from Gentiles wanting to be included in Mark's community. If Van Maaren is correct in his carefully conducted analysis, the Gentile character of Mark's Gospel fades away and the Gospel seems more closely connected to the earliest reception of Mark—the Gospel of Matthew.

The Jewish character of Matthew's Gospel has been recognized since antiquity. Papias's comment in the second century, repeated somewhat later by Irenaeus (*Haer.* 3.1.1.), that the Gospel originally was written in Hebrew assumes that the author was Jewish and that the Gospel was intended for a Jewish audience. Even though attempts have been made to argue that Matthew was a Gentile who wrote for a Gentile audience (Clark 1947) or that Matthew had detached himself from Judaism (see, e.g., Bornkamm 1970–71), today the majority of Matthean scholars would agree on the Jewish nature of Matthew (Evans 2007, 241–45).

The Gentiles in Matthew are, with few exceptions, negatively portrayed. For instance, in Matthew 6:7–8, the audience is warned not to "heap up empty phrases as the Gentiles do" and encouraged not to imitate a Gentile lifestyle; in 6:31–32, the audience is warned not to worry about what to eat, drink, or wear as the Gentiles do; in 7:6, Jesus states that one should "not give what is holy to dogs" or throw "pearls before swine," most likely with Gentiles in mind. According to David C. Sim, the Matthean group "saw the Gentile world as a foreign place, held its religious practices in some contempt, and minimised their contact with their Gentile neighbours" (Sim 2013, 180–81).

Several scholars have reached the conclusion that Matthew's negative view of the Gentile world implies that the Matthean group only accepted *former* Gentiles in their community, that is, Gentiles who had converted to Judaism and thus observed the Torah (Overman 1990; Runesson 2016; Saldarini 1994; Sim 1998). The "believers who belonged to the sect of the Pharisees, who argued that Gentiles had to convert to Judaism" (Acts 15:5) and Paul's "opponents" in Galatians show that such ideas indeed existed within the Jesus movement, and it is entirely feasible that the Gospel of Matthew represents that view.

Whether or not such "Judaizing" entailed male circumcision is in dispute (see discussion in Oliver 2013, 403–10), but Anders Runesson has recently made a compelling argument in favor of male circumcision of Gentiles as an entry requirement to the Matthean group. He has also, however, identified one category of Gentiles who will be saved without converting to Judaism (Runesson 2020). Runesson notices that Gentiles are relatively absent from the narrative and only rarely addressed in their own right. Their main function is to serve as examples of unacceptable behavior—Jews who break the Torah are likened to Gentiles. This indicates that there is a basic distinction between Jews and Gentiles in Matthew's symbolic world.

It is evident from Matthew 28:19–20, Runesson states, that the Matthean Jesus requires complete submission to the Torah, both from his Jewish followers and from Gentiles who are being taught everything Jesus has commanded his disciples, including that "not one stroke of a letter, will pass from the law" (Matt 5:18). The proper term for this is *proselytism*, Runesson concludes, and thus involves a transformation of the status of Gentiles to become Jews. There is, however, one further possibility, according to Runesson, indicated in the parable of the sheep and the goats in Matthew 25:31–46. The "least" (ἐλάχιστος) in the parable refers to followers of Jesus, while "all the nations" (πάντα τὰ ἔθνη) refers to Gentiles, excluding Jews, Runesson maintains. The common denominator of those who are judged (positively or negatively) is that they knew nothing of Jesus or his teaching but are judged solely on how they have interacted with followers of Jesus, thereby activating the blessing or curse connected with Abraham in Genesis 12:3 (on this, see also Runesson 2016, 393–428).

If one accepts Runesson's analysis, the Gospel of Matthew seems to present a salvation economy where humanity finally is redeemed according to the categories Jews (including proselytes) and Gentiles, that is, those Gentiles who have showed compassion for followers of Jesus.

In Luke's Gospel, Jesus's interaction with Gentiles is less emphasized compared to Mark and Matthew. Luke has, for instance, not included two stories involving Gentiles found in Mark: the Syrophoenician woman (Mark 7:24–30) and Mark's second feeding story (8:1–10). It is clear, however, that Gentiles play a significant role in the Lukan vision of the salvation of humanity. Already in the beginning of Luke, Jesus is said to be "a light for revelation to the Gentiles" (Luke 2:32), a clear allusion to Isaiah 49:6. In 3:6, Luke expands his Markan source by adding a verse from Isaiah 40:5 (LXX) "and all flesh [πᾶσα σάρξ] shall see the salvation of God," and in 24:47, the risen Christ says, regarding the Messiah, that "repentance and forgiveness of sins is to be proclaimed in his name to all nations [εἰς πάντα τὰ ἔθνη], beginning from Jerusalem." The Gentiles in Luke's Gospel, Elisabeth Dowling states, are "clearly announced as being included in salvation and Jesus ministers to some Gentiles, but, at the same time, his interactions with Gentiles are far more limited and given less focus" (Dowling 2013, 197).

It seems that Luke has consciously downplayed the presence of Gentiles and instead highlighted the role of the Samaritans, who are never mentioned in Mark's Gospel and only once (negatively) in Matthew: "enter no town of the Samaritans" (Matt 10:5). The fact is that whereas Matthew uses Gentiles as an example of *unacceptable* behavior, Luke uses Samaritans, who certainly are not as bad as Gentiles but still are not regarded as Jewish (Dowling 2013: 198; see Jervell 1972, 113–32), as *positive examples* that Jews should follow. This develops in two key stories: the parable of the Good Samaritan (Luke 10:25–37) and the healing of the ten lepers (Luke 17:11–19), where a Samaritan (called a "stranger"; ἀλλογενής) is the only one who returns to thank Jesus after having been healed.

David Ravens (1995) has suggested that the positive attitude toward the Samaritans is part of Luke's overarching project of restoring Israel, which would involve the reunification of historical Judah and Samaria, thus reestablishing the Davidic kingdom, which is the prerequisite for reaching out to the Gentiles. Luke's missionary strategy is laid out in Acts 1:8, where the risen Christ tells his disciples that they will be his "witnesses in Jerusalem, in all Judea and Samaria, and to the ends of the earth." Consequently, after Pentecost, a proper mission to the Samaritans is introduced in 8:4–25. Luke reports that Philip, Peter, and John successfully bring the gospel to the Samaritans, who have been baptized and received the Holy Spirit. Only hereafter Acts introduces the mission to the Gentiles, possibly through the story of the conversion of the Ethiopian eunuch (Acts 8:26–40)—whose ethnic identity is, perhaps deliberately, not entirely clear (Conzelmann 1987, 314)—but certainly in the story of the conversion of Cornelius (Acts 10:1–11:18). Unlike the Ethiopian eunuch, Cornelius is clearly identified as a Gentile, a centurion, and "a devout man who feared God" (10:2). The lesson Peter learns from his vision of "all kinds of four-footed creatures and reptiles and birds" and the following call to slaughter and eat (Acts 10:9–16) is strangely not connected to food but to the idea that he "should not call anyone profane or unclean" (10:27). Thus, every obstacle, especially moral impurity, preventing close contacts with Gentiles is now removed, and when Peter reports that the Holy Spirit has been poured out also on Gentile believers, even his opponents give in and conclude: "Then God has given even to the Gentiles the repentance that leads to life" (11:18).

In the remaining part of Acts, Paul's role as the apostle to the nations is firmly established. The decisive point in the narrative is Acts 13:44–47. During the so-called first missionary travel, Paul and Barnabas are met with fierce resistance from some Jews in Antioch in Pisidia: the Jews "were filled with jealousy; and blaspheming, they contradicted what was spoken by Paul." To this, Paul and Barnabas respond by stating that it was necessary that the word of God was first spoken to Jews, but since they now reject it, Paul and Barnabas will turn to the Gentiles, which according to the divine plan is predicted already in Luke 1:8 and now repeated: "'I have set you to be a light for the Gentiles, so that you may bring salvation to the ends of the earth.'" With the establishment of the Apostolic Decree in Acts 15, Gentiles have a well-defined position in the salvation economy. They are clearly included in the movement as Gentiles, obliged to observe the Apostolic Decree, thus behaving "Jewishly" to a considerable degree, and they should not be considered profane or unclean.

The Synoptic tradition thus displays a wide range of attitudes toward the Gentiles, who are presented both in negative and positive terms. All Synoptics effectively preserve the distinction between Jews and Gentiles. Tentatively, it is possible to discern two major trajectories. On the one hand Mark and Matthew appear to define a follower of Jesus predominantly in Jewish terms, and Jesus's mission as directed to the Jewish people. To the extent that Gentiles are included, they must become Jews, or at least be obliged to observe the Torah. This seems to be the position of some Jews within the Jesus movement, as evidenced from Paul's "opponents," especially in Galatians, and from Acts 15:5. Matthew, however, seems to be open to the possibility that some Gentiles could be saved, not by putting their trust in Jesus but by showing mercy to followers of Jesus. Thus, Matthew is not completely foreign to the idea that humanity is saved according to the categories Jews and Gentiles.

In Luke-Acts one finds the second major trajectory, already anticipated in the works of Paul. The mission to the Gentiles has always been part of the divine plan for the salvation of humanity, and the salvation of Israel is intimately connected with the salvation of the nations. Jews are supposed to remain Jews, and Gentiles should not become Jews, as this would compromise the idea of God's oneness. One main reason for the emergence of these traditions is most likely the problem of how to deal with the assumed moral impurity of Gentiles. Mark's and Matthew's solution is simply to emphasize the Jewish nature of the movement; Luke (in agreement with Paul) believes that the god of Israel, through Christ, has provided means for Gentiles to be as holy and pure as Israel.

REFERENCES

Barchiesi, Alessandro. 2009. "Roman Perspectives on the Greeks." In *The Oxford Handbook of Hellenic Studies*, edited by George Boys-Stones, Barbara Graziosi, and Phiroze Vasunia, 98–113. Oxford: Oxford University Press.

Barclay, John M. G. 1996. *Jews in the Mediterranean Diaspora: From Alexander to Trajan (323 BCE–117 CE)*. Edinburgh: T&T Clark.

Beard, Mary, John A. North, and Simon R. F. Price. 1998. *Religions of Rome*. Vol. 1. *A History*. Cambridge: Cambridge University Press.

Bornkamm, Günther. 1970–71. "The Authority to 'Bind' and 'Loose' in the Church in Matthew's Gospel: The Problem of Sources in Matthew's Gospel." In *Jesus and Man's Hope*, edited by Donald G Miller and Dikran Y. Hadidian, 37–50. Pittsburgh: Pittsburgh Theological Seminary.

Champion, Craige B. 2017. *The Peace of the Gods: Elite Religious Practices in the Middle Roman Republic*. Princeton: Princeton University Press.

Clark, Kenneth W. 1947. "The Gentile Bias in Matthew." *Journal of Biblical Literature* 66: 165–72.

Conzelmann, Hans. 1987. *Acts of the Apostles: A Commentary on the Acts of the Apostles*. Phildelphia: Fortress.

Cranfield, Charles Ernest Burland. 1959. *The Gospel According to Saint Mark: An Introduction and Commentary*. Cambridge: Cambridge University Press.

Donaldson, Terence L. 2007. *Judaism and the Gentiles: Patterns of Universalism (to 135 CE)*. Waco: Baylor University Press.

Dowling, Elizabeth V. 2013. "Attitudes to Gentiles in Luke-Acts." In *Attitudes to Gentiles in Ancient Judaism and Early Christianity*, edited by David C. Sim and James S. McLaren, 191–208. London: Bloomsbury T&T Clark.

Dunn, James D. G. 1998. *The Theology of Paul the Apostle*. Grand Rapids: Eerdmans.

Dunn, James D. G. 2020. "The New Perspective on Paul." In *Perspectives on Paul: Five Views*, edited by Scot McKnight and B. J. Oropeza, 133–70. Grand Rapids: Baker Academic.

Eisenbaum, Pamela. 2005. "Paul, Polemics, and the Problem of Essentialism." *Biblical Interpretation* 13: 224–38.

Esler, Philip F. 2003. *Conflict and Identity in Romans: The Social Setting in Paul's Letter*. Minneapolis: Fortress.

Evans, Craig A. 2007. "The Jewish Christian Gospel Tradition." In *Jewish Believers in Jesus: The Early Centuries*, edited by Oscar Skarsaune and Reidar Hvalvik, 241–77. Peabody, MA: Hendrickson.

Fredriksen, Paula. 2017. *Paul, the Pagans' Apostle*. New Haven: Yale University Press.

Gambetti, Sandra. 2009. *The Alexandrian Riots of 38 C.E. and the Persecution of the Jews: A Historical Reconstruction*. Leiden: Brill.

Goodman, Martin. 1995. *Mission and Conversion: Proselytizing in the Religious History of the Roman Empire*. Oxford: Oxford University Press.

Gruen, Erich S. 2002. *Diaspora: Jews amidst Greeks and Romans*. Cambridge, MA: Harvard University Press.

Haenchen, Ernst. 1971. *The Acts of the Apostles: A Commentary*. Oxford: Blackwell.

Harland, Philip A. 2003. *Associations, Synagogues, and Congregations: Claiming a Place in Ancient Mediterranean Society*. Minneapolis: Fortress.

Hayes, Christine Elizabeth. 2002. *Gentile Impurities and Jewish Identities: Intermarriage and Conversion from the Bible to the Talmud*. Oxford: Oxford University Press.

Hayes, Christine Elizabeth. 2017. *What's Divine about Divine Law? Early Perspectives*. Princeton: Princeton University Press.

Hedner Zetterholm, Karin. 2015. "The Question of Assumptions: Torah Observance in the First Century." In *Paul within Judaism: Restoring the First-Century Context to the Apostle*, edited by Mark D. Nanos and Magnus Zetterholm, 79–104. Minneapolis: Fortress.

Hirshman, Marc. 2000. "Rabbinic Universalism in the Second and Third Centuries." *Harvard Theological Review* 93: 101–15.

Incigneri, Brian J. 2003. *The Gospel to the Romans: The Setting and Rhetoric of Mark's Gospel*. Leiden: Brill.

Isaac, Benjamin. 2004. *The Invention of Racism in Classical Antiquity*. Princeton: Princeton University Press.

Iverson, Kelly R. 2007. *Gentiles in the Gospel of Mark: "Even the Dogs under the Table Eat the Children's Crumbs."* London: T&T Clark.

Jervell, Jacob. 1972. *Luke and the People of God: A New Look at Luke-Acts*. Minneapolis: Augsburg.

Kloppenborg, John S. 2019. *Christ's Associations: Connecting and Belonging in the Ancient City*. New Haven: Yale University Press.

Last, Richard. 2016a. "The Other Synagogues." *Journal for the Study of Judaism* 47: 330–63.

Last, Richard. 2016b. *The Pauline Church and the Corinthian Ekklēsia: Greco-Roman Associations in Comparative Context*. New York: Cambridge University Press.

Last, Richard, and Philip A. Harland. 2020. *Group Survival in the Ancient Mediterranean: Rethinking Material Conditions in the Landscape of Jews and Christians*. London: T&T Clark.

Livesey, Nina E. 2010. *Circumcision as a Malleable Symbol*. Tübingen: Mohr Siebeck.

McGing, Brian. 2002. "Population and Proselytism: How Many Jews Were There in the Ancient World?" In *Jews in the Hellenistic and Roman Cities*, edited by John R. Bartlett, 88–106. London: Routledge.

Murray, Michele. 2004. *Playing a Jewish Game: Gentile Christian Judaizing in the First and Second Centuries CE*. Waterloo: Wilfred Laurier University Press.

Nanos, Mark D. 1996. *The Mystery of Romans: The Jewish Context of Paul's Letter*. Minneapolis: Fortress.

Nanos, Mark D. 2002. "What Was at Stake in Peter's 'Eating with Gentiles' at Antioch?" In *The Galatians Debate: Contemporary Issues in Rhetorical and Historical Interpretation*, edited by Mark D. Nanos, 282–320. Peabody, MA: Hendrickson.

Nanos, Mark D. 2014. "Paul's Non-Jews Do Not Become 'Jews,' but Do They Become 'Jewish'? Reading Romans 2:25–29 within Judaism, alongside Josephus." *Journal of the Jesus Movement in Its Jewish Setting* 1: 26–53.

Nanos, Mark D., and Magnus Zetterholm, eds. 2015. *Paul within Judaism: Restoring the First-Century Context to the Apostle*. Minneapolis: Fortress.

Novenson, Matthew V. 2022. "Gentile Sinners: A Brief History of an Ancient Stereotype." In *Negotiating Identities: Conflict, Conversion, and Consolidation in Early Judaism and Christianity (200 BCE–400 CE)*, edited by Karin Hedner Zetterholm, Anders Runesson, Cecilia Wassén and Magnus Zetterholm, 159–179. New York: Lexington, Fortress Academic.

Oliver, Isaac W. 2013. *Torah Praxis after 70 CE: Reading Matthew and Luke-Acts as Jewish Texts*. Tübingen: Mohr Siebeck.

Overman, J. Andrew. 1990. *Matthew's Gospel and Formative Judaism: The Social World of the Matthean Community*. Minneapolis: Fortress.

Phang, Sara E. 2016. "Barbarians." In *Conflict in Ancient Greece and Rome: The Definitive Political, Social, and Military Encyclopedia*, edited by Sara E. Phang, Iain Spence, Douglas Kelly, and Peter Londey, 731. Santa Barbara, CA: ABC-CLIO.

Price, Simon. 1999. *Religions of the Ancient Greeks*. Cambridge: Cambridge University Press.

Rajak, Tessa. 1984. "Was There a Roman Charter for the Jews?" *Journal of Roman Studies* 74: 107–23.

Ravens, David. 1995. *Luke and the Restoration of Israel*. Sheffield: Sheffield Academic.

Runesson, Anders. 2016. *Divine Wrath and Salvation in Matthew: The Narrative World of the First Gospel*. Minneapolis: Fortress.

Runesson, Anders. 2020. "Aspects of Matthean Universalism: Ethnic Identity as a Theological Tool in the First Gospel." In *Matthew within Judaism: Israel and the Nations in the First Gospel*, edited by Anders Runesson and Daniel M Gurtner, 103–34. Atlanta: SBL.

Rüpke, Jörg. 2014. "Ethnicity in Roman Religion." In *A Companion to Ethnicity in the Ancient Mediterranean*, edited by Jeremy McInerney, 470–82. London: Blackwell.

Saldarini, Anthony J. 1994. *Matthew's Christian-Jewish Community*. Chicago: University of Chicago Press.

Sanders, Ed Parrish. 1977. *Paul and Palestinian Judaism: A Comparison of Patterns of Religion*. Minneapolis: Fortress.

Sanders, Ed Parrish. 1983. *Paul, the Law, and the Jewish People*. Minneapolis: Fortress.

Sanders, Ed Parrish. 1985. *Jesus and Judaism*. Philadelphia: Fortress.

Schäfer, Peter. 1997. *Judeophobia: Attitudes toward the Jews in the Ancient World*. Cambridge, MA: Harvard University Press.

Sim, David C. 1998. *The Gospel of Matthew and Christian Judaism: The History and Social Setting of the Matthean Community*. Edinburgh: T&T Clark.

Sim, David C. 2013. "The Attitude to Gentiles in the Gospel of Matthew." In *Attitudes to Gentiles in Ancient Judaism and Early Christianity*, edited by David C. Sim and James S. McLaren, 173–90. London: Bloomsbury T&T Clark.

Stowers, Stanley K. 1994. *A Rereading of Romans: Justice, Jews and Gentiles*. New Haven: Yale University Press.

Taylor, Vincent. 1966. *The Gospel According to St. Mark*. London: Macmillan.

Tellbe, Mikael. 2001. *Paul between Synagogue and State: Christians, Jews, and Civic Authorities in 1 Thessalonians, Romans, and Philippians*. Stockholm: Almqvist & Wiksell International.

Thiessen, Matthew. 2011. *Contesting Conversion: Genealogy, Circumcision, and Identity in Ancient Judaism and Christianity*. Oxford: Oxford University Press.

Tomson, Peter J. 1990. *Paul and the Jewish Law: Halakha in the Letters of the Apostle to the Gentiles*. Assen: van Gorcum.

Turcan, Robert. 2000. *The Gods of Ancient Rome*. Edinburgh: Edinburgh University Press.

van de Sandt, Huub, and David Flusser. 2002. *The Didache: Its Jewish Sources and Its Place in Early Judaism and Christianity*. Minneapolis: Fortress.

Van Maaren, John. 2019. "The Gospel of Mark within Judaism: Reading the Second Gospel in Its Ethnic Landscape." PhD diss., McMaster University.

Van Maaren, John. 2022. "Gentile Alterity and Ethnic Solidarity: The Role of Group Categorization in Understanding Mark as Jewish Literature." In *Negotiating Identities: Conflict, Conversion, and Consolidation in Early Judaism and Christianity (200 BCE–400 CE)*, edited by Karin Hedner Zetterholm, Anders Runesson, Cecilia Wassén, and Magnus Zetterholm. 139–158. New York: Lexington, Fortress Academic.

Wagner, J. Ross. 2003. *Heralds of the Good News: Isaiah and Paul in Concert in the Letter to the Romans*. Leiden: Brill.

Wefald, Eric K. 1995. "The Separate Gentile Mission in Mark: A Narrative Explanation of Markan Geography, The Two Feeding Accounts and Exorcisms." *Journal for the Study of the New Testament* 60: 3–26.

Yarbro Collins, Adela. 2007. *Mark: A Commentary*. Minneapolis: Fortress.

Zellentin, Holger. 2018. "Judaeo-Christian Legal Culture and the Qur'an: The Case of Ritual Slaugther and the Consumption of Animal Blood." In *Jewish-Christianity and Origins of Islam: Papers presented at the Colloquium Held in Washington, DC, October 29–31, 2015 (8th ASMEA Conference)*, edited by Francisco del Rio Sanchez. 117–159. Brepols: Turnhout.

Zetterholm, Magnus. 2009. *Approaches to Paul: A Student's Guide to Recent Scholarship*. Minneapolis: Fortress.

Zetterholm, Magnus. 2016. "The Antioch Incident Revisited." *Journal for the Study of Paul and His Letters* 6: 249–59.

Zetterholm, Magnus. 2020. "The Paul within Judaism Perspective." In *Perspectives on Paul: Five Views*, edited by Scot McKnight and B. J. Oropeza, 171–218. Grand Rapids: Baker Academic.

CHAPTER 27

ISRAEL'S SCRIPTURES

SUSAN E. DOCHERTY

INTRODUCTION

THE authors of Mark, Matthew, and Luke evidently held a shared understanding that neither Jesus's ministry nor his death could be fully explained apart from Israel's scriptures, even though the extent of their recourse to them, and the nature of their engagement with them, differs in some respects. This chapter provides an overview of the major features of the use of scripture in each Gospel, followed by a comparative discussion of key issues, such as text form and exegetical method, all set in the wider context of early Jewish interpretation. Mark's account forms the starting point for this review, on the assumption that it served as a primary source for Matthew and Luke. The English translation of the Bible used throughout is the RSV.

The number of direct citations is not necessarily a good indicator of the influence of the scriptures on the evangelists, since their rhetorical and theological aims are often advanced through more implicit reuse of scriptural language, imagery, and narrative models. There are also different ways of counting composite and repeated citations, and of distinguishing between quotations and allusions. However, the following definite and narrowly defined citations can be identified within each of the three Gospels:

Mark: 18 (Torah 7; Psalms 4; Isaiah 6; Zechariah 1)
Matthew: 40 (Torah 12; Psalms 10; Isaiah 9; Jeremiah 1; Hosea 3; Micah 1; Zechariah 3; Malachi 1)
Luke: 20 (Torah 6; Psalms 8; Isaiah 4; Hosea 1; Malachi 1)

These figures reveal some variation in at least the formal presentation of scriptural material. Other, generally more inclusive, summary counts can be found in, for example, Beaton (2002, 17), Kimball (1994, 204–5), Moyise (2001, 34, 45), Pao (2007, 251), Soares Prabhu (1976, 18) and Watts (2007, 111).

The Use of Israel's Scriptures in the Gospels

The Gospel of Mark

Citations

The reader of Mark is immediately struck by the frequency of his appeal to Isaiah, especially in the first half of his narrative. He connects the "good news" of Jesus from the outset to the story of Israel by beginning with a citation of Isaiah 40:3, conflated with Malachi 3:1/Exodus 23:20 (1:2–3). This is the only example of the evangelist employing a scriptural text as editorial comment rather than as spoken directly by Jesus or another character. Its positioning has led many commentators to regard it as programmatic for the Gospel as a whole, indicating Mark's expectation of the imminent realization of the prophetic hopes for future deliverance. In influential studies, Marcus (1992), for example, equates "the way" (8:22–10:52) of Jesus with the fulfillment of the triumphant march of Yahweh through the wilderness, anticipated by Isaiah, but now reinterpreted in the light of the cross, while Watts (1997) characterizes the salvation on offer to those who accept Jesus as an "Isaianic new exodus." Too much weight should not be placed on this single citation, however, since a whole range of scriptural texts and themes are drawn upon in Mark to give expression to his understanding of Jesus.

Further citations from Isaiah follow, including two placed on the lips of Jesus in order to explain the problematic fact that he faced opposition and misunderstanding from his contemporaries (Isa 6:9–10 at Mark 4:12; see Mark 8:17–18; Isa 29:13 at Mark 7:6–7). As the narrative progresses, the Torah is then quoted several times in the context of halakhic disputes between Jesus and the religious leaders (Mark 10:2–12; cf. Gen 1:27; 2:24; 5:2; cf. Deut 24:1–4; 10:17–22; 12:28–34; cf. Exod 20:12–16; Lev 19:18; Deut 5:16–20; 6:4–5). Mark clearly assumes, then, in common with other New Testament authors, that the Jewish law remains the foundation for the ethical practice of his community.

The Psalms of Lament (especially Pss 22, 41, and 69) provide the dominant scriptural backdrop to the Markan account of Jesus's last days. His acknowledgment in Gethsemane of his deep sorrow at his approaching suffering echoes the refrain in Psalms 42–43 (14:34; see Pss 42:5, 11; 43:5), for instance, and his dying words are a citation of Psalm 22:1 (Mark 15:34). This particular psalm is alluded to in several details of Jesus's crucifixion, such as the casting of lots for his garments (Mark 15:24; see Ps 22:18) and the mocking of the bystanders (Mark 15:29–32; see Ps 22:7–8). Stephen Ahearne-Kroll (2007) argues that the assumed Davidic authorship of the psalms is fundamental to their use by the evangelists in this context, as it enables them to surround even Jesus's ignominious death with messianic connotations. Other scriptural passages have also been identified as possible intertexts for the passion narrative, including the depiction of the testing of the righteous one in Wisdom 2:12–20 (e.g., Nickelsburg 1980; see, specifically on Luke's theology of the cross, Doble 1996); the suffering servant of Deutero-Isaiah (e.g., Moo 1983); and Zechariah 13–14 (e.g., Evans 2006b), which sets the future "day of the Lord" on the Mount of Olives (Zech 14:4; see Mark 11:1; 13:3; 14:26), and from which an explicit citation is taken, in Jesus's remark before his arrest: "I will strike the shepherd, and the sheep will be scattered (Mark 14:27; see Zech 13:7).

Allusions

The relative paucity of formal citations in Mark, especially when compared to Matthew, has resulted in an underappreciation of the importance of the scriptures for his narrative and theology (e.g., Suhl 1965). Recent scholarship, however, emphasizes the widespread use of scriptural allusions in this Gospel to disclose Jesus's identity and significance (e.g., Evans 2006a; Hatina 2002; Hays 2016). There are repeated hints, for example, that Jesus is to be understood as the Danielic son of man who comes with the clouds of heaven (Mark 13:26; 14:62; see Dan 7:13; Ps 110:1), and he is also presented as the caring shepherd of God's people (Mark 6:34), imagery applied in scripture to various figures, including Moses's successor Joshua (Num 27:17), the Davidic messiah (Ezek 34:23), and ultimately Israel's God (Ezek 34:11; cf. Zech 10:3). Since the pervasive but indirect reuse of scripture is characteristic of early Jewish apocalyptic writing generally (e.g., 1 Enoch and Revelation), it is perhaps not surprising that allusions to the prophets are especially pronounced in the eschatological discourse (e.g., Mark 13:8 [Isa 19:2]; 13:12 [Mic 7:6]; 13:19 [Dan 12:1]; 13:24–25 [Isa 13:10; Ezek 32:7–8; Joel 2:2, 10, 31; 3:15]; 13:27 [Isa 11:12]). These imply both an exceptional status and an important role for Jesus in the end-times (e.g., Mark 13:26–27), and his unique authority is also demonstrated through the scriptural overtones which color accounts of key episodes in his ministry. The description of the calming of the storm (Mark 4:35–41), for instance, illustrates God's power over nature, celebrated in several psalms (Ps 107:23–32; see Pss 65:7; 89:9). It is not clear, however, that Mark considers Jesus to be divine, so that Hays's claim that he seeks to depict him as "the embodiment of Israel's God" (2016, 97–103) goes beyond the textual evidence.

Scriptural Models

Scriptural patterns and tropes are also employed by Mark in the service of his presentation of Jesus as the successor of Moses and the prophets. Jesus's life, for example, is portrayed as replicating events associated with the Exodus (Perkins 2006; Swartley 1980), including: the testing in the wilderness (Mark 1:12–13); the provision of food in a lonely place (Mark 6:30–44); the experience of divine revelation on a mountain (Mark 9:2–8; see 3:13); and the motif of being on a journey (Mark 8:22–10:52). In keeping with Mark's characteristically understated method of appealing to scripture, however, he neither directly cites the Exodus narratives nor identifies Jesus explicitly as a new Moses. A second noteworthy influence on this Gospel is the Elijah-Elisha cycle (e.g., Kloppenborg and Verheyden 2014). Not only does John the Baptist recall the appearance of Elijah in his leather girdle and garments of animal skin (Mark 1:6; see 2 Kings 1:8), but also several of Jesus's miracles correspond to the mighty works of these former prophets, especially his raising to life of Jairus's daughter (Mark 5:21–24; 35–43; see 2 Kings 4:17–37) and his healing of gentiles like the Syro-Phoenician woman's child (Mark 7:24–30; see 1 Kings 17:17–24). In other similarities with Elisha, Jesus rebuffs his disciples' attempts to prevent people from touching him (Mark 10:13–16; see 2 Kings 4:27), feeds a crowd of people with only a little bread and even has some left over (Mark 6:34–44; see 2 Kings 4:42–44), and heals a boy whom his disciples have been unable to help (Mark 9:14–29; see 2 Kings 4:31–37). While some commentators (e.g., Brodie 2000) may overemphasize the significance of these texts as literary models for the Gospels, it seems clear that they have contributed to shaping both the form and content of the Gospels in places (Vette 2022). The differences between Mark's characters and these scriptural parallels can often be as telling as the resemblances. Herod's act of beheading John the Baptist after his rash oath (Mark 6:14–29), for instance, connects him with the archetypal enemies of Israel when read in the light of the story of Esther and the evil Haman (Esth 5:1–7:10). It also highlights the contrast, however, between the *death*-wish of Herodias and her daughter and Esther's use of the opportunity afforded by a royal vow at a banquet to plead for the *lives* of her people.

The Gospel of Matthew

Citations and Other Explicit Uses of Scripture

Like Mark, Matthew immediately sets his account of Jesus within the larger story of Israel, but he employs the device of an opening genealogy (Matt 1:1–17), which connects Jesus explicitly to that narrative's major figures and events, especially Abraham, David, and the Babylonian exile (Matt 1:1, 6, 11). The scriptures play a visible and pervasive role throughout this Gospel, as all of the citations in the material shared with Mark are included, some of Mark's allusions are formally quoted (e.g., at the entry into Jerusalem; Matt 21:5; cf. Zech 9:9; Mark 11:2; John 12:14–15; cf. the explicit mention of Daniel in connection with the "desolating sacrilege," Matt 24:15; cf. Dan 9:27; cf. Matt 13:14), and at least twenty new texts are introduced, so that there are almost double the total number of quotations. This means that Matthew follows Mark in drawing heavily on Isaiah, on the Psalms, especially in the passion narrative, and on the Torah, particularly in episodes involving conflict, such as in debates with the religious leaders, and at the temptations, where Deuteronomy is cited three times against the devil (Matt 4:1–11; cf. Luke 4:1–13). In addition, greater appeal is made to Jeremiah (Matt 2:18; 16:14; 27:9–10; Knowles 1993) and to the minor prophets. The repetition of Hosea's claim that God prefers mercy to sacrifice (Matt 9:13; 12:7; cf. 23:23; cf. Hos 6:6) demonstrates the importance of this text to the evangelist's thought, and the influence on his understanding of Jesus's death of Zechariah 9–14 is suggested by a cluster of references to these chapters in the latter part of the Gospel (Matt 21:5; 26:31; 27:9; cf. 26:15; Ham 2005). Matthew foregrounds his scriptural material by employing it regularly as editorial comment (eleven times to Mark's one), and by drawing attention to the fact that characters who voice its words are actually quoting what "is written" (Matt 4:4, 7, 10). This frequent and direct manner of engaging with the scriptures implies a religious and social context for Matthew's community in which this was both considered necessary, for teaching and/or apologetic purposes, and was possible, in terms of scribal expertise and access to texts.

The citations common to Matthew and Mark are almost always placed in the same narrative context, but the treatment of the conflated quotation with which Mark's account opens (Mark 1:2–3) is a partial exception. This is divided in Matthew, so that the main text (Isa 40:3) functions to introduce John the Baptist (Matt 3:3), as in Mark, but the reference to his role in preparing the way for the one to come (Mal 3:1 and/or Exod 23:20) is applied to him by Jesus in a later episode which is not included in Mark (Matt 11:10; see Luke 7:27; John 1:23). This seems to be part of a wider intention within this Gospel to clarify John's role in relation to Jesus (e.g. the account of the baptism of Jesus, Matt 3:11–15) and to develop the correspondences between John and Elijah inferred in Mark into a more explicit identification of the two figures (Matt 11:14; 17:12–13; see Mal 4:5).

Introductory Formulae and the "Fulfillment Quotations"

A distinctive feature of Matthew's interpretation of scripture is his use of an introductory formula highlighting the "fulfillment" of certain texts in the life of Jesus. These quotations make up an identifiable group, unique to this Gospel, and are characterized by an unusual text-form, which does not consistently follow known versions of either the Septuagint (LXX) or the Masoretic Text (MT); Soares Prabhu 1976). The citations from Isaiah 9:1–2 at Matthew 4:15–16 and Isaiah 42:1–4 at Matthew 12:18–21 are particularly good illustrations of this textual complexity (e.g., Menken 2004, 15–33, 67–88). It is probable that their form reflects both a Greek translation revised toward the MT and the editorial hand of either the evangelist or members of his community (Stendahl 1968). Matthew's Gospel clearly exemplifies, then, the pluriform state of the scriptural text in the first century CE, as well as the contemporary exegetical practice of the adaptation of sources in quotations.

There are ten definite instances of this fulfillment formula (Matt 1:22–23; 2:15, 17–18, 23; 4:14–16; 8:17; 12:17–21; 13:35; 21:4–5; 27:9–10; cf. 2:5–6, which does not use the term "fulfillment"; Matt 13:14–15 which is introduced slightly differently; and Matt 26:54, 56, which do not refer to a specific text), so it occurs in approximately one-quarter of the total number of citations in Matthew. The first four examples are clustered together in the infancy narrative, and others are related to Jesus's healing ministry (Matt 8:14–17; 12:15–21), his use of parables in teaching (Matt 13:34–35), his entry into Jerusalem (Matt 21:4–5), and his betrayal by Judas (Matt 27:9–10). The formula is applied almost exclusively to passages from the prophetic corpus; the only exceptions are Matthew 2:23, of which the source is uncertain, and Matthew 13:35 (Ps 78:2), but David, the assumed author of the psalms, was widely regarded as a prophet in Second Temple Judaism (e.g., 11Q5 27.11; *Ant.* 8.109–19; cf. Acts 2:30; Subramaniam 2007). Surprisingly, these citations often seem to be employed to support only very minor aspects of the gospel story, such as Jesus's departure from Nazareth to Capernaum (Isa 9:1–2 at Matt 4:13–16); it is perhaps significant that Jesus is also linked with other geographical locations by fulfillment quotations at Matthew 2:15, 17–18, and 23 (cf. 2:5–6). This may indicate that his followers collected scriptural texts which they regarded as fitting every detail of Jesus's life. Beaton (2002; cf. Hays 2016, 176–81), however, argues that these citations actually function bireferentially, both validating the specific incident in view (e.g., the establishment of the Galilean base at Matt 4:13–16) and pointing toward Jesus's wider theological and messianic significance (e.g., in inaugurating the gentile mission by this move).

Soares Prabhu (1976, 59–63) suggests that the model for Matthew's fulfillment formula may be scripture itself (e.g., 1 Kings 2:27; 2 Chron 36:21, 22; Ezra 1:1), although this phrase is not paralleled exactly elsewhere, either in early Jewish or Christian sources. Matthew's singularity should not be overemphasized, though, since the same underlying belief that Jesus's life and death somehow "fulfills" the prophetic hopes for the future salvation of Israel is in evidence across the New Testament (e.g., Mark 14:49; Luke 22:37; 24:44; John 17:12; Acts 1:16; 3:18; 13:27; Rom 1:2; 1 Cor 15:3; 1 Pet 1:10–12). Indeed, Jesus is specifically said to have "fulfilled" (using the same Greek verb πληροῦν) the scriptures several times in the fourth Gospel (John 12:38; 13:18; 15:25; 19:24, 36), and even within the Synoptics, Luke presents Jesus as declaring that a scriptural text is fulfilled in him (Luke 4:21; cf. 21:22). The Qumran community, too, operated within a comparable hermeneutical framework, convinced that they were living on the threshold of the eschatological age, and that the scriptures were direct references to concrete aspects of their history or practice (e.g., Vanderkam 2012, 130–32).

Allusions

Due to the extent of common material, Matthew's Gospel shares numerous scriptural allusions with Mark, including the references to the coming of the son of man with the clouds (Matt 24:30; 25:31; 26:64; cf. Dan 7:13; Ps 110:1; cf. Mark 13:26; 14:62) and to the peoples' need for a shepherd (Matt 9:36; 10:6; 15:24; cf. Num 27:17; 1 Kings 22:17; 2 Chron 18:16; Ezek 34:5–6; Jer 50:6; Zech 10:2; cf. Mark 6:34). Many more are included, however, even in sections of the narrative already dense with scriptural echoes, such as the eschatological discourse (Matt 24:30, 31; Isa 27:13; cf. Zech 12:10). In the passion account, the correspondences between Jesus's death and the Psalms of Lament are drawn out more strongly, in the mocking words of the religious leaders (Matt 27:43; cf. Ps 22:8; cf. Mark 15:32) and in the specific offer to Jesus of "gall" (χολή) to drink (Matt 27:34; see Ps 69:21; cf. Mark 15:23). Matthew's scriptural allusions often serve, as in Mark, to underscore Jesus's significance. The visit of the magi with their gifts (Matt 2:11), for instance, suggests that the birth of this child marks the beginning of the long-awaited acknowledgment by the gentiles of Israel's God (e.g., Ps 72:10–11; Isa 60:5–6), and Jesus's healing ministry recalls the Isaianic promises of future deliverance (e.g., Isa 35:5–6; 61:1). The Gospel's closing words, affirming Jesus's abiding presence with his disciples, reveal him to be the fulfillment of God's own promise through the prophet Haggai: "I am with you, says the Lord" (Matt 28:20; cf. 1:23; see Hag 1:13).

Finally, the extensive teaching sections in this Gospel show influence from the wisdom literature, both in forms like beatitudes (Matt 5:3–11; see Prov 14:21; Sir 25:8–9) and in content: the assurance that the poor and humble will ultimately be rewarded by God

(Matt 5:3, 5) echoes several psalms (e.g., Pss 34:6; 37:11; 73:1; 107:4–7), for example, and the injunctions not to repay evil with evil (Matt 5:38–41) and to lay up treasure in heaven (Matt 6:19–21) are also consonant with Jewish wisdom teaching (e.g., Prov 20:22; 24:29; Sir 28:1–5; 29:10–13). One of Matthew's most memorable images, the self-identification of the son of man at the last judgment with the hungry, the naked, and the stranger (Matt 25:34–45), also reflects ideas found in Proverbs: "He who is kind to the poor lends to the Lord, and he will repay him for his deed" (Prov 19:17). While attempts to claim that Matthew understood Jesus primarily as wisdom incarnate (e.g., Witherington 1994) have not been fully persuasive, the important role of the wisdom tradition in forming the ethical thought of Matthew, and of other New Testament writers like James, should not be underestimated.

Scriptural Models

There are several possible instances of scriptural texts shaping Matthew's narrative, including the notorious example of the introduction of two different animals, an ass and a colt, on which Jesus rides into Jerusalem, in specific fulfillment of the citation of Zechariah 9:9 (Matt 21:4–7). Uniquely in this Gospel, Judas is said to have been paid thirty pieces of silver to betray Jesus (Matt 26:15), a sum which alludes to Zechariah 11:12, a section of scripture which is influential in the wider Matthaean passion narrative. The description of dead saints coming out of their graves at the crucifixion (Matt 27:52–53; cf. John 5:28–29) is also likely to have been inspired by the promise of Ezekiel 37:13.

The clearest case of this operation, however, comes in the development of the theme of Jesus as a new Moses beyond the hints present in Mark's Gospel (Allison 1993). This is evident from the outset, as parts of Matthew's infancy narrative appear to have been intentionally created, or at least molded, to foreground the parallels between the two figures. Details like the visit of wise men from the East to a modest family home in Bethlehem (Matt 2:1–12) or the killing of newborn boys under Herod (Matt 2:16; see Exod 1:15–22), are not attested in any contemporary sources, and seem implausible, but they do connect with early Jewish traditions about Moses. In his rewriting of Exodus, for example, Josephus explains Pharaoh's order to kill the male infant Hebrews as prompted by a prediction by one of his scribes of the birth of a child who would be a threat to Egypt's domination of the Israelites. He then goes on to relate a dream in which Moses's father is assured of divine protection for his unborn son because of his future role as deliverer of Israel (*Ant.* 2.205–20; see Pseudo-Philo 9.1–10; Allison 1993, 144–65). These motifs stem from wider Graeco-Roman cultural expectations about the attendance on the births of heroes of miraculous events and astrological signs. As Matthew's Gospel progresses, Jesus, like Moses, fasts for forty days and nights before beginning his ministry (Matt 4:2; see Deut 9:9), and is presented as an authoritative teacher (e.g., Matt 5:1–7:29). The arrangement of his instruction into five major blocks (Matt 5:1–7:29; 10:5–42; 13:1–52; 18:1–35; 23:1–25:46) is regarded by some commentators (e.g., Donaldson 1985) as a deliberate imitation of the five-book format of the Torah.

It may be that Matthew understands Jesus as recapitulating in his life the entire story of Israel, and not only that of Moses, since it is the people as a whole who are brought safely out of Egypt (Matt 2:13–15, 20–21; see Exod 2:15; 4:19; cf. Hos 11:1) and who are then tempted in the wilderness by hunger to test God and to practise idolatry (e.g., Allison 1993, 165–72; Hays 2016, 108–20).

Nevertheless, neither the Christology nor the literary structure of any Gospel can be explained solely in terms of a single scriptural model, so this emphasis on the Mosaic narratives does not displace Davidic imagery, for instance. Thus Jesus is termed "son of David" in Matthew as in Mark (Matt 20:30–31; 21:9, 15; cf. 12:3–4; 22:41–45; see Mark 2:25–26; 10:47–48; 12:35–37), and this theme is even further amplified in the genealogy and infancy narrative (Matt 1:1, 6, 17, 20), in the acclamation of the crowd as Jesus enters Jerusalem (Matt 21:9; cf. Mark 11:9–10), and perhaps also by the reference to the blind and the lame coming to Jesus in the temple (Matt 21:14), if it is to be understood as signaling a reversal of the situation in David's day when they were forbidden to enter it (2 Sam 5:8).

The Gospel of Luke

Citations

Formal citations of scripture are relatively scarce in Luke's Gospel: Matthew includes almost twice as many, and Mark has approximately the same number but in a considerably shorter work. This is not always because scriptural references in the common material are omitted, however, but because Luke not infrequently chooses to paraphrase rather than directly quote them (e.g., the explanation of the purpose of parables, Luke 8:10; see Matt 13:13–15; Mark 4:11–12; and the debate about resurrection, Luke 20:37–38; see Matt 22:31–32; Mark 12:26–27). In keeping with the practice of both Matthew and Mark, Luke draws conspicuously on Isaiah (e.g., Pao 2000; Mallen 2008) and the Psalms, a pattern repeated in Acts (e.g., Acts 1:20; 2:25–28, 34–35; 4:25–26; 7:49–50; 8:32–33; 13:33–35, 47; 28:26–27). One unique use of scripture at a key point in the narrative, the inauguration of Jesus's Galilean ministry, is widely regarded as particularly indicative of the importance of Isaiah for the Christology of this Gospel (Luke 4:18–19). In a conflated citation (Isa 61:1–2 with a phrase from 58:6, perhaps on the basis of the occurrence of a shared word, ἄφεσις, "release"), Jesus is presented as the one who will fulfill the prophetic hopes for future restoration by liberating the poor and oppressed (e.g., Prior 1995). This passage illustrates the technique of selective or partial quotation, employed by all the evangelists, as one clause, "the day of vengeance of our God" (Isa 61:2), is omitted, so that the whole emphasis falls on the proclamation of good news. On the other hand Luke extends the citation of Isaiah used to introduce John the Baptist (Luke 3:4–6; see Isa 40:3–5; cf. Matt 3:3; Mark 1:3). His additional text includes the line "and all flesh shall see the salvation of God," which fits well with his universalistic theological outlook (see 3:38; Acts 1:8; Mallen 2008, 108–13).

Luke's selection of scriptural texts differs most significantly from Matthew and Mark in the passion account, perhaps an indication of his access to supplementary sources for this section. First, there is no reference to the striking of the shepherd and the scattering of the sheep (Zech 13:7; see Matt 26:31; Mark 14:27; cf. John 16:32). This means that Jesus's death is not connected to the motif of his role as Israel's shepherd, and Zechariah 9–14 exerts less influence on this narrative than on Matthew's version. Second, Jesus's last words on the cross quote Psalm 31:5, rather than Psalm 22:1 (Luke 23:46; see Matt 27:46; Mark 15:34). This text is better suited to Luke's overall presentation of events, in that a cry of abandonment would be inappropriate from one who has just expressed his trusting expectation of a future in paradise (Luke 23:43; Moyise 2001, 48–9). Third, this is the only Gospel to include in the last supper discourse an explicit citation from the so-called fourth servant song of Deutero-Isaiah, "And he was reckoned with transgressors" (Luke 22:37; see Isa 53:12). However, this verse is applied neither to Jesus's death nor to his crucifixion between two criminals (Luke 23:32–33), circumstances which might seem to "fulfill" it more concretely (see its addition at that point in some manuscripts of Mark 15:28) but instead is related to his advice to his disciples to buy swords. This puzzling interpretation might be compared with the way in which a text from this passage is connected in Matthew to Jesus's healings rather than to his atoning death (Matt 12:15–21; see Isa 42:1–4; cf. the use of Isa 53:4 at Matt 8:16–17). The placing of this citation in the context of Jesus's imminent arrest may be intended to serve as a reminder that his disciples must expect to face rejection and opposition as he did (Pao and Schnabel 2007, 385–89), but it does not clearly indicate an understanding of Jesus's sufferings as vicarious. The extent to which the Gospel passion narratives as a whole are shaped by the imagery of the Isaianic servant is a matter of ongoing scholarly debate. The formative influence of this motif is still championed by some (e.g., Moo 1983; Stuhlmacher 2004), but minimized by others (e.g., Juel 1988; Allen 2017), especially following Hooker's (1959) ground-breaking study. The differences between the Gospels at this point illustrate the breadth and variety of early Christian reflection on scripture in the attempt to make sense of Jesus's death.

Allusions

The importance of the scriptures for Luke is confirmed by his extensive employment of allusions to them. Like Matthew, he makes clear from the outset that the Gospel of Jesus is a continuation of the story of Israel (Dahl 1976). His two opening chapters replicate scriptural language and style, and are clearly modeled on the familiar birth and annunciation narratives involving righteous and law-observant women like Sarah (Luke 1:13, 18, 26–38; see Gen 17:15–21), Rachel (Luke 1:25; see Gen 30:23), Hannah (Luke 1:46–55; see 1 Sam 2:1–10), and the unnamed mother of Samson (Luke 1:6–15; see Judg 13:2–25; cf. the presentation in the temple, Luke 2:22–40; see 1 Sam 1:21–28). Three characters, Mary, Zechariah, and Simeon, voice songs of praise (Luke 1:46–55; 1:67–79; 2:29–35), which are composed of a pastiche of references to the Pentateuchal covenant narratives (Litwak 2005, 82–89), as well as to the Psalms (especially Pss 34, 35, 89, 103) and Isaiah (e.g., Luke 1:79; 2:30–32). In form, and in their use of allusions drawn from across the scriptures, they resemble early Jewish prayers in general (Newman 1999) and the Qumran *Hodayot* in particular. These Lukan hymns aim to demonstrate that Jesus reproduces in his life scriptural patterns of God's presence among people (Bock 1987). Thus, just as in the past God acted to "visit" and redeem Israel (Exod 4:31), so in the births of Jesus and John, God's salvation is again at work (Luke 1:68, 71), Elijah has returned (Luke 1:16–17, 76; see Mal 3:1; 4:5–6), a new Davidic ruler is raised up (Luke 1:32–33, 69; see 2 Sam 7:12–16), and the divine promises of mercy and blessing are being brought to completion (Luke 1:50, 54–55, 70–74; 2:30–31). Mary " . . . kept all these things, pondering them in her heart" (Luke 2:19), then, just as Jacob "kept in mind" the dream of the future greatness of his son Joseph (Gen 37:11; cf. Dan 7:28).

Although there is much less direct appeal to scripture in the teaching sections than in other parts of the Gospel, the wisdom literature is an important source of allusions here, both in the material shared with Matthew and in that particular to Luke. The parable of the rich man's barns (Luke 12:16–21), for example, illustrates the common wisdom teaching that riches are transient (e.g., Ps 39:6; Sir 11:19; cf. Jas 4:13–15). Some of the other more significant allusions introduced by Luke include the connecting of further "stone" texts (Isa 8:14–15; cf. Dan 2:34, 44–45; cf. 1 Pet 2:6–8) to the citation about the cornerstone (Ps 118:22) which concludes the parable of the tenants in the vineyard in all three Gospels (Luke 20:17–18; see Matt 21:42; Mark 12:10). The chapter of Isaiah which serves as the source of this parable also offers a parallel in form to the Lukan series of woes (Luke 6:24–26; see Isa 5:8–23).

Scriptural Models

The correspondences between the ministry of Jesus and the stories of Elijah and Elisha, although present in Mark's account, are considered to be strongest in Luke's Gospel (e.g., Brodie 2000). Uniquely in Luke, the beginning of Jesus's mission is explicitly set in the context of the engagement which these early prophets had with non-Israelites (Luke 4:25–27; see 1 Kings 17:8–24; 2 Kings 5:1–14), and he performs a miracle similar to theirs by raising to life the son of the widow of Nain (Luke 7:11–17; see 1 Kings 17:17–24; 2 Kings 4:32–37). In addition, Luke states that Jesus is assumed by some to be Elijah *redivivus* (Luke 9:19), and a plea by a potential disciple to first go and say goodbye to his family echoes Elisha's request to Elijah (Luke 9:59–62; see Matt 8:21–22; see 1 Kings 19:19–21). A further and particularly interesting connection with these narratives comes in the suggestion by James and John that they call down fire from heaven on the Samaritan villagers who refuse to receive Jesus (Luke 9:51–55; see 2 Kings 1:9–12). Unlike Elijah, however, Jesus firmly refuses to allow such an act of revenge. As already observed, then, the differences between Jesus and any scriptural models can be as important as the similarities for understanding an evangelist's Christology (Hays 2016, 202).

Some commentators (e.g., Evans 1955; Moessner 1989) seek to explain the journey framework of Luke's central section (Luke 9:51–19:44) against the backdrop of the book of Deuteronomy. On this reading, Jesus is being presented as the expected prophet like Moses (Deut 18:15–19; see Luke 4:24; 7:16, 39; 9:8, 19; 24:19), who offers life-giving teaching (Deut 30:15–20), works signs and wonders (Deut 34:11–12), converses with God on a mountain (Deut 5:5; 9:9-11; 34:10), and suffers rejection by his people (Deut 1:26-46). Several interesting thematic links with Deuteronomy are surfaced by these studies, but again, it should be stressed that the scriptural interpretation of any Gospel cannot be fully encompassed by reference to a single scriptural book or image.

Synoptic Discussion

The Selection of Texts

The overlap between the scriptural texts cited and alluded to in the Gospels of Matthew, Mark, and Luke is substantial, so in this respect they certainly can be considered synoptic. The extent of their appeal to Isaiah is particularly striking, with the books of Psalms and several of the minor prophets (Hosea, Micah, Zechariah, and Malachi) featuring prominently, too. All three take for granted the continuing ethical validity of the commandments of the Jewish law for the followers of Jesus. The influence of the wisdom literature on the teaching sections of the Gospels has also been highlighted in the discussion here, and is often underestimated. Since the publication of the Dead Sea Scrolls, it has been widely recognized that this "canon within a canon" is remarkably similar to that of the Qumran community, and so reflects wider currents in first-century Judaism (e.g., Brooke 1997; Evans 2015).

The selection of the same scriptural material by the evangelists results, primarily, from their use of common sources, but it also reflects a prior history of exegetical engagement on the part of the early Christian community. It is not necessary to accept in its entirety Dodd's (1952) theory about certain "Old Testament" passages forming the "building blocks" of New Testament thought to recognize that some key texts did quickly become closely associated with aspects of Jesus's life and ministry. The apparent incompatibility of his death with any claim to messianism in particular prompted serious scriptural reflection, as is demonstrated by the high concentration of citations and allusions in the passion narratives of all four Gospels (cf. 1 Cor 15:3-4). Some of the texts that the evangelists applied to Jesus may already have had eschatological associations in Judaism. A messianic interpretation is given to Micah 5:2 (see Matt 2:6) in the targum to the minor prophets, for instance, and to the "cornerstone" of Psalm 118:22 (see Matt 21:42; Luke 20:17) in the targum to Zechariah 4:7 (Blomberg 2007, 74). Similarly, the same verses of Isaiah drawn upon in the Gospels appear in a Qumran document apparently describing the end-times (4Q521 II, 6-13; cf. Matt 11:5; Luke 4:18-19; Vanderkam 2012, 129-30), and the Dead Sea community thought of themselves both as the "cornerstone" (1QS VIII.7) and as those who were preparing the Lord's way in the wilderness (1QS VIII, 13-15; see Isa 40:3; see Matt 3:3; Mark 1:3; Luke 3:4; cf. John 1:23).

Text Form

The differences between the wording of Matthew's "fulfillment quotations" and extant Hebrew and Greek forms of the scriptures have long occasioned particular comment, as discussed earlier. However, in Mark and Luke, too, variations from the LXX occur in citations (e.g., Mark 4:12; Luke 22:37). This is not surprising, in view of the multiple versions in which the scriptures circulated in this period, but does suggest also that key texts may have been transmitted in early Christian circles in a particular (and perhaps adapted) form, both in writing as well as orally. This is further indicated by occasional inaccurate attributions (e.g., Matt 27:9–10) and by the appearance of composite (e.g., Matt 2:6; Mark 1:2–3) and conflated quotations (e.g., Matt 21:5; Luke 4:18–19) and allusions (e.g., Matt 3:17; 17:5; Mark 1:11; Luke 3:22 [Ps 2:7; Isa 42:1]; Matt 26:64; Mark 13:26; 14:62; Luke 21:27 [Dan 7:13; Ps 110:1]). It is, therefore, a distinct possibility that the original source for at least some of the citations in the Gospels may have been something like a testimony book. The practice of making collections of literary extracts is well attested in Graeco-Roman culture, and the Qumran caves have yielded early Jewish examples of scriptural anthologies with a common theme (e.g., 4Q174, 4Q175, 4Q176, 4Q177, 11Q13). The likelihood that early Christians, too, prepared such compilations, either for teaching and apologetic purposes or simply for practical reasons in an age of traveling missionaries and the limited availability of scriptural scrolls, has been persuasively argued, most recently by Albl (1999). Even where the New Testament authors can be assumed to have had direct access to scriptural manuscripts, current scholarship is increasingly emphasizing the importance for their exegesis of the deliberate selection of one form of the text over other available versions (e.g., 1QpHab 11.9–13; see Docherty 2015). This interpretative move may explain some of the unusual features of the citations in Matthew particularly (e.g., Matt 4:15–16; see also his choice of the reading "virgin" (παρθένος) for Isa 7:14 at Matt 1:23). Furthermore, the forms in which the scriptures are quoted in the Gospels may have implications for the Synoptic Problem which warrant further exploration (Goodacre 2011; New 1993)..

Exegetical Techniques

Composite Citation

Combining separate texts in quotation is a technique widely employed in early Jewish sources and in Graeco-Roman literature more widely (Adams and Ehorn 2016). According to the most recent investigation, 16–20 percent of the total number of citations in each of the Synoptic Gospels are composite (Matthew 20 percent, Mark 17.4 percent, Luke-Acts 16.7 percent; Adams and Ehorn 2018, 210). In this form of scriptural reuse, the connected texts become mutually interpretative and so take on a new or expanded meaning: in Luke's Nazareth sermon, for example, the fusing of verses from different chapters of Isaiah makes the liberation of the oppressed a constituent part of

Jesus's proclamation of good news (Luke 4:18–19; see Isa 61:1–2; 58:6). The related exegetical method of adducing two scriptural "proofs" in support of an argument is also present in the Gospels, as in Matthew's account of the controversy over plucking grain on the Sabbath (Matt 12:1–8, citing not only the example of David in 1 Sam 21:1–6, as in the Markan and Lukan versions, but also, uniquely, Hos 6:6; for other New Testament examples see Heb 2:12–13; 4:1–10). Scriptural passages are brought together in other ways, too, in the juxtaposition of quotations from Deuteronomy and Psalms in the temptation narratives (Matt 4:1–11; Luke 4:1–13), for instance, or in the mini-collection of "stone" references in Luke 20:17–18. Passages can also be artfully set in opposition to one another in order to make a point: the temple should be a "house of prayer" (Isa 56:7), for example, but instead is "a den of robbers" (Jer 7:11; Matt 21:13; Mark 11:17; Luke 19:46).

Speaking Scriptural Words

All three Synoptic Gospels present Jesus and other characters as giving voice to scriptural texts, either by quoting them directly (e.g., Jesus in the temptation narratives) or by employing their words without formally signaling a citation. Examples of the latter form of reuse include the crowds welcoming Jesus to Jerusalem with an acclamation drawn from the Psalms (Matt 21:9; Mark 11:9; Luke 19:38; see Ps 118:26) and Jesus's response to a question about dividing a family inheritance, which echoes the retort of the Hebrew slave to Moses: "who made me a judge or divider over you" (Luke 12:14; see Exod 2:14; cf. the dismissal of evildoers at the last judgment, Matt 7:23; 25:41; see Ps 6:8). Scriptural words are freely ascribed to new speakers elsewhere in the New Testament (e.g., John 12:13; Heb 10:5–7; 13:6), a practice also followed in other forms of early Jewish interpretation, including the targumim (Samely 1992) and the rewritten scriptures (Docherty 2018). In Pseudo-Philo's *Biblical Antiquities*, for instance, God promises nourishment to Phinehas in the same terms in which Elijah is addressed in 1 Kings (Pseudo-Philo 48:1; see 1 Kings 17:4), and Gideon's request for a divine sign imitates that of Abraham (Pseudo-Philo 35:6; see Gen 18:30). This technique serves to highlight the correspondences between these figures and stems from an underlying hermeneutical principle that scriptural words, as divine communication with ongoing relevance, are intended to be continually reapplied to new and analogous situations. Their meaning is not exhausted by their original contexts, so that, for example, it is not only the inhabitants of Samaria at the time of Hosea who "will say to the mountains, 'Cover us,' and to the hills, 'Fall upon us'" (Hos 10:8) but also those living in Jerusalem in the approaching end-times (Luke 23:30).

Specifying a General Referent

The Gospels also illustrate the technique of applying a scriptural text with an originally indefinite or ambiguous meaning to a specific person or event. The Psalms are particularly suitable for this operation, as they often readily fit a range of circumstances. In the passion narrative especially, aspects of the generic suffering of the psalmist thus become the precise experience of Jesus: it is he who is betrayed by one who shares his bread (Matt 26:20–25; Mark 14:17–21; see Ps 41:9; cf. 1QH^a 13.23–24), he against whom false witnesses breathe out violence (Matt 26:59–60; Mark 14:56; see Ps 27:12), and it is his companions and relatives who stand at a distance during his crucifixion (Matt 26:58; 27:55; Mark 14:54; 15:40; Luke 22:54; 23:49; see Ps 38:11; cf. his estrangement from his family, Mark 3:21; 6:3; see Ps 69:8). It may be significant that many of these subtle allusions are apparently missed by Luke (e.g. Luke 21:16, 19; 22:27; cf. the removal of the reference to the "desolating sacrilege" of Dan 9:27 at 21:20; see Matt 24:15; Mark 13:14), suggesting either that he and his community were less familiar with the scriptures than the authors of Matthew or Mark or that they perceived less need to connect minor details of Jesus's life to them.

This method is also employed in other New Testament writings (e.g., Acts 1:16–22; Heb 1:6; 5:5–6) and is widespread in early Jewish exegesis. In the *Biblical Antiquities*, for instance, the words of Psalm 42:3—"Where is your God?"—are transformed from a general reproach into a specific taunt directed at Hannah by her rival wife, Peninnah (*Pseudo-Philo* 50.5; compare also *Pseudo-Philo* 35.1 with Judg 6:12; 19:17). Further examples can be found in the rabbinic literature, such as the assumption that the testing of the righteous one in Psalm 11:5 is a reference to Abraham's call to sacrifice Isaac (*Ber. R.* 55.2; see Gen 22:1–14).

Scripturally Shaped Narratives

The authors of the deutero-canonical books and works of rewritten scripture frequently fashion a whole new narrative out of a scriptural text. Pseudo-Philo constructs a story about Abraham escaping a fiery furnace (Pseudo-Philo 6.16–18) which is clearly modeled on the miraculous deliverance of Daniel and his companions (Dan 3:13–30), for instance, and composes a detailed description of Kenaz's victory over the Amorites based on Gideon's rout of the Midianites (*Pseudo-Philo* 27.5–7; see Judg 7:4–23). Similarly, Judith 11–13 is evidently influenced by the narrative of Jael and Sisera (Judg 4–5), and the account of the siege of Ephron in 1 Maccabees 5:45–51 draws freely on the Pentateuch (e.g., Deut 2:26–36; 20:10–14; cf. Num 21:21–24) in order to present this event as replicating Israel's initial conquest of the land. Several examples of this interpretative technique in operation in the Gospels have been discussed here (see further Vette 2022), such as the crafting of the Matthaean infancy narrative to portray Jesus as a new Moses; the shaping of the passion narratives to connect him with the righteous sufferer of the lament psalms; the inclusion of miracle stories relating Jesus to Elijah and Elisha; and the recounting of the calming of the storm (Matt 8:23–27; Mark 4:35–41; Luke 8:22–25) in terms which recall God's power over the forces of nature as celebrated in Psalm 107:23–32.

One particular form of narrative appeal to scriptures within the Gospels is the creation of an episode to show Jesus "fulfilling" specific texts, a practice termed "narrated prophecy" by Krause (1994). Possible examples of this method include the ejection of the money changers from the temple (Matt 21:12–13; Mark 11:15–17; Luke 19:45–46; see Zech 14:21) and the cursing of the fig tree (Matt 21:18–19; Mark 11:12–14; see Hos 9:10, 16–17; cf. the echoes of this text in the parable recounted in Luke 13:6–9). The reference to "green grass" in Mark's account of the feeding of the multitude (6:39) may also indicate that this incident is intended to depict Jesus as the good shepherd described in Psalm 23:2. Several of the parables seem to function in a similar way, as developed illustrations of prophetic oracles. The relationship between the parable of the tenants in the vineyard (Matt 21:33–41; Mark 12:1–9; Luke 20:9–16) and Isaiah 5:1–7 is widely acknowledged, for instance; the allegory of the sower exemplifies scriptural claims that God's word bears fruit (Matt 13:3–9, 18–23; Mark 4:2–20; Luke 8:4–15; see Isa 55:10–11; Jer 17:8); and the parable of the mustard seed similarly picks up the language of the prophets (Matt 13:31–32; Mark 4:30–32; Luke 13:18–19; see Ezek 17:22–23; 31:3–6; Dan 4:10–12). Other parables, especially in Matthew and Luke, expand on motifs present in the wisdom literature, including the search for precious treasure (Prov 2:4; see Matt 13:44–46), the invitation to wisdom's banquet (Prov 9:2–5; see Matt 22:2–4), and the advice to take the lowest place in the presence of the powerful (Prov 25:6–7; see Luke 14:7–11). Israel's scriptures must be recognized as the primary influence on the narrative shape of the Gospels, then, and as a generative source for parts of their content, despite recent interesting attempts to explain them at least partly as Christianized imitations of Homeric epics (MacDonald 2000).

Focus on Key Words

In Jesus's legal debates with the Jewish religious leaders, he is presented as trading scriptural proof-texts and arguing on the same exegetical terms as his opponents. It lies beyond the scope of this essay to assess how accurately this represents the practice of the historical Jesus (see e.g., France 1971; Evans 2015), but the evangelists are evidently familiar with these interpretative methods, which are often described as rabbinic. This kind of detailed engagement with the scriptural text is illustrated particularly clearly in the discussion about resurrection (Matt 22:23–33; Mark 12:18–27; Luke 20:27–40; see Exod 3:6), in which the use of the present tense ("I am the God of Abraham") is taken as implying that the patriarchs are still alive. It often involves a focus on a key word, like "lord" in Psalm 110:1 (Matt 22:41–45; Mark 12:35–37; Luke 20:41–44). This approach derives from an exegetical axiom that every word of scripture is both true and significant, and it is widely exemplified in Jewish sources, including the midrashim (Samely 2002). Elsewhere in the New Testament, the interpretation of Psalm 95:7–11 by the author of Hebrews, for instance, depends on a particular narrow interpretation of selected terms like "rest" and "today" (Heb 3:7–4:10; see also the stress on "old" in Heb 8:13; see Jer 31:31–34).

The Rhetorical Function of Scriptural Reuse

Finally, there is growing scholarly interest in the rhetorical function of appeals to the scriptures within the New Testament writings, and in how these texts are employed to advance the narrative or to persuade the audience of the validity of the author's argument (e.g., Kee 1975; Hatina 2002). This new emphasis owes much to the work of Stanley on Paul's letters (2004), as well as to a fuller appreciation of the active role of the evangelists, especially Mark (e.g., Rhoads et al. 1982), as creators of new literary works, rather than mere redactors and transmitters of traditional material. The particular density of scriptural reuse at the beginning and end of each of the Synoptic Gospels is significant, then, as this connects key moments—Jesus's birth, the start of his ministry, and his death—with the larger story of Israel and the broad sweep of salvation history. Scripture is also employed to signal other important shifts in the narrative, such as the baptism, transfiguration, and entry into Jerusalem, as well as to justify early Christian claims about Jesus's authority through its quotation in situations of conflict with the religious leaders.

Conclusion

The Synoptic evangelists all root their presentation of Jesus firmly in Israel's sacred texts, with the books of Isaiah and Psalms proving especially influential. These scriptures clearly shape, and even generate, key parts of their narratives and provide the major frameworks for their depiction of Jesus and his significance, including the motifs of son of David, new Moses, and rejected prophet. Some of these patterns are reinterpreted in the light of Jesus's life and death, however, and the prophetic hopes of future salvation are sometimes adapted so that they can encompass more unexpected aspects of his ministry, such as the liberation of the sick, the oppressed, and non-Israelites. Attempts to see one overarching model for each Gospel (e.g., Exodus, Deuteronomy, 1–2 Kings) are ultimately unsatisfactory, since all three draw widely on the scriptures as a whole for their language and imagery.

The overlap in the selection of texts and in their application to particular episodes across the Synoptic Gospels is evidence of both the use of common sources and a long history of exegetical activity by the followers of Jesus. Each evangelist exercises some freedom and creativity within this common material, as is seen, for instance, in the infancy narratives of Matthew and Luke, both so rich but so dissimilar in their appeal to the scriptures. There are some surface differences in their use of scripture, such as Mark's preference for allusions over citations, and the uniquely Matthaean fulfillment quotations, but the interpretative techniques and axioms underlying these three Gospels are generally shared, are employed by other New Testament authors, and are part of the broader practice of early Jewish hermeneutics. Reading them synoptically is justified, then, as long as the individual emphases in their treatment of Israel's scriptures are also given due consideration.

References

Adams, Sean A., and Seth M. Ehorn. 2016. *Composite Citations in Antiquity.* Vol. 1. *Jewish, Graeco-Roman and Early Christian Uses.* LNTS 525. London: Bloomsbury T&T Clark.

Adams, Sean A., and Seth M. Ehorn. 2018. *Composite Citations in Antiquity* Vol. 2. *New Testament Uses.* LNTS 593. London: Bloomsbury T&T Clark.

Ahearne-Kroll, Stephen P. 2007. *The Psalms of Lament in Mark's Passion: Jesus' Davidic Suffering.* SNTSMS 142. New York: Cambridge University Press.

Albl, Martin C. 1999. *"And Scripture Cannot Be Broken": The Form and Function of the Early Christian Testimonia Collections.* NovTSup 96. Leiden: Brill.

Allen, David M. 2017. *According to the Scriptures: The Death of Christ in the Old Testament and the New.* London: SCM.

Allison, Dale C. 1993. *The New Moses: A Matthean Typology.* Minneapolis: Augsburg Fortress.

Beaton, Richard. 2002. *Isaiah's Christ in Matthew's Gospel.* SNTSMS 123. Cambridge: Cambridge University Press.

Blomberg, Craig L. 2007. "Matthew." In *A Commentary on the New Testament Use of the Old Testament*, edited by Greg K. Beale and Donald A. Carson, 1–109. Grand Rapids: Baker Academic.

Bock, Darrell L. 1987. *Proclamation from Prophecy and Pattern: Lucan Old Testament Christology.* JSNTSS 12. Sheffield: JSOT Press.

Brodie, Thomas L. 2000. *The Crucial Bridge: The Elijah-Elisha Narrative as an Interpretive Synthesis of Genesis-Kings and a Literary Model for the Gospel.* Collegeville: Michael Glazier.

Brooke, George J. 1997. "'The Canon within the Canon' at Qumran and in the New Testament." In *The Scrolls and the Scriptures: Qumran Fifty Years After*, edited by Stanley E. Porter and Craig A. Evans, 242–66. LSTS 26. Sheffield: Sheffield Academic Press.

Dahl, Nils. 1976. *Jesus in the Memory of the Early Church.* Minneapolis: Augsburg.

Doble, Peter. 1996. *The Paradox of Salvation: Luke's Theology of the Cross.* Cambridge: Cambridge University Press.

Docherty, Susan E. 2015. "New Testament Scriptural Interpretation in Its Early Jewish Context: Reflections on the *Status Quaestionis* and Future Directions." *Novum Testamentum* 57: 1–19.

Docherty, Susan E. 2018. "Exegetical Techniques in the New Testament and 'Rewritten Bible': A Comparative Analysis." In *Ancient Readers and Their Scriptures: Engaging the Hebrew Bible in Early Judaism and Christianity*, edited by Garrick V. Allen and John A. Dunne, 77–97. Leiden: Brill.

Dodd, Charles H. 1952. *According to the Scriptures: The Sub-structure of New Testament Theology.* London: Nisbet.

Donaldson, Terence L. 1985. *Jesus on the Mountain: A Study in Matthean Theology.* JSNTSS 8. Sheffield: JSOT Press.

Evans, Christopher F. 1955. "The Central Section of Luke's Gospel." In *Studies in the Gospels*, edited by Dennis E. Nineham, 37–53. Oxford: Blackwell.

Evans, Craig A. 2006a. "The Beginning of the Good News and the Fulfilment of Scripture in the Gospel of Mark." In *Hearing the Old Testament in the New Testament*, edited by Stanley E. Porter, 83–103. Grand Rapids: Eerdmans.

Evans, Craig A. 2006b. "Zechariah in the Markan Passion Narrative." In *Biblical Interpretation in Early Christian Gospels*, vol. 1, *The Gospel of Mark*, edited by Thomas R. Hatina, 64–80. LNTS 304. London: Bloomsbury T&T Clark.

Evans, Craig A. 2015. "Why Did the New Testament Writers Appeal to the Old Testament?" *Journal for the Study of the New Testament* 38, no. 1: 36–48.

France, Richard T. 1971. *Jesus and the Old Testament.* London: Tyndale.

Goodacre, Mark. 2011. "The Evangelists' Use of the Old Testament and the Synoptic Problem." In *New Studies in the Synoptic Problem. Oxford Conference 2008. Essays in Honour of Christopher M. Tuckett*, edited by Paul Foster, Andrew Gregory, John S. Kloppenborg, and Joseph Verheyden. BETL 239, 281–98. Leuven: Peeters.

Ham, Clay A. 2005. *The Coming King and the Rejected Shepherd: Matthew's Reading of Zechariah's Messianic Hope*. Sheffield: Sheffield Phoenix Press.

Hatina, Thomas R. 2002. *In Search of a Context: The Function of Scripture in Mark's Narrative*. JSNTSS 232/Studies in Early Judaism and Christianity 8. London: Sheffield Academic Press.

Hays, Richard B. 2016. *Echoes of Scripture in the Gospels*. Waco: Baylor University Press

Hooker, Morna D. 1959. *Jesus and the Servant*. London: SPCK.

Juel, Donald. 1988. *Messianic Exegesis: Christological Interpretation of the Old Testament in Early Christianity*. Philadelphia: Fortress.

Kee, Howard C. 1975. "The Function of Scriptural Quotations and Allusions in Mark 11–16." In *Jesus und Paulus: Festschrift für Werner Georg Kümmel zum 70. Geburtstag*, edited by Earle E. Ellis and Erich Grässer, 165–88. Göttingen: Vandenhoeck & Ruprecht.

Kimball, Charles A. 1994. *Jesus' Exposition of the Old Testament in Luke's Gospel*. JSNTSS 94. Sheffield: JSOT Press.

Kloppenborg, John S., and Verheyden, Joseph, eds. 2014. *The Elijah-Elisha Narrative in the Composition of Luke*. LNTS 493. London: Bloomsbury.

Knowles, Michael. 1993. *Jeremiah in Matthew's Gospel: The Rejected Prophet Motif in Matthean Redaction*. JSNTSS 68. Sheffield: Sheffield Academic Press.

Krause, Deborah. 1994. "Narrated Prophecy in Mark 11.12–21: The Divine Authorization of Judgement." In *The Gospels and the Scriptures of Israel*, edited by Craig A. Evans and W. R. Stegner, JSNTSS 104/Studies in Early Judaism and Christianity 3, 235–48. Sheffield: Sheffield Academic Press.

Litwak, Kenneth D. 2005. *Echoes of Scripture in Luke-Acts: Telling the History of God's People Intertextually*. London: Bloomsbury T&T Clark.

MacDonald, Dennis R. 2000. *The Homeric Epics and the Gospel of Mark*. New Haven: Yale University Press.

Mallen, Peter. 2008. *The Reading and Transformation of Isaiah in Luke-Acts*. LNTS 367. London: Bloomsbury T&T Clark.

Marcus, Joel. 1992. *The Way of the Lord: Christological Exegesis of the Old Testament in the Gospel of Mark*. Louisville: Westminster.

Menken, Maarten J. J. 2004. *Matthew's Bible: The Old Testament Text of the Evangelist*. BETL 173. Leuven: Leuven University Press.

Moessner, David P. 1989. *Lord of the Banquet: The Literary and Theological Significance of the Lukan Travel Narrative*. Minneapolis: Augsburg Fortress.

Moo, Douglas J. 1983. *The Old Testament in the Gospel Passion Narratives*. Sheffield: Almond Press.

Moyise, Steve. 2001. *The Old Testament in the New: An Introduction*. London: Continuum.

New, David S. 1993. *Old Testament Quotations in the Synoptic Gospels, and the Two-Document Hypothesis*. SBLSCS 97. Atlanta: Scholars Press.

Newman, Judith H. 1999. *Praying by the Book: The Scripturalization of Prayer in Second Temple Judaism*. Atlanta: Scholars Press.

Nickelsburg, George W. E. 1980. "The Genre and Function of the Markan Passion Narrative." *Harvard Theological Review* 73: 153–84.

Pao, David W. 2000. *Acts and the Isaianic New Exodus*. WUNT 2/130. Tübingen: Mohr Siebeck.

Pao, David W., and Eckhard J. Schnabel. 2007. "Luke." In *A Commentary on the New Testament Use of the Old Testament*, edited by Greg K. Beale and Donald A. Carson, 251–414. Grand Rapids: Baker Academic.

Perkins, Larry. 2006. "Kingdom, Messianic Authority and the Re-Constituting of God's People—Tracing the Function of Exodus Material in Mark's Narrative." In *Biblical Interpretation in Early Christian Gospels*, vol. 1, *The Gospel of Mark*, edited by Thomas R. Hatina, 100–15. LNTS 304. London: Bloomsbury T&T Clark.

Prior, Michael. 1995. *Jesus the Liberator: Nazareth Liberation Theology (Luke 4:16–30)*. Biblical Seminar Series 26. Sheffield: Sheffield Academic Press.

Rhoads, David M., Joanna Dewey, and Donald Michie. 1982. *Mark as Story: An Introduction to the Narrative of a Gospel*. Philadelphia: Fortress.

Samely, Alexander. 1992. *The Interpretation of Speech in the Pentateuch Targums*. TSAJ 27. Tübingen: Mohr Siebeck.

Samely, Alexander. 2002. *Rabbinic Interpretation of Scripture in the Midrashim*. Oxford: Oxford University Press.

Soares Prabhu, George M. 1976. *The Formula Quotations in the Infancy Narrative of Matthew: An Enquiry into the Tradition History of Mt 1–2*. Rome: Biblical Institute Press.

Stanley, Christopher D. 2004. *Arguing with Scripture: The Rhetoric of Quotations in the Letters of Paul*. New York: T&T Clark.

Stendahl, Krister. 1968. *The School of St Matthew and Its Use of the Old Testament*. Lund: Gleerup.

Stuhlmacher, Peter. 2004. "Isaiah 53 in the Gospels and Acts." In *The Suffering Servant: Isaiah 53 in Jewish and Christian Sources*, edited by Bernd Janowski and Peter Stuhlmacher, 147–62. Grand Rapids: Eerdmans.

Subramaniam, J. Samuel. 2007. *The Synoptic Gospels and the Psalms as Prophecy*. LNTS 351. London: Bloomsbury T&T Clark.

Suhl, Alfred. 1965. *Die Funktion der alttestamentliche Zitate und Anspielungen im Markusevangelium*. Gütersloh: Mohn.

Swartley, William. 1980. "The Structural Function of the Term 'Way' (Hodos) in Mark's Gospel." In *The New Way of Jesus: Essays Presented to Howard Charles*, edited by William Klassen, 73–86. Newton, KS: Faith and Life Press.

Vanderkam, James C. 2012. *The Dead Sea Scrolls and the Bible*. Grand Rapids: Eerdmans.

Vette, Nathanael. 2022. *Writing with Scripture: Scripturalized Narrative in the Gospel of Mark*. LNTS 670. London: Bloomsbury T&T Clark.

Watts, Rikk E. 1997. *Isaiah's New Exodus and Mark*. WUNT 2/88. Tübingen: Mohr Siebeck.

Watts, Rikk E. 2007. "Mark." In *A Commentary on the New Testament Use of the Old Testament*, edited by Greg K. Beale and Donald A. Carson, 111–249. Grand Rapids: Baker Academic.

Witherington, Ben. 1994. *Jesus the Sage: The Pilgrimage of Wisdom*. Minneapolis: Fortress.

CHAPTER 28

PORTRAITS OF WOMEN

SUSAN E. MYERS

Representations of Women in the Synoptic Gospels

Women appear on every page of the Gospels of Mark, Matthew, and Luke. Women are among the crowds that greet Jesus, and they are recipients of his teaching and his healings. Women are among Jesus's disciples and appear in the stories he tells. The gospel authors refer to women from the Hebrew tradition, as well as women in the life of Jesus or notable women in society. Several stories feature women prominently, and their interactions with Jesus often contribute to central narratives in the first-century Jesus movement.

Yet women are also hidden, sometimes completely absent from scenes in the gospels or disregarded. In the story of feeding a crowd of 5,000, the Gospel of Matthew specifically counts the men (ἄνδρες) but indicates the presence of women and children, while the Gospels of Mark and Luke explicitly limit the crowd to ἄνδρες only. At other times, the presence of women is missed or ignored in translations and commentary. Women have sometimes been missed because they are part of groups that were assumed, despite an absence of evidence, to be made up solely of men. Since the masculine plural was regularly used to refer to mixed groups, however, it must be understood to be inclusive unless proven otherwise. At other times, figures whose gender is not specified (such as "neighbor"—πλησίον or "child"—παιδίον; both are neuter) have often been assumed to be male, or pronouns used in direct address (the second person, whether singular or plural), although the gender is unspecified, are taken to refer to men. In reality, it is necessary to recognize the presence of multiple genders—or at least to be agnostic regarding gender—in many of these cases.

It is true, however, that ancient authors were living in a patriarchal society and often used exclusive language, assuming that men were the norm. They seem to have adopted a "generic" use of masculine pronouns when referring to an unspecified character in a story (see Smythe 1984: §1015). When care is taken to read a text with as few presuppositions as possible, new options for understanding the characters become available.

This essay examines general considerations regarding characters within the gospels and possible authorship of the gospels, as well as the place of women in ancient society, before turning to individual stories within the gospels themselves. The gospel accounts of the ministry of Jesus were shaped by the authors in order to serve the communities for which they were writing. For the author of Mark, writing at the time of the First Jewish Revolt and the destruction of the Temple in 70 CE, suffering is central, and this Gospel counters a blithe, simplistic, or purely triumphalist understanding of Jesus's significance. Matthew was written approximately one to two decades after Mark and responds to a larger Jewish society unconvinced by messianic claims about Jesus; the author emphasizes Jesus's connection to his Hebrew heritage and the legal traditions of Israel. Luke, perhaps written around the same time as Matthew, also considers the Hebrew tradition to be foundational, but, together with Acts, shows greater focus on Gentiles than does the Gospel of Matthew. With an interest in speaking to concerns of the marginalized, this Gospel also takes care to situate the movement within the specific history of the Roman Empire. These larger concerns both encompass and sometimes interfere with the presentation of women in the Synoptic Gospels.

General Considerations

Characters

In most cases, when Jesus speaks to groups of people, the reader/auditor must conclude that women are present. This includes references to crowds, to disciples, and to other unspecified groups. It also includes reference to any pairs, such as the "two of them" who were traveling to Emmaus in Luke 24:13. The use of the masculine plural suggests only that there was at least one man in the pair, but it does not preclude the presence of a woman. (There may be other reasons, such as the perspective of the author, to suppose that the pair consists of two men.) The masculine plural could refer to a group of men, but it could also refer to a group made up of people of multiple genders. Indeed, after the initial mention of a group, the reader/auditor is sometimes informed later of the presence of a woman or women within the group. See, for example, the women who are among Jesus's entourage in Luke 8:2 (earlier in the Gospel this entourage is referred to as "disciples") or the "crowd" that follows Jesus in Mark 5:21 and 5:24, out of which emerges first a synagogue leader (verse 22, identified as a man by the use of the masculine pronoun) and then a woman (verse 25) to command Jesus's attention. This general rule that the masculine plural is inclusive of gender is true also of "apostles," unless a more limited group is specified. Unlike other authors, the author of Luke/Acts is hesitant to use the term "apostle" of those outside the Twelve, even generally refraining to identify Paul as an apostle. At the same time, there is no reason to think that the seventy (or seventy-two) apostles of Luke 10:1–12, those who are "sent out" in pairs, could not have been understood to include women.

Sometimes, it is simply the case that working with a gendered language creates awkward, although not unclear, situations. For example, the "daughter" whom Jesus declares healed in Mark 7:29 is also called a "child" (neuter), and Jesus and the child's mother engage in extended conversation about food for children (neuter) and for dogs (masculine), when they are actually obliquely discussing the woman's daughter. The use of the masculine plural must, therefore, usually be understood to refer to a mixed group, unless it becomes clear that the group consists only of men. This may be true of groups long assumed to be exclusive of women, such as Pharisees and scribes. When the masculine singular is used, however, the situation is generally—although not always—clearer. The term ἄνθρωπος appears frequently, often referring to humanity in general or to unspecified individual humans. Although grammatically masculine, it could be used with a feminine article to designate a woman. When ἄνθρωπος is used and there is nothing else to specify the gender, the term simply means "person," and could be understood as a man or a woman. There is nothing about the ἄνθρωπος who finds a treasure in a field (Matt 13:44), for example, that suggests that the person is a man.

There was in antiquity a "generic" use of the masculine singular as well as the masculine plural. While ἀδελφοί was clearly used of gender-rich groups (in, for example, Paul's letters), the singular "brother" could also be used to refer to any neighbor or friend. This seems to be operative in the gospel parables, and especially of the term ἄνθρωπος, although the author of Luke often specified an ἀνήρ. Even when a masculine pronoun is used with reference to the ἄνθρωπος, the pronoun may be intended as "generic." The person (identified as "wise" only in Matthew) who builds on a firm foundation (Matt 7:24–27 // Luke 6:48–49) is an ἄνθρωπος in Luke (ἀνήρ in Matthew), and masculine relative pronouns are used, but surely the teaching is intended to apply to anyone. In some stories, the identity of the characters is left ambiguous. The story of the unclean spirit who leaves a "person" only to return later (Matt 12:43–45 // Luke 11:24–26) gives no further identification of the ἄνθρωπος. In the story of the lost sheep (Matt 18:12–14 // Luke 15:1–7), a masculine pronoun is used in Luke but not in Matthew, where the identity of the owner of the sheep is unclear; this parable is followed in Luke by the story of the lost coin, in which the protagonist is clearly a woman, reflecting the Lukan tendency to duplicate stories in order to include an example that features a woman. Finally, the language of teaching materials, as in the Sermon on the Mount/Sermon on the Plain, is less likely to be exclusive, and when masculine pronouns are used, they lend themselves to being understood more generally. A female reader/auditor in the first century would likely see/hear the stories in which an ἄνθρωπος is featured, even when a masculine pronoun is later used, as inclusive of her, even as she may adjust it to apply it to her own circumstance, sometimes understanding it metaphorically or otherwise reinterpreting the specifics of the tale.

Authorship

Because the Synoptic Gospels were written anonymously, it is impossible to know the identity, including the gender, of the authors (with the exception of the Gospel of Luke, in which a self-referential masculine participle in the Greek of the preface suggests a male author). Despite claims to the contrary, some women in the ancient world could read and write. While most people throughout the Mediterranean region were indeed illiterate, members of wealthy and prominent families—of any gender—were educated, as manuscript discoveries and other evidence reveals. Women were largely responsible for educating children and for hiring teachers, and they could serve as formal teachers themselves. Young girls and boys could be educated together, while advanced education in particular signified a family's social standing (Hylen 2019, 119–20). Palestine, as a Roman province that had experienced centuries of Hellenization, shared in many of the features of ancient Mediterranean culture but was also distinctive in many ways as a Jewish region. The trove of second-century documents belonging to Babatha demonstrates that educated Jewish women were also able to navigate a complicated legal system and the social requirements of their time (Kraemer 1999b, 61).

As a result, one cannot disregard the possibility that women were involved in the composition and dissemination of the gospels. Ironically, the gospel that has sometimes been suggested as the writing of a woman is the Gospel of Luke, the only gospel in which the author identifies as a man. But the other gospels, while clearly reflecting a patriarchal social structure, do not give evidence of the gender of the author. To recognize these gospels as anonymous compositions requires an agnostic conclusion regarding their authorship. While there is no clear evidence that a woman was involved in writing any gospel, there is also no clear evidence ruling out that possibility.

Women in Ancient Society

The degree to which a particular region employed androcentric norms varied, although there are some general claims that can be made about the Roman Empire, including the provinces. While it is not typical to find women in positions of power in the ancient world, it is also not unknown. Within Jewish tradition, Queen Alexandra reigned as the last ruler of an independent Jewish state. In the Roman province of Palestine, Berenice ruled jointly with her brother Agrippa II and was the lover of the Roman general Titus (Kraemer 1999b, 54). More significant, some assumptions about women that developed in the early centuries of Christianity, especially in Europe, had not yet developed, and later assertions (for example, that women in the ancient world could not speak with men or could not be seen outside the home) are refuted by the gospels themselves. Later Christian and Jewish writers developed arguments that women were responsible for all evil, that the purpose for women's existence was to bear children, or that women and men could not worship together. While these arguments were sometimes based on biblical texts, such as 1 Timothy 2:8–15, the later writers went well beyond the texts from the biblical Hebrew tradition or the earliest Jesus movement.

In the first-century Roman world, women had freedoms and influence not previously enjoyed. Although the sources are somewhat limited and some, such as those from philosophers, tend to be negative toward women, many women enjoyed considerable autonomy. Women, both Gentile and Jewish and both elite and nonelite, could own and inherit property, and were known to divorce their husbands and remarry (despite the Mosaic injunction that only men could initiate divorce; Cohick 2009, 115–17; Hylen 2019, 81). While the "ideal woman" remained at home, and indeed women could have authority within the household, there is no evidence that women were confined to the home. Stories in the gospels recount Jesus encountering women in crowds, in the Temple, in the synagogue, and in the market. Professions in which women were engaged varied; women served as midwives, clerics, teachers, wet-nurses, and brickmakers and were involved in the production of clothing or other goods. As household managers, women of means often oversaw the workers involved in the family business, whether in farming or finance, and less advantaged women participated in producing the family's goods and selling them in the marketplace (Hylen 2019, 113–30).

Almost all marriages in the first century were *sine manu*, that is, women were not legally under the control of their husbands, although within marriage, a woman was generally considered to be inferior to her husband. As property owners, women could exercise the legal rights of the *paterfamilias*. In general, a woman's ability to act independently was founded more on her wealth and her social standing than on her marital status.

Within religious spheres, Gentile women could sponsor religious festivals and processions. They were expected to take on public religious duties just as men were, and they could be honored for their leadership (LiDonnici 1999, 81). Within Judaism, women could be leaders of synagogues (Brooten 1982; Kraemer 2011, 232–41; Levine 2000, 483). While authors often praise women for their modesty and loyalty to their families and religion, it is precisely these qualities that provide the freedom to be publicly active and respected. The figure of Anna in Luke 2:36–38, for example, is presented as a virtuous widow, and is therefore renowned as a prophet and is able to be active at the Temple.

Stories of Women

The gospels are filled with stories of Jesus interacting with individual women. While in his ministry he exercises the same general reserve in his encounters with Jewish women, especially married Jewish women, that governed the behavior of first-century Jewish men (Kraemer 1999a), he is also seen encountering women in his childhood and interacting with women during his ministry, and he is mourned by women after his death.

Stories of individual women and girls, or groups of women, that appear throughout the Synoptic Gospels far outnumber the stories of women in the Gospel of John (which, however, has lengthier stories, including the longest encounter between Jesus and a woman in the story of the Samaritan woman). The Gospel of Mark includes at least ten scenes or stories of women or girls; there are a few additional stories in the Gospel of Matthew. It is in the Gospel of Luke that the presence of women is especially pronounced; there are extended accounts of women in the infancy narrative, stories unknown elsewhere, and duplications in parables. In general, however, the roles of women in the Gospel of Luke are more restricted, and their authority diminished.

The Syrophoenician/Canaanite Woman

The story of Jesus's encounter with this Gentile woman appears only in the Gospels of Mark and Matthew. Her identity outside the people of Israel is emphasized in several ways in both Gospels: she lives in a Gentile city, she is a "a Greek, a Syrophoenician" (Mark 7:26) or a "Canaanite" (Matt 15:22), and she discusses with Jesus whether her child may be healed of a demon; in Matthew, Jesus explicitly responds that he was sent to "the lost sheep of the house of Israel" and his disciples are less than gracious to her.

At first glance, the story is troubling, for Jesus calls the woman and her family "dogs," and the woman achieves her goal of healing for her daughter by accepting the appellation but arguing that dogs, as well as children, must eat. While the encounter allows the author of Matthew to emphasize the Jewish character of Jesus and his ministry, it is the original story in Mark that is intriguing. The woman has been described as an ultimate outsider—by virtue of her gender, her ethnicity, and her religious identity (Schüssler Fiorenza 1992, 96)—yet she is also a person with whom many of the recipients of the Gospel would have identified (D'Angelo 1999d, 139). She is a Greek-speaking Gentile, and her clash with Jesus signals the author's intent in this gospel to move Jesus to a new phase in his ministry, one not limited only to the people of Israel.

The Anointing Woman

All four canonical gospels have a story of a woman anointing Jesus, but distinctive elements characterize the different narratives. Only in the Gospel of John is the woman identified. In the Synoptics, the Gospel of Mark (followed closely in Matthew) sets the scene in Bethany, at the home of Simon the leper. The woman lavishes expensive ointment on Jesus's head and is criticized (by Jesus's disciples in Matthew) for the waste of money, which could have been used for the poor. It is not clear if the woman is a participant in the meal or intrudes upon the scene. Jesus defends the woman, declaring that she has anointed him for burial, and her story will be told "in memory of her" (Mark 14:9), a striking declaration for an unnamed woman (Schüssler Fiorenza 1983, xiii). Placed as this story is, just before the Passion in Mark and Matthew, the woman's extravagance is contrasted with the greed of Judas in the next scene, and her actions anticipate those of the women who approach the tomb to anoint Jesus's body, a detail removed from the tomb story in Matthew.

The Lukan narrative completely changes the meaning of this woman's actions. The story is moved much earlier in Jesus's ministry, where it offers an opportunity for teaching about forgiveness and where there can be no association with Jesus's death. The woman hears of Jesus's presence at the house of a Pharisee (later identified as Simon, confirming the author's use—and complete overhaul—of the story in Mark), appears with the ointment and, standing behind Jesus, washes his feet with her tears, wipes them with her hair, and anoints them. From the beginning, she is identified as a known sinner, although the precise nature of her sinfulness is never clarified. Despite creative attempts to identify the woman as sexually promiscuous, the narrative simply does not provide enough information to reach this conclusion; there were many "known sinners," including those who dealt regularly with Gentiles (Getty-Sullivan 2001, 109). Although her sinfulness is unknown to Jesus, the host knows of it and questions how Jesus, if he is a "prophet," could be unaware of her past sin. Jesus then responds with a parable about indebtedness and gratitude. As in the other gospels, Jesus rebukes the woman's critic and defends her, while here also offering her forgiveness.

The story of the anointing woman in Luke follows the visit from the messengers of John the Baptist to Jesus. This version includes the narrator's pronouncement that "all the people," even tax collectors (who were considered "known sinners" just like the anointing woman), accepted the baptism of John, and concludes with Jesus's declarations against "the people of this generation." Perhaps the author's intent is, therefore, to demonstrate that the religious leaders, represented here by Simon, were rejecting the divine call that was so appealing to sinners (Kilgallen 1985). To the author and the intended audience, Simon's misunderstanding of Jesus is related to his misunderstanding of the woman (Reid 1996, 110), and the entire scene allows the author to dwell on a valued theme, that of forgiveness. As for the woman, however, her prophetic role of signifying Jesus as the "anointed one" (as maintained in the Gospel of Mark; see Mark 1:1), acting as the Hebrew Bible prophets had toward the rulers (messiahs) of Israel, is absent from the story in Luke.

The Woman with the Flow of Blood and Jairus's Daughter

A key text in the history of feminist biblical criticism, the story of the healing of the daughter of Jairus—interrupted as it is by the healing of the woman with the flow of blood—appears in all of the Synoptic Gospels. The earliest story, that in Mark, is the most interesting.

The story begins with a ruler of the synagogue, Jairus, joining the crowd around Jesus to beseech him for assistance. Declaring that his daughter is dying, he affirms that Jesus can make her well. Into this scene is inserted the saga of a woman who has been suffering for twelve years; her struggles are recounted in detail. She has heard of Jesus and believes that he can heal her; indeed, when she touches his mantle, she recognizes that she has been healed. Jesus, too, recognizes that something has happened and, despite the interference of his disciples, seeks the one who touched him, declaring that her faith has healed her. Once again, the scene shifts, and the synagogue ruler learns that his daughter has died, but Jesus tells him to believe. Approaching the house filled with mourners, Jesus touches the girl and raises her, then instructs everyone not to speak of the incident.

Several standard Markan elements characterize this account. These include the use of chiasm, the importance of faith for healing, the use of physical touch in Jesus's interactions, the ignorance of the disciples, the placement of Palestinian Aramaic on Jesus's lips, and the inclusion of the Messianic Secret. In addition, elements of the narrative create suspense: crowds interfere with the woman's attempt to reach Jesus as well as his effort to identify who has touched him. The story of the woman also creates suspense regarding the child, and the delay lends credence to the idea that the girl has died. While several men in Jesus's entourage are named, the woman and the girl are unnamed, perhaps offering the possibility for other women and girls hearing the story to identify with their plight. Just as the woman and Jairus demonstrate their determination (deemed "faith" in this Gospel), so also the readers/auditors would be encouraged to persevere in their own circumstances.

Although many have claimed to find concerns with ritual purity in this passage, and assume that the woman must be menstruating, the text is silent on these details. Indeed, with the setting in Galilee, the idea that Temple purity is of concern is highly unlikely. Jesus, or any character who encounters the bleeding woman, would have many other opportunities for uncleanliness before reaching the Temple as well as opportunities for ritual purification. Although the text does not specify the source of the bleeding, the possibility that it is menstrual is enhanced by terminology linking the two stories. Not only had the woman experienced bleeding for twelve years, but the girl, aged twelve, had died at the onset of puberty (and the age at which Roman and later rabbinic law declared her to be marriageable), perhaps suggesting that the woman's womb was unnaturally "open" while the girl's was, due to her untimely death, unnaturally "closed" (D'Angelo 1999a, 95; 1999d, 143). The parallels between Jairus's daughter and the woman extend also to the appellation "daughter" used of both. Inexplicable from the perspective of age, Jesus addresses the woman as "daughter." The woman's age is never given but, having suffered for twelve years, she is unlikely to be envisioned as much younger than Jesus, if younger at all. These parallels, however, further link the two female characters together. Both also experience Jesus's healing power as the result of faithfulness: the woman's faith or that of the girl's father.

The recounting of this story in the Gospel of Luke follows that of Mark to a great extent, with a few notable deletions and changes: the woman's internal monologue is silenced, and her afflictions are abridged, as is the scene at Jairus's house; Peter (the leader of the band of Jesus's followers in Luke/Acts) is given voice for the disciples; and Jesus speaks only Greek. It is in the Gospel of Matthew that the most significant changes are made.

First, the account is shorter and more direct in Matthew, not uncommon in stories shared in the Gospels of Mark and Matthew. But there are several other Matthean characteristics that appear as well. The synagogue ruler does not fall before Jesus but kneels, signifying greater reverence. To heighten the drama, and to eliminate the need for a messenger to arrive later, the girl has already died by the time Jairus asks Jesus for help. The story of the bleeding woman is significantly shortened, in large part because Jesus expresses no uncertainty about what has happened or who has touched him. The Messianic Secret is removed, and the story ends with Jesus's deeds being regionally proclaimed.

Although the woman and girl are nameless, and the story is clearly set within a patriarchal culture, there are also elements, especially within the Markan story, that draw attention to the independence and authority of the woman. While Jesus's healing powers are clearly the focus of the narrative, the woman's participation is needed for the miracle to occur. She accomplishes the healing and "brings forth the power of Jesus" (D'Angelo 1998, 37) through her initiative. While the author of Matthew is apparently uncomfortable with Jesus's ignorance, Jesus is left to affirm what has already happened in both Mark and Luke. His power is made evident through the woman's resourcefulness.

Mary Magdalene and the Women at the Tomb

No account of women in the New Testament would be complete without an examination of the figure of Mary Magdalene, the follower of Jesus who appears in all four canonical gospels as present at the crucifixion of Jesus and a visitor to his tomb. Bearing the extremely common Hebrew name Miriam, this woman has throughout history, at least in some areas of Christianity, sometimes been confused with other gospel women. The early traditions, recorded in both biblical and noncanonical sources, about Mary Magdalene suggest that she must have been remembered by the earliest Christian writers as among the first to proclaim the message that death had not conquered Jesus. This is precisely the claim made in the longer ending, added later, to the Gospel of Mark. Her status as witness to Jesus's resurrection and the commission given her to proclaim it, her portrayal as recipient of a resurrection appearance in some gospels, and the memory that she had been a close follower of Jesus, all contributed to her early revered status and the designation "apostle" (Brock 2003).

Only in the Gospel of Luke (8:1–3) is Mary Magdalene introduced prior to the scene at the cross. She is the "one from whom seven demons had gone out," and a member of the group of women, clearly depicted as disciples although not explicitly labeled as such, who provided for Jesus as well as, according to some manuscripts, his companions. In the Gospel of Mark (15:40–41), she is also presented as a disciple who, together with two other named women from Galilee, followed Jesus from the beginning and "ministered" (διακονέω) to him; "many other women" joined them at the cross. Much the same claim, including the use of διακονέω, is made of Mary in the Gospel of Matthew (27:55–56; although her companions differ), and even in Luke, although in the Lukan Passion account the women are not named until after they leave the tomb (24:10), and they are accompanied by "all" Jesus's acquaintances (23:49).

Although all four gospels agree that a group of women, including Mary Magdalene, were faithful to the end and visited the tomb, the gospels differ markedly with respect to the presence of men at the tomb and the authority granted to the women. In Mark and Matthew, the women visit the tomb alone and discover it empty; they are greeted by a figure (an angel in Matthew) who announces that Jesus is risen and, in Matthew, they meet Jesus himself. The Gospel of John grants Mary an audience with Jesus, although the role of being the first to look into the empty tomb is granted to men. But it is the Gospel of Luke that most effectively diminishes the women's role in the eyes of the community, for they are perplexed and disbelieved by the others, and Peter is granted the role of witness (24:12, 34).

The identities of the women who accompany Mary Magdalene to the tomb vary. In Luke, one woman, Joanna, is apparently aristocratic, as identified in 8:3. Unless "Mary the mother of James" (Mark 16:1; "of James the younger and of Joses" in 15:40 and "of Joses" in 15:47) and/or "Mary the mother of James and Joseph" (Matthew 27:56; "of James" in Luke 24:10) is to be understood as the mother of Jesus, the women are largely unknown until their appearance at Jesus's crucifixion.

In the Gospel of Mark, the three women who have remained at the cross, two of whom have witnessed the burial, bring spices to anoint the body of Jesus. This is an intriguing detail in a gospel in which Jesus has said he was already anointed before burial (14:8), but it provides a reason for having the women appear at the tomb. Since there are no resurrection appearances in the Gospel of Mark, the tomb story is a necessary composition to affirm that Jesus is risen. The women find the tomb opened and a young man inside who proclaims that Jesus is risen and gives them a commission to announce to the "disciples and Peter" that Jesus will precede them to Galilee. The astonished women flee, saying nothing to anyone. The abruptness of this ending clearly troubled later Christians, who composed a variety of more suitable closures for this Gospel.

The women in Mark 16:8, therefore, appear in the final scene in a less than flattering light, a depiction that accords with the portrait of Jesus's disciples in this Gospel as faithless and blundering (Kelhoffer 2010; Malbon 1983). These women are not, however, to be dismissed. First, a higher proportion of women are presented as examples of discipleship than are men in this Gospel, setting the stage for these three reliable witnesses who appear at the tomb (Carey 2019). All of Jesus's followers in the Gospel of Mark are unmistakably flawed, yet this presentation in itself is an invitation for others to join them as disciples. The silent flight of the women from the tomb, far from a complete disparagement of the women, serves several purposes in this artfully composed Gospel (written, though it is, with simple language). The author, who makes use of chiasm elsewhere, creates an entire gospel with a chiastic structure in which the ending is paired with early presentations of the Messianic Secret in order to draw attention to the middle of the narrative, in which Peter, as representative of Jesus-followers within the community receiving the Gospel, understands the identity of Jesus as Messiah but does not comprehend the significance of suffering and death entailed in that title. The phenomenon of believers wanting to focus on the spectacular is known already from Paul (see, e.g., 1 Cor 4:8), who insists on preaching the cross; the Markan composer has a similar purpose. Although the women flee the tomb, they are presented as witnesses, and the author may have kept them silent in order to defend against a potential charge that the movement was based on empty words of women, as the author of Luke seems to have done (D'Angelo 2004, 52). Finally, when considering the readers/hearers of this Gospel, the ending at 16:8, following the proclamation that Jesus is risen but closing with women who say nothing, would be experienced as a command and an opportunity to go forth to proclaim the good news of the Jesus movement: that Jesus is risen. The entire scene thus furthers the author's purpose in several ways.

Just as the Gospel of Matthew offers greater reverence for Jesus and for other characters in the Gospel (see, for example, Matt 20:20 and compare with Mark 10:35), it rehabilitates the women at the tomb, offering a bright and joyful scene. The women remain witnesses to the burial and approach the tomb (here, without ointment) to witness an amazing event: a dazzling angel descends, proclaims that Jesus is risen, and gives the women a commission to tell all the disciples. The Matthean women, far from fleeing in silence and fear, joyfully run to tell the others but are interrupted by Jesus, who also gives them a commission (Matt 28:8–10).

While the story in Luke bears neither the gloom of the Markan ending nor the brightness of that in Matthew, it alters the presentation of the women. They witness the location of the tomb and come with spices for the body (the anointing woman in this Gospel had not anointed Jesus for burial) before greeting, in perplexity and terror, two men who announce that Jesus is risen. When they report this to the others, they are not believed; their role as bearers of the good news is stripped from them but without serving the author's intent as in Mark. It takes Peter, and the travelers to Emmaus, to encounter Jesus and to recognize the significance of what has occurred. This presentation accords with the Lukan author's tempering of the authority and independence of women during and after Jesus's ministry, an apparent attempt to provide legitimacy for the movement within the culture of the Roman Empire.

The stature of Mary Magdalene both rose and fell in subsequent literature. She is revered in later centuries as the one whom Jesus loved and the "apostle to the apostles," but legends also developed regarding her travels, her encounter with the emperor, her marriage to Jesus, and her lasciviousness. Over time, her authority is superseded by that of Mary the mother of Jesus, a displacement that begins in the gospels themselves, in particular in the Gospel of Luke.

Mary, the Mother of Jesus

Mary, Jesus's mother, barely appears as a character in the Gospel of Mark. Her name is mentioned after Jesus teaches in the synagogue in his hometown, when the people take offense at him because they know him as "the carpenter, the son of Mary" (Mark 6:3). The author probably intends the reader/auditor to presume that Mary is part of Jesus's "family" who have tried to restrain him in chapter 3. A short time later, Jesus's mother and siblings are outside while he is teaching, and the crowd draws attention to them. Jesus's response is dismissive: "'Who are my mother and my siblings?' And looking at those who sat around him, he said, 'Here are my mother and my siblings. Whoever does the will of God is my brother and sister and mother'" (Mark 3:33–35).

The story in which Jesus's mother and siblings appear while he is preaching (and his dismissive response) is much the same in Matthew as in Mark, and Mary, Jesus's mother, has a minor role in the infancy narrative in Matthew, in which most of the interest is in the figure of Joseph. While she is included in the genealogy (along with other women of questionable sexual renown), it is simply because she is the one "of whom Jesus was born." In Joseph's deliberations over her pregnancy and his encounter with an angel, Mary is mentioned, but she never appears as a character in her own right until after Jesus is born and the magi visit the child who is said to be with her. Joseph is the central figure in the narrative of the flight to Egypt, although he is instructed (again by an angel) to "take the child and his mother" to safety. "Mary the mother of James and Joseph" is again present at the crucifixion and is apparently the "other Mary" who visits the tomb, but the problems of identification of this figure are similar to those in the Gospel of Mark.

It is in the Gospel of Luke that Mary, Jesus's mother, comes into her own in the narrative. In a gospel in which women's prophetic roles are diminished, Mary appears as a woman chosen by God. She notably also encounters other women who bear witness to her part in the divine plan. One of these women is Elizabeth, the mother of John the Baptist, and the other is Anna, a woman who is explicitly identified as a prophet. The Lukan infancy narrative is a highly structured account of the events surrounding Jesus's birth and childhood. There are numerous parallels and contrasts—Zechariah/Elizabeth; Elizabeth/Mary; John/Jesus; Simeon/Anna; Temple/home—as well as various angels, various travels on the part of the major characters, and several poetic songs of praise. Although the parallels between the men and the women cannot be missed, the women claim attention in their own right.

It is Elizabeth, not Mary, who is said to be filled with the Holy Spirit (Luke 1:41), and she is the one who ensures that the statement of the angel regarding her son's name is honored. Unlike her husband, the direct recipient of the angel's words, she apparently trusts those words, retaining her ability to speak and declaring that God has looked on her with favor. Modeled on stories from the Hebrew tradition of parents conceiving a child despite advanced years, especially that of Hannah (1 Sam 1:1–18), the tale of the conception of John serves to highlight divine communication and a woman's response, preparing for the depiction of Mary as faithful servant of God.

Elizabeth's words to Mary (Luke 1:45) could suggest that it is not Mary's role in procreation but rather her faith that distinguishes her. Jesus's response to the woman (Luke 11:27–28) who declares Mary's womb and breasts to be blessed ("Blessed rather are those who hear the word of God and obey it") could perhaps be seen also as affirming the idea that Mary's uniqueness is characterized by discipleship rather than by her identity as Jesus's mother. There are, however, many women—in this Gospel in particular—who follow Jesus or are portrayed as faithful, and the reality is that the story of Mary focuses on her role as mother, just as the blessing of the woman in chapter 11 "focuses solely on the mothering function of the female body: womb and breasts" (Seim 1994b, 733). It is precisely by being willing to give birth to Jesus that Mary takes on the role of disciple. The blessing of Mary spoken by Elizabeth (Luke 1:42–43) focuses on Mary as the "mother of my Lord." Because the women at the tomb are denied a prophetic role in this Gospel, and their words about the empty tomb are disbelieved, Jesus's mother supersedes them in importance. While discipleship is indeed a concern of this author, it seems that being able to bear a child is central to discipleship for this particular woman.

Elizabeth, too, is a mother, but she is also prophetic (filled with the Spirit) and makes the Christological claim that identifies Jesus as "Lord"; despite the range of meanings of that term, it is clearly of consequence for the author and the community(ies) that have received the Gospel. Some manuscripts (although relatively late) place the Canticle of Mary (Luke 1:46–55) on the lips of Elizabeth rather than those of Mary. The origin of this prophetic song of reversal and divine justice, while difficult to pinpoint, bears some resemblance to the song of Hannah in 1 Samuel 2, and Elizabeth's situation more clearly parallels that of Hannah than does Mary's (verse 48 is clearly supplied by the author of the Gospel). Whichever figure is understood to sing this song, she celebrates the revolutionary God of Israel. Although Elizabeth and Zechariah are ultimately less significant for the author than the parents of Jesus, they are accorded far more attention; indeed, Zechariah speaks a canticle of praise while Joseph, in the end, is the one who is mute.

Mary's role, then, is that of the bearer of Jesus, but also the one who "ponders." First troubled by the words of the angel, she comes to accept them. After Jesus's birth, when shepherds encounter an angel who tells of the birth of a "savior, the Messiah," and additional angels proclaim God's greatness, Mary treasures the words of the shepherds and ponders them in her heart. Together with Jesus's father, she is amazed at the words of Simeon, who declares that divine salvation has arrived, with implications for both Israel and the nations, but it is she whom Simeon addresses directly, declaring that her soul will be pierced. She is the one who chastises her child when he causes his parents anxiety, and she is the one who treasures his words in her heart. Mary is the repository of the prophetic declarations of others, and it is she who bears witness to the Christological claims the author wants to reveal.

As for Mary as an actual historical figure, she is somewhat unremarkable, although one can see in her actions some understanding of the lives of women in first-century Palestine. She is a girl or young woman, living in poverty (as attested by the sacrifice of a "pair of turtledoves or two young pigeons" in Luke 2:24; see Lev 14:21–22), who is pregnant with her first child. In the Gospel of Luke, she is presented as traveling some distance to visit a relative, without mention of anyone accompanying her. The two women rejoice to see one another and spend significant time in one another's presence. Together they share the role of mother, which has often drawn disparate women into communion with one another and inspired acts of service for family and community.

The final figure who appears in the Lukan infancy narrative is Anna, the prophet and widow. She was married for seven years, but she has lived as a widow to the age of eighty-four. No child of hers is mentioned, but she is distinguished by her loyalty, both to God and to her husband, and her piety. She is presented as a trustworthy figure in compliance with the cultural expectations of the time. It is precisely her virtuous life that qualifies her to assume the role of prophet (Hylen 2019, 89–90).

These three women—Elizabeth, Mary, and Anna—are given prominent roles in the opening chapters of the Gospel of Luke. This fact becomes even more striking upon reading the rest of the Gospel, a composition that is "perhaps the most dangerous in the Bible" because of its portrayal of women as "models of subordinate service, excluded from the power center of the movement and from significant responsibilities" (Schaberg 1998, 363). Yet these women are active, are often given voice, and serve as prophets of the divine message. Especially conspicuous is the canticle spoken by Mary in chapter 1. Given the ways in which the author of Luke/Acts seeks to present Jesus and his followers as good citizens, unthreatening to Roman rule, this proclamation of divine overthrow is remarkable. Apparently, the author is comfortable presenting women who act with autonomy and authority, even challenging social and political powers, as long as their identity is defined by the domestic sphere and the traditional role of motherhood; the activity of these women also occurs prior to Jesus's birth or during his childhood, long before Jesus himself could be seen as a threat to peace in the empire.

Mary and Martha

The final Mary I will examine is a member of a pair, together with her sister Martha. Although in the Gospel of John she is identified as the woman who anoints Jesus and she hails from Bethany, her only appearance in the Synoptics is a brief one, with her sister, in the Gospel of Luke (Luke 10:38–42). In this passage, Martha is the dominant figure, and Mary, silent, is the subject of the conversation between Jesus and Martha. Both sisters warrant attention.

Often adduced in the history of Christian interpretation, with strikingly different conclusions, this story has been used to pit women (or what these women are understood to represent) against one another with respect to their experiences and choices. Yet the precise nature of Martha's concern and of Jesus's advice is not entirely clear, obfuscated in part by manuscript differences (Schüssler Fiorenza 1986, 25). Central to the story is an understanding of how to engage with Jesus and how to approach the subject of ministry.

The story is brief. At the home of Martha, her sister Mary sits at the feet of their guest, Jesus, in the posture of a disciple, and Martha makes a request of "the Lord" to have Mary assist her. Jesus responds, perhaps in rebuke, perhaps in sympathy, defending Mary's inaction and declining Martha's request.

The story appears sandwiched between the story of the Good Samaritan and that in which Jesus teaches how to pray. The recently begun travel narrative of Jesus on the journey to Jerusalem takes a detour to the home of Martha. The pair of independent women, evocative of missionary couples in the early Jesus movement, here provide respite, revealing the need for itinerant preachers in the movement to seek shelter and support while traveling. As such, the story suggests the importance of the journey and the need of travelers to receive hospitality (Gench 2004, 59, 76).

The language used to describe the women is significant. Mary is called "sister," a term often used to refer to a member of the community of Jesus-followers. Martha is involved in "much service," and the author uses the term for ministry (διακονία), perhaps Eucharistic ministry, within the Jesus movement (see, e.g., the role of Phoebe in Rom 16:1, and the use of the term repeatedly throughout Acts, especially in Acts 6:2–4). In the Gospel of Luke, the only named characters who "serve" are women, while the term is used only of men in Acts. For Martha, this service causes her to be "pulled away," or distracted. Jesus offers either a mild rebuke or a loving reply ("Martha, Martha"), depending on one's perspective, but precisely what his response suggests is obscured by textual variants. The author may mean to indicate that Martha is overzealous in her service and could simplify it (thus "few things are necessary, or only one"). Or the figure of Jesus may be saying that "only one thing" is necessary, and it is Mary who has chosen it. Or, as Meister Eckhart read the story, it is Martha who has the more mature realization of what it is to follow Jesus, but Mary has chosen what for her is the better, foundational role of learning, something Martha has already accomplished (Wyant 2019, 9–10).

While this passage surely reflects the experiences of the early Jesus movement as known to the author, recent scholarship has not agreed on the understanding of the pericope. Perhaps the story reflects tensions in the community regarding the ministerial roles of women, including table ministry (Schüssler Fiorenza 1992, 64–65), or any ministries in which women could participate as a result of discipleship (Alexander 2004, 210; Reid 1996, 157). Perhaps the two women represent historical groups of women who either took on roles of active service or were students, but not preachers, of the gospel (Seim 1994a, 112–18). While Mary's role as learner is affirmed, Martha is the key figure in the story, which may illustrate the perspective of women in ministry that their service was disregarded and that their "sisters" were not fully supportive of their roles (Reid 1996, 157–58), a restriction in women's activities that the author of Luke promotes.

However the story is understood, Mary and Martha were probably remembered as constituting a missionary partnership within the community of Jesus-followers—a phenomenon well attested by the many pairs mentioned in Paul's letters—whose story would suggest, to a first- or second-century reader/auditor, the ministry of hosting a house church (D'Angelo 1990, 78). Although the author of Luke/Acts is happy to allow women to act as patrons, using their resources in support of Jesus (Luke 8:1–3) or of the Jesus community and individuals within it (Acts 9:36–43; 12:12; 16:14–15), the author does not encourage the idea of women in authority. While there are many more women in the Gospel of Luke (and to a lesser extent in Acts) than in the other gospels, women are generally presented in more traditional roles and distanced from ministry (D'Angelo 1999c, 187). Even in telling the story of Prisca, who must have been remembered as a teacher of some renown whose story cannot be ignored, the author chooses to use the diminutive of her name, Priscilla (unlike Paul). Indeed, in the story of Mary and Martha,

Martha's διακονία is unsustainable, while the figure of Mary, who receives approval, is never given voice. There is no question that this author understands women to be part of the Jesus movement, and includes stories to invite and teach more members, but only if the women stay in their place.

CONCLUSION

The Gospels of Mark, Matthew, and Luke include accounts of several women, women who are at the same time both ordinary and significant. Overall, the Gospel of Mark grants these characters greater responsibility and authority, and this trend continues in Matthew. The author of Luke/Acts, while happy to affirm the role of women as patrons and in maternal roles, also recognizes that women can receive and communicate the divine will. Once Jesus's ministry commences for this author, however, women can no longer function as prophetic witnesses or serve in leadership roles.

REFERENCES

Alexander, Loveday C. 2004. "Sisters in Adversity: Retelling Martha's Story." In *A Feminist Companion to Luke*, edited by Amy-Jill Levine, 197–213. Cleveland: Pilgrim.

Brock, Ann Graham. 2003. *Mary Magdalene, the First Apostle: The Struggle for Authority*. Harvard Theological Studies 51. Cambridge, MA: Harvard University Press.

Brooten, Bernadette J. 1982. *Women Leaders in the Ancient Synagogue: Inscriptional Evidence and Background Issues*. Brown Judaic Studies 36. Chico, CA: Scholars Press.

Carey, Holly J. 2019. "Women in Action: Models for Discipleship in Mark's Gospel." *Catholic Biblical Quarterly* 81: 429–48.

Cohick, Lynn H. 2009. *Women in the World of the Earliest Christians: Illuminating Ancient Ways of Life*. Grand Rapids: Baker Academic.

D'Angelo, Mary Rose. 1990. "Women Partners in the New Testament." *Journal of Feminist Studies in Religion* 6: 65–86.

D'Angelo, Mary Rose. 1998. "Gender in the Origins of Christianity: Jewish Hopes and Imperial Exigencies." In *Equal at the Creation: Sexism, Society, and Christian Thought*, edited by Joseph Martos and Pierre Hégy, 25–48. Toronto: University of Toronto Press.

D'Angelo, Mary Rose. 1999a. "Gender and Power in the Gospel of Mark: The Daughter of Jairus and the Woman with the Flow of Blood." In *Miracles in Jewish and Christian Antiquity: Imagining Truth*, edited by John C. Cavadini, 83–109. Notre Dame: University of Notre Dame Press.

D'Angelo, Mary Rose. 1999b. "Reconstructing 'Real' Women in Gospel Literature: The Case of Mary Magdalene." In *Women & Christian Origins*, edited by Ross Shepard Kraemer and Mary Rose D'Angelo, 105–28. Oxford: Oxford University Press.

D'Angelo, Mary Rose. 1999c. "(Re) Presentations of Women in the Gospel of Matthew and Luke-Acts." In *Women & Christian Origins*, edited by Ross Shepard Kraemer and Mary Rose D'Angelo, 171–95. Oxford: Oxford University Press.

D'Angelo, Mary Rose. 1999d. "(Re) Presentations of Women in the Gospels: John and Mark." In *Women & Christian Origins*, edited by Ross Shepard Kraemer and Mary Rose D'Angelo, 129–49. Oxford: Oxford University Press.

D'Angelo, Mary Rose. 2004. "The ANHP Question in Luke-Acts: Imperial Masculinity and the Deployment of Women in the Early Second Century." In *A Feminist Companion to Luke*, edited by Amy-Jill Levine, 44–69. Cleveland: Pilgrim.

Gench, Frances Taylor. 2004. *Back to the Well: Women's Encounters with Jesus in the Gospels*. Louisville: Westminster John Knox.

Getty-Sullivan, Mary Ann. 2001. *Women in the New Testament*. Collegeville: Liturgical Press.

Hylen, Susan E. 2019. *Women in the New Testament World*. Oxford: Oxford University Press.

Kelhoffer, James A. 2010. "A Tale of Two Markan Characterizations: The Exemplary Woman Who Anointed Jesus's Body for Burial (14:3–9) and the Silent Trio Who Fled the Empty Tomb (16:1–8)." In *Women and Gender in Ancient Religions: Interdisciplinary Approaches*, edited by Stephen P. Ahearne-Kroll et al., Wissenschaftliche Untersuchungen zum Neuen Testament 263, 85–98. Tübingen: Mohr Siebeck.

Kilgallen, John J. 1985. "John the Baptist, the Sinful Woman, and the Pharisee." *Journal of Biblical Literature* 104: 675–79.

Kraemer, Ross S. 1999a. "Jewish Women and Christian Origins: Some Caveats." In *Women & Christian Origins*, edited by Ross Shepard Kraemer and Mary Rose D'Angelo, 35–49. Oxford: Oxford University Press.

Kraemer, Ross S. 1999b. "Jewish Women and Women's Judaism(s) at the Beginning of Christianity." In *Women & Christian Origins*, edited by Ross Shepard Kraemer and Mary Rose D'Angelo, 50–79. Oxford: Oxford University Press.

Kraemer, Ross S. 2011. *Unreliable Witnesses: Religion, Gender, and History in the Greco-Roman Mediterranean*. Oxford: Oxford University Press.

Levine, Lee I. 2000. *The Ancient Synagogue: The First Thousand Years*. 2nd ed. New Haven: Yale University Press.

LiDonnici, Lynn R. 1999. "Women's Religions and Religious Lives in the Greco-Roman City." In *Women & Christian Origins*, edited by Ross Shepard Kraemer and Mary Rose D'Angelo, 80–102. Oxford: Oxford University Press.

Malbon, Elizabeth Struthers. 1983. "Fallible Followers: Women and Men in the Gospel of Mark." *Semeia* 28: 29–48.

Reid, Barbara. 1996. *Choosing the Better Part? Women in the Gospel of Luke*. Collegeville: Liturgical Press.

Schaberg, Jane. 1998. "Luke." In *Women's Bible Commentary*, edited by Carol A. Newsom and Sharon H. Ringe, 363–80. Expanded ed. Louisville: Westminster John Knox.

Schottroff, Luise, and Marie-Theres Wacker, eds. 2012. *Feminist Biblical Interpretation: A Compendium of Critical Commentary on the Books of the Bible and Related Literature*. Grand Rapids: Eerdmans.

Schüssler Fiorenza, Elisabeth. 1983. *In Memory of Her: A Feminist Theological Reconstruction of Christian Origins*. New York: Crossroad.

Schüssler Fiorenza, Elisabeth. 1986. "A Feminist Critical Interpretation for Liberation: Martha and Mary: Lk 10:38–42." *Religion and Intellectual Life* 3, no. 2: 21–35.

Schüssler Fiorenza, Elisabeth. 1992. *But She Said: Feminist Practices of Biblical Interpretation*. Boston: Beacon.

Seim, Turid Karlsen. 1994a. *The Double Message: Patterns of Gender in Luke and Acts*. Nashville: Abingdon.

Seim, Turid Karlsen. 1994b. "The Gospel of Luke." In *Searching the Scriptures*, vol. 2, *A Feminist Commentary*, edited by Elisabeth Schüssler Fiorenza, 728–62. New York: Crossroad.
Smythe, Herbert Weir. 1984. *Greek Grammar*. Revised by Gordon M. Messing. Cambridge, MA: Harvard University Press.
Wire, Antoinette Clark. 1978. "The Gospel Miracle Stories and Their Tellers." *Semeia* 11: 83–113.
Wyant, Jennifer S. 2019. *Beyond Mary or Martha: Reclaiming Ancient Models of Discipleship*. Emory Studies in Early Christianity 21. Atlanta: SBL Press.

CHAPTER 29

GENDER

JOSHUA M. RENO AND
STEPHEN P. AHEARNE-KROLL

GENDER IN GREEK AND ROMAN CULTURE

Gender exists at the intersection of numerous societal discourses and inheres idiosyncratically in the very fabric of societies, ancient and modern. However "constructed" gender is within a particular society, or indeed however gender is "constructed," its existence as a discourse fundamentally shapes that society, encouraging taxonomic categorization, fostering differentiation, reifying hierarchy, enforcing protocols, and penalizing deviation, all under the guise of the incontrovertible rubric of *natura*. Gender is ubiquitous, existing in everything from intellectual treatises on proper household management to solecistic screeds scrawled on brothel walls. That is because the performance of gender is under constant scrutiny through self-protecting, reinforcing protocols of propriety and efficacy. Students of antiquity have used gender as a critical, discursive category for literary and historical analysis. Classical antiquity has been both a veil and a foil for modern scholars; simultaneously providing the legendary cultural history for modern conceptions of gender, and serving as the locus classicus for numerous poststructuralist comparative analyses of gender.

The New Testament and its Gospels offer a panoply of vignettes open to critical examination of ancient roles and protocols of gender. Indeed, the history of New Testament scholarship demonstrates the fecundity of this soil as much as the diversity of its fruits. Much like gender itself, the scholarly application of gendered lenses exists outside the binary. Thus, the history of gender studies in the New Testament includes diverse approaches and perspectives ranging from early studies of "Women and Religion," whose aim was to reconstruct the social realities of "real women," to queer and trans perspectives that have illuminated fissures in the façade and deviations from the demands of ancient gender ideologies. Different approaches often highlight interrelated difficulties in examining literary representations. For instance, are the Gospels' women "real" representations of actual women, in historical circumstances, or are they "literary" representations of stylized women, in fictive circumstances? Put another way, to what degree do the depictions of gender within the Gospels represent "real" or "historical" persons?[1] Other questions persist. By what standard(s) of gender should the characters of the Gospels be assessed? Contemporary Roman, historical Hellenic, local Semitic, some combination thereof, or different standards altogether? Societal, geographical, chronological variations all affect what the ancient comparanda offer, not to mention the social status or class of comparative authors and the genre and medium of their art. Furthermore, what is one to make of deviations from "the norm"? In those instances where Jesus deviates from Roman idealized masculinity, how does one address these deviations? Was Jesus simply out of sync with elite Roman paradigms of masculinity as a Jewish peasant from the extremes of the empire? Or was Jesus flagrantly flouting imperial gender norms in acts of defiance? Or should one assume that Jesus adhered to another (Semitic?) standard of masculinity? All too often these questions are overlooked in favor of palatable explanations of Jesus as a radical egalitarian liberator dismantling and subverting hegemonic Roman (or Pharisaic) patriarchy and misogyny.

In spite of these complexities, there are shared currents of thought and frameworks for understanding that undergird ancient Greek, Roman, and Jewish conceptions of gender. This essay (1) will elucidate three convictions that provide ideological foundations for (2) several common expressions of gender discourse that will function as the context in and from which (3) the Synoptic Gospels can be examined.

Sexual Performance

Scholars of Greek antiquity have defined Greek sexual relations, since K. J. Dover's and Michel Foucault's pioneering investigations, around the penetration model. David Halperin (1990, 30–31) provided the clearest exposition of the penetration model:

> [Sex] effectively divides, classifies, and distributes its participants into distinct and radically opposed categories. Sex possesses this valence, apparently, because it is conceived to center essentially on, and to define itself around, an asymmetrical gesture, that of the penetration of the body of one person by the body—and, specifically, by the phallus—of another. Sex is not only polarizing, however; it is also hierarchical.

---

[1] The complexity of the Synoptic Gospels is particularly convoluted. Beyond the question of whether these depictions are "real" or "literary," one must ask: (1) Do the historical figures and the authors of the existing sources share the same gender ideologies? (2) If the gender protocols are literary, whose literary depiction? Mark? Matthew? Luke? Q? Do Matthew and Mark share the same gender ideologies such that Matthew's recapitulation of Mark reproduces Mark's gender protocols? Or do Matthew's subtle alterations indicate subtle differences in his view of gender? (3) How were these gendered narratives received by the diverse audiences of the ancient Mediterranean for whom they were written? While Mark may parse Semiticisms for his readers, how might his Roman (or Galilean or Syrian) readers have understood the gender performance of his characters?

> ... Sexual "activity," moreover, is thematized as domination: the relation between the "active" and the "passive" sexual partner is thought of as the same kind of relation as that obtaining between social superior and social inferior. "Active" and "passive" sexual roles are therefore necessarily isomorphic with superordinate and subordinate social status; hence, an adult, male citizen of Athens can have legitimate sexual relations only with statutory minors ... the citizen's superior prestige and authority express themselves in his sexual precedence—in his power to initiate a sexual act, his right to obtain pleasure from it, and his assumption of an insertive rather than a receptive role.

For Greek men, sexual desire was normally directed toward socially inferior objects irrespective of gender. Wives, slaves male or female, sex workers, freeborn boys were all appropriate sexual objects for Athenian citizen males so long as the social hierarchy was reflected in the sexual act. An Athenian man, in erotic encounters, had to be felt to assume those stylized acts that asserted his dominance and superordination to his partner, chief among these being his insertive role.

The penetration model is felt most pointedly in (purported) deviation. So Jeffrey Henderson (1975, 209) remarks that the most prolific set of insults in Attic comedy was directed against receptive partners, especially men. Of particular note are those references to men with "gaping-assholes" (εὐρύπρωκτοι). Numerous other terms were used—with varying degrees of euphemism—to denigrate the receptive role, many of them relating to a stressed, worn, wide, or used asshole. These insults are coupled with insinuations of political corruption, aristocratic nepotism, and/or sophistic oration (see Skinner 2014, 149; Worman 2008, 64–65). Whatever their encoded meanings, these calumniations derided Athenian men with accusations of receptivity and passivity that by extension undermined their claims to authority and citizenship and even their manhood.

While Hellenists were busy defining the protocols that governed sexual acts at Athens, Latinists took up a similar agenda at Rome. The pioneer's task was undertaken definitively by Amy Richlin. Not insignificantly, Latinists speak of a Roman, "Priapic" model that received its name from Richlin's landmark work on Roman sexual humor, *The Garden of Priapus*. The god Priapus, known for his gargantuan, erect phallus, represented the sexually threatening male in Roman literature. Thus, according to Richlin (1992, 58), "normal male sexuality at Rome was aggressive and active" whether directed at females or other males. Craig Williams (2010) argues that this is the "prime directive" of Roman masculinity as explicitly stated in the *Carmina Priapea*: "my dick will go through the middle of boys and the middle of girls, but with bearded men it will aim only for the top" (74; trans. Williams 2010, 27). The foremost protocol of masculinity was to ensure that the Roman man dominated and penetrated his sexual objects. Sex was an instantiation of masculine sexual persona, of sociosexual dominance: the ability to assert penetrative power over another person (29). This principle is seen in a wide range of Roman literature, ranging from oratory to history to elegy, as well as material evidence, for example Pompeiian graffiti. Time and again the principle remains the same: a Roman man was expected to position himself in a penetrative role vis-à-vis his sexual object, irrespective of gender.[2]

Ancient Medical Perspectives

Surveying medical and philosophical treatises from antiquity, Thomas Laqueur argued that, beginning with Aristotle, Greek and Roman theorists understood male and female not as polar opposites; rather, material bodies were understood under the rubric of one sex, namely the male. The phenotypological phenomena that divided male and female were, according to these writers, distortions or aberrations in a perfect and perfectly male system. According to Laqueur, the one-sex model arrayed "men and women... according to their degree of metaphysical perfection, their vital heat, along an axis whose telos was male" (1990, 5). For Galen, then, the female reproductive system was literally an inverted, internalized version of the male system (*De usu part.* 2.628–29; see Aristotle *Gen. an.* 737a26–30). The catalyst for these divergences of anatomy was vital heat.[3] In ancient conception, males were intrinsically warmer than females (Aristotle *Gen. an.*775a; Galen *De usu part.* 2.630). The difference between male and female, according to medical theorists, was not dimorphic genitalia or other phenotypological markers; rather, what separated male and female was the presence or absence of adequate heat. This difference again served the "male norm." The female body was, in ancient conception, an inversion of the male's, and as such the female body was a cooler, less potent, ultimately imperfect version of the "canonical body."

One-sex theory incited an acute anxiety in ancient men: fear of gender slippage. John Winkler (1990, 50) noted that there was "this odd belief in the reversibility of the male person, always in peril of slipping into the servile or the feminine." Ancient Greek and Roman men always stood at the precipice of a steep hill that rolled down to effeminacy. There were no constant, incontrovertible biological facts to avert this precarious position.[4] If the female marked simply an imperfect version of the male, the corollary was the traversability of that distance which separated the two. Fluidity, Holmes (2012, 50–55) elucidates, affects both soul and body; that is, "the physical body is not quarantined from culture" (55).[5] It, too, in ancient conception, might slip. So the paths between

---

[2] Here, of course, there were exceptions, as Williams (*Homosexuality*, 103–36) notes in his chapter on *stupra*. Among Romans, freeborn Roman boys and girls were off limits. Williams concludes that Roman men were encouraged to see wives, slaves of any gender and any age, sex workers of any gender and any age, boys (so long as not freeborn), and in some cases men (so long as not freeborn) as potential sexual objects.

[3] Heat is intimately tied to dryness and impermeability, other hallmarks of the male constitution in ancient thought. See Holmes 2012, 29–31.

[4] Holmes (2012, 44) helpfully corrects Winkler, noting that this path is one-way. Men are in danger of slippage; however, women are not in the reverse position.

[5] Holmes sets out a needed corrective to Laqueur's work. Whereas Laqueur imagines an inversion of modern ideology whereby the ancients conceived of gender as metaphysically determined while sex was fluid, Holmes insists that this is an anachronistic ideological imposition. For the ancients, Holmes

male and female, between masculine and feminine, between men and women were numerous, and intermediate positions are readily identifiable. Castrates, slaves, and boys stand out as intermediary figures, persons whose genitalia might suggest manhood but whose social positions in Greco-Roman culture decidedly did not. Disease too opened paths to effeminacy, through loss of vital heat, aridity, or impermeability. Worse still than disease were men who willingly disposed of masculinity through effeminate activity. However the distance was crossed, the specter of lost masculinity was the consequence of the material body's indeterminacy. Manhood, therefore, without the ability to appeal to the body, had to be achieved through decisive masculine comportment.

Agonizing Gender

In the hierarchical, if inconstant, one-sex model, the fear of the feminine was deeply ingrained in discourses of masculinity. The dread of being robbed of your manhood, or being struck with an effeminizing disease, was no doubt cause for the strident and rancorous denigration of all things effeminate, only outdone by the valorization of all that was masculine. In this context, Maud Gleason (1995, xxii) has proven, "manhood was not a state to be definitively and irrefutably achieved, but something always under construction and constantly open to scrutiny, [such that] adults needed to keep practicing the arts that made them men." Gender was remarkably isolated from anatomy, even if they slid on parallel spectra. Gleason's insight extends from Judith Butler's (1990) realization that gender is performative, the repetition of stylized acts. So, in antiquity, one witnesses that masculinity was not a default state; rather, manhood must be achieved through a set of masculine acts and *critically* the avoidance of effeminate acts. Everything from clothes and gait to a trill of the voice or a furtive glance, every manner of physical comportment was organized and categorized according to an asymmetrical system of social relations. Comportment was a cipher that communicated the internal reality of one's gender identity to those versed in the physiognomic science (Gleason 1995, xxvi–xxvii). Physiognomy taught its ancient practitioners how to look past deceptive phenotypes and scrutinize the gender quality of another's countenance and comportment, enabling them to expose surreptitious effeminacy in rivals and crucially identify precisely who was a real man (Williams 2010, 208–9).

In this cultural milieu men had to demonstrate—publicly and with regularity—their manhood. Orators had to avoid frivolous hand gestures and a shrill tone. Soldiers were expected to demonstrate courage in adversity. Fathers and husbands were responsible for the moral discipline of children, wives, and slaves. All men were required to exhibit self-control, too, for the state of the soul was thought to be reflected in the body, and vice versa (Gleason 1995, 71). Perhaps most crucially, men must never be thought to subvert

---

demurs, sex and gender were not dichotomous opposites aligned with fixity and fluidity. Instead, ancient authors demonstrate both fluidity and fixity to varying extents with respect to both. The material body and gender identity are plastic and malleable, though the latter seems to move more freely.

or invert the penetrative model. The most notorious foil for proper masculinity were those men who failed to penetrate during sex. Taking a receptive role was tantamount to acting womanly; those men who acted as women in a very real sense became (more) woman(ly) (Conway 2008, 18). Passivity or receptivity amounted to nothing less than the complete abandonment of masculinity. In this respect, to be labeled a *cinaedus* was the ultimate mark of effeminacy, the worst form of gender deviance. The *cinaedus* stood for dreaded gender-liminality, with a penchant for receptive sexual encounters, cunnilingus, adultery, and utter lack of self-control (*egkrateia/akrateia*). To call the *cinaedus* a man would already be a misnomer, for manhood—acting male—was the precise failure of such a person (Williams 2010, 232–33). A real man in Greco-Roman antiquity was charged first and foremost with guarding his reputation from legitimate or credible allegations of such behavior. To do so he had not only to safeguard against all such accusations but also to present himself in the whole spectrum of his daily life as a man.

The Gift of *Logos*

However the one-sex model of gender was received by nonphysicians, its influence is felt in larger worldviews about gender and the differences between men and women. Not all ancients considered why these differences existed, but one expects that all ancients were aware of ubiquitous stereotypes. The literature of antiquity, almost invariably written by men, assumes a long list of correlated oppositional pairs among which gender was taxonomized. As already mentioned, the hot/cold spectrum and male/female spectrum are correlated. Craig Williams (2010, 156) illuminates the situation: "in short, the oppositional pair masculine/effeminate can be aligned with a set of others: moderation/excess; hardness/softness; courage/timidity; strength/weakness; activity/passivity; sexually penetrating/being sexually penetrated; and, encompassing all of these, domination/submission. If a man is associated with the second term in any one of these antitheses, he is *ipso facto* effeminate." Masculinity was an all-or-nothing endeavor. Either a man was courageous, temperate, strong, and active, in other words, masculine, or, lacking any one of these, he was effeminate. This prejudice explains how a woman, slave, or *cinaedus* could exhibit masculine comportment or male phenotypes and yet still be considered on the whole effeminate. While temperance may be a laudable quality for a woman to have, it does not make her a man.

Among these oppositional pairs, one might list *logos/alogos*. In Greco-Roman thinking, *logos* was that principle via which God endowed humanity with (among other qualities) reason, speech, *philanthropia*, and self-control. In short, *logos* separated humanity from beasts, granting humans the capacity to live morally, to speak intelligibly, and to desire to form societies. However, *logos* was not equally distributed; rather, social status correlated with *logos* status. In general, *logos* was considered to be conferred on free, adult, citizen men to a greater degree than slaves, children, foreigners, and women. With great power, however, comes great responsibility, at least according to those with power. Thus, ancient society was predicated on a benevolent patriarchy (or *kyriarchy*) within which men were encouraged to aid their statutory inferiors in living lives suitable to respective statuses. Thus, the *kyrios* or *paterfamilias* was responsible for the moral education of sons, the chastity of daughters, the loyalty of his wife (and his paramours), and the discipline of slaves. Failure or abdication of this duty heaped shame not only on the errant party but the family as a whole and especially the head of household himself.

In homosocial settings, *logos* became a matter of contest. Agonistic strife defined the zero-sum game of ancient Greek and Roman societies. Status, including a man's claim to masculinity, was fought for and indeed wrestled from rivals. Off the battlefield, masculinity began to be contested in the arenas of speech and comportment (McDonnell 2006). In classical Athens and republican Rome, politicians and orators famously faced off and vied for public acclaim. During the Roman Principate, this practice continued, as evidenced by public speakers, for example Dio Chrysostom, or the notorious rivalry of Polemo and Favorinus. Eloquent, persuasive (public) speech became a hallmark of masculinity, and verbal contests allowed rivals to challenge each other not merely for political supremacy but sociogender dominance. Verbal performance became as indicative of masculinity as sexual performance. Public performances of speech, whether agonistic or not, were scrutinized by ancient audiences so as to assess and assign the quality of masculinity performed and achieved by the speaker (Gleason 1995). In essence, the word became en-gendered.

Ancient Bodily Autonomy

Today's neoliberal (sexual) ethics are (at least ostensibly) predicated on bodily autonomy: the right of the individual to choose the if, who, how, when, and where of sexual encounters. In short, consent undergirds nearly all of today's discussions of sexual and corporeal ethics. Ancient Greek and Roman societies functioned on a fundamentally different set of principles. Classicists have identified complete bodily autonomy, or inviolability, as a privilege granted only to adult, free, citizen men (Walters 1997). Access to bodies descended from the top downward. Put another way, in ancient Greece and Rome, consent was the prerogative of the highest echelon of society, and was unilaterally granted. Free men had consent to advance sexually on statutory inferiors. Furthermore, statutory inferiors' sexuality was conceptualized as ideally governed by a statutory superior. Thus, a wife's body was conceptualized as "belonging to" her husband (i.e., chastity, fidelity, fecundity), a daughter's body to her father (i.e., chastity, virginity, dowry), a slave's body to their master (i.e., productivity, commodification). This belonging was not reciprocal; for example, husbands did not owe fidelity to their wives. Indeed, free men rather freely enjoyed sexual liaisons with slaves, sex workers, young boys, et alii provided access to their bodies was granted by a governing figure (i.e., by another free man).

Bodily autonomy also protected men from undue violence. This social belief extends from ancient medical theory that positioned permeability/impermeability along gender lines. Thus, the female's body was permeable, the male's was not. Proofs of this fact were allegedly natural: menstruation and impregnation via male ejaculate.[6] Her body allowed passage from without to within and vice versa. The male's body, it was claimed, did not. In this context, men were by nature impermeable and therefore (legally) protected from bodily violation/domination. Sexual penetration as a form of physical dominance was idealized as the prerogative of free men, performed on objects of lower sociogender status: women, boys, foreigners, slaves. Violence, as another form of physical dominance, was also idealized as a protected action performed on statutory inferiors. To become the object of violence was to suffer effeminacy. Violence, insofar as it involved one dominating the body of the other, was an attack on masculinity. Thus in late Republican and early Principate law, Roman citizen men were inviolable, that is, not subject to beatings (e.g., Acts 22:22–29).[7] To beat a man robbed him of (some of) his claim to masculinity. In short, corporeal punishment was emasculating. However, fortitude and a stoic demeanor in the face of suffering were considered emblematic of masculinity (Conway 2008, 29–30). Mastering the body through self-control was paradigmatic of man's status as *logikos*, or imbued with *logos*. So the true man endures suffering bravely without complaint and anguish, and through reason dominates his baser instincts, facing unavoidable pain and suffering willingly and reservedly.

The Gender of Virtue and the Virtues of Genders

Virtue was intrinsically masculine in ancient thought. Among antiquity's moral philosophers, virtue, stative qualities or actions that result in *eudaimonia* ("happiness"), were the prerogative of men. The Greek concept, *aretē*, was gendered from the Homeric period, where it denoted manliness or valor performed by individual warriors on the battlefield. Classical Greek, especially philosophical literature, adopts the term for ethical—and therefore foundationally mental—excellence.[8] The influence of this term on its Latin equivalent, *virtus*, is well established, as a strictly martial denotation slowly takes on primarily political and ethical meanings (McDonnell 2006, 110–34).[9] Further, virtue was considered a proper mental response to external stimulus and as such was achieved only by creatures endowed with *logos*. In this respect, ancient ethical treatises treat men as rational actors whose ethical responsibility is to achieve and perform virtue

---

[6] Critically, permeability was considered something over which women had no control. Menstruation, penetration, impregnation happened whether willing or not. Men's bodies on the other hand were idealized as self-controlled. Put more accurately, masculinity was associated with full mastery of one's body and complete bodily autonomy.

[7] Walters 1997, 38–39. It is important to note that Roman citizens could lose this status for various offenses (e.g., sex work, adultery).

[8] It is worth noting that *aretē* is etymologically a mental quality or action, a point made clear by the Italic cognate *ratus*.

[9] Latin's association of virtue with manliness is all the more self-evident. *Virtus* (*vir* [man] + *tus* [abstract noun suffix]) is properly more equivalent to the Greek *andreia* (*anēr* [man] + *ios* [adj. suffix] + *ē* [abstract noun suffix]).

through the proper ordering of the mind and in turn through self-controlled, temperate action. Conversely, when women were not ignored entirely, they often appeared as the subjects of texts directed from men to men: how ought a man handle or treat his wife. Women were seldom the audience of ethical treatises; rather, ancient Greco-Roman patriarchy assumed that women were the responsibility of men to govern, control, and protect.

This is not to say, nevertheless, that women were not extolled for virtuous behavior or expected to perform womanhood along gendered protocols. Whereas men, for instance, were expected to engage in sexual intercourse with self-restraint (*egkrateia*), society restricted a woman's sexuality to her husband. Thus, outside Greek novels, virginity (*parthenia, koreia, virginitas*) was a strictly feminine quality. In Greek and Roman societies, virginity was confined to women insofar as it confined women. The power of this discourse exists in the fact that its gender specificity was unacknowledged in antiquity and continues to go *unmarked* among many scholars. One only need consider how *marked* celibacy was as a decided masculine quality in antiquity to see the disparity. That a woman should abstain from sex outside marriage was presumed, and any delay of or abstention from marriage was scrutinized uncharitably for sexual defilement. A man who abstained from sex and marriage was remarkable. Not only might his self-control be considered praiseworthy, but his abstention might be lauded as a Cynic's rejection of societal *mores*, though even among the Cynic-Stoics of the early Principate, Augustan procreationism and "traditional" families were favored (Wheeler-Reed 2017, 1–62). Indeed, the Stoic Musonius Rufus rejects all nonprocreative forms of sexual intercourse, including those liaisons that result in illegitimate children, and extols those laws that penalize abortions and childlessness (*Fr.* XII, XIIIA, XIIIB, XV). In this respect, women were praised for their virginity until marriage and chastity within it, for only through fidelity came fecundity, apart from which ancient women could not hope to attain prized epithets such as *matrona* or *mater* (*familias*).

Failure to protect virginity, or dereliction of chastity, in other words adultery,[10] was grounds for divorce. Adulterers were subject to egregious penalties under both Athenian and Roman law, including potentially fines, beatings, death, exile, and even public anal rape by radish (*rhaphandiosis*). Adulteresses were similarly liable to religious excommunication, exile, and death. Ancient Roman society valued a woman's fidelity so highly that it valorized lifelong commitment to one's husband, dead or alive. The epithet *univira* indicated a woman had only ever belonged to one man and stood in stark relief with that of the *scorta*, whose body was open to any person with money. Unsurprisingly, adultery and sex work were coextensive in ancient rhetorical practice, and the adulteress often figured as the "whore" in public discourse (Glazebrook 2006, 130–35; Strong 2016).[11] Husbands could divorce wives on account of adultery; in fact, Augustan law

---

[10] Traditionally understood, adultery (*moicheia, adulterium*) was a criminal act performed by one man against another through a woman. In other words, women were the means through which a man violated another man's rights.

[11] This does not hold true for adulterers seemingly because the offense of an adulterer is the violation of another man, while a male sex worker is detestable on the assumption that he has become subordinate

penalized husbands who did not divorce adulterous wives. Adultery was not the only grounds for divorce; indeed, ancient evidence indicates that either party could submit a no-fault divorce decree against his/her spouse. However, only women suffered for remarriage, as this precluded them from the title *univira*.

Ancient men considered a virtuous woman to be one who represented the household well and whose actions contributed to the socioeconomic welfare thereof. While strict, procrustean dichotomies, for example public/private,[12] misrepresent ancient society, there is some truth to the distribution of gender roles along domestic and political lines. Both husband and wife worked toward the prosperity of the household. Women contributed to the financial stability of the household through domestic industries (e.g., wool-work) and domestic management, including managing slaves and free workers and regulating consumption and expenses. And, much as in modern society, women performed enormous amounts of "invisible labor," for example childrearing and education. Women were also integral to the social welfare of the household through networking—exploiting and maintaining social connections, including extended family, whose social and financial support were critical for the domestic economy and society. Hylen (2019, 50–54) identifies the performance of these activities as the desirable quality, "industry," a virtue for which wives were praised and a trait that men sought in contracting marriage alliances.

With all of these ideals, it should be remembered that Judea of the Roman Principate period was far removed, both geographically and chronologically, from classical Athens and to greater and lesser degrees from Rome. However, with the Synoptic Gospels the greatest distance may be that of class. Simply put, the authors and audiences, characters and historical personages reflected and depicted in these texts were not (predominantly)[13] those of an elite, wealthy, predominantly male upper echelon of an expanding imperial power. Rather, the Gospels reflect and depict colonized, marginalized, and oppressed characters and perspectives, whose realities diverge significantly from the plutocrats of Athens and Rome. The realities of the poorer classes of ancient societies precluded the idealized gender roles of Greek and Roman elite households. Perhaps the most obvious low-hanging fruit of an intersectional analysis of gender in the Gospels is that lower-class women were not secluded indoors, as Thucydides might have encouraged.[14] Class as a measure of one's distance from subsistence living precluded ancient persons from enacting idealized gendered norms. Slaves, for instance, did not have the bodily autonomy to protect themselves from being made to endure degrading

---

to his clients, presumably for penetration, though even without it he has still debased his body as dominable and commodifiable. Both client and sex worker lack *self*-control, the former in surrendering to his passions, the latter in being bought by his client.

[12] Antiquity's shame-based society functionally excludes the modern dichotomy public/private.

[13] Of course, the specter of Roman authority is ever-present, through figures like Pontius Pilate, Herod the Great, his relatives, and Roman centurions.

[14] There were also difference of opinions among the educated elite; see Plutarch, *Mul. virt.* 242e. For more see Hylen 2019, 25–41.

actions or perform them. Poverty-stricken women were known to subsist through sex work. The calculus that prioritized an honorable death (so-called) over a life of infamy was not solved by all women as Lucretia and her apologists solved it. Thus, it must be recognized that not all women (or indeed all men) operated under a set of universal, uncontested gender protocols (Kamen and Levin-Richardson 2015; Levin-Richardson 2013). The intersection of varied identities affected how gender functioned for any given person in antiquity. Gender-critical lenses need an intersectional framework to suss out how other identities affect and influence any ancient person's capacity to act along idealized gender lines.

Gender in the Synoptics

With every analytical exercise with the Synoptic Gospels, it is not a question of the uniqueness of perspective each author has but of each contribution to the Venn diagram that is the Synoptics. The same holds for gender analysis; what follows is a series of treatments of three passages from the Synoptics viewed through the theoretical lenses of gender to show the importance of gender when reading each Gospel and how complex the social dynamics can be in overly familiar passages.

Mark's Syrophoenician Mother (Mark 7:24–30)

This complex story of a grief-stricken mother who advocates for her dying daughter is ripe for feminist interpretation, and indeed it has been approached with these lenses quite often (Ringe 1985; Schüssler Fiorenza 1983; Tolbert 1989, 185–86). But a gender analysis of this passage focuses on the dynamics of gender between Jesus and the unnamed woman, dynamics which in turn are affected by the social realities of both characters. In Mark 7:26 she is identified as a Greek (Ἑλληνίς, the only time this word is used by Mark) and a Syrophoenician "by kin" (τῷ γένει), which is a very interesting compound social identification—a hybrid identity, as Leander says (2013, 221)—that has a significant impact on how one teases out the dimensions of gender within this story.

Jesus's encounter with the Syrophoenician woman occurs after his debating the Pharisees and scribes about the traditions of purification and eating (7:1–23). The issue does not seem to be a legal but a political one—who has the power to determine ritual practices and their interpretation? This scene is just the latest in a number of political power struggles or depictions of political power in Mark (all through 1:1–3:6; 6:1–5, 17–44, e.g.) and it becomes a dominant theme in the next section (8:22–10:52). The scene in 7:1–23 sets the stage for another power struggle with the Greek, Syrophoenician woman, one where Jesus's authority is not so unimpeachable and his masculinity does not exactly match the ancient ideal.

After his interchange with the Pharisees, Jesus retreats to Tyre, seemingly to get a break from the crowds, but that is not in the cards. "Gentile" is too general a term for the woman (contra Taylor 1953, 349; Hooker 1991, 183; van Iersel 1998, 248; and Yarbro Collins 2007, 366), and one should take the lead of Mark, who identifies her more specifically as a Greek Syrophoenician. Phoenicians were a Semitic people who were extremely influential in the ancient Mediterranean world before the rise of Rome as the dominant power. By the first century, Rome had diminished Phoenician influence significantly (Pliny, *Nat.* 5.75–76). The fact that this woman was identified as a Syrophoenician insinuates a dominated status, like many other peoples under Rome's power. But within her dominated status, she is also identified as Greek, which means that she is not a typical Phoenician. By the Roman period, Greek and Latin (to a lesser extent) had become the dominant languages of the region, so much so that Phoenician became almost nonexistent in the surviving evidence of elite culture (coins, inscriptions), and "we cannot be sure that the Phoenician language was spoken in the east after the first century CE" (Kaldellis 2019, 687; see Alliquot 2019, 115–16). But it seems identifying this woman as a Greek sets her apart from other Phoenicians; otherwise, why mention it? Perhaps it indicates a higher social status among Phoenicians in the region of Tyre (Leander 2013, 224). Leander also points to the term used for her daughter's bed as a social indicator of her status—κλίνη (a couch or bed with legs), rather than κράβαττος (a simple floor mat or pallet) (224).

So here is a probably higher status Tyrian woman meeting Jesus, a Galilean male Jew, probably a craftsperson, so definitely on the lower end of the social makeup of the region. Galilean rural or village life was probably cooperative in nature, but not lucrative, and a craftsperson like Jesus probably would have earned enough for a relatively stable life. But there was little hope or expectation for such people to climb the social ladder to significantly higher levels. Rural Galilean life probably also depended on trade with more urban areas, like Tyre, but the political status of both Tyrians and Galileans were subject to the dominant Roman Empire. While both Jesus and the woman were part of subjugated populations, the woman in this story—urban, Greek, higher status, and female—was on the opposite side of social life from Jesus: rural/village, Jewish Galilean, lower status, and male. The gender dynamics in this story are complicated because of these interwoven social forces of economy, social status, and politics.

As the woman approaches Jesus in 7:25, one might expect her to act as she did by approaching him in a subservient way (falling prostrate at Jesus's feet), but her higher social status and her urban sophistication complicates matters. Her prostration might be more natural, or at least not unusual, for a Galilean village woman in need of help from Jesus. But for a higher status Greek from Tyre, woman or man, this would be a noticeable act of obeisance, one where the woman lowers herself beyond what the social norms might call for. The gesture, and the fact that she knows about Jesus, not only communicates her desperation to help her dying daughter but also elevates Jesus beyond his expected social status as a male Galilean villager. Jesus wants no part of her and dismisses her with the slanderous κυνάριον (little dog), placing her not only below him but even below children (7:27).

Up to this point in Mark, Jesus has a limited but ambiguous relationship with females. There are three episodes where women are featured at all. The first is when his family members come to him "at home" (εἰς οἶκον, 3:20) to try to restrain him, following on the accusation that he is going out of his mind. His mother and brothers (and sisters, in some manuscripts) eventually stand outside and send for him to come out of the overcrowded house (3:31); he refuses to go out to them and even disowns them. But he does not exclude the idea of being with women, because he redefines his followers as his true mother and brothers, asserting his authority to determine the constitution of the household, even if God's will is the ultimate arbiter of the household (3:35). So Jesus's expected dominant, authoritative gender role is reinforced here, but in 5:21–43 that role is called into question because of his interaction with a woman with a flow of blood. As mentioned earlier, the penetration model of gender has been developed to describe ideal ancient masculinity. A man's "natural" role to penetrate and not to be penetrated marked his masculinity. Included in this model is the relative porosity of men and women, with men being on the less porous side of the spectrum (thus unable to be penetrated). The ideal is for a man to be in control of himself, his body, and his household (including women). In Jesus's interaction with the struggling woman in 5:24–34, his power is drained from him without his permission. The women crosses his physical boundary (i.e. penetrates him), takes his power, and wields it to be healed. (See Moss 2010 for a compelling reading of the porosity of Jesus's body.) Jesus does not even know who performs this act, fruitlessly looking around in the crowd. It is not a picture of ideal masculinity for a woman to covertly take one's power for her healing. Jesus does somewhat redeem himself as the woman reveals herself and then later in the episode by raising Jairus's daughter. But even there, he does not control the crowd and is thus mocked at his declaration of the daughter's status as asleep and not dead. He turns out to be correct, but only after being shamed. An ideal man would not have performed so poorly in public. The final episode (6:1–6) only briefly mentions women (Jesus's sisters) as among those who are called to mind by those in his hometown synagogue when they question Jesus's authority to teach. Their unbelief limited Jesus's power, again, not a quality of an ideal man. One further note to set up 7:24–30: In none of these episodes are women's speech with Jesus reported directly (Leander 2013 233–34). Jesus's mother and brothers stand outside the house and send for him in 3:31; the struggling woman tells Jesus the whole truth in 5:33, but her words are not expressed; and no women act in 6:1–6.

So when the Greek Syrophoenician woman encounters Jesus, one does not have much expectation that their interaction will reveal Jesus as an ideal man, by any means. His actions try to assert as much when he shuts down the woman's request by pulling "rank" on her as a male, but he quickly loses control. After his derogatory term, the woman leans into the depiction and plays out the metaphor brilliantly by turning it back on Jesus, coopting "dogs" catachrestically, "stripping it of stigmatization" (Leander 2014, 235). But she also logically outduels Jesus: crumbs (or more accurately things considered below human palatability) were the reserve of dogs in Greek/Roman culture. Dogs sat below/beneath the table precisely for "scraps." So in a sense, Jesus offers common-sense logic about dogs ("you don't give them people food") and the woman responds with the exception to his rule ("unpalatable food waste was reserved for dogs"). She forces him to see her and her daughter, invisible to him as anything but Tyrian dogs not worthy of even crumbs from his purportedly superior masculine Jewish table. Jesus falls into stereotypical dichotomous rivalries (urban/rural, high-status/low-status, Tyrian/Galilean, feminine/masculine), which the woman initially resists with her voluntary obeisance and then undermines by negotiating with Jesus as a "dog." She takes control, both in the performance of wit, and in the deployment of logic, and Jesus loses control. Jesus's attempt at performing his masculinity is undone by the woman when she shames him into an empathetic response (5:29). In the end, she gets what she wants, despite Jesus's failed attempt to perform in a masculine way. Clearly, Mark's Jesus is the hero of the Gospel, but this episode questions whether or not his heroism is tied to his masculinity. Here, it seems subservient to the social forces of a socially superior Greek Syrophoenician woman and leaves Jesus as a victim of the social circumstances of his Galilean roots. Perhaps this is a foreshadowing of the events that await him in Jerusalem.

A Tale of Two Kings: Jesus and Herod in Matthew's Infancy Story

Kendra Allison Mohn's recent dissertation on the construction of masculinities in the Gospel of Matthew has an insightful analysis of Joseph's masculinity in Matthew 1–2. In particular, she argues that Joseph's masculinity in Matthew is constructed through three categories of ancient masculinity—wealth, dominating control over self and others, and divine service—and primarily in terms of divine service (Mohn 2018, 66). More to the point of this essay, she argues that Joseph's masculinity is constructed in contrast to that of Herod the Great, in the pattern of the ancient rhetorical concept of σύγκρισις, "used to point out difference or superiority" (66–67; see also Stanton 1992, 77–84). While this comparison between Joseph and Herod the Great is instructive and is one fruitful way to approach these chapters in Matthew from the point of view of gender, I wish to make a different comparison—that of Jesus and Herod. Here is a would-be king in his conception and infancy who is invested with power from God through Israel's heritage, contrasted with a Roman client king who is invested with power from the emperor. The gender constructs depict two extremes that are instructive for understanding the claims made in Matthew's Gospel.

Matthew starts the construction of Jesus's character with a genealogy, a standard tool in the belts of ancient authors who wish to tell the stories of important figures, including the gods (throughout Hesiod, *Theogony*; *Catalogue of Women*; Homer, *Il.* 6.145–211; Plato, *Alc.* 1.121a; Polybius 9.1.4; Genesis 5; 11:10–32; see Thomas 1996). The genealogies often traced the ancestry of important figures to heroes, demigods, or even gods themselves. In Matthew, a similar genealogical statement is made of Jesus, whose identity is summarized in 1:1 as χριστός (anointed one), son of David, and son of Abraham. Jesus's ancestry is then traced in detail, starting with the founding patriarch of Israel, Abraham, through many great figures in Israel's history (including several women similar to Mary; Kampen 2019, 192) as well as through the royal line of David (Israel's greatest king), Solomon (builder of the first Jerusalem temple), Josiah (who renovated the temple and found "the book of the Law" in the process; 2 Kings 22:8–11), and Zerubbabel (the administrator who was credited with beginning the reconstruction of the Second Temple after the return from exile). Matthew establishes Jesus's solid pedigree through this genealogy in order to establish his credentials as a significant figure in Israel's history. Herod, by contrast, has no reported genealogy, no pedigree for his claim to kingship.

Matthew then narrates Jesus's conception and birth through miraculous means in 1:18–25, again starting the narration by identifying Jesus as χριστός, the royally anointed one. In this story, some key bells and whistles of ancient masculinity complement the strong genealogy from 1:1–17. Jesus's conception has its origins in the divine world ("from the Holy Spirit" ἐκ πνεύματος ἁγίου, 1:18) and is affirmed by a divine messenger (1:20), and he is given a name by that messenger (1:21; related to the Hebrew for "he saves"; σωτήρ ["savior"] is a common epithet for gods and rulers in the ancient world), and his arrival is grounded in the sacred prophecies of Israel (1:23). The first crack appears in Jesus's masculinity, however, and that is his parents. Jesus's conception happens while Joseph and Mary are betrothed but not married. The cultural assumption of betrothal in Judaism was that a couple would not have sex until marriage, so Jesus's conception raises the potential to soil his pedigree. Matthew works to preserve it, however, by reporting the virtuousness of Joseph, who stays betrothed to Mary despite his initial instinct and does not have sex with her until Jesus is born (1:24–25). Anointed before birth, Matthew's Jesus, so far, firmly stands on the foundations of Israel and God as future king.

Then King Herod appears for the first time, in chapter 2, where his presence is announced not because of his pedigree or greatness but merely as a marker of time relative to Jesus, who was born "in the days of King Herod" (2:1). Herod is not included in Jesus's genealogy, which, along with the royal identification of Jesus by the magi, signals Herod as an illegitimate king of Israel in the face of Jesus's advent. This is Matthew's narrative way of negatively commenting on the status of leadership in Israel at the time, with Herod not being appointed in the line of the great kings of Israel (as Jesus is) but being installed as a client king of Rome. He serves at the pleasure of the emperor and is thus beholden to him, rather than serving at the pleasure of God (see Carter 2000, esp. 73–89). Herod's authority is demonstrably derivative and contingent, whereas Jesus's is inherent and divinely determined. Herod's actions inform his status, as well. He fails to recognize Jesus as a divinely appointed king and instead "was thrown into disorder and all of Jerusalem with him" (ἐταράχθη καὶ πᾶσα Ἱεροσόλυμα μετ' αὐτοῦ, 2:3). Ταράσσω has the overtone of physical shaking or stirring or troubling; it can indicate fear, but not in the same way that φοβέομαι might. This is also the term in Hellenistic philosophy for being (passionally) disturbed; compare *ataraxia*. In addition, the term can be used in sociopolitical contexts for people who disturb or rouse a social body. Either way, it stresses that Herod's lack of mental tranquility is responsible for social upheaval, too. Herod is shaken by Jesus's birth, and the fact that he reacts the same way as "all Jerusalem" portrays him not as a strong, calm leader of his people but as a weak man who buckles at the first sign of challenge. And the challenge is from an infant, further diminishing his masculinity. Herod then quickly calls a council of chief priests and scribes to find out the birthplace of the anointed one (2:4); next, he attempts to trick the magi into giving Jesus away to him (2:7–8), but the magi follow a dream oracle to avoid him on their return (2:12).

Even if one needed no further confirmation of Jesus's divinely established royalty, even at the stage of infancy, the magis' reaction to him provides it (Kampen 2019, 192). Not only do they travel from a great distance but also they discern Jesus's star, follow it faithfully, and find him. When the star stops, they "rejoiced exceedingly." (With its cognate accusative and double modifier, ἐχάρησαν χαράν μεγάλην σφόδρα is hard to convey in proper English.) They enter the house where Jesus is and pay him the homage due to a king. They also offer him three valuable gifts, befitting a king (2:7–12).

Herod "is greatly enraged" (ἐθυμώθη λίαν, 2:16) at being mocked by the magi and responds irrationally by ordering the death of all the children under age two in Bethlehem and its surroundings. Although he has the authority to do so, to control his charges to act in this barbaric way, his act shows his lack of self-control, a far better indicator of one's masculinity than unbridled power. Herod's actions are hypermasculine, a brutal abuse of his masculine authority, revealing him to be an aberration rather than a model of masculinity. He acts as a tyrant, not a king. Furthermore, Matthew marks Herod's behavior not just as a petulant king with too much power but by quoting Jeremiah 31:15 so as to loop Herod's actions in with one of the lowest moments in the history of Israel, the exile of the Northern tribes to Assyria in the eighth century BCE. This quotation lowers Herod to the level of national enemy rather than just rival king to the infant Jesus, thus raising Jesus to the level of national hero and future benevolent ruler of Israel.

The masculinity of two kings could not be in greater contrast: Herod—volatile, unreasonable, violent client of Rome, and a tyrant—on the one hand and Jesus—divinely conceived and anointed, legitimate heir to David's throne, protected by divine messengers, recognized by the nations, and an infant—on the other. As an infant, Jesus does not even act on his own accord, yet he still far outstrips Herod in every way in his royalty and masculinity. Although the contrast is stark—Rome's king on one side and God's king on the other—this is not a simple dichotomy, since Jesus's origins are somewhat questionable (conceived out of wedlock) and his future purpose (saving the people from their sins) is not that of a typical king, even the greatest of Israel. Violence will shroud Jesus, as it did in his first year, until the end of his life, and he will die the shameful death of a slave. With the clear contrast that Matthew presents with Herod in the beginning of Jesus's story, however, perhaps Jesus's masculinity is predicated on a competing set of categories determined instead by divine presence and faithfulness.

Talking Back to an Angel: Zechariah and Mary in Luke's Annunciation Scenes

The annunciation scenes in Luke 1:5–38 provide another interesting contrast in characters ripe for gender analysis. John the Baptist and Jesus—the two most consequential male characters in Luke's conception, birth, and infancy narrative—both have miraculous beginnings, and their parents (Zechariah and Mary, respectively) both have encounters with Gabriel, the angel or divine messenger. But Zechariah's and Mary's encounters are significantly different, even though their verbal exchanges with Gabriel are remarkably similar. Gender might play a role in this difference.

At the outset, Zechariah and Elizabeth are portrayed as ideal Jews. Zechariah, an ordinary priest from a legitimate priestly line (that of Abijah, one of the twenty-four classes of priesthood mentioned in 1 Chr 24:7–19) and Elizabeth (a descendant of Aaron and so also from a priestly background) "were both righteous before God, walking without blame in all the commandments and decrees of the Lord" (1:6). Zechariah's credentials as a man were unimpeachable, and he and Elizabeth were ideal Israelites, in other words; the only problem was that they did not have any children because of Elizabeth's sterility. This righteous standing for both of them should translate into a bit of leeway when it comes to Zechariah's pending interaction with Gabriel, but it does not seem to matter much.

Amid Zechariah's scheduled service in the temple, and in the presence of the prayers of the whole assembly during his incense offering, an angel of the Lord appears to him (1:8–11). Zechariah's response is similar to Herod's in Matthew when he learns of Jesus's birth; he is "thrown into confusion" (ἐταράχθη), and "a great fear fell upon him" (φόβος ἐπέπεσεν ἐπ᾽ αὐτόν). While Herod's fear is implicit, Zechariah's is very clear. Gabriel, for his part, recognizes Zechariah's fear and attempts to reassure him with his oracle about John's birth and ensuing significance for the fulfillment of the hopes of Israel, and how he will prepare the people for the Lord in the image of Elijah (1:13–17). Zechariah replies with a simple follow-up question, "How will I know this? For I am old and my wife is advanced in her years" (1:18), pointing out the life circumstances that would prevent Elizabeth from conceiving and giving birth. Gabriel does not receive his question well and takes it as a lack of faith and challenge to his authority by Zechariah, resulting in the muting of Zechariah until after John is born (1:19–20). When Zechariah regains his ability to speak, he gives a remarkable speech about God announcing the mercy of God and the fulfillment of the promises God made to Israel, setting the stage for John's life and work and Jesus's advent.

At the outset, Zechariah's masculinity is ideal in many ways. He is married and so the typical head of his household. He is blameless before God and so virtuous and self-controlled. He is a leader in Israel as a priest and so is a member in one of the groups who occupy the higher status roles in Jerusalem and so probably wealthy, as well. The only exception to his strong masculine characteristics is displayed in his reaction to Gabriel's appearance. As noted, ταράσσω does not betray the stability an ideal man would show in the face of adversity, nor does the great fear that befalls him. He is shaken and disturbed, although his subsequent actions are very different from what is shown in Matthew's Herod, who acts irrationally to eliminate the threat he fears. In addition, Gabriel takes Zechariah's question "How can I know this?" as an act of unbelief, thrusting him into Gabriel's disfavor (and by implication, God's). His fall from grace results in a punishment of silence, which—Brittany Wilson (whose analysis we follow here) points out—has serious gender ramifications in the ancient world and, for Zechariah, marks his emasculation (Wilson 2015, 94–105).

As a brief reminder of the relationship between gender and speech, we point to Wilson: "in the Greco-Roman world, discourse—in both the spoken and written sense—was emblematic of power and inextricably connected to masculinity" (2015, 94). The literary evidence for speech overwhelmingly presents it as the purview of powerful men, even if there are occasional exceptions. Wilson points to Libanius, who sums up the relationship between speech and power this way: "those who speak 'hold power because they speak' (Libanius, *Or.* 35.12)" (94; with many ancient references from Greek and Latin literature).[15] When Zechariah's power of speech is taken from him, and made known publicly (1:21–22), he is not just temporarily chastised for challenging Gabriel. He is emasculated, stripped of one key power of his masculinity. In the interim between Zechariah's emasculation and the restoration of his speech, Elizabeth and Mary are endowed with the power that was stripped from Zechariah (91–94), reversing the focus on Zechariah's masculinity and turning it to Elizabeth and Mary. Elizabeth is the first to speak (1:25) even though she has remained in seclusion for five months, declaring a removal of her "disgrace" (ὄνειδος) long endured publicly ("among people" ἐν ἀνθρώποις). Then, during Mary's visit, Elizabeth feels the fetus of John stir at Mary's arrival and "proclaims with a loud shout, 'Blessed are you among women, and blessed is the fruit of your womb!'" (1:42) and follows with a description of what happened when Mary arrived. Mary, in response, speaks what will become the most famous speech in the New Testament in 1:46–55. Finally, Elizabeth speaks again, after the birth of John, naming her child John in obedience to Gabriel's wishes, and over the objections of those present (1:59–61). Traditionally, this is an operation of the patriarch of a household both in choosing a name and thereby officially recognizing the child as a member of his household. Elizabeth makes a public stand against the wishes of those asserting their influence to name the boy after Zechariah. These are not just mundane conversations included in Luke's narrative but powerful statements that outstrip Zechariah's speech, even when he had it, and elevate Mary and Elizabeth to very high levels, according to ancient norms around gender and speech.

Zechariah is restored, however, starting with the birth of John. His climb back up begins with his confirmation of Elizabeth's wishes, which he carries out through writing, restoring his speech in the process. Once he can speak again, he launches into a speech

---

[15] Also see Lincoln 1999, 3–46, for an excellent treatment of the power of speech in ancient Greece, as well as Lincoln 2014 for a comparative treatment of the relationship between discourse and power.

second only to Mary's in grandeur, one that marks him as a gifted and inspired orator, as he skillfully weaves the events at hand into the traditions of Israel after being filled with the Holy Spirit (1:67–79), reminiscent of the prophets of old.

One must contrast Mary's interaction with Gabriel with Zechariah's. Gabriel visits Mary, who is described as a *parthenos*, an idealized feminine identity, betrothed to Joseph "from the house of David" (ἐξ οἴκου Δαυίδ, 1:27), an identity that trumps that of Zechariah because of the connection with the greatest king in Israel's history. She is also from Nazareth, a village in rural Galilee, marking her as fairly low status by normal measures, and certainly so compared to Zechariah. After Gabriel greets Mary, her reaction is almost identical to Zechariah's: she is thrown into confusion (διαταράσσω) just as Zechariah is (ταράσσω), even though some standard translations indicate a significant difference. (NRSV has Zechariah "terrified," but Mary is "much perplexed"; the two Greek words are cognates and virtually identical in meaning, even if διαταράσσω is less common.) Gabriel reassures Mary just as he does with Zechariah, even starting each of his responses with μὴ φοβοῦ (1:13 and 30). Mary then questions Gabriel very similarly to the way Zechariah does, explaining that her life circumstance prevent Gabriel's prediction from being possible (1:18 [Zechariah] and 34 [Mary]). But Gabriel's response to Mary elevates her above Zechariah because he does not take offense at Mary's question as he does with Zechariah. He accuses Zechariah of unbelief, whereas he simply answers Mary's concerns by describing the mechanism by which she will become pregnant. (The Holy Spirit will "come upon" her and "overshadow" her; ἐπέρχομαι and ἐπισκιάζω, 1:35.) No silencing, no rebuke, even using Elizabeth as proof for the veracity of his claims. Mary even has the final word, one of obedience and consent (1:37).

The contrast with Zechariah could not be starker. He starts as a high-status, righteous Israelite priest whose masculinity is intact, falls by his emasculation at Gabriel's hand, and then rises higher than he started by uttering inspired speech, masculinity more strongly secured as a result. Mary is righteous but a low-status rural girl, but she is given a direct speaking voice, has unquestioned faithfulness even in the face of her challenge to Gabriel, and has oratorical skills to produce and deliver a speech unrivaled by any male in Luke-Acts. By ancient gender standards, she has no business speaking with the authority and prominence she does. But Luke has other ideas, apparently. As Wilson argues throughout her book, this gender contrast reflects a pattern of recasting traditional categories of masculinity in Luke-Acts, a "refiguration of elite masculine norms" (2015, 112), recasting not just the role of women in Luke but perhaps also how to think about ancient femininity.

Conclusion

The theoretical foundations of gender analysis of the Synoptic Gospels rightly focus on masculinity because of the evidence from ancient sources. They overwhelmingly talk about what it means to be an ideal man and how to maintain one's status as a man through performance of certain actions that ensure one remains a masculine man rather than slipping into becoming an effeminate man. Where there is talk about what it means to be an ideal woman in ancient evidence, it is invariably written by men and defined as the opposite of what it means to be an ideal man. In other words, masculinity is the norm by which femininity is defined. Such is life in a patriarchy. But some interesting work has been done recently that tries to expand the evidence base beyond ancient literature written by men. Sarah Levin-Richardson and Deborah Kamen's research on female agency in ancient Rome (Kamen and Levin-Richardson 2015; Levin-Richardson 2013) has fascinating ramifications for expanding the field of inquiry and reconsidering the alternate ways that nonelites lived out their genders in antiquity. Our earlier observation bears repeating here: "class as a measure of one's distance from subsistence living precluded ancient persons from enacting idealized gendered norms." Intersectional lenses are needed to more fully understand how gender worked, especially for ancient nonelites, and this holds true for gender analysis of the Synoptic Gospels as well.

References

Ahearne-Kroll, Stephen P. 2022. "Mark." In *The Jerome Biblical Commentary for the Twenty-First Century*, 3rd rev. ed., edited by John J. Collins, et al. 1238–88, New York: Bloomsbury Academic.

Aliquot, Julien. 2019. "Phoenicia in the Roman Empire." In *The Oxford Handbook of the Phoenician and Punic Mediterranean*, edited by Brian R. Doak and Carolina López-Ruiz, 111–24, . Oxford: Oxford University Press.

Bonnet, Corinne. 2019. "The Hellenistic Period and Hellenization in Phoenicia." In *The Oxford Handbook of the Phoenician and Punic Mediterranean*, edited by Brian R. Doak and Carolina López-Ruiz, 99–110. Oxford: Oxford University Press.

Butler, Judith. 1990. *Gender Trouble: Feminism and the Subversion of Identity*. 2nd ed. New York: Routledge.

Carter, Warren. 2000. *Matthew and the Margins: A Sociopolitical and Religious Reading*. Maryknoll, NY: Orbis.

Conway, Colleen M. 2008. *Behold the Man: Jesus and Greco-Roman Masculinity*. New York: Oxford University Press.

Dover, Kenneth J. 1989. *Greek Homosexuality*. Cambridge: Harvard University Press.

Foucault, Michel. 1990. *The History of Sexuality*. 3 vols. Trans. Robert Hurley. New York: Vintage Books.

Glazebrook, Allison. 2006. "The Bad Girls of Athens: The Image and Function of *Hetairai* in Judicial Oratory." In *Prostitutes and Courtesans in the Ancient World*, edited by Christopher A. Faraone and Laura K. McClure, 125–38. Madison: University of Wisconsin Press.

Gleason, Maud W. 1995. *Making Men: Sophists and Self-Presentation in Ancient Rome*. Princeton: Princeton University Press.

Halperin, David M. 1990. *100 Years of Homosexuality: And Other Essays on Greek Love*. New Ancient World. New York: Routledge.

Henderson, Jeffrey. 1975. *The Maculate Muse: Obscene Language in Attic Comedy*. New York: Oxford University Press.

Holmes, Brooke. 2012. *Gender: Antiquity and Its Legacy*. Ancients and Moderns. New York: Oxford University Press.

Hooker, Morna D. 1991. *A Commentary on the Gospel According to St. Mark*. London: Black.

Hylen, Susan E. 2019. *Women in the New Testament World*. Essentials of Biblical Studies. New York: Oxford University Press.

Kaldellis, Anthony. 2019. "Neo-Phoenician Identities in the Roman Empire." In *The Oxford Handbook of the Phoenician and Punic Mediterranean*, edited by Brian R. Doak and Carolina López-Ruiz, 685–96. Oxford: Oxford University Press.

Kamen, Deborah, and Sarah Levin-Richardson. 2015. "Revisiting Roman Sexuality: Agency and the Conceptualization of Penetrated Males." In *Sex in Antiquity: Exploring Gender and Sexuality in the Ancient World*, edited by Mark Masterson, Nancy Sorkin Rabinowitz, and James Robson, 449–60. New York: Routledge.

Kampen, John. 2019. *Matthew within Sectarian Judaism*. New Haven: Yale University Press.

Laqueur, Thomas. 1990. *Making Sex: Body and Gender from the Greeks to Freud*. Cambridge: Harvard University Press.

Leander, Hans. 2013. *Discourses of Empire: The Gospel of Mark from a Postcolonial Perspective*. Atlanta: Society of Biblical Literature.

Levin-Richardson, Sarah. 2013. "*Fututa Sum Hic*: Female Subjectivity and Agency in Pompeiian Graffiti." *CJ* 108: 319–45.

Lincoln, Bruce. 2014. *Discourse and the Construction of Society: Comparative Studies of Myth, Ritual, and Classification*. Second Edition. Oxford: Oxford University Press.

Lincoln, Bruce. 1999. *Theorizing Myth: Narrative, Ideology, and Scholarship*. Chicago: University of Chicago Press.

McDonnell, Myles. 2006. *Roman Manliness:* Virtus *and the Roman Republic*. New York: Cambridge University Press.

Mohn, Kendra Allison. 2018. "Real Men: Masculinities in the Gospel of Matthew." PhD diss., Texas Christian University.

Moss, Candida R. 2010. "The Man with the Flow of Power: Porous Bodies in Mark 5:25–34." *JBL* 129: 507–19.

Richlin, Amy. 1992. *The Garden of Priapus: Sexuality and Aggression in Roman Humor*. Rev. ed. New York: Oxford University Press.

Ringe, Sharon H. 1985. "A Gentile Woman's Story." In *Feminist Interpretation of the Bible*, edited by Letty M. Russell, 65–72. Philadelphia: Westminster.

Schüssler Fiorenza, Elisabeth. 1983. *In Memory of Her: A Feminist Theological Reconstruction of Christian Origins*. New York: Crossroads.

Skinner, Marilyn B. 2014. *Sexuality in Greek and Roman Culture*. 2nd ed. Malden, MA: Wiley-Blackwell.

Stanton, Graham. 1992. *A Gospel for a New People: Studies in Matthew*. Edinburgh: T&T Clark.

Strong, Anise K. 2016. *Prostitutes and Matrons in the Roman World*. New York: Cambridge University Press.

Taylor, Vincent. 1953. *The Gospel According to St. Mark*. 3rd. ed. London: Macmillan.

Thomas, Rosalind. 1996. "Genealogy." *OCD* 3rd ed. Oxford. Oxford University Press.

Tolbert, Mary Ann. 1989. *Sowing the Gospel: Mark's World in Literary-Historical Perspective*. Minneapolis: Fortress.

van Iersel, Bas M. F. 1998. *Mark: A Reader-Response Commentary*. JSNTSS 164. Sheffield: Sheffield Academic Press.

Walters, Jonathan. 1997. "Invading the Roman Body: Manliness and Impenetrability in Roman Thought." In *Roman Sexualities*, edited by Judith P. Hallett and Marilyn B. Skinner, 29–43. Princeton: Princeton University Press.

Wheeler-Reed, David. 2017. *Regulating Sex in the Roman Empire: Ideology, the Bible, and the Early Christians*. Synkrisis: Comparative Approaches to Early Christianity in Greco-Roman Culture. New Haven: Yale University Press.

Williams, Craig A. 2010. *Roman Homosexuality*. 2nd ed. New York: Oxford University Press.

Wilson, Brittany. 2015. *Unmanly Men: Reconfigurations of Masculinity in Luke-Acts*. Oxford: Oxford University Press.

Winkler, John J. 1990. *The Constraints of Desire: The Anthropology of Sex and Gender in Ancient Greece*. New Ancient World. New York: Routledge.

Worman, Nancy. 2008. *Abusive Mouths in Classical Athens*. New York: Cambridge University Press.

Yarbro Collins. 2007. *Mark: A Commentary*. Hermeneia. Minneapolis: Fortress.

CHAPTER 30

BODY

STEPHEN D. MOORE

INSUBSTANTIAL ANCIENT BODIES

THE body in the Synoptic Gospels—what a daunting topic, and one that has become more, not less, unwieldy with the passage of time. Half a century ago, one might have been content to take one's lead from works like John A. T. Robinson's *The Body: A Study in Pauline Theology* (1952) or Robert H. Gundry's *Sōma in Biblical Theology* (1976), their enviable erudition and tidy taxonomies dictating the section titles of one's essay: "The Body in Greco-Roman Literature"; "The Body in the Septuagint"; "The Body in New Testament Literature outside the Synoptic Gospels"; "The Body in Mark"; "The Body in Matthew"; "The Body in Luke." The body would flicker ambiguously at times as the reader was whisked across the vast expanse of extrabiblical Greek literature. Arriving at the Septuagint, however, the reader would be confidently informed that the preeminent Greek body-word, *sōma*, was used to translate the Hebrew noun *bāśār* only when the latter denoted the physical body, as opposed, say, to the "whole person" (so Gundry 1976, 23). From there it would be but a short step to the Synoptics, where *sōma* would also be said to possess exclusively physical connotations. The essay would mull over *sōma*'s five occurrences in Mark, all but one of them (Mark 5:29) references to Jesus's body—specifically, his soon-to-be-dead (Mark 14:8, 22) or already dead body (Mark 15:43, 45); *sōma*'s twelve occurrences in Matthew, six of them in Jesus's discourse (Matt 5:29–30; 6:22–23, 25; 10:28; for the remaining instances, see 14:12; 26:12, 26; 27:52, 58–59); and its eleven occurrences in Luke (Luke 11:34, 36; 12:4, 22–23; 17:37; 22:19; 23:52, 55; 24:3, 23), all but four of them with Matthean parallels, and accompanied by a lone occurrence of *sōma* in Acts 9:40, and a yet more lonely occurrence of *sōmatikos* ("bodily") in Luke 3:22, the sole instance of this adjective in the canonical gospels or Acts. Again and again, the sheer physicality, the fleshly solidity, of the Synoptic *sōma* would be emphasized. By the end of the essay, one could practically reach out and prod it.

If the foregoing flirts with caricature, it is only because the deficiencies of a "word study" approach (see also Schweizer [1964] 1971) to the topic are by now glaringly obvious. If the only human bodies to be considered in Mark's narrative, say, were those of Jesus and the hemorrhaging woman (the only bodies that explicitly receive the *sōma* designation), then Mark would be a curious narrative indeed. Most of the human bodies in Mark (to focus only on human bodies for now) are implied bodies (more on which later) but no less consequential for that.

There are also other reasons why "the Synoptic body" is a less than solid entity, not easily grasped. The Synoptic body is vulnerable to a highly contagious condition that currently threatens all ancient bodies. The ancient body in general has been gradually dissolving in recent decades, its surfaces and contours becoming ever more indistinct, rather than ever more distinct, as scholars have crowded curiously around it, instruments in hand. Already in 1998, classicist Dominic Montserrat could write: "recent studies on the ancient body are withdrawing from the idea of 'the body' as an undifferentiated, nomothetic category," akin to the category of "woman" in second-wave feminism. The ancient body is better regarded both as a "plurality" and "as a means of conveying ideologies—of status and control, of gender and ethnicity, of nature and culture" (1998, 1–2).

It is not only classicists who have been voicing such deliquescing views of the ancient body. Mira Balberg has recently argued that ancient rabbinic discourse "compel[s] us to think of the body as an entity whose boundaries and constituent elements are not stable, but are rather constantly mutating. The rabbinic impurity discourse, which habitually parses the body into parts and fragments, does not put forth any coherent notion of *the* body as a single self-explanatory unit, but rather depicts a complex web of organs, limbs, and visceral components, a web in which different bodies are connected and then separated, and in which bodies are continually being remolded and redefined" (2014, 9). Such a discourse does not confront one "with the body as a biosocial given"; rather, it confronts one "time and again with the question of *what* the body *is*: where does it begin and end, what does it consist of, and what makes a body into a person" (9).

This mutable, malleable body is no stranger to New Testament studies either—at least in the field of Pauline studies. The Pauline body has always demanded superlative efforts from New Testament body analysts. In 1 Corinthians, in particular, Paul's body discourse runs exhilaratingly wild, extending to the pneumatic body (6:19–20), the gendered body (7:4, 34), the ascetic body (9:27; see also 13:3), the transpersonal Eucharistic body (10:16–17, 24, 27, 29), the yet more transcendent Body of Christ (12:12–27), and the risen body (15:35–44), along with the celestial and terrestrial bodies (15:40; see also 15:44), the nonhuman animal body (15:39), and even the plant body (15:36–38). Small wonder that the bulk of the body work undertaken in New Testament studies has been done on the Pauline letters.

Dale B. Martin rose splendidly to the concept-bending body challenge posed by Paul in *The Corinthian Body* (1995). Martin's extended detour in the introductory chapter of his book through ancient philosophical, medical, magical, and physiognomic discourses on the body led him to conclude: "for most people of Greco-Roman culture ... the self was a precarious, temporary state of affairs, constituted by forces surrounding and pervading the body, like the radio waves that bounce around and through the bodies of modern urbanities. In such a maelstrom of cosmological forces, the individualism of modern conceptions disappears, and the body is perceived as a location in a continuum of cosmic movement. The body—or the 'self'—is an unstable point of transition, not a discrete, permanent, solid entity" (25).

The ancient body, then, as conceived by Robinson, Gundry, and an entire earlier generation of New Testament scholars, has been, since the 1990s, intermittently and unevenly, the subject of a theoretical makeover, influenced by fields such as classics, in which that transformation has been more insistent and more evident. The ancient body has been reconceived and remolded by gender theory, but also by queer theory (more on which later). More generally, it has been reshaped by diffuse, widely disseminated versions of poststructuralist theory. Most of all, it has been Foucault-ized.

Introducing yet another ancient body book, this one in classics, Gloria Ferrari ponders how and why it was that the human body in general became "an important topic" in the humanities and social sciences in the latter decades of the twentieth century (2009, 1). Among the catalysts, she identifies feminist studies, queer theory, and postcolonial theory, all fields that demonstrate how "dominant ideologies identify, shape and control particular bodies." But if one were to single out the primary catalyst, she continues, "most would agree that it was the work of Michel Foucault." Foucault's distinctive brand of body constructionism—his radical reconception of the body as a discursive object, culturally constituted from head to toe—uncoupled debate on the ontological and epistemological status of the body from the field of philosophy, enabling it to become "a central concern in studies of culture and society and the proper subject of historical inquiry" (2009, 1). Because the second and third volumes of Foucault's *History of Sexuality* dealt with Greek and Roman antiquity, respectively (Foucault [1984] 1985; [1984] 1986), Foucault's impact on the field of classics in particular "has been considerable" (Ferrari 2009, 1). Many classicists would concur with this judgment. Maud W. Gleason, for example, had already claimed that Foucault "put on the scholarly map a whole archipelago of concerns about the [ancient] self, the body, and sexuality that were either invisible before, or but little visited by persons of repute" (1995, xi). Never mind that Foucault was seen by many traditionally minded classicists as a bull in the disciplinary china shop, or that feminist classicists quickly (and rightly) took Foucault to task for his egregious androcentrism. Foucault intensified an already incipient interest in the body in the field of classics, provoked a sweeping reappraisal of what a body, not least an ancient body, is—or, more precisely, what it could be—and modeled a sophisticated methodology for analyzing that newly complexified object.

Because classics has always been the primary interdisciplinary field for New Testament and early Christian studies, it did not take long for the Foucauldian body to migrate into the latter fields, unobtrusively at first. Martin's *The Corinthian Body* barely mentions Foucault explicitly, but its assumptions about what ancient bodies, or any bodies, are—assumptions transmitted in part by Foucault-informed classicists such as David Halperin and John Winkler—are Foucauldian through and through. The first sentence of Martin's first chapter reads: "different societies construct the human body differently" (1995, 3). He continues: "in this chapter I will attempt to show how

Greco-Roman constructions of the body were significantly different from our own" (3). Such assumptions about the body would soon come to be dubbed "alteritism" in the historical fields, and would routinely be traced back to Foucault's *History of Sexuality*. But Martin's approach to the ancient body also puts one in mind of Foucault's "archaeological" project of excavating the unspoken and unwritten rules, the hidden logics, that regulate discourses of all kinds. Martin states (again without explicit reference to Foucault; the ether of influence is diffuse here, wafted through many intermediaries): "my goal is to sketch the logic underlying these ancient discourses about the body" (xiii). He is seeking to uncover "unspoken logics of corporeal construction" and "in particular ideologies that construe the body in certain ways as a result of certain societal interests" (xiii).

Much that is still implicit in *The Corinthian Body* is fully explicit in a more recent Corinthian body book: Brian J. Robinson's *Being Subordinate Men: Paul's Rhetoric of Gender and Power in 1 Corinthians* (2019). "I seek the excavation of Paul's body," Robinson announces at the outset (1) and later indicates that Foucault will be a crucial resource for the project (12). However, Judith Butler (unmentioned in Martin's much earlier monograph) is also a fundamental influence on Robinson's sensibilities as a gender analyst (see esp. 40; also 24–25). This Robinson shares in common with many gender analysts in classics. Butler's theory of gender performativity effectively extended and further intensified the sex-disassembling and gender-deessentializing project of Foucault's *History of Sexuality*. Famously for Butler, gender is the cumulative product of a socially scripted set of stylized actions, which combine and conspire to generate retroactively the illusion that gender is natural and innate, "expressed" by the speech, gestures, and other behaviors that in fact engender it (Butler 1990, 128–41). In short, gender is performative, "a practice of improvisation within a scene of constraint" (Butler 2004, 1).

PERFORMED SYNOPTIC BODIES

Performativity, whether explicitly named or not, is key for much biblical work on the body. *The Oxford Handbook of Biblical Narrative* (Fewell 2016) is illuminating in this regard. Part 3 of this tome is titled "The Bible and Bodies"; yet other than Jeremy Schipper's opening essay, "Plotting Bodies in Biblical Narrative" (Schipper 2016), none of its eight essays grapple centrally with the body, or bodies, as such. What they mainly discuss are gender, sex, and sexuality, and the cultural scripts that enable and constrain their enactment.

Indeed, in much biblical work on how bodies act and interact, the body as such tends to be a curiously effaced entity. Symptomatically, Patrick Schreiner's *The Body of Jesus: A Spatial Analysis of the Kingdom in Matthew* (2016), a rare example of a book on a Synoptic Gospel with the word "body" in its title, turns out to be primarily about space and only secondarily about the body—a problematic phrasing of the issue, admittedly, since Schreiner contends that space and body are indissociable concepts. The Matthean Jesus's mission, as Schreiner understands it, "is the reordering of the earth with [Jesus's] body as the nucleus" (2016, 5). Nevertheless, *The Body of Jesus* is not a book about Jesus's body, ultimately, or about any body, or bodies, as such. Even when the body is determinedly kept in focus, as it is in Jin Young Choi's *Postcolonial Discipleship of Embodiment: An Asian and Asian American Feminist Reading of the Gospel of Mark* (2015), it is anything but solid. For Choi, the Markan Jesus's body is immensely fluid and thoroughly fragmented, as epitomized by—but by no means confined to—the broken-bread symbolism of the Last Supper. "Mark presents the body of Jesus as fluid when it touches other bodies and is consumed by others. In this way Jesus's body, which lives on in death and is present in absence, disrupts the power and presence of the imperial body" (2015, 10). Jesus's body continually slips away in Mark, ultimately slipping the control imposed by the Roman Empire on its subject peoples through the instrumentality of the body, not least the crucified body (50, 61, 106–7).

The eclipse of the ancient body is also conspicuous in the ever-expanding corpus of body/sex/gender work in New Testament and early Christian studies inspired by comparable work in the field of classics. That eclipse comes to explicit expression in Colleen M. Conway's *Behold the Man: Jesus and Greco-Roman Masculinity* (2008). A section of the book, aptly titled "The Paradoxical Body," begins with an ostensible truism: "the body is perhaps the most obvious entrée into issues of sexuality and gender" (2008, 16). Nevertheless, continues Conway, "what has become increasingly clear" (clear in the field of classics first and foremost, one might add, and primarily as a result of the Foucault effect) "is that ancient masculinity was constituted more by the shape of one's life than the shape of one's body" (16). Indeed, "the body was ultimately not of primary importance in the achievement of ideal masculinity" (17). Why not? Because "the core of masculine identity resided not in the body per se but rather in what one did with, and allowed to be done to, one's body" (21). To rephrase this statement in Butlerian terms (and Butler does make cameo appearances in Conway's monograph), the core of masculine identity resided not in the body per se but rather in bodily performativity.

Like most sophisticated contemporary analysts of early Christian masculinities, Conway is primarily concerned with the performance of masculinity in the New Testament texts she explores. Jesus is the gender performer who is Conway's principal focus, and she ascribes intriguingly different performances to each of the Synoptic Jesuses. At one end of the spectrum—more specifically, at the "lower" end of that ancient gender gradient that ascended precipitously from femininity to masculinity—Conway sets the Markan Jesus, whose masculinity she finds to be the most conflicted and ambivalent of the three Synoptic Jesuses. To be sure, Mark's Jesus styles himself ὁ ἰσχυρός, "the strong man" (Mark 3:27; see also 5:4, 15), and has earlier been hailed by John the Baptist as ὁ ἰσχυρότερός μου, "the one who is stronger than I" (1:7; Conway 2008, 90). It is not bodily strength, however, that is in view here. The Markan Jesus is no megawarrior—no Hercules, no Achilles. He overcomes his opponents through verbal prowess or by supernatural means.

What of the Markan Jesus's self-mastery, that trait being the preeminent index of masculinity in so many of the philosophical and literary texts that survive from antiquity? Here Conway finds him curiously lacking. Jesus's first passion prediction (8:31) does seem to set up the expectation that his impending execution will adhere closely to the Greco-Roman manly, noble-death script. But already in 8:38 Jesus seems to be warding off the shameful specter of emasculation associated with death by crucifixion in the ancient Mediterranean world (2008, 97). Moreover, "nothing in the Gospel prepares the audience for the Gethsemane scene" (100). Jesus barely squeaks through it with his masculine honor intact. Later at the cross, that already brittle masculinity seems to shatter completely. In place of a triumphant and transcendent speech from the cross (in the mode of, say, the martyrs of 4 Maccabees), all one hears is an emasculating cry of desolation (Mark 15:34). All told, as Conway reads it, the Markan Jesus's relationship with hegemonic masculinity on the Roman model is inconsistent and conflicted—which, of course, is what makes it interesting.

The Matthean Jesus, while still a marginal man in certain respects, nonetheless manages to pull off a more manly performance than his Markan counterpart, for Conway, not least because the Matthean Jesus is a consummate public speaker and "the role of public speaker/teacher was a decidedly masculine one in the ancient world" (2008, 114). But it is the Lukan Jesus who is the most manly of the three Synoptic Jesuses, Conway contends. The heroes one encounters in the narrative world of Luke-Acts in general—"Jesus, Stephen, Peter, Paul—are portrayed as educated, articulate, reasonable, self-controlled, pious men, fully capable of holding their own in the upper echelons of the masculine world of the Roman Empire" (127). Mind you, the Lukan Jesus is barely tested in that regard. He does interact with a Roman prefect (Luke 23:1–5), a Roman client king (23:6–11), a Roman centurion (7:1–10), and a Jewish "ruler" (ἄρχων; 18:18–23). In general, however, upper-echelon males are in short supply in Jesus's story as even Luke tells it.

Classicist Maud Gleason pinpoints the problem with styling Luke's Jesus, or any Gospel Jesus, a polished performer of Roman masculinity:

> For one thing, Jesus had no *paideia*. He ... could control the attention of a large crowd, but most of his crowds were composed of rustics. Greco-Roman gentlemen had no use for such persons: they cut their gender-teeth discoursing with others of their own social kind, in a literary dialect that was probably over the heads of even those rustics whose native language was some kind of Greek. Indeed, while the ability to dominate a crowd verbally may well have been part of a pan-Mediterranean koine of masculinity, educated elites who excelled at *paideia* were actually suspicious of speakers who were excessively popular with audiences of low degree.... In the eyes of the educated, Jesus's public-speaking ability would have been at best an ambiguous component of his masculinity. (2003, 325–26)

Jesus's public performances in the Gospels, then, do not conjure up or construct an elite masculinity. What of Jesus's body? Here Gleason is equally incisive: "Jesus clearly did not control . . . the boundaries of his own body. This inability, in the eyes of educated men and those who accepted their value system, was related to his educational limitations: one of the chief benefits of *paideia* was its power to protect the body-boundaries of the educated person from violation, particularly from violations by the agents of the imperial criminal justice system. The only thing that the Gospel narratives tell us about Jesus' body is that it was thus violated" (2003, 326).

Among the Synoptic evangelists, Luke discloses the violability of Jesus's body with the most obvious reluctance, famously glossing over Jesus's flogging. (Pilate twice announces that he will have Jesus flogged [Luke 23:16, 22] and Jesus himself earlier predicted the flogging [18:33], but Luke declines to say that it actually occurred: compare 23:25 with Mark 15:15 and Matt 27:26.) Yet even the Lukan Jesus ends up as a brute slab of meat cruelly pinioned to a wooden cross (Luke 23:33; 24:39a), an utterly emasculating condition that Luke must work hard to counter, assiduously placing noble-death utterances on the lips of his expiring hero (23:28, 34, 43, 46). But is the Lukan Jesus's abjected body thereby successfully covered over?

Among scholarly spectators of the Lukan Jesus's demise, Brittany E. Wilson is the least convinced that the cover does not slip, that his emasculating shame does not peek through. When Wilson in her monograph on masculinity in Luke-Acts (2015) comes to take the measure of the Lukan Jesus's manliness against the inflexible yardstick of Greco-Roman gender protocols, she is immediately drawn to the Lukan passion narrative. Indeed, Wilson's chapter on the Lukan Jesus's masculinity is primarily a chapter on the fate of the Lukan Jesus's body during his final hours. And Wilson's verdict on that publicly displayed body? "It is above all a passive body," she concludes (2015, 227). It "is led around, beaten, blindfolded, mocked, abandoned, stripped naked, made a spectacle, and penetrated with nails" (234). The owner of this body fails abysmally to protect its boundaries; as such, his status as a man is fatally undermined (234–35). What is more, even the Lukan Jesus's resurrection does not effect a manly metamorphosis, for Wilson (239). Uniquely among the Synoptic Jesuses, the Lukan Jesus even in his risen state continues to bear on his body the shameful marks of his emasculating demise: "They were startled and terrified, and thought that they were seeing a ghost. He said to them, 'Why are you frightened . . . ? Look at my hands and my feet [ἴδετε τὰς χεῖράς μου καὶ τοὺς πόδας μου]; see that it is I myself'" (24:37–39; see also John 20:24–27).

Yet even though Wilson homes in with laser-sharp focus on the Lukan Jesus's body in her critical appraisal of his masculinity, the body that appears in her lens is an overwritten body, an inscribed body, an encoded body. Wilson is able to read it, to decipher it, only by overlaying it with the ancient Mediterranean gender scripts that classicists have meticulously reconstructed. Undeniably, much of importance may be decrypted in the overwritten literary bodies of antiquity. The arrival of disability studies in New Testament studies makes this importance particularly plain. Louise J. Lawrence's *Sense and Stigma in the Gospels* (2013), a seminal instance of New Testament disability studies, illustrates the social constructionist assumptions about the body that have subtended this emerging field (see also Avalos, Melcher, and Schipper 2007, 1–2;

Moss and Schipper 2011, 4, 6; Solevåg 2018, 1–2). Lawrence identifies "embodiment" and "performance" as two crucial concepts that she will "think with" throughout her book. For her, as for the disability theorists who have informed her, the body is not a "static fact"; rather, when it comes to the body, there is only "purposefully enacted role-play" (2013, 3). Moreover, for Lawrence, bodily performers, not least the blind, deaf, leprous, "demon-possessed," and other disabled characters in the Synoptic Gospels, can subtly subvert and tactically convert the stereotypes and stigmas that prop up the biopolitical binaries of physiological normality and abnormality, ability and disability that construct and contain them (2–3, 20–21).

And yet, many currents in contemporary theory (not least post-Butlerian queer theory and nonrepresentational narratology; see, for example, Nigianni and Storr 2009, 3, 5; Ruffolo 2016, 8–10; Askin 2016, 8–16) compel one to ask in response: Is performativity the only reality that can be imagined for bodies, whether ancient or contemporary? Is reading and counterreading representations the only theoretical or methodological game in town when it comes to the analysis of literary bodies? Is the encoded body, the constructed body, the only body that theory and criticism are equipped to access? Intriguingly, analogous questions have been voiced by at least one prominent analyst of ancient social body-scripts, gender scripts in particular.

Jennifer A. Glancy has been one of the most incisive decrypters of ancient Christian corporeality, most of all in her *Corporal Knowledge: Early Christian Bodies* (2010). Interestingly, Glancy too reveals that "Foucault's influence" on her project has been "pervasive but diffuse" (2010, 4). Yet hers "is not a book about Foucault. After we have said everything about early Christian bodies that Foucault helps us say, those bodies will still have more stories to tell" (4). The latter statement gestures to a highly pertinent problem that Glancy has set herself in this book. Even her failures to surmount the conundrum are instructive. Already in her first chapter, Glancy is worried that "at this point in [her] discussion, early Christian bodies may seem remote, more ghost than matter" (15). Attempting to flesh out these spectral bodies, she turns to "the corporal vernacular at work in the Gospel of Mark" (15). Detailed analysis of Mark's representations of bodily gestures, bodily deportment, and other revealing bodily movements and dispositions then follows. In particular, Glancy ponders the action of various Markan characters, most notably the Syrophoenician woman (Mark 7:24–30), of throwing themselves at Jesus's feet or otherwise abasing themselves before him. "Although the varying postural descriptions may evoke somewhat different images, each is an act of self-lowering that participates in a corporal vernacular expressing emotion, social location, and perception of power" (15–16). Through these stylized actions, the characters enact a nonverbal sociocultural script that would have been readily legible to ancient Mediterranean audiences. "Such negotiations of the hierarchies of power would have been familiar to Mark's readers and indeed throughout the Roman Empire" (19).

But in focusing on these formulaic movements does Glancy really succeed in fleshing out the bodies that enact or perform them? Or is the body still a secondary effect of a primary regimen of socially scripted gestures and dispositions, the paradoxical product of the actions it ostensibly enables? In other words, has Glancy really exited the

Foucauldian-Butlerian paradox of a body that has no articulable existence anterior to the discourses that bestow legible form on it or "enflesh" it, no expressible essence apart from the performativity that conjures it into being?

Even Glancy herself seems less than satisfied with her corporeal analysis of Markan characters. Following the exercise summarized here, and another on the Johannine episode of the man born blind (John 9:1–12), she confesses: "I have a long-standing frustration with analyses of bodies that tell us nothing about what it means to be a body.... In focusing on the ... body of John's vision-impaired beggar, for example, we overlook the question of whether the world was blear or crisp when the beggar first glimpsed it; what visual sense he made of a world he had previously known through hearing and touch; whether the mud Jesus rubbed into the blind man's eyes was gritty and slimy on the thin flesh of his eyelids" (21).

The same line of questioning could, of course, be put to an entire throng of newly sighted bodies in the Synoptic Gospels (Matt 9:27–31; 12:22; 15:30–31; 20:29–34; 21:14; Mark 8:22–26; 10:46–52; Luke 4:18; 7:21–22; 18:35–43). "If we think about such questions at all," Glancy reflects, "we bracket them as homiletic" (2010, 21). She promises that the final chapter of her book, "an extended treatment of Mary's body in childbirth," will finally press beyond "a semiotic or representational approach to bodies" to what she terms "a phenomenological approach" (22). The experiment turns out to be an intriguing one, although—disappointingly for my project here—the laboring body of the Matthean and even the Lukan Mary are absent from it, as Glancy opts to focus instead on the *Infancy Gospel of James* and other extracanonical sources.

There are, in any case, ways other than the phenomenological of pressing beyond "a semiotic or representational approach to bodies." Glancy's monograph is titled *Corporal Knowledge*, but the early Christian narratives with which it wrestles contain no corporeal entities, no bodies as such to know, only incorporeal bodies, which demand a different kind of knowing, an incorporeal knowledge, and a return to theoretical first principles.

Incorporeal Synoptic Bodies

What is a body when it is incorporeal? How might one write about such a paradoxical nonobject? Specifically (since it is my topic), how might one write about the incorporeal bodies of the Synoptic Gospels? For there are, of course, no bodies in the Synoptics, strictly speaking: no human bodies, no animal bodies, no bodies of any kind. There are only representations of bodies in the Synoptics, one might say (the concept of representation is a mystification, but let it stand for now)—and representations more abstract, more oblique than any modern or postmodern work of visual art. As literary representations, the words in the Synoptics that denote or connote bodies are necessarily devoid of any relation of resemblance to physical bodies. Visual representation (sculpture, painting, drawing, photography, film) ordinarily entails a relation of resemblance to the object represented. Even the Alexamenos graffito, a crude drawing of two figures, one of them a crucified donkey-headed man—possibly the earliest extant visual depiction of Jesus—may be classified as representational, notwithstanding the fact that the caricatured anthropoid at its center has an animal head: nonexistent entities lend themselves as readily as existent entities to visual representation. Linguistic representation, in contrast, including literary representation (at least when conducted in nonpictographic alphabets), entails no relation of resemblance between the word and its referent: the word "Jesus," in any language, is precisely as like or unlike the historical person or the literary characters who bore or bear that name as the words "James," "Jacqueline," or "jack-in-the box."

The example of the name is not incidental to my elusive topic, the body in the Synoptic Gospels. In common with much ancient literature (not least the literature of the Hebrew Bible, as Erich Auerbach [1946] 1953, 7–11, long ago observed), and in contrast with most modern literature, the Synoptics are almost entirely devoid of descriptions of human bodies. Proper names and personal pronouns are employed to fill that void. Undescribed bodies dangle pendulously from appellative hooks: "Jesus," "Peter," "Mary," "the Pharisee," "the leper," "the women".... Physical portraiture in antiquity, both verbal and visual, tended to be bound up with physiognomy: interpreting physical characteristics as expressive of moral character. It has been argued that the Synoptic evangelists were not enamored of physiognomy (is that why none of their Gospels contains a physical description of their protagonist?), and that at least one of them, Luke, sought to subvert physiognomic conventions (Parsons 2006; Lamb 2017). Further engagement with physiognomics, however, will not defamiliarize the phenomenon of literary representation; for physiognomy was representational through and through. In physiognomy, outward aspect (straight eyebrows, outward-curving eyebrows, downward-curving eyebrows . . .) was relentlessly made to represent inner disposition (gentleness, cynicism, irascibility . . .). Framing the dearth of physical descriptions in my target texts by means of different, more recent conceptual resources yields this heuristic proposition: the Synoptic Gospels are largely innocent of the ruse of resemblance.

The ruse of resemblance: *What you see on the surface of this ceiling mural from the Catacomb of Callixtus is not a maze of lines, a chaos of colors. Rather, it is a young man bearing a sheep on his shoulders, his left hand firmly gripping its legs. It is, indeed, Jesus as Good Shepherd. He stands foregrounded in an illusory space whose imagined depths seem (to our modern, perspective-accustomed eyes, at least) to contain foreshortened trees toward which we might casually stroll in our imaginations, picking our way around the immobile youth and the other sheep at his feet.* (See Foucault [1968] 1983, 43, whose ruminations on representation I'm loosely paraphrasing here.) Revelation 1:12–16, the book's head-to-toe description of the glorified Son of Man (physiognomy in a Jewish apocalyptic register?), spectacularly enacts the ruse of resemblance: *What is present to your mind as you pore over this text or hear it declaimed aloud is not a muddle of random squiggles on papyrus or paper, nor a cacophony of arbitrary sounds emitted by a human vocal apparatus, but an anthropomorphic entity whose divine nimbus and consequent anomalous corporeal composition presses your imagination to its limits (and beyond).*

In the Synoptic Gospels, in contrast, nobody—and, more to the point, no body—is accorded a remotely comparable description. And it is not only detailed descriptions of glorious bodies—angelic, transfigured, risen, returning on the clouds—that are lacking in these narratives. (Matt 17:2, hardly ample, comes closest: "and his face shone like the sun, and his clothes became dazzling white"; see also Mark 9:3; Luke 9:29; Exod 34:29; Dan 10:5–6.) Descriptions of inglorious bodies are equally lacking, which is to say that there is also nothing comparable in the Synoptics to the arrestingly ordinary (and consummately physiognomic) description of Paul found in the *Acts of Paul and Thecla* 3.3: "a man small of stature, with a bald head and crooked legs, in a good state of body, with eyebrows meeting and nose somewhat hooked, full of friendliness; for now he appeared like a man, and now he had the face of an angel" (trans. from Schneemelcher 1992).

In the Synoptic Gospels, in contrast, there are only proper names and personal pronouns; condensed descriptive tags; and sporadic mentions of specific body parts. Regarding Mark's "John the Baptizer," for instance, there is mention only of a "waist," which is wrapped with "a leather belt," which in turn serves to accessorize "clothing made of camel's hair" (Mark 1:6; see also Matt 3:4). This, however, is considerably more than is told about Jesus's appearance when he arrives on the scene (Mark 1:9), or about Simon, Andrew, James, or John, his first followers (1:16–20), or about most of the characters in this narrative. To these minimalistic verbal indexes, implied bodies are appended by audiences. How else might the matter be phrased? The main catalyst for the reflections that follow is the para-poststructuralist philosophy of Gilles Deleuze, whose impact on critical theory in the opening decades of the twenty-first century has been comparable to that of Jacques Derrida and Michel Foucault on it in the closing decades of the twentieth. Why Deleuzian theory, even when applied to literature, is resolutely nonrepresentational will emerge in due course.

Synoptic bodies are Janus-faced entities that, like all literary bodies, turn in two directions simultaneously. One face is turned to the verbal fragments that tether the bodies to their respective narratives. One face is turned to the word, so to speak. Another face, meanwhile, is turned to the world, meaning the world "outside" the text—the world of which the text is, however, a moving part, a cog in a complex sociopolitical machine, and in relation to which it assumes agency. Incorporeal literary bodies, including Synoptic bodies, shimmer, specter-like, along the surface, the boundary, that simultaneously separates and conjoins word and world (see Deleuze [1969] 1990, 166–67).

In the world, corporeal bodies exist in multitude. Synoptic audiences possess knowledge of innumerable corporeal bodies, beginning with their own, and it is that encyclopedic body-knowledge, at once intimate and abstract, that enables these audiences to ascribe phantom substance to the implied, incorporeal bodies of the Synoptic narratives. These incorporeal bodies do not exist so much as insist: they press insistently upon the imagination, the emotions, the intellect. Although incorporeal, they exercise agency in the corporeal realm. They cause events to occur not just in the world of words but also in the world of things. Most obviously, the incorporeal bodies of the Synoptic Jesuses have, through the ages and in alliance with the incorporeal bodies of other New Testament Jesuses, created entire worlds of things, while obliterating other worlds of things. In the process, they have moved countless corporeal bodies in ways that have been sublimely life-transforming, horrifyingly destructive, or stultifyingly mundane.

Because these incorporeal, undescribed Synoptic bodies can always be—indeed, must always be—actualized differently by different readers or hearers, they may also be categorized as virtual bodies (see Deleuze [1968] 1994, 208–14). But because these virtual Synoptic bodies are minimally defined—line drawings of the most rudimentary kind, figuratively speaking—their capacity for variant actualizations is multiplied exponentially. They can be fleshed out in endless variations and through infinite permutations, as the history of Christian art alone superabundantly testifies. As such, whereas the bodies in the Synoptic Gospels—whether cursorily described, conspicuously underdescribed, or altogether undescribed—constitute a finite series, limited in number, the incorporeal bodies assembled on the innumerable borders between the words of those Gospels and the worlds in and through which those incorporeal bodies assume imagined flesh, and thereby live and act, constitute an infinite series. These virtual bodies have inestimable effects and generate incalculable affects in the local communities and wider worlds that ceaselessly and compulsively actualize them.

The incorporeal human bodies of the Synoptic Gospels travel, then. They travel in the narrative wor(l)ds of those Gospels, and, far more extensively, in their extratextual worlds. But they do not travel alone. Most often they are coupled with, or conjoined to, incorporeal nonhuman bodies: animal bodies and further other-than-human bodies, including "inanimate" bodies—although the latter often exercise as much agency as so-called animate bodies. The Markan account of Jesus's postbaptismal *peirasmos*, for instance (Mark 1:12–13), is a scene with six actors (or, better, actants), only one of which is human. "The Spirit" thrusts Jesus into "the wilderness" (the latter an important actant in Mark, one with the uncanny capacity to cause the remote past to reactualize transformatively in the present: see 1:2–4; 6:31–44; 8:1–9, together with Isa 40:3; Exod 16; Num 11; 2 Kgs 4:42–44), where he is "tempted by Satan" and is "with the wild beasts," and where "the angels minster to him." The human being is a notably passive player, a relatively inert body, in this transspecies, interbeing drama.

Human bodies in the Synoptics, as this scene illustrates, frequently exist in symbiotic, temporary relationships with nonhuman bodies. Such examples abound; what follows is but a sample of them. A "paralytic" (παραλυτικός) is accompanied not by any physical description but by a "pallet" (κράβατον), which, when the man is lying prone on it, announces that he is a disabled body, but when he is carrying it, that he is able-bodied (Mark 2:3–12; see also Matt 9:2–8; Luke 5:18–26). The ancient grammar of disability here employs things in apposition to words. The Matthean Peter is presented with keys—"the keys of the kingdom of heaven" (Matt 16:19)—that will shadow him through the history of Christian art, distinguishing him from every other generic, male, bearded Christ follower in that tradition (such as Paul with his sword). The anointing woman is nameless, faceless, and wordless in each of her Synoptic appearances. She would be nothing whatsoever, however, a perfect blank, were it not for her alabaster jar of ointment, which confers agency on her (Mark 14:3–9; Matt 26:6–13; see also Luke 7:36–50).

Jesus is also coupled with agential objects. In all three Synoptics, he is clothed with a cloak of healing, which exercises agency independently of him, curing those who touch it (Mark 5:27–30; see also Mark 6:56; Matt 9:20–22; 14:35–36; Luke 8:43–44; Acts 19:11–12). To be a true Jesus-follower, as later emerges, is to be a cross-bearer (Mark 8:34; Matt 16:24; Luke 14:27)—to carry one's cross around "daily" (καθ' ἡμέραν), indeed, adds Luke's Jesus (9:23), plunging from the grotesque into the surreal. The Synoptic Jesuses themselves are, of course, never unaccompanied by their crosses, even when those crosses are not invoked by name. Each Synoptic Jesus casts a cruciform shadow. Jesus Triumphant, meanwhile, in all three Synoptics is as blank affectively as a freshly scrubbed slate, but symbiotically, and semiotically, supplemented by a colt (Mark 11:1–10; Luke 19:28–38) or a colt together with an ass (Matt 21:1–9; see Zech 9:9), which, singly or in tandem, declaim to the multitude the message Jesus himself need not speak. Postresurrection, finally, Jesus Triumphant is conjoined with the throne into which his cross has morphed—"the throne of his glory [ὁ θρόνος δόξης αὐτοῦ]" (Matt 19:28; 25:31; see also Mark 14:62; Luke 1:32; 22:69).

In contemporary theoretical parlance, human bodies in the Synoptics live, move, and have their being in "assemblages" (see Deleuze and Guattari [1980] 1987, 3–4, 88–90, 323–37, 503–5; DeLanda 2016). These Synoptic bodies are incorporeal entities, as I have shown. But Deleuze and Guattari's assemblage theory also enables one to consider where and how the corporeal interacts with the incorporeal in the actualizing act of reading.

Deleuze and Guattari distinguish "assemblages of enunciation" from "machinic assemblages" (1987, esp. 88–90). The former pertain to the interconnections of words, propositions, and discourses, while the latter pertain to the interactions of material bodies, both human and nonhuman. Assemblages of enunciation interlock intricately, and productively, with machinic assemblages. For example, a human reader (a corporeal body) reads a Synoptic Gospel (another corporeal body) aloud to a human audience (an assembly of further corporeal bodies), and in the machinic conjoining of these different corporeal entities, incorporeal bodies, both human and nonhuman, are produced, and interact in turn: Jesus, John the Baptizer, the Jordan river, the Spirit, the heavenly voice, the wilderness, Satan, the wild beasts, the angels....

Incorporeal bodies, Synoptic or otherwise, are not as different from corporeal bodies as one may be inclined to imagine. The corporeal/incorporeal distinction does not imply a solidity, a fixity on the part of corporeal bodies (those of readers or hearers, for example) in contrast to the fluidity, the mutability of incorporeal bodies (those of the Synoptic Jesuses, for example, or the other human characters who constellate around them). The corporeal body, too, is a creature of flux, caught up in perpetual becoming, incessantly changing. In the event of reading, corporeal bodies-in-process intermingle with incorporeal bodies-in-process. The incorporeal body acts upon the corporeal body even as the corporeal body acts upon the incorporeal body. Something passes from one to the other—and is immediately passed back in a different form, in a recursive loop.

Agency is exercised on both sides of this instantaneous exchange. On the side of the reader, however, it is an agency that exceeds the individual, since nothing that the reader encounters in the text, nothing that she projects onto it, originates absolutely with the reader; rather, it passes through her from elsewhere. On the side of the text, too, agency insistently exceeds whatever intentions may have animated the author as he penned the text. The text is "a little machine" (Deleuze and Guattari 1987, 4) that now exercises agency independently of its manufacturer, and exercises it intensely and unremittingly. For the text is ceaselessly caught up in "a collective assemblage of enunciation," which is to say, "of acts and statements, of incorporeal transformations attributed to bodies" (88).

Incorporeal transformations must be distinguished from corporeal transformations. The latter abound in the Synoptics; they are the indispensable stuff of its multitudinous miracle tales: "'Be made clean!' Immediately his leprosy was cleansed"; "'Go; let it be done for you according to your faith.' And the servant was healed in that hour"; "he touched her hand, and the fever left her" (Matt 8:3, 13, 15). *Incorporeal* transformations operate differently; the changes they bring about do not entail bodily alterations but are equally real nonetheless: "the judge's sentence . . . transforms the accused into a convict," just as the words "I love you" transform the utterer into a lover, and the words "Nobody move!" transform airline passengers into hostages (Deleuze and Guattari 1987, 80–81). Incorporeal transformations also occur within the narrative worlds of the Synoptics: "Your sins are forgiven"; "Today salvation has come to this house"; "Then he took a loaf of bread . . . and gave it to them, saying, 'This is my body'" (Luke 7:48; 19:9; 22:19). But these Synoptic narratives, both in their constituent components and in their entirety, are themselves immensely powerful machines for producing incorporeal transformations in the extranarrative worlds in which their ever-changing audiences live processually, move incessantly, and have their being-as-becoming.

All this is to say that the Synoptic narratives intervene in the worlds of their audiences—although not as agents external to those worlds. They are themselves material and hence worldly as well as word-ly, fully implicated in sociopolitical realities, folded into them. Furthermore and relatedly, the Synoptic narratives do not exercise agency through strategies of representation—specifically, through representing bodies, both human and nonhuman, in a nonbodily medium; for what are called "literary representations" are themselves bodies (Deleuze and Guattari 1987, 86) and, as such, possess bodily agency. They are material objects in the material world: inked letters on papyrus, printed letters on paper, electronic letters on a visual display terminal. Unhindered by their absolute nonresemblance to our organic bodies, these bodies of inscription act on, move, attract, repel us—viscerally, affectively, and, above all, instantaneously. There is no perceptible interval between visual or aural decoding of a written or spoken word in the semantically seething sentence of a Synoptic narrative, or any narrative, and being affected by that word (187). One does not need to put the sentence on hold or hit a mental pause button while one rummages through one's immense inner encyclopedia for the appropriate referent of the word. Rather, the word, whatever it may be—loaves . . . fish . . . broke . . . ate . . . filled—immediately, and autonomously, generates an incorporeal body that affects one's own body as reader or hearer, that corporeal body acting, reacting, "before the mind moves it" (Deleuze [1993] 1997, 123).

The foregoing assertion, moreover, can be made without ever leaving the material plane, without ever levitating above it. The incorporeal body is not a bodiless ghost or spirit that wafts out of the text, hovers over it, and only then enters the body of the reader, possessing it. Like the Synoptic superdemon Legion (Mark 5:1–20; Matt 8:28–34; Luke 8:26–39), who can exit the demoniac's body only by entering the bodies of the "great herd of swine," incorporeal bodies require corporeal bodies in order to exist. Like Legion, too, now careening suicidally toward the Sea of Galilee in multiple porcine bodies, incorporeal bodies also have the capacity to inhabit more than one body at once: the textbody, the readerbody, the multibody of a liturgical audience. While the corporeal bodies remain separate entities in the text-audience commingling, the incorporeal bodies that emerge from this coupling manifest themselves in a nonspace that is neither one nor the other: neither the space of the text nor yet the space of the reader or hearer. Channeling Deleuze, one might say that the textbody and the reader/hearerbody form "a zone of indistinction, of indiscernibility," as though, unaccountably, they had somehow "reached the point immediately preceding their respective differentiation" (Deleuze [1993] 1997, 78). This is the mundane miracle of reading, everywhere enacted daily. And whereas corporeal bodies are mortal or otherwise finite, incorporeal bodies are, in principle, potentially eternal, available for infinite actualizations, each one different, as they manifest themselves in, through, and beyond corporeal entities (Bryant 2012).

The Synoptic Jesus's dogged refusal to die, the megatrope with which each of the three Synoptics ends, makes him a particularly apt emblem of the incorporeal body, all the more so since his risen body also resists knowability. "We know nothing about a body until we know what it can do," Deleuze and Guattari insist (1987, 257), echoing Spinoza ([1677] 2002, 280). "We know nothing about a body until we know . . . what its affects are" (Deleuze and Guattari 1987, 257)—by which they do not mean a body's emotional capacity so much as its capacity to act upon other bodies (whether corporeal or incorporeal, human or nonhuman), thereby augmenting or diminishing their power to act in turn. "We know nothing about a body until we know . . . how [its affects] can or cannot enter into composition with . . . the affects of another body, either to . . . exchange actions and passions with it or to join with it in composing a more powerful body" (257).

The Synoptic Gospels have been particularly potent bodies of this kind (for a text is a body, too, as noted, with both corporeal and incorporeal dimensions), embedded in infinitely open-ended, intricately nested assemblages of heterogeneous bodies and forces. Each Synoptic Gospel interacts continually with its two Synoptic companions, thereby augmenting or diminishing its individual power. The immense power of the Synoptic Gospels in human history, however, derives from another relationship—a relationship of intimate proximity, of immediate contiguity—to another body. Each Synoptic Gospel is, first and foremost, the surface, the skin, connecting the corporeal body of "the Jesus behind the Gospels" (as some like to say) with the boundless multiplicity of the incorporeal Jesuses incessantly actualized by the inexhaustible heterogeneity of hearers and readers. But things are considerably more complex even than that, and not only because the once corporeal Jesus now possesses the power to manifest himself incorporeally and hence multiplicitously. New Testament scholars are fastidious curators of the differences *between* the Synoptic Jesuses. They are less attentive to the differences *within* each Synoptic Jesus—not to mention the differences within the Composite Christ, the

Synoptic (and Johannine) amalgam with whom the rest of the gospel-reading world is content to commune.

Channeling Deleuze once more, one might affirm that "two bodies coexist" within the Pan-Synoptic Composite Christ, "each of which reacts upon and enters into the other: a body of judgment, with its ... differentiations ... its hierarchies"—

> "For the Son of Man is to come with his angels in the glory of his Father, and then he will repay everyone for what has been done" (Matt 16:27)

> "All the nations will be gathered before him, and he will separate people one from another as a shepherd separates the sheep from the goats" (Matt 25:32)

> "I confer on you, just as my Father has conferred on me, a kingdom ... and you will sit on thrones judging the twelve tribes of Israel" (Luke 22:29–30)

"but also a body of justice in which the ... differentiations [are] lost, and the hierarchies thrown into confusion"—

> "Among the Gentiles ... their rulers lord it over them, and their great ones are tyrants over them. But it is not so among you.... For the Son of Man came not to be served but to serve" (Mark 10:41–45)

> "I was hungry and you gave me food ... thirsty and you gave me something to drink ... naked and you gave me clothing ... in prison and you visited me.... Truly I tell you, just as you did it to one of the least of these ... you did it to me" (Matt 25:35–36, 40)

> "Blessed are you who are poor.... But woe to you who are rich" (Luke 6:20, 24)

"a body that retains nothing but intensities that make up uncertain zones"—

> "He broke it ... and said, 'Take; this is my body.' Then he took a cup, and ... all of them drank from it. He said ... 'This is my blood' " (Mark 14:22–24);

> "Jesus himself came near and went with them, but their eyes were kept from recognizing him" (Luke 24:15–16);

> "Why are you frightened, and why do doubts arise in your heart? Look at my hands and my feet; see that it is I myself " (Luke 24:38–39)

"[a body] that traverse[s] these zones ... and confront[s] the powers in them, [an] anarchic body" (Deleuze [1993] 1997, 131). These two incorporeal Jesus bodies—the body of judgment and the body of justice—perpetually confront and constrain each other within and across the Synoptic Gospels. And each reader actualizes both of them simultaneously and incompletely, and lives both of them in contradiction.

I turn back, finally, to the intricate, occluded operations of the textbody-readerbody assemblage. What kind of conjoined body or symbiotic entity does a Synoptic Gospel and its reader form? "With what can we compare [it], or what parable will we use for it?" (Mark 4:30; see also Luke 13:18). A Synoptic Gospel—like any canonical gospel, like any scriptural text, bloated with readings, insatiable for interpretations—may be likened to a tick. "Attracted by the light, [it] hoists itself up to the tip of a branch; it is sensitive to the smell of mammals, and lets itself fall when one passes beneath . . . ; it digs into its skin, at the least hairy place it can find. Just three affects; the rest of the time the tick sleeps . . . indifferent to all that goes on in the immense forest" (Deleuze and Guattari 1987, 257). But perhaps Deleuze and Guattari's parable of the orchid and the wasp (10) better captures the intricate interactivity of the Gospel-reader assemblage. Let the orchid be the Gospel and let the wasp be the reader. Certain orchids cunningly simulate the body parts and pheromones of female wasps, impelling maddened male wasps to attempt copulation with them, the males thereby becoming unwitting vehicles for the orchid's pollen as they visit, and fertilize, other orchids. Effectively, the wasp becomes a cog in an alien organic machine: the orchid's reproductive apparatus. Analogously, the unwitting reader mistakes the Synoptic Gospel for something human (it's not; it's nonsentient matter through and through) and attempts to unite with it—to enter it, or, alternatively, to draw it into her body: interspecies copulation. In the process, the Gospel propagates, ensures its perpetuation. Manifested in this unnatural mating dance and its consummation, especially when viewed in the longue durée of Christian history, is the "aparallel evolution" of two bodies "that have absolutely nothing to do with each other" (10).

And that, ultimately, is why there are no human bodies in the Synoptic Gospels, or even any representations of human bodies: the very concept of "representation" blindly glosses over the irreducible difference between text and reader. The abstract surface squiggles that constitute the Synoptic Gospels have even less to do with human bodies, ontologically speaking, than orchids have to do with wasps. Wasps and orchids, readers and texts, Gospels and communities of reception are all "interkingdoms, unnatural participations" (Deleuze and Guattari 1987, 242). They can be understood only in terms of symbiosis. And in this ceaseless symbiotic process, each unalike body—the textual body, the readerly body (never as solitary as it feels itself to be), the corporate body of readers-in-community (often pack-like and prone to contagion)—constantly becomes more and other than what it was, and always in communion with what it is not.

References

Askin, Ridvan. 2016. *Narrative and Becoming*. Plateaus—New Directions in Deleuze Studies. Edinburgh, UK: Edinburgh University Press.

Auerbach, Erich. [1946] 1953. *Mimesis: The Representation of Reality in Western Literature*. Translated by Willard R. Trask. Princeton: Princeton University Press.

Avalos, Hector, Sarah J. Melcher, and Jeremy Schipper. 2007. Introduction to *This Abled Body: Rethinking Disabilities in Biblical Studies*, edited by Hector Avalos, Sarah J. Melcher, and Jeremy Schipper, 1–11. Semeia Studies 55. Atlanta: Society of Biblical Literature.

Balberg, Mira. 2014. *Purity, Body, and Self in Early Rabbinic Literature*. Berkeley: University of California Press.

Bryant, Levi R. 2012, October 18. "The Strange Ontology of Incorporeal Machines: Writing." *Larval Subjects*. https://larvalsubjects.wordpress.com/2012/10/18/the-strange-ontology-of-incorporeal-machines-writing/.

Butler, Judith. 1990. *Gender Trouble: Feminism and the Subversion of Identity*. New York: Routledge.

Butler, Judith. 2004. *Undoing Gender*. New York: Routledge.

Choi, Jin Young. 2015. *Postcolonial Discipleship of Embodiment: An Asian and Asian American Feminist Reading of the Gospel of Mark*. Postcolonialism and Religions. New York: Palgrave Macmillan.

Conway, Colleen M. 2008. *Behold the Man: Jesus and Greco-Roman Masculinity*. New York: Oxford University Press.

DeLanda, Manuel. 2016. *Assemblage Theory*. Speculative Realism. Edinburgh, UK: Edinburgh University Press.

Deleuze, Gilles. [1968] 1994. *Difference and Repetition*. Translated by Paul Patton. European Perspectives. New York: Columbia University Press.

Deleuze, Gilles. [1969] 1990. *The Logic of Sense*. Edited by Constantin V. Boundas. Translated by Mark Lester with Charles Stivale. New York: Columbia University Press.

Deleuze, Gilles. [1993] 1997. *Essays Critical and Clinical*. Translated by Daniel W. Smith and Michael A. Greco. Minneapolis: University of Minnesota Press.

Deleuze, Gilles, and Félix Guattari. [1980] 1987. *A Thousand Plateaus: Capitalism and Schizophrenia*. Translated by Brian Massumi. Minneapolis: University of Minnesota Press.

Ferrari, Gloria. 2009. Introduction to *Bodies and Boundaries in Graeco-Roman Antiquity*, edited by Thorsten Fögen and Mireille M. Lee, 1–9. Berlin: De Gruyter.

Fewell, Danna Nolan, ed. 2016. *The Oxford Handbook of Biblical Narrative*. New York: Oxford University Press.

Foucault, Michel. [1968] 1983. *This Is Not a Pipe*. Translated and edited by James Harkness. Berkeley: University of California Press.

Foucault, Michel. [1984] 1985. *The History of Sexuality*. Vol. 2. *The Use of Pleasure*. Translated by Robert Hurley. New York: Pantheon Books.

Foucault, Michel. [1984] 1986. *The History of Sexuality*. Vol. 3. *The Care of the Self*. Translated by Robert Hurley. New York: Pantheon Books.

Glancy, Jennifer A. 2010. *Corporal Knowledge: Early Christian Bodies*. New York: Oxford University Press.

Gleason, Maud W. 1995. *Making Men: Sophists and Self-Presentation in Ancient Rome*. Princeton: Princeton University Press.

Gleason, Maud W. 2003. "By Whose Gender Standards (If Anybody's) Was Jesus a Real Man?" In *New Testament Masculinities*, edited by Stephen D. Moore and Janice Capel Anderson, 325–27. Semeia Studies 45. Atlanta: Society of Biblical Literature.

Gundry, Robert H. 1976. *Sōma in Biblical Theology: With Emphasis on Pauline Anthropology*. Society for New Testament Studies Monograph Series 29. Cambridge: Cambridge University Press.

Lamb, Gregory E. 2017. "Sinfully Stereotyped: Jesus's Desire to Correct Ancient Physiognomic Assumptions in the Gospel According to Luke." *Word & World* 37, no. 2: 177–85.

Lawrence, Louise J. 2013. *Sense and Stigma in the Gospels: Depictions of Sensory-Disabled Characters*. Biblical Refigurations. New York: Oxford University Press.

Martin, Dale B. 1995. *The Corinthian Body*. New Haven: Yale University Press.

Montserrat, Dominic. 1998. Introduction to *Changing Bodies, Changing Meanings: Studies on the Human Body in Antiquity*, edited by Dominic Montserrat, 1-9. New York: Routledge.

Moss, Candida R., and Jeremy Schipper. 2011. Introduction to *Disability Studies and Biblical Literature*, edited by Candida R. Moss and Jeremy Schipper, 1–12. New York: Palgrave Macmillan.

Nigianni, Chrysanthi, and Merl Storr. 2009. "Introduction . . . So as to Know 'Us' Better." In *Deleuze and Queer Theory*, edited by Chrysanthi Nigianni and Merl Storr, 1–10. Deleuze Connections. Edinburgh: Edinburgh University Press.

Parsons, Mikeal C. 2006. *Body and Character in Luke and Acts: The Subversion of Physiognomy in Early Christianity*. Grand Rapids: Baker Academic.

Robinson, Brian J. 2019. *Being Subordinate Men: Paul's Rhetoric of Gender and Power in 1 Corinthians*. Lanham, MD: Lexington Books.

Robinson, John A. T. 1952. *The Body: A Study in Pauline Theology*. Studies in Biblical Theology 5. London: SCM Press.

Ruffolo, David V. 2016. *Post-queer Politics*. Queer Interventions. New York: Routledge.

Schipper, Jeremy. 2016. "Plotting Bodies in Biblical Narrative." In *The Oxford Handbook of Biblical Narrative*, edited by Danna Nolan Fewell, 389-97. New York: Oxford University Press.

Schneemelcher, Wilhelm, ed. 1992. *New Testament Apocrypha*, vol. 2, *Writings Relating to the Apostles; Apocalypses and Related Subjects*. Translated by R. McL. Wilson. Rev. ed. Louisville: Westminster John Knox.

Schreiner, Patrick. 2016. *The Body of Jesus: A Spatial Analysis of the Kingdom in Matthew*. Library of New Testament Studies 555. New York: Bloomsbury T&T Clark.

Schweizer, Eduard. [1964] 1971. "Sōma, ktl." In *Theological Dictionary of the New Testament*, edited by Gerhard Kittel and Gerhard Friedrich, translated by Geoffrey W. Bromiley, vol. 7, 1024–93. Grand Rapids: Eerdmans.

Solevåg, Anna Rebecca. 2018. *Negotiating the Disabled Body: Representations of Disability in Early Christian Texts*. Early Christianity and Its Literature 23. Atlanta: SBL Press.

Spinoza, Baruch. [1677] 2002. *Ethics*. In *Spinoza: The Complete Works*, edited by Michael L. Morgan, translated by Samuel Shirley, 213-382. Indianapolis: Hackett.

Wilson, Brittany E. 2015. *Unmanly Men: Refigurations of Masculinity in Luke-Acts*. New York: Oxford University Press.

Index

For the benefit of digital users, indexed terms that span two pages (e.g., 52–53) may, on occasion, appear on only one of those pages.

Tables and figures are indicated by *t* and *f* following the page number

Acts of John, 205, 206–12, 213, 214–15
Acts of John by Prochorus, 214–15
Acts of John in Rome, 205, 213–15, 214*t*
Acts of Peter, 206–7
Acts of Thomas, 206–7
Acts of Timothy, 197, 205, 216–20
afterlife. *See* resurrection and afterlife
Against Heresies (Irenaeus), 181–82, 192, 194
agency, 115, 146, 285, 368, 561–62, 575–78
Ahearne-Kroll, Stephen, 250–51, 507–8
Aichele, George, 144
Aland, Barbara, 166–67
Aland, Kurt, 18, 154n.5, 166–67
Albl, Martin, 517
Alexander the Great, 338–39, 394, 395
Allison, Dale C., 380, 383, 436–37
allusions, 54, 72–73, 232–33, 250, 363, 476, 500, 508, 511–12, 514–15, 517, 518–19, 521
ancient composition sources. *See* sources in ancient compositions
Ancient Literacy (Harris), 120–21
ancient rhetoric. *See also* oral tradition and writing
  activities and forms in, 65–66, 69–71
  Bartimaeus healed and, 67–68, 68*t*, 72–73, 76–77
  biblical rhetoric and, 67–69, 68*t*
  biographical portrayal and, 74
  blind men healed and, 69–78, 70*t*
  cautions for, 77–78
  clarity in, 75–76
  conciseness in, 75–76
  education in, 64–65
  epideictic form in, 72

  FH and, 63–64, 66–67, 76–77
  gender and, 551–52, 556
  Greek rhetoric in, 64–67
  imitation and, 66–67
  including everything necessary and, 76–77
  Israel's Scriptures and, 520–21
  literary dependence and, 63–64, 65–67, 68–78
  Mark and, 69–77
  Markan priority and, 69, 77–78
  Matthew and, 69–77
  narrative design and, 69–71, 72, 75
  oral performance and, 120–21, 127–28
  overview of, xv–xvi, 63–64
  Paul and, 64, 84
  petitio/δεήσις form in, 72
  plausibility in, 75–76
  progymnasmata texts and, 64–65, 69
  reasons for selecting specific forms in, 65–66
  rhetorical criticism and, 64, 68–69, 78
  Roman rhetoric in, 64–67
  Synoptic Problem and, xv–xvi, 20, 63–69
  2DH and, 73–74, 76–77
  utilitas causae principle in, 71
Antiquities (Josephus), 48–50, 309–10, 384–85, 489–90
Apocalypse of Peter, 206, 426
Apocalypse of Weeks, 423
apocalyptic eschatology
  definition of, 412–14
  determinism and, 415, 418, 423
  dualism and, 415, 418–20, 425
  future orientation of, 416

apocalyptic eschatology (*cont.*)
  judgment and, 420–21, 425–26
  Kingdom of God and, 416–17, 424–25
  Luke and, 416–24
  Mark and, 416–24
  Matthew and, 416–24
  messianic expectation and, 421–24, 426
  overview of, 412
  parousia and, 422–24
  Paul and, 413, 424
  precursors to, 414–15
  punishment and, 420–21, 425–26
  resurrection and afterlife and, 440–43
  reward and, 420–21, 425–26
  Son of Man and, 419, 421–24, 426–27
  Thomas and, 236–37
  wider context of, 424–27
apocryphal narratives. *See also* Thomas
  as analogies, 212–15
  compositional processes and, 204–5, 212–15
  fluidity of, 204–5, 216
  literary dependence and, 214–15
  Luke and, 204–12
  Mark and, 204–12
  Matthew and, 204–12
  overview of, 204–5
  reception of, 204–12
  redaction and, 204–5, 212–13, 214–15, 216–20
  Synoptic Problem and, 215
  transfiguration narrative and, 205–12
Apostolic Decree, 494–97, 501
Aquila, 48
Aristarchus of Samothrace, 189–90
Aristotle, 68–69, 140–41, 297, 301, 546
Arnal, William, 304, 324–25
assemblages, 577, 581
Augustine
  canons and, 3–4
  literary dependence and, 3–4, 6
  Synoptic Problem and, 3–5, 6, 18
authored texts, Gospels as, 175–76, 192–96, 197
authority. *See* kingdom, authority, and power
Avalos, Hector, 267–68

Bailey, Kenneth, 129
Bainbridge, William, 470–71
Balberg, Mira, 566

Bang, Peter, 300
baptism of Jesus, 32, 140–41, 373, 510
Barrett, C. K., 383
Barthes, Roland, 144
Bartimaeus healed, 67–68, 68t, 72–73, 76–77, 361, 362
Bartlet, Vernon, 37
Bauckham, Richard, 177
Baum, Armin, 113–14
Baumgarten, Albert, 470
Baur, F. C., 7–8, 12–13
Bazzana, Giovanni, 304, 305, 324–26
Beardsley, Monroe, 138
Beatitudes, 227, 228, 256, 304–5, 310–11, 421, 511–12
Behind the Third Gospel (Taylor), 37
Behold the Man (Conway), 569
Being Subordinate Men (Robinson), 568
Ben Sira, 186, 190–91, 305
Bergemann, Thomas, 111–12
Berger, Klaus, 72
Berrigan, Daniel, 284–85
Bible in Ancient and Modern Media Group, 120, 123, 125
biblical performance criticism, 123–25
biblical rhetoric, 67–69, 68t
Black, Max, 443–44
Blenkinsopp, J., 469–70
blind men healed, 69–78, 70t
Blinzler, Joseph, 206–7, 211
Bock, Darrell, 139
Body, The (Robinson), 565
the body
  agency and, 575–78
  ancient bodies, 565–68
  assemblages and, 577, 581
  autonomy and, 549–50
  constructionism and, 567–68, 571–72
  education and, 571
  gender and, 569–72
  healing and exorcism and, 365–67
  incorporeal bodies, 573–81
  insubstantial bodies, 565–68
  overview of, 565–66
  Paul and, 566–67
  performativity of, 568–73
Body of Jesus, The (Schreiner), 568–69

INDEX

Bogel, Fredric, 139, 144
Boismard, Marie-Emile, 18, 114
Book of Watchers, 415
books, Gospels as, 176–77, 192–96, 197
Books and Readers in the Early Church (Gamble), 177, 180
Boomershine, Thomas, 120, 121, 125
Botha, Pieter, 126
Bovon, François, 91–92, 204–6, 212–13, 252
Bremmer, Jan, 217n.21, 345
Brinkema, Eugenie, 146
Brookins, Timothy, 298–99
Bruster, Douglas, 137n.3
Bultmann, Rudolf, 365, 468
Burkett, Delbert, 114–15, 206
Burridge, Richard, 145n.11
Burton, Ernest DeWitt, 28–30, 32, 33–35
Butler, B. C., 14–15, 18–19, 568
Butler, Judith, 547, 568, 569

Campbell, Douglas, 456–57
Cancik, Hubert, 395
canon incorporation, 194–96
Capper, Brian, 456n.4
Carey, Greg, 56n.26
Carruthers, Mary, 54
Carter, Warren, 260n.1, 261, 267–68, 286–87
Cavallin, H. C. C., 434–35
Cerquiglini, Bernard, 185
Chaniotis, Angelos, 394
Choi, Young, 568–69
Christian history, 399–407
Christology, 39, 82, 291, 350, 426, 513, 515
Cicero, 69, 127–28, 254, 489
Clement of Alexandria, 194–95
Codex Bezae, 46, 166, 166t, 169–72, 185
Codex Bobiensis, 194, 198–99
Codex Ephraemi Syri Rescriptus, 163, 170–71
Codex Fuldensis, 51
Codex Sinaiticus, 164–66, 165t, 165f, 168–69, 170–71
Codex Vaticanus, 168–69, 170–72
Codex Washingtonianus, 185
Coffman, Kristofer, xviii
Collins, Adela Yarbro, 51, 303, 413n.1, 418–19, 458–59, 479–80
Collins, John J., 414, 435

composition, 204–5, 212–15. *See also* sources in ancient compositions
Conquergood, Dwight, 122, 131
Conservation and the Gospel of Efficiency (Hays), 451
Constitution and Law of the Church in the First Two, The (Harnack), 452–53
constructionism, 567–68, 571–72
Context Group, 120
Conway, Colleen, 569–70
Conzelmann, Hans, 422–23
Corinthian Body, The (Martin), 566–68
Corley, Kathleen, 344–45
Corporal Knowledge (Glancy), 572–73
Crabbe, Kylie, 423, 423n.5
Creed, J. M., 39–40
criticism. *See* form criticism; redaction criticism; source criticism; text criticism
Crossan, John, 269–70
Cullmann, Oscar, 431

Dalman, Gustaf, 376, 381
Damm, Alexander, 20, 65n.2, 113
dating. *See* publication and dating
Davies, Margaret, 379
Davies, W. D., 380, 383, 384
Davis, Philip, 254
Dead Sea Scrolls, 47, 415, 474, 516
De consensu evangelistarum (Augustine), 3–4
Deines, Roland, 306
Deleuze, Gilles, 575, 577, 578–81
Delling, Gerhard, 456n.4
de Man, Paul, 137
Denaux, Adelbert, 63n.1
De oratorio (Cicero), 127–28
Der Einfluss paulinischer Theologie im Markusevangelium (Werner), 82
Derrenbacker, Robert, 48–49
Derrida, Jacques, 144, 286, 575
design of narratives. *See* narrative design
Desjardins, Michel, 268, 270–71
de Ste. Croix, G. E. M., 145
determinism, 415, 418, 423
Deutero-Markus, 15–16, 17–18
De Wette, Wilhelm, 7
Dewey, Joanna, 126
Diatessaron (Tatian), 50–52

Dibelius, Martin, 247n.2, 253
Didache, 21, 191, 323–24, 330, 407, 497
Die synoptischen Evangelien
  (Holtzmann), 8–9
Dinkler, Michal Beth, xv–xvi, 231–32
Dio Cassius, 488–89
Dodd, C. H., 83–84, 267–68, 516
Donaldson, Terence, 488
double tradition, 9, 11–12, 13–14, 29–30,
  31–32, 36–37, 41–42, 102, 108–9,
  111–12, 115
Dover, K. J., 544
Dowling, Elisabeth, 500
Downing, F. Gerald, 20, 48, 49, 50, 53n.15
Draper, Jonathan, 129
Droysen, Johann G., 394
dualism, 367, 368, 382–83, 415, 418–20, 425. *See also* media dualism
Dube, Musa, 287–90, 293, 325–26
Dubrow, Heather, 137n.3
Dunn, James D. G., 87n.5, 112, 129, 479, 493

Ebner, Markus, 345
Ebner, Martin, 348
economy. *See* wealth, poverty, and economy
education, 44–45, 64–65, 120–21, 324, 375, 386, 395, 398, 570–71
Ehrman, Bart, 167
Eichhorn, Johann Gottfried, 5–6, 7, 100–1, 102–6, 107–8, 112, 114–15
Eisenbaum, Pamela, 493–94
Eliade, Mircea, 382–83
Elliott, J. Keith, 163n.20, 205–6
Elliott, Scott, 147
embodiment. *See* the body
empire-critical approaches, 283–86, 287–90, 292–93
Endsjø, Dag Øistein, 431–32
Enneads (Plotinus), 189
Ennulat, Andreas, 15–16, 17–18
Enoch, 433–35, 441, 445
envoys of God, 261–66, 274
Epic Cycle, 52–53
Epp, Eldon, 182, 185
eschatology. *See* apocalyptic eschatology
Esler, Philip, 469–70, 493
Eubank, Nathan, 308

Eusebius
  composition of Synoptic Gospels and, 3–4, 216, 219–20
  discrepancies among Gospels and, 3–4
  influence of, 4
  on Origen's early education and scriptorium, 46
  sources in ancient compositions and, 46
  Synoptic Problem and, 3–4
Eve, Eric, 54, 129
Ewald, Heinrich, 9
Exegeses of the Dominical Logia
  (Papias), 192–93
exorcism. *See* healing and exorcism

Fanning, Buist, 139
Farmer, William, 10, 14–15, 113
Farrer, Austin, 14
Farrer Hypothesis (FH)
  ancient rhetoric and, 63–64, 66–67, 76–77
  challenges to, 16–17, 19, 20
  development of, 14
  diagram of, 161f
  imitation and, 66–67
  manuscripts and, 171
  media dualism and, 115
  oral tradition and writing and, 115
  revival of, 14, 15–16
  Synoptic Problem and, 15–16, 18–19, 57, 115, 160, 161f
Fauconnier, Gilles, 443–44
Federico, Annette, 137–38, 145
Feine, Paul, 36–37, 41
feminist interpretations, 278, 283, 287–89
Ferrari, Gloria, 567
FH. *See* Farrer Hypothesis (FH)
Finkelberg, Margalit, 189–90
"First Century Mark," 176–77
Flavian period, 396, 398
Fleddermann, Harry, 304–5
Fletcher-Louis, Crispin H. T., 435, 441
flow of blood woman, 531–33
Foley, John Miles, 116, 121, 129
food and meals
  beginnings and, 343–44
  communal meals, 338–39, 341–42, 343, 344–45, 346–49, 352–53

Galilean ministry and, 344–46
Gentile regions ministry and, 346–47
Greek and Roman culture and, 338–40
Jerusalem journey and, 347–48
Last Supper tradition and, 350–51
Luke and, 341–43
Mark and, 341–43
Matthew and, 341–43
overview of, 338
Passion and death of Jesus and, 348–49
resurrection and ascension of Jesus and, 352
similarities and differences between Gospels and, 343–52
women and, 344–45
form criticism, 110–11, 119–20, 130, 227, 356
Foster, Paul, 472
Foster, Robert, 381–82
Foucault, Michel, 544, 567–68, 572, 575
Four Gospels, The (Streeter), 13–14, 27, 30, 111
Four-Source Hypothesis, 27–28, 28f, 158, 158f, 479–80
France, R. T., 88
Fredriksen, Paula, 495
Friesen, Steven, 298–300
Friesen-Longnecker economic scale, 298–300, 298t, 302, 313, 314–15
From Gospels to Garbage (Luijendijk), 185
Funk, Robert, 120

Galen, 187–89, 356–57, 546
Galilean ministry, 344–46
Galilee, 321–23
Gamble, Harry, 177, 180
Gathercole, Simon, 191–92
gender. *See also* women
    agonizing of, 547–48
    ancient medical perspectives and, 546–47
    ancient rhetoric and, 551–52, 556
    bodily autonomy and, 549–50
    body and, 569–72
    gift of *Logos* and, 548–49
    Greek and Roman culture and, 543–53
    Herod and, 556–58
    Jesus and, 556–58
    Luke and, 559–61
    Mark and, 553–56
    Mary and, 559–61
    Matthew and, 556–58
    overview of, 543–44
    sexual performance and, 544–46, 549
    virtue and, 550–53
    Zechariah and, 559–61
Gentile-Jewish relations
    early Jesus movement and, 492–97
    general situation during first century of, 486–89
    historical Jesus and, 492
    Jewish privileges and, 489–91
    Luke and, 497–502
    Mark and, 497–502
    Matthew and, 497–502
    overview of, 486–89
    Paul and, 492–97
    spaces of interaction and, 491–92
Gentile regions ministry, 346–47
Gerhardsson, Birger, 113–14
GH. *See* Griesbach Hypothesis (GH)
Gieseler, Carl Udwig
    feste Form and, 105–6
    media dualism and, 100–1, 107
    minor agreements and, 105–6
    oral tradition and writing and, 105–7
    Synoptic Problem and, 105–6
    translation variant hypothesis and, 106
    updating of, 113–14
    Urgospel of, 100–1, 105–7
Gillihan, Yonder, 472–73
Glancy, Jennifer A., 572–73
Gleason, Maud, 547, 567, 570–71
Goodacre, Mark, 16–17, 115, 154n.5, 161–62, 231
Goody, Jack, 120–21
Gorman, Heather, 65n.2
Gospel, meaning of
    etymology and, 451
    following rise of Christianity, 452–54
    in the Gospels, 458–64
    Luke and, 461–62
    Mark and, 458–61
    Matthew and, 462–64
    new way forward on question of, 454–58
    overview of, 451
    Paul as founder and proprietor, 454–58
    prior to rise of Christianity, 452
    Q and, 453, 459

Gospel and the Land (Davies), 384
Gospel harmonies, 3, 4–6, 50–52, 91, 92–93, 95, 166–67, 172
Gospel of Luke. *See* Luke
Gospel of Mark. *See* Mark
Gospel of Matthew. *See* Matthew
Gospel of Thomas. *See* Thomas
Gospel origins. *See* Gospel, meaning of; oral tradition and writing
Gospels as authored texts, 175–76, 192–96, 197
Gospels as books, 176–77, 192–96, 197
Gospels as published books, 177–78, 192–96
Goulder, Michael, 15–16, 19, 20, 115
Grant, F. C., 33
Great Commission, 89–90, 289
Greatest Commandment, 215
Greek and Roman culture, xvi–xvii, 64–67, 338–40, 392–98, 472–73, 487, 528–29, 543–53, 567
Greek rhetoric, 64–67
Gribetz, Sarit Kattan, 330
Griesbach, Johann Jakob
　harmonies and, 6
　literary dependence and, 6–7, 8
　Synoptic Problem and, 6–8, 19
　three-gospel synopsis of, 6–7
Griesbach Hypothesis (GH). *See also* Two Gospel Hypothesis (2GH)
　challenges to, 10
　decline in, 12–13
　diagram of, 58f
　media dualism and, 110–11, 113
　oral tradition and writing and, 105–7, 113
　revival of, 7, 14–15
　sources in ancient compositions and, 57
　Synoptic Problem and, 113
　theological development exemplified by, 7
Gruen, Erich, 489
Guattari, Félix, 54–577, 579–81
Gundry, Robert, 73, 73n.11, 74, 75–77, 75n.18, 76n.20, 565, 567

Halperin, David, 544–45, 567–68
harmonies of the Gospels, 3, 4–6, 50–52, 91, 92–93, 95, 166–67, 172
Harnack, Adolf von, 13, 323, 355, 359, 452–53, 464

Harris, William, 120–21
Hawkins, John, 27, 110–11
Hayes, Christine, 496
Hays, Richard B., 84
Hays, Samuel, 451
healing and exorcism
　allegiance demonstrations and, 363–65
　embodiment and, 365–67
　kingdom, authority, and power and, 291–92
　overview of, 355–63
　power demonstrations and, 363–65
　Q and, 357–58
　tyranny of transformation and, 365–67
Henderson, Jeffrey, 545
Hengel, Martin, 431–32, 463n.12
Herder, Johann Gottfried, 10, 100–2
hermeneutics, 83–89, 95, 119–20, 121, 122, 131–32, 228, 366, 367–68, 399, 402
Herod Antipas, 51–52, 262–63
Herod the Great, 126–27, 279–80, 281, 303, 345–46, 405–6, 508–9, 512–13, 556–58, 559–60
Herzog, William, 264, 267–70
Ḥever, Naḥal, 47
Hill, Charles, 182
Hippocrates, 188–89, 191, 359n.2, 364–65
historical Jesus. *See also* Jesus
　authenticity and, 129–30
　Gentile-Jewish relations and, 492
　Israel's Scriptures and, 520
　Jewish sectarianism and, 479, 481
　minor sources and, 27–28, 37
　oral performance and, 119–20, 129–30
　Q and, 13
　Synoptic Problem and, 5, 12–13, 152–53, 155
　Thomas and, 224–25
　travel and itinerancy and, 321–22
　violent imaginaries and, 271
historiography, 393–94, 395–96
history
　birth of Christian history, 399–407
　disclosing the past and, 399–400
　Greek and Roman culture and, 392–94, 396–98
　historian's task then and now and, 399–400
　historiography and, 393–94, 395–96
　literary invention of, 402–4

Luke's transformation of Mark and, 404–6
Mark and, 400–7
Matthew's transformation of Mark
    and, 406–7
oral tradition and writing and, 403
overview of, 392
Paul and, 400–2
periodization and, 394
prehistoriographical accounts and, 395–98
Q and, 401–2, 403
shaping and transforming literary memory
    and, 392, 393–94, 395–96, 400–4
time mastery and, 399–407
writing history, 392–94
History of Sexuality (Foucault), 567–68
Hobsbawm, Eric, 399–400
Holleman, Joost, 433–34, 436–37
Holmes, Brooke, 546–47
Holmes, Michael W., 182–83
Holtzmann, Heinrich Julius
    A and, 11–13
    criticism of, 10–11
    Hebrew Bible citations of, 11
    historical Jesus of, 12–13
    influences on, 9
    literary dependence and, 9–12
    Markan priority and, 11–12
    oral tradition and writing and, 110
    2DH established by, 8–9, 11–12
    Ur-Markus and, 9–10, 11–12
    utilization hypotheses and, 10
Holy Spirit, 94, 284, 290–91, 343–44, 423, 500–1, 536, 560–61
Homer, 52, 121, 189–90, 195
Homilies on Luke (Origen), 195–96
Hooker, Morna, 514
Horsley, Richard, 129–30, 285, 287, 323–24, 384, 468–69
Huck, Albert, 163
Huck-Greeven *Synopsis*, 163, 164–65, 164*t*, 167–69, 167*t*, 170–71
Hurtado, Larry, 182
Hylen, Susan, 552
hypotheses. *See* Farrer Hypothesis (FH); Four-Source Hypothesis; Griesbach Hypothesis (GH); Two Document Hypothesis (2DH),

Iamblichus, 479–80
Iliad (Homer), 52–53
illness, 76, 246–47, 360, 365
imaginaries. *See* violent imaginaries
imitation, 44–45, 53, 66–67, 84, 255
In Catena in Marcum, 196
Incigneri, Brian, 303
infancy narratives, 36, 37, 38–39, 40, 284, 417, 419, 422, 510–11, 512–13, 519, 521, 530, 536, 537–38
Ingold, Tim, 375
Insights from Performance Criticism (Perry), 122
Institutio Oratoria (Quintilian), 44–45, 53, 127–28, 397
International Q Project, 324
Irenaeus of Lyons, 181–82, 191, 192, 195–96
Israel's Scriptures
    allusions to, 508, 511–12, 514–15, 517, 518–19, 521
    ancient rhetoric and, 520–21
    citations of, 507–8, 509–10, 513–15, 517–18
    composite citation of, 517–18
    discussion of, 516–21
    exegetical techniques for, 517–21
    explicit uses of, 509–10
    focus on key words in, 520
    fulfillment quotations and, 510–11
    historical Jesus and, 520
    introductory formulae and, 510–11
    Luke and, 513–16
    Mark and, 507–9
    Matthew and, 509–13
    overview of, 506
    scripturally shaped narratives and, 519–20
    scriptural models and, 508–9, 512–13, 515–16
    selection of, 516
    speaking scriptural words and, 518
    specifying a general referent and, 518–19
    Synoptic Problem and, 517
    text form and, 517–18
itinerancy. *See* travel and itinerancy
Iverson, Kelly R., 498

Jerome, 195–96
Jerusalem journey, 347–48
Jerusalem school, 17

Jesus. *See also* historical Jesus
  baptism of, 32, 140–41, 373, 510
  character of, 229–30
  food and meals and, 348–49, 352
  gender and, 556–58
  Gentile-Jewish relations and, 492–97
  Passion and death of, 35–36, 38, 40, 348–49, 435–36, 498
  resurrection and ascension of, 352, 435–39
  suffering and sacrifice of, 247–54
  violent imaginaries and, 261–66
Jesus Remembered (Dunn), 129
Jesus Seminar, 120
Jewett, Robert, 456–57
Jewish-Gentile relations. *See* Gentile-Jewish relations
Jewish-Roman War (66–70 CE), 89, 145, 393, 490–91
Jewish sectarianism
  definition of, 469–73
  Greek and Roman culture and, 472–73
  historical Jesus and, 479, 481
  Luke and, 478–81
  Mark and, 478–81
  Matthew and, 473–78
  overview of, 468–69
  Paul and, 471–72
  Q and, 479
  Thomas and, 479
  2DH and, 473
Jewish War (Josephus), 190–91
Johnson, Benton, 470
Johnson, Mark, 443–44
Johnson, William, xv–xvi
John the Baptist, 9–10, 18, 126–27, 156–58, 225, 262–63, 265, 273, 282–83, 284, 343–44, 345–46, 352–53, 403–4, 405, 416, 421–22, 439, 508–9, 510, 559
Jokiranta, Jutta, 471
Jonge, Marinus de, 435–36
Josephus
  Gentiles-Jewish relations and, 488, 489–92
  history and, 393, 394, 396, 398
  Israel's Scriptures and, 512–13
  Jewish sectarianism and, 469, 479–81
  resurrection and afterlife and, 432
  sources in ancient compositions and, 48–50
Judas, 5, 11, 147, 282, 510–11, 512

judgment, 420–21, 425–26
Junod, Eric, 210n.8, 214–15

Kaestli, Jean-Daniel, 210n.8, 214–15
Kähler, Martin, 145
Käsemann, Ernst, 454
Kay, Philip, 300
Keddie, Anthony, 305
Keith, Chris, 130–31, 132
Kelber, Werner, 119–20, 126
Kellermann, Ulrich, 433–34
Kilpatrick, M., 33
kingdom, authority, and power
  earthly power and, 279–80
  empire-critical approaches to, 283–86, 287–90, 292–93
  feminist interpretations of, 278, 283, 287–89
  future directions for, 292–93
  healing and exorcism and, 291–92
  heavenly power and, 279–80
  imperial power and, 281–83
  Mark and, 284–86
  Matthew and, 286–90
  overview of, 278–79
  resistance to, 281–83
  spiritual power and, 290–92
Kingdom of God, 92–93, 223–24, 247, 278, 373, 376–84, 416–17, 424–25, 441–42, 492–93
Kingdom of Heaven, 380–82
Kingdom of Satan, 382–84
Kingsbury, Jack Dean, 140–41
Kinzig, Wolfram, 194–95
Kirk, Alan, xv–xvi, 20, 54, 56
Klinghardt, Matthias, 338–40
Kloppenborg, John, 63–64, 113, 158n.9, 271–72, 302, 304, 324–26, 479, 492
Knott, Kim, 375
Koester, Helmet, 182, 479
Koppe, J. B., 6
Kotrosits, Maia, 145
Krause, Deborah, 519–20

L
  coherence and unity of, 35–37, 41
  decreased scholarly interest in, 40, 41–42
  estimates of, 27, 35–36, 40
  Four-Source Hypothesis and, 27–28
  infancy narratives in, 40

Jewish Christian character of, 36–37, 41
oral tradition and writing and, 39–40, 41
origin of, 35–37, 41
overview of, 35–41
Q and, 36–37
reconstructions of, 35–36, 40–41
renewed scholarly interest in, 40
Synoptic Problem and, 36–37, 41–42
theological character of, 36
wealth, poverty, and economy and, 311–14
Lachmann, Karl, 7–8
Lachmann fallacy, 14–15
Lakoff, George, 443–44
Lamb, William R. S., 196
Laqueur, Thomas, 546
Larsen, Matthew, xvi, 143–44
Last, Richard, 491
Last Supper, 91–94, 350–51, 568–69
Leander, Hans, 289
Lee, Kristi, xviii
Lehtipuu, Outi, 431–32, 441, 442
Lessing, Gottfried
  harmonies criticized by, 5–6
  Matthew and, 5–6
  media dualism and, 100–1
  Synoptic Problem and, 5–6, 7
  Urgospel and, 10, 100–2
Levine, Caroline, 140
Levinson, Marjorie, 137–38
Liew, Tat-siong Benny, 146, 147, 148, 285–86
Life of Apollonius (Philostratus), 192–93
Lipsius, R. A., 214–15
literary dependence. *See also* Markan priority
  ancient rhetoric and, 63–64, 65–67, 68–78
  apocryphal narratives and, 214–15
  challenges to, 153
  consensus on, 10
  Gospel harmonies and, 5
  manuscripts and, xvi, 152–53
  oral tradition and writing and, xv–xvi, 7, 10
  overview of, xv–xvi
  Paul and, 7, 82
  publication and dating and, 182–83, 198
  traditional assumptions about, xvi
  Urgospel and, 5–6, 7
  utilization hypotheses and, 7, 10
literary memory, 392, 393–94, 395–96, 400–4
Liu, Jinyu, 297

Logos, 548–49
Lord, Alfred, 121
Lord's Prayer, 305, 417
Lotman, Jurij, 141n.6
Luedemann, Gerd, 456–57
Luke. *See also* Proto-Luke
  apocalyptic eschatology and, 416–24
  apocryphal narratives and, 204–12
  food and meals and, 341–43
  gender and, 559–61
  Gentile-Jewish relations and, 497–502
  Gospel and, meaning of, 461–62
  history and, 404–6
  Israel's Scriptures and, 513–16
  Jewish sectarianism and, 478–81
  Lukan priority not defended for, 10
  narrative design and, 140–42
  oral performance and, 125–30
  Paul's influence on, 91–95
  sacred space and, 387–88
  sources in ancient compositions and, 52–54
  suffering and sacrifice and, 252–54
  travel and itinerancy and, 331–34
  wealth, poverty, and economy and, 310–11
Luz, Ulrich, 73, 74n.12, 74n.15, 75–76, 89–90, 112

M
  as adulterated source, 32
  anti-Gentile aspects of, 33
  decreased scholarly interest in, 33–34, 41–42
  estimates of, 27, 31–32, 33
  Four-Source Hypothesis and, 27–28
  humility as a result of approaching, 34–35
  Judaistic sayings in, 30–32, 33, 34–35
  lack of coherence in, 32
  list of contents of, 29–30, 29t
  micro-conflation in, 32
  oral tradition and writing and, 32, 33–34
  origin of, 28–29, 30–31, 32–33
  overview of, 28–35
  Paul and, 30–31, 32
  pro-Gentile aspects of, 33
  Q and, 28–32, 33
  reconstructions of, 31–33
  Synoptic Problem and, 41–42
Maccabees, 245, 433–35, 440–41, 445
MacCormack, E. R., 443–44

Magness, J. Lee, 143
Malbon, Elizabeth Struthers, 375
Manson, T. W.
  commentary by, 31–32
  influence of, 34–35
  L and, 39–40
  M and, 31–32, 33–35
  micro-conflation and, 32
  oral tradition and writing and, 32, 39–40
  Proto-Luke and, 39–40
  Q and, 32
  reconstruction of, 31–32
manuscripts
  FH and, 171
  Gospel harmonies and, 167–70
  instability of Greek in, 163–64
  literary dependence and, xvi, 152–53
  overview of, 152–53
  parallels in, 153–72, 155t, 156t, 157t, 159t, 162t, 164t, 165f, 165t, 166t, 167t, 168t, 169t
  problem of, 161–71
  stable texts tradition and, 152–53, 161–62, 163–64, 171–72
  Synoptic Problem and, 152–61, 171–72
  textual fluidity and, 152–53, 163–64
  2DH and, 171
Marcion, 7, 21, 464
Marcus, Joel, 72–73, 81, 82–83, 377–78, 380, 383, 418–19, 507
Marguerat, Daniel, 142–43
Mark. See also Proto-Mark
  ancient rhetoric and, 69–77
  apocalyptic eschatology and, 416–24
  apocryphal narratives and, 204–12
  food and meals and, 341–43
  gender and, 553–56
  Gentile-Jewish relations and, 497–502
  Gospel and, meaning of, 458–61
  history and, 400–6
  Israel's Scriptures and, 507–9
  Jewish sectarianism and, 478–81
  kingdom, authority, and power and, 284–86
  Luke's transformation of, 404–6
  Matthew's transformation of, 69–77, 406–7
  narrative design and, 140–48
  oral performance and, 126–28
  Paul's influence on, xv–xvi, 82–89, 95
  sacred space and, 387–88
  sources in ancient compositions and, 52–54
  suffering and sacrifice and, 250–52
  travel and itinerancy and, 326–28
  wealth, poverty, and economy and, 301–4
Markan posteriority, 7, 14–15
Markan priority
  ancient rhetoric and, 69, 77–78
  oral tradition and writing and, 113–14
  proto-Mark and, 13–14
  Q and, 14
  questioning of, 14–15
  sources in ancient compositions and, 54, 56
  Synoptic Problem and, 13, 18, 21
  2DH and, 13–14
  Urgospel and, 7
Mark as Story (Rhoads, Dewey, and Michie), 126, 143
Marks, Susan, 344–45
Marshall, I. Howard, 382–83
Martha, 538–40
Martial, 53–54, 297–98
Martin, Dale B., 566–68
Martyrdom of Polycarp, The, 191
Mary, mother of Jesus, 535–38, 559–61
Mary Magdalene, 533–35
Mason, Steve, 454–55
Matthaean posteriority, 17
Matthew. See also Proto-Matthew
  ancient rhetoric and, 69–77
  apocalyptic eschatology and, 416–24
  apocryphal narratives and, 204–12
  food and meals and, 341–43
  gender and, 556–58
  Gentile-Jewish relations and, 497–502
  Gospel and, meaning of, 462–64
  history and, 406–7
  Israel's Scriptures and, 509–13
  Jewish sectarianism and, 473–78
  kingdom, authority, and power and, 286–90
  Mark transformed by, 69–77, 406–7
  narrative design and, 140–42
  oral performance and, 128–30
  Paul's influence on, xv–xvi, 89–90, 95
  sacred space and, 387–88
  sources in ancient compositions and, 52–54
  travel and itinerancy and, 328–30
  wealth, poverty, and economy and, 307–10
McAdon, Brad, 66–67

meals. *See* food and meals
meaning of Gospel. *See* Gospel, meaning of
media dualism
  FH and, 115
  GH and, 110–11, 113
  multiple-source hypothesis and, 114–15
  oral hypothesis and, 113–14
  oral tradition and writing and, 100–1, 107–8, 110, 111–17
  overcoming of, 115–17
  persistence of, 111–15
  Q and, 111–12, 114
  Synoptic Problem and, 112–15
  2DH and, 111–13
  Urgospel and, 100–2
Meijboom, Hajo Uden, 7n.4, 12
messianic expectation, 421–24, 426
Metzger, Bruce, 167, 168–69
Meynet, Roland, 67–69, 67n.5, 69n.6, 72–73
Michie, Donald, 126
minor agreements (MAs), 9, 11–12, 15–16, 17–18, 376
minor sources. *See also* L; M; Q; sources in ancient compositions
  demise of, 41–42
  historical Jesus and, 27–28, 37
  overview of, 27–28
  Synoptic Problem and, 28, 41–42
  terminology of, 27
miracles, xvi–xvii, 82, 87, 93–94, 140–41, 210–11, 217–18, 347, 355–56, 439, 508–9
Mission Discourse, 32
Mitchell, Margaret M., 84–86, 177
Moessner, David, 215n.15
Mohn, Kendra Allison, 556
Montserrat, Dominic, 566
Moore, Stephen, 286, 287
Moxne, Halvor, 325, 378, 383–84
Mroczek, Eva, 186
Muratorian canon, 193
Murphy-O'Connor, Jerome, 456–57
Musonius Rufus, 551

narrative design
  affordances and, 144
  agency and, 146
  ancient rhetoric and, 69–71, 72, 75
  distributional matrix and, 146
  fallacy of formal generalization and, 144
  Freytag's pyramid and, 140–41
  literary turn and, 136
  Luke and, 140–42
  Mark and, 140–48
  Matthew and, 140–42
  New Criticism and, 136–37, 138, 145
  New Formalism and, 137–40, 142–48
  oral performance and, 127
  overview of, 136–37
  poststructuralism and, 144
  sense of suspended endings and, 142–48
  story and discourse distinguished in, 141–42
Narrative Space and Mythic Meaning in Mark (Malbon), 375
Neirynck, Franz, 7, 15–16, 41–42, 112
Nestle-Aland, 163, 164–65, 168–70, 168*t*, 169*t*
Network of Biblical Storytellers, 125
Neusner, Jacob, 469–70
New, David, 9n.5
New Criticism, 136–37, 138, 145
New Formalism, xv–xvi, 137–40, 142–48
New Testament in the Original Greek, The (Westcott and Hort), 179
Nickelsburg, George W. E., 433–34, 435–36
Nolland, John, 436–37
Nongbri, Brent, xvi, 191–92, 194

O'Brien, Kelli, 136
Odyssey (Homer), 52–53
Ong, Walter, 119
On My Own Books (Galen), 187–88
oral performance
  ancient rhetoric and, 120–21, 127–28
  applause markers and, 127–28
  authenticity and, 129–30, 131–32
  biblical performance criticism and, 123–25
  exegetical ethos and, 131
  historical Jesus and, 119–20, 129–30
  impact and influence of criticism of, 130–32
  literacy and, 120–21
  Luke and, 128–30
  Mark and, 126–28
  Matthew and, 128–30
  narrative design and, 127
  overview of, xv–xvi, 119
  performance criticism and, 121–26, 127, 128–29, 130–32

oral performance (*cont.*)
    problem of, 119
    Q and, 129–30
    redaction and, 128–29, 130
    response to problem of, 119–21
    sources in ancient compositions and, 52
    steps in performance of biblical texts and, 123–25
    Synoptic Problem and, 128–29
    Thomas and, 130
oral tradition and writing. *See also* ancient rhetoric
    early synoptic scholarship and, 100–11
    Eichhorn and, 100–1, 102–5
    evangelists as redactors and, 107–10
    FH and, 115
    GH and, 105–7, 113
    Herder and, 100–2
    history and, 403
    informal and controlled theory of, 129
    L and, 39–40, 41
    Lessing and, 100–2
    literary dependence and, xv–xvi, 7, 10
    M and, 32, 33–34
    Markan priority and, 113–14
    media dualism and, 100–1, 107–8, 110, 111–17
    memory and, 110
    oral hypothesis and, 107, 109, 110, 113–14
    overview of, xv–xvi, 100–1
    primordiality and, 110
    redaction and, 100–1, 107–10, 111
    sources in ancient compositions and, 54
    Synoptic Problem and, xv–xvi, 100–1, 113–14
    translation variant hypothesis and, 103–4, 106
    2DH and, 111–13
    Urgospel and, 5–6, 10, 100–7
    utilization hypotheses and, 100–1
    Wilke and, 100–1, 107–10
Origen
    conflations by, 54
    education and scriptorium of, 46
    publication and dating and, 194–96
    sources in ancient compositions and, 46
    Synoptic Problem and, 3
Osiander, Alfons, 5
Ottenheijm, Eric, 347–48

Overman, J. Andrew, 469–70, 471–72
Oxford Handbook of Biblical Narrative, The (Fewell), 568
Oxford Studies in the Synoptic Problem (Sanday), 12, 37

Paffenroth, K., 40–41, 42
Pamment, Margaret, 381
Papias, 7–8, 9–10, 194
"Papyri, Ethics, and Economics" (Mazza), 185
Parker, David, 161n.17, 179, 182, 186, 193
Parker, P., 33
parousia, 206, 327–28, 402, 421–24, 426–27
Parry, Milman, 121
Parsons, Mikeal, 461n.9
Passion narratives, 35–36, 38, 40, 348–49, 435–36, 498
Paul
    accidental Paulism, 89–90, 95
    ancient rhetoric and, 64, 84
    anticipation and, 86–89
    apocalyptic eschatology and, 413, 424
    body and, 566–67
    etiological hermeneutic of, 83–89
    exorcism and, 88–89
    as founder and proprietor of Gospel, 454–58
    Gentile-Jewish relations and, 492–97
    Great Commission and, 89–90
    history and, 400–2
    Jewish sectarianism and, 471–72
    Last Supper and, 91–94
    literary dependence and, 7, 82
    Luke influenced by, 91–95
    M and, 30–31, 32
    Mark influenced by, xv–xvi, 82–89, 95
    Matthew influenced by, xv–xvi, 89–90, 95
    overview of, xv–xvi, 81
    self-understanding of, 86–87
    suffering and sacrifice and, 249–50
performance, oral. *See* oral performance
performance criticism, 121–26, 127, 128–29, 130–32
performativity, 568–73
periodization, 394, 415, 423
Periodoi of Leucius, 214–15
Perry, Peter, 122, 123–24, 125, 132
Person, Raymond, 132

Pervo, Richard I., 461n.9
Petersen, William L., 182
Phaedo (Plato), 253
Pharisees, 16–17, 51–52, 303, 309, 329–30, 333–34, 346–47, 349, 379, 469–70, 472, 474, 480, 494–95, 497, 499, 527, 553
Philo, 72, 235–36, 254, 385, 432, 440, 479–80
Pilate, 247, 248, 284, 286–87, 498
Plato, 431–32
Pliny the Younger, 45, 190, 305
Plotemy, 195–96
Plotinus, 189, 195
Plutarch, 72, 190–91, 254, 452
Poirier, John, 53
Porphyry, 3, 189, 195
portraits of women. *See* women
Postcolonial Discipleship of Embodiment (Choi), 568–69
Postcolonial Feminist Interpretation of the Bible (Dube), 287–89
poststructuralism, 144, 543, 567, 575
poverty. *See* wealth, poverty, and economy
Powell, Mark Allen, 139
power. *See* kingdom, authority, and power
Prabhu, Soares, 506, 511
priority of Mark. *See* Markan priority
progymnasmata, 64–65, 69, 395, 398
Protevangelium of James, 205–6
Proto-Luke
  author of, 37–39
  challenges to, 39–40
  Christology in, 39
  coherence and unity of, 41
  decreased scholarly interest in, 41–42
  eschatology in, 39
  estimations of, 38
  formation of, 36–37
  Four-Source Hypothesis and, 27–28
  historical Jesus and, 37
  infancy narratives in, 38–39
  as intermediary source, 35
  Kingdom of God in, 39
  L and, 35
  origin of, 35, 36–39
  overview of, 36–40
  Passion narrative in, 38
  Paul and, 39–40
  Q and, 35
  reconstruction of, 38–39
  scholarly interest in decreased, 40
  Synoptic Problem and, 41–42
  theological character of, 39
Proto-Mark, 10, 13–14, 114–15
Proto-Matthew, 5–6, 10, 31–32
Pseudo-Philo, 518, 519
publication and dating
  adding taxis and, 194–95
  advances in gospel studies and adjacent fields and, 183–87
  alternative model proposed for, 197
  architecture of synoptic studies and, 178–79
  assumptive building blocks of, 175–78
  authored texts and, 175–76, 192–96, 197
  books and, Gospels as, 176–77, 192–96, 197
  canon incorporation and, 194–96
  chapter divisions and, 195
  Christian origins to early Christianity shift and, 184
  commentary and, 195–96
  as complex social process, 187–98
  earliest evidence in, 181–82, 191
  Enlightenment thinkers and, 175–76
  external markings of texts and, 189–90
  "First Century Mark" and, 176–77
  future research on, 198–99
  internal markings of texts and, 187–89
  literary dependence and, 182–83, 198
  overview of, xvi, 175–78
  prefaces and, 192–93
  problems with current architecture and, 180–83
  process of the Gospel publication, 190–92
  published books and, Gospels as, 177–78, 192–96
  redaction and, 177, 179
  SBL Handbook of Style and, 176
  Synoptic Problem and, xvi, 178–79, 198
  synthesizing remarks on, 186–87
  text criticism and, 179, 182
  textual unfinishedness and, 180–81
  tradition philology to new philology of variance shift and, 185
  variance and instability and, 182–83
  writing as contained to open-ended process shift and, 186

published books, Gospels as, 177–78, 192–96
punishment, 420–21, 425–26

Q
    challenges to, xv, 41–42
    diagram of, 160f
    estimates of, 27
    Gospel and, meaning of, 453, 459
    healing and exorcism and, 357–58
    historical Jesus and, 13
    history and, 401–2, 403
    Jewish sectarianism and, 479
    L and, 36–37
    literary dependence and, 13
    M and, 28–32, 33
    Markan priority and, 14
    media dualism and, 111–12, 114
    minor agreements and, 159–60
    oral performance and, 129–30
    oral tradition and writing and, 37, 111–12
    origin of, 13, 30, 33
    pro-Gentile aspects of, 33
    Proto-Luke and, 35
    Synoptic Problem and, xv, 13, 36–37, 158–60, 160f, 161f
    Thomas and, 227–28, 237–38
    travel and itinerancy and, 323–26, 333
    2DH and, 13–14, 15–16, 41–42, 159–60
    violent imaginaries and, 261–63, 268, 270–71, 273–74
    wealth, poverty, and economy and, 304–6
Q in Matthew (Kirk), 56
Quintilian, 44–45, 53, 68–69, 127–28, 393, 397

Ravens, David, 500–1
redaction
    apocryphal narratives and, 204–5, 212–13, 214–15, 216–20
    oral performance and, 128–29, 130
    oral tradition and writing and, 100–1, 107–10, 111
    publication and dating and, 177, 179
    suffering and sacrifice and, 255
    Synoptic Problem and, 128–29
redaction criticism, xv–xvi, 14, 33, 40, 111–12, 119–20, 130, 179, 468
Reed, Jonathan, 321–22

references to Scripture. *See* scriptural references
Reid, Duncan, 65n.2, 113
Reimarus, Herrmann Samuel, 5
resurrection and afterlife
    ambiguity of, 443–46
    apocalyptic eschatology and, 440–43
    cognitive approach to, 443–46
    corporeality of, 440–43
    difficulties in defining, 430–32
    food and meals and, 352
    incorporeality of, 440–43
    Jesus and, 435–39
    overview of, 430–32
    types of, 433–35
rhetoric in the ancient world. *See* ancient rhetoric
Rhoads, David, 121, 123, 125–27
the rich. *See* wealth, poverty, and economy
Richards, I. A., 443–44
Richlin, Amy, 545–46
Robbins, Vernon, 68, 126
Rodriguez, Rafael, 129–30, 132
Rohde, Erwin, 431–32
Roller, Matthew, 344–45
Roman and Greek culture, xvi–xvii, 64–67, 338–40, 392–98, 472–73, 487, 528–29, 543–53, 567
Roman Empire, 64, 128, 148, 267–68, 283, 320–23, 526, 528–29, 568–69
Roman-Jewish War (66–70 CE), 89, 145, 393, 490–91
Roman rhetoric, 64–67
Rothschild, Clare K., 193
Ruge-Jones, Phil, 125–26
Runesson, Anders, 472, 499–500

sacred space
    architecture and, 374–76
    cities and, 379–80
    doors and, 379–80
    inside/outside and, 377–78
    Kingdom of God as, 373, 376–84
    Kingdom of Heaven as, 380–82
    Kingdom of Satan and, 382–84
    land as common feature of, 384–85
    location of the sacred and, 386–87

Luke and, 387–88
Mark and, 387–88
Matthew and, 387–88
negative sacred space, 382–84
organic growth and, 378
overview of, 372–74
point of entry and, 377–78
sense experience and, 378
Synoptic Problem and, 374–75
temple and, 386–87
sacrifice. *See* suffering and sacrifice
Saldarini, Anthony, 471–72
salvation, 82–83, 86–87, 89, 235–36, 247,
    286–87, 405, 416–17, 418–19, 420, 422–23,
    441–42, 452–53, 457–58, 492, 494, 500,
    507, 514–15, 521
Sanday, William, 12, 37
Sanders, E. P., 160, 492, 493–94
SBL Handbook of Style, 176
Schäfer, Peter, 487
Schechner, Richard, 122, 125, 130–31
Scheidel, Walter, 299–300
Schipper, Jeremy, 568
Schleiermacher, Friedrich, 7–8, 9–10
Schmidt, Karl, 119–20, 253
Schuller, Eileen, 250–51
Schweitzer, Albert, 12–13, 284–85
scriptural models, 508–9, 512–13, 515–16
scriptural references
    Exodus
        21:29, 249
        23:20, 507
    Leviticus
        17–18, 495
    2 Samuel, 48–50
        5
            6-10, 50
            13–16, 49
    1 Chronicles
        3:5-9, 49
        11:4-9, 50
        14:3-7, 49
    Psalms
        6, 250–51
        11:5, 519
        21:2a, 251–52
        22:1, 514
        23:2, 519–20
        31
            5, 514
            6, 253
        37, 385
        41-42, 250–51
        42-43, 507–8
        104:27-28, 306
        118, 170
        22, 516
    Proverbs
        1:1-6, 477
        21:1, 214–15
    Isaiah
        2:2-4, 492–93
        3:6, 500
        5, 232–33
        5:1-7, 519–20
        6:9-10, 54
        7:11, 386–87
        9:1-2, 510
        24:47, 500
        26:19, 433
        40:3, 18, 331–32, 507
        42:1-4, 510
        49:6, 500
        51:17, 251
        52-53, 433–34
        53:10b-12, 248–49
        56:7, 386–87
        58, 290–91
            6, 310
        61, 290–91
            1-2, 310
    Jeremiah
        31:15, 558
    Ezekiel
        37, 414–15
            1-14, 433–34
        13, 512
    Daniel
        3, 433–34
        6, 433–34
        7, 426
            9-14, 421–22
            13-14, 421, 422
        7-12, 271–72

scriptural references (*cont.*)
    12
        2, 414–15
        2-3, 433–35, 445
    Hosea
        6:2, 248
    Jonah
        4:9, 250–51
    Micah
        5:2, 516
    Habakkuk
        2
            7, 47
            18, 47
        3:14, 47
    Zechariah
        1:3, 47
        4:7, 516
        9-14, 509–10
        9:9, 512
        11:12, 512
    Malachi
        3:1, 478–79, 507
        4:5-6, 478–79
    Matthew
        1
            1-17, 557
            18-25, 557
        1-2, 556
        3
            4, 343–44
            7-10, 18, 156, 157*t*
        3-28, 33
        4
            15-16, 510
            16, 16–17
        5, 474–75
            1-7:27, 19, 29
            3-5, 473–74
            3-12, 475–76
            10, 474
            11-12, 475–76
            17-20, 472
            18, 236–37
            20, 474
            23, 32
            42, 20
            46-48, 20
        5-7, 7–8, 16, 223–24
        6
            7-8, 499
            19-21, 308–9
            31-32, 499
        7
            2, 20
            5b, 223–24
            6, 499
            12, 20
            15-20, 330
        8
            1-9:26, 56
            18-22, 328–29
        8-9, 362
        9
            9, 155, 155*t*, 161–66, 162*t*, 164*t*, 165*t*,
                165*f*, 166*t*
            20, 15–16
            25, 345
            35, 362
            35-11:1, 328–29
            36-10:42, 29
        10, 7–8
            1-42, 16
        11
            25-27, 476
            25-30, 477
        12
            8, 167–69, 167*t*, 168*t*
            18, 510
            22-24, 358
            32, 418
            41-42, 440
        13
            1-52, 7–8, 16
            1-53, 29
            24-30, 307
            31-32, 159*t*
            44, 308–9
            45-46, 308–9
            47-50, 231
            51-52, 309
        14
            21, 344–45
        15
            38, 344–45
            46, 308

16, 128, 130–31
  19, 477
  20, 379
17
  15, 246–47
  22-18:35, 29
  24-27, 309
18, 7–8
  1-35, 16
  15-20, 477
  18, 379, 477
  23-24, 29–30
  23-25, 307–8
  23-35, 266–67
19, 329
  17, 308
  21, 308
20
  1-15, 29–30
  1-16, 308
  20-28, 348
  29-34, 69–77, 70t
  31, 75
  32, 75–76
  34, 74
21-25, 477
21:42-46, 169–71, 169t
22, 348–49
  11, 348–49
  34-40, 215
23, 16–17
  1-25:46, 29
  1-37, 349
  15, 328–29
  16-17, 309–10
  18-19, 309–10
  23, 309
23-25, 7–8
24, 21, 273
  14, 463
  36-44, 349
  37-44, 349
  45-51, 349
24-25, 16
25, 420, 421
  31-46, 499–500
26
  5-13, 344–45

  26-29, 343
  55-56, 156, 157t
27
  43, 435–36
  52-53, 436–37, 445
  69, 15–16
28
  2, 438
  16-20, 438
  19-20, 499–500
29
  22, 400
40, 506
Mark
  1, 404
  1, 393
  2-6, 18
  5, 18
  6, 301, 343–44
  8, 506
  16-18, 302
  21, 18
  26, 359
  29-31, 302
  32, 302–3
  34, 360
  35, 302–3
  39, 18
2, 127–28
  1-12, 55
  13-17, 344–45
  14, 155, 155t, 161–66, 162t, 164t, 165t, 166t
  23-28, 301
  28, 167–69, 167t, 168t
3
  19, 9, 18
  22-30, 68
  31, 555
4
  1-9, 301
  14-20, 226
  30-32, 159t
  40, 459–60
5
  1, 301, 326–27
  21, 526–27
  21-43, 555
  24, 526–27

scriptural references (*cont.*)
    24-34, 555
    25-34, 123–24
    33, 555
  5-10, 361
  6
    1-6, 555
    3, 302
    10, 302–3
    11, 56
    21-29, 303
    37, 459–60
    41, 93–94
    52, 459–60
  7
    1-23, 460
    19, 480
    24-30, 553–56
    26, 553
    29, 527
  8, 130–31
    1, 326–27
    4, 459–60
    6, 93–94
    22-10:52, 255
    22-26, 156*t*
    27-33, 459–60
    38, 570
  9
    1, 400
    14-29, 358
    27-31, 76–77
    30-32, 459–60
    31, 248
    38-40, 88–89
    42, 301
  10, 255
    30, 418
    33-45, 459–60
    35-45, 348
    38, 251
    38-40, 400
    45, 251
    46-52, 69–77, 70*t*
    49-50, 75–76
  10:46-52, 67–69, 68*t*
  11
    27-33, 232
    32, 11
  12
    1, 232
    1-12, 263–64, 301
    10-12, 169–71, 169*t*
    13-17, 303
    25, 440, 441
    28-37, 215
    41-44, 299
  13, 12–13, 21, 248, 256, 272, 273, 286, 327–28, 398
    9, 56
    9-10, 498
  14
    3-9, 344–45
    9, 400, 463
    22-25, 343
    24, 251
    36, 250–51
    48-52, 156, 156*t*, 157*t*
  15
    16-20, 248
    39, 127
  16
    1-8, 142–48, 438
    8, 85–86, 534–35
    14-15, 438
    14-18, 352
Luke
  1
    1-4, 234
    5-38, 559
    75, 474
  2
    36-38, 529
    40-42, 386
  3
    7-9, 8, 18, 156, 157*t*
    7-17, 9
    16-17, 8
  4, 359–60
    1-13, 8, 9
    16, 16–17
    31-37, 358–59
    33-37, 141
    39, 344–45
    4-8, 362
    5, 358–59

24, 422
27-28, 155, 155t, 161–66, 162t, 164t,
  165t, 166t
6, 223–24
  5, 167–69, 167t, 168t
  17-49, 473
  20, 313
  20-49, 9, 11–12, 19
  38, 311–12
7
  1-10, 9–10
  18-35, 9–10, 11–12
  22, 310
  36-50, 344–45
8, 363
  2, 526–27
  44, 15–16, 21
9
  23, 109–10
  51-18:13, 16
  60, 441–42
10
  1-12, 526–27
  25-28, 215, 312
  25-37, 331–32
  30-37, 312
  40, 344–45
11, 333–34
  37-54, 346–47
12
  13-15, 312
  15-21, 231
  33, 313
  35-39, 347–48
  40-48, 347–48
13
  2, 247
  6-9, 519–20
  18-19, 159t
14, 348–49, 363
  7-11, 341
  7-14, 347–48
  12, 312
  14, 312–13, 440
  15-24, 347–49
  16-24, 314
15
  11-32, 347–48

16
  16, 405
  23, 445–46
17:7-8, 313
20, 506
  17-19, 169–71, 169t
  27-38, 441
  35-36, 440
  36b, 440
  38, 440–41
  38b, 441
  45-47, 16–17
22
  1-14, 348–49
  15-20, 343
  19, 91–92, 351
  20, 92
  52-53, 156, 157t
  64, 15–16
24
  13, 526–27
  30-35, 352
  33-43, 352
  36-43, 438, 445
  42, 352
  27:39, 430–31
John
  3, 236
  6:51, 46
  12:45, 46, 54
  14:9c, 46, 54
  16:8, 474
  20:19-23, 438
  21:24-25, 234
Acts
  1:8, 500–1
  8:4-25, 500–1
  11:19-20, 491–92
  13:44-47, 501
  14:26-16:10, 462
  15, 501
    5, 501
    7, 461
  17:32, 437
  23:6, 437
  24
    10-21, 440
    15, 440

scriptural references (*cont.*)
    21, 437
    26:23, 437
    27:35, 352
  Romans
    3:24-25, 249
  1 Corinthians
    1:17-2:5, 84
    10:17, 93
    11
      4, 458
      24, 351
    15
      1-3, 455
      3-7, 455
      3-8, 86
      4, 248
      5, 438
      12-19, 436-37
  2 Corinthians
    4:10, 85
  Galatians
    1
      6-9, 458
      16, 85
    2
      1-10, 494-95
      7-9, 455-56
      11-14, 462
  Philippians
    1:5, 456
    4:15, 456
  1 Thessalonians
    2:14-16, 265
    4:17, 426-27
  2 Timothy
    2:17-18, 427
  Revelation
    1:12-16, 574
Scriptures, Israel's. *See* Israel's Scriptures
sectarianism. *See* Jewish sectarianism
Seim, Turid Karlsen, 441
Sellew, Melissa Harl, xvi
Seneca, 190-91, 254, 297-98, 306, 399, 488-89
Sense and Stigma in the Gospels (Lawrence), 571-72
Sense of an Ending, The (Kermode), 143

Sermon on the Mount, 9, 16-17, 18, 20, 51, 55, 112, 142, 260, 361-62, 385, 473-74, 481, 527
sexuality, 544-46, 549
Shiner, Whitney, 121, 125-26, 127-28
Shively, Elizabeth, 143-44
Sim, David C., 86n.4, 471-72, 499
Simon, Ulrich, 382
Singer of Tales, The (Lord), 121
Smith, Daniel, 21
Smith, Dennis, 338-39, 343, 344-45, 350
Smith, Jonathan Z., 386
Smith, Morton, 469
Society of Biblical Literature, 120, 121, 123, 125
Socrates, 253-54
Sōma in Biblical Theology (Gundry), 565
Son of Man, 41, 167, 247-49, 270-71, 419, 421-24, 426-27, 479
source criticism, xv-xvi, 39, 41-42, 100-1, 108, 110-12, 116-17, 119, 120, 196, 198, 225, 226
sources in ancient compositions. *See also* minor sources
  combination of sources and, 48, 49-50, 52, 55, 57
  GH and, 57
  Homer and, 52-53
  imitation and, 44-45, 53
  inexact quotations and, 54
  Josephus's *Antiquities* and, 48-50
  kaige and, 46-48
  Luke and, 52-54
  Mark and, 52-54
  Markan priority and, 54, 56
  Matthew and, 52-54
  minor agreements and, 55
  oral performance and, 52
  oral tradition and writing and, 54
  overview of, xv-xvi, 44-46
  relative degrees of difficulty for use of, 57, 58*t*
  Septuagint recensions and, 46-48, 59
  Sermon on the Mount and, 55
  Synoptic Problem and, xv-xvi, 51, 57-59
  Tatian's Diatessaron and, 50-52, 59
  theories of synoptic relations and, 57, 58*f*
  translation and, 48
  2DH and, 56
  visual contact with sources and, 55-57
  writing materials and processes in, 44-46

Spittler, Janet, xvi
Spivak, Gayatri, 146, 286
stable texts tradition, xv, 152–53, 161–62, 163–64, 171–72, 189–90
Stanton, Graham N., 453–54, 472
Stanton, V. H., 37
Stark, Rodney, 470–71
Sterling, Gregory, 253, 253n.13
Stewart, Eric, 384–85
Storr, Gottlob Christian, 6–7
Streeter, B. H.
   Four-Source Hypothesis and, 27
   influence of, 31–32, 34–35
   Judaistic sayings and, 30–32
   L and, 27, 35, 36, 37, 40, 41
   M and, 27, 30–31, 32, 33–35
   minor sources and, 27
   oral tradition and, 110–11
   Paul and, 30–31
   Proto-Luke and, 37
   Q and, 27, 30–31, 111
   Synoptic Problem and, 13–14
   2DH and, 111
Strier, Richard, 137
Structuring Early Christian Memory (Rodríguez), 129–30
"Studying Snapshots" (Lied and Lunghaug), 185
suffering and sacrifice
   endurance of, 246–47
   eschatology and, 256
   followers of Jesus and, 254–56
   illness as suffering, 246–47
   imitation and, 255
   Jesus and, 247–54
   Luke and, 252–54
   Mark and, 250–52
   Messianic Secret and, 247
   overview of, 245–46
   Paul and, 249–50
   predictions of, 247–49, 254–56
   redaction and, 255
Suggs, M. Jack, 456n.4
Symmachus, 46–47, 48
Synoptic Gospels. *See* Luke; Mark; Matthew
Synoptic Problem
   ancient rhetoric and, xv–xvi, 20, 63–69
   apocryphal narratives and, 215
   challenges to, xvi, 18, 153
   coherence arguments and, 19–20
   complexity of, xvi, 18–19
   current study of, 15–17
   decreased scholarly interest in, 41–42
   definition of, 3–5, 155, 161–62
   diagrams of Gospel overlap and, 153–54, 154f, 159–60, 160f, 161f
   early history of, 3–5
   expanding of, 21
   FH and, 15–16, 18–19, 57, 115, 160, 161f
   GH and, 113
   Gospel harmonies and, 4–6
   historical Jesus and, 5, 12–13, 152–53, 155
   Israel's Scriptures and, 517
   L and, 36–37, 41–42
   M and, 41–42
   manuscripts and, 152–61, 171–72
   Markan priority and, 13, 18, 21
   media dualism and, 112–15
   minor agreements and, 17–18, 158–60, 159t
   minor sources and, 28, 41–42
   multiple-source hypothesis and, 114–15
   oral performance and, 128–29
   oral tradition and writing and, xv–xvi, 100–1, 113–14
   overview of, xv–xvii, 3–5, 152–61, 155t, 156t, 157t, 159t, 160f, 161f
   Proto-Luke and, 41–42
   publication and dating and, xvi, 178–79, 198
   Q and, xv, 13, 36–37, 158–60, 160f, 161f
   recent scholarship on, xv–xvii
   redaction and, 128–29
   sacred space and, 374–75
   sixteenth to nineteenth century history of, 5–13, 100–1
   solutions to, xv, 4–8, 18–20, 57–59, 128–29, 156
   sources in ancient compositions and, xv–xvi, 51, 57–59
   stable texts tradition and, xv–xvi, 161–62
   stages in discussion of, 18–19
   thematic studies in, xv
   theories of Synoptic relations and, 58f
   Thomas and, xvi, 21
   twentieth century history of, 13–14

Synoptic Problem (*cont.*)
  2DH and, 8–9, 17, 19, 21, 111–13, 158, 158*f*
  Urgospel and, 5–6
  Ur-Markus and, 8
  utilization hypotheses and, 4, 7, 10
  ways forward on, 17–21
Synoptic Problem, The (Farmer), 14–15
Syrophoenician woman, 141, 357, 358–59, 498, 553–56, 572

Tacitus, 487, 488–89
Tacoma, Laurens, 320–21, 322–23
Tappenden, Frederick, 445
Tatian, 50–52
Taussig, Hal, 145, 339–40, 341, 351
Taylor, Vincent
  Christology and, 39
  infancy narratives and, 38–39
  influence of, 39
  L and, 37–38, 40, 41
  origin and author of Proto-Luke and, 38–39
  Proto-Luke hypothesis and, 38–40
  theological character of Proto-Luke and, 39
Tertullian, 251n.10
text criticism, xvi, 114–15, 178, 179, 182
textual fluidity, 152–53, 163–64
textual unfinishedness, 180–81
Theissen, Gerd, 323–24, 325, 355n.1, 367, 468–69
Theological Tendency of Codex Bezae Cantabrigiensis in Acts (Epp), 185
Theophilus of Antioch, 191, 195–96
Thiessen, Matthew, 496
Thomas
  authentic human existence in, 235–36
  character of Jesus in, 229–30
  disciples in, 233–35
  discovery of, 223–24
  distinctness of, 223–24
  divine mysteries in, 229–30
  eschatology in, 236–37
  future directions in study of, 238
  genre of, 227–29
  historical Jesus and, 224–25
  Jewish sectarianism and, 479
  oral performance and, 130
  overview of, xvi, 223–24

  parables in, 230–33
  patterns of familiarity and independence in, 224–27
  Q and, 227–28, 237–38
  relevance of, 223–24, 237–38
  salvation in, 235–36
  Synoptic Problem and, xvi, 21
Thucydides, 143n.9, 552–53
time mastery, 399–407
To Cast the First Stone (Knust and Wasserman), 185
tomb woman, 533–35
transfiguration narrative, 205–12, 372, 373–74, 376, 378, 381, 387
translation variant hypothesis, 7, 103–4, 106
travel and itinerancy
  Galilee and, 321–23
  historical Jesus and, 321–22
  Luke and, 331–34
  Mark and, 326–28
  Matthew and, 328–30
  mission and, 328–30
  overview of, 320–21
  Q and, 323–26, 333
  Roman Empire and, 321–23
  universality and, 331–34
triple tradition, 29–30, 104–5, 108, 111, 113, 114–15, 156, 160, 163–64, 167
Trobisch, David, 192, 193
Troeltsch, Ernst, 470
Tübingen school, 7–8
Tuckett, Christopher, 374–75
Turner, Mark, 443–44
Tweed, Thomas, 373
Two Document Hypothesis (2DH)
  ancient rhetoric and, 73–74, 76–77
  challenges to, 14–15, 16, 19, 159–60
  diagram of, 158*f*
  establishment of, 8–9, 13–14
  Jewish sectarianism and, 473
  Lachmann fallacy and, 14–15
  legacy of, 12–13, 15–16, 17
  manuscripts and, 171
  Markan priority and, 13–14
  media dualism and, 111–13
  minor agreements evidence against, 15–16, 21, 159–60

oral tradition and writing and, 111–13
precursor to, 8
privileged position of, 15–16
Q and, 13–14, 15–16, 41–42, 159–60
sources in ancient compositions and, 56
Synoptic Problem and, 8–9, 17, 19, 21, 111–13, 158, 158*f*
Two Gospel Hypothesis (2GH), 14–15, 16–17, 19–20, 76–77
Two Spirits Treatise, 415
Tynjanov, Yury, 139, 139n.5

Udoh, Fabian, 303
Urgospel
criticism of, 10
formation of, 101–2
literary dependence and, 5–6, 7
Markan priority and, 7
media dualism and, 100–2
oral tradition and writing and, 5–6, 10, 100–7
oral *Urgospel*, 100–2, 105–7
positing of, 5–6
Synoptic Problem and, 5–6
Ur-Markus, 5–6, 8, 9–10, 11–12
utilization hypotheses, 4, 7, 10, 100–1, 113

Valerius Maximus, 254, 395–96, 397
Van Maaren, John, 498–99
Van Segbroeck, Frans, 7
Victor of Antioch, 196
violent imaginaries
definition of, 261
envoys of God and, 261–66, 274
eschatology and, 271–74
historical Jesus and, 271
Jesus and, 261–66
overview of, 260–61
parables and, 266–71
Q and, 261–63, 268, 270–71, 273–74
virtue, 20, 72, 496, 550–53

Waters, Kenneth L., 436–37
Watson, Francis, 16–17, 18–19, 51, 55, 184
Weaks, Joe, 154n.5
wealth, poverty, and economy
amassing treasure in heaven and, 308
ancient economy and, 300–1
Friesen-Longnecker economic scale and, 298–300, 298*t*
hoarding and hiding of, 308–9
L and, 311–14
Luke and, 310–11
Mark and, 301–4
Matthew and, 307–10
multivalent definitions of, 296–98
overview of, 296–98
Q and, 304–6
slaves, tenants, and daily wage earners and, 307–8
survey of direct addresses and, 311–14
temple economy and, 309–10
Weber, Max, 323–24, 470
Wefald, Eric K., 498
Weiss, Johannes
apocalyptic thinking and, 13
L and, 35–37, 41
Proto-Luke hypothesis and, 36–37
Q and, 13
Weisse, C. H., 8–10
Weissenrieder, Annette, 355–56
Werner, Martin, 81–83, 459n.5
Wernle, Paul, 12, 13, 110
What is Redaction Criticism? (Perrin), 179
Whitaker, C. R., 299
Wilke, Christian Gottlob
Markan priority and, 108–9
media dualism and, 107–8
oral tradition and writing and, 100–1, 107–10
redaction and, 100–1, 107–10
Synoptic Problem and, 108–10
Urtext and, 108
Williams, Craig, 545–46, 548
Williams, Joel, 146
Wilson, Britney, 559–61, 571
Wilson, Walter, 356–57
Wimsatt, William, 138
Winkler, John, 546–47, 567–68
Wire, Antoinette Clark, 126, 128
Woloch, Alex, 146
women. *See also* gender
ancient society and, 528–29
anointing woman, 530–31

women (*cont.*)
  authorship and, 528
  characters and, 526–27
  flow of blood woman, 531–33
  food and meals and, 344–45
  general considerations
    of, 526–29
  Jairus's daughter, 531–33
  Martha and Mary, 538–40
  Mary, mother of Jesus, 535–38
  Mary Magdalene, 533–35
  overview of, 525–26
  stories of, 529–40
  Syrophoenician/Canaanite woman, 530
  tomb woman, 533–35
Woolf, Greg, 314
Wrede, Wilhelm, 12–13, 247
writing. *See* oral tradition and writing

Yarbrough, Robert, 381–82
Yoder Neufeld, Thomas, 268, 270–71

Zamagni, Claudio, 216n.17
Zechariah, 559–61